Marketing Management
Knowledge and Skills 6/e

J. Paul Peter
James R. McManus-Bascom
Professor in Marketing
University of Wisconsin—Madison

James H. Donnelly, Jr.
Thomas C. Simons Professor of Business
University of Kentucky

Irwin
McGraw-Hill

Boston   Burr Ridge, IL   Dubuque, IA   Madison, WI   New York San Francisco   St. Louis
Bangkok   Bogotá   Caracas   Kuala Lumpur   Lisbon   London   Madrid   Mexico City
Milan   Montreal   New Delhi   Santiago   Seoul   Singapore   Sydney   Taipei   Toronto

McGraw-Hill Higher Education

A Division of The **McGraw-Hill** Companies

MARKETING MANAGEMENT: KNOWLEDGE AND SKILLS
International Edition 2001

Exclusive rights by McGraw-Hill Book Co – Singapore, for manufacture and export. This book cannot be re-exported from the country to which it is sold by McGraw-Hill. The International Edition is not available in North America.

10   09 08 07 06   05 04 03 02 01
20   09 08 07 06   05   04 03 02 01 00
CTP   SLP

Library of Congress Cataloging-in-Publication Data

Peter, J. Paul.
   Marketing management : knowledge and skills / J. Paul Peter, James H. Donnelly, Jr.—
6th ed.
   p.   cm.
   ISBN 0-07-231557-1
   1.   Marketing—Management. 2. Marketing—Management—Case studies. I. Donnelley,
James H. II. Title
HF5415.13.P387 2000
658.8—dc21   00-026735

www.mhhe.com

When ordering this title, use ISBN 0-07-118130-X

Printed in Singapore

Dedication

To Gayla Donnelly
   —Jim Donnelly

To Rose and Angie
   —J. Paul Peter

Preface

Our goal in the first edition of *Marketing Management: Knowledge and Skills* was to develop and offer a complete student resource for marketing management education. Our goal remains the same for this, the sixth edition. However, the resources students and instructors need have changed and thus, this edition has changed. Our focus, however, remains the same. We seek to enhance student *knowledge* of marketing management and to develop their *skills* in using this knowledge to develop and maintain successful marketing strategies.

■ Changes in This Edition

The basic structure of our text has been expanded in this edition and the following changes have been made:

1. The text chapters are an important part of our book. Accordingly, they have been completely updated and revised for this edition. Several chapter title changes from the previous edition reflect these revisions. Some specific content changes include new coverage of the cross-functional aspects of strategic marketing planning, product management, and new product development and sales; an expanded discussion of the marketing research process and sources of marketing research information; expanded coverage of consumer decision making, vendor analysis, and organizational purchasing policies and procedures; additional discussion of geodemographic segmentation and product positioning; new discussions of integrated market communications, strategic partnerships, and strategic alliances; new coverage of wholesaling and store and nonstore retailing; and an entirely rewritten global marketing chapter with expanded coverage of global marketing research.

2. A new section in this edition provides eleven Internet exercises for those instructors wishing to add them to the skill development component of their course. These exercises were developed to relate specifically to the content of the text chapters. The exercises are all strategic in focus and allow students to relate the concepts in the text to the challenges of marketing on the Internet.

3. Finding relevant new cases is always a challenge. We have been fortunate to continue to locate truly outstanding new cases. Combining this and the previous edition, 39 new cases have been included, 14 of which are specific to this edition. Our emphasis continues to be on well-known companies, including both domestic and global companies, high-tech companies, consumer and organizational products, small and large businesses, products and services, and manufacturers and channel members.

   Some of the popular cases in the book can truly be considered "classics." But whether new or 10 years old, these "snapshots in time" enable students to analyze the situation within the time period the case was written and/or bring the situation up-to-date with their own research and analyses.

4. A new resource has been added which presents an annotated bibliography of the major on-line databases used in marketing. This new resource replaces our previous "Secondary Data Sources" section. It is an up-to-date resource for students to use in the analysis of Internet exercises, cases, and the development of marketing plans. It is included in Section IV immediately following the Internet exercises.

5. Several of the cases include in-class exercises that provide the instructor with additional means of enhancing student learning, participation, analysis, and team building.

6. A number of the cases include video introductions and discussion questions to enhance student interest, thinking, and analysis.

■ Structure of the Book

We have experimented over many years with various teaching philosophies. The structure of this book evolved and continues to evolve from these experiments. Currently, our six-stage learning approach includes (1) learning basic marketing principles, (2) learning approaches and tools for performing marketing analyses, (3) analyzing Internet exercises, (4) analyzing marketing management cases, (5) analyzing strategic marketing cases, and (6) developing marketing plans.

Our six-stage learning approach is the focus of the seven book sections. Each section has as its objective both *knowledge enhancement* and *skill development*. The framework and structure of our book is presented in the following diagram, which will be used throughout the text to integrate various sections.

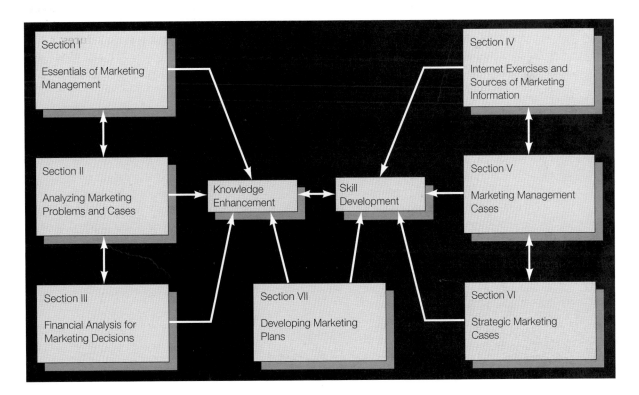

Stage 1: Learning Basic Marketing Principles

It is clearly necessary for students to learn and understand basic definitions, concepts, and marketing logic before they can apply them in the analysis of marketing problems or development of marketing plans. Section 1 of the book contains 13 chapters which present the essentials of marketing management. One problem we continually face in more advanced case-oriented courses is that most students have long ago discarded or sold their basic marketing texts. Consequently, when they are faced with case problems they have nothing to rely on but their memories. We believe this seriously detracts from the usefulness of case analysis. Thus, we include this section as a reference source for key marketing concepts. Our objective in this section is to focus on material that is relevant primarily for analyzing marketing problems and cases.

Stage 2: Learning Approaches and Tools for Problem Analysis

The second stage in our approach involves offering students basic tools and approaches for solving marketing problems. Section II, "Analyzing Marketing Problems and Cases" is a widely praised approach to analyzing, writing, and presenting case analyses. Section III, "Financial Analyses for Marketing Decisions," presents some important financial calculations that can be useful in evaluating the financial position of a firm and the financial impact of various marketing strategies. Section IV includes an annotated bibliography of some of the most widely used marketing databases. It will assist students in researching a particular industry or firm and can greatly improve the analysis of exercises and cases.

Stage 3: Analyzing Internet Exercises

As a way of introducing students to the challenges of case analysis, some instructors utilize Internet exercises. They find that these exercises are an especially useful way to integrate text material with case work. Accordingly, Section IV provides 11 such exercises that are new to this edition. Other instructors, especially those with more advanced marketing students, find their students are fully prepared to tackle case analyses. For these instructors, this section is optional.

Stage 4: Analyzing Marketing Management Cases

It has been our experience that few students have the confidence and experience necessary to analyze complex strategic marketing cases in their first exposure to this type of learning. We believe it is far better for them to apply their skills by analyzing cases for which traditional marketing principles can be applied somewhat directly before they attempt more challenging problems. Accordingly, Section V of the book has been expanded to include 33 marketing management cases, organized into six groups: market opportunity analysis, product strategy, promotion strategy, distribution strategy, pricing strategy, and social and ethical issues in marketing management. Within each group, cases are sequenced so that later cases contain more information and typically require higher levels of marketing management analysis skills than earlier ones.

Stage 5: Analyzing Strategic Marketing Cases

Once students have developed sufficient skills to provide thoughtful analyses of marketing management cases, they are prepared to tackle strategic marketing cases. These cases go beyond traditional marketing principles and focus on the role of marketing in cross-functional business or organization strategies. Section VI of our book contains 11 such cases. They are sequenced so that the latter cases contain more information and require higher skill levels to analyze them properly.

Stage 6: Developing Marketing Plans

The final stage in our approach involves the development of an original marketing plan. We believe that after a two-course sequence in marketing management, students should be able to do one thing very well and should know that they can do it well: Students should be able to construct a quality marketing plan for any product or service. Section VII provides a framework for developing such a plan. Instructors can consult the *Instructors Manual* which accompanies this book for alternative ways to incorporate this stage into their course.

We have found that this six-stage process is very flexible and can easily be adapted to student needs and instructor objectives. For example, if the course is the first learning experience in marketing, then emphasis could be placed on the first four stages. If students progress well through these stages, then marketing management cases can be assigned on an individual or group basis.

If the course is for students with one or more previous courses in marketing or is the capstone marketing management course, then major attention should shift to stages 2 through 6. In this instance, Section I becomes a resource for review and reference and the course focuses more on skill development.

Finally, the text can be used for a two-course sequence in marketing management. The first course can emphasize stages 1 through 4 and the second can concentrate on stages 5 and 6.

■ Acknowledgments

Our heartfelt thanks go to all of the case and exercise writers who contributed their work to help others better educate marketing students. Each of the contributors names and affiliations appear in the Contents and at the point in the book where their contribution appears.

Many thanks to the users who responded to our survey. Your responses were valuable because they were used in planning this edition, and in making the hard choices involved in replacing cases, selecting new cases, and deciding on which of the "classic" cases remain. Again, thank you for your help.

We also want to acknowledge those colleagues who provided detailed reviews of previous editions:

Sammy G. Amin
Frostburg State State University
V. Glenn Chappell
Meredith College
Henry Chen
University of West Florida
John Considine
LeMoyne College
Randall Ewing
Ohio Northern University

Renee Foster
Delta State University
John Gauthier
Gateway Technical College
Anne B. Lowery
University of Mobile
Gregory Martin
University of West Florida
Wendy Martin
Judson College

Mary K. McManamon
Lake Erie College
William F. Schoell
University of Southern Mississippi
Anusorn M. Singhapakdi
Old Henry Dominion University
Jean Shaneyfelt
Edicon Community College

John Shaw
Providence College
Charlotte Smedberg
Florida Metropolitan University System
Joseph R. Stasio
Merrimack College
Albert J. Taylor
Austin Peay State University

For reviewing the present edition we want to thank:

Andrew Bergstein
Pennsylvania State University
Newell Chiesl
Indiana State University
Mike Dailey
University of Texas, Arlington
David Griffith
University of Oklahoma
Jack Healey
Golden Gate University

JoAnne S. Hooper
Western Carolina University
Benoy Joseph
Cleveland State University
Donald J. Messmer
College of William & Mary
Kevin Webb
Drexel University
Dale Wilson
Michigan State University

Rick Adams, Senior Sponsoring Editor, Christine Parker, Developmental Editor, and Craig Leonard, Project Manager, provided the leadership required to bring this edition to print. Thanks to each of you.

Andrew Policano, Dean of the School of Business at the University of Wisconsin, and Richard Furst, Dean of the Gatton College of Business and Economics at the University of Kentucky, have always supported our efforts and we are very grateful to them.

Finally, we want to thank Charles Heath and Geoffrey Gordon of Northern Illinois who have contributed to this edition and its predecessors.

J. Paul Peter
James H. Donnelly, Jr.

Contents

Chapter Nine
Personal Selling   136

Chapter Ten
Distribution Strategy   154

Chapter Eleven
Pricing Strategy   170

Section I

Essentials of Marketing Management

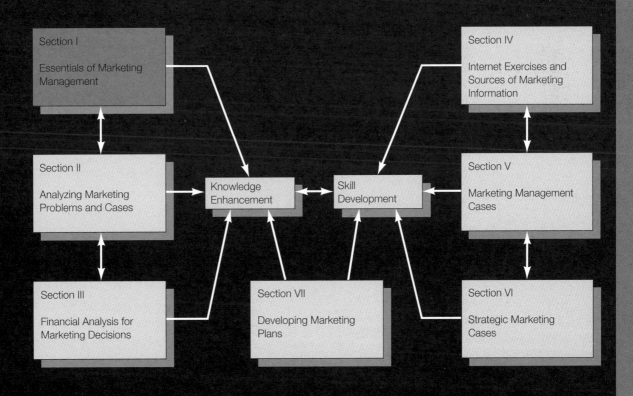

Part A

Introduction

Chapter One
Strategic Planning and the Marketing
Management Process

Chapter One

Strategic Planning and the Marketing Management Process

The purpose of this introductory chapter is to present the marketing management process and outline what marketing managers must *manage* if they are to be effective. In doing so, it will also present a framework around which the remaining chapters are organized. Our first task is to review the organizational philosophy known as the marketing concept, since it underlies much of the thinking presented in this book. The remainder of this chapter will focus on the process of strategic planning and its relationship to the process of marketing planning.

■ The Marketing Concept

Simply stated, the marketing concept means that *an organization should seek to make a profit by serving the needs of customer groups.* The concept is very straightforward and has a great deal of commonsense validity. Perhaps this is why it is often misunderstood, forgotten, or overlooked.

The purpose of the marketing concept is to rivet the attention of marketing managers on serving broad classes of customer needs (customer orientation), rather than on the firm's current products (production orientation) or on devising methods to attract customers to current products (selling orientation). Thus, effective marketing starts with the recognition of customer needs and then works backward to devise products and services to satisfy these needs. In this way, marketing managers can satisfy customers more efficiently in the present and anticipate changes in customer needs more accurately in the future. This means that organizations should focus on building long-term customer relationships in which the initial sale is viewed as a beginning step in the process, not as an end goal. As a result, the customer will be more satisfied and the firm will be more profitable.

The principal task of the marketing function operating under the marketing concept is not to manipulate customers to do what suits the interests of the firm, but rather to find effective and efficient means of making the business do what suits the interests of customers. This is not to say that all firms practice marketing in this way. Clearly, many firms still emphasize only production and sales. However, effective marketing, as defined in this text, requires that consumer needs come first in organizational decision making.

One qualification to this statement deals with the question of a conflict between consumer wants and societal needs and wants. For example, if society deems clean air and water as necessary for survival, this need may well take precedence over a consumer's want for goods and services that pollute the environment.

■ What Is Marketing?

One of the most persistent conceptual problems in marketing is its definition.[1] The American Marketing Association has recently defined marketing as "the process of planning and executing conception, pricing, promotion, and distribution of ideas, goods, and services to create exchanges that satisfy individual and organizational goals."[2] This definition takes into account all parties involved in the marketing effort: members of the producing organization, resellers of goods and services, and customers or clients. While the broadness of the definition allows the inclusion of nonbusiness exchange processes, the primary emphasis in this text is on marketing in the business environment. However, this emphasis is not meant to imply that marketing concepts, principles, and techniques cannot be fruitfully employed in other areas of exchange. In fact, some discussions of nonbusiness marketing take place later in the text.

■ What Is Strategic Planning?

Before a production manager, marketing manager, and personnel manager can develop plans for their individual departments, some larger plan or blueprint for the *entire* organization should exist. Otherwise, on what would the individual departmental plans be based?

In other words, there is a larger context for planning activities. Let us assume that we are dealing with a large business organization that has several business divisions and several product lines within each division (e.g., General Electric, Philip Morris). Before any marketing planning can be done by individual divisions or departments, a plan has to be developed for the entire organization.[3] This means that senior managers must look toward the future and evaluate their ability to shape their organization's destiny in the years and decades to come. The output of this process is objectives and strategies designed to give the organization a chance to compete effectively in the future. The objectives and strategies established at the top level provide the context for planning in each of the divisions and departments by divisional and departmental managers. It is worth noting that, depending on the environmental challenges faced by the organization, different planning approaches may be called for.

Marketing
Highlight 1–1

Basic Elements of the Marketing Concept

1. Companywide managerial awareness and appreciation of the consumer's role as it is related to the firm's existence, growth, and stability. As Drucker has noted, business enterprise is an organ of society; thus, its basic purpose lies outside the business itself. And the valid definition of business purpose is the creation of customers.

2. Active, companywide managerial awareness of, and concern with, interdepartmental implications of decisions and actions of an individual department. That is, the firm is viewed as a network of forces focused on meeting defined customer needs, and comprising a system within which actions taken in one department or area frequently result in significant repercussions in other areas of the firm. Also, it is recognized that such actions may affect the company's equilibrium with its external environment, for example, its customers, its competitors.

3. Active, companywide managerial concern with innovation of products and services designed to solve selected consumer problems.

4. General managerial concern with the effect of new products and service introduction on the firm's profit position, both present and future, and recognition of the potential rewards that may accrue from new product planning, including profits and profit stability.

5. General managerial appreciation of the role of marketing intelligence and other fact-finding and reporting units within and adjacent to the firm in translating the general statements presented above into detailed statements of profitable market potentials, targets, and action. Implicit in this statement is not only an expansion of the traditional function and scope of formal marketing research, but also assimilation of other sources of marketing data, such as the firm's distribution system and its advertising agency counsel, into a potential marketing intelligence service.

6. Companywide managerial effort, based on participation and interaction of company officers, in establishing corporate and departmental objectives that are understood by and acceptable to these officers and that are consistent with enhancement of the firm's profit position.

SOURCES: For an up-to-date discussion of the marketing concept, see Frederick E. Webster, Jr., "Defining the New Marketing Concept," *Marketing Management* 2, no. 4 (1994), pp. 22–31. For a classic discussion, see Robert L. King, "The Marketing Concept: Fact or Intelligent Platitude," *The Marketing Concept in Action,* Proceedings of the 47th National Conference (Chicago: American Marketing Association, 1964), p. 657.

Strategic Planning and Marketing Management

Some of the most successful business organizations are here today because many years ago they offered the right product at the right time to a rapidly growing market. The same can also be said for nonprofit and governmental organizations. Many of the critical decisions of the past were made without the benefit of strategic thinking or planning. Whether these decisions were based on wisdom or were just luck is not important; they worked for these organizations. However, a worse fate befell countless other organizations. Over three-quarters of the 100 largest U.S. corporations of 70 years ago have fallen from the list. These corporations at one time dominated their markets, controlled vast resources, and had the best-trained workers. In the end, they all made the same critical mistake. Their managements failed to recognize that business strategies need to reflect changing environments and emphasis must be placed on developing business systems that allow for continuous improvement. Instead, they attempted to carry on business as usual.

Present-day managers are increasingly recognizing that wisdom and innovation alone are no longer sufficient to guide the destinies of organizations, both large and small. These same managers also realize that the true mission of the organization is to provide value for three key constituencies: customers, employees, and investors. Without this type of outlook, no one, including shareholders, will profit in the long run.

Strategic planning includes all the activities that lead to the development of a clear organizational mission, organizational objectives, and appropriate strategies to achieve the objectives for the entire organization. The form of the process itself has come under criticism in some quarters for being too structured; however, strategic planning, if performed successfully, plays a key role in achieving an equilibrium between the short and the long term by balancing acceptable financial performance with preparation for inevitable changes in markets, technology, and competition, as well as in economic and political arenas. Managing principally for current cash flows, market share gains, and earnings trends can mortgage the firm's future. An intense focus on the near term can produce an aversion to risk that dooms a business to stagnation. Conversely, an overemphasis on the long run is just as inappropriate. Companies that overextend themselves betting on the future may penalize short-term profitability and other operating results to such an extent that the company is vulnerable to takeover and other threatening actions.

The strategic planning process is depicted in Figure 1–1. In the strategic planning process the organization gathers information about the changing elements of its environment. Managers from all functional areas in the organization assist in this information-gathering process. This information is useful in aiding the organization to adapt better to these changes through the process of strategic planning. The strategic plan(s)[4] and supporting plan are then implemented in the environment. The end results of this implementation are fed back as new information so that continuous adaptation and improvement can take place.

■ **Figure 1–1** The Strategic Planning Process

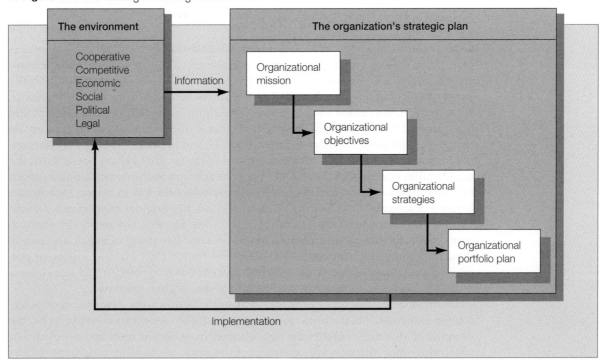

Marketing
Highlight 1–2

Mission Statements

Organization	Mission
Goodyear	Our mission is constant improvement in products and services to meet our customers' needs. This is the only means to business success for Goodyear and prosperity for its investors and employees.
Intel Corporation	Do a great job for our customers, employees, and stockholders by being the preeminent building block supplier to the computing industry.
Levi Strauss & Co.	The mission of Levi Strauss & Co. is to sustain responsible commercial success as a global marketing company of branded casual apparel. We must balance goals of superior profitability and return on investment, leadership market positions, and superior products and service. We will conduct our business ethically and demonstrate leadership in satisfying our responsibilities to our communities and to society. Our work environment will be safe and productive and characterized by fair treatment, teamwork, open communications, personal accountability, and opportunities for growth and development.
Merck & Co., Inc.	The mission of Merck & Co., Inc., is to provide society with superior products and services—innovations and solutions that satisfy customer needs and improve their quality of life—to provide employees with meaningful work and advancement opportunities and investors with a superior rate of return.
Marriott	Grow a worldwide lodging business using total quality management (TQM) principles to continuously improve preference and profitability. Our commitment is that *every guest leaves satisfied.*

SOURCE: Patricia Jones and Larry Kahaner, *Say It and Live It: The 50 Corporate Mission Statements That Hit the Mark* (New York: Doubleday, 1995).

The Strategic Planning Process

The output of the strategic planning process is the development of a strategic plan. Figure 1–1 indicates four components of a strategic plan: mission, objectives, strategies, and portfolio plan. Let us carefully examine each one.

Organizational Mission. The organization's environment provides the resources that sustain the organization, whether it is a business, a college or university, or a government agency. In exchange for these resources, the organization must supply the environment with quality goods and services at an acceptable price. In other words, every organization exists to accomplish something in the larger environment and that purpose, vision, or mission usually is clear at the organization's inception. As time passes, however, the organization expands, and the environment and managerial personnel change. As a result, one or more things are likely to occur. First, the organization's original purpose may become irrelevant as the organization expands into new products, new markets, and even new industries. For example, Levi Strauss began as a manufacturer of work clothes. Second, the original mission may remain relevant, but managers begin to lose interest in it. Finally, changes in the environment may make the original mission inappropriate. The result of any or all three of these conditions is a "drifting" organization, without a clear mission, vision, or purpose to guide critical decisions. When this occurs, management must search for a purpose or emphatically restate and reinforce the original purpose.

The mission statement, or purpose, of an organization is the description of its reason for existence. It is the long-run vision of what the organization strives to be, the unique aim that differentiates the organization from similar ones and the means by which this differentiation will take place. In essence, the mission statement defines the direction in which the organization is heading and how it will succeed in reaching its desired goal. While some argue that vision and mission statements differ in their purpose, the perspective we will take is that both reflect the organization's attempt to guide behavior, create a culture, and inspire commitment.[5] However, it is more important that the mission statement comes from the heart and is practical, easy to identify with, and easy to remember so that it will provide direction and significance to all members of the organization regardless of their organizational level.

The basic questions that must be answered when an organization decides to examine and restate its mission are What is our business? Who is the customer? What do customers value? and What will our business be?[6] The answers are, in a sense, the assumptions on which the organization is being run and from which future decisions will evolve. While such questions may seem simplistic, they are such difficult and critical ones that the major responsibility for answering them must lie with top management, not planning gurus. In fact, the mission statement remains the most widely used management tool in business today. In developing a statement of mission, management must take into account three key elements: the organization's history, its distinctive competencies, and its environment.[7]

1. *The organization's history.* Every organization—large or small, profit or nonprofit—has a history of objectives, accomplishments, mistakes, and policies. In formulating a mission, the critical characteristics and events of the past must be considered.

2. *The organization's distinctive competencies.* While there are many things an organization may be able to do, it should seek to do what it can do best. Distinctive competencies are things that an organization does well: so well in fact that they give it an advantage over similar organizations. For Honeywell, it's their ability to design, manufacture, and distribute a superior line of thermostats.[8] Similarly, Procter & Gamble's distinctive competence is its knowledge of the market for low-priced, repetitively purchased consumer products. No matter how appealing an opportunity may be, to gain advantage over competitors, the organization must formulate strategy based on distinctive competencies.

3. *The organization's environment.* The organization's environment dictates the opportunities, constraints, and threats that must be identified before a mission statement is developed. For example, managers in any industry that is affected by technology breakthroughs should continually be asking, How will the changes in technology affect my customers' behavior and the means by which we need to conduct our business?

However, it is extremely difficult to write a useful and effective mission statement. It is not uncommon for an organization to spend one or two years developing a useful mission statement. When completed, an effective mission statement will be *focused on markets rather than products, achievable, motivating, and specific.*[9]

Focused on Markets rather than Products. The customers or clients of an organization are critical in determining its mission. Traditionally, many organizations defined their business in terms of what they made ("our business is glass") and in many cases they named the organization for the product or service (e.g., National Cash Register, Harbor View Savings and Loan Association). Many of these organizations have found that, when products and technologies become obsolete, their mission is no longer relevant and the name of the organization may no longer describe what it does. Thus, a more enduring way of defining the mission is needed.

In recent years, therefore, a key feature of mission statements has been an *external* rather than *internal* focus. In other words, the mission statement should focus on the broad class of needs that the organization is seeking to satisfy (external focus), not on the physical product or service that the organization is offering at present (internal focus). These market-driven firms stand out in their ability to continuously anticipate market opportunities and respond before their competitors. This has been clearly stated by Peter Drucker:

> A business is not defined by the company's name, statutes, or articles of incorporation. It is defined by the want the customer satisfies when he buys a product or service. To satisfy the customer is the mission and purpose of every business. The question "What is our business?" can, therefore, be answered only by looking at the business from the outside, from the point of view of customer and market.[10]

While Drucker was referring to business organizations, the same necessity exists for both nonprofit and governmental organizations. That necessity is to state the mission in terms of serving a particular group of clients or customers and meeting a particular class of need.

Achievable.   While the mission statement should stretch the organization toward more effective performance, it should, at the same time, be realistic and achievable. In other words, it should open a vision of new opportunities but should not lead the organization into unrealistic ventures far beyond its competencies.

Motivational.   One of the side (but very important) benefits of a well-defined mission is the guidance it provides employees and managers working in geographically dispersed units and on independent tasks. It provides a shared sense of purpose outside the various activities taking place within the organization. Therefore, such end results as sales, patients cared for, and reduction in violent crimes can then be viewed as the result of careful pursuit and accomplishment of the mission and not as the mission itself.

Specific.   As we mentioned earlier, public relations should not be the primary purpose of a statement of mission. It must be specific to provide direction and guidelines to management when they are choosing between alternative courses of action. In other words, "to produce the highest-quality products at the lowest possible cost" sounds very good, but it does not provide direction for management.

Organizational Objectives.   *Organizational objectives* are the end points of an organization's mission and are what it seeks through the ongoing, long-run operations of the organization. The organizational mission is distilled into a finer set of specific and achievable organizational objectives. These objectives must be *specific, measurable, action commitments* by which the mission of the organization is to be achieved.

As with the statement of mission, organizational objectives are more than good intentions. In fact, if formulated properly, they can accomplish the following:

1. They can be converted into specific action.
2. They will provide direction. That is, they can serve as a starting point for more specific and detailed objectives at lower levels in the organization. Each manager will then know how his or her objectives relate to those at higher levels.
3. They can establish long-run priorities for the organization.
4. They can facilitate management control because they serve as standards against which overall organizational performance can be evaluated.

■ **Figure 1–2**
Sample Organizational
Objectives (manufac-
turing firm)

Area of Performance	Possible Objective
1. Market standing	To make our brands number one in their field in terms of market share.
2. Innovations	To be a leader in introducing new products by spending no less than 7 percent of sales for research and development.
3. Productivity	To manufacture all products efficiently as measured by the productivity of the workforce.
4. Physical and financial resources	To protect and maintain all resources—equipment, buildings, inventory, and funds.
5. Profitability	To achieve an annual rate of return on investment of at least 15 percent.
6. Manager performance and responsibility	To identify critical areas of management depth and succession.
7. Worker performance and attitude	To maintain levels of employee satisfaction consistent with our own and similar industries.
8. Social responsibility	To respond appropriately whenever possible to societal expectations and environmental needs.

Organizational objectives are necessary in all areas that may influence the performance and long-run survival of the organization. As shown in Figure 1–2, objectives can be established in and across many areas of the organization. The list provided in Figure 1–2 is by no means exhaustive. For example, some organizations are specifying the primary objective as the attainment of a specific level of quality, either in the marketing of a product or the providing of a service. These organizations believe that objectives should reflect an organization's commitment to the customer rather than its own finances. Obviously, during the strategic planning process conflicts are likely to occur between various functional departments in the organization. The important point is that management must translate the organizational mission into specific objectives that support the realization of the mission. The objectives may flow directly from the mission or be considered subordinate necessities for carrying out the mission. As discussed earlier, the objectives are specific, measurable, action commitments on the part of the organization.

Organizational Strategies.   Hopefully, when an organization has formulated its mission and developed its objectives, it knows where it wants to go. The next managerial task is to develop a "grand design" to get there. This grand design constitutes the organizational strategies. Strategy involves the choice of major directions the organization will take in pursuing its objectives. Toward this end, it is critical that strategies are consistent with goals and objectives and that top management ensures strategies are implemented effectively. As many as 60 percent of strategic plans have failed because the strategies in them were not well defined and, thus, were unable to be implemented effectively.[11] What follows is a discussion of various strategies organizations can pursue.

Marketing
Highlight 1–3

**Potential Sources of Cross-Functional
Conflict for Marketers**

Functions	What They May Want to Deliver	What Marketers May Want Them to Deliver
Research and development	Basic research projects	Products that deliver customer value
	Product features	Customer benefits
	Few projects	Many new products
Production/ operations	Long production runs	Short production runs
	Standardized products	Customized products
	No model changes	Frequent model changes
	Long lead times	Short lead times
	Standard orders	Customer orders
	No new products	Many new products
Finance	Rigid budgets	Flexible budgets
	Budgets based on return on investment	Budgets based on need to increase sales
	Low sales commissions	High sales commissions
Accounting	Standardized billing	Custom billing
	Strict payment terms	Flexible payment terms
	Strict credit standards	Flexible credit standards
Human resources	Trainable employees	Skilled employees
	Low salaries	High salaries

SOURCE: G. A. Churchill, Jr., and J. Paul Peter, *Marketing: Creating Value for Customers* (Burr Ridge, IL: Irwin/McGraw-Hill, 1998), p. 15.

Organizational Strategies Based on Products/Markets. One means to develop organizational strategies is to focus on products offered and markets served. Using this focus, organizations can achieve their objectives in two ways. They can better manage what they are presently doing or find new things to do. In choosing either or both of these paths, the organization then must decide whether to concentrate on present customers or to seek new ones, or both. Figure 1–3 presents the available strategic choices. This figure is known as a product-market matrix and indicates the strategic alternatives available to an organization for achieving its objectives. It indicates that an organization can grow in a variety of ways by concentrating on present or new products and on present or new customers.[12]

■ **Figure 1–3**
Organizational Growth Strategies

Products / Markets	Present Products	New Products
Present Customers	Market penetration	Product development
New Customers	Market development	Diversification

Market Penetration Strategies. These organizational strategies focus on improving the position of the organization's present products with its present customers. For example:

- A snack products company concentrates on getting its present customers to purchase more of its products.
- A charity seeks ways to increase donations from present supporters.
- A bank concentrates on getting present credit card customers to use their cards more frequently.

A market penetration strategy might involve devising a marketing plan to encourage customers to purchase more of a product. Tactics used to carry out the strategy could include price reductions, advertising that stresses the many benefits of the product, packaging the product in different-sized packages, or making the product available at more locations. For example, Procter & Gamble decided to implement an everyday low-pricing strategy, slashing prices on over 40 percent of its product offerings, in order to stimulate consumer demand. Likewise, a production plan might be developed to produce more efficiently what is being produced at present. Implementation of such a plan could include increased production runs, the substitution of preassembled components for individual product parts, or the automation of a process that previously was performed manually. In other words, market penetration strategies concentrate on improving the efficiency of various functional areas in the organization.

Market Development Strategies. Following this strategy, an organization would seek to find new customers for its present products. For example:

- A manufacturer of industrial products may decide to develop products for entrance into consumer markets.
- A governmental social service agency may seek individuals and families who have never utilized the agency's services.
- A manufacturer of automobiles decides to sell automobiles in eastern Europe because of the recent transition to a free market system.
- An athletic clothing and footwear company decides to develop a line of fitness clothing for children.

Market development strategies involve much more than simply getting the product to a new market. Before considering marketing techniques such as packaging and promotion, companies often find they must establish a foothold in the market, sometimes spending millions of dollars simply to educate consumers as to why they should consider purchase of the product.

Product Development Strategies. In choosing either of the remaining two strategies, the organization in effect seeks new things to do. With this particular strategy, the new products developed would be directed to present customers. For example:

- A candy manufacturer may decide to offer a fat-free candy.
- A social service agency may offer additional services to present clients.
- A college or university may develop programs for nontraditional students.
- A soft drink manufacturer may develop a midcalorie or clear cola.

Diversification. An organization diversifies when it seeks new products for customers it is not serving at present. For example:

- A cigarette manufacturer diversifies into real estate development.
- A college or university establishes a corporation to find commercial uses for the results of faculty research efforts.
- A cosmetics manufacturer acquires a baby care products company.

Organizational Strategies Based on Competitive Advantage.

Michael Porter developed a model for formulating organizational strategy that is applicable across a wide variety of industries.[13] The focus of the model is on organizations devising means to gain competitive advantage. Porter's generic strategy model suggests that firms should first analyze their industry and then develop either a *cost leadership strategy* or a *strategy based on differentiation*. These strategies can be utilized on a marketwide basis or in a niche (segment) contained within the total market. Businesses using a cost leadership strategy focus on being the low-cost company in their industry. They attempt to be efficient and offer a standard, no-frills product. They can accomplish this through efficiencies in production, product design, manufacturing, distribution, technology, or some other means. To succeed, an organization must continually strive to be the cost leader in the industry or market segment it competes in. However, even a cost leader must offer products or services that are acceptable to customers when compared to competitors' offerings. Wal-Mart, Southwest Airlines, and Timex Group Ltd. are examples of companies that have succeeded with this approach.

Second, an organization may pursue a competitive advantage through differentiation. With a differentiation strategy, a company attempts to be unique in its industry or market segment along some dimensions that customers value. These dimensions might pertain to design, quality, service, variety of offerings, brand name, or some other factor. Because of the uniqueness of the product or service, companies can charge a premium price. L. L. Bean, Rolex, Coca-Cola, and Microsoft are all examples of companies that have successfully employed this strategy.

Organizational Strategies Based on Value Disciplines.

More recently, Michael Treacy and Fred Wiersema developed a model for devising organizational strategy that is based on three core value disciplines that organizations can strive to achieve.[14] Their contention is that no firm in today's complex environment can succeed by trying to be all things to all people. Instead, the firm must find the unique value that it alone can deliver to a given market. The first value discipline, *operational excellence,* is pursued by companies that are not product or service innovators, nor do they cultivate deep, one-to-one relationships with customers. Instead, operationally excellent companies provide middle-of-the-road products (in terms of quality) at the best price with the least inconvenience. Their proposition to customers is simple: low price or hassle-free service, or both. Price/Costco and Dell Computer are examples of this type of company.

The second value discipline, *product leadership,* is pursued by companies that push performance boundaries. Their proposition to customers is that they offer the best product or service, period. These companies continually innovate year after year. For these product leaders, competition is not about price or customer service (although those can't be ignored), it's about product performance. Johnson &

Johnson, Nike, and Rubbermaid are examples of companies following this discipline. The final value discipline, *customer intimacy,* is adhered to by companies not interested in what the entire market wants; rather, the focus is on providing what specific customers want. Customer-intimate companies do not pursue one-time transactions; they cultivate relationships. These companies specialize in satisfying unique needs that are often only recognized by developing close relationships with and intimate knowledge of select customers. Their proposition to customers is, "We have the best products for you, and we provide all the support you need to achieve optimum results." Airborne Express, Roadway, and Cott Corp. are examples of companies pursuing this final discipline.

Choosing an Appropriate Strategy.　On what basis does an organization choose one (or all) of its strategies? Of extreme importance are the directions set by the mission statement. Management should select those strategies consistent with its mission and capitalize on the organization's distinctive competencies that will lead to a sustainable competitive advantage. A sustainable competitive advantage can be based on either the assets or skills of the organization. Technical superiority, low-cost production, customer service/product support, location, financial resources, continuing product innovation, and overall marketing skills are all examples of distinctive competencies that can lead to a sustainable competitive advantage. For example, Honda is known for providing quality automobiles at a reasonable price. Each succeeding generation of Honda automobiles has shown marked quality improvements over previous generations. Likewise, VF Corporation, manufacturer of Wrangler and Lee jeans, has formed "quick response" partnerships with both discounters and department stores to ensure the efficiency of product flow. The key to sustaining a competitive advantage is to continually focus and build on the assets and skills that will lead to long-term performance gains.

Organizational Portfolio Plan.　The final phase of the strategic planning process is the formulation of the organizational portfolio plan. In reality, most organizations at a particular time are a portfolio of businesses, that is, product lines, divisions, schools. To illustrate, an appliance manufacturer may have several product lines (e.g., televisions, washers and dryers, refrigerators, stereos) as well as two divisions, consumer appliances and industrial appliances. A college or university will have numerous schools (e.g., education, business, law, architecture) and several programs within each school. Some widely diversified organizations such as Philip Morris are in numerous unrelated businesses, such as cigarettes, food products, land development, and industrial paper products.

Managing such groups of businesses is made a little easier if resources are plentiful, cash is plentiful, and each is experiencing growth and profits. Unfortunately, providing larger and larger budgets each year to all businesses is seldom feasible. Many are not experiencing growth, and profits and resources (financial and nonfinancial) are becoming more and more scarce. In such a situation, choices must be made, and some method is necessary to help management make the choices. Management must decide which businesses to build, maintain, or eliminate, or which new businesses to add. Indeed, much of the recent activity in corporate restructuring has centered on decisions relating to which groups of businesses management should focus on.

Obviously, the first step in this approach is to identify the various division's product lines and so on that can be considered a "business." When identified, these are referred to as *strategic business units* (SBUs) and have the following characteristics:

- They have a distinct mission.
- They have their own competitors.
- They are a single business or collection of related businesses.
- They can be planned independently of the other businesses of the total organization.

Thus, depending on the type of organization, an SBU could be a single product, product line, or division; a college of business administration; or a state mental health agency. Once the organization has identified and classified all of its SBUs, some method must be established to determine how resources should be allocated among the various SBUs. These methods are known as *portfolio models*. For those readers interested, the appendix of this chapter presents two of the most popular portfolio models, the Boston Consulting Group model and the General Electric model.

The Complete Strategic Plan

Figure 1–1 indicates that at this point the strategic planning process is complete, and the organization has a time-phased blueprint that outlines its mission, objectives, and strategies. Completion of the strategic plan facilitates the development of marketing plans for each product, product line, or division of the organization. The marketing plan serves as a subset of the strategic plan in that it allows for detailed planning at a target market level. This important relationship between strategic planning and marketing planning is the subject of the final section of this chapter.

■ The Marketing Management Process

Marketing management can be defined as "the process of planning and executing the conception, pricing, promotion, and distribution of goods, services, and ideas to create exchanges with target groups that satisfy customer and organizational

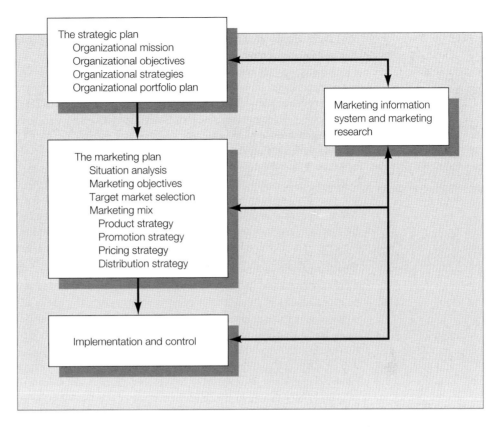

objectives."[15] It should be noted that this definition is entirely consistent with the marketing concept, since it emphasizes the serving of target market needs as the key to achieving organizational objectives. The remainder of this section will be devoted to a discussion of the marketing management process in terms of the model in Figure 1–4.

Situation Analysis

With a clear understanding of organizational objectives and mission, the marketing manager must then analyze and monitor the position of the firm and, specifically, the marketing department, in terms of its past, present, and future situation. Of course, the future situation is of primary concern. However, analyses of past trends and the current situation are most useful for predicting the future situation.

The situation analysis can be divided into six major areas of concern: (1) the cooperative environment; (2) the competitive environment; (3) the economic environment; (4) the social environment; (5) the political environment; and (6) the legal environment. In analyzing each of these environments, the marketing executive must search both for opportunities and for constraints or threats to achieving objectives. Opportunities for profitable marketing often arise from changes in these environments that bring about new sets of needs to be satisfied. Constraints on marketing activities, such as limited supplies of scarce resources, also arise from these environments.

The Cooperative Environment.   The cooperative environment includes all firms and individuals who have a vested interest in the firm accomplishing its objectives. Parties of primary interest to the marketing executive in this environment are (1) suppliers; (2) resellers; (3) other departments in the firm; and (4) subdepartments and employees of the marketing department. Opportunities in this environment are primarily related to methods of increasing efficiency. For example, a company might decide to switch from a competitive bid process of obtaining materials to a single source that is located near the company's plant. Likewise, members of the marketing, engineering, and manufacturing functions may utilize a teamwork approach to developing new products versus a sequential approach. Constraints consist of such things as unresolved conflicts and shortages of materials. For example, a company manager may believe that a distributor is doing an insufficient job of promoting and selling the product, or a marketing manager may feel that manufacturing is not taking the steps needed to produce a quality product.

The Competitive Environment.   The competitive environment includes primarily other firms in the industry that rival the organization for both resources and sales. Opportunities in this environment include such things as (1) acquiring competing firms; (2) offering demonstrably better value to consumers and attracting them away from competitors; and (3) in some cases, driving competitors out of the industry. For example, one airline purchases another airline, a bank offers depositors a free checking account with no minimum balance requirements, or a grocery chain engages in an everyday low-price strategy that competitors can't meet. The primary constraints in these environments are the demand stimulation activities of competing firms and the number of consumers who cannot be lured away from competition.

The Economic Environment.   The state of the macroeconomy and changes in it also bring about marketing opportunities and constraints. For example, such factors as high inflation and unemployment levels can limit the size of the market that can afford to purchase a firm's top-of-the-line product. At the same time, these factors may offer a profitable opportunity to develop rental services for such products or to develop less expensive models of the product. In addition, changes in technology can provide significant threats and opportunities. For example, in the communications industry, technology has developed to a level where it is now possible to provide cable television using phone lines. Obviously such a system poses a severe threat to the existence of the cable industry as it exists today.

The Social Environment.   This environment includes general cultural and social traditions, norms, and attitudes. While these values change slowly, such changes often bring about the need for new products and services. For example, a change in values concerning the desirability of large families brought about an opportunity to market better methods of birth control. On the other hand, cultural and social values also place constraints on marketing activities. As a rule, business practices that are contrary to social values become political issues, which are often resolved by legal constraints. For example, public demand for a cleaner environment has caused the government to require that automobile manufacturers' products meet certain average gas mileage and emission standards.

The Political Environment.   The political environment includes the attitudes and reactions of the general public, social and business critics, and other organizations, such as the Better Business Bureau. Dissatisfaction with such business and marketing practices as unsafe products, products that waste resources, and unethical sales procedures can have adverse effects on corporation image and customer loyalty. However, adapting business and marketing practices to these attitudes can be an opportunity. For example, these attitudes have brought about markets for such products as unbreakable children's toys, high-efficiency air conditioners, and more economical automobiles.

The Legal Environment.   This environment includes a host of federal, state, and local legislation directed at protecting both business competition and consumer rights. In past years, legislation reflected social and political attitudes and has been primarily directed at constraining business practices. Such legislation usually acts as a constraint on business behavior, but again can be viewed as providing opportunities for marketing safer and more efficient products. In recent years, there has been less emphasis on creating new laws for constraining business practices. As an example, deregulation has become more common as evidenced by recent events in the airlines, financial services, and telecommunications industries.

Marketing Planning

In the previous sections it was emphasized that (1) marketing activities must be aligned with organizational objectives; and (2) marketing opportunities are often found by systematically analyzing situational environments. Once an opportunity is recognized, the marketing executive must then plan an appropriate strategy for taking advantage of the opportunity. This process can be viewed in terms of three interrelated tasks: (1) establishing marketing objectives; (2) selecting the target market; and (3) developing the marketing mix.

Establishing Objectives.   Marketing objectives usually are derived from organizational objectives; in some cases where the firm is totally marketing oriented, the two are identical. In either case, objectives must be specified and performance in achieving them should be measurable. Marketing objectives are usually stated as standards of performance (e.g., a certain percentage of market share or sales volume) or as tasks to be achieved by given dates. While such objectives are useful, the marketing concept emphasizes that profits rather than sales should be the overriding objective of the firm and marketing department. In any case, these objectives provide the framework for the marketing plan.

Selecting the Target Market.   The success of any marketing plan hinges on how well it can identify customer needs and organize its resources to satisfy them profitably. Thus, a crucial element of the marketing plan is selecting the groups or segments of potential customers the firm is going to serve with each of its products. Four important questions must be answered:

1. What do customers want or need?
2. What must be done to satisfy these wants or needs?
3. What is the size of the market?
4. What is its growth profile?

Marketing
Highlight 1–5

Key Issues in the Marketing Planning Process That Need to Be Addressed

Speed of the Process. There is the problem of either being so slow that the process seems to go on forever or so fast that there is an extreme burst of activity to rush out a plan.

Amount of Data Collected. Sufficient data are needed to properly estimate customer needs and competitive trends. However, the law of diminishing returns quickly sets in on the data-collection process.

Responsibility for Developing the Plan. If planning is delegated to professional planners, valuable line management input may be ignored. If the process is left to line managers, planning may be relegated to secondary status.

Structure. Many executives believe the most important part of planning is not the plan itself but the structure of thought about the strategic issues facing the business. However, the structure should not take precedence over the content so that planning becomes merely filling out forms or crunching numbers.

Length of the Plan. The length of a marketing plan must be balanced between being so long it is ignored by both staff and line managers and so brief that it ignores key details.

Frequency of Planning. Too frequent reevaluation of strategies can lead to erratic firm behavior. However, when plans are not revised frequently enough, the business may not adapt quickly enough to environmental changes and thus suffers a deterioration in its competitive position.

Number of Alternative Strategies Considered. Discussing too few alternatives raises the likelihood of failure, whereas discussing too many increases the time and cost of the planning effort.

Cross-Functional Acceptance. A common mistake is to view the plan as the proprietary possession of marketing. Successful implementation requires a broad consensus including other functional areas.

Using the Plan as a Sales Document. A major but often overlooked purpose of a plan and its presentation is to generate funds from either internal or external sources. Therefore, the better the plan, the better the chance of gaining desired funding.

SOURCE: Donald R. Lehmann and Russell S. Winer, *Analysis for Marketing Planning,* 4th ed., chap. 1. © Richard D. Irwin, Inc., 1997.

Present target markets and potential target markets are then ranked according to (*a*) profitability; (*b*) present and future sales volume; and (*c*) the match between what it takes to appeal successfully to the segment and the organization's capabilities. Those that appear to offer the greatest potential are selected. One cautionary note on this process involves the importance of not neglecting present customers when developing market share and sales strategies. In a recent study, it was found that for every 10 companies that develop strategies aimed at increasing the number of first-time customers, only 4 made any serious effort to develop strategies geared toward retaining present customers and increasing their purchases.[16] Chapters 3, 4, and 5 are devoted to discussing consumer behavior, industrial buyers, and market segmentation.

Developing the Marketing Mix. The marketing mix is the set of controllable variables that must be managed to satisfy the target market and achieve organizational objectives. These controllable variables are usually classified according to four major decision areas: product, price, promotion, and place (or channels of distribution). The importance of these decision areas cannot be overstated, and in fact, the major portion of this text is devoted to analyzing them. Chapters 6 and 7 are devoted to product and new product strategies; Chapters 8 and 9 to promotion strategies in terms of both nonpersonal and personal selling; Chapter 10 to distribution strategies; and Chapter 11 to pricing strategies. In addition, marketing mix variables are the focus of analysis in two chapters on marketing in special fields, that

Marketing
Highlight 1–6

Criteria for Setting Marketing Objectives

Criteria	Poor Goal	Good Goal
Overall marketing objectives are clearly stated.	To get people to buy our new Betty Crocker Microwave Bread Shop products.	To obtain 5 percent of the fresh-baked bread market in 12 months.
Behavioral objectives are clearly stated.	To have sales increase.	To stimulate 30 percent of all U.S. households to try one loaf of Betty Crocker Microwave bread.
Expectations are realistic.	To obtain half the fresh-baked bread market.	Given the strong name of Betty Crocker in the baked bread goods market and that Americans consume 50 lbs. of bread a year, we hope to achieve an 18 percent share of the fresh-baked bread market.
Adequate support exists for the program.	No mention of budget dollars in the program statement. No check to make sure the program meshes with corporate goals.	Given the commitment by General Mills to grow in the baked goods market, the budget for Betty Crocker's Microwave Bread Shop over the next three years is $45 million, $41 million, and $35 million, respectively.

SOURCE: Charles W. Lamb, Jr., Joseph F. Hair, Jr., and Carl McDaniel, *Principles of Marketing*, p. 27. Reproduced with the permission of the South-Western Publishing Co. © 1992, Cincinnati, by South-Western Publishing Co. All rights reserved.

is, the marketing of services (Chapter 12) and international marketing (Chapter 13). Thus, it should be clear to the reader that the marketing mix is the core of the marketing management process.

The output of the foregoing process is the marketing plan. It is a formal statement of decisions that have been made on marketing activities; it is a blueprint of the objectives, strategies, and tasks to be performed.

Implementation and Control of the Marketing Plan

Implementing the marketing plan involves putting the plan into action and performing marketing tasks according to the predefined schedule. Even the most carefully developed plans often cannot be executed with perfect timing. Thus, the marketing executive must closely monitor and coordinate implementation of the plan. In some cases, adjustments may have to be made in the basic plan because of changes in any of the situational environments. For example, competitors may introduce a new product. In this event, it may be desirable to speed up or delay implementation of the plan. In almost all cases, some minor adjustments or fine-tuning will be necessary in implementation.

Controlling the marketing plan involves three basic steps. First, the results of the implemented marketing plan are measured. Second, these results are compared with objectives. Third, decisions are made on whether the plan is achieving objectives. If serious deviations exist between actual and planned results, adjustments may have to be made to redirect the plan toward achieving objectives.

■ **Figure 1–5** The Cross-Functional Perspective in Planning

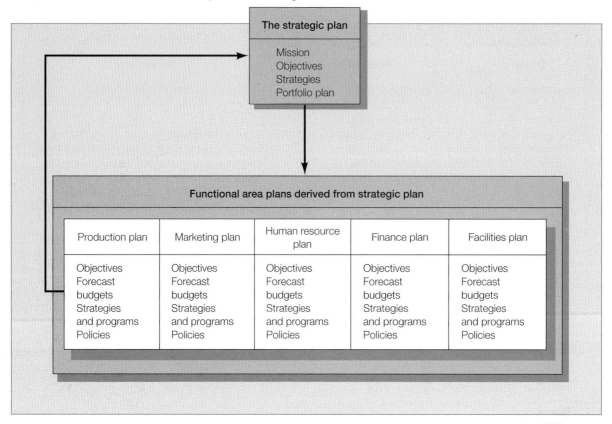

Marketing Information Systems and Marketing Research

Throughout the marketing management process, current, reliable, and valid information is needed to make effective marketing decisions. Providing this information is the task of the marketing information system and marketing research. These topics are discussed in detail in Chapter 2.

■ The Strategic Plan, the Marketing Plan, and Other Functional Area Plans

Strategic planning is clearly a top management responsibility. In recent years, however, there has been an increasing shift toward more active participation by marketing managers in strategic analysis and planning. This is because, in reality, nearly all strategic planning questions have marketing implications. In fact, the two major strategic planning questions—What products should we make? and What markets should we serve?—are clearly marketing questions. Thus, marketing executives are involved in the strategic planning process in at least two important ways: (1) they influence the process by providing important inputs in the form of information and suggestions relating to customers, products, and middlemen; and (2) they must always be aware of what the process of strategic planning involves as well as the results because everything they do, the marketing objectives and strategies they develop, must be derived from the strategic plan. In fact, the planning done in all functional areas of the organization should be derived from the strategic plan.

■ **Figure 1–6** A Blueprint for Management Action: Relating the Marketing Plan to the Strategic Plan and the Production Plan

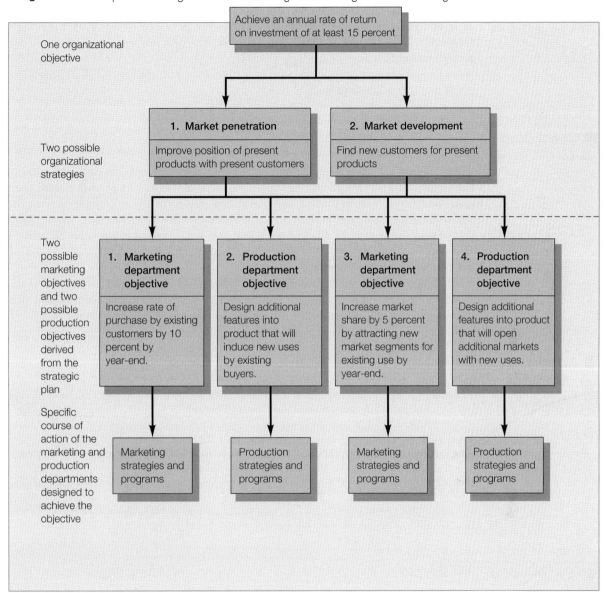

In well-managed organizations, therefore, a direct relationship exists between strategic planning and the planning done by managers at all levels. The focus and time perspectives will, of course, differ. Figure 1–5 illustrates the cross-functional perspective of strategic planning. It indicates very clearly that all functional area plans should be derived from the strategic plan while at the same time contributing to the achievement of the strategic plan.

If done properly, strategic planning results in a clearly defined blueprint for management action in all functional areas of the organization. Figure 1–6 clearly illustrates this blueprint using only one organizational objective and two strategies from the strategic plan (above the dotted line) and illustrating how these are translated into elements of the marketing department plan and the production department plan (below the dotted line). Note that in Figure 1–6, all objectives and strategies are related to other objectives and strategies at higher and lower levels in the organization, that is, a hierarchy of objectives and strategies exists. We have illustrated only two possible marketing objectives and two possible production objectives. Obviously, many others could be developed, but our purpose is to illustrate the cross-functional nature of strategic planning and how objectives and strategies from the strategic plan must be translated into objectives and strategies for all functional areas including marketing.

■ Conclusion

This chapter has described the marketing management process in the context of the organization's overall strategic plan. Clearly, marketers must understand their cross-functional role in joining the marketing vision for the organization with the financial goals and manufacturing capabilities of the organization. The greater this ability, the better the likelihood is that the organization will be able to achieve and sustain a competitive advantage, the ultimate purpose of the strategic planning process.

At this point it would be useful to review Figures 1–4, 1–5, and 1–6 as well as the book's Contents. This review will enable you to better relate the content and progression of the material to follow to the marketing management process.

■ Additional Readings

Avlonitis, George J., and Spiros P. Gounaris. "Market-Orientation and Company Performance: Industrial vs. Consumer Goods Companies." *Industrial Marketing Management,* September 1997, pp. 385–402.

Reichheld, Frederick F. *The Loyalty Effect.* Boston: HBS Press, 1996.

Shaw, Gordon; Robert Brown; and Philip Bromiley. "How 3M Is Rewriting Business Planning." *Harvard Business Review,* May–June 1998, pp. 41–50.

Slywotzky, Adrian J. *Value Migration: How to Think Several Moves Ahead of the Competition.* Boston: HBS Press, 1996.

Appendix

Portfolio Models

Portfolio models remain a valuable aid to marketing managers in their efforts to develop effective marketing plans. The use of these models can aid managers who face situations that can best be described as "more products, less time, and less money." More specifically, (1) as the number of products a firm produces expands, the time available for developing marketing plans for each product decreases; (2) at a strategic level, management must make resource allocation decisions across lines of products and, in diversified organizations, across different lines of business; and (3) when resources are limited (which they usually are), the process of deciding which strategic business units (SBUs) to emphasize becomes very complex. In such situations, portfolio models can be very useful.

Portfolio analysis is not a new idea. Banks manage loan portfolios seeking to balance risks and yields. Individuals who are serious investors usually have a portfolio of various kinds of investments (common stocks, preferred stocks, bank accounts, and the like), each with different characteristics of risk, growth, and rate of return. The investor seeks to manage the portfolio to maximize whatever objectives he or she might have. Applying this same idea, most organizations have a wide range of products, product lines, and businesses, each with different growth rates and returns. Similar to the investor, managers should seek a desirable balance among alternative SBUs. Specifically, management should seek to develop a business portfolio that will assure long-run profits and cash flow.

Portfolio models can be used to classify SBUs to determine the future cash contributions that can be expected from each SBU as well as the future resource requirement that each will require. Remember, depending on the organization, an SBU could be a single product, product line, division, or a distinct business. While there are many different types of portfolio models, they generally examine the competitive position of the SBU and the chances for improving the SBU's contribution to profitability and cash flow.

There are several portfolio analysis techniques. Two of the most widely used are discussed in this appendix. To truly appreciate the concept of portfolio analysis, however, we must briefly review the development of portfolio theory.

■ A Review of Portfolio Theory

The interest in developing aids for managers in the selection of strategy was spurred by an organization known as the Boston Consulting Group (BCG) over 25 years ago. Its ideas, which will be discussed shortly, and many of those that followed were based on the concept of experience curves.

Experience curves are similar in concept to learning curves. Learning curves were developed to express the idea that the number of labor hours it takes to produce one unit of a particular product declines in a predictable manner as the number of units produced increases. Hence, an accurate estimation of how long it takes to produce the 100th unit is possible if the production time for the 1st and 10th units are known.

The concept of experience curves was derived from the concept of learning curves. Experience curves were first widely discussed in the ongoing Profit Impact of Marketing Strategies (PIMS) study conducted by the Strategic Planning Institute. The PIMS project studies 150 firms with more than 1,000 individual business units. Its major focus is on determining which environmental and internal firm variables influence the firm's return on investment (ROI) and cash flow. The researchers have concluded that seven categories of variables appear to influence the return on investment: (1) competitive position; (2) industry/market environment; (3) budget allocation; (4) capital structure; (5) production processes; (6) company characteristics; and (7) "change action" factors.[17]

The experience curve includes all costs associated with a product and implies that the per-unit costs of a product should fall, due to cumulative experience, as production volume increases. In a given industry, therefore, the producer with the largest volume and corresponding market share should have the lowest marginal cost. This leader in market share should be able to underprice competitors, discourage entry into the market by potential competitors, and, as a result, achieve an acceptable return on investment. The linkage of experience to cost to price to market share to ROI is exhibited in Figure A–1. The Boston Consulting Group's view of the experience curve led the members to develop what has become known as the BCG Portfolio Model.

◼ The BCG Model

The BCG is based on the assumption that profitability and cash flow will be closely related to sales volume. Thus, in this model, SBUs are classified in terms of their relative market share and the growth rate of the market the SBU is in. Using these dimensions, products are either classified as stars, cash cows, dogs, or question marks. The BCG model is presented in Figure A–2.

- *Stars* are SBUs with a high share or a high-growth market. Because high-growth markets attract competition, such SBUs are usually cash users because they are growing and because the firm needs to protect their market share position.

◼ **Figure A–1** Experience Curve and Resulting Profit Curve

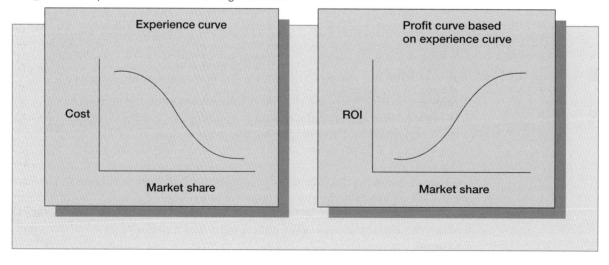

- *Cash cows* are often market leaders, but the market they are in is not growing rapidly. Because these SBUs have a high share of a low-growth market, they are cash generators for the firm.
- *Dogs* are SBUs that have a low share of a low-growth market. If the SBU has a very loyal group of customers, it may be a source of profits and cash. Usually, dogs are not large sources of cash.
- *Question marks* are SBUs with a low share of a high-growth market. They have great potential but require great resources if the firm is to successfully build market share.

As you can see, a firm with 10 SBUs will usually have a portfolio that includes some of each of the above. Having developed this analysis, management must determine what role each SBU should assume. Four basic objectives are possible:

1. *Build share.* This objective sacrifices immediate earnings to improve market share. It is appropriate for promising question marks whose share has to grow if they are ever to become stars.
2. *Hold share.* This objective seeks to preserve the SBU's market share. It is very appropriate for strong cash cows to ensure that they can continue to yield a large cash flow.
3. *Harvest.* Here, the objective seeks to increase the product's short-term cash flow without concern for the long-run impact. It allows market share to decline in order to maximize earnings and cash flow. It is an appropriate objective for weak cash cows, weak question marks, and dogs.
4. *Divest.* This objective involves selling or divesting the SBU because better investment opportunities exist elsewhere. It is very appropriate for dogs and those question marks the firm cannot afford to finance for growth.

There have been several major criticisms of the BCG Portfolio Model, revolving around its focus on market share and market growth as the primary indicators of

■ **Figure A–2**
The Boston Consulting
Group Portfolio Model

preference. First, the BCG model assumes market growth is uncontrollable.[18] As a result, managers can become preoccupied with setting market share objectives instead of trying to grow the market. Second, assumptions regarding market share as a critical factor affecting firm performance may not hold true, especially in international markets.[19] Third, the BCG model assumes that the major source of SBU financing comes from internal means. Fourth, the BCG matrix does not take into account any interdependencies that may exist between SBUs, such as shared distribution.[20] Fifth, the BCG matrix does not take into account any measures of profits and customer satisfaction.[21] Sixth, and perhaps most important, the thrust of the BCG matrix is based on the underlying assumption that corporate strategy begins with an analysis of competitive position. By its very nature, a strategy developed entirely on competitive analysis will always be a reactive one.[22] While the above criticisms are certainly valid ones, managers (especially of large firms) across all industries continue to find the BCG matrix useful in assessing the strategic position of SBUs.[23]

■ The General Electric Model

Although the BCG model can be useful, it does assume that market share is the sole determinant of an SBU's profitability. Also, in projecting market growth rates, a manager should carefully analyze the factors that influence sales and any opportunities for influencing industry sales.

Some firms have developed alternative portfolio models to incorporate more information about market opportunities and competitive positions. The GE model is one of these. The GE model emphasizes all the potential sources of strength, not just

■ **Figure A–3** The General Electric Portfolio Model

market share, and all of the factors that influence the long-term attractiveness of a market, not just its growth rate. As Figure A–3 indicates, all SBUs are classified in terms of *business strength* and *industry attractiveness*. Figure A–4 presents a list of items that can be used to position SBUs in the matrix.

Industry attractiveness is a composite index made up of such factors as those listed in Figure A–4. For example: *market size*—the larger the market, the more attractive it would be; *market growth*—high-growth markets are more attractive than low-growth markets; *profitability*—high-profit-margin markets are more attractive than low-profit-margin industries.

Business strength is a composite index made up of such factors as those listed in Figure A–4. For example: *market share*—the higher the SBU's share of market, the greater its business strength; *quality leadership*—the higher the SBU's quality compared to competitors, the greater its business strength; *share compared with leading competitor*—the closer the SBU's share to the market leader, the greater its business strength.

Once the SBUs are classified, they are placed on the grid (Figure A–3). Priority "A" SBUs (often called *the green zone*) are those in the three cells at the upper left, indicating that these are SBUs high in both industry attractiveness and business strength, and that the firm should "build share." Priority "B" SBUs (often called *the yellow zone*) are those medium in both industry attractiveness and business strength. The firm will usually decide to "hold share" on these SBUs. Priority "C" SBUs are those in the three cells at the lower right (often called *the red zone*). These SBUs are low in both industry attractiveness and business strength. The firm will usually decide to harvest or divest these SBUs.

Whether the BCG model, the GE model, or a variation of these models is used, some analyses must be made of the firm's current portfolio of SBUs as part of any strategic planning effort. Marketing must get its direction from the organization's strategic plan.

■ **Figure A–4**
Components of
Industry Attractiveness
and Business Strength
at GE

Industry Attractiveness	Business Strength
Market Size	Market position
Market growth	Domestic market share
Profitability	World market share
Cyclicality	Share growth
Ability to recover from inflation	Share compared with leading competitor
World scope	
	Competitive strengths
	Quality leadership
	Technology
	Marketing
	Relative profitability

Part B

Marketing Information, Research, and Understanding the Target Market

Chapter Two

Marketing Research: Process and Systems for Decision Making

Marketing managers require current, reliable, useful information to make effective decisions. In today's highly competitive global economy, marketers need to exploit opportunities and avoid mistakes if they are to survive and be profitable. Not only is sound marketing research needed but also a system that gets current, valid information to the marketing decision maker in a timely manner.

This chapter is concerned with the marketing research process and information systems for decision making. It begins by discussing the marketing research process that is used to develop useful information for decision making. Then, marketing information systems are briefly discussed. The chapter is intended to provide a detailed introduction to many of the important topics in the area, but it does not provide a complete explanation of the plethora of marketing research topics.

The Role of Marketing Research

Marketing research is the process by which information about the environment is generated, analyzed, and interpreted for use in marketing decision making.[1] It cannot be overstated that *marketing research is an aid to decision making and not a substitute for it*. In other words, marketing research does not make decisions, but it can substantially increase the chances that good decisions are made. Unfortunately, too many marketing managers view research reports as the final answer to their problems; whatever the research indicates is taken as the appropriate course of action. Instead, marketing managers should recognize that (1) even the most carefully executed research can be fraught with errors; (2) marketing research does not forecast with certainty what will happen in the future; and (3) they should make decisions in light of their own knowledge and experience as no marketing research study includes all of the factors that could influence the success of a strategy.

Although marketing research does not make decisions, it can reduce the risks associated with managing marketing strategies. For example, it can reduce the risk of introducing new products by evaluating consumer acceptance of them prior to full-scale introduction. Marketing research is also vital for investigating the effects of various marketing strategies after they have been implemented. For example, marketing research can examine the effects of a change in any element of the marketing mix on customer perceptions and behavior.

At one time, marketing researchers were primarily engaged in the technical aspects of research but were not heavily involved in the strategic use of research findings. Today, however, many marketing researchers work hand-in-hand with marketing managers throughout the research process and have responsibility for making strategic recommendations based on the research.

■ The Marketing Research Process

Marketing research can be viewed as systematic processes for obtaining information to aid in decision making. There are many types of marketing research, and the framework illustrated in Figure 2–1 represents a general approach to the process. Each element of this process is discussed next.

■ **Figure 2–1**
The Five Ps of the
Research Process

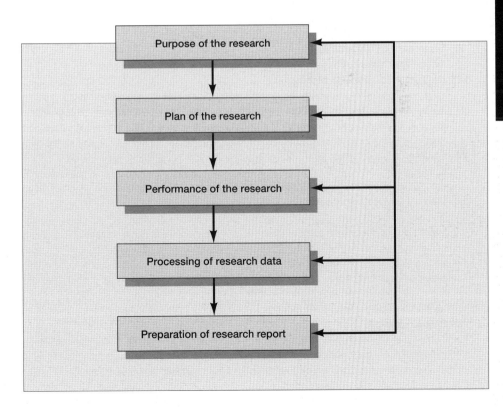

Purpose of the Research

The first step in the research process is to determine explicitly why the research is needed and what it is to accomplish. This may be much more difficult than it sounds. Quite often a situation or problem is recognized as needing research, yet the nature of the problem is not clear or well defined nor is the appropriate type of research evident. Thus, managers and researchers need to discuss and clarify the current situation and develop a clear understanding of the problem. At the end of this stage, managers and researchers should agree on (1) the current situation involving the problem to be researched; (2) the nature of the problem; and (3) the specific question or questions the research is designed to investigate. This step is crucial since it influences the type of research to be conducted and the research design.

Plan of the Research

Once the specific research question or questions have been agreed upon, a research plan can be developed. A research plan spells out the nature of the research to be conducted and includes an explanation of such things as the sample design, measures, and analysis techniques to be used. Figure 2–2 presents a sample research plan. Three critical issues that influence the research plan are (1) whether primary or secondary data are needed; (2) whether qualitative or quantitative research is needed; and (3) whether the company will do its own research or contract with a marketing research specialist.

■ **Figure 2–2** Sample Sections of a Research Plan

   I. **Tentative projective title**
  II. **Statement of the problem**
      One or two sentences describing the general problem under consideration.
 III. **Define and delimit the problem**
      Here the writer states the purpose(s) and scope of the problem. *Purpose* refers to goals or objectives. Closely related to this is *justification.* Sometimes this is a separate step, depending on the urgency of the task. *Scope* refers to the limits of the research effort; in other words, what *is* and *is not* going to be investigated. Here is the point where the researcher spells out the various hypotheses to be investigated or the questions to be answered.
  IV. **Outline**
      Generally, this is a tentative framework for the entire project. It should be flexible enough to accommodate unforeseen difficulties, show statistical tables in outline form, and also show planned graphs.
   V. **Method and data sources**
      The types of data to be sought (primary, secondary) are briefly identified. A brief explanation of how the necessary information or data will be gathered (e.g., surveys, experiments, library sources) is given. *Sources* refer to the actual depositories for the information, whether from government publications, company records, actual people, and so forth. If measurements are involved, such as consumers' attitudes, the techniques for making such measurements are stated. The relevance of all techniques (qualitative and quantitative) should be discussed. The nature of the problem will probably indicate the types of techniques to be employed, such as factor analysis, depth interviews, or focus groups.
  VI. **Sample design**
      This provides a description of the population to be studied and how it will be defined. The researcher specifies the population, states the desired sample size, and discusses how nonresponse and missing data are to be handled. If a nonrandom sample is to be used, the justification and type of sampling strategy to be employed, such as convenience sample, are stated.

(continued)

■ **Figure 2–2** Sample Sections of a Research Plan (*concluded*)

VII. Data collection forms

The forms to be employed in gathering the data are discussed here. For surveys, this involves either a questionnaire or an interview schedule. For other research, the forms could include inventory forms, psychological tests, and so forth. The plan should state how these instruments have been or will be validated, and the reader should be given any evidence of their reliability and validity.

VIII. Personnel requirements

This provides a complete list of all personnel who will be required, indicating exact jobs, time duration, and expected rate of pay. Assignments should be made indicating each person's responsibility and authority.

IX. Phases of the study with a time schedule

This is a detailed outline of the plan to complete the study. The study should be divided into workable pieces. Then, considering the persons involved in each phase, their qualifications and experience, and so forth, the time for the job is estimated. Some jobs may overlap. This plan will help in estimating the time required.

    Illustration:

A. Preliminary investigation—two weeks.

B. Final test of questionnaire—one week.

C. Sample selection—one week.

D. Mail questionnaires, field follow-up, and so forth—two months.

E. Additional tasks.

X. Analysis plans

This is a discussion of editing and proofreading of questionnaires, coding instructions, and the type of data analysis. An outline of some of the major tables that will appear in the report should be presented.

XI. Cost estimate for doing the study

Personnel requirements are combined with time on different phases to estimate total personnel costs. Estimates on travel, materials, supplies, drafting, computer charges, and printing and mailing costs must also be included. If an overhead charge is required, it should be calculated and added to the subtotal of the above items.

Primary versus Secondary Data. Given the information needed and budget constraints, a decision must be made as to whether primary data, secondary data, or some combination of the two are needed. *Primary data* are data collected specifically for the research problem under investigation; *secondary data* are those that have previously been collected for other purposes but can be used for the problem at hand. For example, if a company wanted to know why users of a competitive brand didn't prefer its brand, it may have to collect primary data to find out. On the other hand, if a company wanted to know the population size of key global markets that it might enter, it could find this information from secondary sources. Secondary information has the advantage of usually being cheaper than primary data, although it is not always available for strategy-specific research questions.

There are many sources of secondary data for use in marketing research. Research services such as A. C. Nielsen Co, Arbitron Co., IMS International, and Information Resources, Inc., sell a variety of useful data to companies. Business and industry publications such as the *Million Dollar Directory* or the *Encyclopedia of Associations* provide useful information for decision making, as do government reports such as *Statistical Abstracts of the United States* or the *Survey of Current Business.* Trade groups such as the American Medical Association or the National Association of Retail Dealers of America can also be contacted for information relevant to their industries.[2]

Qualitative versus Quantitative Research. Given a research question, a decision must be made whether qualitative or quantitative research would be a better approach. Qualitative research typically involves face-to-face interviews with respondents designed to develop a better understanding of what they think and feel concerning a research topic, such as a brand name, a product, a package, or an advertisement. The two most common types of qualitative research in marketing are focus groups and long interviews. *Focus groups* involve discussions among a small number of individuals led by an interviewer; they are designed to generate insights and ideas. *Long interviews* are conducted by an interviewer with a single respondent for several hours. They are designed to find out such things as the meanings various products or brands have for an individual or how a product influences a person's life.

Quantitative research involves more systematic procedures designed to obtain and analyze numerical data. Four common types of quantitative research in marketing are observation, surveys, experiments, and mathematical modeling.

Observational research involves watching people and recording relevant facts and behaviors. For example, retail stores may use observational research to determine what patterns customers use in walking through stores, how much time they spend in various parts of the store, and how many items of merchandise they examine. This information can be used to design store layouts more effectively. Similarly, many retail marketers do traffic counts at various intersections to help determine the best locations for stores.

Survey research involves the collection of data by means of a questionnaire either by mail, phone, or in person. Surveys are commonly used in marketing research to investigate customer beliefs, attitudes, satisfaction, and many other issues. Mail surveys are useful for reaching widely dispersed markets but take more time to get responses than telephone surveys; personal surveys involving structured questions are useful but expensive.

Experimental research involves manipulating one variable and examining its impact on other variables. For example, the price of a product in one test store could be changed while left the same in other stores. By comparing sales in the test store with those in other stores, evidence can be obtained about the likely impact of a price change in the overall market. Experiments are useful for getting a better idea of the causal relationships among variables, but they are often difficult to design and administer effectively in natural settings. Thus, many marketing research experiments are conducted in laboratories or simulated stores to carefully control other variables that could impact results.

Mathematical modeling research often involves secondary data, such as scanner data collected and stored in computer files from retail checkout counters. This approach involves the development of equations to model relationships among variables and uses econometric and statistical techniques to investigate the impact of various strategies and tactics on sales and brand choices. Math modeling is useful because it provides an efficient way to study problems with extremely large secondary data sets.

Choosing which of these types of research is best for particular research questions requires considerable knowledge of each of them. Often, qualitative research is used in early stages of investigating a topic to get more information and insight about it. Then, quantitative approaches are used to investigate the degree to which the insights hold across a larger sample or population.

Company versus Contract Research.　　Most large consumer goods companies have marketing research departments that can perform a variety of types of research. However, there are many marketing research firms, advertising agencies, and consulting companies that do marketing research on a contract basis. Some marketing research suppliers have special expertise in a particular type of research that makes them a better choice than doing the research internally. A decision has to be made as to whether the marketing research department has the ability to do a particular type of research itself or whether all or part of the research should be contracted with a research supplier. In either case, schedules for task completion, the exact responsibilities of all involved parties, and cost need to be considered.

Performance of the Research

Performance of the research involves preparing for data collection and actually collecting them. The tasks at this stage obviously depend on the type of research that has been selected and the type of data needed. If secondary data are to be used, they must be located, prepared for analysis, and possibly paid for. If primary data are to be collected, then observational forms, questionnaires, or other types of measures must be designed, pretested, and validated. Samples must be drawn and interviews must be scheduled or preparations must be made for mailing or phoning selected individuals.

In terms of actual data collection, a cardinal rule is to obtain and record the maximal amount of useful information, subject to the constraints of time, money, and respondent privacy. Failure to obtain and record data clearly can obviously lead to a poor research study, while failure to consider the rights of respondents raises both practical and ethical problems. Thus, both the objectives and constraints of data collection must be closely monitored.

Marketing
Highlight 2–2

Types of Questions that Marketing Research Can Help Answer

I. **Planning**
- A. What types of people buy our product? Where do they live? How much do they earn? How many of them are there?
- B. Is the market for our product increasing or decreasing? Are there promising markets that we have not yet reached?
- C. Are there markets for our products in other countries?

II. **Problem solving**
- A. Product
  1. Which, of various product designs, is likely to be the most successful?
  2. What kind of packaging should we use?
- B. Price
  1. What prices should we charge for our products?
  2. As production costs decline, should we lower our prices or try to develop a higher-quality product?

C. Place
  1. Where, and by whom, should our product be sold?
  2. What kinds of incentives should we offer to induce the trade to push our product?

D. Promotion
  1. How effective is our advertising? Are the right people seeing it? How does it compare with the competition's advertising?
  2. What kinds of sales promotional devices—coupons, contests, rebates, and so forth—should we employ?
  3. What combination of media—newspapers, radio, television, magazines and Internet—should we use?

III. **Control**
- A. What is our market share overall? In each geographic area? By each customer type?
- B. Are customers satisfied with our product? How is our record for service? Are there many returns?
- C. How does the public perceive our company? What is our reputation with the trade?

SOURCE: Table from Gilbert A. Churchill, Jr., *Marketing Research: Methodological Foundations,* 7th ed. © 1999, Fort Worth, TX, Dryden Press. Reproduced by permission of the publisher.

Processing Research Data

Processing research data includes the preparation of data for analysis and the actual analysis of them. Preparations include such things as editing and structuring data and coding and preparing them for analysis. Data sets should be clearly labeled to ensure they are not misinterpreted or misplaced.

The appropriate analysis techniques for collected data depend on the nature of the research question and the design of the research. Qualitative research data consist of interview records that are content analyzed for ideas or themes. Quantitative research data may be analyzed in a variety of ways depending on the objectives of the research. Figure 2–3 lists a number of data analysis methods used in marketing research.

A critical part of this stage is interpreting and assessing the research results. Seldom, if ever, do marketing research studies obtain findings that are totally unambiguous. Usually, relationships among variables or differences between groups are small to moderate, and judgment and insight are needed to draw appropriate inferences and conclusions. Marketing researchers should always double-check their analysis and avoid overstating the strength of their findings. The implications for developing or changing a marketing strategy should be carefully thought out and tempered with judgment about the overall quality of the study.

■ **Figure 2–3** Some Statistical Techniques Used in Marketing Research

Marketing researchers use many statistical techniques to analyze data and obtain insights for strategy. In many cases, researchers are interested in investigating the impact of one or more variables (called *independent variables* or *predictor variables*) on another variable (called the *dependent variable* or *criterion variable*). In other types of marketing research, the goals are to investigate differences between groups of consumers on various measures or to group variables or people into smaller sets. Below are brief descriptions of a number of statistical techniques used in the field. More information on these techniques can be found in the texts listed in the Additional Readings for this chapter.

Analysis of variance (ANOVA). A statistical procedure for examining whether different samples came from populations with equal means. This procedure is commonly used to compare the average or mean scores for different groups in experiments to determine the impact of a particular variable.

Conjoint analysis. A statistical technique in which respondents' valuations of attributes are inferred from the preferences they express for various combinations of these attributes. This technique is commonly used to determine the most important attributes to build into new products or to enhance in existing products.

Cluster analysis. A body of statistical techniques concerned with developing empirical groupings of objects based on a set of measures. These techniques are used in market segmentation to form groups of similar people that could be treated as target markets.

Correlation analysis. A statistical technique that determines the linear relationship between two variables. Correlations range from $+1.0$, for a perfect positive linear relationship, to 0.0, no linear relationship, to -1.0, a perfect negative linear relationship.

Cross tabulation. A technique that involves counting the number of cases (usually people) that fall into each of several categories when the categories are based on two or more variables considered at the same time. For example, a cross tabulation may compare the number of cars owned in different income groups to investigate the effects of income on car ownership.

Discriminant analysis. A statistical technique used to model the relationships between a criterion and a set of predictor variables. The criterion variable is a category (such as buyers and nonbuyers) in this procedure.

Factor analysis. A body of statistical techniques concerned with the study of interrelationships among a set of variables. It is commonly used to reduce a large set of variables into a smaller set of factors that can be meaningfully interpreted.

Multidimensional scaling. An approach in which people's perceptions of the similarity of objects and their preferences among them are measured and plotted in a multidimensional space.

Regression analysis. A statistical technique used to derive an equation that relates a single criterion variable to one or more predictor variables. It is commonly used in many types of marketing research that investigate the impact of various strategic elements on such things as sales, profits, overall customer satisfaction, and purchase intentions.

SOURCES: Based on definitions in Gilbert A. Churchill, Jr., *Marketing Research: Methodological Foundations,* 7th ed. (Fort Worth, TX: Dryden Press, 1999); and Peter D. Bennett, ed., *Dictionary of Marketing Terms,* 2nd ed. (Chicago: American Marketing Association, 1995).

Preparation of Research Report

The research report is a complete statement of everything done in a research project and includes a write-up of each of the previous stages as well as the strategic recommendations from the research. The limitations of the research should be carefully noted. Figure 2–4 illustrates the types of questions marketing researchers and managers should discuss prior to submitting the final research report.

■ **Figure 2–4**
Eight Criteria for
Evaluating Marketing
Research Reports

1. Was the type of research appropriate for the research questions?
2. Was the research well designed?
   a. Was the sample studied appropriate for the research questions?
   b. Were measures well developed, pretested, and validated?
   c. Were the data analysis techniques the best ones for the study?
3. Was there adequate supervision of data collection, editing, and coding?
4. Was the analysis conducted according to standards accepted in the field?
5. Do the findings make sense given the research question and design, and were they considered in light of previous knowledge and experience?
6. Are the limitations of the study recognized and explained in detail?
7. Are the conclusions appropriately drawn or are they over- or understated?
8. Are the recommendations for marketing strategy clear and appropriate?

Research reports should be clear and unambiguous with respect to what was done and what recommendations are made. Often research reports must trade off the apparent precision of scientific jargon for everyday language that managers can understand. Researchers should work closely with managers to ensure that the study and its limitations are fully understood.

Limitations of the Research Process

Although the foregoing discussion presented the research process as a set of simple stages, this does not mean that conducting quality marketing research is a simple task. There are many problems and difficulties that must be overcome if a research study is to provide valuable information for decision making.[3] For example, consider the difficulties in one type of marketing research, *test marketing.*

The major goal of most test marketing is to measure new product sales on a limited basis where competitive retaliation and other factors are allowed to operate freely. In this way, future sales potential can often be estimated reasonably well. Listed below are a number of problems that could invalidate test marketing study results.

1. Test market areas are not representative of the market in general in terms of population characteristics, competition, and distribution outlets.
2. Sample size and design are incorrectly formulated because of budget constraints.
3. Pretest measurements of competitive brand sales are not made or are inaccurate, limiting the meaningfulness of market share estimates.
4. Test stores do not give complete support to the study such that certain package sizes may not be carried or prices may not be held constant during the test period.
5. Test market products are advertised or promoted beyond a profitable level for the market in general.
6. The effects of factors that influence sales, such as the sales force, season, weather conditions, competitive retaliation, shelf space, and so forth, are ignored in the research.
7. The test market period is too short to determine whether the product will be repurchased by customers.

Marketing
Highlight 2–3

Ethical Responsibilities of Marketing Researchers

Marketing researchers have ethical responsibilities to the respondents who provide them primary data, clients for whom they work, and subordinates who work under them. Below are a number of ethical responsibilities to these groups.

Responsibilities to Respondents

1. *Preserving respondent anonymity.* Marketing researchers should ensure that respondents' identities are safe from invasion of privacy.
2. *Avoiding mental stress for respondents.* Marketing researchers should minimize the mental stress placed on respondents.
3. *Avoiding questions detrimental to respondents.* Marketing researchers should avoid asking questions for which the answers conflict with the self-interest of the respondents.
4. *Avoiding the use of dangerous equipment or techniques.* Physical or reputational harm to respondents based on their participation in marketing research should not occur. Respondents should be informed of any other than minimal risks involved in the research and be free to self-determine their participation.
5. *Avoiding deception of respondents.* Respondents should not be deceived about the purpose of the study in most cases. Many consider deception acceptable in research where it is needed to obtain valid results, there is minimal risk to respondents,

and respondents are debriefed explaining the real purpose of the study.
6. *Avoiding coercion of respondents.* Marketing researchers should avoid coercing or harassing people to try to get them to agree to be interviewed or fill out questionnaires.

Responsibilities to Clients

1. *Providing confidentiality.* Marketing researchers are obliged not to reveal information about a client to competitors and should carefully consider when a company should be identified as a client.
2. *Providing technical integrity.* Marketing researchers are obliged to design efficient studies without undue expense or complexity and accurately report results.
3. *Providing administrative integrity.* Marketing researchers are obliged to price their work fairly without hidden charges.
4. *Providing guidance on research usage.* Marketing researchers are obliged to promote the correct usage of research and to prevent the misuse of findings.

Responsibilities to Subordinate Employees

1. *Creating an ethical work environment.* Marketing research managers are obliged to create an ethical work environment where unethical behavior is not encouraged or overlooked.
2. *Avoiding opportunities for unethical behavior.* Marketing research managers are obliged to avoid placing subordinates in situations where unethical behavior could be concealed but rewarded.

SOURCE: Based on Gilbert A. Churchill, Jr., *Marketing Research: Methodological Foundations,* 7th ed. (Fort Worth, TX: Dryden Press, 1999), Appendix 2A.

A list of such problems could be developed for any type of marketing research. However, careful research planning, coordination, implementation, and control can help reduce such problems and increase the value of research for decision making.

■ Marketing Information Systems

Most marketers use computer-based systems to help them gather, sort, store, and distribute information for marketing decisions.[4] A popular form of marketing information system is the marketing decision support system, which is a coordinated collection of data, tools, and techniques involving both computer hardware and software by which marketers gather and interpret relevant information for decision making. These systems require three types of software:

1. Database management software for sorting and retrieving data from internal and external sources.
2. Model base management software that contains routines for manipulating data in ways that are useful for marketing decision making.
3. A dialog system that permits marketers to explore databases and use models to produce information to address their decision-making needs.

Marketing decision support systems are designed to handle information from both internal and external sources. Internal information includes such things as sales records, which can be divided by territory, package size, brand, price, order size, or salesperson; inventory data that can indicate how rapidly various products are selling; or expenditure data on such things as advertising, personal selling, or packaging. Internal information is particularly important for investigating the efficiency and effectiveness of various marketing strategies.

External information is gathered from outside the organization and concerns changes in the environment that could influence marketing strategies. External information is needed concerning changes in global economies and societies,

■ **Figure 2–5** Global Information Sources for Marketing Information Systems

Information Source	Types of Data
The Export Connection, a National Trade Databank service of the U.S. Department of Commerce (Washington, DC)	Monthly series of CD-ROM disks containing data from 15 U.S. government agencies, including marketing research reports, information about specific countries and their economies, and a listing of foreign importers of U.S. products
Global Market Surveys	Detailed surveys for given industries such as graphics, computers, medical equipment, industrial equipment
Dun & Bradstreet's *Principal International Business*	Names, addresses, number of employees, products produced, and chief executive officer, up to 6 SIC classifications (4-digit) for each organization; over 144,000 business units classified by 4-digit SIC and alphabetical order
Moody's International Manual	Company histories, descriptions of business, financial statistics, management personnel
Overseas Business Reports	Monthly reports provide information for marketing to specific countries (e.g., "Marketing in Pakistan," "Marketing in Nigeria")
The Exporter's Guide to Federal Resources for Small Business (Washington, DC: U.S. Government Printing Office)	Reference guide to export assistance available from the U.S. government
Automated Trade Locator Assistance System (district offices of the Small Business Administration)	Results of current marketing research about world markets
Small Business Foundation of America, export opportunity hotline: 800-243-7232	Answers to questions from small businesses interested in exporting
Hotline sponsored by AT&T and seven other organizations: 800-USA-XPORT	Free exporter's kit and data on 50 industries and 78 countries
International trade fairs (sponsored by many industry organizations and national governments, including the U.S. Small Business Administration)	Products and needs of existing and potential buyers and competitors from around the world

SOURCE: Gilbert A. Churchill, Jr., and J. Paul Peter, *Marketing: Creating Value for Customers,* 2nd ed. (Burr Ridge, IL: Irwin/McGraw-Hill, 1998), p. 135.

competitors, customers, and technology. Figure 2–5 lists a sample of sources of external information that could help global marketers make better decisions. Of course, information from marketing research studies conducted by an organization is also put into marketing information systems to improve marketing strategy development.

■ Conclusion

This chapter emphasized the importance of marketing research for making sound marketing strategy decisions. The chapter discussed marketing research as a process involving several stages, which include determining the purpose of the research, designing the plan for the research, performing the research, processing research data, and preparing the research report. Then, marketing information systems were discussed and one type, the marketing decision support system, was explained. Such systems provide decision makers with the right information, at the right time, in the right way, to make sound marketing decisions.

■ Additional Readings

Aaker, David A.; V. Kumar; and George S. Day. *Marketing Research.* 6th ed. New York: Wiley, 1998.

Burns, Alvin C., and Ronald F. Bush. *Marketing Research.* 2nd ed. Englewood Cliffs, NJ: Prentice Hall, 1998.

Churchill, Gilbert A., Jr. *Basic Marketing Research.* 3rd ed. Ft. Worth, TX: Dryden Press, 1996.

———. *Marketing Research: Methodological Foundations.* 7th ed. Fort Worth, TX: Dryden Press, 1999.

Crask, Melvin; Richard J. Fox; and Roy G. Stout. *Marketing Research: Principles and Applications.* Englewood Cliffs, NJ: Prentice Hall, 1995.

Dillon, William R.; Thomas J. Madden; and Neil H. Firtle. *Marketing Research in a Marketing Environment.* 3rd ed. Burr Ridge, IL: Irwin, 1994.

Lehmann, Donald R.; Sunil Gupta; and Joel H. Steckel. *Marketing Research.* Reading, MA: Addison-Wesley, 1998.

Malhotra, Naresh K. *Marketing Research: An Applied Orientation.* Englewood Cliffs, NJ: Prentice Hall, 1993.

O'Brien, James A. *Management Information Systems.* Homewood, IL: Richard D. Irwin, 1993.

Sudman, Seymour, and Edward Blair. *Marketing Research: A Problem-Solving Approach.* Boston: Irwin/McGraw-Hill, 1998.

Zikmund, William G. *Exploring Marketing Research.* 6th ed. Fort Worth, TX: Dryden Press, 1997.

Chapter Three

Consumer Behavior

The marketing concept emphasizes that profitable marketing begins with the discovery and understanding of consumer needs and then develops a marketing mix to satisfy these needs. Thus, an understanding of consumers and their needs and purchasing behavior is integral to successful marketing.

Unfortunately, there is no single theory of consumer behavior that can totally explain why consumers behave as they do. Instead, there are numerous theories, models, and concepts making up the field. In addition, the majority of these notions have been borrowed from a variety of other disciplines, such as sociology, psychology, anthropology, and economics, and must be integrated to understand consumer behavior.

In this chapter, some of the many influences on consumer behavior will be examined in terms of consumer decision making. The reader may wish to examine Figure 3–1 closely, since it provides the basis for this discussion.

The chapter will proceed by first examining consumer decision making and then discussing the social, marketing, and situational influences on this process.

■ Consumer Decision Making

The process by which consumers recognize a need for a product, search for information about alternatives to meet the need, evaluate the information, make purchases, and evaluate the decision after the purchase can be viewed as consumer decision making. In general, there are three types of decision making, which vary in terms of how complex or expensive a product is and how involved a consumer is in purchasing it.

Extensive decision making requires the most time and effort since the purchase involves a highly complex or expensive product that is important to the consumer.

■ **Figure 3–1** An Overview of the Buying Process

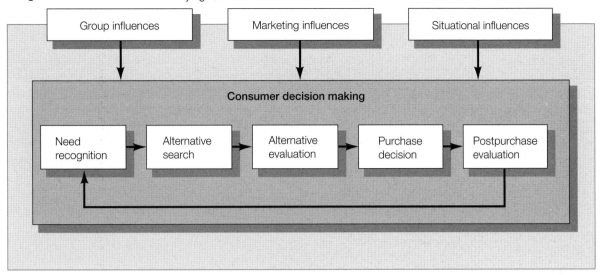

For example, the purchase of a car, house, or computer often involves considerable time and effort comparing alternatives and deciding on the right one. In terms of the number of purchases a consumer makes, extensive decision making is relatively rare, but it is critical for marketers of highly complex or expensive products to understand that consumers are willing to process considerable information to make the best choice. Thus, marketers should provide consumer factual information that highlights competitive advantages for such high-involvement products.

Limited decision making is more moderate but still involves some time and effort searching for and comparing alternatives. For example, when buying shirts or shorts, consumers may shop several stores and compare a number of different brands and styles. Marketers of products for which consumers usually do limited decision making often use eye-catching advertising and in-store displays to make consumers aware of their products and encourage consumers to consider buying them.

Routine decision making is the most common type and the way consumers purchase most packaged goods. Such products are simple, inexpensive, and familiar, and consumers often have developed favorite brands that they purchase without much deliberation. For example, consumers often make habitual purchases of soft drinks, candy bars, or canned soup without carefully comparing the relative merits of different brands. Marketers of such products need to have them readily available for purchase in a variety of outlets and price them competitively if price is an important criterion to consumers. Marketers of these low-involvement products often use celebrity spokespeople and other non-product-related cues to encourage purchases.

Need Recognition

The starting point in the buying process is the recognition of an unsatisfied need by the consumer. Any number of either internal or external stimuli may activate needs or wants and recognition of them. Internal stimuli are such things as feeling hungry and wanting some food, feeling a headache coming on and wanting some Excedrin, or feeling bored and looking for a movie to go to. External stimuli are such things as seeing a McDonald's sign and then feeling hungry or seeing a sale sign for winter parkas and remembering that last year's coat is worn out.

It is the task of marketing managers to find out what needs and wants a particular product can and does satisfy and what unsatisfied needs and wants consumers have for which a new product could be developed. In order to do so, marketing managers should understand what types of needs consumers may have. A well-known classification of needs was developed many years ago by Abraham Maslow and includes five types.[1] Maslow's view is that lower-level needs, starting with physiological and safety, must be attended to before higher-level needs can be satisfied. Maslow's hierarchy is described below.

> *Physiological needs.* This category consists of the primary needs of the human body, such as food, water, and sex. Physiological needs will dominate when all needs are unsatisfied. In such a case, none of the other needs will serve as a basis for motivation.
> *Safety needs.* With the physiological needs met, the next higher level assumes importance. Safety needs consist of such things as protection from physical harm, ill health, economic disaster, and avoidance of the unexpected.
> *Belongingness and love needs.* These needs are related to the social and gregarious nature of humans and the need for companionship. This level in the hierarchy is the point of departure from the physical or quasi-physical needs of the two previous levels. Nonsatisfaction of this level of need may affect the mental health of the individual.
> *Esteem needs.* These needs consist of both the need for the self-awareness of importance to others (self-esteem) and actual esteem from others. Satisfaction of these needs leads to feelings of self-confidence and prestige.
> *Self-actualization needs.* This need can be defined as the desire to become more and more what one is, to become everything one is capable of becoming. This means that the individual will fully realize the potentialities of given talents and capabilities. Maslow assumes that satisfaction of these needs is only possible after the satisfaction of all the needs lower in the hierarchy.

While the hierarchy arrangement of Maslow presents a convenient explanation, it is probably more realistic to assume that the various need categories overlap. Thus, in affluent societies, many products may satisfy more than one of these needs. For example, gourmet foods may satisfy both the basic physiological need of hunger as well as esteem and status needs for those who serve gourmet foods to their guests.

Alternative Search

Once a need is recognized, the individual then searches for alternatives for satisfying the need. There are five basic sources from which the individual can collect information for a particular purchase decision.

1. *Internal sources.* In most cases the individual has had some previous experience in dealing with a particular need. Thus, the individual will usually "search" through whatever stored information and experience is in his or her mind for dealing with the need. If a previously acceptable product for satisfying the need is remembered, the individual may purchase with little or no additional information search or evaluation. This is quite common for routine or habitual purchases.

Marketing
Highlight 3–1

Ethical Conduct toward Customers

The marketing profession has long recognized the need to uphold its integrity, honor, and dignity. Part of this obligation is to treat customers fairly and honestly. In the American Marketing Association Code of Ethics, a number of issues are concerned with this obligation. Below is a list of some of the Code of Ethics responsibilities that bear directly or indirectly on exchanges with consumers and organizational buyers.

Product Development and Management Area

Products and services offered should be safe and fit for their intended use.

All substantial risks associated with product or service usage should be disclosed.

Product component substitutions that might materially change the product or impact the buyer's decision should be disclosed.

Extra-cost added features should be identified.

Promotion Area

Communication about offered products and services should not be deceptive.

False and misleading advertising should be avoided.

High-pressure manipulation or misleading sales tactics should be avoided.

Sales promotions that use deception or manipulation should be avoided.

Distribution Area

The availability of a product should not be manipulated for the purpose of exploitation.

Coercion in the marketing channel should not be used.

Undue influence over the resellers' choice to handle products should be avoided.

Pricing Area

Price fixing should not be practiced.

Predatory pricing should not be practiced.

The full price associated with any purchase should be disclosed.

SOURCE: Adapted from the American Marketing Association Code of Ethics.

2. *Group sources.* A common source of information for purchase decisions comes from communication with other people, such as family, friends, neighbors, and acquaintances. Generally, some of these (i.e., relevant others) are selected that the individual views as having particular expertise for the purchase decision. Although it may be quite difficult for the marketing manager to determine the exact nature of this source of information, group sources of information often are considered to be the most powerful influence on purchase decisions.

3. *Marketing sources.* Marketing sources of information include such factors as advertising, salespeople, dealers, packaging, and displays. Generally, this is the primary source of information about a particular product. These sources of information will be discussed in detail in the promotion chapters of this text.

4. *Public sources.* Public sources of information include publicity, such as a newspaper article about the product, and independent ratings of the product, such as *Consumer Reports.* Here product quality is a highly important marketing management consideration, since such articles and reports often discuss such features as dependability and service requirements.

5. *Experiential sources.* Experiential sources refer to handling, examining, and perhaps trying the product while shopping. This usually requires an actual shopping trip by the individual and may be the final source consulted before purchase.

Information collected from these sources is then processed by the consumer.[2] However, the exact nature of how individuals process information to form evaluations of products is not fully understood. In general, information processing is viewed as a four-step process in which the individual is (1) exposed to information; (2) becomes attentive to the information; (3) understands the information; and (4) retains the information.[3]

Alternative Evaluation

During the process of collecting information or, in some cases, after information is acquired, the consumer evaluates alternatives on the basis of what he or she has learned. One approach to describing the evaluation process can be found in the logic of attitude modeling.[4] The basic logic can be described as follows:

1. The consumer has information about a number of brands in a product class.
2. The consumer perceives that at least some of the brands in a product class are viable alternatives for satisfying a recognized need.
3. Each of these brands has a set of attributes (color, quality, size, and so forth).
4. A set of these attributes is relevant to the consumer, and the consumer perceives that different brands vary in how much of each attribute they possess.
5. The brand that is perceived as offering the greatest number of desired attributes in the desired amounts and desired order will be the brand the consumer will like best.
6. The brand the consumer likes best is the brand the consumer will intend to purchase.

Purchase Decision

If no other factors intervene after the consumer has decided on the brand that is intended for purchase, the actual purchase is a common result of search and evaluation. Actually, a purchase involves many decisions, which include product type, brand, model, dealer selection, and method of payment, among other factors. In addition, rather than purchasing, the consumer may make a decision to modify, postpone, or avoid purchase based on an inhibitor to purchase or a perceived risk.

Traditional risk theorists believe that consumers tend to make risk-minimizing decisions based on their *perceived* definition of the particular purchase. The perception of risk is based upon the possible consequences and uncertainties involved. Consequences may range from economic loss, to embarrassment if a new food product does not turn out well, to actual physical harm. Perceived risk may be either functional (related to financial and performance considerations) or psychosocial (related to whether the product will further one's self- or reference group image). The amount of risk a consumer perceives in a particular product depends on such things as the price of the product and whether other people will see the individual using it.

The perceived risk literature emphasizes that consumers generally try to reduce risk in their decision making. This can be done by either reducing the possible negative consequences or by reducing the uncertainty. The possible consequences of a purchase might be minimized by purchasing in small quantities or by lowering the individual's aspiration level to expect less in the way of results from the product. However, this cannot always be done. Thus, reducing risk by attempting to increase the certainty of the purchase outcome may be the more widely used strategy. This can be done by seeking additional information regarding the proposed purchase. In general, the more information the consumer collects prior to purchase, the less likely postpurchase dissonance is to occur.

Marketing
Highlight 3–2

Factors Affecting Information Search by Consumers

Influencing Factor	Increasing the Influencing Factor Causes Search to:
I. Market characteristics	
A. Number of alternatives	Increase
B. Price range	Increase
C. Store concentration	Increase
D. Information availability	Increase
1. Advertising	
2. Point-of-purchase	
3. Sales personnel	
4. Packaging	
5. Experienced consumers	
6. Independent sources	
II. Product characteristics	
A. Price	Increase
B. Differentiation	Increase
C. Positive products	Increase
III. Consumer characteristics	
A. Learning and experience	Decrease
B. Shopping orientation	Mixed
C. Social status	Increase
D. Age, gender, and household life cycle	Mixed
E. Perceived risk	Increase
IV. Situational characteristics	
A. Time availability	Increase
B. Purchase for self	Decrease
C. Pleasant surroundings	Increase
D. Social surroundings	Mixed
E. Physical/mental energy	Increase

SOURCE: Del I. Hawkins, Kenneth A. Coney, and Roger Best, Jr., *Consumer Behavior: Implications for Marketing Strategy,* 7th ed. (Burr Ridge, IL: Richard D. Irwin, 1998), p. 534.

Postpurchase Evaluation

In general, if the individual finds that a certain response achieves a desired goa
or satisfies a need, the success of this cue-response pattern will be remembered
The probability of responding in a like manner to the same or similar situation
in the future is increased. In other words, the response has a higher probability
of being repeated when the need and cue appear together again, and thus i
can be said that learning has taken place. Frequent reinforcement increases
the habit potential of the particular response. Likewise, if a response does no
satisfy the need adequately, the probability that the same response will be re
peated is reduced.

For some marketers this means that if an individual finds a particular product fulfills the need for which it was purchased, the probability is high that the individual will repurchase the product the next time the need arises. The firm's promotional efforts often act as the cue. If an individual repeatedly purchases a product with favorable results, loyalty may develop toward the particular product or brand. This loyalty can result in habitual purchases, and such habits are often extremely difficult for competing firms to alter.

Although many studies in the area of buyer behavior center on the buyer's attitudes, motives, and behavior before and during the purchase decision, emphasis has also been given to study of behavior after the purchase. Specifically, studies have been undertaken to investigate postpurchase dissonance, as well as postpurchase satisfaction.

The occurrence of postdecision dissonance is related to the concept of *cognitive dissonance.* This theory states that there is often a lack of consistency or harmony among an individual's various cognitions, or attitudes and beliefs, after a decision has been made—that is, the individual has doubts and second thoughts about the choice made. Further, it is more likely that the intensity of the anxiety will be greater when any of the following conditions exist:

1. The decision is an important one psychologically or financially, or both.
2. There are a number of forgone alternatives.
3. The forgone alternatives have many favorable features.

These factors can relate to many buying decisions. For example, postpurchase dissonance might be expected to be present among many purchasers of such products as automobiles, major appliances, and homes. In these cases, the decision to purchase is usually an important one both financially and psychologically, and there are usually a number of favorable alternatives available.

These findings have much relevance for marketers. In a buying situation, when a purchaser becomes dissonant it is reasonable to predict such a person would be highly receptive to advertising and sales promotion that support the purchase decision. Such communication presents favorable aspects of the product and can be useful in reinforcing the buyer's wish to believe that a wise purchase decision was made. For example, purchasers of major appliances or automobiles might be given a phone call or sent a letter reassuring them that they have made a wise purchase.

As noted, researchers have also studied postpurchase consumer satisfaction. Much of this work has been based on what is called the *disconfirmation paradigm.* Basically, this approach views satisfaction with products and brands as a result of two other variables. The first variable is the expectations a consumer has about a product before purchase. These expectations concern the beliefs the consumer has about the product's performance.

The second variable is the difference between expectations and postpurchase perceptions of how the product actually performed. If the product performed as well as expected or better than expected, the consumer will be satisfied with the product. If the product performed worse than expected, the consumer will be dissatisfied with it.

One implication of this view for marketers is that care must be taken not to raise prepurchase expectations to such a level that the product cannot possibly meet them. Rather, it is important to create positive expectations consistent with the product's likely performance.[5]

Marketing
Highlight 3–3

A Summary of American Cultural Values

Value	General Features	Relevance to Marketing
Achievement and success	Hard work is good; success flows from hard work	Acts as a justification for acquisition of success goods ("You deserve it")
Activity	Keeping busy is healthy and natural	Stimulates interest in products that are time-savers and enhance leisure-time activities
Efficiency and practicality	Admiration of things that solve problems (e.g., save time and effort)	Stimulates purchase of products that function well and save time
Progress	People can improve themselves; tomorrow should be better	Stimulates desire for new products that fulfill unsatisfied needs; acceptance of products that claim to be "new" or "improved"
Material comfort	"The good life"	Fosters acceptance of convenience and luxury products that make life more enjoyable
Individualism	Being one's self (e.g., self-reliance, self-interest, and self-esteem)	Stimulates acceptance of customized or unique products that enable a person to express his or her own personality
Freedom	Freedom of choice	Fosters interest in wide product lines and differentiated products
External conformity	Uniformity of observable behavior; desire to be accepted	Stimulates interest in products that are used or owned by others in the same social group
Humanitarianism	Caring for others, particularly the underdog	Stimulates patronage of firms that compete with market leaders
Youthfulness	A state of mind that stresses being young at heart or appearing young	Stimulates acceptance of products that provide the illusion of maintaining or fostering youth
Fitness and health	Caring about one's body, including the desire to be physically fit and healthy	Stimulates acceptance of food products, activities, and equipment perceived to maintain or increase physical fitness

SOURCE: Leon G. Schiffman and Leslie Lazar Kanuck, *Consumer Behavior*, 5th ed., p. 437 © 1994. Reprinted by permission of Prentice Hall, Inc., Upper Saddle River, NJ.

■ Social Influences on Consumer Behavior

Behavioral scientists have become increasingly aware of the powerful effects o the social environment and personal interactions on human behavior. In terms o consumer behavior, culture, social class, and reference group influences have been related to purchase and consumption decisions. It should be noted tha these influences can have both direct and indirect effects on the buying process By direct effects we mean direct communication between the individual and othe members of society concerning a particular decision. By indirect effects we mean the influence of society on an individual's basic values and attitudes as well as the important role that groups play in structuring an individual's personality.

Culture and Subculture

Culture is one of the most basic influences on an individual's needs, wants, and behavior, since all facets of life are carried out against the background of the society in which an individual lives. Cultural antecedents affect everyday behavior, and there is empirical support for the notion that culture is a determinant of certain aspects of consumer behavior.

Cultural values are transmitted through three basic organizations: the family, religious organizations, and educational institutions; and in today's society, educational institutions are playing an increasingly greater role in this regard. Marketing managers should adapt the marketing mix to cultural values and constantly monitor value changes and differences in both domestic and global markets. To illustrate, one of the changing values in America is the increasing emphasis on achievement and career success. This change in values has been recognized by many business firms that have expanded their emphasis on time-saving, convenience-oriented products.

In large nations such as the United States, the population is bound to lose a significant amount of its homogeneity, and thus subcultures arise. In other words, there are subcultures in the American culture where people have more frequent interactions than with the population at large and thus tend to think and act alike in some respects. Subcultures are based on such things as geographic areas, religions, nationalities, ethnic groups, and age. Many subcultural barriers are decreasing because of mass communication, mass transit, and a decline in the influence of religious values. However, age groups, such as the teen market, baby boomers, and the mature market, have become increasingly important for marketing strategy. For example, since baby boomers (those born between 1946 and 1962) make up about a third of the U.S. population and soon will account for about half of discretionary spending, many marketers are repositioning products to serve them. Snickers candy bars, for instance, used to be promoted to children as a treat but are now promoted to adults as a wholesome, between-meals snack.

Social Class

While many people like to think of America as a land of equality, a class structure can be observed. Social classes develop on the basis of such things as wealth, skill, and power. The single best indicator of social class is occupation. However, interest at this point is in the influence of social class on the individual's behavior. What is important here is that different social classes tend to have different attitudinal configurations and values, which influence the behavior of individual members. Figure 3–2 presents a social class hierarchy developed specifically for marketing analysis and describes some of these important differences in attitudes and values.

For the marketing manager, social class offers some insights into consumer behavior and is potentially useful as a market segmentation variable. However, there is considerable controversy as to whether social class is superior to income for the purpose of market segmentation.

Reference Groups and Families

Groups that an individual looks to (uses as a reference) when forming attitudes and opinions are described as reference groups.[6] Primary reference groups include family and close friends, while secondary reference groups include fraternal organizations and professional associations. A buyer may also consult a single individual about decisions, and this individual would be considered a reference individual.

A person normally has several reference groups or reference individuals for various subjects or different decisions. For example, a woman may consult one reference group when she is purchasing a car and a different reference group for lingerie. In other words, the nature of the product and the role the individual is

■ **Figure 3–2**
Social Class Groups
for Marketing Analysis

Upper Americans (14 percent of population). This group consists of the upper-upper, lower-upper, and upper-middle classes. They have common goals and are differentiated mainly by income. This group has many different lifestyles, which might be labeled post-preppy, conventional, intellectual, and political, among others. The class remains the segment of our society in which quality merchandise is most prized, special attention is paid to prestige brands, and the self-image is "spending with good taste." Self-expression is more prized than in previous generations, and neighborhood remains important. Depending on income and priorities, theater, books, investment in art, European travel, household help, club memberships for tennis, golf, and swimming, and prestige schooling for children remain high consumption priorities.

Middle class (32 percent of population). These consumers definitely want to "do the right thing" and buy "what's popular." They have always been concerned with fashion and following recommendations of "experts" in print media. Increased earnings result in better living, which means a "nicer neighborhood on the better side of town with good schools." It also means spending more on "worthwhile experiences" for children, including winter ski trips, college educations, and shopping for better brands of clothes at more expensive stores. Appearance of home is important, because guests may visit and pass judgment. This group emulates upper Americans, which distinguishes it from the working class. It also enjoys trips to Las Vegas and physical activity. Deferred gratification may still be an ideal, but it is not often practiced.

Working class (38 percent of population). Working-class Americans are "family folk" depending heavily on relatives for economic and emotional support (e.g., tips on job opportunities, advice on purchases, help in times of trouble). The emphasis on family ties is only one sign of how much more limited and different working-class horizons are socially, psychologically, and geographically compared to those of the middle class. In almost every respect, a parochial view characterizes this blue-collar world. This group has changed little in values and behaviors in spite of rising incomes in some cases. For them, "keeping up with the times" focuses on the mechanical and recreational, and thus, ease of labor and leisure is what they continue to pursue.

Lower Americans (16 percent of population). The men and women of lower America are no exception to the rule that diversities and uniformities in values and consumption goals are to be found at each social level. Some members of this world, as has been publicized, are prone to every form of instant gratification known to humankind when the money is available. But others are dedicated to resisting worldly temptations as they struggle toward what some believe will be a "heavenly reward" for their earthly sacrifices.

SOURCE: Richard P. Coleman, "The Continuing Significance of Social Class to Marketing," *Journal of Consumer Research,* December 1983, pp. 265–80. © 1983 by the University of Chicago Press. Reprinted with permission.

playing during the purchasing process influence which reference group will be consulted. Reference group influence is generally considered to be stronger for products that are "public" or conspicuous—that is, products that other people see the individual using, such as clothes or automobiles.

As noted, the family is generally recognized to be an important reference group, and it has been suggested that the household, rather than the individual, is the relevant unit for studying consumer behavior.[7] This is because within a household the purchaser of goods and services is not always the user of these goods and services. Thus, it is important for marketing managers to determine not only who makes the actual purchase but also who makes the decision to purchase. In addition, it has been recognized that the needs, income, assets, debts, and expenditure patterns change over the course of what is called the *family life cycle*. The family life cycle can be divided into a number of stages ranging from single, to married, to married with children of different age groups, to older couples, to solitary survivors. It may also include divorced people, both with and without children. Because the life cycle combines trends in earning power with demands placed on income, it is a useful way of classifying and segmenting individuals and families.[8]

■ Marketing Influences on Consumer Behavior

Marketing strategies are often designed to influence consumer decision making and lead to profitable exchanges. Each element of the marketing mix (product, price, promotion, place) can affect consumers in various ways.

Product Influences

Many attributes of a company's products, including brand name, quality, newness, and complexity, can affect consumer behavior. The physical appearance of the product, packaging, and labeling information can also influence whether consumers notice a product in-store, examine it, and purchase it. One of the key tasks of marketers is to differentiate their products from those of competitors and create consumer perceptions that the product is worth purchasing.

Price Influences

The price of products and services often influences whether consumers will purchase them at all and, if so, which competitive offering is selected. Stores, such as Wal-Mart, that are perceived to charge the lowest prices attract many consumers based on this fact alone. For some offerings, higher prices may not deter purchase because consumers believe that the products or services are higher quality or are more prestigious. However, many of today's value-conscious consumers may buy products more on the basis of price than other attributes.

Promotion Influences

Advertising, sales promotions, salespeople, and publicity can influence what consumers think about products, what emotions they experience in purchasing and using them, and what behaviors they perform, including shopping in particular stores and purchasing specific brands. Since consumers receive so much information from marketers and screen out a good deal of it, it is important for marketers to devise communications that (1) offer consistent messages about their products and (2) are placed in media that consumers in the target market are likely to use. Marketing communications play a critical role in informing consumers about products and services, where they can be purchased, and in creating favorable images and perceptions.

Place Influences

The marketer's strategy for distributing products can influence consumers in several ways. First, products that are convenient to buy in a variety of stores increase the chances of consumers finding and buying them. When consumers are seeking low-involvement products, they are unlikely to engage in extensive search, so ready availability is important. Second, products sold in exclusive outlets, such as Nordstrom, may be perceived by consumers as higher quality. In fact, one of the ways marketers create brand equity, that is, favorable consumer perceptions of brands, is by selling them in prestigious outlets. Third, offering products by nonstore methods, such as on the Internet or in catalogs, can create consumer perceptions that the products are innovative, exclusive, or tailored for specific target markets.

■ Situational Influences on Consumer Behavior

Situational influences can be defined as all those factors particular to a time and place of observation that have a demonstrable and systematic effect on current behavior. In terms of purchasing situations, five groups of situational influences have been identified.[9] These influences may be perceived either consciously or subconsciously and may have considerable effect on product and brand choice.

1. *Physical surroundings* are the most readily apparent features of a situation. These features include geographic and institutional location, decor, sounds, aromas, lighting, weather, and visible configurations of merchandise or other material surrounding the stimulus object.
2. *Social surroundings* provide additional depth to a description of a situation. Other persons present, their characteristics, their apparent roles and interpersonal interactions are potentially relevant examples.

55

3. *Temporal perspective* is a dimension of situations that may be specified in units ranging from time of day to season of the year. Time also may be measured relative to some past or future event for the situational participant. This allows such conceptions as time since last purchase, time since or until meals or paydays, and time constraints imposed by prior or standing commitments.

4. *Task definition* features of a situation include an intent or requirement to select, shop for, or obtain information about a general or specific purchase. In addition, task may reflect different buyer and user roles anticipated by the individual. For instance, a person shopping for a small appliance as a wedding gift for a friend is in a different situation than when shopping for a small appliance for personal use.

5. *Antecedent states* make up a final feature that characterizes a situation. These are momentary moods (such as acute anxiety, pleasantness, hostility, and excitation) or momentary conditions (such as cash on hand, fatigue, and illness) rather than chronic individual traits. These conditions are further stipulated to be immediately antecedent to the current situation to distinguish the states the individual brings to the situation from states of the individual resulting from the situation. For instance, people may select a certain motion picture because they feel depressed (an antecedent state and a part of the choice situation), but the fact that the movie causes them to feel happier is a response to the consumption situation. This altered state then may become antecedent for behavior in the next choice situation encountered, such as passing a street vendor on the way out of the theater.

■ Conclusion

This chapter presented an overview of consumer behavior. Consumer decision making, which can be extensive, limited, or routine, was viewed as a series of five stages: need recognition, alternative search, alternative evaluation, purchase decision, and postpurchase evaluation. This process is influenced by social, marketing, and situational factors. Clearly, understanding consumers is a prerequisite for developing successful marketing strategies.

■ Additional Readings

Assael, Henry. *Consumer Behavior and Marketing Action.* 6th ed. Cincinnati: South-Western College, 1998.

Engel, James F.; Roger D. Blackwell; and Paul W. Miniard. *Consumer Behavior.* 8th ed. Fort Worth, TX: Dryden Press, 1995.

Hawkins, Del; Kenneth A. Coney; and Roger Best, Jr. *Consumer Behavior: Building Marketing Strategy.* 7th ed. Burr Ridge, IL: Irwin/McGraw-Hill, 1998.

Hoyer, Wayne D., and Deborah J. MacInnis. *Consumer Behavior.* Boston: Houghton Mifflin, 1997.

Mowen, John C., and Michael Minor. *Consumer Behavior.* 5th ed. New York: Macmillan, 1998.

Onkvisit, Sak, and John J. Shaw. *Consumer Behavior: Strategy and Analysis.* New York: Macmillan, 1994.

Peter, J. Paul, and Jerry C. Olson. *Consumer Behavior and Marketing Strategy.* 5th ed. Burr Ridge, IL: Irwin/McGraw-Hill, 1999.

———— and ———— . *Understanding Consumer Behavior.* Burr Ridge, IL: Richard D. Irwin, 1994.

Schiffman, Leon G., and Leslie Kanuck. *Consumer Behavior.* 6th ed. Englewood Cliffs, NJ: Prentice Hall, 1997.

Solomon, Michael R. *Consumer Behavior.* 4th ed. Boston: Allyn & Bacon, 1999.

Wells, William D., and David Prensky. *Consumer Behavior.* New York: Wiley, 1996.

Appendix

Selected Consumer Behavior Data Sources

1. Demographic Information

U.S. Census of Population, www.census.gov.
Marketing Information Guide.
A Guide to Consumer Markets.
State and city government publications.
Media (newspapers, magazines, television, and radio stations) make demographic data about their readers or audiences available.

2. Consumer Research Findings

Advances in Consumer Research
American Demographics
Journal of the Academy of Marketing Science
Journal of Advertising
Journal of Advertising Research
Journal of Applied Psychology
Journal of Consumer Marketing
Journal of Consumer Research
Journal of Marketing
Journal of Marketing Research
Marketing Science

3. Marketing Applications

Advertising Age
Business Week
Forbes
Fortune
Marketing Communications
Nation's Business
Sales & Marketing Management

Chapter Four

Organizational Buying

Organizational buyers include individuals involved in purchasing products and services for businesses, government agencies, and other institutions and agencies. Those who purchase for businesses include industrial buyers who purchase goods and services to aid them in producing other goods and services for sale, and resellers who purchase goods and services to resell at a profit. Government agencies purchase products and services to carry out their responsibilities to society, and other institutions and agencies, such as churches and schools, purchase to fulfill their organizational missions.

The purpose of this chapter is to examine the organizational buying process and the factors that influence it. Figure 4–1 provides a model of the organizational buying process that will be used as a framework for discussion in this chapter.

■ Figure 4–1 A Model of Organizational Buying Process

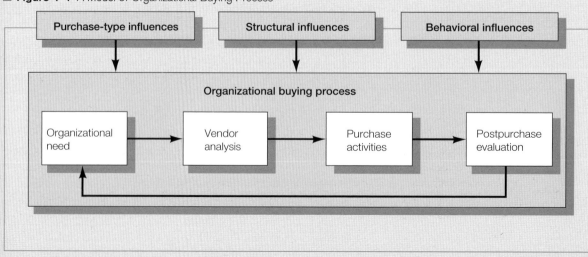
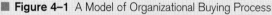

■ Purchase-Type Influences on Organizational Buying

A major consideration that affects the organizational buying process is the complexity of the purchase that is to be made. Three types of organizational purchase based on their degree of complexity include the straight rebuy, modified rebuy, and new task purchase.[1]

Straight Rebuy

The simplest and most common type of purchase is called a *straight rebuy*. This type of purchase involves routinely reordering from the same supplier a product that has been purchased in the past. Organizations use a straight rebuy when they are experienced at buying the product, have an ongoing need for it, and have regular suppliers of it. In many cases, organizations have computer systems that automatically reorder certain commonly used products. Organizations use this simple approach to purchasing because it is fast and requires relatively few employees.

Straight rebuys are common among organizations that practice *just-in-time inventory,* which is a system of replenishing parts or goods for resale just before they are needed. Such buyers do not have time to hunt around for potential suppliers and solicit bids. Instead they regularly place their orders with a supplier whose quality and timely delivery can be counted on. If a supplier delivers items that are late or of unacceptable quality, these buyers will not have a reserve in inventory to draw on. Therefore, organizations that use just-in-time inventory tend to favor suppliers with a strong commitment to quality.

To retain customers who use straight rebuys, the marketer needs to maintain high-quality products and reliable service so that the customers will continue to be satisfied with their purchases.

Modified Rebuy

When some aspects of the buying situation are unfamiliar, the organization will use a *modified rebuy*. This type of purchase involves considering a limited number of alternatives before making a selection. Organizational buyers follow this approach rather than a straight rebuy when a routine purchase changes in some way; for example, a supplier discontinues a product or stops satisfying the customer, the price of a usual product rises, or a new product becomes available to meet the same need.

In such situations, the organizational buyer considers the new information and decides what changes to make. If the change proves satisfactory and the product is one needed routinely, the buyer may then make it a straight rebuy. Marketers seek to win new organizational customers by giving them reasons to change from a straight rebuy to a modified rebuy in which the marketer's products are considered.

New Task Purchase

Organizations purchase some products only occasionally, especially in the case of large investments such as machinery, equipment, and real estate. In these cases, the organization may use a *new task purchase*. This type of purchase involves an extensive search for information and a formal decision process.

New task purchases are most often used for big-ticket items, so the cost of a mistake is great. Therefore, a new task purchase is time consuming and involves a

Part B   Marketing Information, Research, and Understanding the Target Market

■ **Figure 4–2** Differences in Types of Organizational Purchases

Purchase Type	Complexity	Time Frame	Number of Suppliers	Applications
Straight rebuy	Simple	Short	One	Frequently purchased, routine products, such as printer paper and toner
Modified rebuy	Moderate	Medium	Few	Routine purchase that has changed in some way, such as air travel (new fares, flights, destinations)
New task purchase	Complex	Long	Many	Expensive, seldom-purchased products, such as a new location for a department store

relatively large number of decision makers, who may consider many alternatives. This is the type of purchase decision that is most likely to involve joint decision making because many kinds of expertise are required to make the best decision.

A new task purchase is an opportunity for the marketer to learn about the needs of the organizations in its target market and to discuss ways to meet organizational needs, such as through the use of new products and technology. Figure 4–2 summarizes the differences in the three types of purchases.

■ Structural Influences on Organizational Buying

The term *structural influences* refers to the design of the organizational environment and how it affects the purchasing process. Three important structural influences on organizational buying are purchasing roles, organization-specific factors, and purchasing policies and procedures.

Purchasing Roles

It is common in organizational buying for more than one department and several persons to be involved in the purchasing process. These people may also play a variety of different roles in arriving at a purchase decision. These roles include:

1. *Users,* who are the people in the organization who actually use the product, for example, an assistant who would use a new word processor.
2. *Influencers,* who affect the buying decision, usually by helping define the specifications for what is bought. For example, an information systems manager would be a key influencer in the purchase of a new computer system.
3. *Buyers,* who have the formal authority and responsibility to select the supplier and negotiate the terms of the contract. For example, in the purchase of a computer system, the purchasing manager would likely perform this role.
4. *Deciders,* who have the formal or informal power to select or approve the supplier that receives the contract. For important technical purchases, deciders may come from R&D, engineering, or quality control.
5. *Gatekeepers,* who control the flow of information in the buying center. Purchasing personnel, technical experts, and assistants can all keep marketers and their information from reaching people performing the other four roles.[2]

Major Differences between Organizational Buyers and Final Consumers

Differences in Purchases

1. Organizational buyers acquire for further production, use in operations, or resale to other consumers. Final consumers acquire only for personal, family, or household use.
2. Organizational buyers commonly purchase installations, raw materials, and semifinished materials. Final consumers rarely purchase these goods.
3. Organizational buyers purchase on the basis of specifications and technical data. Final consumers frequently purchase on the basis of description, fashion, and style.
4. Organizational buyers utilize multiple-buying and team-based decisions more often than final consumers.
5. Organizational buyers are more likely to apply value and vendor analysis.

6. Organizational buyers more commonly lease equipment.
7. Organizational buyers more frequently employ competitive bidding and negotiation.

Differences in the Market

1. The demand of organizational buyers is derived from the demand of final consumers.
2. The demand of organizational buyers is more subject to cyclical fluctuations than final-consumer demand.
3. Organizational buyers are fewer in number and more geographically concentrated than final consumers.
4. Organizational buyers often employ buying specialists.
5. The distribution channel for organizational buyers is shorter than for final consumers.
6. Organizational buyers may require special services.
7. Organizational buyers are more likely than final consumers to be able to make goods and services as alternatives to purchasing them.

SOURCE: Joel R. Evans and Barry Berman, *Marketing*, 5th ed., p. 174. © 1992. Reprinted by permission of Prentice Hall, Inc., Upper Saddle River, NJ.

When several persons are involved in the organizational purchase decision, marketers may need to use a variety of means to reach each individual or group. Fortunately, it is often easy to find which individuals in organizations are involved in a purchase because such information is provided to suppliers. Organizations do this because it makes suppliers more knowledgeable about purchasing practices, thus making the purchasing process more efficient.[3] Also a number of firms have developed closer channel relationships that facilitate these transactions, as discussed in Chapter 10.

Organization-Specific Factors

There are three primary organization-specific factors that influence the purchasing process: orientation, size, and degree of centralization. First, in terms of orientation, the dominant function in an organization may control purchasing decisions. For example, if the organization is technology oriented, it is likely to be dominated by engineering personnel, and buying decisions will be made by them. Similarly, if the organization is production oriented, production personnel may dominate buying decisions.

Second, the size of the organization may influence the purchasing process. If the organization is large, it will likely have a high degree of joint decision making for other than straight rebuys. Smaller organizations are likely to have more autonomous decision making.

Finally, the degree of centralization of an organization influences whether decisions are made individually or jointly with others. Organizations that are highly centralized are less likely to have joint decision making. Thus, a privately owned, small company with technology or production orientations will tend toward autonomous decision making, while a large-scale, public corporation with considerable decentralization will tend to have greater joint decision making.

Purchasing Policies and Procedures

Organizations typically develop a number of policies and procedures for various types of purchases. These policies and procedures are designed to ensure that the appropriate products and services are purchased efficiently and that responsibility for buying is assigned appropriately. Often a purchasing department will be assigned the task of centralized buying for the whole organization, and individuals within this department will have authority to purchase particular types of products and services in a given price range.

A current trend in many organizations is *sole sourcing*, in which all of a particular type of product is purchased from a single supplier. Sole sourcing has become more popular because organizational buyers have become more concerned with quality and timely delivery and less likely to purchase only on the basis of price. Sole sourcing is advantageous for suppliers because it provides them with predictable and profitable demand and allows them to build long-term relationships with organizational buyers. It is advantageous for organizational buyers because it not only increases timely delivery and quality of supplies but also allows the buyers to work more closely with suppliers to develop superior products that meet their needs and those of their customers. The use of sole sourcing also simplifies the buying process and can make what were formally modified rebuys into simpler straight rebuys.

Of course, many organizational purchases are more complicated and require policies and procedures to direct the buying process. In many cases, organizations will develop a list of approved vendors from which buyers have authorization to purchase particular products. The buyer's responsibility is to select the vendor that will provide the appropriate levels of quality and service at the lowest cost. These policies and procedures also specify what positions in the purchasing department or buying center have authority to make purchases of different types and dollar amounts.

For large onetime projects, such as the construction of a building, organizations may seek competitive bids for part or all of the project. The development of policies and procedures for handling such purchases is usually complex and involves a number of criteria and committees.

■ Behavioral Influences on Organizational Buying

Organizational buyers are influenced by a variety of psychological and social factors. We will discuss two of these, personal motivations and role perceptions.

Personal Motivations

Organizational buyers are, of course, subject to the same personal motives or motivational forces as other individuals. Although these buyers may emphasize nonpersonal motives in their buying activities, it has been found that organizational buyers often are influenced by such personal factors as friendship, professional pride, fear and uncertainty (risk), and personal ambitions in their buying activities.

Marketing
Highlight 4–2

**Twenty Potential Decisions Facing
Organizational Buyers**

1. Is the need or problem pressing enough that it must be acted upon now? If not, how long can action be deferred?
2. What types of products or services could conceivably be used to solve our need or problem?
3. Should we make the item ourselves?
4. Must a new product be designed, or has a vendor already developed an acceptable product?
5. Should a value analysis be performed?
6. What is the highest price we can afford to pay?
7. What trade-offs are we prepared to make between price and other product/vendor attributes?
8. Which information sources will we rely on?
9. How many vendors should be considered?
10. Which attributes will be stressed in evaluating vendors?
11. Should bids be solicited?
12. Should the item be leased or purchased outright?
13. How far can a given vendor be pushed in negotiations? On what issues will that vendor bend the most?
14. How much inventory should a vendor be willing to keep on hand?
15. Should we split our order among several vendors?
16. Is a long-term contract in our interest?
17. What contractual guarantees will we require?
18. How shall we establish our order routine?
19. After the purchase, how will vendor performance be evaluated?
20. How will we deal with inadequate product or vendor performance?

SOURCE: Michael H. Morris, *Industrial and Organizational Marketing* (Columbus, OH: Charles E. Merrill Publishing, 1988), p. 87. © 1988. Reprinted by permission of Prentice Hall, Inc., Upper Saddle River, NJ.

For example, professional pride often expresses itself through efforts to attain status in the firm. One way to achieve this might be to initiate or influence the purchase of goods that will demonstrate a buyer's value to the organization. If new materials, equipment, or components result in cost savings or increased profits, the individuals initiating the changes have demonstrated their value at the same time. Fear and uncertainty are strong motivational forces on organizational buyers, and reduction of risk is often important to them. This can have a strong influence on purchase behavior. Marketers should understand the relative strength of personal gain versus risk-reducing motives and emphasize the more important motives when dealing with buyers.

Thus, in examining buyer motivations, it is necessary to consider both personal and nonpersonal motivational forces and to recognize that the relative importance of each is not a fixed quantity. It will vary with the nature of the product, the climate within the organization, and the relative strength of the two forces in the particular buyer.

Role Perceptions

A final factor that influences organizational buyers is their own perception of their role. The manner in which individuals behave depends on their perception of their role, their commitment to what they believe is expected of their role, the "maturity" of the role type, and the extent to which the institution is committed to the role type.

Different buyers will have different degrees of commitment to their buying role, which will cause variations in role behavior from one buyer to the next. By *commitment* we mean willingness to perform their job in the manner expected by the organization. For example, some buyers seek to take charge in their role as buyer and have little commitment to company expectations. The implication for marketers is that such buyers expect, even demand, that they be kept constantly advised of all

An Operational View of the Organizational Buying Process

Although there is no single format dictating how organizations actually purchase goods and services, a relatively standard process is followed in most cases:

1. A department discovers or anticipates a problem in its operation that it believes can be overcome with the addition of a certain product or service.
2. The department head draws up a requisition form describing the desired specifications he or she believes the product or service must have to solve the problem.
3. The department head sends the requisition form to the firm's purchasing department.
4. Based on the specifications required, the purchasing department conducts a search for qualified sources of supply.
5. Once sources have been located, proposals based on the specifications are solicited, received, and analyzed for price, delivery, service, and so on.
6. Proposals are compared with the cost of producing the product in-house in a make-or-buy decision: if it is decided that the buying firm can produce the product more economically, the buying process for the product in question is terminated; however, if the opposite is true, the process continues.
7. A source or sources of supply is selected from those who have submitted proposals.
8. The order is placed, and copies of the purchase order are sent to the originating department, accounting, credit, and any other interested departments within the company.
9. After the product is shipped, received, and used, a follow-up with the originating department is conducted to determine if the purchased product solved the department's problem.

Although there are many variations of this process in actual operation, this is typical of the process by which organizational goods and services are purchased. It must be understood that in actual practice these steps are combined, not separate.

SOURCE: Robert W. Hass, *Business Marketing Management,* 5th ed., p. 174. Reproduced with the permission of South-Western College Publishing. © 1992 PWS-Kent Publishing Co. All rights reserved.

new developments to enable them to more effectively shape their own role. On the other hand, other buyers may have no interest in prescribing their role activities and accept their role as given to them. Such a buyer is most concerned with merely implementing prescribed company activities and buying policies with sanctioned products. Thus, some buyers will be highly committed to play the role the firm dictates (i.e., the formal organization's perception of their role) while others might be extremely innovative and uncommitted to the expected role performance. Obviously, roles may be heavily influenced by the organizational climate existing in the particular organization.[4]

Organizations can be divided into three groups based on differences in degree of employee commitment. These groups include innovative, adaptive, and lethargic firms. In *innovative firms,* individuals approach their occupational roles with a weak commitment to expected norms of behavior. In an *adaptive organization,* there is a moderate commitment; in a *lethargic organization,* individuals express a strong commitment to traditionally accepted behavior and behave accordingly. Thus, a buyer in a lethargic firm would probably be less innovative in order to maintain acceptance and status within the organization and would keep conflict within the firm to a minimum.

Buyers' perception of their role may differ from the perception of their role held by others in the organization. This difference can result in variance in perception of the actual purchase responsibility held by the buyer. One study involving purchasing agents revealed that, in every firm included in the study, the purchasing agents believed they had more responsibility and control over certain decisions than the other influential purchase decision makers in the firm perceived them as having. The decisions were (1) design of the product, (2) cost of the product, (3) performance life, (4) naming of the specific supplier, (5) assessing the amount of engineering help available from the supplier, and (6) reduction of rejects. This variance in role perception held true regardless of the size of the firm or the significance of the item purchased to the overall success of the firm. It is important, therefore, that the marketer be aware that such perceptual differences may exist and to determine as accurately as possible the amount of control and responsibility over purchasing decisions held by each purchase decision influencer in the firm.

■ Stages in the Organizational Buying Process

As with consumer buying, most organizational purchases are made in response to a particular need or problem. Ideally, the products or services purchased will meet the organizational need and improve the organization's efficiency, effectiveness, and profits. The organizational buying process can be analyzed as a series of four stages: organizational need, vendor analysis, purchase activities, and postpurchase evaluation.

Organizational Need

Organizations have many needs for products and services to help them survive and meet their objectives. For example, a manufacturer may need to purchase new machinery to increase its production capacity and meet demand; a retailer may need to purchase services from a marketing research firm to better understand its market; a government agency may need to purchase faster computers to keep up with growing demand for its services; a hospital may need to purchase more comfortable beds for its patients. Recognizing these needs, and a willingness and ability to meet them, often results in organizational purchases. For straight rebuys, the purchase process may involve little more than a phone call or a few clicks on a computer to order products and arrange payment and delivery. For modified rebuys or new task purchases, the process may be much more complex.

Vendor Analysis

Organizational buyers must search for, locate, and evaluate vendors of products and services to meet their needs. Searching for and locating vendors is often easy since they frequently make sales calls on organizations that might need their products. Vendors also advertise in trade magazines or on the Internet and have displays at industry trade shows to increase their visibility to organizational buyers. For products and services that the organization has previously purchased, a list of approved vendors may have already been developed by the organization.

Organizational buyers often use a vendor analysis to evaluate possible suppliers. A *vendor analysis* is the process by which buyers rate each potential supplier on various performance measures such as product quality, on-time delivery, price, payment terms, and use of modern technology. Figure 4–3 presents a sample vendor analysis form that lists a number of purchase criteria and the weights one organization used to compare potential suppliers.

■ **Figure 4–3** Sample Vendor Analysis Form

Supplier Name: _____   Type of Product: _____
Shipping Location: _____   Annual Sales Dollars: _____

	5 Excellent	4 Good	3 Satisfactory	2 Fair	1 Poor	0 N/A
Quality (45%)						
Defect rates	____	____	____	____	____	____
Quality of sample	____	____	____	____	____	____
Conformance with quality program	____	____	____	____	____	____
Responsiveness to quality problems	____	____	____	____	____	____
Overall quality	____	____	____	____	____	____
Delivery (25%)						
Avoidance of late shipments	____	____	____	____	____	____
Ability to expand production	____	____	____	____	____	____
Performance in sample delivery	____	____	____	____	____	____
Response to changes in order size	____	____	____	____	____	____
Overall delivery	____	____	____	____	____	____
Price (20%)						
Price competitiveness	____	____	____	____	____	____
Payment terms	____	____	____	____	____	____
Absorption of costs	____	____	____	____	____	____
Submission of cost savings plans	____	____	____	____	____	____
Overall price	____	____	____	____	____	____
Technology (10%)						
State-of-the-art components	____	____	____	____	____	____
Sharing research & development capability	____	____	____	____	____	____
Ability and willingness to help with design	____	____	____	____	____	____
Responsiveness to engineering problems	____	____	____	____	____	____
Overall technology	____	____	____	____	____	____

Buyer: _____ Date: _____
Comments: _____

SOURCE: Gilbert A. Churchill, Jr., and J. Paul Peter, *Marketing: Creating Value for Customers,* 2nd ed. (Burr Ridge, IL: Irwin/McGraw-Hill, 1998), p. 186.

A formal vendor analysis can be used for at least three purposes. First, it can be used to develop a list of approved vendors, all of which provide acceptable levels of products and services. Organizational buyers can then select any company on the list, simplifying the purchase process. Second, a vendor analysis could be used to compare competing vendors; the buyers then select the best one on the basis of the ratings. This could help the organization pare down vendors to a single supplier for which a long-term, sole-sourcing relationship could be developed. Third, a vendor analysis can be done both before and after purchases to compare performance on evaluation criteria and evaluate the process of vendor selection.

Purchase Activities

Straight rebuys may involve a quick order to an approved vendor or sole-source supplier. However, other types of organizational purchases can involve long time periods with extensive negotiations on price and terms and formal contracts stating quality, delivery, and service criteria. The complexity of the product or service, the number of suppliers available, the importance of the product to the buying organization, and pricing all influence the number of purchase activities to be performed and their difficulty. For example, an airline buying a fleet of jumbo jets or a car rental agency buying a fleet of cars may take months or years to negotiate and make purchases. While such buyers may have considerable leverage in negotiating, it should be remembered that these organizations need the products just as badly as the sellers need to sell them. Thus, there is often more collaboration among organizational buyers and sellers than in the consumer market.

Postpurchase Evaluation

Organizational buyers must evaluate both the vendors and the products they purchase to determine whether the products are acceptable for future purchases or whether other sources of supply should be found. A comparison of the performance of the vendor and products with the criteria listed on the prior vendor analysis can be useful for this purpose. If the purchase process went smoothly and products meet price and quality criteria, then the vendor may be put on the approved list or perhaps further negotiations can be made to sole-source with the supplier.

One problem in judging the acceptability of suppliers and products is that different functional areas may have different evaluation criteria. Figure 4–4 presents several functional areas of a manufacturing company and their common concerns in purchasing. Clearly, these concerns should be considered both prior to purchasing from a particular supplier and after purchase to ensure that every area's needs are being met as well as possible.

■ Conclusion

Organizational buyers include individuals involved in purchasing products and services for businesses, government agencies, and other institutions and agencies. The organizational buying process is influenced by whether the purchase is a straight rebuy, modified rebuy, or new task purchase. It is also influenced by people

■ Figure 4–4
Functional Areas and
Their Key Concerns in
Organizational Buying

Functional Areas	Key Concerns
Design and development engineering	Name reputation of vendor; ability of vendors to meet design specifications
Production	Delivery and reliability of purchases such that interruption of production schedules is minimized
Sales/marketing	Impact of purchased items on marketability of the company's products
Maintenance	Degree to which purchased items are compatible with existing facilities and equipment; maintenance service offered by vendor; installation arrangements offered by vendor
Finance/accounting	Effects of purchases on cash flow, balance sheet, and income statement positions; variances in costs of materials over estimates; feasibility of make-or-buy and lease options to purchasing
Purchasing	Obtaining lowest possible price at acceptable quality levels; maintaining good relations with vendors
Quality control	Assurance that purchased items meet prescribed specifications and tolerances, governmental regulations, and customer requirements

SOURCE: Michael H. Morris, *Industrial and Organizational Marketing* (Columbus, OH: Merrill Publishing, 1989), p. 81.

in various purchasing roles, the orientation, size, and degree of centralization of the organization, the organization's purchasing policies and procedures, and individuals' motivations and perceived roles. The organizational buying process can be viewed as a series of four stages ranging from organizational need, to vendor analysis, to purchase activities, to postpurchase evaluation. It is important for companies marketing to organizations to understand the influences and process by which organizations buy products and services so that their needs can be met fully and profitably.

■ Additional Readings

Bingham, Frank G., and Barney T. Raffield III. *Business to Business Marketing Management.* Homewood, IL: Irwin, 1990.

Bunn, Michele. "Taxonomy of Buying Decision Approaches." *Journal of Marketing,* January 1993, pp. 38–56.

Corey, E. Raymond. *Industrial Marketing: Cases and Concepts.* 4th ed. Englewood Cliffs, NJ: Prentice Hall, 1991.

Drumwright, Minette E. "Socially Responsible Organizational Buying: Environmental Concern as a Noneconomic Buying Criterion." *Journal of Marketing,* July 1994, pp. 1–19.

Eckles, Robert W. *Business Marketing Management.* Englewood Cliffs, NJ: Prentice Hall, 1990.

Hayes, H. Michael; Per V. Jenster; and Nils-Erik Aaby. *Business Marketing: A Global Perspective.* Boston: Irwin/McGraw-Hill, 1996.

Ramaswamy, Venkatram; Hubert Gatignon; and David J. Reibstein. "Competitive Marketing Behavior in Industrial Markets." *Journal of Marketing,* April 1994, pp. 45–55.

Sherlock, Paul. *Rethinking Business to Business Marketing.* New York: Free Press, 1991.

Ward, Scott, and Frederick E. Webster, Jr. "Organizational Buying Behavior." In *Handbook of Consumer Behavior,* eds. T. S. Robertson and H. H. Kassarjian. Englewood Cliffs, NJ: Prentice Hall, 1991, pp. 419–58.

Weiss, Allen M., and Jan B. Heide. "The Nature of Organizational Search in High Technology Markets." *Journal of Marketing Research,* May 1993, pp. 220–33.

Wilson, Elizabeth J.; Gary L. Lilien; and David T. Wilson. "Developing and Testing a Contingency Paradigm of Group Choice in Organizational Buying." *Journal of Marketing Research,* November 1991, pp. 452–66.

Chapter Five

Market Segmentation

Market segmentation is one of the most important concepts in marketing. In fact, a primary reason for studying consumer and organizational buyer behavior is to provide bases for effective segmentation, and a large portion of marketing research is concerned with segmentation. From a marketing management point of view, selection of the appropriate target market is paramount to developing successful marketing programs.

The logic of market segmentation is quite simple and is based on the idea that a single product item can seldom meet the needs and wants of *all* consumers. Typically, consumers vary as to their needs, wants, and preferences for products and services, and successful marketers adapt their marketing programs to fulfill these preference patterns. For example, even a simple product like chewing gum has multiple flavors, package sizes, sugar contents, calories, consistencies (e.g., liquid centers), and colors to meet the preferences of various consumers. While a single product item cannot meet the needs of all consumers, it can almost always serve more than one consumer. Thus, there are usually *groups of consumers* who can be served well by a single item. If a particular group can be served *profitably* by a firm, it is a viable market segment. In other words, the firm should develop a marketing mix to serve the group or market segment.

In this chapter we consider the process of market segmentation. We define *market segmentation* as the process of dividing a market into groups of similar consumers and selecting the most appropriate group(s) for the firm to serve. We break down the process of market segmentation into six steps, as shown in Figure 5–1. While we recognize that the order of these steps may vary, depending on the firm and situation, there are few if any times when market segmentation analysis can be ignored. In fact, even if the final decision is to "mass market" and not segment at all, this decision should be reached only *after* a market segmentation analysis has been conducted. Thus, market segmentation analysis is a cornerstone of sound marketing planning and decision making.

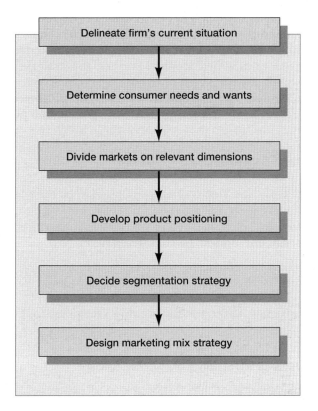

■ Delineate the Firm's Current Situation

As emphasized in Chapter 1, a firm must do a complete situational analysis when embarking on a new or modified marketing program. At the marketing planning level, such an analysis aids in determining objectives, opportunities, and constraints to be considered when selecting target markets and developing marketing mixes. In addition, marketing managers must have a clear idea of the amount of financial and other resources that will be available for developing and executing a marketing plan. Thus, the inclusion of this first step in the market segmentation process is intended to be a reminder of tasks to be performed prior to marketing planning.

■ Determine Consumer Needs and Wants

As emphasized throughout this text, successful marketing strategies depend on discovering and satisfying consumer needs and wants. In some cases, this idea is quite operational. To illustrate, suppose a firm has a good deal of venture capital and is seeking to diversify its interest into new markets. A firm in this situation may seek to discover a broad variety of unsatisfied needs. However, in most situations, the industry in which the firm operates specifies the boundaries of a firm's need satisfaction activities. For example, a firm in the communication industry may seek more efficient methods for serving consumers' long-distance telephone needs.

As a practical matter, new technology often brings about an investigation of consumer needs and wants for new or modified products and services. In these situations, the firm is seeking the group of consumers whose needs could best be satisfied by the new or modified product. Further, at a strategic level, consumer needs and wants usually are translated into more operational concepts. For instance, consumer attitudes, preferences, and benefits sought, which are determined through marketing research, are commonly used for segmentation purposes.

■ Divide Markets on Relevant Dimensions

In a narrow sense, this step is often considered to be the whole of market segmentation (i.e., consumers are grouped on the basis of one or more similarities and treated as a homogeneous segment of a heterogeneous total market). There are three important questions to be considered here:

1. Should the segmentation be a priori or post hoc?
2. How does one determine the relevant dimensions or bases to use for segmentation?
3. What are some bases for segmenting consumer and organizational buyer markets?

A Priori versus Post Hoc Segmentation

Real-world segmentation has followed one of two general patterns. An *a priori segmentation* approach is one in which the marketing manager has decided on the appropriate basis for segmentation in advance of doing any research on a market. For example, a manager may decide that a market should be divided on the basis of whether people are nonusers, light users, or heavy users of a particular product. Segmentation research is then conducted to determine the size of each of these groups and their demographic or psychographic profiles.

Post hoc segmentation is an approach in which people are grouped into segments on the basis of research findings. For example, people interviewed concerning their attitudes or benefits sought in a particular product category are grouped according to their responses. The size of each of these groups and their demographic and psychographic profiles are then determined.

Both of these approaches are valuable, and the question of which to use depends in part on how well the firm knows the market for a particular product class. If through previous research and experience a marketing manager has successfully isolated a number of key market dimensions, then an a priori approach based on them may provide more useful information. In the case of segmentation for entirely new products, a post hoc approach may be useful for determining key market dimensions. However, even when using a post hoc approach, some consideration must be given to the variables to be included in the research design. Thus, some consideration must be given to the relevant segmentation dimensions regardless of which approach is used.

Relevance of Segmentation Dimensions

Unfortunately, there is no simple solution for determining the relevant dimensions for segmenting markets. Certainly, managerial expertise and experience are needed for selecting the appropriate dimensions or bases on which to segment particular

Marketing
Highlight 5–1

Developing Market Segments for Women's Apparel

Marketers often use a variety of dimensions to develop an overall description of their markets. Below are descriptions of J. C. Penney's three major markets for women's apparel.

	Conservative	Traditional	Update
Size	23% of population	38% of population	16% of population
	16% of total sales	40% of total sales	24% of total sales
Age	35–55 years old	25–49 years old	25–49 years old
Values	Conservative values	Traditional values	Contemporary values
	Satisfied with present status	Active, busy, independent, self-confident	Active, busy, independent, very self-confident
Employment	Has job, or career	Family- and job/career-oriented	Family- and job/career-oriented
Income	Limited disposable income	Considerable income	Considerable income
Benefits sought	Price-driven, reacts to sales	Quality-driven, will pay a little more	Fashion-driven, expresses self through apparel
	Wants easy care and comfort	Wants traditional styling, seeks clothes that last	Wants newness in color and style
	Not interested in fashion	Interested in newness	Shops often
	Defines value as	Defines value as	Defines value as
	price	quality	fashion
	quality	fashion	quality
	fashion	price	price

SOURCE: Michael Levy and Barton A. Weitz, *Retailing Management,* 3d ed. (Boston, MA: Irwin/McGraw-Hill, 1998), p. 148.

markets. In most cases, however, at least some initial dimensions can be determined from previous research, purchase trends, and managerial judgment. For instance, suppose we wish to segment the market for all-terrain vehicles. Clearly, several dimensions come to mind for initial consideration, including sex (male), age (18 to 35 years), lifestyle (outdoorsman), and income level (perhaps $25,000 to $40,000). At a minimum, these variables should be included in subsequent segmentation research. Of course, the most market-oriented approach to segmentation is on the basis of what benefits the potential consumer is seeking. Thus, consideration and research of sought benefits is a strongly recommended approach in the marketing literature. This approach will be considered in some detail in the following section.

Bases for Segmentation

A number of useful bases for segmenting consumer and organizational markets are presented in Figure 5–2. This is by no means a complete list of possible segmentation variables but represents some useful bases and categories. Two commonly used approaches for segmenting markets include benefit segmentation and psychographic segmentation. We will discuss these two in some detail. We will also discuss geodemographic segmentation, a recent development with a number of advantages for marketers.

■ **Figure 5–2** Useful Segmentation Bases for Consumer and Organizational Buyer Markets

Consumer Markets	
Segmentation Base	**Examples of Market Segments**
Geographic	
Continents	Africa, Asia, Europe, North America, South America
Global regions	Southeast Asia, Mediterranean, Caribbean
Countries	China, Canada, France, United States, Brazil
Country regions	Pacific Northwest, Middle Atlantic, Midwest
City, county, or SMSA size	Under 5,000 people, 5,000–19,999, 20,000–49,999, 50,000+
Population density	Urban, suburban, rural
Climate	Tropical, temperate, cold
Demographic	
Age	Under 6 years old, 6–12, 13–19, 20–29, 30–39, 40–49, 50+
Gender	Male, female
Family size	1–2 persons, 3–4 persons, more than 4 persons
Family life cycle	Single, young married, married with children, sole survivor
Income	Under $10,000 per year, $10,000–$19,999, $20,000–$29,999, $30,000–$39,999, $40,000–$49,999, $50,000+
Education	Grade school or less, some high school, graduated from high school, some college, graduated from college, some graduate work, graduate degree
Marital status	Single, married, divorced, widowed
Social	
Culture	American, Hispanic, African, Asian, European
Subculture	
Religion	Jewish, Catholic, Muslim, Mormon, Buddhist
Race	European-American, Asian-American, African-American, Hispanic-American
Nationality	French, Malaysian, Australian, Canadian, Japanese
Social class	Upper class, middle class, working class, lower class
Thoughts and feelings	
Knowledge	Expert, novice
Involvement	High, medium, low
Attitude	Positive, neutral, negative
Benefits sought	Convenience, economy, prestige
Innovativeness	Innovator, early adopter, early majority, late majority, laggards, nonadopter
Readiness stage	Unaware, aware, interested, desirous, plan to purchase
Perceived risk	High, moderate, low
Behavior	
Media usage	Newspaper, magazine, TV, Internet
Specific media usage	*Sports Illustrated, Life, Cosmopolitan*
Payment method	Cash, Visa, MasterCard, American Express, check
Loyalty status	None, some, total
Usage rate	Light, medium, heavy
User status	Nonuser, ex-user, current user, potential user
Usage situation	Work, home, vacation, commuting
Combined approaches	
Psychographics	Achievers, strivers, strugglers
Person/situation	College students for lunch, executives for business dinner
Geodemography	Blue Blood Estates, Towns and Gowns, Hispanic Mix

(*Continued*)

■ **Figure 5–2**   Useful Segmentation Bases for Consumer and Organizational Buyer Markets (*concluded*)

Organizational Buyer Markets	
Segmentation Base	**Examples of Market Segments**
Source loyalty	Purchases product from one, two, three, four, or more suppliers
Company size	Small, medium, large relative to industry
Purchase quantity	Small, medium, large account
Product application	Production, maintenance, product component
Organization type	Manufacturer, retailer, government agency, hospital
Location	North, south, east, west sales territory
Purchase status	New customer, occasional purchaser, frequent purchaser, nonpurchaser
Attribute importance	Price, service, reliability of supply

Benefit Segmentation.   The belief underlying this segmentation approach is that the benefits people are seeking in consuming a given product are the basic reasons for the existence of true market segments.[1] Thus, this approach attempts to measure consumer value systems and consumer perceptions of various brands in a product class. To illustrate, the classic example of a benefit segmentation was provided by Russell Haley and concerned the toothpaste market. Haley identified four basic segments, which are presented in Figure 5–3. Haley argued that this segmentation could be very useful for selecting advertising copy, media, commercial length, packaging, and new product design. For example, colorful packages might

■ **Figure 5–3** Toothpaste Market Benefit Segments

	Sensory Segment	Sociable Segment	Worrier Segment	Independent Segment
Principal benefit sought	Flavor and product appearance	Brightness of teeth	Decay prevention	Price
Demographic strengths	Children	Teens, young people	Large families	Men
Special behavioral characteristics	Users of spearmint-flavored toothpaste	Smokers	Heavy users	Heavy users
Brands disproportionately favored	Colgate	Macleans, Ultra Brite	Crest	Cheapest brand
Lifestyle characteristics	Hedonistic	Active	Conservative	Value oriented

SOURCE: Adapted from Russell I. Haley, "Benefit Segmentation: A Decision-Oriented Research Tool," *Journal of Marketing,* July 1968, pp. 30–35.

**Want to Know Your VALS Category?
Check It Out on the Internet**

You can find your VALS classification by filling out a questionnaire on the Internet. The Web address is http://future.sri.com/vals/valshome.html. The ques-

tionnaire takes about 10 minutes to complete, and your lifestyle will take about 10 seconds to compute. You will get a report that includes both your primary and secondary VALS type. The VALS website has a lot of information describing the program and different types of VALS segments.

be appropriate for the sensory segment, perhaps aqua (to indicate fluoride) for the worrier group, and gleaming white for the social segment because of this segment's interest in white teeth.

Calantone and Sawyer also used a benefit segmentation approach to segment the market for bank services.[2] Their research was concerned with the question of whether benefit segments remain stable across time. While they found some stability in segments, there were some differences in attribute importance, size, and demographics at different times. Thus, they argue for ongoing benefit segmentation research to keep track of any changes in a market that might affect marketing strategy.

Benefit segmentation is clearly a market-oriented approach to segmentation that seeks to identify consumer needs and wants and to satisfy them by providing products and services with the desired benefits. It is clearly very consistent with the approach to marketing suggested by the marketing concept.

Psychographic Segmentation. Whereas benefit segmentation focuses on the benefits sought by the consumer, psychographic segmentation focuses on the personal attributes of the consumer. The psychographic or lifestyle approach typically follows a post hoc model of segmentation. Generally, a large number of questions are asked concerning consumers' activities, interests, and opinions, and then consumers are grouped together empirically based on their responses. Although questions have been raised about the validity of this segmentation approach, it provides much useful information about markets.[3]

A well-known psychographic segmentation was developed at SRI International in California. The original segmentation divided consumers in the United States into nine groups and was called VALS™, which stands for "values and lifestyles." However, while this segmentation was commercially successful, it tended to place the majority of consumers into only one or two groups, and SRI felt it needed to be updated to reflect changes in society. Thus, SRI developed a new typology called VALS 2™.[4]

VALS 2 is based on two national surveys of 2,500 consumers who responded to 43 lifestyle questions. The first survey developed the segmentation, and the second validated it and linked it to buying and media behavior. The questionnaire asked consumers to respond to whether they agreed or disagreed with statements such as "My idea of fun at a national park would be to stay at an expensive lodge and dress up for dinner" and "I could stand to skin a dead animal." Consumers were then clustered into eight groups, shown and described in Figure 5–4.

■ Figure 5–4
VALS 2 Eight
American Lifestyles

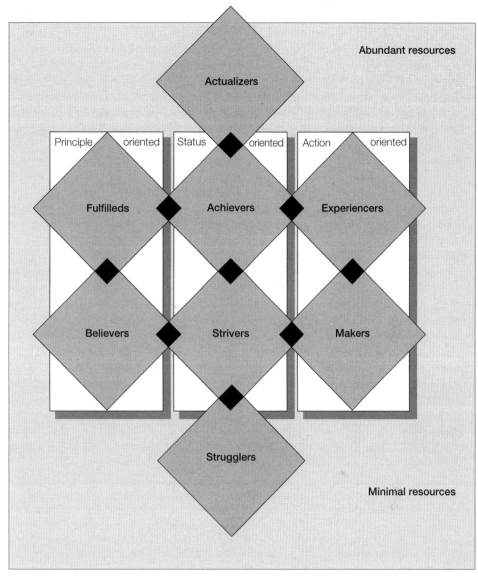

(continued)

The VALS 2 groups are arranged in a rectangle and are based on two dimensions. The vertical dimension represents resources, which include income, education, self-confidence, health, eagerness to buy, intelligence, and energy level. The horizontal dimension represents self-orientations, and includes three different types. *Principle-oriented consumers* are guided by their views of how the world is or should be; *status-oriented consumers* by the action and opinions of others; and *action-oriented consumers* by a desire for social or physical activity, variety, and risk taking.

Each of the VALS 2 groups represents from 9 to 17 percent of the U.S. adult population. Marketers can buy VALS 2 information for a variety of products and can have it tied to a number of other consumer databases.

■ **Figure 5–4**   VALS 2 Eight American Lifestyles (*concluded*)

Actualizers. These consumers have the highest incomes and such high self-esteem and abundant resources that they can indulge in any or all self-orientations. They are located above the rectangle. Image is important to them as an expression of taste, independence, and character. Their consumer choices are directed toward the finer things in life.

Fulfilleds. These consumers are the high-resource group of those who are principle oriented. They are mature, responsible, well-educated professionals. Their leisure activities center on their homes, but they are well-informed about what goes on in the world and open to new ideas and social change. They have high incomes but are practical consumers.

Believers. These consumers are the low-resource group of those who are principle oriented. They are conservative and predictable consumers who favor American products and established brands. Their lives are centered on family, church, community, and the nation. They have modest incomes.

Achievers. These consumers are the high-resource group of those who are status oriented. They are successful, work-oriented people who get their satisfaction from their jobs and families. They are politically conservative and respect authority and the status quo. They favor established products and services that show off their successes to their peers.

Strivers. These consumers are the low-resource group of those who are status oriented. They have values very similar to achievers but have fewer economic, social, and psychological resources. Style is extremely important to them as they strive to emulate people they admire and wish to be like.

Experiencers. These consumers are the high-resource group of those who are action oriented. They are the youngest of all the segments with a median age of 25. They have a lot of energy, which they pour into physical exercise and social activities. They are avid consumers, spending heavily on clothing, fast foods, music, and other youthful favorites—with particular emphasis on new products and services.

Makers. These consumers are the low-resource group of those who are action oriented. They are practical people who value self-sufficiency. They are focused on the familiar—family, work, and physical recreation—and have little interest in the broader world. As consumers, they appreciate practical and functional products.

Strugglers. These consumers have the lowest incomes. They have too few resources to be included in any consumer self-orientation and are thus located below the rectangle. They are the oldest of all the segments with a median age of 61. Within their limited means, they tend to be brand-loyal consumers.

SOURCE: Martha Farnsworth Riche, "Psychographics for the 1990s," *American Demographics,* July 1989, pp. 24ff.

Geodemographic Segmentation.   One problem with many segmentation approaches is that while they identify types or categories of consumers, they do not identify specific individuals or households within a market. *Geodemographic segmentation* does identify specific households in a market by focusing on local neighborhood geography (such as zip codes) to create classifications of actual, addressable, mappable neighborhoods where people live and shop. One geodemographic system created by Claritas, Inc., is called PRIZM, which stands for Potential Ranking Index by Zip Markets. This system classifies every U.S. neighborhood into one of 62 distinct types or clusters of consumers. Each PRIZM cluster is based on ZIP codes, demographic information from the U.S. census, and information on product usage, media usage, and lifestyle preferences to create profiles of the people who live in specific neighborhoods. Figure 5–5 shows a sample cluster profile. The PRIZM system includes maps of different areas that rank neighborhoods on their potential to purchase specific products or services.

The PRIZM system is based on the assumptions that consumers in particular neighborhoods are similar in many respects and that the best prospects are those

■ Figure 5–5
Claritas PRIZM Cluster
36—Towns and
Gowns

The "towns and gowns" cluster describes most of our college towns and university campus neighborhoods. With a typical mix of half locals (towns) and half students (gowns), it is wholly unique, with thousands of penniless 18- to 24-year-old kids, plus highly educated professionals, all with a taste for prestige products beyond their evident means.

Predominant characteristics

• Households (% U.S.):	1,290,200 (1.4%)
• Population:	3,542,500
• Demographic caption:	College-town singles
• Ethnic diversity:	Dominant white, high Asian
• Family type:	Singles
• Predominant age ranges:	Under 24, 25–34
• Education:	College graduates
• Employment level:	White collar/service
• Housing type:	Renters/multiunit 10+
• Density percentile:	58 (1 = sparse, 99 = dense)

More likely to:

Lifestyle

Go to college football games
Play racquetball
Go skiing
Play billiards/pool
Use cigarette rolling paper
Use a charter/tour bus

Products and services

Have a personal education loan
Use an ATM card
Own a Honda
Buy 3+ pairs of jeans annually
Drink Coca-Cola Classic
Eat Kraft Macaroni and Cheese

Radio/TV

Watch VH1
Listen to alternative rock music
Watch "Jeopardy"
Listen to variety radio
Watch "The Simpsons"

Print

Read *Self*
Read newspaper comics section
Read *Rolling Stone*
Read *GQ*

SOURCE: Valarie Walsh and J. Paul Peter, "Claritas Inc.: Using Compass and PRIZM," in *Marketing Management: Knowledge and Skills,* 5th ed., eds. J. Paul Peter and James H. Donnelly, Jr. (Burr Ridge, IL: Irwin/McGraw-Hill, 1998), p. 334.

who actually use a product or other consumers like them. Marketers use PRIZM to better understand consumers in various markets, what they're like, where they live, and how to reach them. These data help marketers with target market selection, direct-marketing campaigns, site selection, media selection, and analysis of sales potential in various areas.

■ Develop Product Positioning

By this time, the firm should have a good idea of the basic segments of the market that could potentially be satisfied with its product. The current step is concerned with positioning the product favorably in the minds of customers relative to competitive products. There are several different positioning strategies that can be used. First, products can be positioned by focusing on their superiority to competitive products based on one or more attributes. For example, a car could be positioned as less expensive (Hyundai), safer (Volvo), higher quality (Toyota), or more prestigious (Lexus) than other cars. Second, products can be positioned by use or application. For example, Campbell's soup is positioned not only as a lunch item but also for use as a sauce or dip or as an ingredient in main dishes. Third, products can be positioned in terms of particular types of product users. For example, sales for Johnson's Baby Shampoo increased dramatically after the company positioned the product not only for babies but also for active adults who need to wash their hair frequently. Fourth, products can be positioned relative to a product class. For example, Caress soap was positioned by Lever Brothers as a bath oil product rather than as a soap. Finally, products can be positioned directly against particular competitors. For example, Coke and Pepsi and McDonald's and Burger King commonly position directly against each other on various criteria, such as taste. The classic example of positioning is of this last type: Seven-Up positioned itself as a tasty alternative to the dominant soft drink, colas.

One way to investigate how to position a product is by using a *positioning map,* which is a visual depiction of customer perceptions of competitive products, brands, or models. It is constructed by surveying customers about various product attributes and developing dimensions and a graph indicating the relative position of competitors. Figure 5–6 presents a sample positioning map for automobiles that offers marketers a way of assessing whether their brands are positioned appropriately. For example, if Chrysler or Buick wants to be positioned in the minds of consumers as serious competitors to Lexus, then their strategies need to be changed to move up on this dimension. After the new strategies are implemented, a new positioning map could be developed to see if the brands moved up as desired.

Some experts argue that different positioning strategies should be used depending on whether the firm is a market leader or follower and that followers usually should not attempt to position directly against the industry leader.[5] The main point

■ **Figure 5–6**
Positioning Map for Automobiles

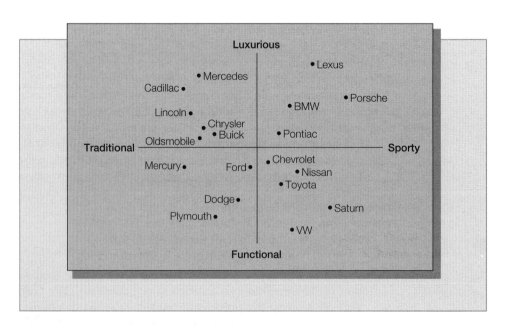

SOURCE: Gilbert A. Churchill, Jr., and J. Paul Peter, *Marketing: Creating Value for Customers,* 2nd ed. (Burr Ridge, IL: Irwin/McGraw-Hill, 1998), p. 221.

here is that in segmenting markets, some segments might have to be forgone because a market-leading competitive product already dominates in sales and in the minds of customers. Thus, a smaller or less desirable target market may have to be selected since competing with market leaders is costly and not often successful.

■ Decide Segmentation Strategy

The firm is now ready to select its segmentation strategy. There are four basic alternatives. First, the firm may decide not to enter the market. For example, analysis to this stage may reveal there is no viable market niche for the firm's offering. Second, the firm may decide not to segment but to be a mass marketer. There are at least three situations when this may be the appropriate decision for the firm:

1. The market is so small that marketing to a portion of it is not profitable.
2. Heavy users make up such a large proportion of the sales volume that they are the only relevant target.
3. The brand is the dominant brand in the market, and targeting to a few segments would not benefit sales and profits.

Third, the firm may decide to market to one segment. And fourth, the firm may decide to market to more than one segment and design a separate marketing mix for each. In any case, the firm must have some criteria on which to base its segmentation strategy decisions. Three important criteria on which to base such decisions are that a viable segment must be (1) measurable, (2) meaningful, and (3) marketable.

1. *Measurable.* For a segment to be selected, the firm must be capable of measuring its size and characteristics. For instance, one of the difficulties with segmenting on the basis of social class is that the concept and its divisions are not

Marketing
Highlight 5–4

Differences in Marketing Strategy for Three Segmentation Alternatives

Strategy Elements	Mass Marketing	Single Market Segmentation	Multiple Market Segmentation
Market definition	Broad range of consumers	One well-defined consumer group	Two or more well-defined consumer groups
Product strategy	Limited number of products under one brand for many types of consumers	One brand tailored to one consumer group	Distinct brand for each consumer group
Pricing strategy	One "popular" price range	One price range tailored to the consumer group	Distinct price range for each consumer group
Distribution strategy	All possible outlets	All suitable outlets	All suitable outlets—differs by segment
Promotion strategy	Mass media	All suitable media	All suitable media—differs by segment
Strategy emphasis	Appeal to various types of consumers through a uniform, broad-based marketing program	Appeal to one specific consumer group through a highly specialized, but uniform marketing program	Appeal to two or more distinct market segments through different marketing plans catering to each segment

SOURCE: Joel R. Evans and Barry Berman, *Marketing,* 5th ed. (New York: Macmillan, 1992), p. 219. © 1992. Reprinted by permission of Prentice Hall, Inc., Upper Saddle River, NJ.

clearly defined and measured. Alternatively, income is a much easier concept to measure.

2. *Meaningful.* A meaningful segment is one that is large enough to have sufficient sales and growth potential to offer long-run profits for the firm.
3. *Marketable.* A marketable segment is one that can be reached and served by the firm in an efficient manner.

Segments that meet these criteria are viable markets for the firm's offering. The firm must now give further attention to completing its marketing mix offering.

■ Design Marketing Mix Strategy

The firm is now in a position to complete its marketing plan by finalizing the marketing mix or mixes to be used for each segment. Clearly, selection of the target market and designing the marketing mix go hand in hand, and thus many marketing mix decisions should have already been carefully considered. To illustrate, the target market selected may be price sensitive, so some consideration has already been given to price levels, and clearly product positioning has many implications for promotion and channel decisions. Thus, while we place marketing mix design at the end of the model, many of these decisions are made in *conjunction* with target market selection. In the next six chapters of this text, marketing mix decisions will be discussed in detail.

■ Conclusion

The purpose of this chapter was to provide an overview of market segmentation. Market segmentation was defined as the process of dividing a market into groups of similar consumers and selecting the most appropriate group(s) for the firm to serve. Market segmentation was analyzed as a six-stage process: (1) to delineate the firm's current situation; (2) to determine consumer needs and wants; (3) to divide the market on relevant dimensions; (4) to develop product positioning; (5) to decide segmentation strategy; (6) to design marketing mix strategy.

■ Additional Readings

Chintagunta, Pradeep K. "Heterogeneous Logit Model Implications for Brand Positioning." *Journal of Marketing Research*, May 1994, pp. 304–11.

Dickson, Peter R., and James L. Ginter. "Market Segmentation, Product Differentiation, and Marketing Strategy." *Journal of Marketing*, April 1987, pp. 1–10.

Green, Paul E., and Abba M. Krieger. "Segmenting Markets with Conjoint Analysis." *Journal of Marketing*, October 1991, pp. 20–31.

Gupta, Sachin, and Pradeep K. Chintagunta. "On Using Demographic Variables to Determine Segment Membership in Logit Mixture Models." *Journal of Marketing Research*, February 1994, pp. 128–36.

Kamakura, Wagner A., and Thomas P. Kovak. "Value-System Segmentation: Exploring the Meaning of LOV." *Journal of Consumer Research*, June 1992, pp. 119–32.

Myers, James H. *Segmentation and Positioning for Strategic Marketing Decisions.* Chicago: American Marketing Association, 1996.

Pechmann, Cornelia, and S. Ratneshwar. "The Use of Comparative Advertising for Brand Positioning: Association versus Differentiation." *Journal of Consumer Research*, September 1991, pp. 145–60.

Rangan, V. Kasturi; Rowland T. Moriarty; and Gordon S. Swartz. "Segmenting Customers in Mature Industrial Markets." *Journal of Marketing*, October 1992, pp. 72–82.

Part C

The Marketing Mix

Section I
Essentials of Marketing Management

Chapter Six

Product
Strategy

Product strategy is a critical element of marketing and business strategy, since it is through the sale of products and services that companies survive and grow. This chapter discusses four important areas of concern in developing product strategies. First, some basic issues are discussed, including product definition, product classification, product quality and value, product mix and product line, branding and brand equity, and packaging. Second, the pro- duct life cycle and its implications for product strategy are explained. Third, the product audit is reviewed, and finally, three ways to organize for product management are outlined. These include the marketing manager system, brand manager system, and cross-functional teams.

■ Basic Issues in Product Management

Successful marketing depends on understanding the nature of products and basic decision areas in product management. In this section, we discuss the definition and classification of products, the importance of product quality and value, and the nature of a product mix and product lines. Also considered is the role of branding and packaging.

Product Definition

The way in which the product variable is defined can have important implications for the survival, profitability, and long-run growth of the firm. For example, the same product can be viewed at least three different ways. First, it can be viewed in terms of the *tangible product*—the physical entity or service that is offered to the buyer. Second, it can be viewed in terms of the *extended product*—the tangible product along with the whole cluster of services that accompany it. For example, a manufacturer of computer software may offer a 24-hour hotline to answer questions users may have about free or reduced-cost software updates, free replacement of damaged software, and a subscription to a newsletter that documents new applications of the software. Third, it can be viewed in terms of the *generic product*—the essential benefits the buyer expects to receive from the product. For example, many personal care products bring to the purchaser feelings of self-enhancement and security in addition to the tangible benefits they offer.

From the standpoint of the marketing manager, to define the product solely in terms of the tangible product is to fall into the error of "marketing myopia." Executives who are guilty of committing this error define their company's product too narrowly, since they overemphasize the physical object itself. The classic example of this mistake can be found in railroad passenger service. Although no amount of product improvement could have staved off its decline, if the industry had defined itself as being in the transportation business, rather than the railroad business, it might still be profitable today. On the positive side, toothpaste manufacturers have been willing to exercise flexibility in defining their product. For years toothpaste was an oral hygiene product where emphasis was placed solely on fighting tooth decay and bad breath (e.g., Crest with fluoride). More recently, many manufacturers have recognized the need to market toothpaste as a cosmetic item (to clean teeth of stains), as a defense against gum disease (to reduce the buildup of tartar above the gumline), as an aid for denture wearers, and as a breath freshener. As a result, special purpose brands have been designed to serve these particular needs, such as Ultra Brite, Close-Up, Aqua-Fresh, Aim, Dental Care, and the wide variety of baking soda, tartar-control formulas, and gel toothpastes offered under existing brand names.

In line with the marketing concept philosophy, a reasonable definition of product is that it is *the sum of the physical, psychological, and sociological satisfactions the buyer derives from purchase, ownership, and consumption.* From this standpoint, products are customer-satisfying objects that include such things as accessories, packaging, and service.

Product Classification

A product classification scheme can be useful to the marketing manager as an analytical device to assist in planning marketing strategy and programs. A basic assumption underlying such classifications is that products with common attributes can be marketed in a similar fashion. In general, products are classed according to two basic criteria: (1) end use or market; and (2) degree of processing or physical transformation.

1. *Agricultural products and raw materials.* These are goods grown or extracted from the land or sea, such as iron ore, wheat, sand. In general, these products are fairly homogeneous, sold in large volume, and have low value per unit or bulk weight.
2. *Organizational goods.* Such products are purchased by business firms for the purpose of producing other goods or for running the business. This category includes the following:
   a. Raw materials and semifinished goods.
   b. Major and minor equipment, such as basic machinery, tools, and other processing facilities.
   c. Parts or components, which become an integral element of some other finished good.
   d. Supplies or items used to operate the business but that do not become part of the final product.

3. *Consumer goods.* Consumer goods can be divided into three classes:
   a. Convenience goods, such as food, which are purchased frequently with minimum effort. Impulse goods would also fall into this category.
   b. Shopping goods, such as appliances, which are purchased after some time and energy are spent comparing the various offerings.
   c. Specialty goods, which are unique in some way so the consumer will make a special purchase effort to obtain them.

In general, the buying motive, buying habits, and character of the market are different for organizational goods vis-à-vis consumer goods. A primary purchasing motive for organizational goods is, of course, profit. As mentioned in a previous chapter, organizational goods are usually purchased as means to an end and not as an end in themselves. This is another way of saying that the demand for goods is a derived demand. Organizational goods are often purchased directly from the original source with few middlemen, because many of these goods can be bought in large quantities; they have high unit value; technical advice on installation and use is required; and the product is ordered according to the user's specifications. Many organizational goods are subject to multiple-purchase influence and a long period of negotiation is often required.

The market for organizational goods has certain attributes that distinguish it from the consumer goods market. Much of the market is concentrated geographically, as in the case of steel, auto, or shoe manufacturing. For certain products there are a limited number of buyers; this is known as a *vertical market,* which means that (1) it is narrow, because customers are restricted to a few industries; and (2) it is deep, in that a large percentage of the producers in the market use the product. Some products, such as office supplies, have a *horizontal market,* which means that the goods are purchased by all types of firms in many different industries. In general, buyers of organizational goods are reasonably well informed. As noted previously, heavy reliance is often placed on price, quality control, and reliability of supply source.

In terms of consumer products, many marketing scholars have found the convenience, shopping, and specialty classification inadequate and have attempted to either refine it or to derive an entirely new typology. None of these attempts appears to have met with complete success. Perhaps there is no best way to deal with this problem. From the standpoint of the marketing manager, product classification is useful to the extent that it assists in providing guidelines for developing an appropriate marketing mix. For example, convenience goods generally require broadcast promotion and long channels of distribution as opposed to shopping goods, which generally require more targeted promotion and somewhat shorter channels of distribution.

Product Quality and Value

Quality can be defined as the degree of excellence or superiority that an organization's product possesses.[1] Quality can encompass both the tangible and intangible aspects of a firm's products or services. In a technical sense, quality can refer to physical traits such as features, performance, reliability, durability, aesthetics, serviceability, and conformance to specifications. Although quality can be evaluated from many perspectives, the customer is the key perceiver of quality because his or her purchase decision determines the success of the organization's product or service and often the fate of the organization itself.

Many organizations have formalized their interest in providing quality products by undertaking total quality management (TQM) programs. TQM is an organizationwide commitment to satisfying customers by continuously improving every business process involved in delivering products or services. Instead of merely correcting defects when they occur, organizations that practice TQM train and commit employees to continually look for ways to do things better so defects and problems don't arise in the first place. The result of this process is higher-quality products being produced at a lower cost. Indeed, the emphasis on quality has risen to such a level that over 70 countries have adopted the ISO 9000 quality system of standards, a standardized approach for evaluating a supplier's quality system, which can be applied to virtually any business.[2]

The term quality is often confused with the concept of value. Value encompasses not only quality but also price. *Value* can be defined as what the customer gets in exchange for what the customer gives. In other words, a customer, in most cases, receives a product in exchange for having paid the supplier for the product. A customer's perception of the value associated with a product is generally based both on the degree to which the product meets his or her specifications and the price that the customer will have to pay to acquire the product. Some organizations are beginning to shift their primary focus from one that solely emphasizes quality to one that also equally encompasses the customer's viewpoint of the price/quality trade-off. Organizations that are successful at this process derive their competitive advantage from the provision of customer value. In other words, they offer goods and services that meet or exceed customer needs at a fair price. Recall that Chapter 1 described various strategies based on value disciplines.

Product Mix and Product Line

The *product mix* is the composite of products offered for sale by the firm; *product line* refers to a group of products that are closely related, either because they satisfy a class of need, are used together, are sold to the same customer groups, are marketed through the same types of outlets, or fall within given price ranges. There are three primary dimensions of a firm's product mix: (1) width of the product mix, which refers to the number of product lines the firm handles; (2) depth of the product mix, which refers to the average number of products in each line;

Marketing
Highlight 6–2

A. Classes of Consumer Goods—Some Characteristics and Marketing Considerations

	Type of Product		
	Convenience	**Shopping**	**Specialty**
Examples:	Canned fruit	Furniture	Expensive Suits
Characteristics:			
Time and effort devoted by consumer to shopping	Very little	Considerable	Cannot generalize*
Time spent planning the purchase	Very little	Considerable	Considerable
How soon want is satisfied after it arises	Immediately	Relatively long time	Relatively long time
Are price and quality compared?	No	Yes	No
Price	Usually low	High	High
Frequency of purchase	Usually frequent	Infrequent	Infrequent
Importance	Unimportant	Often very important	Cannot generalize
Marketing considerations:			
Length of channel	Long	Short	Short to very short
Importance of retailer	Any single store is relatively unimportant	Important	Very important
Number of outlets	As many as possible	Few	Few; often only one in a market
Stock turnover	High	Lower	Lower
Gross margin	Low	High	High
Responsibility for advertising	Producer	Retailer	Joint responsibility
Importance of point-of-purchase display	Very important	Less important	Less important
Brand or store name important	Brand name	Store name	Both
Importance of packaging	Very important	Less important	Less important

*Consumer may go to by store and buy with minimum effort or may have to go to distant store and spend much time and effort.

SOURCE: Michael J. Etzel, Bruce J. Walker, and William J. Stanton, *Fundamentals of Marketing,* 11th ed. © 1997, New York, McGraw-Hill, Inc., pp. 195, 198. Reproduced by permission of The McGraw-Hill Companies.

(continued)

Marketing
Highlight 6–2

B. Classes of Organizational Products—
Some Characteristics and Marketing

	Raw Materials	Fabricating Parts and Materials	Installations	Accessory Equipment	Operating Supplies
Examples:	Iron ore	Engine blocks	Blast furnaces	Storage racks	Paper clips
Characteristics:					
Unit price	Very low	Low	Very high	Medium	Low
Length of life	Very short	Depends on final product	Very long	Long	Short
Quantities purchased	Large	Large	Very small	Small	Small
Frequency of purchase	Frequent delivery; long-term purchase contract	Infrequent purchase, but frequent delivery	Very infrequent	Medium frequency	Frequent
Standardization of competitive products	Very much; grading is important	Very much	Very little; custom-made	Little	Much
Quantity of supply	Limited; supply can be in-creased slowly or not at all	Usually no problem	No problem	Usually no problem	Usually no problem
Marketing considerations:					
Nature of channel	Short; no middlemen	Short; middle-men for small buyers	Short; no middlemen	Middlemen used	Middlemen used
Negotiation period	Hard to generalize	Medium	Long	Medium	Short
Price competition	Important	Important	Not important	Not main factor	Important
Presale/post-sale service	Not important	Important	Very important	Important	Very little
Promotional activity	Very little	Moderate	Sales people very important	Important	Not too important
Brand preference	None	Generally low	High	High	Low
Advance buying contract	Important; long-term contracts used	Important; long-term contracts used	Not usually used	Not usually used	Not usually used

Table header spanning: Type of Product

and (3) consistency of the product mix, which refers to the similarity of product lines. Thus, McDonald's hamburgers represent a product item in its line of sandwiches, whereas hotcakes or Egg McMuffins represent items in a different line, namely, breakfast foods.

An integral component of product line planning revolves around the question of how many product variants should be included in the line.[3] Manufacturing costs are usually minimized through large-volume production runs, and distribution costs tend to be lower if only one product is sold, stocked, and serviced. At a given level of sales, profits will usually be highest if those sales have been achieved with a single product. However, many product variants are offered by many firms.

There are three reasons organizations offer varying products within a given product line. First, potential customers rarely agree on a single set of specifications regarding their "ideal product," differing greatly in the importance and value they place on specific attributes. For example, in the laundry detergent market, there is a marked split between preferences for powder versus liquid detergent. Second, customers prefer variety. For example, a person may like Italian food but does not want to only eat spaghetti. Therefore, an Italian restaurant will offer the customer a wide variety of Italian dishes to choose from. Third, the dynamics of competition lead to multiproduct lines. As competitors seek to increase market share, they find it advantageous to introduce new products that subsegment an existing market segment by offering benefits more precisely tailored to the specific needs of a portion of that segment. For example, Procter & Gamble offers Jif peanut butter in a low-salt version to target a specific subsegment of the peanut butter market.

All too often, organizations pursue product line additions with little regard for consequences.[4] However, in reaching a decision on product line additions, organizations need to evaluate whether (1) total profits will decrease or (2) the quality/value associated with current products will suffer. If the answer to either of the above is yes, then the organization should not proceed with the addition. Closely related to product line additions are issues associated with branding. These are covered next.

Branding and Brand Equity

For some organizations, the primary focus of strategy development is placed on brand building, developing, and nurturing activities.[5] Many other companies use branding strategies in order to increase the strength of the product image. Factors that serve to increase the brand image strength include[6] (1) product quality when products do what they do very well (e.g., Windex and Easy-Off); (2) consistent advertising and other marketing communications in which brands tell their story often and well (e.g., Pepsi and Visa); (3) distribution intensity whereby customers see the brand wherever they shop (e.g., Marlboro); and (4) brand personality where the brand stands for something (e.g., Disney). The strength of the Coca-Cola brand, for example, is widely attributed to its universal availability, universal awareness, and trademark protection, which came as a result of strategic actions taken by the parent organization.[7]

The brand name is perhaps the single most important element on the package, serving as a unique identifier. Specifically, a *brand* is a name, term, design, symbol, or any other feature that identifies one seller's good or service as distinct from those of other sellers. The legal term for brand is *trademark*.[8] A good brand name can evoke feelings of trust, confidence, security, strength, and many other desirable characteristics.[9] To illustrate, consider the case of Bayer aspirin. Bayer can be sold at up to two times the price of generic aspirin due to the strength of its brand image.

Many companies make use of manufacturer branding strategies in carrying out market and product development strategies. The *line extension* approach uses a brand name to facilitate entry into a new market segment (e.g., Diet Coke and Liquid Tide). An alternative to line extension is brand extension. In *brand extension,* a current brand name is used to enter a completely different product class (e.g., Jello pudding pops, Ivory shampoo).[10]

A third form of branding is *franchise extension* or *family branding,* whereby a company attaches the corporate name to a product either to enter a new market segment or a different product class (e.g., Honda lawnmower, Toyota Lexus). A final type of branding strategy that is becoming more and more common is dual branding. A *dual branding* (also known as joint or cobranding) strategy is one in which two or more branded products are integrated (e.g., Bacardi rum and Coca-Cola, Archway cookies and Kellogg cereal, US Airways and NationsBank Visa). The logic behind this strategy is that if one brand name on a product gives a certain signal of quality, then the presence of a second brand name on the product should result in a signal that is at least as powerful, if not more powerful than, the signal in the case of the single brand name. Each of the preceeding four approaches is an attempt by companies to gain a competitive advantage by making use of its or others' established reputation, or both.

Companies may also choose to assign different or multiple brand names to related products. By doing so, the firm makes a conscious decision to allow the products to succeed or fail on their own merits. Major advantages of using multiple brand names are that (1) the firm can distance products from other offerings it markets; (2) the image of one product (or set of products) is not associated with other products the company markets; (3) the product(s) can be targeted at a specific market segment; and (4) should the product(s) fail, the probability of failure impacting on other company products is minimized. For example, many consumers are unaware that Dreft, Tide, Oxydol, Bold, Cheer, and Dash laundry detergents are all marketed by Procter & Gamble. The major disadvantage of this strategy is that because new names are assigned, there is no consumer brand awareness and significant amounts of money must be spent familiarizing customers with new brands.

Increasingly, companies are finding that brand names are one of the most valuable assets they possess. Successful extensions of an existing brand can lead to additional loyalty and associated profits. Conversely, a wrong extension can cause damaging associations, as perceptions linked to the brand name are transferred back from one product to the other.[11] *Brand equity* can be viewed as the set of assets (or liabilities) linked to the brand that add (or subtract) value.[12] The value of these assets is dependent upon the consequences or results of the marketplace's relationship with a brand. Figure 6–1 lists the elements of brand equity. Brand equity is determined by the consumer and is the culmination of the consumer's assessment of the product, the company that manufactures and markets the product, and all other variables that impact on the product between manufacture and consumer consumption.

Before leaving the topic of manufacturer brands, it is important to note that, as with consumer products, organizational products also can possess brand equity. However, several differences do exist between the two sectors.[13] First, organizational

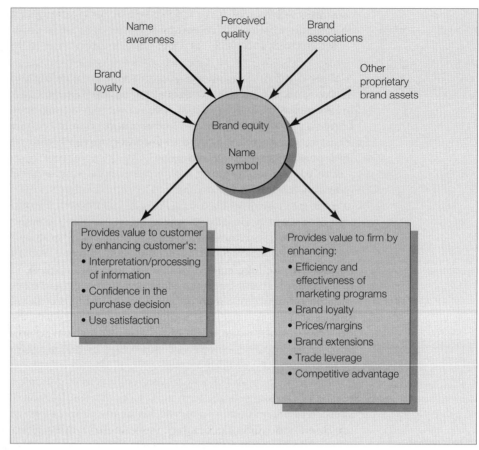

SOURCE: David A. Aaker, *Managing Brand Equity.* © 1991, New York, by David A. Aaker. Reprinted with the permission of The Free Press, a division of Simon & Schuster.

products are usually branded with firm names. As a result, loyalty (or disloyalty) to the brand tends to be of a more global nature, extending across all the firm's product lines. Second, because firm versus brand loyalty exists, attempts to position new products in a manner differing from existing products may prove to be difficult, if not impossible. Finally, loyalty to organizational products encompasses not only the firm and its products but also the distribution channel members employed to distribute the product. Therefore, attempts to establish or change brand image must also take into account distributor image.

As a related branding strategy, many retail firms produce or market their products under a so-called private label. For example, Kmart has phased in its own store-brand products to compete with the national brands. There's Nature's Classics, a line of fancy snacks and cookies; Oral Pure, a line of dental care products; Prevail house cleaners; B.E., a Gap-style line of weekend wear; and Benchmark, a line of "made in the U.S.A." tools. Such a strategy is highly important in industries where middlemen have gained control over distribution to the consumer. The growth of the large discount and specialty stores, such as Kmart, Wal-Mart, Target, The Gap, Limited, and others, has accelerated the development of private brands. If a manufacturer refuses to supply certain middlemen with private branded merchandise, the alternative is for these middlemen to go into the manufacturing busines. in the case of Kroger supermarkets.

Private label products differ markedly from so-called generic products that sport labels such as "beer," "cigarettes," and "potato chips." Today's house brands are packaged in distinctively upscale containers. The quality of the products utilized as house brands equals and sometimes exceeds those offered by name brands. While generic products were positioned as a means for consumers to struggle through recessionary times, private label brands are being marketed as value brands, products that are equivalent to national brands but are priced much lower. Private brands are rapidly growing in popularity. For example, it took J. C. Penney only five years to nurture its private label jeans, the Arizona brand, into a powerhouse with annual sales surpassing $500 million.

Consolidation within the supermarket industry, growth of "super centers," and heightened product marketing are poised to strengthen private brands even further.[14] However, these gains will not come without a fight from national manufacturers who are undertaking aggressive actions to defend their brands' market share. Some have significantly rolled back prices, while others have instituted increased promotional campaigns. The ultimate winner in this ongoing battle between private (store) and manufacturer (national) brands, not surprisingly, should be the consumer who is able to play off these store brands against national brands. By shopping at a mass merchandiser like Wal-Mart or Walgreens, consumers are exposed to and able to choose from a wide array of both national and store brands, thus giving them the best of both worlds: value and variety.

Packaging

Distinctive or unique packaging is one method of differentiating a relatively homogeneous product. To illustrate, shelf-stable microwave dinners, pumps rather than tubes of toothpaste or bars of soap, and different sizes and designs of tissue packages are attempts to differentiate a product through packaging and to satisfy consumer needs at the same time.

In some cases, companies have begun utilizing packaging strategies to strengthen their brands by updating the look. For example, in the cold pill product segment, there are over 240 varieties of products consumers can choose from.[15] SmithKline Beecham, the maker of Contac, saw its share of this market had been slipping steadily. To combat increasing competition, especially from private brands, SmithKline decided to radically redesign the package. The formerly white background is now blue, with the color growing darker from the bottom of the box to the top. A clock in the bottom right corner, indicating 12-hour relief, was replaced by a globe, also meant to represent the passage of time. The Contac logo was maintained, but underneath it was placed a yellow banner that indicated what cold symptoms each formula is for. There were two equally important net results of these changes. First, the new packaging made it very obvious to the consumer that they were purchasing the Contac brand. Second, due to all the color schemes, the package was very expensive to replicate, thus decreasing the likelihood of a look-alike private brand emerging.

In other cases, packaging changes have succeeded in creating new attributes of value in a brand. A growing number of manufacturers are using green labels or packaging their products totally in green wrap to signify low or no fat content.[16] Frito-Lay, Quaker Oats, ConAgra, Keebler, Pepperidge Farm, Nabisco, and Sunshine Biscuits are all examples of companies involved in this endeavor.

Finally, packaging changes can make products urgently salable to a targeted segment. For example, the products in the Gillette Series grooming line, including shave cream, razors, aftershave, and skin conditioner, come in ribbed, rounded, metallic-gray shapes, looking at once vaguely sexual and like precision engineering.[17]

Marketing managers must consider both the consumer and costs in making packaging decisions. On one hand, the package must be capable of protecting the product through the channel of distribution to the consumer. In addition, it is desirable for packages to have a convenient size and be easy to open for the consumer. For example, single-serving soups and zip-lock packaging in cereal boxes are attempts by manufacturers to serve consumers better. Hopefully, the package is also attractive and informative, capable of being used as a competitive weapon to project a product's image. However, maximizing these objectives may increase the cost of the product to such an extent that consumers are no longer willing to purchase it. Thus, the marketing manager must determine the optimal protection, convenience, positioning, and promotional strengths of packages, subject to cost constraints.

■ Product Life Cycle

A firm's product strategy must take into account the fact that products have a life cycle. Figure 6–2 illustrates this life-cycle concept. Products are introduced, grow, mature, and decline. This cycle varies according to industry, product, technology, and market. Marketing executives need to be aware of the life-cycle concept because it can be a valuable aid in developing marketing strategies.

■ **Figure 6–2**
The Product Life Cycle

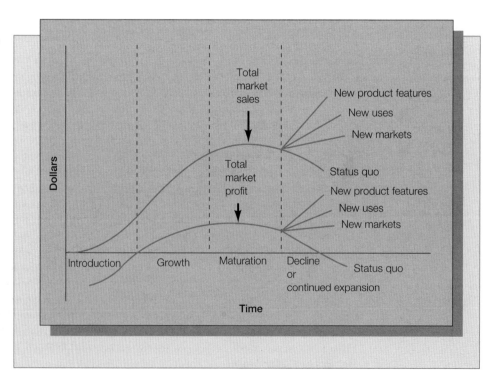

During the introduction phase of the cycle, there are usually high production and marketing costs, and since sales are only beginning to materialize, profits are low or nonexistent. Profits increase and are positively correlated with sales during the growth stage as the market begins trying and adopting the product. As the product matures, profits for the initiating firm do not keep pace with sales because of competition. Here the seller may be forced to "remarket" the product, which may involve making price concessions, increasing product quality, or expanding outlays on advertising and sales promotion just to maintain market share. At some time sales decline, and the seller must decide whether to (1) drop the product; (2) alter the product; (3) seek new uses for the product; (4) seek new markets; or (5) continue with more of the same.

The usefulness of the product life-cycle concept is primarily that it forces management to take a long-range view of marketing planning. In doing so, it should become clear that shifts in phases of the life cycle correspond to changes in the market situation, competition, and demand. Thus, the astute marketing manager should recognize the necessity of altering the marketing mix to meet these changing conditions. It is possible for managers to undertake strategies that, in effect, can lead to a revitalized product life cycle. For example, past advancements in technology led to the replacement of rotary dial telephones by touch-tone, push-button phones. Today, newer technology is allowing the cordless and cellular phone to replace the traditional touch-tone, push-button phone. When applied with sound judgment, the life-cycle concept can aid in forecasting, pricing, advertising, product planning, and other aspects of marketing management. However, the marketing manager must also recognize that the life cycle is purely a tool for assisting in strategy development and not let the life cycle dictate strategy development.[18]

■ The Product Audit

The product audit is a marketing management technique whereby the company's current product offerings are reviewed to ascertain whether each product should be continued as is, improved, modified, or deleted. The audit is a task that should be carried out at regular intervals as a matter of policy. Product audits are the responsibility of the product manager unless specifically delegated to someone else.

Deletions

In today's environment, there are a growing number of products being introduced each year that are competing for limited shelf space. This growth is primarily due to (1) new knowledge being applied faster, and (2) the decrease in time between product introductions (by a given organization).[19] In addition, companies are not consistently removing products from the market at the same time they are introducing new products. The result is a situation in which too many products are fighting for too little shelf space. One of the main purposes of the product audit is to detect sick products and then bury them. Rather than let the retailer or distributor decide which products should remain, organizations themselves should take the lead in developing criteria for deciding which products should stay and which should be deleted. Some of the more obvious factors to be considered are

Marketing
Highlight 6–3

**Marketing Strategy Implications
of the Product Life Cycle**

Strategy Dimension	Life-Cycle Stage			
	Introduction	**Growth**	**Maturity**	**Decline**
Basic objectives	Establish a market for product type; persuade early adopters to buy	Build sales and market share; develop preference for brand	Defend brand's share of market; seek growth by luring customers from competitors	Limit costs or seek ways to revive sales and profits
Product	Provide high quality; select a good brand; get patent or trademark protection	Provide high quality; add services to enhance value	Improve quality; add features to distinguish brand from competitors	Continue providing high quality to maintain brand's reputation; seek ways to make the product new again
Pricing	Often high to recover development costs; sometimes low to build demand rapidly	Somewhat high because of heavy demand	Low, reflecting heavy competition	Low to sell off remaining inventory or high to serve a niche market
Channels	Limited number of channels	Greater number of channels to meet demand	Greater number of channels and more incentives to resellers	Limited number of channels
Communication	Aimed at early adopters; messages designed to educate about product type; incentives such as samples and coupons to induce trial	Aimed at wider audience; messages focus on brand benefits; for consumer products, emphasis on advertising	Messages focus on differentiating brand from its competitors; heavy use of incentives such as coupons to induce buyers to switch brands	Minimal, to keep costs down

SOURCE: Gilbert A. Churchill, Jr., and J. Paul Peter, *Marketing: Creating Value for Customers,* rev. ed. (Burr Ridge, IL: Irwin/McGraw-Hill, 1998), p. 238.

Sales trends. How have sales moved over time? What has happened to market share? Why have sales declined? What changes in sales have occurred in competitive products both in our line and in those of other manufacturers?

Profit contribution. What has been the profit contribution of this product to the company? If profits have declined, how are these tied to price? Have selling, promotion, and distribution costs risen out of proportion to sales? Does the product require excessive management time and effort?

Product life cycle. Has the product reached a level of maturity and saturation in the market? Has new technology been developed that poses a threat to the product?

Are there more effective substitutes on the market? Has the product outgrown its usefulness? Can the resources used on this product be put to better use?
Customer migration patterns. If the product is deleted, will customers of this product switch to other substitute products marketed by our firm? In total, will profits associated with our line increase due to favorable switching patterns?

The above factors should be used as guidelines for making the final decision to delete a product. Deletion decisions are very difficult to make because of their potential impact on customers and the firm. For example, eliminating a product may force a company to lay off some employees. There are other factors to consider, such as keeping consumers supplied with replacement parts and repair service and maintaining the goodwill of distributors who have an inventory of the product. The deletion plan should provide for clearing out of stock in question.

Product Improvement

One of the other important objectives of the audit is to ascertain whether to alter the product in some way or to leave things as they are. Altering the product means changing one or more of its attributes or marketing dimensions. *Attributes* refer mainly to product features, design, package, and so forth. *Marketing dimensions* refer to such things as price, promotion strategy, and channels of distribution.

It is possible to look at the product audit as a management device for controlling the product strategy. Here, control means feedback on product performance and corrective action in the form of product improvement. Product improvement is a top-level management decision, but the information needed to make the improvement decision may come from the consumer or the middlemen. Suggestions are often made by advertising agencies or consultants. Reports by the sales force should be structured in a way to provide management with certain types of product information; in fact, these reports can be the firm's most valuable product improvement tool. Implementing a product improvement decision will often require the coordinated efforts of several specialists, plus some research. For example, product design improvement decisions involve engineering, manufacturing, accounting, and marketing. When a firm becomes aware that a product's design can be improved, it is not always clear how consumers will react to the various alterations. To illustrate, in blind taste tests, the Coca-Cola Company found that consumers overwhelmingly preferred the taste of a reformulated, sweeter new Coke over old Coke. However, when placed on the market in labeled containers, new Coke turned out to be a failure due to consumers' emotional attachments to the classic Coke. Consequently, it is advisable to conduct some market tests in realistic settings.

It would be remiss on our part if the discussion on product improvement was closed without taking into account the benefits associated with benchmarking, especially as they relate to the notion of the extended product.[20] The formal definition of *benchmarking* is the continuous process of measuring products, services, and practices against those of the toughest competitors or companies renowned as leaders. In other words, benchmarking involves learning about best practices from best-performing companies—how they are achieving strong performance. It is an effective tool being used by organizations to improve on existing products, activities, functions, or processes. Major corporations, such as IBM, AT&T, DuPont, Ford, Eastman Kodak, Miliken, Motorola, and Xerox, all have numerous benchmarking studies in progress. For example, IBM has already performed more than 500 benchmarking studies. Benchmarking can assist companies in many product improvement efforts, including (1) boosting product quality, (2) developing more user-friendly products, (3) improving customer order-processing activities, and (4) shortening delivery lead times. In the case of benchmarking, companies can achieve great success by copying others. Thus, by its very nature, benchmarking becomes an essential element in the ongoing product auditing process.

■ Organizing for Product Management

Whether managing existing products or developing new products (the subject of the next chapter), organizations that are successful have one factor in common, they actively manage both types. Obviously, if a firm has but one product it gets everyone's attention. But as the number of products grows and the need to develop new products becomes evident, some rational management system is necessary.

Under a *marketing manager system,* one person is responsible for overseeing an entire product line with all of the functional areas of marketing such as research, advertising, sales promotion, sales, and product planning. This type of system is popular in organizations with a line or lines of similar products or one dominant product line. Sometimes referred to as category management, the marketing-manager system is seen as being superior to a brand manager system because one manager oversees all brands within a particular line, thus avoiding brand competition. Organizations such as PepsiCo, Purex, Eastman Kodak, and Levi Strauss use some form of marketing manager system.

Under a *brand manager system,* there is a manager who focuses on a single product or a very small group of new and existing products. Typically, this person is responsible for everything from marketing research and package design to advertising. Often called a product management system, the brand manager system has been criticized on several dimensions. First, brand managers often have difficulty because they do not have authority commensurate with their responsibilities. Second, they often pay inadequate attention to new products. Finally, they are often

■ **Figure 6–3** Some Requirements for the Effective Use of Cross-Functional Teams in Product Management and New Product Development

A growing number of organizations have begun utilizing cross-functional teams for product management and new product development. Having representatives from various departments clearly has its advantages; but most important, effective teams must have the nurture and support of management. Some requirements for effective teams are

1. *Commitment of top management and provision of clear goals.* Organizations that successfully use cross-functional teams in product management or development have managers who are deeply committed to the team concept. As a result, high-performance teams have a clear understanding of the product management and development goals of the organization. The importance of these goals encourages individuals to defer their own functional or departmental concerns to team goals.
2. *Trust among members.* For cross-functional teams to work, a high level of trust must exist among members. The climate of trust within a team seems to be highly dependent on members' perception of management's trust of the group as a whole.
3. *Cross-functional cooperation.* If a team is to take responsibility and assume the risk of product development, its members will need detailed information about the overall operation of the organization. It often requires that functional units be willing to share information that previously was not shared with other departments.
4. *Time and training.* Effective cross-functional teams need time to mature. They require massive planning and intense and prompt access to resources, financial and other. Because members have to put aside functional and departmental loyalties and concerns, training is usually necessary.

more concerned with their own brand's profitability than with the profitability of all of the organization's brands. These criticisms are not aimed at people but at the system itself, which may force brand managers into the above behaviors. Despite its drawbacks, organizations such as RJR Nabisco and Black & Decker have utilized that system.

Successful *new* products often come from organizations that try to bring all of the capabilities of the organization to bear on the problems of customers. Obviously, this requires the cooperation of all of the various functional departments in the organization. Thus, the use of *cross-functional teams* has become an important way to manage the development of new products. A *venture team* is a popular method utilized in such organizations as Xerox, Polaroid, Exxon, IBM, Monsanto, and Motorola. A venture team is a cross-functional team responsible for all the tasks involved in the development of a new product. Once the new product is already launched, the team may turn over responsibility for managing the product to a brand manager or product manager or it may manage the new product as a separate business.

The use of cross-functional teams in product management and new product development is increasing for a very simple reason; organizations need the contributions of all functions and therefore require their cooperation. Cross-functional teams operate independently of the organization's functional departments but include members from each function. A team might include a member from engineering, marketing, finance, service, and designers. Some organizations even include important outsiders (e.g., parts suppliers) on cross-functional teams. Figure 6–3 presents some important prerequisites for the use of cross-functional teams in managing existing products and developing new products.

■ Conclusion

This chapter has been concerned with a central element of marketing management—product strategy. The first part of the chapter discussed some basic issues in product strategy, including product definition and classification, product quality and value, product mix and product lines, branding and brand equity, and packaging. The product life cycle was discussed as well as the product audit. Finally, three methods of organizing for product management were presented. Although product considerations are extremely important, remember that the product is only one element of the marketing mix. Focusing on product decisions alone, without consideration of the other marketing mix variables, would be an ineffective approach to marketing strategy.

■ Additional Readings

Aaker, David. "Should You Take Your Brand to Where the Action Is?" *Harvard Business Review,* September–October 1997, pp. 135–43.

Cespedes, Frank. "Beyond Teamwork: How the Wise Can Synchronize." *Marketing Management,* Spring 1996, pp. 25–37.

Keller, Kevin Lane. *Strategic Brand Management: Building, Measuring, and Managing Brand Equity.* Upper Saddle River, NJ: Prentice Hall, 1998.

Lehman, Donald R., and Russell S. Winer. *Product Management.* Burr Ridge, IL: Irwin/ McGraw-Hill, 1997.

Mudambi, Susan McDowell; Peter Doyle; and Veronica Wong. "An Exploration of Branding in Industrial Markets." *Industrial Marketing Management,* September 1997, pp. 433–46.

Tulin, Erden. "An Empirical Analysis of Umbrella Branding." *Journal of Marketing Research,* August 1998, pp. 339–51.

Upshaw, Lynn B. *Building Brand Identity,* New York: Wiley, 1995.

Chapter Seven

New Product Planning and Development

New products are a vital part of a firm's competitive growth strategy. Leaders of successful firms know that it is not enough to develop new products on a sporadic basis. What counts is a climate of product development that leads to one triumph after another. It is commonplace for major companies to have 50 percent or more of their current sales in products introduced within the last 10 years. For example, the 3M Company derives 30 percent of its revenues from products less than four years old.[1]

Some additional facts about new products are:

- Many new products are failures. Estimates of new product failures range from 33 percent to 90 percent, depending on industry.
- New product sales grow far more rapidly than sales of current products, potentially providing a surprisingly large boost to a company's growth rate.
- Companies vary widely in the effectiveness of their new product programs.
- A major obstacle to effectively predicting new product demand is limited vision.
- Common elements appear in the management practices that generally distinguish the relative degree of efficiency and success between companies.

In one recent year, almost 22,000 products were introduced in supermarkets, drugstores, mass merchandisers, and health food stores.[2] Of these, only a small percentage (less than 20 percent) met sales goals. The cost of introducing a new brand in some consumer markets can range from $50 million to hundreds of millions of dollars. In addition to the outlay cost of product failures, there are also opportunity costs. These opportunity costs refer not only to the alternative uses of funds spent on product failures but also to the time spent in unprofitable product development.

Product development can take many years. For example, Hills Brothers (now owned by Nestlé) spent 22 years in developing its instant coffee, while it took General Foods (now owned by Philip Morris) 10 years to develop Maxim. However, the success of one new product is no guarantee that the way will be paved for additional and successful low-cost brand extensions. For example, on the positive side, Gillette was able to leverage the research and monies spent on the original Sensor to successfully develop and launch the Sensor razor for women and the Sensor Excel razor. On the negative side, Maxwell House (Philip Morris), Folgers (Procter & Gamble), and Nestlé are still struggling to develop commercially successful lines of fresh whole bean coffee, having been beaten to the punch by smaller companies such as Millstone Coffee, Inc., and Brothers Gourmet Coffees.[3]

Good management, with heavy emphasis on planning, organization, and interaction among the various functional units (e.g., marketing, manufacturing, engineering, R&D), seems to be the key factor contributing to a firm's success in launching new products. The primary reason found for new product failure is an inability on the part of the selling company to match up its offerings to the needs of the customer. This inability to satisfy customer needs can be attributed to three main sources: inadequacy of upfront intelligence efforts, failure on the part of the company to stick close to what the company does best, and the inability to provide better value than competing products and technologies.

■ New Product Strategy

In developing new products, the first question a marketing manager must ask is, In how many ways can a product be new? C. Merle Crawford developed a definition of new products based on the following five different categories:[4]

1. *New-to-the-world products.* Products that are inventions, for example, Polaroid camera, the first car, rayon, the laser printer, in-line skates.
2. *New category entries.* Products that take a firm into a category new to it. Products are not new to the world, for example, P&G's first shampoo, Hallmark gift items, AT&T's Universal Card.
3. *Additions to product lines.* Products that are line extensions, flankers, and so on, to the firm's current markets, for example, Tide Liquid detergent, Bud Light, Apple's Power Mac.
4. *Product improvements.* Current products made better; virtually every product on the market has been improved, often many times.
5. *Repositionings.* Products that are retargeted for a new use or application; a classic case is Arm & Hammer baking soda, which was repositioned several times as drain deodorant, refrigerator freshener, toothpaste, deodorant, and so on.

The new product categories listed above raise the issue of imitation products, strictly me-too or improved versions of existing products. If a firm introduces a form of dry beer that is new to them but is identical or similar to those on the market, is it a new product? The answer is yes because it is new to the firm. Managers should not get the idea that to imitate is bad and to innovate is good, for most of the best-selling products on the market today are improvements over another company's original invention. The best strategy is the one that will maximize company goals. It should be noted that Crawford's categories don't encompass variations such as new to a country, new channel of distribution, packaging improvement, and different resources or method of manufacture, which he considers to be variations of the five categories, especially as they relate to additions to product lines.

A second broader approach to the new product question is the one developed by H. Igor Ansoff in the form of growth vectors.[5] This is the matrix first introduced in

Marketing Highlight 7–1

Three Common Misconceptions about the New Product Development Process

Since successful new product development is of vital importance to an organization, corporations are searching for numerous methods to improve the NPD process. However, in the mad rush, managers can overlook their greatest ally, common sense. What follows are three misconceptions that are commonly held by managers involved in the new product development process.

1. *It worked there; it will work here.* What works well at one company may not be as easily transferable with equal success to another company. There is no one common formula to the new product development process.
2. *It worked once; it will work again.* There will be peaks and valleys in every new product development process. Failure, as well as success, should be viewed as a common outcome.
3. *The cart can come before the horse.* Successful implementation of a means to improve the new product development process is heavily dependent on assumed conditions already existing within the corporation. Before the process can be improved, other organizational changes may have to be implemented.

SOURCE: Adapted from Geoffrey Gordon, Douglas Ayers, Nessim Hanna, and Rick Ridnour, "The Product Development Process: Three Misconceptions Which Can Derail Even the 'Best-Laid' Plans," *Journal of Product and Brand Management* 4, no. 1 (1995), pp. 7–17.

Chapter 1 that indicates the direction in which the organization is moving with respect to its current products and markets. It is shown again in Figure 7–1.

Market penetration denotes a growth direction through the increase in market share for present product markets. *Product development* refers to creating new products to replace existing ones. Firms utilizing either market penetration or product development strategies are attempting to capitalize on existing markets and combat competitive entry and/or further market incursions. *Market development* refers to finding new customers for existing products. *Diversification* refers to developing new products and cultivating new markets. Firms utilizing market development and diversification strategies are seeking to establish footholds in new markets or preempt competition in emerging market segments.

As shown in Figure 7–1, market penetration and market development strategies utilize present products. A goal of these types of strategies is to either increase frequency of consumption or increase the number of customers utilizing the firm's product(s). A strategic focus is placed on altering the breadth and depth of the firm's existing product lines. Product development and diversification can be characterized as product mix strategies. New products, as defined in the growth vector matrix, usually require the firm to make significant investments in research and development and may require major changes in its organizational structure. Firms are not confined to pursuing a single direction. For example, Miller Brewing Co. has decided four key strategies should dictate its activities for the next decade, including (1) building its premium-brand franchises through investment spending, (2) continuing to develop value-added new products with clear consumer benefits, (3) leveraging local markets to build its brand franchise, and (4) building business

Figure 7–1
Growth Vector Components

	Products	
Markets	**Present**	**New**
Present	Market penetration	Product development
New	Market development	Diversification

Ten Factors Associated with New Product Success

1. *Product superiority/quality.* The competitive advantage the product has by virtue of features, benefits, quality, uniqueness, and so on.
2. *Economic advantage to user.* The product's quality for the customer's money.
3. *Overall company/project fit.* The product's synergy with the company—marketing, managerial, business fit.
4. *Technological compatibility.* The product's technological synergy with the company—R&D, engineering, production fit.
5. *Familiarity to the company.* How familiar or "close to home" the product is to the company's current products and markets (as opposed to being targeted at new customers or markets).
6. *Market need, growth, and size.* The magnitude of the market opportunity.
7. *Competitive situation.* How easy the market is to penetrate from a competitive standpoint.
8. *Defined opportunity.* Whether the product has a well-defined category and established market to enter.
9. *Market-driven process.* The new product process is well planned and executed receiving adequate resources suited to the customer's needs, wants, and buying behavior.
10. *Customer service.* The product is supported by friendly, courteous, prompt, and efficient customer service.

SOURCES: Based on research conducted by Robert G. Cooper, "What Distinguishes the Top Performing New Products in Financial Services," *Journal of Product Innovation Management,* September 1994, pp. 281–99; and "The NewProd System: The Industry Experience," *Journal of Product Innovation Management,* June 1992, pp. 113–27.

globally.[6] Success for Miller depends on pursuing strategies that encompass all areas of the growth vector matrix.

It has already been stated that new products are the lifeblood of successful business firms. Thus, the critical product policy question is not whether to develop new products but in what direction to move. One way of dealing with this problem is to formulate standards or norms that new products must meet if they are to be considered candidates for launching. In other words, as part of its new product policy, management must ask itself the basic question, What is the potential contribution of each anticipated new product to the company?

Each company must answer this question in accordance with its long-term goals, corporate mission, resources, and so forth. Unfortunately, some of the reasons commonly given to justify the launching of new products are so general that they become meaningless. Phrases such as *additional profits, increased growth,* or *cyclical stability* must be translated into more specific objectives. For example, one objective may be to reduce manufacturing overhead costs by utilizing plant capacity better. This may be accomplished by using the new product as an off-season filler. Naturally, the new product proposal would also have to include production and accounting data to back up this cost argument.

In every new product proposal some attention must be given to the ultimate economic contribution of each new product candidate. If the argument is that a certain type of product is needed to keep up with competition or to establish leadership in the market, it is fair to ask, Why? To put the question another way, top management can ask: What will be the effect on the firm's long-run profit picture if we do not develop and launch this or that new product? Policy-making criteria on new products should specify (1) a working definition of the profit concept acceptable to top management; (2) a minimum level or floor of profits; (3) the availability and cost of capital to develop a new product; and (4) a specified time period in which the new product must recoup its operating costs and begin contributing to profits.

It is critical that firms not become solely preoccupied with a short-term focus on earnings associated with new products. For example, in some industrial markets, there has been found to be a 20-year spread between the development and wide-spread adoption of products, on average. Indeed, an advantage Japanese firms possess is that their management is free from the pressure of steady improvement in earnings per share that plagues American managers who emphasize short-term profits. Japanese managers believe that market share will lead to customer loyalty, which in turn will lead to profits generated from repeat purchases. Through a continual introduction of new products, firms will succeed in building share. This share growth will then ultimately result in earnings growth and profitability that will be supported by the stock market in terms of higher share prices over the long term.

■ New Product Planning and Development Process

Ideally, products that generate a maximum dollar profit with a minimum amount of risk should be developed and marketed. However, it is very difficult for planners to implement this idea because of the number and nature of the variables involved. What is needed is a systematic, formalized process for new product planning. Although such a process does not provide management with any magic answers, it can increase the probability of new product success. Initially, the firm must establish some new product policy guidelines that include the product fields of primary

■ **Figure 7–2**
The New Product
Development Process

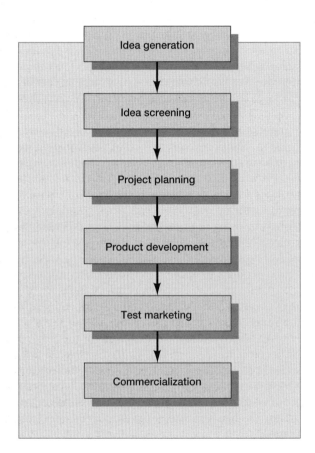

Idea generation

Idea screening

Project planning

Product development

Test marketing

Commercialization

interest, organizational responsibilities for managing the various stages in new product development, and criteria for making go-ahead decisions. After these guidelines are established, a process such as the one shown in Figure 7–2 should be useful in new product development.

Idea Generation

Every product starts as an idea. But all new product ideas do not have equal merit or potential for economic or commercial success. Some estimates indicate that as many as 60 or 70 ideas are necessary to yield one successful product. This is an average figure, but it serves to illustrate that new product ideas have a high mortality rate. In terms of money, almost three-fourths of all the dollars of new product expense go to unsuccessful products.

The problem at this stage is to ensure that all new product ideas available to the company at least have a chance to be heard and evaluated. Ideas are the raw materials for product development, and the whole planning process depends on the quality of the idea generation and screening process. Since idea generation is the least costly stage in the new product development process (in terms of investment in funds, time, personnel, and escalation of commitment), it makes sense that an emphasis be placed first on recognizing available sources of new product ideas and then on funneling these ideas to appropriate decision makers for screening.

Top management support is critical to providing an atmosphere that stimulates new product activity. Many times, great ideas come from some very unusual sources. A top management structure that is unwilling to take risks will avoid radical, new product and other innovation activities and instead solely concentrate on minor areas of improvement such as line extensions. To facilitate top management support, it is essential that new product development be focused on meeting market needs.

Both technology push and market pull research activities play an important role in new product ideas and development. By taking a broad view of customer needs and wants, basic and applied research (technology push) can lead to ideas that will yield high profits to the firm. For example, Compaq bet millions (and won) on PC network servers in the early 1990s even though business customers said they would never abandon their mainframes. In a similar vein, Chrysler forged ahead with the original minivan despite research showing people disliked the odd-looking vehicle.[7] Marketing, on the other hand, is more responsible for gathering and disseminating information gained from customer and other contacts. This information relates mainly to specific features and functions of the product that can be improved upon or market needs that current products are not satisfying. For example, product ideas at Rubbermaid often come from employees roaming the aisles at hardware stores and conversations with family and friends.[8] Both technology push and market pull approaches are essential to the generation of new product ideas.

Some firms use mechanisms such as "out-rotation," outsider involvement, and rewards for boundary-spanning to foster cooperation between design engineers and marketers.[9] Out-rotation involves placing employees in positions that require direct contact with customers, competitors, and other key outside groups. For example, Hewlett-Packard regularly rotates design engineers to retail sales positions on a temporary basis. Other organizations actively involve "outsiders" in planning or reward engineers for making external customer contacts. Regardless of method used, the primary lesson is to keep the communications flow going in all directions throughout the organization.

Idea Screening

The primary function of the idea screening process is twofold: first, to eliminate ideas for new products that could not be profitably marketed by the firm, and second, to expand viable ideas into full product concepts. New product ideas may be eliminated either because they are outside the fields of the firm's interest or because the firm does not have the necessary resources or technology to produce the product at a profit. Generally speaking, the organization has to consider three categories of risk (and its associated risk tolerance) in the idea screening phase prior to reaching a decision. These three risk categories are:[10]

1. *Strategic risk.* Strategic risk involves the risk of not matching the role or purpose of a new product with a specific strategic need or issue of the organization. If an organization feels it necessary to develop certain types of radical innovations or products new to the company in order to carry out long-term strategies, then management must be willing to dedicate necessary resources and time to pursue these type projects.
2. *Market risk.* Market risk is the risk that a new product won't meet a market need in a value-added, differentiated way. As products are being developed, customer requirements change and new technologies evolve. Management must be willing and able to shift its new product efforts to keep pace with change.
3. *Internal risk.* Internal risk is the risk that a new product won't be developed within the desired time and budget. Up front, management must decide the level of commitment it will extend in terms of time and budgetary expenditures to adequately ensure the completion of specific projects. Concurrently, progress goals must be established so that "proceed" or "do not proceed" decisions can be reached regarding continuation of projects.

In evaluating these risks, firms should not act too hastily in discounting new product ideas solely because of a lack of resources or expertise. Instead, firms should consider forming joint or strategic alliances with other firms. Potential benefits to be gained from alliances include (1) increased access to technology, funding, and information; (2) market expansion and greater penetration of current markets; and (3) de-escalated competitive rivalries. Motorola is a company that has prospered by forming numerous joint ventures with both American and foreign companies.[11]

Ideas that appear to have adequate profit potential and offer the firm a competitive advantage in the market should be accepted for further study.

Project Planning

This stage of the process involves several steps. It is here that the product proposal is evaluated further and responsibility for the project is assigned to a project team. The proposal is analyzed in terms of production, marketing, financial, and competitive factors. A development budget is established, and some preliminary marketing and technical research is undertaken. The product is actually designed in a rough form. Alternative product features and component specifications are outlined. Finally, a project plan is written up, which includes estimates of future development, production, and marketing costs along with capital requirements and manpower needs. A schedule or timetable is also included. Finally, the project proposal is given to top management for a go or no-go decision.

Various alternatives exist for creating and managing the project teams. Two of the better-known methods are the establishment of a skunkworks, whereby a project team can work in relative privacy away from the rest of the organization, and a rugby or relay approach, whereby groups in different areas of the company are simultaneously working on the project.[12] The common tie that binds these and other successful approaches together is the degree of interaction that develops between the marketing, engineering, production, and other critical staff. The earlier in the process that interactive, cooperative efforts begin, the higher the likelihood is that development efforts will be successful. A key component contributing to the success of many companies' product development efforts relates to the emphasis placed on creating *cross-functional teams* early in the development process. Members from many different departments come together to jointly establish new product development goals and priorities and to also develop new product development schedules. Frequently, marketing and/or sales personnel are called in to lead these teams.[13]

Product Development

At this juncture, the product idea has been evaluated from the standpoint of engineering, manufacturing, finance, and marketing. If it has met all expectations, it is considered a candidate for further research and testing. In the laboratory, the product is converted into a finished good and tested. A development report to management is prepared that spells out in fine detail: (1) the results of the studies by the engineering department; (2) required plan design; (3) production facilities design; (4) tooling requirements; (5) marketing test plan; (6) financial program survey; and (7) an estimated release date.[14]

Test Marketing

Up until now the product has been a company secret. Now management goes outside the company and submits the product candidate for customer approval. Test

The New Product Team

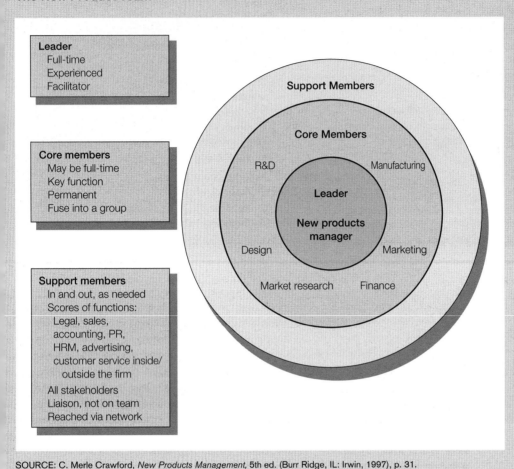

Leader
- Full-time
- Experienced
- Facilitator

Core members
- May be full-time
- Key function
- Permanent
- Fuse into a group

Support members
- In and out, as needed
- Scores of functions:
  - Legal, sales, accounting, PR, HRM, advertising, customer service inside/ outside the firm
- All stakeholders
- Liaison, not on team
- Reached via network

Diagram labels: Support Members · Core Members · R&D · Manufacturing · Leader · New products manager · Design · Marketing · Market research · Finance

SOURCE: C. Merle Crawford, *New Products Management,* 5th ed. (Burr Ridge, IL: Irwin, 1997), p. 31.

market programs are conducted in line with the general plans for launching the product. Several of the more commonly utilized forms of test marketing are:[15]

1. *Pseudo sales.* Potential buyers are asked to answer survey questions or pick items off a shelf in a make-believe store. The key factor is that no spending or risk for the consumer takes place.
2. *Controlled sale.* Here the buyer must make a purchase. The sale may be quite formal or informal, but it is conducted under controlled conditions. The product has not been released for regular sale.
3. *Full sale.* In this case, the firm has decided to fully market the product (not so in the above methods). But it wants to do so on a limited basis first, to see if everything is working right.
4. *National launch.* Here the firm just launches the product on a national scale and makes adjustments as needed.

Marketing
Highlight 7–5

Measurements of New Product Performance

Financial Criteria

Return on investment (ROI)
Various profit margin measures
Sales and sales growth
Various profit measures
Payback and payback period
Internal rate of return (IRR)
Return on assets (ROA)
Return on equity (ROE)
Breakeven and breakeven point

Share and market share
Return on sales
Net present value (NPV)

Nonfinancial Criteria

Performance of new products
Market share achieved
Satisfy customer needs
Other market-related benefits
Strategic issues/fit/synergy
Technical aspects of production
Uniqueness of the new products

SOURCE: Albert L. Page, "Assessing New Product Development Practices and Performance: Establishing Crucial Norms," *Journal of Product Innovation Management,* September 1993, pp. 273–90. ©1993 by Elsevier Science Inc. Reprinted by permission of the publisher.

The main goal of a test market is to evaluate and adjust, as necessary, the general marketing strategy to be used and the appropriate marketing mix. Additionally, producers can utilize the early interaction with buyers, occurring in test markets, to begin exploration of issues related to the next generation of product development.[16] Especially in cases where new technologies and markets are emerging, firms can benefit greatly from knowledge gained in test markets. Throughout the test market process, findings are being analyzed and forecasts of volume developed. In summary, a well-done test market procedure can reduce the risks that include not only lost marketing and sales dollars but also capital—the expense of installing production lines or building a new factory. Upon completion of a successful test market phase, the marketing plan can be finalized and the product prepared for launch.

Commercialization

This is the launching step. During this stage, heavy emphasis is placed on the organization structure and management talent needed to implement the marketing strategy. Emphasis is also given to following up such things as bugs in the design, production costs, quality control, and inventory requirements. Procedures and responsibility for evaluating the success of the new product by comparison with projections are also finalized.

The Importance of Time

Over the course of the last five years, companies have placed an increasing emphasis on shortening their products' time to market. *Time to market* can be defined as the elapsed time between product definition and product availability. It has been well documented that companies that can bring their products to market first enjoy a competitive advantage both in terms of profits and market share.[17] Successful time-based innovations can be attributed to the use of short production runs whereby products can be improved on an incremental basis, the use of cross-functional teams, decentralized work scheduling and monitoring, and a responsive system for gathering and analyzing customer feedback.

Several U.S. companies, including Procter & Gamble, have taken steps to speed up the new product development cycle by giving managers, at the product class and brand family level, more decision-making power. Increasingly, companies are bypassing time-consuming regional test markets, when feasible, in favor of national launches. It is becoming important, more than ever, that firms do a successful job of developing new products right the first time. To accomplish this, companies must have the right people with the right skills and talents in key positions within the new product framework.

Causes of New Product Failure

Many new products with satisfactory potential have failed to make the grade. Many of the reasons for new product failure relate to execution and control problems. The following is a brief list of some of the more important causes of new product failures after they have been carefully screened, developed, and marketed.[18]

1. No competitive point of difference, unexpected reactions from competitors, or both.
2. Poor positioning.
3. Poor quality of product.
4. Nondelivery of promised benefits of product.
5. Too little marketing support.
6. Poor perceived price/quality (value) relationship.
7. Faulty estimates of market potential and other marketing research mistakes.
8. Faulty estimates of production and marketing costs.

9. Improper channels of distribution selected.
10. Rapid change in the market (economy) after the product was introduced.

Some of these problems are beyond the control of management; but it is clear that successful new product planning requires large amounts of reliable information in diverse areas. Each department assigned functional responsibility for product development automatically becomes an input to the information system needed by the new product decision maker. For example, when a firm is developing a new product, it is wise for both engineers and marketers to consider both the kind of market to be entered (e.g., consumer, organizational, international) and specific target segments. These decisions will be of paramount influence on the design and cost of the finished good, which will, of course, directly influence price, sales, and profits.

Need for Research

In many respects it can be argued that the keystone activity of any new product planning system is research—not just marketing research, but technical research as well. Regardless of the way in which the new product planning function is organized in the company, new product development decisions by top management require data that provide a base for making more intelligent choices. New product project reports ought to be more than a collection of "expert" opinions. Top management has a responsibility to ask certain questions, and the new product planning team has an obligation to generate answers to these questions based on research that provides marketing, economic, engineering, and production information. This need will be more clearly understood if some of the specific questions commonly raised in evaluating product ideas are examined:

1. What is the anticipated market demand over time? Are the potential applications for the product restricted?
2. Can the item be patented? Are there any antitrust problems?
3. Can the product be sold through present channels and sales force? What will be the number of new salespersons needed? What additional sales training will be required?
4. At different volume levels, what will be the unit manufacturing costs?
5. What is the most appropriate package to use in terms of color, material, design, and so forth?
6. What is the estimated return on investment?
7. What is the appropriate pricing strategy?

While this list is not intended to be exhaustive, it serves to illustrate the serious need for reliable information. Note, also, that some of the essential facts required to answer these questions can only be obtained through time-consuming and expensive marketing research studies. Other data can be generated in the engineering laboratories or pulled from accounting records. Certain types of information must be based on assumptions, which may or may not hold true, and on expectations about what will happen in the future, as in the case of anticipated competitive reaction or the projected level of sales.

Another complication is that many different types of information must be gathered and formulated into a meaningful program for decision making. To illustrate, in trying to answer questions about return on investment of a particular project, the analyst must know something about (1) the pricing strategy to be used and (2) the investment outlay. Regardless of the formula used to measure the investment worth of a new product, different types of information are required. Using one of the simplest approaches—the payback method (the ratio of investment outlay to annual cash flow)—one needs to estimate the magnitude of the product investment outlay and the annual cash flow. The investment outlay requires estimates of such things as production equipment, R&D costs, and nonrecurring introductory marketing expenditures; the annual cash flow requires a forecast of unit demand and price. For development projects that are dealing with more radical innovations, the difficulty in estimating cash flows in future years is immense due to the uncertainty of demand and competitive reaction(s).[19] In cases where uncertainty exists, more sophisticated analytical methods, including those which incorporate sensitivity analysis, must be utilized.

■ Conclusion

This chapter has focused on the nature of new product planning and development. Attention has been given to the management process required to have an effective program for new product development. It should be obvious that this is one of the most important and difficult aspects of marketing management. The problem is so complex that, unless management develops a plan for dealing with the problem, it is likely to operate at a severe competitive disadvantage in the marketplace.

■ Additional Readings

Crawford, C. Merle. *New Products Management.* 5th ed. Burr Ridge, IL: Irwin/McGraw-Hill, 1997.

Hanna, Nessim; Douglas J. Ayers; Rick E. Ridnour; and Geoffrey L. Gordon. "New Product Development Practices in Consumer versus Business Products Organizations." *Journal of Product and Brand Management,* 1995, pp. 33–35.

Moorman, Christine, and Anne A. Miller. "The Convergence of Planning and Execution: Improvisation in New Product Development." *Journal of Marketing,* July 1998, pp. 1–20.

Sobek, Durwood K. II; Jeffrey K. Liker; and Allen C. Ward. "Another Look at How Toyota Integrates Product Development." *Harvard Business Review,* July–August 1998, pp. 36–48.

Chapter Eight

Integrated Marketing Communications: Advertising and Sales Promotion

To simplify the discussion of the general subject of promotion, the topic has been divided into two basic categories, personal selling and nonpersonal selling. Personal selling will be discussed in detail in the next chapter, and this chapter will be devoted to nonpersonal selling.

Nonpersonal selling includes all demand creation and demand maintenance activities of the firm other than personal selling. It is mass selling. In more specific terms, nonpersonal selling includes (1) advertising, (2) sales promotion, and (3) publicity. For purposes of this text, primary emphasis will be placed on advertising and sales promotion. Publicity is a special form of promotion that amounts to free advertising, such as a write-up about the firm's products in a newspaper article. It will not be dealt with in detail in this text.

■ The Promotion Mix

The promotion mix concept refers to the combination and types of promotional effort the firm puts forth during a specified period. In developing product strategy, marketers strive for the right mix of promotional elements to make sure that their product is well received.[1] If the product is new, the promotional effort will probably rely heavily on advertising, sales promotion, and publicity in order to (1) make potential buyers aware of the product, (2) inform these buyers about the benefits associated with the product, (3) convince buyers the product possesses high value, and (4) entice buyers to purchase the product. If the product is more established but the objective is to stabilize sales during a weak season, the promotional mix will most likely contain short-term incentives (sales promotion) for people to buy the product immediately. If the product is highly technical and needs a lot of explanation, the promotional mix will probably contain more personal selling, so that potential buyers can ask questions of a salesperson.

As seen by the previous examples, a firm's promotion mix is likely to change over time. The mix will need continual altering and adapting to reflect changes in the market, competition, the product's life cycle, and the adoption of new strategies. In essence, the firm should take into account three basic factors when devising its promotion mix: (1) the role of promotion in the overall marketing mix, (2) the nature of the product, and (3) the nature of the market. Highlight 8–1 provides an overview of the major advantages and disadvantages associated with the elements of the promotion mix.

Integrated Marketing Communications

In many organizations, elements of the promotion mix are often managed by specialists in different parts of the organization or, in some cases, outside the organization when an advertising agency is used. For example, advertising plans might be done jointly by the advertising department and the advertising agency; plans for the sales force might be done by managers of the sales force; and sales promotions might be developed independent of the advertising and sales plans. Thus, it is not surprising that the concept of *integrated marketing communications* has evolved in recent years.

The idea of integrated marketing communications is easy to understand and certainly has a great deal of commonsense validity. But like so many concepts in marketing, it is difficult to implement. The goal of integrated marketing communications is to develop marketing communications programs that coordinate and integrate all elements of promotion—advertising, sales promotion, personal selling, and publicity—so that the organization presents a consistent message. Integrated marketing communication seeks to manage all sources of brand or company contacts with existing and potential customers.

The concept of integrated marketing communication is illustrated in Figure 8–1. It is generally agreed upon that potential buyers generally go through a process of (1) *awareness* of the product or service; (2) *comprehension* of what it can do and its important features; (3) *conviction* that it has value for them; and (4) *ordering* on the part of a sufficient number of potential buyers. Consequently, the firm's marketing communication tools must encourage and allow the potential buyer to experience the various stages. Figure 8–1 illustrates the role of various marketing communication tools for a hypothetical product.

The goal of integrated marketing communication is an important one, and many believe it is critical for success in today's crowded marketplace. As with many management concepts, implementation is slower than many would like to see. Internal "turf" battles within organizations and the reluctance of some advertising agencies to willingly broaden their role beyond advertising are two factors that are hindering the successful implementation of integrated marketing communication.

Advertising: Planning and Strategy

Advertising seeks to promote the seller's product by means of printed and electronic media. This is justified on the grounds that messages can reach large numbers of people and inform, persuade, and remind them about the firm's offerings. The traditional way of defining advertising is as follows: It is any paid form of nonpersonal presentation of ideas, goods, or services by an identified sponsor.[2]

Part C   -The Marketing Mix

Marketing
Highlight 8–1

**Some Strengths and Weaknesses of the
Major Promotion Elements**

Element	Strengths	Weaknesses
Advertising	Efficient for reaching many buyers simultaneously, effective way to create image of the brand, flexible, variety of media to choose from	Reaches many people who are not potential buyers, ads are subject to much criticism, exposure time is usually short, people tend to screen out advertisements, total cost may be high
Personal selling	Salespeople can be persuasive and influential, two-way communication allows for questions and other feedback, message can be targeted to specific individuals	Cost per contact is high, salespeople may be hard to recruit and motivate, presentation skills vary among salespeople
Sales promotion	Supports short-term price reductions designed to stimulate demand, variety of sales promotion tools available, effective in changing short-term behavior, easy to link to other communications	Risks inducing brand-loyal customers to stock up while not influencing others, impact may be limited to short term, price-related sales promotion may hurt brand image, easy for competitors to copy
Publicity	Total cost may be low; media-generated messages seen as more credible than marketer-sponsored messages	Media may not cooperate, heavy competition for media attention, marketer has little control over message

SOURCE: Gilbert A. Churchill, Jr., and J. Paul Peter, *Marketing: Creating Value for Customers,* rev. ed. (Burr Ridge, IL: Irwin/McGraw-Hill, 1998), p. 453.

From a management perspective, advertising is a strategic device for maintaining or gaining a competitive advantage in the marketplace. For example, in a recent year, Procter & Gamble spent $1.5 billion advertising its products. On an individual brand basis, Ralston Purina spent approximately $62 million solely to advertise its Eveready line of batteries.[3]

For manufacturers and resellers alike, advertising budgets represent a large and growing element in the cost of goods and services. As part of the seller's promotion mix, advertising dollars must be appropriated and budgeted according to a marketing plan that takes into account such factors as

1. Nature of the product, including life cycle.
2. Competition.
3. Government regulations.
4. Nature and scope of the market.
5. Channels of distribution.
6. Pricing strategy.
7. Availability of media.
8. Availability of funds.
9. Outlays for other forms of promotion.

■ Figure 8–1
How Various
Promotion Tools Might
Contribute to the
Purchase of a
Hypothetical Product

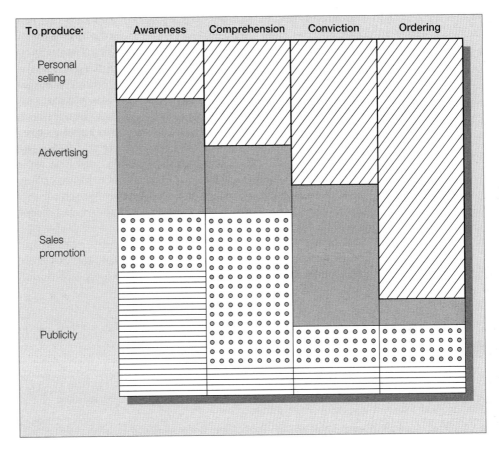

Objectives of Advertising

There are at least three different viewpoints taken in attempts to evaluate the contribution of advertising to the economic health of the firm. The generalist viewpoint is primarily concerned with sales, profits, return on investment, and so forth. At the other extreme, the specialist viewpoint is represented by advertising experts who are primarily concerned with measuring the effects of specific ads or campaigns; here primary attention is given to such matters as the Nielsen Index, Starch Reports, Arbitron Index, Simmons Reports, copy appeal, and so forth. A middle view, one that might be classified as more of a marketing management approach, understands and appreciates the other two viewpoints but, in addition, sees advertising as a competitive weapon. Emphasis in this approach is given to the strategic aspects of the advertising function.[4]

Building on what was said earlier, objectives for advertising can be assigned that focus on creating *awareness,* aiding *comprehension,* developing *conviction,* and encouraging *ordering.* Within each category, more specific objectives can be developed that take into account time and degree of success desired. Obviously, compared to the large number of people advertising makes aware of the product or service, the number actually motivated to purchase is usually quite small.

In the long run and often in the short run, advertising is justified on the basis of the revenue it produces. Revenue in this case may refer either to sales or profits.

Economic theory assumes that firms are profit maximizers, and the advertising outlays should be increased in every market and medium up to the point where the additional cost of gaining more business equals the incremental profits. Since most business firms do not have the data required to use the marginal analysis approach, they usually employ less sophisticated decision-making models. There is also evidence to show that many managers advertise to maximize sales on the assumption that higher sales mean more profits (which may or may not be true).

The point to be made here is that the ultimate objective of the business advertiser is to make sales and profits. To achieve this objective, the actions taken by customers must encompass purchase and continued repurchases of the advertised product. Toward this end, an approach to advertising is needed that provides for intelligent decision making. This approach must recognize the need for measuring the results of advertising, and these measurements must be as valid and reliable as possible. Marketing managers must also be aware that advertising not only complements other forms of communication but is subject to the law of diminishing returns. This means that for any advertised product, it can be assumed a point is eventually reached at which additional advertising produces little or no additional sales.

■ Advertising Decisions

In line with what has just been said, the marketing manager must make two key decisions. The first decision deals with determining the size of the advertising budget, and the second deals with how the advertising budget should be allocated. Although these decisions are highly interrelated, we deal with them separately to achieve a better understanding of the problems involved. Today's most successful brands of consumer goods were built by heavy advertising and marketing investment long ago.[5] Recently, many marketers have lost sight of the connection between advertising spending and market share. They practice the art of discounting: cutting ad budgets to fund price promotions or fatten quarterly earnings. Companies employing these tactics may benefit in the short term but may be at a severe competitive disadvantage in the long term.

Marketers at some companies, however, know that brand equity and consumer preference for brands drive market share. They understand the balance of advertising and promotion expenditures needed to build brands and gain share, market by market, regardless of growth trends in the product categories where they compete. For example, Procter & Gamble has built its Jif and Folger's brands from single-digit shares to being among category leaders. In peanut butter and coffee, P&G invests more in advertising and less in discounting than its major competitors. What P&G and other smart marketers such as Kellogg, General Mills, Coke, and PepsiCo hold in common is an awareness of a key factor in advertising: consistent investment spending. They do not raid their ad budgets to increase earnings for a few quarters, nor do they view advertising as a discretionary cost.

Marketing
Highlight 8–2

Developing Advertising Objectives: Nine Questions

1. Does the advertising aim at *immediate sales*? If so, objectives might be:
   - Perform the complete selling function.
   - Close sales to prospects already partly sold.
   - Announce a special reason for buying now (price, premium, and so forth).
   - Remind people to buy.
   - Tie in with special buying event.
   - Stimulate impulse sales.

2. Does the advertising aim at *near-term sales*? If so, objectives might be:
   - Create awareness.
   - Enhance brand image.
   - Implant information or attitude.
   - Combat or offset competitive claims.
   - Correct false impressions, misinformation.
   - Build familiarity and easy recognition.

3. Does the advertising aim at building a *long-range consumer franchise*? If so, objectives might be:
   - Build confidence in company and brand.
   - Build customer demand.
   - Select preferred distributors and dealers.
   - Secure universal distribution.
   - Establish a "reputation platform" for launching new brands or product lines.
   - Establish brand recognition and acceptance.

4. Does the advertising aim at helping *increase sales*? If so, objectives would be:
   - Hold present customers.
   - Convert other users to advertiser's brand.
   - Cause people to specify advertiser's brand.
   - Convert nonusers to users.
   - Make steady customers out of occasional ones.
   - Advertise new uses.
   - Persuade customers to buy larger sizes or multiple units.
   - Remind users to buy.
   - Encourage greater frequency or quantity of use.

5. Does the advertising aim at some specific step that leads to a sale? If so, objectives might be:
   - Persuade prospect to write for descriptive literature, return a coupon, enter a contest.
   - Persuade prospect to visit a showroom, ask for a demonstration.
   - Induce prospect to sample the product (trial offer).

6. How important are supplementary benefits of advertising? Objectives would be:
   - Help salespeople open new accounts.
   - Help salespeople get larger orders from wholesalers and retailers.
   - Help salespeople get preferred display space.
   - Give salespeople an entrée.
   - Build morale of sales force.
   - Impress the trade.

7. Should the advertising impart information needed to consummate sales and build customer satisfaction? If so, objectives may be to use:
   - "Where to buy it" advertising.
   - "How to use it" advertising.
   - New models, features, package.
   - New prices.
   - Special terms, trade-in offers, and so forth.
   - New policies (such as guarantees).

8. Should advertising build confidence and goodwill for the corporation? Targets may include:
   - Customers and potential customers.
   - The trade (distributors, dealers, retail people).
   - Employees and potential employees.
   - The financial community.
   - The public at large.

9. What kind of images does the company wish to build?
   - Product quality, dependability.
   - Service.
   - Family resemblance of diversified products.
   - Corporate citizenship.
   - Growth, progressiveness, technical leadership.

SOURCE: William Arens, *Contemporary Advertising*, 7th ed. (Burr Ridge, IL: Irwin/McGraw-Hill, 1999), p. R18.

The Expenditure Question

Most firms determine how much to spend on advertising by one of the following methods:

Percent of Sales.   This is one of the most popular rule-of-thumb methods, and its appeal is found in its simplicity. The firm simply takes a percentage figure and applies it to either past or future sales. For example, suppose next year's sales are estimated to be $1 million. Using a 2-percent-of-sales criterion, the ad budget would be $20,000. This approach is usually justified by its advocates in terms of the following argument: (1) advertising is needed to generate sales; (2) a number of cents, that is, the percentage used, out of each dollar of sales should be devoted to advertising in order to generate needed sales; and (3) the percentage is easily adjusted and can be readily understood by other executives. The percent-of-sales approach is popular in retailing.

Per-unit Expenditure.   Closely related to the above technique is one in which a fixed monetary amount is spent on advertising for each unit of the product expected to be sold. This method is popular with higher priced merchandise, such as automobiles or appliances. For instance, if a company is marketing color televisions priced at $500, it may decide that it should spend $30 per set on advertising. Since this $30 is a fixed amount for each unit, this method amounts to the same thing as the percent-of-sales method. The big difference is in the rationale used to justify each of the methods. The per unit expenditure method attempts to determine the retail price by using production costs as a base. Here the seller realizes that a reasonably competitive price must be established for the product in question and attempts to cost out the gross margin. All this means is that, if the suggested retail price is to be $500 and manufacturing costs are $250, there is a gross margin of $250 available to cover certain expenses, such as transportation, personal selling, advertising, and dealer profit. Some of these expense items are flexible, such as advertising, while others are nearly fixed, as in the case of transportation. The basic problem with this method and the percentage-of-sales method is that they view advertising as a function of sales, rather than sales as a function of advertising.

All You Can Afford.   Here the advertising budget is established as a predetermined share of profits or financial resources. The availability of current revenues sets the upper limit of the ad budget. The only advantage to this approach is that it sets reasonable limits on the expenditures for advertising. However, from the standpoint of sound marketing practice, this method is undesirable because there is no necessary connection between liquidity and advertising opportunity. Any firm that limits its advertising outlays to the amount of available funds will probably miss opportunities for increasing sales and profits.

Competitive Parity.   This approach is often used in conjunction with other approaches, such as the percent-of-sales method. The basic philosophy underlying this approach is that advertising is defensive. Advertising budgets are based on those of competitors or other members of the industry. From a strategy standpoint, this is a "followership" technique and assumes that the other firms in the industry know what they are doing and have similar goals. Competitive parity is not a preferred method, although some executives feel it is a safe approach. This may or may not be true depending in part on the relative market share of competing firms and their growth objectives.

The Research Approach. Here the advertising budget is argued for and presented on the basis of research findings. Advertising media are studied in terms of their productivity by the use of media reports and research studies. Costs are also estimated and compared with study results. A typical experiment is one in which three or more test markets are selected. The first test market is used as a control, either with no advertising or with normal levels of advertising. Advertising with various levels of intensity are used in the other markets, and comparisons are made to see what effect different levels of intensity have. The marketing manager then evaluates the costs and benefits of the different approaches and intensity levels to determine the overall budget. Although the research approach is generally more expensive than some other models, it is a more rational approach to the expenditure decision.

The Task Approach. Well-planned advertising programs usually make use of the task approach, which initially formulates the advertising goals and defines the tasks to accomplish these goals. Once this is done, management determines how much it will cost to accomplish each task and adds up the total. This approach is often in conjunction with the research approach.

The Allocation Question

This question deals with the problem of deciding on the most effective way of spending advertising dollars. A general answer to the question is that management's choice of strategies and objectives determines the media and appeals to be used. In other words, the firm's or product division's overall marketing plan will function as a general guideline for answering the allocation question.

From a practical standpoint, however, the allocation question can be framed in terms of message and media decisions. A successful ad campaign has two related tasks: (1) say the right things in the ads themselves, and (2) use the appropriate media in the right amounts at the right time to reach the target market.

Message Strategy.   The advertising process involves creating messages with words, ideas, sounds, and other forms of audiovisual stimuli that are designed to affect consumer (or distributor) behavior. It follows that much of advertising is a communication process. To be effective, the advertising message should meet two general criteria: (1) it should take into account the basic principles of communication, and (2) it should be predicated upon a good theory of consumer motivation and behavior.

The basic communication process involves three elements: (1) the sender or source of the communication, (2) the communication or message, and (3) the receiver or audience. Advertising agencies are considered experts in the communications field and are employed by most large firms to create meaningful messages and assist in their dissemination. Translating the product idea or marketing message into an effective ad is termed *encoding*. In advertising, the goal of encoding is to generate ads that are understood by the audience. For this to occur, the audience must be able to *decode* the message in the ad so that the perceived content of the message is the same as the intended content of the message. From a practical standpoint, all this means is that advertising messages must be sent to consumers in an understandable and meaningful way.

Advertising messages, of course, must be transmitted and carried by particular communication channels commonly known as advertising media. These media or channels vary in efficiency, selectivity, and cost. Some channels are preferred to others because they have less "noise," and thus messages are more easily received and understood. For example, a particular newspaper ad must compete with other ads, pictures, or stories on the same page. In the case of radio or TV, while only one firm's message is usually broadcast at a time, there are other distractions (noise) that can hamper clear communications, such as driving while listening to the radio.

The relationship between advertising and consumer behavior is quite obvious. For many products and services, advertising is an influence that may affect the consumer's decision to purchase a particular product or brand. It is clear that consumers are subjected to many selling influences, and the question arises about how important advertising is or can be. Here is where the advertising expert must operate on some theory of consumer behavior. The reader will recall from the discussion of consumer behavior that the buyer was viewed as progressing through various stages from an unsatisfied need through and beyond a purchase decision. The end goal of an advertisement and its associated campaign is to make the consumer feel that, "Hey, this brand is right for me."[6] By doing so, the advertisement will have succeeded in moving the consumer to the trial and repeat purchase stage of the consumer behavior process, which is the end goal of advertising strategy.

The planning of an advertising campaign and the creation of persuasive messages require a mixture of marketing skill and creative know-how. Relative to the dimension of marketing skills, there are some important pieces of marketing information needed before launching an ad campaign. Most of this information must be generated by the firm and kept up to date. Listed below are some of the critical types of information an advertiser should have.

1. *Who* the firm's customers and potential customers are; their demographic, economic, and psychological characteristics; and any other factors affecting their likelihood of buying.
2. *How many* such customers there are.

3. *How much* of the firm's type and brand of product they are currently buying and can reasonably be expected to buy in the short-term and long-term future.
4. *Which* individuals, other than customers and potential customers, *influence* purchasing decisions.
5. *Where* they buy the firm's brand of product.
6. *When* they buy, and frequency of purchase.
7. *Which* competitive brands they buy and frequency of purchase.
8. *How* they use the product.
9. *Why* they buy particular types and brands of products.

Media Mix. Media selection is no easy task. To start with, there are numerous types and combinations of media to choose from. Highlight 8–4 presents a brief summary of the advantages and disadvantages of some of the major advertising media.

Although the number of media and media combinations available for advertising is overwhelming at first glance, four interrelated factors limit the number of practical alternatives:

1. *The nature of the product* limits the number of practical and efficient alternatives. For instance, a radically new and highly complex product could not be properly promoted using billboard advertisements. Instead, the company may choose to develop an *infomercial,* a program-length ad that mixes information and entertainment with sales pitches. Infomercials can either be carried on broadcast media or put on videotapes that are then mailed to targeted customers. Indeed, a growing amount of money is being spent on this medium to promote automobiles and computers.
2. *The nature and size of the target market* also limits appropriate advertising media. For example, it is generally inefficient to advertise organizational products in mass media publications.
3. *The advertising budget* may restrict the use of expensive media, such as television.
4. *The availability* of some media may be limited in particular geographic areas.

Although these factors reduce media alternatives to a more manageable number, specific media must still be selected. A primary consideration at this point is media effectiveness or efficiency.

In the advertising industry, a common measure of efficiency or productivity is cost per thousand, or CPMs. This figure generally refers to the dollar cost of reaching 1,000 prospects, and its chief advantage lies in its simplicity and allowance for a common base of comparison between differing media types. The major disadvantage of the use of CPMs also relates to its simplicity. For example, the same commercial placed in two different television programs, having the same viewership and the same audience profile, may very well generate different responses depending on the level of viewer involvement. This "positive effects" theory states that the more viewers are involved in a television program, the stronger they will respond to commercials. In essence, involving programs produce engaged respondents who demonstrate more favorable responses to advertising messages.

Generally, such measures as circulation, audience size, and sets in use per commercial minute are used in the calculation. Of course, different relative rankings of media can occur, depending on the measure used. A related problem deals with what is meant by "effectively reaching" the prospect.[7] *Reach,* in general, is the number of different targeted audience members exposed at least once to the advertiser's message within a predetermined time frame. As important as the number

Marketing
Highlight 8–4

Some Relative Merits of Major Advertising Media

Newspapers

Advantages
1. Flexible and timely.
2. Intense coverage of local markets.
3. Broad acceptance and use.
4. High believability of printed word.

Disadvantages
1. Short life.
2. Read hastily.
3. Small "pass-along" audience.

Radio

Advantages
1. Mass use (over 25 million radios sold annually).
2. Audience selectivity via station format.
3. Low cost (per unit of time).
4. Geographic flexibility.

Disadvantages
1. Audio presentation only.
2. Less attention than TV.
3. Chaotic buying (nonstandardized rate structures).
4. Short life.

Outdoor

Advantages
1. Flexible.
2. Relative absence of competing advertisements.
3. Repeat exposure.
4. Relatively inexpensive.

Disadvantages
1. Creative limitations.
2. Many distractions for viewer.
3. Public attack (ecological implications).
4. No selectivity of audience.

Television

Advantages
1. Combination of sight, sound, and motion.
2. Appeals to senses.
3. Mass audience coverage.
4. Psychology of attention.

Disadvantages
1. Nonselectivity of audience.
2. Fleeting impressions.
3. Short life.
4. Expensive.

Magazines

Advantages
1. High geographic and demographic selectivity.
2. Psychology of attention.
3. Quality of reproduction.
4. Pass-along readership.

Disadvantages
1. Long closing periods (six to eight weeks prior to publication).
2. Some waste circulation.
3. No guarantee of position (unless premium is paid).

Direct Mail

Advantages
1. Audience selectivity.
2. Flexible.
3. No competition from competing advertisements.
4. Personalized.

Disadvantages
1. Relatively high cost.
2. Consumers often pay little attention and throw it away.

Internet

Advantages
1. Interactive.
2. Low cost per exposure.
3. Ads can be placed in interest sections.
4. Timely.
5. High information content possible.
6. New favorable medium.

Disadvantages
1. Low attention getting.
2. Short message life.
3. Reader selects exposure.
4. May be perceived as intruding.
5. Subject to download speeds.

Marketing
Highlight 8–5

Procedures for Evaluating Advertising Programs and Some Services Using the Procedures

Procedures for Evaluating Specific Advertisements

1. *Recognition tests:* Estimate the percentage of people claiming to have read a magazine who recognize the ad when it is shown to them (e.g., Starch Message Report Service).
2. *Recall tests:* Estimate the percentage of people claiming to have read a magazine who can (unaided) recall the ad and its contents (e.g., Gallup and Robinson Impact Service, various services for TV ads as well).
3. *Opinion tests:* Potential audience members are asked to rank alternative advertisements as most interesting, most believable, best liked.
4. *Theater tests:* Theater audience is asked for brand preferences before and after an ad is shown in context of a TV show (e.g., Schwerin TV Testing Service).

Procedures for Evaluating Specific Advertising Objectives

1. *Awareness:* Potential buyers are asked to indicate brands that come to mind in a product category. A message used in an ad campaign is given and buyers are asked to identify the brand that was advertised using that message.
2. *Attitude:* Potential buyers are asked to rate competing or individual brands on determinant attributes, benefits, characterizations using rating scales.

Procedures for Evaluating Motivational Impact

1. *Intention to buy:* Potential buyers are asked to indicate the likelihood they will buy a brand (on a scale from "definitely will not" to "definitely will").
2. *Market test:* Sales changes in different markets are monitored to compare the effects of different messages, budget levels.

SOURCE: Joseph Guiltinan and Gordon Paul, *Marketing Management,* 6th ed., © 1997, New York, McGraw-Hill, Inc., p. 274. Reproduced by permission of The McGraw-Hill Companies.

of different people exposed (reach) is the number of times, on average, that they are exposed to an advertisement within a given time period. This rate of exposure is called *average frequency.* Since marketers all have budget constraints, they must decide whether to increase reach at the expense of average frequency or average frequency at the expense of reach. In essence, the marketer's dilemma is to develop a media schedule that both (1) exposes a sufficient number of targeted customers (reach) to the firm's product and (2) exposes them enough times (average frequency) to the product to produce the desired effect. The desired effect can come in the form of reaching goals associated with any or all of the categories of advertising objectives (prospect becomes aware of the product, takes action, etc.) covered earlier in the chapter.

■ Sales Promotion

In marketing, the word *promotion* is used in many ways. For instance, it is sometimes used to refer to a specific activity, such as advertising or publicity. In the general sense, promotion has been defined as any identifiable effort on the part of the seller to persuade buyers to accept the seller's information and store it in retrievable form. However, the term *sales promotion* has a more restricted and technical meaning and has been defined by the American Marketing Association as follows:[8]

> Media and nonmedia marketing pressure applied for a predetermined, limited period of time at the level of consumer, retailer, or wholesaler in order to stimulate trial, increase consumer demand, or improve product availability.

Marketing
Highlight 8–6

Some Objectives of Sales Promotion

When Directed at Consumers

1. To obtain the trial of a product.
2. To introduce a new or improved product.
3. To encourage repeat or greater usage by current users.
4. To bring more customers into retail stores.
5. To increase the total number of users of an established product.

When Directed at Salespeople

1. To motivate the sales force.
2. To educate the sales force about product improvements.
3. To stabilize a fluctuating sales pattern.

When Directed at Resellers

1. To increase reseller inventories.
2. To obtain displays and other support for products.
3. To improve product distribution.
4. To obtain more and better shelf space.

SOURCE: Steven J. Skinner, *Marketing*, 2nd ed., p. 673. ©1994 by Houghton Mifflin Company. Adapted with permission.

The popularity of sales promotion has been increasing. Since 1983, the promotion-to-advertising expenditure ratio increased from a 57 percent to 43 percent split to a 75 percent to 25 percent level.[9] Dollars spent on trade promotions accounted for about 63 percent of all promotional dollars spent. Reasons for this growth of sales promotion include a shifting emphasis from pull to push marketing strategies by many firms, a widening of the focus of advertising agencies to include promotional services to firms, an emphasis on the part of management towards short-term results, and the emergence of new purchase tracking technology. For example, many supermarket cash registers are now equipped with a device that dispenses coupons to a customer at the point of purchase. The type, variety, and cash amount of the coupon will vary from customer to customer based on their purchases. In essence, it is now possible for the Coca-Cola Company to dispense coupons to only those customers who purchase Pepsi, thus avoiding wasting promotional dollars on already-loyal Coke drinkers. Figure 8–2 presents some popular targets of sales promotion and the methods used.

■ **Figure 8–2** Example of Sales Promotion Activities

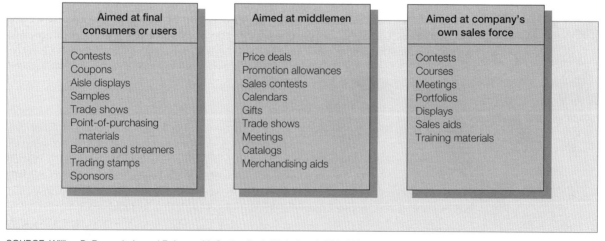

Aimed at final consumers or users	Aimed at middlemen	Aimed at company's own sales force
Contests	Price deals	Contests
Coupons	Promotion allowances	Courses
Aisle displays	Sales contests	Meetings
Samples	Calendars	Portfolios
Trade shows	Gifts	Displays
Point-of-purchasing materials	Trade shows	Sales aids
Banners and streamers	Meetings	Training materials
Trading stamps	Catalogs	
Sponsors	Merchandising aids	

SOURCE: William D. Perreault, Jr., and E. Jerome McCarthy, *Basic Marketing: A Global Managerial Approach*, 12th ed. (Burr Ridge, IL: Irwin/McGraw-Hill, 1996), p. 422.

4. *Rebates and refunds.* Consumers, either on the spot or through the mail, are given cash reimbursements for purchasing products. For example, consumers are offered a $3 mail-in rebate for purchasing a Norelco coffee maker.

5. *Sweepstakes and contests.* Consumers can win cash or prizes either through chance selection or games of skill.

6. *Premiums.* A premium is a reward or gift that comes from purchasing a product.

7. *Coupons.* Probably the most familiar and widely used of all consumer promotions, coupons are cents-off or added-value incentives. Because of the high incidence of coupon fraud, manufacturers, including Royal Crown Cola and General Mills, are now experimenting with the use of personalized checks as an alternative to coupons. An added advantage of this alternative is a quicker redemption for retailers. Point-of-purchase coupons are becoming an increasingly efficient way for marketers to target their promotional efforts at specific consumers.

What Sales Promotion Can and Can't Do

Advocates of sales promotion often point to its growing popularity as a justification for the argument that we don't need advertising; sales promotion itself will suffice. Marketers should bear in mind that sales promotion is only one part of a well-constructed integrated marketing communications program. While proven to be effective in achieving the objectives listed in the previous sections, there are several compelling reasons why sales promotion should not be utilized as the sole promotional tool. These reasons include sales promotion's inability to (1) generate long-term buyer commitment to a brand in many cases; (2) change, except on a temporary basis, declining sales of a product; (3) convince buyers to purchase an otherwise unacceptable product; and (4) make up for a lack of advertising or sales support for a product. In addition, promotions can often fuel the flames of competitive retaliation far more than other marketing activities.[13] When the competition gets drawn into the promotion war, the effect can be a significant slowing of the sharp sales increases predicted by the initiator of the promotion. Worse yet, promotions can often devalue the image of the promoted brand in the consumer's eyes.

The dilemma faced by marketers, as shown in Figure 8–3, is how to cut back on sales promotions without losing market share to competitors. In an effort to overcome this problem, some consumer products companies are instituting new pricing policies to try to cut back on the amount of sales promotions used. For example, Procter & Gamble and General Mills have instituted everyday low-price strategies for many of their products. The intent of this type of policy is to give retailers a lower list price in exchange for the cutting of trade promotions. While the net cost of the product to retailers remains unchanged, retailers are losing promotional dollars that they controlled. In many situations, although trade allowances are supposed to be used for encouraging retail sales, it is not uncommon for retailers to take a portion of the trade allowance money as profit. The rationale behind companies' (such as Procter & Gamble and General Mills) efforts to cut back on trade and other promotions is to (1) not force brand-loyal customers to pay unusually high prices when a product isn't on special, (2) allow consumers to benefit from a lower average shelf price since retailers will no longer have discretion over the use of allowance dollars, and (3) improve efficiencies in manufacturing and distribution systems because retailers will lose the incentive to do heavy forward buying of discounted items.

■ **Figure 8–3** The Sales Promotion Dilemma

SOURCE: George E. Belch and Michael A. Belch, *Introduction to Advertising and Promotion: An Integrated Communications Perspective,* 4th ed. (Burr Ridge, IL: Irwin/McGraw-Hill, 1998), p. 509.

In addition to developing pricing policies to cut back on short-term promotions, some consumer products companies are starting to institute *frequency marketing programs* in which they reward consumers for purchases of products or services over a sustained period of time.[14] These programs are not technically considered sales promotions because of their ongoing nature. Frequency marketing originated in 1981 when American Airlines launched its frequent-flyer program with the intention of securing the loyalty of business travelers. Since that time, American has awarded over 14 million free flights. In fact, among all airlines, there are an estimated 34 million individuals holding frequent-flyer cards.

■ Conclusion

This chapter has been concerned with integrated marketing communications. Remember that advertising and sales promotion are only two of the ways by which sellers can affect the demand for their product. Advertising and sales promotion are only part of the firm's promotion mix and, in turn, the promotion mix is only part of the overall marketing mix. Thus, advertising and sales promotion begin with the marketing plan and not with the advertising and sales promotion plans. Ignoring this point can produce ineffective and expensive promotional programs because of a lack of coordination with other elements of the marketing mix.

■ Additional Readings

Duncan, T., and Sandra Moriarity. *Driving Brand Value: Using Integrated Marketing to Manage Profitable Stakeholder Relationships.* New York: McGraw-Hill, 1997.

Gilly, Mary C., and Mary Wolfinberger. "Advertising's Internal Audience." *Journal of Marketing,* January 1998, pp. 69–88.

Keller, Kevin Lane; Susan E. Heckler; and Michael J. Houston. "The Effects of Brand Name Suggestiveness on Advertising Recall." *Journal of Marketing,* January 1998, pp. 48–57.

McArthur, D. N., and T. Griffin. "A Marketing Management View of Integrated Marketing Communications." *Journal of Advertising Research,* September–October 1997, pp. 19–26.

Appendix

Major Federal Agencies Involved in Control of Advertising

Agency	Function
Federal Trade Commission	Regulates commerce between states; controls unfair business practices; takes action on false and deceptive advertising; most important agency in regulation of advertising and promotion.
Food and Drug Administration	Regulatory division of the Department of Health, Education, and Welfare; controls marketing of food, drugs, cosmetics, medical devices, and potentially hazardous consumer products.
Federal Communications Commission	Regulates advertising indirectly, primarily through the power to grant or withdraw broadcasting licenses.
Postal Service	Regulates material that goes through the mails, primarily in areas of obscenity, lottery, and fraud.
Alcohol and Tobacco Tax Division	Part of the Treasury Department; has broad powers to regulate deceptive and misleading advertising of liquor and tobacco.
Grain Division	Unit of the Department of Agriculture responsible for policing seed advertising.
Securities and Exchange Commission	Regulates advertising of securities.

Information Source	Description
Patent Office	Regulates registration of trademarks.
Library of Congress	Controls protection of copyrights.
Department of Justice	Enforces all federal laws through prosecuting cases referred to it by other government agencies.

Chapter Nine

Personal Selling

Personal selling, unlike advertising or sales promotion, involves direct relationships between the seller and the prospect or customer. In a formal sense, personal selling can be defined as a two-way flow of communication between a potential buyer and a salesperson that is designed to accomplish at least three tasks: (1) identify the potential buyer's needs; (2) match those needs to one or more of the firm's products or services; and (3) on the basis of this match, convince the buyer to purchase the product.[1] The personal selling element of the promotion mix can encompass diverse forms of direct interaction between a salesperson and potential buyer, including face-to-face, telephone, written, and computer communication. The behavioral scientist would most likely characterize personal selling as a type of personal influence. Operationally, it is a complex communication process, one still not fully understood by marketing scholars.

■ Importance of Personal Selling

The importance of the personal selling function depends partially on the nature of the product. As a general rule, goods that are new and different, technically complex, or expensive require more personal selling effort. The salesperson plays a key role in providing the consumer with information about such products to reduce the risks involved in purchase and use. Insurance, for example, is a complex and technical product that often needs significant amounts of personal selling. In addition, many organizational products cannot be presold, and the salesperson has a key role to play in finalizing the sale.

It is important to remember that, for many companies, the salesperson represents the customer's main link to the firm. In fact, to some, the salesperson is the company. Therefore, it is imperative that the company take advantage of this unique link. Through the efforts of the successful salesperson, a company can build relationships with customers that continue long beyond the initial sale. It is the salesperson who serves as the conduit through which information regarding product flaws, improvements, applications, or new uses can pass from the customer to the marketing department. To illustrate the importance of using salespeople as an information resource, consider this fact: In some industries, customer information serves as the source for up to 90 percent of new product and process ideas.[2] Along with techniques described in the previous chapter, personal selling provides the push needed to get middlemen to carry new products, increase their amount of goods purchased, and devote more effort in merchandising a product or brand.[3]

In summary, personal selling is an integral part of the marketing system, fulfilling two vital duties (in addition to the core sales task itself): one for customers and one for companies.[4] First, the salesperson dispenses knowledge to buyers. Lacking relevant information, customers are likely to make poor buying decisions. For example, computer users would not learn about new equipment and new programming techniques without the assistance of computer sales representatives. Doctors would have difficulty finding out about new drugs and procedures were it not for pharmaceutical salespeople. Second, salespeople act as a source of marketing intelligence for management. Marketing success depends on satisfying customer needs. If present products don't fulfill customer needs, then profitable opportunities may exist for new or improved products. If problems with a company's product exist, then management must be quickly apprised of the fact. In either situation, salespeople are in the best position to act as the intermediary through which valuable information can be passed back and forth between product providers and buyers.

◼ The Sales Process

Personal selling is as much an art as it is a science. The word *art* is used to describe that portion of the selling process that is highly creative in nature and difficult to explain. This does not mean there is little control over the personal selling element in the promotion mix. It does imply that, all other things equal, the trained salesperson can outsell the untrained one.

Before management selects and trains salespeople, it should have an understanding of the sales process. Obviously, the sales process will differ according to the size of the company, the nature of the product, the market, and so forth, but there are some elements common to almost all selling situations that should be understood. For the purposes of this text, the term *sales process* refers to two basic factors: (1) the objectives the salesperson is trying to achieve while engaged in selling activities, and (2) the sequence of stages or steps the salesperson should follow in trying to achieve the specific objectives (the relationship-building process).

Objectives of the Sales Force

Much like the concepts covered in the previous chapter, personal selling can be viewed as a strategic means to gain competitive advantage in the marketplace. For example, most organizations include service representatives as part of their sales team to ensure that customer concerns with present products are addressed and remedied at the same time new business is being solicited.

In a similar manner, marketing management understands that, while ultimately, personal selling must be justified on the basis of the revenue and profits it produces,

Marketing
Highlight 9–1

Information the Sales Force Can Obtain from Organizational Customers

a. Problems with current products.
b. Cost-reduction needs of customer.
c. Unmet needs or wishes of customer.
d. Superior features of competitive products.
e. Changes in technology/industry standards.
f. Additions needed for service(s) accompanying the product.
g. Changes in the regulatory environment.
h. Other manufacturers' (competitors') products currently used by customers.

i. Customer's level of satisfaction with products currently used.
j. Product features evaluated by customers in choosing another manufacturer's product.
k. Customer's ideal products according to relevant choice criteria.
l. Customer's criteria for rating products.
m. Customer's order of preference for competing products.
n. Customer's likely demand for products in the future.

SOURCE: Adapted from Geoffrey Gordon, Denise Schoenbachler, Peter Kaminski, and Kimberly Brouchous, "The Use of the Sales Force in the Opportunity Identification Phase of the New Product Development Process," *Journal of Business and Industrial Marketing*, 12, no. 1 (1997), pp. 33–48.

there are two major categories of objectives generally assigned to the personal selling function as part of the overall promotion mix.[5] These objectives can be categorized as either image or demand oriented. Although many companies have some interest in image-oriented selling efforts, the primary emphasis is placed on achieving demand-oriented objectives. A brief description of each category follows.

Image-Oriented Objectives. When personal selling objectives are image oriented, they usually involve public relations. Public relations, in general, can be considered the use of communication that is designed to foster a favorable image for goods, services, or organizations. Needless to say, when personal selling is utilized as part of a public relations effort, it is initiated and paid for by the sponsoring firm. The specific objectives of image-oriented personal selling efforts can be to utilize the sales force (1) as public role models in displaying the firm's commitment to ethical behavior through the employment of acceptable sales practices; (2) to portray the firm's upstanding image by having salespeople maintain a good appearance in all customer contacts; or (3) to show the firm's commitment to relationship building by having the sales force follow practices aimed at gaining the respect of customers, employees, and other public entities.

Demand-Oriented Objectives. When personal selling objectives are demand oriented, the overriding goal is to convert customer interest into first, an initial sale and, subsequently, repeat purchases. To achieve this goal, three major categories of objectives are pursued:

1. *Information provision.* Especially in the case of new products or customers, the salesperson needs to fully explain all attributes of the product or service, answer any questions, and probe for additional questions.
2. *Persuasion.* Once the initial product or service information is provided, the salesperson needs to focus on the following objectives:
   - Clearly distinguish attributes of the firm's products or services from those of competitors.
   - Maximize the number of sales as a percent of presentations.
   - Convert undecided customers into first-time buyers.
   - Convert first-time customers into repeat purchasers.

- Sell additional or complementary items to repeat customers.
- Tend to the needs of dissatisfied customers.

3. *After-sale service.* Whether the sale represents a first-time or repeat purchase, the salesperson needs to ensure the following objectives are met:
- Delivery or installation of the product or service that meets or exceeds customer expectations.
- Immediate follow-up calls and visits to address unresolved or new concerns.
- Reassurance of product or service superiority through demonstrable actions.

The Sales Relationship-Building Process

For many years, the traditional approach to selling emphasized the first-time sale of a product or service as the culmination of the sales process. As emphasized in Chapter 1, the marketing concept and accompanying approach to personal selling views the initial sale as merely the first step in a long-term relationship-building process, not as the end goal. As we shall see later in this chapter, long-term relationships between the buyer and seller can be considered partnerships because the buyer and seller have an ongoing, mutually beneficial affiliation, with each party having concern for the other party's well-being.[6] The relationship-building process is designed to meet the objectives listed in the previous section and contains six sequential stages (see Figure 9–1). These stages are (1) prospecting, (2) planning the sales call,

■ **Figure 9–1**
The Sales Relationship-Building Process

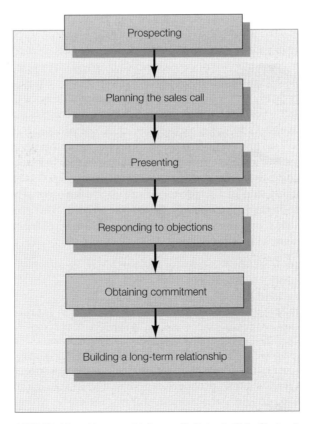

SOURCE: Adapted from material discussed in Barton A. Weitz, Stephen B. Castleberry, and John F. Tanner, *Selling: Building Partnerships,* 3rd ed. (Burr Ridge, IL: Irwin/McGraw-Hill, 1998), p. 187.

(3) presenting, (4) responding to objections, (5) obtaining commitment/closing the sale, and (6) building a long-term relationship. What follows is a brief description of each of the stages.

Prospecting.   The process of locating potential customers is called *prospecting*. The prospecting activity is critical to the success of organizations in maintaining or increasing sales volume. Continual prospecting is necessary for several reasons, including the fact that customers (1) switch to other suppliers, (2) move out of the organization's market area, (3) go out of business because of bankruptcy, (4) are acquired by another firm, or (5) have only a one-time need for the product or service. In addition, the organization's buying contracts with present customers may be replaced and organizations who wish to grow must increase their customer base. Prospecting in some fields is more important than in others. For example, a stockbroker, real estate agent, or partner in an accounting firm with no effective prospecting plan usually doesn't last long in the business. In these positions, it may take as many as 100 contacts to gain 10 prospects who will listen to presentations from which one to two sales may result. On the other hand, a Procter & Gamble sales representative in a certain geographic area would likely know all the potential retailers for Crest toothpaste.

The prospecting process usually involves two major activities that are undertaken on a continual, concurrent basis. First, prospects must be located. When names and addresses of prospects are not available, as is usually the case when firms enter new markets or a new salesperson is hired, they can be generated by randomly calling on businesses or households or by employing mass appeals (through advertising). This process is called *random lead* or *blind searching* and usually requires a high number of contacts to gain a sale. A *lead* is a potential prospect that may or may not have the potential to be a true prospect, a candidate, to whom a sale could be made.

For most professional, experienced salespeople, a more systematic approach to generating leads from predetermined target markets is utilized. This approach, aptly named *selected-lead searching*, utilizes existing contacts and knowledge to generate new prospects. In general, the best source of prospects is referrals from satisfied customers. The more satisfied one's customers are, the higher the quality of leads a salesperson will receive from them. Highlight 9–2 lists some common sources of leads and how they are used to generate new contacts.

The second step in the prospecting process involves screening. Once leads are generated, the salesperson must determine whether the prospect is a true prospect. This qualifying process usually entails the gathering of information, which leads to the answering of five questions:

1. Does the lead have a want or need that can be satisfied by the purchase of the firm's products or services?
2. Does the lead have the ability to pay?
3. Does the lead have the authority to pay?
4. Can the lead be approached favorably?
5. Is the lead eligible to buy?

Depending on the analysis of answers to these questions, the determination of whether a lead is a true prospect can be made. In seeking and qualifying leads, it is important to recognize that responsibility for these activities should not be totally assumed by individual salespeople. Rather, companies should develop a consistent, organized program, recognizing that the job of developing prospects belongs to the entire company not just the sales force.

Common Sources of Sales Leads

Source	How Used
Satisfied customers	Current and previous customers are contacted for additional business and leads.
Endless chain	Salesperson attempts to secure at least one additional lead from each person he or she interviews.
Center of influence	Salesperson cultivates well-known, influential people in the territory who are willing to supply lead information.
Promotional activities	Salesperson ties into the company's direct mail, telemarketing, and trade shows to secure and qualify leads.
Lists and directories	Salesperson uses secondary data sources, which can be free or fee-based.
Canvassing	Salesperson tries to generate leads by calling on totally unfamiliar organizations.
Spotters	Salesperson pays someone for lead information.
Telemarketing	Salesperson uses phone and/or telemarketing staff to generate leads.
Sales letters	Salesperson writes personal letters to potential leads.
Other sources	Salesperson uses noncompeting salespeople, people in his or her own firm, social clubs, and so forth, to secure lead information.

SOURCE: Adapted from material discussed in Barton A. Weitz, Stephen B. Castleberry, and John F. Tanner, *Selling: Building Partnerships*, 3rd ed. (Burr Ridge, IL: Irwin/McGraw-Hill, 1998), p. 191.

Planning the Sales Call. Salespeople will readily admit that their number one problem is getting through the door for an appointment with a prospect. Customers have become sophisticated in their buying strategies. Consequently, salespeople have to be equally sophisticated in developing their selling strategies.

While a full discussion on the topic of planning sales calls is beyond the scope of this text, what follows are brief descriptions of some key areas of knowledge salespeople should possess prior to embarking on sales calls.

1. They should have thorough knowledge of the company they represent, including its past history. This includes the philosophy of management as well as the firm's basic operating policies.
2. They should have thorough knowledge of their products and/or product lines. This is particularly true when selling organizational products. When selling very technical products, many firms require their salespeople to have training as engineers.
3. They should have good working knowledge of competitors' products. This is a vital requirement because the successful salesperson will have to know the strengths and weaknesses of those products that are in competition for market share.
4. They should have in-depth knowledge of the market for their merchandise. *The market* here refers not only to a particular sales territory but also to the general market, including the economic factors that affect the demand for their goods.
5. They should have accurate knowledge of the buyer or the prospect to whom they are selling. Under the marketing concept, knowledge of the customer is a vital requirement.

Presenting.   Successful salespeople have learned the importance of making a good impression. One of the most important ways of improving the buyer's impression is for the salesperson to be well-prepared in the knowledge areas discussed above. Some salespeople actually develop a checklist of things to take to the presentation so that nothing is forgotten. Just as important is the development of good interpersonal skills; they are a key ingredient of effective selling. Salespeople who can adapt their selling style to individual buyer needs and styles have a much stronger overall performance than less flexible counterparts.

While much goes into planning and delivering sales presentations, 14 core principles for presentation success stand out.[7] Successful salespeople

1. Are prepared.
2. Believe what they have to say is important.
3. Know their call's purpose and make sure it fits the buyer's reality.
4. Identify the fundamental message and associated key points.
5. Know their audience and speak only to issues of concern for them.
6. Summarize at the start of the presentation.
7. Throughout the presentation, continually reinforce ideas and key points.
8. Pay close attention to details when making presentations.
9. Test presentations by performing dry runs.
10. Make their presentation a performance.
11. Remain flexible, being able to adjust the presentation as it evolves.
12. Remain ready for questions.
13. Keep their perspective and enjoy the presentation.
14. Always remember that they are selling, not conversing.

Responding to Objections.   To assume the buyer will passively listen and positively respond to a sales presentation by placing an immediate order would be unrealistic. Salespeople can expect to hear objections (issues or concerns raised by the buyer) at any time during the presentation and subsequent relationship. Objections can be raised when the salesperson attempts to secure appointments, during the presentation, when the salesperson attempts to obtain commitment, or during the after-sale follow-up. Prospects raise many kinds of objections although the following are the most common. The prospect

1. Has no need for the product or service.
2. Needs more information.
3. Has never done it this way before.
4. Is just not interested.
5. Doesn't understand what is being communicated.
6. Doesn't like the product or service features, the salesperson's company, or even the salesperson him- or herself.
7. Has no money or believes the value does not exceed the cost.
8. Expects a discount or other price concession.
9. Is used to dealing with a competitor.
10. Needs more time to think about the offer.

When sales prospects raise an objection, it is a sign that they are not ready to buy and need an acceptable response to the objection before the buying decision can be made. In response to an objection, the salesperson should not challenge the respondent. Rather, the salesperson's objective should be to present the necessary information so that the prospect is able to make intelligent decisions based on that information.

Obtaining Commitment. At some point, if all objections have been resolved, the salesperson must ask for commitment. It's a rare moment when a customer will ask to buy.[8] Consequently, knowing how and when to close a sale is one of a salesperson's most indispensable skills. What follows are some basic guidelines for closing sales.

1. The salesperson should ask for the order as it is the salesperson's, not the customer's responsibility.
2. The salesperson should be persistent as customers usually will not say yes the first time they are asked to commit.
3. The salesperson should review with the customer the benefits and drawbacks associated with saying yes.
4. Once the salesperson asks for the sale, he or she should wait for the customer to respond.
5. After the customer says yes, the salesperson should immediately assure the customer he or she made the right decision.
6. The salesperson should, after commitment has been obtained, show sincere appreciation for the order as well as develop the relationship.

It should be noted that not all sales calls end in commitment, a successful closing. If commitment is not obtained, salespeople should analyze the reasons and determine if (1) more sales calls are necessary to obtain commitment; or (2) currently, there just does not exist a good match between customer needs and seller offerings. If the salesperson determines more calls are necessary, then he or she should leave the meeting with a clear action plan, which is agreeable to the customer, for the next visit.

Building a Long-Term Relationship. Developing long-term relationships with customers has become increasingly important for salespeople and their firms. It costs substantially more to win a new customer than to keep a current customer—from 5 to 10 times as much.[9] Many marketers continue to overlook the fundamental idea that the longer they keep a customer, the more profitable the customer becomes. The focus of attention and effort on current customers to maximize their satisfaction with an organization is called *aftermarketing*. Successful aftermarketing efforts require many specific activities be undertaken by the salesperson and other organizational members. These activities include

1. Establishing and maintaining a customer information file.
2. Monitoring order processing.
3. Ensuring initial proper use of the purchased product or service.
4. Providing ongoing guidance and suggestions on the use of the purchased product or service.
5. Analyzing customer feedback and responding quickly to customer questions and complaints.
6. Continually conducting customer satisfaction research and responding to it.

As seen by the preceeding discussion, there are no magic secrets of successful selling. The difference between good salespeople and mediocre ones is often the result of training plus experience. Training is no substitute for experience; the two complement each other. The difficulty with trying to discuss the selling job in terms of basic principles is that experienced, successful salespeople will always be able to find exceptions to these principles.

Relationships Can Lead to Partnerships.   When the interaction between a salesperson and a customer does not end with the sale, the beginnings of a relationship are present. Many salespeople are finding that building relationships and even partnering with customers is becoming increasingly important.

When a buyer and a salesperson have a close personal relationship, they both begin to rely on each other and communicate honestly. When each has a problem they work together to solve it. Such market relationships are known as *functional relationships.* An important trust begins to exist between each party. As with any relationship, each often gives and takes when the situation calls for it in order to keep the relationship intact. The reader may have such a relationship with a long-term medical or dental practitioner or hair cutter.

When organizations move beyond functional relationships, they develop *strategic partnerships,* or *strategic alliances.* These are long-term, formal relationships in which both parties make significant commitments and investments in each other in order to pursue mutual goals and to improve the profitability of each other. While a functional relationship is based on trust, a strategic partnership or alliance moves beyond trust. The partners in the relationship actually invest in each other. Obviously, the reasons for forming strategic partnerships vary. Some do it because they see joint opportunities (banks, insurance companies, and brokerage firms), to gain access to new markets (United Parcel Service of America and Mail Boxes Etc.), to develop new technology or exploit joint opportunities (IBM and Apple), or to gain a marketing advantage over competitors (United Airlines and Starbucks Coffee, American Airlines and Career Track).

People Who Support the Sales Force

In many instances, sales personnel will require some assistance at various stages of the sales process. These support personnel do not seek the order. Their purpose is to focus on the long-term relationship and increase the likelihood of sales in the long run.

Missionary salespeople are used in certain industries such as pharmaceuticals to focus solely on promotion of existing products and introduction of new products. They may call on physicians to convince them to prescribe a new drug or on pharmacies to convince them to promote a new cold remedy with a large display during the cold and flu season.

A *technical sales specialist* supports the sales staff by providing training or other technical assistance to the prospect. This individual may follow up an expression of interest to the salesperson from a prospect, especially when the product is to be used to solve certain technical problems of the buyer. Some organizations will provide training to the front-line staff of the buying organization who will be expected to sell the product to their customers.

Finally, when the product is extremely high priced and is being sold to the whole organization, *cross-functional sales teams* are often used. As products increase in technical complexity, and specialized knowledge is required by units of the buying organization before a buying decision can be made, team selling has increased in popularity. For example, a manufacturer's sales team might be made up of people from

Why Cross-Functional Sales Teams Are Growing in Popularity

1. *Improved sales productivity.* When the product or system being purchased is for the whole organization, different specialists handle different parts of the job. This usually results in a more effective and efficient sales process.
2. *More flexibility and quicker decisions.* To thrive in today's increasingly competitive markets, buying organizations often require selling organizations to produce small runs of tailored products on a very tight schedule. Cross-functional sales teams enable sellers to be more flexible because all functional units are involved in the sales process, which also enables the seller to make quicker decisions in response to buyer demands.
3. *Better decisions.* In most cases, the use of cross-functional teams composed of individuals with varied backgrounds in the company will lead to more innovative forms of thought and superior decisions than would be the case of an individual acting alone. Improved decisions would benefit both the buyer and the seller.
4. *Increased customer satisfaction.* The ultimate measure of the success of cross-functional sales teams comes with increased customer satisfaction, cemented relationships, and repeat business. The energy, flexibility, and commitment associated with cross-functional sales teams has led many organizations to adopt the approach.

sales, engineering, customer service, and finance, depending on the needs of the customer. A bank's sales team might consist of people from the commercial lending, investments, small business, and trust departments.

■ Managing the Sales and Relationship-Building Process

Every personal sale can be divided into two parts: the part done by the salespeople and the part done for the salespeople by the company. For example, from the standpoint of the product, the company should provide the salesperson with a product skillfully designed, thoroughly tested, attractively packaged, adequately advertised, and priced to compare favorably with competitive products. Salespeople have the responsibility of being thoroughly acquainted with the product, its selling features, and points of superiority, and a sincere belief in the value of the product. From a sales management standpoint, the company's part of the sale involves the following:

1. Efficient and effective sales tools, including continuous sales training, promotional literature, samples, trade shows, product information, and adequate advertising.
2. An efficient delivery and reorder system to ensure that customers will receive the merchandise as promised.
3. An equitable compensation plan that rewards performance, motivates the salesperson, and promotes company loyalty. It should also reimburse the salesperson for all reasonable expenses incurred while doing the job.
4. Adequate supervision and evaluation of performance as a means of helping salespeople do a better job, not only for the company but for themselves as well.

Being a successful sales manager is much different from being a successful salesperson.[10] Reports, budgets, meetings, and other tasks take on new importance as the focus changes from getting an order to running an entire department or division. Indeed, the role of the sales manager can be likened to that of a good coach.[11] The sales manager must possess a variety of skills including those related to (1) problem solving, (2) interpersonal relations, (3) written and oral communication, (4) persuasion, and (5) technology.[12] The sales manager must continually remind the sales force of selling fundamentals, constantly encourage peak efforts, consistently praise effective performance, and, perhaps most important, do as much listening as speaking.[13] Simultaneously, the sales manager is charged with developing an effective overall sales plan so that organizational goals can be realized. An important key to maximizing sales productivity and end performance is the ability of the sales manager to give good coaching to the many and not to rely on the individual efforts of the few.

The Sales Management Task

Since the advent of the marketing concept, a clear-cut distinction has been made between marketing management and sales management. Marketing management refers to all activities in the firm that have to do with satisfying demand. Sales management is a narrower concept dealing with those functions directly related to personal selling. Generally speaking, sales managers are in middle management and report directly to the vice president of marketing. Their basic responsibilities can be broken down into at least seven major areas: (1) developing an effective sales organization for the company, (2) formulating short-range and long-range sales programs, (3) recruiting, training, and supervising the sales force, (4) formulating sales budgets and controlling selling expenses, (5) coordinating the personal selling effort with other forms of promotional activities, (6) maintaining lines of communication among the sales force, customers, and other relevant parts of the organization, such as advertising, production, and logistics, and, in some firms, (7) developing sales forecasts and other types of relevant marketing studies to be used in sales planning and control.

Sales managers are line officers whose primary responsibility is establishing and maintaining an active sales organization. In terms of authority, they usually have equivalent rank to that of other marketing executives who manage aspects of the marketing program, such as advertising, product planning, or logistics. The sales organization may have separate departments and department heads to perform specialized tasks, such as training, personnel, promotion, and forecasting. Figure 9–2 is an example of such a sales organization.

■ **Figure 9–2** An Example of a Sales Organization

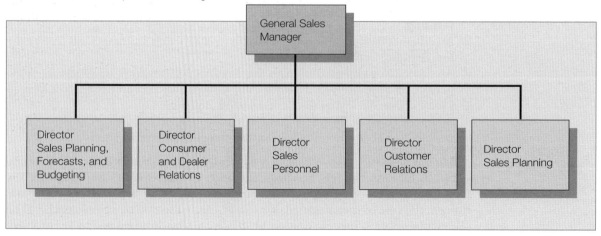

In other cases, a general marketing manager may have product managers or directors reporting to them. This is common in cases where the firm sells numerous products and each product or product line is handled by a separate manager. Another common arrangement is to have sales managers assigned to specific geographic regions or customer groups. This type of specialization enables the sales force to operate more efficiently and effectively by avoiding overlaps.

Toward this end, more and more organizations are embracing the concept of national account management programs. National account management programs allow firms to identify and target their largest and most important customer accounts and provide these accounts with special treatment in order processing, and service.[14] Specific sales personnel are assigned to handle each national account regardless of geographic location where individual offices and facilities of the account may reside. National accounts differ from traditional customers in that they tend to have more centralized purchasing processes and purchase a much larger volume of products. National account management programs provide a number of benefits for both the selling organization and the customer. For the selling firm, there is the potential to develop better, closer relationships with the customer, which can give the firm a competitive advantage through increased profit margins, increased communication between the buying and selling firm, and the maintenance of a stable customer base among a firm's national accounts. From the customer's perspective two benefits are that fewer mistakes are likely to occur during processing and servicing orders due to fewer points of contact with the selling firm, and customer needs can be addressed more immediately than if they were processed through more traditional channels.

Controlling the Sales Force

There are two obvious reasons why it is critical that the sales force be properly controlled. First, personal selling can be the largest marketing expense component in the final price of the product. Second, unless the sales force is somehow directed, motivated, and audited on a continual basis, it is likely to be less efficient than it is capable of being. Controlling the sales force involves four key functions: (1) forecasting sales, (2) establishing sales territories and quotas, (3) analyzing expenses, and (4) motivating and compensating performance.

Forecasting Sales.   Sales planning begins with a forecast of sales for some future period or periods. From a practical standpoint, these forecasts are made on a short-term basis of a year or less, although long-range forecasts of one to five years are made for purposes other than managing the sales force, such as financing, production, and development. Generally speaking, forecasting is the marketing manager's responsibility. In large firms, because of the complexity of the task, it is usually delegated to a specialized unit, such as the marketing research department. Forecast data should be integrated into the firm's marketing information system for use by sales managers and other executives. For many companies, the sales forecast is the key instrument in the planning and control of operations.

The *sales forecast* is an estimate of how much of the company's output, either in dollars or in units, can be sold during a specified future period under a proposed marketing plan and under an assumed set of economic conditions. A sales forecast has several important uses: (1) it is used to establish sales quotas; (2) it is used to plan personal selling efforts as well as other types of promotional activities in the marketing mix; (3) it is used to budget selling expenses; and (4) it is used to plan and coordinate production, logistics, inventories, personnel, and so forth.

Sales forecasting has become very sophisticated in recent years, especially with the increased availability of computer software. It should be mentioned, however, that a forecast is never a substitute for sound business judgment. At the present time there is no single method of sales forecasting known that gives uniformly accurate results with infallible precision. Outlined below are some commonly used sales forecasting methods.[15]

1. *Jury of executive opinion method.* This combines and averages the views of top management representing marketing, production, finance, purchasing, and administration.
2. *Sales force composite method.* This is similar to the first method in that it obtains the combined views of the sales force about the future outlook for sales. In some companies all salespeople, or district managers, submit estimates of the future sales in their territory or district.
3. *Customer expectations method.* This approach involves asking customers or product users about the quantity they expect to purchase.
4. *Time-series analysis.* This approach involves analyzing past sales data and the impact of factors that influence sales (long-term growth trends, cyclical fluctuations, seasonal variations).
5. *Correlation analysis.* This involves measuring the relationship between the dependent variable, sales, and one or more independent variables that can explain increases or decreases in sales volumes.
6. *Other quantitative techniques.* Numerous statistical and mathematical techniques can be used to predict or estimate future sales. Two of the more important techniques are *(a)* growth functions, which are mathematical expressions specifying the relationship between demand and time; and *(b)* simulation models, where a statistical model of the industry is developed and programmed to compute values for the key parameters of the model.

Establishing Sales Territories and Quotas.   The establishment of sales territories and sales quotas represents management's need to match personal selling effort with sales potential (or opportunity). Soundly designed sales territories can improve how the market is served.[16] It is much easier to pinpoint customers and prospects and to determine who should call on them when the market is geographically divided than when the market is considered as a large aggregate of potential accounts. The geographic segments should represent small clusters of customers or prospects within some physical proximity. Implied here is the notion that there are some distinct economic advantages to dividing the market into smaller segments. Salespeople restricted to a geographic area are likely to get more sales in the territory. Instead of simply servicing the "easy" and larger accounts, they are prone to develop small accounts. Of course, there are criteria other than geography for establishing territories. One important criterion is that of product specialization. In this case, salespeople are specialists relative to particular product or customer situations.

The question of managing sales territories cannot be discussed meaningfully without saying something about sales quotas. In general, quotas represent goals assigned to salespeople. As such, quotas provide three main benefits. First they provide incentives for salespeople. For example, the definite objective of selling $500,000 worth of computer equipment is more motivation to most salespeople

Marketing
Highlight 9–4

Technology and the Sales Force

In today's information-driven business environment, companies are looking to their sales force as a vital source of customer information. In a recent survey of sales executives, sales representatives, and information systems managers from large corporations, more than 80 percent admitted to some form of technology to gather customer data. Pen-based computers and contact databases are examples of the technology being utilized by salespeople across the globe. Listed below are a few examples of the benefits companies are experiencing from technology.

I. Tangible benefits
  A. Increased time spent with customers/clients.
  B. Higher levels of customer satisfaction.
  C. Increased numbers of promising prospects.
  D. Consistent and prompt follow-up correspondence.
  E. Increased revenue per salesperson.
  F. Increased customer service.
  G. Better time management by both salespeople and managers.
  H. Improved communication within the organization.
  I. Better business results companywide.
  J. Increased favorable exposure of the company name.

II. Intangible benefits
  A. Smoother functioning within the company.
  B. Increased employee motivation and satisfaction.
  C. Better trained salespeople and marketing personnel.
  D. More efficient use of field force equipment.
  E. More recent and pertinent information with easier access.
  F. Improved responsiveness to customer and prospect needs.
  G. Enhancement of corporate image.
  H. Corporate differentiation and competitive advantage.
  I. Smoother, more efficient organizational change.
  J. Improved control and understanding of selling and marketing expenses.

than the indefinite charge to go out and sell computer equipment. Sales bonuses and commissions based on quotas can also be motivational. Second, quotas provide a quantitative standard against which the performance of individual sales representatives or other marketing units can be measured. They allow management to pinpoint individuals and units that are performing above average and those experiencing difficulty. Third, quotas can be used not only to evaluate salespersons' performance but also to evaluate and control their efforts. As part of their job, salespeople are expected to engage in various activities besides calling on established accounts. These activities might include calling on new accounts, collecting past-due accounts, and planning and developing sales presentations. Activity quotas allow the company to monitor whether salespeople are engaging in these activities to the extent desired.

Sales quotas represent specific sales goals assigned to each territory or unit over a designated time period. The most common method of establishing quotas for territories is to relate sales to forecasted sales potential. For example, if the Ajax Drug Company's territory M has an estimated industry sales potential for a particular product of $400,000 for the year, the quota might be set at 25 percent of that potential, or $100,000. The 25 percent figure represents the market share Ajax estimates to be a reasonable target. This $100,000 quota may represent an increase of $20,000 in sales over last year (assuming constant prices) that is expected from new business.

In establishing sales quotas for its individual territories or sales personnel, management needs to take into account three key factors. First, all territories will not have equal potential and, therefore, compensation must be adjusted accordingly.

Second, all salespeople will not have equal ability, and assignments may have to be made accordingly. Some companies adjust quotas up or down depending on the specific salesperson's (1) years of experience with the company, (2) past sales performance, and (3) need for organizational resources to support his or her efforts.[17] Third, the sales task in each territory may differ from time period to time period. For instance, the nature of some territories may require that salespeople spend more time seeking new accounts, rather than servicing established accounts, especially in the case of so-called new territories. The point to be made here is that quotas can vary, not only by territory but also by assigned tasks. The effective sales manager should assign quotas not only for dollar sales but also for each major selling function. Figure 9–3 is an example of how this is done for the Medi-test Company, where each activity is assigned a quota and a weight reflecting its relative importance.

Analyzing Expenses.   Sales forecasts should include a sales expense budget. In some companies, sales expense budgets are developed from the bottom up. Each territorial or district manager submits estimates of expenses and forecasted sales quotas. These estimates are usually prepared for a period of a year and then broken down into quarters and months. The sales manager then reviews the budget requests from the field offices and from staff departments. Expenses may be classified as fixed, semivariable or variable, and direct or indirect. Certain items, such as rent or administrative salaries, are fixed. In field offices, employee compensation is the principal expense, and it may be fixed or semivariable, depending on the compensation plan. Other items, such as travel, samples, or other promotional material, are variable in nature. Some expenses are directly traceable to the sale of specific products, such as samples or displays, while other expenses are indirect, as in the case of administrative salaries and rent. Sales commissions and shipping expenses tend to vary in direct proportion to sales, while travel expense and entertainment may not be tied to sales volume in any direct proportion.

■ **Figure 9–3**
Medi-test Company
Sales Activity
Evaluation

Territory: Southern
Salesperson: Marsha Smith

Functions	(1) Quota	(2) Actual	(3) Percent (2 ÷ 1)	(4) Weight	(5) Score (3 × 4)
Sales volume					
Old business	$380,000	$300,000	79	0.7	55.7
New business	$ 20,000	$ 20,000	100	0.5	50.0
Calls on prospects					
Doctors	20	15	75	0.2	15.0
Druggists	80	60	75	0.2	15.0
Wholesalers	15	15	100	0.2	20.0
Hospitals	10	10	100	0.2	20.0
				2.0	175.7

Performance index = 175.7

Motivating and Compensating Performance. The sales manager's personnel function includes more than motivating and compensating the sales force; but from the vantage point of sales force productivity, these two tasks are of paramount importance. Operationally, it means that the sales manager has the responsibility of keeping the morale and efforts of the sales force at high levels through supervision and motivation. These closely related tasks are accomplished through interaction with the sales force by (1) spending time in the field visiting customers, (2) communicating on a frequent basis via E-mail, telephone, or in-person meetings, (3) giving credit and praise for work well done, (4) providing performance feedback on a regular basis, and (5) developing incentive schemes through which greater opportunity for earnings (as in sales contests) or job promotion can be achieved.[18]

Compensation is a principal method by which firms are able to recruit, motivate, and retain their sales forces. Devising a compensation plan for a company is a technical matter, but there are some general guidelines in formulating such a plan. First, a firm should be mindful of any modifications necessary to meet its particular needs when adopting another company's compensation plan. Second, the plan should make sense (i.e., should have a logical rationale) to both management and the sales force. Third, the plan should not be so overly complex that it cannot be understood by the average salesperson. Fourth, as suggested in the section on quotas, the plan should be fair and equitable to avoid penalizing the sales force because of factors beyond their control; conversely, the plan should ensure rewards for performance in proportion to results. Fifth, the plan should allow the sales force to earn salaries that permit them to maintain an acceptable standard of living. Sixth, the plan should attempt to minimize attrition by giving the sales force some incentive, such as a vested retirement plan, for staying with the company. Finally, and perhaps most important, the individual compensation plan must be tied to the overall sales and marketing plans.[19]

There are two basic types of compensation: salary and commission. *Salary* usually refers to a specific amount of monetary compensation at an agreed rate for definite time periods. *Commission* is usually monetary compensation provided for

■ **Figure 9–4** Types of Incentives and Their Possible Performance Outcomes

Types of Incentives	Performance Outcomes
• Positive feedback on salesperson performance evaluation	• Sell a greater dollar volume
• Company praise (e.g., recognition in a newsletter)	• Increase sales of more profitable products
• Bonus (e.g., cash, merchandise, or travel allowances)	• Push new products
	• Push selected items at designated seasons
• Salary increase	• Achieve a higher degree of market penetration by products, kinds of customers, or territories
• Pay for performance for specific new product idea	• Increase the number of calls made
• Paid educational allowance	• Secure large average orders
• Earned time off	• Secure new customers
• Fringe benefits	• Service and maintain existing business
• Stock options	• Reduce turnover of customers
• Vested retirement plan	• Achieve full-line (balanced) selling
• Profit sharing	• Reduce direct selling costs
	• Submit reports and other data promptly

SOURCE: Some of the material was adapted from Gilbert A. Churchill Jr., Neil M. Ford, and Orville C. Walker, *Sales Force Management,* 5th ed. (Burr Ridge, IL: Irwin/McGraw-Hill, 1997), p. 490.

each unit of sales and expressed as a percentage of sales. The base on which commissions are computed may be volume of sales in units of product, gross sales in dollars, net sales after returns, sales volume in excess of a quota, and net profits. Very often, several compensation approaches are combined. For example, a salesperson might be paid a base salary, a commission on sales exceeding a volume figure, and a percentage share of the company's profits for that year.

In addition to straight dollar compensation, there are numerous other forms of incentives that can be used to motivate the sales force. Some of these types of incentives and their potential performance outcomes are listed in Figure 9–4.

■ Conclusion

This chapter has attempted to outline and explain the personal selling aspect of the promotion mix. An emphasis was placed on describing the importance of the relationship-building aspect of the personal selling process. For organizations that wish to continue to grow and prosper, personal selling plays an integral part in the marketing of products and services. As long as production continues to expand through the development of new and highly technical products, personal selling will continue to be an important part of marketing strategy.

■ Additional Readings

Duboff, Robert S., and Lori Underwood Sherer. "Customized Customer Loyalty." *Marketing Management,* Summer 1997, pp. 21–27.

Fournier, Susan; Susan Dobscha; and David Glen Mick. "Preventing the Premature Death of Relationship Marketing." *Harvard Business Review,* January–February 1998, pp. 42–53.

Gardner, Alston; Stephen J. Bistritz; and Jay Klopmaker. "Selling to Senior Executives, Part I." *Marketing Management,* Summer 1998, pp. 10–21.

Lambert, Douglas M.; Margaret E. Emmelhainz; and John T. Gardner. "So You Think You Want a Partner." *Marketing Management,* Summer 1996, pp. 24–41.

McIntyre, Roger P., and Martin S. Meloche. "Psychological Determinants of Effective Sales Presentations." *Journal of Marketing Management,* Fall–Winter 1994, pp. 23–36.

Chapter Ten

Distribution Strategy

Channel of distribution decisions involve numerous interrelated variables that must be integrated into the total marketing mix. Because of the time and money required to set up an efficient channel, and since channels are often hard to change once they are set up, these decisions are critical to the success of the firm.

This chapter is concerned with the development and management of channels of distribution and the process of goods distribution in complex, highly competitive, and specialized economies. It should be noted at the outset that channels of distribution provide the ultimate consumer or organizational buyer with time, place, and possession utility. Thus, an efficient channel is one that delivers the product when and where it is wanted at a minimum total cost.

■ The Need for Marketing Intermediaries

A *channel of distribution* is the combination of institutions through which a seller markets products to the user or ultimate consumer. The need for other institutions or intermediaries in the delivery of goods is sometimes questioned, particularly since the profits they make are viewed as adding to the cost of the product. However, this reasoning is generally fallacious, since producers use marketing intermediaries because the intermediary can perform functions more cheaply and more efficiently than the producer can. This notion of efficiency is critical when the characteristics of advanced economies are considered.

For example, the U.S. economy is characterized by heterogeneity in terms of both supply and demand. In terms of numbers alone, there are nearly 6 million establishments comprising the supply segment of the economy, and there are close to 100 million households making up the demand side. Clearly, if each of these units had to deal on a one-to-one basis to obtain needed goods and services, and there were no intermediaries to collect and disperse assortments of goods, the system would be totally inefficient. Thus, the primary role of intermediaries is to bring supply and demand together in an efficient and orderly fashion.

■ Classification of Marketing Intermediaries and Functions

There are a great many types of marketing intermediaries, many of which are so specialized by function and industry that they need not be discussed here. Figure 10–1 presents the major types of marketing intermediaries common to many industries. Although there is some overlap in this classification, these categories are based on the marketing functions performed. That is, various intermediaries perform different marketing functions and to different degrees. Figure 10–2 is a listing of the more common marketing functions performed in the channels.

It should be remembered that whether or not a manufacturer utilizes intermediaries to perform these functions, the functions have to be performed by someone. In other words, the managerial question is not whether to perform the functions but who will perform them and to what degree.

■ **Figure 10–1** Major Types of Marketing Intermediaries

Middleman—an independent business concern that operates as a link between producers and ultimate consumers or organizational buyers.

Merchant middleman—a middleman who buys the goods outright and takes title to them.

Agent—a business unit that negotiates purchases, sales, or both but does not take title to the goods in which it deals.

Wholesaler—a merchant establishment operated by a concern that is primarily engaged in buying, taking title to, usually storing and physically handling goods in large quantities, and reselling the goods (usually in smaller quantities) to retailers or to organizational buyers.

Retailer—a merchant middleman who is engaged primarily in selling to ultimate consumers.

Broker—a middleman who serves as a go-between for the buyer or seller. The broker assumes no title risks, does not usually have physical custody of products, and is not looked upon as a permanent representative of either the buyer or the seller.

Manufacturers' agent—an agent who generally operates on an extended contractual basis, often sells within an exclusive territory, handles noncompeting but related lines of goods, and possesses limited authority with regard to prices and terms of sale.

Distributor—a wholesale middleman especially in lines where selective or exclusive distribution is common at the wholesaler level in which the manufacturer expects strong promotional support; often a synonym for wholesaler.

Jobber—a middleman who buys from manufacturers and sells to retailers; a wholesaler.

Facilitating agent—a business firm that assists in the performance of distribution tasks other than buying, selling, and transferring title (i.e., transportation companies, warehouses, etc.)

SOURCE: Based on Peter D. Bennett, ed., *Dictionary of Marketing Terms,* 2nd ed. (Chicago: American Marketing Association, 1995).

Part C The Marketing Mix

■ **Figure 10–2**
Marketing Functions
Performed in Channels
of Distribution

Buying—purchasing products from sellers for use or for resale.

Selling—the personal or impersonal process whereby the salesperson ascertains, activates, and satisfies the needs of the buyer to the mutual continuous benefit of both buyer and seller.

Sorting—a function performed by intermediaries to bridge the discrepancy between the assortment of goods and services generated by the producer and the assortment demanded by the consumer. This function includes four distinct processes: sorting out, accumulation, allocation, and assorting.

Sorting out—a sorting process that breaks down a heterogeneous supply into separate stocks that are relatively homogeneous.

Accumulation—a sorting process that brings similar stocks from a number of sources together into a larger homogeneous supply.

Allocation—a sorting process that consists of breaking a homogeneous supply down into smaller and smaller lots.

Assorting—a sorting process that consists of building an assortment of products for use in association with each other.

Concentration—the process of bringing goods from various places together in one place.

Financing—providing credit or funds to facilitate a transaction.

Storage—maintaining inventories and protecting products to provide better customer service.

Grading—the classifying of a product by examining its quality. It is often done with a program of grade labeling, though individual firms can grade their own products by a private system if they wish, for example, good, better, best.

Transportation—a marketing function that adds time and place utility to the product by moving it from where it is made to where it is purchased and used. It includes all intermediate steps in the process.

Risk-taking—taking on business risks involved in transporting and owning products.

Marketing research—collecting information concerning such things as market conditions, expected sales, consumer trends, and competitive forces.

SOURCE: Based on Peter D. Bennett, ed., *Dictionary of Marketing Terms,* 2nd ed. (Chicago: American Marketing Association, 1995).

■ Channels of Distribution

As previously noted, a channel of distribution is the combination of institutions through which a seller markets products to the user or ultimate consumer. Some of these links assume the risks of ownership; others do not. The conventional channel of distribution patterns for consumer goods markets are shown in Figure 10–3.

Some manufacturers use a *direct channel,* selling directly to a market. For example, Gateway 2000 sells computers through the mail without the use of other intermediaries. Using a direct channel, called *direct marketing,* increased in popularity as marketers found that products could be sold directly using a variety of media. These media include direct mail, telemarketing, direct-action advertising, catalog selling, cable selling, on-line selling, and direct selling through demonstrations at home or place of work.

■ **Figure 10–3** Conventional Channels of Distribution of Consumer Goods

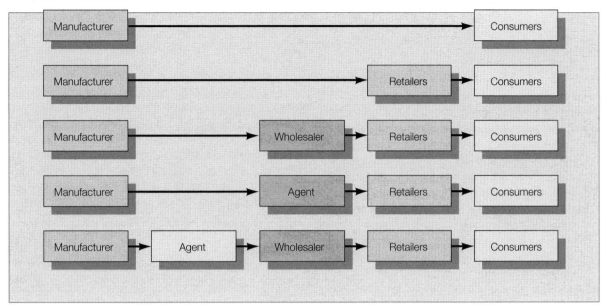

In other cases, one or more intermediaries may be used in the distribution process. For example, Hewlett-Packard sells its computers and printers through retailers such as Best Buy and Office Max. A common channel for consumer goods is one in which the manufacturer sells through wholesalers and retailers. For instance, a cold remedy manufacturer may sell to drug wholesalers who, in turn, sell a vast array of drug products to various retail outlets. Small manufacturers may also use agents, since they do not have sufficient capital for their own sales forces. Agents are commonly used intermediaries in the jewelry industry. The final channel in Figure 10–3 is used primarily when small wholesalers and retailers are involved. Channels with one or more intermediaries are referred to as *indirect channels.*

In contrast to consumer products, the direct channel is often used in the distribution of organizational goods. The reason for this stems from the structure of most organizational markets, which often have relatively few but extremely large customers. Also, many organizational products, such as computer systems, need a great deal of presale and postsale service. Distributors are used in organizational markets when there is a large number of buyers but each purchases a small amount of a product. As in the consumer market, agents are used in organizational markets in cases where manufacturers do not wish to have their own sales forces. Such an arrangement may be used by small manufacturers or when the market is geographically dispersed. The final channel arrangement in Figure 10–4 may also be used by a small manufacturer or when the market consists of many small customers. Under such conditions, it may not be economical for sellers to have their own sales organization.

■ **Figure 10–4** Conventional Channels of Distribution for Organizational Goods

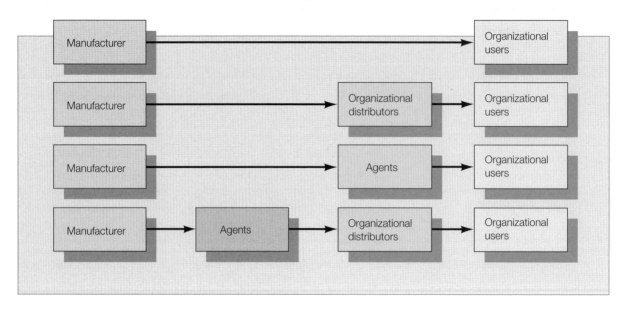

■ Selecting Channels of Distribution

Given the numerous types of channel intermediaries and functions that must be performed, the task of selecting and designing a channel of distribution may at first appear to be overwhelming. However, in many industries, channels of distribution have developed over many years and have become somewhat traditional. In such cases, the producer may be limited to this type of channel to operate in the industry. This is not to say that a traditional channel is always the most efficient and that there are no opportunities for innovation, but the fact that such a channel is widely accepted in the industry suggests it is highly efficient. A primary constraint in these cases and in cases where no traditional channel exists is that of *availability* of the various types of middlemen. All too often in the early stages of channel design, executives map out elaborate channel networks only to find out later that no such independent intermediaries exist for the firm's product in selected geographic areas. Even if they do exist, they may not be willing to accept the seller's products. In general, there are six basic considerations in the initial development of channel strategy. These are outlined in Figure 10–5.

It should be noted that for a particular product any one of these characteristics greatly influences choice of channels. To illustrate, highly perishable products generally require direct channels, or a firm with little financial strength may require intermediaries to perform almost all of the marketing functions.

Specific Considerations

The above characteristics play an important part in framing the channel selection decision. Based on them, the choice of channels can be further refined in terms of (1) distribution coverage required, (2) degree of control desired, (3) total distribution cost, and (4) channel flexibility.

■ **Figure 10–5** General Considerations in Channel Planning

1. **Customer characteristics**
   a. Number
   b. Geographic dispersion
   c. Preferred channels and outlets for purchase
   d. Purchasing patterns
   e. Use of new channels (e.g., on-line purchasing)
2. **Product characteristics**
   a. Unit value
   b. Perishability
   c. Bulkiness
   d. Degree of standardization
   e. Installation and maintenance services required
3. **Intermediary characteristics**
   a. Availability
   b. Willingness to accept product or product line
   c. Geographic market served
   d. Marketing functions performed
   e. Potential for conflict
   f. Potential for long-term relationship
   g. Competitive products sold
   h. Financial condition
   i. Other strengths and weaknesses

4. **Competitor characteristics**
   a. Number
   b. Relative size and market share
   c. Distribution channels and strategy
   d. Financial condition and estimated marketing budget
   e. Size of product mix and product lines
   f. Overall marketing strategy employed
   g. Other strengths and weaknesses
5. **Company characteristics**
   a. Relative size and market share
   b. Financial condition and marketing budget
   c. Size of product mix and product lines
   d. Marketing strategy employed
   e. Marketing objectives
   f. Past channel experience
   g. Marketing functions willing to perform
   h. Other strengths and weaknesses
6. **Environmental characteristics**
   a. Economic conditions
   b. Legal regulations and restrictions
   c. Political issues
   d. Global and domestic cultural differences and changes
   e. Technological changes
   f. Other opportunities and threats

Distribution Coverage Required.   Because of the characteristics of the product, the environment needed to sell the product, and the needs and expectations of the potential buyer, products will vary in the intensity of distribution coverage they require. Distribution coverage can be viewed along a continuum ranging from intensive to selective to exclusive distribution.

Intensive Distribution.   Here the manufacturer attempts to gain exposure through as many wholesalers and retailers as possible. Most convenience goods require intensive distribution based on the characteristics of the product (low unit value) and the needs and expectations of the buyer (high frequency of purchase and convenience).

Selective Distribution.   Here the manufacturer limits the use of intermediaries to the ones believed to be the best available in a geographic area. This may be based on the service organization available, the sales organization, or the reputation of the intermediary. Thus, appliances, home furnishings, and better clothing are usually distributed selectively. For appliances, the intermediary's service organization could be a key factor, while for better clothing and home furnishings, the intermediary's reputation would be an important consideration.

Exclusive Distribution.   Here the manufacturer severely limits distribution, and intermediaries are provided exclusive rights within a particular territory. The characteristics of the product are a determining factor here. Where the product requires certain specialized selling effort or investment in unique facilities or large inventories, this arrangement is usually selected. Retail paint stores are an example of such a distribution arrangement.

Degree of Control Desired.   In selecting channels of distribution, the seller must make decisions concerning the degree of control desired over the marketing of the firm's products. Some manufacturers prefer to keep as much control over their products as possible. Ordinarily, the degree of control achieved by the seller is proportionate to the directness of the channel. One eastern brewery, for instance, owns its own fleet of trucks and operates a wholly owned delivery system direct to grocery and liquor stores. Its market is very concentrated geographically, with many small buyers, so such a system is economically feasible. However, all other brewers in the area sell through distributors.

When more indirect channels are used, the manufacturer must surrender some control over the marketing of the firm's product. However, attempts are commonly made to maintain a degree of control through some other indirect means, such as sharing promotional expenditures, providing sales training, or other operational aids, such as accounting systems, inventory systems, or marketing research data on the dealer's trading area.

Total Distribution Cost.   The total distribution cost concept has developed out of the more general topic of systems theory. The concept suggests that a channel of distribution should be viewed as a total system composed on interdependent subsystems, and that the objective of the system (channel) manager should be to optimize total system performance. In terms of distribution costs, it generally is assumed that the total system should be designed to minimize costs, other things being equal. The following is a representative list of the major distribution costs to be minimized.

1. Transportation
2. Order processing
3. Cost of lost business (an opportunity cost due to inability to meet customer demand)
4. Inventory carrying costs, including
   a. Storage-space charges
   b. Cost of capital invested
   c. Taxes
   d. Insurance
   e. Obsolescence and deterioration
5. Packaging
6. Materials handling

The important qualification to the total cost concept is the statement "other things being equal." The purpose of the total cost concept is to emphasize total system performance to avoid suboptimization. However, other important factors must be considered, not the least of which are level of customer service, sales, profits, and interface with the total marketing mix.

Channel Flexibility.   A final consideration relates to the ability of the manufacturer to adapt to changing conditions. To illustrate, much of the population has moved from inner cities to suburbs and thus make most of their purchases in shopping centers and malls. If a manufacturer had long-term, exclusive dealership with retailers in the inner city, the ability to adapt to this population shift could have been severely limited.

■ Managing a Channel of Distribution

Once the seller has decided on the type of channel structure to use and selected the individual members, the entire coalition should operate as a total system. From a behavioral perspective, the system can be viewed as a social system since each member interacts with the others, each member plays a role vis-à-vis the others, and each has certain expectations of the other. Thus, the behavioral perspective views a channel of distribution as more than a series of markets or participants extending from production to consumption.

Relationship Marketing in Channels

For many years in theory and practice, marketing has taken a competitive view of channels of distribution. In other words, since channel members had different goals and strategies, it was believed that the major focus should be on concepts such as power and conflict. Research interests focused on issues concerning bases of power, antecedents and consequences of conflict, and conflict resolution.

More recently, however, a new view of channels has developed. Perhaps because of the success of Japanese companies in the 1980s, it was recognized that much could be gained by developing long-term commitments and harmony among channel members. This view is called *relationship marketing,* which can be defined as "marketing with the conscious aim to develop and manage long-term and/or trusting relationships with customers, distributors, suppliers, or other parties in the marketing environment."[1]

It is well documented in the marketing literature that long-term relationships throughout the channel often lead to higher-quality products with lower costs. These benefits may account for the increased use of vertical marketing systems.[2]

Vertical Marketing Systems

To this point in the chapter the discussion has focused primarily on conventional channels of distribution. In conventional channels, each firm is relatively independent of the other members in the channel. However, one of the important developments in channel management in recent years is the increasing use of vertical marketing systems.

Vertical marketing systems are channels in which members are more dependent on one another and develop long-term working relationships in order to improve the efficiency and effectiveness of the system. Figure 10–6 shows the major types of vertical marketing systems, which include administered, contractual, and corporate systems.[3]

Administered Systems.   Administered vertical marketing systems are the most similar to conventional channels. However, in these systems there is a higher degree of interorganizational planning and management than in a conventional channel. The dependence in these systems can result from the existence of a strong channel leader such that other channel members work closely with this company in order to maintain a long-term relationship. While any level of channel member may be the leader of an administered system, Wal-Mart, Kmart, and Sears are excellent examples of retailers that have established administered systems with many of their suppliers.

Contractual Systems.   Contractual vertical marketing systems involve independent production and distribution companies entering into formal contracts to

■ **Figure 10–6**
Major Types of Vertical
Marketing Systems

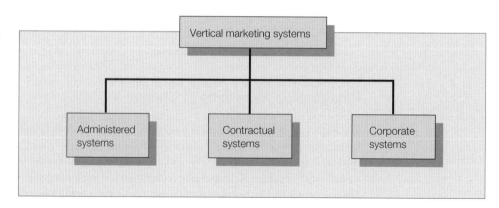

Marketing
Highlight 10–2

Franchising: An Alternative to Conventional Channels of Distribution

A franchise is a means by which a producer of products or services achieves a direct channel of distribution without wholly owning or managing the physical facilities in the market. In effect, the franchisor provides the franchisee with the franchisor's knowledge, manufacturing, and marketing techniques for a financial return.

Ingredients of a Franchised Business

Six key ingredients should be included within a well-balanced franchise offered to a franchisee. These are given in order of importance.

- *Technical knowledge* in its practical form is supplied through an intensive course of study.
- *Managerial techniques* based on proven and time-tested programs are imparted to the franchisee on a continuing basis, even after the business has been started or taken over by the franchisee.
- *Commercial knowledge* involving prescribed methods of buying and selling is explained and codified. Most products to be obtained, processed, and sold to the franchisee are supplied by the franchisor.
- *Financial instruction* on managing funds and accounts is given to the franchisee during the indoctrination period.
- *Accounting controls* are set up by the franchisor for the franchisee.

- *Protective safeguards* are included in the intensive training of the franchisee for employees and customers, including the quality of the product, as well as the safeguards for assets through adequate insurance controls.

Elements of an Ideal Franchise Program

- *High gross margin.* In order for the franchisee to be able to afford a high franchise fee (which the franchisor needs), it is necessary to operate on a high gross margin percentage. This explains the widespread application of franchising in the food and service industries.
- *In-store value added.* Franchising works best in those product categories where the product is at least partially processed in the store. Such environments require constant on-site supervision—a chronic problem for company-owned stores using a hired manager. Owners simply are willing to work harder over longer hours.
- *Secret processes.* Concepts, formulas, or products that the franchisee can't duplicate without joining the franchise program.
- *Real estate profits.* The franchisor uses income from ownership of property as a significant revenue source.
- *Simplicity.* The most successful franchises have been those that operate on automatic pilot: All the key decisions have been thought through, and the owner merely implements the decisions.

SOURCES: Partially adapted from Phillip D. White and Albert D. Bates, "Franchising Will Remain Retailing Fixture, but Its Salad Days Have Long Since Gone," *Marketing News*, February 17, 1984, p. 14; and Scott Shane and Chester Spell, "Factors for New Franchise Success," *Sloan Management Review*, Spring 1998, pp. 43–50.

perform designated marketing functions. Three major types of contractual vertical marketing systems are the retail cooperative organization, wholesaler-sponsored voluntary chain, and various franchising programs.

In a retail cooperative organization, a group of independent retailers unite and agree to pool buying and managerial resources to improve competitive position. In a wholesaler-sponsored voluntary chain, a wholesaler contracts with a number of retailers and performs channel functions for them. Usually, retailers agree to concentrate a major portion of their purchasing with the sponsoring wholesaler and to sell advertised products at the same price. The most visible type of contractual vertical marketing systems involves a variety of franchise programs. Franchises involve a parent company (the franchisor) and an independent firm (the franchisee) entering into a contractual relationship to set up and operate a business in a particular way. Many products and services reach consumers through franchise systems, including automobiles (Ford), gasoline (Mobil), hotels and motels (Holiday

Inn), restaurants (McDonald's), car rentals (Avis), and soft drinks (Pepsi). In fact, some analysts predict that within the next 10 years, franchises will account for 50 percent of all retail sales.

Corporate Systems.   Corporate vertical marketing systems involve single ownership of two or more levels of a channel. When a manufacturer purchases wholesalers or retailers, it is called *forward integration*. When wholesalers or retailers purchase channel members above them, it is called *backward integration*. Firms may choose to develop corporate vertical marketing systems in order to compete more effectively with other marketing systems, to obtain scale economies, and to increase channel cooperation and avoid channel conflict.

■ Wholesaling

As noted, wholesalers are merchants that are primarily engaged in buying, taking title to, usually storing and physically handling goods in large quantities, and re-selling the goods (usually in smaller quantities) to retailers or to industrial or business users.[4] Wholesalers are also called *distributors* in some industries, particularly when they have exclusive distribution rights, such as in the beer industry. Other wholesalers that do not take title to goods are called *agents, brokers,* or *manufacturers' representatives* in various industries. There are over 490,000 wholesalers in the United States.

Wholesalers create value for suppliers, retailers, and users of goods by performing distribution functions efficiently and effectively. They may transport and warehouse goods, exhibit them at trade shows, and offer advice to retailers concerning which lines of products are selling best in other areas. Producers use wholesalers to reach large markets and extend geographic coverage for their goods. Wholesalers may lower the costs for other channel members by efficiently carrying out such activities as physically moving goods to convenient locations, assuming the risk of managing large inventories of diverse products, and delivering products as needed to replenish retail shelves.

While producers may actively seek out wholesalers for their goods, wholesalers also try to attract producers to use their services. To do so, they may offer to perform all the distribution functions or tailor their services to include only the functions that producers do not have the ability to perform effectively. Naturally, wholesalers especially seek producers of major brands for which sales and profit potential are likely to be the greatest. Wholesalers may compete with other wholesalers to attract producers by offering lower costs for the functions they perform. Wholesalers with excellent track records that do not carry directly competing products and brands, that have appropriate locations and facilities, and that have relationships with major retail customers can more easily attract manufacturers of successful products. Also, wholesalers that serve large markets may be more attractive since producers may be able to reduce the number of wholesalers they deal with and thereby lower their costs. Long-term, profitable producer–wholesaler relationships are enhanced by trust, doing a good job for one another, and open communication about problems and opportunities.

Wholesalers also need to attract retailers and organizational customers to buy from them. In many cases, wholesalers have exclusive contracts to distribute products in a particular trading area. For popular products and brands with large market

Some Benefits of Wholesalers for Various Channel Members

Benefits for Manufacturers

- Provides the ability to reach diverse geographic markets cost-effectively.
- Provides information about retailers and end users in various markets.
- Reduces costs through greater efficiency and effectiveness in distribution functions performed.
- Reduces potential losses by assuming risks and offering expertise.

Benefits for Retailers

- Provides potentially profitable products otherwise unavailable for resale in retail area.
- Provides information about industries, manufacturers, and other retailers.
- Reduces costs by providing an assortment of goods from different manufacturers.
- Reduces costs through greater efficiency in distribution functions performed.

Benefits for End Users

- Increases the product alternatives available in local markets.
- Reduces retail prices by the efficiency and effectiveness contributed to the channel.
- Improves product selection by providing information to retailers about the best products to offer end users.

shares, the wholesaler's task is simplified because retailers want to carry them. For example, distributors of Coke and Pepsi can attract retailers easily because the products sell so well and consumers expect to find them in many retail outlets. Retail supermarkets and convenience stores would be at a competitive disadvantage without these brands.

However, for new or small market-share products and brands, particularly those of less well known manufacturers, wholesalers may have to do considerable marketing to get retailers to stock them. Wholesalers may get placement for such products and brands in retail stores because they have previously developed strong long-term working relationships with them. Alternatively, wholesalers may have to carefully explain the marketing plan for the product, why it should be successful, and why carrying the product will benefit the retailer.

While there are still many successful wholesalers, the share of products sold by them is likely to continue to decrease. This is because large retail chains like Wal-Mart have gained such market power that they can buy directly from manufacturers and bypass wholesalers altogether. The survival of wholesalers depends on their ability to meet the needs of both manufacturers and retailers by performing distribution functions more efficiently and effectively than a channel designed without them.

■ Store and Nonstore Retailing

As noted, retailers are merchants that are primarily engaged in selling to ultimate consumers. The more than 1.4 million retailers in the United States can be classified in many ways. For example, they are broken down in the Standard Industrial Classification (SIC) codes into eight general categories and a number of subcategories based on the types of merchandise they sell.[5]

Marketers have a number of decisions to make to determine the best way to retail their products. For example, decisions have to be made as to whether to use stores to sell merchandise, and if so, whether to sell through company-owned stores, franchised outlets, or through independent stores or chains. Decisions have to be made as to whether to sell through nonstore methods, such as the Internet, and if so, which methods of nonstore retailing should be used. Each of these decisions brings about a number of others such as what types of stores to use, how many of them, what locations should be selected, and what specific types of nonstore retailing to use.

Store Retailing

Over 90 percent of retail purchases are made through stores, which makes them an appropriate retail method for most types of products and services. Retailers vary not only in the types of merchandise they carry but also in the breadth and depth of their product assortments and the amount of service they provide. In general, *mass merchandisers* carry broad product assortments and compete on two bases. Supermarkets (Kroger), department stores (Marshall Fields), and catalog showrooms (Service Merchandise) compete with other retailers on the basis of offering a good selection in a number of different product categories, whereas superstores (Cub Foods), hypermarkets (Bigg's), discount stores (Wal-Mart), warehouse stores (Price Club), variety stores (Woolworth), and off-price retailers (T. J. Maxx) compete more on the basis of offering lower prices on products in their large assortments. Manufacturers of many types of consumer goods must get distribution in one or more types of mass merchandisers to be successful.

Specialty stores handle deep assortments in a limited number of product categories. Specialty stores include limited-line stores that offer a large assortment of a few related product lines (The Gap), single-line stores that emphasize a single product (Batteries Plus), and category killers (Circuit City), which are large, low-priced limited-line retail chains that attempt to dominate a particular product category. If a product type is sold primarily through specialty stores and sales are concentrated in category killer chains, manufacturers may have to sell through them to reach customers.

Convenience stores (7-Eleven) are retailers whose primary advantage to consumers is location convenience, close-in parking, and easy entry and exit. They stock products that consumers want to buy in a hurry, such as milk or soft drinks, and charge higher prices for the purchase convenience. They are an important retail outlet for many types of convenience goods.

In selecting the types of stores and specific stores and chains to resell their products, manufacturers (and wholesalers) have a variety of factors to consider. They want stores and chains that reach their target market and have good reputations with consumers. They want stores and chains that handle distribution functions efficiently and effectively, order large quantities, pay invoices quickly, display their merchandise well, and allow them to make good profits. Selling products in the right stores and chains increases sales, and selling in prestigious stores can increase the equity of a brand and the price that can be charged. The locations of retail stores, the types of people who shop at them, and the professionalism of the salespeople and clerks who work in them all affect the success of the stores and the products they sell. In addition to the merchandise offered, store advertising and price levels, the characteristics of the store itself—including layout, colors, smells, noises, lights, signs, and shelf space and displays—influence the success of both the stores and the products they offer.

Nonstore Retailing

Although stores dominate sales for most products, there are still opportunities to market products successfully in other ways. Five nonstore methods of retailing include catalogs and direct mail, vending machines, television home shopping, direct sales, and electronic exchanges.[6]

Catalogs and Direct Mail.   As shown in Figure 10–7, catalogs and direct mail dominate nonstore retailing. The advantages of this type of nonstore retailing for marketers are that consumers can be targeted effectively and reached in their homes or at work, overhead costs are decreased, and assortments of specialty merchandise can be presented with attractive pictures and in-depth descriptions of features and benefits. Catalogs can also remain in homes or offices for a lengthy time period, making available potential sales. Catalogs can offer specialty products for unique markets that are geographically dispersed in a cost-effective manner. Although consumers cannot experience products directly as they can in stores, catalog retailers with reputations for quality and generous return policies can reduce consumers' risks. For example, Levenger, which sells pens, desks, and "other tools for serious readers," sends consumers a postage-paid label to return unwanted merchandise. Many consumers enjoy the time savings of catalog shopping and are willing to pay higher prices to use it.

■ **Figure 10–7**
Annual Nonstore Retail
Sales, 1996

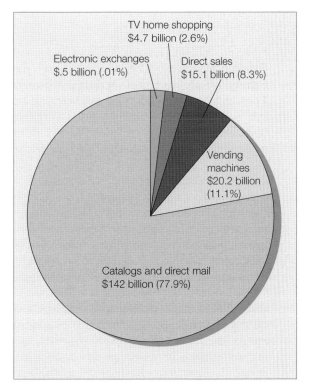

SOURCE: Michael Levy and Barton A. Weitz, *Retail Management,* 3rd ed.
(Burr Ridge, IL: Irwin/McGraw-Hill, 1998), p. 68.

Recommendations for Developing Successful Commercial Websites

Because electronic commerce is expected to grow dramatically, many companies are spending heavily to develop effective websites. One study found that 32 percent of the companies it polled were spending from $500,000 to over $5 million to create a commerce-based website. Like most marketing strategies, designing successful websites requires careful analysis of consumers. Below are five recommendations for designing websites that consumers will be able to use efficiently and effectively.

1. Make sure the site has contact information that is accurate and complete. Many websites lack basics such as postal address, phone and fax numbers, and e-mail addresses. Don't hide this stuff five levels deep in a back corner; make it easy to find.

2. Don't make factual information, such as product updates and prices, hard to come by. Someone other than the Webmaster should be responsible for tracking this information and keeping it up to date.

3. Make sure users can find the site with straightforward key words. Make it simple to find the site via the various search engines. Work on improving the search function on the site itself.

4. Make it just as easy for consumers to exit the site as it is for them to find and use it. The layout and design of the site should be fairly obvious to viewers no matter where they land inside.

5. Create a good table of contents and index. Most consumers do not want to start at the front door and proceed in an orderly fashion through the entire site. Keep the number of screens and subscreens for contents and site organization down to a bare minimum. Put links both to the table of contents and to an index on the front page so that consumers can find them quickly.

To find more information about site usability, see the Alertbox written by Jakob Nielsen of SunSoft (www.useit.com/alertbox/) or read *Understanding Electronic Commerce* by David Kosiur available through www.amazon.com.

SOURCES: Adapted from Mark Halper, "So Does Your Website Pay?" *Forbes ASAP*, August 25, 1997, pp. 117–18, and David Strom, "Five Steps for Site Success," *Forbes ASAP*, August 25, 1997, p. 118.

Vending Machines.   Vending machines are a relatively limited method of retail merchandising, and most vending machine sales are for beverages, food, and candy. They have the advantage for marketers of being available for sales 24 hours a day, can be placed in a variety of high-traffic locations, and can charge higher prices. While uses of vending machines for such things as airline insurance and concert and game tickets are not unusual, this method has limited potential for most products.

Television Home Shopping.   Television home shopping includes cable channels dedicated to shopping, infomercials, and direct-response advertising shown on cable and broadcast networks. Home Shopping Network and QVC are the leaders in this market, and the major products sold are inexpensive jewelry, apparel, cosmetics, and exercise equipment. While this method allows better visual display than catalogs, potential customers must be watching at the time the merchandise is offered; if not, they have no way of knowing about the product or purchasing it.

Direct Sales.   Direct sales are made by salespeople to consumers in their homes or offices or by telephone. The most common products purchased this way are cosmetics, fragrances, decorative accessories, vacuum cleaners, home appliances, cooking utensils, kitchenware, jewelry, food and nutritional products, and educational materials. Avon, Mary Kay, and Tupperware are probably the best-known retail users of this channel. Salespeople can demonstrate products effectively and provide detailed feature and benefit information. A limitation of this method is that consumers are often too busy to spend their time this way and do not want to pay the higher prices needed to cover the high costs of this method of retailing.

Electronic Exchanges. Electronic exchanges involve consumers collecting information, shopping, and purchasing from websites on the Internet. It is the fastest growing nonstore method of retailing, although still a small share of retail sales. Most companies have websites in case electronic exchanges become more common as they are predicted to do. This method of retailing has a number of advantages for marketers. It eliminates the need for expensive stores, paper catalogs, or salespeople and is available 24 hours a day. It can provide good visual presentation and extended description of features and benefits. It allows a company to offer a vast product assortment to a geographically dispersed market. However, it is limited to computer literate consumers who are willing to purchase this way and possibly pay higher prices; in addition, for some consumers, Internet purchases carry the perceived risk of buying from a fraudulent company or having a hacker get their credit card number. An important limitation is that consumers have to come to the website, whereas catalogs can be sent to them as can advertisements for stores.

■ Conclusion

This chapter introduced the distribution of goods and services in a complex, highly competitive, highly specialized economy. It emphasized the vital need for marketing intermediaries to bring about exchanges between buyers and sellers in a reasonably efficient manner. The chapter examined various types of intermediaries and the distribution functions they perform as well as topics in the selection and management of distribution channels. Finally, both wholesaling and store and nonstore retailing were discussed.

■ Additional Readings

Agrawal, Deepak, and Rajiv Lal. "Contractual Arrangements in Franchising: An Empirical Investigation." *Journal of Marketing Research,* May 1995, pp. 213–21.

Berman, Barry. *Marketing Channels.* New York: Wiley, 1996.

Bowersox, Donald J., and M. Bixby Cooper. *Strategic Marketing Channel Management.* New York: McGraw-Hill, 1992.

Lambert, Douglas M.; James R. Stock; and Lisa M. Ellram. *Fundamentals of Logistics Management.* Burr Ridge, IL: Irwin/McGraw-Hill, 1998.

Levy, Michael, and Burton A. Weitz. *Retailing Management.* 3d ed. Burr Ridge, IL: Irwin/McGraw-Hill, 1998.

Pelton, Lou E.; David Strutton; and James R. Lumpkin. *Marketing Channels: A Relationship Management Approach.* Burr Ridge, IL: Irwin, 1997.

Rosenbloom, Bert. *Marketing Channels: A Management View.* 6th ed. Fort Worth: Dryden Press, 1999.

Stern, Louis W.; Adel I. El-Ansary; and Anne T. Coughlin. *Marketing Channels.* 5th ed. Englewood Cliffs, NJ: Prentice Hall, 1996.

Chapter Eleven

Pricing Strategy

One of the most important and complex decisions a firm has to make relates to pricing its products or services. If consumers or organizational buyers perceive a price to be too high, they may purchase competitive brands or substitute products, leading to a loss of sales and profits for the firm. If the price is too low, sales might increase, but profitability may suffer. Thus, pricing decisions must be given careful consideration when a firm is introducing a new product or planning a short- or long-term price change.

This chapter discusses demand, supply, and environmental influences that affect pricing decisions and emphasizes that all three must be considered for effective pricing. However, as will be discussed in the chapter, many firms price their products without explicitly considering all of these influences.

Demand Influences on Pricing Decisions

Demand influences on pricing decisions concern primarily the nature of the target market and expected reactions of consumers to a given price or change in price. There are three primary considerations here: demographic factors, psychological factors, and price elasticity.

Demographic Factors

In the initial selection of the target market that a firm intends to serve, a number of demographic factors are usually considered. Demographic factors that are particularly important for pricing decisions include the following:

1. Number of potential buyers, and their age, education, and gender.
2. Location of potential buyers.

3. Position of potential buyers (resellers or final consumers).
4. Expected consumption rates of potential buyers.
5. Economic strength of potential buyers.

These factors help determine market potential and are useful for estimating expected sales at various price levels.

Psychological Factors

Psychological factors related to pricing concern primarily how consumers will perceive various prices or price changes. For example, marketing managers should be concerned with such questions as

1. Will potential buyers use price as an indicator of product quality?
2. Will potential buyers be favorably attracted by odd pricing?
3. Will potential buyers perceive the price as too high relative to the service the product gives them?
4. Are potential buyers prestige oriented and therefore willing to pay higher prices to fulfill this need?
5. How much will potential buyers be willing to pay for the product?

While psychological factors have a significant effect on the success of a pricing strategy and ultimately on marketing strategy, answers to the above questions may require considerable marketing research. In fact, a review of buyers' subjective perceptions of price concluded that very little is known about how price affects buyers' perceptions of alternative purchase offers and how these perceptions affect purchase response.[1] However, some tentative generalizations about how buyers perceive price have been formulated. For example, research has found that persons who choose high-priced items usually perceive large quality variations within product categories and see the consequences of a poor choice as being undesirable. They believe that quality is related to price and see themselves as good judges of product quality. In general, the reverse is true for persons who select low-priced items in the same product categories. Thus, although information on psychological factors involved in purchasing may be difficult to obtain, marketing managers must at least consider the effects of such factors on their desired target market and marketing strategy.[2]

There are three types of psychological pricing strategies. First there is *prestige pricing*, in which a high price is charged to create a signal that the product is exceptionally fine. Prestige pricing is commonly used for some brands of cars, clothing, perfume, jewelry, cosmetics, wine and liquor, and crystal and china. Second, there is *odd pricing*, or odd-even pricing, in which prices are set a few dollars or a few cents below a round number. For example, Frito-Lay's potato chips are priced at 69 cents a bag rather than 70 cents to encourage consumers to think of them as less expensive (60 some-odd cents) rather than 70 cents. Hertz economy cars are rented for $129 rather than $130 to appear less expensive. Third, there is *bundle pricing*, in which several products are sold together at a single price to suggest a good value. For example, travel agencies offer vacation packages that include travel, accommodations, and entertainment at a single price to connote value and convenience for customers.

Price Elasticity

Both demographic and psychological factors affect price elasticity. Price elasticity is a measure of consumers' price sensitivity, which is estimated by dividing relative changes in the quantity sold by the relative changes in price:

$$e = \frac{\text{percent change in quantity demanded}}{\text{percent change in price}}$$

Although difficult to measure, there are two basic methods commonly used to estimate price elasticity. First, price elasticity can be estimated from historical data or from price/quantity data across different sales districts. Second, price elasticity can be estimated by sampling a group of consumers from the target market and polling them concerning various price/quantity relationships. Both of these approaches provide estimates of price elasticity; but the former approach is limited to the consideration of price changes, whereas the latter is often expensive and there is some question as to the validity of subjects' responses. However, even a crude estimate of price elasticity is a useful input to pricing decisions.[3]

■ Supply Influences on Pricing Decisions

For the purpose of this text, supply influences on pricing decisions can be discussed in terms of three basic factors. These factors relate to the objectives, costs, and nature of the product.

Pricing Objectives

Pricing objectives should be derived from overall marketing objectives, which in turn should be derived from corporate objectives. Since it is traditionally assumed that business firms operate to maximize profits in the long run, it is often thought that the basic pricing objective is solely concerned with long-run profits. However, the profit maximization norm does not provide the operating marketing manager with a single, unequivocal guideline for selecting prices. In addition, the marketing manager does not have perfect cost, revenue, and market information to be able to evaluate whether or not this objective is being reached. In practice, then, many other objectives are employed as guidelines for pricing decisions. In some cases, these objectives may be considered as operational approaches to achieve long-run profit maximization.

Marketing
Highlight 11–2

Retail Pricing Strategies: EDLP or High/Low?

There are two common pricing strategies at the retail level: EDLP, which stands for "everyday low pricing," and high/low, which means that the retailer charges prices that are sometimes above competitors but promotes frequent sales that lowers prices below them. Four of the most successful U.S. retailers—Home Depot, Wal-Mart, Office Depot, and Toys 'R' Us—have adopted EDLP, while many fashion, grocery, and drugstores use high/low. Below is a list of the advantages of each of these pricing strategies.

Advantages of EDLP

1. *Reduces price wars*—If consumers believe that the store's prices are low, the retailer can avoid getting into price wars with competitors.
2. *Reduces advertising*—Since prices are relatively stable using EDLP, weekly advertisements promoting sales are unnecessary.
3. *Improves customer service*—Since customer flow is more steady without sales-stimulating throngs of shoppers, in-store salespeople and clerks can spend more time with each customer.
4. *Reduces stockouts and improves inventory management*—Since large variations in demand created by sales are eliminated, necessary inventory can be kept on the shelf to avoid stockouts; inventory ordering, delivery, and handling are more efficient.

5. *Increases overall profit margins*—Even though prices are generally lower using EDLP, overall profit margins can increase since merchandise is no longer sold at large price reductions and some costs are reduced.

Advantages of High/Low

1. *Helps segment the market*—Since different groups of customers are willing to pay different prices for products, high/low allows stores to receive higher prices from the first people to buy and still serve hard-core bargain hunters at the end of the fashion cycle.
2. *Creates excitement*—Sales can draw crowds and create an exciting buying experience for shoppers. This exciting experience may bring shoppers back for other sales.
3. *Moves merchandise*—Frequent sales enable retailers to move merchandise, even though profits are lower on sale merchandise.
4. *Emphasizes product quality and store service*—The high initial price sends a signal to customers that a product is high quality or the store provides excellent service, or both.
5. *Is easier to use*—Most retailers have a difficult time using EDLP since they must convince customers that the store's prices are relatively low on most products. High/low, on the other hand, offers customers a means of assessing how low prices are since the original and sale price are readily available and can be compared.

SOURCE: Based on Michael Levy and Barton A. Weitz, *Retailing Management,* 3rd ed. (Burr Ridge, IL: Irwin/McGraw-Hill, 1998), pp. 441–43.

Research has found that the most common pricing objectives are (1) pricing to achieve a target return on investment, (2) stabilization of price and margin, (3) pricing to achieve a target market share, and (4) pricing to meet or prevent competition.

Cost Considerations in Pricing

The price of a product usually must cover costs of production, promotion, and distribution, plus a profit for the offering to be of value to the firm. In addition, when products are priced on the basis of costs plus a fair profit, there is an implicit assumption that this sum represents the economic value of the product in the marketplace.

Cost-oriented pricing is the most common approach in practice, and there are at least three basic variations: markup pricing, cost-plus pricing, and rate-of-return

Basic Break-Even Formulas

The following formulas are used to calculate break-even points in units and in dollars:

$$BEP_{(in\ units)} = \frac{FC}{(SP-VC)}$$

$$BEP_{(in\ dollars)} = \frac{FC}{1-(VC/SP)}$$

where

$$
\begin{aligned}
FC &= \text{fixed cost} \\
VC &= \text{variable cost} \\
SP &= \text{selling price}
\end{aligned}
$$

If, as is generally the case, a firm wants to know how many units or sales dollars are necessary to generate a given amount of profit, profit (P) is simply added to fixed costs in the formulas. In addition, if the firm has estimates of expected sales and fixed and variable costs, the selling price can be solved for. (A more detailed discussion of break-even analysis is provided in the financial analysis section of this book.)

pricing. *Markup pricing* is commonly used in retailing, where a percentage is added to the retailer's invoice price to determine the final selling price. Closely related to markup pricing is *cost-plus pricing,* where the costs of producing a product or completing a project are totaled and a profit amount or percentage is added on. Cost-plus pricing is most often used to describe the pricing of jobs that are non-routine and difficult to "cost" in advance, such as construction and military weapon development.

Rate-of-return or *target pricing* is commonly used by manufacturers. In this method, price is determined by adding a desired rate of return on investment to total costs. Generally, a break-even analysis is performed for expected production and sales levels and a rate of return is added on. For example, suppose a firm estimated production and sales to be 75,000 units at a total cost of $300,000. If the firm desired a before-tax return of 20 percent, the selling price would be (300,000 + 0.20 × 300,000) ÷ 75,000 = $4.80.

Cost-oriented approaches to pricing have the advantage of simplicity, and many practitioners believe that they generally yield a good price decision. However, such approaches have been criticized for two basic reasons. First, cost approaches give little or no consideration to demand factors. For example, the price determined by markup or cost-plus methods has no necessary relationship to what people will be willing to pay for the product. In the case of rate-of-return pricing, little emphasis is placed on estimating sales volume. Even if it were, rate-of-return pricing involves circular reasoning, since unit cost depends on sales volume but sales volume depends on selling price. Second, cost approaches fail to reflect competition adequately. Only in industries where all firms use this approach and have similar costs and markups can this approach yield similar prices and minimize price competition. Thus, in many industries, cost-oriented pricing could lead to severe price competition, which could eliminate smaller firms. Therefore, although costs are a highly important consideration in price decisions, numerous other factors need to be examined.

Product Considerations in Pricing

Although numerous product characteristics can affect pricing, three of the most important are (1) perishability, (2) distinctiveness, and (3) stage in the product life cycle.

Perishability.   Goods that are very perishable in a physical sense must be priced to promote sales without costly delays. Foodstuffs and certain types of raw materials tend to be in this category. Products can be considered perishable in two other senses. High fashion, fad, and seasonal products are perishable not in the sense that the product deteriorates but that demand for the product is confined to a specific time period. Perishability also relates to consumption rate, which means that some products are consumed very slowly, as in the case of consumer durables. Two important pricing considerations here are that (1) such goods tend to be expensive because large amounts of service are purchased at one time; and (2) the customer has a certain amount of discretionary time available in making replacement purchase decisions.

Distinctiveness.   Products can be classified in terms of how distinctive they are. Homogeneous goods are perfect substitutes for each other, as in the case of bulk wheat or whole milk, while most manufactured goods can be differentiated on the basis of certain features, such as package, trademark, engineering design, and chemical features. Thus, few consumer goods are perfectly homogeneous, and one of the primary marketing objectives of most firms is to make their products and brands distinctive in the minds of buyers. Large sums of money are often invested to accomplish this task, and one of the payoffs for such investments is the seller's ability to charge higher prices for distinctive products.

Life Cycle.   The stage of the life cycle that a product is in can have important pricing implications. With regard to the life cycle, two approaches to pricing are skimming and penetration price policies. A *skimming* policy is one in which the seller charges a relatively high price on a new product. Generally, this policy is used when the firm has a temporary monopoly and when demand for the product is price inelastic. In later stages of the life cycle, as competition moves in and other market factors change, the price may then be lowered. Digital watches and calculators are examples of this. A *penetration* policy is one in which the seller charges a relatively low price on a new product. Generally, this policy is used when the firm expects competition to move in rapidly and when demand for the product is, at least in the short run, price elastic. This policy is also used to obtain large economies of scale and as a major instrument for rapid creation of a mass market. A low price and profit margin may also discourage competition. In later stages of the life cycle, the price may have to be altered to meet changes in the market.

■ Environmental Influences on Pricing Decisions

Environmental influences on pricing include variables that are uncontrollable by the marketing manager. Two of the most important of these are competition and government regulation.

Competition

In setting or changing prices, the firm must consider its competition and how competition will react to the price of the product. Initially, consideration must be given to such factors as:

1. Number of competitors.

2. Size of competitors.
3. Location of competitors.
4. Conditions of entry into the industry.
5. Degree of vertical integration of competitors.
6. Number of products sold by competitors.
7. Cost structure of competitors.
8. Historical reaction of competitors to price changes.

These factors help determine whether the firm's selling price should be at, below, or above competition. Pricing a product at competition (i.e., the average price charged by the industry) is called *going-rate pricing* and is popular for homogeneous products, since this approach represents the collective wisdom of the industry and is not disruptive of industry harmony. An example of pricing below competition can be found in *sealed-bid pricing*, where the firm is bidding directly against competition for project contracts. Although cost and profits are initially calculated, the firm attempts to bid below competitors to obtain the job contract. A firm may price above competition because it has a superior product or because the firm is the price leader in the industry.

Government Regulations

Prices of certain goods and services are regulated by state and federal governments. Public utilities are examples of state regulation of prices. However, for most marketing managers, federal laws that make certain pricing practices illegal are of primary consideration in pricing decisions. The list below is a summary of some of the more important legal constraints on pricing. Of course, since most marketing managers are not trained as lawyers, they usually seek legal counsel when developing pricing strategies to ensure conformity to state and federal legislation.

1. Price fixing is illegal per se. Sellers must not make any agreements with competitors or distributors concerning the final price of the goods. The Sherman Antitrust Act is the primary device used to outlaw horizontal price fixing. Section 5 of the Federal Trade Commission Act has been used to outlaw price fixing as an unfair business practice.
2. Deceptive pricing practices are outlawed under Section 5 of the Federal Trade Commission Act. An example of deceptive pricing would be to mark merchandise with an exceptionally high price and then claim that the lower selling price actually used represents a legitimate price reduction.
3. Price discrimination that lessens competition or is deemed injurious to it is outlawed by the Robinson-Patman Act (which amends Section 2 of the Clayton Act). Price discrimination is not illegal per se, but sellers cannot charge competing buyers different prices for essentially the same products if the effect of such sales is injurious to competition. Price differentials can be legally justified on certain grounds, especially if the price differences reflect cost differences. This is particularly true of quantity discounts.
4. Promotional pricing, such as cooperative advertising, and price deals are not illegal per se; but if a seller grants advertising allowances, merchandising service, free goods, or special promotional discounts to customers, it must do so on proportionately equal terms. Sections 2(d) and 2(e) of the Robinson-Patman Act are designed to regulate such practices so that price reductions cannot be granted to some customers under the guise of promotional allowances.[4]

■ A General Pricing Model

It should be clear that effective pricing decisions involve considerations of many factors, and different industries may have different pricing practices. Although no single model will fit all pricing decisions, Figure 11–1 presents a general model for developing prices for products and services.[5] While all pricing decisions cannot be made strictly on the basis of this model, it does break pricing strategy into a set of manageable stages that are integrated into the overall marketing strategy.

■ **Figure 11–1**
A General Pricing Model

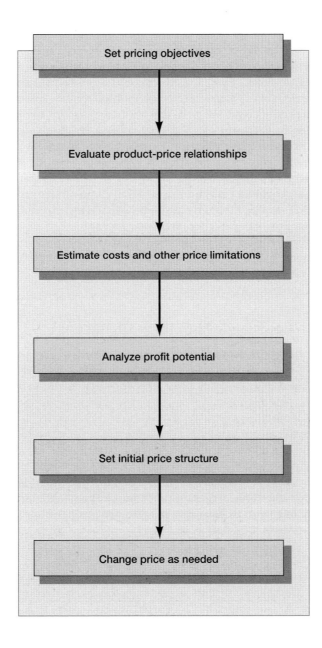

Set pricing objectives

Evaluate product-price relationships

Estimate costs and other price limitations

Analyze profit potential

Set initial price structure

Change price as needed

Set Pricing Objectives

Given a product or service designed for a specific target market, the pricing process begins with a clear statement of the pricing objectives. These objectives guide the pricing strategy and should be designed to support the overall marketing strategy. Because pricing strategy has a direct bearing on demand for a product and the profit obtained, efforts to set prices must be coordinated with other functional areas. For example, production will have to be able to meet demand at a given price, and finance will have to manage funds flowing in and out of the organization at predicted levels of production.

Evaluate Product-Price Relationships

As noted, the distinctiveness, perishability, and stage of the life cycle a product is in, all affect pricing. In addition, marketers need to consider what value the product has for customers and how price will influence product positioning. There are three basic value positions. First, a product could be priced relatively high for a product class because it offers value in the form of high quality, special features, or prestige. Second, a product could be priced at about average for the product class because it offers value in the form of good quality for a reasonable price. Third, a product could be priced relatively low for a product class because it offers value in the form of acceptable quality at a low price. A Porsche or Nike Air Jordans are examples of the first type of value; a Honda Accord or Keds tennis shoes are examples of the second; and Hyundai cars and private label canvas shoes are examples of the third. Setting prices so that targeted customers will perceive products to offer greater value than competitive offerings is called *value pricing*.

In addition, research is needed to estimate how much of a particular product the target market will purchase at various price levels—price elasticity. This estimate provides valuable information about what the target market thinks about the product and what it is worth to them.

Estimate Costs and Other Price Limitations

The costs to produce and market products provide a lower bound for pricing decisions and a baseline from which to compute profit potential. If a product cannot be produced and marketed at a price to cover its costs and provide reasonable profits in the long run, then it should not be produced in its designed form. One possibility is to redesign the product so that its costs are lower. In fact, some companies first determine the price customers are willing to pay for a product and then design it so that it can be produced and marketed at a cost that allows targeted profits.

Other price limitations that need to be considered are government regulations and the prices that are charged by competitors for similar and substitute products. Also, likely competitive reactions that could influence the price of a new product or a price change in an existing one need to be considered.

Analyze Profit Potential

Analysis in the preceding stages should result in a range of prices that could be charged. Marketers must then estimate the likely profit in pricing at levels in this range. At this stage, it is important to recognize that it may be necessary to

Marketing
Highlight 11–4

Some Short-Term Price Reduction Tactics

1. *Cents-off deals:* "Package price is 20¢ off."
2. *Special offers:* "Buy one, get one free"; "Buy three tires and get the fourth free."
3. *Coupons:* Store or manufacturer coupons in newspaper, magazines, flyers, and packages.

4. *Rebates:* Mail-in proof-of-purchase seals for cash or merchandise.
5. *Increase quantity for same price:* "2 extra ounces of coffee free."
6. *Free installation or service for a limited time period.*
7. *Reduce or eliminate interest charges for a limited time:* "90 days same as cash."
8. *Special sales:* "25 percent off all merchandise marked with a red tag."

offer channel members quantity discounts, promotional allowances, and slotting allowances to encourage them to actively market the product. *Quantity discounts* are discounts for purchasing a large number of units. *Promotional allowances* are often in the form of price reductions in exchange for the channel member performing various promotional activities, such as featuring the product in store advertising or on in-store displays. *Slotting allowances* are payments to retailers to get them to stock items on their shelves. All of these can increase sales but also add marketing cost to the manufacturer and affect profits.

Set Initial Price Structure

Since all of the supply, demand, and environmental factors have been considered, a marketer can now set the initial price structure. The price structure takes into account the price to various channel members, such as wholesalers and retailers, as well as the recommended price to final consumers or organizational buyers.

Change Price as Needed

There are many reasons why an initial price structure may need to be changed. Channel members may bargain for greater margins, competitors may lower their prices, or costs may increase with inflation. In the short term, discounts and allowances may have to be larger or more frequent than planned to get greater marketing effort to increase demand to profitable levels. In the long term, price structures tend to increase for most products as production and marketing costs increase.

■ Conclusion

Pricing decisions that integrate the firm's costs with marketing strategy, business conditions, competition, demand, product variables, channels of distribution, and general resources can determine the success or failure of a business. This places a very heavy burden on the price maker. Modern-day marketing managers cannot ignore the complexity or the importance of price management. Pricing strategies must be continually reviewed and must take into account that the firm is a dynamic entity operating in a very competitive environment. There are many ways for money to flow out of a firm in the form of costs, but often there is only one way to bring in revenues and that is by the price-product mechanism.

■ Additional Readings

Dolan, Robert J., and Hermann Simon. *Power Pricing.* New York: Free Press, 1996.

Kalwani, Manohar U., and Chi Kin Yim. "Consumer Price and Promotion Expectations: An Experimental Study." *Journal of Marketing Research,* February 1992, pp. 90–100.

Lichtenstein, Donald R.; Nancy M. Ridgway; and Richard G. Netemeyer. "Price Perceptions and Consumer Shopping Behavior: A Field Study." *Journal of Marketing Research,* May 1993, pp. 234–45.

Mafzumdar, Tridib, and Sung Youl Jun. "Consumer Evaluations of Multiple versus Single Price Change." *Journal of Consumer Research,* December 1993, pp. 441–50.

Mayhew, Glenn E., and Russell S. Winer. "An Empirical Analysis of Internal and External Reference Prices Using Scanner Data." *Journal of Consumer Research,* June 1992, pp. 62–70.

Monroe, Kent B. *Pricing: Making Profitable Decisions,* 2nd ed. New York: McGraw-Hill, 1990.

Nagle, Thomas T., and Reed K. Holden. *The Strategy and Tactics of Pricing,* 2nd ed. Englewood Cliffs, NJ: Prentice Hall, 1995.

Rajengran, K. N., and Gerard J. Tellis. "Contextual and Temporal Components of Reference Price." *Journal of Marketing,* January 1994, pp. 22–34.

Rao, Askay R., and Mark E. Bergen. "Price Premium Variations as a Consequence of Buyers' Lack of Information." *Journal of Consumer Research,* December 1992, pp. 412–23.

Simon, Hermann, and Robert J. Dolan. "Price Customization." *Marketing Management,* Fall 1998, pp. 11–17.

Part D

Marketing in Special Fields

Chapter Twelve

The Marketing of Services

Over the course of the past 15 years, the fastest growing segment of the American economy has not been the production of tangibles but the performance of services. Spending on services has increased to such an extent that today it captures more than 50 cents of the consumer's dollar. Meanwhile, the service sector has also grown steadily in its contribution to the U.S. gross domestic product and now generates 74 percent of the gross domestic product and accounts for 79 percent of all jobs.[1] In addition, the service sector in the United States produces a balance-of-trade surplus of approximately $58 billion annually (versus a deficit of $132 billion for goods) and is expected to be responsible for all net job growth through the year 2005. And the dominance of the service sector is not limited to the United States. The service sector accounts for more than half the GNP and employs more than half the labor force in most Latin American and Caribbean countries. Over the course of the next decade, the service sector will spawn whole new legions of doctors, nurses, medical technologists, physical therapists, home health aids, and social workers to administer to the needs of an aging population, along with armies of food servers, childcare providers, and cleaning people to cater to the wants of two-income families. Also rising to the forefront will be a swelling class of technical workers, including computer engineers, systems analysts, and paralegals.

Many marketing textbooks still devote little attention to program development for the marketing of services, especially those in the rapidly changing areas of health care, banking, and travel. This omission is usually based on the assumption that the marketing of products and services is basically the same, and, therefore, the techniques discussed under products apply as well to the marketing of services. Basically, this assumption is true. Whether selling goods or services, the marketer must be concerned with developing a marketing strategy centered on the four controllable decision variables that comprise the marketing mix: the product (or service), the price, the distribution system, and promotion. In addition, the use of marketing research is as valuable to service marketers as it is to product marketers.

However, because services possess certain distinguishing characteristics, the task of determining the marketing mix ingredients for a service marketing strategy may raise different and more difficult problems than those encountered in marketing products. For example, many consumers believe that all services associated with their credit card are provided by just one company: the bank that they send their payment to. In reality, there are numerous unseen companies, such as First Data Corp. (the largest credit transaction processor), that form the nucleus of the credit card transaction process.

The purpose of this chapter is fourfold. First, the reader will become acquainted with the special characteristics of services and their strategy implications. Second, key concepts associated with providing quality services will be discussed. Third, obstacles will be described that, in the past, impeded and still continue to impede development of services marketing. Finally, current trends and strategies of innovation in services marketing will be explored. Using this approach, the material in the other chapters of the book can be integrated to give a better understanding of the marketing of services.

Before proceeding, some attention must be given to what we refer to when using the term *services*. Probably the most frustrating aspect of the available literature on services is that the definition of what constitutes a service remains unclear. The fact is that no common definition and boundaries have been developed to delimit the field of services. The American Marketing Association has defined services as follows:

1. *Service products,* such as a bank loan or home security, that are intangible, or at least substantially so. If totally intangible, they are exchanged directly from producer to user, cannot be transported or stored, and are almost instantly perishable. Service products are often difficult to identify, since they come into existence at the same time they are bought and consumed. They are comprised of intangible elements that are inseparable; they usually involve customer participation in some important way, cannot be sold in the sense of ownership transfer, and have no title. Today, however, most products are partly tangible and partly intangible, and the dominant form is used to classify them as either goods or services (all are products). These common, hybrid forms, whatever they are called, may or may not have the attributes just given for totally intangible services.
2. *Services,* as a term, is also used to describe activities performed by sellers and others that accompany the sale of a product, and aid in its exchange or its utilization (e.g., shoe fitting, financing, an 800 number). Such services are either presale or postsale and supplement the product but do not comprise it. If performed during sale, they are considered to be intangible parts of the product.[2]

The first definition includes what can be considered almost pure services such as insurance, banking, entertainment, airlines, health care, telecommunications, and hotels; the second definition includes such services as wrapping, financing an automobile, and providing warranties on computer equipment and the like because these services exist in connection with the sale of a product or another service. This suggests that marketers of goods are also marketers of services. For example, one could argue that McDonald's is not in the hamburger business. Its hamburgers are actually not very different from those of the competition. McDonald's is in the service business: "You deserve a break today, . . . we do it all for you."[3] In fact, a recent study found that the quality of a company's service can cause it to gain or lose as much as 10 percent in sales revenue.[4] Services that accompany products can affect sales in two ways: (1) directly, by enhancing the reliability of product availability, and (2) indirectly, by increasing a buyer's preference for and loyalty to a supplier that provides reliable service with fewer problems.[5] Honda and Merck are prime examples of companies that build their strategies not around products but around deep knowledge of highly developed core service strategies, such as (1) stressing senior management involvement with customers, (2) going all out to resolve customer complaints, and (3) placing an emphasis on retaining current customers.[6]

More and more manufacturers are also exploiting their service capabilities as stand-alone revenue producers. For example, General Motors, Ford, and Chrysler all offer financing services. Ford and General Motors have extended their financial services offerings to include a MasterCard, which offers discounts on purchases of their automobiles. Likewise, Sears introduced the Discover Card, which was positioned as a direct competitor to Visa and MasterCard.

The reader can imagine from his or her own experience that some purchases are very tangible (a coffee maker) while others are very much intangible (a course in marketing). Others have elements of both (lunch on a flight from New York to Chicago). In other words, in reality there is a goods-service continuum, with many purchases including both tangible goods and intangible services. Figure 12–1 illustrates such a continuum. On the goods side of the continuum, the buyer owns an object after the purchase. On the services side of the continuum, when the transaction is over, the buyer leaves with an experience and a feeling. When the course in marketing is over or the flight from New York to Chicago is completed, the student or passenger leaves with a feeling.

The examples of services on the right side of Figure 12–1 are mostly or entirely intangible. They do not exist in the physical realm. They cannot appeal to the five senses.

■ Important Characteristics of Services

Services possess several unique characteristics that often have a significant impact on marketing program development. These special features of services may cause unique problems and often result in marketing mix decisions that are substantially different from those found in connection with the marketing of goods. Some of the more important of these characteristics are intangibility, inseparability, perishability and fluctuating demand, highly differentiated marketing systems, and a client relationship.

■ **Figure 12–1**
The Goods-Service Continuum

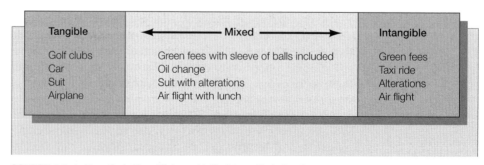

Tangible	◀——————— Mixed ———————▶	Intangible
Golf clubs	Green fees with sleeve of balls included	Green fees
Car	Oil change	Taxi ride
Suit	Suit with alterations	Alterations
Airplane	Air flight with lunch	Air flight

SOURCE: Adapted from G. A. Churchill, Jr., and J. Paul Peter, *Marketing: Creating Value for Customers* (Burr Ridge, IL: Irwin/McGraw-Hill, 1998), p. 290.

Intangibility

The obvious basic difference between goods and services is the intangibility of services, and many of the problems encountered in the marketing of services are due to intangibility. To illustrate, how does an airline make tangible a trip from Philadelphia to San Francisco? These problems are unique to service marketing.

The fact that many services cannot appeal to a buyer's sense of touch, taste, smell, sight, or hearing before purchase places a burden on the marketing organization. For example, hotels that promise a good night's sleep to their customers cannot actually show this service in a tangible way. Obviously, this burden is most heavily felt in a firm's promotional program, but as will be discussed later, it may affect other areas. Depending on the type of service, the intangibility factor may dictate use of direct channels because of the need for personal contact between the buyer and seller. Since a service firm is actually selling an idea or experience, not a product, it must tell the buyer what the service will do because it is often difficult to illustrate, demonstrate, or display the service in use. For example, the hotel must somehow describe to the consumer how a stay at the hotel will leave the customer feeling well rested and ready to begin a new day.

The above discussion alludes to two strategy elements firms should employ when trying to overcome the problems associated with service intangibility. First, tangible aspects associated with the service should be stressed. For example, advertisements for airlines should emphasize (through text and visuals) the newness of the aircraft, the roominess of the cabin, and the friendliness of the flight attendants. Second, end benefits resulting from completion of the service encounter should be accentuated. In the case of air travel, an individual's ability to make an important meeting or arrive home in time for a special occasion could be the derived benefit.

Inseparability

In many cases, a service cannot be separated from the person of the seller. In other words, the service must often be produced and marketed simultaneously. Because of the simultaneous production and marketing of most services, the main concern of the marketer is usually the creation of time and place utility. For example, the bank teller produces the service of receiving a deposit and markets other appropriate bank services at the same time. Many services, therefore, are tailored and not mass-produced. Often, because a company's employees are "the company" at the point of contact, they must be given wide latitude and assistance in determining how best to tailor a specific service to meet customer needs.[7]

The implication of inseparability on issues dealing with the selection of channels of distribution and service quality is quite important. Inseparable services cannot be inventoried, and thus direct sale is the only feasible channel of distribution. Service quality is sometimes unable to be completely standardized because of the inability to completely mechanize the service encounter. However, some industries, through innovative uses of technology, have been able to overcome or, at least, alleviate challenges associated with the inseparability characteristic.

For example, in the financial services industry, automated teller machines (ATMs) and home banking, through use of computers and telephones, have contributed greatly to eliminating the need for the customer to directly interact with a bank teller. Further, many banks are developing computer applications to allow tellers and other service representatives to think like expert problem solvers. These

Marketing
Highlight 12–1

Ten of the Most Critical Differences between Products and Services

Products

1. The customer owns an object.
2. The goal of producing a product is uniformity—all widgets are alike.
3. A product can be put into inventory; a sample can be sent in advance for the customer to review.
4. The customer is an end user who is not involved in the production process.
5. One conducts quality control by comparing output to specifications.
6. If improperly produced, the product can be pulled off the line or recalled.
7. The morale of production employees is important.
8. Customer can determine level of quality by comparing product to other products.
9. Low level of collaboration between the buyer and the seller.
10. Greater number and variety of product brands available to customers.

Services

1. The customer owns a memory. The experience cannot be sold or passed on to a third party.
2. The goal of service is uniqueness; each customer and each contact is special.
3. A service happens at the moment. It cannot be stockpiled or saved to be used at a later date.
4. The customer is a coproducer who is a partner in creating the service.
5. Customers conduct quality control by comparing expectations to experience.
6. If improperly performed, apologies and reparations are the only means of recourse.
7. The morale of service employees is critical.
8. Customer can determine level of quality throughout the delivery of the service.
9. High level of collaboration between the buyer and the seller.
10. Fewer brands of services available to customer.

SOURCES: Ron Zemke, "The Emerging Art of Service Management," *Training*, January 1992, pp. 36–42; and Ralph W. Jackson, Lester A. Neidell, and Dale A. Lunsford, "An Empirical Investigation of the Differences in Goods and Services as Perceived by Organizational Buyers," *Industrial Marketing Management* 24 (1995), pp. 99–108.

applications allow for platform banking, a means of enabling bank representatives in any location to bring up on a screen all the information the bank has about the customer. Every face-to-face contact with a customer can mean an opportunity to make a sale and, more important, further the relationship with the customer. Of course, the bank representative is still of critical importance as the one who might recognize by the customer's expression or words that this visit is not the appropriate time to be marketing additional services.

In addition to technology, tangible representations of the service can serve to overcome the inseparability problem. For example, in the insurance industry, a contract serves as the tangible representation of the service. The service itself remains inseparable from the seller (insurance provider), but the buyer has a tangible representation of the service in the form of a policy. This enables the use of intermediaries (agents) in the marketing of insurance. Another example would be in the use of a credit card—the card itself is a tangible representation of the service that is being produced and consumed each time the card is being used.

Perishability and Fluctuating Demand

Services are perishable and markets for most services fluctuate either by season (tourism), days (airlines), or time of day (movie theaters). Unused telephone capacity and electrical power; vacant seats on planes, trains, buses, and in stadiums; and time spent by catalog service representatives waiting for customers to reach them all represent business that is lost forever.

Marketing
Highlight 12–2

**Expectations of Service Customers
in Selected Industries**

Type of Service	Type of Customer	Principal Expectations
Automobile repair	Consumers	*Be competent.* Fix it right the first time. *Explain things.* Explain why the customer needs the suggested repairs—provide an itemized list. *Be respectful.* "Don't treat me like an idiot."
Automobile insurance	Consumers	*Keep me informed.* "I shouldn't have to learn about insurance law changes from the newspaper." *Be on my side.* "I don't want them to treat me like I am a criminal just because I have a claim." *Play fair.* "Don't drop me when something goes wrong." *Protect me from catastrophe.* "Make sure my estate is covered in the event of a major accident." *Provide prompt service.* "I want fast settlement of my claims."
Hotel	Consumers	*Provide a clean room.* "Don't have a deep-pile carpet that can't be completely cleaned. . . . You can literally see germs down there." *Provide a secure room.* Good bolts and a peephole on the door. *Treat me like a guest.* "It is almost like they're looking you over to decide whether or not they're going to let you have a room." *Keep your promise.* "They said the room would be ready at the promised time, but it wasn't."
Property and casualty insurance	Business customers	*Fulfill obligations.* Pay up. *Learn my business and work with me.* "I expect them to know me and my company." *Protect me from catastrophe.* Cover risk exposure so there is no single big loss. *Provide prompt service.* Fast claim service.
Equipment repair	Business customers	*Share my sense of urgency.* Speed of response. "One time I had to buy a second piece of equipment because of the huge downtime with the first piece." *Be prepared.* Have all the parts ready.
Truck and tractor rental/leasing	Business customers	*Keep the equipment running.* Have equipment working all the time—that is the key. *Be flexible.* "The leasing company should have the leasing flexibility to rent us equipment when we need it." *Provide full service.* Get rid of all the paperwork and headaches.

SOURCE: A. Parasuraman, Leonard L. Berry, and Valarie A. Zeithaml, "Understanding Customer Expectations of Service," *Sloan Management Review,* Spring 1991, pp. 39–48.

The combination of perishability and fluctuating demand has created many problems for marketers of services. Specifically, in the areas of staffing and distribution, avenues must be found to have the services available for peak periods, and new strategies need to be developed to make use of the service during slack periods. Some organizations are attempting to cope with these problems through the use of pricing strategy. *Off-peak pricing* consists of charging different prices during different times or days in order to stimulate demand during slow periods. Discounts given for weekend calling, Saturday night stayovers, early-bird dinners, or winter cruises are all examples of efforts made by service providers to redistribute demand.

Other organizations are dealing with issues related to peak period demand through the use of technology. To illustrate, a well-designed voice mail system allows companies and callers to cut down on missed phone calls, eliminates long waits on hold, and delivers clear, consistent messages. In the catalog industry, automated call routing (ACR) is used to route incoming calls to available service representatives in the order in which they were received. Finally, in the utilities industry, many electric utilities no longer have to generate capacity that will meet peak electrical demand. Instead, they rely on buying unused power from other utilities in other regions of the country.

Highly Differentiated Marketing Systems

Although the marketer of a tangible product is not compelled to use an established marketing system, such systems are often available and may be the most efficient. If an established system is not available, the marketer can at least obtain guidelines from the systems used for similar products. In the case of services, however, there may be little similarity between the marketing systems needed and those used for other services. To illustrate, the marketing of banking and other financial services bears little resemblance to the marketing of computer services or telecommunications. The entire area of services marketing, therefore, demands creativity and ingenuity on the part of marketing management. For example, trucking companies are now making arrangements with railways to combine forces on some routes. This form of intermodal transportation allows the trucking companies' customers to take advantage of the cheaper fuel and labor associated with rail transport, coupled with the faster, more reliable service offered by trucks. Likewise, the U.S. Postal Service, due to the heavy volume of mail processed, knows that some of its staff is at work every day of the week. As a result, they instituted Sunday delivery on Express Mail packages to gain an advantage over Federal Express and other private carriers that shut down on Sundays. Conversely, Federal Express, as a result of its efficient delivery processes, is able to now provide same-day delivery of packages on Mondays through Fridays.

Client Relationship

In the marketing of a great many services, a client relationship, as opposed to a customer relationship, exists between the buyer and the seller. In other words, the buyer views the seller as someone who has knowledge that is of value to them. Examples of this type of relationship are the physician–patient, college professor–student, accountant–small business owner, and broker–investor. The buyer, many times, abides by the advice offered or suggestions provided by the seller, and these relationships may be of an ongoing nature. Also, since many service firms are client-serving organizations, they may approach the marketing function in a more professional manner, as seen in health care, finance, and legal, governmental, and educational services.

There appear to be at least two marketing challenges that professionals face. First, in many cases, fear or hostility is brought to the transaction because the customer is uncertain about how genuine the professional's concern for his or her satisfaction is. For example, many unpleasant reasons exist for consulting doctors, lawyers, bankers, or even visiting a college professor. These could include having surgery, being sued, having to take out a loan, or doing poorly on an exam. Second, even high-quality service delivery by the professional can lead to dissatisfied customers. For a physician, the ability to provide high-quality medical care may be overshadowed by a brusque, unfriendly personality. For a college professor, the demand on students to only contact or visit him or her during office hours, coupled with students' own hectic work schedules, can diminish the impact of the professor's classroom presentations. It is vitally important that the professional service provider strive to build long-term positive relationships with clients. Highlight 12–3 illustrates the use of unconditional guarantees, which are one way to help build such a relationship.

■ Providing Quality Services

In today's increasingly competitive environment, quality service is critical to organizational success. In a study on the importance of service quality, more than 40 percent of all customers surveyed listed poor service as the number one reason for switching to the competition, while only 8 percent listed price.[8] As a result, delivering high-quality service is closely linked to profits, cost savings, and market share.[9] Thus, retaining current customers and building their loyalty is of great importance.[10] Unlike products where quality is often measured against standards, service quality is measured against performance.[11] Since services are frequently produced in the presence of a customer, are labor intensive, and are not able to be stored or objectively examined, the definition of what constitutes good service quality can be difficult and, in fact, continually changes in the face of choices.[12] Customers determine the value of service quality in relation to available alternatives and their particular needs. In general, problems in the determination of good service quality are attributable to differences in the expectations, perceptions, and experiences regarding the encounter between the service provider and consumer. These gaps can be classified as

1. The gap between consumer expectations and management perceptions of consumer expectations.
2. The gap between management perceptions of consumer expectations and the firm's service quality specifications.
3. The gap between service quality specifications and actual service quality.
4. The gap between actual service delivery and external communications about the service.

In essence, the customer perceives the level of service quality as being a function of the magnitude and direction of the gap between expected service and perceived service. Management of a company may not even realize that they are delivering poor-quality service due to differences in the way managers and consumers view acceptable quality levels. To overcome this problem and to avoid losing customers, firms must be aware of the determinants of service quality. A brief description of these determinants follows.

1. *Tangibles* include the physical evidence of the service. For example, employees are always visible in a hotel lobby dusting, emptying ash trays, or otherwise cleaning up. Likewise, clean, shiny, up-to-date medical equipment or aircraft are examples of tangible elements.
2. *Reliability* involves the consistency and dependability of the service performance. For example, does a bank or phone company always send out accurate customer statements? Likewise, does the plumber always fix the problem on his or her first visit?
3. *Responsiveness* concerns the willingness or readiness of employees or professionals to provide service. For example, will a physician see patients on the same day they call in to say they are ill? Will a college professor return a student's call the same day?
4. *Assurance* refers to the knowledge and competence of service providers and the ability to convey trust and confidence. This determinant encompasses the provider's name and reputation; possession of necessary skills; and trustworthiness, believability, and honesty. For example, a bank will guarantee same-day loan processing; a doctor is highly trained in a particular specialty.
5. *Empathy* refers to the service provider's efforts to understand the customer's needs and then to provide, as best as possible, individualized service delivery. For example, flight attendants on a customer's regular route learn what type of beverages the customer drinks and what magazines the customer reads.

Each of the determinants on the previous page plays an important role in how the customer views the service quality of a firm. Turning service quality into a powerful competitive weapon requires continuously striving for service superiority—consistently performing above the adequate service level and capitalizing on opportunities for exceeding the desired service level. Relentless efforts to continually improve service performance may well be rewarded by improvements in customer attitudes toward the firm: from customer frustration to customer preference to customer loyalty. What should be obvious is that to be successful, a service firm must have both an effective means to measure customer satisfaction and dedicated employees to provide high-quality service.

Customer Satisfaction Measurement

As mentioned above, satisfied customers can become loyal customers. Service quality and customer satisfaction are of growing concern to business organizations throughout the world, and research on these topics generally focuses on two key issues: (1) understanding the expectations and requirements of the customer and (2) determining how well a company and its major competitors are succeeding in satisfying these expectations and requirements.[13]

As such, an organization's approach to measuring service quality through customer satisfaction measurement (CSM) and effectively implementing programs derived from results of such studies can spell the difference between success and failure. Research on market leaders' CSMs found they had the following aspects in common:

1. Marketing and sales employees were primarily responsible (with customer input) for designing CSM programs and questionnaires.
2. Top management and the marketing function championed the programs.
3. Measurement involved a combination of qualitative and quantitative research methods that primarily included mail questionnaires, telephone surveys, and focus groups.
4. Evaluations included both the company's and competitor's satisfaction performance.
5. Results of all research were made available to employees, but not necessarily to customers.
6. Research was performed on a continual basis.
7. Customer satisfaction was incorporated into the strategic focus of the company via the mission statement.
8. There was a commitment to increasing service quality and customer satisfaction from employees at all levels within the organization.

The Importance of Internal Marketing

Properly performed customer satisfaction research can yield a wealth of strategic information about customers, the sponsoring company, and competitors. However, service quality goes beyond the relationship between a customer and a company. Rather, as shown by the last aspect listed, it is the personal relationship between a customer and the particular employee that the customer happens to be dealing with at the time of the service encounter that ultimately determines service quality. The importance of having customer-oriented, frontline people cannot be overstated.[14] If frontline service personnel are unfriendly, unhelpful, uncooperative, or uninterested in the customer, the customer will tend to project that same attitude to the company as a whole. The character and personality of an organization reflects the character and personality of its top management. Management must develop programs that will stimulate employee commitment to customer service. To be successful, these programs must contain five critical components:

1. *A careful selection process in hiring frontline employees.* To do this, management has to clearly define the skills the service person must bring to the job.[15] For example, Fairfield Inn often considers as many as 25 candidates for each housekeeping or front-desk position.[16]

2. *A clear, concrete message* that conveys a particular service strategy that frontline people can begin to act on. People delivering service need to know how their work fits in the broader scheme of business operations.[17] They need to have a cause because servicing others is just too demanding and frustrating to be done well each day without one.[18]

3. *Significant modeling by managers,* that is, managers demonstrating the behavior that they intend to reward employees for performing. For example, Virgin Atlantic Airways chairman Richard Branson regularly travels economy class on his airline to talk to customers and solicit ideas for improvement.[19]

4. *An energetic follow-through process,* in which managers provide the training, support, and incentives necessary to give the employees the capability and willingness to provide quality service. For example, AT&T Universal Card Services has set up an umbrella organization, aptly called Universal Card University, to give all of its employees a single point of reference in their training.[20]

5. *An emphasis on teaching employees to have good attitudes.* This type of training usually focuses on specific social techniques, such as eye contact, smiling, tone of voice, and standards of dress.

However, organizing and implementing such programs will only lead to temporary results unless managers practice a strategy of internal marketing. We define *internal marketing* as the continual process by which managers actively encourage, stimulate, and support employee commitment to the company, the company's goods and services, and the company's customers. Emphasis should be placed on the word *continual.* Managers who consistently pitch in to help when needed, constantly provide encouragement and words of praise to employees, strive to help employees understand the benefits of performing their jobs well, and emphasize the importance of employee actions on both company and employee results are practitioners of internal marketing. In service marketing, successful internal marketing efforts, leading to employee commitment to service quality, are a key to success.

Federal Express serves as a prime example of the benefits accruing to a company that successfully practices internal marketing.[21] Earlier this decade, Federal Express became the first service organization to win the Malcolm Baldrige National Quality Award. The company's motto is "people, service, and profits." Behind its purple, white, and orange planes and uniforms are self-managing work teams, gainsharing plans, and empowered employees seemingly consumed with providing flexible and creative services to customers with varying needs. Federal Express is a high-involvement, horizontally coordinated organization that encourages employees to use their judgment above and beyond the rulebook.

■ Overcoming the Obstacles in Service Marketing

The factors of intangibility and inseparability, as well as difficulties in coming up with objective definitions of acceptable service quality make comprehension of service marketing difficult. However, in view of the size and importance of services in our economy, considerable innovation and ingenuity are needed to make high-quality services available at convenient locations for consumers as well as businesspeople. In fact, the area of service marketing probably offers more opportunities for imagination and creative innovation than does product marketing. Unfortunately, many service firms still lag in the area of creative marketing. Even today, those service firms that have done a relatively good job have been slow in recognizing opportunities in all aspects of their marketing programs. Four reasons, connected to past practices, can be given for the lack of innovative marketing on the part of service marketers: (1) a limited view of marketing, (2) a lack of strong competition, (3) a lack of creative management, and (4) no obsolescence.

Limited View of Marketing

Because of the nature of their service, many firms depended to a great degree on population growth to expand sales. A popular example here is the telephone company, which did not establish a marketing department until 1955. It was then that the company realized it had to be concerned not only with population growth but also with meeting the needs of a growing population. Increases in educational levels and the standard of living also bring about the need for new and diversified services. A study conducted by *American Demographics* concluded that college-educated householders are much more likely to buy services—from dry cleaning to financial services—than those with less education.[22] As a well-educated, younger generation replaces the less educated, older one, the demand for services should only increase.

Service firms must meet these changing needs by developing new services and new channels and altering existing channels to meet the changing composition and needs of the population. For many service industries, growth has come as a result of finding new channels of distribution. For example, some banks and other financial service companies were able to grow and tap into new markets by establishing limited-service kiosks in malls and supermarkets. Airlines have successfully brought in a whole new class of travelers by offering advance-purchase discounted fares. Traditionally, users of these fares either drove or utilized other means of transportation in order to reach their destination.

While many service firms have succeeded in adopting a marketing perspective, others have been slow to respond. It was not until deregulation of the telecommunications industry took place in 1984 that the telephone companies began taking a broadened view of marketing. Even today, critics point to the obsession with inventing new technology versus using current technology in meeting customer needs as a weakness of these companies.

Limited Competition

A second major cause of the lack of innovative marketing in many service industries was due to the lack of competition. Many service industries, like banking, railroads, and public utilities have, throughout most of their histories, faced very little competition; some have even been regulated monopolies. Obviously, in an environment characterized by little competition, there was not likely to be a great deal of innovative marketing. However, two major forces have changed this situation. First, in the past two decades the banking, financial services, railroad, cable, airline, and telecommunications industries have all been deregulated in varying degrees. With deregulation has come a need to be able to compete effectively. For example, AT&T was once the sole provider of long-distance telephone service. Now, AT&T has to compete not only against such companies as MCI and Sprint but also against the regional Bell operating companies such as Ameritech and US West, which once were part of AT&T. Second, service marketing has taken on an international focus. Today, many foreign companies are competing in domestic service markets. Foreign interests own several banks, many hotels (including Holiday Inn), and shares in major airlines (including Northwest and US Airways). Likewise, American companies are expanding overseas as markets open up. For example, Merrill Lynch & Co. purchased Smith New Court PLC, a large British security firm, to become the world's largest brokerage firm.

Noncreative Management

For many years, the managements of service industries have been criticized for not being progressive and creative. Railroad management was criticized for many years for being slow to innovate. More recently, however, railroads have become leading innovators in the field of freight transportation, introducing such innovations as piggyback service and containerization, and in passenger service, introducing luxury overnight accommodations on trains with exotic names such as the Zephyr. Some other service industries, however, have been slow to develop new services or to innovate in the marketing of their existing services. In fact, as a whole, U.S. firms lag behind their Japanese and German competitors not only in collecting customer satisfaction data but also in designing services that address customers' needs.[23]

No Obsolescence

A great advantage for many service industries is the fact that many services, because of their intangibility, are less subject to obsolescence than goods. While this is an obvious advantage, it has also led some service firms to be sluggish in their approach to marketing. Manufacturers of goods may constantly change their marketing plans and seek new and more efficient ways to produce and distribute their products. Since service firms are often not faced with obsolescence, they often failed to recognize the need for change. This failure has led to wholesale changes in many industries as new operators, who possessed marketing skills, revolutionized the manner in which the service is performed and provided. Many a barbershop and hair dresser have gone out of business because of an inability to compete against hairstyling salons. Many accountants have lost clients to tax preparation services, such as H&R Block, that specialize in doing one task well and have used technology, including computerized filing services, to their advantage. Likewise, the old, big movie house has become a relic of the past as entrepreneurs realized the advantages to be gained from building and operating theater complexes that contain several minitheaters in or near suburban malls.

■ The Service Challenge

Despite traditional thinking and practices on the part of many marketing managers and writers concerning the similarities between the operation of manufacturing and services organizations, the past decade has seen the growth of many innovative ways of meeting the service challenge. The service challenge is the quest to (1) constantly develop new services that will better meet customer needs, (2) improve on the quality and variety of existing services, and (3) provide and distribute these services in a manner that best serves the customer. This next section illustrates the challenges facing companies in various service industries and examples of marketing strategies employed by them to meet the service challenge.

Banking

"Banking is vital to a healthy economy. Banks are not." This is the message that a banking expert delivered to an industry group recently.[24] Needless to say, the days when banking was considered a dead-end career, but one that offered stable employment for marketers, is long gone. Perhaps banking best exemplifies the changes that are taking place as service organizations strive to become practitioners of the "marketing concept." Buy or be bought is the new watchword in the banking industry, which is experiencing the biggest wave of consolidation in its history. Experts predict that in the next 10 to 15 years, the United States' 10,200 banks may consolidate into as few as 4,000, a process expedited by the recent clearance for interstate banking.[25] While past bank deals have been mainly predicated on cost savings, today's deals are made to enable surviving banks to effectively compete as major players in the industry.

Banking is becoming an increasingly technology-driven business. The main reason is that more and more financial services, from loans to credit cards, are being marketed through computers and telephones instead of through branches. Banks large enough to afford big technology investments can reach customers nationwide even though their physical franchise may be limited. For example, most consumers possess credit cards from banks they have never physically visited. Further, the advent of new electronic delivery systems (via computer) for consumer and small business banking could, within the next decade, greatly reduce the number of branch banks needed. To prevent a loss of a large portion of their customer base, many of the leading banks, such as Chase Manhattan and Citibank, are aligning themselves with software and hardware manufacturers to develop home banking systems.

Banks have also learned the value of bundling services. Many now offer an account that combines checking, savings, credit card, and auto loan features. Benefits to the customer include free ATM transactions, interest-bearing checking accounts, no-fee credit cards, and the convenience of one-stop banking. In addition, they offer preapproved auto loans and cash-flow statements. Most banks also target some marketing activities toward senior citizens, which may include discount coupons for entertainment, travel newsletters, and lower monthly minimum required balances.

Competition between banks and other financial institutions will continue to intensify. The survivors will be those that have best mastered the art of services marketing. Toward this end, every bank must understand the needs and expectations of its customers and then design efficient delivery systems that meet those requirements.[26]

Health Care

The distribution of health care services is of vital concern. In health care delivery, the inseparability characteristic presents more of a handicap than in other service industries because users (patients) literally place themselves in the hands of the seller. Although direct personal contact between producer and user is often necessary, new and more efficient means of distribution seem to be evolving.

Up until the past few decades, medical care has been traditionally associated with the solo practice, fee-for-service system. Recently, several alternative delivery systems have been developed, most notably the health maintenance organization (HMO). This type of delivery system stresses the creation of group health care clinics using teams of salaried health practitioners (physicians, pharmacists, technicians, and so forth) that serve a specified, enrolled membership on a prepaid basis. The primary benefits to the customer (patient) from membership in an HMO are (1) the ability to have all ailments treated at one facility, (2) payment of a fixed fee for services, and (3) the encouragement of preventive versus remedial treatments. The success of the HMO concept in traditional medical care has inspired similar programs to be developed for dental and eye care.

As with banking, the hospital segment of the health care industry has become extremely competitive with for-profit hospitals competing among themselves and against nonprofit organizations. Although facing some serious ethics charges and management changes in the late '90s, one of the leading hospitals in terms of growth and stock appreciation has been Columbia/HCA (CHCA).[27] In less than three years, CHCA grew from a hospital chain of around 20 facilities to one of approximately 320. The ultimate goal of CHCA is to own 1,200 to 1,300 hospitals, or about 25 percent of the nongovernment hospitals in the United States. CHCA's success is largely due to its acumen in carrying out operations and marketing strategy. CHCA buys hospitals and, by consolidating activities, gets rid of redundancies, thereby reducing its cost structure. As a result, CHCA can price its services below competition and gain contractual arrangements to service large HMOs. As described by one hospital official, "Columbia/HCA is the self-proclaimed Wal-Mart of health care," offering quality service at an affordable price.

In the pharmaceutical field, Chronimed of Minnetonka, Minnesota, has focused on providing great customer service as its avenue to success.[28] The company supplies 100,000 patients across the United States with specialized medications that local pharmacies can't afford to stock. Chronimed's skill is twofold. First, it provides needed drugs by mail to organ transplant recipients and patients with diabetes or AIDS. Second, it employs a team of 50 pharmacists and assistants who provide much-needed information about the medications they dispense, such as details about drug interaction and side effects. As evidenced by the above examples, health care companies, regardless of what specific area in which they compete, are becoming more and more market-oriented as they try to differentiate their offerings from those of the competition.

Insurance

In recent years, the insurance industry has exploded with new product and service offerings. Not too long ago, customers were faced with limited options in choosing life, hospital, or auto insurance. Now, there is a wide array of insurance policies to choose from, including universal life policies, which double as retirement savings; nursing care insurance; reversible mortgages, which allow people to take equity from their house while still living in it; and other offerings aimed at serving an aging population. To illustrate, Prudential Insurance Company offers a program whereby terminally ill policyholders are allowed to withdraw funds against the face value of their policy while still alive. In addition to insurance services, most insurance companies now offer a full range of financial services, including auto loans, mortgages, mutual funds, and certificates of deposit.

Distribution of insurance services has also been growing. The vending machines found in airports for flight insurance have been finding their way into other areas. Travel auto insurance is now available in many motel chains and through the AAA. Group insurance written through employers and labor unions also has been extremely successful. In each instance, the insurance industry has used intermediaries to distribute its services.

Travel

The travel industry, most notably the airlines, has been a leader in the use of technology. Computerized reservation systems allow customers to book plane tickets from home or work. Nearly all airlines are using Internet sites to dispense flight and fare information. Airlines are in the midst of implementing ticketless travel programs in which passengers purchase tickets, select their seats, and pick up boarding passes and luggage tags at machines resembling ATMs.[29] Technology has also allowed airlines to make strategic pricing decisions through the use of yield management. In yield management, certain seats on aircraft are discounted and certain ones aren't. Through the use of elaborate computer programs, managers are able to determine who their customer segments are and who is likely to purchase airline tickets when and to where.

Despite its success in employing technology to attract additional customers and offer added convenience, the airline industry has operated in somewhat dire straits, plagued by problems associated with overcapacity, high labor costs, and low perceived service quality. The recent period from 1990 through 1995 could be considered the most turbulent ever encountered by U.S. commercial airlines.[30] During this time, some airlines either went out of business (Midway, Eastern, and Pan Am) or were in and out of bankruptcy proceedings (Continental, America West, and TWA); and most others operated at a loss. Fortunately, in the last five years, good news came to the industry in the form of decreased fuel prices, the abandoning of some hub-and-spoke operations, and other events leading to cost decreases.

A notable exception to the fate that befell most carriers is Southwest Airlines, which has finally convinced its peers that a carrier can be consistently profitable by offering cheap fares on short-distance routes. Now, big carriers such as Continental and United have created their own Southwest look-alikes to supplement their long-haul, full-service, high-fare operations. Southwest's secret to success (which other airlines may or may not be able to imitate) is the high level of employee morale exhibited by everyone associated with the company. This has come as a direct result of upper management's internal marketing efforts.

Recent experiences in the lodging industry point out potential opportunities and pitfalls in service branding strategies.[31] Marriott, one of the most respected names in the lodging industry, is generally regarded as one of the more prestigious hotels. When Marriott decided to enter the lower-priced segment of the hotel market, it did so with new brands. By altering the physical appearance and changing the names of its new motels to Courtyard by Marriott, Comfort Inn, and Marriott Resorts, Marriott was able to distinguish between its upscale offerings and those that were moderately priced. Holiday Inn, on the other hand, has experienced difficulty in trying to change from its middle-class image. It created Hampton Inns and Holiday Express for the budget segment, and Crowne Plaza and Embassy Suites for the upscale market. Because of overlapping between segments, Holiday Inn had difficulties in differentiating between the brands, especially in instances when two of the brands were located in the same city. By far, the most confused brand strategy relates to the use of the Ramada name. The Ramada Renaissance is a 16-unit chain of four-star hotels owned and operated in the United States by Ramada International Hotels & Resorts. Concurrently, there exists the 600-unit Ramada Hotel and Inn chain, which is owned and operated by Hospitality Franchise Systems, a privately held company that also manages the Howard Johnson and Days Inn franchises. As a result, much confusion reigns in consumers' minds when asked to define what type of hotel the Ramada name brings to mind. The examples point out the necessity of multiple brands for service marketers when practicing market segmentation.

Implications for Service Marketers

The preceding sections emphasized the use of all components of the marketing mix. Many service industries have been criticized for an overdependence on advertising. The overdependence on one or two elements of the marketing mix is a mistake that service marketers cannot afford. The sum total of the marketing mix elements represents the total impact of the firm's marketing strategy. The slack created by severely restricting one element cannot be compensated by heavier emphasis on another, since each element in the marketing mix is designed to address specific problems and achieve specific objectives.

Services must be made available to prospective users, which implies distribution in the marketing sense of the word. The revised concept of the distribution of services points out that service marketers must distinguish conceptually between the production and distribution of services. The problem of making services more widely available must not be ignored.

The above sections also pointed out the critical role of new service development. In several of the examples described, indirect distribution of the service was made possible because "products" were developed that included a tangible representation of the service. This development facilitates the use of intermediaries, because the service can now be separated from the producer. In addition, the development of new services paves the way for companies to expand and segment their markets. With the use of varying service bundles, new technology, and alternative means of distributing the service, companies are now able to practice targeted marketing.

■ Conclusion

This chapter has dealt with the complex topic of service marketing. While the marketing of services has much in common with the marketing of products, unique problems in the area require highly creative marketing management skills. Many of the problems in the service area can be traced to the intangible and inseparable nature of services and the difficulties involved in measuring service quality. However, considerable progress has been made in understanding and reacting to these difficult problems, particularly in the area of distribution. In view of the major role services play in our economy, it is important for marketing practitioners to better understand and appreciate the unique problems of service marketing.

■ Additional Readings

Berry, Leonard L. "Retailers with a Future." *Marketing Management,* Spring 1996, pp. 38–46.

Price, B. Joseph, III, and James Gilmore. "Welcome to the Experience Economy." *Harvard Business Review,* July–August 1998, pp. 97–105.

"Services Marketing at the Turn of the Century." *Marketing Management,* Special Issue, (Fall 1997), pp. 9–39.

van Biema, Michael, and Bruce Greenwold. "Managing Our Way to Higher Service-Sector Productivity." *Harvard Business Review,* July–August 1997, pp. 87–95.

Chapter Thirteen

Global Marketing

A growing number of U.S. corporations have transversed geographical boundaries and become truly multinational in nature. For most other domestic companies, the question is no longer, Should we go international? Instead, the questions relate to when, how, and where the companies should enter the international marketplace. The past 15 years have seen the reality of a truly world market unfold. In today's world, the global economy is becoming almost totally integrated, versus 25 percent integrated in 1980 and 50 percent integrated in the early 1990s. Primary reasons for previously separated, individual markets evolving to a network of interdependent economies include

1. The growing influence and economic development of lesser developed countries. In years to come, the real battleground for the two trade powers, the United States and Japan, will take place in the developing world. Containing 80 percent of the world's population and with growth rates nearly double those of industrial nations, these countries have emerged as the "fourth engine in the world economy" (following the United States, Japan, and Europe).[1]
2. The integration of world financial markets. For example, changes in currency exchange rates between the yen and the dollar greatly influence issues relating to import and export activities for all countries.
3. Increased efficiencies in transportation and telecommunication and data communication networks. To illustrate, consider the cases of Eastern Europe, China, and Russia. In these countries, technological advances have allowed the emergence of stock exchanges on which brokers throughout the world can trade.
4. The opening of new markets. For example, recent political events in Vietnam have led to the opening of a market that for decades (since the end of the Vietnam War) was closed to U.S. companies.

Multinational firms invest in foreign countries for the same basic reasons they invest in their own country. These reasons vary from firm to firm but fall under the categories of achieving offensive or defensive goals. Offensive goals are to (1) increase long-term growth and profit prospects, (2) maximize total sales revenue, (3) take advantage of economies of scale, and (4) improve overall market position. As many American markets reach saturation, American firms look to foreign markets as outlets for surplus production capacity, sources of new customers, increased profit margins, and improved returns on investment. For example, the ability to expand the number of locations of McDonald's restaurants in the United States is becoming severely limited. Yet, on any given day, only 0.5 percent of the world's population visits McDonald's. This fact illustrates the vast potential markets still open to the company.[2] Indeed, in the recent past, of the 50 most profitable McDonald's outlets, 25 were located in Hong Kong. For PepsiCo, the results are similar. Its restaurant division operates 7,400 Kentucky Fried Chicken, Pizza Hut, and Taco Bell outlets abroad, deriving over $5.6 billion in sales from these foreign locations.

Multinational firms also invest in other countries to achieve defensive goals. Chief among these goals are the desire to (1) compete with foreign companies on their own turf instead of in the United States, (2) have access to technological innovations that are developed in other countries, (3) take advantage of significant differences in operating costs between countries, (4) preempt competitors' global moves, and (5) not be locked out of future markets by arriving too late.

Such well-known companies as Zenith, Pillsbury, A&P, Shell Oil, CBS Records, and Firestone Tire & Rubber are now owned by non-U.S. interests. Since 1980, the share of the U.S. high-tech market held by foreign products has grown from less than 8 percent to close to 25 percent. In such diverse industries as power tools, tractors, television, and banking, U.S. companies have lost the dominant position they once held. By investing solely in domestic operations or not being willing to adapt products to foreign markets, U.S. companies are more susceptible to foreign incursions. For example, there has been a great uproar over Japan's practice of not opening up its domestic automobile market to U.S. companies. However, as of 1996, a great majority of the American cars shipped to Japan still had the steering wheel located on the left side of the vehicle—the opposite of where it should be for the Japanese market.

In many ways, marketing globally is the same as marketing at home. Regardless of which part of the world the firm sells in, the marketing program must still be built around a sound product or service that is properly priced, promoted, and distributed to a carefully analyzed target market. In other words, the marketing manager has the same controllable decision variables in both domestic and nondomestic markets.

Although the development of a marketing program may be the same in either domestic or nondomestic markets, special problems may be involved in the implementation of marketing programs in nondomestic markets. These problems often arise because of the environmental differences that exist among various countries that marketing managers may be unfamiliar with.

In this chapter, marketing management in a global context will be examined. Methods of organizing global versus domestic markets, global market research tasks, methods of entry strategies into global markets, and potential marketing strategies for a multinational firm will be discussed. In examining each of these areas, the reader will find a common thread—knowledge of the local cultural environment—that appears to be a major prerequisite for success in each area.

With the proper adaptations, many companies have the capabilities and resources needed to compete successfully in the global marketplace. To illustrate, companies

Marketing
Highlight 13–1

**The Decision Process Involved in Determining
Whether to Compete in Global Markets**

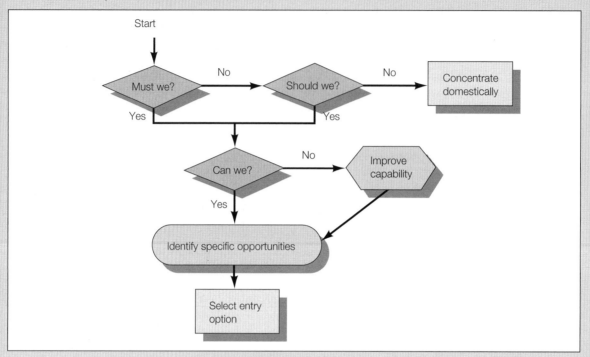

SOURCE: Betty Jane Punnett and David A. Ricks, *International Business* (Boston: PWS-Kent Publishing Co., 1992), p. 257.

as diverse as Kellogg's, Avon, Eli Lilly, and Sun Microsystems each generates over 40 percent of sales from foreign operations.[3] Smaller companies can also be successful. For example, Nemix, Inc., of Bell Gardens, California, is a franchisee of Church's Fried Chicken with $91 million in annual sales. Small by world standards, this company has succeeded in developing a fully vertical operation in Poland, doing everything from raising chickens to operating restaurants.[4]

■ Organizing for Global Marketing

When compared with the tasks it faces at home, a firm attempting to establish a global marketing organization faces a much higher degree of risk and uncertainty. In a foreign market, management is often less familiar with the cultural, political, and economic situation. Many of these problems arise as a result of conditions specific to the foreign country. Managers are also faced with the decisions concerning how to organize the multinational company.

Problems with Entering Foreign Markets

While numerous problems could be cited, attention here will focus on those firms most often face when entering foreign markets.

Marketing
Highlight 13–2

Examples of Cultural Differences That Could Lead to Marketing Problems

Body Language

- Standing with your hands on your hips is a gesture of defiance in Indonesia.
- Carrying on a conversation with your hands in your pockets makes a poor impression in France, Belgium, Finland, and Sweden.
- Shaking your head from side to side means yes in Bulgaria and Sri Lanka.
- Crossing your legs to expose the sole of your shoe is really taboo in Muslim countries. In fact, to call a person a "shoe" is a deep insult.

Physical Contact

- Patting a child on the head is a grave offense in Thailand or Singapore, since the head is revered as the location of the soul.
- In an Oriental culture, touching another person is considered an invasion of privacy; in southern European and Arabic countries, it is a sign of warmth and friendship.

Promptness

- Be on time when invited for dinner in Denmark or in China.
- In Latin countries, your host or business associate would be surprised if you arrived at the appointed hour.

Eating and Cooking

- It is rude to leave anything on your plate when eating in Norway, Malaysia, or Singapore.
- In Egypt, it is rude *not* to leave something.
- In Italy and Spain, cooking is done with oil.
- In Germany and Great Britain, margarine and butter are used.

Other Social Customs

- In Sweden, nudity and sexual permissiveness are quite all right, but drinking is really frowned on.
- In Spain, there is a very negative attitude toward life insurance. By receiving insurance benefits, a wife feels that she is profiting from her husband's death.
- In western European countries, many consumers still are reluctant to buy anything (other than a house) on credit. Even for an automobile, they will pay cash.

SOURCE: William J. Stanton, Michael J. Etzel, and Bruce J. Walker, *Fundamentals of Marketing*, 11th ed. © 1997, New York, McGraw-Hill, Inc., p. 544. Reproduced by permission of The McGraw-Hill Companies.

Cultural Misunderstanding. Differences in the cultural environment of foreign countries may be misunderstood or not even recognized because of the tendency for marketing managers to use their own cultural values and priorities as a frame of reference. Some of the most common areas of difference lie in the way dissimilar cultures perceive time, thought patterns, personal space, material possessions, family roles and relationships, personal achievement, competitiveness, individuality, social behavior, and other interrelated issues.[5] Another important source of misunderstandings is in the perceptions of managers about the people with whom they are dealing. Feelings of superiority can lead to changed communication mannerisms.

American managers must make the necessary efforts to learn, understand, and adapt to the cultural norms of the managers and customers they deal with in other parts of the world. Failure to do so will result in missed market opportunities. Highlight 13–2 provides further examples of cultural differences that could lead to marketing problems.

On the other hand, companies should not shy away from attempting to enter global markets because conventional wisdom says that products and service will not succeed in some regions purely because of cultural reasons. For example, PepsiCo's Pepsi division entered into a $500 million offensive to try to grab a larger share of the $6 billion Brazilian soft-drink market.[6] Understanding the dramatic changes that had taken place in Brazil, Pepsi repositioned itself as the choice of a new Brazil. Advertisements for the Pepsi brand feature young people enumerating recent changes in Brazil, such as perhaps the devaluation of its currency in 1999. Does this campaign sound familiar? It should since it's a takeoff on the popular "Pepsi, the choice of a new generation" theme utilized in the United States. Actions taken by PepsiCo's Frito-Lay unit serve as another example of a successful adaptation to cultural differences.[7] In China, Frito-Lay recently introduced its popular Cheetos snack food. The twist to this effort lies in the fact that the Chinese are not big consumers of dairy products. In China, Cheetos are cheeseless, instead consisting of flavors such as "Savory American Cream" and "Zesty Japanese Steak." As a result of these and other adaptations, it's no wonder that PepsiCo ranks among the leaders in the global food and beverage industry.

Political Uncertainty.   Governments are unstable in many countries, and social unrest and even armed conflict must sometimes be reckoned with. Other nations are newly emerging and anxious to seek their independence. These and similar problems can greatly hinder a firm seeking to establish its position in foreign markets. For example, firms scaled back their investment plans in Russia due to, among other reasons, (1) a business environment plagued by mobsters, (2) politics badly corrupted by the botched invasion of Chechnya, and (3) an economy troubled by runaway inflation and a plummeting ruble.[8] This is not to say investment in Russia is a poor choice. Rather, in situations like this, caution must be utilized and companies must have a keen understanding of the risks involved in undertaking sizable investments.

Import Restrictions.   Tariffs, import quotas, and other types of import restrictions hinder global business. These are usually established to promote self-sufficiency and can be a huge roadblock for the multinational firm. For example, a number of countries, including South Korea, Taiwan, Thailand, and Japan, have placed import restrictions on a variety of goods produced in America, including telecommunications equipment, rice, wood products, automobiles, and produce. In other cases, governments may not impose restrictions that are commonly adhered to in the United States. For example, Chrysler pulled out of a proposed investment deal in China, worth billions of dollars, because the Chinese government refused to protect its right to limit access to technological information.

Exchange Controls and Ownership Restrictions.   Some nations establish limits on the amount of earned and invested funds that can be withdrawn from it. These exchange controls are usually established by nations that are experiencing balance-of-payment problems. In addition, many nations have a requirement that the majority ownership of a company operating there be held by nationals. These and other types of currency and ownership regulations are important considerations in the decision to expand into a foreign market. For example, up until 1990, foreign holdings in business ventures in India were limited to a maximum of 40 percent. Once this ban was lifted, numerous global companies such as Sony, Whirlpool, JVC, Grundig, Panasonic, Kellogg's, Levi Strauss, Pizza Hut, and Domino's rushed to invest in this market.[9]

Economic Conditions.　As noted earlier, nations' economies are becoming increasingly intertwined, and business cycles tend to follow similar patterns. However, there are differences, mainly due to political upheaval or social changes, and these may be significant. In determining whether to invest, marketers need to perform in-depth analyses of a country's stage of economic development, the buying power of its populace, and the strength of its currency. For example, when the North American Free Trade Agreement (NAFTA) was signed, many American companies rushed to invest in Mexico, building production facilities and retail outlets. These companies assumed that the signing of the agreement would stabilize Mexico's economy. In the long term, these investments may pay off. However, many companies lost millions of dollars there due to the devaluation of the peso. Indeed, the crash of the peso caused the retail giant Wal-Mart to scale back a $1 billion investment project to open stores throughout Mexico.

Organizing the Multinational Company

There are two kinds of multinational corporations—the *multidomestic corporation* and the *global corporation*.[10] The *multidomestic company* pursues different strategies in each of its foreign markets. Each overseas subsidiary is autonomous. A company's management tries to operate effectively across a series of worldwide positions with diverse product requirements, growth rates, competitive environments, and political risks. Local managers are given the authority and control to make the necessary decisions; however, they are also held responsible for results. In effect, the company competes on a market-by-market basis. Honeywell and General Foods are examples of two American companies that have operated well in this manner.

The *global company,* on the other hand, pits its entire resources against the competition in an integrated fashion. Foreign subsidiaries and divisions are largely interdependent on both operations and strategy. These "stateless" corporations standardize manufacturing, regularly offer innovative solutions to the market, and seek creative collaborations with other firms to merge complementary skills and gain access to new markets. The global company operates as though the world were one large market, not a series of individual countries. Since there is no one clear-cut way to organize a global company, three alternative structures are normally used: (1) worldwide product divisions, each responsible for selling its own products throughout the world, (2) divisions responsible for all products sold within a geographic area, and (3) a matrix system that combines elements of both these arrangements. Many multinational companies already have structured their organization in a global fashion including IBM, Caterpillar, Timex, General Electric, Siemens, and Mitsubishi.

Most companies are realizing the need to take a global approach to managing their businesses. However, recognizing the need and actually implementing a truly global approach are two different tasks. For some companies, industry conditions dictate that they take a global perspective. The ability to actually implement a global approach to managing international operations, however, largely depends on factors unique to the company. Globalization, as a competitive strategy, is inherently more vulnerable to risk than a multidomestic or domestic strategy, due to the relative permanence of the organizational structure once established.[11]

In determining whether or not to globalize a particular business, managers should look first at their industry.[12] Market, economic, environmental, and competitive factors all influence the potential gains to be realized by following a global strategy. Factors constituting the external environment that are conducive to a global strategy are

1. *Market factors.* Homogeneous market needs, global customers, shortening product life cycles, transferable brands and advertising, and the ability to globalize distribution channels.
2. *Economic factors.* Worldwide economies of scale in manufacturing and distribution, steep learning curves, worldwide sourcing efficiencies, rising product development costs, and significant differences in host-country costs.
3. *Environmental factors.* Improving communications, favorable government policies, and the increasing speed of technological change.
4. *Competitive factors.* Competitive interdependencies among countries, global moves of competitors, and opportunities to preempt a competitor's global moves.[13]

Many of the reasons given in the first part of the chapter as to why a domestic company should become a multinational can also be used to support the argument that a firm should take a global perspective. This is because the integration of markets is forcing companies that wish to remain successful to not only become multinationals but also to take a global perspective in doing so. In the past, companies had the option of remaining domestic or going multinational due to the separation of markets. This is no longer the case.

There are several internal factors that can either facilitate or impede a company's efforts to undertake a global approach to marketing strategies. These factors and their underlying dimensions are

1. *Structure.* The ease of installing a centralized global authority and the absence of rifts between present domestic and international divisions or operating units.
2. *Management processes.* The capabilities and resources available to perform global planning, budgeting, and coordination activities, coupled with the ability to conduct global performance reviews and implement global compensation plans.
3. *Culture.* The ability to project a global versus national identity, a worldwide versus domestic commitment to employees, and a willingness to tolerate interdependence among business units.
4. *People.* The availability of employable foreign nationals and the willingness of current employees to commit to multicountry careers, frequent travel, and having foreign superiors.

Overall, whether a company should undertake a multidomestic or global approach to organizing its international operations will largely depend on the nature of the company and its products, how different foreign cultures are from the domestic market, and the company's ability to implement a global perspective. Many large brands have failed in their quest to go global. The primary reason for this failure is rushing the process. Successful global brands carefully stake out their markets, allowing plenty of time to develop their overseas marketing efforts and evolve into global brands.

Indeed, in many cases, firms do not undertake either purely multidomestic or global approaches to marketing. Instead, a hybrid approach is developed whereby these global brands carry with them the same visual identity, the same strategic positioning, and the same advertising. In addition, local characteristics are factored in. Regardless of the approach undertaken, management and organizational skills that emphasize the need to handle diversity are the critical factors that determine the long-term success of any company's endeavors in the global marketplace.

Programming for Global Marketing

In this section of the chapter, the major areas in developing a global marketing program will be examined. As was mentioned at the outset, marketing managers must organize the same controllable decision variables that exist in domestic markets. However, many firms that have been extremely successful in marketing in the United States have not been able to duplicate their success in foreign markets.

Global Marketing Research

Because the risks and uncertainties are so high, marketing research is equally important (and probably more so) in foreign markets than in domestic markets. Many companies encounter losing situations abroad because they do not know enough about the market.[14] They don't know how to get the information or find the cost of collecting the information too high. To be successful, organizations must collect and analyze pertinent information to support the basic go/no-go decision before getting to the issues addressed by conventional market research. Toward this end, in attempting to analyze foreign consumers and markets, at least four organizational issues must be considered.

Population Characteristics.   Population characteristics are one of the major components of a market, and significant differences exist between and within foreign countries. If data are available, the marketing manager should be familiar with the total population and with the regional, urban, rural, and interurban distribution. Other demographic variables, such as the number and size of families, education, occupation, and religion, are also important. In many markets, these variables can have a significant impact on the success of a firm's marketing program. For example, in the United States, a cosmetics firm can be reasonably sure of the desire to use cosmetics being common among women of all income classes. However, in Latin America the same firm may be forced to segment its market by upper-, middle-, and lower-income groups, as well as by urban and rural areas. This is because upper-income women want high-quality cosmetics promoted in prestige media and sold through exclusive outlets. In some rural and less prosperous areas, cosmetics must be inexpensive; in other rural areas, women do not accept cosmetics.

Ability to Buy.   To assess the ability of consumers in a foreign market to buy, four broad measures should be examined: (1) gross national product or per capita national income, (2) distribution of income, (3) rate of growth in buying power, and (4) extent of available financing. Since each of these varies in different areas of the world, the marketing opportunities available must be examined closely.

Willingness to Buy.   The cultural framework of consumer motives and behavior is integral to the understanding of the foreign consumer. If data are available, cultural values and attitudes toward the material culture, social organizations, the supernatural, aesthetics, and language should be analyzed for their possible influence on

Marketing
Highlight 13–3

Tips for Global Consumer Marketing Research

Many consumer goods companies have sought growth by expanding into global markets. For U.S. companies, this is sound strategy since 95 percent of the world's population and two-thirds of its purchasing power are located outside their country. The potential for success in global markets is enhanced when companies carefully research and analyze consumers in foreign countries, just as it is in domestic markets. Below are some suggestions for companies seeking to successfully market to global consumers.

- Research the cultural nuances and customs of the market. Be sure that the company and brand name translate favorably in the language of the target country, and if not, consider using an abbreviation or entirely different brand name for the market. Consider using marketing research firms or ad agencies that have detailed knowledge of the culture.
- Determine whether the product can be exported to the foreign country as is or whether it has to be modified to be useful and appealing to targeted consumers. Also, determine what changes need to be made to packaging and labeling to make the product appealing to the market.
- Research the prices of similar products in the target country or region. Determine the necessary retail price

to make marketing it profitable in the country, and research whether a sufficient number of consumers would be willing to pay that price. Also, determine what the product has to offer that should make consumers willing to pay a higher price.
- On the basis of research, decide whether the targeted country or region will require a unique marketing strategy or whether the same general strategy can be used in all geographic areas.
- Research the ways consumers purchase similar products in the targeted country or region and whether the company's product can be sold effectively using this method of distribution. Also, determine if a method of distribution not currently being used in the country could create a competitive advantage for the product.
- Pretest integrated marketing communication efforts in the targeted country to ensure that not only are messages translated accurately but that subtle differences in meaning are not problematic. Also, research the effectiveness of planned communication efforts.

Marketing consumer goods successfully in global markets requires a long-term commitment as it may take time to establish an identity in new markets. However, with improving technology and the evolution of a global economy, both large and small companies have found global marketing both feasible and profitable.

SOURCE: Dom Del Prete, "Winning Strategies Lead to Global Marketing Success," *Marketing News*, August 18, 1997, pp. 1, 2.

each of the elements in the firm's marketing program. It is easy to see that such factors as the group's values concerning acquisition of material goods, the role of the family, the positions of men and women in society, and the various age groups and social classes can have an effect on marketing, because each can influence consumer behavior.

In some areas there appears to be a convergence of tastes and habits, with different cultures becoming more and more integrated into one homogeneous culture, although still separated by national boundaries. This appears to be the case in western Europe, where consumers are developing into a mass market. This obviously will simplify the task for a marketer in this region. However, cultural differences still prevail among many areas of the world and strongly influence consumer behavior. However, marketing organizations may have to do primary research in many foreign markets to obtain usable information about these issues.

Differences in Research Tasks and Processes. In addition to the dimensions mentioned above, the processes and tasks associated with carrying out the market research program may also differ from country to country. Many market researchers count on census data for in-depth demographic information. However, in foreign countries there are a variety of problems the market researcher is likely to encounter in using census data. These include[15]

1. *Language.* Some nations publish their census reports in English. Other countries offer census reports only in their native language; some do not take a census.
2. *Data content.* Data contained in a census will vary from country to country and often omit items of interest to researchers. For example, most foreign nations do not include an income question on their census. Others do not include such items as marital status or education levels.
3. *Timeliness.* The United States takes a census every 10 years. Japan and Canada conduct one every five years. However, some northern European nations are abandoning the census as a data-collection tool and instead are relying on population registers to account for births, deaths, and changes in marital status or place of residence.
4. *Availability in the United States.* If a researcher requires detailed household demographics on foreign markets, the cost and time required to obtain the data will be significant. Unfortunately, census data for many countries do not exist. For some it will be difficult to obtain, although others can be found on the Internet.

Global Product Strategy

Global marketing research can help determine whether (1) there is an unsatisfied need for which a new product could be developed to serve a foreign market or (2) there is an unsatisfied need that could be met with an existing domestic product, either as is or adapted to the foreign market. In either case, product planning is necessary to determine the type of product to be offered and whether there is sufficient demand to warrant entry into a foreign market.

Most U.S. firms would not think of entering a domestic market without extensive product planning. However, some marketers have failed to do adequate product planning when entering foreign markets. An example of such a problem occurred when American manufacturers began to export refrigerators to Europe. The firms exported essentially the same models sold in the United States. However, the refrigerators were the wrong size, shape, and temperature range for some areas and had weak appeal in others—thus failing miserably. Although adaptation of the product to local conditions may have eliminated this failure, this adaptation is easier said than done. For example, even in the domestic market, overproliferation of product varieties and options can dilute economies of scale. This dilution results in higher production costs, which may make the price of serving each market segment with an adapted product prohibitive.

The solution to this problem is not easy. In some cases, changes need not be made at all or, if so, can be accomplished rather inexpensively. In other cases, the sales potential of the particular market may not warrant expensive product changes. For example, Pepsi's Radical Fruit line of juice drinks has been introduced without adaptation on three continents.[16] On the other hand, U.S. companies wishing to market software in foreign countries must undertake painstaking and costly efforts to convert the embedded code from English to foreign languages. This undertaking severely limits the potential markets where individual software products can be profitably marketed. In any case, management must examine these product-related problems carefully prior to making foreign market entry decisions.

■ **Figure 13–1**
Common Distribution
Channels for Global
Marketing

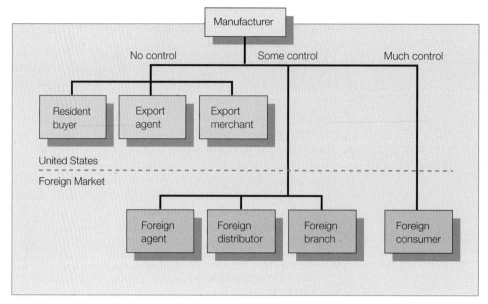

Global Distribution Strategy

The role of the distribution network in facilitating the transfer of goods and titles and in the demand stimulation process is as important in foreign markets as it is at home. Figure 13–1 illustrates some of the most common channel arrangements in global marketing. The continuum ranges from no control to almost complete control of the distribution system by manufacturers.

The channel arrangement where manufacturers have the least control is shown at the left of Figure 13–1. These are the most indirect channels of distribution. Here manufacturers sell to resident buyers, export agents, or export merchants located in the United States. In reality, these are similar to some domestic sales, since all of the marketing functions are assumed by intermediaries.

Manufacturers become more directly involved and, hence, have greater control over distribution when agents and distributors located in foreign markets are selected. Both perform similar functions, except that agents do not assume title to the manufacturers' products, while distributors do. If manufacturers should assume the functions of foreign agents or distributors and establish their own foreign branch, they greatly increase control over their global distribution system. Manufacturers' effectiveness will then depend on their own administrative organization rather than on independent intermediaries. If the foreign branch sells to other intermediaries, such as wholesalers and retailers, as is the case with most consumer goods, manufacturers again relinquish some control. However, since the manufacturers are located in the market area, they have greater potential to influence these intermediaries. For example, Volkswagen, General Motors, Anheuser-Busch, and Procter & Gamble have each made substantial investments in building manufacturing facilities in Brazil. These investments allow the companies to begin making direct sales to dealers and retailers in the country.

The channel arrangement that enables manufacturers to exercise a great deal of control is shown at the right of Figure 13–1. Here, manufacturers sell directly to organizational buyers or ultimate consumers. Although this arrangement is most common in the sale of organizational goods, some consumer goods companies have also pursued this arrangement.

Global Pricing Strategy

In domestic markets, pricing is a complex task. The basic approaches used in price determination in foreign markets are the same as those discussed earlier in the chapter on pricing. However, the pricing task is often more complicated in foreign markets because of additional problems associated with tariffs, antidumping laws, taxes, inflation, and currency conversion.

Import duties are probably the major constraint for global marketers and are encountered in many markets. Management must decide whether import duties will be paid by the firm, by the foreign consumer, or shared by both. This and similar constraints may force the firm to abandon an otherwise desirable pricing strategy or may force the firm out of a market altogether.

Another pricing problem arises because of the rigidity in price structures found in many foreign markets. Many foreign intermediaries are not aggressive in their pricing policies. They often prefer to maintain high unit margins at the expense of low sales volume rather than develop large sales volume by means of lower prices and smaller margins per unit. Many times this rigidity is encouraged by legislation that prevents retailers from cutting prices substantially at their own discretion. These are only a few of the pricing problems encountered by foreign marketers.

Global Advertising and Sales Promotion Strategy

When expanding their operations into the world marketplace, most firms are aware of the language barriers that exist and realize the importance of translating their messages into the proper idiom. However, there are numerous other issues that must be resolved, such as selecting appropriate media and advertising agencies in foreign markets.

There are many problems in selecting media in foreign markets. Often the media that are traditionally used in the domestic market are not available. For example, it was not until recently that national commercial TV became a reality in the former Soviet Union. If media are available, they may be so only on a limited basis or they may not reach the potential buyers. In addition to the problem of availability, other difficulties arise from the lack of accurate media information. There is no rate and data service or media directory that covers all the media available throughout the world. Where data are available, their accuracy is often questionable.

Another important promotion decision that must be made is the type of agency used to prepare and place the firm's advertisements. Along with the growth in multinational product companies, more multinational advertising agencies are available. Among the top 15 global advertising agencies, less than half are U.S. owned. Alliances and takeovers have served to stimulate growth in the formation of global agencies. For the U.S. company, there are two major approaches to choosing an agency. The first is to use a purely local agency in each area where the advertisement is to appear. The rationale for this approach is that a purely local agency employing only local nationals can better adapt the firm's message to the local culture.

Marketing
Highlight 13–4

Checklist of Country Selection Criteria for Companies Considering Investment in Eastern Europe

Overall Economic and Political Conditions

- What is the foreign debt service expense as a percentage of hard currency foreign exchange earnings?
- What is the inflation rate? If hyperinflation exists, are appropriate fiscal and monetary policies being implemented to bring it under control?
- How substantial are raw material reserves that can be converted to hard currency?
- Are state subsidies, cheap credits, and tax concessions for state enterprises being phased out?
- Does the government intend to sell stakes in state enterprises to foreign investors?
- Is there an emerging capital market based on real interest rates?
- What progress is being made toward developing a code of company law?
- Is political decision-making authority centralized or fragmented?
- How rapid and sustainable is continued progress toward democracy and a free market economy? Is there any historical tradition to support such trends?

Climate for Foreign Investment

- What percentage ownership may foreign companies have in joint ventures? Is government approval required, and if so, how long does it take to obtain?
- Is private ownership of property recognized?
- Are intellectual property rights upheld?
- Can foreign investors obtain premises easily? Can they own real estate?
- Can an initial capital investment by a foreign company be held in hard currency?
- Can a foreign investor sell its stake in a joint venture?
- Can hard currency be used to pay for imported raw materials or to repatriate profits?
- What is the tax rate on business enterprise profits?

Market Attractiveness

- What is the sales potential in this country?
- Do the country's geographical location and political relations permit it to serve as a gateway to other East European markets?
- How well developed are the necessary managerial and technical skills?
- How skilled is the labor pool? What are labor costs?
- Can continued supply of the raw materials required for production be assured?
- What is the quality of the transportation and telecommunications infrastructure?
- Will Western executives accept being located in the country?
- To what degree have government officials developed a familiarity with Western business practices?

SOURCE: John A. Quelch, Erich Joachimsthaler, and Jose Luis Nueno, "After the Wall: Marketing Guidelines for Eastern Europe," *Sloan Management Review,* Winter 1991, p. 85.

The other approach is to use either a U.S.–based multinational agency or a multinational agency with U.S. offices to develop and implement the ad campaign. For example, the Coca-Cola Company uses one agency to create ads for the 80 nations in which Diet Coke is marketed. The use of these so-called super agencies is increasing (annual growth rates averaging over 30 percent in the last decade). By using global advertising agencies, companies are able to take advantage of economies of scale and other efficiencies. However, global agencies are not without their critics. Many managers believe that small, local agencies in emerging markets take a more entrepreneurial and fresher approach to advertising than do global agencies. Much discussion has developed over which approach is best, and it appears that both approaches can be used successfully by particular firms.

The use of sales promotion can also lead to opportunities and problems for marketers in foreign markets. Sales promotions often contain certain characteristics that are more attractive than other elements of the promotion mix.[17] In less wealthy countries, consumers tend to be even more interested in saving money through price discounts, sampling, or premiums. Sales promotion can also be used as a strategy for bypassing restrictions on advertising placed by some foreign governments. In addition, sales promotion can be an effective means for reaching people who live in rural locations where media support for advertising is virtually nonexistent.

■ Entry and Growth Strategies for Global Marketing

A major decision facing companies that desire either to enter a foreign market or pursue growth within a specific market relates to the choice of entry or growth strategy. What type of strategy to employ depends on many factors, including the analysis of market opportunities, company capabilities, the degree of marketing involvement and commitment the company is willing to make, and the amount of risk that the company is able to tolerate.[18] A company can decide to (1) make minimal investments of funds and resources by limiting its efforts to exporting, (2) make large initial investments of resources and management effort to try to establish a long-term share of global markets, or (3) take an incremental approach whereby the company starts with a low-risk mode of entry that requires the least financial and other resource commitment and gradually increases its commitment over time. All three approaches can be profitable. In general, there are six ways by which a company can initially enter a global market and, subsequently, pursue growth in the global marketplace:

1. *Exporting.* Exporting occurs when a company produces the product outside the final destination and then ships it there for sale. It is the easiest and most common approach for a company making its first international move. Exporting has two distinct advantages. First, it avoids the cost of establishing manufacturing operations in the host country; second, it may help a firm achieve experience-curve and location economies. By manufacturing the product in a centralized location and exporting it to other national markets, the firm may be able to realize substantial scale economies from its global sales volume. This method is what allowed Sony to dominate the global TV market. The major disadvantages related to exporting include (1) the sometimes higher cost associated with the process; (2) the necessity of the exporting firm to pay import duties or face trade barriers; and (3) the delegation of marketing responsibility for the product to foreign agents who may or may not be dependable.

2. *Licensing.* Companies can grant patent rights, trademark rights, and the right to use technological processes to foreign companies. This is the most common strategy for small and medium-sized companies. The major advantage to licensing is that the firm does not have to bear the development costs and risks associated with opening up a foreign market. In addition, licensing can be an attractive option in unfamiliar or politically volatile markets. The major disadvantages are that (1) the firm does not have tight control over manufacturing, marketing, and strategy that is required for realizing economies of scale; and (2) there is the risk that the licensed technology may be capitalized on by foreign companies. RCA Corporation, for example, once licensed its color TV technology to a number of Japanese firms. These firms quickly assimilated the technology and used it to enter the U.S. market.

3. *Franchising.* Franchising is similar to licensing but tends to involve longer-term commitments. Also, franchising is commonly employed by service as opposed to manufacturing firms. In a franchising agreement, the franchisor sells limited rights to use its brand name in return for a lump sum and share of the franchisee's future profits. In contrast to licensing agreements, the franchisee agrees to abide by strict operating procedures. Advantages and disadvantages associated with franchising are primarily the same as with licensing except to a lesser degree. In many cases, franchising offers an effective mix of centralized and decentralized decision making.

4. *Joint ventures.* A company may decide to share management with one or more collaborating foreign firms. Joint ventures are especially popular in industries that call for large investments, such as natural gas exploration and automobile manufacturing. Control of the joint venture may be split equally, or one party may control decision making. Joint ventures hold several advantages. First, a firm may be able to benefit from a partner's knowledge of the host country's competitive position, culture, language, political systems, and so forth. Second, the firm gains by sharing costs and risks of operating in a foreign market. Third, in many countries, political considerations make joint ventures the only feasible entry mode. Finally, joint ventures allow firms to take advantage of a partner's distribution system, technological know-how, or marketing skills. For example, General Mills teamed up with CPC International in an operation called International Dessert Partners to develop a major baking and dessert-mix business in Latin America. The venture combines General Mills' technology and Betty Crocker dessert products with CPC's marketing and distribution capabilities in Latin America. The major disadvantages associated with joint ventures are that (1) a firm may risk giving up control of proprietary knowledge to its partner, and (2) the firm may lose the tight control over a foreign subsidiary needed to engage in coordinated global attacks against rivals.

5. *Strategic alliances.* Although considered by some to be a form of joint venture, we consider strategic alliances to be a distinct entity for two reasons. First, strategic alliances are normally partnerships entered into by two or more firms to gain a competitive advantage on a worldwide as opposed to local basis. Second, strategic alliances are usually of a much longer-term nature than are joint ventures. In strategic alliances, the partners share long-term goals and pledge almost total cooperation. Strategic alliances can be used to reduce manufacturing costs, accelerate technological diffusion and new product development, and overcome legal and trade barriers.[19] The major disadvantage associated with formation of a strategic alliance is the increased risk for competitive conflict between the partners. Indeed, a recent study showed that strategic alliances have grown at a 25 percent average annual rate, but the median life span of such alliances is only about seven years.[20]

6. *Direct ownership.* Some companies prefer to enter or grow in markets either through establishment of a wholly owned subsidiary or through acquisition. In either case, the firm owns 100 percent of the stock. The advantages to direct ownership are that the firm has (1) complete control over its technology and operations, (2) immediate access to foreign markets, (3) instant credibility and gains in the foreign country when acquisitions are the mode of entry or growth, and (4) the ability to install its own management team. Of course, the primary disadvantages of direct ownership are the huge costs and significant risks associated with this strategy. These problems may more than offset the advantages depending upon the country entered.

Regardless of the choice of methods used to gain entry into and grow within a foreign marketplace, companies must somehow integrate their operations. The complexities involved in operating on a worldwide basis dictate that firms decide on operating strategies. A critical decision that marketing managers must make relates to the extent of adaptation of the marketing mix elements for the foreign country in which the company operates. Depending on the area of the world under consideration and the particular product mix, different degrees of standardization/adaptation of the marketing mix elements may take place. As a guideline, standardization of one or more parts of the marketing mix is a function of many factors that individually and collectively affect companies in their decision making.[21] These factors and their resulting influences are

1. When markets are economically alike, standardization is more practical.
2. When worldwide customers, not countries, are the basis for segmenting markets, a standardization strategy is more effective.
3. The greater the degree of similarity in the markets in terms of customer behavior and lifestyle, the more effective a standardization strategy is.
4. The higher the cultural compatibility of the product across the host countries, the more appropriate is standardization.
5. When a firm's competitive position is similar in different markets, standardization is more practical.
6. When competing against the same adversaries, with similar share position, in different countries, standardization is more appropriate than when competing against purely local companies.
7. Organizational and high-technology products are more suitable for standardization than consumer products.
8. The greater the differences in physical, political, and legal environments between home and host countries, the greater will be the necessary degree of adaptation.
9. The more similar the marketing infrastructure in the home and host countries, the more likely is the effectiveness of standardization.

The decision to adapt or standardize marketing should be made only after a thorough analysis of the product-market mix has been undertaken. The company's end goal is to develop, manufacture, and market the products best suited to the actual and potential needs of the local (wherever that may be) customer and to the social and economic conditions of the marketplace. There can be subtle differences from country to country and from region to region in the ways a product is used and what customers expect from it.

■ Conclusion

The world is truly becoming a global market. Many companies that avoid operating in the global arena are destined for failure. For those willing to undertake the challenges and risks necessary to become multinational corporations, long-term survival and growth are likely outcomes. The purpose of this chapter was to introduce the reader to the opportunities, problems, and challenges involved in global marketing.

■ Additional Readings

Burnstein, Daniel, and Arne de Keigzer. *Big Dragon China's Future: What It Means for Business, the Economy, and the Global Order.* New York: Simon and Schuster, 1998.

Ho, Suk-ching. "The Emergence of Consumer Power in China." *Business Horizons,* September–October 1997, pp. 15–21.

Tong, Lewis. "Consumerism Sweeps the Mainland." *Marketing Management,* Winter 1998, pp. 32–35.

Yoshimura, Noboru, and Philip Anderson. *Inside the Kaisha: Demystifying Japanese Business Behavior.* Boston: Harvard Business School Press, 1997.

Section II

Analyzing Marketing Problems and Cases

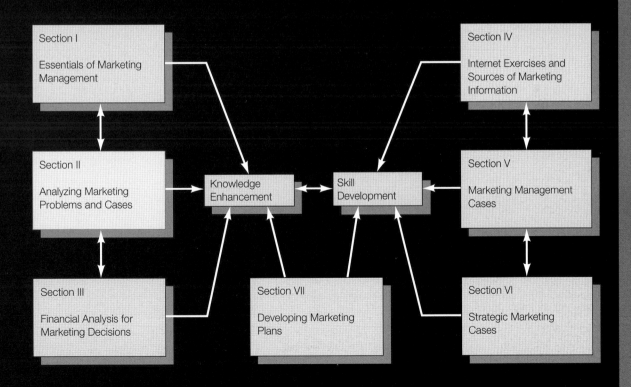

A Case for Case Analysis

Cases assist in bridging the gap between classroom learning and the so-called real world of marketing management. They provide us with an opportunity to develop, sharpen, and test our analytical skills at

- Assessing situations.
- Sorting out and organizing key information.
- Asking the right questions.

- Defining opportunities and problems.
- Identifying and evaluating alternative courses of action.
- Interpreting data.
- Evaluating the results of past strategies.
- Developing and defending new strategies.
- Interacting with other managers.
- Making decisions under conditions of uncertainty.
- Critically evaluating the work of others.
- Responding to criticism.

SOURCE: David W. Cravens and Charles W. Lamb, Jr., *Strategic Marketing: Cases and Applications,* 4th ed. (Burr Ridge, IL: Irwin/McGraw-Hill, 1993), p. 95.

The use of business cases was developed by faculty members of the Harvard Graduate School of Business Administration in the 1920s. Case studies have been widely accepted as one effective way of exposing students to strategic marketing processes.

Basically, cases represent detailed descriptions or reports of business problems. They are often written by a trained observer who was actually involved in the firm or organization and had some dealings with the problems under consideration. Cases generally entail both qualitative and quantitative data, which the student must analyze to determine appropriate alternatives and solutions.

The primary purpose of the case method is to introduce a measure of realism into marketing management education. Rather than emphasizing the teaching of concepts, the case method focuses on application of concepts and sound logic to real-world business problems. In this way, students learn to bridge the gap between abstraction and application and to appreciate the value of both.

The primary purpose of this section is to offer a logical format for the analysis of case problems. Although there is no one format that can be successfully applied to all cases, the following framework is intended to be a logical sequence from which to develop sound analyses. This framework is presented for analysis of comprehensive marketing cases; however, the process should also be useful for shorter marketing cases, incidents, and problems.

◼ A Case Analysis Framework

A basic approach to case analysis involves a four-step process. First, the problem is defined. Second, alternative courses of action are formulated to solve the problem. Third, the alternatives are analyzed in terms of their strengths and weaknesses. And fourth, an alternative is accepted, and a course of action is recommended. This basic approach is quite useful for students well versed in case analysis, particularly for shorter cases or incidents. However, for the newcomer, this framework may be oversimplified. Thus, the following expanded framework and checklists are intended to aid students in becoming proficient in case and problem analysis.

1. Analyze and Record the Current Situation

Whether the analysis of a firm's problems is done by a manager, student, or paid business consultant, the first step is to analyze the current situation. This does not mean writing up a history of the firm but entails the type of analysis described below. This approach is useful not only for getting a better grip on the situation but also for discovering both real and potential problems—central concern of any case analysis.

Phase 1: The Environment.   The first phase in analyzing a marketing problem or case is to consider the environment in which the firm is operating. The environment can be broken down into a number of different components such as the economic, social, political, and legal areas. Any of these may contain threats to a firm's success or opportunities for improving a firm's situation.

Phase 2: The Industry.   The second phase involves analyzing the industry in which the firm operates. A framework provided by Michael Porter includes five competitive forces that need to be considered to do a complete industry analysis.[1] The framework is shown in Figure 1 and includes rivalry among existing competitors, threat of new entrants, and threat of substitute products. In addition, in this framework, buyers and suppliers are included as competitors since they can threaten the profitability of an industry or firm.

While rivalry among existing competitors is an issue in most cases, analysis and strategies for dealing with the other forces can also be critical. This is particularly so when a firm is considering entering a new industry and wants to forecast its potential success. Each of the five competitive forces is discussed below.

■ **Figure 1**
Competitive Forces
in an Industry

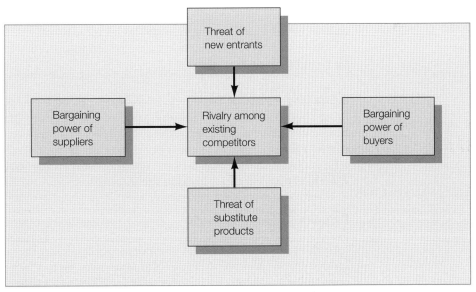

SOURCE: Adapted from Michael E. Porter, "Industry Structure and Competitive Strategy: Keys to Profitability," *Financial Analysts Journal,* July–August 1980, p. 33.

Rivalry among Existing Competitors.   In most cases and business situations a firm needs to consider the current competitors in its industry in order to develop successful strategies. Strategies such as price competition, advertising battles, sales promotion offers, new product introductions, and increased customer service are commonly used to attract customers from competitors.

To fully analyze existing rivalry, it is important to determine which firms are the major competitors and what are their annual sales, market share, growth profile, and strengths and weaknesses. Also, it is useful to analyze their current and past marketing strategies to try to forecast their likely reactions to a change in a competitive firm's strategy. Finally, it is important to consider any trends or changes in government regulation of an industry or changes in technology that could affect the success of a firm's strategy.

Threat of New Entrants.   It is always possible for firms in other industries to try to compete in a new industry. New entrants are more likely in industries that have low entry barriers. *Entry barriers* include such things as a need for large financial resources, high brand equity for existing brands in an industry, or economies of scale obtained by existing firms in an industry. Also, existing firms in an industry may benefit from experience curves; that is, their cumulative experience in producing and marketing a product may reduce their per unit costs below those of inexperienced firms. In general, the higher the entry barriers, the less likely outside firms are to enter an industry. For example, the entry barriers for starting up a new car company are much higher than for starting up an on-line software company.

Threat of Substitute Products.   In a broad sense, all firms in an industry compete with industries producing substitute products. For example, in cultures where bicycles are the major means of transportation, bicycle manufacturers compete with substitute products such as motor scooters and automobiles. Substitutes limit the potential return in an industry by placing a ceiling on the prices a firm in the industry can profitably charge. The more attractive the price-performance alternative offered by substitutes, the tighter the lid on industry profits. For example, the price of candy, such as Raisinets chocolate-covered raisins, may limit the price that can be charged for granola bars.

Bargaining Power of Suppliers.   Suppliers can be a competitive threat in an industry because they can raise the price of raw materials or reduce their quality. Powerful suppliers can reduce the profitability of an industry or firm if companies cannot raise their prices to cover price increases by suppliers. Also, suppliers may be a threat because they may forward integrate into an industry by purchasing a firm that they supply or other firms in the industry.

Bargaining Power of Buyers.   Buyers can compete with an industry by forcing prices down, bargaining for higher quality or more services, and playing competitors off against each other. All of these tactics can lower the profitability of a firm or industry. For example, because Wal-Mart sells such a large percentage of many companies' products, it can negotiate for lower prices than smaller retailers can. Also, buyers may be a threat because they may backward integrate into an industry by purchasing firms that supply them or other firms in the industry.

Phase 3: The Firm.   The third phase involves analysis of the firm itself not only in comparison with the industry and industry averages but also internally in terms of both quantitative and qualitative data. Key areas of concern at this stage are such factors as objectives, constraints, management philosophy, financial condition, and the organizational structure and culture of the firm.

Phase 4: The Marketing Strategy.   Although there may be internal personnel or structural problems in the marketing department that need examination, typically an analysis of the current marketing strategy is the next phase. In this phase, the objectives of the marketing department are analyzed in comparison with those of the firm in terms of agreement, soundness, and attainability. Each element of the marketing mix as well as other areas, like marketing research and information systems, is analyzed in terms of whether it is internally consistent, synchronized with the goals of the department and firm, and focused on specific target markets. Although cases often are labeled in terms of their primary emphasis, such as "pricing" or "advertising," it is important to analyze the marketing strategy and entire marketing mix, since a change in one element will usually affect the entire marketing program.

In performing the analysis of the current situation, the data should be analyzed carefully to extract the relevant from the superfluous. Many cases contain information that is not relevant to the problem; it is the analyst's job to discard this information to get a clearer picture of the current situation. As the analysis proceeds, a watchful eye must be kept on each phase to determine (1) symptoms of problems; (2) current problems; and (3) potential problems. Symptoms of problems are indicators of a problem but are not problems in and of themselves. For example, a symptom of a problem may be a decline in sales in a particular sales territory. However, the problem is the root cause of the decline in sales—perhaps the field representative quit making sales calls and is relying on phone orders only.

The following is a checklist of the types of questions that should be asked when performing the analysis of the current situation.

Checklist for Analyzing the Current Situation
Phase 1: The environment
1. What is the state of the economy and are there any trends that could affect the industry, firm, or marketing strategy?
2. What are current trends in cultural and social values and how do these affect the industry, firm, or marketing strategy?
3. What are current political values and trends and how do they affect the industry, firm, or marketing strategy?
4. Is there any current or pending federal, state, or local legislation that could change the industry, firm, or marketing strategy?
5. Overall, are there any threats or opportunities in the environment that could influence the industry, firm, or marketing strategy?

Phase 2: The industry
1. What industry is the firm in?
2. Which firms are the major competitors in the industry and what is their annual sales, market share, and growth profile?
3. What strategies have competitors in the industry been using, and what has been their success with them?

Marketing
Highlight 2

What Does Case "Analysis" Mean?

A common criticism of prepared cases goes something like this: "You repeated an awful lot of case material, but you really didn't analyze the case." Yet, at the same time, it is difficult to verbalize exactly what *analysis* means—that is, "I can't explain exactly what it is, but I know it when I see it!"

This is a common problem since the term *analysis* has many definitions and means different things in different contexts. In terms of case analysis, one thing that is clear is that analysis means going beyond simply describing the case information. It includes determining the implications of the case information for developing strategy. This determination may involve careful financial analysis of sales and profit data or thoughtful interpretation of the text of the case.

One way of thinking about analysis involves a series of three steps: synthesis, generalizations, and implications. A brief example of this process follows.

The high growth rate of frozen pizza sales has attracted a number of large food processors, including Pillsbury (Totino's), Quaker Oats (Celeste), American Home Products (Chef Boy-ar-dee), Nestlé (Stouffer's), General Mills (Saluto), and H. J. Heinz (La Pizzeria). The major independents are Jeno's, Tony's, and John's. Jeno's and Totino's are the market leaders, with market shares of about 19 percent each. Celeste and Tony's have about 8 to 9 percent each, and the others have about 5 percent or less.

The frozen pizza market is a highly competitive and highly fragmented market.

In markets such as this, attempts to gain market share through lower consumer prices or heavy advertising are likely to be quickly copied by competitors and thus not be very effective.

Lowering consumer prices or spending more on advertising are likely to be poor strategies. Perhaps increasing freezer space in retail outlets could be effective (this might be obtained through trade discounts). A superior product, for example, better-tasting pizza, microwave pizza, or increasing geographic coverage of the market, may be better strategies for obtaining market share.

Note that none of the three analysis steps includes any repetition of the case material. Rather, they involve abstracting a meaning of the information and, by pairing it with marketing principles, coming up with the strategic implications of the information.

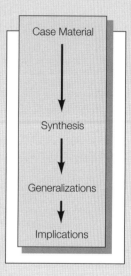

Case Material

↓

Synthesis

↓

Generalizations

↓

Implications

4. What are the relative strengths and weaknesses of competitors in the industry?
5. Is there a threat of new competitors coming into the industry, and what are the major entry barriers?
6. Are there any substitute products for the industry, and what are their advantages and disadvantages compared to this industry's products?
7. How much bargaining power do suppliers have in this industry, and what is its impact on the firm and industry profits?
8. How much bargaining power do buyers have in this industry, and what is its impact on the firm and industry profits?

Phase 3: The firm

1. What are the objectives of the firm? Are they clearly stated? Attainable?
2. What are the strengths of the firm? Managerial expertise? Financial? Copyrights or patents?
3. What are the constraints and weaknesses of the firm?
4. Are there any real or potential sources of dysfunctional conflict in the structure of the firm?
5. How is the marketing department structured in the firm?

Phase 4: The marketing strategy

1. What are the objectives of the marketing strategy? Are they clearly stated? Are they consistent with the objectives of the firm? Is the entire marketing mix structured to meet these objectives?

2. What marketing concepts are at issue in the current strategy? Is the marketing strategy well planned and laid out? Is the strategy consistent with sound marketing principles? If the strategy takes exception to marketing principles, is there a good reason for it?

3. To what target market is the strategy directed? Is it well defined? Is the market large enough to be profitably served? Does the market have long-run potential?

4. What competitive advantage does the marketing strategy offer? If none, what can be done to gain a competitive advantage in the marketplace?

5. What products are being sold? What is the width, depth, and consistency of the firm's product lines? Does the firm need new products to fill out its product line? Should any product be deleted? What is the profitability of the various products?

6. What promotion mix is being used? Is promotion consistent with the products and product images? What could be done to improve the promotion mix?

7. What channels of distribution are being used? Do they deliver the product at the right time and right place to meet customer needs? Are the channels typical of those used in the industry? Could channels be made more efficient?

8. What pricing strategies are being used? How do prices compare with similar products of other firms? How are prices determined?

9. Are marketing research and information systematically integrated into the marketing strategy? Is the overall marketing strategy internally consistent?

The relevant information from this preliminary analysis is now formalized and recorded. At this point the analyst must be mindful of the difference between facts and opinions. Facts are objective statements, such as financial data, whereas opinions are subjective interpretations of facts or situations. The analyst must make certain not to place too much emphasis on opinions and to carefully consider any variables that may bias such opinions.

Regardless of how much information is contained in the case or how much additional information is collected, the analyst usually finds that it is impossible to specify a complete framework for the current situation. At this point, assumptions must be made. Clearly, since each analyst may make different assumptions, it is critical that assumptions be explicitly stated. When presenting a case, the analyst may wish to distribute copies of the assumption list to all class members. In this way, confusion is avoided in terms of how the analyst perceives the current situation, and others can evaluate the reasonableness and necessity of the assumptions.

2. Analyze and Record Problems and Their Core Elements

After careful analysis, problems and their core elements should be explicitly stated and listed in order of importance. Finding and recording problems and their core elements can be difficult. It is not uncommon on reading a case for the first time for the student to view the case as a description of a situation in which there are no problems. However, careful analysis should reveal symptoms, which lead to problem recognition.

Recognizing and recording problems and their core elements is most critical for a meaningful case analysis. Obviously, if the root problems are not explicitly stated and understood, the remainder of the case analysis has little merit, since the true issues are not being dealt with. The following checklist of questions is designed to assist in performing this step of the analysis.

Marketing
Highlight 3

Understanding the Current Situation through SWOT Analysis

A useful approach for gaining an understanding of the situation an organization is facing at a particular time is called *SWOT analysis*. SWOT stands for the organization's *s*trengths and *w*eaknesses and the *o*pportunities and *t*hreats it faces in the environment. Below are some issues an analyst should address in performing a SWOT analysis.

Potential Internal Strengths

- Core competencies in key areas.
- Adequate financial resources.
- Well thought of by buyers.
- An acknowledged market leader.
- Well-conceived functional area strategies.
- Access to economies of scale.
- Insulated (at least somewhat) from strong competitive pressures.
- Proprietary technology.
- Cost advantages.
- Better advertising campaigns.
- Product innovation skills.
- Proven management.
- Ahead on experience curve.
- Better manufacturing capability.
- Superior technological skills.
- Other?

Potential External Opportunities

- Serve additional customer groups.
- Enter new markets or segments.
- Expand product line to meet broader range of customer needs.
- Diversify into related products.

- Vertical integration (forward or backward).
- Falling trade barriers in attractive foreign markets.
- Complacency among rival firms.
- Faster market growth.
- Other?

Potential Internal Weaknesses

- No clear strategic direction.
- Obsolete facilities.
- Subpar profitability because . . .
- Lack of managerial depth and talent.
- Missing some key skills or competencies.
- Poor track record in implementing strategy.
- Plagued with internal operating problems.
- Falling behind in R&D.
- Too narrow a product line.
- Weak market image.
- Weak distribution network.
- Below-average marketing skills.
- Unable to finance needed changes in strategy.
- Higher overall unit costs relative to key competitors.
- Other?

Potential External Threats

- Entry of lower-cost foreign competitors.
- Rising sales of substitute products.
- Slower market growth.
- Adverse shifts in foreign exchange rates and trade policies of foreign governments.
- Costly regulatory requirements.
- Vulnerability to recession and business cycle.
- Growing bargaining power of customers or suppliers.
- Changing buyer needs and tastes.
- Adverse demographic changes.
- Other?

SOURCE: Adapted from Arthur A. Thompson, Jr., and A. J. Strickland III, *Strategic Management: Concepts and Cases,* 6th ed. (Burr Ridge, IL: Irwin/McGraw-Hill, 1992), p. 88. Reprinted by permission.

Checklist for Analyzing Problems and Their Core Elements

1. What is the primary problem in the case? What are the secondary problems?
2. What proof exists that these are the central issues? How much of this proof is based on facts? On opinions? On assumptions?
3. What symptoms are there that suggest these are the real problems in the case?
4. How are the problems, as defined, related? Are they independent, or are they the result of a deeper problem?
5. What are the ramifications of these problems in the short run? In the long run?

3. Formulate, Evaluate, and Record Alternative Courses of Action

This step is concerned with the question of what can be done to resolve the problem defined in the previous step. Generally, a number of alternative courses of action are available that could potentially help alleviate the problem condition. Three to seven is usually a reasonable number of alternatives to work with. Another approach is to brainstorm as many alternatives as possible initially and then reduce the list to a workable number.

Sound logic and reasoning are very important in this step. It is critical to avoid alternatives that could potentially alleviate the problem, but would create a greater new problem or require greater resources than the firm has at its disposal.

After serious analysis and listing of a number of alternatives, the next task is to evaluate them in terms of their costs and benefits. Costs are any output or effort the firm must exert to implement the alternative. Benefits are any input or value received by the firm. Costs to be considered are time, money, other resources, and opportunity costs; benefits are such things as sales, profits, brand equity, and customer satisfaction. The following checklist provides a guideline of questions to be used when performing this phase of the analysis.

Checklist for Formulating and Evaluating Alternative Courses of Action

1. What possible alternatives exist for solving the firm's problems?
2. What limits are there on the possible alternatives? Competence? Resources? Management preference? Ethical responsibility? Legal restrictions?
3. What major alternatives are now available to the firm? What marketing concepts are involved that affect these alternatives?
4. Are the listed alternatives reasonable, given the firm's situation? Are they logical? Are the alternatives consistent with the goals of the marketing program? Are they consistent with the firm's objectives?
5. What are the financial and other costs of each alternative? What are the benefits? What are the advantages and disadvantages of each alternative?
6. Which alternative best solves the problem and minimizes the creation of new problems, given the above constraints?

4. Select and Record the Chosen Alternative and Implementation Details

In light of the previous analysis, the alternative is now selected that best solves the problem with a minimum creation of new problems. It is important to record the logic and reasoning that precipitated the selection of a particular alternative. This includes articulating not only why the alternative was selected but also why the other alternatives were not selected.

No analysis is complete without an action-oriented decision and plan for implementing the decision. The accompanying checklist indicates the type of questions that should be answered in this stage of analysis.

Checklist for Selecting and Implementing the Chosen Alternative

1. What must be done to implement the alternative?
2. What personnel will be involved? What are the responsibilities of each?
3. When and where will the alternative be implemented?
4. What will be the probable outcome?
5. How will the success or failure of the alternative be measured?

■ Pitfalls to Avoid in Case Analysis

Below is a summary of some of the most common errors analysts make when analyzing cases. When evaluating your analysis or those of others, this list provides a useful guide for spotting potential shortcomings.

1. *Inadequate definition of the problem.* By far the most common error made in case analysis is attempting to recommend courses of action without first adequately defining or understanding the core problems. Whether presented orally or in a written report, a case analysis must begin with a focus on the central issues and problems represented in the case situation. Closely related is the error of analyzing symptoms without determining the root problem.

2. *The search for "the answer."* In case analysis, there are usually no clear-cut solutions. Keep in mind that the objective of case studies is learning through discussion and exploration. There is usually no one "official" or "correct" answer to a case. Rather, there are usually several reasonable alternative solutions.

3. *Not enough information.* Analysts often complain there is not enough information in some cases to make a good decision. However, there is justification for not presenting *all* of the information in a case. As in real life, a marketing manager or consultant seldom has all the information necessary to make an optimal decision. Thus, reasonable assumptions have to be made, and the challenge is to find intelligent solutions in spite of the limited information.

4. *Use of generalities.* In analyzing cases, specific recommendations are necessarily not generalities. For example, a suggestion to increase the price is a generality; a suggestion to increase the price by $1.07 is a specific.

5. *A different situation.* Considerable time and effort are sometimes exerted by analysts contending that "If the situation were different, I'd know what course of action to take" or "If the marketing manager hadn't already fouled things up so badly, the firm wouldn't have a problem." Such reasoning ignores the fact that the events in the case have already happened and cannot be changed. Even though analysis or criticism of past events is necessary in diagnosing the problem, in the end, the present situation must be addressed and decisions must be made based on the given situations.

6. *Narrow vision analysis.* Although cases are often labeled as a specific type of case, such as "pricing," "product," and so forth, this does not mean that other marketing variables should be ignored. Too often analysts ignore the effects that a change in one marketing element will have on the others.

7. *Realism.* Too often analysts become so focused on solving a particular problem that their solutions become totally unrealistic. For instance, suggesting a $1 million advertising program for a firm with a capital structure of $50,000 is an unrealistic solution.

8. *The marketing research solution.* A quite common but unsatisfactory solution to case problems is marketing research; for example, "The firm should do this or that type of marketing research to find a solution to its problem." Although marketing research may be helpful as an intermediary step in some cases, marketing research does not solve problems or make decisions. In cases where marketing research is recommended, the cost and potential benefits should be fully specified in the case analysis.

9. *Rehashing the case material.* Analysts sometimes spend considerable effort rewriting a two- or three-page history of the firm as presented in the case. This is unnecessary since the instructor and other analysts are already familiar with this information.

10. *Premature conclusions.* Analysts sometimes jump to premature conclusions instead of waiting until their analysis is completed. Too many analysts jump to conclusions upon first reading the case and then proceed to interpret everything in the case as justifying their conclusions, even factors logically against it.

■ Communicating Case Analyses

The final concern in case analysis deals with communicating the results of the analysis. The most comprehensive analysis has little value if it is not communicated effectively. There are two primary media through which case analyses are communicated—the written report and the oral presentation.

The Written Report

Since the structure of the written report will vary by the type of case analyzed, the purpose of this section is not to present a "one and only" way of writing up a case. The purpose of this section is to present some useful generalizations to aid analysts in case write-ups.

A good written report starts with an outline that organizes the structure of the analysis in a logical manner. The following is a general outline for a marketing case report.

    I. *Title Page*
    II. *Table of Contents*
    III. *Executive Summary* (one- to two-page summary of the analysis and recommendations)
    IV. *Situation Analysis*
        A. Environment
           1. Economic conditions and trends
           2. Cultural and social values and trends
           3. Political and legal issues
           4. Summary of environmental opportunities and threats
           5. Implications for strategy development

    B. Industry
- **1.** Classification and definition of industry
- **2.** Analysis of existing competitors
- **3.** Analysis of potential new entrants
- **4.** Analysis of substitute products
- **5.** Analysis of suppliers
- **6.** Analysis of buyers
- **7.** Summary of industry opportunities and threats
- **8.** Implications for strategy development

    C. Firm
- **1.** Objectives and constraints
- **2.** Financial condition
- **3.** Management philosophy
- **4.** Organizational structure
- **5.** Organizational culture
- **6.** Summary of the firm's strengths and weaknesses
- **7.** Implications for strategy development

    D. Marketing strategy
- **1.** Objectives and constraints
- **2.** Analysis of sales, profits, and market share
- **3.** Analysis of target market(s)
- **4.** Analysis of marketing mix variables
- **5.** Summary of marketing strategy's strengths and weaknesses
- **6.** Implications for strategy development

V. *Problems Found in Situation Analysis*

    A. Statement of primary problem(s)
- **1.** Evidence of problem(s)
- **2.** Effects of problem(s)

    B. Statement of secondary problem(s)
- **1.** Evidence of problem(s)
- **2.** Effects of problem(s)

VI. *Strategic Alternatives for Solving Problems*

    A. Description of strategic alternative 1
- **1.** Benefits of alternative 1
- **2.** Costs of alternative 1

    B. Description of strategic alternative 2
- **1.** Benefits of alternative 2
- **2.** Costs of alternative 2

    C. Description of strategic alternative 3
- **1.** Benefits of alternative 3
- **2.** Costs of alternative 3

VII. *Selection of Strategic Alternative and Implementation*

    A. Statement of selected strategy

    B. Justification for selection of strategy

    C. Description of implementation of strategy

VIII. *Summary*

IX. *Appendices*

    A. Financial analysis

    B. Technical analysis

Writing the case report entails filling out the details of the outline in prose form. Of course, not every case report requires all the headings listed above and different headings may be required for some cases. Like any other skill, it takes practice to determine the appropriate headings and approach for writing up particular cases. However, good case reports flow logically from topic to topic, are clearly written, are based on solid situation analysis, and demonstrate sound strategic thinking.

The Oral Presentation

Case analyses are often presented by an individual or team. As with the written report, a good outline is critical, and it is often useful to hand out the outline to each class member. Although there is no best way to present a case or to divide responsibility between team members, simply reading the written report is unacceptable since it encourages boredom and interferes with all-important class discussion.

The use of visual aids can be quite helpful in presenting class analyses. However, simply presenting financial statements contained in the case is a poor use of visual media. On the other hand, graphs of sales and profit curves can be more easily interpreted and can be quite useful for making specific points.

Oral presentation of cases is particularly helpful to analysts for learning the skill of speaking to a group. In particular, the ability to handle objections and disagreements without antagonizing others is a skill worth developing.

■ Conclusion

From the discussion it should be obvious that good case analyses require a major commitment of time and effort. Individuals must be highly motivated and willing to get involved in the analysis and discussion if they expect to learn and succeed in a course where cases are utilized. Persons with only passive interest who perform "night before" analyses cheat themselves out of valuable learning experiences that can aid them in their careers.

■ Additional Readings

Bernhardt, Kenneth L., and Thomas C. Kinnear. *Cases in Marketing Management*. 6th ed. Burr Ridge, IL: Irwin/McGraw-Hill, 1994, chap. 2.

Cravens, David W., and Charles W. Lamb, Jr. *Strategic Marketing Management Cases*. 4th ed. Burr Ridge, IL: Irwin/McGraw-Hill, 1993, pp. 94–108.

O'Dell, William F.; Andrew C. Ruppel; Robert H. Trent; and William J. Kehoe. *Marketing Decision Making: Analytic Framework and Cases*. 4th ed. Cincinnati: South-Western Publishing, 1988, chaps. 1–5.

Section III

Financial Analysis for Marketing Decisions

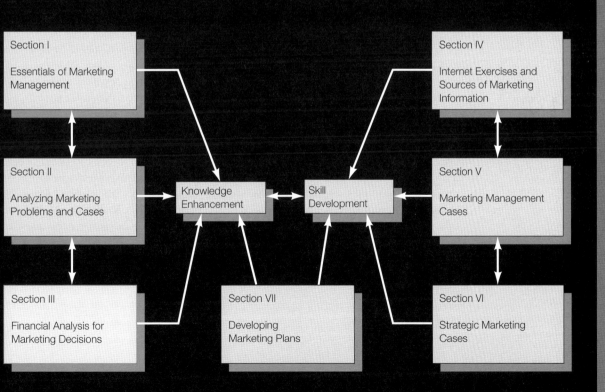

Section I

Essentials of Marketing Management

Section II

Analyzing Marketing Problems and Cases

Section III

Financial Analysis for Marketing Decisions

Knowledge Enhancement

Section VII

Developing Marketing Plans

Skill Development

Section IV

Internet Exercises and Sources of Marketing Information

Section V

Marketing Management Cases

Section VI

Strategic Marketing Cases

■ Financial Analysis

Financial analysis is an important aspect of strategic marketing planning and should be an integral part of marketing problem and case analysis. In this section, we present several financial tools that are useful for analyzing marketing problems and cases. First, we investigate break-even analysis, which is concerned with determining the number of units or dollar sales, or both, necessary to break even on a project or to obtain a given level of profits. Second, we illustrate net present value analysis, which is a somewhat more sophisticated tool for analyzing marketing alternatives. Finally, we investigate ratio analysis, which can be a useful tool for determining the financial condition of the firm, including its ability to invest in a new or modified marketing program.

Break-Even Analysis

Break-even analysis is a common tool for investigating the potential profitability of a marketing alternative. The *break-even point* is that level of sales in either units or sales dollars at which a firm covers all of its costs. In other words, it is the level at which total sales revenue just equals the total costs necessary to achieve these sales.

To compute the break-even point, an analyst must have or be able to obtain three values. First, the analyst needs to know the selling price per unit of the product (SP). For example, suppose the Ajax Company plans to sell its new electric car through its own dealerships at a retail price of $5,000. Second, the analyst needs to know the level of fixed costs (FC). Fixed costs are all costs relevant to the project that do not change regardless of how many units are produced or sold. For instance, whether Ajax produces and sells 1 or 100,000 cars, Ajax executives will receive their salaries, land must be purchased for a plant, a plant must be constructed, and machinery must be purchased. Other fixed costs include such things as interest, lease payments, and sinking fund payments. Suppose Ajax has totaled all of its fixed costs and the sum is $1.5 million. Third, the analyst must know the variable costs per unit produced (VC). As the name implies, variable costs are those that vary directly with the number of units produced. For example, for each car Ajax produces, there are costs for raw materials and components to build the car, such as batteries, electric motors, steel bodies and tires; there are labor costs for operating employees; there are machine costs, such as electricity and welding rods. Suppose these are totaled by Ajax, and the variable costs for each car produced equal $3,500. With this information, the analyst can now determine the break-even point, which is the number of units that must be sold to just cover the cost of producing the cars. The break-even point is determined by dividing total fixed costs by the *contribution margin*. The contribution margin is simply the difference between the selling price per unit (SP) and variable costs per unit (VC). Algebraically,

$$BEP_{(in\ units)} = \frac{Total\ fixed\ costs}{Contribution\ margin}$$

$$= \frac{FC}{SP - VC}$$

Substituting the Ajax estimates,

$$BEP_{(in\ units)} = \frac{1,500,000}{5,000 - 3,500}$$

$$= \frac{1,500,000}{1,500}$$

$$= 1,000\ units$$

In other words, the Ajax Company must sell 1,000 cars to just break even (i.e., for total sales revenue to cover total costs).

Alternatively, the analyst may want to know the break-even point in terms of dollar sales volume. Of course, if the preceding analysis has been done, one could simply multiply the $BEP_{(in\ units)}$ times the selling price to determine the break-even sales volume (i.e., 1,000 units $\times$ \$5,000/unit = \$5 million). However, the $BEP_{(in\ dollars)}$ can be computed directly, using the formula below:

$$BEP_{(in\ dollars)} = \frac{FC}{1 - \dfrac{VC}{SP}}$$

$$= \frac{1,500,000}{1 - \dfrac{3,500}{5,000}}$$

$$= \frac{1,500,000}{1 - .7}$$

$$= \$5,000,000$$

Thus, Ajax must produce and sell 1,000 cars, which equals \$5 million sales, to break even. Of course, firms do not want to just break even but want to make a profit. The logic of break-even analysis can easily be extended to include profits (P). Suppose Ajax decided that a 20 percent return on fixed costs would make the project worth the investment. Thus, Ajax would need 20% $\times$ \$1,500,000 = \$300,000 before-tax profit. To calculate how many units Ajax must sell to achieve this level of profits, the profit figure (P) is added to fixed costs in the above formulas. (We will label the break-even point as BEP' to show that we are now computing unit and sales levels to obtain a given profit level.) In the Ajax example:

$$BEP'_{(in\ units)} = \frac{FC + P}{SP - VC}$$

$$= \frac{1,500,000 + 300,000}{5,000 - 3,500}$$

$$= \frac{1,800,000}{1,500}$$

$$= 1,200\ units$$

In terms of dollars,

$$BEP'_{(in\ dollars)} = \frac{FC + P}{1 - \dfrac{VC}{SP}}$$

$$= \frac{1{,}500{,}000 + 300{,}000}{1 - \dfrac{3{,}500}{5{,}000}}$$

$$= \frac{1{,}800{,}000}{1 - .7}$$

$$= \$6{,}000{,}000$$

Thus, Ajax must produce and sell 1,200 cars (sales volume of $6 million) to obtain a 20 percent return on fixed costs. Analysis must now be directed at determining whether a given marketing plan can be expected to produce sales of at least this level. If the answer is yes, the project would appear to be worth investing in. If not, Ajax should seek other opportunities.

Net Present Value Analysis

The profit-oriented marketing manager must understand that the capital invested in new products has a cost. It is a basic principle in business that whoever wishes to use capital must pay for its use. Dollars invested in new products could be diverted to other uses—to pay off debts, pay dividends to stockholders, or buy U.S. Treasury bonds that would yield economic benefits to the corporation. If, on the other hand, all of the dollars used to finance a new product have to be borrowed from lenders outside the corporation, interest has to be paid on the loan.

One of the best ways to analyze the financial aspects of a marketing alternative is *net present value* analysis. This method employs a discounted cash flow, which takes into account the time value of money and its price to the borrower. The following example will illustrate this method.

To compute the net present value of an investment proposal, the cost of capital must be estimated. The cost of capital can be defined as the required rate of return on an investment that would leave the owners of the firm as well off as if the project was not undertaken. Thus, it is the minimum percentage return on investment that a project must make to be worth undertaking. There are many methods of estimating the cost of capital. However, since these methods are not the concern of this text, we will simply assume that the cost of capital for the Ajax Corporation has been determined to be 10 percent.[1] Again, it should be noted that once the cost of capital is determined, it becomes the minimum rate of return required for an investment—a type of cutoff point. However, some firms in selecting their new product investments select a minimum rate of return that is above the cost of capital figure to allow for errors in judgment or measurement.

The Ajax Corporation is considering a proposal to market instant developing movie film. After conducting considerable marketing research, sales were projected to be $1 million per year. In addition, the finance department compiled the following information concerning the projects:

New equipment needed	$700,000
Useful life of equipment	10 years
Depreciation	10% per year
Salvage value	$100,000
Cost of goods and expenses	$700,000 per year
Cost of capital	10%
Tax rate	50%

To compute the net present value of this project, the net cash flow for each year of the project must first be determined. This can be done in four steps:

1. Sales − Cost of goods and expenses = Gross income or

$$\$1,000,000 - 700,000 = \$300,000$$

2. Gross income − Depreciation = Taxable income or

$$\$300,000 - (10\% \times 600,000) = \$240,000$$

3. Taxable income − Tax = Net income or

$$\$240,000 - (50\% \times 240,000) = \$120,000$$

4. Net income + Depreciation = Net cash flow or

$$\$120,000 + 60,000 = \$180,000 \text{ per year}$$

Since the cost of capital is 10 percent, this figure is used to discount the net cash flows for each year. To illustrate, the $180,000 received at the end of the first year would be discounted by the factor $1/(1 + 0.10)$, which would be $180,000 \times 0.9091$ = $163,638; the $180,000 received at the end of the second year would be discounted by the factor $1/(1 + 0.10)^2$ which would be $180,000 \times 0.8264 = \$148,752$, and so on. (Most finance textbooks have present value tables that can be used to simplify the computations.) The table that follows shows the present value computations for the 10-year project. It should be noted that the net cash flow for year 10 is $280,000 since there is an additional $100,000 inflow from salvage value.

Year	Net Cash Flow	0.10 Discount Factor	Present Value
1	$ 180,000	0.9091	$ 163,638
2	180,000	0.8264	148,752
3	180,000	0.7513	135,234
4	180,000	0.6830	122,940
5	180,000	0.6209	111,762
6	180,000	0.5645	101,610
7	180,000	0.5132	92,376
8	180,000	0.4665	83,970
9	180,000	0.4241	76,338
10	280,000	0.3855	107,940
Total	$1,900,000		$1,144,560

Marketing
Highlight 1

Selected Present Value Discount Factors

Years	8%	10%	12%	14%	16%	18%
1	.9259	.9091	.8929	.8772	.8621	.8475
2	.8573	.8264	.7972	.7695	.7432	.7182
3	.7938	.7513	.7118	.6750	.6407	.6086
4	.7350	.6830	.6355	.5921	.5523	.5158
5	.6806	.6209	.5674	.5194	.4761	.4371
6	.6302	.5645	.5066	.4556	.4104	.3704
7	.5835	.5132	.4523	.3996	.3538	.3139
8	.5403	.4665	.4039	.3506	.3050	.2660
9	.5002	.4241	.3606	.3075	.2630	.2255
10	.4632	.3855	.3220	.2697	.2267	.1911

Thus, at a discount rate of 10 percent, the present value of the net cash flow from new product investment is greater than the $700,000 outlay required, and so the decision can be considered profitable by this standard. Here the net present value is $444,560, which is the difference between the $700,000 investment outlay and the $1,144,560 discounted cash flow. The *present value ratio* is nothing more than the present value of the net cash flow divided by the cash investment. If this ratio is 1 or larger than 1, the project would be profitable for the firm to invest in.

There are many other measures of investment worth, but only one additional method will be discussed. It is the very popular and easily understood payback method. *Payback* refers to the amount of time required to pay back the original outlay from the cash flows. Staying with the example, the project is expected to produce a stream of cash proceeds that is constant from year to year, so the payback period can be determined by dividing the investment outlay by this annual cash flow. Dividing $700,000 by $180,000, the payback period is approximately 3.9 years. Firms often set a maximum payback period before a project will be accepted. For example, many firms refuse to take on a project if the payback period exceeds three years.

This example should illustrate the difficulty in evaluating marketing investments from a profitability or economic worth standpoint. The most challenging problem is that of developing accurate cash flow estimates because there are many possible alternatives, such as price of the product and channels of distribution, and the consequences of each alternative must be forecast in terms of sales volumes, selling costs, and other expenses. In spite of all the problems, management must evaluate the economic worth of new product and other decisions, not only to reduce some of the guesswork and ambiguity surrounding marketing strategy development but also to reinforce the objective of making profits.

Ratio Analysis

Firms' income statements and balance sheets provide a wealth of information that is useful for developing marketing strategies. Frequently, this information is included in marketing cases, yet analysts often have no convenient way of interpreting the financial position of the firm to make sound marketing decisions. Ratio analysis provides the analyst an easy and efficient method for investigating a firm's financial position by comparing the firm's ratios across time or with ratios of similar firms in the industry or with industry averages.

Ratio analysis involves four basic steps:

1. Choose the appropriate ratios.
2. Compute the ratios.
3. Compare the ratios.
4. Check for problems or opportunities.

1. Choose the Appropriate Ratios. The five basic types of financial ratios are (1) liquidity ratios; (2) asset management ratios; (3) profitability ratios; (4) debt management ratios; and (5) market value ratios.[2] While calculating ratios of all five types is useful, liquidity, asset management, and profitability ratios provide information that is most directly relevant for marketing decision making. Although many ratios can be calculated in each of these groups, we have selected two of the most commonly used and readily available ratios in each group to illustrate the process.

Liquidity Ratios. One of the first considerations in analyzing a marketing problem is the liquidity of the firm. *Liquidity* refers to the ability of the firm to pay its short-term obligations. If a firm cannot meet its short-term obligations, there is little that can be done until this problem is resolved. Simply stated, recommendations to increase advertising, to do marketing research, or to develop new products are of little value if the firm is about to go bankrupt.

The two most commonly used ratios for investigating liquidity are the *current ratio* and the *quick ratio* (or "acid test"). The current ratio is determined by dividing current assets by current liabilities and is a measure of the overall ability of the firm to meet its current obligations. A common rule of thumb is that current ratio should be about 2:1.

The quick ratio is determined by subtracting inventory from current assets and dividing the remainder by current liabilities. Since inventory is the least liquid current asset, the quick ratio deals with assets that are most readily available for meeting short-term (one-year) obligations. A common rule of thumb is that the quick ratio should be at least 1:1.

Asset Management Ratios.   Asset management ratios investigate how well the firm handles its assets. For marketing problems, two of the most useful asset management ratios are concerned with *inventory turnover* and *total asset utilization*. The inventory turnover ratio is determined by dividing sales by inventories.[3] If the firm is not turning its inventory over as rapidly as other firms, it suggests that too much money is being tied up in unproductive or obsolete inventory. In addition, if the firm's turnover ratio is decreasing over time, it suggests that there may be a problem in the marketing plan, since inventory is not being sold as rapidly as it had been in the past. One problem with this ratio is that, since sales usually are recorded at market prices and inventory usually is recorded at cost, the ratio may overstate turnover. Thus, some analysts prefer to use cost of sales rather than sales in computing turnover. We will use cost of sales in our analysis.

A second useful asset management ratio is total asset utilization. It is calculated by dividing sales by total assets and is a measure of how productively the firm's assets have been used to generate sales. If this ratio is well below industry figures, it suggests that the firm's marketing strategies are less effective than those of competitors or that some unproductive assets need to be eliminated.

Profitability Ratios.   Profitability is a major goal of marketing and is an important measure of the quality of a firm's marketing strategies. Two key profitability ratios are *profit margin on sales* and *return on total assets*. Profit margin on sales is determined by dividing profit before tax by sales. Serious questions about the firm and marketing plan should be raised if profit margin on sales is declining across time or is well below other firms in the industry. Return on total assets is determined by dividing profit before tax by total assets. This ratio is the return on the investment for the entire firm.

2. Compute the Ratios.   The next step in ratio analysis is to compute the ratios. Figure 1 presents the balance sheet and income statement for the Ajax Home Computer Company. These six ratios can be calculated from the Ajax balance sheet and income statement as follows:

Liquidity ratios:

$$\text{Current ratio} = \frac{\text{Current assets}}{\text{Current liabilities}} = \frac{700}{315} = 2.2$$

$$\text{Quick ratio} = \frac{\text{Current assets} - \text{Inventory}}{\text{Current liabilities}} = \frac{270}{315} = .86$$

Asset management ratios:

$$\text{Inventory turnover} = \frac{\text{Cost of sales}}{\text{Inventory}} = \frac{2,780}{430} = 6.5$$

$$\text{Total asset utilization} = \frac{\text{Sales}}{\text{Total assets}} = \frac{3,600}{2,400} = 1.5$$

Profitability ratios:

$$\text{Profit margin on sales} = \frac{\text{Profit before tax}}{\text{Sales}} = \frac{300}{3,600} = 8.3\%$$

$$\text{Return on total assets} = \frac{\text{Profit before tax}}{\text{Total assets}} = \frac{300}{2,400} = 12.5\%$$

■ **Figure 1** Balance Sheet and Income Statement for Ajax Home Computer Company

Ajax Home Computer Company
Balance Sheet
March 31, 1999
(in thousands)

Assets		Liabilities and Stockholders' Equity	
Cash	$ 30	Trade accounts payable	$ 150
Marketable securities	40	Accrued	25
Accounts receivable	200	Notes payable	100
Inventory	430	Accrued income tax	40
Total current assets	700	Total current liabilities	315
Plant and equipment	1,000	Bonds	500
Land	500	Debentures	85
Other investments	200	Stockholders' equity	1,500
Total assets	$2,400	Total liabilities and stockholders' equity	$2,400

Ajax Home Computer Company
Income Statement
for the 12-Month Period Ending March 31, 1999
(in thousands)

Sales	$3,600
Cost of sales	
Labor and materials	2,000
Depreciation	200
Selling expenses	500
General and administrative expenses	80
Total cost	2,780
Net operating income	820
Less interest expense	
Interest on notes	20
Interest on debentures	200
Interest on bonds	300
Total interest	520
Profit before tax	300
Federal income tax (@40%)	120
Net profit after tax	$ 180

3. Compare the Ratios.   While rules of thumb are useful for analyzing ratios, it cannot be overstated that comparison of ratios is always the preferred approach. The ratios computed for a firm can be compared in at least three ways. First, they can be compared over time to see if there are any favorable or unfavorable trends in the firm's financial position. Second, they can be compared with the ratios of other firms in the industry of similar size. Third, they can be compared with industry averages to get an overall idea of the firm's relative financial position in the industry.

Figure 2 provides a summary of the ratio analysis. The ratios computed for Ajax are presented along with the median ratios for firms of similar size in the industry and the industry median. The median is often reported in financial sources, rather than the mean, to avoid the strong effect of outliers.[4]

■ **Figure 2**
Ratio Comparison for
Ajax Home Computer
Company

	Ajax	Industry Firms Median ($1–10 Million in Assets)	Overall Industry Median
Liquidity ratios			
Current ratio	2.2	1.8	1.8
Quick ratio	.86	.9	1.0
Asset management ratios			
Inventory turnover	6.5	3.2	2.8
Total assets utilization	1.5	1.7	1.6
Profitability ratios			
Profit margin	8.3%	6.7%	8.2%
Return on total assets	12.5%	15.0%	14.7%

4. Check for Problems or Opportunities. The ratio comparison in Figure 2 suggests that Ajax is in reasonably good shape financially. The current ratio is above the industry figures, although the quick ratio is slightly below them. However, the high inventory turnover ratio suggests that the slightly low quick ratio should not be a problem, since inventory turns over relatively quickly. Total asset utilization is slightly below industry averages and should be monitored closely. This, coupled with the slightly lower return on total assets, suggests that some unproductive assets should be eliminated or that the production process needs to be made more efficient. While the problem could be ineffective marketing, the high profit margin on sales suggests that marketing effort is probably not the problem.

■ **Conclusion**

This section has focused on several aspects of financial analysis that are useful for marketing decision making. The first, break-even analysis, is commonly used in marketing problem and case analysis. The second, net present value analysis, is quite useful for investigating the financial impact of marketing alternatives, such as new product introductions or other long-term strategic changes. The third, ratio analysis, is a useful tool sometimes overlooked in marketing problem solving. Performing a ratio analysis as a regular portion of marketing problem and case analysis can increase the understanding of the firm and its problems and opportunities.

■ **Additional Readings**

Brealey, Richard A., and Stewart C. Myers. *Principles of Corporate Finance*. 5th ed. New York: McGraw-Hill, 1996.

Day, George, and Liam Fahay. "Valuing Market Strategies." *Journal of Marketing*, July 1988, pp. 45–57.

Ross, Stephen A.; Randolph W. Westerfield; and Jeffrey F. Jaffe. *Corporate Finance*. 5th ed., Burr Ridge, IL: Irwin/McGraw-Hill, 1999.

Ross, Stephen A.; Randolph W. Westerfield; and Bradford D. Jordan. *Fundamentals of Corporate Finance*. 4th ed. Burr Ridge, IL: Irwin/McGraw-Hill, 1998.

Section IV

Internet Exercises and Sources of Marketing Information

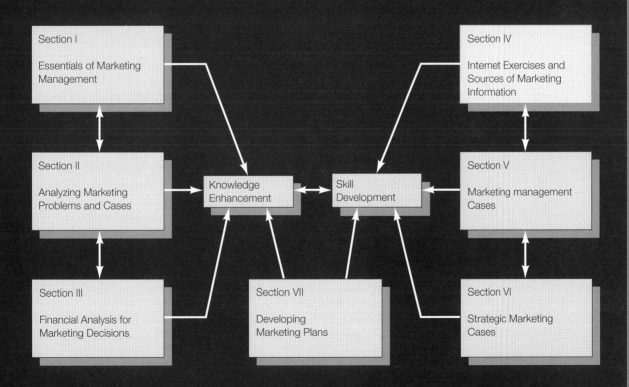

■ **Part A   Internet Exercises**

Charles Heath
Xavier University

Exercise 1. Corporate Websites

Every major corporation has a corporate website. For the most part, the primary purpose of the corporate website is to communicate with current and potential customers, investors, and channel partners. Because they are used to attract new business, corporate websites are good places to determine what customers see as their mission and primary purpose.

IBM www.ibm.com	*Cisco Systems* www.cisco.com
Microsoft www.microsoft.com	*Ben and Jerry's* www.benjerry.com

For this assignment, visit the corporate websites listed above and look for the following pieces of business information.

1. Look for a statement of mission.
2. Investigate their history and changes.
3. Look for what they claim to be strengths (what are they selling to their investors) and distinctive competencies.
4. Organizational objectives—do they make statements resembling those in Figure 1–2, page 11?
5. Look at their product lines and business units.

Exercise 2. On-line vs. Off-line Retail Experiences

The growth of E-commerce has brought about a whole new shopping experience. It is easy to see that shopping on-line is different from shopping at a traditional "brick and mortar" store. But how is it different? What are companies doing to make the shopping experience similar or different?

Find two retail sites on the World Wide Web (WWW) that have famous "real-world" counterparts. For example:

Barnes & Noble www.bn.com	*Montgomery Wards* www.wards.com
Best Buy www.bestbuy.com	*Nordstroms* www.nordstrom.com/Shop/
Bloomingdales www.bloomingdales.com	*Sears* www.sears.com
Eddie Bauer www.eddiebauer.com	*Toys "R" Us* www.toysrus.com
The Gap Online www.gap.com	*Victoria's Secret* www.victoriassecret.com
Jewel/Osco www.jewelosco.com	*Wal-Mart* www.walmart.com
Macy's www.macys.com	

1. Compare shopping at the virtual retailer to the physical version. What about the shopping experience is similar?
2. Now, contrast the two experiences. What does the on-line store offer that the "brick and mortar" store cannot? What does the "brick and mortar" store offer that the virtual store cannot?
3. What value does the on-line site add to the retailer as a corporation?
4. Will the on-line site ever completely replace the "brick and mortar" store? Why or why not?

Exercise 3. Consumer Decision-Making Process

When consumers make a purchase they progress through a series of behaviors in five stages. The consumer decision-making (CDM) process describes those behaviors and the activities that take place at each stage. In order to increase sales, marketers are looking at the five stages discussed below and trying to find ways to influence the consumer as they progress through the CDM process.

The Internet is the most recent tool that marketers are using to influence consumers. Discuss the impact of the Internet on the five stages of the CDM process. What happens differently, or how does the Internet use these processes to sell more efficiently?

Need Recognition.   During the first stage, the consumer recognizes a need that can be satisfied by a purchase. What are ways that internet marketers are attempting to trigger consumers' recognition of needs? What are some things that Amazon.com **www.amazon.com** is doing to activate need recognition?

Alternative Search.   Once a consumer realizes a need he or she begins to search for potential ways to satisfy that need. There are five primary sources of information: internal, group, marketing, public, and experimental. How can the Internet provide information for consumers? Which of the sources can the Internet influence? What impact does the information available at Edmunds **www.edmunds.com** have on consumers' alternative search?

Alternative Evaluation.   All the viable alternatives that can satisfy the need are evaluated and compared against each other. The consumer selects the brand that best satisfies the need as the intended purchase. Many times comparing products is difficult because of complex product features, numerous available choices, and physical distance between products in stores. Visit iQVC **www.iqvc.com** and select any product category of your choice. How does this website help consumers compare product alternatives?

Purchase Decision.   The consumer decides to make a purchase of the intended brand, purchase a different brand, or postpone the purchase. The Internet plays a major role in consumers' purchase decisions. What are some Internet features that influence the purchase decisions? Revisit Amazon.com and discuss some of the ways they influence the consumer's purchase decision. What role does UPS **www.ups.com** play in the purchase decision?

Post-Purchase Evaluation.   The consumer reviews the purchase and the entire purchase process of the product. If consumers have doubts or second thoughts about purchases they experience post-purchase dissonance. What are Internet marketers doing on-line to help customers avoid dissonance? Go to the Ford website **www.ford.com.** If you had a problem with the purchase of a Ford Explorer what does the site do to help you alleviate or avoid dissonance? How does eBay.com **www.ebay.com** allow consumers to review the purchase process?

Exercise 4. Discovering Product Assortments On-line

Most companies manufacture a wide range of products that they then offer to consumers. How companies that offer multiple products and product lines manage those offerings is of extreme importance to the overall success of the company.

General Motors **www.gm.com**   *General Mills* **www.generalmills.com**
Proctor & Gamble **www.pg.com**   *Gillette* **www.gillette.com**
Nabisco **www.nabisco.com**

Using the Internet, visit one of the corporate sites listed above. Browse through the site and find where product offerings are discussed. How has the product mix been defined? How many different product lines are offered? Discuss both the breadth and depth of the product mix. Pick three products and tell which type of product they are (convenience, shopping, or specialty) and why the company produces that type of product.

Exercise 5. Brand Equity on the Internet

Branding issues are of extreme importance to manufacturers, traditional retailers, and customers. The growth of the Internet has lead to the increased importance of a strong product brand name. The brand name is used to differentiate products in both traditional and on-line retail situations. On-line, there is increased importance because of trust and security issues. Pick a company from the list below and write a few words that describe your thoughts about the company whose website you are about to visit.

Ben and Jerry's **www.benjerry.com**   *L. L. Bean* **www.llbean.com**
CD-Now **www.cdnow.com**   *McDonald's* **www.mcdonalds.com**
Coke **www.coke.com**   *Ragu* **www.eat.com**
IBM **www.ibm.com**   *Reebok* **www.reebok.com**

Now, browse the company's website and get a good feeling for what information is presented at the site, how the site is organized, how the designers have chosen the theme, color scheme, images, and so on.

1. What is the main purpose for the website?
2. Briefly discuss what messages the website is trying to convey.
3. Compare what you thought about the company before visiting the website to the message that was conveyed by the material on the website. Does the Web material match what you thought or is it different?
4. What is it about the company's website that is helping it build brand equity?

Exercise 6. The Impact of Communities on Marketing

Communities are areas on-line where consumers who share interests gather and interact. There are a number of virtual areas that function as a community including discussion lists, chat rooms, and message boards. The unique properties of on-line communities offer marketers a number of opportunities to reach their customers in ways that never existed before.

1. Go to the Amazon.com **www.amazon.com** homepage and click on the community button. Discuss how Amazon uses reference groups to influence consumers at its website.

2. Go to one of the following sites: iVillage.com **www.ivillage.com** or Women.com **www.women.com**. How can a sponsor benefit by being associated with a community?

3. Read about Ford's OwnerConnection at the Ford website **www.ownerconnection.com** and click "About OwnerConnection". What ways can a company use community to develop new products or change existing ones?

Exercise 7. Branding for Pure Plays

Barnes & Noble.com (BN.com) entered the E-commerce arena in 1997 and has grown to become the fifth largest on-line retailer. When it began to operate on-line, Barnes & Noble already had an established brand name while Amazon.com, a "pure play" (a company that exists only in an on-line form), did not.

Brand equity is determined by the consumer and is the sum of all of the consumer's assessments of the product. Visit both Amazon.com **www.amazon.com** and BN.com **www.bn.com**. Describe the different elements of the brand equity of each (see p. 94, Figure 6–1 for help). How did Amazon develop such a strong brand name? What issues will B & N have to deal with that Amazon did not?

"Brick and Mortar" Retailer		"Pure Play" Retailer
Toys "R" Us **www.toysrus.com**	vs.	*eToys* **www.etoys.com**
Musicland/ Sam Goody **www.musicland.com** then go to **www.samgoody.com**	vs.	*CDNow* **www.cdnow.com**
Joseph-Beth **www.josephbeth.com**	vs.	*Amazon.com* **www.amazon.com**
Jewel/Osco **www.jewelosco.com**	vs.	*Peapod.com* **www.peapod.com**
Blockbuster Video **www.blockbuster.com**	vs.	*Reel.com* **www.reel.com**

Pick a pair of retailers from the list above and answer the following questions.

1. Compare the purpose of the two sites. How are they similar/different?
2. Which of the two do you think has the advantage in the future and why?
3. What strategic advantage does the "brick and mortar" retailer have that the "pure play" retailer does not?
4. Does the "pure play" retailer have any strategic advantages that the "brick and mortar" retailer does not?

Exercise 8. Pricing Issues on the Internet

One of the easiest places to see the impact of the Internet on marketing is by looking at its effect on pricing decisions and consumers' perceptions of prices. Over just the last five years, the World Wide Web (WWW) has developed the reputation as being *the* place to shop to get the lowest prices.

1. Why has this reputation developed?
2. Why might it be possible to charge lower prices on-line?
3. Are products really cheaper?

To answer this last question, choose two products and find them for sale on-line (books, CDs, and software work very well). Calculate the total price that would be charged to your credit card, then go to a "brick and mortar" retailer and find prices for the same product there. Make your comparisons.

1. Where is the cheapest place to buy the products you have selected?
2. What costs go into determining which place you buy your product?
3. Are there any nonfinancial costs to shopping on-line? To off-line shopping?

Exercise 9. Selecting the Internet as a Distribution Channel

One very important decision that marketers need to make is which channel of distribution to use for its products or services. There are four primary considerations that need to be analyzed before making the distribution choice.

Distribution coverage required
Degree of control desired
Total distribution cost
Channel flexibility

Discuss the implications of using the Internet on these four considerations. To help analyze the possible implications of the Internet on these elements, visit the following sites and consider how they distribute their products differently than traditional manufacturers.

Dell Computers **www.dell.com**   *Peapod Groceries* **www.peapod.com**
Gateway Computers **www.gateway.com**   *Amazon.com* **www.amazon.com**

Also visit these sites and think about the role they play in the new breed of channel intermediaries.

Federal Express (FedEx) **www.fedex.com**   *Yahoo.com* **www.yahoo.com**
United Parcel Service (UPS) **www.ups.com**   *IBM eBusiness* **www.ibm.com/ebusiness/**
Roadway Express **www.roadway.com**

Exercise 10. Internet Advertising

Marketers need to decide the best possible way to get the message about their products to those consumers who would be interested in making a purchase. Advertising is one of the most popular methods companies use to deliver their product messages. However, the marketing communications manager must decide not only where to advertise, but also how to communicate that message. There are four primary objectives that marketers wish to accomplish with advertising.

Awareness
Comprehension
Conviction
Ordering

Discuss how Internet advertising can be used to accomplish these four objectives.

Awareness.   Visit both PriceWonders.com **www.pricewonders.com** and Amazon.com **www.amazon.com.** What features of their homepages are attempting to trigger awareness in the consumer?

Comprehension.   Go to the Sony website **www.sony.com,** select electronics, electronics again, then choose televisions from the drop-down list. How does this site help comprehension of the product offering?

Conviction.   Go to CDnow.com **www.cdnow.com** and select the artist and title of your choice. What does CDnow do to try to convince customers to purchase a CD?

Ordering. Go to Yahoo.com **www.yahoo.com** and select computers and Internet. At the top of the page, click on the banner ad. How is this banner ad different from TV ads and magazine ads?

Exercise 11. The Adaptation of Services to the Internet

The way that services are offered to consumers is changing drastically because of the impact of the Internet. How have the following industries had to change to adapt to this technological change?

Banking. Go to the Bank One homepage **www.bankone.com** and select Internet banking. Take a look at CyberCash **www.cybercash.com** and eMortgages.com **www.emortgages.com**

Insurance. Log on to Instant Quote **www.instantquote.com** and click on "how it works." How does this compare to the "old" way of buying insurance?

Travel. Visit one of the following travel sites: Trip.com **www.trip.com**, Travelocity.com **www.travelocity.com**, Expedia **www.expedia.com**. How have the growth of these on-line reservation sites affected the travel agencies? What role do Travel agencies *now* play in the marketplace?

■ **Part B   Internet Sources of Marketing Information**

Charles Heath
Xavier University

When doing research on a company, there are thousands of sites on the World Wide Web (WWW) that can contain information about your company of choice. For example, a search conducted on Altavista in November of 1999 found 11,681,605 websites that contain the word Microsoft on their pages! A similar search found 79,160 pages for Monsanto, a life sciences company. Although far fewer results would occur, it would be impossible to search 79,000 websites for information about the company you are writing your marketing plan about. In fact, a very small percentage of those pages would contain information that would be of any use.

This section is designed to provide you with a list of sources that would be helpful in uncovering the information necessary to write an insightful marketing plan. The list is not in any order and each company will have different levels of information available at some of these sites. In addition, there are plenty of business resources that are not listed here. Please look beyond this list during your research while utilizing these sources. Hopefully this list will help you save hours of time and eliminate the frustration sometimes associated with searching the Internet.

Search Engines and Directories. The enormous growth of the Web has placed a growing strain on the ability of search engines to adequately represent the total number of Web pages. In fact, search engines cover only 42 percent of the Web pages that exist on-line, and the best search engines retrieve information from only about 16 percent of them![1] Despite all this, the search engine can be your friend if you use very specific queries. For help don't hesitate to visit the help section that each search site offers.

www.yahoo.com	Best directory with categorized and indexed results.
www.altavista.com	Provides tons of possible results and has a new easy-to-use search tool.
www.northernlight.com	Very good for research purposes and covers the greatest percentage of websites.
www.hotbot.com	Relevance-related results that are usually very relevant!
www.google.com	Started as a project at Stanford, now it keeps producing relevant results!

Corporate Websites.   When looking for information, you have to look at the company's own website! It can provide a wealth of information about what the company is currently doing in the marketplace. Remember that corporate websites are also designed to lure investors and often provide a great deal of investment-level information just for that purpose. Don't expect to find any company secrets though!

The vast majority of corporate sites have bought their own corporation domain name **www.microsoft.com**, **www.abc.com**, **www.ibm.com**. Others use abbreviated versions of the company name (Procter & Gamble is **www.pg.com** and Ben and Jerry's is **www.benjerry.com**)

Government.   The government, both federal and state levels, collects a great deal of information about companies and industries. This information has always been available in the government references section of your university library. Now, the government has done an admirable job of creating access to this information via Internet sources! Here are a few of the useful government sites.

www.doc.gov	The Commerce Department website contains useful legislative information pertinent to the external environment.
www.odci.gov	The CIA World Factbook is an excellent resource for international information.
www.census.gov	The Census bureau details economic and social descriptors.
www.fedstats.gov	Fedstats offers statistics from over 70 federal agencies at one location!
www.loc.gov	The Library of Congress is a vault of information about a great many subjects.
www.dol.gov	The Department of Labor homepage links to labor information including the Bureau of Labor Statistics.

Business Publications.   Because business publications focus their reporting eyes on the business world, they are an excellent source for information about companies and today's marketplace. Almost all the major business publications have websites that include stories from the current issue as well as some archives that can be searched. A few of the sites do require a membership to search their archives.

---

[1]Sirapyan, Nancy. *Search Sites*. ZDNet.com, September 6, 1999.

www.forbes.com	Access to the type of news, articles, and information that *Forbes* is known for.
www.pathfinder.com	Links to the *Time* magazine homepage, but also links to the Fortune.com and Money.com homepages.
www.adage.com	The world of advertising is at your mouse click with *Advertising Age*'s website.
www.adweek.com	Home of *Adweek* and linked to its partners *Brandweek* and *Mediaweek*.
www.demographics.com	*American Demographics* magazine and its wealth of statistical data can be found here.
www.dowjones.com	The publishers of *The Wall Street Journal* bring you business news in the WSJ tradition.
www.salesandmarketing.com	The popular sales publication offers articles online. However, a magazine subscription is needed to search the archives.
www.business2.com	Internet-related issues are featured in the Web version of the E-commerce magazine.
www.businessweek.com	Some of the articles are subscription only, but there is some good free information as well.
www.usnews.com	More than just college rankings, the on-line version of the *U.S. News and World Report* is a wealth of information.
www.barrons.com	*Barrons* on-line presents some market information for free and full text versions of the print version to subscribers.
www.companiesonline.com	Enter a company name into the search box on the Companies Online site and get information about the company plus a series of links that relate to the company and its products.

Newspapers.   Major newspapers have also made their presence known on the World Wide Web. Because they focus exclusively on news, they are an excellent on-line source of business information. While the major newspapers carry a good deal of national information, more regionalized newspapers focus on the business news in their immediate geographic region. Matching a company's headquarters with its local newspaper may result in more information than looking only at the large national papers.

National Papers

www.usatoday.com	America's newspaper has a user-friendly site that contains all the major business news.
www.wsj.com	The business newspaper is a subscription-based service that has archives of its articles on-line. It might be a good idea to subscribe while you are in college.
www.newsindex.com	This news-only search engine looks through more than 250 newspapers on-line and retrieves all matches to your search request.

Large City Papers

www.nyt.com — *The New York Times* maintains its class and informative content on-line.

www.chicagotribune.com — The windy city's newspaper makes it easy to search and find corporate information.

www.washingtonpost.com — From the nation's capital, the *Washington Post* is rich in politically-based business news.

International Papers

www.sunday-times.co.uk — Get an international flavor by searching through London's source of business information.

www.financialtimes.com — If you want international business information you must look at the *Financial Times*.

Regional Papers

http://dir.yahoo.com/News_and_Media/Newspapers/By_Region/U_S__States/
Regional newspapers are listed by the state in which they are published.

General Business Sites.   In addition to print media and newspapers, there are a number of websites that provide researchers and investors with very timely and in-depth business information. These sites provide news headlines and also allow the researcher to search the site using key words.

www.hoovers.com — Possibly the best business information site on the Web. Great information from the business search function plus a business directory that links the researcher to even more business information!

www.cnnfn.com — The financial branch of the news network provides up-to-the-minute information about the marketplace and companies.

www.msnbc.com — This joint venture between Microsoft and NBC television has both event news and business information.

www.moneynet.com — Reuters MoneyNet is an excellent source of business information with a market focus.

www.zdnet.com — ZDNet provides business information that focuses on technology firms and advances.

Compilation Sites.   The following are sites that have been created and maintained as resources for business-based research.

www.ciber.bus.msu.edu/busres.htm — The Michigan State University Center for International Business Education and Research (CIBER) maintains a directory of international Web resources.

www.lib.umich.edu/libhome/Documents.center/stats.html
The University of Michigan's Document Center maintains a listing of Web-based statistical resources.

Section V

Marketing Management Cases

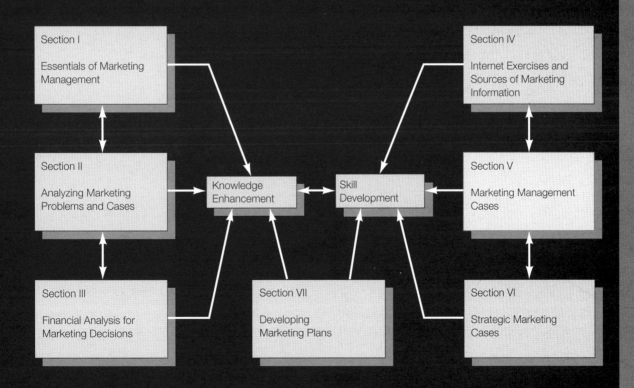

Section I Essentials of Marketing Management			**Section IV** Internet Exercises and Sources of Marketing Information
Section II Analyzing Marketing Problems and Cases	Knowledge Enhancement	Skill Development	**Section V** Marketing Management Cases
Section III Financial Analysis for Marketing Decisions	**Section VII** Developing Marketing Plans		**Section VI** Strategic Marketing Cases

■ Note to the Student

The primary emphasis of the 33 cases in this section is on marketing as a functional business or organizational area. As such, much of the analysis in these cases involves research and selection of appropriate target markets and the development and management of marketing mix variables.

We have divided these cases into six groups to help focus your analysis. These six groups include cases dealing with market opportunity analysis, product strategy, promotion strategy, distribution strategy, pricing strategy, and selected issues in marketing management. However, keep in mind that regardless of how the case is classified, you should not become too focused on a single issue or marketing mix variable and ignore other elements of marketing strategy.

Case Group A
Marketing Opportunity Analysis

▪ Case 1   Campus Calendar

William R. Wynd
Eastern Washington University

Eastern Washington University is one of four regional universities in Washington State. Operated on a quarter system, enrollment is around 8,200 students, most of whom are residents of Spokane County. Academic programs at Eastern feature liberal arts, education, business, and science.

Spokane, Washington's second largest city, is 16 miles east. The county is a metro area with over 356,000 people. It is a banking, health care, and distribution center for a portion of three states designated as the "Inland Empire."

As part of a class in basic marketing, eight junior students became so interested in marketing that they banded together for the purpose of applying what they were learning. With the help of their instructor they formed a partnership called CI (Collegiate Images). They sought to develop and market a product for the express purpose of making enough money to fund their senior year tuition of $500 per quarter and gain some practical experience in business.

Over a period of several weeks in the fall quarter they sought to narrow a list of potential products. Three limitations helped purge their list almost immediately. First, each could raise no more than $500 for start-up capital. Second, the venture could require no more than an average of about 15 hours per week per student. Third, if they were to market a product the following fall, only nine months remained for planning and production. Applying these criteria they screened a list and determined that a calendar featuring Eastern students posed in campus settings would be a likely candidate.

The idea of a campus calendar is not new. Several other schools in the Pacific Northwest had produced calendars at one time or another. Since the marketing research section of their beginning course had taught them to start by finding out what others had done, they developed a questionnaire and conducted a telephone survey; the results of that survey are in Table 1. Based on the results of the survey, the students concluded that quality was particularly important. Visual inspection of

---

This case was prepared by William R. Wynd of Eastern Washington University as a basis for class discussion rather than to illustrate either effective or ineffective handling of a managerial situation.

■ **Table 1** Comparison of Calendars

Questions	U of M	OSU	U of O	USC
1. Size of market	18,000	15,000	18,000	International Market
2. What type of calendar did you produce? M—Male F—Female B—Both on same page.	F	F	F	M & F
3. Was it a: B—full-body shot S—swimsuit M—mixed	M	M	M	F—swimsuit M—head
4. Did you produce in: B/W—blk/white C—color	C	C	B/W	C
5. Who did your photography? T—themselves C—contracted out	C	C	T	C
6. What calendar year did you use? S—school year C—calendar year	C	C	C	C
7. Did you put advertising on the calendar?	Yes	No	Yes	No
8. What was your unit price?	$3–$4	$6.95	$5–$6	$7.95 $8.95—$9.95
9. How many did you sell?	3,300	6,500	1,000	International Market
10. How did you sell them? R—retail W—wholesale B—both	W	W	W	B
11. Sponsor?	Miller Beer	Several Businesses	Coors Beer	No sponsor

sample calendars sent by the survey respondents emphasized that the quality of printing, paper, and photography contributed greatly to the product image. The size of the calendar varied from a folded size of 8½ " × 11", which was considered small, to 12" × 12", which was considered large. The large size calendar produced at USC on heavyweight stock was the most attractive. But the survey left many unanswered questions about what was wanted in a product and what information was needed to develop strategies for pricing, promotion, and distribution.

Several focus groups were held to determine how students use a calendar and what they wanted in terms of quality, price, and character of poses. The focus groups revealed that students need a place to write notes and reminders. Normally they try to find a calendar with a date page that is large enough for this purpose. However, most students receive free calendars and so may not specifically purchase a calendar with a large date page. In addition most students, particularly full-time students living on campus or off campus in Cheney, said they would be interested in a calendar featuring Eastern students indicating some school spirit. Older students and many of those who commuted, however, were not interested. They came to Eastern for an education, worked in their spare time, and did not come to the campus except for their classes.

We are students in a marketing class at Eastern Washington University. We are conducting a survey to decide the possibility of a campus calendar. We would appreciate your answer to the following questions. Please answer fully and honestly; all information is anonymous. Thank you for your time and trouble.

1. We would like to produce a quality E.W.U. campus calendar for the year 1989–1990. We plan to use students from the campus as models. Would you be interested in a calendar with only E.W.U. students in it?
   253 (a) yes   76 (b) no
2. What kind of models would you prefer in a single calendar?
   49 (a) all male   62 (c) alternating males and females
   110 (b) all female   108 (d) male & female on the same page
3. What kind of photo poses would you prefer? (Check all that apply):
   107 (a) fully clothed body shot   36 (c) face and chest shot
   12 (b) swimsuit body shot   86 (d) partially clothed
4. What starting date would you prefer?
   132 (a) a calendar year, starting in January
   181 (b) school year, starting in September
5. Would you buy the calendar?
   105 (a) for yourself   32 (b) as a gift   192 (c) not at all
6. If we produce a calendar which is pleasing to you what is the most you would be willing to pay?
   0 (a) $12   19 (b) $10   48 (c) $8   70 (d) $6
7. What is your age?
   135 (a) 18–21   80 (b) 22–24   54 (c) 25–29   60 (d) over 29
8. What is your sex?
   150 (a) male   179 (b) female
9. Where do you reside?
   161 (a) off campus, commute   61 (b) on campus
   107 (c) off campus (Cheney)
10. What is your class standing?
    41 (a) freshman   55 (b) sophomore   82 (c) junior   151 (d) senior

Women said they would like a calendar featuring men, and men said they would like a calendar featuring women in swimsuits. Most said they would prefer a fairly large calendar, especially if it featured attractive pictures.

Information from the focus groups was used to generate a measurement instrument. This one-page questionnaire was administered to 329 students in classes selected at random at a time and on a day when most students attended classes. Results of the survey are shown in Exhibit 1. A check with records in the Office of the Registrar indicated that the proportion of sexes, ages, and class standings in the sample closely matched that of the student body. Ninety-three percent of the student body was classified as full time.

Several cross tabulations were run on the data. These revealed that 54 percent of the students who expressed interest in the calendar were male. In addition, 68 percent of those who said they were interested lived on campus or in Cheney. Seniors were less interested than underclassmen. Student preferences for poses are shown in Table 2. Most males preferred females in swimsuits, where most females preferred males with their clothes on.

Pose	Male	Female
Fully clothed body shot	42	63
Swimsuit body shot	70	52
Face and chest shot	21	14
Partially clothed shot	45	38

| | Size of Calendar | |
Weight of Cover Stock	Small	Large
Light	$6,920	$ 9,829
Heavy	8,000	12,040

Several printers were contacted to obtain quotes. There were variations in both price and quality. Production quotes for the best quality and price combination are shown in Table 3.

There was a minimum order of 2,000, and 15 percent for each additional 500. Production costs included paper, printing, and binding. Typesetting was an extra $1,000.

Since the pictures were the central part of the product they had to be of good quality. A number of professional photographers were asked to submit their portfolios. The best work was far ahead of the rest. Their charge was $250 per setting with a minimum of 12 settings. This price included travel, set-up charges, several negatives, and a final camera-ready print.

Selecting the students to pose for the pictures was a problem. One idea was to have students nominate whom they wanted in the pictures. One of the student partners in Collegiate Images was an amateur photographer and agreed to take the preliminary snapshots that would later be screened by another group of students. Film and developing costs were estimated at $75.

Distribution was also a problem. The campus bookstore offered to take 1,000 calendars at a markup on the cost of 40 percent. A booth in a high traffic area of the Student Union Building could be rented for $2 per day as long as it was connected with a student project. A booth could also be set up in the stadium at the homecoming football game. There were other possibilities but a strategy decision would have to be made about intensive, selective, or exclusive distribution before outlets could be selected.

Promotion possibilities included interviews with the local student newspaper and announcements in the *FOCUS,* a daily flyer available to all students in all buildings on campus. A member of Collegiate Images could also appear as a guest on a talk show aired by the student radio station. None of these activities cost money. On the other hand, an ad in the student newspaper about the size of the date page of the large-size calendar would cost $140. The *Easterner* is published weekly with a press run of 6,000. Flyers about the same size were estimated to cost about $2.50 in quantities of 100.

By this time it was evident that there was not enough money available to meet start-up costs even at the minimum order of 2,000. Someone suggested that an advertiser might be interested in sponsoring a portion of the calendar. Three of the other universities surveyed had sponsors. Advertising consisted of a corporate logo in the background of the date page. Students felt that if accepted, advertisements should be tasteful.

There was a lot of work to be done before attempting to secure sponsorship. A business plan would have to be made on how many calendars to produce, the exact composition of poses, the calendar start date, price, distribution, and promotion strategy. A price for advertising sponsorship for all or a portion of the calendar would have to be established. Everyone knew that the success of the project depended on the amount of creativity used in developing and implementing a marketing strategy.

■ Case 2   McDonald's Corporation

Henry C. K. Chen
University of West Florida

■ Introduction

During the winter of 1990, James Fletcher, who is currently vice president of marketing for McDonald's Corporation, became concerned about the company's recent performance. Careful market expansion, new products, and special promotional strategies have made McDonald's Corporation the leader of the fast-food industry. However, sales per McDonald's store in the United States plummeted to an inflation-adjusted 6 percent during the second quarter of 1989. Fletcher was trying to decide on a set of appropriate marketing strategies for the 1990s in order to stay ahead of competition.

■ The Fast-Food Industry

The $60 billion fast-food industry reached a saturation point in the late 1980s. Fletcher expected sales to grow at an inflation-adjusted 2 percent in 1990—down from the double-digit growth rate in the 1970s and early 1980s.

The burger sector accounted for $31 billion of the $60 billion fast-food industry and was growing at 8 percent annually. The pizza sector accounted for $20 billion and had grown 11 percent annually over the past five years. Although fast-food restaurants' sales had slowed, the number of fast-food outlets had increased steadily at a rate of 5 percent annually.

Trends

In recent years, several environmental forces have adversely affected the fast-food industry, especially the burger sector. The traditional frequent users of fast-food restaurants—the 75 million baby boomers, who are now in their 40s and are well established economically—are looking toward the higher-quality and higher-priced entries into the fast-food market. To meet their needs, General Mills, Inc., launched the Olive Garden Italian Restaurant chain in 1982. Red Lobster and other fast-food chains have invested heavily to upgrade their menus.

Over the last decade, consumers' eating habits have changed noticeably. Marketing research findings reveal that American consumers are becoming more health conscious. Nearly 50 percent of U.S. adults are watching their weight. They are seeking fast foods high in nutritional value and low in saturated fats and cholesterol. Consumers eat less red meat and greasy foods. Per capita consumption of poultry products increased from 49.8 pounds in 1980 to 62.7 pounds in 1987. Ethnic food preparation at home has also increased rapidly—a 40 percent increase in sales in Italian food, a 21 percent increase in Oriental food, and a 14 percent increase in Mexican food.

This case was prepared by Henry C. K. Chen of The University of West Florida.

Consumers increasingly prefer the convenience of eating quality foods and having a good selection of meals at home. Take-out and home delivery services have therefore emerged as the most rapidly growing business in the fast-food industry. Home delivery has gained widespread acceptance by consumers and has become a formidable competitive strategy in pizza restaurants. Many other fast-food outlets are also experimenting with home delivery. In the Bay Area and in New York City, frazzled two-income families can order their preferred dinners to their tastes and have them delivered to their homes seven days a week. Many small restaurants have experienced great success with this strategy.

In addition, while coping with the consumer's desire for healthier and higher-quality food, fast-food restaurants have been frustrated by rising wholesale food prices and labor costs. Food costs represent approximately 40 to 45 percent of sales in a typical U.S. fast-food restaurant, and labor costs represent about 25 percent of sales. In 1989, beef prices rose 10 percent, and analysts expect beef, wheat, and coffee prices to increase anywhere from 3 to 6 percent in 1990.

The increase in the minimum wage from $3.35 an hour in 1989 to $3.80 in 1990, and to $4.25 in 1991, further squeezed fast-food restauranteurs' profit margins. Labor costs will go even higher if Congress mandates health insurance coverage for part-time employees.

Fast-food restaurants also face a shortage of workers. The primary labor pool for the industry is declining. The 16- to 24-year-old population, which stood at 20 percent in 1990, is expected to shrink to 15 percent of the total population by the year 2000, and there is no sign of relief in the near future. Many areas of the country have already felt this pinch. Consequently, fast-food outlets have to pay higher wages and develop innovative benefit packages in order to attract workers.

Although the domestic market is reaching a saturation level, one bright spot is the international market, which is growing at a rate almost double that of the United States. The international market was much like that of the United States in the 1960s and 1970s—a period of customer acceptance and rapid economic growth. Major players in the fast-food industry such as McDonald's, Burger King, Wendy's, Pizza Hut, and Kentucky Fried Chicken have aggressively made inroads into these fertile markets.

■ The Competitive Environment

The fierce competition among fast-food chains and from the nonfood outlets in a saturated market forces fast-food chains to frantically woo customers away from each other.

Competition among fast-food restaurants comes from a long list of hamburger and nonhamburger fast-food chains and also from a variety of ethnic food chains and quick-service family restaurants. Major players in the hamburger sector include Burger King, Wendy's, and Hardee's. In the nonhamburger segment, players include Pizza Hut, Kentucky Fried Chicken, Taco Bell, Church's Chicken, and Rax. In recent years, sales of the nonburger segment have outgrown the hamburger segment. Quick-service family dining chains such as Morrison's, Shoney's, Red Lobster, and Roy Rogers have also steadily increased their shares in the industry.

Competition also comes from nonrestaurant stores. Delicatessens and food services are inching their way into supermarkets and traditional nonfood retail outlets. Consumers now can conveniently pick up sandwiches for lunch at supermarkets, convenience stores, and even gas stations. A great variety of microwave oven-ready meals is also available in supermarkets and small grocery stores.

Direct Competition

McDonald's was the leading fast-food restaurant chain in the hamburger segment with a 1988 sales volume exceeding $5.56 billion. Burger King holds the number two position with 1988 sales of approximately $1.4 billion followed by Wendy's, with 1988 sales of about $1.06 billion. In the nonburger sector, Pizza Hut is the world's leading pizza restaurant chain with a 1988 sales volume of $2.8 billion (more than 20 percent of the $13.5 billion U.S. pizza industry). Kentucky Fried Chicken is the world's largest chicken restaurant system. Of the $6.2 billion U.S. segment, it holds a 46 percent market share with 1988 sales of just under $2.9 billion. Taco Bell is the leading quick-service Mexican food chain with sales of $1.6 billion in 1988.

McDonald's Marketing Strategy

Product. In the 1960s, the McDonald's menu mainly consisted of hamburgers and french fries. Recognizing changing consumer lifestyles and eating habits, development of new and innovative menu items became McDonald's major focus.

During the 1970s, McDonald's created the breakfast sandwich, which has become a big success. In the early 1980s, McDonald's introduced the Chicken Biscuit Sandwich and McNuggets. McD.L.T. moved nationally in 1985. Salads, introduced in 1987, now bring in about 7 percent of McDonald's total revenue. In 1989, McDonald's introduced McRib in several regional markets and test marketed a 14-inch pizza. The results of the test market are not yet known. Adding menu items is not a panacea for success. McDonald's management is aware that new product introduction is always a gamble; it takes years to develop a new product and millions of dollars to launch it into the market. The failure of the McChicken sandwich is an example of the risk of introducing a new product.

Market Selection. In addition to developing new products, McDonald's has employed an aggressive market expansion strategy. In 1989, McDonald's had 10,513 outlets and was planning to add 650 new outlets in 1990.

The location of its outlets is one of the pivotal factors that makes McDonald's so successful. McDonald's had typically expanded into suburban areas during the 1960s, and into the crowded downtown markets in the 1970s and 1980s; but now it is opening restaurants in airports and even hospitals. The international market represents an especially lucrative opportunity. In 1988, McDonald's had 2,600 outlets outside the United States. After a 14-year negotiation, McDonald's completed its first 20 restaurants in the Commonwealth of Independent States. In the U.S. market, the average annual store sales are about $1.6 million.

Promotion. McDonald's promotional message focuses on tasty and nutritious food, friendly folks, and fun. To accomplish these goals McDonald's has invested heavily in promoting its brand awareness and improving its public image. McDonald's annual Charity Christmas Parade in Chicago and its Ronald McDonald House charity provide the company with beneficial exposure and publicity. A large amount of its market budget is spent on well-planned special promotional programs, including Monopoly II, Scrabble, Kraft salad dressing give-away, Happy Meals, Plush toys, in-store kid videos, and various Big Mac–related promotions.

In 1989, McDonald's spent about $1 billion on marketing and promotion, and the company experimented with music and dim lighting in several test markets.

Pricing.

Because price slashing could cheapen the image of fast-food restaurants, discounts have not been widely employed in the industry. However, confronting the intraindustry rivalries and competition from quick-service restaurants and nonfood stores, fast-food chains have no choice but to engage grudgingly in short-term discounts. Discounts of major fast-food chains in late 1989 are shown below:

McDonald's: Offered 99¢ quarter-pound cheeseburgers and Big Macs and 50¢ cheeseburgers, which were regularly $1.90 and 79¢, respectively.

Wendy's: Super Value Menu featuring 99¢ junior bacon cheeseburgers and a 99¢ bowl of chili, which were regularly $1.05 and $1.15, respectively.

Kentucky Fried Chicken: A $1.99 special on chicken sandwiches and french fries, which was regularly $2.44.

Hardee's: A $1.99 special on a regular roast beef sandwich and medium soft drink, which was regularly $2.39.

Taco Bell: Tacos and burritos for 59¢ per shell, compared with the regular prices of 79¢ and $1.07 per shell.

Burger King's Strategy

In the late 1980s, Burger King experienced four years of flat sales and a 49 percent decline in profit. In the hope of reversing that trend, Burger King introduced several new menu items, including a salad bar, Chicken Fingers, Chicken Tenders, and Fish Tenders. Burger King was also the first fast-food chain to provide a nutrition guide that includes information on the calories, fats, salt, and protein content of Burger King's foods. To attract new market segments, Häagen-Dazs ice cream bars and broiled chicken made their debut at Burger King in 1989. Like McDonald's, Burger King has aggressively expanded its markets in the United States and abroad. In 1986, Burger King began operating 20 mobile food service vehicles to bring its menus to remote locations, such as military bases and national parks. In 1989, Burger King had 5,737 restaurants in the United States.

Some industry analysts believe that Burger King's poor sales were caused by a lack of focus in its advertising campaigns and abrupt changes in promotional strategies. From 1974 to 1989, Burger King changed its advertising themes eight times. Some of its early memorable messages include, "Have It Your Way" (1974–76), "Battle of the Burgers" (1983–86), "We Do It Like You'd Do It" (1988–89), and "Sometimes You've Gotta Break the Rules" (1989–90). Many franchisees were unhappy about the last campaign theme and criticized the rules-breaking theme as ill-focused and incomprehensible.

In 1989, Burger King's marketing budget was about $250 million, of which $215 million was spent on advertising. Gary Langstaff, vice president of marketing, who left Hardee's in April 1989, indicated that Burger King would place more emphasis on special market segments and brand image and less on product promotion. In order to penetrate the minority markets, Spanish-language songs have been aired in several major Hispanic markets such as Miami, Los Angeles, and San Antonio. However, Burger King once again changed its promotion strategy by pulling its corporate image commercial spots in early 1990.

Hardee's Strategy

To keep abreast of McDonald's and Burger King, Hardee's has diversified and up-graded its limited menu featuring specialty sandwiches—Big Roast Beef sandwich, hamburgers, and soft drinks. In 1984, the chain added three entree salads—garden, chef, and shrimp. In 1987, Hardee's rolled out a soft-serve ice cream program in a bid to attract more women, and in 1988, Chicken Stix was introduced. The acquisition of Roy Rogers not only gives Hardee's greater presence in the Northwest but also adds boned chicken to its menu. In June 1990, Hardee's announced the debut of a light hamburger sandwich called "Lean 1" that has about 30 percent less total fat than the chain's other quarter-pound hamburgers.

Founded in 1960, Hardee's has been aggressively expanding into the national market through franchising and acquisitions. Hardee's purchased the 650-unit Burger Chef chain from General Foods Corporation in 1962. Traditionally, Hardee's market strategy focused on small towns, thereby avoiding fierce battles with McDonald's and other major fast-food chains. Now, however, Hardee's is inching into big cities. In 1986, Hardee's signed a contract with Southland, the owner of the largest convenience store chain, to distribute Hardee's sandwiches in Southland's 7,636 Seven-Eleven stores. In April 1990, Hardee's acquired the 638-unit Roy Rogers chain. This move gives the number four fast-food chain a total of 3,968 units and also enables Hardee's to gain vital market in the northwest United States.

As a small regional fast-food chain in the 1970s, Hardee's had wisely utilized sales promotion and community relations to build its image and sales. Hardee's has sponsored many community events in small towns, such as offering free meals to local high schoolers who make a 3.0 average, and giving special price breaks to bowlers for high scores. In order to transform its small-town appeal into a big-city image, and to differentiate itself from other fast-food chains, Hardee's launched a low-key spot advertising campaign in 1990. The spot commercials make no mention of price cutting and product promotion. They just talk about Hardee's new Grilled Chicken sandwich—in a casual tone directed to consumers as individuals. The only carry-over of the past advertising theme is, "We're out to win you over."

Some industry analysts consider Hardee's to be the most aggressive fast-food chain. Its goal is to pass number two Burger King.

Wendy's Strategy

In the mid-1980s, Wendy's added its very popular Super Bar—a hot and cold buffet. In 1988, Super Bars accounted for about 20 percent of sales in the restaurants carrying it. In 1989, Wendy's tested a new grilled chicken sandwich—the third chicken product, and continued to revamp its breakfast menu. In 1990, the chain publicized using pure vegetable oil for its fried items.

Market segmentation has been Wendy's strategic focus. Its goal is to build sales volume by broadening the base of targeted consumers. For example, in the late 1980s Wendy's experimented with family, weekend, and dinner markets, and added drive-through windows and takeout menus. Although Wendy's has steadily added restaurants in traditional locations, it is now opening restaurants in Sears and even in supermarkets. In 1989, Wendy's had 3,762 outlets in the domestic United States and 241 outlets abroad. The average annual sales volume per U.S. outlet was about $750,000.

Wendy's has consistently promoted an image of quality food, excellent service, and dining ambience. Its national advertising theme has been, "The Best Burger in the Business and a Whole Lot More." Wendy's has been perceived as a chain at the higher end of the fast-food price spectrum. In order to eliminate the high-price image and expand its customer base, Wendy's launched a new ad campaign in 1990 touting the company's Super Value Menu—an array of 99-cent items. In 1988, service enhancement programs included updating crew and manager training, adding headsets and timers for the drive-through windows, and introducing customer comment cards.

Indirect Competition

The Nonhamburger Fast-Food Chains.
The gradual shift of consumer preference toward hamburger substitutes presents strong competition for hamburger fast-food restaurants. The nonburger fast-food sector grew by about 11 percent in 1989. Pizza and fried chicken had taken the lion's share of this sector.

In the United States, Pizza Hut, Kentucky Fried Chicken, and Taco Bell restaurants held leading positions in their respective segments with total sales in 1988 amounting to $7.3 billion.

Pizza Hut.
Pizza Hut is the leading pizza restaurant chain in the world with 1988 U.S. sales volume of $2.8 billion. Internationally, there are Pizza Hut restaurants in over 50 countries, including two in the Commonwealth of Independent States.

In the early 1980s the five-minute personal pan pizza was introduced. Hand-tossed traditional pizza was introduced during 1988 and now accounts for about 20 percent of Pizza Hut's total pizza sales.

New Pizza Huts are opening in hospitals, airports, universities, and shopping malls. Pizza Hut Express units, where customers can purchase a personal pan pizza in seconds, have opened in high-traffic areas. Delivery has taken off since mid-1987, and annual sales are growing at double-digit rates. A Pairs Program—offering two pizzas for one low price—is very attractive to both carry-out and delivery customers.

Kentucky Fried Chicken.
Kentucky Fried Chicken is the world's largest quick-service chicken restaurant chain. In 1989, U.S. sales were $2.1 billion, and $2.1 billion in 57 other countries.

New value-oriented products were introduced in the late 1980s, including Chicken Little sandwiches for lunch or snacks, chicken filet burgers, and grilled chicken.

New outlets are opening in shopping malls and other high-traffic areas. Home delivery was tested in several markets in 1989.

Taco Bell.
Taco Bell is the leading U.S. chain in the quick-service Mexican category. Sales in 1988 in the United States and six international markets amounted to $1.6 billion.

In 1987 Taco Bell introduced Steak Fajitas and Chicken Fajitas. In 1988 they introduced Meximelt, a tortilla with melted cheese, a low-cost item that can be eaten either as a main dish or as a side dish.

PepsiCo, the parent company of Kentucky Fried Chicken, Pizza Hut, and Taco Bell, is experimenting with the concept of combining them into one store to provide customers with a greater selection while cutting down on operating expenses.

Sales of major nonburger, fast-food, and quick service family-dining restaurants are given in Exhibit 1.

■ The McDonald's Corporation

McDonald's Corporation was incorporated in Delaware on March 1, 1965. McDonald's operates in one industry segment. Substantially all revenues result from the sale of menu products, regardless of whether the restaurants are operated by the company, its franchisees, or affiliates. As of January 1990, McDonald's had 11,300 restaurants. Exhibit 2 shows the geographic location of these outlets.

Sales outside of the United States continue to be strong, despite weaker foreign currencies. During the past five years, 41 percent of systemwide restaurants have been added outside of the United States. The major company-operated markets are located in England, Canada, and West Germany. Restaurants operated by affiliates are located primarily in Japan and other Pacific countries due to local business and political conditions.

Sales and profit information by geographic segments are shown in Exhibit 3. Financial statements from 1986 to 1989 are shown in Exhibit 4.

Although Fletcher was satisfied with McDonald's profit margins in recent years, the future prospects for the fast-food industry appear dreadful. Price, product, and locational competition have become so fierce that profit growth may be impossible. How can McDonald's attract health-conscious consumers? What new products should be introduced? Should it go with a McPizza and McRib? Should it expand its menu into new areas? What operational problems may it encounter? Should it discount? What market expansion and locational strategies should be used in the U.S. market and in the international markets? Which international regions should it focus on? Can it improve profitability in European markets? Fletcher's plan of action would have to convince top management that the new program could be successfully implemented despite a hostile environment.

■ **Exhibit 1**
Sales of Major Nonburger and Family Dining Restaurants (in thousands of dollars)

	1987	1988
Kentucky Fried Chicken		$6,000,000
Pizza Hut		2,800,000
Taco Bell		1,600,000
Church's Fried Chicken	$400,525	419,600
Morrison's	689,277	829,158
Shoney's	671,124	752,134
Rax	52,825	62,462

SOURCE: Moody's.

■ **Exhibit 2**
Geographic Locations of McDonald's Restaurants

Location	Year					
	1985	1986	1987	1988	1989	1990[a]
U.S.				7,567		
Outside U.S.A.						
Canada				515		
W. Europe				665		
Pacific				873		
Latin America				85		
Other				462		
Total	8,901	9,410	9,911	10,167	10,513	11,300

[a]Up to February 1990.
SOURCE: InfoTrac.

■ **Exhibit 3**
McDonald's Sales and
Profits by Geographic
Segment (in millions of
dollars)

	Year			
	1986	**1987**	**1988**	**1989**
Revenue				
U.S.	$3,077	$3,437	$3,716	$3,923
Europe	557	767	1,015	1,168
Canada	435	468	540	621
Other (Pacific and Latin American)	172	221	295	430
Total revenue	$4,240	$4,893	$5,566	$6,142
Operating Income				
U.S.	$ 809	$ 883	$ 909	$ 995
Europe	70	109	164	204
Canada	84	91	109	118
Other	59	79	102	143
Total operating income	1,021	1,162	1,284	1,459
Interest expense	(173)	(203)	(237)	(302)
Income before provision for income taxes	848	959	1,047	1,157
Assets				
U.S.	$4,218	$4,509	$5,148	$5,846
Europe	996	1,460	1,703	2,063
Canada	358	422	511	562
Other	397	591	798	904
Total assets	$5,969	$6,982	$8,160	$9,175

SOURCE: InfoTrac.

■ **Exhibit 4**
McDonald's Profit
and Loss Statement,
1986–89 (in millions
of dollars)

	1986	1987	1988	1989
Net sales	$4,143	$4,894	$5,566	$6,142
Cost of goods	1,808	3,013	2,377	2,581
Gross profit	2,336	1,880	3,189	3,561
Sell gen. & admin. expenses	1,175	525	1,581	1,873
Income before dep. & amort.	1,161	1,355	1,608	1,688
Depreciation and amort.	236	193	324	229
Nonoperating income	97	—	—	—
Interest expenses	173	203	237	302
Net income before taxes	848	959	1,046	1,157
Provision for inc. taxes	368	410	401	430
Net inc. bef. ex. items	480	549	646	727
Ex. items & disc. ops.	—	47	—	—
Net income	$ 480	$ 596	$ 646	$ 727
Outstanding shares	126,985	207,567	207,567	362,000

SOURCE: InfoTrac.

■ Case 3   South Delaware Coors, Inc.

James E. Nelson and Eric J. Karson
University of Colorado

Larry Brownlow was just beginning to realize the problem was more complex than he thought. The problem, of course, was giving direction to Manson and Associates regarding which research should be completed by February 20, 1989, to determine market potential of a Coors beer distributorship for a two-county area in southern Delaware. With data from this research, Larry would be able to estimate the feasibility of such an operation before the March 5 application deadline. Larry knew his decision on whether or not to apply for the distributorship was the most important career choice he had ever faced.

Larry Brownlow

Larry was just completing his M.B.A. and, from his standpoint, the Coors announcement of expansion into Delaware could hardly have been better timed. He had long ago decided the best opportunities and rewards were in smaller, self-owned businesses and not in the jungles of corporate giants. Because of a family tragedy some three years ago, Larry found himself in a position to consider small business opportunities such as the Coors distributorship. Approximately $500,000 was held in trust for Larry, to be dispersed when he reached age thirty. Until then, Larry and his family lived on an annual trust income of about $40,000. It was on this income that Larry decided to leave his sales engineering job and return to graduate school for his M.B.A.

The decision to complete a graduate program and operate his own business had been easy to make. While he could have retired and lived off investment income, Larry knew such a life would not be to his liking. Working with people and the challenge of making it on his own, Larry thought, were far more preferable to enduring an early retirement.

Larry would be thirty in July, about the time money would actually be needed to start the business. In the meantime, he had access to about $15,000 for feasibility research. While there certainly were other places to spend the money, Larry and his wife agreed the opportunity to acquire the distributorship could not be overlooked.

■ Coors, Inc.

Coors's history dates back to 1873, when Adolph Coors built a small brewery in Golden, Colorado. Since then, the brewery has prospered and become the fourth-largest seller of beer in the country. Coors's operating philosophy could be summed

This case was written by Professor James E. Nelson and Doctoral Student Eric J. Karson, University of Colorado. This case is intended for use as a basis for class discussion rather than to illustrate either effective or ineffective administrative decision making. Some data are disguised. © 1989 by the Business Research Division, College of Business and Administration and the Graduate School of Business Administration, University of Colorado, Boulder, Colorado 80309–0419.

up as "hard work, saving money, devotion to the quality of the product, caring about the environment, and giving people something to believe in." Company operation is consistent with this philosophy. Headquarters and most production facilities are still located in Golden, Colorado, with a new Shenandoah, Virginia, facility aiding in nationwide distribution. Coors is still family operated and controlled. The company issued its first public stock, $127 million worth of nonvoting shares, in 1975. The issue was received enthusiastically by the financial community despite its being offered during a recession.

Coors's unwillingness to compromise on the high quality of its product is well known both to its suppliers and to its consuming public. Coors beer requires constant refrigeration to maintain this quality, and wholesalers' facilities are closely controlled to ensure proper temperatures are maintained. Wholesalers are also required to install and use aluminum can recycling equipment. Coors was one of the first breweries in the industry to recycle its cans.

Larry was aware of Coors's popularity with many consumers in adjacent states. However, Coors's corporate management was seen by some consumers to hold antiunion beliefs (because of a labor disagreement at the brewery some ten years ago and the brewery's current use of a nonunion labor force). Some other consumers perceived the brewery to be somewhat insensitive to minority issues, primarily in employment and distribution. The result of these attitudes—plus many other aspects of consumer behavior—meant that Coors's sales in Delaware would depend greatly on the efforts of the two wholesalers planned for the state.

■ Manson Research Proposal

Because of the press of his studies, Larry had contacted Manson and Associates in January for their assistance. The firm was a Wilmington-based general research supplier that had conducted other feasibility studies in the south Atlantic region. Manson was well known for the quality of its work, particularly with respect to computer modeling. The firm had developed special expertise in modeling population and employment levels for cities, counties, and other units of area for periods of up to 10 years into the future.

Larry had met John Rome, senior research analyst for Manson, and discussed the Coors opportunity and appropriate research extensively in the January meeting. Rome promised a formal research proposal (Exhibits 1 and 2) for the project, which Larry now held in his hand. It certainly was extensive, Larry thought, and reflected the professionalism he expected. Now came the hard part, choosing the more relevant research from the proposal, because he certainly couldn't afford to pay for it all. Rome had suggested a meeting for Friday, giving Larry only two more days to decide.

Larry was at first overwhelmed. All the research would certainly be useful. He was sure he needed estimates of sales and costs in a form allowing managerial analysis, but what data in what form? Knowledge of competing operations' experience, retailer support, and consumer acceptance also seemed important for feasibility analysis. For example, what if consumers were excited about Coors and retailers indifferent or the other way around? Finally, several of the studies would provide information that could be useful in later months of operation in the areas of promotion and pricing, for example. The problem now appeared more difficult than before!

It would have been nice, Larry thought, to have had some time to perform part of the suggested research himself. However, there was just too much in the way of class assignments and other matters to allow him that luxury. Besides, using Manson and Associates would give him research results from an unbiased source.

■ **Exhibit 1** Manson and Associates Research Proposal

Mr. Larry Brownlow   January 16, 1989
1198 West Lamar
Chester, PA 12345

Dear Larry:

It was a pleasure meeting you last week and discussing your business and research interests in Coors wholesaling. After further thought and discussion with my colleagues, the Coors opportunity appears even more attractive than when we met.

Appearances can be deceiving, as you know, and I fully agree some formal research is needed before you make application. Research that we recommend would proceed in two distinct stages and is described below:

Stage One Research Based on Secondary Data and Manson Computer Models:

Study A: National and Delaware per Capita Beer Consumption for 1988–1992.
   Description: Per capita annual consumption of beer for the total population and population aged 21 and over is provided in gallons.
   Source: Various publications, Manson computer model
   Cost: $1,000

Study B: Population Estimates for 1985–1995 for two Delaware Counties in Market Area.
   Description: Annual estimates of total population and population aged 21 and over is provided for the period 1985–1995.
   Source: U.S. Bureau of Census, Sales Management Annual Survey of Buying Power, Manson computer model
   Cost: $1,500

Study C: Coors Market Share Estimates for 1990–1995.
   Description: Coors market share for the two-county market area based on total gallons consumed is estimated for each year in the period 1990–1995. This data will be projected from Coors's nationwide experience.
   Source: Various publications, Manson computer model
   Cost: $2,000

Study D: Estimated Liquor and Beer Licenses for the Market Area, 1990–1995.
   Description: Projections of the number of on-premise sale operations and off-premise sale operations is provided.
   Source: Delaware Department of Revenue, Manson Computer Model
   Cost: $1,000

Study E: Beer Taxes Paid by Delaware Wholesalers for 1987 and 1988 in the Market Area.
   Description: Beer taxes paid by each of the six presently operating competing beer wholesalers is provided. This can be converted to gallons sold by applying the state gallonage tax rate (6 cents per gallon).
   Source: Delaware Department of Revenue
   Cost: $200

Study F: Financial Statement Summary of Wine, Liquor, and Beer Wholesalers for Fiscal Year 1986.
   Description: Composite balance sheets, income statements, and relevant measures of performance provided for 510 similar wholesaling operations in the United States is provided.
   Source: Robert Morris Associates Annual Statement Studies 1987 ed.
   Cost: $49.50

(continued)

■ **Exhibit 1** (*concluded*)

Stage Two Research Based on Primary Data:

Study G: Consumer Study
            Description: Study G involves focus group interviews and a mail questionnaire to determine
                consumer past experience, acceptance, and intention to buy Coors beer. Three focus group
                interviews would be conducted in the two counties in the market area. From these data, a
                mail questionnaire would be developed and sent to 300 adult residents in the market area,
                utilizing direct questions and semantic differential scale to measure attitudes toward Coors
                beer, competing beers, and an ideal beer.
            Source: Manson and Associates
            Cost: $6,000

Study H: Retailer Study
            Description: Group interviews would be conducted with six potential retailers of Coors beer in
                one county in the market area to determine their past beer sales and experience and their
                intention to stock and sell Coors. From these data, a personal interview questionnaire would
                be developed and executed at all appropriate retailers in the market area to determine
                similar data.
            Source: Manson and Associates
            Cost: $4,800

Study I: Survey of Retail and Wholesale Beer Prices
            Description: Study I involves in-store interviews with a sample of 50 retailers in the market area
                to estimate retail and wholesale prices for Budweiser, Miller Lite, Miller, Busch, Bud Light,
                Old Milwaukee, and Michelob.
            Source: Manson and Associates
            Cost: $2,000

Examples of the form of final report tables are attached [Exhibit 2]. This should give you a better idea of the
data you will receive.

As you can see, the research is extensive and, I might add, not cheap. However, the research as outlined will
supply you with sufficient information to make an estimate of the feasibility of a Coors distributorship, the investment for which is substantial.

I have scheduled 9:00 next Friday as a time to meet with you to discuss the proposal in more detail. Time is
short, but we firmly feel the study can be completed by February 20, 1989. If you need more information in the
meantime, please feel free to call.

Sincerely,

John

John Rome
Senior Research Analyst

■ **Exhibit 2** Examples of Final Research Report Tables

(A) National and Delaware Resident Annual Beer Consumption per Capita, 1988–1992 (Gallons)

	U.S. Consumption		Delaware Consumption	
Year	Based on Entire Population	Based on Population over Age 21	Based on Entire Population	Based on Population over Age 21
1988				
1989				
1990				
1991				
1992				

SOURCE: Study A.

(B) Population Estimates for 1986–1996 for Two Delaware Counties in Market Area

Entire Population

County	1986	1988	1990	1992	1994	1996
Kent						
Sussex						

Population Age 21 and Over

County	1986	1988	1990	1992	1994	1996
Kent						
Sussex						

SOURCE: Study B.

(C) Coors Market Share Estimates for 1990–1995

Year	Market Share (%)
1990	
1991	
1992	
1993	
1994	
1995	

SOURCE: Study C.

(continued)

■ **Exhibit 2** *(continued)*

(D) Liquor and Beer License Estimates for Market Area for 1990–1995

Type of License	1990	1991	1992	1993	1994	1995
All beverages						
Retail beer and wine						
Off-premises beer only						
Veterans beer and liquor						
Fraternal						
Resort beer and liquor						

SOURCE: Study D.

(E) Beer Taxes Paid by Beer Wholesalers in the Market Area, 1987 and 1988

Wholesaler	1987 Tax Paid ($)	1988 Tax Paid ($)
A		
B		
C		
D		
E		
F		

SOURCE: Study E.
NOTE: Delaware beer tax is 6 cents per gallon.

(F) Financial Statement Summary for 510 Wholesalers of Wine, Liquor, and Beer in Fiscal Year 1986

Assets		Percentage
Cash and equivalents		
Accounts and notes receivable net		
Inventory		
All other current		
Total current		
Fixed assets net		
Intangibles net		
All other noncurrent		
Total	100.0	
	Ratios	
	Quick	
	Current	
	Debts/worth	

(continued)

■ **Exhibit 2** (*continued*)

(F) Financial Statement Summary for 510 Wholesalers of Wine, Liquor, and Beer in Fiscal Year 1986 (continued)

Liabilities		**Percentage**
Notes payable—short-term		Sales/receivables
Current maturity long-term debt		Cost sales/inventory
Accounts and notes payable—trade		Percentage profit before taxes
Accrued expenses		based on total assets
All other current		
Total current		
Long-term debt		
All other noncurrent		
Net worth	———	
Total liabilities and net worth	100.0	
Income Data		
Net sales	100.0	
Cost of sales		
Gross profit		
Operating expenses		
Operating profit		
All other expenses net	———	
Profit before taxes		

SOURCE: Study F (Robert Morris Associates, © 1987)

Interpretation of Statement Studies Figures

RMA recommends that Statement Studies data be regarded only as general guidelines and not as absolute industry norms. There are several reasons why the data may not be fully representative of a given industry:

1. The financial statements used in the *Statement Studies* are not selected by any random or statistically reliable method. RMA member banks voluntarily submit the raw data they have available each year, with these being the only constraints: (a) The fiscal year-ends of the companies reported may not be from April 1 through June 29, and (b) their total assets must be less than $100 million.

2. Many companies have varied product lines; however, the *Statement Studies* categorize them by their primary product Standard Industrial Classification (SIC) number only.

3. Some of our industry samples are rather small in relation to the total number of firms in a given industry. A relatively small sample can increase the changes that some of our composites do not fully represent an industry.

4. There is the chance that an extreme statement can be present in a sample, causing a disproportionate influence on the industry composite. This is particularly true in a relatively small sample.

5. Companies within the same industry may differ in their method of operations which in turn can directly influence their financial statements. Since they are included in our sample, too, these statements can significantly affect our composite calculations.

6. Other considerations that can result in variations among different companies engaged in the same general line of business are different labor markets; geographical location; different accounting methods; quality of products handled; sources and methods of financing; and terms of sale.

For these reasons, RMA does not recommend the Statement Studies *figures be considered as absolute norms for a given industry. Rather the figures should be used only as general guidelines and in addition to the other methods of financial analysis. RMA makes no claim as to the representativeness of the figures printed in this book.*

(*continued*)

■ **Exhibit 2** (*continued*)

(G) Consumer Questionnaire Results

	Yes	No		Yes	No
Consumed Coors in the Past:	%	%	**Usually Buy Beer at:**	%	
Attitudes toward Coors:	%				
Strongly like			Liquor stores		
Like			Taverns and bars		
Indifferent/no opinion			Supermarkets		
Dislike			Corner grocery		
Strongly dislike			Total	100.0	
Total	100.0				
			Features Considered Important		
Weekly Beer Consumption:	%		**When Buying Beer:**	%	
Less than 1 can			Taste		
1–2 cans			Brand name		
3–4 cans			Price		
5–6 cans			Store location		
7–8 cans			Advertising		
9 cans and over			Carbonation		
Total	100.0		Other		
			Total	100.0	
Intention to Buy Coors:	%				
Certainly will					
Maybe will					
Not sure					
Maybe will not					
Certainly will not					
Total	100.0				

Semantic Differential Scale-Consumers*

	Extremely	Very	Somewhat	Somewhat	Very	Extremely	
Masculine	____	____	____	____	____	____	Feminine
Healthful	____	____	____	____	____	____	Unhealthful
Cheap	____	____	____	____	____	____	Expensive
Strong	____	____	____	____	____	____	Weak
Old-fashioned	____	____	____	____	____	____	New
Upper-class	____	____	____	____	____	____	Lower-class
Good taste	____	____	____	____	____	____	Bad taste

SOURCE: Study G.
*Profiles would be provided for Coors, three competing beers, and an ideal beer.

(*continued*)

■ Exhibit 2 (concluded)

(H) Retailer Questionnaire Results

Brands of Beer Carried:	%	Beer Sales:	%
Budweiser		Budweiser	
Miller Lite		Miller Lite	
Miller		Miller	
Busch		Busch	
Bud Light		Bud Light	
Old Milwaukee		Old Milwaukee	
Michelob		Michelob	
		Others	
		Total	100.0

Semantic Differential Scale-Retailers*

	Extremely	Very	Somewhat	Somewhat	Very	Extremely	
Masculine	___	___	___	___	___	___	Feminine
Healthful	___	___	___	___	___	___	Unhealthful
Cheap	___	___	___	___	___	___	Expensive
Strong	___	___	___	___	___	___	Weak
Old-fashioned	___	___	___	___	___	___	New
Upper-class	___	___	___	___	___	___	Lower-class
Good taste	___	___	___	___	___	___	Bad taste

Intention to Sell Coors: %

Certainly will	
Maybe will	
Not sure	
Maybe will not	
Certainly will not	
Total	100.0

SOURCE: Study G.
*Profiles would be provided for Coors, three competing beers, and an ideal beer.

(I) Retail and Wholesale Prices for Selected Beers in the Market Area

Beer	Wholesale* Six-Pack Price (dollars)	Retail† Six-Pack Price (dollars)
Budweiser		
Miller Lite		
Miller		
Busch		
Bud Light		
Old Milwaukee		
Michelob		

SOURCE: Study I.
*Price that the wholesaler sold to retailers.
†Price that the retailer sold to consumers.

■ Investing and Operating Data

Larry was not completely in the dark regarding investment and operating data for the distributorship. In the past two weeks he had visited two beer wholesalers in his hometown of Chester, Pennsylvania, who handled Anheuser-Busch and Miller beer, to get a feel for their operation and marketing experience. It would have been nice to interview a Coors wholesaler, but Coors management had strictly informed all of their distributors to provide no information to prospective applicants.

While no specific financial data was discussed, general information had been provided in a cordial fashion because of the noncompetitive nature of Larry's plans. Based on his conversations, Larry made the following estimates:

Inventory		$240,000
Equipment		
Delivery trucks	$150,000	
Forklift	20,000	
Recycling and miscellaneous equipment	20,000	
Office equipment	10,000	
Total equipment		200,000
Warehouse		320,000
Land		40,000
Total investment		$800,000

A local banker had reviewed Larry's financial capabilities and saw no problem in extending a line of credit on the order of $400,000. Other sources also might loan as much as $400,000 to the business.

As a rough estimate of fixed expenses, Larry planned on having four route salespeople, a secretary, and a warehouse manager. Salaries for these people and himself would run about $160,000 annually plus some form of incentive compensation he had yet to determine. Other fixed or semifixed expenses were estimated at:

Equipment depreciation	$35,000
Warehouse depreciation	15,000
Utilities and telephone	12,000
Insurance	10,000
Personal property taxes	10,000
Maintenance and janitorial	5,600
Miscellaneous	2,400
	$90,000

According to the wholesalers, beer in bottles and cans outsold keg beer by a three-to-one margin. Keg beer prices at the wholesale level were about 45 percent of prices for beer in bottles and cans.

■ Meeting

The entire matter deserved much thought. Maybe it was a golden opportunity, maybe not. The only thing certain was that research was needed, Manson and Associates was ready, and Larry needed time to think. Today is Tuesday, Larry thought—only three days until he and John Rome would get together for direction.

■ Case 4　Claritas Inc.: Using Compass and PRIZM

Valerie Walsh and J. Paul Peter
University of Wisconsin–Madison

■ Introduction

Managers are often faced with the task of making tough decisions regarding their marketing strategies. To make effective decisions, they need to understand their markets. In order to do so, they rely on marketing research. Some firms have their own marketing research departments while other firms rely on companies that specialize in analyzing markets. Many firms have found it useful to use technology-driven, desktop marketing information systems, such as Claritas's Compass and PRIZM systems.

■ Industry Background

The modern marketing information analysis industry was born in the 1970s, after the completion of the first computer-accessible census. Electronic census access made it possible to tabulate demographic data by geographic boundaries. During the 1970s, data (including demographics) were stored on large mainframes as opposed to personal computers. Marketers who wanted to analyze census data either needed a mainframe nearby or a connection to a mainframe via a modem, which used a commercial time-sharing service. Either way, data access was relatively slow and expensive.

One solution to the problem was to reduce the amount of data being analyzed by focusing on neighborhoods rather than individual census households. To accomplish this, a Harvard-educated social scientist named Jonathan Robbin developed the first "geodemographic" segmentation system, PRIZM (Potential Ranking Index by ZIP Market), in 1974. By analyzing neighborhoods, Robbin was able to convey a great deal about their character and market potential without using a large set of descriptive variables. "Geodemography" was the term given to the linking of demographic data and local neighborhood geography (such as ZIP codes, ZIP + 4 codes, Census Tracts and Block Groups) to create classifications of actual, addressable, mappable neighborhoods where people live and shop.

Implementing Geodemographic Analysis

There are two main types of geography used for marketing applications of data: Census and Postal. The specifications for census geography were created by the U.S. Department of the Census to aid the collection of census data. The specifications for postal geography are developed and maintained by the U.S. Postal Service to aid

This case was prepared by Valerie Walsh, Nielsen Scholar at the University of Wisconsin–Madison, under the supervision of J. Paul Peter. Information provided by Claritas Inc. Special thanks to Jeremy Schwarz of Claritas Inc. Copyright by J. Paul Peter.

■ **Exhibit 1** Geography Definitions

Census Geography Definitions

- **USA:** The United States is comprised of the 50 states and the District of Columbia.
- **State**: A two-digit Federal Information Processing Standards (FIPS) code uniquely identifies each state; codes follow the alphabetic sequence of the states.
- **MSA:** Metropolitan Statistical Areas consist of one or more entire counties that meet specified standards pertaining to population, commuting ties and metropolitan character. The total population is at least 100,000 and includes a city of 50,000+. MSAs are designated and defined by the federal Office of Management and Budget (OMB) and do not cover the entire United States. There are 358 MSAs in the United States.
- **County:** The primary political and administrative subdivision of a state. There are 3,141 counties in the United States.
- **Census Tract:** A subdivision of a county that is designed to be a relatively homogeneous area of 1,200–2,500 people. As of the 1990 census, the entire country is tracted, and there are 61,258 tracts in the United States.
- **Block Group:** A subdivision of a census tract that is approximately four blocks or 400–800 individuals. There are approximately 226,399 block groups in the United States.
- **Block:** Blocks are the smallest census geographic entity, usually bounded by prominent physical features such as streets, roads, streams, railroad tracks, and the like. A block generally contains 18–22 households, and there are 6,961,697 blocks in the United States.

Postal Geography Definitions

- **ZIP Codes:** Established by the U.S. Postal Service for the distribution of mail, ZIP code boundaries do not follow census boundaries and are subject to constant change. Each ZIP code is assigned to one county; actual ZIP boundaries can cross county and state lines.
- **ZIP+4:** A subdivision of a ZIP code, but not every ZIP code is divided. ZIP+4s are used for more detailed mail routing definition and do not cover the entire United States. Some ZIP+4s are a street block, while others are a floor in a city office building.
- **Carrier Route:** A three-digit code used by the U.S. Postal Service to specify mail delivery routes. Routes vary in size and cross over ZIP and ZIP+4 boundaries.

the delivery of U.S. mail. Exhibit 1 describes the different levels of census and postal geography from the largest to the smallest geographic area for which PRIZM and other data systems are available.

It was not long before census data and geodemography were married to a wealth of survey data. Independent research organizations, such as A. C. Nielsen, R. L. Polk, and Mediamark Research Inc. (MRI) collect and sell television rating data, vehicle registration data, and consumer product consumption and media habit data, respectively. Data can be purchased in raw electronic format or in a prespecified report format.

The system that Robbin developed in 1974 ran on a mainframe, and it was not until 1984 that PRIZM was used on a personal computer. A geodemographic segmentation system links vast amounts of demographic and lifestyle data to actual, mappable neighborhoods. Every U.S. neighborhood is classified into a segment based on demographic characteristics of the people who live there. For an example of how a company would use a segmentation system, consider Jane Smith as one of its best customers. By knowing Jane's ZIP+4 code, the company can find out the demographic and lifestyle profile of Jane's neighborhood. The company can then find out where other neighborhoods like Jane's are located by searching for neighborhoods with Jane's same segment assignment, and can then target those neighborhoods through direct mail or other types of promotion.

In 1987, National Decision Systems (NDS) combined independent survey data and census data with geographic boundaries to create the first desktop marketing information system, Infomark, for the personal computer. This revolutionized the marketing information industry, and other companies quickly followed with their own systems. A desktop marketing information system is a software and data package which allows the users to create reports (see Exhibit 2) and maps (see Exhibit 3) that are used to understand markets and make effective marketing decisions. Today's systems have been enhanced by a greater amount of data, industry-specific geographic boundaries (such as telephone system boundaries), and availability of roads and landmarks for map enhancement. Claritas's Compass and NDS's Infomark are examples of desktop marketing information systems.

Marketing information and segmentation systems are used in many different industries to solve industry specific marketing problems. Some of the main industries using marketing information analysis are financial services, retail, advertising, telecommunications, and print media. As the use of marketing information services increases, companies are demanding that client service representatives have in-depth industry knowledge to help solve their problems. Some of the cross-industry uses of marketing information are:

- **Target selection:** Through the use of demographic and lifestyle data, clients can determine who their best prospects are.
- **Direct marketing:** Use of lifestyle data tied to geography can help clients create a promotional mail campaign to target their best prospects.
- **Site selection:** A profile of customers who frequent clients' most profitable stores or branches can be created, and then more customers of the same demographic and lifestyle makeup can be located. This can help clients determine where to open a new retail store or bank branch.
- **Media selection:** Once clients have identified their best prospects, independent survey data can help determine which magazines or television shows to advertise in/on to reach these consumers.
- **Market potential:** Based on past sales, clients can map the sales potential of a specific product within any given market in the United States. This can help them forecast whether the product will be profitable within given markets.

Competitive Environment

Claritas and NDS are the two main competitors in the desktop marketing information analysis industry. Both companies sell desktop marketing information systems, segmentation systems, and industry specific applications, and both systems operate in an IBM-compatible Windows environment. A third competitor, Strategic Mapping Inc. (SMI), was purchased by Claritas in 1996. With the acquisition of SMI, Claritas gained SMI's Windows-based desktop marketing information system along with a variety of other products. Exhibit 4 lists the systems of the two main competitors.

■ **Exhibit 2** Market Potential Index (MPI) Report for Alternative Rock Music in the District of Columbia

ZIP Code & Post Office Name	Households	MPI	Median Household Income
20050- Washington	880	316	$30,563
20006- Twentieth Street	772	316	26,979
20336- Bolling AFB Quarter	1,144	247	42,409
MPI of 200+	**2,796***	**288****	
20037- Watergate	5,422	185	44,446
20038- Washington	1,058	175	35,754
20088- Washington	228	165	98,214
20033- Washington	287	161	39,028
20036- Twentieth Street	3,164	160	40,095
20015- Northwest	5,522	155	82,879
20035- Washington	1,046	151	51,129
20016- Eagle	11,397	146	67,081
20007- Calvert	10,639	146	58,292
20057- Georgetown Univ	63	141	41,821
20012- Walter Reed	4,785	138	54,038
20008- Cleveland Park	13,817	137	57,602
20009- Kalorama	19,854	125	36,398
MPI of 200–120	**77,282***	**143****	
20026- Washington	1,731	118	39,391
20024- L'Enfant Plaza	5,264	114	43,155
20013- Washington	3,364	114	53,045
20017- Brookland	6,036	110	47,453
20005- Central	4,787	107	29,308
20003- Southeast	8,103	102	48,313
20011- Brightwood	20,657	91	37,658
20004- Benjamin Franklin	628	84	11,623
MPI of 120–80	**50,570***	**101****	
20002- Kendall Green	19,923	72	32,360
20056- Washington	1,292	69	27,101
20010- Columbia Heights	9,194	68	30,338
20018- Customs House	6,553	67	30,771
20020- Anacostia	17,197	67	30,038
20090- Washington	2,606	55	33,839
20001- Le Droit Park	9,594	51	24,373
20032- Congress Heights	12,036	46	26,016
20019- Benning	19,920	45	27,578
20039- Washington	648	40	40,089
20077- Washington	8	40	20,000
20044- Washington	2,396	40	8,013
20515- Washington	8	40	16,250
20043- Washington	345	40	26,289
20091- Washington	736	36	28,188
20030- Washington	943	36	26,477
20029- Washington	1,521	33	35,819
20064- Catholic Univ	0	0	0
20301- Dept of Defense	0	0	0
20059- Howard Univ	0	0	0
MPI of < 80	**104,920***	**58****	

*Total number of households in each of these ZIP code groups.
**Weighted average MPI for each of these ZIP code groups.

NOTE: Any MPI above 100 is considered to be above average.

SOURCE: Claritas, Inc.

A market potential index (MPI) is used to identify geographic areas with high usage potential for a given product. The example above shows that the ZIP code 20050 has the highest market potential index for alternative rock music. In addition, the above report lists the number of households and the median household income in each ZIP code.

■ **Exhibit 3** Market Potential for Alternative Rock Music in the District of Columbia

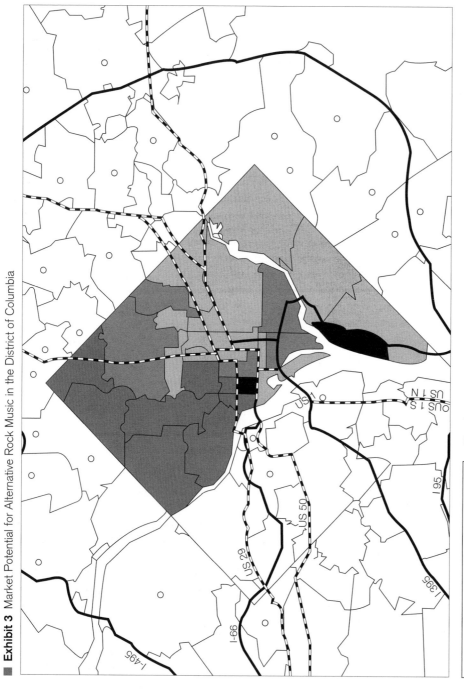

The above map displays the market potential for alternative rock in the Washington D.C. area. The map is another way to view the data (as opposed to looking at a report) and is often easier for clients to analyze.

ZIP MPI for Alternative Rock Music
District of Columbia

■ Highest Potential (3 ZIP codes)
▨ Medium–High Potential (13 ZIP codes)
▨ Medium–Low Potential (8 ZIP codes)
▨ Lowest Potential (20 ZIP codes)

SOURCE: Claritas, Inc.

■ **Exhibit 4** Products of Major Competitors in the Desktop Marketing Information Industry

Products	Claritas	NDS
Desktop Marketing Information System	Compass Conquest (an acquired SMI product)	Infomark
Segmentation System	PRIZM ClusterPLUS 2000 (an acquired SMI product)	MicroVision

In addition to the three main players in the market, secondary competition comes from geographic information system (GIS) companies. These companies include MapInfo, ESRI, and Tactician. The GIS companies produce and sell mapping software that is used in many industries, including law enforcement, emergency services, and marketing. The problem with GIS software is that data are not conveniently bundled with the software, forcing marketers to build their own system. The advantage to GIS systems is that they have more detailed mapping capabilities, which are useful for activities that involve in-depth mapping of a geographic area. The desktop marketing systems in Exhibit 4 all use one of the main GIS systems for their mapping engine. Claritas uses MapInfo's MapInfo, while NDS uses ESRI's ArcView. Although a GIS system is used for the mapping engine, the geographic detail is greater in a GIS system alone than in a desktop marketing information system.

■ Company Overview

Claritas was founded in 1971 by Jonathan Robbin, a computer scientist. The word "claritas" is Latin for clarity and it inspired Robbin through a James Joyce book, *A Portrait of the Artist as a Young Man,* in which claritas is cited as one of the three essential elements of great art.

The 1970s were a decade of growth for Claritas, as the company introduced its first version of PRIZM, the segmentation system that would become the backbone of the company. The initial marketing challenge was to create an awareness and acceptance of the new marketing information analysis industry. The company had to convince the business world of the inherent value of purchasing market segmentation information for making marketing decisions, as opposed to the traditional use of primary research.

Claritas is owned by VNU Business Information Services (VNU BIS) which is owned by VNU United Dutch Publishing Companies, a $1.6 billion publishing and information services company based in the Netherlands. Approximately 2,000 people are employed by VNU BIS and the company has annual revenues of more than $150 million. In addition to Claritas, VNU owns seven other U.S. marketing companies. The companies complement each other in many ways, but do not work together very often. The company that is most similar to Claritas is Spectra Marketing. An agreement between Claritas and Spectra grants Spectra the right to sell Claritas's products, however, Spectra customizes the Claritas core segmentation and software products to focus on the packaged goods industry.

Products

Claritas's two main areas of business are: (1) nonlicensed data sales and projects, and (2) licensed data and software. Nonlicensed data are typically smaller in quantity and lower in price (under $5,000) and are mostly sold via telephone through Claritas's Data Services Group. These data include demographic market area reports, ZIP code reports, and various other forms of ad-hoc data. Nonlicensed projects are often sold through the consultative field sales force as a stepping stone toward licensing a full software system.

The majority of Claritas's business is licensed data and software sold to clients for a period of one to three years. Selling of these products is the main focus of Claritas's sales and client service staff, and their responsibilities include sales and consulting support of client applications using Claritas data.

PRIZM.   PRIZM is a market segmentation system that classifies every U.S. neighborhood into one of 62 distinct types or "clusters." Each PRIZM cluster combines detailed demographics with product, media, and lifestyle preferences to create a profile of the people in these neighborhoods (see the three cluster profiles in Exhibits 5–7). The PRIZM system uses the following assumptions to help identify target markets:

1. **Birds of a feather flock together:** meaning that people living in the same types of neighborhoods tend to be more similar to each other than people in different types of neighborhoods.
2. **The best customers for your product are existing customers:** describing the people who already use your product or a similar one, or other people like your existing customers, as the best prospects.

Marketers use PRIZM to segment customers into groups to better understand customer lifestyles and behavior and then target their best prospects. PRIZM cluster reports can be run to identify clusters with heaviest product usage for specific products (see Exhibit 8). As seen in Exhibits 5–7, different PRIZM clusters contain different types of people. With the identification of which clusters to target comes an identification of what type of person to target. For example, people in the Hispanic Mix cluster have different backgrounds and culture than people in the Blue Blood Estates cluster, hence different marketing strategies might be needed to reach each group. The PRIZM system is rarely licensed alone, but is licensed as an integrated part of Claritas's Compass system.

Compass.   Compass is a PC-based marketing workstation used to integrate, analyze, and map demographic, consumer demand and usage, site, and geographic data. Industry-specific applications, such as Compass/Agency (for advertising agencies), Compass/Banking (for banking and insurance companies), and Compass/Cable (for Cable TV companies) are used to address the unique marketing needs of individual industries. Compass also includes dozens of demographic, product usage, media, business, and site databases. Many clients use Compass to help understand their customers by answering the following questions:

• **Who are my target consumers?** The different databases available in Compass allow clients to link their own customer data with neighborhood demographics, PRIZM lifestyle segments, syndicated data, or survey research data. By linking customer data with Compass data, clients can understand exactly what type of consumer is most likely to use their product or service.

■ **Exhibit 5** Sample Cluster Profile from the PRIZM System (Cluster 01—Blue Blood Estates)

The **Blue Blood Estates** cluster contains America's wealthiest suburbs, populated by super-upper established executives, professionals, and heirs to "old money" who are accustomed to privilege and live in luxury, supported by servants. One in ten residents is a multi-millionaire, and there is a sharp drop from these heights to the next level of affluence.

Predominant Characteristics
- Households (%U.S.):   729,500 (0.8%)
- Population: 2,181,400
- Demographic caption: Elite super-rich families
- Ethnic diversity: Dominant White, High Asian
- Family type: Married couples w/children
- Predominant age ranges: 35–54
- Education: College graduates
- Employment level: Professional
- Housing type: Owners/Single Unit
- Density centile: 66 (1= sparse, 99=dense)

More Likely To:

Lifestyle	*Products and Services*
Belong to a country club	Purchase a car phone
Travel to Japan/Asia	Eat pita bread
Contract home improvement	Drink imported wine
Go sailing	Own a Lexus
Use maid/housekeeper	Spend 250+ on business suit
Lease car for personal use	Buy Montblanc/Waterman pen
Radio/TV	*Print*
Watch Arts & Entertainment	Read *National Geographic Travel*
Listen to news/talk radio	Read newspaper business section
Watch "Seinfeld"	Read *Elle*
Listen to soft contemp radio	Read *Food & Wine*
Watch Masters (Golf)	Read *Fortune*

■ **Exhibit 6**   Sample Cluster Profile from the PRIZM System   (Cluster 36—Towns and Gowns)

    The **Towns and Gowns** cluster describes most of our college towns and university campus neighborhoods. With a typical mix of half locals (Towns) and half students (Gowns), it is wholly unique, with thousands of penniless 18–24-year-old kids, plus highly educated professionals, all with a taste for prestige products beyond their evident means.

Predominant Characteristics
- Households (%U.S.):   1,290,2000 (1.4%)
- Population: 3,542,500
- Demographic caption: College town singles
- Ethnic diversity: Dominant White, High Asian
- Family type: Singles
- Predominant age ranges: Under 24, 25–34
- Education: College graduates
- Employment level: White-Collar/Service
- Housing type: Renters/Multi-Unit 10+
- Density centile: 58 (1=sparse, 99=dense)

More Likely To:

Lifestyle	*Products and Services*
Go to college football games	Have a personal education loan
Play racquetball	Use an ATM card
Go skiing	Own a Honda
Play billiards/pool	Buy 3+ pairs of jeans annually
Use cigarette rolling paper	Drink Coca-Cola Classic
Use a charter/tour bus	Eat Kraft Macaroni and Cheese
Radio/TV	*Print*
Watch VH1	Read *Self*
Listen to alternative rock music	Read newspaper comics section
Watch "Jeopardy"	Read *Rolling Stone*
Listen to variety radio	Read *GQ*
Watch "The Simpsons"	

■ **Exhibit 7** Sample Cluster Profile from the PRIZM System (Cluster 46—Hispanic Mix)

The **Hispanic Mix** cluster collects the nation's bilingual, Hispanic barrios, which are chiefly concentrated in the Atlantic metro corridor, Chicago, Miami, Texas, Los Angeles, and the Southwest. The neighborhoods are populated by large families with many small children. They rank second in percent foreign-born, first in transient immigration.

Predominant Characteristics:
- Households (%U.S.):   1,420,100 (1.5%)
- Population: 4,473,100
- Demographic caption: Urban Hispanic singles & families
- Ethnic diversity: Dominant Hispanic
- Family type: Singles, parents, married couples
- Predominant age ranges: Under 24, 25–34
- Education: Grade school
- Employment level: Blue-Collar/Service
- Housing type: Renters/Multi-Unit 10+
- Density centile: 91 (1=sparse, 99=dense)

More Likely To:

Lifestyle	*Products and Services*
Go to pro basketball games	Use postal money orders
Go roller skating	Buy stereo equipment
Go to truck & tractor pull races	Own a Mazda
Buy dance music	Eat canned hashes
Smoke regular cigarettes	Eat children's frozen dinners
Rent foreign videos	Drink imported beer often
Radio/TV	*Print*
Watch "Cops"	Read *Jet*
Listen to Spanish radio	Read newspaper classified section
Watch "Geraldo"	Read *Weight Watchers*
Listen to urban contemp radio	Read the *National Enquirer*
Watch "Married with Children"	Read *Motor Trend*

■ **Exhibit 8**

1995 Clusters Ranked by Propensity to Listen to Alternative Rock Music

Cluster #	Cluster Nickname	Propensity to Listen Index
36	Towns & Gowns	317
40	Military Quarters	247
01	Blue Blood Estates	182
18	Young Influentials	173
46	Hispanic Mix	168
27	Urban Achievers	161
10	Bohemian Mix	161
31	Latino America	157
22	Blue-Chip Blues	149
08	Young Literati	141
07	Money & Brains	134
23	Upstarts & Seniors	132
24	New Beginnings	131
33	Boomtown Singles	129
17	Greenbelt Families	128
28	Big City Blend	126
11	Second City Elite	126
02	Winner's Circle	125
06	Urban Gold Coast	124
12	Upward Bound	124
38	Middle America	123
35	Sunset City Blues	121
04	Pools & Patios	120
42	New Eco-topia	120
13	Gray Power	120
05	Kids & Cul-de-Sacs	119
03	Executive Suites	117
16	Big Fish, Small Pond	115
60	Back Country Folks	111
21	Suburban Sprawl	108
55	Mines & Mills	104
43	River City, USA	104
26	Gray Collars	104
50	Family Scramble	102
37	New Homesteaders	95
09	American Dreams	94
15	God's Country	92
61	Scrub Pine Flats	82
19	New Empty Nests	82
49	Hometown Retired	81
20	Boomers & Babies	79
39	Red, White & Blues	76
62	Hard Scrabble	74
25	Mobility Blues	73
14	Country Squires	72
32	Middleburg Managers	71
52	Golden Ponds	69

(continued)

■ **Exhibit 8**
(*concluded*)

Cluster #	Cluster Nickname	Propensity to Listen Index
45	Single City Blues	65
56	Agri-Business	65
51	Southside City	63
29	Old Yankee Rows	63
41	Big Sky Families	63
34	Starter Families	59
54	Norma Rae-ville	58
59	Rustic Elders	57
48	Smalltown Downtown	45
58	Blue Highways	43
53	Rural Industria	41
47	Inner Cities	40
44	Shotguns & Pickups	38
57	Grain Belt	35
30	Mid-City Mix	29

The above report is used to identify PRIZM clusters with high propensity to listen to alternative rock music. A propensity score above 100 is considered to be above average.

SOURCE: Claritas, Inc.

- **What are they like?** Once clients have identified their consumer targets, a thorough lifestyle profile can be created. A profile will answer questions like: How do best prospects spend their leisure time? What products do they buy? Where do they travel? How do they invest their money?

- **Where do they live?** Since Compass links demographics and PRIZM clusters to geography, clients can find out where their best customers or prospects live and find more people like them. Once geographic areas of interest are identified, Compass allows the client to print a detailed, full-color map shaded by demographic characteristic or product potential.

- **How can I reach them?** With their best customer targets in mind, clients can use Compass to evaluate the best ways to reach those customers. Clients can find out what magazines and newspapers their target consumers read and what TV, cable, or radio shows they tune in. Compass information is also used to plan in-store promotions and merchandise mixes.

Pricing

Pricing of Claritas licensed products is very complex and is determined by:

- Requested market coverage (national, regional, or market level).
- Requested geographic level (ZIP code, block group, etc.).
- Requested databases (MRI, Nielsen, R. L. Polk, etc.).
- Requested segmentation systems (PRIZM or P$YCLE, a segmentation system for the financial industry).
- Requested length of the license (one to three years).

Customer Satisfaction

Claritas has a long list of satisfied customers who have used Compass and PRIZM to make effective marketing decisions in a variety of areas. Reasons for such satisfaction include positive results such as increased response rates from targeted direct mail campaigns, profitable placement of new store sites, and increased sales of consumer products in various markets. Quotes from satisfied customers include:

- "Before using the Claritas system, we were ordering basic reports from a vendor, pulling out Rand McNally maps and photocopying them. We would mark stores and trace ZIP Code areas by hand. By mapping and using more specialized data from Claritas, we are making educated decisions on where to locate our stores and how to better serve our customers. This allows us to be more professional—and profitable."—Rob Groscup, Eddie Bauer Sportswear.

- "This (segmentation) program helps Perdue Farms and our retailers clear out the less desirable products and put in the fast-moving products, but what's less desirable and what's fast-moving varies from store to store. We've never been able to identify that on a per-store basis, and PRIZM has allowed us to do that."—James Mendelsohn, Perdue Farms.

- "The response rates (to our direct mail program) have improved dramatically since implementing the Claritas program and the cost per loan, which had risen as high as $550–$800 variance based on market and time of year, dropped to a consistent $295–$350 per loan, and is headed even lower."—Clare Erlander, Security Pacific Financial Services.

- "We feel we'd be remiss to not use a tool like PRIZM to go after additional ad dollars. The difference it has made is significant."—Walter Rodgers, The Eagle–Tribune.

Discussion Questions

1. What is geodemography and why is it useful?
2. Using Exhibits 2 and 3 in the case, answer the following questions:
   a. What information do the market potential index (MPI) scores in Exhibit 2 provide, how is this information useful, and who would use it?
   b. Who should be targeted based on the alternative rock music MPI?
   c. What is the relationship between median household income and potential alternative rock listeners in Exhibit 2?
   d. How would marketers use the map in Exhibit 3 to target alternative rock listeners?
3. Name three products or services that you think would vary in demand across the three clusters in Exhibits 5, 6, and 7. How would you change the marketing mix for these products or services to appeal to each cluster?
4. Using Exhibits 5, 6, 7, and 8, answer the following questions:
   a. From Exhibit 8, which cluster has the highest index? What is the meaning of the index?
   b. What additional information do Exhibits 5, 6, and 7 provide that would help market an alternative rock music magazine?
   c. How could the report in Exhibit 8 be used for a direct mailing?

5. Suppose you own a chain of computer stores in the state of Massachusetts. Recently you have noticed an increase in sales and a high demand for your products. Your industry is forecasted to continue growing for the next ten years. You decide that you want to expand your business and open more stores. Unfortunately, you are unsure of where to locate them. How could Claritas's Compass system help you?

6. What are the strengths of Claritas's PRIZM segmentation system?

7. Based on information given about the marketing information analysis industry, how should Claritas organize its internal sales and client-service staff to best sell its Compass and PRIZM software? Discuss the advantages and disadvantages of organizing geographically, by industry group, or by product.

Case 5   The Quaker Oats Company, Gatorade, and Snapple Beverage

Arthur A. Thompson, Jr.   John E. Gamble
The University of Alabama   Auburn University–Montgomery

In November 1994, Quaker Oats Co. negotiated a deal to acquire iced tea and fruit drink marketer Snapple Beverage Corp. for $1.7 billion in cash, a move that took Quaker off the list of rumored takeover targets and greatly strengthened its position as a producer-marketer of beverage substitutes for soft drinks. Quaker's Gatorade brand commanded 85 percent of the sports drink segment in the United States, generated worldwide sales of almost $1.2 billion, and was Quaker's fastest-growing, most lucrative product. Snapple had 1993 sales of $516 million, up from $95 million in 1991, and was the clear-cut market leader in New Age or alternative beverages, with national distribution capability and growing brand awareness among consumers. Quaker's acquisition of Snapple elevated it into a nonalcoholic beverage powerhouse, with nearly $2 billion in sales, trailing only Coca-Cola and PepsiCo.

Quaker agreed to pay Snapple shareholders $14 a share for the 121,620,000 shares outstanding, a price roughly equal to the $13.75–$14.25 trading range of Snapple stock in the few days before the agreement was announced. Shares of Snapple, which had traded in the $28–$32 range in late 1993 and early 1994, had fallen in recent months when its sales growth during the first three quarters of 1994 slowed significantly, and ready-to-drink tea products carrying the Lipton and Nestea brands began to capture almost 50 percent of sales in supermarkets. The Lipton line was jointly produced and marketed by PepsiCo and Unilever's Thomas J. Lipton subsidiary; the Nestea line was the product of an alliance between Coca-Cola and Nestlé (Nestlé was the world's largest food products company and the producer of Nestea-brand teas).

Hours before the Quaker–Snapple agreement was announced, Snapple reported a third-quarter earnings drop of 74 percent, which analysts attributed to oversized inventories and intensifying competition. In NYSE trading on the following day, Quaker's stock fell nearly 10 percent, from $74.50 to $67.125. The drop in price was said to be a combination of Snapple's poor earnings report, the reduced likelihood that Quaker would be a takeover target, and the rich acquisition price Quaker was paying for Snapple. Wall Street analysts regarded the outlook for Snapple's future sales and earnings as very uncertain. Whereas Snapple management indicated in May 1994 that it was comfortable with a 1994 earnings per share projection of 86 cents a share, the confidential business plan Snapple gave Quaker during their negotiations contained a projection of only 55 cents a share; in a filing with the Securities and Exchange Commission in the week following the acquisition announcement, Snapple indicated that 1994 earnings of 40 cents a share appeared more reasonable.[1] The $14 acquisition price represented a multiple of 35 times Snapple's latest 40 cents per share earnings projection and a multiple of nearly 20 times Snapple's estimated 1994 operating earnings (the latter multiple was well above the multiples of 10 and 11 that other recently acquired beverage companies had commanded).[2]

This case was prepared by Arthur A. Thompson Jr., The University of Alabama, and John E. Gamble, Auburn University of Montgomery. Copyright © 1995 by Arthur A. Thompson, Jr.

[1]Reported in *The Wall Street Journal*, November 7, 1994, p. A4.
[2]*The Wall Street Journal*, November 3, 1994, pp. A3 and A4.

To finance the Snapple acquisition, Quaker borrowed $2.4 billion from Nations-Bank. Quaker planned to use the loan proceeds to (1) make cash payments of $1.7 billion to Snapple's shareholders for the outstanding 121,620,000 shares, (2) pay off $100 million in Snapple debt, (3) refinance $350 million in Quaker's debt, and (4) retain $250 million for working capital. Quaker management was reportedly seeking buyers for its European pet foods business and Mexican chocolate subsidiary (combined sales of $900 million) as part of an ongoing restructuring of its food products lineup and, presumably, to raise cash to pay down debt associated with the Snapple acquisition.

■ The Quaker Oats Company

In 1994, Quaker Oats was the 12th largest food and beverage company in the United States, with worldwide sales of $6 billion (see Exhibit 1). The company operated 54 manufacturing plants in 16 states and 13 foreign countries and had distribution centers and sales offices in 21 states and 18 foreign countries. Nearly one-third of corporate revenues came from sales outside the United States. Quaker's worldwide grocery product portfolio included such well-known brands as Quaker Oats, Cap'n Crunch, Rice-A-Roni, Gatorade, Aunt Jemima, Ken-L Ration pet foods, and Van Camp's bean products; 81 percent of the company's sales came from brands holding the number one or number two position in their respective categories.

■ **Exhibit 1**
The 25 Largest Food and Beverage Companies in the United States (ranked by 1993 food and beverage sales, in millions of dollars)

Company	1992	1993
1. Philip Morris	$33,024	$34,526
2. ConAgra Inc.	16,201	16,499
3. PepsiCo	13,738	15,665
4. Coca-Cola	13,039	13,937
5. IBP Inc.	11,128	11,671
6. Anheuser-Busch	10,741	10,792
7. Sara Lee	6,622	7,206
8. H. J. Heinz	6,582	7,103
9. RJR Nabisco	6,707	7,025
10. Campbell Soup	6,263	6,586
11. Kellogg	6,191	6,295
12. Quaker Oats	5,576	5,731
13. CPC International	5,502	5,636
14. General Mills	5,234	5,397
15. Seagram Company	5,214	5,227
16. Tyson Foods	4,169	4,707
17. Ralston Purina	4,558	4,526
18. Borden Inc.	4,056	3,674
19. Hershey Foods	3,220	3,488
20. Procter & Gamble	3,709	3,271
21. Dole Foods	3,120	3,108
22. Hormel Food	2,814	2,854
23. Chiquita Brands	2,723	2,522
24. Dean Foods	2,220	2,243
25. International Multifoods	2,281	2,224

SOURCE: The Food Institute.

Moreover, 82 percent of Quaker's worldwide sales came from brands positioned in categories where sales volumes were growing. Hot cereals were Quaker's oldest, best-known, and most profitable products. Of the top-25-selling cereal brands, Quaker had four: Instant Quaker Oatmeal, Cap'n Crunch, Old Fashioned and Quick Quaker Oats, and Life Cereal.

Quaker's top management was committed to achieving real earnings growth of 7 percent and providing total shareholder returns (dividends plus share price appre-

■ **Exhibit 2** Financial Summary for Quaker Oats Company, 1984–1994 (Dollars in millions, except per share data)

Year Ended June 30	5-Year CAGR*	10-Year CAGR*	1994	1993	1992	1991
Operating Results, †						
Net sales	4.1%	7.7%	$5,955.0	$5,730.6	$5,576.4	$5,491.2
Gross profit	6.3%	10.8%	3,028.8	2,860.6	2,745.3	2,652.7
Income from continuing operations before income taxes and cumulative effect of accounting changes	9.6%	6.0%	378.7	467.6	421.5	411.5
Provision for income taxes	10.3%	4.0%	147.2	180.8	173.9	175.7
Income from continuing operations before cumulative effect of account changes	9.2%	7.5%	231.5	286.8	247.6	235.8
Income (loss) from discontinued operations—net of tax			—	—	—	(30.0)
Income from the disposal of discontinued operations—net of tax			—	—	—	—
Cumulative effect of accounting changes—net of tax			—	(115.5)	—	—
Net income	2.7%	5.3%	$ 231.5	$ 171.3	$ 247.6	$ 205.8
Per common share:						
Income from continuing operations for cumulative effect of accounting changes	12.3%	9.5%	$ 3.36	$ 3.93	$ 3.25	$ 3.05
Income (loss) from discontinued operations			—	—	—	(0.40)
Income from the disposal of discontinued operations			—	—	—	—
Cumulative effect of accounting changes			—	(1.59)	—	—
Net income	5.6%	7.2%	$ 3.36	$ 2.34	$ 3.25	$ 2.65
Dividends declared:						
Common stock	8.1%	12.2%	$ 140.6	$ 136.1	$ 128.6	$ 118.7
Per common share	12.1%	14.4%	$ 2.12	$ 1.92	$ 1.72	$ 1.56
Convertible preferred and redeemable preference stock			$ 4.0	$ 4.2	$ 4.2	$ 4.3
Average number of common shares outstanding (in thousands)			67,618	71,974	74,881	75,904
Financial Statistics†, §						
Current ratio			1.0	1.0	1.2	1.3
Working capital			$ (5.5)	$ (37.5)	$ 168.7	$ 317.8
Property, plant and equipment—net			$1,214.2	$1,228.2	$1,273.3	$1,232.7
Depreciation expense			$ 133.3	$ 129.9	$ 129.7	$ 125.2
Total assets			$3,043.3	$2,815.9	$3,039.9	$3,060.5
Long-term debt			$ 759.5	$ 632.6	$ 688.7	$ 701.2

ciation) that exceeded the S&P 500 stock index over time. Management also believed it could enhance shareholder value by prudently using leverage. Prior to the Snapple acquisition, Quaker issued $200 million in medium-term notes, increasing total debt to $1 billion. In fiscal 1994, Quaker used its debt proceeds and cash flows from operations to repurchase 3 million shares of common stock, make four small acquisitions, extend the company's record of consecutive dividend increases to 27 years, and make $175 million in capital investments to support growth and efficiency improvements. Exhibit 2 provides a 10-year financial summary of Quaker Oats corporate performance.

1990	1989	1988	1987	1986	1985	1984
$5,030.6	$4,879.4	$4,508.0	$3,823.9	$2,968.6	$2,925.6	$2,830.9
2,350.3	2,229.0	2,114.6	1,750.7	1,298.7	1,174.7	1,085.7
382.4	239.1	314.6	295.9	255.8	238.8	211.3
153.5	90.2	118.1	141.3	113.4	110.3	99.0
228.9	148.9	196.5	154.6	142.4	128.5	112.3
(59.9)	54.1	59.2	33.5	37.2	28.1	26.4
—	—	—	55.8	—	—	—
—	—	—	—	—	—	—
$ 169.0	$ 203.0	$ 255.7	$ 243.9	$ 179.6	$ 156.6	$ 138.7
$ 2.93	$ 1.88	$ 2.46	$ 1.96	$ 1.77	$ 1.53	$ 1.35
(0.78)	0.68	0.74	0.43	0.47	0.35	0.32
—	—	—	—	0.71	—	—
—	—	—	—	—	—	—
$ 2.15	$ 2.56	$ 3.20	$ 3.10	$ 2.24	$ 1.88	$ 1.67
$ 106.9	$ 95.2	$ 79.9	$ 63.2	$ 55.3	$ 50.5	$44.4
$ 1.40	$ 1.20	$ 1.00	$ 0.80	$ 0.70	$ 0.62	$0.55
$ 3.6	—	—	—	$ 2.3	$ 3.6	$3.9
76,537	79,307	79,835	78,812	79,060	81,492	80,412
1.3	1.8	1.4	1.4	1.4	1.7	1.6
$ 342.8	$ 695.8	$ 417.5	$ 507.9	$ 296.8	$ 400.7	$ 316.8
$1,154.1	$ 959.6	$ 922.5	$ 898.6	$ 691.0	$ 616.5	$ 650.1
$ 103.5	$ 94.2	$ 88.3	$ 81.6	$ 59.1	$ 56.3	$ 57.4
$3,377.4	$3,125.9	$2,886.1	$3,136.5	$1,944.5	$1,760.3	$1,726.5
$ 740.3	$ 766.8	$ 299.1	$ 527.7	$ 160.9	$ 168.2	$ 200.1

(continued)

■ **Exhibit 2** (*concluded*)

Year Ended June 30	5-Year CAGR*	10-Year CAGR*	1994	1993	1992	1991
Financial Statistics[+], [§] (*Continued*)						
Preferred stock (net of deferred compensation) and redeemable preference stock			$ 15.3	$ 11.4	$ 7.9	$ 4.8
Common shareholders' equity			$ 445.8	$ 551.1	$ 842.1	$ 901.0
Net cash provided by operating activities			$ 450.8	$ 558.2	$ 581.3	$ 543.2
Operating return on assets"			19.9%	21.1%	18.9%	18.8%
Gross profit as a percentage of sales			50.9%	49.9%	49.2%	48.3%
Advertising and merchandising as a percentage of sales			26.6%	25.7%	26.0%	25.6%
Income from continuing operations before cumulative effect of accounting changes as a percentage of sales			3.9%	5.0%	4.4%	4.3%
Total debt-to-total capitalization ratio[#]			68.8%	59.0%	48.7%	47.4%
Common dividends as a percentage of income available for common shares (excluding cumulative effect of accounting changes)			63.1%	48.9%	52.9%	58.9%
Number of common shareholders			28,197	33,154	33,580	33,603
Number of employees worldwide			20,000	20,200	21,100	20,900
Market price range of common stock—High			$ 82	$ 77	$ 75 1/4	$ 64 7/8
—Low			$ 61 7/8	$ 56 1/8	$ 50 1/4	$ 41 3/4

*CAGR—compound average growth rate.

**Fiscal 1994 results include a pretax restructuring charge of $118.4 million, or $1.09 per share, for workforce reductions, plant consolidations, and product discontinuations and a pretax gain of $9.8 million, or $0.13 per share, for the sale of a business in Venezuela.

[+]Fiscal 1989 results include a pretax restructuring charge of $124.3 million, or $1.00 per share, for plant consolidations and overhead reductions and a pretax charge of $25.6 million, or $0.20 per share, for a change to the LIFO method of accounting for the majority of U.S. Grocery Products inventories.

[‡]Income-related statistics exclude the results of businesses reported as discontinued operations. Balance sheet amounts and related statistics have not been restated for discontinued operations, other than Fisher-Price, due to materiality.

[§]Effective fiscal 1991, common shareholders' equity and number of employees worldwide were reduced as a result of the Fisher-Price spinoff.

"Operating income divided by average identifiable assets of U.S. and Canadian and International Grocery Products.

[#]Total debt divided by total debt plus total shareholders' equity including preferred stock (net of deferred compensation) and redeemable preference stock.

SOURCE: 1994 Annual Report.

Quaker's Corporate Organization and Brand Portfolio

Quaker Oats's worldwide production and sales operations were structured around two broad geographic groups: U.S. and Canadian Grocery Products and International Grocery Products. The U.S. and Canadian Grocery group was subdivided into four product divisions: Breakfast Foods, Gatorade Worldwide, Diversified Grocery Products (pet foods and grain products), and Convenience Foods. The International Grocery Products group had three geographic operating divisions: Europe, Latin America, and Pacific. Exhibit 3 shows the financial performance of the two major product groups. Exhibit 4 shows the brands and sales of the divisional units.

1990	1989	1988	1987	1986	1985	1984
$ 1.8	—	—	—	—	$ 37.9	$ 38.5
$1,017.5	$1,137.1	$ 1,251.1	$1,087.5	$ 831.7	$ 786.9	$ 720.1
$ 460.0	$ 408.3	$ 320.8	$ 375.1	$ 266.9	$ 295.5	$ 263.6
20.4%	14.4%	18.3%	22.1%	25.8%	24.5%	24.4%
46.7%	45.7%	46.9%	45.8%	43.7%	40.2%	38.4%
23.8%	23.4%	24.9%	22.9%	21.7%	19.4%	18.4%
4.6%	3.1%	4.4%	4.0%	4.8%	4.4%	4.0%
52.3%	44.2%	33.8%	50.2%	35.7%	28.9%	35.4%
65.1%	46.9%	31.3%	25.9%	31.2%	33.0%	32.9%
33,859	34,347	34,231	32,358	27,068	26,670	26,785
28,200	31,700	31,300	30,800	29,500	28,700	28,400
$ 68 1/8	$ 66 1/4	$ 57 1/8	$ 57 5/8	$ 39 1/4	$26 1/8	$ 16 1/8
$ 45 1/8	$ 42 5/8	$ 31	$ 32 5/8	$ 23 1/2	$14 1/4	$ 10 3/4

■ **Exhibit 3** Financial Performance of Quaker's Two Major Grocery Products Groups, 1989–1994 (dollars in millions)

Product Group	Fiscal Year Ended June 30					
	1989	1990	1991	1992	1993	1994
U.S. and Canadian Grocery Products						
Net sales	$3,630	$3,610	$3,860	$3,842	$3,930	$4,253
Operating income	256	373	429	435	447	431
Identifiable assets	2,055	2,150	2,229	1,998	1,877	1,999
Return on net sales	7.1%	10.3%	11.1%	11.3%	11.4%	10.1%
Return on assets	13.1%	17.7%	19.6%	20.6%	23.1%	22.2%
International Grocery Products						
Net sales	$1,250	$1,421	$1,631	$1,734	$1,800	$1,702
Operating income	93	172	104	105	128	106
Identifiable assets	482	638	656	842	745	786
Return on net sales	7.5%	12.1%	6.4%	6.1%	7.1%	6.2%
Return on assets	20.0%	30.7%	16.1%	14.0%	16.2%	13.9%

SOURCE: 1994 Annual Report.

■ **Exhibit 4** Quaker's Brands and Sales by Division, 1989–1994 (dollars in millions)

Division/Category	Brands/Products	Sales in Fiscal Year Ending June 30					
		1989	1990	1991	1992	1993	1994
Breakfast foods	Quaker Oatmeal, Cap'n Crunch, Life, Quaker rice cakes, Quaker Chewy granola bars, Quaker grits, Aunt Jemima cornmeal	$1,292	$1,280	$1,322	$1,313	$1,425	$1,573
Pet foods	Ken-L Ration, Gaines, Kibbles'n Bits, Puss'n Boots, Cycle	608	518	531	531	529	539
Golden Grain	Rice-A-Roni, Noodle Roni, Near East Golden Grain, Mission	283	275	297	309	269	305
Convenience foods	Aunt Jemima breakfast products, Celeste frozen pizza, Van Camp's canned beans, Wolf chili, Burry cookies, Maryland Club coffee, Proof & Bake frozen products, Petrofsky's bakery products	857	901	978	953	949	924
Gatorade (U.S. and Canada)	Gatorade	584	630	724	727	750	906
Europe	Quaker cereals, Gatorade, Felix cat food, Bonzo dog food, Cuore corn oil	969	1,085	1,326	1,355	1,336	1,164
Latin America and Pacific	Quaker cereals, Gatorade	281	336	305	380	465	538

SOURCE: 1994 Annual Report.

The Gatorade Worldwide Division

Gatorade was developed in 1965 for the University of Florida Gators; it was sold to Stokely-Van Camp in 1967. Quaker acquired the Gatorade brand in 1983 when it bought Stokely-Van Camp. At the time, Gatorade sales were about $100 million. Since the acquisition, sales of Gatorade had grown at an average annual compound rate of 22 percent, spurred by the addition of flavor and package-size variety as well as wider geographic distribution. Worldwide sales were just over $1.1 billion in 1994, up 21 percent over fiscal 1993. U.S. and Canadian volume increased 19 percent; international volume was up 31 percent. According to Quaker estimates, Gatorade held a 77 percent share of the $1.3 billion U.S. sports beverage category as of mid-1994 (down from 90 percent-plus in 1990–91) and more than 40 percent of the global sports drink market. Quaker management believed that Gatorade's science-based rehydration capability to replace salts and fluids lost during exercise, its strong identity with sports, and its leading position domestically and globally made it an exceptionally profitable growth opportunity worldwide. Gatorade was Quaker's number-one growth priority, and the stated mission of the Gatorade Worldwide division was "to quench hot and thirsty consumers in every corner of the world."

Gatorade's Market Scope.   In 1994, Gatorade was marketed in 26 countries on five continents and had the leading market position in most locations. The brand's biggest markets in 1994 were the United States, Mexico, South Korea, Canada, Venezuela, Italy, Germany, and Taiwan. In 1994, sales of Gatorade totaled nearly $900 million in the United States and approximately $220 million in the remaining 25 countries where it was marketed. Management's objective was to increase sales in Latin America, Europe, and the Pacific to $1 billion by the year 2000.

In Latin America, Gatorade's share of the sports beverage segment was in the 90 percent range in all countries where it was available. Mexico was Gatorade's second largest market after the United States. In 1994, sales in Brazil increased fourfold as Gatorade was successfully relaunched in the Sao Paulo region. Sales volumes continued to rise in Venezuela and the Caribbean, and Gatorade was introduced into Chile. To meet the growing sales volume in Latin America, Quaker was investing in additional production facilities.

Competition in the sports beverage market in Europe was fierce because in a number of important countries the market was already developed. When Gatorade was introduced in these country markets, it had to win sales and market share away from established brands. Quaker had pulled Gatorade out of the competitive U.K. and French markets. Given the varying competitive intensity from country to country, Quaker's Gatorade division was focusing its marketing resources on the most promising European country markets. Sales were currently biggest in Germany and Italy. In 1994, Gatorade was introduced in Holland and Austria. Quaker management anticipated that Gatorade sales in Europe would evolve more slowly than other global locations. In 1994, volume grew 9 percent in Europe but sales revenue was lower because of weaker European currencies against the U.S. dollar.

Throughout most of the Pacific, Gatorade was sold primarily via licensing agreements. Quaker's most successful licensing agreement was with Cheil Foods in South Korea, where Gatorade was a strong second in the sports beverage segment. Gatorade volume in South Korea ranked third, behind the United States and Mexico. In fiscal 1994, Gatorade was introduced in Australia (where the brand was sold through an arrangement with Pepsi-Cola bottlers of Australia), Singapore, and Hong Kong. Although Gatorade was not the first sports drink marketed in Australia, the brand captured the leading share by mid-1994, less than 12 months after it was introduced.

The expense of underwriting Gatorade's entry into new country markets had pinched Gatorade's international profit margins. Quaker's profits from international sales of Gatorade were expected to remain subpar as the company pushed for expanded penetration of international markets. Quaker management believed that increased consumer interest in healthy foods and beverages, growing sports participation, expanded sports competition in the world arena, increasing acceptance of international brands, and a growing population in warm climate countries and in youthful age segments—especially in Latin America and the Asian Pacific—all bode well for Gatorade's continued sales growth in international markets.

The U.S. Market Situation. The Gatorade brand was coming under increased competition pressure in the U.S. market as a number of companies introduced their own sports beverage brand:

Brand	Marketer
Powerade	Coca-Cola Co.
All Sport	Pepsi-Cola Co.
10-K	Suntory (Japan)
Everlast	A&W Brands
Nautilus Plus	Dr Pepper/Seven-Up
Snap-Up (renamed Snapple Sport in April 1994)	Snapple Beverage Co.

Soft-drink companies were looking for new market segments because the $47 billion retail soft-drink market had grown less than 3 percent annually since 1980. Both Coca-Cola and Pepsi were moving to market their brands directly against Gatorade's well-developed connections to sports teams, coaches, trainers, and celebrity athletes (Michael Jordan was Gatorade's athlete spokesman). Coca-Cola had maneuvered successfully to get Powerade named as the official sports drink of the 1996 Olympic Games in Atlanta and was running Powerade ads to sponsor World Cup Soccer. Coca-Cola's Powerade ads on local TV and radio carried the tag line "More power to ya." Coca-Cola had signed pro basketball–football star Deion Sanders to appear in Powerade ads. Pepsi-Cola's commercials for All Sport touted the theme "Fuel the fire" and showed gritty scenes of youths playing fast-action sports like blacktop basketball. Pepsi had also enlisted pro basketball's Shaquille O'Neal to appear in its ads and was sponsoring telecasts of NCAA basketball games. Snapple's ads for Snap-Up/Snapple Sport featured tennis celebrities Ivan Lendl and Jennifer Capriati. Suntory was seeking to attract preteens to its 10-K brand with ads featuring a 12-year-old boy who played five sports. Gatorade rivals were expected to spend $30 million to $40 million advertising their brands in 1994. Pepsi's All Sport and Coca-Cola's Powerade were considered particularly formidable brands because they were backed by nationwide networks of local soft-drink bottlers who delivered daily to major supermarkets (and at least weekly to other soft-drink retailers and vending machine outlets) and who typically stocked the shelves of retailers and set up in-store aisle displays. With such distribution muscle both Powerade and All Sport could gain market exposure everywhere soft drinks were available.

To counter rivals' efforts to horn in on Gatorade's market share, Quaker doubled its 1994 ad budget to nearly $50 million and created ads that reduced Michael Jordan's role in favor of product-benefit claims. Quaker also expanded Gatorade's line to eight flavors, compared to four for Powerade and All Sport. Still, Gatorade's estimated market share was five percentage points lower in fall 1994 than a year earlier.

In an attempt to develop a new beverage category, the Gatorade division was test-marketing a new product named SunBolt Energy Drink, designed for morning consumption or any time consumers wanted a "pick-me-up." Sunbolt contained three carbohydrate sources, caffeine, and vitamin C equivalent to a whole orange; it was offered in four flavors. SunBolt was positioned in juice aisles of grocery stores where Gatorade was shelved.

Despite the entry of other sports beverages, Quaker management regarded water as Gatorade's biggest competitor as a "thirst quencher." Moreover, in many supermarkets, Gatorade was located alongside fruit juices, whereas Powerade and All Sport were often located in the soft-drink section, something Gatorade executives believed was an advantage. Gatorade executives also believed that the entry of competing sports drink brands would help grow the category enough so that Gatorade sales would grow despite a declining market share. According to Quaker President Phil Marineau:[3]

> When you have a 90 percent share of a category and competitors like Coke and Pepsi moving in, you're not foolish enough to think you won't lose some market share. But we're going to keep our position as the dominant force among sports drinks. Greater availability is the key to the U.S. success of Gatorade.

---

[3]As quoted in "Gatorade Growth Seen Outside U.S.," *Advertising Age,* November 15, 1993, p. 46.

Gatorade's Marketing and Distribution Strategies.

Quaker executives concluded as of early 1994 that U.S. sales of Gatorade were approaching the limits of its traditional grocery channel delivery system—Gatorade was shipped from plants to retailer warehouses, and stores ordered what they needed to keep shelves stocked. Sustaining Gatorade's sales growth in the United States meant stretching the distribution strategy for Gatorade to include other channels. Donald R. Uzzi, a Pepsi executive, was hired in March 1994 as president of Gatorade's U.S. and Canada geographic unit. Uzzi's top strategic priority was to develop additional sales outlets for Gatorade; the options included fountain service for restaurants and fast-food outlets, vending machines, direct deliveries to nongrocery retail outlets, and point-of-sweat locations such as sports gyms and golf courses. The customary way of accessing such outlets was by building a network of independent distributors who would market to and service such accounts. In 1994, Gatorade's strongest markets were in the South and Southwest.

In foreign markets, Gatorade relied on several strategies to establish its market presence:

- Shipping the product in, handling the marketing and advertising in-house, and partnering with a local distributor to sell retail accounts, gain shelf space, and make deliveries. This approach was being utilized in Greece with a food distribution company.
- Handling the marketing and advertising in-house and having a local partner take care of manufacturing, sales, and distribution. This approach was being used in Australia.
- Contracting with a soft-drink bottler to handle production, packaging, and distribution, with Gatorade taking care of marketing functions and supervising the contractor. This strategy was used in Spain, where the contractor was a Pepsi-owned bottler.
- Handling all functions in-house—manufacturing, marketing, sales, and distribution. Such was the case in Venezuela where Quaker had built facilities to produce Gatorade.

■ Snapple Beverage Corp.

Snapple Beverage Corp. originated as a subchapter S corporation in 1972. The company, operating as Mr. Natural, Inc., was the brainchild of three streetwise entrepreneurs: Leonard Marsh, Arnold Greenberg, and Hyman Golden. Marsh and Greenberg were lifelong friends, having gone to grade school and high school together; Golden was Marsh's brother-in-law. Mr. Natural, headquartered in Brooklyn, marketed and distributed a line of specialty beverages for the New York City area; the company's products were supplied by contract manufacturers and bottlers. The company's sales and operating scope grew gradually. Its all-natural products sold well in health food stores; later, delicatessens and convenience stores began to take on the line. By 1988, the company had become a regional distributor and headquarters operations were moved to East Meadow on Long Island, New York. Exhibit 5 summarizes key events in the company's history.

Capitalizing on consumers' growing interest in natural and healthy beverage products, the three entrepreneurs launched an all-natural beverage line under the Snapple name in 1980. Over the years, more flavors and varieties were added; Snapple iced teas were introduced in 1987. Introduction of the Snapple iced tea line was supported with a creative and catchy advertising campaign stressing the message, "Try this, you'll love the taste, and it's good for you." Snapple's recipe for making a

■ **Exhibit 5**   Summary of Key Events in Snapple Beverage Corporation's History

---

1972
Marsh, Golden, and Greenberg formed a company in association with a California juice manufacturer to distribute 100% natural fruit juices in New York City, primarily via health food distributors.

1979
A production plant is purchased in upstate New York to produce a line of pure, natural fruit juices.

1980
The name "Snapple" makes its first appearance when Snapple Beverage Corporation became the first company to manufacture a complete line of all-natural beverages.

1982
Snapple introduces Natural Sodas and pioneers the natural soft drink category.

1986
All Natural Fruit Drinks join the Snapple family, including Lemonade, Orangeade, Grapeade, and more.

1987
Snapple launches its All Natural Real Brewed Ice Tea and revolutionizes the beverage industry with the first tea to be brewed hot instead of mixed from cold concentrate. Snapple's signature wide-mouth bottle also makes its first appearance.

1990
Snapple introduces Snapple Sport, the first isotonic sports drink with the great taste of Snapple.

1991
Snapple recruits its first international distributor in Norway.

1992
The Thomas H. Lee Investment Company buys Snapple and leads an effort to take the company public. The stock triples in the first three months and is listed among the hottest stocks in the country. The three co-founders retain 23.1% of Snapple's common stock and Thomas H. Lee ends up owning 47.5% of Snapple's common shares.

1992/1993
Fruit Drink line expands to include such exotic flavors as Kiwi-Strawberry Cocktail, Mango Madness Cocktail, and Melonberry Cocktail.

1993
Snapple goes international, signing on distributors in the United Kingdom, Canada, Mexico, the Caribbean, Hong Kong, and elsewhere.

1994
Snapple introduces seven new products including Guava Mania Cocktail, Mango Tea, Amazin Grape Soda, Kiwi Strawberry Soda, and Mango Madness Soda as well as new diet versions of some bestsellers—Diet Kiwi Strawberry Cocktail, Diet Mango Madness Cocktail, and Diet Pink Lemonade.

SOURCE: Company promotional materials.

good-tasting iced tea involved making it hot and then bottling it; artificial preservatives or colors were avoided. Snapple's strategy was simple: make all-natural beverages that taste great, and keep introducing new and exciting flavors. As sales grew (principally because devoted health-conscious consumers spread the word among friends and acquaintances), company principals Marsh, Greenberg, and Golden plowed their profits back into the Snapple brand. Wider geographic distribution was attained by signing new distributors and granting them exclusive rights to distribute the Snapple line across a defined territory.

By 1991, sales had reached $95 million. Revenues jumped to $205.5 million in 1992 and to $516.0 million in 1993, as distribution widened and more consumers were attracted to try the line. Snapple's sales in 1993 ranked it no. 35 on the top 50 beverage companies list. Exhibits 6 and 7 present Snapple's financial statements.

■ **Exhibit 6**   Snapple's Income Statement, 1992 and 1993

	1992	1993
Net sales	$205,465,595	$516,005,327
Cost of goods sold	127,098,086	298,724,646
Gross profit	78,367,509	217,280,681
Selling, general, and administrative expenses	45,455,818	105,693,741
Nonoperating expenses	10,626,742	9,116,664
Interest expense	19,086,213	2,459,297
Income before tax	3,198,736	100,010,070
Provisions for income taxes	1,262,919	32,387,498
Net income before extraordinary items	1,935,817	67,623,481
Extraordinary item	(2,632,904)	0
Net income	$ (697,087)	$ 67,623,481

SOURCE: Company annual report.

■ **Exhibit 7**   Snapple Beverage Corporation Balance Sheet, 1992 and 1993

	1992	1993
Assets		
Cash	$ 97,486,632	$ 13,396, 949
Receivables	17,428,379	53,010,325
Inventories	16,166,183	40,922,888
Other current assets	6,788,585	4,192,759
Total current assets	137,869,779	111,522,921
Net property, plant, and equipment	1,053,399	10,751,597
Deferred charges	3,705,001	18,552,625
Intangibles	82,770,827	97,819,997
Other assets	1,338,166	304,745
Total assets	$226,737,172	$238,951,885
Liabilities and Shareholders' Equity		
Accounts payable	$ 6,100,345	$ 7,326,411
Current long-term debt	150,469	8,949,665
Accrued expenses	16,999,258	17,573,454
Income taxes	446,892	6,034,860
Other current liabilities	90,000,000	3,860,844
Total current liabilities	113,696,964	43,745,234
Long-term debt	18,226,138	26,218,911
Other long-term liabilities	4,000,000	5,011,000
Total liabilities	135,923,102	74,975,145
Minority interest	0	1,499,717
Common stock net	1,213,766	1,216,096
Capital surplus	90,297,391	94,334,533
Retained earnings	(697,087)	66,926,394
Total shareholders' equity	90,814,070	162,477,023
Total liabilities and shareholders' equity	$226,737,172	$238,951,885

SOURCE: Company annual report.

The company went public in December 1992 as Snapple Beverage Corp., with the three founders retaining 23.1 percent of the stock (7.7 percent each). After the initial public offering at a split-adjusted price of $5, the stock traded as high as $32.25 in late 1993 before trading as low as $11.50 in mid-1994. Responding to concerns of investors and Wall Street analysts as to whether the company's rapid growth was sustainable, Marsh said:

> For those of you who might have heard mumblings that we've grown too far, too fast, I suggest you consider Snapple in the proper context. The average American drank 500 soft drinks last year (1993) . . . and the average American drank only five Snapples last year. That's a 1 percent share of a $64 billion pie.[4]

During the summer months of 1994, Snapple marketed 75 varieties and flavors in five categories (ready-to-drink iced teas, fruit drinks, natural sodas and seltzers, fruit juices, and sports drinks) and had distributors in all 50 states. Despite sales of more than $500 million, Snapple had fewer than 200 employees; production, bottling, packaging, and distribution were handled by contractors and independent distributors. Company activities were focused on marketing, new product development (the company had expertise in flavor technology), and overall management of contractors and distributors. In May 1994, however, management initiated construction of the company's first production facility—a $25 million plant in Arizona, scheduled to begin operations in 1995 and employ 100 people.

Snapple was widely credited with catalyzing a more pronounced consumer trend toward New Age beverages, spurring added sales growth in bottled waters, sports drinks, and juices as well as its own line of flavored teas and fruit drinks. In 1993, New Age or "alternative" beverages constituted a $3 billion product category. Exhibit 8 shows trends in the per capita consumption of liquid beverages in the United States during the 1983–94 period.

■ **Exhibit 8**   Per Capita Consumption of Liquid Beverages in the United States, 1983–1994 (in gallons)

	1983	1984	1985	1986	1987	1988	1989	1990	1991	1992	1993E	1994P
Soft drinks	37.0	38.8	41.0	42.3	44.3	46.2	46.7	47.6	47.8	48.0	48.9	49.6
Coffee*	26.1	26.3	26.8	27.1	27.1	26.5	26.4	26.4	26.5	26.1	25.9	26.0
Beer	24.3	23.9	23.9	24.2	24.0	23.8	23.6	24.0	23.3	23.0	22.8	22.5
Milk	19.7	19.8	20.0	19.9	19.8	19.4	19.6	19.4	19.4	19.1	18.9	19.1
Tea*	7.2	7.2	7.3	7.3	7.3	7.4	7.2	7.0	6.7	6.8	6.9	7.0
Bottled water	3.4	4.0	5.2	5.8	6.4	7.3	8.1	9.2	9.6	9.9	10.5	11.2
Juices	8.2	7.0	7.9	7.8	8.3	7.7	8.0	7.1	7.6	7.1	7.0	7.0
Powdered drinks	6.5	6.4	6.3	5.2	4.9	5.3	5.4	5.7	5.9	6.1	6.0	5.9
Wine†	2.2	2.3	2.4	2.4	2.4	2.3	2.1	2.0	1.9	2.0	1.7	1.6
Distilled spirits	1.9	1.9	1.8	1.8	1.6	1.5	1.5	1.5	1.4	1.3	1.3	1.3
Subtotal	136.5	137.6	142.6	142.6	146.1	147.4	148.6	149.9	150.1	149.4	149.9	151.2
Imputed water consumption‡	46.0	44.9	39.9	39.9	36.4	35.1	33.9	32.6	32.4	33.1	32.6	31.3
Total	182.5	182.5	182.5	182.5	182.5	182.5	182.5	182.5	182.5	182.5	182.5	182.5

*Coffee and tea data are based on a three-year moving average to counterbalance inventory swings, thereby portraying consumption more realistically.
†Includes wine coolers beginning in 1984.
‡Includes all others.
E = estimated; P = projected.
SOURCE: John C. Maxwell, "Annual Soft Drink Report," *Beverage Industry Supplement*, March 1994, p. 6.

---

[4]As quoted in Beverage World's *Periscope*, February 28, 1994, p.21.

Snapple's Marketing and Distribution Strategies

In Snapple's early days, the product wasn't selling well; market research revealed consumers thought the bottles were ugly and difficult to store. A packaging re-design followed, resulting in the use of clear wide-mouth 16-ounce glass bottles—a container that management said was "perfectly suited to the hot-brewed process we use to make Snapple beverages." The new bottles were affixed with redesigned labels. Sales perked up quickly, buoyed by an offbeat and catchy media campaign.

The company sparked demand for Snapple products with offbeat, witty ads and catchy themes. Snapple had gotten the greatest mileage out of an ad featuring a stereotypical receptionist, "Wendy the Snapple Lady" (who was actually employed in the company's marketing department), responding to customer inquiries. Snapple ads sometimes poked fun at things. Print ads compared Snapple sales to "hot cakes" and "greased lightning" with "more flavors than you can shake a stick at." Ivan Lendl and Rush Limbaugh appeared in Snapple TV ads as celebrity endorsers. Most of Snapple's distributors were local soft drink bottlers/distributors who had third-place or fourth-place market shares (usually behind Coca-Cola and Pepsi) and who were eager to take on product lines where competition was less intense and profit margins were bigger. The average price per case for New Age beverages was around $9 to $11 versus $5 to $6 per case for soft drinks. On average, soft drinks offered bottlers and distributors $1 margin per case compared with about $3 per case for New Age products. These distributors delivered Snapple directly to supermarkets, convenience stores, delicatessen outlets, and up-and-down the street retailers, on trucks carrying an assortment of branded beverages (low-volume soft drink brands, bottled waters, club soda, tonic water, ginger ale, and perhaps canned Gatorade). Snapple's distributors were responsible for everything—selling retail accounts, keeping shelves stocked, handling point-of-sale displays, and setting prices. Retail prices for a 16-ounce bottle were typically around 75 cents. Snapple's surging sales in 1992 and 1993—a boom that reportedly began in convenience stores and delicatessens where trend-setting consumers bought Snapple from the cooler and drank it straight from the bottle—helped it recruit distributors willing to commit time and resources to the Snapple line. Snapple established a nationwide network of distributors in a matter of months—something few alternative beverage brands had been able to do. The attractive profit margins distributors earned on Snapple sales were a key factor underlying the company's ability to recruit distributors willing to invest time and resources in building the Snapple brand. Snapple's market research showed that half the U.S. population had tried Snapple by the end of October 1993. Snapple's sales were biggest in California and the Northeast; sales were weakest in the South and Southwest. By mid-1994, Snapple had begun introducing its brands in Europe. Launches in Britain, Ireland, and Norway came first, followed by Sweden and Denmark. Test-marketing was underway in France and Spain. As of November 1994, only 1 percent of Snapple's sales were derived from overseas markets.

In April 1994, Snapple announced it had developed an exclusive, glass-front vending machine capable of offering 54 different flavors simultaneously; the machine held 18 cases of the company's 16-ounce wide-mouth bottles. The company expected to place 10,000 units in service by year-end to broaden its distribution beyond supermarkets, convenience stores, and delicatessens.

Competition in the Iced Tea/New Age Segment

Snapple's success in developing consumer interest in ready-to-drink iced teas and teas spiked with fruit juices attracted other competitors quickly. In 1993, Coca-Cola, Pepsi-Cola, Dr Pepper/Seven-Up, and Cadbury Schweppes/A&W Beverages all launched New Age offerings. Several regional products, most notably Arizona Iced Tea (packaged in distinctive tall cans with a Southwestern motif), also entered the market. As of 1994, the major players in the ready-to-drink iced tea segment were:

Brand	Marketer
Snapple	Snapple Beverage Corp.
Lipton	Pepsi-Cola and the Thomas J. Lipton division of Unilever
Nestea	Coca-Cola Nestlé Refreshments (a joint venture of the Coca-Cola Company and Nestlé)
Tetley	A&W Brands and Tetley Tea Co. partnership
Luzianne	Barq's Inc. and Wm. B. Reily partnership
All Seasons	Cadbury Beverages and Omni Industries
Celestial Seasonings	Perrier Group of America and Celestial Seasonings
Arizona	Ferolito, Vultaggio and Sons

Besides the major players, there were 5 to 10 niche brands of bottled teas. In addition, Pepsi-Cola had teamed with Ocean Spray Cranberries, Inc., to introduce a line of juices and lemonade. Minute Maid had announced a new line of juices, Very Fine and Tradewinds were planning lemonade entries, and Gatorade introduced its eighth flavor, Gatorade Iced Tea Cooler. An Information Resources survey of supermarket sales of canned and bottled iced teas during the 12 weeks ended April 17, 1994, showed the following:[5]

Brand	Case Volume (in millions)	Dollar Volume (in millions)
Snapple	2.5	$22.3
Lipton	2.3	14.9
Nestea	1.0	7.8
Arizona	0.5	5.0

Snapple's market share (based on dollars) was 17 percentage points lower in this survey than the comparable year-earlier period. The Arizona brand was gaining share and had edged out Snapple as the market leader in several markets in the West. However, Snapple's market share of convenience store sales was estimated to be in the 75 percent range. Exhibit 9 presents estimated case sales of alternative beverage companies.

Industry analysts estimated that wholesale volume for iced tea flavors grew from $500 million in 1992 to more than $1 billion in 1993. Alternative beverage sales were breaking out into 40 percent take-home purchases and 60 percent single-service and on-premise consumption. Ready-to-drink teas and juice-based drinks were the fastest-growing products in the New Age category, while sales of "clear" products

---

[5]As reported in *The Wall Street Journal,* June 9, 1994, p. B6.

■ **Exhibit 9**   Estimated Case Sales of Alternative Beverage Companies, 1992–1993

Company/Brand	Case Sales (in millions)	
	1992	1993
Snapple Beverage Company		
Snapple Iced Tea	28.33	52.63
Snapple drinks	19.73	45.41
Snapple sodas	1.52	3.10
Snapple Snap-Up/Sport	0.51	1.03
Snapple juices	0.51	1.03
Total	50.60	103.20
Coca-Cola Company		
Nestea	14.00	33.00
Powerade	1.20	10.00
Minute Maid Juices-to-Go	5.00	15.00
Total	20.20	58.00
PepsiCo		
Ocean Spray	6.50	16.00
Litpon	—	33.00
All Sport	2.00	3.00
H2 Oh!	0.50	0.63
Total	9.00	52.63
Perrier Group		
15-Brand totals	30.40	36.70
Cadbury beverages/A&W brands		
Tetley	2.90	4.30
Everlast	—	—
Others	17.30	17.30
Total	20.20	21.60
Ferolito, Vultaggio and Sons		
Arizona	—	2.00
All others	169.60	175.37
Segment totals	300.00	449.50

SOURCE: Compiled from "Annual Soft Drink Report," *Beverage Industry Supplement*, March 1994, pp. 22–23.

dropped to the 8 to 9 percent range (down from 44 percent growth in 1992). Analysts were divided in their assessments about how long the booming growth in ready-to-drink teas and fruit beverages would last. Some analysts believed that teas and fruit drinks would enjoy continued growth because of their healthy, "all-natural" image with consumers and because the proliferation of brands and varieties would help develop greater buyer interest. Others were skeptical, observing that trendy products had comparatively short life-cycles and that three or four growth years were all many product categories ever experienced. While some cola bottlers had derisively referred to Snapple as a member of the "brand of the day" club, unconvinced of its power to sustain broad consumer interest, market research indicated that younger consumers (who had fueled the growth in New Age beverages) had gravitated to Snapple, Arizona, and unusual niche brands with distinctive packaging and a certain mystique. In fall 1994, industry observers saw bottled tea as becoming increasingly complex to market successfully because the market was overcrowded, costs to support a brand were rising, shelf space was harder to obtain, and image was such a dominant factor in a brand's success or failure.

In late August 1994, Coca-Cola and Nestlé unexpectedly announced dissolution of their iced tea alliance; Nestea sales had been disappointing, falling well behind supermarket sales of both Snapple and Lipton. It was not clear whether Nestlé would continue to market Nestea bottled teas on its own. Meanwhile, Pepsi-Lipton had begun running a series of radio ads attacking Snapple as being "mixed up from a tea powder." The announcer said, "Snapple. Isn't that a cute name. Kinda snappy. I bet they call it Snapple ˌcause it's iced tea made in a snap." The spot went on to boast that Lipton Original varieties were "real brewed," a trait that Pepsi-Lipton believed was its best weapon against rivals.[6] Pepsi had also run Super Bowl ads for Lipton Original and promoted Lipton Original heavily in supermarkets, including a 99-cent value pack containing one bottle each of Lipton Original, All Sport, and Ocean Spray Lemonade.

Snapple management indicated its iced teas were made from "the finest tea leaves in India" but wouldn't specify how it was produced. Arnold Greenberg said:

> Pepsi would die to make tea taste so great. People don't care how it's made. They just care that it tastes good.[7]

Snapple management also pointed out that the less expensive Lipton Brisk varieties, sold in cans and 64-ounce bottles, were not "real brewed." Analysts estimated that during the first five months of 1994, about 60 percent of Pepsi's prepared iced teas were Lipton Brisk varieties. To counter the increased competition from rival teas, Snapple more than doubled its 1994 advertising budget and launched a new $65 million media campaign in April 1994.

---

[6]As quoted in *The Wall Street Journal,* June 9, 1994, p. B6.

[7]Ibid.

Case 6   Circus Circus Enterprises, Inc., 1998

John K. Ross III, Michael J. Keeffe, and Bill J. Middlebrook
Southwest Texas State University

> We possess the resources to accomplish the big projects: the know-how, the financial power and the places to invest. The renovation of our existing projects will soon be behind us, which last year represented the broadest scope of construction ever taken on by a gaming company. Now we are well-positioned to originate new projects. Getting big projects right is the route to future wealth in gaming; big successful projects tend to prove long staying power in our business. When the counting is over, we think our customers and investors will hold the winning hand.[1]

Big projects and a winning hand. Circus Circus does seem to have both. And big projects they are, with huge pink and white striped concrete circus tents, a 600-foot-long river boat replica, a giant castle, and a great pyramid. It's latest project, Mandalay Bay, will include a 3,700 room hotel/casino, an 11-acre aquatic environment with beaches, a snorkeling reef and a swim-up shark exhibit.

Circus Circus Enterprises, Inc. (hereafter Circus) describes itself as in the business of entertainment, and has been one of the innovators in the theme resort concept popular in casino gaming. Their areas of operation are the glitzy vacation and convention meccas of Las Vegas, Reno, and Laughlin, Nevada, as well as other locations in the U.S. and abroad. Historically, Circus's marketing of its products has been called "right out of the bargain basement," and has catered to "low rollers." Circus has continued to broaden its market and now aims more at the middle income gambler and family-oriented vacationers as well as the more upscale traveler and player.

Circus was purchased in 1974 for $50,000 as a small and unprofitable casino operation by partners William G. Bennett, an aggressive cost-cutter who ran furniture stores before entering the gaming industry in 1965, and William N. Pennington (see Exhibit 1 for Board of Directors and top managers). The partners were able to rejuvenate Circus with fresh marketing, went public with a stock offering in October 1983, and experienced rapid growth and high profitability over time. Within the five year period between 1993–1997 the average return on invested capital was 16.5 percent and Circus had generated over $1 billion in free cash flow. Today, Circus is one of the major players in the Las Vegas, Laughlin, and Reno markets in terms of square footage of casino space and number of hotel rooms—despite the incredible growth in both markets. For the first time in company history, casino gaming operations in 1997 provided slightly less than one half of total revenues and that trend continued into 1998 (see Exhibit 2). On January 31, 1998, Circus reported a net income of approximately $89.9 million on revenues of $1.35 billion. This was down slightly from 1997's more than $100 million net income on revenues of $1.3 billion. During that same year Circus invested over $585.8 million in capital expenditures and another $663.3 million was invested in fiscal year 1998.

This case was prepared by Professors John K. Ross III, Michael J. Keeffe, and Bill J. Middlebrook of Southwest Texas State University. The case was prepared for classroom purposes only, and is not designed to show effective or ineffective handling of administrative situations.

Dr. Bill Middlebrook, Dr. Michael J. Keeffe, and Dr. John K. Ross III are all of the Department of Management and Marketing, Southwest Texas State University.

[1]Annual Report, 1997.

■ **Exhibit 1**   Circus Circus Enterprises, Inc.

Directors		
Name	**Age**	**Title**
Clyde T. Turner	59	Chairman of the Board and CEO Circus Circus Enterprises
Michael S. Ensign	59	Vice Chairman of the Board and COO Circus Circus Enterprises
Glenn Schaeffer	43	President, CFO Circus Circus Enterprises
William A. Richardson	50	Vice Chairman of the Board and Executive Vice President Circus Circus Enterprises
Richard P. Banis	52	Former President and COO Circus Circus Enterprises
Arthur H. Bilger	44	Former President and COO New World Communications Group International
Richard A. Etter	58	Former Chairman and CEO Bank of America–Nevada
William E. Bannen, M.D.	48	Vice President/Chief Medical Officer, Blue Cross Blue Shield of Nevada
Donna B. More	40	Partner, Law Firm of Freeborn & Peters
Michael D. McKee	51	Executive Vice President The Irving Company
Officers		
Clyde T. Turner		Chairman of the Board and Chief Executive Officer
Michael S. Ensign		Vice Chairman of the Board and Chief Operating Officer
Glenn Schaeffer		President, Chief Financial Officer and Treasurer
William A. Richardson		Vice Chairman of the Board and Executive Vice President Circus Circus Enterprises
Tony Alamo		Senior Vice President, Operations
Gregg Solomon		Senior Vice President, Operations
Kurt D. Sullivan		Senior Vice President, Operations
Steve Greathouse		Senior Vice President, Operations
Yvett Landau		Vice President, General Counsel and Secretary
Les Martin		Vice President and Chief Accounting Officer

SOURCE: Annual Report 1998; Proxy Statement May 1, 1998.

■ **Exhibit 2**
Circus Circus Enterprises, Inc.—Sources of Revenues as a Percentage of Net Revenues

	1998	1997	1996	1995
Casinos	46.7%	49.2%	51.2%	52.3%
Food & Beverage	15.9	15.8	15.5	16.2
Hotel	24.4	22.0	21.4	19.9
Other	10.5	11.0	12.2	14.2
Unconsolidated	7.3	6.5	3.5	.5
Less: Complimentary Allowances	4.8	4.5	3.8	3.1

SOURCE: Circus Circus 10-K, January 31, 1995–1998.

■ Circus Circus Operations

Circus defines entertainment as pure play and fun, and it goes out of the way to see that customers have plenty of opportunities for both. Each Circus location has a distinctive personality. Circus Circus–Las Vegas is the world of the Big Top, where live circus acts perform free every 30 minutes. Kids may cluster around video games while the adults migrate to nickel slot machines and dollar game tables. Located at the north end of the Vegas strip, Circus Circus–Las Vegas sits on 69 acres of land with 3,744 hotel rooms, shopping areas, two specialty restaurants, a buffet with seating for 1,200, fast food shops, cocktail lounges, video arcades, 109,000 square feet of casino space, and includes the Grand Slam Canyon, a five-acre glass enclosed theme park including a four-loop roller coaster. Approximately 384 guests may also stay at nearby Circusland RV Park. For the year ending January 31, 1997, $126.7 million was invested in this property for new rooms and remodeling with another $35.2 million in fiscal year 1998.

Luxor, an Egyptian-themed hotel and casino complex, opened on October 15, 1993, when 10,000 people entered to play the 2,245 slot and video poker games and 110 table games in the 120,000-square-foot casino in the hotel atrium (reported to be the world's largest). By the end of the opening weekend 40,000 people per day were visiting the 30-story bronze pyramid that encases the hotel and entertainment facilities.

Luxor features a 30-story pyramid and two new 22-story hotel towers including 492 suites and is connected to Excalibur by a climate-controlled skyway with moving walkways. Situated at the south end of the Las Vegas strip on a 64-acre site adjacent to Excalibur, Luxor features a food and entertainment area on three different levels beneath the hotel atrium. The pyramid's hotel rooms can be reached from the four corners of the building by state-of-the-art "inclinators" which travel at a 39-degree angle. Parking is available for nearly 3,200 vehicles, including a covered garage which contains approximately 1,800 spaces.

The Luxor underwent major renovations costing $323.3 million during fiscal 1997 and another $116.5 million in fiscal 1998. The resulting complex contains 4,425 hotel rooms, extensively renovated casino space, an additional 20,000 square feet of convention area, an 800 seat buffet, a series of IMAX attractions, five theme restaurants, seven cocktail lounges, and a variety of specialty shops. Circus expects to draw significant walk-in traffic to the newly refurbished Luxor and is one of the principal components of the Masterplan Mile.

Located next to the Luxor, Excalibur is one of the first sights travelers see as they exit Interstate Highway 15 (management was confident that the sight of a giant, colorful medieval castle would make a lasting impression on mainstream tourists and vacationing families arriving in Las Vegas). Guests cross a drawbridge, with moat, onto a cobblestone walkway where multicolored spires, turrets and battlements loom above. The castle walls are four 28-story hotel towers containing a total of 4,008 rooms. Inside is a medieval world complete with a Fantasy Faire inhabited by strolling jugglers, fire eaters and acrobats, as well as a Royal Village complete with peasants, serfs, and ladies-in-waiting around medieval theme shops. The 110,000 square-foot casino encompasses 2,442 slot machines, more than 89 game tables, a sports book, and a poker and keno area. There are twelve restaurants, capable of feeding more than 20,000 people daily, and a 1,000-seat amphitheater. Excalibur, which opened in June 1990, was built for $294 million and primarily financed with internally generated funds. In the year ending January 31, 1997, Excalibur contributed 23 percent of the organization's revenues, down from 33 percent in 1993. Yet 1997 was a record year, generating the company's highest margins and over $100 million in operating cash flow. In fiscal 1998 Excalibur underwent $25.1 million in renovations and was connected to the Luxor by enclosed, moving walkways.

Situated between the two anchors on the Las Vegas strip are two smaller casinos owned and operated by Circus. The Silver City Casino and Slots-A-Fun primarily depend on the foot traffic along the strip for their gambling patrons. Combined, they

■ **Exhibit 3**   Circus Circus Enterprises, Inc.—Properties and Percent of Total Revenues

Properties	Percent Revenues			
	1998	**1997**	**1996**	**1995**
Las Vegas				
Circus Circus–Las Vegas	25[1]	24[1]	27[1]	29[1]
Excalibur	21	23	23	25
Luxor	23	17	20	24
Slots-A-Fun and Silver City				
Reno				
Circus Circus–Reno				
Laughlin				
Colorado Bell	12[2]	12[2]	13[2]	16[2]
Edgewater				
Jean, Nevada				
Gold Strike	6[3]	6[3]	4[3]	NA
Nevada Landing				
Henderson, Nevada				
Railroad Pass				
Tunica, Mississippi				
Gold Strike	4	4	5	3
50% ownership:				
Silver Legacy, Reno, Nevada	7.3	6.5[4]	3.5[4]	.5[4]
Monte Carlo, Las Vegas, Nevada				
Grand Victoria Riverboat Casino, Elgin Illinois				

[1]Combined with revenues from Circus Circus–Reno.

[2]Colorado Bell and Edgewater have been combined.

[3]Gold Strike and Nevada Landing have been combined.

[4]Revenues of unconsolidated affiliates have been combined.

Revenues from Slots-A-Fun and Silver City, management fees and other income was not separately reported.

offer more than 1,202 slot machines and 46 gaming tables on 34,900 square feet of casino floor.

Circus owns and operates ten properties in Nevada, one in Mississippi and has a 50 percent ownership in three others (see Exhibit 3).

All of Circus's operations do well in the city of Las Vegas. However, Circus Circus 1997 operational earnings for the Luxor and Circus Circus–Las Vegas were off 38 percent from the previous year. Management credits the disruption in services due to renovations for this decline.

However, Circus's combined hotel room occupancy rates had remained above 90 percent due, in part, to low room rates ($45 to $69 at Circus Circus–Las Vegas) and popular buffets. Each of the major properties contain large, inexpensive buffets that management believe make staying with Circus more attractive. Yet, recently results show a room occupancy rate of 87.5 percent, due in part to the building boom in Las Vegas.

The company's other big-top facility is Circus Circus–Reno. With the addition of Skyway Tower in 1985, this big top now offers a total of 1,605 hotel rooms, 60,600 square feet of casino, a buffet which can seat 700 people, shops, video arcades, cocktail lounges, midway games, and circus acts. Circus Circus–Reno had several marginal years, but has become one of the leaders in the Reno market. Circus anticipates that recent remodeling, at a cost of $25.6 million, will increase this property's revenue generating potential.

The Colorado Belle and The Edgewater Hotel are located in Laughlin, Nevada, on the banks of the Colorado River, a city 90 miles south of Las Vegas. The Colorado Belle, opened in 1987, features a huge paddle wheel riverboat replica, buffet, cocktail lounges, and shops. The Edgewater, acquired in 1983, has a southwestern motif, a 57,000 square-foot casino, a bowling center, buffet and cocktail lounges. Combined, these two properties contain 2,700 rooms and over 120,000 square feet of casino. These two operations contributed 12 percent of the company's revenues in the year ended January 31, 1997, and again in 1998, down from 21 percent in 1994. The extensive proliferation of casinos throughout the region, primarily on Indian land, and the development of mega-resorts in Las Vegas have seriously eroded outlying markets such as Laughlin.

Three properties purchased in 1995 and located in Jean and Henderson, Nevada, represent continuing investments by Circus in outlying markets. The Gold Strike and Nevada Landing service the I-15 market between Las Vegas and southern California. These properties have over 73,000 square feet of casino space, 2,140 slot machines, and 42 gaming tables combined. Each has limited hotel space (1,116 rooms total), and depend heavily on I-15 traffic. The Railroad Pass is considered a local casino and is dependent on Henderson residents as its market. This smaller casino contains only 395 slot machines and 11 gaming tables.

Gold Strike–Tunica (formally Circus Circus–Tunica) is a dockside casino located in Tunica, Mississippi, opened in 1994 on 24 acres of land located along the Mississippi River, approximately 20 miles south of Memphis. In 1997 operating income declined by more than 50 percent due to the increase in competition and lack of hotel rooms. Circus decided to renovate this property and add a 1,200 room tower hotel. Total cost for all remodeling was $119.8 million.

Joint Ventures

Circus is currently engaged in three joint ventures through the wholly owned subsidiary Circus Participant. In Las Vegas, Circus joined with Mirage Resorts to build and operate the Monte Carlo, a hotel-casino with 3,002 rooms designed along the lines of the grand casinos of the Mediterranean. It is located on 46 acres (with 600 feet on the Las Vegas strip) between the New York–New York casino and the soon to be completed Bellagio, with all three casinos to be connected by monorail. The Monte Carlo features a 90,000-square-foot casino containing 2,221 slot machines and 95 gaming tables, along with a 550 seat bingo parlor, high tech arcade rides, restaurants and buffets, a microbrewery, approximately 15,000 square feet of meeting and convention space and a 1,200 seat theater. Opened on June 21, 1996, the Monte Carlo generated $14.6 million as Circus's share in operating income for the first seven months of operation.

In Elgin, Illinois, Circus is in a 50 percent partnership with Hyatt Development Corporation in The Grand Victoria. Styled to resemble a Victorian riverboat, this floating casino and land-based entertainment complex includes some 36,000 square feet of casino space, containing 977 slot machines and 56 gaming tables. The adjacent land-based complex contains two movie theaters, a 240 seat buffet, restaurants and parking for approximately 2,000 vehicles. Built for a total of $112 million, The Grand Victoria returned to Circus $44 million in operating income in 1996.

The third joint venture is a 50 percent partnership with Eldorado Limited in the Silver Legacy. Opened in 1995, this casino is located between Circus Circus–Reno and the Eldorado Hotel and Casino on two city blocks in downtown Reno, Nevada. The Silver Legacy has 1,711 hotel rooms, 85,000 square feet of casino, 2,275 slot machines and 89 gaming tables. Management seems to believe that the Silver Legacy holds promise; however the Reno market is suffering and the opening of the Silver Legacy has cannibalized the Circus Circus–Reno market.

Circus engaged in a fourth joint venture to penetrate the Canadian market, but on January 23, 1997, announced they had been bought out by Hilton Hotels Corporation, one of three partners in the venture.

Circus has achieved success through an aggressive growth strategy and a corporate structure designed to enhance that growth. A strong cash position, innovative ideas, and attention to cost control have allowed Circus to satisfy the bottom line during a period when competitors were typically taking on large debt obligations to finance new projects (See Exhibits 4, 5, 6, & 7). Yet the market is changing. Gambling of all kinds has spread across the country; no longer does the average individual need to go to Las Vegas or New Jersey. Instead, gambling can be found as close as the local quick market (lottery), bingo hall, many Indian reservations, the Mississippi River and others. There are now almost 300 casinos in Las Vegas alone, 60 in Colorado and 160 in California. In order to maintain a competitive edge, Circus has continued to invest heavily in renovation of existing properties (a strategy common to the entertainment/amusement industry) and continues to develop new projects.

■ **Exhibit 4**   Selected Financial Information

	FY 98	**FY 97**	**FY 96**	**FY 95**	**FY 94**	**FY 93**	**FY 92**	**FY 91**
Earnings per share	0.40	0.99	1.33	1.59	1.34	2.05	1.84	1.39
Current ratio	.85	1.17	1.30	1.35	.95	.90	1.14	.88
Total liabilities/total assets	.65	.62	.44	.54	.57	.48	.58	.77
Operating profit margin	17.4%	17%	19%	22%	21%	24.4%	24.9%	22.9%

SOURCE: Circus Circus Annual Reports and 10K's, 1991–1998.

■ **Exhibit 5**
Twelve Year Summary

	Revenues (in 000)	**Net Income**
FY 98	$1,354,487	$ 89,908
FY 97	1,334,250	100,733
FY 96	1,299,596	128,898
FY 95	1,170,182	136,286
FY 94	954,923	116,189
FY 93	843,025	117,322
FY 92	806,023	103,348
FY 91	692,052	76,292
FY 90	522,376	76,064
FY 89	511,960	81,714
FY 88	458,856	55,900
FY 87	373,967	28,198
FY 86	306,993	37,375

SOURCE: Circus Circus Annual Reports and 10K's, 1986–1998.

■ **Exhibit 6**   Circus Circus Enterprises, Inc., Annual Income, Year ended January 31 (in thousands)

Fiscal Year Ending	1/31/98	1/31/97	1/31/96	1/31/95	1/31/94
Revenues					
Casino	$ 632,122	$ 655,902	$ 664,772	$ 612,115	$538,813
Rooms	330,644	294,241	278,807	232,346	176,001
Food and beverage	215,584	210,384	201,385	189,664	152,469
Other	142,407	146,554	158,534	166,295	117,501
Earnings of unconsolidated affiliates	98,977	86,646	45,485	5,459	—
	1,419,734	1,393,727	1,348,983	1,205,879	984,784
Less complimentary allowances	(65,247)	(59,477)	(49,387)	(35,697)	(29,861)
Net revenue	1,354,487	1,334,250	1,299,596	1,170,182	954,923
Costs and expenses					
Casino	316,902	302,096	275,680	246,416	209,402
Rooms	122,934	116,508	110,362	94,257	78,932
Food and beverage	199,955	200,722	188,712	177,136	149,267
Other operating expenses	90,187	90,601	92,631	107,297	72,802
General and administrative	232,536	227,348	215,083	183,175	152,104
Depreciation and amortization	117,474	95,414	93,938	81,109	58,105
Preopening expense	3,447	—	—	3,012	16,506
Abandonment loss		48,309	45,148	—	—
	1,083,435	1,080,998	1,021,554	892,402	737,118
Operating profit before corporate expense	271,052	223,252	278,042	277,780	217,805
Corporate expense	34,552	31,083	26,669	21,773	16,744
Income from operations	236,500	222,169	251,373	256,007	201,061
Other income (expense)					
Interest, dividends and other income (Loss)	9,779	5,077	4,022	225	(683)
Interest income and guarantee fees from unconsolidated affiliate	6,041	6,865	7,517	992	—
Interest expense	(88,847)	(54,681)	(51,537)	(42,734)	(17,770)
Interest expense from unconsolidated affiliate	(15,551)	(15,567)	(5,616)	—	—
	(88,578)	(58,306)	(45,614)	(41,517)	(18,453)
Income before provision for income tax	147,922	163,863	205,759	214,490	182,608
Provision for income tax	58,014	63,130	76,861	78,204	66,419
Income before extraordinary loss	—	—	—	—	116,189
Extraordinary loss	—	—	—	—	—
Net income	89,908	100,733	128,898	136,286	116,189
Earnings per share					
Income before extraordinary loss	.95	.99	1.33	1.59	1.34
Extraordinary loss	.01	—	—	—	—
Net income per share	.94	.99	1.33	1.59	1.34

SOURCE: Circus Circus Annual Reports and 10K's, 1994–1998.

■ **Exhibit 7**   Circus Circus Enterprises Inc., Consolidated Balance Sheets (in thousands)

Assets	1/31/98	1/31/97	1/31/96	1/31/95	1/31/94
Current assets					
Cash and cash equivalents	58,631	69,516	$62,704	$53,764	$39,110
Receivables	33,640	34,434	16,527	8,931	8,673
Inventories	22,440	19,371	20,459	22,660	20,057
Prepaid expenses	20,281	19,951	19,418	20,103	20,062
Deferred income tax	7,871	8,577	7,272	5,463	
Total current	142,863	151,849	124,380	110,921	87,902
Property, equipment					
Other assets					
Excess of purchase price over fair market value	375,375	385,583	394,518	9,836	10,200
Notes receivable	1,075	36,443	27,508	68,083	
Investments in unconsolidated affiliates	255,392	214,123	173,270	74,840	
Deferred charges and other assets	21,995	21,081	17,533	9,806	16,658
Total other	653,837	657,230	612,829	162,565	26,858
Total assets	3,263,548	2,729,111	2,213,503	1,512,548	1,297,924
Liabilities and Stockholders Equity					
Current liabilities					
Current portion of long-term debt	3,071	379	863	106	169
Accounts and contracts payable					
Trade	22,103	22,658	16,824	12,102	14,804
Construction	40,670	21,144	—	1,101	13,844
Accrued liabilities					
Salaries, wages and vacations	36,107	31,847	30,866	24,946	19,650
Progressive jackpots	7,511	6,799	8,151	7,447	4,881
Advance room deposits	6,217	7,383	7,517	8,701	6,981
Interest payable	17,828	9,004	3,169	2,331	2,278
Other	33,451	30,554	28,142	25,274	25,648
Income tax payable	—	—	—	—	3,806
Total current liabilities	166,958	129,768	95,532	82,008	92,061
Long-term debt	1,788,818	1,405,897	715,214	632,652	567,345
Other liabilities					
Deferred income tax	175,934	152,635	148,096	110,776	77,153
Other long-term liabilities	8,089	6,439	9,319	988	1,415
Total other liabilities	184,023	159,074	157,415	111,764	78,568
Total liabilities	2,139,799	1,694,739	968,161	826,424	737,974
Redeemable preferred stock	—	17,631	18,530		
Temporary equity	—	44,950			
Commitments and contingent liabilities					
Stockholders equity					
Common stock	1,893	1,880	1,880	1,607	1,603
Preferred stock					
Additional paid-in capital	558,658	498,893	527,205	124,960	120,135
Retained earnings	1,074,271	984,363	883,630	754,732	618,446
Treasury stock	(511,073)	(513,345)	(185,903)	(195,175)	(180,234)
Total stockholders equity	1,123,749	971,791	1,226,812	686,124	559,950
Total liabilities and stockholders equity	3,263,548	2,729,111	2,213,503	1,512,548	1,297,924

SOURCE: Circus Circus Annual Reports and 10K's, 1994–1998.

New Ventures

Circus currently has three new projects planned for opening in the near future. The largest project, named "Mandalay Bay," is scheduled for completion in the first quarter of 1999, and is estimated to cost $950 million (excluding land). Circus owns a contiguous mile of the southern end of the Las Vegas strip which they call their "Masterplan Mile" and which currently contains the Excalibur and Luxor resorts. Located next to the Luxor, Mandalay Bay will aim for the upscale traveler and player and will be styled as a South Seas adventure. The resort will contain a 43-story hotel–casino with over 3,700 rooms and an 11-acre aquatic environment. The aquatic environment will contain a surfing beach, swim up shark tank, and snorkeling reef. A Four Seasons Hotel with some 400 rooms will complement the remainder of Mandalay Bay. Circus anticipates that the remainder of the Masterplan Mile will eventually be comprised of at least one additional casino resort and a number of stand alone hotels and amusement centers.

Circus also plans three other casino projects, provided all the necessary licenses and agreements can be obtained. In Detroit, Michigan, Circus has combined with the Atwater Casino Group in a joint venture to build a $600 million project. Negotiations with the city to develop the project have been completed, however, the remainder of the appropriate licenses will need to be obtained before construction begins.

Along the Mississippi Gulf, at the north end of the Bay of St. Louis, Circus plans to construct a casino resort containing 1,500 rooms at an estimated cost of $225 million. Circus has received all necessary permits to begin construction, however these approvals have been challenged in court, delaying the project.

In Atlantic City, Circus has entered into an agreement with Mirage Resorts to develop a 181-acre site in the Marina District. Land title has been transferred to Mirage; however, Mirage has purported to cancel its agreement with Circus. Circus has filed suit against Mirage seeking to enforce the contract, while others have filed suit to stop all development in the area.

Most of Circus's projects are being tailored to attract mainstream tourists and family vacationers. However the addition of several joint ventures and the completion of the Masterplan Mile will also attract the more upscale customer.

■ The Gaming Industry

By 1997 the gaming industry had captured a large amount of the vacation/leisure time dollars spent in the U.S. Gamblers lost over $44.3 billion on legal wagering in 1995 (up from $29.9 billion in 1992) including wagers at racetracks, bingo parlors, lotteries, and casinos. This figure does not include dollars spent on lodging, food, transportation, and other related expenditures associated with visits to gaming facilities. Casino gambling accounts for 76 percent of all legal gambling expenditures, far ahead of second place Indian Reservation at 8.9 percent and lotteries at 7.1 percent. The popularity of casino gambling may be credited to a more frequent and somewhat higher pay out as compared to lotteries and racetracks; however, as winnings are recycled, the multiplier effect restores a high return to casino operators.

Geographic expansion has slowed considerably as no additional states have approved casino type gambling since 1993. Growth has occurred in developed locations, with Las Vegas, Nevada, and Atlantic City, New Jersey, leading the way.

Las Vegas remains the largest U.S. gaming market and one of the largest convention markets with more than 100,000 hotel rooms hosting more than 29.6 million visitors in 1996, up 2.2 percent over 1995. Casino operators are building to take advantage of this continued growth. Recent projects include the Monte Carlo ($350 million), New York–New York ($350 million), Bellagio ($1.4 billion), Hilton Hotels ($750 million), and Project Paradise ($800 million). Additionally, Harrah's is adding a 989-room tower and remodeling 500 current rooms, and Caesar's Palace has expansion plans to add 2,000 rooms. Las Vegas hotel and casino capacity is expected to continue to expand with some 12,500 rooms opening within a year, beginning late 1998. According to the Las Vegas Convention and Visitor Authority, Las Vegas is a destination market with most visitors planning their trip more than a week in advance (81 percent), arriving by car (47 percent) or airplane (42 percent), and staying in a hotel (72 percent). Gamblers are typically return visitors (77 percent) averaging 2.2 trips per year who like playing the slots (65 percent).

For Atlantic City, besides the geographical separation, the primary differences in the two markets reflect the different types of consumers frequenting these markets. While Las Vegas attracts overnight resort-seeking vacationers, Atlantic City's clientele are predominantly day-trippers traveling by automobile or bus. Gaming revenues are expected to continue to grow, perhaps to $4 billion in 1997 split between ten casino/hotels currently operating. Growth in the Atlantic City area will be concentrated in the Marina section of town where Mirage Resorts has entered into an agreement with the city to develop 150 acres of the Marina as a destination resort. This development will include a resort wholly owned by Mirage, a casino/hotel developed by Circus, and a complex developed by a joint venture with Mirage and Boyd Corp. Currently in Atlantic City, Donald Trump's gaming empire holds the largest market share with Trump's Castle, Trump Plaza, and the Taj Mahal (total market share is 30 percent). The next closest in market share is Caesar's (10.3 percent), Tropicana and Bally's (9.2 percent each), and Showboat (9.0 percent).

There remain a number of smaller markets located around the U.S., primarily in Mississippi, Louisiana, Illinois, Missouri, and Indiana. Each state has imposed various restrictions on the development of casino operations within their states. In some cases, for example Illinois where there are only ten gaming licenses available, this has severely restricted the growth opportunities and hurt revenues. In other states, Mississippi and Louisiana, revenues are up 8 percent and 15 percent, respectively, in riverboat operations. Native American casinos continue to be developed on federally controlled Indian land. These casinos are not publicly held but do tend to be managed by publicly held corporations. Overall these other locations present a mix of opportunities and generally constitute only a small portion of overall gaming revenues.

■ Major Industry Players

Over the past several years there have been numerous changes as mergers and acquisitions have reshaped the gaming industry. As of year end 1996, the industry was a combination of corporations ranging from those engaged solely in gaming to multi-national conglomerates. The largest competitors, in terms of revenues, combined multiple industries to generate both large revenues and substantial profits (see Exhibit 8). However, those engaged primarily in gaming could also be extremely profitable.

■ **Exhibit 8**   Major U.S. Gaming, Lottery, and Pari-mutuel Companies—1996 Revenues and Net Income (in millions)

	1997 Revenues	1997 Income	1996 Revenues	1996 Income
Starwood/ITT			$6,597.0	$249.0
Hilton Hotels	5,316.0	250.0	3,940.0	82.0
Harrah's Entertainment	1,619.0	99.3	1,586.0	98.9
Mirage Resorts	1,546.0	207.0	1,358.3	206.0
Circus Circus	1,354.4	89.9	1,247.0	100.7
Trump Hotel and Casino, Inc.	1,399.3	−42.1	976.3	−4.9
MGM Grand	827.5	111.0	804.8	74.5
Aztar	782.3	4.4	777.5	20.6
Int. Game Technology	743.9	137.2	733.5	118.0

SOURCE: Individual companies annual reports and 10K's, 1996.

In 1996 Hilton began a hostile acquisition attempt of ITT Corporation. As a result of this attempt, ITT has merged with Starwood Lodging Corporation and Starwood Lodging Trust. The resulting corporation is one of the world's largest hotel and gaming corporations, owning the Sheraton, The Luxury Collection, the Four Points Hotels, Caesar's, as well as communications and educational services. In 1996 ITT hosted approximately 50 million customer nights in locations worldwide. Gaming operations are located in Las Vegas, Atlantic City, Halifax and Sydney (Nova Scotia), Lake Tahoe, Tunica (Mississippi), Lima (Peru), Cairo (Egypt), Canada, and Australia. In 1996 ITT had net income of $249 million on revenues of $6.579 billion. In June 1996, ITT announced plans to join with Planet Hollywood to develop casino/hotels with the Planet Hollywood theme in both Las Vegas and Atlantic City. However, these plans may be deferred as ITT becomes fully integrated into Starwood and management has the opportunity to refocus on the operations of the company.

Hilton Hotels owns (as of February 1, 1998) or leases and operates 25 hotels and manages 34 hotels partially or wholly owned by others along with 180 franchised hotels. Eleven of the hotels are also casinos, six of which are located in Nevada, two in Atlantic City, with the other three in Australia and Uruguay. In 1997 Hilton had net income of $250.0 million on $5.31 billion in revenues. Hilton receives some 38 percent of total operating revenues from gaming operations and continues to expand in the market. Recent expansions include the Wild Wild West theme hotel/casino in Atlantic City, the completed acquisition of all the assets of Bally's, and construction on a 2,900-room Paris Casino resort located next to Bally's Las Vegas.

Harrah's Entertainment, Inc., is primarily engaged in the gaming industry with casino/hotels in Reno, Lake Tahoe, Las Vegas, and Laughlin, Nevada; Atlantic City, New Jersey; riverboats in Joliet, Illinois; and Vicksburg and Tunica, Mississippi; Shreveport, Louisiana; Kansas City, Kansas; two Indian casinos and one in Auckland, New Zealand. In 1997 they operated a total of approximately 774,500 square feet of casino space with 19,835 slot machines and 934 table games. With this and some 8,197 hotel rooms they had a net income of $99.3 million on $1.619 billion in revenues.

All of Mirage Resorts, Inc.'s gaming operations are currently located in Nevada. It owns and operates the Golden Nugget–Downtown, Las Vegas, the Mirage on the strip in Las Vegas, Treasure Island, and the Golden Nugget–Laughlin. Additionally they are a 50 percent owner of the Monte Carlo with Circus Circus. Net income for Mirage Resorts in 1997 was $207 million on revenues of $1.546 billion. Current expansion plans include the development of the Bellagio in Las Vegas ($1.6 billion estimated cost) and the Beau Rivage in Biloxi, Mississippi ($600 million estimated cost). These two properties would add a total of 265,900 square feet of casino space to the current Mirage inventory and an additional 252 gaming tables and 4,746 slot machines. An additional project is the development of the Marina area in Atlantic City, New Jersey, in partnership with Boyd Gaming.

MGM Grand Hotel and Casino is located on approximately 114 acres at the northeast corner of Las Vegas Boulevard across the street from New York–New York Hotel and Casino. The casino is approximately 171,500 square feet in size, and is one of the largest casinos in the world with 3,669 slot machines and 157 table games. Current plans call for extensive renovation costing $700 million. Through a wholly-owned subsidiary, MGM owns and operates the MGM Grand Diamond Beach Hotel and a hotel/casino resort in Darwin, Australia. Additionally, MGM and Primadonna Resorts, Inc., each own 50 percent of New York–New York Hotel and Casino, a $460 million architecturally distinctive, themed destination resort which opened on January 3, 1997. MGM also intends to construct and operate a destination resort hotel/casino, entertainment and retail facility in Atlantic City on approximately 35 acres of land on the Atlantic City Boardwalk.

■ The Legal Environment

Within the gaming industry all current operators must consider compliance with extensive gaming regulations as a primary concern. Each state or country has it's own specific regulations and regulatory boards requiring extensive reporting and licensing requirements. For example, in Las Vegas, Nevada, gambling operations are subject to regulatory control by the Nevada State Gaming Control Board, the Clark County Nevada Gaming and Liquor Licensing Board, and by city government regulations. The laws, regulations, and supervisory procedures of virtually all gaming authorities are based upon public policy primarily concerned with the prevention of unsavory or unsuitable persons from having a direct or indirect involvement with gaming at any time or in any capacity and the establishment and maintenance of responsible accounting practices and procedures. Additional regulations typically cover the maintenance of effective controls over the financial practices of licensees, including the establishment of minimum procedures for internal fiscal affairs and the safeguarding of assets and revenues, providing reliable record keeping and requiring the filing of periodic reports, the prevention of cheating and fraudulent practices, and providing a source of state and local revenues through taxation and licensing fees. Some restrictive laws, regulations and procedures could have an adverse effect on any gaming operations. All gaming companies must submit detailed operating and financial reports to authorities. Nearly all financial transactions, including loans, leases and the sale of securities must be reported. Some financial activities are subject to approval by regulatory agencies. As Circus moves into other locations outside of Nevada, it will need to adhere to local regulations.

■ Future Considerations

Circus Circus states that it is "in the business of entertainment, with . . . core strength in casino gaming," and that it intends to focus its efforts in Las Vegas, Atlantic City, and Mississippi. Circus further states that the "future product in gaming, to be sure, is the entertainment resort" (Circus Circus 1997 Annual Report).

Circus was one of the innovators of the gaming resort concept and has continued to be a leader in that field. However the mega-entertainment resort industry operates differently than the traditional casino gaming industry. In the past consumers would visit a casino to experience the thrill of gambling. Now they not only gamble, but expect to be dazzled by enormous entertainment complexes that are costing billions of dollars to build. The competition has continued to increase at the same time revenue growth rates have been slowing.

For years analysts have questioned the ability of the gaming industry to continue high growth in established markets as the industry matures. Through the 1970s and '80s the gaming industry experienced rapid growth. Through the 1990s the industry began to experience a shake out of marginal competitors and a consolidation phase. Circus Circus has been successful through this turmoil but now faces the task of maintaining high growth in a more mature industry.

■ Bibliography

Circus Circus Announces Promotion, *PR Newswire,* June 10, 1997.

Industry Surveys–Lodging and Gaming, *Standard and Poors Industry Surveys,* June 19, 1997.

"Casinos Move into New Areas," *Standard and Poors Industry Surveys,* March 11, 1993, pp. L35–L41.

Circus Circus Enterprises, Inc., *Annual Report to Shareholders,* January 31, 1989; January 31, 1990; January 31, 1993; January 31, 1994; January 31, 1995; January 31, 1996.

Circus Circus Enterprises, Inc., *Annual Report to Shareholders,* January 31, 1997.

Circus Circus Enterprises, Inc., *Annual Report to Shareholders,* January 31, 1998.

Corning, Blair, "Luxor: Egypt Opens in Vegas," *San Antonio Express News,* October 24, 1993.

Lalli, Sergio, "Excalibur Awaiteth," *Hotel and Motel Management,* June 11, 1990.

"Economic Impacts of Casino Gaming in the United States," by Arthur Anderson for the American Gaming Association, May 1997.

"Harrah's Survey of Casino Entertainment," Harrah's Entertainment, Inc., 1996.

"ITT Board Rejects Hilton's Offer as Inadequate, Reaffirms belief that ITT's Comprehensive Plan is in the best Interest of ITT shareholders," Press Release, August 14, 1997.

Mirage Resorts, Inc., *1997 and 1998 10K,* and retrieved from EDGAR Data Base, www.sec.gov/Archives/edgar/data/.

Hilton Hotels Corp. *1997 and 1998 10K,* retrieved from EDGAR Data Base, www.sec.gov/Archives/edgar/data/.

Aztar Corp. *1997 and 1998 10K,* retrieved from EDGAR Data Base, www.sec.gov/Archives/edgar/data/.

ITT Corp. *1997 10K,* retrieved from EDGAR Data Base, www.sec.gov/Archives/edgar/data/.

Harrah's Entertainment, Inc., *1997 and 1998 10K,* retrieved from EDGAR Data Base, www.sec.gov/Archives/edgar/data/.

MGM Grand, Inc., *1997 and 1998 10K,* retrieved from EDGAR Data Base, www.sec.gov/Archives/edgar/data/.

Case Group B
Product Strategy

■ Case 7   Pfizer, Inc., Animal Health Products[1]

Jakki J. Mohr and Sara Streeter
Both of the University of Montana

Gail Oss, Territory Manager of Pfizer, Inc., Animal Health Group in western Montana and southeastern Idaho, was driving back to her home office after a day of visiting cattle ranchers in her territory. The combination of the spring sunshine warming the air and the snow-capped peaks of the Bitterroot Mountains provided a stunningly beautiful backdrop for her drive. But, the majestic beauty provided little relief to her troubled thoughts.

The NAFTA agreement with Canada and Mexico had hit local ranchers particularly hard. The influx of beef cattle into the U.S. market from these countries, as well as beef from other countries (e.g., Australia) had wreaked havoc over the past year. Prices of beef had declined precipitously from the prior year. Ranchers in the past had retained sufficient cash reserves to come back from a bad year, but this year, things were particularly bad. The prices being offered for the calves by the feedlot operators were, in many cases, less than the costs of raising them. Ranchers' objectives had changed from making some modest income off their cattle operations to minimizing their losses.

In this environment, ranchers were actively seeking ways to cut costs. Gail sold high-quality animal health products, oftentimes at a premium price. One way in which ranchers could cut costs was either to scrimp on animal health care products, such as vaccines and antibiotics, or to switch to a lower-cost alternative. The current environment posed a particularly severe threat, not only to Gail's company, but also to her very livelihood. Gail had spent a substantial amount of time and effort cultivating long-term relationships with many of these ranchers—many of whom she had had to convince of her credibility, given her gender. Given the time and effort she had spent cultivating these relationships, as well as the camaraderie she felt with her customers, she did not want to see the ranchers in her territory go under. Ranching was an important part of the history of Montana; many ranchers had ties to the land going back generations. They took pride in producing the food for many

[1]Some of the information in this case has been modified to protect the proprietary nature of firms' marketing strategies. The case is intended to be used as a basis for class discussion rather than to illustrate either effective or ineffective marketing strategies.

© Copyright Jakki J. Mohr, 1999. All Rights Reserved. Support from The Institute for the Study of Business Markets, Pennsylvania State University, is greatly appreciated.

tables in the U.S. and other areas of the world. Gail felt that Pfizer could use its fairly significant resources in a very influential manner to help these ranchers. Merely lowering the price on her products (if that was even possible) was merely a band-aid solution to the problem.

As part of Gail's weekly responsibilities, she communicated via an automated computer system to her sales manager, Tom Brooks (also in Montana), and to the marketing managers at headquarters (in Exton, Pennsylvania). She knew she needed to report the severity of the situation, but more importantly, she wanted to encourage headquarters to take the bull by the horns, so to speak. So, she was pondering the message she would write that evening from her kitchen table.

■ Industry Background

The supply chain (Exhibit 1) for beef begins with the cow/calf producer (the commercial rancher). Commercial ranchers are in the business of breeding and raising cattle for the purpose of selling them to feedlots. Ranchers keep a herd of cows that are bred yearly. The calves are generally born in the early spring, weaned in October, and shipped to feedlots generally in late October/early November. The ranchers' objectives are (1) to minimize death loss in their herd, (2) to breed cows that give birth to low birth-weight calves (for calving ease), (3) to produce beef that will grade choice by having a good amount of marbling, and (4) to produce calves that gain weight quickly. Success measures include: conception rate of cows exposed to bulls; live birth rates, birth weights, weaning weights, death loss, and profitability. By the time a rancher sells his or her calves to the feedlot, the name of the game is pounds. The rancher generally wants the biggest calves possible by that time.

■ **Exhibit 1**
Supply Chain for Beef

Cow/Calf Producers → Feedlot → Meat Packer → Customers (food service, retail, etc.)

Within a commodity market, basic laws of supply and demand are influenced by those in a position to control access to the markets. Four meatpackers control roughly 80 percent of the industry. Meatpackers act as an intermediary between the meat consumer and the meat producer. This situation has not facilitated a free flow of information throughout the supply chain, and therefore, the industry has not been strongly consumer-focused.

Exhibit 2 traces the market share for beef, pork, and poultry from 1970–1997, and projects changes in the market through 2003. The market share for beef has fallen from 44 percent in 1970 to 32 percent in 1997, a 27 percent drop. Some of the reasons for the decline in beef demand included:

- Changes in consumer lifestyles (less time spent in preparing home-cooked meals); 66 percent of all dinner decisions are made on the same day and of those, 75 percent of dinner preparers don't know what they're going to make at 4:30 P.M.

■ **Exhibit 2**
Per Capita Meat
Consumption %
Market Share (Retail
Weight)

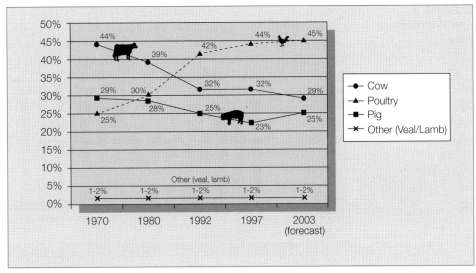

SOURCE: USDA & NCBA

- Health/nutritional issues (dietary considerations involving cholesterol, fat content, food-borne diseases, etc.).
- Switching to alternative meat products.

In addition, the pork and poultry industries have done a better job of marketing their products. During 1997, the number of new poultry products (for example, stuffed chicken entrees, gourmet home meal replacements) introduced to the market increased 13 percent from the prior year, compared to an increase of only 3.5 percent for new beef products. Retail pricing for beef also remained high (although this high price did not translate into higher prices for the calves to the ranchers).

As shown in Exhibit 3, the beef production cycle spans a twelve-year period in which production levels expand and contract. The amount of beef produced (bars in the chart, millions of pounds on the left-hand scale) increased through the mid-90s—despite declining beef consumption in the U.S. This relationship between production and consumption is consistent with other commodity markets where there exists an inverse relationship between supply and demand.

Some of the reasons for increased beef production in the mid-90s included:

- Herd liquidation: low cattle prices, coupled with the high cost of feed drove some producers out of business.
- Improved genetics and animal health/nutrition increased production yields; although cow numbers had decreased by 10 percent since 1985 productivity per cow increased by 29 percent.
- Export of beef increased seven-fold since 1985 (to 2 billion pounds); key markets include Japan (54 percent of export volume), Canada (16 percent), Korea (11 percent), and Mexico (9 percent).

Exhibit 3 also shows that the price the ranchers received for their beef cattle varied inversely with production (right-hand scale). Although calf prices were expected to rise slightly through the late '90s and early 2000s, the prices paid ranchers were

■ **Exhibit 3**
Beef Production and
Price

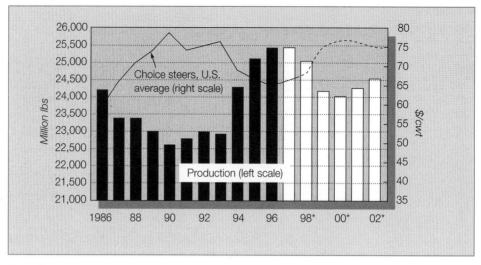

*forecast

still far below the relatively high prices consumers paid at retail. One of the reasons given for the relatively low prices paid to ranchers was the high degree of concentration at the meat packer level of the supply chain. As noted previously, four packing houses controlled access to the market. Some ranchers believed this gave the packing houses near-monopoly power in setting prices (both for what they would pay feedlot operators for the calves, and in charging prices to their downstream customers (e.g., the grocery store chains). Although the U.S. government had investigated the possibility of collusion among packers, the evidence was not sufficient to draw any firm conclusions.

To further complicate matters, the NAFTA agreement passed in 1989 gave open access to the U.S. markets from Mexican and Canadian ranchers. The lowering of trade barriers, coupled with weakness in the Canadian dollar and the Mexican peso, made imported livestock cheap, compared to U.S.–grown animals. As a result, thousands of cattle came streaming across the borders.

During the summer of 1998, ranchers became quite vocal in drawing attention to the influx of cattle from Canada. Local governments were somewhat responsive to their concerns. Indeed, trucks carrying Canadian cattle had been turned back at the U.S./Canadian border for minor infractions, such as licensing problems. In addition, the trucks were pulled over for inspections. A private coalition of ranchers, calling itself the Ranchers-Cattlemen Action Legal Foundation (R-CALF) filed three separate petitions with the U.S. International Trade Commission (ITC) on October 1, 1998, two against Canada and one against Mexico, asking for U.S. government trade investigations. The group requested that anti-dumping duties be levied on meat or livestock imports from the two countries. The Montana Stockgrowers Association had been an early and steadfast supporter of R-CALF.

The ITC determined that there was evidence to support the charge that Canadian cattle imports caused material injury to U.S. domestic cattle producers. The Department of Commerce began to collect information on Canadian subsidies and the prices at which cattle are sold in Canada and in the United States. In the case against Mexico, the ITC determined that there was no indication that imports of live cattle

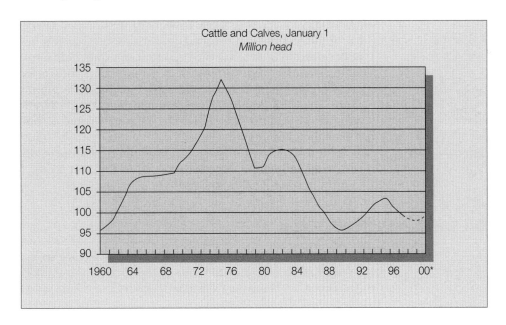

Cattle and Calves, January 1
Million head

from Mexico were causing "material injury" to the domestic industry in the U.S. Dissatisfied with the response, R-CALF decided to appeal the case to the Court of International Trade.

Ranchers were doing what they could to minimize the impact of the NAFTA agreement on their livelihoods, however, some could not sustain their operations because of the low prices. The number of cattle operations was declining. In many cases, smaller ranchers were selling out to their larger neighbors. This reality was reflected in the cattle inventory statistics, shown in Exhibit 4.

The number of cattle kept by U.S. ranchers had declined from a high of approximately 132 million head in 1975, to just under 100 million head in 1998. As noted previously, improvements in genetics and animal health and nutrition allowed ranchers to increase production yields, even with fewer head.

■ Additional Industry Changes

Some of the changes that occurred in the poultry and pork industries, including more ready-to-eat products and branded products, were expected to diffuse into the cattle industry. Industry analysts believed that the beef industry would need to develop products that could be more easily prepared, and to develop branded products that consumers could recognize and rely on for quality and convenience. In addition, industry analysts believed that the beef industry would need to improve the quality of its products (in terms of more consistent taste and tenderness), as only 25 percent of the beef produced met quality targets.

The development of branded beef would require a tracking system from "birth-to-beef" in the supply chain. Such tracking would allow standardized health, quality, and management protocols, as well as improved feedback through the production chain. This change would also necessitate that producers become more closely linked to the feedlots to improve beef quality. Branded beef production would move the industry from a cost-based (production) approach to a value-added approach. Better coordination along the supply chain would help ensure an increased flow of information from the consumer to the producer. Alliances between the cow/calf producer and the feedlots would allow ranchers to better track the success of their calves (based on health and weight gain). Such data could help ranchers to further improve the genetics of their herd by tracking which cow/bull combinations had delivered the higher-yield calves. As part of these trends, some degree of integration or vertical coordination would occur in the beef industry. Ranchers would need to participate in order to ensure market access for their product. Ranchers would have to think beyond the boundaries of their own ranches.

■ Pfizer Animal Health Group

Pfizer Inc. is a research-based, diversified health care company with global operations. Pfizer Animal Health is one of the corporation's three major business groups (the other two being the Consumer Health Care Group, and U.S. Pharmaceuticals). The Animal Health Products Group accounted for roughly 12 percent of the company's revenues in 1998.

Pfizer Animal Health products are sold to veterinarians and animal health distributors in more than 140 countries around the world for use by livestock producers, and horse and pet owners; the products are used on more than 30 animal species. Pfizer Animal Health is committed to providing high-quality, research-based health products for livestock and companion animals. The company invests heavily in research and development. As a result, Pfizer has many new animal health products in its research pipeline, a number of which have already been introduced in international markets and would become available in the United States in the next several years.

As Exhibit 5 shows, the Animal Health Group is divided in the North American Region into a U.S. Livestock Division, a U.S. Companion Animal Division (cats, dogs, etc.), and Canada. The Cow/Calf Division falls under the Cattle Business Unit within the Livestock Division. That Division is organized further by product type.

■ **Exhibit 5** Pfizer Animal Health Organization

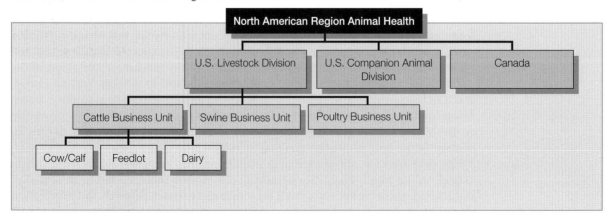

The marketing managers for each cattle market segment work closely with product managers and sales managers to ensure timely, accurate information back from the field. Territory managers responsible for all sales activities report to an area sales manager, who in turn reports to the national sales and marketing manager. Territory managers are typically compensated on a roughly 80 percent salary/20 percent commission basis. This breakdown varies by salesperson by year: in a good year the commission might be a much higher percentage of overall earnings, while in a bad year, the salary component might be a greater percentage of the salesperson's overall earnings.

■ Marketing Strategy

Pfizer's Cow/Calf Division offers a full range of products to cattle ranchers, including vaccines for both new-born calves and their mothers, medications (for example, de-wormers, anti-diarrheals), and antibiotics (for pneumonia and other diseases). Pfizer's sophisticated research-and-development system produced a number of new and useful products for the market. For example, Pfizer developed a long-lasting de-wormer that was simply poured over the cow's back. This technology was a significant time-saver to the rancher, eliminating the need to administer either an oral medication or an injection.

Pfizer offered a diverse product line to cow/calf ranchers. Pfizer segmented ranchers in the cow/calf business on the basis of herd size, as shown in Exhibit 6.

"Hobbyists" are so called because in many cases, these ranchers run their cattle as a sideline to some other job. "Traditionalists'"main livelihood is their cattle operation. The "Business" segment operations are large ranches, owned either by a family or a corporation.

Pfizer's extensive network of field sales representatives visits ranchers to inform them about new and existing products. Time spent with accounts was typically allocated on the basis of volume of product purchased.

Pfizer positioned its products on the combination of superior science (resulting from its significant R&D efforts) and high-quality production/quality control techniques. For example, although other companies in the market (particularly generics) used similar formulations in their products, on occasion they did not have good quality control in the production line, resulting in batches of ineffective vaccines and recalls. Pfizer backed its products completely with a Technical Services Department. If ranchers had any kind of health or nutritional problem with their herds, they could call on a team of Pfizer technical specialists who would work with the local veterinarian utilizing blood and other diagnostics to identify the problem and suggest a solution.

■ **Exhibit 6**
Pfizer Market
Segments, 1998

Segment	# of Cattle	# of Operations	% of National Cattle Inventory
Hobbyist	<100	808,000	50%
Traditionalist	100–499	69,000	36%
Business	500+	5,900	14%

Pfizer also was involved in the cattle industry itself. Each territory manager was given an annual budget that included discretionary funds to be spent in his/her territory to sponsor industry activities such as seminars on herd health, stock shows, 4-H, and so forth. Gail Oss, for example, chose to spend a significant portion of her discretionary funds sponsoring meetings and conferences for the Montana Stockgrower's Association, which might include a veterinarian or a professor from the Extension Office of a state university speaking on issues pertinent to ranchers.

The majority of Pfizer's trade advertising was focused on specific products and appeared in cattle industry publications, such as *Beef Magazine* and *Bovine Veterinarian*. One ad read, "More veterinarians are satisfied with [Pfizer's] Dectomax Pour-On," and went on to describe veterinarians' superior satisfaction and greater likelihood of recommending Dectomax compared to a key competitor, Ivomec.

> Eighty-four percent of veterinarians who recommended Dectomax Pour-On said they were satisfied or very satisfied with its performance—compared to only 51 percent who were satisfied or very satisfied with Ivomec Eprinex Pour-On. . . . If choosing only between Dectomax and Ivomec, over three out of four veterinarians would choose to recommend Dectomax Pour-On.

Another ad read, "Calf Health Program Boosts Prices by Up to $21 more per Head." The data in the copy-intensive ad highlighted that "cow-calf producers enrolled in value-added programs like Pfizer Select Vaccine programs are being rewarded for their efforts with top-of-the-market prices." Such programs are based on consistent vaccination of animals with specific products, and provide optimal disease protection. The programs result in cattle that perform more consistently and predictably in terms of weight gain and beef quality—resulting in higher prices at sale time.

Although the territory managers called on ranchers (as well as the veterinarians, distributors, dealers) in their territories, they did not sell directly to ranchers. Ranchers could buy their animal health products from either a local veterinarian or a distributor or dealer (such as a feed-and-seed store). The percentage of product flowing through vets or distributors and dealers varied significantly by region. In areas where feedlots (vs. cow/calf ranchers) were the predominant customers, 95 percent of the product could flow through distributors. In areas where ranchers are the predominant customers, vets could sell 50 percent of the product, depending upon customer preferences.

Vets were particularly important given that the overwhelming majority of ranchers said that the person they trusted the most when it came to managing the health of their herd was their veterinarian. Pfizer capitalizes on this trust in the vet in its marketing program. When the vet consults and recommends a Pfizer product to a rancher, the vet gives the rancher a coded coupon which may be redeemed at either a vet clinic or supply house. When the coupon is sent back to Pfizer for reimbursement, the vet is credited for servicing that product, regardless of where the product is purchased.

Pfizer offers some trade promotions to vets and distributors, including volume rebate programs, price promotions on certain products during busy seasonal periods, and so forth. However, Pfizer's competitors oftentimes gave much more significant discounts to distributors. As a result, when a rancher goes to a distributor to buy a product which the vet had recommended, the distributor might switch the rancher to a similar product for which the distributor was making more profit. If it was a Pfizer product which the vet had recommended, the distributor might switch the rancher to a competitors' product. Pfizer had historically avoided competing on the basis of such promotional tactics, feeling instead that investing funds into R&D resulted in better long-term benefits for its customers.

So, as Gail pondered these various facets of the company's market position and strategies, she decided to take a strong stance in her weekly memo. It was time to cut the bull.

Discussion Questions

1. Evaluate the trends affecting the cattle ranching industry.
2. To what degree is a high quality/premium price position a strength or a liability during an industry downturn? What are the various ways Pfizer could handle this situation?
3. Evaluate the various dimensions of Pfizer's marketing strategy: Market segmentation and positioning, product/price, distribution, trade advertising and trade promotion, personal selling, public relations and sponsorships. What makes sense and what doesn't? Why or why not?
4. Would Pfizer benefit from a relationship marketing focus? How would its marketing strategy need to be modified to take such a focus?
5. When an industry is in decline, to what extent should a supplier be involved in ensuring its customers' livelihoods?

Case 8   Valley BancSystem, Inc.

James E. Nelson
University of Colorado

Chuck Smith walked briskly across the lobby of the Broadmoor bank to his office. It was 7:30 on a chilly morning in November 1992. He would have at least an hour before the rush of Friday customers would begin. Friday always meant a great deal of public relations for Smith in terms of exchanging greetings and small talk with customers. Today I could do without it, Smith thought, I'd rather work on what the marketing committee discussed yesterday. However, he knew that customers expected to see his door open and his face break into a smile whenever they voiced a greeting. The hour or so would be enough time to get his thoughts down on the Shop and Save proposal. The other topics that he had discussed with the committee would have to wait.

■ Valley BancSystem, Inc.

Valley Bank and Trust Company of Broadmoor was one of eight members of Valley BancSystem, Inc., a multibank holding company under the laws of the state of Illinois. Seven of the eight subsidiaries were located within 25 miles of each other in Polk and Madison counties. The sixth, Valley Bank and Trust Company of Columbus, was almost 80 miles south in Jackson County. Polk and Madison counties were due west of Chicago.

Valley BancSystem, Inc., was formed on April 30, 1982, about one year after enactment of an Illinois law permitting multibank holding companies. Earlier, the eight subsidiaries were considered "affiliated" in the sense that they shared several officers and directors. The holding company provided auditing, investment, and accounting services for its subsidiaries. It contracted with an outside organization for computer services and managed the ATM service. The holding company had authority and responsibility for major financial and marketing decisions for all subsidiaries. As an example of financial decision making, senior management had decided in late 1991 to charge off about $4.7 million in loans (primarily agricultural). The action had produced a net loss of $25,000 (see Exhibit 1).

Now that financial matters had been resolved, the attention of senior management turned to marketing. A marketing committee had been formed at the request of the new chairman of the board and president, James Kuhn. Kuhn had joined the holding company in late 1989, replacing John Charles who had served as chairman and president since 1958. Kuhn's previous experience included positions as senior vice president of Essex County Bank and Trust, senior vice presi-

This case was written by Prof. James E. Nelson, University of Colorado. It is intended for use as a basis for class discussion rather than to illustrate either effective or ineffective decision making. Data and case location are disguised. © 1993 by Prof. James E. Nelson, College of Business and Administration, University of Colorado, Boulder, Colorado 80309.

■ **Exhibit 1**
Financial Data*

	1989	1990	1991	1992†
Assets	$308,339	$321,067	$312,104	$318,093
Liabilities	283,268	295,415	289,872	294,312
Stockholders' equity	25,071	25,652	22,232	23,781
Interest income	32,687	33,399	30,807	26,871
Interest expense	20,300	21,460	18,871	16,051
Net interest income	12,387	11,939	11,936	10,820
Provision for possible loan losses	285	309	4,140	258
Net interest income after provision for possible loan losses	12,102	11,630	7,796	10,562
Other income	1,676	1,685	661	1,758
Other expenses	7,473	7,924	8,482	6,242
Income (loss) before income taxes and extraordinary item	6,305	5,391	(25)	6,078
Deposit growth (%)	3.9	6.2	−2.0	−1.5
Return on assets (%)	1.0	0.6	−0.0	1.0
Return on equity (%)	12.6	8.6	−0.1	14.4
Capital to assets (%)	7.6	7.4	6.1	6.6

*All data are stated in thousands of dollars except data for Deposit Growth, Return on Assets, Return on Equity, and Capital to Assets.

†As of September.

dent of the Bank Marketing Association, and vice president of Beverly Bankcorporation. Kuhn held an M.S. in marketing and took a keen interest in the marketing issues facing Valley BancSystem.

■ Marketing Issues

Smith settled into his chair and read the five marketing issues he had summarized last night:

1. What should be our response to the Shop and Save proposal to put four or five full service branch offices in their supermarkets in Polk and Madison counties?
2. How can we capitalize and build on the sales training program?
3. How should we organize for the marketing function—at the holding company and at each subsidiary? What should be the authority and responsibility at each level?
4. How do we translate corporate financial goals into marketing goals? How do we make marketing goals part of the management process?
5. What should be Valley's marketing strategy over the next five years?

Smith knew the senior management considered all issues to be high priority items.

The Shop and Save Proposal

Early in October the Broadmoor bank president had paid a call on the manager of a Shop and Save supermarket located in nearby Ridgeway, Illinois. The purpose of the call was to inquire into the possibility of placing a Valley branch facility in the store. The timing could not have been better—the store was soon to begin a remodeling project and could easily accommodate the facility. Further discussion between Valley officers and Shop and Save's executive committee had led to the latter group's offer last month of leases at four stores.

Smith and the marketing committee had discussed the proposal at length. Branches would occupy about 500 square feet at each location (sites to be identified later and to be mutually acceptable to both parties). Costs to Valley for the space would be $15 per square foot. Other costs would include wages and benefits for the two tellers expected to staff the branch and the manager (who might be responsible for all four locations). If branches proved popular with Shop and Save customers, Smith thought that each might generate some $2–$4 million in deposits in a year. As much as $1 or $2 million in loans per branch should also be possible.

The entire matter deserved much analysis but Smith and the committee were unsure about how to proceed. What they needed most was a framework for their analysis, what to examine, what to forecast, what to summarize and present to the board. Each member had promised to spend some time on this issue before the next meeting. Once they had a good framework for the decision, data collection and analysis would be much easier.

The Sales Training Program

Early in 1992 Kuhn and the marketing committee had seen the need for a comprehensive sales training program for all 250 Valley employees. Actually, Valley preferred to call its employees "associates" to highlight the common interest that all had in the success of the organization. All associates were to receive 20 hours of sales training.

The training was intended to improve Valley's performance by developing associates' customer relations and customer development skills. Training for customer relations skills included lectures, discussion, and exercises on such topics as, what customers expect from a bank and its employees, how to deal effectively with customers, and what to avoid as customer service mistakes. Training for customer development skills covered the seeking of new business both on and off bank premises. While the training would show direct effects on performance, Kuhn and the marketing committee felt that an equal, if not more important benefit was that the training would raise an awareness that selling was an important part of *everyone's* job description.

Presidents, other officers, and some selected associates would receive advanced training on customer relations and customer development in 20 hours of sessions held separately from those for most associates. Presidents and selected officers were also to receive eight more hours of training on sales management and planning. All sessions would be held at Valley facilities. A Chicago consultant who specialized in sales training would conduct the sessions, during late afternoon hours from October 1992 through March 1993. The consultant's fee was $45,000.

Already Smith thought he could see some effects of the first two and one-half hour session. For example, many tellers and new accounts people had worn costumes on Halloween to represent bank products. The best, in his mind, was a teller dressed as a house with dollar bills protruding from her doors and windows. A sign by the house urged customers to get money from their houses by signing up for an Equity Plus loan. The teller had gotten seven referrals. If all resulted in a booked loan, the teller would receive $350 from Valley for her efforts. Apart from Halloween costumes, Smith had noticed a general improvement in associates' attitudes and behavior toward customers. However, a few associates thought that acquiring customer development skills was a bit distasteful and probably unnecessary. Some officers at one or two banks felt the same way.

The marketing committee wanted to change this attitude and keep the momentum begun by the training. Several things seemed to be needed. One consisted of motivational mechanisms or systems to encourage selling activity by associates and officers. Kuhn had told the committee that he could support most any type of reward including money, recognition, and career advancement. All he wanted was an effective, ethical, and simple approach. Another need was for control procedures to make sure associates and officers performed as expected. Kuhn's expectations here were for a system that allowed for a great deal of individuality; he wanted no associate or officer to feel that someone was constantly looking over his or her shoulder. Another need was for networking or communication systems to facilitate the sharing of sales problems and opportunities.

Smith's thoughts went back to his conversation yesterday with Kuhn. The two had compared their impressions of the early effects of the sales training. Kuhn had ended the exchange stating that "The way banking is going, the only potential advantages a bank can have over its competitors are its location and its people. I want you and the marketing committee to recommend everything we need to do to make sure our people are effective salespeople."

Organizing for the Marketing Function

The third major issue facing the committee was how to organize for marketing at Valley. Right now the marketing organization consisted of the three-member committee which reported directly to Kuhn. Members of the committee were Chuck Smith, executive vice president of the Broadmoor bank; R.J. Day, president and director of the New Richmond bank; and Thomas Charles, president and director of the Alden bank. Smith chaired the committee because of his greater interest in marketing and his experience as a correspondent banker for a St. Louis bank before joining Valley some eight years ago. Day had the most banking experience of the three (23 years with Valley), primarily in commercial and mortgage lending. Charles had about the same number of years of banking experience as Smith, again with an emphasis on lending. The committee had been meeting about once a month since its beginning in early 1991. However, Smith and Day usually met with Kuhn about once a week to discuss marketing topics.

The committee's accomplishments to date included implementation of the training program and formulation of the first-ever promotion budget. The promotion budget planned for 1992 currently stood at $420,000. All but $50,000 of this amount had been carefully allocated by the committee and an advertising agency to various advertising and promotion activities. Each month in 1992 was scheduled for a major promotion (IRA, home improvement loan, ATM, for example), a statement stuffer coordinated with the promotion, a newsletter, and several news releases. Major promotions always included newspaper advertising, lobby posters, teller cards (drive-up and counter), and brochures. Radio advertising would be added for June and October. The remaining $50,000 was available to satisfy requests by subsidiaries for local market promotions.

Accomplishments illustrated the committee's responsibilities. That is, the committee managed existing services and recommended, developed, and priced new services. It ensured that appropriate personnel were trained to sell all services. It budgeted and coordinated most of the advertising and promotion efforts. In short, the marketing committee was charged with setting marketing objectives; investigating, recommending, and implementing marketing strategies; and monitoring marketing results.

To do all of this took a great deal of time and effort. Each committee member spent several hours per week on marketing matters yet each felt it was not enough. The investment of time and effort was doubly frustrating because it took away from each member's ability to do his primary job. However, the committee seemed a good way to organize for marketing because it made the acceptance of marketing activities relatively easy at each subsidiary.

An alternative to the committee organization would be to employ a full-time marketing director at the holding company. One committee member had noted that a marketing director could provide leadership and needed expertise on marketing matters. A director would also have more credibility, Smith thought, even though some subsidiaries might not like the idea of yet another staff person at the holding company. A good marketing director with experience would probably cost around $80,000 per year in salary and benefits.

The committee had discussed marketing organization for several minutes in yesterday's meeting. Members finally decided to give the matter more thought before they met again, concluding that there probably were other advantages and disadvantages of either type of organization. "There might even be some other ways of organizing," one of the members had said, "ways that would combine the best features of a committee and a director."

The committee also had discussed the organization for marketing at each subsidiary bank. No subsidiary could justify hiring a full-time marketing officer given its size and the marketing efforts planned at the holding company. Yet it seemed unwise to have no formal marketing authority and responsibility at each subsidiary. Committee members had agreed that a marketing orientation at the subsidiary was crucial to the success of a subsidiary. The problem was how to achieve this orientation because subsidiary officers generally lacked marketing backgrounds.

Marketing Goals

The lack of marketing backgrounds made marketing goal setting difficult at both the holding company and subsidiary levels. However, Kuhn and the committee felt it important that the holding company and each subsidiary have marketing goals. Marketing goals would encourage marketing thinking and focus marketing efforts. Marketing goals would also form a standard against which performance could be measured.

This was the first time that the holding company and subsidiaries had ever set marketing goals. Most officers were familiar with financial goal setting and the holding company's financial goals for 1992: 8 percent growth in deposits; 1.2 percent return on assets; 16 percent return on equity; and a 7 percent capital to assets ratio. Each subsidiary's financial goals departed somewhat from these figures, dependent on local market conditions and forecasts.

Neither the holding company nor the subsidiaries had translated financial goals into marketing goals. The committee had discussed some criteria for the translation, concluding that marketing goals should be consistent with financial goals and be stated in specific and measurable terms at realistic levels. The committee had even tried to write some marketing goals:

Obtain 200 Vacation Club accounts by October 1993.
Increase IRA deposits by 15 percent.
Book 350 Equity Plus loans by the end of 1993.

Each member had promised to spend more time thinking about marketing goals after yesterday's meeting. Each was also to produce a more complete list of goals by the end of next week, send it to other committee members, and be ready for a discussion at the next meeting. It would be important to get some marketing goals approved at the holding company level before expecting each subsidiary to write its own.

Marketing Strategy

The last major issue discussed by the marketing committee was Valley's marketing strategy over the next five years. Kuhn had requested that the committee study this topic and propose two options, each with clearly identified strengths and weaknesses. He had also asked for the committee's choice between the options.

The first strategic option was growth via market development. This strategy would emphasize the marketing of existing financial services to new markets defined in terms of either geographic areas or market segments. Growth via new geographic areas could be done three ways. The first would be to stay in Polk and Madison counties and locate in one or more of several growing communities. The second would be to expand westward and southward to other Illinois counties. The third would be to cross the state line and enter the Wisconsin market about 20 miles north of Alden. Valley could move into Wisconsin by its directors establishing a Wisconsin corporation in the banking industry. Alternatively, it could enter Wisconsin by offering a limited service bank that would provide all of Valley's services except commercial loans.

Kuhn and the directors wanted any new market area chosen to show a deposit growth potential in excess of 8 percent per year; any new facility should show an operating profit within the first five years. Committee members thought that careful selection of new market areas could meet these criteria. However, the consequences of a mistake in their judgment could be substantial.

Less risky was a market development strategy based not on new geographic areas but on new market segments. These new segments would be in the local community where Valley's reputation was strongest. Examples of possible new segments were professionals, commercial accounts (mostly retailing and light industry), and young marrieds. Potential here was probably not as great as with geographic expansion.

The second strategic option was growth via service development. This strategy would emphasize the marketing of new financial services to existing markets. New services could be aimed at either existing consumer or commercial accounts with the goal of increasing deposits, loans, or service fees. There were literally hundreds of new services that Valley could add. Some of the more promising ones had been mentioned in yesterday's meeting. In-home banking would allow customers to link their home computers with the bank's system and pay bills, transfer funds, and check on account balances. Optimistic forecasts here called for about 10 percent of U.S. households to use some form of home banking by the mid 1990s. Auto leasing would have Valley as lessor to individual customers. Experts forecast a 6 to 10 percent annual growth rate for the service, reaching a level of about 40 percent of all new car deliveries in the late 1990s. Personal financial planning would use financial advisers at the bank to investigate middle-aged customers' financial objectives and resources and then recommend a financial program. A "prestige" credit card would provide increased services and higher loan limits to upscale customers. The committee recognized the need for careful research before recommending one new service over another.

The committee also recognized that a recommendation to market any new service would subject Valley to the chance of failure. Costs associated with failure depended on the new service. However, in no case did the committee think that a major new service could be introduced for less than $100,000 in training, marketing, and other start-up costs.

Finally, the committee recognized that growth objectives could be met by either strategy and that Valley almost certainly would not pursue one strategy to the exclusion of the other. A mix between the two would be best; the issue really was which of the two strategies should be emphasized. Further, adoption of either strategy would not mean abandonment of existing customer segments. All Valley subsidiaries would be expected to continue to show growth via penetrating existing segments through the offering of present services.

■ Holding Company Strategy

Choosing between a market development and a product development strategy was the final decision in formulating the holding company's strategy. Earlier in the year, Kuhn and the directors had agreed on other strategic components: profitable growth, liquidity, active asset/liability management, financial and marketing control over subsidiaries, capable personnel, and market leadership. All components were tied to a community bank orientation: suburban locations, a high profile in local community affairs, personal relationships with customers, and deposits and loans generated in the local community.

"For the next few years, our strategy could also be described as conservative," Kuhn had told the committee. He had gone on to explain that a conservative approach was called for because it would avoid risks and produce profits (important because of last year's loss), allow Valley time to train and develop its associates and officers, and minimize the risk of any costly mistakes. The net effect of a conservative approach should be intermediate and long-term profitability. However, Kuhn noted that in the short term the approach might mean some missed opportunities and some stronger competitors.

Topics for Discussion

1. Devise a framework the committee could use in making a decision on the Shop and Save proposal. Be complete.
2. Develop an action plan that would motivate selling activity by associates and officers, control their efforts, and make possible the sharing of selling problems and opportunities.
3. Propose four marketing goals for Valley. Support your choice of each goal with a brief discussion. What uses should be made of these goals?
4. Analyze the strategic options facing Valley. Specifically, what are each option's strengths and weaknesses?

■ Case 9 Salomon: The Monocoque Ski

Francis Bidault
International Management Development Institute

> Yes, it's excellent . . . I really love this prototype. You have all done a truly superb job! But, we are still only half way into this venture. There is a lot more work to do. . . . I would say you will probably need another four years before we can see Salomon skis, as well as boots and bindings, on the slopes. But, it is time to discuss an action plan and I would like to present it at next month's New Product Committee meeting! So, I'd appreciate it if you could let us have your plan a few days beforehand.

Georges Salomon, the 62-year-old president of Salomon S.A., was stroking, with visible excitement, the new prototype that the development team had just presented during one of his regular meetings with them. It was November 15, 1987, and he was glad to see the progress made by the team on this truly strategic project which he had initiated in July 1984: to design a Salomon ski as an addition to the company's successful product portfolio.

As Georges Salomon was making his concluding comments, the project team had mixed feelings. They were happy that their work had gained such positive recognition from the president, but they also felt under pressure, knowing what remained to be done. Until now, the development of the first Salomon ski had been a very exciting adventure: unlimited creativity, daring solutions, and generous support. That was the easy part. Now, the time had come to try and make the "dream" come true: They would have to work hard to complete the development and prepare a commercial launch. The real challenge was still ahead.

As they were leaving the meeting room, each member of the team was recollecting the key events that had led to this development and considering the significance of this project for the company and for the overall ski market.

■ Salomon S.A.

Salomon, a fast-growing company with headquarters in Annecy in the French Rhône-Alpes region, was proud of being the world leader (based on its sales) in winter sports equipment (refer to Exhibits 1–3). The company, always aiming for the top, had regularly improved its position in each of its market areas: number one in ski bindings with a 46 percent market share; number one in cross-country ski boot-bindings with a 30 percent market share; and number two in alpine ski boots where it was just a few percentage points behind Nordica. A line of accessories—clothes, bags, caps, and such ("Club-Line")—completed its winter sports offerings. In addition, Salomon owned Taylor-Made, a successful firm in the golf equipment business (clubs and accessories).

■ **Exhibit 1**
Salomon S.A. Sales
and Profits (FF Million)

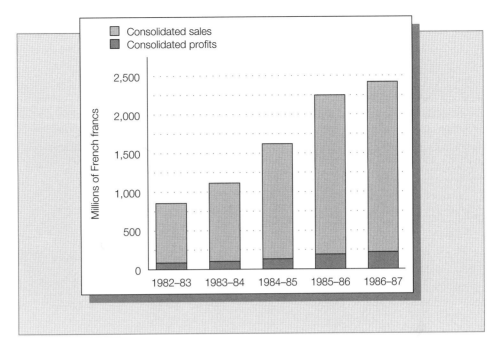

■ **Exhibit 2**
Growth of Sales and
R&D Expenditures

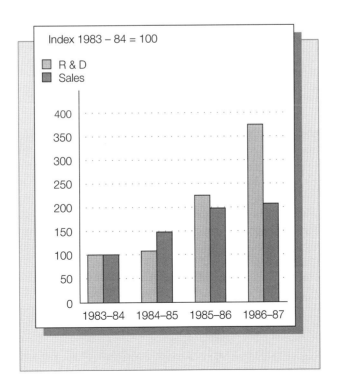

■ **Exhibit 3**   Salomon S.A. Five-Year Financial Summary, 1983–1987 (Thousands of French francs)

			Year Ended March 31		
Operations	**1983**	**1984**	**1985**	**1986**	**1987**
Net sales	FF817,170	FF1,109,263	FF1,666,277	FF2,220,686	FF2,241,700
Other revenues	8,656	22,182	19,462	25,200	21,307
Total revenues	825,826	1,131,445	1,685,739	2,245,886	2,443,077
Cost of sales—materials	(271,272)	(351,540)	(578,712)	(772,247)	(869,233)
Payroll expenses	(165,757)	(209,256)	(250,565)	(303,253)	(346,977)
Depreciation charge	(33,870)	(49,553)	(66,354)	(108,338)	(128,585)
Other operating expenses	(188,466)	(274,867)	(379,315)	(526,268)	(569,116)
Operating profit	166,461	246,229	410,793	535,780	529,166
Interest expense, net	(36,965)	(38,385)	(47,368)	(84,361)	(90,959)
Nonoperating items	(10,383)	(10,487)	(38,124)	(38,759)	(79,407)
Pretax net income	119,113	197,357	325,301	414,660	358,800
Provision for income taxes	(53,700)	(96,651)	(156,655)	(197,625)	(135,637)
Net income	FF 65,143	FF100,706	FF168,646	FF217,035	FF223,163
Financial Position					
Cash and marketable securities	FF169,037	FF 263,258	FF 363,854	FF 830,126	FF 656,544
Accounts receivable	174,527	185,191	279,927	350,293	414,537
Inventories	158,951	260,536	381,093	562,221	601,505
Other current assets	37,382	157,758	58,414	77,719	195,184
Total current assets	539,897	866,743	1,083,288	1,820,359	1,877,770
Property, plant and equipment, net	94,666	145,575	197,614	364,432	445,694
Other noncurrent assets	5,993	5,493	47,100	13,645	12,134
Total assets	640,556	1,017,811	1,328,002	2,196,436	2,325,598
Loans payable	108,893	300,230	302,329	646,597*	532,222*
Accounts payable and accrued expenses	326,462	300,943	381,830	496,495	568,546
Other liabilities	13,055	4,231	49,144	55,634	42,067
Shareholders' equity	192,146	412,407	594,699	97,710	1,182,763
Total liabilities and shareholders' equity	FF640,556	FF1,017,811	FF1,328,002	FF2,196,436	FF2,325,598

*Including capital lease obligations.

SOURCE: Company annual report for 1987.

Salomon's sales were distributed around the globe: 30 percent in North America, 22 percent in Japan, 40 percent in Europe, and 8 percent in the rest of the world. Salomon had fully owned subsidiaries in 12 countries, including Japan, which was the largest in terms of sales.

The company was heavily involved in competitive events in winter sports as well as in golf. Success in competition was considered very important for establishing the credibility and reputation of Salomon and Taylor-Made products. The company invested a significant amount of money (some FF 50 million annually) in amateur and professional sporting events.

Salomon's management philosophy revolved around three basic principles:

• Partnership with employees.
• Cooperation with suppliers and distributors.
• Innovation for customers.

The partnership with the company's workforce was founded on the premise that success could only come if the employees were competent and felt associated with the future of the firm. Therefore, training was regarded as a key driver in the company's effectiveness, with over 5 percent of the payroll "invested" in this activity. In addition, employees benefited from the company's success by receiving bonuses, based on annual results, and a regular distribution of shares. The 1986–1987 annual report[1] mentioned that 3 percent of the company's common stock was held by its employees.

Salomon recognized that cooperation with suppliers and distributors was needed in order to have effective high-quality support for delivering its products. The company relied on numerous subcontractors to manufacture up to 60 percent of its production of bindings and boots, and all of its "Club-Line" products. There was also a worldwide network of retailers offering the necessary service to the customer (advice, testing, adjustments, etc.). For both the subcontractors and the retailers, Salomon provided continuous information and training to ensure the quality of their contribution. Recently, the company had taken a further step by introducing the concept of the "Salomon Authorized Dealer," whereby the rights and duties of retailers vis-à-vis the company were specified.

The third principle was no less essential: ongoing innovation and investment in new technology that would serve the needs of sports enthusiasts in increasingly better ways! Salomon spent some 4 percent of its consolidated sales on research and development, and registered around 100 patents worldwide every year. From the very beginning, innovation had always been a key word at Salomon.

■ Salomon: The First Forty Years

In 1947, François Salomon and his wife, Jeanne, set up a small firm that performed metal processing activities. Initially, it made saw blades and steel edges for skis, a technology for which François owned a patent. At that time, the edges were attached to the wooden skis by the retailers.

The Salomons' son Georges decided to give up his job as a schoolmaster and to join the family firm. Soon afterward, Georges invented a machine to improve the processing of steel for ski edges.[2] However, in only a few years, the Salomons realized that the ski manufacturers were integrating this process and that they needed to look for other activities to prepare for the future.

In the early '50s, Georges was approached by a Parisian inventor with a new type of ski binding that no manufacturer was interested in. Georges immediately saw its potential and decided to buy the technology. This innovative device filled a real need at a time when the market was developing quickly. Orders came soon and sales grew fast, particularly in North America. Thus, the firm was able to benefit from the post-World War II growth of skiing as a major leisure activity, at an international level right from the beginning. In 1962, Georges realized that the growth of his company needed to address the world market. From then on, the commercial development of Salomon S.A. was based on two pillars: new products and international presence.

Georges, however, did not become complacent with success and systematically continued to look for ways to improve the protection of skiers against accidents. In 1967, he introduced the first ski binding without a cable. This innovation was a real breakthrough, one that radically changed skiing safety and comfort, and also resulted in a profound restructuring of the bindings industry. Such an

---

[1]Salomon's annual report covered the time period from April 1 to March 31 of the following year.

[2]Salomon S.A., Case Study, Jim Whyte, Department of Management, Napier College, Edinburgh, 1986.

accomplishment had only occurred because Georges was determined to concentrate on product innovation, devoting much of his time to it—as he preferred that activity to administrative tasks.

By 1972, Salomon had gained a real presence in foreign markets, surpassing Tyrolia and Marker to become the world leader in bindings—a position the company has since maintained.

In the early '70s, Salomon began to look for new products beyond ski bindings. Several options were studied, among them the markets for ski boots and skis. In 1974, the decision was made to pursue the former. Georges Salomon had a clear objective: to come up with a boot that was not only better but would also offer a significant and visible improvement. In 1979, Salomon introduced a truly innovative boot design—the rear-entry boot—which addressed a key frustration for skiers: lack of comfort. This "revolutionary" ski boot concept was reasonably well accepted. However, in spite of success with Giradelli, the industry (racers, journalists, ski instructors, etc.) gave it a lukewarm welcome. They claimed that it was not tight enough on the foot and gave it the uncomplimentary nickname, "*la pantoufle.*"[3] Even though sales were significant, they did not develop as quickly as expected. Salomon gradually adapted its design, keeping rear entry for only one part of the line and, in this way, eventually was able to gain a steady market share. By 1987, the company held second place, close behind Nordica (of Italy).

During this same time period, starting in 1978, Salomon undertook to enter the cross-country ski market. Again, the ambition was to offer a clearly superior product. In 1980, Salomon made the headlines when it introduced a unique system: a cross-country boot and binding combination. This was definitely a superior concept, which took off very quickly and put Salomon at the top with an amazing 30 percent of the market in 1987.

Meanwhile, being dependent on winter sports had become a major concern for Salomon's management. The company considered several activities that could provide a counterbalance. One option was windsurfing, which was turned down because it did not offer enough potential and was already suffering from a huge overcapacity. Eventually, the golfing business was chosen, an industry twice as big as winter sports: about FF 12 billion. In 1984, Salomon purchased the entire shareholdings of the American company, Taylor-Made, which manufactured and sold upmarket golf clubs. The choice of Taylor-Made was based on its similarity to Salomon: the philosophy of providing excellence through innovation.

Over the years, Salomon's progressive product diversification reflected ambitious goals for each market entry, which had its roots in the corporate culture and, especially, in the personality of the president.

■ Management, Structure, and Culture

In the mid-'80s, Salomon had become a mini-multinational with subsidiaries in 12 countries. The headquarters in the suburb of Annecy also had a definite international feeling, with managers coming from around the world (Canada, Norway, the United States). Like Philips and Bosch, Salomon had a matrix organization that was structured around its products (bindings, shoes, cross-country equipment, etc.) and their respective markets (using national sales organizations). The company had

---

[3]"The slipper."

come a long way from the little workshop that made ski edges to become a multi-line sports equipment firm.

At Salomon S.A., recruitment was considered a particularly important task. The company was very demanding and therefore selective, and could afford to be so because its sporty and dynamic image made it a very attractive employer. Early on, it had recruited engineers and technicians from the best schools. It also was able to attract the most senior managers from top companies. The majority of the people working at Salomon had a double profile: highly skilled in their discipline and expert in a sport. Indeed, several of them were former ski champions. Consequently, Salomon was managed with state-of-the-art technology and highly skilled motivated teams who, literally, "loved" their products.

The personality of Georges Salomon as an individual had a big impact on the culture of the company. Even though he did not have a technical education, he spent a lot of his time looking for ways that new technology could bring value to products. He had personally developed several products, which gave him credibility with his team. He was the one mainly responsible for the goal to launch only products that were clearly and visibly superior. Also essential to the company's successful product development record was its impeccable use of extreme caution in all decision making. This prudence came, in large part, from Georges's anxiety about the outcome of each company product. Everyone who managed a major project knew that he must be thoroughly prepared with an answer for all of Georges's concerns. Above all, Georges was a mountaineer and a careful climber who was aware that "rushing tends to be dangerous."

Georges Salomon's daily behavior also carried some messages to his organization; he made no secret about where his priorities were. Even though he had received countless awards in Paris for the company's performance (in design, innovation, exports), Georges avoided personal publicity. He did not care much about pleasing the establishment, either. He much preferred walking around the company's workshops discussing new products, contributing ideas, even occasionally drawing a quick sketch. When he had to meet with bankers or high-ranking officials, he would insist on inviting them to the company canteen.

Georges's personal life-style reflected his passion for his job and dedication to the company. In his dress, he was informal and casual—preferring mountaineer clothing. For a long time, he drove a rusty Renault 5, which was a frequent topic of discussion. His chalet, on a slope overlooking Annecy, was considered spacious but not luxurious.

He played a central role in company strategy, particularly when it came to market entry decisions. Georges was very demanding, systematically wanting to ensure that every product would really make a difference and that the strategy concerning its development and launch was optimal. He often reminded the project team that he would "pull the plug" at any time if he had any doubts about the project's success. And he meant it; indeed, he had actually canceled some projects a few weeks before their official launch.

■ The Decision to Enter the Ski Market

By 1984, Georges Salomon had come to the conclusion that it was time to enter the ski market. In his view, Salomon, the world's largest company in the winter sports industry, could no longer ignore such an essential piece of equipment for skiers.

Skis, as a product, had several characteristics that made them attractive to Salomon. First of all, they were the most visible piece of equipment. In practical terms, in a photograph of a skier in action, it was the skis that one could see most clearly; the boot and the binding were usually not so easily distinguishable. Hence, from a communication point of view, skis offered better support to the brand name. Secondly, skis were the most expensive item bought by skiers and, therefore, the market size was bigger (about twice the amount of the bindings market). Finally, skis were the piece of equipment most talked about by skiers, the focus of an enthusiast's passion, in a way that boots and bindings could not equal. Consequently, skis were a powerful contributor to brand awareness. As Georges Salomon explained to his staff: "Ski companies that are much smaller than Salomon in terms of sales enjoy a greater brand recognition by the public . . . which is why this ski development challenge is so important for our firm."

Salomon's management felt that it had the capability to enter the ski market successfully. The company had adequate experience, it was argued, to take on this new activity, given its track record and current situation. For example, Salomon had:

- A **mastery of innovation,** thanks to the most advanced design tools, and databases on skiers' needs and desires, and on the behavior and reaction of various materials.
- A **know-how in automation,** which allowed it to achieve higher quality levels and competitive production costs.
- A **financially healthy situation,** which made it possible for the corporation to afford the high R&D expenditures and the necessary financial investment at the manufacturing stage.
- A **strong brand image and distribution network,** which could quickly promote sales of this new ski and generate economies of scale at the same time.

In a survey conducted in 1984 to learn about Salomon's brand image, it appeared that the market was definitely anticipating such a move: in fact, a significant proportion of interviewees believed that Salomon was already making skis! This surprising piece of information provided even more motivation to enter this market, in spite of the risks.

Salomon's management was conscious that moving into skis was not a risk-free operation. After all, the company's bindings were being mounted on other manufacturers' skis. Even though the ski-binding assembly was done at the retail level, some feared that large ski competitors might try to retaliate by joining forces with some other bindings producers—for example, "ski X prefers bindings Y." Also, this move could prompt a countermove into Salomon's own territory, with other ski manufacturers deciding to compete in bindings and boots. Finally, the issue of branding was also raised. Salomon was planning to offer all three products (skis, bindings, and boots) under its own brand name. It would be the first company to make such an offering. Clearly, there were some risks associated with this strategy—that is, if a customer had a bad experience with one of the products, the other products could be affected as well.

These concerns, however, did not prevent the company from going ahead with the diversification. By 1985, Salomon's top management had set up ambitious objectives for the ski business:

1. To become a world leader, in five or six years, in the medium to top segments of the market.

2. To reach, at "cruising speed," a net profitability of the same order of magnitude as bindings and boots (around 9 percent of sales).

In order to pursue these demanding objectives, the following strategic principles were established:

- To give skiers a piece of equipment with a "plus," based on some visible innovation that would be identified through market surveys and technical research.
- To emphasize partnership with distributors in order to provide optimal quality service.
- To gain recognition through success in competition, with the Winter Olympics in Albertville (Winter 1992) being used to enhance the impact.

■ The Ski Market in 1987

There were some 55 million skiers in the world in 1987. Most of them were in Western Europe (around 30 million), North America (9 million), and Japan (the single largest national market with over 12 million skiers). There were also some minor markets in Eastern Europe (particularly Yugoslavia, Poland, Czechoslovakia, and the USSR) and in Australia. The proportion of skiers to the total population varied tremendously from country to country and was partly a function of local skiing possibilities. Switzerland was clearly the highest (with a ratio of 30.4 percent), followed by Austria (27.7 percent) and Sweden (23.8 percent), then Germany, Italy, and France (in the 10–12 percent range). The United States, although a large market of 5.4 million skiers, had a very low ratio (2.2 percent) compared to Japan (9.9 percent).

Skiing as a sport was being influenced by several important trends. First of all, skiing had become affordable and accessible to an increasing number of consumers, but the relative time spent participating in winter sports had been diminishing. Secondly, skiers tended to be less "fanatic" than in the past, especially as the competitive pressure of other leisure activities (golfing, cruising, tourism in exotic countries) grew stronger. Thirdly, skiing had become an increasingly diversified sport—with "off-piste" (off the official groomed trails), mogul, freestyle, acrobatic, and speed skiing, as well as the introduction of new types of equipment (monoskis and surfboards). The final factor was fashion: Colors in equipment and clothing were becoming brighter and more dramatic, and styles and shapes were ever changing.

The Market

The international ski market was already mature. It was expected to plateau at around 6.5 million pairs (refer to Exhibit 4) with possible ups and downs following business cycles and the amount of snowfall. The world market was estimated at FF 4.5 billion, compared to FF 3.5 billion for ski boots and FF 2 billion for bindings. The largest national markets were (in rank order) Japan, the United States, Germany, and France (refer to Exhibit 5). Some markets still seemed to be growing (North America), while others were flattening (Japan, Western Europe) or even declining (Scandinavia) over the short to medium term.

The price structure of the market was somewhat peculiar. In most markets, the distribution of sales along the price range could be seen as a pyramid, with sales of the most expensive segment being the smallest. The ski market, however, presented a

■ **Exhibit 4**   Ski Sales in the 1980s

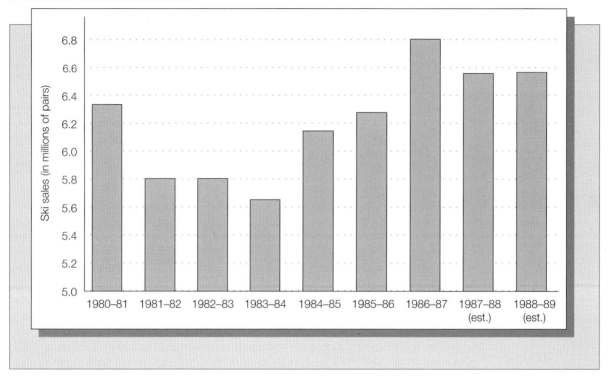

■ **Exhibit 5**   Sales of Skis, by Country, 1986–1987 Winter Season

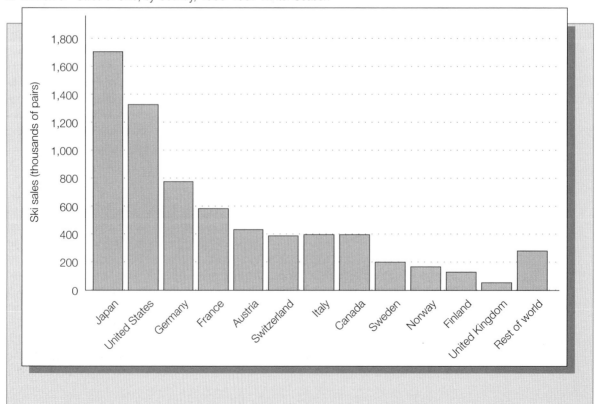

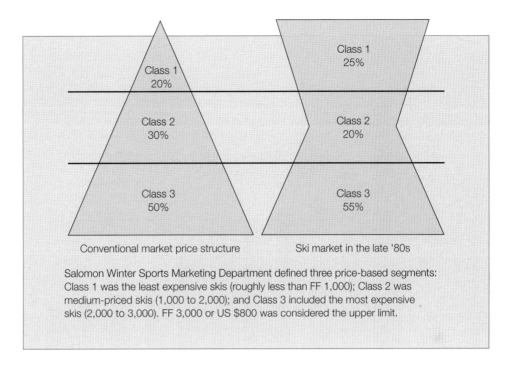

Conventional market price structure   Ski market in the late '80s

Salomon Winter Sports Marketing Department defined three price-based segments:
Class 1 was the least expensive skis (roughly less than FF 1,000); Class 2 was
medium-priced skis (1,000 to 2,000); and Class 3 included the most expensive
skis (2,000 to 3,000). FF 3,000 or US $800 was considered the upper limit.

different pattern, as the most expensive products sold more than the medium-priced ones (refer to Exhibit 6).

The traditional market segmentation made a first distinction between rental (10 percent of the volume), junior (another 20 percent) and adult (the remainder). Within the adult segment, there were three types of users: leisure (55 percent of the volume), sport (20 percent) and performance (25 percent). Leisure skiers tended to be people who skied for recreation and to have fun, not for "records." The second segment included skiers that were more "aggressive" on the slopes, but not competing in any way. The last segment were those skiers who were involved in some form of competition. The last two segments (sport and performance), sometimes called "medium" and "top," represented around 2 million pairs of skis.

The Competitors

The number of competitors was much higher in skis than in bindings or boots. Some 80 different brands were competing worldwide (21 in Japan, 15 in the United States, 12 in Austria, 6 in France, and 20 more in other countries). Most companies owned one brand, except large players like the world leader Rossignol (France) which controlled Dynastar (also in France). On the average, the number of brands present in each country was about twice as large as in bindings.

In addition, skis were sold under private label. The estimate was that, worldwide, this represented around 50 percent of volume, with the proportion varying considerably from country to country.

The market was dominated by Rossignol (France), Atomic (Austria), Elan (Yugoslavia), Head (United States), Dynastar (France), and Blizzard (Austria), which all sold more than half a million pairs every year (refer to Exhibit 7). Most Japanese manufacturers were relatively small (100 to 150,000 pairs), except for Yamaha,

■ **Exhibit 7**   Sales by Manufacturers

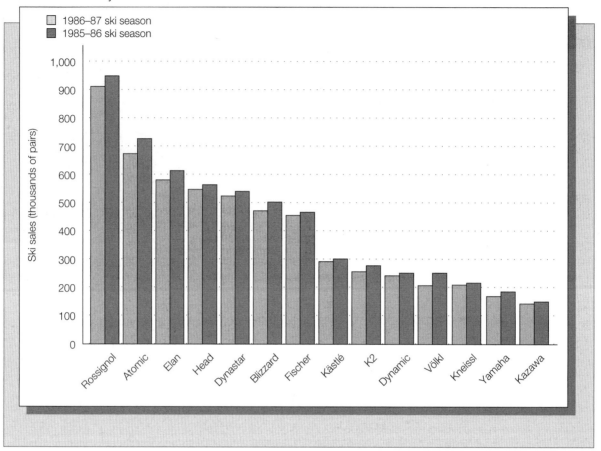

which barely passed the 200,000 pair threshold. While the Western brands were present in Europe, the Japanese producers were virtually nonexistent outside Japan.

Competitors differed in their approach to the ski market in many ways. A few strategic dimensions seemed to be critical in discriminating among industry players. The first dimension was overall product positioning. Some companies, such as Rossignol and Atomic, offered skis for all levels—from beginners to racers—while others focused on a specific market niche (the upmarket: Völkl, Fischer, K2; the low to medium end: Head, Elan). Participation in ski competition also affected a company's positioning. Brands that addressed the top end of the market (Rossignol, Völkl, K2) sponsored ski racers in an effort to enhance the visibility of their products, while companies focusing on the lower niches did not pursue this activity. Another important dimension was the scope of market presence. Most of the 80 ski manufacturers around the world were only local players that marketed their products in their own country. This situation was particularly true for the Japanese brands. Among the companies that had "gone international," the scope of market coverage differed. The leaders (Rossignol, Atomic, Elan, Head, Dynastar) were present in all significant markets; other companies (like Blizzard) had substantial international sales, but were not represented in all national markets.

■ **Exhibit 8**
Types of Ski Structures

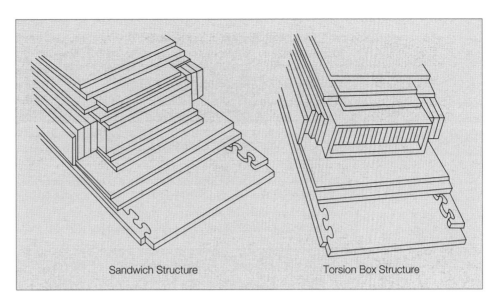

Sandwich Structure   Torsion Box Structure

The Manufacturing of Skis

Skis, which had been in existence for at least 5,000 years, only were considered "sports equipment" at the beginning of the 20th century, when they were brought to Switzerland by British tourists. The first skis were very simple, made out of ordinary wood. In order to achieve a more solidly constructed ski, one of the first innovations was to use laminates of wood that were glued together, thus gaining greater flexibility and a longer ski. Metal edges were introduced later in order to reduce deterioration of the sole of the ski and provide a better grip. After World War II, plastic soles were added to enhance the ski's sliding capability. In 1950, Head introduced the metal sandwich ski, which irreversibly changed ski technology. Metal was later replaced by the various plastic and composite materials that dominated the market in the '80s.

At this point in time, several types of design were used in the construction of skis. The most common structures were the sandwich ski and the torsion box ski (refer to Exhibit 8). A sandwich ski was essentially made of various materials arranged in layers, with the more rigid and resistant layers on the top and the bottom of the ski. This technology, which increased resistance to flexion and shock absorption, was the most widely used (75 percent of skis). In a torsion box ski, the resistance was obtained from a box located in the core of the ski. It gave a better grip in the snow, as well as a quicker reaction. Together, the sandwich and torsion box technologies represented 90 percent of the skis manufactured. There were a few other technologies—for example, the "omega" structure—but most of them had only a very limited production.

The Production Cycle

The production of skis started a full year before the winter season, in November. For instance, skis sold by retailers between November 1985 and March 1986 had been produced between November 1984 and November 1985. This production phase had been preceded by development work on shape, materials, and art work. The duration of the development phase depended on the importance of the work involved, from four years for a major ski innovation to a few months for a cosmetic change, which was being done every year in recent years (colors and art work).

The production plan, initially made during the preceding summer, could be adjusted at three points. The first occasion was ISPO, the annual sports industry exhibition in Munich, in the second part of February every year when distributors started to order. Later, in May, when the number of orders was better known, a second adjustment would be made. Lastly, in September–October, as orders were being completed, it was possible to fine-tune production to market demand (volume and mix).

Over time, manufacturing had become a complex process. In the '80s, it involved the assembly of several kinds of material (steel, fibers, resins, plastic sheets) which represented around 13 percent of the retail price. Each material was carefully selected, as it played a role in the performance of the ski. Production workers would typically put together the different materials needed (the sole, the edges, the various layers, polyester resin, the upper platform) into a mold, which would then be put into a press with warm plates. Because of the material and equipment involved, which generated both heat and odor, working conditions were difficult. Manufacturing costs represented 19.5 percent of the retail price.

Distribution

Skis were sold through a network of wholesalers and retailers, which was organized by the manufacturers. Small brands tended to rely on local independent distributors (one per country), while large manufacturers often had their own sales organization for major countries. It was estimated that the cost of the wholesale function amounted to 17.5 percent of the retail price.

Retailing was shared between independent outlets and distribution chains. In ski resorts, independent retailers—usually also managing a large rental activity—were dominant. In major towns and cities, large retail chains (such as Intersport in Germany and Decathlon in France) represented the major portion of the market. Non-specialized chains (hypermarkets) had a limited participation, mostly selling inexpensive products. On average, the retailers' margin was 50 percent of the final price, including sales tax.

Depending on the country, retailers offered 5 to 10 different brands,[4] with 4–5 models in each one. There were some real technical differences, in terms of materials, structure, and shape, that needed to be evaluated in the selection process, along with more superficial considerations. Consumers thus had an enormous choice. The selection of a ski was often made through the recommendation of a salesperson, on the basis of physical characteristics, skiing style, ability, and budget (refer to Exhibit 9).

Therefore, the sales process required having capable, often technical, explanations by the retail staff, a situation which called for training. Although makers of the best-selling brands made a genuine effort to provide technical information to their network, product descriptions and performance data provided to retailers sometimes tended to be unclear, with an overemphasis on jargon. Ill-founded rumors and myths were not uncommon.

---

[4]Except in Japan, where retailers typically stored 25 different brands.

■ **Exhibit 9**   The Ski Purchasing Process

The following table presents the distribution of answers to the question below asked to a sample of ski buyers. "What do you think is the best way to choose skis when buying them?" Respondents could give more than one answer so the percentages do not add to 100%.

	Total	France	Germany	United States	Japan
1. Pick a brand with a good reputation.	26%	27%	21%	31%	25%
2. Select a brand you have already used.	17	16	27	15	9
3. Listen to other people's advice.	44	35	45	39	56
4. Be guided by a ski salesman.	26	31	30	15	28
5. It is a personal decision. Choose the ski you like.	16	12	5	19	26
6. Gather information, read reviews, study technical tests.	20	14	23	23	18
7. Follow advice from ski instructors.	8	12	8	4	7
8. Rent a ski and test it before buying.	16	16	23	18	6
9. Pick the brand a champion uses.	2%	*%	2%	5%	*%
Sample size (total respondents)	n=1,444	n=350	n=373	n=361	n=360

*Negligible.

Communication with the consumer was done through advertising in specialized magazines and point-of-sale material (catalogs, leaflets). In addition, magazines published articles appraising new products coming onto the market and were another channel of information, mostly for the high end of the market.

■ The Monocoque Project

The origin of the monocoque[5] project could be traced to early 1984 when Georges Salomon entered the office of Roger Pascal, the director of the Bindings Division, and said: "Pascal, you have to make me a ski!"

Roger Pascal, then 46 years old, had worked with Salomon since 1969. He was an engineer by training (INSA, Lyon), but he was also an expert skier, having been a ski instructor (École du Ski Français) while he was a student. He had started in the engineering department and eventually had become manager, before heading the ski boot engineering department.

Initial Steps

Georges Salomon and Roger Pascal agreed that there could be no meaningful entry into the ski business without an in-depth knowledge of the ski market and industry. They reckoned that, even though Salomon was selling in related markets, its information on consumers' needs, technological solutions, and marketing processes was not sufficient to make a difference in the ski market.

The ski project got underway with the appointment of Jean-Luc Diard in July 1984. Jean-Luc had just completed his studies at the ESC Paris, one of the top business schools in France. He was also an excellent skier, having won the annual French student ski championship. Recruited as a special kind of trainee,[6] he was sent to

---

[5]Pronounced *mon-oh-caulk.*

[6]A program that allowed a graduate to be a trainee in a French firm or public organization outside of France, as a replacement for military service.

Salomon's Austrian subsidiary to study the ski market and industry. He focused on making an international study of the best products available at the time, and traveled extensively to meet and interview the world's experts. The information he gathered was encouraging for Salomon: There were still ways to improve on existing ski technologies.

At the same time, a series of market surveys were launched in order to appraise the level of satisfaction among skiers. The first results came as a surprise. While Salomon had detected significant frustration with ski boots in earlier surveys, it seemed that consumers were generally satisfied with skis. These results renewed Georges Salomon's conviction that the new ski must be radically better if it were to make a difference in the marketplace. In order to have a specific goal and objective for the team, Georges and Roger agreed that the ski should be able to sell at a 15 percent premium above the market price.

The Project Team

In the summer of 1985, Georges Salomon was able to convince two technology experts—Maurice Legrand and Yves Gagneux—to join the ski development team. Maurice Legrand, the former head of Rossignol's engineering department, was in charge of product technology. Yves Gagneux, the former head of manufacturing at Dynamic, was made responsible for process technology.

The team—Roger, Jean-Luc, Maurice, and Yves—functioned like a "commando operation"—that is, a group of highly skilled volunteers who were totally devoted to their "secret mission." The team was maintained out of the normal organization, in an effort to preserve confidentiality as long as possible. Their work was kept secret, even to insiders, as Salomon did not want its competitors to know about it. Also, like a commando group, there was a sense of close community among the members, with each one knowing what the others were doing. Indeed, the competence of all the team members was truly exceptional: each individual was outstanding in his field and all were excellent skiers as well. In addition, the interaction was so interconnected that their disciplinary boundaries were blurred. Thus, Jean-Luc, in charge of marketing, also contributed technical solutions, while Maurice came up with marketing ideas.

Project Management

The activity of the ski development team was characterized by a high energy level, thanks to the enthusiasm and the sense of challenge that surrounded their mission. This project, however, was not a "skunk works" operation.[7] Quite the contrary. Yves Gagneux explained: "Maurice Legrand and myself were able to bring the technical knowledge that Salomon was lacking. But, Salomon provided us with a superb project management approach without which our expertise, as good as it was, would have been a lot less effective. Clearly, that was a strong point at Salomon!"

The management of the project actually used the whole gamut of modern techniques. At the very beginning, Georges Salomon had set the goal: to introduce a ski in five or six years, with excellent and visible advantages over existing products. The team translated this objective into a very detailed action plan, specifying the milestones, the resources needed, the tools used—Quality Function Deployment, Design

---

[7]A "skunk works" project typically operated with a minimum budget and no real facilities.

to Manufacturing, Consumer Clinics. Early on, the team had worked on a business plan that outlined expenditures and income on a yearly basis, from the project's inception to the "cruising speed" period in the mid-'90s.

The team reported regularly to the Executive Committee for major investment or expenditure decisions. It also presented a progress report to the New Model Committee on implementation issues. However, more important than the formal reporting were the team's meetings, which Georges Salomon personally attended. In summing up his style, one individual commented: "Georges Salomon isn't usually found behind his desk . . . he is more likely to be in the product development lab . . . clomping around in ski boots and baggy sweater . . . doing what he likes best . . . devising ways to frustrate his competition."[8] In order to answer all the probing questions that an anxious Georges Salomon inevitably asked, the team had to be well prepared—an exercise that obviously took time. "*Se hâter lentement*"[9] could have been the motto for this project.

The Concept Development

Between July 1985 and January 1987, Roger Pascal asked the team, which over time had progressively been enlarged, to systematically study all aspects of ski technology: measurements, the core, the sole, printing techniques, the spatula, edges, polishing, wax. The mandate was for each team member to come up with two or three ideas for improving every aspect studied. The team leaders would meet regularly to review these ideas and seek ways to incorporate them into a concept. In fact, they succeeded in producing the first plaster model by the second semester of 1985.

The shape of the ski gradually emerged as a result of these systematic experiments. The team realized early on that little could be done to the shape of the sole, which had been already optimized over time to the point where skiers were accustomed to it. However, alternatives for the walls on both sides and for the surface of the ski could be considered. The team started to challenge the verticality of the side walls. Were they optimum? Could other settings be better? In a very creative fashion, they explored the various options: from being slanted outward to slanted inward. A close examination revealed that the best solution was actually a progressive profile, with nearly vertical walls under the ski boots to provide an optimum grip where it was most needed, and side walls slanted inward to ensure optimum cutting into the snow at both extremes. These changes, in addition, had the required characteristics of being visible, one of the conditions set clearly by Georges Salomon (refer to Exhibit 10).

This initial idea naturally led to another important discovery: the side walls and surface of the ski should be made of a unique shell that would carry a major part of the stress. In conventional skis, the action of the skier passed from the steel edges through a succession of layers, particularly in the sandwich ski. This method of transmission was more indirect and resulted in less precision. The monocoque structure (the unique piece linking the surface to the edges) would thus provide a better control of the ski.

The team was supplied with the best computer-assisted design (CAD) system available in the industry at the time (ComputerVision and Sun Microsystems). The ideas were quickly converted into drawings in the engineering lab. Molds for prototypes

---

[8]*Business Week,* April 19, 1989.

[9]A French saying that means "rushing slowly."

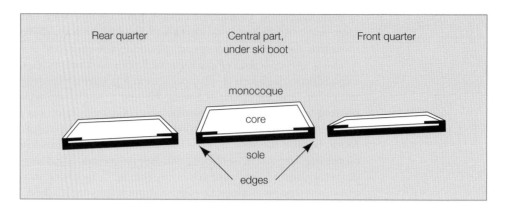

were machined directly from the CAD system, which allowed them to create a large number of shapes for testing. By the middle of 1986, the first prototypes were available. They were tested in labs as well as on the snow, with test engineers and expert skiers hired as consultants with a confidentiality agreement. The team at that time comprised around 35 people.

Several ideas for improving the manufacturing process were conceived. While most ski manufacturers applied composite material in a tacky state, the team found a new way to handle this step more satisfactorily. Yves Gagneux explored the "dry process," which consisted of using fibers that had already been impregnated with resin and dried, which were therefore not only much easier to manipulate but had the additional advantage of not smelling strongly, as the "wet process" did. It was expected that these enhanced working conditions would produce a much higher level of quality as well.

By November 1987, the engineering studies were providing interesting results. The team had developed a detailed understanding of the ski market. It knew the strengths and weaknesses of the best competitors. It had identified a long list of possible improvement areas. It had even singled out the particular areas where it wanted the new ski to make a difference. The prototypes that had been developed, through numerous trials and tests, were showing very promising potential.

■ The Decision

There were, of course, still a number of issues that needed to be clarified. In one sense, it was obvious that the team had done a good job, considering that the project had started from scratch in 1984. They had gone a long way toward the development of a radically new ski. Some of the detailed engineering still needed for the ski's final development was clearly going to be even more demanding. In order to proceed, the New Product Committee would have to release a budget for engineering work, testing, and for the construction of a new plant. Given the technology required, some of it actually calling for custom-made equipment, the budget would amount to some FF 300 million. Additionally, using a full-time team that would be expanded to 50 people would increase the operating costs.

The team's next challenge was to prepare a clear action plan for finalizing the development of Salomon's monocoque ski and launching it into the already crowded and mature ski market.

Case 10   Nike, Inc.

Randall K. White
Auburn University–Montgomery

Introduction

In his letter to shareholders in the 1991 annual report, Philip H. Knight, Chairman and CEO, projected his outlook for the company:

> Around the world, people of all cultures are increasing their participation in fitness activities. All are motivated by the common desire for athletic and personal excellence.
>
> Nike—a simple sneaker company to many newspaper readers—is transforming into an international consumer products company. Companies attacking international markets generally will take one of two approaches: (1) lay a solid infrastructure and build off of it forever, or (2) cream it without regard to the long term. Obviously, we have chosen the first approach.
>
> Specifically, over the past decade, we have built an international management team of more than 1,500 people. In Western Europe, we own the distribution rights over 90 percent of our sales. Nike has hired more than 1,000 people in the last 12 months, mostly dictated by our desire to service and support our international growth.
>
> Shortly after the middle of the decade, Nike will be a bigger company outside the United States than inside. Given the speed and power of global communications, there will no longer be a different brand leading the market in each hemisphere. There will be one world leader in sports and fitness. You can easily guess which brand gets my vote.
>
> The payoff from overcoming all these challenges can be seen in our 1991 international growth of 80 percent to $862 million in revenues. We are at last, after many sometimes comical fits and starts, after 10 years of hard work, a serious threat not only in Europe, but in Asia as well.

Reflecting Knight's comments, Nike experienced continued growth in net income, from $167 million in 1989 to $243 million in 1990 to over $287 million in 1991, an increase of over 71 percent since 1989. This impressive growth was in sharp contrast to the reported income of $36 million in 1987. The company reported that the decline in 1987 was due to three factors: the "decrease in volume of Air Jordan basketball products, the elimination in 1987 revenues from the company's unprofitable Japanese subsidiary which was sold, and increased competition."[1] However, profits rebounded to over $101 million in 1988 partly because of a swing in buyers' tastes. After years of preferring stylish Reeboks, the trendsetters are now clamoring for "performance" shoes such as Nike's.[4] Sales followed a relatively similar pattern. From 1989 to 1990, revenues climbed from over $1.7 billion to about $2.2 billion, a 29 percent increase. The following year, 1991, revenues exceeded $3 billion, a 34 percent increase.

The company's inventory position increased from $309 million in 1990 to about $586 million in 1991, a $277 million increase. Approximately $157 million of this increase was in domestic footwear, while international inventories increased $102 million to handle the increased demand.

Courtesy of Randall K. White, Auburn University–Montgomery.

Nevertheless, as it faced stiff challenges in its various market segments, the question remained whether Nike could respond fast enough to remain a top athletic shoe manufacturer. Other strategic questions were facing the company. (*a*) Nike was a low-cost producer with overseas manufacturing facilities in Asia—notably South Korea, Thailand, and Taiwan where 51 percent, 15 percent, and 13 percent, respectively, of shoes were produced. About 43 percent of the company's apparel production was also located in Asia and in South America. Could the potential political risks, increasing costs, and a declining U.S. dollar compel the company to retrench and make other sourcing arrangements? (*b*) Did it have the financial muscle and customer franchise to counter such strong competitors as Reebok, L.A. Gear, and others? (*c*) Would the intense competition in the industry compel the company to sell its high-quality athletic footwear as private-branded products for major retailing chains? Or, should it position itself as the premier athletic shoe company?

■ Brief History

Incorporated in 1968 in Oregon, Nike began years earlier "when Knight, a former college miler, sold running shoes from the back of his station wagon at track meets."[2] A native of Oregon and born in 1938, Knight graduated from the University of Oregon in 1959 with a BBA and later received his MBA from Stanford in 1962. His interests in running shoes remained strong during this period after visiting Japan, which he felt would become a major player in the athletic shoe market. Knight joined Coopers & Lybrand as an accountant from 1963 to 1964 and then moved to Price Waterhouse from 1964 to 1967. He later became an assistant professor in business administration at Portland State University from 1967 to 1969. Both *Fortune* and *Business Week* magazines provided interesting personal glimpses of Knight:

> He is no match for Bo Jackson, the pro football and baseball player who displays a stunning athletic versatility in the ubiquitous TV ads for Nike shoes. But for a middle-aged CEO who gently complains about "old bones," Phil Knight, 51, does all right. He runs 18 to 30 miles a week, lifts weights, plays tennis.[4]
>
> Philip H. Knight, shy? In private, yes. A foot twitches nervously while the blond, bearded chief executive officer of Nike Inc. talks about himself. But watch the former college runner in competition, and "shy" is not a word anyone would dare hang on Phil Knight. He is emotional about Nike, even prone to watery eyes during his employee pep talks. And when a guy like that gets beat, he usually gets even.[4]

Knight and his track coach, William Bowerman of the University of Oregon, formed Blue Ribbon Sports on an initial investment of $500 each and began importing Tiger brand shoes from Japan. The venture enjoyed considerable success as sales surged from its modest beginning of $3 million in 1972 to fiscal year-end 1988, when sales exceeded $1 billion. However, disputes with the company's large supplier led the company to design and market its own shoes, which the founders named Nike, after the Greek goddess of victory.

Highly regarded within the company as the driving entrepreneurial force that ultimately transformed Nike into a world-class athletic footwear manufacturer, Knight visualized the company focusing on three core areas: shoes, related clothing, and accessories. At the same time, he viewed timely acquisitions as a way to strengthen the company's position in the highly competitive athletic footwear market. Moreover, Knight envisioned the company primarily as a producer of performance-oriented shoes, not a fashion shoe company.

■ **Exhibit 1**　Nike Management Organization Chart

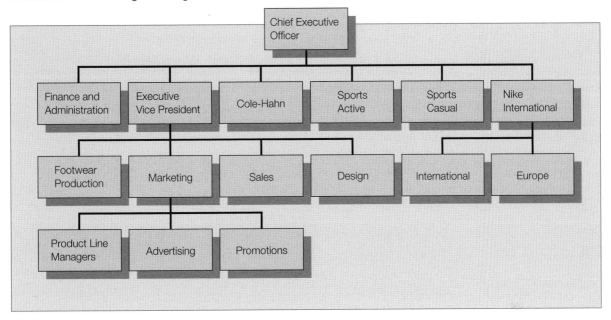

■ Organization

Nike's organizational structure is shown in Exhibit 1. Although generally regarded as a company with a deliberately lean structure intended to foster autonomy and an entrepreneurial climate, Nike has a formalized management structure that defines accountability and responsibility. This presumably freed Knight to deal with long-term strategic issues.

The company's experienced executive officers and the board of directors are listed in Exhibit 2. Outsiders accounted for one-half of the board membership; in addition, six of its officers, including Knight, are CPAs.

Nike's basic mission is the design, development, and worldwide merchandising of high-quality footwear and apparel products for a wide range of sport, athletic, and leisure activities. Nike does not see itself as a manufacturer but more a market-driven company. Consequently, it does a number of things very well—for example, maintaining and nurturing the ability to pinpoint future trends in the industry, continuing to strengthen its R&D capability for new and technologically superior athletic footwear, and cultivating its existing and potential relationships with its various domestic and international contract manufacturers in order to ensure product quality.

In effect, Nike, as well as many other U.S. companies, has essentially become a marketer for foreign producers; that is, a company such as Nike, which designs, develops, and markets products worldwide, does not manufacture anything! In contrast to traditional manufacturers, these firms are labeled "hollow corporations."[14] As many U.S. firms move to low-cost overseas producers (Taiwan, South Korea, and others), this continued outsourcing could bring about a decline in U.S. manufacturing capability. Some see these "hollow corporations" as "network companies"—that is, companies that depend on other firms for manufacturing and other functional support.

■ **Exhibit 2** Nike, Inc., Officers and Directors

Name	Age	Position with Nike, Principal Occupation, and Business Experience
Philip H. Knight*,**(1) Chairman and CEO	50	Cofounder of the company and has served as its Chairman of the Board and, except for the period June 1983 through September 1984, as its President since its organization in 1968.
Richard K. Donahue*,**(1) President and Chief Operating Officer	n/a	Partner, Donahue & Donahue, Attorneys, Lowell, Massachusetts.
William J. Bowerman*,**(2) Deputy Chairman of the Board of Directors and Senior Vice President	77	Cofounder of the company, has served as Sr. Vice President and a Director since 1968 and was elected Senior Vice President and Deputy Chairman of the Board in 1980.
Delbert J. Hayes*,**(4) Executive Vice President	53	Joined the company as Treasurer and Executive and became a Director in 1975. He thereafter served as Treasurer and in a number of executive positions, primarily in manufacturing, until his election as Executive Vice President in 1980. He is a certified public accountant.
Thomas E. Clarke* General Manager and Vice President	n/a	n/a
Harry C. Carsh* Vice President	49	Joined the company in 1977 and was elected Vice President in June 1984. Mr. Carsh has held executive positions in accounting, manufacturing, and European marketing. He has served as Vice President in charge of the International Division and is currently Vice President in charge of merchandising operations. Prior to joining the company, he served for four years as Vice President of Finance for Laneet Medical Industries. He is a certified public accountant.
Nicholas Kartalis* Vice President	n/a	n/a
Ronald E. Nelson* Vice President	45	Has been employed by the company since 1976, with primary responsibilities in finance, marketing, and production. He is currently Vice President in charge of the company's footwear production operations. He was elected Vice President in 1983. He is a certified public accountant.
Mark G. Parker*	n/a	n/a

(continued)

■ Marketing

Product

Although the company's footwear products are targeted for athletic use, many buyers tend to wear them also for casual and leisure purposes. To complement its footwear merchandise and round out its athletic image, Nike produces a variety of accessory and apparel items such as athletic bags, hats, socks, jackets, warm-up suits, shorts, T-shirts, and tank tops. The company also introduced the Nike Monitor, an electronic monitoring training aid.

■ **Exhibit 2** (concluded)

Name	Age	Position with Nike, Principal Occupation, and Business Experience
George E. Porter* Vice President—Finance	57	Joined the company as Vice President in 1982 and has held executive positions in administration, research and development, and footwear. He became Vice President—Finance in February 1985. Prior to joining the company, he was employed for nine years by Evans Products Company, Portland, Oregon, as Vice President and Controller. He is a certified public accountant.
David B. Taylor* Vice President	n/a	n/a
John E. Jaqua*,**(3)(5) Secretary	67	Has been Secretary and a Director of the company since 1968. He has been a principal in the law firm of Jaqua, Wheatley, Gallagher and Holland, P.C., Eugene, Oregon since 1962.
Lindsay D. Stewart* Vice President & Corporate Counsel	n/a	n/a
Thomas Niebergall* Assistant Secretary	n/a	n/a
Jill K. Conway**(2)	n/a	Visiting Scholar, Massachusetts Institute of Technology, Boston, Massachusetts.
Robert T. Davis**(2)	n/a	Professor of Marketing, Stanford University, Palo Alto, California.
Robert D. DeNuncio**(3)(4)(5)	n/a	n/a
Douglas G. Houser**(2)	n/a	Assistant Secretary, Nike, Inc.; Partner—Bullivant, Houser, Bailey, Pendergrass & Hoffman, Attorneys, Portland, Oregon.
Thomas O. Paine**(3)(5)	n/a	Chairman, Thomas Paine Associates, Los Angeles, California.
Charles W. Robinson**(4)	n/a	Chairman, Energy Transition Corporation, Santa Fe, New Mexico.
John R. Thompson, Jr.**(3)	n/a	Head Basketball Coach, Georgetown University.

* Officers, annual report.
** Directors
(1) Member—Executive Committee
(2) Member—Audit Committee
(3) Member—Personnel Committee
(4) Member—Finance Committee
(5) Member—Stock Option Committee

Jones[2] reported that Nike may need to diversify to stay ahead in the highly competitive and mature running shoe market, and perhaps, "to change its image from a running shoe company to a total-fitness–oriented operation." However, it was unlikely it would abandon the running shoe market—a unique Nike strength.

To protect its market share from fast-growing fashion-oriented competitors such as Reebok and L.A. Gear, Nike introduced, in late 1988, a new line called Side One, a nontechnical shoe for teenage girls who buy athletic, or athletic-looking shoes, to make a fashion statement. Those customers are the core of Keds' and L.A. Gear's business.[7] The company missed the shift in consumer preferences toward fashion and sport-styled shoes, and consumer desire to stay fit through a variety of such activities as running, weightlifting, aerobics, tennis, and other sports activities.[3] To meet this need, Nike developed the cross-training shoe, which was a natural product evolution for the company, whose prime attention was directed toward specialized products. The company pinpointed the product's marketing message toward the shoe's economy and the convenience of buying, wearing, and carrying only one pair of shoes for diverse fitness activities. The shoe was a result of the company's commitment to thorough research of the foot's biomechanical movements. To convey the cross-trainer's technical qualities, Nike contracted with 100 of the top U.S. fitness instructors and provided them with samples of the product to influence their students as well as to take part in trade shows and other sales activities.[15]

To further expand its product lines, Nike acquired, in May 1988, Cole-Hahn Holdings, Inc., "a leading designer and marketer of high quality casual and dress shoes." Nike paid for the acquisition with $89.2 million in cash and the issuance of 243,713 shares of Nike stock, which had a market value of $5.8 million, for the remainder.[1] Knight estimated the company's efforts to broaden its lines would increase sales by $150 million and would position Nike with the "most prestigious brands at both ends of the footwear spectrum."[8] Knight added that about "69 percent of the company's shoe sales come from models costing between $44 and $73 a pair."[8]

Promotion

Advertising and promotion expenditures steadily increased, from $135 million in 1989 to $190 million in 1990 (a 40 percent increase), then doubled from 1989 to 1991, to $286 million. Promotional activities include brochures, print and TV advertising, as well as point-of-purchase displays. Posters are used to depict new footwear models promoted by the company.

Other promotional efforts have included publication of the book *Walk On,* which was co-authored by a former sports research laboratory director and a senior editor of *American Health Magazine.* Containing extensive information on walking—a potentially large growth area for the company—the book provided relevant consumer and product information. Back-to-school campaigns broadened the children's line of such new products as the Air Jordan, Air Max, and the Air Trainer; these were competitively promoted in the $50 range. Other new children's shoes were designed exclusively for children's activities such as skateboarding and biking. In addition, a licensing arrangement with Major League Baseball allowed the company to market specially designed baseball apparel; this unique opportunity would enable Nike to transfer its favorable sports image both on and off the field.

Nike has also developed a co-op advertising program whereby a retailer can accumulate a 1 to 3 percent credit allowance based on its total footwear purchases. For example, assuming a 1 percent allowance on $100,000 of footwear purchases, the retailer could build up $1,000 of credit with Nike, which it could use to buy certain promotional items such as watches, sunglasses, and ankle weights. The applicable percentage for the retailer is based on population and buying power data.

To a large extent, Nike relies heavily on endorsements by prominent athletes from a variety of sports such as running, walking, track, tennis, basketball, football, baseball, and racquetball, and from such general fitness activities as aerobics. Hence, the high performance of Nike is consistently advertised by these top athletes. The company's Air Ace tennis shoe achieved a milestone when it received the first endorsement of a U.S.-based shoe manufacturer by a Soviet sports federation; this allowed the company to introduce its products into the Soviet Union. The company has also promoted the higher-priced cross-training shoe, the Air Trainer, as one shoe for all purposes. To further develop this concept, the company signed Bo Jackson, the versatile NFL (Los Angeles Raiders) and Major League Baseball (Chicago White Sox) superstar to endorse the cross-training line.[6]

The company achieved a milestone in 1985, when it signed Chicago Bulls basketball star Michael Jordan to a contract. Jordan, who had just completed an outstanding rookie year in the National Basketball Association, was hired to introduce the new Air Jordan leather basketball shoe.[9] This shoe, which had a special gas pocket in its sole, provided extra spring and better protection from serious injuries usually encountered by the professional basketball athlete to the foot, leg, and back. The Air Jordan was cited as one of several new products for the year by *Fortune* magazine.[10] Nike also signed Charles Barkley of the Phoenix Suns.[9]

Distribution

Domestic.   The company's approximately 17,000 retail accounts racked up over $2 billion in sales in 1991, about 71 percent of total revenues. Retailers included department, footwear, and sporting goods stores as well as tennis and golf shops and other specialty retailers. The three largest retail customers accounted for about 30 percent of domestic sales; military sales were handled in-house.

Independent regional sales representatives are assigned several associate representatives and specific accounts within their jurisdictions. These associate representatives, who work solely on commission, are especially careful to ensure that retailer orders are handled promptly and within monthly deadlines. To establish and maintain a solid loyal dealer network as well as control the demands placed on the company's transportation and delivery system, Nike set up its innovative Futures ordering program whereby retailers could place their orders five to six months in advance and Nike would guarantee that 90 percent of their orders would be delivered on a set date at a fixed price. The Futures program has had some success in controlling inventory; for example, 81 percent of domestic footwear shipments in 1991 (excluding Cole-Hahn) were made under this program compared to 82 percent and 79 percent in 1990 and 1989, respectively.[1] As ocean and air carriers are used to transport products produced overseas into the United States, Nike exerts much effort to work closely with the U.S. Customs Service to avoid the inspections and seizures other importers face. This working relationship also helps the company to detect counterfeiters of athletic footwear, apparel, and sports bags.[16] Additionally, imported products are subject to duties collected by the Customs Service.

Another innovation is Nike's next-day guarantee shipment for certain team accounts such as colleges and universities. According to one source, if the university faces an emergency when a few athletes require a certain size or type of shoe, the institution can contact Nike's promotional division for a special shipment of this equipment. The shoes are shipped via Federal Express. The program is reported to be very successful because of the high degree of loyalty these accounts provide Nike. Team accounts also have access to Nike's Futures program; for example, orders placed in December will be delivered by June or July of the following year. Regional distribution centers for footwear are located in Wilsonville and Beaverton, Oregon; Memphis, Tennessee; Greenland, New Hampshire; and Yarmouth, Maine. Apparel goods are shipped exclusively from Memphis.

The company also has 40 wholly owned retail outlets. *Chain Store Age Executives*, a trade publication, described one of Nike's innovative retail outlets. It cited the store's attractive display of styles and colors for footwear and clothing, which are geared toward a variety of sports. Knowledgeable sales personnel staff the store; they know the product, can explain it, and use it themselves. Shoes are turned upside down to show their soles, thus differentiating the various types of athletic footwear. Apparently, Nike capitalized on the simple idea that customers prefer to buy from salespeople who really know what they sell.[17]

Twenty-two outlets sell primarily "B grade" and closeout merchandise. "B grade" merchandise has "cosmetic" defects such as discoloration, poor stitching, and so on, and is therefore not first quality. As this merchandise is not first line, these products are sold in plain white boxes marked "blemished."

Foreign.   Nike markets its products through independent distributors, licensees, subsidiaries, and branch offices located in about 66 countries outside the United States. Foreign sales accounted for 29 percent of revenues in 1991, compared to 21 percent and 20 percent for 1990 and 1989, respectively. Branch offices are located in Canada, Brazil, Belgium, Denmark, France, Great Britain, Hong Kong, Italy, Norway, South Korea, Spain, Sweden, Taiwan, West Germany, the Netherlands, Indonesia, Malaysia, Singapore, and Thailand. Since 1972, the Japanese trading company Nissho Iwai American Corporation (NIAC) has provided Nike with substantial financing and export-import services, enabling Nike to buy through NIAC almost all of its athletic footwear and apparel for U.S. and European sales. Nike also bought goods for other foreign sales through NIAC. In 1991, the largest single foreign supplier outside the United States accounted for about 7 percent of total production.

■ Research and Development

The company takes an aggressive stance in designing and marketing innovative footwear products based on such customer benefits as performance, reliability, quality, and reduction or prevention of injury—factors that appeal to both the professional and nonprofessional athlete. In-house specialists come from a variety of such backgrounds as "biomechanics, exercise physiology, engineering, industrial design and related fields."[1] The company set up advisory boards and research committees to review designs, materials, and product concepts; these groups included a broad range of experts such as athletes, coaches, trainers, equipment managers, orthopedists, podiatrists, and other professionals. R&D expenditures averaged over $8.4 million from 1989 to 1991.

Its Sports Research Lab, reputedly one of the most sophisticated among shoe manufacturers, is equipped to do biomechanical and anatomical checks on footwear "using the latest traction-testing devices and high-speed video cameras." Through careful testing procedures, Nike evaluates shoes in diverse locations under varying climatic conditions. Over a 90-day period, testers log reports of "total miles and terrain traversed, reporting every two weeks on cushioning, flexibility, perception of weight, and durability."[18] The company's advanced product engineers, regarded as the cornerstone of their R&D efforts, "devised the multisport cross-trainer shoe and conceived what became the aqua sock," now used widely by swimmers. Compounds and molds for footwear are also tested in a rubber laboratory; the molds for soles are constructed in a model shop, after which samples are manufactured by a small-scale shoe factory. A physical testing lab also evaluates shoe tension and adhesion.

Nike has an exclusive worldwide license to manufacture and sell footwear using its technology to deliver the ultimate cushioning agent: compressed air. According to *Science Digest,* Nike Air shoes feature gas-filled mattresses encapsulated in polyurethane. The walls of the mattress's inflated plastic tubes are supposed to be virtually leak-proof. The gas never breaks down, and it returns to the foot much of the energy of additional impact, acting somewhat like a trampoline.[19] Additional stability for the shoe is provided by using denser polyurethane, which collars the heel, plus a wider sole "along the inside of the foot near the arch." This feature helps to prevent the "foot's natural tendency to roll inward after landing," a tendency called pronation. E. C. Frederick, Nike's former director of the Sports Research Lab, called pronation the " 'herpes' of the running crowd."[20] This Air Revolution, as Nike called it, helped to introduce twelve new Nike-Air models. The research lab also pioneered other new materials such as durathane, a synthetic, and washable leather.

To protect itself from patent infringement, the company registered its Nike trademark and the well-known "Swoosh" design in over 70 countries. The company felt that these distinctive marks were important in marketing its products as well as distinguishing them from competitors' goods.

■ Manufacturing

In fiscal 1991, about 47 percent of Nike's apparel production was manufactured in the United States, by independent contract manufacturers located primarily in the southern states. The balance was manufactured by independent contractors in Asia and in South America, mainly in Hong Kong, Malaysia, Singapore, Taiwan, Thailand, Chile, and Peru. Almost all of its footwear is produced by Asian contractors in Taiwan, Indonesia, South Korea, and Thailand. Management contracts also exist with independent factories in Brazil, Hungary, Italy, Mexico, and the United States. Nike also has a management contract with the People's Republic of China (PRC) and has experienced no stoppages at these plants. The Chinese produce about 11 percent of its shoes.[8,1]

As mentioned earlier, South Korean, Thai, and Taiwanese contractors account for 51, 15, and 13 percent, respectively, of the company's total footwear production. Considering the magnitude of the company's dependence on Korean manufacturers, Nike's financial condition could be seriously affected by any disruptions in delivery of their products. However, the company has indicated that it has the ability to develop over a period of time alternative sources of supply for its products. Moreover, Nike claims that at the present time, it is not materially affected by this risk. Still another risk Nike faces with certain Asian manufacturers is increasing labor costs.

Management contracts are a critical part of Nike's overall strategy to provide its 17,000 retail accounts with a reliable delivery system. Moreover, these contracts allow the company to solidify its Futures program and enable Nike to guarantee retailers' orders by a set date and a fixed price. Additionally, the company is better able to refine its sales forecasts and, equally important, control inventory buildup and the subsequent costs. These independent domestic and foreign contractors provide Nike with two advantages: greater flexibility to take advantage of low-cost foreign labor and less capital requirements. Yet, foreign sourcing could cause the company a number of problems such as political instability, currency fluctuations, and the inability to repatriate profits.

Because of the volume of overseas production, Nike maintains a keen interest regarding any legislation passed by Congress that would impose quotas on certain countries that have been cited as having unfair trading practices. For example, Japan has been cited as having restrictive trade barriers that deny U.S. firms access to the

Japanese market. Hence, the U.S. could assess an increase in duty rates on certain Japanese products imported into the United States. In addition, legislation has been introduced that could revoke the "most favored nation" status of the PRC and, consequently, result in a significant increase in tariffs on goods imported from China.

Raw materials such as canvas, rubber, nylon, and leather used in Nike's footwear products are purchased in bulk and are generally available in the countries where these products are manufactured. The company also acquired Tetra Plastics, Inc., in 1991, its only supplier for the air-sole cushioning components used in footwear. Hence, Nike encounters little difficulty in meeting its raw materials requirements. Moreover, to assure uniform product quality, Nike provides its contractors with exacting product guidelines, which, according to one source, are closely monitored through on-site expatriate quality control personnel. It should be noted that there is an industry trend to move from relatively high labor cost countries such as Taiwan and South Korea to other low-cost Asian countries.

■ The Competition

Several firms can be identified as competitors in the U.S. athletic shoe market (see Exhibits 3 and 4). This $5.8 billion wholesale market in 1991 was characterized as one with a shoe for any occasion. According to *Marketing and Media Decisions,* about 80 percent of the athletic shoes purchased are not used for the activity they are designed for; hence, the shoes' look counts. Moreover, basketball shoes are the largest segment, with a 28 percent share of the market, claimed the Sporting Goods Manufacturers Association.[21] Exhibits 5 through 9 show the financial picture for Nike, followed by Exhibits 10 through 13, which detail the financial picture for its competitors.

Reebok International, Ltd.

A closely held firm (about 60 percent) and a major competitor of Nike, Reebok was founded in 1979 when it acquired exclusive use of the name in North America—it brought the original English Reebok firm later, in mid-1985. The company was incorporated in Massachusetts to design, develop, and market athletic shoes and related accessories. It was initially a successful marketer of women's fashion aerobic shoes; however, in order to grow, the company needed to expand into men's performance athletic footwear such as basketball and tennis shoes. Exhibits 10 and 11 provide financial and operating data.

According to Steve Race, its general manager of athletic footwear, a shoe could have fashion and performance; moreover, fashion is "a very important function of our performance shoes. And in fashion shoes, performance in terms of comfort is a very important element."[21] To stress performance, the company contracted with such professional athletes as Dominique Wilkins of the NBA's Atlanta Hawks and PGA professional Greg Norman. The company also added children's shoes to its product lines.

Reebok acquired the Rockport Company, a major walking and leisure shoe manufacturer, for about $119 million cash in late 1986 and followed with another major acquisition, for about $180 million in early 1987, of Avia Group International, a premium priced athletic footwear and hiking shoes producer. Other acquisitions included the North American operations of the Italian Ellesses International for

■ **Exhibit 3**
Athletic Footwear
World Market Share,
1991

Nike*	20.72%
Reebok*	16.18
Adidas	9.89
L.A. Gear*	5.23
ASICS (Tiger)	4.95
Aritmos (includes Etonic, Puma)	3.51
Keds*	3.14
Converse*	3.09
Others (includes licenses)	33.29

*U.S.-based company.
SOURCE: *Sporting Goods Intelligence,* as cited in *The Wall Street Journal,* July 11, 1992, p. 417.

■ **Exhibit 4**   Financial Data, 1989–1991 (in millions)

	1989	1990	1991
Net Sales			
Nike	$1710.8	$2235.2	$3003.6
Reebok	1822.1	2159.2	2734.5
L.A. Gear	617.1	902.2	618.1
Net Income			
Nike	167.1	243.0	287.1
Reebok	175.0	176.6	234.7
L.A. Gear	55.1	31.3	45.0
Net Profit Margin			
Nike	9.8%	10.9%	9.6%
Reebok	9.6%	8.2%	8.6%
L.A. Gear	8.9%	3.5%	NMF
Earned Net Worth			
Nike	29.7%	31.0%	27.8%
Reebok	20.7%	17.7%	28.5%
L.A. Gear	32.7%	15.2%	NMF

SOURCE: Value Line.

■ **Exhibit 5**   Nike Revenues by Product Categories for the Fiscal Years Ended May 31, 1991, 1990, 1989

	1991	Percent Change	1990 (in thousands)	Percent Change	1989	Percent Change
Domestic footwear	$1,676,400	22	$1,368,900	29	$1,058,400	40
Domestic apparel	325,700	22	266,100	28	208,200	46
Other brands	139,400	16	120,500	26	95,500	—
Total United States	$2,141,500	22	$1,755,500	29	$1,362,100	51
International						
Europe	$ 664,700	99	$ 334,300	38	$ 241,400	3
Canada	98,100	7	92,100	76	52,200	66
Other	99,300	86	53,300	(3)	55,100	45
Total International	862,100	80	479,700	38	348,700	15
Total Nike	$3,003,600	34	$2,235,200	31	$1,710,800	42

SOURCE: 1991 Annual Report.

■ **Exhibit 6**   Nike, Inc. Consolidated Balance Sheet as of Fiscal Years May 31, 1991, 1990 (in thousands)

	1991	1990
Assets		
Current Assets		
Cash and equivalents	$ 119,804	$ 90,449
Accounts receivable, less allowance for doubtful accounts of $14,288 and $10,624	521,588	400,877
Inventories	586,594	309,476
Deferred income taxes	25,536	17,029
Prepaid expenses	26,738	19,851
Total current assets	1,280,260	837,682
Property, plant and equipment	397,601	238,461
Less accumulated depreciation	105,138	78,797
	292,463	159,664
Goodwill	114,710	81,021
Other assets	20,997	16,185
	$ 1,708,430	$ 1,094,552
Liabilities and Shareholders' Equity		
Current Liabilities		
Current portion of long-term debt	$ 580	$ 8,792
Notes payable	300,364	31,102
Accounts payable	165,912	107,423
Accrued liabilities	115,824	94,939
Income taxes payable	45,792	30,905
Total current liabilities	628,472	273,161
Long-term debt	29,992	25,941
Non-current deferred income taxes and purchased tax benefits	16,877	10,931
Commitments and contingencies	—	—
Redeemable preferred stock	300	300
Shareholders' equity		
Common Stock at stated value:		
Class A convertible—27,438 and 28,102 shares outstanding	164	168
Class B—47,858 and 46,870 shares outstanding	2,712	2,706
Capital in excess of stated value	84,681	78,582
Foreign currency translation adjustment	(4,428)	1,035
Retailed earnings	949,660	701,728
	1,032,789	784,219
	$ 1,708,430	$ 1,094,552

SOURCE: 1991 Annual Report.

about $60 million; Ellesses manufactures premium-priced tennis shoes and ski fashions. Other acquisitions were the John A. Frye Company, a boot and loafer manufacturer, and Boston Whaler, a power boat firm.[11,12]

Six plants are located in Massachusetts and one in Oregon, the home state of Nike. The company sources over 70 percent of its footwear with contract manufacturers in South Korea, in addition to other plants located in Taiwan and the Philippines.

■ **Exhibit 7**   Nike, Inc., Consolidated Statement of Income Fiscal Years Ended May 31, 1989, 1990, and 1991 (in thousands, except per share data)

	1991	1990	1989
Revenues	$3,003,610	$2,235,244	$1,710,803
Costs and expenses:			
Cost of sales	1,850,530	1,384,172	1,074,831
Selling and administrative	664,061	454,521	354,825
Interest	12,316	10,457	13,949
Other (income) expense	(43)	(7,264)	(3,449)
	2,541,864	1,841,886	1,440,156
Income before income taxes	461,746	393,358	270,647
Income taxes	174,700	150,400	103,600
Net income	$ 287,046	$ 242,958	$ 167,047
Net income per common share	$3.77	$3.21	$2.22
Average number of common and common equivalent shares	76,067	75,668	75,144

SOURCE: 1991 Annual Report.

■ **Exhibit 8**   Nike, Inc., Selected Financial Data Year Ended May 31, 1987 through 1991 (in thousands, except per share data)

	1991	1990	1989	1988	1987
Revenues	$3,003,610	$2,235,244	$1,710,803	$1,203,440	$887,357
Net income	287,046	242,958	167,047	101,695	35,879
Net income per common share	3.77	3.21	2.22	1.35	.46
Cash dividends declared per common share	.52	.38	.27	.20	.20
Working capital	$ 651,788	$ 564,521	$ 422,478	$ 298,816	$325,200
Total assets	1,708,430	1,094,552	825,410	709,095	511,843
Long-term debt	29,992	25,941	34,051	30,306	35,202
Redeemable preferred stock	300	300	300	300	300
Common shareholders' equity	1,032,789	784,219	561,804	411,774	338,017

SOURCE: 1991 Annual Report.

NOTE: All per common share amounts have been adjusted to reflect the 2-for-1 stock split paid October 5, 1990. The company's class B common stock is listed on the New York and the Pacific Stock Exchanges and trades under the symbol NKE. At May 31, 1991, there were approximately 4,500 shareholders of record.

Sales grew steadily, from over $1.7 billion in 1988 to about $1.8 billion in 1989, then exceeded to $2.1 billion in 1990. Net income increased from $137 million in 1988 to over $174 million in 1989, a 20 percent increase; this was followed by another increase of over 18 percent from 1989 to 1990.

L.A. Gear, Inc.

Robert Y. Greenberg, CEO and owner of 25 percent of the company's stock, founded L.A. Gear in 1985. L.A. Gear carved its niche as a developer, designer, and marketer of stylish, high-quality, and youthful shoes for aerobics, athletics, and leisure. The line was later expanded to include a variety of other footwear, such as walking,

■ **Exhibit 9** Nike, Inc., Operations by Geographic Areas Fiscal Years Ended May 31, 1991, 1990, and 1989 (in thousands)

	1991	1990	1989
Revenues from unrelated entities			
United States	$2,141,461	$1,755,496	$1,362,148
Europe	664,747	334,275	241,380
Other international	197,402	145,473	107,275
	$3,003,610	$2,235,244	$1,710,803
Intergeographic revenues			
United States	$ 9,111	$ 4,765	$ 1,757
Europe	—	—	—
Other international	11,892	5,628	4,323
	$ 21,003	$ 10,393	$ 6,080
Total revenues			
United States	$2,150,572	$1,760,261	$1,363,905
Europe	664,747	334,275	241,380
Other international	209,294	151,101	111,598
Less intergeographic revenues	(21,003)	(10,393)	(6,080)
	$3,003,610	$2,235,244	$1,710,803
Operating income			
United States	$ 325,257	$ 315,246	$ 230,156
Europe	134,069	55,098	35,376
Other international	51,745	42,880	30,173
Less corporate, interest, and other income (expense) and eliminations	(49,325)	(19,866)	(25,058)
	$ 461,746	$ 393,358	$ 270,647
Assets			
United States	$1,156,091	$ 786,775	$ 600,629
Europe	370,104	162,383	102,744
Other international	94,212	74,329	50,756
Total identifiable assets	1,620,407	1,023,487	754,129
Corporate cash and eliminations	88,023	71,065	71,281
	$1,708,430	$1,094,552	$ 825,410

SOURCE: 1991 Annual Report.

tennis, and overall fitness shoes, for children and men. Sales surged from over $223 million in 1988 to $902 million in 1990, a threefold increase. Although net income rose 15 percent, from $22 million in 1988 to over $55 million in 1989, it then declined 43 percent from 1989 to 1990. Exhibits 12 and 13 provide financial and operating data.

The company moved into the highly competitive "60 percent chunk of the $4.2 billion U.S. athletic-shoe market" in basketball and running, a market dominated by Nike and Reebok. Skeptics were doubtful about the success of L.A. Gear's shoes for the male-dominated basketball segment, as males typically paid less attention to style and leaned more toward the inner structure of the shoe supporting the feet. Commented a competitor, technology was the fashion. However, to promote its acceptance in this market, the company signed 42-year-old Kareem Abdul-Jabbar, the retired superstar of the Los Angeles Lakers. As one analyst remarked, this was a move

■ **Exhibit 10**
Reebok International,
Ltd., Consolidated
Balance Sheet As of
December 31, 1990
($000)

	1990	1989
Assets		
Cash & cash equivalents	$ 227,140	$ 171,424
Accounts receivable, net	391,288[a]	289,363[a]
Inventory	367,233	276,911
Deferred income taxes	31,673	34,845
Prepaid expenses	12,328	11,735
Total current assets	$1,029,662	$ 784,278
Gross property & equipment	$ 160,132	$ 136,776
Less: Accumulated depreciation & amortization	49,017	30,542
Property & equipment, net	111,115	106,234
Intangibles, net of amortization	255,051	261,398
Other noncurrent assets	7,397	14,457
Total noncurrent assets	373,563	382,089
Total assets	$1,403,225	$1,166,367
Liabilities		
Notes payable to banks	$ 8,855	$ 1,651
Commercial paper	59,805	—
Current maturity of long-term debt	1,411	598
Accounts payable & accrued expenses	166,061	148,360
Income taxes payable	49,071	43,834
Dividends payable	8,576	8,538
Total current liabilities	$ 293,779	$ 202,981
Long-term debt, net current maturity	$ 105,752	$ 110,302
Deferred income taxes	6,975	7,788
Common stock	1,144[b]	1,139[b]
Additional paid-in capital	281,478	275,336
Retained earnings	707,336	564,987
Unearned compensation	dr 191	dr 524
Foreign currency translation adjusted	cr 6,962	cr 3,358
Stockholders' equity	996,729	844,296
Total liability and stockholders' equity	$1,403,225	$1,166,367
Net current assets	$ 735,883	$ 581,297
Book value	$6.48	$5.12

[a]Allowance for doubtful accounts: 1990, $33,730,000; 1989, $28,704,000.
[b]Par value $.01; Auth shs: 1990, 250,000,000; 1989, 250,000,000.
SOURCE: Reebok Annual Reports.

to the "geriatric crowd." Later, other notable basketball athletes were signed to con-tracts—Akeem Alajuwan of the Houston Rockets and Karl Malone of the Utah Jazz. Michael Jackson was also contracted to design shoes and apparel.[21]

The company's footwear is sold principally in department, shoe, sporting goods, and athletic footwear stores, while its apparel is distributed through department, specialty, and sporting goods stores. Products are also distributed through inde-pendent distributors in 20 countries, primarily in Japan, Canada, and West Ger-many. Manufacturing is done by 13 suppliers in South Korea and 2 in Taiwan; both countries also manufacture Nike footwear. The company maintains offices in both countries.

To further expand its product offerings, L.A. Gear has ventured into the jeans and watch markets where, presumably, its brand name and distribution network will enhance its market position.

■ **Exhibit 11**

Reebok International, Ltd., Consolidated Income Account Years Ended December 31, 1990, 1989, 1988 ($000)

	1990	1989	1988[a]
Net sales	$2,159,243	$1,822,092	$1,785,935
Other income (exp)	dr 893	11,377	dr 1,351
Gross operating revenues	2,158,350	1,833,469	1,784,584
Cost of sales	1,288,314	1,071,751	1,122,226
Selling expenses	353,983	278,939	260,891
General & administrative expenses	202,352	174,972	149,195
Amortization of intangibles	15,646	14,427	14,216
Interest expense	18,857	15,554	14,129
Interest income	15,637	12,953	6,633
Total costs & expenses	1,863,515	1,542,690	1,554,024
Income before income taxes	294,835	290,779	230,560
Income taxes	118,229	115,781	93,558
Net income	176,606	174,998	137,002
Previous retained earnings	564,987	424,002	320,886
Dividends declared	34,257	34,013	33,886
Retained earnings	707,336	564,987	424,002
Earnings per common share	$1.54	$1.53	$1.20
Common shares (000):			
Year-end	114,428	113,856	112,951
Average	114,654	114,176	113,757
Depreciation & amortization	20,156	13,512	8,850

[a]Reclassified to conform to current presentation.
SOURCE: Reebok Annual Reports.

■ **Exhibit 12**

L.A. Gear, Inc., Consolidated Balance Sheet As of November 30, 1990, 1989 (in thousands of dollars)

	1990	1989
Assets		
Cash	$ 3,291	$ 353
Accounts receivable, net	156,391	100,290
Inventory	160,668	139,516
Prepaid expenses & other current assets	16,912	12,466
Deferred tax charges	1,097	4,589
Total current assets	338,359	257,214
Gross property & equipment	28,599	9,888
Accumulated depreciation	4,975	1,809
Property & equipment, net	23,624	8,079
Other assets	1,972	1,265
Total assets	$363,955	$266,558
Liabilities		
Line of credit	$ 94,000	$ 37,400
Accounts payable	22,056	25,619
Accrued expenses & other current liability	39,672	17,627
Accrued compensation	2,350	16,906
Income taxes payable	—	783
Total current liabilities	158,078	98,335
Common stock	91,179[a]	84,363[a]
Retained earnings	114,698	83,360
Total shareholders' equity	205,877	168,223
Total liabilities & stock equity	$363,955	$266,558
Net current assets	$180,281	$158,879
Book value	$10.61	$ 8.80

[a]No par value: Auth shs: 1990, 80,000,000; 1989, 80,000,000.
SOURCE: L.A. Gear Annual Reports.

■ **Exhibit 13**
L.A. Gear, Inc.,
Consolidated Income
Statement Years
Ended November 30,
1990, 1989, 1988 (in
thousands of dollars)

	1990	1989	1988
Net sales	$902,225	$617,080	$223,713
Cost of sales	591,740	358,482	129,103
Gross profit	310,485	258,598	94,610
Sell, general & administrative expenses	240,596	154,449	53,168
Interest expense, net	18,515	12,304	4,102
Earned income before taxes	51,374	91,845	37,340
Income tax expense	20,036	36,786	15,310
Net earnings	31,338	55,059	22,030
Previous retained earnings	83,360	28,301	6,271
Retained earnings	114,698	83,360	28,301
Earnings per common share	$1.56	$3.01[a]	$1.29[b]
Common shares (000):			
Year-end	19,395	19,109[a]	16,374[b]
Average	20,041	18,308[a]	17,110[b]

[a]2-for-1 stock split, 9/25/89.
[b]Reclassified to conform to 1989 presentation.
SOURCE: L.A. Gear Annual Reports.

■ **Exhibit 14**
Selected Industry
Composite Indicators,
1989–1992

	1989	1990	1991[a]	1992[a]
Sales ($ Mil)	7762.8	8905.2	10365.0	11250.0
Operating margin (%)	12.7	12.1	10.5	11.0
Net profit margin (%)	6.7	6.2	5.9	6.5
Return on net worth (%)	20.9	19.1	20.5	21.0

[a]Estimated.

■ The Industry

Exhibit 14 depicts a growing sales trend for the shoe industry from 1989 to 1992. Other data in the exhibit show varying performances for this same period.

Generally regarding athletic footwear as discretionary items, consumers would be likely to limit their spending for these products during an economic downturn. Moreover, with rising consumer debt and decreasing personal savings, buyers' confidence could be seriously affected. At the same time, buyers would prefer footwear that is not only durable but also suitable for a variety of activities.

The long-term prospects for the industry appear promising. The trend toward physical fitness should accelerate as it becomes a pastime for increasing numbers of buyers. Also, certain demographic changes favor continued industry growth; for example, Census Bureau projections for adults in the 25–44 age segment—major buyers for sporting and athletic equipment—are estimated to approximate 82 million people by 1992, about one-third of the total population. Moreover, this age group is forecasted to grow at twice the rate for the total population. Another important buyer segment is the 45–54 age group, projected to increase annually by 3.6 percent between 1987 and 1992 in contrast to a 1 percent growth for the total population.

Other key growth indicators include the increasing participation of women in sports, not only to improve their physical fitness, but also for recreation and competition. According to a National Sporting Goods Association study, women were the major participants in 10 of 45 activities it surveyed; these activities include aerobic exercise, gymnastics, and exercise walking. Additionally, the increasing presence of women in the work force and decisions to delay childbearing and have fewer children, should bring about higher household incomes, thus allowing for more discretionary spending and more leisure time available for recreation. In essence, greater emphasis may be directed toward fitness-related products.

As mentioned earlier in the case, there is a continuing movement by U.S. manufacturers to produce overseas through manufacturing contracts. However, as these newly industrialized countries become more developed—which exerts upward pressure on production costs—manufacturers will be compelled to seek other low-cost producer countries.

■ The Future

Nike management faces a number of challenges for the future. Can Nike move fast enough in a rapidly changing market with strong competitors such as Reebok, L.A. Gear, and others to remain the premier athletic shoe manufacturer? Given Nike's low-cost production in Taiwan, South Korea, and the People's Republic of China, will recent political demonstrations in the latter two countries compel Nike to seek other low-cost Asian producers or increase its U.S. domestic manufacturing? Should Nike consider manufacturing private-branded products for major retailing chains?

■ References

1. Annual Reports, various years, and Forms 10–K.
2. Lynn Strong in Dodds, "Heading Back on the Fast Track," *Financial World,* August 21–September 3, 1985, p. 90. See also *Who's Who in Finance & Industry,* 1983–84, p. 431.
3. Sheryl Franklin, "The Other Side," *Bank Marketing,* August 1987, p. 62.
4. Barbara Buell, "Nike Catches Up with the Trendy Frontrunner," *Business Week,* October 24, 1988, p. 88. See also "Walking on Air at Nike," *Fortune,* January 1, 1990, p. 72.
5. See reference 11.
6. Marcy Magiera, and Pat Sloan, "Sneaker Attack," *Advertising Age,* June 20, 1988, p. 3.
7. Marcy Magiera, ". . . As Nike Flexes Its Fashion Sense," *Advertising Age,* January 30, 1989, p. 76.
8. James P. Miller, "Nike Chairman Concurs with Estimates of Net Rise for Year of as Much as 65%," *The Wall Street Journal,* July 7, 1989, p. A5A. See also "Increase in Sales Expected by Nike," *New York Times,* February 11, 1989, p. 37; Dori Jones Yang, "Setting Up Shop in China: Three Paths to Success," *Business Week,* October 19, 1987, p. 74.
9. "Nike Pairs Michael Jordan with a Down-to-Earth Guy," *New York Times,* February 14, 1989, p. D7.

10. Carri Gottlieb, "Products of the Year," *Fortune,* December 9, 1985, p. 112. See also Jon Wiener, "Exploitation and the Revolution," *Advertising Age,* June 29, 1987, p. 18.

11. Douglas C. McGill, "Reebok's New Models, Fully Loaded," *New York Times,* February 14, 1989, pp. D1–D2.

12. Christopher Chipello, "Reebok to Buy CML Unit for $42 Million, Signalling Expansion of Product Line," *The Wall Street Journal,* August 8, 1989, p. A4.

13. Kathleen Kerwin, "L.A. Gear Is Going Where the Boys Are," *Business Week,* June 19, 1989, p. 54. See also "The Best of 1989 so Far," *Business Week,* June 26, 1989, p. 112.

14. "The Hollow Corporation," *Business Week,* March 3, 1986, pp. 57–85.

15. Sheryl Franklin, "'Word of Foot' Helps Nike Stay One Step Ahead," *Bank Marketing,* August 1987, p. 62.

16. "Nike Outdoes Competition in Delivery to Customers," *Global Trade,* March 1988, p. 8. See also *U.S. Industrial Outlook,* 1988, pp. 49–59.

17. "The Nike Store Breaks New Ground," *Chain Store Age Executive,* July 1990, pp. 90–91.

18. Dori Jones Yang, "Step by Step with Nike," *Business Week,* August 13, 1990, pp. 116–117. See also "When Your Feet Are Spending the Day Underwater," *Business Week,* February 27, 1989, p. 136.

19. Tom Yulsman, "Anatomy of the High-Tech Running Shoe," *Science Digest,* April 1985, pp. 46, 80, 83. See also Jean Sherman, "No Pain, No Gain," *Working Woman,* May 1987, p. 82.

20. Ibid.

21. Brian Bagot, "Shoeboom!" *Marketing and Medium Decisions,* June 1990, pp. 61–65.

Case 11   GM Tries to Sharpen Its Car Images

Joseph Wolfe
University of Tulsa

In late 1990 Lloyd Reuss, soon to be president of General Motors, asked a customer how she liked her recently-purchased Chevrolet Beretta. Although somewhat embarrassed by the question she answered the car had some quality problems, one of which was having a front door fall off. Without a blush, Reuss responded, "Well, how's your gas mileage?"*

In the early 1920s Alfred Sloan announced, "A car for every purpose, a car for every pocketbook." Thus was born the cornerstone of General Motors' marketing philosophy, an approach that took a nearly bankrupt firm and turned it into the world's largest automobile producer. It also set the tone for all competitive practices in the American automobile industry.

The young Chrysler Motors Corporation, started in 1924 by an ex-GM executive Walter P. Chrysler, copied the same market segmentation approach. He created the Chrysler motor car for the market's prestige segment or affluent customers and then filled out his car line through an acquisition and the creation of new makes. In 1928 the Dodge was acquired so Chrysler could offer a middle-priced car as well as trucks. In the same year it created the Plymouth for the market's low-budget or entry-level segment and the DeSoto as a step-up from the Dodge. Ford, after swimming upstream for a number of years, ultimately bowed to GM's way of doing business. Although it had built its fortunes on the marketing philosophy of a standard, utilitarian car for everyone in dependable Japan Black, it acquired the Lincoln as its prestige nameplate in 1922 and created the Mercury in 1939 to serve as its middle-price offering. Thus General Motors (GM) established the industry's tenor by using a marketing strategy that squeezed out rivals such as Reo, Chalmers, Studebaker, Hudson, Packard, Nash and others, who did not or could not match its segment coverage strategy.

While GM (SIC 3711) has had many glory years, that was then but this is now. The era of the 1990s has sorely tested the company. After having attained at least 50 percent car and light truck market shares in the mid-1950s and early 1960s, its shares for 1992–1994 have respectively been 33.9 percent, 33.2 percent and 32.9 percent. And the downward trend continued in 1995. While it is still the world's largest automobile producer, GM has also become the industry's greatest money loser. See Exhibit 1; the company racked up losses of over $23 billion in 1992.

■ **Exhibit 1**
GM Sales and Net Profits ($000,000)

Year	Sales	Net Profit
1995	$163,861.0	$ 6,933.0
1994	154,219.5	4,900.6
1993	138,219.5	2,465.8
1992	132,242.2	−23,498.3
1991	123,108.8	−4,452.8
1990	124,705.1	−1,985.7

SOURCE: *Hoover's Company Profile Database.* Austin, TX: The Reference Press, Inc., 1996 for 1995 results, company 10–Ks for all other years.

This case was prepared by Joseph Wolfe of the University of Tulsa. Copyright Joseph Wolfe, 1995.

*From *Collision Course: Inside the Battle for General Motors* by Micheline Maynard.

Company	1993	1994	1995
General Motors	$2,180	$2,060	$1,980
Chrysler	1,920	1,820	1,855
Ford	1,660	1,650	1,630

SOURCE: Derived from data collected by Harbour & Associates presented in Bill Vlasic, "The Saginaw Solution," *Business Week,* July 15, 1996, p. 78.

The culprit in its downfall has been its North American automobile operations where it has been marketing a large number of look-alike cars that were poorly defined in the public's mind, poorly marketed, and badly made at high costs. Accordingly, these operations lost money from 1989–1993 and drastic measures were finally taken by a dissatisfied board of directors.

GM stalwarts Lloyd Reuss and Robert C. Stempel, who held the respective offices of President, and Chairman of the Board and CEO, were fired for moving too slowly. An entirely new management team, comprised of outsider John Smale from Procter & Gamble (P&G) and John (Jack) Smith, head of GM's international operations, was installed and drastic cost-cutting and quality control measures were undertaken. Twenty-one plants and facilities were closed with attendant layoffs and early retirements of 74,000 people. Supply costs were slashed by hard-bargaining its parts supplier network. GM also spent billions of dollars cleaning up its balance sheet including its pension fund, which was underfunded by $22.3 billion in 1993 and was causing the company to earn poor credit ratings.

These moves began to show results in 1994 and beyond. While its labor costs per vehicle are still higher than those of either Ford or Chrysler, Exhibit 2 shows it was making progress. Because of its reduced direct and indirect expenses North American automobile operations turned a small profit of $362 million in 1994 and its 1995 earnings are expected to be about $1.4 billion. With GM's financial and production houses beginning to show some order, top management next turned its attention to the marketing of its cars and light trucks. Asked how GM went wrong, Jack Smith acknowledged, "We lost touch with the customer would probably be the kindest way to say it."

In mid-1994, the automobile industry's embarrassed giant began to initiate its era of the marketing manager by again going outside the industry to solve its sales problems. It was looking for a top marketing person, "a brand guy" who would bring a fresh approach to how GM decided what cars to produce and how to promote them. After a five-month search, Ronald L. Zarrella, a top executive who had previously dealt with Playtex panties and had sold contact lenses and Ray-Ban sunglasses for Bausch & Lomb, was made "czar" over North American sales, service and marketing with far-reaching powers. Reporting to Zarrella were all car and truck divisions, advertising, service parts, Canadian sales and numerous support operations. The problem then was to create a top-notch marketing organization, and Zarrella had a strong mandate for change.

■ GM Searches for Talent

When GM went outside its organization and tapped John Smale, a consumer-goods executive from P&G, two strong signals were sent through the company. First, those inside GM would not automatically get the first crack at any job openings, which had always been the case. Second, GM was looking for people with different perspectives, where having an automobile background, with strong loyalties and long service to only one company could serve more as liabilities than as assets.

The search for the company's new marketing czar was conducted by James Carpenter of the executive search firm Russell Reynolds Associates, Inc. Given GM's new chairman John Smale had been hired from P&G, various candidates for the position were thought to be coming from Smale's alma mater. Frequently-mentioned P&G alumni were William B. Connell, a former vice president for beauty care, and another vice president, Charles A. Lieppe. Carpenter's search passed over such highly-touted GM insiders as the Pontiac division's John G. Middlebrook and Buick's Edward H. Mertz.

Although P&G people were often mentioned for the job, GM went further afield and hired Ron Zarrella from Bausch & Lomb on November 16, 1994. He had been serving as its president and CEO since 1993 after joining the company in international sales in 1985. His executive experience entailed stints at Bristol-Myers from 1971–1979 and the Playtex FP Group Inc. from 1979–1985 after receiving training as an engineer at Worcester Polytechnic Institute in 1971 and a New York University MBA in 1978.

When Zarrella arrived at GM in mid-December, he wasted no time in attending to matters, although some insiders doubted he would last very long due to corporate infighting. His extroverted personality, candor and marketing horse-sense, however, served him well and gave him instant credibility. Buick's general marketing manager Mike O'Malley found with Zarrella, "There's an instant rapport, because when you talk about the business with him, you talk about it from a marketing and brand management perspective" while John D. Rock, Oldsmobile's general manager, found, "he has survived the GM immune system."

■ Attending to Marketing Matters

GM's marketing czar Ron Zarrella believed his first priority, within his overall job of creating his company's marketing strategies, was to focus the images of GM's muddled nameplates. At the time of Zarrella's appointment, industry watcher Christopher W. Cedergren noted, "The problem GM is having is that their division chiefs want their divisions to be all things to all people." As examples of this phenomenon, GM was offering in late November 1994 the Saturn, Chevrolet Cavalier, Pontiac Sunfire and the Geo Prizm. These cars were cannibalizing each other to some degree, as they appealed to overlapping sets of customers. GM had also added vehicles to different division lineups, although the divisions had no expertise in selling them. For example, the Bravada sport utility vehicle had been put into Oldsmobile showrooms, where salespeople had been trained to sell cars and not light trucks.

Much overlap was also found regarding the physical nature of the vehicles themselves and the prices charged for each division's cars. Exhibit 3 illustrates the degree that GM was violating Alfred Sloan's "A car for every pocketbook" dictum, where one car badged a Chevrolet sells for more than a Cadillac, and various Pontiacs, Oldsmobiles and Buicks could be purchased for almost the same price. Exhibits 4–6 also demonstrate how Sloan's "A car for every purpose" was also being violated, as a number of brands were using the same engines and platforms or chassis. The use of shared components and platforms, while allowing GM to spread its developmental costs over more brands and to achieve manufacturing economies of scale at various

■ **Exhibit 3**
GM's 1995 Make and
Model List Price
Ranges

Saturn	$ 9,995–$12,995
Chevrolet	$10,060–$68,043
Pontiac	$11,074–$27,139
Oldsmobile	$13,500–$33,680
Buick	$13,700–$33,084
Cadillac	$34,900–$45,935

SOURCE: Abstracted from information in "Profiles of the 1995 Cars,"
Consumer Reports (April 1995), pp. 231–234, 249, 250–251; and "Upscale
Sedans," *Consumer Reports* (May 1995), p. 366.

■ **Exhibit 4**
GM Automobile Makes
and Models by Shared
Platforms

Platform	Makes and Models
A	Oldsmobile Ciera and Ciera wagon Buick Century
B	Chevrolet Caprice and Caprice wagon Buick Roadmaster sedan and Roadmaster Estate wagon
C	Oldsmobile Ninety-Eight Buick Park Avenue
D	Cadillac Fleetwood
F	Chevrolet Camaro Pontiac Firebird
G	Oldsmobile Aurora Buick Riviera
H	Pontiac Bonneville Oldsmobile Eighty-Eight Buick LeSabre
J	Chevrolet Cavalier and Cavalier wagon Pontiac Sunfire
K	Cadillac Eldorado, Seville, DeVille and DeVille Concours
L	Chevrolet Corsica and Beretta
M	Chevrolet Geo Metro
N	Pontiac Grand Am Oldsmobile Achieva Buick Skylark
S	Chevrolet Geo Prizm
W	Chevrolet Lumina and Monte Carlo Pontiac Grand Prix Oldsmobile Cutlass Supreme Buick Regal
Y	Chevrolet Corvette
Z	Saturn SC1/SC2 coupe, SL/SL1/SL2 sedan and SW1/SW2 wagon

SOURCE: "1995 General Motors Car Platforms," *1995 Market Data Book,* Detroit: Crain Communications, Inc., p. 58.

■ **Exhibit 5**
GM Light Truck Makes
and Models by Shared
Platforms

Platform	Makes and Models
U	Chevrolet Lumina minivan Oldsmobile Silhouette Pontiac Trans Sport
M	Chevrolet Astro GMC Safari Oldsmobile Bravada
C/K	Chevrolet C/K pickup, Tahoe and Suburban GMC Sierra, Yukon and Suburban
G	Chevrolet Van and Sportvan GMC Vandura and Rally Van
P	Chevrolet P-model chassis GMC P-model chassis
S/T	Chevrolet S pickup and Blazer GMC Sonoma and Jimmy
Suburban	Chevrolet Suburban GMC Suburban
W	Chevrolet Tiltmaster
CE	Chevrolet Geo Tracker 2wd
CJ	Chevrolet Geo Tracker 4wd
C5-7	Chevrolet Topkick GMC Kodiak

SOURCE: "1995 General Motors Truck Platforms," 1995 Market Data Book, Detroit: Crain Communications, Inc., p. 58.

assembly plants, made it very difficult to truly differentiate each division's cars. Accordingly, the previously cited Bravada was badged the Blazer in Chevrolet showrooms and the Jimmy at GMC Truck dealerships. Regarding sedans, the same body was being used for five different cars, Chevrolet's Lumina and Monte Carlo, Pontiac's Grand Prix, Oldsmobile's Cutlass Supreme and Buick's Regal.

Not only was this inbreeding of platforms and engines producing confusion in the marketplace, it was also causing delays in the design and production of the cars themselves. At the time of Zarrella's arrival GM was selling 77 different car and truck models. Crucial launch date delays of up to six months had occurred costing the company as much as $500 million in profits. Monies spent on previously-scheduled advertising programs were wasted, dealers counting on selling new models while trying to clear out old inventories were frustrated and many customers were losing their faith in GM's dependability. Even when cars were launched on time, many plants were slow in producing cars of reliable quality. Even though Chevrolet's Oshawa, Ontario, factory had been producing its new Lumina since February 14, 1994, it still was not up to full speed by late July 1994. Exhibit 7 summarizes GM launch-date delays.

■ **Exhibit 6**
GM Automobile Makes
and Models by Shared
Engines

Engine	Displacement	Makes and Models
LKO	1.9 Liters	Saturn
LLO	1.9 Liters	Saturn
LE4	2.0 Liters	Pontiac Sunbird
LN2	2.2 Liters	Buick Century Chevrolet Cavalier, Corsica and Beretta Oldsmobile Cutlass Ciera
LGO	2.3 Liters	Chevrolet Corsica and Beretta Oldsmobile Achieva Pontiac Grand Am
LD2	2.3 Liters	Oldsmobile Achieva Pontiac Grand Am
L40	2.3 Liters	Buick Skylark Oldsmobile Achieva Pontiac Grand Am
LG7	3.1 Liters	Buick Skylark
L82	3.1 Liters	Buick Century Oldsmobile Cutlass Ciera, Cutlass Supreme
LHO	3.1 Liters	Buick Regal Chevrolet Cavalier, Corsica, Lumina and Beretta Pontiac Sunbird
L82	3.1 Liters	Oldsmobile Achieva Pontiac Grand Am and Grand Prix
L32	3.4 Liters	Chevrolet Camaro Pontiac Firebird
LQ1	3.4 Liters	Chevrolet Lumina Oldsmobile Cutlass Supreme Pontiac Grand Prix
L27	3.8 Liters	Buick Regal, LeSabre and Park Avenue Oldsmobile Eighty-Eight and Ninety-Eight Pontiac Bonneville
L67	3.8 Liters	Buick Park Avenue Oldsmobile Ninety-Eight Pontiac Bonneville
LB4	4.3 Liters	Chevrolet Caprice
LD8	4.6 Liters	Cadillac Seville and Eldorado
L37	4.6 Liters	Cadillac Seville and Eldorado
L26	4.6 Liters	Cadillac DeVille
LT1	5.7 Liters	Buick Roadmaster Cadillac Fleetwood Chevrolet Camaro and Corvette Pontiac Firebird
LO5	5.7 Liters	Chevrolet Caprice
LT5	5.7 Liters	Chevrolet Corvette

SOURCE: "Equipment Installations," *1995 Market Data Book*, Detroit: Crain Communications, Inc., pp. 68–69.

■ **Exhibit 7**   Original and Delayed Launch Dates for GM Vehicles

Model	Original Date	Revised Date
Chevrolet cargo van	October 1995	March–April 1996
Chevrolet Sportvan (to be renamed the Express)	October 1995	March–April 1996
GMC Vandura	October 1995	March–April 1996
Rally full-size van	October 1995	March–April 1996
Chevrolet Lumina minivan (to be renamed Venture)	April 1996	October 1996 or later
Pontiac Transport minivan	April 1996	October 1996 or later
Oldsmobile Silhouette	April 1996	October 1996 or later
Pontiac Grand Prix	April 1996	October 1996
Chevrolet Malibu	October–November 1996	February–March 1997
Oldsmobile Cutlass Ciera (to be renamed Cutlass)	October–November 1996	February–March 1997
Oldsmobile Cutlass Supreme (to be renamed Intrigue)	October 1996	June 1997
Oldsmobile Achieva (to be renamed Allero)	October 1997	Spring or Fall 1998
Pontiac Grand AM	October 1997	Spring or Fall 1998
GMX160 (an unnamed Oldsmobile)	Fall 1997	Spring or Fall 1999

■ Developing the New Aurora

GM's experience with creating Oldsmobile's new Aurora illustrated the product development problems Zarrella had to solve to be successful in creating marketable cars. The Aurora, or G-car project, was the company's first attempt to develop a car under a new product development structure created in 1993, called the Five-Phase Vehicle Development Process. This process was part of a new company structure which was just one of a series of restructurings that had occurred at GM between 1988 and 1992. In 1993 the company created a major new company called GM North American Operations. This company was created by rearranging the firm's American- and Canadian-market cars into two major groups comprising the following corporations and divisions:

> Small Car Group—The Saturn Corporation and the Lansing Automotive Division Midsize and Luxury Car Group—The Midsize Car Division and the Cadillac Luxury Car Division

General Motors said the new structure's purpose was "to have a clear market-driven focus, retain the uniqueness of its products and take advantage of North American Operations-wide economies of scale facilitated by the use of common parts, processes, and systems throughout the operations."

■ **Exhibit 8**

GM's Five-Phase
Vehicle Development
Process

1. Determine what customers want in a car.
2. Develop the car's concept based on customer wants.
3. Convert the car's concept into a specific car's styling and configuration.
4. Develop any new manufacturing processes demanded by the car's styling and configuration.
5. Redesign and/or adapt manufacturing equipment to produce the new car.

SOURCE: Adapted from Kathleen Kerwin, "GM Finally Faces Up to the Dangers of Inbreeding," *Business Week,* August 29, 1994, p. 36.

Within this new North American structure GM placed the new Five-Phase Vehicle Development Process shown in Exhibit 8. With this process the company wanted to preserve the power of its functional departments believing this was the best way to nurture and capitalize on its technical expertise. Thus the Aurora development team had GM design engineers from Flint, Michigan, working with Oldsmobile's marketing group in Lansing, Michigan, and GM factory managers at its Lake Orion, Michigan, plant. While other automobile companies, such as Honda and Chrysler, place nearly all product development decisions in the hands of a single, autonomous product team, president and CEO Jack Smith expressed satisfaction with his company's system saying, "What's important now is that everyone is tied together."

Exhibit 9 summarizes the events occurring in and around the Aurora project since its inception in 1988. Information on the marketability and quality of the car produced by the design process employed by General Motors is presented in Exhibit 10. During its development, the Aurora endured one and one-half year's worth of product development suspensions for cost-cutting purposes, the turnover of the company's top managers, the threatened elimination of its entire division, a switch-over on where the car was manufactured and a conversion of its dealership network's selling techniques.

■ Some Short-Term Decisions

Before turning his attention to some of GM's longer-term, product development problems, Ron Zarrella had to face a number of decisions regarding the number of brands to continue, given some were deteriorating badly in the marketplace, while others were due for a new design cycle. As a product management philosophy, Zarrella believed it was easier to rejuvenate a fading brand than to create a new one. Consequently, when John Rock wanted to drop the Cutlass name from its 1996 replacement model Oldsmobile, Zarrella vetoed the idea. On the other hand, he ordered the discontinuance of the timeworn Cadillac Fleetwood, Chevrolet Impala SS, Buick Roadmaster and Chevrolet Caprice.

Of even greater importance, Zarrella axed Cadillac's desires for a luxury sport-utility vehicle (SUV) in early June 1995. Since peaking with sales of 351,000 units in 1978, the division's sales fell to about 175,000 units in 1995 with its share of the luxury market amounting to 15 percent, down from a 24 percent market share in 1989. In the face of these falling sales and the fact that some of its major competitors would soon be entering the marketplace with the luxury SUVs shown in Exhibit 11, Cadillac wanted to put a nameplate of its own on one of GM's big trucks. Rather than allowing the division to get into luxury trucks, Zarrella defined

■ **Exhibit 9** Oldsmobile Develops the Aurora

Date	Event
February 1988	Oldsmobile Division begins to consider a successor to the fading Toronado Coupe which had been created in 1966. It was determined through 20 nationwide focus groups comprised of owners of European luxury cars such as Mercedes-Benz and BMW, and over 4,200 consumer interviews, that customers wanted a quality, high performance four-door sporty sedan. The car's details should include leather seats and wood interior trim, a multivalve engine for smooth acceleration and four-wheel disk brakes.
Autumn 1988	GM designer Bud Chandler makes his first sketches of the car which is dubbed the "tube car" after its cylindrical conformation entailing prominent wheels and no grille.
March 1989	A fiberglass mock-up of the "tube car" is shown to a Los Angeles focus group. After receiving positive reactions the design is altered slightly and then "locked in" for the duration of the car's development. Engineers begin experimenting with an extremely rigid framework to give the Aurora stability but quiet, nimble handling.
July 1989	GM's corporate level approves the continuation of the Aurora project as well as the development of its sister car, the Buick Riviera. The development of these two cars will ultimately cost about $823 million.
Autumn 1989	Pressure builds on the Aurora development team as the Lexus LS 400 and Nissan Infiniti Q45 come to market.
January 1990	GM, in an economy move, suspends the funding of engineering developmental work on the Aurora. Roger Masch, GM's luxury car chief engineer, continues minimal developmental work on the car. Engineers from manufacturing work on rear quarter panel joining problems.
January 1991	Engineering work on the Aurora resumes. Chairman Roger B. smith steps down and is succeeded by Robert C. Stempel as Chairman and CEO. Lloyd E. Reuss designated GM President.
December 1991	Stempel and Reuss announce their cost-cutting plan that entails the shuttering of 21 plants and the elimination of 74,000 jobs.
Early 1992	The design team reluctantly jettisons Oldsmobile's famous "rocket" logotype when market research shows the logo is a liability rather than serving as a reminder of the division's glory days as a technological innovator.
Early 1992	Tool and die work on the Aurora delayed for six months as spending on the project is suspended for six months in another economy move.
April 1992	Reuss replaced by John (Jack) F. Smith Jr., former head of GM's international operations.
September 1992	John D. Rock, Oldsmobile's General Manager, obtains renewed approval from GM's North American Strategy Board to continue the development of the Aurora.
November 1992	Stempel removed by the board of directors for not moving fast enough with his reforms.
January 1993	The Aurora unveiled at automobile shows in Los Angeles and Detroit. No official launch date for the car is announced.
August 1993	GM's Lake Orion, Michigan, plant starts pilot production of the Aurora. The 1995 Auroras will be made at Buick City in Flint, Michigan, and the 1996 cars will be made at the Lake Orion plant.
October 1993	After the Oldsmobile Division loses $552 million in 1992 rumors circulate that GM will discontinue the entire division due to these losses and faltering sales which have dropped from over 1 million in the mid-1980s to 381,000 in 1992. Rock saves the division with a plan to "Saturnize" it with the Aurora as its centerpiece. The division will subsequently offer a trimmed-down line of cars which have an import feel and advanced engine technology.
April–May 1994	First Auroras arrive in dealer showrooms. A $30 million advertising campaign begins and $20 million is spent on a dealer-training program designed to help dealers emulate Saturn's low-keyed, no-haggle, one-price sales method.

SOURCE: Timeline adapted from Kathleen Kerwin, "GM Finally Faces Up to the Dangers of Inbreeding," *Business Week,* August 29, 1994, p.36; and Automotive News *1996 Market Data Book,* April 24, 1996, pp.132 and 138.

■ **Exhibit 10**   Summary *Consumer Reports* Comments

Comparing the Aurora to similar-priced, "European style" cars such as the Toyota Avalon XLS, Volvo 850 Turbo, Mazda Millenia S, Lexus ES300, Saab 9000 and Mercedes-Benz C280, *Consumer Reports* noted "The Oldsmobile Aurora's best features are its Northstar V8 engine, smooth transmission, and excellent climate-control system. But beyond that, the Aurora just does not cut it in this company. It's a heavy, cumbersome car that's unpleasant to ride in and to drive."

In *Consumer Reports*' frequently-referenced annual automobile issue its summary review on the Aurora reads as follows:

Predicted reliability: Less than average. This is GM's answer to the imported sports sedans. A sophisticated, 250 hp aluminum "Northstar" V8 similar to Cadillac's is the Aurora's best feature. Handling is ponderous. The ride is harsh on bumpy roads, especially with the optional performance tires. A low roof and high dash compromise the driver's view. The safety belts can be uncomfortable for tall people. The controls work well, once you learn their haphazard layout. The climate-control system is close to ideal. The front seats are lumpy. The rear seat comfortably holds two tall people, but a middle passenger won't be happy. The trunk is roomy but awkward to load.

Regarding the Aurora's potential reliability *Consumer Reports* commented that ". . . our Aurora left us wary. The car arrived with its radiator overflow hose disconnected. Early in the course of our testing, the engine-coolant thermostat, the front-seat lumbar support adjustments, and the glovebox light failed."

Based on reader-owner surveys for 1993–1995 cars the 1995 Aurora's reliability scored as follows against various European style benchmark cars:

Automobile	Percent of Group Average
Lexus ES300	+55.0%
Mazda Millenia S	+44.0%
Volvo 850	+35.0%
Toyota Avalon XLS	+31.0%
BMW 3-Series	+23.0%
Aurora	−18.0%
Mercedes-Benz C280	−22.0%

SOURCE: "Upscale Sedans," *Consumer Reports*, May 1995, pp. 361 and 365; "1996 Cars Reliability," *Consumer Reports*, April 1996, p. 50; and "New Cars," *Consumer Reports*, April 1996, p. 41.

■ **Exhibit 11**
New Luxury Sport-
Utility Entrants

Vehicle	Arrival	Price Range
Acura SLX	Spring 1996	$24,000–$35,000
BMW SUV	Spring/Fall 1999	$35,000–$45,000
Jaguar SUV	Fall 1999	$40,000–$50,000
Infiniti SUV	Fall 1996	$33,000–$39,000
Lexus LX450	Spring 1996	$40,000–$45,000
Lincoln Navigator	Spring 1997	$40,000–$45,000
Mercedes-Benz AAV	Spring 1997	$33,000–$45,000

SOURCE: "GM Picks GMC Over Cadillac for Utility Vehicle," *The Wall Street Journal,* June 13, 1995, p. A2.

Cadillac as a producer of cars. He told Cadillac to put its efforts behind its new entry-level Catera, which would be inaugurated in mid-1996. Based on GM's European Opel division's Omega MV6, it had been designed to appeal to 40ish baby boomers. Given the buyers of some Cadillac models average almost 70 years of age, many felt this was a badly-needed car. Christopher J. MacConnell, president of Cincinnati's Thomson-MacConnell Cadillac, said that "Cadillac dealers often joke that instead of a first-time-buyer program, we need a last-time-buyer program."

Zarrella's Brand Management System

After much internal study and discussions with other firms who had successfully used brand managers, Ron Zarrella announced GM's version of its brand management system on August 10, 1995. Exhibit 12 presents the new structure which employed 36 brand managers, each responsible for marketing one or more particular brands. These brand managers worked laterally with a brand product development manager who had been assigned to him or her by a vehicle line engineer (VLE), under whom the brand was being developed. This new system had been designed to bring marketers and product designers closer. The goal was to define distinct images for each brand and model, engineer those cars to meet customer needs and then

Exhibit 12
GM's New Brand Manager System

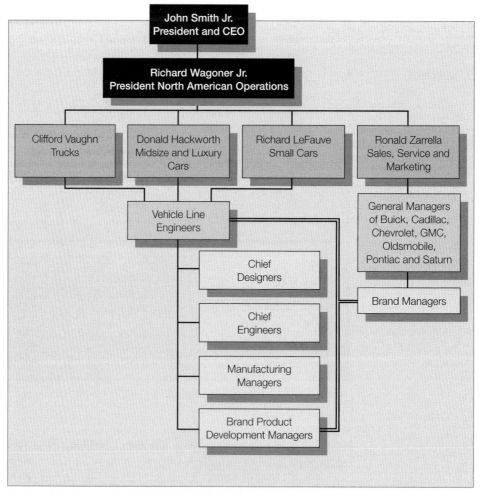

SOURCE: Keith Naughton and Kathleen Kerwin, "At GM, Two Heads May Be Worse Than One," *Business Week,* August 14, 1995, p. 46.

effectively market the cars and trucks to the target customers. The system's VLEs were top engineers, responsible for developing the platform or chassis on which individual models were to be built.

As an example of how the VLE and brand managers interacted, a VLE was put in charge of the "J" platform on which the Chevrolet Cavalier and Pontiac Sunfire are built. In turn, the Cavalier and Sunfire each had its own brand manager. These brand managers channeled marketing ideas, such as how a particular model should look and what accessories it should contain to the VLE, while reporting back to his or her respective Chevrolet and Pontiac divisions.

As observed by Jeff Hurlbert, Chevrolet's general marketing manager, "The brand manager was to be a very powerful individual within the divisions." Because brand managers report directly to the division's general manager, GM's decision making pyramid was flattened. This flattening should speed the development of new models, shorten GM's replacement cycle and accomplish these two goals at a lower cost. Zarrella's goal was to develop the average new model in 36 months, a 12 month reduction in its development time requirement, while slashing engineering costs by 30 percent. GM's new brand manager system also required 5,000 fewer engineers, whereas it had 30,000 working on product development in August 1995. Richard Wagoner Jr., President of North American Operations, has acknowledged that GM had been inclined to let some of its models get too old. GM's average replacement cycle had been around eight years and he wanted to cut that to six, although most Japanese carmakers replace their cars every four years or less. With the shorter replacement cycles Zarrella aimed to give each division two new models a year, despite eliminating some of its platforms and brands.

■ GM Recruits Its New Brand Managers

As soon as Ron Zarrella's brand manager system was approved, he retained the services of Russell Reynolds Associates to help him find six outside brand managers to go along with the 28 he wanted to hire from within GM. By September he had begun interviewing candidates for the new positions. Aspirants underwent an all-day session, where they created a marketing plan for a hypothetical model. Once hired for their positions, it was expected they would stay in the same job for 8–10 years, or two model cycles. This was a much longer than normal time period for a fast-tracking executive at GM. During the process of hiring new brand managers and moving other executives to new positions, at least 500 GM "dead-ended" middle-management types were offered buyouts or were encouraged to retire. Exhibit 13 presents the names, brand assignments and backgrounds of Zarrella's six outside hires. Exhibit 14 lists those who were hired as brand managers from inside GM. By mid-October 1995 nearly all positions had been filled.

■ The Visioning Process Began

With his brand managers now in place, their task was to lead 10-member brand management teams, drawn from such areas as customer satisfaction, public relations, engineering, and sales, service and distribution. In this role, they had profit and loss responsibilities for the brands they managed. Rather than marketing Pontiacs, Chevrolets and Cadillacs, or an entire division's cars, they focused on

■ **Exhibit 13**   GM's "Outside" Brand Managers

Brand	Brand Manager and Business Background
GMC Jimmy Blazer sport-utility	Jeffrey B. Cohen. Served as Nabisco's senior business director for breakfast aisle and variety salty snack products and as brand manager of SnackWell cereal bars. Also managed a number of different product categories at Johnson & Johnson.
Oldsmobile Bravada sport-utility and Oldsmobile Silhouette minivan	Michael F. McEnaney. Formerly executive vice president of marketing for Ralcorp Holdings' $350 million cereal and snack business as well as Tender Vittles and Purina Cat Chow.
Cadillac Seville and Eldorado	Robert Baird. Previously category general manager for Scott Paper's Wet Wipes division. Also worked at Bristol-Myers Squibb and Procter & Gamble.
Pontiac Grand Am	Lisa Baird. Managed the introduction of Cool Mint Listerine toothpaste while serving as vice president for personal care at Warner Lambert. Earlier worked at Procter & Gamble, Johnson & Johnson and Bristol-Myers Squibb.
Buick Regal	Roger Adams. Formerly vice president of marketing and R&D at United Biscuits Holdings PLC's Keebler Company. Also worked for J. H Heinz, PepsiCo and RJR Nabisco.
Chevrolet Venture	Karen Francis. Vice president of marketing for the Newall Corporation handling the company's consumer writing business. Worked on the Crest brand while at Procter & Gamble. Left this position mid-summer 1996.

SOURCE: Chad Rubel, "GM Breaks Tradition, Hires Outsiders as Brand Managers," *Marketing News,* April 8, 1996, p. 7.

■ **Exhibit 14**   GM's "Inside" Brand Managers

Division/Brand	Manager	Division/Brand	Manager
Cadillac:		Oldsmobile:	
Catera	David Nottoli	Achieva	Bob Clark
DeVille	Janet Eckhoff	Ciera Cutlass 88	John Gatt
Chevrolet:		98 Aurora	
Camaro	Dick Allman	Cutlass Supreme	Ken Stewart
Corvette		Intrigue	
Cavalier	Steve Wagg		
Lumina	Don Parkinson		
Monte Carlo			
Malibu	Jim Heckert		
Astro	John Gaydash	Pontiac–GMC:	
Venture		Bonneville	Mark LaNeve
Blazer	Russ Clark	Grand Prix	William E. Heugh
C/K Truck	Curt Ritter	Firebird	James D. Murray
S-Series	Ron Stanley	TransAm	
Tahoe	Steven Ramsey	Transport	
Suburban		Sunfire	Jim Bunnell
Buick:		GMC Yukon	Dennis J. O'Connell
Century	A. H. "Tony" Derhake	GMC Suburban	
Park Avenue	Kathryn Benoit	GMC Safari	Cheryl Caeton
LeSabre	J. J. "Joe" Fitzsimmins, Jr.	GMC Sonoma	Lou Elbert
Riviera	Michael Wright	GMC Sierra	Jim Kornas
Skylark	Ed Berger	Commercial trucks	Dick Pennell

■ **Exhibit 15**   Zarrella's Vision for GM's Car Divisions

> **Chevrolet**—GM's high volume car and light truck division. The cars produced by this division "should offer affordability, dependability, reliability and (the) widest range of models."
>
> **Pontiac**—Will be the division marketing GM's sportiest cars. They will stand for youthfulness and high spirits; will feature racy, aggressive "in-your-face styling."
>
> **Saturn**—Will continue to build small cars targeted towards those who traditionally buy foreign cars. Its cars will stand for reliability and intelligent design with a focus on a pleasurable and gratifying "shopping, buying and ownership experience."
>
> **Oldsmobile**—The car-owner's next step for ex-Saturn owners as they become wealthier and want a bigger, average-priced car. Oldsmobile's cars should be competitive against Audi, Acura, and the entry-level Infiniti G20 and Lexus ES300.
>
> **Buick**—This division's cars will be GM's "premium American car" and will be targeted at baby boomers in their 50s. Its cars will be sophisticated, large, comfortable and well-powered and its dealerships should have a distinct "country club" feel.
>
> **Cadillac**—Will continue to be GM's luxury car division. Its cars will be innovative, highly-engineered and will compete favorably with all the world's premium cars such as Mercedes, BMW and Lexus.

SOURCE: Gabriella Stern, "GM's New Marketing Chief Seeks Clarity Amid Muddle of Overlapping Car Lines," *The Wall Street Journal,* May 1, 1995, p. A3; and Gabriella Stern, "Buick Confronts Its Fuddy-Duddy Image," *The Wall Street Journal,* June 19, 1995, p. B1.

marketing Grand Ams, Corvettes and DeVilles based on the belief that customers buy individual models or brands. As the teams began their work, Zarrella's vision for each division's cars is shown in Exhibit 15. The identities of particular brands were evolving but certain ones, such as the following somewhat amorphous forms, were already in place:

> Chevrolet Malibu vision—Aimed at "hard working people" seeking value and functionality.
>
> Oldsmobile Intrigue—For "highly discriminating" import-car buyers searching out a "rewarding driving experience."
>
> Buick Century—For buyers who are "sensible by nature and committed to domestic brands."
>
> Cadillac Eldorado—Intended for 40-year-old-plus men who seek a feeling of escape in their cars.
>
> Cadillac Seville—Meant for affluent, highly educated men and women under 50 who are proud of their accomplishments.
>
> Cadillac DeVille—For the 50-somethings, especially affluent women and African-American buyers who want a traditional large luxury car with contemporary touches.

■ Should Zarrella's New System Work?

As 1996 began GM was looking to improve its performance with the introduction of its new Chevy Venture minivan, the Buick Regal and Pontiac Grand Prix. Although Zarrella's VLE concept was borrowed from Toyota, and the brand manager concept was imported from P&G, he believed what he had designed would be effective.

Moreover, the industry's outlook was positive as analysts believed 1996s sales would be about 15.1 million units, or a 2 percent increase from 1995's sales.

Viewing the new organization Zarrella had created for GM, however, a former Chrysler executive says the new system "is bound to cause turf battles. Under the new system GM's powerful heads of its car and truck divisions will lose much of their power. GM still seems to want an adversarial relationship between the guys who build 'em and the guys who sell 'em." Interestingly, under the new brand manager system two of GM's insiders who were passed over in favor of Zarrella, now report to him in his new position. Zarrella himself admits, "Behaviors are going to have to change if this is going to work."

Looking at the mechanics of the brand management structure, Joseph Phillippi, an analyst at Lehman Brothers Inc., commented, "Why did they have to make it so complex? Why not just have one chief engineer with profit and loss responsibility, like Toyota?" In response, GM's vice president of vehicle development, Arvin Mueller, said his company's vast size requires the creation of a complex structure. More importantly he reasoned, "We used to have hundreds of people making these decisions, and now we've got it down to two," while Jeffrey Liker, an industry expert at the University of Michigan says, "They're moving in the right direction."

Others observed that while GM made a bold move within the context of its own development, it will still be far behind the industry even if the reorganization is successful. While it has taken the goal of cutting its average development time to 36 months, some projects could take as much as 50 months to complete. More importantly, Toyota can bring out a new car in 30 months and Ford has set its development-time goal to 24 months. Regarding the use of brand managers, GM was pitted against similar systems at Ford and Chrysler. Chrysler has had a brand manager heading each of its divisions for a number of years while Ford's program began January 1, 1996, with five brand managers.

In the past the automotive industry has designed cars that matched up against the competition, and those that had more technology were considered "superior." More recently, the emphasis is on what the customer wants rather than what the company's engineers want. Zarrella takes solace that the Chevrolet Lumina, while not technically sophisticated, has been successful because it delivers the three most important elements GM found midsize car buyers want—price, space and quality. With his brand managers now in place he now hopes to design and market cars that North America wants.

■ Secondary Quote Sources

1994 Company 10–K.

Kerwin, Kathleen, "A Caddy That's Not For Daddy," *Business Week,* December 18, 1995, pp. 87–88.

Kerwin, Kathleen, "GM Finally Faces Up to the Dangers of Inbreeding," *Business Week,* August 29, 1994, p. 36.

Naughton, Keith and Kathleen Kerwin, "At GM, Two Heads May Be Worse Than One," *Business Week,* August 14, 1995, p. 46.

Rubel, Chad, "GM Breaks Tradition, Hires Outsiders as Brand Managers," *Marketing News,* April 8, 1996, pp. 7, 10.

Serafin, Raymond, "Brand Guy Zarrella 'Catalyst Making Things Happen,' " *Advertising Age,* October 23, 1995, p. 4.

Serafin, Raymond, "Saturn's Shannon to Boost Olds Team," *Advertising Age,* July 17, 1995, p. 8.

Taylor, III, Alex, "GM's $11,000,000,000 Turnaround," *Fortune,* October 17, 1994, p. 56.

Suggested Assignments/Study Questions

1. What does the case's opening anecdote about Lloyd Ruess and a Chevrolet customer say about General Motors?

2. What were the historical elements or roots of GM's market segmentation approach? To what degree is that approach being practiced by GM today? What elements or factors have acted to destroy the implementation of its long-held ideal of distinctive cars for definable segments?

3. What culture clashes do you believe occurred when Lloyd Reuss and Robert Stempel were fired and the "marketing types" John Smale and Ron Zarrella were brought into GM? What values were associated with or prized by the traditional GM types? What values do the new marketing types bring to GM?

4. Did Ron Zarrella have to overcome any credibility problems when he arrived at GM in December 1994? What credibility problems do the "outside" brand managers he has hired possess? In bringing about a marketing revolution within GM, from what power bases can Zarrella and his new "outside" hires operate?

5. What problems have been caused within GM due to its need to share chassis and components?

6. What factors within GM will serve to frustrate the effectiveness of its new Five-Phase Vehicle Development Process as a new product development concept?

7. What are the crucial steps in GM's Five-Phase Vehicle Development Process as presented in case Exhibit 8? How were these steps implemented in the development of the Oldsmobile Aurora as outlined in case Exhibit 9?

8. Reviewing the 1995 Oldsmobile Aurora's test reports in case Exhibit 10, what kind of car was ultimately produced by GM? Does this car appeal to the target market's customer? Is the Aurora competitive with the other cars in its intended class?

Case Group C
Promotion Strategy

■ **Case 12** **harley-davidson.com and the Global Motorcycle Industry**

J. Paul Peter
University of Wisconsin–Madison

Harley-Davidson, Inc., achieved its thirteenth consecutive year of record revenue and earnings and a 74 percent increase in the value of the firm in 1998. The company had previously divested interests in other industries and focused its efforts exclusively on the motorcycle industry, including accessories and financing. It strengthened its presence in the industry by obtaining full ownership in Buell Motorcycle Company, a manufacturer of sport motorcycles based on Harley-Davidson components and previously established Eaglemark Financial Services, Inc., to provide financial services to dealers and customers.

The company completed a new 479,200-square-foot facility near Milwaukee in 1998 which manufactures engines and transmissions and finished a 330,000-square-foot facility in Kansas City, Missouri, which produces all six models of Sportsters, Harley's 833cc and 1200cc bikes. The company also introduced a new engine, the Twin Cam 88, a more powerful one to compete with the larger engines in some competitive motorcycles. Overall, it sold 157,152 motorcycles in 1998, a 15 percent increase over the previous year, achieved net sales of over $2 billion, a 17 percent increase over 1997, and gross profits of $104.5 million, a 17.8 percent increase over the previous year.

Chairman and CEO Jeffrey L. Bleustein believed that the phenomenal success of Harley could be attributed to four major factors:

- A powerful and much admired brand centered around the experiences of motorcycling; its attributes of freedom, adventure, and individuality that appeal to people across a wide variety of demographic segments.
- Strong relationships with all of its stakeholders including dealers, customers, employees, suppliers, governments, society, and shareholders.
- A proven management team and empowered employees committed to sustaining steady, manageable growth in a worldwide motorcycle market.
- Harley-Davidson's mystique . . . the ability of the brand to bring together in unique and surprising ways seemingly disparate combinations of products, people, processes, and experiences.

A final measure of the success of Harley-Davidson can be seen in the growth of its Harley Owners Group or H.O.G., started in 1983 with 33,000 members, all in the U.S. In 1997, it had 380,000 members in 105 countries and grew to 430,000 members in 115 countries by 1998. Clearly, the company had made a number of excellent management decisions and had built a large group of satisfied, involved, loyal customers around the world.

Global Competition

Exhibit 1 presents motorcycle registrations in three major regions where Harley competes. All three areas show solid growth which demonstrates, in part, the success of motorcycle manufacturers in generating demand for their products.

Exhibit 2 presents a breakdown of market shares by competitors in three regions. While Harley-Davidson dominates the market in North America, it has the smallest market share of major competitors in Europe and is fourth in the Asia/Pacific region which is dominated by Japanese brands. Part of the reason for Harley's smaller market share in Europe and the Asia/Pacific region is that the company cannot produce enough motorcycles to meet demand and its prices tend to be higher than competitive models. Overall, Harley-Davidson and Buell together achieved 25.2 percent of the global heavyweight motorcycle market.

Product quality for Harley and its major competitors is excellent although competitive bikes are often more technologically advanced. Competition in the industry is based on such things as styling, engine displacement (power), features (e.g., cruise control, fuel injection), availability, brand equity and price. Shortages of Harleys lead many consumers to purchase competitive bikes as there are two-year waiting lists for some Harley models.

■ **Exhibit 1**
New Heavyweight Motorcycle (651 cc+) Registrations in Three Global Regions (in 000's)

Year	North America[1]	Europe[2]	Asia/Pacific[3]	Total
1998	246.2	270.5	69.2	585.6
1997	205.4	250.3	58.9	514.6
1996	178.5	224.7	37.4	440.6
1995	163.1	207.2	39.4	409.7
1994	150.4	201.9	39.1	391.4

[1]Includes United States and Canada.
[2]Includes Austria, Belgium, France, Germany, Italy, Netherlands, Spain, Switzerland and United Kingdom.
[3]Includes Japan and Australia.
SOURCE: Adapted from Harley-Davidson, Inc., *1998 Annual Report,* p. 52.

■ **Exhibit 2**
1998 Heavyweight Motorcycle (651 cc+) Market Shares by Global Regions

Company	North America	Europe	Asia/Pacific
BMW	2.7%	13.4%	4.3%
Harley-Davidson/Buell	48.5	6.4	15.6
Honda	20.5	24.1	28.0
Kawasaki	10.2	10.7	22.1
Suzuki	10.3	17.2	7.9
Yamaha	4.8	16.3	16.6
Other	3.0	11.9	5.5

NOTE: Regions defined as in Exhibit 1.
SOURCE: Adapted from Harley-Davidson, Inc., *1998 Annual Report,* p. 52.

All of the major competitors produce touring and custom (cruiser) motorcycles that compete directly with Harley and sport bikes that compete with Buell's offerings. BMW's R and K series of bikes; Honda's Gold Wing, ST1100, Shadow, Valkyrie, and Pacific Coast; Kawasaki's Vulcan series and Concours; Yamaha's Venture, Road Star, Royal Star, Virago, and Vstar; and Suzuki's Marauder and Intruder series are some of the major models competing with Harley-Davidson. In addition, most of the major competitors have full lines of smaller motorcycles with engine displacements of less than 651 ccs, a market in which Harley does not compete.

New Competition

In addition to established competitors, there are a number of new competitors entering the market. Polaris, the snowmobile manufacturer, converted an assembly line in its Spirit Lake, Iowa, facility to produce the Polaris Victory Y9ZC, a retro-look, V-twin cruiser. This bike is targeted to Polaris's existing snowmobile customers, 30 percent of whom are also motorcycle enthusiasts. Excelsior-Henderson, once one of the big three motorcycle manufacturers (along with Harley and Indian), has been resurrected in Belle Plaine, Minnesota, to produce the Super X, a direct Harley competitor. A California company purchased the Indian trademark and plans to build a limited edition Indian Chief motorcycle. All of these companies are seeking to capitalize on the demand for heavyweight bikes, particularly Harleys.

Competitive Remakes and Accessories

Big Dog Motorcycles of Sun Valley, Idaho, produces the Big Dog Aerosport Cruiser, a customized Harley selling for thousands over the stock Harley price. A variety of other companies, such as Titan, Ultra Kustom, Illusion, and California Motorcycle Co. make non-Harley Harleys with their own parts. S&S Cycle produces performance parts that compete directly with Harley parts as do other manufacturers who produce seats, exhaust pipes, saddlebags, and windshields that some customers prefer over Harley offerings.

Motorcycle Buyers

The demographic profile of motorcycle buyers has changed over the years. According to the Motorcycle Industry Council, 61 percent of buyers are over 35 years old whereas in 1980, only 27 percent had reached this age. In 1980, only 2.4 percent of motorcycle buyers had incomes of $50,000 or higher, whereas in 1998, over one third were in this income group. White-collar professionals are the largest group of new bike riders, accounting for 36 percent. Many are former riders now stepping up to their dream machines and state that motorcycle riding helps reduce stress in their lives.

Motorcycle Company Websites

Harley-Davidson's management believes that the Internet is a powerful marketing tool. Its website is affectionately called the "anti-website" since it encourages visitors to get off-line and onto their Harleys. The website includes detailed information on the company and its products and had nearly 1.5 million visitors in 1997 alone.

All of Harley's major competitors have products other than motorcycles on their websites including cars (Honda, Acura, Suzuki, BMW), outboard motors (Honda, Yamaha, Suzuki), jet skis (Kawasaki), snowmobiles (Yamaha), boats (Yamaha), generators and power equipment (Honda, Yamaha). However, Harley-Davidson's website is devoted exclusively to motorcycle-related information about Harley's products, experience, and the company itself, including financial data. This may be a competitive advantage for Harley because it illustrates that the company is focused only in the motorcycle industry.

Discussion Questions

1. Why is the Internet a particularly good promotion medium for Harley-Davidson?
2. What different roles could Harley-Davidson's website play for Harley owners, for people shopping for a motorcycle, and for people just interested in motorcycles in general?
3. Visit Harley-Davidson's website (www.harley-davidson.com) and evaluate it on the following criteria:

   a. Home page quality
   b. Site map quality
   c. Ease of browsing
   d. Image speed
   e. Attractiveness
   f. Product information
   g. Dealer information
   h. Company information
   i. Ease of exiting
   j. Overall evaluation (sum of above)

   Rate each dimension on a scale from one (poor) to five (excellent). What do you conclude about the quality of Harley's website as a marketing tool?
4. Evaluate Harley-Davidson's website from a promotion strategy point of view. What role does it play in Harley's promotion mix?
5. Compare Harley-Davidson's website with those of its major competitors on the criteria listed in Question 3 above. Focus only on the motorcycle portion of these websites:

   www.bmw.com
   www.honda.com
   www.kawasaki.com
   www.suzuki.com
   www.yamaha-motor.com

   Overall, what are the strengths and weaknesses of each website?
6. Visit the Polaris website at **www.victory-usa.com**. What is your evaluation of this website and the Polaris Victory Y9ZC?
7. Why do you think the heavyweight motorcycle market has grown so much in recent years?
8. How many motorcycles did each company sell globally in 1998? What accounts for Honda's success?

■ References

Brown, Stuart F., "The Company That Out-Harleys Harley," *Fortune*, September 28, 1998, pp. 56–57.

della Cava, Marco R., "Motorcycle Maker Caters to the Continent," *USA Today*, April 22, 1998, p. 8B.

Eldridge, Earle, "Motorcycling Passion Climbs the Corporate Ladder," *USA Today*, May 7, 1999, pp. B1–B2.

Harley-Davidson, Inc., 1997 *Annual Report*.

Harley-Davidson, Inc., 1998 *Annual Report*.

Machan, Dyan, "Is the Hog Going Soft?" *Forbes*, March 10, 1997, pp. 114–119.

Melcher, Richard A., "Tune-Up Time for Harley," *Business Week*, April 8, 1996, pp. 90–94.

Motorcycle Cruiser, Los Angeles, CA: Peterson Publishing Company, April 1999.

Stevens, Karen, and Dale Kurschner, "That Vroom! You Hear May Not Be a Harley," *Business Week*, October 1997, pp. 159–160.

Case 13   Hanover-Bates Chemical Corporation

Robert E. Witt
University of Texas–Austin

James Sprague, newly appointed northeast district sales manager for the Hanover-Bates Chemical Corporation, leaned back in his chair as the door to his office slammed shut. "Great beginning," he thought. "Three days in my new job and the district's most experienced sales representative is threatening to quit."

On the previous night, James Sprague, Hank Carver (the district's most experienced sales representative), and John Follet, another senior member of the district sales staff, had met for dinner at Jim's suggestion. During dinner Jim had mentioned that one of his top priorities would be to conduct a sales and profit analysis of the district's business in order to identify opportunities to improve the district's profit performance. Jim had stated that he was confident that the analysis would indicate opportunities to reallocate district sales efforts in a manner that would increase profits. As Jim had indicated during the conversation, "My experience in analyzing district sales performance data for the national sales manager has convinced me that any district's allocation of sales effort to products and customer categories can be improved." Both Carver and Follet had nodded as Jim discussed his plans.

Hank Carver was waiting when Jim arrived at the district sales office the next morning. It soon became apparent that Carver was very upset by what he perceived as Jim's criticism of how he and the other district sales representatives were doing their jobs—and, more particularly, how they were allocating their time in terms of customers and products. As he concluded his heated comments, Carver said:

> This company has made it darned clear that 34 years of experience don't count for anything . . . and now someone with not much more than two years of selling experience and two years of pushing paper for the national sales manager at corporate headquarters tells me I'm not doing my job. . . . Maybe it's time for me to look for a new job . . . and since Trumbull Chemical [Hanover-Bates's major competitor] is hiring, maybe that's where I should start looking . . . and I'm not the only one who feels this way.

As Jim reflected on the scene that had just occurred, he wondered what he should do. It had been made clear to him when he had been promoted to manager of the northeast sales district that one of his top priorities should be improvement of the district's profit performance. As the national sales manager had said, "The northeast sales district may rank third in dollar sales, but it's our worst district in terms of profit performance."

Prior to assuming his new position, Jim had assembled the data presented in Exhibits 1 through 6 to assist him in analyzing district sales and profits. The data had been compiled from records maintained in the national sales manager's office. Although he believed the data would provide a sound basis for a preliminary analysis of district sales and profit performance, Jim had recognized that additional data would probably have to be collected when he arrived in the northeast district (District 3).

In response to the national sales manager's comment about the northeast district's poor profit performance, Jim had been particularly interested in how the district had performed on its gross profit quota. He knew that the district gross

---

This case was prepared by Professor Robert E. Witt, University of Texas, Austin, and is intended to serve as a basis for class discussion rather than to illustrate effective or ineffective management.

■ **Exhibit 1**   Hanover-Bates Chemical Corporation: Summary Income Statements, 1981–1985

	1981	1982	1983	1984	1985
Sales	$19,890,000	$21,710,000	$19,060,000	$21,980,000	$23,890,000
Production expenses	11,934,000	13,497,000	12,198,000	13,612,000	14,563,000
Gross profit	7,956,000	8,213,000	6,862,000	8,368,000	9,327,000
Administrative expenses	2,606,000	2,887,000	2,792,000	2,925,000	3,106,000
Selling expenses	2,024,000	2,241,000	2,134,000	2,274,000	2,399,000
Pretax profit	3,326,000	3,085,000	1,936,000	3,169,000	3,822,000
Taxes	1,512,000	1,388,000	790,000	1,426,000	1,718,000
Net profit	$ 1,814,000	$ 1,697,000	$ 1,146,000	$ 1,743,000	$ 2,104,000

■ **Exhibit 2**   District Sales Quota and Gross Profit Quota Performance, 1985

District	Number of Sales Reps	Sales		Gross Profit	
		Quota	Actual	Quota*	Actual
1	7	$ 3,880,000	$ 3,906,000	$1,552,000	$1,589,000
2	6	3,750,000	3,740,000	1,500,000	1,529,000
3	6	3,650,000	3,406,000	1,460,000	1,239,000
4	6	3,370,000	3,318,000	1,348,000	1,295,000
5	5	3,300,000	3,210,000	1,320,000	1,186,000
6	5	3,130,000	3,205,000	1,252,000	1,179,000
7	5	2,720,000	3,105,000	1,088,000	1,310,000
		$23,800,000	$23,890,000	$9,520,000	$9,327,000

*District gross profit quotas were developed by the national sales manager in consultation with the district managers and took into account price competition in the respective districts.

■ **Exhibit 3**   District Selling Expenses, 1985

District	Sales Rep Salaries*	Sales Commission	Sales Rep Expenses	District Office	District Manager Salary	District Manager Expenses	Sales Support	Total Selling Expenses
1	$177,100	$19,426	$56,280	$21,150	$33,500	$11,460	$69,500	$ 388,416
2	143,220	18,700	50,760	21,312	34,000	12,034	71,320	351,346
3	157,380	17,030	54,436	22,123	35,000†	12,382	70,010	368,529
4	150,480	16,590	49,104	22,004	32,500	11,005	66,470	348,153
5	125,950	16,050	42,720	21,115	33,000	11,123	76,600	326,558
6	124,850	16,265	41,520	20,992	33,500	11,428	67,100	315,655
7	114,850	17,530	44,700	22,485	31,500	11,643	58,750	$300,258
								$2,398,915

*Includes cost of fringe-benefit program, which was 10 percent of base salary.
†Salary of Jim Sprague's predecessor.

profit quotas were assigned in a manner that took into account variation in price competition. Thus he felt that poor performance in the gross profit quota area reflected misallocated sales efforts either in terms of customers or in the mix of product line items sold. To provide himself with a frame of reference, Jim had also requested data on the north-central sales district (District 7). This district was

■ **Exhibit 4**   District Contribution to Corporate Administrative Expense and Profit, 1985

District	Sales	Gross Profit	Selling Expenses	Contribution to Administrative Expense and Profit
1	$ 3,906,000	$1,589,000	$ 388,416	$1,200,544
2	3,740,000	1,529,000	351,346	1,177,654
3	3,406,000	1,239,000	368,529	870,471
4	3,318,000	1,295,000	348,153	946,847
5	3,210,000	1,186,000	326,558	859,442
6	3,205,000	1,179,000	315,376	863,624
7	3,105,000	1,310,000	300,258	1,009,742
	$23,890,000	$9,327,000	$2,398,636	$6,928,324

■ **Exhibit 5**   Northeast (#3) and North-Central (#7) District Sales and Gross Profit Performance by Account Category, 1985

District	(A)	(B)	(C)	Total
	Sales by Account Category			
Northeast	$915,000	$1,681,000	$810,000	$3,406,000
North-central	751,000	1,702,000	652,000	3,105,000
	Gross Profit by Account Category			
Northeast	$356,000	$ 623,000	$260,000	$1,239,000
North-central	330,000	725,000	255,000	1,310,000

■ **Exhibit 6**   Notential Accounts, Active Accounts, and Account Call Coverage: Northeast and North-Central Districts, 1985

District	Potential Accounts			Active Accounts			Account Coverage (total calls)		
	(A)	(B)	(C)	(A)	(B)	(C)	(A)	(B)	(C)
Northeast	90	381	635	53	210	313	1,297	3,051	2,118
North-central	60	286	499	42	182	218	1,030	2,618	1,299

generally considered to be one of the best, if not the best, in the company. Further-more, the north-central district sales manager, who was only three years older than Jim, was highly regarded by the national sales manager.

■ The Company and Industry

The Hanover-Bates Chemical Corporation was a leading producer of processing chemicals for the chemical plating industry. The company's products were pro-duced in four plants located in Los Angeles, Houston, Chicago, and Newark, New Jersey. The company's production process was, in essence, a mixing operation. Chemicals purchased from a broad range of suppliers were mixed according to a variety of user-based formulas. Company sales in 1985 had reached a new high of $23.89 million, up from $21.98 million in 1984. Net pretax profit in 1985 had been

$3.822 million, up from $3.169 million in 1984. Hanover-Bates had a strong balance sheet, and the company enjoyed a favorable price-earnings ratio on its stock, which traded on the OTC market.

Although Hanover-Bates did not produce commodity-type chemicals (e.g., sulfuric acid and others), industry customers tended to perceive minimal quality differences among the products produced by Hanover-Bates and its competitors. Given the lack of variation in product quality and the industrywide practice of limited advertising expenditures, field sales efforts were of major importance in the marketing programs of all firms in the industry.

Hanover-Bates's market consisted of several thousand job-shop and captive (in-house) plating operations. Chemical platers process a wide variety of materials including industrial fasteners (e.g., screws, rivets, bolts, washers, and others), industrial components (e.g., clamps, casing, coupling, and others), and miscellaneous items (e.g., umbrella frames, eyelets, decorative items, and others). The chemical plating process involves the electrolytic application of metallic coatings such as zinc, cadmium, nickel, brass, and so forth. The degree of required plating precision varies substantially, with some work being primarily decorative, some involving relatively loose standards (e.g., 0.0002 zinc, which means that anything over two ten-thousandths of an inch of plate is acceptable), and some involving relatively precise standards (e.g., 0.0003–0.0004 zinc).

Regardless of the degree of plating precision involved, quality control is of critical concern to all chemical platers. Extensive variation in the condition of materials received for plating requires a high level of service from the firms supplying chemicals to platers. This service is normally provided by the sales representatives of the firm(s) supplying the plater with processing chemicals.

Hanover-Bates and the majority of the firms in its industry produced the same line of basic processing chemicals for the chemical plating industry. The line consisted of a trisodium phosphate cleaner (SBX), anesic aldehyde brightening agents for zinc plating (ZBX), cadmium plating (CBX), and nickel plating (NBX), a protective post-plating chromate dip (CHX), and a protective burnishing compound (BUX). The company's product line is detailed as follows:

Product	Container Size	List Price	Gross Margin
SPX	400-lb. drum	$ 80	$28
ZBX	50-lb. drum	76	34
CBX	50-lb. drum	76	34
NBX	50-lb. drum	80	35
CHX	100-lb. drum	220	90
BUX	400-lb. drum	120	44

■ Company Sales Organization

Hanover-Bates's sales organization consisted of 40 sales representatives operating in seven sales districts. Sales representatives' salaries ranged from $14,000 to $24,000, with fringe-benefit costs amounting to an additional 10 percent of salary. In addition to their salaries, Hanover-Bates's sales representatives received commissions of 0.5 percent of their dollar sales volume on all sales up to their sales quotas. The commission on sales in excess of quota was 1 percent.

In 1983 the national sales manager of Hanover-Bates had developed a sales program based on selling the full line of Hanover-Bates products. He believed that if the sales representatives could successfully carry out his program, benefits would accrue to both Hanover-Bates and its customers:

1. Sales volume per account would be greater and selling costs as a percentage of sales would decrease.
2. A Hanover-Bates sales representative could justify spending more time with such an account, thus becoming more knowledgeable about the account's business and becoming better able to provide technical assistance and identify selling opportunities.
3. Full-line sales would strengthen Hanover-Bates's competitive position by reducing the likelihood of account loss to other plating chemical suppliers (a problem that existed in multiple-supplier situations).

The national sales manager's 1983 sales program had also included the following account call-frequency guidelines:

- A accounts (major accounts generating $12,000 or more in yearly sales)—two calls per month.
- B accounts (medium-sized accounts generating $6,000–$11,999 in yearly sales)—one call per month.
- C accounts (small accounts generating less than $6,000 yearly in sales)—one call every two months.

The account call-frequency guidelines were developed by the national sales manager after discussions with the district managers. The national sales manager had been concerned about the optimum allocation of sales effort to accounts and felt that the guidelines would increase the efficiency of the company's sales force, although not all of the district sales managers agreed with this conclusion.

It was common knowledge in Hanover-Bates's corporate sales office that Jim Sprague's predecessor as northeast district sales manager had not been one of the company's better district sales managers. His attitude toward the sales plans and programs of the national sales manager had been one of reluctant compliance rather than acceptance and support. When the national sales manager succeeded in persuading Jim Sprague's predecessor to take early retirement, he had been faced with the lack of an available qualified replacement.

Hank Carver, who most of the sales representatives had assumed would get the district manager job, had been passed over in part because he would be 65 in three years. The national sales manager had not wanted to face the same replacement problem again in three years and also had wanted someone in the position who would be more likely to be responsive to the company's sales plans and policies. The appointment of Jim Sprague as district manager had caused considerable talk, not only in the district but also at corporate headquarters. In fact, the national sales manager had warned Jim that "a lot of people are expecting you to fall on your face . . . they don't think you have the experience to handle the job, in particular, and to manage and motivate a group of sales representatives, most of whom are considerably older and more experienced than you." The national sales manager had concluded by saying, "I think you can handle the job, Jim. . . . I think you can manage those sales reps and improve the district's profit performance . . . and I'm depending on you to do both."

Case 14 Wind Technology

Ken Manning
University of South Carolina

Jakki J. Mohr
University of Montana

Kevin Cage, general manager of Wind Technology, sat in his office on a Friday afternoon watching the snow fall outside his window. It was January 1991 and he knew that during the month ahead he would have to make some difficult decisions regarding the future of his firm, Wind Technology. The market for the wind profiling radar systems that his company designed had been developing at a much slower rate than he had anticipated.

■ The Situation

During Wind Technology's 10-year history, the company had produced a variety of weather-related radar and instrumentation. In 1986, the company condensed its product mix to include only wind-profiling radar systems. Commonly referred to as wind profilers, these products measure wind and atmospheric turbulence for weather forecasting, detection of wind direction at NASA launch sites, and other meteorological applications (i.e., at universities and other scientific monitoring stations). Kevin had felt that this consolidation would position the company as a leader in what he anticipated to be a high-growth market with little competition.

Wind Technology's advantages over Unisys, the only other key player in the wind-profiling market, included the following: (1) The company adhered stringently to specifications and quality production; (2) Wind Technology had the technical expertise to provide full system integration. This allowed customers to order either basic components or a full system including software support; (3) Wind Technology's staff of meteorologists and atmospheric scientists provided the customer with sophisticated support, including operation and maintenance training and field assistance; (4) Finally, Wind Technology had devoted all of its resources to its wind-profiling business. Kevin believed that the market would perceive this as an advantage over a large conglomerate like Unisys.

Wind Technology customized each product for individual customers as the need arose; the total system could cost a customer from $400,000 to $5 million. Various governmental entities, such as the Department of Defense, NASA, and state universities had consistently accounted for about 90 percent of Wind Technology's sales. In lieu of a field sales force, Wind Technology relied on top management and a team of engineers to call on prospective and current customers. Approximately $105,000 of their annual salaries was charged to a direct selling expense.

This case was prepared by Ken Manning of the University of South Carolina and Jakki J. Mohr, University of Montana. This case is intended for use as a basis for class discussion rather than to illustrate either effective or ineffective administrative decision making. Some data are disguised. Copyright © by Jakki Mohr 1990. All rights reserved.

The Problem

The consolidation strategy that the company had undertaken in 1986 was partly due to the company being purchased by Vaitra, a high-technology European firm. Wind Technology's ability to focus on the wind-profiling business had been made possible by Vaitra's financial support. However, since 1986 Wind Technology had shown little commercial success, and due to low sales levels, the company was experiencing severe cash-flow problems. Kevin knew that Wind Technology could not continue to meet payroll much longer. Also, he had been informed that Vaitra was not willing to pour more money into Wind Technology. Kevin estimated that he had from 9 to 12 months (until the end of 1991) in which to implement a new strategy with the potential to improve the company's cash flow. The new strategy was necessary to enable Wind Technology to survive until the wind-profiler market matured. Kevin and other industry experts anticipated that it would be two years until the wind-profiling market achieved the high growth levels that the company had initially anticipated.

One survival strategy that Kevin had in mind was to spin off and market component parts used in making wind profilers. Initial research indicated that, of all the wind-profiling system's component parts, the high-voltage power supply (HVPS) had the greatest potential for commercial success. Furthermore, Kevin's staff on the HVPS product had demonstrated knowledge of the market. Kevin felt that by marketing the HVPS, Wind Technology could reap incremental revenues, with very little addition to fixed costs. (Variable costs would include the costs of making and marketing the HVPS. The accounting department had estimated that production costs would run approximately 70 percent of the selling price, and that 10 percent of other expenses—such as top management direct-selling expenses—should be charged to the HVPS.)

High-Voltage Power Supplies

For a vast number of consumer and industrial products that require electricity, the available voltage level must be transformed to different levels and types of output. The three primary types of power supplies include linears, switchers, and converters. Each type manipulates electrical current in terms of the type of current (AC or DC) and/or the level of output (voltage). Some HVPS manufacturers focus on producing a standardized line of power supplies, while others specialize in customizing power supplies to the user's specifications.

High-voltage power supplies vary significantly in size and level of output. Small power supplies with relatively low levels of output (under 3 kV[1]) are used in communications equipment. Medium-sized power supplies that produce an output between 3 and 10 kV are used in a wide range of products including radars and lasers. Power supplies that produce output greater than 10 kV are used in a variety of applications, such as high-powered X rays and plasma-etching systems.

Background on Wind Technology's HVPS

One of Wind Technology's corporate strategies was to control the critical technology (major component parts) of its wind-profiling products. Management felt that this control was important since the company was part of a high-technology indus-

---

[1]kV (kilovolt): 1,000 volts.

try in which confidentiality and innovation were critical to each competitor's success. This strategy also gave Wind Technology a differential advantage over its major competitors, all of whom depended on a variety of manufacturers for component parts. Wind Technology had successfully developed almost all of the major component parts and the software for the wind profiler, yet the development of the power supply had been problematic.

To adhere to the policy of controlling critical technology in product design (rather than purchasing an HVPS from an outside supplier), Wind Technology management had hired Anne Ladwig and her staff of HVPS technicians to develop a power supply for the company's wind-profiling systems. Within six months of joining Wind Technology, Anne and her staff had completed development of a versatile power supply which could be adapted for use with a wide variety of equipment. Some of the company's wind-profiling systems required up to ten power supplies, each modified slightly to carry out its role in the system.

Kevin Cage had delegated the responsibility of investigating the sales potential of the company's HVPS to Anne Ladwig since she was very familiar with the technical aspects of the product and had received formal business training while pursuing an MBA. Anne had determined that Wind Technology's HVPS could be modified to produce levels of output between 3 and 10 kV. Thus, it seemed natural that if the product was brought to market, Wind Technology should focus on applications in this range of output. Wind Technology also did not have the production capabilities to compete in the high-volume, low-voltage segment of the market, nor did the company have the resources and technical expertise to compete in the high-output (10 kV +) segment.

The Potential Customer

Power supplies in the 3–10 kV range could be used to conduct research, to produce other products, or to place as a component into other products such as lasers. Thus, potential customers could include research labs, large end-users, OEMs, or distributors. Research labs each used an average of three power supplies; other types of customers ordered a widely varying quantity.

HVPS users were demanding increasing levels of reliability, quality, customization, and system integration. *System integration* refers to the degree to which other parts of a system are dependent upon the HVPS for proper functioning, and the extent to which these parts are combined into a single unit or piece of machinery.

Anne had considered entering several HVPS market segments in which Wind Technology could reasonably compete. She had estimated the domestic market potential of these segments at $237 million. To evaluate these segments, Anne had compiled growth forecasts for the year ahead and had evaluated each segment in terms of the anticipated level of customization and system integration demanded by the market. Anne felt that the level of synergy between Wind Technology and the various segments was also an important consideration in selecting a target market. Exhibit 1 summarizes this information. Anne believed that if the product was produced, Wind Technology's interests would be best served by selecting only one target market on which to concentrate initially.

Competition

To gather competitive information, Anne contacted five HVPS manufacturers. She found that the manufacturers varied significantly in terms of size and marketing

■ **Exhibit 1**   HVPS Market Segments in the 3–10 kV Range

Application	Forecasted Annual Growth (%)	Level of Customization/ Level of System Integration*	Synergy Rating**	Percent of $237 Million Power Supply Market***
General/Univ. laboratory	5.40	Medium/medium	3	8
Lasers	11.00	Low/medium	4	10
Medical equipment	10.00	Medium/medium	3	5
Microwave	12.00	Medium/high	4	7
Power modulators	3.00	Low/low	4	25
Radar systems	11.70	Low/medium	5	12
Semiconductor	10.10	low/low	3	23
X-ray systems	8.60	Medium/high	3	10

* The level of customization and system integration generally in demand within each of the applications is defined as low, medium, or high.

** Synergy ratings are based on a scale of 1 to 5; 1 is equivalent to a very low level of synergy and 5 is equivalent to a very high level of synergy. These subjective ratings are based on the amount of similarities between the wind-profiling industry and each application.

*** Percentages total 100 percent of the $237 million market in which Wind Technology anticipated it could compete.

NOTE: This list of applications is not all-inclusive.

■ **Exhibit 2**   Competitor Profile (3–10 kV range)

Company	Gamma	Glassman	Kaiser	Maxwell*	Spellman
Approximate annual sales	$2 million	$7.5 million	$3 million		$7 million
Market share	1.00%	3.00%	1.50%		2.90%
Price**	$5,830	$5,590	$6,210	$5,000–$6,000	$6,360
Delivery	12 weeks	10 weeks	10 weeks	8 weeks	12 weeks
Product customization	No	Medium	Low	Medium	Low
System integration experience	Low	Low	Low	Medium	Low
Customer targets	Gen. lab.	Laser	Laser	Radar	Capacitors
	Space	Medical	Medical	Power mod.	Gen. lab.
	Univ. lab.	X ray	Microwave	X ray	Microwave
			Semiconductor	Medical equip.	X ray

*Maxwell was in the final stages of product development and stated that the product would be available in the spring. Maxwell anticipated that the product would sell in the $5,000–$6,000 range.

** Price quoted for an HVPS with the same specifications as the "standard" model developed by Wind Technology.

strategy (see Exhibit 2). Each listed a price in the $5,500–$6,500 range on power supplies with the same features and output levels as the HVPS that had been developed for Wind Technology. After she spoke with these firms, Anne had the feeling that Wind Technology could offer the HVPS market superior levels of quality, reliability, technical expertise, and customer support. She optimistically believed that a one-half percent market share objective could be achieved the first year.

Promotion

If Wind Technology entered the HVPS market, they would require a hard-hitting, thorough promotional campaign to reach the selected target market. Three factors made the selection of elements in the promotion mix especially important to Wind Technology: (1) Wind Technology's poor cash flow, (2) the lack of a well-developed marketing department, and (3) the need to generate incremental revenue from sales of the HVPS at a minimum cost. In fact, a rule of thumb used by Wind Technology was that all marketing expenditures should be about 9 to 10 percent of sales. Kevin and Anne were contemplating the use of the following elements:

1. Collateral Material.
Sales literature, brochures, and data sheets are necessary to communicate the product benefits and features to potential customers. These materials are designed to be (1) mailed to customers as part of direct-mail campaigns or in response to customer requests, (2) given away at trade shows, and (3) left behind after sales presentations.

Because no one in Wind Technology was an experienced copywriter, Anne and Kevin considered hiring a marketing communications agency to write the copy and to design the layout of the brochures. This agency would also complete the graphics (photographs and artwork) for the collateral material. The cost for 5,000 pieces (including the 10 percent markup for the agency) was estimated to be $5.50 each.

2. Public Relations.
Kevin and Anne realized that one very cost-efficient tool of promotion is publicity. They contemplated sending out new product announcements to a variety of trade journals whose readers were part of Wind Technology's new target market. By using this tool, interested readers could call or write to Wind Technology, and the company could then send the prospective customers collateral material. The drawback of relying too heavily on this element was very obvious to Kevin and Anne—the editors of the trade journals could choose not to print Wind Technology's product announcements if their new product was not deemed newsworthy.

The cost of using this tool would include the time necessary to write the press release and the expense of mailing the release to the editors. Direct costs were estimated by Wind Technology to be $500.

3. Direct Mail.
Kevin and Anne were also contemplating a direct-mail campaign. The major expenditure for this option would be buying a list of prospects to whom the collateral material would be mailed. Such lists usually cost around $5,000, depending upon the number of names and the list quality. Other costs would include postage and the materials mailed. These costs were estimated to be $7,500 for a mailing of 1,500.

4. Trade Shows.
The electronics industry had several annual trade shows. If they chose to exhibit at one of these trade shows, Wind Technology would incur the cost of a booth, the space at the show, and the travel and incidental costs of the people attending the show to staff the booth. Kevin and Anne estimated these costs at approximately $50,000 for the exhibit, space, and materials, and $50,000 for a staff of five people to attend.

5. Trade Journal Advertising.
Kevin and Anne also contemplated running a series of ads in trade journals. Several journals they considered are listed in Exhibit 3, along with circulation, readership, and cost information.

■ **Exhibit 3** Trade Publications

Trade Publication	Editorial	Cost per Color Insertion (1 page)	Circulation
Electrical Manufacturing	For purchasers and users of power supplies, transformers, and other electrical products.	$4,077	35,168 nonpaid
Electronic Component News	For electronics OEM's. Products addressed include work stations, power sources, chips, etc.	$6,395	110,151 nonpaid
Electronic Manufacturing News	For OEM's in the industry of providing manufacturing and contracting of components, circuits, and systems.	$5,075	25,000 nonpaid
Design News	For design OEM's covering components, systems, and materials.	$8,120	170,033 nonpaid
Weatherwise	For meteorologists covering imaging, radar, etc.	$1,040	10,186 paid

NOTE: This is a partial list of applicable trade publications. Standard Rate and Data Service lists other possible publications.

6. Personal Selling. **(a)** *Telemarketing* (Inbound/Inside Sales).[2] Kevin and Anne also considered hiring a technical salesperson to respond to HVPS product inquiries generated by product announcements, direct mail, and advertising. This person's responsibilities would include answering phone calls, prospecting, sending out collateral material, and following up with potential customers. The salary and benefits for one individual would be about $50,000.

(b) *Field Sales.* The closing of sales for the HVPS might require some personal selling at the customer's location, especially if Wind Technology pursued the customized option. Kevin and Anne realized that potentially this would provide them with the most incremental revenue, but it also had the potential to be the most costly tool. Issues such as how many salespeople to hire, where to position them in the field (geographically), and so on, were major concerns. Salary plus expenses and benefits for an outside salesperson were estimated to be about $80,000.

Decisions

As Kevin sat in his office and perused the various facts and figures, he knew that he would have to make some quick decisions. He sensed that the decision about whether or not to proceed with the HVPS spin-off was risky, but he felt that to not do something to improve the firm's cash flow was equally risky. Kevin also knew that if he decided to proceed with the HVPS, there were a number of segments in that market in which Wind Technology could position its HVPS. He mulled over which segment appeared to be a good fit for Wind Technology's abilities (given Anne's recommendation that a choice of one segment would be best). Finally, Kevin was concerned that if they entered the HVPS market, that promotion for their product would be costly, further exacerbating the cash flow situation. He knew that promotion would be necessary, but the exact mix of elements would have to be designed with financial constraints in mind.

---

[2]"Inbound" refers to calls that potential customers make to Wind Technology, rather than "outbound," in which Wind Technology calls potential customers (i.e., solicits sales).

Case 15   Longevity Healthcare Systems, Inc.

Lawrence M. Lamont and Elizabeth W. Storey
both of Washington and Lee University

■ Introduction

Kathryn Hamilton, President of Longevity Healthcare Systems, Inc., located in Grand Rapids, Michigan, was reviewing the 1993 annual statements. "We concluded another terrific year," she commented. "Our sales and earnings exceeded expectations, but I'm concerned about the next few years." Although Longevity was successful, it was beginning to experience competition and the uncertainty of health care reform. In February, 1994, a large hospital in Grand Rapids, Michigan had converted an entire wing to a long-term care facility. The hospital also initiated an aggressive sales and advertising campaign and was competing with Longevity for new nursing home residents.

Longevity's recent acquisition of seven nursing homes in Toledo, Ohio, was also proving to be an unprofitable venture. Many of the residents were on Medicare and Medicaid and these health insurance programs generally did not reimburse the full costs of care. Additionally, the families of the Toledo residents were becoming value conscious and they frequently commented about the quality and cost of nursing care. Kathryn realized that to improve the profitability, attention would have to be given to customer satisfaction and attracting more profitable private-pay residents. Health care reform was also a source of concern. It was her belief that reform of the health care industry would be comprehensive with increased emphasis on cost control, competitive pricing and quality of care. She wondered what effect reform would have on Longevity and what the timetable for legislative action would be.

While increased competition and health care reform seemed certain, the most profitable path for future growth was not clear because several marketing opportunities existed. An aging population had created a strong demand for long-term care in nursing homes. Alzheimer's disease was also becoming more common and Longevity had recently lost some nursing home residents to Alzheimer's treatment centers because the company did not offer a specialized facility. Kathryn had to decide whether offering Alzheimer's treatment would be desirable.

Opportunities to expand existing businesses were also an option. The Grand Rapids pharmacy acquired in 1992 had been successfully phased into Longevity and Kathryn was wondering if a similar acquisition would work in Toledo. However, she was concerned about the impact of reform on the pricing of prescription drugs and medical supplies. To date, the pharmacy had been very profitable, but what would the future hold?

Geographic expansion of the firm's nursing and subacute care facilities might also be a profitable avenue for growth. Industry consolidation was making it possible to acquire nursing homes and unprofitable hospitals that could be converted to health care facilities. However, Kathryn envisioned that a future industry trend might be toward vertical integration of health care services. If so, it might make sense to further integrate Longevity's business in the Grand Rapids and Toledo markets before committing to additional geographic expansion.

Beyond decisions on the future direction of Longevity, Kathryn wondered if it was time to begin thinking about a more formal approach to marketing. "I really need to get some ideas about marketing in our different businesses down on paper so I can see how they fit with my views on an overall corporate marketing strategy," she remarked.

■ History of Longevity Healthcare Systems, Inc.

In 1972, Kathryn Hamilton, R.N., was searching for a nursing home for her mother in Grand Rapids, Michigan. Discouraged by a six-month wait for admission, she decided to move her into the home she occupied with her husband, Richard Hamilton, M.D., who enjoyed a medical practice in Grand Rapids specializing in care for older adults.

A Nursing Home Business

In 1974, Richard's mother and father joined the household, and Kathryn and Richard continued to learn how to care for older adults. In 1976, the Hamiltons leased a small, outdated 40-bed hospital in a nearby suburb and converted it into a long-term care facility. Following certification, the facility was opened in 1977 as the Longevity Nursing Home. In addition to their parents, 10 other adults over 65 entered the home during the year. All were "private pay," meaning they paid directly for services with personal assets, but without government assistance. By 1979, the nursing facility was fully occupied with private pay residents. Longevity was incorporated and Kathryn Hamilton became the President and its Director of Nursing, while her husband, Richard, provided medical services and continued his practice. The leased facility was purchased in 1979.

New Nursing Services

By 1980, Longevity found it necessary to add additional nursing services for aging residents. Two levels of care were added and professional nurses were hired to provide the services. The new services were favorably received and the referrals from residents and physicians kept the facility filled.

Expansion by Acquisition, 1980–85

The demand for nursing care was strong in the early 1980s and Longevity expanded. Eight unprofitable nursing homes with a total of 480 beds were acquired in Grand Rapids and nearby communities. All of the homes were licensed, certified by Medicare and Medicaid, and occupied by residents requiring a variety of nursing services. Shortly after the acquisition, Dr. Hamilton left his medical practice to join Longevity full-time as its Medical Director. He added skilled nursing care for residents requiring 24-hour-a-day care and rehabilitation services for those needing physical, speech, and occupational therapy.

Nursing Home Construction

From 1986–1988, Longevity expanded by constructing three 70-bed nursing homes in nearby communities.[1] Each provided the full range of nursing and rehabilitation services and was licensed for Medicare and Medicaid patients. The homes were quickly filled, and by the end of 1988 Longevity operated 12 nursing homes with a total of 730 beds. Employment had grown to 1,200 full-time and part-time employees.

New Business Opportunities

During a medical convention in 1990, Kathryn Hamilton noted a growing concern over the escalating costs of hospital care and the desire of insurance providers to shorten the hospitalization of patients requiring medical supervision, but not the other services traditionally provided by hospitals. Sensing an opportunity, the Hamiltons converted a 30-bed wing of one of the Grand Rapids nursing homes to a subacute care facility for patients that did not need the full services of a licensed acute care hospital. For patients moved from a hospital to the Longevity facility, the needed care was provided for about half the cost. The subacute care facility was licensed in 1991, and it quickly filled with referrals from hospitals, physicians and health care insurers.

The growing recognition that treating patients requiring subacute care in low overhead nursing facilities was a cost effective alternative, substantially increased the demand for Longevity's subacute care.[2] In 1992, following marketing research, Longevity constructed a 50-bed subacute care facility near one of its nursing homes. It was completed in 1993 and, within a few months, operated at capacity with patients referred from insurance companies, physicians, and Longevity nursing homes.

As the demand for specialized nursing and medical care expanded, it became apparent that profitability could be improved by operating a pharmacy. In 1992, Longevity acquired a retail pharmacy in Grand Rapids from a retiring pharmacist. It was converted into an institutional pharmacy to provide prescriptions, medical equipment and supplies, and consulting services to Longevity facilities.

---

[1]By 1988, all Longevity nursing homes were certified to receive Medicare and Medicaid patients. Medicare is a federally funded and administered health insurance program that reimburses health care facilities for nursing and medical services. Medicaid is a state-administered reimbursement program that covers skilled and intermediate long-term care for the medically indigent. The benefits paid by Medicaid programs vary from state-to-state.

[2]Medical services fall along a continuum from intensive care, acute care, subacute care, nursing care and home health care. Hospitals offer intensive and acute care for patients with complex medical conditions. They have fully equipped operating and recovery rooms, radiology services, intensive and coronary care units, pharmacies, clinical laboratories, therapy services and emergency services. Subacute care facilities owned by nursing homes serve the needs of patients who require nursing and medical care, but not many of the specialized services and equipment provided by an acute care hospital.

Geographic Expansion

Late in 1992, what appeared to be an exceptional business opportunity came to the attention of Kathryn and Richard Hamilton. A few hundred miles away, in Toledo, Ohio, a large health care company was selling seven unprofitable nursing homes with a total of 280 beds for $12,000,000. The homes were occupied primarily by Medicare and Medicaid patients and operated at 70 percent of capacity. The Hamiltons decided to take a one year option on the facilities while they raised the money to complete the purchase. Eventually, 40 percent of Longevity's common stock was sold to a large insurance company and some of the proceeds were used to exercise the purchase option. Kathryn Hamilton hired an experienced administrator and assigned him the task of returning the nursing homes to profitability. To reflect the company's broadening scope in the health care industry, the Hamiltons decided to change its name to Longevity Healthcare Systems, Inc. As shown in Exhibits 1 and 2, Longevity ended 1993 with 12 nursing homes, two subacute care facilities and a pharmacy located in Michigan, and 7 nursing homes located in Ohio. Exhibits 3 and 4 contain the financial statements for the year ending December 31, 1993. Exhibit 5 presents a five-year sales and earnings history, while Exhibit 6 provides some financial information for the pharmacy.

■ Longevity Marketing

Marketing was used to promote high occupancy in Longevity facilities, expand the percentage of private pay residents, and increase the profits of its institutional pharmacy.[3] Operating information for the health care facilities is shown in Exhibit 7 and the products and services marketed by Longevity are summarized in Exhibit 8.

Nursing care was marketed locally. The administrator and admissions director of each facility designed a marketing strategy to increase awareness of the nursing home and its services in the market it served. Personal selling using telemarketing and direct contact was targeted to referral sources such as physicians, hospital administrators, home health agencies, community organizations and churches, senior citizens groups, retirement communities, and the families of prospective residents. Longevity also distributed promotional literature discussing its philosophy of care, services, and quality standards. Frequently the literature was provided to prospective residents and their families when they inquired about nursing or toured the facilities.

Marketing for subacute care was directed by Kathryn Hamilton, who contacted insurance companies, managed care organizations such as HMOs, hospital administrators, and other third-party payors to promote Longevity's services. Kathryn also attended professional meetings where she maintained contact with the various referral sources.

---

[3]Managed care organizations provide health care products that integrate financing and management with the delivery of health care services through a network of providers (such as nursing homes and hospitals) who share financial risk or who have incentives to deliver cost-effective services. An HMO (Health Maintenance Organization) provides prepaid health care services to its members through physicians employed by the HMO at facilities owned by the HMO or through a network of independent physicians and facilities. They actively manage patient care to maximize quality and cost effectiveness.

■ **Exhibit 1**

Longevity Healthcare Systems, Inc., Historical Development, 1972–1993

Date	Activity
1972–75	Nursing care for parents.
1976–77	Leased a 40-bed hospital and converted it to a nursing home.
1979	Business incorporated as Longevity Nursing Home.
1979	Corporation purchased leased nursing home.
1980–85	Acquired 8 nursing homes in Grand Rapids area, 480 beds.
1986–88	Constructed 3 nursing homes in Grand Rapids area, 210 beds.
1990–91	Converted a 30-bed wing of Grand Rapids nursing home into subacute care.
1992–93	Constructed a 50-bed subacute care facility in Grand Rapids area.
1992	Acquired a retail pharmacy in Grand Rapids.
1992–93	Acquired 7 nursing homes in Toledo area, 280 beds.
1993	Corporation name changed to Longevity Healthcare Systems, Inc.

■ **Exhibit 2**

Longevity Healthcare Systems, Inc., Geographic Location of Longevity Healthcare Facilities

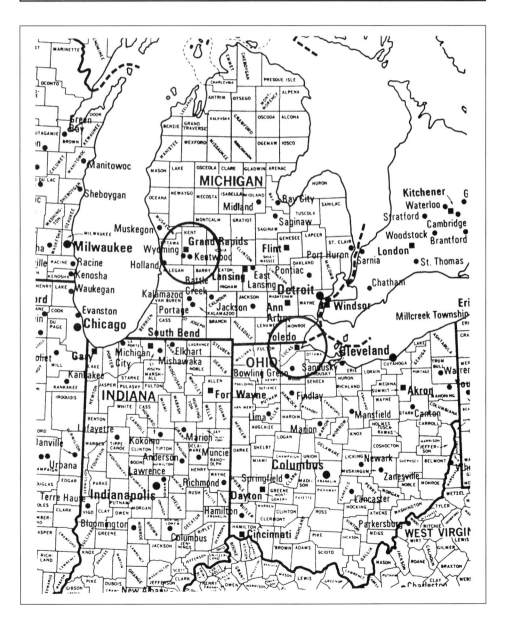

■ Exhibit 3

Longevity Healthcare Systems, Inc., Income Statement (Year Ending 12-31-93)

Net Revenues	
Basic LTC services	$45,500,000
Subacute medical services	9,000,000
Pharmacy services	3,000,000
Total revenues	$57,500,000
Operating Expenses	
Salaries, wages and benefits	$20,125,000
Patient services	21,275,000
Administrative and general	3,450,000
Depreciation and amortization	575,000
Total costs and expenses	$45,425,000
Income from operations	$12,075,000
Interest expense	1,726,111
Earnings before taxes	$10,348,889
Income taxes	4,139,555
Net income	$ 6,209,334
Net income per share	$ 0.78

■ Exhibit 4

Longevity Healthcare Systems, Inc., Balance Sheet (Years Ending 12-31-93 and 12-31-92)

Assets	1993	1992
Current Assets		
Cash and equivalents	$ 841,770	$ 501,120
Accounts receivable	3,265,584	2,702,552
Inventory	2,262,816	1,624,399
Property, Plant and Equipment		
Land	$ 9,959,051	$ 7,690,249
Buildings and improvements	27,002,416	13,622,079
Equipment	2,917,136	2,179,842
Accumulated depreciation	(4,028,149)	(2,464,535)
Other Assets		
Goodwill	$ 791,794	$ 655,278
Other long-term assets	5,163,275	4,063,190
Total Assets	$45,175,693	$30,574,174
Liabilities and Shareholders' Equity		
Current Liabilities		
Accounts payable	$ 1,250,201	$ 1,043,648
Accrued expenses	708,447	586,301
Accrued compensation	416,734	344,883
Current portion of long-term debt	2,041,995	2,700,120
Accrued interest	196,694	203,954
Long-term debt (net)	$10,506,622	$12,871,452
Shareholders' Equity		
Common stock, $.01 par value	$ 50,000	$ 50,000
Additional paid-in capital	17,870,666	3,848,816
Retained earnings	15,134,334	8,925,000
Total Liabilities and Shareholders' Equity	$45,175,693	$30,574,174

■ **Exhibit 5**
Longevity Healthcare
Systems Inc.,
Historical Revenues
and Net Income

Year	Revenues	Net Income
1993	$57,500,000	$6,209,334
1992	46,575,000	5,029,560
1991	37,260,000	3,017,736
1990	26,715,420	2,987,692
1989	21,799,783	1,334,147

■ **Exhibit 6**
Longevity Healthcare
Systems Inc., Selected
Pharmacy Information
(Year Ending 12-31-93)

Income Statement	1993
Net revenue	$3,000,000
Operating expenses	2,430,000
Operating income	570,000
Net income	390,000
Financial ratios	
Current ratio	1.94
Inventory turnover	4.20
Profit margin (%)	13.00
Return on assets (%)	9.29

■ **Exhibit 7**
Longevity Healthcare
Systems Inc., Operat-
ing Information for
Longevity Healthcare
Facilities (Year Ending
12-31-93)

Payor Mix	Grand Rapids	Toledo	Total
Private and other	69.7%	18.7%	44.2%
Medicare	8.4	17.8	13.1
Medicaid	21.9	63.5	42.7
Occupancy	96.4%	81.2%	88.8%
No. of beds	780	280	1,060

■ **Exhibit 8**
Longevity Healthcare
Systems Inc., Products
and Services

Business	Products/Services
Nursing care	Custodial care
	Assisted living
	Intermediate nursing care
	Skilled nursing care
Subacute care for	Lung and heart disease
	Coma, pain, and wound care
	Spinal cord injuries
	Head injuries
	Intravenous therapy
	Joint replacements
Rehabilitation services	Occupational therapy
	Physical therapy
	Speech therapy
Institutional pharmacy	Prescription drugs
	Nonprescription drugs
	Medical supplies
	Medical equipment
	Consulting services

Semi-private room, $105.00 per day	$3,150.00 per month
Basic telephone service	15.00
Rehabilitation therapy, 7.0 hours per month	840.00
Pharmacy and other specialized services	360.00
Miscellaneous personal expenses	50.00
Total	$4,415.00
Per day	147.17

[1]Based on private pay. Includes room and board, 24-hour professional nursing care, meals, housekeeping and linen services. Social and recreational activity programs are also included.

The products and services of the institutional pharmacy were marketed by the pharmacy manager and his assistant by direct contact with Longevity facilities, other nursing homes, hospitals, clinics and home health agencies. In addition to drugs and medical supplies, management also provided consulting services to help ensure quality patient care. These services were especially valuable because they enabled the nursing homes to admit patients that required more complex and profitable medical services.

Nursing Home Services

Longevity nursing homes provided room and board, dietary services, recreation and social activities, housekeeping and laundry services, four levels of nursing care, and numerous specialized services. Custodial care was provided to residents needing minimal care. Assisted living was used by persons needing some assistance with personal care such as bathing and eating. Intermediate care was provided to residents needing more nursing and attention, but not continual access to nurses. Finally, skilled nursing care was available to residents requiring the professional services of a nurse on a 24-hour-a-day basis. Rehabilitation therapy was also available for residents who had disabilities or were returning from hospitalization for surgery or illness. Rehabilitation was an important part of Longevity's care because it helped residents improve their quality of life.

Most of the residents in Longevity nursing homes were female and over 65. Although rates depended on accommodations and the services used, a typical nursing home bed generated monthly revenues of $4,415. It was common for residents to initially enter the nursing home needing only custodial care or assisted living and to progress to higher levels of nursing care as they aged. Exhibit 9 provides a typical schedule of monthly charges for a resident in a semiprivate room with seven hours of therapy.

All of the Longevity nursing homes were licensed in their respective states. Generally, the licenses had to be renewed annually. For renewal, state health care agencies considered the physical condition of the facility, the qualifications of the administrative and medical staff, the quality of care, and the facilities compliance with the applicable laws and regulations.

Subacute Care

Longevity marketed subacute care for patients with more complex medical needs that required constant medical supervision, but not the expensive equipment and services of an acute care hospital. Subacute care generated higher profit margins than nursing care, although patient stays in the facility were usually shorter.[4] Daily patient rates varied from $250 to $750 depending on the services and equipment required. Longevity's services included care for patients with lung and heart disease, spinal cord and head injuries, joint replacements, coma, pain and wound care, and intravenous therapy. Services at the subacute care facilities were not limited to the elderly. Younger patients discharged from hospitals were attractive because of their longer life expectancy and eventual need for nursing and rehabilitation. Based on an average rate of $1,000 per day charged by acute care hospitals, Longevity knew that its prices were substantially lower for comparable services. Like the nursing homes, the subacute care facilities were subject to licensing by the state health care agencies and certification by Medicare. All Longevity subacute care facilities were licensed and certified.

Pharmacy Products and Services

Longevity provided pharmacy products and services to nursing homes, retirement communities, and other health care organizations. The pharmacy's products were frequently customized with special packaging and dispensing systems and delivered daily. The pharmacy also consulted on medications and long-term care regulations and provided computerized tracking of medications, medical records processing, and 24-hour emergency services.

■ The Market for Long-Term Health Care

Long-term health care includes basic health care (such as that provided in nursing homes), rehabilitation therapy and Alzheimer's care, institutional pharmacy services, subacute care, and home health care. In recent years, spending for these and other health care services has increased significantly. For example, in 1993, one out of every seven dollars that Americans spent went to purchase health care. Total expenditures are projected to increase from $585.3 billion in 1990 to $3,457.7 billion in 2010; an annual growth rate of over 9 percent.

Nursing homes are important providers of long-term health care. Expenditures for nursing home care are expected to increase at a comparable rate, from $53.1 billion in 1990 to $310.1 billion in 2010. This industry consists of about 16,000 licensed facilities with a total of 1,700,000 beds. It includes a large number of small, locally owned nursing homes and a growing number of regional and national companies. The industry is undergoing restructuring in response to stricter regulation, increasing complexity of medical services, and competitive pressures. Smaller, local operators who lack sophisticated management and financial resources are being acquired by larger, more established companies. At present, the 20 largest firms operate about 18 percent of the nursing facilities. Consolidation is expected to continue, but the long-term outlook is extremely positive for the businesses that survive. Nursing home revenues increased by about 12 percent in 1993 and they are expected to experience similar gains in 1994. Several factors account for the optimistic outlook:

---

[4]Longevity profit margins for subacute care facilities were about 25 percent higher than for nursing care facilities. The length of stay was usually 20 to 45 days versus 8 months for private pay nursing care and 2 years for Medicaid patients.

Favorable Demographic Trends

Demographic trends, namely growth in the elderly segment of the population, are increasing the demand for health care and the services of nursing homes. Most of the market for nursing care consists of men and women 65 years of age and older. Their number was approximately 25 million in 1980 and is projected to increase to 35 million by 2000 and to 40 million by the year 2010. The 65-and-over segment suffers from a greater incidence of chronic illnesses and disabilities and currently accounts for about two thirds of the health care expenditures in the United States.

Pressures to Control Costs

Government and private payers have adopted cost control measures to encourage reduced hospital stays. In addition, private insurers have begun to limit reimbursement to "reasonable" charges, while managed care organizations are limiting hospitalization costs by monitoring utilization and negotiating discounted rates. As a result, hospital stays have been shortened and many patients are discharged with a continuing need for care. Because nursing homes are able to provide services at lower prices, the cost pressures have increased the demand for nursing home services and subacute care following hospital discharge.

Advances in Medical Technology

Advances in technology leading to improved medications and surgical procedures have increased life expectancies. Adults over age 85 are now the fastest growing segment of the population and their numbers are expected to double over the next 20 years. Many require skilled care and the medical equipment traditionally available only in hospitals. Nursing homes are acquiring some of the specialty medical equipment and providing skilled nursing care to older adults through subacute care facilities.

Limited Supply of Nursing Beds

The supply of nursing home beds has been limited by the availability of financing and high construction and start-up expenses. Additionally, the supply has been constrained by legislation limiting licenses for new nursing beds in states that require a demonstration of need. The effect has been to create a barrier to market entry and conditions where demand for nursing home services exceeds the available supply in many states.

◼ National Health Care Reform

The next decade will be a period of reform for the health care system. Although it is not clear how comprehensive the reform will be and how it will be financed, the focus will be to control costs and provide universal access to quality health care. The most likely plan will probably reform the health insurance industry, build on the current employer-financed approach and call for market incentives to control costs. To ensure universal access, insurance and managed care companies will be prohibited from dropping, rejecting, or pricing out of the market anyone with an expensive medical condition.

Reform will affect long-term care providers, such as nursing homes, in several ways. It will regulate the insurance companies to make health insurance more price competitive and affordable. This change will favorably impact long-term health care providers by increasing the number of residents paying with insurance benefits. Reform may also extend Medicare coverage for home health care. A change such as this would encourage more older adults to receive health care at home instead of at a nursing facility, resulting in an unfavorable impact.

Employers will also have incentives to control costs and deliver quality care. Increasingly they will rely on managed care organizations, such as HMO's, who are likely to contract lower cost providers, such as nursing homes, for subacute care and other cost effective services. Companies capable of providing a variety of health care services at attractive prices should see opportunities to expand demand.

Institutional pharmacies will also be impacted by health care reform. President Clinton's Health Security Act called for the addition of prescription drug coverage to the Medicare program. If adopted, this provision would probably decrease prices of prescription drugs by regulation of pharmaceutical manufacturers. Price decreases, either legislated or achieved through managed care and the market system, may allow institutional pharmacies to enjoy higher profit margins while still providing medications at affordable prices to patients.

■ Regulation and Competition

Health care providers are regulated at the state and federal levels. Regulation impacts financial management and the quality and safety of care. Ensuring that health care facilities are in compliance with regulatory standards is an important aspect of managing a health care business. In addition, management is increasingly confronted with competition. Nursing homes and subacute care facilities compete for patients who are able to select from a variety of alternatives to meet their needs. Managed care and insurance organizations also negotiate aggressively with health care providers to ensure quality care at attractive prices.

Financial Regulation

The Health Care Financing Administration (HCFA) is the federal regulatory agency for Medicare and Medicaid. Both programs are cost-based and use a per-diem payment schedule that reimburses the provider for a portion of the costs of care. Each facility must apply to participate in the Medicare and Medicaid programs and then have its beds certified to provide skilled nursing, intermediate, or other levels of care. A nursing home may have a mix of beds at any time, but it must match patient services to each bed. A facility cannot place a Medicare patient requiring skilled nursing care in a bed certified for intermediate care without recertifying the bed for skilled care. Recertification often required a month or more.

Quality and Safety of Care

Much of the current regulation facing nursing homes was developed in the Omnibus Budget Reconciliation Act of 1987 (OBRA 87). Facilities that participate in Medicare and Medicaid must be regularly inspected by state survey teams under contract with HCFA to ensure safety and quality of care. OBRA 87 also established a resident "bill of rights" that essentially converted nursing homes from merely custodial facilities into centers for rehabilitation. Nursing homes are now required to establish a care plan for patients and conduct assessments to ensure that the facility achieves the highest practical well-being for each resident.

Competition

Longevity competes with acute care and rehabilitation hospitals, other nursing and subacute care facilities, home health care agencies, and institutional pharmacies. Some offer services and prices which are comparable to those offered by Longevity.

Nursing homes compete on the basis of their reputation in the community, the ability to meet particular needs, the location and appearance of the facility, and the price of services. When a nursing facility is being selected, members of a prospective resident's family usually participate by visiting and evaluating nursing homes over a period of several weeks.

Some of the competing nursing homes in Grand Rapids and Toledo are operated by nonprofit organizations (churches and fraternal organizations) that can finance capital expenditures on a tax-exempt basis or receive charitable contributions to subsidize their operations. They compete with Longevity on the basis of price for private pay residents.

Longevity competes for subacute care patients with acute care and rehabilitation hospitals, nursing homes, and home health agencies. The competition is generally local or regional and the competitive factors are similar to those for nursing care, although more emphasis is placed on support services such as third-party reimbursement, information management, and patient record keeping. Insurance and managed care organizations exert considerable influence on the decision and increase the competition by negotiating with several health care providers.

The institutional pharmacy market has no dominant competitor in the markets served by Longevity. Twenty percent of the market is accounted for by the institutional pharmacies owned by nursing homes. Independent institutional pharmacies control about 35 percent of the market and retail pharmacies supply the remainder. Retail pharmacies are steadily being acquired by nursing homes and independents to gain market share and achieve economies of scale in purchasing prescriptions and medical supplies. Institutional pharmacies compete on the basis of fast, customer-oriented service, price, and the ability to provide consulting and information management services to customers.

■ Marketing Issues and Opportunities

Kathryn Hamilton believed that Longevity could improve its marketing. She was concerned about the efforts of individual nursing homes and the need to improve the marketing of subacute care to managed care providers. Finally, she believed that customer satisfaction would become an important competitive factor and Longevity would need to assess the reactions of nursing home residents and their families to the quality of its services.

Continued growth was also on Kathryn's mind. Population demographics and health care reform would create outstanding opportunities for businesses that could design and implement successful marketing strategies. For some time, she had been thinking about expanding into Alzheimer's treatment because of the demographics and the growing need for facilities in the Grand Rapids area. Additionally, she saw an opportunity to further integrate Longevity by establishing a pharmacy in Toledo or by acquiring nursing homes in a new market such as South Bend, Indiana. Each marketing opportunity seemed to make sense, so the final choices would be difficult.

Local Marketing of Health Care Services

Although local marketing had worked well, duplication of effort and overlapping market areas were becoming problems as the number of nursing homes in a market increased. Kathryn wondered what the marketing strategy for nursing home services should be and whether the marketing efforts of the Grand Rapids and Toledo nursing homes could be coordinated in each area to eliminate duplication and preserve local identity. One approach she was considering was to hire a marketing specialist to work with the nursing homes to attract more private pay customers. Advertising was a related issue because it had not been used, and Kathryn questioned whether it should be part of the marketing strategy. Should an advertising campaign be created for all of the nursing homes in a market, or should it be left to nursing home administrators to decide if advertising was appropriate in their strategy? If advertising was to be used, then a decision would have to be made on the type of advertising, the creative strategy, and the appropriate media.

Marketing Subacute Care

Subacute care was viewed as an attractive marketing opportunity because of the profit margins. However, to further penetrate the market, a marketing strategy would have to be developed. Kathryn noted that managed care organizations and other referral sources were like organizational buyers as they made decisions on subacute care for the cases they managed. Instead of marketing the service to physicians and patient families, Longevity would negotiate directly with HMOs and insurance companies to determine services and a rate structure based on the patient's medical needs. Personal selling would be used to build a relationship with the case managers for both the insurance company and the hospital. The marketing objective was to convince the insurance companies that the subacute unit could achieve the same patient outcomes at a lower cost than a hospital. If a marketing strategy could be developed along with appropriate staffing, it might be desirable to expand this part of Longevity's business. Economics favored conversion of a wing of an existing nursing home into a subacute care facility at a cost of $25,000 per bed. One possibility existed in Toledo where an unprofitable 80-bed facility was operating at 60 percent of capacity. If part of the facility was upgraded to subacute care, she expected that within a short time, it would operate at capacity.

Customer Satisfaction

Occasional complaints from nursing home residents about the price and quality of care were of concern to management. Since Longevity depended on referrals, customer satisfaction was an important element of a successful marketing strategy. In thinking about the issue, Kathryn noted that the license renewal process generally assured the maintenance of high standards in each facility, but it focused heavily on the inputs necessary to provide quality nursing care and not on customer satisfaction. Kathryn needed to decide what should be done to monitor individual nursing homes to assure customer satisfaction with Longevity's services.

Acquisition of a Toledo Pharmacy

One marketing opportunity being considered was the acquisition of a Toledo pharmacy. From management's perspective, an acquisition was interesting because it further integrated the existing health care operations and provided an incremental source of earnings from the Toledo market.

Management had identified an institutional pharmacy serving 15 nursing homes with 700 beds. It was offered at a cash price of $1,050,000 and generated annual revenues of approximately $1,450 per bed served. The pharmacy was quite profitable, with an average profit margin of 12.5 percent over the past five years. To consider the profitability of the acquisition, Kathryn believed it was reasonable to assume that the pharmacy would be able to support the Longevity facilities in Toledo and retain 60 percent of the nursing home beds it presently served if it was staffed with appropriate marketing support.

One concern was the impact of health care reform. Most of the nursing homes served by the pharmacy had a high percentage of Medicare and Medicaid patients. If the reimbursement rates for prescription drugs and medical supplies were to decline, then what seemed to be an attractive opportunity could quickly change.

Alzheimer's Treatment

Alzheimer's treatment was being considered because the demand for care was not being met and the development of a cure or drug therapy for the disease was progressing slowly. Kathryn believed that the demand for Alzheimer's treatment would grow at least as fast as the over-65 population. Projections from the U.S. Department of Health and Human Services indicated that by the year 2000, the Alzheimer's care market would increase by 50 percent from the present base of 4,000,000 presently suffering from the disease.

Longevity was considering establishing an Alzheimer's wing in two of the Grand Rapids nursing homes that served areas near older community residents. Each unit would serve 30 patients, and it would be self-contained and secured to protect residents against their wandering habits. The furniture and fixtures would also be renovated to meet the needs of the Alzheimer's patient, including softer colors, more subdued lighting, a separate nurses' station and a secured entrance. If an existing facility was converted, about six nursing rooms would have to be taken out of service to provide a separate activity and dining space. However, management reasoned that the revenue loss would be offset by average monthly revenues of $3,400 per patient and 15 percent lower costs than those for the average nursing home resident. Alzheimer's patients frequently required less costly care because of their younger age, better health, and a tendency to use fewer services. Longevity management had secured cost estimates that indicated the conversion costs would be $2,000 to $3,000 per bed.

In thinking about the opportunity Kathryn also recalled that Alzheimer's units typically had occupancy levels above 95 percent. Patients averaged a three-year length of stay and were almost always private pay. The marketing for Alzheimer's units focused on Alzheimer's associations, Alzheimer support groups, and church groups. Kathryn would have to decide how to position and market the Alzheimer's units so they would not appear to conflict with or be confused with the nursing home services. This would be a difficult but important marketing challenge because nursing homes that were known to operate Alzheimer's units tended to have better relationships with referral sources. Apparently they were perceived as providing an important community service.

■ Toward a Comprehensive Marketing Strategy

As Kathryn Hamilton completed her review of the financial statements, she was reminded of the need to make improvements in Longevity's marketing strategies. "I wish I could just write a one-paragraph statement of the corporate marketing strategy for this company. Then I could address each of the marketing issues and opportunities using my corporate strategy as a guide," she remarked.

Certainly one issue was improving existing marketing efforts. Marketing of nursing care, subacute care and the institutional pharmacy had been reasonably successful, but Kathryn felt uneasy about going another year without making needed changes. Since most of Kathryn's time was now needed to manage the business, additional marketing personnel would be necessary to develop and implement the marketing strategies for the various services. How many people would be needed and how the marketing effort would be organized also had to be decided.

Because Longevity was still evolving as a company with an uncertain marketing strategy, the most profitable direction for future growth was also important. Selecting attractive marketing opportunities was complicated because the choice depended on financial resources. Should Longevity expand the institutional pharmacy business, the subacute care business, or would resources be better utilized by offering Alzheimer's care? Each would bring Longevity closer to becoming an integrated health care provider.

Just as Kathryn moved to turn her personal computer off for the day, she noticed an electronic mail message from the administrator of the Toledo nursing homes. It said that for the first quarter of 1994, the seven nursing homes were breaking even at 81 percent occupancy and 25 percent private pay residents. When she arrived home that evening, she was greeted by her husband, Richard, who mentioned that

■ **Exhibit 10**   Longevity Healthcare Systems, Inc., Selected Demographic Information

	Grand Rapids[1]		**Toledo**		**South Bend**[2]	
Retired	235,513	18.9%	161,630	19.9%	119,401	20.0%
Age, Household Head						
55–64	77,383	12.4	54,421	13.2	40,661	13.4
65–74	71,142	11.4	52,772	12.8	39,448	13.0
75 and older	56,165	9.0	40,816	9.9	30,951	10.2
Median Age		44.5		46.1		46.7
Lifecycle Stage						
Married, 45–64	87,992	14.1	58,544	14.2	44,910	14.8
Married, 65 +	61,157	9.8	42,053	10.2	34,289	11.3
Single, 45–64	44,932	7.2	31,746	7.7	23,365	7.7
Single, 65 +	56,789	9.1	43,702	10.6	30,951	10.2
Median income	$ 32,928		$ 32,194		$ 31,264	
Adult population	1,246,101		812,212		597,003	
Nursing facilities[3]	439		988		590	
Total Nursing beds	49,927		92,518		64,263	

[1]Includes Kalamazoo and Battle Creek, Michigan.
[2]Includes Elkhart, Indiana.
[3]Statewide statistics for certified Medicare and Medicaid facilities and beds.

SOURCE: The Lifestyle Market Analyst, 1993. Health Care Financing Administration, 1991.

she had received a telephone call from a commercial real estate broker in South Bend, Indiana. The broker had located five nursing homes with a total of 450 beds that were being sold in a bankruptcy proceeding for $5,000,000. During dinner that evening, Richard mentioned that they needed to discuss the South Bend opportunity because the homes were attractively priced in a desirable market. It was his belief that in the future, the most profitable health care businesses would be vertically integrated and geographically diversified. Kathryn nodded in agreement as he handed her the summary information provided in Exhibit 10 and mentioned that a decision would have to be made in five days. She thought to herself, I wonder if it's financially possible?

Case 16　Virgin Atlantic Airways: Ten Years After

Pantéa Denoyelle and Jean-Claude Larréché
both of INSEAD

June 1994. Virgin Atlantic Airways celebrated the 10th anniversary of its inaugural flight to New York. Richard Branson, the airline's chairman and founder, reminisced about its tremendous growth. In 10 short years, he had established Virgin Atlantic as Britain's second largest long-haul airline, with a reputation for quality and innovative product development. Richard Branson turned his thoughts to the challenges that lay ahead.

■ The Origins of the Virgin Group

"Branson, I predict you will either go to prison, or become a millionaire." These were the last words that the 17-year-old Richard Branson heard from his headmaster as he left school. Twenty-five years later, Richard Branson ruled over a business empire whose 1993 sales exceeded £1.5 billion[1.] He had started his first entrepreneurial business at the age of 12, selling Christmas trees. Soon after leaving school, he set up *Student,* a national magazine, as "a platform for all shades of opinion, all beliefs and ideas . . . a vehicle for intelligent comment and protest." The magazine, whose editorial staff had an average age of 16, featured interviews by Richard Branson with celebrities, and articles on controversial issues.

In 1970, Richard Branson founded a mail-order record business—called Virgin to emphasize his own commercial innocence. The first Virgin record shop was opened in London's Oxford Street in 1971, soon followed by a recording studio and a label which produced records for performers such as Phil Collins, Genesis and Boy George. The Venue nightclub opened in 1978. In 1980, Virgin Records began expanding overseas, initially on a licensing basis; it later set up its own subsidiaries. Virgin Vision was created in 1983, followed by Virgin Atlantic Airways and Virgin Cargo in 1984, and Virgin Holidays in 1985.

In November 1986, the Virgin Group, which included the Music, Communication, and Retail divisions, was floated on the London stock exchange. The airline, clubs, and holidays activities remained part of the privately-owned Voyager Group Ltd. In its first public year, Virgin Group Plc had profit of £13 million on £250 million turnover(sales)—far beyond expectations. Its public status, however, was short lived: Richard Branson believed he could not be an entrepreneur while chairing a public company. In October 1988, he regained full control by buying back all outstanding shares. The constraints that he had struggled with during the company's public life were replaced by an overwhelming sense of relief and freedom. A partnership with Seibu Saison International, one of Japan's largest retail and travel groups, was equally brief. In 1990, Richard Branson sold 10 percent of the equity of

---

This case was prepared by Pantéa Denoyelle, Research Associate, under the supervision of Jean-Claude Larréché, Alfred H. Heineken Professor of Marketing at INSEAD. It is intended to be used as a basis for class discussion rather than to illustrate either effective or ineffective handling of an administrative situation.

[1]In June 1994, one pound sterling (£) = 1.51 US dollar ($).

■ **Exhibit 1**　The Virgin Group of Companies

Virgin consists of 3 wholly owned separate holding companies involved in distinct business areas from media and publishing to retail, travel and leisure. There are over 100 operating companies across the 3 holding companies in 12 countries worldwide.

Virgin Retail Group	Virgin Communication	Voyager Investments		
		Virgin Group	Voyager Group	Virgin Travel Group
Operates a chain of megastores in the UK, Continental Europe, Australia and Pacific selling music, video and other entertainment products.	Publishing of computer entertainment software	Investments: joint-ventures	Clubs & Hotels	UK's second largest long-haul international airline: Virgin Atlantic Airways
	Management of investments in broadcasting including Music Box. Investments in related publishing and entertainment activities, television post production services	Property developments	Airship and balloon operations	Freight handling and packaging
Operates game stores in the UK. Wholesale record exports and imports		Magnetic media distribution	Storm model agency	Inclusive tour operations: Virgin Holidays
Note:		Management and corporate finance services to the Virgin organization		
Marui of Japan own 50% of Virgin Megastores Japan	Book publishing			
WH Smith own 50% of Virgin Retail UK	Virgin Radio, Britain's first national commercial contemporary music station			

SOURCE: Virgin Atlantic.

Voyager Travel Holdings, the holding company for Virgin Atlantic, to the Japanese group in return for an injection of £36 million of equity and convertible loan capital—only to buy out his Japanese partner for £45 million in 1991.

In 1992, Richard Branson sold Virgin Music (by then the world's sixth largest record company) to Thorn EMI for £560 million. By 1994, the Virgin Group consisted of three holding companies: Virgin Retail Group, Virgin Communication, and Virgin Investments which controlled over 100 entities in 12 countries. Exhibit 1 summarizes the groups' activities.

■ The Creation of Virgin Atlantic Airways

In 1984, Richard Branson was approached by Randolph Fields, a 31-year-old lawyer who wanted to start a transatlantic airline. Fields' plan was to operate a business class-only B747 service to New York. Richard Branson quickly made up his mind. He announced that the new airline, to be named Virgin Atlantic Airways, would be operational within three months. Needless to say, his decision struck Virgin's senior management as completely insane.

Richard Branson, who knew nothing about the airline business, set out to learn from the downfall of Laker Air, an airline launched in 1970 by Freddie Laker with six planes and 120 employees. Laker Air was originally designed as a low-risk business, flying under contract for package-holiday firms; in 1971, however, it introduced a low-budget, no-frills service between London and New York. Laker's overconfidence led to several mistakes, including purchasing three DC-10s before the U.S. government had approved his London-New York line, and generally ordering more aircraft than he could afford. He accumulated a £350 million debt while the big transatlantic carriers slashed prices. This eventually led to Laker Airways' demise in 1981.

Richard Branson hired two former Laker executives, Roy Gardner (who later became Virgin Atlantic's co-managing director) and David Tait. Branson decided that his new airline should not be all business class, but combine an economy section with a first class section at business class prices. His goal was clear: "To provide all classes of travellers with the highest quality travel at the lowest cost." Richard Branson also leased a second-hand 747. The contract he negotiated with Boeing had a sell-back option at the end of the first, second or third year; a clause protected Virgin against currency fluctuations. Another priority was to recruit air crew. Fortunately, British Airways had recently lowered the optional retirement age for its crew, creating a pool of experienced pilots from which Virgin could draw; this gave it the most experienced crew of any British airline.

Obtaining permission to fly to New York from American regulatory bodies was not easy; authorization to land at Newark was granted only three days before Virgin's first flight was scheduled. Forbidden to advertise in the U.S. until the approval, Virgin decided to launch a teaser campaign. Skywriters festooned the Manhattan sky with the words "WAIT FOR THE ENGLISH VIRGI. . . ."

Virgin Atlantic's inaugural flight took off from London on June 22, 1984, packed with friends, celebrities, reporters, and Richard Branson wearing a World War I leather flight helmet. Once the plane had taken off, passengers were surprised to see the cockpit on the video screen, where the crew—Richard Branson and two famous cricket players—greeted them. Although this was obviously a recording, it was a memorable moment for passengers.

Early Years (1984–89)

Virgin Atlantic's early years were slightly chaotic. "I love the challenge," Richard Branson said. "I suspect that before I went into the airline business, a lot of people thought I would never be able to make a go of it. It made it even more challenging to prove them wrong." Richard Branson's determination and enthusiasm, as well as the experienced management team that he assembled, made up for the initial amateurism.

Virgin Atlantic extended its operations progressively. Its early routes, all from London, were to New York (Newark since 1984 and John F. Kennedy airport since 1988), Miami (1986), Boston (1987), and Orlando (1988). Flights to Tokyo and Los Angeles were added in 1989 and 1990. In 1987, Virgin celebrated its one millionth transatlantic passenger. Until 1991, all Virgin flights left from London's Gatwick airport, which was much smaller than Heathrow. Virgin countered this commercial disadvantage with a free limousine service for Upper Class passengers and a Gatwick Upper Class lounge, inaugurated in 1990.

While Richard Branson had always befriended rock stars, he had otherwise kept a low profile. This changed when he launched the airline: "I knew that the only way of competing with British Airways and the others was to get out there and use myself to promote it," he explained. Richard made a point of being accessible to reporters and never missed an opportunity to cause a sensation, wearing a stewardess's uniform or a bikini on board, or letting himself be photographed in his bath. What really caught the public's attention were his Atlantic crossings. In 1986, his "Virgin Atlantic Challenger II" speedboat recorded the fastest time ever across the Atlantic with Richard Branson on board. Even more spectacular was the 1987 crossing of the "Virgin Atlantic Flyer"—the largest hot-air balloon ever flown and the first to cross the Atlantic. Three years later Richard Branson crossed the Pacific in another balloon from Japan to Arctic Canada, a distance of 6,700 miles, breaking all existing records with speeds of up to 245 miles per hour.

The Years of Professionalization (1989–94)

The professionalization of Virgin Atlantic's management began in 1989. Until then Virgin Atlantic had had a flat structure, with 27 people reporting to Richard Branson directly. As the airline expanded, it had outgrown its entrepreneurial ways, and needed to become customer-driven.

Richard Branson asked Syd Pennington, a veteran Marks & Spencer retailer, to look into the airline's duty-free business in addition to his other responsibilities at Virgin Megastores. Some time later, while coming back from a trip, Pennington learned that he had been promoted to co-managing director of the airline. When Pennington expressed his surprise, Richard explained: "It's easier to find good retail people than good airline people." Syd Pennington saw that Virgin Atlantic lacked controls and procedures, and he devoted himself to professionalizing its management. His objective was to infuse the business with Richard Branson's charisma and energy while also making it effective enough to succeed. Exhibit 2 has a five-year summary of Virgin Atlantic's financial performance and labor force. Exhibit 3 shows the three year evolution of passengers carried and market shares.

After years of campaigning, Virgin Atlantic was granted the right to fly out of Heathrow in 1991. Heathrow, Britain's busiest airport, handled 100,000 passengers a day—a total of 40 million in 1990, compared with 1.7 million at Gatwick. Virgin Atlantic was assigned to Heathrow's Terminal 3, where it competed with 30 other airlines serving over 75 destinations on five continents. In Richard Branson's eyes, gaining access to Heathrow was a "historic moment and the culmination of years of struggle." His dream to compete with other long-haul carriers on an equal footing had come true. A new era began for Virgin. Flying from Heathrow enabled it to have high load factors all year and to attract more business and full-fare economy passengers. It could also carry more interline flyers and more cargo, since Heathrow was the UK's main air freight center. On the morning of the airline's first flight from Heathrow, a Virgin 'hit squad' encircled the model British Airways Concorde at the airport's entrance and pasted it over with Virgin's logo. Richard Branson, dressed up as a pirate, was photographed in front of the Concorde before security forces could reach the site. A huge party marked the end of the day.

In April 1993, Virgin ordered four A340s from Airbus Industries, the European consortium in which British Aerospace had a 20 percent share. The order, worth over £300m, reflected the airline's commitment to new destinations. "We are proud to buy an aircraft which is in large part British-built, and on which so many jobs in

■ **Exhibit 2**
Financial Results and
Labor Force of Virgin
Atlantic Airways

Financial Year	Turnover (£m)	Profit (Loss) before Tax (£m)
1988/89	106.7	8.4
1989/90	208.8	8.5
1990/91	382.9	6.1
1991/92	356.9	(14.5)
1992/93	404.7	0.4

NOTE: The reporting year ends on 31 July until 1990, and on 31 October as of 1991. The 1990/91 period covers 15 months.

Year	Number of Employees*
1988	440
1989	678
1990	1104
1991	1591
1992	1638
1993	1627
1994	2602

*As of 31 December (31 May for 1994).
SOURCE: Virgin Atlantic.

■ **Exhibit 3**
Market Shares of
Virgin Atlantic Airways
(revenue passengers)

Route	1993	1992	1991
New York (JFK & Newark)	19.6%	17.2%	18.0%
Florida (Miami & Orlando)	33.2%	30.6%	25.2%
Los Angeles	23.6%	21.8%	25.8%
Tokyo	18.4%	15.5%	16.0%
Boston	22.2%	20.0%	15.3%
Total Passengers Carried	1,459,044	1,244,990	1,063,677

NOTE: Flights from Gatwick and LHR.
SOURCE: Virgin Atlantic.

the UK depend," said Richard Branson. The A340, the longest range aircraft in the world, accommodated 292 passengers in three cabins, and had key advantages such as low fuel consumption and maintenance costs. When the first A340 was delivered in December, Virgin became the first UK carrier to fly A340s. Virgin also ordered two Boeing 747-400s and took options on two others. It also placed a $19 million order for the most advanced in-flight entertainment system available, featuring 16 channels of video, which it planned to install in all three sections. In keeping with the airline's customization efforts, the new aircraft's cabin was redesigned. Upper Class passengers would find electronically operated 54-inch seats with a 55 degree recline and an onboard bar. There was a rest area for flight and cabin crew.

In June 1993, Virgin scheduled a second daily flight from Heathrow to JFK. "We've given travellers a wider choice on their time of travel," said Richard Branson. "The early evening departure is timed to minimize disruption to the working day, a welcome bonus to both busy executives and leisure travellers." In March 1994, Virgin put an end to British Airways' and Cathay Pacific's long-standing duopoly on the London-Hong Kong route, launching its own A340 service.

17th May 1994

NEW SAN FRANCISCO ROUTE MARKS CONTINUED EXPANSION
FOR VIRGIN ATLANTIC

A new service to San Francisco, its sixth gateway to the US, was launched today (17th
    May 1994), by Virgin Atlantic Airways, marking another stage in the airline's devel-
    opment as it approaches its tenth anniversary.

The daily Boeing 747 service from London's Heathrow airport follows further route
    expansion in February 1994 when the airline introduced a daily service to Hong
    Kong, using two of four recently acquired Airbus A340 aircraft.

Virgin Atlantic Chairman Richard Branson said: "San Francisco was always on our list
    of the 15 or so great cities of the world that we wanted to fly to, so it's a very proud
    moment for us finally to be launching this new service today.

"We regularly receive awards for our transatlantic flights so I hope that this new service
    will be able to provide consumers on both sides of the Atlantic with a better alterna-
    tive to the current duopoly which exists on the San Francisco/London route.

"Today's launch is also the culmination of a number of significant developments at
    Virgin Atlantic, not least of which is our recent acquisition of two new Boeing 747-
    400s and four Airbus A340s. This comes on the back of our $19 million investment in
    new 14 channel in-flight entertainment, which, unlike other airlines, we have made
    available to all of our passengers."

Mr. Branson added that it was the airline's intention to have one of the most modern
    and passenger-friendly fleets in the world. Virgin's current fleet comprises: eight
    B747s, three A340s, and an A320 and two BAe 146 Whisper Jets which are jointly
    operated with franchise partners in Dublin and Athens.

A daily service will depart Heathrow at 11.15, arriving in San Francisco at 14.05 local
    time. Flights leave San Francisco at 16.45, arriving in the UK the following day at
    10.45. For reservations call 0293 747747.

For further information:

James Murray
Virgin Atlantic Airways
Tel: 0293 747373

Virgin's first Boeing 747-400 was delivered in May 1994. Only days later, Virgin
opened its San Francisco line (until then a British Airways-United duopoly). In a
press release shown in Exhibit 4, Virgin emphasized the continuation of its expansion plans, the renewal of its fleet, and the "better alternative" that it offered
customers on both sides of the Atlantic. During the inaugural flight 150 guests—and
some fare-paying flyers who had been warned that it would not be a quiet flight—
were entertained with a fashion show and a jazz band. In San Francisco the aircraft
stopped near a giant taximeter. The door opened, Richard Branson appeared, and
inserted a huge coin in the taximeter, out of which popped the Virgin flag. Airport
authorities offered Richard Branson a giant cake decorated with a miniature Golden
Gate Bridge. Guests were entertained for a whirlwind five days which included a tour
of the Napa Valley and a visit to Alcatraz prison where Richard Branson was jailed in
a stunt prepared by his team. Virgin also took advantage of the launch to unveil a recycling and environmental program. A stewardess dressed in green—rather than the
usual red Virgin uniform—gave passengers information on the program, which had
delivered savings of £500,000 since it was launched in late 1993.

At the time of Virgin's 10th anniversary, its fleet comprised eight B747-200s, a B747-400 and three A340s. The airline awaited delivery of its second B747-400 and fourth A340 and also planned to retire two older B747-200s by the end of 1994. By then, half of its fleet would be brand new. By comparison, the average age of British Airways' fleet was eight years.[2] Richard Branson planned to expand his fleet to 18 planes which would serve 12 or 15 destinations by 1995. Proposed new routes included Washington D.C., Chicago, Auckland, Singapore, Sydney, and Johannesburg. The London–Johannesburg license, granted in 1992, had been a major victory for Virgin: when exploited, it will end a 50-year duopoly enjoyed by British Airways and South African Airways.

All Virgin Atlantic planes were decorated with a Vargas painting of a red-headed, scantily dressed woman holding a scarf. The names of most Virgin aircraft evoked the 'Vargas Lady' theme, starting with its first aircraft, "Maiden Voyager." (Exhibit 5 lists the aircraft's names). The first A340, inaugurated by the Princess of Wales, was christened "The Lady in Red."

Virgin Classes

Richard Branson originally proposed to call Virgin's business and economy classes Upper Class and Riff Raff respectively; in the latter case, however, he bowed to the judgment of his managers, who urged him to desist. Virgin Atlantic strove to offer the highest quality travel to all classes of passengers at the lowest cost, and to be flexible enough to respond rapidly to their changing needs. For instance, Virgin catered to the needs of children and infants with special meals, a children's channel, pioneering safety seats, changing facilities, and baby food.

"Offering a First Class service at less than First Class fares" had become a slogan for Virgin Atlantic. Marketed as a first class service at business class prices, Upper Class competed both with other carriers' first class and business class. Since its 1984 launch, this product had won every major travel industry award.

The Economy Class promised the best value for money, targeting price-sensitive leisure travellers who nevertheless sought comfort. It included three meal options, free drinks, seat-back video screens, and ice cream during movies on flights from London.

After years of operating only two classes, business and economy, Virgin had introduced its Mid Class in 1992 after realizing that 23 percent of Economy passengers travelled for business. Mid Class was aimed at cost-conscious business travellers who required enough space to work and relax. This full fare economy class offered flyers a level of service usually found only in business class, with separate check-in and cabin, priority meal service, armrest or seat-back TVs, and the latest in audio and video entertainment. Exhibit 6 shows Virgin's three sections: Upper Class, Mid Class and Economy.

Virgin's B747 configuration on the Heathrow/JFK route consisted of 50 seats in Upper Class, 38 in Mid Class, and 271 in Economy. The typical British Airways B747 configuration on the same route was 18 First Class seats, 70 seats in Club World, and 282 in World Traveller Class[3].

---

[2]BA's fleet had 240 aircraft, including some 180 Boeings, 7 Concordes, 10 A320s, 15 BAe ATPs, and 7 DC10s.

[3]As of April 1994, the Club World and World Traveller—Euro Traveller for flights within Europe—were the names given to British Airways' former Business and Economy Classes respectively.

■ **Exhibit 5**
Virgin Atlantic Fleet

Aircraft	Type	Name	Into Service
G-VIRG	B747-287B	Maiden Voyager	1984
G-VGIN	B747-243B	Scarlet Lady	1986
G-TKYO	B747-212B	Maiden Japan	1989
G-VRGN	B747-212B	Maid of Honour	28/08/89
G-VMIA	B747-123	Spirit of Sir Freddy	09/05/90
G-VOYG	B747-283B	Shady Lady	10/03/90
G-VJFK	B747-238B	Boston Belle	06/03/91
G-VLAX	B747-238B	California Girl	28/05/91
G-VBUS	A340-311	Lady in Red	16/12/93
G-VAEL	A340-311	Maiden Toulouse	01/01/94
G-VSKY	A340-311	China Girl	21/03/94
G-VFAB	B747-4Q8	Lady Penelope	19/05/94
G-VHOT	B747-4Q8		delivery 10/94
G-VFLY	A340-311		delivery 10/94

SOURCE: Virgin Atlantic.

■ **Exhibit 6**
Virgin Atlantic's
Three Classes

UPPER CLASS

- Reclining sleeper seat with 15″ more legroom than other airlines
- Latest seat arm video/audio entertainment
- Unique Clubhouse lounge at Heathrow featuring health spa (includes hair salon, library, music room, games room, study and brasserie)
- Virgin Arrival Clubhouse with shower, sauna, swimming pool and gym
- Inflight beauty therapist on most flights
- Onboard lounges and stand up bars
- "Snoozzone" dedicated sleeping section with sleeper seat, duvet and sleep suit
- Complimentary airport transfers including chauffeur-driven limousine or motorcycle to and from airport
- Free confirmable Economy ticket for round trip to US/Tokyo

(continued)

Service the Virgin Way

Virgin Atlantic wanted to provide the best possible service while remaining original, spontaneous and informal. Its goal was to turn flying into a unique experience, not to move passengers from one point to another. It saw itself not only in the airline business but also in entertainment and leisure. According to a staff brochure:

> We must be memorable, we are not a bus service. The journeys made by our customers are romantic and exciting, and we should do everything we can to make them feel just that. That way they will talk about the most memorable moments long after they leave the airport.

Virgin Atlantic saw that as it became increasingly successful, it risked also becoming complacent. The challenge was to keep up customers' interest by keeping service at the forefront of activities. Virgin was often distinguished for the quality and consistency of its service (as shown in Exhibit 7); it won the Executive Travel Airline of the Year award for an unprecedented three consecutive years. Service delivery, in other words 'getting it right the first time' was of key importance. The airline was also perceived to excel in the art of service recovery, where it aimed to be proactive,

■ **Exhibit 6**
(*concluded*)

MID CLASS

- Separate check-in and cabin
- Most comfortable economy seat in the world with 38″ seat pitch (equivalent to many airlines' business class seat)
- Complimentary pre-take off drinks and amenity kits
- Frequent Flyer programme
- Priority meal service
- Priority baggage reclaim
- Armrest/seatback TVs and latest audio/video entertainment

ECONOMY CLASS

- Contoured, space-saving seats, maximizing legroom, seat pitch up to 34″
- Three meal option service (including vegetarian) and wide selection of free alcoholic and soft drinks
- Seatback TVs and 16 channels of the latest inflight entertainment
- Pillow and blankets
- Advance seat selection
- Complimentary amenity kit and ice cream (during movies on flights from London)

SOURCE: Virgin Atlantic.

■ **Exhibit 7**   Awards Won by Virgin Atlantic

1994	**Travel Weekly** Best Transatlantic Airline	**The Travel Organization** Best Long Haul Airline	**Business Traveller** Best Business Class-Long Haul
Executive Travel Best Transatlantic Airline Best Business Class Best Inflight Magazine	**Travel Trade Gazette** Best Transatlantic Airline	**Conde Nast Traveller** In the Top Ten World Airlines	**World Airline Entertainment Awards** Best Overall Inflight Entertainment Best Inflight Audio Entertainment
	Courvoisier Book of the Best Best Business Airline	**Air Cargo News** Cargo Airline of the Year	Best Inflight Entertainment Guide (Outside Magazine)
Travel Weekly Best Transatlantic Airline	**ITV Marketing Awards** Brand of the Year—Service		**Onboard Services Magazine** Overall Onboard Service Award (Upper
1993	**Frontier Magazine**	**1990**	Class)
Executive Travel Airline of the Year	Best Airline/Marine Duty Free	**Executive Travel** Airline of the Year	**Which Holiday?** Best Transatlantic Airline
Best Transatlantic Carrier Best Business Class	**BPS Teleperformance** **UK Winner**	Best Transatlantic Carrier Best Inflight Entertainment	**Nihon Keizai Shimbun (Japan)**
Best Cabin Staff Best Food and Wine	Overall European Winner	**Business Traveller**	Best Product in Japan—for Upper Class
Best Inflight Entertainment Best Airport Lounges	**Meetings and Incentive Travel** Best UK Base Airline	Best Business Class—Long Haul	**1988**
Best Inflight Magazine Best Ground/Check-in Staff	**Ab-Road Magazine**	**Travel News (now Travel Weekly)**	**Executive Travel** Best Business Class—North Atlantic
Travel Weekly	Airline "Would most like to fly" Best Inflight Catering	Best Transatlantic Airline Special Merit Award to Richard	**Business Traveller**
Best Transatlantic Airline		Branson	Best Business Class—Long Haul
Travel Trade Gazette Best Transatlantic Airline	**1991**	**Travel Trade Gazette** Best Transatlantic Airline	**Travel Trade Gazette** Best Transatlantic Airline
TTG Travel Advertising Awards Best Direct Mail Piece	**Executive Travel** (Awards Given in 1992)	Travel Personality—Richard Branson	**1986**
	Business Traveller Best Business Class—Long Haul	**Avion World Airline Entertainment Awards**	**The Marketing Society** Consumer Services Awards
1992	**Travel Weekly**	Best Overall Inflight Entertainment	**What to Buy for Business**
Executive Travel (Awards given for 91/92) Airline of the Year	Best Transatlantic Airline	Best Video Programme Best Inflight Entertainment Guide	Business Airline of the Year
Best Transatlantic Carrier Best Long Haul Carrier	**Travel Trade Gazette** Best Transatlantic Airline	**Onboard Services Magazine**	
Best Business Class Best Inflight Food	Most Attentive Airline Staff	Outstanding Inflight Enter- tainment Programme	
Best Inflight Entertainment Best Ground/Check-in Staff	**Avion World Airline Entertainment Awards**	Outstanding Entertainment (for Sony Video Walkmans)	
Business Traveller	Best Inflight Videos—Magazine Style Best Inflight Audio—Programming	**The Travel Organization** Best Long Haul Airline	
Best Airline for Business Class- Long Haul	Best Inflight Audio of an Original Nature		
	Which Airline?	**1989**	
	Voted by the Reader as one of the Top Four Airlines in the World (the only British Airline amongst these four)	**Executive Travel** Best Transatlantic Airline Best Business Class in the World Best Inflight Entertainment	

SOURCE: Virgin Atlantic.

not defensive. It handled complaints from Upper Class passengers within 24 hours, those from Economy Class flyers within a week. If a flight was delayed, passengers received a personalized fax of apology from Richard Branson or a bottle of champagne. Passengers who had complained were occasionally upgraded to Upper Class.

Innovation

Virgin's management, who wanted passengers never to feel bored, introduced video entertainment in 1989. They chose the quickest solution: handing out Sony Watchmans on board. Virgin later pioneered individual video screens for every seat, an idea that competitors quickly imitated. In 1994, Virgin's onboard entertainment offered up to 20 audio channels and 16 video channels including a shopping channel and a game channel. A gambling channel would be introduced at year end. In the summer, a 'Stop Smoking Program' video was shown on all flights—Virgin's contribution to a controversy over whether smoking should be permitted on aircraft.

The presence of a beauty therapist or a tailor was an occasional treat to passengers. The beautician offered massages and manicures. On some flights to Hong Kong, the tailor faxed passengers' measurements so that suits could be ready on arrival. In 1990, Virgin became the only airline to offer automatic defibrillators on board and to train staff to assist cardiac arrest victims. A three-person Special Facilities unit was set up in 1991 to deal with medical requests. Its brief was extended to handle arrangements for unaccompanied minors or unusual requests such as birthday cakes, champagne for newlyweds, public announcements, or midflight marriage proposals. The unit also informed passengers of flight delays or cancellations, and telephoned clients whose options on tickets had expired without their having confirmed their intention to travel. Another service innovation was motorcycle rides to Heathrow for Upper Class passengers. The chauffeur service used Honda PC800s with heated leather seats. Passengers wore waterproof coveralls and a helmet with a built-in headset for a cellular phone.

In February 1993, Britain's Secretary of State for Transport inaugurated a new Upper Class lounge at Heathrow: the Virgin Clubhouse. The £1 million Clubhouse, shown in Exhibit 8, had an unusual range of facilities: Victorian style wood-panelled washrooms with showers and a grooming salon offering massages, aromatherapy and hair cuts; a 5,000-volume library with antique leather armchairs; a game room with the latest computer technology; a music room with a CD library; a study with the most recent office equipment. Many of the furnishings came from Richard Branson's own home: a giant model railway, the Challenger II Trophy, a three-meter galleon model. A two-ton, five-meter table, made in Vienna from an old vessel, had to be installed with a crane. Upon the opening of the Hong Kong route, a blackjack table was added at which visitors received 'Virgin bills' that the dealer exchanged for tokens. There was also a shoe shine service. Passengers seemed to enjoy the lounge. One remarked in the visitors' book: "If you have to be delayed more than two hours, it could not happen in a more pleasant environment."

Customer Orientation, Virgin Style

Virgin tried to understand passengers' needs and go beyond their expectations. While it described itself as a "niche airline for those seeking value-for-money travel", its standards and reputation could appeal to a broad spectrum of customers. It managed to serve both sophisticated, demanding executives and easygoing, price-sensitive leisure travellers in the same aircraft. According to Marketing Director

■ **Exhibit 8**   Virgin Atlantic Clubhouse

SOURCE: Virgin Atlantic.

Steve Ridgeway, Virgin attracted a broader range of customers than its competitors because it managed this coexistence between passenger groups better. This had enabled the airline to reach high load factors soon after opening new lines, as shown in Exhibit 9.

Virgin Atlantic initially had marketed itself as an economical airline for young people who bought Virgin records and shopped at Virgin stores, but gradually its target shifted. The danger, which Richard Branson saw clearly, was that people would perceive it as a 'cheap and cheerful' airline, a copy of the defunct Laker Airways. Richard Branson knew that his airline's survival depended on high yield business travellers. After establishing a strong base in leisure traffic, Virgin turned to the corporate segment and strove to establish itself as a sophisticated, business-class airline that concentrated on long-haul routes. The idea of fun and entertainment, however, was not abandoned. Upper Class was upgraded and incentives were added to attract the business traveller. By 1991, 10 percent of the airline's passengers and 35 to 40 percent of its income came from the business segment. Virgin's competitive advantage was reinforced through the combination of corporate travel

■ **Exhibit 9**

Load Factors of Virgin
Atlantic Airways

Year	Newark	Miami	Tokyo	JFK	Los Angeles	Boston
1990–1991	82.0%	89.5%	65.9%	76.9%	84.5%	83.3%
1989–1990	83.3%	92.1%	68.3%	74.2%	79.8%	
1988–1989	82.8%	86.7%	52.4%			
1987–1988	77.1%	85.0%				
1986–1987	74.4%	76.4%				
1985–1986	72.9%					
1984–1985	72.0%					

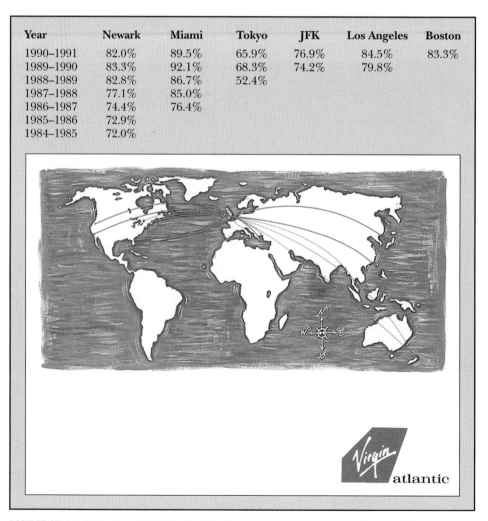

SOURCE: Virgin Atlantic promotional materials. This information is no longer made public since 1991.

buyers' price consciousness and the rising service expectations of travellers. Richard Branson actively wooed business customers by regularly inviting corporate buyers to have lunch at his house and seeking their comments.

As part of Virgin's drive to meet customers' standards, on each flight 30 passengers were asked to fill out a questionnaire. Their answers formed the basis of widely distributed quarterly reports. Virgin's senior managers flew regularly, interviewing passengers informally, making critical comments on the delivery of service and circulating their reports among top management. Richard Branson himself, who welcomed every opportunity to obtain feedback from customers, took time to shake hands and chat with passengers. The preoccupation with service was so strong that staff were often more exacting in their evaluation of each other than the customers were.

Business executives, unlike younger leisure travellers, did not readily relate to other aspects of the Virgin world: the records, the Megastores, the daredevil chairman. Their good feelings about Virgin stemmed mainly from their positive experiences with the airline. These tough and demanding customers appreciated Virgin's style, service, innovations and prices. Some were enthusiastic enough to rearrange their schedules in order to fly Virgin despite punctuality problems. Aside from complaints about flight delays, their only serious criticism was that Virgin did not serve enough destinations.

Virgin's People

Virgin Atlantic attracted quality staff despite the relatively low salaries it paid. In management's eyes, the ideal employee was 'informal but caring:' young, vibrant, interested, courteous and willing to go out of his or her way to help customers. Richard Branson explained:

> We aren't interested in having just happy employees. We want employees who feel involved and prepared to express dissatisfaction when necessary. In fact, we think that the constructively dissatisfied employee is an asset we should encourage and we need an organization that allows us to do this—and that encourages employees to take responsibility, since I don't believe it is enough for us simply to give it.

Richard Branson believed that involving management and staff was the key to superior results: "I want employees in the airline to feel that it is *they* who can make the difference, and influence what passengers get," he said. He wrote to employees regularly to seek their ideas and to ensure that relevant news was communicated to them. His home phone number was given to all staff, who could call him at any time with suggestions or complaints.

Virgin Atlantic's philosophy was to stimulate the individual. Its dynamic business culture encouraged staff to take initiatives and gave them the means to implement them. Staff often provided insights into what customers wanted or needed—sometimes anticipating their expectations better than the customers themselves. Virgin Atlantic had a formal staff suggestion scheme and encouraged innovation from employees, both in project teams and in their daily work. Employees' suggestions were given serious consideration; many were implemented, such as the idea of serving ice cream as a snack, although formal marketing research had never shown the need for such a service.

Richard Branson himself was open to suggestions and innovations. He talked to everyone and was a good listener, inquisitive and curious about all aspects of the business. He spent time with passengers, and visited the lounge without any advance notice. While he personified a "hands-on" approach to management, he never appeared controlling or threatening. His constant presence was a sign of involvement and a source of motivation for staff, who felt a lot of affection for him. It was not unusual to hear crew discuss his recent decisions or activities, mentioning "Mr. Branson" or "Richard" with admiration and respect.

In the difficult environment of the late 1980s and early 1990s, most airline employees were eager to keep their jobs. With most operating costs—fuel prices, aircraft prices, insurance, landing and air traffic control fees—beyond management's control, labor costs were the main target of cutbacks. In 1993, the world's top 20 airlines cut 31,600 jobs, or 3.6 percent of their workforce, while the next 80 airlines added nearly 14,000, or 2.4 percent. That same year, Virgin Atlantic maintained its labor force, and was in the process of recruiting at the end of the year. In June 1994, Virgin Atlantic had 2,602 employees and recruited 880 cabin crew members. Opening a single long-haul line required hiring about 400 people.

■ The Airline Industry

Deregulation of the U.S. air transport industry in 1978 had reduced the government's role and removed protective rules, thereby increasing competition among American airlines. A decade later, deregulation hit Europe. The liberalization movement began in an effort to end monopolies and bring down prices. In fact, European carriers had been engaged in moderate competition in transatlantic travel while the domestic scheduled market remained heavily protected through bilateral agreements. European airlines were mostly state-owned, in a regulated market where access was denied to new entrants. In April 1986, the European Court of Justice ruled that the Treaty of Rome's competition rules also applied to air transportation. Deregulation took place in three phases between 1987—when price controls were relaxed and market access was opened—and 1992, when airlines were allowed to set their own prices, subject to some controls.

In this atmosphere of deregulation and falling prices, traffic revenue grew briskly until 1990, when a global recession and the Gulf War plunged airlines in their worst crisis since World War II. The 22-member association of European airlines saw the number of passengers plummet by 7 million in 1991. Traffic recovered in 1992, when the world's 100 largest airlines saw their total revenue, measured in terms of tonnage or passengers, increase by just over 10 percent. However, the airlines recorded a net loss of $8 billion in 1992, after losses of $1.84 billion in 1991 and $2.66 billion in 1990. Some experts believed that the industry would ultimately be dominated by a handful of players, with a larger number of mid-size carriers struggling to close the gap. Exhibits 10 and 11 show financial and passenger load data for some international airlines, while Exhibit 12 ranks Europe's top 20 airlines.

Virgin's Competitors

Virgin's direct competitor was British Airways (BA). Both carriers were fighting each other intensely on the most attractive routes out of London. BA, the number-one British airline, was 15 times the size of second-placed Virgin. Exhibits 13 and 14 compare Virgin's and British Airways' flights and fares.

■ **Exhibit 10** Financial Results of Selected International Airlines

Airline Company	Ranking 92	Ranking 91	Sales US$ Million 1992	Sales % Change	Operating Results US$Million	Net Results US$Million 1992	Net Results US$Million 1991	Net Margin % 1992	Jet and Turbo Fleet	Total Employees	Productivity Sales/Employee ($000)
American	1	1	14,396	11.7	(25.0)	(935.0)	(239.9)	−6.5	672	102,400	140
United	2	2	12,889	10.5	(537.8)	(956.8)	(331.9)	−7.4	536	84,000	153
Delta	3	4	11,639	15.7	(825.5)	(564.8)	(239.6)	−4.9	554	79,157	147
Lufthansa	4	5	11,036	7.1	(198.5)	(250.4)	(257.7)	−2.3	302	63,645	173
Air France	5	3	10,769	−1.1	(285.0)	(617.0)	(12.1)	−5.7	220	63,933	168
British Airways	6	6	9,307	6.5	518.4	297.7	687.3	3.2	241	48,960	190
Swissair	16	16	4,438	7.0	152.8	80.7	57.9	1.8	60	19,025	233
TWA Inc	18	18	3,634	−0.7	(404.6)	(317.7)	34.6	−8.7	178	29,958	121
Singapore	19	19	3,443	5.4	548.0	518.5	558.4	15.1	57	22,857	150
Qantas	20	20	3,099	2.9	79.1	105.7	34.6	3.4	46	14,936	207
Cathay Pacific	21	21	2,988	11.3	464.0	385.0	378.0	12.9	49	13,240	225
Southwest	34	41	1,685	28.3	182.6	103.5	26.9	6.1	141	11,397	148
Virgin Atlantic	62	62	626	7.3	(22.0)	Not Reported	3.8	Not Reported	8	2,394	261

SOURCE: *Airline Business*, "Much Pain, No Gain," September 1993. Productivity computed for this exhibit.

■ **Exhibit 11** Passenger Load Factors of Selected International Airlines

Airline Company	1992 Revenue Tonne Km Million			1992 Revenue Passenger Km		1992 Passengers		Passenger Load Factor			1992
	Passenger	Freight	Total	% Change	Million	% Change	Million	% Change	1992 %	1991 %	Year End	Rank
American	14,223	2,176	16,399	19.7	156,786	18.3	86.01	13.3	63.7	61.7	Dec. 92	1
United	13,489	2,522	16,010	12.0	149,166	12.6	67.00	8.1	67.4	66.3	Dec. 92	2
Delta	11,761	1,765	13,525	20.2	129,632	19.6	82.97	11.8	61.3	60.3	Dec. 92	3
Lufthansa	5,882	4,676	10,725	14.4	61,274	17.1	33.70	14.2	65.0	64.0	Dec. 92	4
Air France	5,238	3,970	9,208	5.3	55,504	4.0	32.71	3.4	67.4	66.8	Dec. 92	5
British Airways	7,622	2,691	10,313	13.2	80,473	15.6	28.10	10.5	70.8	70.2	Mar. 93	6
Swissair	1,573	1,063	2,684	9.1	16,221	7.0	8.01	0.4	60.3	61.6	Dec. 92	16
TWA Inc	4,258	734	4,992	1.4	46,935	1.8	22.54	8.5	64.7	64.7	Dec. 92	18
Singapore Air.	3,675	2,412	6,086	14.2	37,861	8.5	8.64	6.3	71.3	73.5	Mar. 93	19
Qantas	2,684	1,220	3,904	4.9	28,836	7.2	4.53	9.4	66.2	66.0	Jun. 92	20
Cathay Pacific	2,695	1,671	4,366	13.3	27,527	12.7	8.36	13.1	73.5	73.6	Dec. 92	21
Southwest Air.	2,032	49	2,082	23.4	22,187	22.0	27.84	22.6	64.5	61.1	Dec. 92	34
Virgin Atlantic	984	285	1,269	27.4	9,001	8.7	1.23	5.6	76.1	81.6	Oct. 92	62

SOURCE: "Much Pain, No Gain," *Airline Business*, September 1993.

Rank	Airline Company	Sales US$ million	Global Rank
1	Lufthansa	11,036.5	4
2	Air France Group	10,769.4	5
3	British Airways	9,307.7	6
4	SAS Group	5,908.2	12
5	Alitalia	5,510.7	14
6	KLM Royal Dutch	4,666.3	15
7	Swissair	4,438.5	16
8	Iberia	4,136.7	17
9	LTU/LTU Sud	1,836.1	31
10	Sabena	1,708.3	33
11	Aer Lingus	1,381.0	38
12	Aeroflot	1,172.1	43
13	Finnair	1,132.2	45
14	TAP Air Portugal	1,110.1	47
15	Austrian Airlines	1,003.8	49
16	Britannia Airways	924.0	53
17	Olympic Airways	922.5	54
18	Turkish Airlines	736.5	59
19	Airlines of Britain Hldgs	687.7	61
20	Virgin Atlantic	626.5	62

SOURCE: "Much Pain, No Gain," *Airline Business,* September 1993.

British Airways became the state owned British airline in 1972 as the result of a merger between British European Airways and British Overseas Airways Corporation. In the early 80s, it was the clear leader in the highly lucrative and regulated transatlantic route, where operating margins were approximately 15 percent of sales. However, its overall profitability was shaky when Lord King became Chairman in 1981. He transformed BA into a healthy organization and prepared it for its successful privatization in 1987. Since this time, BA has remarkably out-performed its European rivals.

British Airways traditionally benefited from a strong position at Heathrow, but competition toughened in 1991 when TWA and Pan Am sold their slots to American and United Airlines for $290 million and $445 million respectively. In the same year, Virgin also received slots at Heathrow. These slot attributions so infuriated Lord King that he scrapped its annual £40,000 donation to Britain's ruling Conservative Party. At the time of the Heathrow transfer, BA scheduled 278 flights a week across the Atlantic from London, with 83,000 seats, while American had 168 flights with 35,000 seats and United 122 with 30,000. Virgin had 84 flights with 30,000 seats.

Despite these competitive pressures and the recent airline recession, British Airways remained one of the world's most profitable airlines. The largest carrier of international passengers, serving 150 destinations in 69 countries, it was making continuous progress in terms of cost efficiency, service quality and marketing. BA recruited marketing experts from consumer goods companies who implemented a brand approach to the airline's classes. Some of the actions undertaken by BA in the early nineties included the relaunching of its European business class Club Europe with £17.5 million and spending £10 million on new lounges (with a traditional British feel), check-in facilities and ground staff at Heathrow. It was also rumored that BA was preparing to spend nearly £70 million on an advanced in-flight entertainment and information system for its long-haul fleet before the end of 1994.

■ **Exhibit 13** Virgin Atlantic and British Airways: Comparison of Routes

Destination From London to:	Airline	Frequency	Departure-Arrival (local times)	Aircraft
New York (JFK)	Virgin Atlantic	Daily (LHR)	14:00-16:40	747
			18:35-20:55	
	British Airways	Daily (LHR)	10:30-09:20	Concorde
			11:00-13:40	747
			14:00-16:40	747
			18:30-21:10	747
			19:00-17:50	Concorde
	Daily (Gat)		10:40-13:20	D10
New York (Newark)	Virgin Atlantic	Daily (LHR)	16:00-18:40	747
	British Airways	Daily (LHR)	14:45-17:40	747
Boston	Virgin Atlantic	Daily (Gat.)	15:00-17:10	A340
	British Airways	Daily (LHR)	15:45-18:00	747
		Daily (LHR)	09:55-12:30	767
Los Angeles	Virgin Atlantic	Daily (LHR)	12:00-15:10	747
	British Airways	Daily (LHR)	12:15-15:15	747-400
		Daily (LHR)	15:30-18:30	747-400
Miami	Virgin Atlantic	W,F,S,Su (Gat.)	11:15-15:45	747
		Th (Gat.)	11:15-15:45	
	British Airways	Daily (LHR)	11:15-15:40	747
		Daily (LHR)	14:30-18:55	747
Orlando	Virgin Atlantic	Daily (Gat.)	12:30-16:40	747
	British Airways	Tu,W,Su (LHR)	11:15-19:15	747
		M,Th,F,S (Gat.)	11:00-15:10	747
San Francisco	Virgin Atlantic	Daily (LHR)	11:15-14:05	747
	British Airways	Daily (LHR)	13:15-16:05	747-400
		Daily (LHR)	10:50-13:40	747
Tokyo	Virgin Atlantic	M,T,Th,F,S,Su (LHR)	13:00-08:55 (next day)	747/A340
	British Airways	Daily (LHR)	12:55-08:45 (next day)	747-400
		M,T,Th,F,S,Su (LHR)	16:30-12:15 (next day)	747-400
Hong Kong	Virgin Atlantic	Daily	20:30-16:35 (next day)	A340
	British Airways	F	13:55-09:55 (next day)	747-400
		M,T,W,Th,S,Su.	14:30-10:30 (next day)	747-400
		Daily	21:30-17:30 (next day)	747-400

SOURCES: *The Guide to Virgin Atlantic Airways,* Issue May/June 1994; *British Airways Worldwide Timetable,* 27 March–29 October 1994.

British Airways and Virgin had fiercely competed against one another from the onset. One major incident that marked their rivalry was what became known as the "Dirty Tricks Campaign." In 1992, Virgin Atlantic filed a lawsuit against BA, accusing it of entering Virgin's computer system and spreading false rumors. In January 1993, Virgin won its libel suit against BA in London. The wide press coverage caused much embarrassment to British Airways. Later that year, Virgin filed a $325 million lawsuit in the Federal Court of New York, accusing BA of using its monopoly power to distort competition on North American routes.

■ **Exhibit 14**   Virgin Atlantic and British Airways Fares (£)

Route	Virgin Atlantic			British Airways			
	Upper Class[1]	Economy Mid Class[1]	21 Day Apex[2]	First Class[1]	Club[1]	Economy	21 Day Apex[3]
New York	1195	473	489	1935	1061	620	538
San Francisco	1627	595	538[4]	2179	1627	920	638
Los Angeles	1627	604	538	2179	1627	920	638
Tokyo	1806	783	993	2751	1806	1580	993
Hong Kong	979	600	741	3280	2075	1808	741
Boston	1082	473	439	1935	1061	620	538
Miami	1144	529	498	2085	1144	780	598
Orlando	1144	529	498	2085	1144	780	598

[1]One-way weekend peak-time fares in Pounds Sterling (£).
[2]Economy fare for Virgin is "Economy 21 day Apex" (reservation no later than 21 days prior to departure).
[3]21 day Apex round trip ticket.
[4]Between May 17 and June 30, 1994 a special launch fare round trip ticket was sold at £299.

In addition to British Airways, Virgin competed with at least one major carrier on each of its destinations. For instance, it was up against United Airlines to Los Angeles, American Airlines to New York and Cathay Pacific to Hong Kong. Most of its competitors surpassed Virgin many times in terms of turnover, staff and number of aircraft. Yet, Virgin was not intimidated by the size of its competitors; it saw its modest size as an advantage that enabled it to react quickly and remain innovative.

■ Virgin Atlantic's Management Structure

Virgin Atlantic's headquarters was in Crawley, a suburb near Gatwick. The airline had a loose organization combined with a high level of dialogue and involvement, as well as strong controls. A senior manager explained: "Our business is about independence, entrepreneurial flair, and people having autonomy to make decisions; yet we pay a great deal of attention to overhead and cost levels." Members of the management team, whose structure is shown in Exhibit 15, came from other airlines, other industries, or other divisions of the Virgin Group. The three top executives—co-managing directors Roy Gardner and Syd Pennington and finance director Nigel Primrose—reported directly to Richard Branson.

Gardner had joined Virgin Airways as technical director in 1984 after working at Laker Airways and British Caledonian Airways. He was responsible for the technical aspects of operations: quality, supplies, maintenance, emergency procedures. Pennington oversaw commercial operations, marketing, sales and flight operations. Primrose, a chartered accountant with 20 years of international experience, had

■ **Exhibit 15**   Virgin Atlantic Airways Ltd., Organizational Structure May 1994

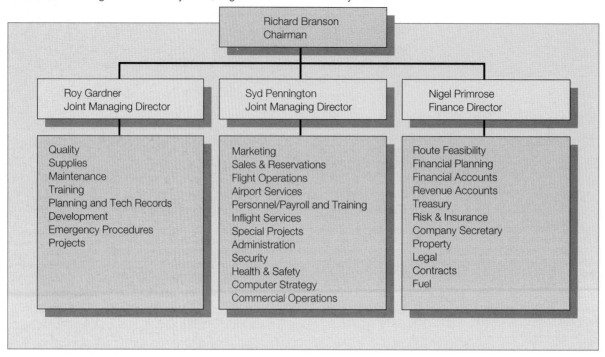

SOURCE: Virgin Atlantic.

been part of the senior team that setup Air Europe in 1978 and Air UK in 1983 before joining Virgin Atlantic in 1986. He was Virgin Atlantic's company secretary with responsibility for route feasibility, financial planning, financial accounts, treasury, and legal affairs.

Steve Ridgeway headed the marketing department. After assisting Richard Branson in several projects, including the Transatlantic Boat Challenge, he had joined the airline in 1989 to develop its frequent traveller program, becoming head of marketing in 1992. Paul Griffiths, who had 14 years of commercial aviation experience, became Virgin Atlantic's Director of Commercial Operations after spending two years designing and implementing its information management system. Personnel Director Nick Potts, a business studies graduate, had been recruited in 1991 from Warner Music UK where he was the head of the personnel department.

■ Marketing Activities

Steve Ridgeway's marketing department covered a variety of activities, as shown in Exhibit 16. Some traditional marketing disciplines, such as advertising, promotions, planning and the Freeway frequent flyer program, reported to Ruth Blakemore, Head of Marketing. Catering, retail operations (for example, duty free sales), product development and public relations reported directly to Steve Ridgeway.

Virgin Atlantic spent 2 percent of turnover on advertising, well below the 5 to 7 percent industry norm. Virgin's advertising had featured a series of short campaigns

■ **Exhibit 16**   Virgin Atlantic: Marketing Department

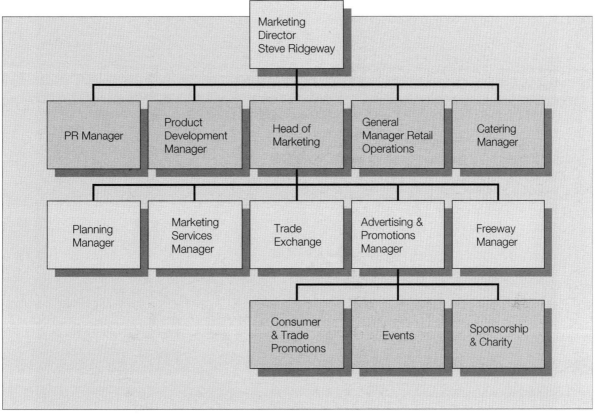

SOURCE: Virgin Atlantic.

handled by various agencies. The winning of a quality award was often a campaign opportunity, as in Exhibit 17, as was the opening of a new line. On one April Fool's Day, Virgin announced that it had developed a new bubble-free champagne. It also launched ad-hoc campaigns in response to competitors' activities, as in Exhibit 18. The survey in Exhibit 19 shows that Virgin Atlantic enjoyed a strong brand equity, as well as a high level of spontaneous awareness and a good image in the United Kingdom. In order to increase the trial rate, its advertising had evolved from a conceptual approach to more emphasis on specific product features.

In 1990, the airline launched its Virgin Freeway frequent travellers program in Britain (it started in the U.S. in 1992). While Virgin Freeway was an independent division of the Virgin Travel Group, it operated within the airline's marketing department. Freeway miles were offered to members who flew Mid Class or Upper Class or who used the services of international companies such as American Express, Inter-Continental Hotels, British Midland, SAS and others. Miles could be exchanged for free flights to Europe, North America and Japan, as well as a wide range of activities: hot air ballooning, polo lessons, rally driving, luxury country getaways for two, five days skiing in the U.S. As part of the Freeway Program, Virgin offered a free standby ticket for every Upper Class ticket purchased.

■ **Exhibit 17**   Virgin Atlantic Advertising (1990)

The world's favourite airline?

They must be on a different planet.

It's a brave airline that claims to be the world's favourite.

Now it seems the world has a different idea.

For at the 1989 Executive Travel Airline of the Year Awards, Virgin Atlantic have emerged victorious.

Those most demanding and, dare one say, discerning of people, the readers of Executive Travel Magazine voted Virgin Atlantic, Best Transatlantic Carrier.

It's not just over the Atlantic that they hold sway.

For Virgin were also named Best Business Class in the World, above airlines they admire such as Singapore and Thai.

A choice that was quickly seconded by Business Traveller Magazine.

It's not hard to see why Virgin's Upper Class commands such respect.

AIRLINE OF THE YEAR AWARDS 1989

VIRGIN ATLANTIC AIRWAYS
EXECUTIVE TRAVEL MAGAZINE

Best Transatlantic Carrier
Best Business Class in the World
World's Best Inflight Entertainment

BUSINESS TRAVELLER MAGAZINE

World's Best Business Class

Passengers enjoy a free chauffeur driven car* to and from the airport plus a free economy stand-by ticket.†

On the plane there are first class sleeper seats that, miraculously, you can actually sleep in and on-board bars and lounges.

And your own personal Sony Video Walkman with a choice of 100 films.

As you might expect from Virgin, this entertainment is truly award winning. It helped scoop a third major award. Best In-Flight Entertainment.

So the next time you want to travel across the world in style, you know who to favour.

For details call *0800 800 400* or for reservations *0293 551616*, or see your travel agent.

*First 40 miles with our compliments. †Not available on Tokyo route.

LONDON   ·   NEW YORK JFK AND NEWARK   ·   MIAMI   ·   MOSCOW   ·   TOKYO

■ **Exhibit 18**   Virgin Atlantic Advertising (Spring 1994) Response to a British Airways Campaign

The world's favourite airline?
Not in our book.

BEATS THE PANTS OFF BA!
VERY GOOD SERVICE.

JAMES ARMSTRONG
B. S. LIMITED

Excellent.
Keep BA on the run!

JEREMY HATTON
NORWICH CRUISE CENTRE

The best service from the best airline in the World!
Absolutely Fabulous - !!

VINCE CRAWLEY
COUNTRY CASUALS LTD

With a deal like this,
who the hell wants to
fly BA anyway!!

BOB BROWN
FILMCO EUROFORM

A previously dedicated and loyal
British Airways customer, now
a dedicated and loyal Virgin
customer!

ROBERT CASSON
PFIZER INC

Best Business Class price
service in the air.

GEOFF TOVEY
SMITHKLINE BEECHAM

Such a refreshing change from BA! Great
entertainment & service! - Looking forward
to another flight!

ANDREW TURNER
REED TRAVEL GROUP

I am your biggest fan -
I promise never to fly
another airline if I can
help it. It is always
a pleasure on Virgin!

KATHY BRADY
BANKERS TRUST

As ever, Virgin
leads the field.

PAUL JACKSON
CARLTON TV

My first time too on Virgin Atlantic and it's
unquestionably better than the equivalent BA.
The service, for example, was first class.

SHERBAN CANTACUZINO
ROYAL FINE ART COMMISSION

Virgin Atlantic's Upper Class costs the same as BA Club Class. And it's not just
the comments in our visitors' book that are better. Hope to see you soon.

	British Airways	**Virgin Atlantic**	**American**	**United**
Perceived strongest brand name in transatlantic travel (% of respondents)	70	24	2	1
Spontaneous awareness (%)	96	74	49	22
Usage (%)	93	48	44	23
Rating of brand names (0-100 scale)	85	80	61	58

SOURCE: Business Marketing Services Limited (BMSL). Based on 141 interviews of executives from the UK's top 500 organisations.

The Virgin Freeway was run in partnership with SAS and other international groups which, according to Ruth Blakemore, enabled it to compete with British Airways. Virgin also had ties with SAS through another Freeway partner, British Midland, wholly-owned by Airlines of Britain in which SAS had a 35 percent stake. Virgin delivered significant interline traffic to British Midland, and Blakemore believed that there was a useful common ground for all three to join forces against British Airways.

In May 1993, Virgin Atlantic unveiled a promotional campaign targeted at BA passengers who had never tried Virgin. Members of BA's Executive Club USA program who had accumulated 50,000 miles or more qualified for a free Upper Class Companion ticket on Virgin; those with 10,000 to 49,999 miles qualified for a free Mid Class ticket. The campaign was launched with a radio commercial in which Richard Branson said: "In recent years, Virgin has done about everything we can think of to get those remaining British Airways' passengers to try Virgin Atlantic."

The marketing department handled the franchising of the Virgin Atlantic brand, which included two routes. London-Athens, launched from Gatwick in March 1992 in partnership with South East European Airlines of Greece, was transferred to Heathrow seven months later. London City Airport–Dublin, with City Jet, was launched in January 1994. In both cases, the aircraft and crew bore Virgin's name and colors, but Virgin's partner was the operator and paid royalties to Virgin for the use of its brand, marketing and sales support, and for assistance in the recruitment and training of flight staff.

In April 1994, Virgin announced a partnership with Delta Air Lines—its first alliance with a major international airline. Delta would purchase a set percentage of seats on Virgin flights between London and Los Angeles, New York (Newark and JFK), Miami, San Francisco, Orlando, and Boston which it would price and sell independently. The alliance, which increased Virgin's annual revenue by $150 million and gave Delta access to Heathrow, had received the blessing of the British government and was awaiting US approval.

Virgin Atlantic's public relations department, known as 'the press office' and led by James Murray, played an important role. "We are not here just to react to press inquiries," explained Murray. "We also try to gain publicity for the airline's products and services and to show how much better we are than the competition." Virgin Atlantic enjoyed excellent relations with the media—not the rule in the airline industry—because of a combination of factors: Richard Branson's persona, the airline's openness in dealing with the press, its "David vs. Goliath" quality, the news value of its innovations, and a good management of media relationships.

For instance, Virgin had readily accepted an invitation to participate in BBC television's prime time "Secret Service" series, in which investigators posing as customers test service at well-known firms. Failures in service delivery were exposed and discussed. British Airways, which the BBC had approached first, had declined. While the program did identify some shortcomings in Virgin's operations, including delays in meal service (due to oven problems) and in answering passenger calls, it gave a lively demonstration of the quality of service in Upper Class and of Virgin's willingness to take corrective action.

The public relations department comprised three people in Crawley and two in the group press office, where James Murray spent two days a week. Originally set up in Richard Branson's own house, the group press office had to move next door as the amount of work increased. Staff were on call round-the-clock, sometimes taking calls from journalists in the middle of the night. During a one-hour car ride with James Murray, the casewriters watched him handle a constant flow of requests ranging from invitations to the inaugural San Francisco flight to questions on Virgin's position on privatizing the Civil Aviation Agency or the possible banning of peanuts on flights after reports of allergy risks—all on the car phone.

A five-member Product Development department evaluated and developed innovations. It handled a broad range of new product activities—a new identity program for the aircraft, selection of seat design and internal decoration, the catering system, or new lounges—and coordinated the input from other departments. Typically, the marketing, engineering, commercial and sales departments also participated in developing new products. For example, Airport Services played a crucial role in setting up the Clubhouse lounge.

By June 1994, Virgin had taken steps to correct its main weaknesses: the age of its fleet and its punctuality problems. More than half the fleet would be renewed by the end of the year, and Virgin was undertaking an "On-Time Initiative" in which cabin crew were to shut doors exactly 10 minutes before departure time, even if late passengers had not boarded—even Richard Branson, who was notorious for being late. Virgin was also implementing a new corporate identity program. In addition to the Virgin logo and the "Vargas Lady," all aircraft would bear the words "virgin atlantic" in large grey letters, as shown in Exhibit 20.

■ Challenges for the Future

During its first decade Virgin Atlantic had confronted great challenges and survived the worst recession in the history of air transportation. Amidst rumors over the airline's financial health, Richard Branson had always stressed his personal commitment. "I would put everything I had into making sure that Virgin Atlantic was here in twenty years time," he said.

Virgin Atlantic had demonstrated its capacity to innovate, to satisfy customers, and to be financially viable in difficult times. As the world economy began to recover, the airline was poised for a quantum leap in the scale of its operations. When Richard Branson had founded it in 1984, his ambition had been to build an airline unlike any other. Ten years later, what set Virgin apart was its reputation for giving customers what they wanted at prices they could afford, pioneering new concepts in

Exhibit 20 Virgin Atlantic Aircraft after New Corporate Identity Program (1994)

service and entertainment, and restoring a sense of pleasure and excitement to long distance travel.

The main challenge the airline faced as it celebrated its 10th anniversary was to foster this difference throughout the 1990s. What sort of airline should it be? How could it achieve that goal? How could it remain profitable? How could it retain its competitive edge in innovations? Was it possible to grow while retaining the organizational advantages of a small entrepreneurial company? How could it keep employees motivated and enthusiastic? How would it keep the momentum of its success? These were some of the questions that went through Richard Branson's mind as his 400 guests and himself watched a Virgin 747 Jumbo fly over the Thames and Westminster to mark Virgin's first decade.

Case Group D
Distribution Strategy

■ **Case 17   Tupperware 1999**

J. Paul Peter
University of Wisconsin–Madison

In 1958 Justin Dart purchased Tupperware from former DuPont chemist Earl Tupper for $10 million. From that time until 1980 Tupperware earned an estimated $1.5 billion pretax and had a phenomenal 25-year record of doubling sales and earnings every 5 years. In 1983, Tupperware sales slipped 7 percent and operating profits sank 15 percent. In 1992, sales for the second quarter fell 33 percent from the same period a year before. That quarter also saw a 20 percent decline in the number of active U.S. dealers. As shown in Exhibit 1, changes in families and households contributed to the loss of business.

Traditionally, Tupperware plastic products were sold at in-home parties. These parties now are held not only in homes but also in offices and other locations convenient for people going home from work. These parties consist of a part-time salesperson inviting friends and acquaintances to the location and displaying the many varieties of plastic products. The parties typically include refreshments, a free sample of Tupperware, casual conversation, games in which participants can win pieces of Tupperware, and formal offering of Tupperware products. Customers order at the party and pay for the products on delivery by the salesperson.

In order to try to curb the decline, Tupperware offered a variety of new products. These included Modular Mates, which defend against cabinet clutter; TupperWave, which microwaves an entire dinner in 30 minutes; and the Earth Pack, a set of containers in a washable green lunch bag. Many consumers resisted the Earth Pack since they prefer a Ziploc bag to washing it out.

Selling Tupperware might be a lot easier except that most women (55 percent by Tupperware's estimate) either have no idea how to find Tupperware or no desire to go to a Tupperware party. Some 40 percent of Tupperware's sales are from people who skip the parties but send orders along with friends who attend.

This case was prepared by J. Paul Peter, James R. McManus-Bascom Professor in Marketing at the University of Wisconsin–Madison.

Sources: Peter Spiegel, "Party On," *Forbes,* May 3, 1999, p. 76; Laurie M. Grossman, "Families Have Changed but Tupperware Keeps Holding Its Parties," *The Wall Street Journal,* July 21, 1992, pp. A1, A13; Kerry Hannon, "Party Animal," *Forbes,* November 16, 1987, pp. 262–68.

■ **Exhibit 1** Changing U.S. Lifestyles Have Hurt Tupperware

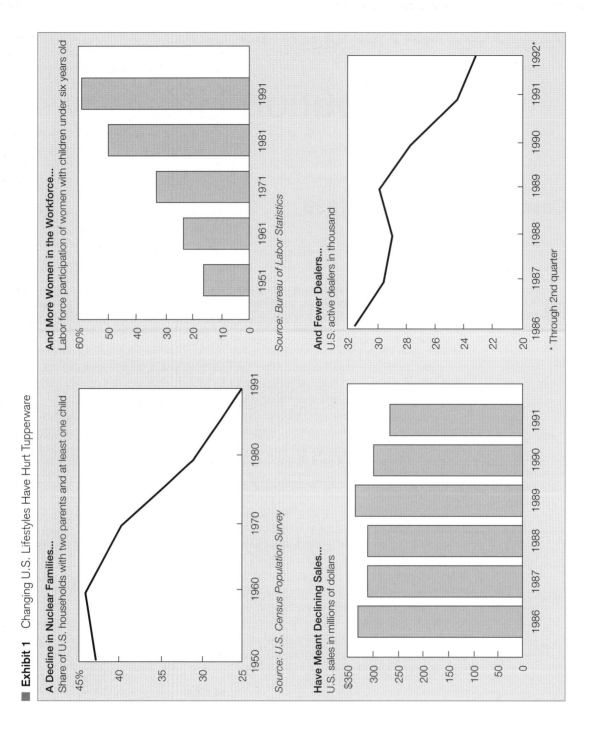

A Decline in Nuclear Families...
Share of U.S. households with two parents and at least one child

Source: U.S. Census Population Survey

And More Women in the Workforce...
Labor force participation of women with children under six years old

Source: Bureau of Labor Statistics

Have Meant Declining Sales...
U.S. sales in millions of dollars

And Fewer Dealers...
U.S. active dealers in thousand

* Through 2nd quarter

454

Tupperware relies heavily on overseas markets to generate sales growth. However, its sales were brutalized by the economic downturns in Asia and Latin America in the late 1990s and revenues dropped by more than one third. In the U.S., the company sold only $166 million worth of containers and cookware in 1998. However, its gross margin on these sales was over 60 percent.

Tupperware's major competitor, Rubbermaid, reaches consumers by selling in discount stores and supermarkets. Rubbermaid's products sell at substantially lower prices. For example, a two-quart Tupperware pitcher sells for $10.50 while one from Rubbermaid sells for about one fourth that amount. Lower prices and the convenience of having its products readily available in stores has led Rubbermaid to sales of $1.9 billion annually.

Tupperware's plans for 1999 include two new strategies. First, it plans to sell Tupperware on cart-like kiosks in malls across the country. It tested the idea in five malls and the results were promising. Second, it plans to sell products on the Internet. While the company does not expect this channel to improve sales substantially, it does expect some incremental sales.

In-home parties will continue to be a major part of Tupperware's strategy. The company insists that the in-home party is not an outdated concept since its products are of such high quality that a trained Tupperware lady (the party-givers are almost all women) is needed to explain product advantages.

Discussion Questions

1. Why has direct selling using in-home parties been such an effective channel for Tupperware historically?
2. The data shown in the exhibit suggest a number of social changes that took place in the 1990s. What impact do they have on Tupperware's strategy to use in-home parties to sell its products?
3. Evaluate Tupperware's strategies of using kiosks in malls and the Internet to sell its products.
4. What opportunities are there for Tupperware to curb the decline and increase its sales and profits?

Case 18   Sears, Roebuck Inc.

Sara L. Pitterle and J. Paul Peter

both of the University of Wisconsin–Madison

Sears, Roebuck Inc., for many years the number one retailer in America, has fallen on hard times. The company, which once was able to brag that its sales represented 1 percent of the U.S. Gross National Product, was surpassed in 1991 by both Kmart and Wal-Mart (see Exhibit 1). Moreover, both Kmart and Wal-Mart remained profitable in 1992 while Sears posted a loss of $3.93 billion, its first loss since 1933.[1] The loss did not surprise either Sears' shareholders or company observers. Sears' core retailing business has been stagnating since the late 1970s and the company has remained profitable until now only because of the earnings of its financial services unit.

Because of the difficulties in its merchandising unit and pressure from shareholder groups, Sears was forced to downsize. First, in mid-1992, the company announced plans to sell off parts of its financial services network. Then, in January 1993, with the previous year's disastrous results in hand, Sears announced the closing of its catalog unit and 113 unprofitable stores.[2] These closings meant that 50,000 people would eventually lose their positions. These people join the 48,000 who were laid off in previous restructuring attempts.[3]

While Sears prospered during much of this century, it did not respond to the environmental changes which took place in the 1970s and '80s. Sears ignored the emergence of national discount chains and specialty stores and appeared to concentrate primarily on growing the financial services division. Even with these recent changes, many analysts doubt whether Sears' executives have the ability and foresight necessary to lead the company through restructuring.

Sears, Roebuck Inc., started in 1886 when Richard Sears, a freight agent in North Redwood, Minnesota, realized that there was more money to be made in sales than there was in working for the railroad. Sears got his start when a jeweller in North Redwood refused a shipment of "yellow watches" which had been sent on consignment from a watch company in Chicago. The factory offered the watches to him at

■ Exhibit 1

Company	1990	1991	% Change
Wal-Mart	$32.6	$43.9	34.7
Kmart	32.0	34.6	8.1
Sears	32.0	31.4	−1.8

This case was prepared by Sara L. Pitterle, Nielsen Fellow at the University of Wisconsin-Madison, under the supervision of J. Paul Peter.

[1] Gregory Patterson, "Sears Registers Quarterly Loss of $1.8 Billion," *The Wall Street Journal,* February 19, 1993, pp. A3, A4.

[2] Gregory Patterson, "Sears Trims Operations, Ending an Era," *The Wall Street Journal,* January 26, 1993, p. B1.

[3] Kate Fitzgerald, "Brennan Will Have to Answer to Upset Sears Shareholders," *Advertising Age,* 63 (April 20, 1992), p. 42.

$12 dollars apiece, and he in turn offered them at $14 dollars each to the freight agents further down the line. The other agents could keep whatever they made for selling the watches which were retailing for $25 in most local stores. Thus, the other freight agents made a nice profit by underselling their competition, and Sears made a profit with little or no risk. With this one order, Richard Sears was hooked on the mail-order business.

Sears ordered additional watches "Cash on Delivery" but since he was a freight agent, was not required to pay to take delivery. Therefore, Sears was able to resell these watches to other freight agents at a profit and only settle his account after receiving payment from buyers. Within six months, he had made $5,000, a fortune at that time, without taking any risk. He left the railroad and moved to Minneapolis where he founded the R. W. Sears Watch Company. He began advertising the Chicago-made watches in local newspapers and orders poured in. Within a matter of months, the company had outgrown Minneapolis, and Sears began looking to bigger cities for more opportunities.

On March 1, 1887, Sears set up shop in Chicago and immediately began advertising watches for a deposit of fifty cents or a dollar. Sears and his staff of three knew nothing about watch repair, but so many people had heard of the R. W. Sears Watch Company that repair orders began to stream in. Sensing a new way to make a profit, Sears hired a young watchmaker, Alvah Roebuck, in April of 1887.

In the late 1800s, 72 percent of the United States was rural and agriculture was the biggest single source of national wealth. Richard Sears' advertising was aimed at these rural Americans who had limited shopping options. Sears' lower prices, his willingness to send watches on approval for just the payment of a deposit, and the company's policy of guaranteed satisfaction convinced the nation's farm families to order from Sears.

Sears sold the company a year later because he wanted to retire in a smaller town. Within weeks of his "retirement," he was restless and started a new watch company called the Warren Company, so named because of his pledge not to use the Sears name for three years. He sold this company to Roebuck in 1891 to again try retirement, but quickly decided he wanted back in and convinced Roebuck to sell him half share again. This company became the Sears, Roebuck Company. It published a 52-page catalog of watches the first year, a 100-page catalog of watches, charms, rings and other goods the following year. In 1893, the catalog had expanded to 322 pages and included sewing machines, bicycles, organs, pianos, and men's and boys' clothing. The satisfaction guarantee on all products, which had been so successful for Sears in his previous ventures, was an integral part of this strategy.[4]

As Sears, Roebuck Inc., began to expand, Alvah Roebuck decided to leave the company, and Julius Rosenwald was brought in. Rosenwald brought strict management procedures to the growing company. His philosophy of merchandising which would guide Sears through many successful years was "sell honest merchandise for less money and more people will buy it."[5] To this general philosophy three supporting directives were added: (1) sell for less by purchasing in bulk; (2) sell for less by reducing the expenses associated with moving products from producer to consumer; and (3) make less profit on individual items so as to move more items,

---

[4]Gordon L. Weil, *Sears Roebuck, U. S.A.* (New York: Stein and Day Publishers, 1977), p. 66.

[5]James C. Worthy, *Shaping an American Institution* (Urbana & Chicago: University of Illinois Press, 1984), p. 27.

increasing total profits. With this general philosophy, Rosenwald changed the perspective of the company from "Seller to America's Farmers" to "Buyer for America's Farmers."[6]

By the 1970s, the Sears organization felt secure in its position as the largest retailer in the United States. The company had prospered during economic growth and recession because of the vision and direction of its early leaders. Sears had been able to perceive and react to consumer trends quicker than its competition. The company was a trusted part of most Americans' lives and appeared to be indomitable. The company's stock was selling at 30 times annual earnings, and investors perceived Sears to be a growth company which would continue to respond to changing market trends.

At this point, Sears began to change its selling strategy. The company promoted more expensive brand names and encouraged its loyal customers to trade up to these products. The company pursued this strategy so aggressively that in 1974, the Federal Trade Commission (FTC) reprimanded the company for using "bait and switch" techniques as a means of increasing sales on these higher margin products.[7] Sears not only incurred the wrath of the FTC, but customers began to buy at emerging discount chains such as Kmart.

In 1976, Sears realized its customer base was declining. The company tried to reposition and compete directly with the discount chains simply by reducing prices. Since no attempt was made to reduce administrative and selling expenses, this new strategy resulted in a serious decline in both income and profit margins during 1977. Ed Telling, Sears' chairman and CEO at this time, then declared that the company was going back to basics. The company was not going to try to compete with the discounters but once again sell to middle class Americans who wanted quality products at reasonable prices.

■ Sears in the 1980s

While Sears decided to pursue growth and profitability by going back to its historic selling strategy, many analysts felt it had grown too big to be managed effectively. The company had 1,700 catalog offices, 900 stores, 13 regional distribution centers, and 124 warehouses.[8] As analysts worried about the company's future in retailing, Sears' executives began to aggressively pursue growth through diversification into financial services. Under Mr. Telling's direction, Sears focused on becoming America's one stop shop for consumer financial services.

In 1981, Sears acquired the Dean Witter Reynolds securities brokerage business and the Coldwell Banker real-estate operation for $812 million. Sears' senior executives were more interested in these new ventures and their associated potential than with the retailing business, which accounted for half of the company's profits at this point.

---

[6]Ibid., p. 28.

[7]Bait and switch techniques involve a company extensively advertising a reduced price on some product, but when customers try to purchase it, salespeople aggressively recommend purchasing an alternative product at a higher price and profit margin. Often the sale item isn't even available if the customer insists on purchasing it.

[8]J. Worthy, p. 261.

Sears did not expand store space aggressively during the 1970s and 1980s when retail space doubled nationwide. During this time, Sears was actually closing unproductive stores while Kmart, Wal-Mart, and other new competitors built stores in prime locations. The company did not react as Wal-Mart pursued its strategy of locating large discount stores in rural communities. These new discount stores contributed to the erosion of Sears' catalog sales in rural sections of America. Sears, whose Homart real-estate unit is one of the nation's largest shopping center developers, could have built new stores in these profitable rural locations as well if senior executives had approved expansion plans.

Sears' executives appeared oblivious to the threat posed by both discount chains and specialty stores. In fact, senior executives began to seriously analyze these competitors only after they had successfully attracted large numbers of Sears' customers. As described below, these stores offered desirable combinations of products and services which were not available from Sears.

Discount Stores

Emerging discount chains provided a major threat to Sears. In the late 1970s, Sears' executives identified Kmart as a possible threat to market share. While Sears identified the threat, effective counter strategies were never developed. Discount chains were carrying extensive assortments of merchandise and locating in convenient areas. Most important, these chains were selling desired brand name merchandise at prices below those charged by Sears. These retailers were able to sell profitably at lower prices because they had successfully reduced selling and administrative expenses.

For example, Wal-Mart is estimated to have selling expenses of only 14 percent and distribution costs under 3 percent of sales revenue. Wal-Mart's efficiencies are built around easily accessed strategic information. Whenever a customer purchases an item from Wal-Mart, that information goes to the manufacturer's plant in "real time" and is used to establish appropriate manufacturing, shipping, and delivery schedules.[9] Advanced technology is also utilized at Wal-Mart's fourteen distribution centers; laser scanners route the goods along conveyor belts which move products from suppliers' trailers to Wal-Mart's store delivery trucks. This technology is used by many companies; however, only Wal-Mart appears to have implemented the technology so as to gain a strategic advantage.[10] These efficiencies have contributed to Wal-Mart's ability to undersell competitors while maintaining healthy profit margins.

While Kmart's selling and administrative expenses were higher than Wal-Mart's at 20 percent, Kmart was still able to sell cheaper than Sears.[11] In addition, Kmart recognized that to remain competitive with Wal-Mart, it had to cut costs. The company instituted the "Classification and Assignment System" (CLAS) which allows Kmart to ship products to different stores based on the actual volume being sold.[12] With this system, the chain is able to accurately predict the sales volume of products at different pricing and promotion levels and adjust the product mix at each store accordingly. The chain also developed a relational merchandise database which

[9]Ibid,. p. A16

[10]John Huey, "Wal-Mart, Will It Take Over the World?" *Fortune,* January 30, 1989, p. 54.

[11]Susan Caminiti, "Sears' Need: More Speed," *Fortune,* July 15, 1991, p. 89.

[12]Bruce Fox, "Kmart Tackles Distribution with 'CLAS,'" *Chain Store Age Executive,* January 1991, p. 60.

reflects actual customer purchases in different stores. This database allows managers to accurately track the products which are moving through individual stores throughout the country. With these systems, Kmart maintained a profitable position as the second largest retailer.

Alternatively, Sears had been able to prosper with higher average costs because of its unique retailing strategy. Sears developed corporate brand names which could be sold at higher prices than similar unbranded products and advertised these exclusive brands extensively to generate volumes equal to those of low margin/low price products. Exclusive brand-name products like Kenmore, Craftsman, and Diehard brought customers to Sears. The company's emphasis on quality and customer satisfaction kept customers coming back to Sears year after year. Because of the perceived high quality, Sears was able to maintain margins that were 50 percent higher than the competition's and yet continue to generate higher volumes.[13] The strategy while successful, was able to cover the higher selling and administrative costs incurred by Sears which ran about 22 percent. In fact, as a result of this strategy's success, Sears was able to ignore its uncompetitive cost structure for many years.

Specialty Stores

Specialty stores are defined as retailers that carry a broad selection of goods in a limited number of product lines. During the 1980s, these stores focused their marketing strategies on target markets for particular products. Since specialty stores are able to stock only limited product lines, products chosen must turn over quickly. To ensure that items being stocked did in fact have the required turnover level, these specialty stores invested in advanced information systems. These systems provide instantaneous feedback to the organization's management on the items which were moving. Products not selling were pulled and replaced by others. Some specialty stores, such as Toys 'R' Us, were so effective that they became known as "category killers" since general merchandise companies could hardly compete with them.

Specialty stores, especially those competing in fashion product lines, also developed reorder systems which significantly reduced the time taken for an order with a manufacturer to be translated into delivered goods at the retail outlet. This time delay between order placement and delivered goods is a critical issue for fashion merchandisers. Trends change rapidly and stores cannot afford to be late in bringing out new styles. Many of the specialty stores carrying such fashion merchandise have reduced the time between order placement and delivery to four weeks by utilizing computer technology.

In contrast to these fast-reacting specialty stores, Sears was a lumbering giant. Sears' buyers did not have access to timely information on product turnover in individual Sears stores. Sears did not invest in advanced point-of-sale terminals which provide this information until the end of the 1980s. In addition, Sears did not attempt to reduce the time between order placement with suppliers and delivery at the retail stores. While specialty clothing stores were hanging new merchandise on the racks after only four to six weeks, Sears stores were waiting 18 weeks for an order to be turned into clothing on the racks.[14] Moreover, once merchandise arrived at Sears stores, store personnel were inept at creating appealing merchandise displays. Thus, Sears became known for its utilitarian and dowdy atmosphere.

---

[13]Henry H. Beam, "Strategic Discontinuities," *Business Horizons,* July–August 1990, p. 11.

[14]Barry Stavro, "Minding the Store," *Forbes,* April 7, 1986, p. 31.

■ Challenges and Changes

While outside observers recognized in the '70s that the big store was in trouble, only cosmetic changes in Sears' retailing division were made during the first half of the 1980s. Innovative and creative marketing strategies were being implemented exclusively in the new financial services division. In the merchandising division, confidence had become complacency. Finally, in the second half of the 1980s, as discounters and specialty stores took ever greater parts of the company's retail market share, the company recognized that its merchandising operation was in serious trouble.

In 1988, the company saw that it was in danger of losing its coveted position as America's number one retailer and began to make changes. Many of these changes were forced upon it by disgruntled shareholders who were tired of Sears' poor performance. In a move designed to appease disgruntled shareholders and prohibit a corporate asset breakup, Sears' chairman and CEO, Ed Brennan, announced a restructuring plan that included the sale of the Sears Tower, a stock buy-back plan, and a new pricing strategy for the entire retail operation. Of these programs, only the stock buy-back program was a success. No acceptable offers were received for the Sears Tower and the new pricing strategy did not succeed in raising sales revenue for the retailing unit.

The new pricing strategy failed for a number of reasons. Because Sears traditionally sold on high margins, the retailer often reduced prices on remaining inventory when new stock arrived. Sales became so predictable that customers simply put off purchases until items went on sale. Before the new pricing strategy was announced, 60 percent of Sears' sales were on promotion items. The new pricing strategy was extensively promoted as a change to "Everyday Low Pricing" which would eliminate the necessity of sales. Sears' executives believed the company could remain profitable on the lower margins because of the reduction in advertising expenses. However, Sears' customers actually wanted the regular sales. Also, Sears could not compete profitably with the prices being offered by both Kmart and Wal-Mart. The company began to review its cost structure and merchandising philosophy.

As Sears examined its expenses, one of the changes implemented was vertical profit and loss statements. Before 1989, Sears had apportioned costs based on company averages for each business. Managers were not able to assess the actual warehouse or distribution costs for any single product category; therefore, the profitability of individual products being sold was not known.[15] Once costs were broken out separately, the company was able to begin addressing its uncompetitive selling and administrative expenses and attempt to make necessary adjustments.

Changes Implemented in the Stores

Sears reacted to the challenges posed by specialty stores through a comprehensive store remodeling program. Specifically, Sears remodeled its stores into seven power formats: women's apparel, appliances and electronics, home improvements, children's clothes, automotive, men's fashion, and furniture.[16] In a radical departure from Sears' tradition, each of these power formats stocked and sold not only Sears' brand names but national brands as well. In each of the power formats, a more inviting and alluring atmosphere was created. By introducing these formats, Sears desperately attempted to shake its dowdy and utilitarian image.

---

[15]Susan Caminiti, "Sears' Need: More Speed," *Fortune,* July 15, 1991, p. 89.

[16]Johnathon R. Laing, "Can You Count on Sears?" *Barron's,* May 18, 1992, p. 10.

When Sears decided to begin carrying national brands in addition to its own brands, stores were forced to reduce the amount of floor space being used for inventory storage. Sears stores had been using as much as 50 percent of available selling space as storage and administrative areas. (The industry average is approximately 20 percent of retail selling space being used for storage and administrative purposes.)[17] As more products were added to each category, stores had to find space to display the new merchandise. The company cut the amount of inventory held at each store without increasing out-of-stock occurrences through a restructuring program in its distribution and warehousing procedures. Stores were then able to use approximately 70 percent of floor space for merchandise display and selling.[18] A definite improvement, but still below industry leaders.

In addition, Sears reorganized its buying procedures to support the new power formats. Traditionally, Sears' buyers purchased products from suppliers, and then resold the merchandise to store managers. The result was disagreement on the appropriate product mix for different stores and diffused responsibility for inventory levels. After the change to power formats, buyers were responsible for pricing and merchandising for one format nationwide.[19] A national business manager was appointed to oversee buyers and other staff connected with each power format. This business manager was responsible for developing strategies to successfully compete against specialty stores operating in similar merchandise categories. Sears' senior management hoped that the smaller, more focused units would be able to react more quickly to changing market conditions.

While power formats had positive effects, Sears was slow to remodel its 868 retail stores in the United States. As of May 1992, only the new automotive and appliance formats were in place nationwide. The home furnishings and apparel units had reached only 20 percent of the stores. Because these changes were being implemented so slowly, many analysts called for Sears to downsize. Some of these analysts suggested that Sears should get out of the fashion merchandise and home furnishing businesses altogether and concentrate exclusively on appliances and hardware where it had a competitive advantage.[20]

In January 1993, the company announced plans to close 113 unprofitable stores. Instead of focusing on hardware and appliances, though, Sears announced plans to invest even more floor space and company resources in promoting fashion merchandise. Sears' 1992 revenue and profit figures support the move to a fashion merchandise focus since, while apparel contributed only 24 percent of the company's retail revenue, it accounted for 64 percent of this division's profit (see Exhibit 2).

Sears' move into fashion merchandise categories was facilitated by computerized point-of-sale registers. Although the company was slow to take advantage of information technology, it finally recognized the strategic advantage of timely information and upgraded its point-of-sale registers. These registers perform credit checks, automatic price lookup functions, inventory adjustment functions, and schedule replacement deliveries. Furthermore, bar-code scanners have tied stores, warehouses, home office, and suppliers together in a "seamless web."[21] These systems

---

[17]Kevin Kelly, "At Sears, the More Things Change . . .," *Business Week*, November 12, 1990, p. 66.

[18]Ibid.

[19]Caminiti, S., op. cit., p. 89.

[20]Johnathon R. Laing, "Can You Count on Sears?" *Barron's*, May 18, 1992, p. 10.

[21]Ibid., p. 11.

■ **Exhibit 2**
Sears Revenue
Breakdown[22]

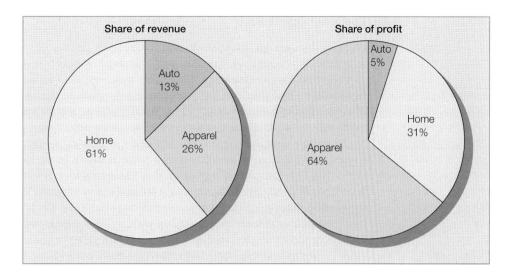

enable Sears to react more quickly to changing fashion trends, remove items which are not selling and thus, compete more effectively with specialty stores. However, while these systems are the best available, Sears' competitors utilize comparable systems. Thus, Sears' massive investment in technology only enabled it to keep abreast of its competitors; these systems did not provide a strategic advantage over competitors.

While no cost advantage was obtained from the new register system, Sears did surpass competitors in the area of retail space planning. The company developed the Merchandise Assortment Planning System (MAPS) software for planning assortments in stores. MAPS is space management, a technology commonly associated with supermarkets. Sears developed the software in partnership with Logistics Data Systems.[23] The space management system simulates all store fixtures and product properties. The appropriate displays for merchandise can be constructed on computer and transferred electronically throughout the organization. When the displays are finalized, the data is passed not only to store managers but to the Sears replenishment system, thereby starting off the reorder system. When new merchandise arrives at the store, a manager constructs displays based on store-specific planograms received from the head office. The process of planning a new assortment used to take four months but with the MAPS program, the time was cut in half.

In summary, Sears began restructuring its retail stores into seven captive "specialty stores" to entice customers back from specialty and discount stores. The change in management structure was designed to enable each format to develop a more focused marketing strategy. Furthermore, the introduction of new computerized registers was designed to enable the company to better track product movement. While these changes were implemented in the retail unit, the company also had major problems with its floundering catalog unit.

---

[22]Ellen Neuborne, "Streamlined Sears Shopping for New Image," *USA Today,* October 17, 1992 p. 7B.

[23]"Sears 'MAPS' Customized Assortments," *Chain Store Age Executive,* October 1990, p. 62.

Catalog Operations

In 1991 the catalog division was separated from the retail store operations for the first time. When managers assessed the catalog business by itself, they discovered the division had lost money since 1985. The unit lost $145 million in 1991 followed by $165 million in 1992.[24] These losses were tallied while the mail-order industry grew to over $200 billion per year.[25] The Sears' catalog, which was once the envy of the mail-order industry, had lost touch with modern direct mail practices.

Other direct-mail companies developed specialty catalogs targeted to specific consumers but Sears continued to mail a huge book to every household that ordered regularly. The company did mail smaller catalogs which it labeled "specialty books," but these were simply sections taken from the big catalog. While other companies purchased demographic information and mailing lists for targeting markets, Sears had invaluable customer information within the company which apparently it overlooked. It was estimated that 40 percent of American households had a Sears credit card.[26] From these credit records, the company could have developed mailing lists for multiple specialty catalogs, but failed to do so.

Sears also failed to introduce services which other direct-mail companies were offering, such as a toll-free 800 number, 24 hour order entry, and home delivery. Customers were required to come to Sears' stores to pick up merchandise or pay a penalty charge for home delivery. In 1992, Sears finally recognized that in-store pick up was enormously expensive because of the space these operations occupy, space more profitably used as selling and display areas. The retailer cut 6,900 jobs by phasing out in-store catalog service desks and hoped to save $50 million annually.[27]

Soon after these interim changes, the company decided to close the entire catalog unit. The company finally realized the complexity of trying to make the unit profitable again, and decided that resources could be better applied to restructuring retail operations. The closure of catalog operations at the end of 1993 meant the forced termination of 50,000 employees.

As Sears examined its entire merchandising unit's operations, it became obvious that along with major restructuring in the stores and catalog unit, the distribution and transportation systems within the retail operations had to be restructured. Distribution costs were placing the organization at a competitive disadvantage.

Transportation and Distribution

While Sears was slow to make changes in the organization's distribution and transportation systems, the change to power formats revealed the necessity of drastic changes. Sears reduced logistics costs through a partnership with a company specializing in efficient logistics systems.

In 1990, Sears spun off its transportation and logistics operations as a separate company called Sears Logistics Services (SLS). The separate organization was charged with handling the needs of the merchandise division. Sears Logistics contracted with third-party partners to handle certain operations involved with ware-

[24]Patterson, February 10, 1993, p. A3.

[25]"Mail-Order Top 250+," *Direct Marketing*, July 1991, p. 29.

[26]John Berry, "Can Brennan Save the Big Store?" *Adweek*, February 18, 1991, p. 5.

[27]Francine Schwadel, "Retailing: Sears Roebuck to Streamline Catalog Business," *The Wall Street Journal*, January 8, 1992, p. B1.

housing and freight distribution. The partnership with Menlo Logistics, a subsidiary of Consolidated Freightways, handled all the "Less than Full Truck Load" (LTL) freight transportation from Sears' 4,000 vendors to the company's distribution centers.[28]

After the implementation of the logistic partnership with Menlo, stores no longer had to perform a receiving function. All goods went through one of the Sears replenishment centers, and the receiving activity at stores was limited to unloading, scanning, and placing merchandise on racks. Sears Logistics had on-line access to the Menlo computer systems to check on inbound merchandise and verify shipment from suppliers. In addition, with electronic data interchange (EDI), the partnership created a paperless environment. Where Sears used to receive and process freight bills from 100 different carriers, the company now received electronic freight bills from one company.

While the Sears' alliance with Menlo was perhaps the company's biggest step in reducing distribution costs, the company made other tough decisions in order to reduce costs. The company closed five of twelve distribution centers and laid off the 5,700 people employed at them.[29] The centers were antiquated, multilevel complexes which were labor intensive and difficult to streamline.

The restructuring of the Sears merchandise group required other changes in the distribution system. The first power format to be implemented, appliances and electronics, was supported by completely separate distribution centers. The company built six new warehouses across the country to support the new "Brand Central" appliance format exclusively. When an appliance is ordered in the store, the order is checked by computer, shipped immediately from the closest distribution center, and installed in the customer's home within three days.[30]

Information and Systems Technology

Sears tried to make electronic data interchange (EDI) a precondition for gaining supply contracts with the merchandise division.[31] Through EDI, Sears attempted to reduce distribution expenses through reduced inventory levels and a reduction in time taken to turn merchandise orders into goods on the racks. Sears still could not bring fashion goods to retail racks as quickly as some of the specialty stores. To address this problem, the company signed special partnerships with 94 vendors representing 138 different products.[32] The partnerships emphasized information exchange and a relationship built on mutual goals and objectives. The agreements formally recognized that each party's success depended on the full cooperation of the partners. These partnerships were designed to enable Sears to bring new products onto the selling floor much more quickly.

In addition to EDI, Sears developed and implemented a computer system to streamline distribution functions and reduce reaction time. The Sears Distribution

---

[28]Thomas A. Foster, "How Sears Leverages Its LTL," *Distribution*, September 1992, p. 46.

[29]Michael Oneal, "Sears: Trimming the Worst of the Corporate Fat," *Business Week*, March 16, 1987, p. 3.

[30]Michael Oneal, "Shaking Sears Right Down to Its Work Boots," *Business Week*, October 17, 1988, p. 87.

[31]Michael Fitzgerald, " 'When?' Is Now at Sears," *Computerworld*, October 8, 1990, p. 71.

[32]Bernie Knill, "QuickResponse 90: Manufacturing Gets More Respect," *Material Handling Engineering*, June 1990, p. 48.

Operating System (DOS) integrated Sears' distribution sites with all of the 868 stores through the in-store point-of-sale systems.[33] The Distribution Operating System replaced the traditional automated and manual functions used to manage the movement of merchandise throughout the Sears organization. The system allowed managers to see individual turnover rates, inventory levels, and reorder cycles at any particular moment. This system enabled Sears to reduce inventory levels without increasing in-store stock outs.

Changes in Financial Services Division

In 1992, Sears announced plans to sell the Dean Witter Financial Services Group which includes the Discover credit card operation. The divestiture of this subsidiary was slated for completion by late 1993. In addition, the company planned to sell the Coldwell Banker residential real-estate business but retain the Homart Development Corporation. Sears also offered 20 percent of the Allstate Insurance Group to the public in a new stock offering. These divestitures were forced upon Sears by agitated shareholders who wanted Sears to concentrate on the merchandise unit exclusively. Furthermore, most investors believe that each of the subsidiaries will be even more profitable once separated from the bureaucracy at Sears.

By eliminating the Sears Financial Network, the company returned to where it was twelve years earlier, except that it was no longer the number one retailer. Sears planned to focus on its stores, which ironically had become the company's weakest business unit. The divestitures, along with the restructuring of the stores and closure of the catalog unit, were enormous changes that may not return the company to retailing prominence or even profitability. While Sears once had an advertising slogan of "Sears, Where America Shops," it now seems that Sears is where America *used to* shop.

---

[33]Ibid.

Case 19 Lands' End

Peter G. Goulet and Lynda L. Goulet
both of the University of Northern Iowa

Lands' End, Inc. (LEI), was founded in 1963 by Gary C. Comer, an avid sailor and an award-winning copywriter with the advertising agency of Young & Rubican. LEI was founded to sell equipment to racing sailors by direct mail. Its unique name was the result of a mistake in its first printed mailing piece. Lands' End was meant to be Land's End, the name of a famous English seaport. The error was left uncorrected and the firm was off and running. Mr. Comer has said, "For me Lands' End is a dream that came true. I always wanted to create a company of my own and here it is."

From its founding until 1976, LEI emphasized the sales of sailing gear while gradually adding related traditional recreational clothing and soft luggage to its product line. The clothing and luggage became so popular among the firm's upscale clientele that by 1976, LEI shifted its focus entirely to these more popular items. In 1979, having outgrown its Chicago location, LEI moved to its current headquarters in Dodgeville, Wisconsin. The Chicago facility which once housed the whole firm was retained as the location of its marketing creative staff of 35 people.

In its first 25 years Lands' End has grown to sales of over $335 million, making it one of the nation's largest merchants selling entirely through the medium of the direct-mail catalog. In the five years between 1982 and 1987, LEI's sales more than tripled and the firm set a goal of doubling fiscal 1986 sales by 1991. LEI went public in October 1986, achieving listing on the New York Stock Exchange in late 1987. LEI's 20,040,000 shares had a market value of $560 million in September 1988. For the fiscal year ending in January 1989, Lands' End is expected to circulate 72 million catalogs, achieve sales of $388 million, and earn profits of $26 million, or $1.30 per share.[1] Further financial information is presented in Exhibits 1–3.

Business and Customers

Lands' End is a clothing retailer serving the market by direct mail through its extensive catalog of traditional clothing and related items. The main types of products sold include men's dress shirts, slacks, ties, and accessories, as well as sport clothes such as sweaters, shoes, jogging suits, and "sweats," and a myriad of styles of knit shirts. The women's line includes similar sport clothing, as well as traditional natural fiber shirts, skirts, slacks, shoes, and accessories. The firm also offers a limited, but growing, line of children's clothing in styles similar to the adult lines. Finally, the firm manufactures and sells a line of soft luggage products and has recently introduced a line of linen and bedding.

This case was prepared by Peter G. Goulet and Lynda L. Goulet of the University of Northern Iowa and is intended to be used as a basis for class discussion rather than to illustrate either effective or ineffective handling of an administrative situation. The authors thank Julie Coppock, a UNI graduate student, and Stephen Ashley of Blunt, Ellis, and Loewi for their help in the preparation of this case.

Presented to and accepted by the refereed Midwest Society for Case Research. All rights reserved to the authors and to the MSCR. © 1988 by Peter G. Goulet and Lynda L. Goulet.

[1]All financial data in this case comes from Lands' End annual reports and analytical reports prepared by Stephen Ashley of Blunt, Ellis, and Loewi, Inc. (August 4, 1987 and November 23, 1987).

■ **Exhibit 1** Income Statements for the Fiscal Years Ended January 31 (thousands of dollars), Lands' End

	1988	Percent	1987	Percent	1986	Percent	1985	Percent
Net sales	$336,291	100.0%	$265,058	100.0%	$227,160	100.0%	$172,241	100.0%
Cost of sales	190,348	56.6%	152,959	57.7%	135,678	59.7%	101,800	59.1%
Gross profit	145,943	43.4%	112,099	42.3%	91,482	40.3%	70,441	40.9%
Operating expense	104,514	31.0%	80,878	30.5%	67,781	29.9%	55,431	32.2%
Depreciation	3,185	1.0%	2,576	1.0%	1,867	.8%	1.435	.8%
Operating income	38,244	11.4%	28,645	10.8%	21,834	9.6%	13,575	7.9%
Interest expense	(1,357)	−0.4%	(1,488)	−0.6%	(1,579)	−0.7%	(1,697)	−1.0%
Other income	1,441	0.4%	1,329	0.5%	1,329	0.6%	938	0.5%
Income before tax	38,328	11.4%	28,486	10.7%	21,584	9.5%	12,816	7.4%
Income tax (1)	15,523	4.6%	13,881	5.2%	10,314	4.5%	6,076	3.5%
Net income	22,805	6.8%	14,605	5.5%	11,270	5.0%	6,740	3.9%
Per share (2)	$ 1.14		$ 0.73		$ 0.56			
Catalogs mailed	63.5 mil.		50.0 mil.		44.0 mil.		29.0 mil.	
Quarterly percents	Sales	Gr. Pr.	Sales	Gr. Pr.	Sales	Gr. Pr.		
Feb–Apr	18.0%	17.6%	17.8%	16.7%	19.1%	19.5%		
May–July	19.0	18.8	19.9	18.7	19.4	18.1		
Aug–Oct	23.8	24.1	24.5	25.3	23.7	24.4		
Nov–Jan	39.1	39.4	37.8	39.3	37.8	38.0		

Lands' End was a Subchapter S corporation through part of 1987. Therefore: (1) Income taxes from 1985–87 are estimated to reflect a normal corporate structure. (2) Earnings per share are estimated based on shares outstanding in 1988.

■ **Exhibit 2** Statement of Changes in Working Capital for Fiscal Years Ended (thousands of dollars), Lands' End

	1988	Percent	1987	Percent	1986	Percent	1985	Percent
Sources:								
Operations (1)	$25,668		$21,804		$23,451		$14,251	
Long-term debt			264		316			
Sale of stock			22,584				520	
Fixed assets, net	776		38		243		205	
Total sources	$26,444		$44,690		$24,010		$14,976	
Uses:								
Dividends (2)	$ 4,008		$28,000		$13,775		$11,755	
Fixed assets	5,862		9,595		6,631		2,658	
Reduce L. T. debt	1,918						478	
Other			40		24			
Total uses	$11,788		$37,635		$20,430		$14,891	
Net incr. w. cap.	$14,656		$ 7,055		$ 3,580		$ 85	

(1) Cash flow from operations consists of net income, depreciation, and additions to deferred taxes. (2) Lands' End was a subchapter S corporation through part of 1987. Therefore, dividends from 1985–87 are subchapter S distributions.

	1988	1987	1986
Current assets			
Cash & m. secur.	$ 28,175	$ 16,032	$ 3,578
Receivables	274	238	319
Inventories	46,444	40,091	31,057
Other	3,363	1,299	733
Total current	$ 78,256	$ 57,660	$35,687
Plant & equipment			
Land & buildings	15,114	13,809	9,499
Equipment	21,974	19,667	13,266
Leasehold improv.	908	661	584
Other	674		1,250
Total	38,670	34,137	24,599
Depreciation	9,947	7,315	4,758
Net fixed assets	28,723	26,822	19,841
Total assets	$106,979	$ 84,482	$55,528
Current liabilities			
Curr. portion long-term debt	$ 1,918	$ 321	$ 193
Accounts payable	21,223	16,791	13,927
Order advances	453	449	193
Accruals	7,226	4,394	2,589
Profit sharing	2,646	1,707	830
Taxes payable	5,394	9,258	
Total current	38,860	32,920	18,002
Long-term debt	8,667	10,585	10,321
Deferred inc. tax	2,778	3,100	
	50,305	46,605	28,323
Stockholders' equity			
Common stock	200	100	95
Paid-in-capital	22,308	22,408	73
Retained earnings	34,166	15,369	27,037
Total equity	56,674	37,877	27,205
Total debt and owners' equity	$106,979	$ 84,482	$55,528

	Median Household Income	Women, Percent Employed	Percent, Ages 25–49	Growth 25–49 >$30K*	Percent Employed Professionals
LEI	$46,000	75%	69%	3.2%	70%
U.S.	24,500	<50%	50%	<1.0%	<25%

*Annual growth expected from 1985 to 1995 for the population group with incomes over $30,000, and from 25 to 49 years of age.

The Lands' End customer is reasonably affluent. Sixty percent have incomes in excess of $35,000. Most have been to college and are employed in professional or managerial jobs. Exhibit 4 compares the typical Lands' End customer to its counterpart in the population as a whole. In 1986, LEI estimated that there were 23 million households in the United States that met its typical customer characteristics. Moreover, this group was growing more than three times as fast as the population as a whole. Further, it typically spends a larger proportion of its income on apparel than the average for the population.

The Direct Marketing Association (DMA) estimated that 10.1 percent of the total female population and 5.4 percent of the male population ordered at least one item of clothing from a catalog or other direct-mail merchant in 1986. On average, between 9 percent and 10 percent of all the people with incomes over $30,000 made a direct-mail clothing purchase. In addition, DMA has estimated that 10.7 percent of college graduates and 10.5 percent of professional/managerial households made such a purchase. Overall, it would appear that about 10 percent of the group Lands' End considers to be its prime customers can be expected to make a direct-mail clothing purchase from some firm in a given year. Out of the base of 23 million customers, this would imply an average of 2.3 million active customers per year. In fact, LEI estimates that in the 36 months preceding February 1988, it had made at least one sale to 3.4 million different persons.

■ Industry Environment

Lands' End is part of the catalog apparel industry, which accounts for approximately 10 percent of all apparel sales. Recent data for these markets is shown in Exhibit 5. In 1988 the firm held about a 4 percent share of the catalog apparel market, making it the seventh largest direct-market or catalog-apparel retailer (see Exhibit 6 for a list of selected competitors). This market has enjoyed recent growth of 8.6 percent per year and is expected to continue to grow at 10 percent per year through 1991. Lands' End has grown roughly two to three times as fast as the market since calendar 1985.

Though catalog retailing is expected to grow faster than retailing in general, there are some clouds on the horizon. The prospects for growth have caused a sharp increase in the number of catalogs directed to the buying public. In 1985, a total of 10 billion catalogs were mailed, rising to 11.8 billion in 1987.[2] In addition, poor service on the part of some catalog merchants may help create a negative image for the segment in general. *Consumer Reports* has recently published ratings of catalog retailers to help consumers determine the relative service quality of many of the larger firms, including Lands' End. Lands' End was beaten only by L. L. Bean in these initial consumer ratings.

■ **Exhibit 5**
Retail Sales Data
($ billions)

	1985	1986	1987E	1988E	Growth Rate†
Retail sales	1374.0	1454.0	1541.0	1633.0	5.9%
Retail apparel	74.0	81.0	86.7	92.8	7.8
Catalog sales*	26.0	27.5	29.7	32.1	7.3
Catalog apparel*	7.5	8.2	8.9	9.6	8.6
Lands' End	.23	.26	.34	.39	19.2
share cat. app'l.	3.1%	3.1%	3.8%	4.1%	

*Estimated.
†Average annual growth, 1985–88.

SOURCE: U.S. Commerce Department.

---

[2]A. Hagedorn, " 'Tis the Season for Catalog Firms," *The Wall Street Journal,* November 24, 1987, p. 6.

Another threat to catalog retailers is the rising cost of shipping goods and mailing catalogs. Early in 1988, the postal service raised postage rates for catalogs 25 percent and U.P.S. raised surface shipping costs as well. In addition, catalog production costs are also rising, as are catalog sizes. The typical cost for a catalog the size and quality of that published by Lands' End can run as high as $750–$800 per thousand, exclusive of mailing and handling costs. A typical 64-page catalog in two or four colors costs around $350–$400 per thousand. To partially offset these rising costs, some catalog retailers—such as Bloomingdale's—have begun to sell their catalogs in major chain bookstores and to sell advertising space in the catalogs.

Finally, most states do not require catalog retailers to charge sales tax on catalog sales outside of the states in which the firm operates. Recently, however, states are beginning to view this practice as a significant source of lost revenue. In 1988, Iowa was added to a small but growing list of states which will require catalog firms to remit sales tax on all purchases made from catalogs by residents of the state, regardless of where the catalog firm is located. If all states move to this type of policy it will reduce one of the key advantages to catalog retailers and could create significant overhead expenses for keeping the records required to satisfy each state.

A segment of the direct-market retailing industry outside of the catalog segment may also pose a threat to catalog retailers. Home shopping directed through cable television was expected to generate an estimated $1.75 billion in sales in 1987. The companies in this segment, of which the largest is the Home Shopping Network, Inc., were estimated to have reached over 40 million households in that year. Further, though some view the cable shopping phenomenon as a fad, DMA estimates that by 1992 this industry segment could be generating $5.6 billion in sales and be reaching nearly 80 million households. If this is true it represents a 26 percent average annual growth rate for the period. Given the growth of retail sales in general and forecasts for direct-market retailing, this would seem to be growth that could easily come at the expense of other direct marketers.

Though entry into direct marketing does not demand the same level of investment required to generate similar sales in the normal retail market, the costs may still be significant. To provide sufficient service requires expertise and may involve a large equipment investment. To develop a mailing list is also important and expensive. Name rental may run anywhere from $60–$100 per thousand names annually, or upwards of $100,000 for a million quality, proven names. As established firms such as Lands' End and L. L. Bean become large, economies of scale and learning curve effects may make it difficult for new firms to enter the business in all but small niche markets.

Pure catalog retailers have a number of significant advantages over conventional retailers. The most obvious of these is that they have no stores to operate and have, therefore, lower costs. Passing on some of these cost savings can create a competitive advantage. Yet in spite of this inherent advantage, several major catalog competitors have chosen to operate store locations in addition to their catalog operation. What these firms have attempted to do is improve their performance as traditional retailers by using higher-profit catalog sales as an adjunct to normal store-based selling. The Limited, Eddie Bauer, Talbots, J.C. Penney, and Sears, for example, operate anywhere from several dozen to several hundred stores each.

In addition to lower costs and prices, catalog retailers offer the customer the advantage of convenience. Being able to shop through a catalog and call in an order even in the middle of the night may be of great benefit to households where, for example, both spouses work outside the home. Using a catalog also allows the consumer to think about the purchase and compare alternate sources without costly transportation and sales pressure. Finally, catalog shopping is a convenience for people who live in smaller communities where a variety of upscale goods, in particular, is not typically available; obtaining such goods from a conventional store would be even more inconvenient than purchasing through a catalog.

The biggest weaknesses of catalog shopping involve the inability to see an item before buying it and the cost and inconvenience of having to return an unsatisfactory purchase. In spite of these issues, however, a Gallup poll reported by the DMA in 1987 shows that two-thirds of the population would consider making a direct/catalog purchase even if the item were available in conventional stores.

■ Lands' End Strategy

Catalog retailers must adhere to most of the principles that govern traditional store-based retailers. Merchandise must be fresh, varied, and of satisfactory quality. By maintaining itself as a retailer of traditional clothing, Lands' End does not have the concerns with fad and fashion faced by such combination in-store and direct-mail retailers as the Limited and Bloomingdales, for example. However, the firm does have to offer new merchandise regularly. Its most recent introductions have been its lines of linens and children's clothing. Other featured items include its knit shirts and rugby shirts, the latter having been chosen by the U.S. National Rugby Team as their official jersey.

All Lands' End merchandise carries the firm's private label. All catalog items except luggage are produced by outside vendors. The luggage is manufactured by the firm at its plant in West Union, Iowa. Product quality is assured by frequent inspections of goods, both at the manufacturer's facility and at the company. The firm even maintains a Lear jet to fly its staff of quality assurance personnel to the factories of domestic manufacturers to direct production according to Lands' End specifications. Further, 10 percent of every shipment received at Dodgeville is inspected to assure continuing quality. Critical products are purchased from more than one vendor and consistency between them is maintained by strict specifications. To further assure quality and service from vendors, officers of these companies are regularly brought to Dodgeville to see the Lands' End operation.

Lands' End understands that catalog retailing is a difficult business in which to create a competitive advantage. Its catalogs, therefore, are produced with what the firm calls an "editorial" approach. Goods are not merely described in short, dry prose. Rather, key product lines are given half- or full-page descriptions designed to be interesting, appealing, and original. The catalog also contains several pages devoted to editorials, essays, and witty commentary dealing with a variety of subjects of interest to the firm's clientele. Two pages in the April 1988 issue described glass blowing. This kind of content is not unique to Lands' End. The catalog issued by the trendy Banana Republic employs a similar approach. However, because different writers and subjects are involved in each catalog, Lands' End catalogs are unique and difficult to copy.

The quality and presentation of the Lands' End catalog is tightly controlled and merchandise is presented in "life-style" settings designed to appeal to the firm's clientele. Merchandise is grouped in "programs" to promote multiple-item sales. This magazine-style approach is further supported by the use of product teams: new items are studied by a team consisting of a writer, an artist, and a buyer to make certain that each item is presented properly in the catalog.

To interest prospective customers, Lands' End utilizes print advertising. The cost of this national campaign in selected upscale publications such as *The Wall Street Journal* and the *New Yorker* is approximately 1 percent of sales. The campaign is designed to be compatible with the firm's editorial catalog structure and contains copy in a similar style.

Lands' End considers itself a "direct merchant" and summarizes its marketing and operations strategy as:

1. Establishing a strong, unique consumer brand image.
2. Placing an emphasis on product quality and value.
3. Identifying and expanding an active customer base.
4. Creating a continuous relationship with active customers.
5. Building customer confidence and convenience through service.

■ Service

At least part of the success of Lands' End has been attributed to its customer-oriented marketing philosophy. This customer orientation is reflected in a number of ways. Prompt service is supported by rapid response and personal attention. The firm claims its 24-hour-a-day 800 number—which is the source of 73 percent of all incoming orders—rarely requires more than two rings before it is answered. In addition, 99 percent of its orders are shipped within 24 hours of receipt. This level of service is facilitated by a dedicated staff, a sophisticated computerized operating system, and a distribution center recently doubled in size to 275,000 square feet. The DMA reports in its 1987 survey of customer attitudes that 83 percent of all direct-mail customers have some sort of complaint about direct-mail purchasing. Though the most common complaints center on the inability to tell what one is likely to receive, or that one will have been deceived by the merchandise, a significant percentage either object to poor service (20 percent) or inconvenience of some kind (16 percent). In addition, over half of consumers surveyed by DMA say they would buy more from direct marketers who provide prompt delivery.

Lands' End deals with customer complaints with the same commitment they have to customers placing orders. This is essential if the firm is to retain its strong group of dedicated customers. The DMA reports that though a high proportion of customers may have some complaint with mail order, 73 percent will become repeat customers if the complaint is satisfactorily handled, compared to 17 percent if it is not.

Lands' End sums up its marketing and service philosophy through its "Principles of Doing Business." These principles have been published in the catalog, annual reports, and advertising copy produced by the company:

Principle 1. We do everything we can to make our products better. We improve material, and add back features and construction details that others have taken out over the years. We never reduce the quality of a product to make it cheaper.

Principle 2. We price our products fairly and honestly. We do not, have not, and will not participate in the common retail practice of inflating markups to set up a future phony "sale."

Principle 3. We accept any return, for any reason, at any time. Our products are guaranteed. No fine print. No arguments. We mean exactly what we say: GUAR-ANTEED. PERIOD.

Principle 4. We ship faster than anyone we know of. We ship items in stock the day we receive the order. At the height of the last Christmas season the longest time an order was in the house was 36 hours, excepting monograms which took an-other 12 hours.

Principle 5. We believe that what is best for our customer is best for all of us. Every-one here understands that concept. Our sales and service people are trained to know our products, and to be friendly and helpful. They are urged to take all the time necessary to take care of you. We even pay for your call, for whatever rea-son you call.

Principle 6. We are able to sell at lower prices because we have eliminated middle-men; because we don't buy branded merchandise with high protected markups; and because we have placed our contracts with manufacturers who have proved they are cost conscious and efficient.

Principle 7. We are able to sell at lower prices because we operate efficiently. Our people are hard working, intelligent, and share in the success of the company.

Principle 8. We are able to sell at lower prices because we support no fancy empo-riums with their high overhead. Our main location is in the middle of a 40-acre cornfield in rural Wisconsin. We still operate our first location in Chicago's Near North tannery district.

■ Operations

The heart of any catalog retailing operation is, of course, the catalog itself. Lands' End currently mails thirteen 140-page (average) catalogs a year to its proven cus-tomers. In all, the firm circulated a total of 50 million catalogs in fiscal 1987. That number is expected to rise to 63.5 million in 1988 and is expected to reach 72 mil-lion in 1989, up from 18 million in 1984, the firm's most productive year in terms of sales per catalog mailed.

Another key to effective catalog retailing is the mailing list. Firms the size of Lands' End commonly maintain lists of 5 million or more names. The firm itself maintains a proprietary list of 7.8 million names. Although many catalog retailers obtain names from mailing-list brokers and even competitors, Lands' End has attempted to build its list internally, as much as possible, as a source of competitive advantage. It has also reduced its participation in the mailing-list rental market.

Catalog retailing also depends on order fulfillment and service. Merchandise is stored in and distributed from the firm's 275,000-square-foot distribution center. In spite of the size of this facility, however, it is only expected to be able to satisfy the firm's needs through 1989, when another 250,000-square-foot addition is expected to be completed. Through this center, Lands' End processed approximately 31,000 orders per day in 1987, with a high of 75,000 orders on its peak day. The center has the capacity to process 35,000 orders per nine-hour shift.

To facilitate the function of the distribution center, manage inventories, and min-imize shipping costs, the firm utilizes an optical-scanning sorting system. Orders are processed through the firm's mainframe computer system, based on three very large

Series 3090 IBM computers. Through this computer system, management can obtain real-time information on any part of its current operation status. In addition, during 1987, the firm installed a new computer-controlled garment-moving system and an inseaming system as part of $6 million in capital expenditures. Finally, an automated receiving system installed during 1987, has increased the firm's receiving capacity from 4,000 to 10,000 boxes per day.

Phone service is maintained through company phone centers. This service was recently enlarged by the addition of an auxiliary center designed to handle seasonal overload traffic. The phone system now operates on a fiber-optic cable system to increase communication quality. Through the computer system, each operator has access to customer records and past sales history, as well as a fact file on each catalog item. In normal times, it is not unusual for this system to handle 75 calls at a time, around the clock, with a much higher load during the Christmas season.

Though 95 percent of all sales are through the catalog, and Lands' End operates no retail stores, it does maintain nine "outlet stores" at various locations in Chicago and Wisconsin. The firm also utilizes a "Lands' End Outlet" section in its catalog to help dispose of overstocks.

As the firm has grown, so has the number of employees. The firm now employs more than 2,200 people, with as many as 1,200 added to handle the extra load during the busy fourth quarter. Both the founder and the current president have extensive advertising experience as well as considerable experience with the company. New additions to the list of top managers include experts in catalog merchandising, quality assurance, and other related specialties.

Lands' End realizes the importance of a quality work force. It has worked with the University of Wisconsin, Platteville, to set up an extension in Dodgeville to help workers increase their skills at company expense. Part-time workers earn full-time benefits after they work 1,040 hours in a year. All workers receive the right to an employee discount on the firm's products and they share in LEI's profits. The firm also plans to provide a $5 million employee fitness center in 1988. Overall, wage levels in this industry average approximately $5.75 per hour.

■ Competitors

Dozens of catalog retailers sell apparel, even in the market dominated by Lands' End. However, in its specific target market, LEI has apparently become the market leader. LEI's competitors can be classified into several basic categories. Firms such as the J. Crew unit of Popular Services, Inc. (men's clothing), Talbots (women's clothing, formerly owned by General Mills), and The Company Store (linens), compete directly with a product segment served by Lands' End. Other firms, such as Hanover House, produce multiple catalogs serving a wide variety of customer product and demographic segments. Some of these segments may overlap with those served by LEI. Major retailers such as Sears, J.C. Penney, and Spiegel produce large, seasonal, full-line catalogs selling a wide variety of merchandise, of which apparel is only a part. These large firms, as well as other smaller catalog retailers who also operate retail stores, tend to compete more closely with traditional retailers. Exhibit 6 identifies a number of major catalog retailers and competitors for LEI. Exhibit 7 describes and contrasts several operating characteristics of LEI's closest competitors.

■ **Exhibit 6**
Direct/Catalog Sales,
1985 Largest Direct-
Mail/Catalog-Apparel
Firms

Firm	Direct/Catalog Total 1985 Sales
Fingerhut Corp/Cos.	$1,485 million
Spiegel	847 million
Sears	695 million
The Limited/Brylane	612 million
J. C. Penney	510 million
New Process	330 million
Combined International	227 million
Lands' End	227 million
L. L. Bean	220 million
Hanover House	212 million
Avon Direct Response	205 million
Bear Creek	130 million
General Mills	104 million
CML Group	55 million
Popular Services	40 million

SOURCE: *Inside the Leading Mail Order Houses,* Maxwell Sroge Publishing, 1985.

■ **Exhibit 7**
Competitor
Characteristics, 1985
Lands' End

Company	Catalog Sales ($ mil.)	Catalogs Mailed (mil.)	Sales per Catalog	Active Buyers (mil.)	Stores and/or Catalogs
Lands' End	$227	44	$5.16	3.43	9 outlets
Hanover House	212	250	0.85	4.00	20 catalogs
L. L. Bean	221	68	3.25	2.15	1 store
Popular Services:					
J. Crew	30	7	4.29	.45	
Cliff & Wills	10	2	5.00	.20	
CML Group	55	25	2.20	.49	5 catalogs
					100 stores
General Mills (1985)					
Talbots	47	38	1.25	.47	59 stores
Eddie Bauer	57	25	2.28	.72	39 stores
General Mills (1987)					
Talbots	84	60+	<1.40	.65+	109 stores
Eddie Bauer	76	N/A	N/A	1.00	39 stores

■ **Performance**

Since 1984, when Lands' End achieved sales of $123.4 million and net profits of $7.3 million, the firm's sales and profits have grown annually at 22.2 percent and 25.6 percent, respectively. Sales and profit growth in the first half of fiscal 1989 were 33.7 percent and 64.6 percent higher than the same period in 1988, respectively. Gross margins have improved steadily and may be compared to a level of approximately 42.5 percent typical for apparel retailers in general. Net profit margins have also improved and may be compared to a recent level of about 3.5 percent for large retailers. The percentage of debt to equity has declined steadily throughout the period. The net profit to total assets measure of return on investment has averaged 21 percent over the last five years, compared to 4.4 percent for the nation's 33 largest value retail firms (including LEI) in 1988, and approximately 7.5 percent for all retail establishments. LEI's return on stockholders' equity has averaged 40.4 percent since 1984, having earned 40.2 percent in 1988, compared to 15.4 percent for the 33 largest firms. Financial results for Lands' End are presented in Exhibits 1–3.

Although Lands' End's recent performance is spectacular and far exceeds industry standards, it remains to be seen how long their growth and margins can be maintained. As the catalog market becomes increasingly competitive, new products and marketing methods will have to be developed. In spite of the prospect of future pressures, the sale of General Mills' catalog operations in 1988 brought the firm $585 million, or about 19 times the pretax operating earnings of this unit.

■ References

1987 Supplement to the Fact Book. New York: Direct Marketing Association, 1987.

Inside the Leading Mail-Order Houses. 3rd ed. Colorado Springs: Maxwell Sroge Publishing, 1987.

Lands' End Annual Reports, 1987 and 1988.

1988 Industrial Outlook. U.S. Department of Commerce.

Case 20 Blockbuster Entertainment Corporation

James A. Kidney
Southern Connecticut State University

Introduction

Seated at his desk in a rented two-story stucco executive office building in downtown Fort Lauderdale, Florida, H. Wayne Huizenga prepared to announce record revenues and net income for his chain of Blockbuster Video stores. His mid-April 1992 announcement would attribute those results to "increasing market penetration, gains in same-store revenue, and continued emphasis on cost control and increased productivity."[1] As Blockbuster Entertainment Corporation's Chairman of the Board and Chief Executive Officer, he also prepared to announce that it was now possible to pay a cash dividend to the company's 8,000 stockholders—something that had not been done before.

At the end of 1991, having achieved a 13 percent share of market, the company announced that its goal was to reach a 20 percent share of the U.S. home video market and have 3,000 Blockbuster Video stores operating in North America by 1995.[2] In some of its most mature markets, such as Atlanta, Chicago, Dallas, Detroit, and South Florida, that would mean market shares well in excess of 30 percent. Such a high share of market has been rare in specialty retailing. However, Blockbuster was the only U.S. video rental chain operating on a nationwide basis. Its next largest competitor was a regional chain, less than one-tenth its size.

External Challenges and Opportunities

As Huizenga optimistically pondered the company's strategic situation over the next five to seven years, there were several interesting external challenges and opportunities lurking on the horizon:

- With a higher market share than all of its 300 closest competitors combined, how much further could the company's market penetration grow?
- Could any significant technological changes in home entertainment alter the video rental industry's attractiveness?
- What were the future implications of Philips Electronics N.V.'s recent investment in Blockbuster stock?

This case was prepared by Dr. James A. Kidney, Management Department, School of Business, Southern Connecticut State University, New Haven, CT 06515.

[1] Corporate news release dated April 21, 1992.

[2] The total population of video rental stores operating throughout the U.S. ranged between 25,000 and 29,000, and turnover of individual store locations was quite high during the late 1980s and early 1990s.

■ Company History

David P. Cook, a 31-year-old Texas entrepreneur, founded the company in December 1982 as Cook Data Services, Inc., a provider of software and computer services to the oil and gas industries. Facing a sagging market for such services, Cook decided to switch over to a new, rapidly growing niche in specialty retailing—video rental stores. Cook's first store was opened during 1985, and the present corporate name was adopted one year later. From the outset, Cook recognized that an innovative superstore concept would draw many customers away from typical mom-and-pop rental stores and that well-designed computerized information systems would be advantageous for inventory planning and control as well as for customer information.

The typical mom-and-pop store had a spartan, nondescript atmosphere; short hours; a selection of fewer than 3,000 titles stressing recent hits; and empty boxes to be brought to a clerk who would have to find appropriate tapes—provided they were then in stock. Many mom-and-pops obtained significant rental revenues from X-rated videos, and that occasionally created an unwholesome image.

In comparison, Cook's idea was to have a family-oriented atmosphere with an extensive selection of children's videos, longer, more convenient hours, improved layout, quality service, faster check-in/check-out, state-of-the-art real time computer information systems, and a thoroughly trained professional staff.

■ Attracting Huizenga's Attention

After only two years of operation, Blockbuster's latent potential attracted the attention of Huizenga. By that time, Cook owned 8 stores and franchised 11 more in the Dallas area. Huizenga, then 48 years old, was restless, looking for a way to come back from early retirement, after having successfully made a small fortune from several companies.

Huizenga's previous experience had been in building up businesses in a variety of dissimilar industries, such as trash bin rentals and garbage hauling, dry cleaning, lawn care, portable toilet rentals, water cooler rentals and sale of bottled water. His most notable success was Waste Management, Inc., which he had honed into the world's largest waste collection and disposal company.

There was a common denominator running throughout his past entrepreneurial ventures. Each had rendered relatively basic services, had repeat customers, required little employee training, earned a steady cash flow, and was able to expand within an industry filled with small, undercapitalized competitors. Usually, the fragmented industries he entered were ripe for consolidation, because greater firm size led to economies of scale in marketing, distribution, computerized information systems, and/or potential clout in purchasing products and services.

■ Expansion and Acquisition of Store Locations

During 1987 Huizenga and a couple of close business associates bought out Blockbuster's founders and franchise holders for $18 million, and soon thereafter began acquiring small regional chains, such as Southern Video Partnership and Movies to Go. To help him run the new business, Huizenga hired several former upper level managers from McDonald's Corporation. His upper management group adopted the view that Blockbuster's target audience should be very similar to McDonald's broad-based restaurant clientele. Thus, Blockbuster's national expansion of its retail business was based upon McDonald's well-established growth philosophy, namely: blitz major markets, add stores quickly, use franchising to speed the process of obtaining managerial talent and operating capital, and never admit that the market is saturated.

Facing a rapid rise in VCR ownership, management tried to combine careful planning with opportunistic risk taking. An aggressive acquisition program was financed by new equity capital, in order to avoid burdensome long-term debt. Over the following four years, additional regional chains, such as Video Library Inc., Major Video Corp., Oklahoma Entertainment Inc., Vector Video Inc., Video Superstores Venture L.P., and Erol's Inc. were eagerly gobbled up.

A major international thrust was launched in early 1992, with the acquisition of Cityvision plc, the largest home video retailer in the U.K. Operating under the "Ritz" name and enjoying a 20 percent share of market, this firm had roughly 800 small stores and was considered to be an underperformer.

Around the same time, several Blockbuster Video stores were opened in Japan in a joint-venture with Fujita & Co., a retailer running over 800 McDonald's restaurants and holding a stake in Toys 'R' Us Japan, Ltd. Jointly they hoped to open 1,000 stores over the next ten years.

Describing the hectic, and occasionally disorganized, rush to add store locations Huizenga explained, "We felt we had to go fast because we had nothing proprietary. We had to get the locations in each area before somebody else moved in. It was a mistake, but it turned out okay. We have the locations, the people are trained, and the customers are ours. Now if somebody else comes in, they have to take it away from us."[3]

■ Blockbuster Video's Profile as of 1992

Blockbuster Video was a membership only club, serving more than 29 million members worldwide, who rented more than 1 million of the company's video-cassettes daily. Without incurring any membership fees, patrons were provided with bar-coded membership cards which allowed for speedy computerized check-out from the issuing store. Cards were sometimes honored at other locations in the chain as well. By requiring personal photo identification and an application for membership, rather than dealing with anonymous walk-ins, the rental store was able to secure an extra measure of control over tapes which left the premises. A major credit card also had to be presented, so that the store could charge members for lost or damaged inventory.

The typical Blockbuster Video store was located in a free-standing building of approximately 6,000 square feet (560 square meters) and was open from 10:00 am to midnight, seven days per week, 365 days per year. The atmosphere was bright and wholesome. Aisles were clearly marked and divided into more than 30 categories to distribute customer traffic and encourage browsing. Video boxes with tapes inside were openly displayed within easy reach. Similar categories were placed adjacent to

---

[3] *The New York Times Business World Magazine,* June 9, 1991.

■ **Exhibit 1**

Blockbuster Entertainment Corporation
(number of Blockbuster video stores, by
ownership type)

Date	Company	Franchised	Total
December 31, 1985	1	0	1
December 31, 1986	19	0	19
December 31, 1987	112	126	238
December 31, 1988	341	248	589
December 31, 1989	561	518	1,079
December 31, 1990	787	795	1,582
December 31, 1991	1,025	1,003	2,028
March 31, 1992	1,805	1,024	2,829

NOTE: The surge in company stores during the first quarter of 1992 is attributable to the Cityvision plc acquisition.

SOURCE: Blockbuster's 1991 Annual Report and 1992 press releases.

one another, thereby increasing the potential for increase rentals. Blockbuster's superstores typically carried a comprehensive selection of 10,000 prerecorded videocassettes, consisting of more than 8,000 titles. The strongest months for video store rentals tended to be December through March and June through August, with Hollywood's release schedule being a crucial variable.

Blockbuster Video stores proudly claimed to offer "More Movies Than Anyone In The World." Additionally, their relatively weak, fragmented rivals were seldom able to match Blockbuster's advertising clout and wide array of attractions, such as: computer-driven movie selection aids; a three-evening rental policy; an attractive overnight pricing policy for new hit releases which improved turnover and in-stock positions; a state-of-the-art management information system which tracked rentals and market trends; microwave popcorn and other snack foods; promotional tie-ins with Domino's Pizza, Pepsi-Cola, Pizza Hut, Subway, U.S. Air, and Universal Studios; drop-off boxes for fast returns; and publicity from an annual Blockbuster Bowl football game. Nevertheless, some competitors clearly differentiated themselves from Blockbuster by offering lower prices, reservations, home delivery, or hard core "adult" videos.

As of March 31, 1992, there were 2,829 Blockbuster Video stores, worldwide, up from 19 just five years earlier (Exhibit 1).

■ Locations and Operations

By the first quarter of 1992, 68 percent of Blockbuster's stores were located in 46 of America's 50 states, with the remaining 32 percent located in Austria, Australia, Canada, Chile, Guam, Japan, Mexico, Puerto Rico, Spain, the United Kingdom, and Venezuela. Nearly all of the company's retail, distribution, and administrative facilities were rented under non-cancellable operating leases, which in most cases contained renewal options. Blockbuster employed approximately 12,500 individuals.

There had historically tended to be a 50–50 balance between company-owned and franchised locations. Although franchising remained beneficial in foreign countries, where local partners made it easier to conduct business, franchising within the U.S. became less essential once the company had an ample cash flow and employed many competent people who could help manage ongoing growth.

The usual initial investment (i.e., franchise fee, inventory, equipment, and start-up capital) for a franchised location ranged from $700,000 to $1,000,000. Annual

■ **Exhibit 2**   Blockbuster Entertainment Corporation (selected annual financial data)

	1991	1990	1989	1988	1987
Income Data (Million $)					
Systemwide revenue	1,520	1,133	663	284	98
Company revenue	868	633	402	136	43
Operating costs & expenses	714	514	326	110	37
Operating income	154	119	76	26	6
Net income	94	69	44	17	3
Depreciation & amortization	189	124	76	22	5
Cash flow	283	193	120	39	8
Balance Sheet Data (Million $)					
Total assets	804	608	417	235	105
Cash & cash equivalents	48	49	40	9	7
Current assets	163	116	93	39	27
Current liabilities	164	110	83	49	17
Long-term debt	134	169	118	39	22
Shareholders' equity	483	315	208	124	59
Per Share Data ($)					
Earnings per share	.56	.42	.28	.12	.04
Tangible book value	2.35	1.65	1.18	.75	.41
Stock price—high	15.12	13.37	10.81	6.25	2.63
Stock price—low	7.75	6.75	4.87	1.06	.75
Common Stock and Equivalents (Millions)					
Average shares outstanding	168	162	155	142	75

NOTES: Systemwide revenues include franchise store revenues, while company revenues do not. Operating costs and expenses include depreciation and amortization. Cash flow is net income plus depreciation and amortization. Tangible book value excludes cost of purchased businesses in excess of market value of tangible assets acquired (unamortized goodwill).

SOURCES: Blockbuster's 1991 Annual Report and Standard & Poor's Stock Report.

operating costs per location fell in the $400,000 to $500,000 range. Franchisees were provided extensive guidelines for site selection, store design and product selection, as well as customer service, and management training programs. In addition, the company furnished national and local advertising and promotional programs for the entire system. Franchisees paid royalties and other fees for those services and also routinely paid Blockbuster Entertainment for videocassette inventories, computer hardware and software.

For a typical Blockbuster Video store, cash flow payback on initial store investment occurred rapidly—generally in under three years. The average new store attained monthly revenues of $70,000 within twelve months of opening date.

Systemwide revenues, for company-owned and franchise-owned operations combined, as well as other selected financial data are shown in Exhibit 2.

■ Sources of Revenues

During 1991, 5 percent of company revenues were derived from franchise royalties and fees, 20 percent from product sales mainly to franchisees, and 75 percent from rentals. Other than low-priced used products, outright sales of home videos were never emphasized prior to late 1991, because the largest sellers were highly competitive national discount chains like Wal-Mart and Kmart. As a growing portion of consumer spending went towards videocassette and laser disc purchases, it became logical for video rental stores to begin taking the sell-through market more seriously.

Mr. Joseph Baczko, who headed the highly successful International Division of Toys 'R' Us, Inc. for eight years, was hired in 1991 as Blockbuster's new President and Chief Operating Officer. To carry out a process of "retailizing" as well as internationalizing the company, he brought several executives with significant retailing experience into the firm. Promotional and display efforts to stimulate sell-through transactions were given added emphasis under Baczko's direction. Given his background in toys, he was interested in treating child oriented movies, such as *Batman, Bambi, The Little Mermaid,* and *101 Dalmatians,* mainly as sell-through rather than rental products. Blockbuster's stores also began renting Nintendo and Sega Genesis video game products.

■ Industry Environment

Rentals and sales of home videos in the U.S. amounted to a mere $700 million in 1982. By 1991, domestic revenue for the video rental industry reached $11 billion, and Americans were spending more than twice as much to watch movies at home as they did to watch them in movie theaters. Within the marketplace for prerecorded videocassettes, movies accounted for more than 80 percent of rental revenues and at least 50 percent of dollars spent on purchases. Blockbuster Entertainment estimated that the U.S. video rental market for movies would reach $19.3 billion by the turn of the century (Exhibit 3).

In 1980, the percentage of U.S. households owning at least one television set reached 98 percent and remained at that level thereafter. By 1995, there were expected to be almost 100 million households in the U.S., and 98 percent of them were likely to own at least one color TV set. Blockbuster Entertainment expected 91 percent of those TV owning households also to own VCRs (Exhibit 4), with more than 35 percent of them owning at least two machines.

VCR ownership in Europe also was growing rapidly, with household penetration rates in individual countries lagging behind the U.S. anywhere from two to five years. Total 1991 worldwide spending for home video rental and sales was $21.2 billion (Exhibit 5). Licensing, sale, and rental practices differed from one product/market to another, and in some countries most of the television viewing population remained unaware that movie videos could be rented instead of being purchased.

■ **Exhibit 3**
Estimated and Projected Annual U.S. Movie Revenues, by Viewing Method ($ billions)

Viewing Method	1990	1995	2000
Video	10.3	15.2	19.3
Movie theater	5.1	6.9	7.4
Pay cable (premium channels)	5.1	6.2	7.6
Pay-per-view	.01	0.5	2.0
Total	20.6	28.8	36.3

SOURCE: Blockbuster's 1991 Annual Report.

■ **Exhibit 4**
Estimated and Pro-
jected VCR and Cable
TV Penetration among
U.S. TV Owning
Households (millions
of TV owning house-
holds, percent with
VCRs, percent with
cable TV, and percent
with additional pay-
per-view or pay cable
services, by year)

Year	No. of TV Owning Households	Percent with		
		VCR	**Cable**	**Pay Cable**
1980	76	1	20	7
1981	78	3	22	10
1982	82	6	30	16
1983	83	10	34	19
1984	84	17	39	24
1985	85	30	43	26
1986	86	42	46	27
1987	87	53	48	26
1988	89	62	49	27
1989	90	68	53	29
1990	92	72	56	29
1991	92	77	58	30
1992	93	82	61	31
1993	95	86	64	32
1994	96	89	67	34
1995	97	91	70	36

NOTE: From 1982 through 1995, it's assumed that 98 percent of all U.S. households own televisions.

SOURCE: Blockbuster's 1991 Annual Report, the Universal Almanac, and author's estimates.

■ **Exhibit 5**
Estimated Population,
Home Video Spend-
ing, VCR Penetration
and Basic Cable
Penetration by
Country, as of 1991

Country	Population (millions)	Video Spending ($ billions)	VCRs (% of households)	Cable (% of households)
Australia	17	0.7	70	0
Canada	27	1.2	65	69
France	56	0.7	40	10
Germany	79	0.7	46	32
Italy	58	0.6	38	1
Japan	124	2.6	70	20
United Kingdom	57	1.4	70	2
United States	250	11.0	75	57
Others	4,732	2.3	n.a.	n.a.
Worldwide total	5,400	21.2	n.a.	n.a.

NOTE: n.a. = not available

SOURCES: Blockbuster's 1991 Annual Report, *This Business of Television*, and 1992 *World Almanac*.

■ Movie Production and Distribution

Approximately 390 to 450 new feature films were released annually in the United States. Eight of the largest distributors accounted for more than 90 percent of movie theater film rentals in the United States and Canada. Most of them, such as Paramount, Universal, Warner, Fox, Columbia, and Disney, had been in business for more than 50 years. Leading producers and distributors of videos were usually subsidiaries of large companies which owned other leisure-time businesses. Large distributors also had prime access to international channels for distributing American-made films in foreign countries. Musical, cultural, educational, exercise programs, instructional, and documentary videos tended to be handled by smaller distributors.

The time span from the point when work began on a new movie to the point when its revenue stream was largely realized often was five years or longer. Over that period, producers and distributors attempted to play out their products in a manner which gave them an optimum revenue stream.

By 1991, home video had become a major ancillary source of revenue for movie studios. For example, *Nothing But Trouble* (directed by Dan Aykroyd, 1991) grossed $8.5 million in box office receipts. The studio's share was roughly 50 percent. When released on videocassette, the same movie earned an additional $9.6 million in revenue for the studio.[4]

The sequence of each film's release depended on the nature of individual deals made by the distributor. Domestic release usually occurred somewhat ahead of international release. A typical major studio's United States release tended to be rolled out in the following illustrative manner:

Theatrical showings: January through April, 1992
Home video: Mid-Summer, 1992
Airline: Mid-Summer, 1992
Pay-per-view: Late-Summer or Fall, 1992
Pay cable (premium channels): Winter, 1992–93

If attractively priced, popular movies that were developed for young children were likely to achieve a sell-through market of 1.5 million or more copies. Movies that had been adult hits at the box office within the latest year were the ones most in demand for rentals, and 100,000 to 500,000 copies of them were generally sold, mostly to video rental stores. Assuming a $3 charge per rental, it normally took anywhere from 13 to 19 rentals to recover a store's initial investment in a hit movie tape.

Distributors set high initial suggested retail prices (roughly $80 to $100 on box office hits) for videotaped films they expected consumers to rent and low prices (roughly $20 to $30) for those they expected consumers to buy. Each videocassette cost distributors about $2 to manufacture and $2 to market. Wholesale prices paid by Blockbuster were generally 55 to 65 percent of suggested retail prices.

■ Wholesalers

Despite the fact that movies were the mainstay of the home video business, Blockbuster Entertainment traditionally purchased its movie rental inventory from wholesalers rather than film distributors. Having achieved nationwide scope, the company could decide to bypass regional wholesalers and purchase its movies more economically directly from motion picture distributors.

■ Technological Threats

During the decade from 1982 through 1991 Americans purchased 1.2 billion prerecorded and 2.2 billion blank videocassettes. They also built up a $32 billion investment in VCR equipment. This burgeoning consumer commitment to VCR

---

[4]Source: Blockbuster Entertainment 1991 Corp. Annual Report.

technology seemed to assure long-range demand for videocassettes. Nevertheless, the ease of duplicating and pirating videocassettes was a matter of some concern to movie producers. As laser discs began to attract a modest following, rentals and sales of video discs were being added to many video store's product offerings.

No one knew precisely when new types of home entertainment might begin to undermine home videotape viewing. Cable television was expected to become a more and more serious threat. Even though three out of five TV owning households subscribed to cable service as of 1991, only one third of those subscribers had access to movies on pay cable (e.g. HBO, Showtime, Cinemax, The Disney Channel, The Movie Channel) or pay-per-view channels.

Employing "addressable technology," pay-per-view service allowed customers to call in and have a movie, concert, or sporting event broadcast on their TV for a fee. Being transaction based, pay-per-view depended upon impulse buying. It was sold by direct mailings, advertisements, bill stuffers, and 24 hour "barker" promotional channels.

In 1992, sporting events generated almost twice as much pay-per-view business as other alternatives. As pay-per-view's market potential continued to develop, the Summer of 1992 was regarded as an important psychological turning point. Cable operators were seeking broadcasting rights for live coverage of the Olympic Games in Atlanta, Georgia, hoping that such coverage would significantly boost the number of new subscribers for pay-per-view services.

While viewers had to watch pay-per-view at a scheduled time, this service certainly provided greater convenience than having to make two round trips to a video store. The competitive threat was moderated by the fact that most new movies were released on videocassettes before they appeared on pay-per-view services or pay cable. However, that disparity could disappear rapidly, if movie distributors were enticed by cable's potential for licensing and revenue sharing arrangements.

■ Interactive Television

Over the long-term, advances in satellite and cable television technology and entry of regional telephone companies into the electronic home delivery arena were other potential concerns, within the U.S. market. With new developments in fiber optics and digital signal compression, expansion to 500 channels could become feasible for video delivery systems. Thus, there was a possibility that "video-on-demand" could become a reality on cable or telephone systems by the mid 1990s.

Anticipating major advances in communications, IBM and Time Warner Corp. had begun discussing ways to combine data processing and transmitting expertise with cable TV systems, TV shows, and movies. IBM believed interactive television would eventually encroach upon a wide array of existing entertainment and information product/markets, including catalog shopping, broadcast and cable advertising, home video, information services, theater, video games, electronic messaging, videoconferencing, photography, records, tapes, and CDs. Furthermore, the Federal Communications Commission (FCC) had allocated a portion of the broadcast spectrum to interactive television and intended to award licenses to investors who could serve large markets.

■ Nervous Investors

Had the video rental market remained extremely fragmented, it might not have become so large and well-established. Some industry watchers predicted that Blockbuster's success in becoming a high quality specialty retail chain might impair the development of innovative competing technologies for accessing home entertainment.

Recognizing that other forms of retailing were withstanding competition from television, Baczko made the following point, "Home shopping has not taken the store away, and pay-per-view is not going to do so to video. I don't think you can ever beat a retailing environment."[5]

Nevertheless, newspaper reports of questionable depreciation accounting practices, bankruptcy filings by sizable video retailers, and media hype of future electronic home delivery systems, from time to time, stirred predictions of impending disaster for the video rental industry. Consequently, Blockbuster's common stock attracted speculators and short sellers, and the market price per share plunged every so often as frightened investors hastily bailed out to "take profits" or "stop losses." For example, the price per share reached a high of $15.125 and a low of $7.75 on the New York Stock Exchange during the first half of 1991.

■ Strategic Alliance with Philips Electronics

During 1992, an intriguing strategic alliance began to emerge between Blockbuster Entertainment Corp. and Philips Electronics, N.V. Headquartered in the Netherlands, Philips was the world's second largest consumer electronics company after Japan's Matsushita Electric Industrial Co. Philips' decision to purchase 13 million newly issued common shares (nearly 7.2 percent of outstanding shares) suggested that the two companies might be heading toward a close working relationship.[6]

In 1991 consumer products accounted for 47 percent of Philips' $33 billion in sales revenues. The early 1990s found the U.S., Canada, Australia, the United Kingdom, and Japan all experiencing economic downturns and declining consumer confidence. Stagnant demand and bloody price wars were curbing profits throughout the consumer electronics industry. Battered by stagnant demand and stiff price competition from its Japanese competitors, Philips reported a $3 billion loss in 1990. Philips' new President, Jan D. Timmer, was struggling to slash the payroll, close inefficient plants, and divest unprofitable operations. A streamlining and restructuring process initiated by Timmer, provided a $210 million profit on sales of $33 billion in 1991. Recent sales data are shown in Exhibit 6.

Some analysts, suspecting that Huizenga might be ready to move on to another new venture, speculated that Philips might be interested in acquiring a controlling interest in Blockbuster Entertainment Corp. Others expressed doubts that outright ownership and management of a captive group of rental stores would serve Philips' best interest.

Having pioneered such consumer electronics products as the videocassette recorder, audio compact disc, digital compact cassette, and high-definition televi-

---

[5] *The New York Times,* February 21, 1992.

[6] These funds have been used by Blockbuster to help pay for the Cityvision plc acquisition.

■ **Exhibit 6**
Philips Electronics
N.V., Net Sales by
Product Sector and
Geographical Area
(millions of Guilders)

	1991	1990
Product Sector		
Lighting	7,351	7,026
Consumer products	26,861	25,856
Professional products and systems	12,510	12,400
Components and semiconductors	7,844	7,953
Miscellaneous	2,420	2,529
Net sales	56,986	55,764
Geographical Area		
Netherlands	3,206	3,604
Rest of Europe	30,433	30,366
U.S.A. and Canada	12,833	11,819
Latin America	3,142	3,361
Africa	730	772
Asia	5,565	4,770
Australia and New Zealand	1,077	1,072
Net sales	56,986	55,764

NOTE: On December 31, 1991 and 1990, respectively, one U.S. dollar equaled 1.71 and 1.69 Dutch Guilders.

SOURCE: Philips' 1991 Annual Report.

sion, Philips had long been a superior technological leader. Marketing agility and competitive pricing had never been Philips' strengths. Philips conceivably might be aiming for a reliable international retail base for rapid, broad distribution of future hardware and software products.

Philips owned 51 percent of Super Club Holding & Finance S.A., a poorly performing music and video retail chain. With store locations in Europe and the United States, Super Club might benefit from a tie-in with Blockbuster. Philips also owned 80 percent of PolyGram, one of the three largest music publishing, production, marketing, and distribution companies in the world, and a major European manufacturer of compact discs. Recognizing the increasingly complementary natures of the audio and video fields, Polygram had begun producing and distributing filmed entertainment, as part of its strategy to become a multicultural, global entertainment company.

■ Philips' Multimedia Systems

Potentially even more relevant were Philips' plans for a new Imagination Machine. Philips had developed a new Compact Disk Interactive (CD-I) entertainment system that could turn the family TV into a terminal through which one could play regular music CDs, view photo CD disks, and interact with programs rather than just watch them. Touted as the "VCR of the 21st century," Philips' Imagination Machine was one of the products that Timmer was counting on heavily to revive depressed earnings. Blending text, full-motion video, and stereo-quality sound, it called up sports statistics during live broadcasts, displayed digital snapshots, played karaoke sing-along discs, used Nintendo's new games and played movies and music videos. While CD-I had been promoted primarily to the consumer market, it was also highly suited to the educational market.

Philips utilized a special format for its CD-ROM, which was supported by several other electronics firms as well. Commodore, Apple, Toshiba, and Tandy were offering multimedia equipment with different CD formats. Sony and Panasonic (Matsushita) had not yet revealed the type of standard they might support. Having witnessed the VHS/Beta wars of the late 1970s, Philips recognized the need to insure that its CD-I standard won out over its rivals. Ultimately, the availability of appealing multimedia software would help determine which compact disc standard would dominate.

■ Potential New Undertakings

As Blockbuster entered numerous foreign markets, its employees started to acquire increasing familiarity with markets for movies and home entertainment within many different cultures and political jurisdictions. Blockbuster's increasing knowledge of ways to formalize and expand global rental markets could help foster widespread acceptance of the rental concept for expensive multimedia CDs, such as encyclopedias, music libraries, and games. Blockbuster could thus become a leading worldwide distributor of a new generation of home entertainment products, perhaps selling and/or renting Philips' Imagination Machines and CDs.

Reacting to investor skepticism a year earlier, Huizenga had optimistically asserted, "We have the best locations in town. We've got a plain vanilla box. We can sell shoes there if we want to. Maybe we'll build a music store that's green and white. We could call it Chartbusters."[7] Such remarks indicate that someday Blockbuster Entertainment Corporation could be attracted to retailing opportunities elsewhere within the diverse, yet more and more intertwined, marketplace for home entertainment products.

---

[7] *The New York Times Business World Magazine,* June 9, 1991.

Case 21 Liz Claiborne, 1993: Troubled Times for the Woman's Retail Giant

Sharon Ungar Lane, Patricia Bilafer, Mary Fandel, Barbara Gottfried, and Alan N. Hoffman
Bentley College

In 1986, Liz Claiborne, Inc., became the first company started by a woman to make the Fortune 500. Described by Working Woman magazine as "the wizard of the working woman's wardrobe," Liz Claiborne, Inc., provides quality career and casual clothing, accessories, and fragrances at prices working women can afford. In fact, the company's philosophy, to produce "simple, straightforward fashion designed for women who have more important things to think about than what to wear," has made it the largest women's apparel manufacturer in the world. In 1993, Liz Claiborne sold 65 million garments, and more than 20 million accessories.

The Early Years

The daughter of a banker at Morgan Guaranty Trust Company, Liz Claiborne spent her early childhood in Brussels before moving with her family to New Orleans in 1934. She never finished high school, but after the war, her father sent her to Europe to study at the Art School in Brussels, and then to the Academie in Nice, France to study fine arts. She returned to the United States only to discover that her family opposed her desire to work in the fashion industry. Nevertheless, Liz entered a sketch of a woman's high-collared coat in a design contest sponsored by Harper's Bazaar, and won. At twenty-one, she began her career as a sketcher, model, and later, designer on "Fashion Avenue," the insiders' name for New York's Seventh Avenue garment district, where much of America's ready-to-wear is designed, and was, at one time, produced. Soon afterward, while working at Rhea Manufacturing Company in Milwaukee, she met Arthur Ortenberg, a design executive, whom she married in 1957.

In 1960, Liz Claiborne embarked on a fifteen-year career as the chief designer for Youth Guild, the junior dress division of Jonathan Logan. It was during these years that the seeds of Liz Claiborne, Inc., were sown: more and more women were entering the work force, and Liz perceived that there was an opening in the market for tasteful, moderately priced career clothes. She could not sell Youth Guild on her vision of a mix-and-match sportswear line to fill that gap, so she decided to set up her own company.

This case prepared by Sharon Ungar Lane, Patricia Bilafer, Mary Fandel, Barbara Gottfried, and Alan N. Hoffman, Bentley College.

The authors would like to thank Jane Moreno, Jeffrey Shuman, and Sally Strawn for their valuable contributions to this case. Photographic contribution by Scott Lane.

Please address all correspondence to Dr. Alan N. Hoffman, Department of Management, AGC320, Bentley College, 175 Forest Street, Waltham, MA 02154–4705.

Liz Claiborne, Inc., was launched on January 19, 1976. Financed by $50,000 in personal savings and $200,000 from family, friends, and business associates, the company began small, with Liz Claiborne as President and head designer, and her husband, Arthur Ortenberg, an expert in textiles and business administration, as Secretary and Treasurer of the corporation, and later, Chairman. A third partner, Leonard Boxer, contributed production expertise, and in 1977, Jerome Chazen, a personal friend, was named Vice President of Marketing. Within its first year, the company was operating in the black, with sales of over $2 million. In 1985, sales reached the half billion dollar mark; the next year, retail sales surpassed $1.2 billion, and Liz Claiborne, Inc., made it into the Fortune 500.

In February 1989, Liz Claiborne and Arthur Ortenberg announced their retirement from active management of the company to pursue environmental, social, and other interests. Jerome Chazen, one of the company's original partners was named CEO, and Jay Margolis was hired as Vice Chair and President of Women's Sportswear, Liz Claiborne, Inc.'s core division. Committed to taking Liz Claiborne into the 1990's debt-free, they and a team of designers have expanded product lines, adding accessories and fragrances to meet customer demand. They also purchased Russ Togs company to sustain company growth. Today Liz Claiborne can claim a full 2 percent of the women's apparel market—more than any other publicly held company.

■ The Fashion Industry

The fashion industry is highly competitive. The maturing market for women's clothing is dominated by Liz Claiborne and its major competitors: Jones New York, Chaus, Evan Picone, JH Collectibles, and VF Corporation. Retailers, the interface between the fashion industry and the consumer, have suffered in recent years from the recession and volatile consumer tastes, necessitating major restructuring which has had a significant impact on the fashion industry. Mergers, acquisitions, and bankruptcies of major retailers have created powerful retail rivals with the financial resources to create large economies of scale and withstand new entrants, strict governmental regulation, and technological advances. For instance, when Macy's, which had accounted for a significant percentage of Liz Claiborne sales, went bankrupt in 1992, Liz Claiborne's sales figures suffered in the ensuing bankruptcy settlement.

The retail clothing industry is also highly vulnerable to shifting tastes. Predicting fashion is risky and expensive because what is considered stylish today may be out tomorrow. Yet significant lead time is required to bring new styles to market. A company may invest a year or more in the design and production stages of a new design concept only to have the line fail upon introduction. In fact, clothing lines are usually either complete successes or fail altogether, yet at the same time, inventory levels for successful lines must be adequate to meet consumer demand, which doesn't leave much margin for error. Establishing name recognition is a priority for designers. Consumers consistently shop their favorite designers, and remain loyal to those whose clothes fit best. Indeed, strong designer loyalty dominates the retail industry. Thus fashion industry marketing strategies must take many contingencies into account at all times, while remaining flexible enough to respond to continually shifting consumer tastes.

■ Product Lines

Liz Claiborne's principal lines are designed to meet the work and leisure clothing needs of working women. Today 57.7 percent of all women in the United States work outside the home; and women with children under the age of six are the fastest growing segment of the workforce. The dual income family has become the norm, and stay-at-home moms the exception rather than the rule. Consequently many women no longer have the kind of leisure time they once had to shop; rather they prefer to maximize any shopping outing. Liz Claiborne, Inc., has carved out a niche for itself by targeting these women as its primary constituency, designing mix-and-match coordinating outfits, rather than separates, that can be variously combined to suit individual needs and tastes, simplifying both shopping and dressing for the busy lifestyles of working women. To market this concept, Liz Claiborne was one of the first companies to merchandise their clothing lines as outfits rather than single items, arranging them on the display floor to demonstrate that they can dress the customer from head to toe, rather than displaying single garments by classification. Furthermore, the clothes are modern classic rather than trendy, designed with practicality, style and fashion longevity in mind. Liz Claiborne's goal is to offer clothing and accessories that are not only aesthetically and technically well designed, but which make the customer feel confident, addressing all the needs of her busy life.

As of 1993, Liz Claiborne, Inc., had 14 divisions (Exhibit 1) offering various products aimed at specific target markets and covering a wide gamut of career, active wear and accessories for women, as well as for men. Liz Claiborne is continually adding new products to their apparel line, such as the women's suits introduced in 1991, not simply to increase sales, but to garner more department store space. Their perfume, "Liz Claiborne," has been particularly successful. The versatile scent was conceived to be worn around the clock, at work or out on the town, and based on Liz Claiborne's instinctive preferences rather than on market research, as was the triangle-shaped logo and the red, yellow and blue color scheme for the packaging. The company also carved out a niche for itself marketing to the "forgotten" woman. Over 30 percent of adult women are overweight. Liz Claiborne, Inc., entered the large-sized women's clothing market with its "Elisabeth" line, which successfully serves a long-neglected group of consumers by offering large-sized sportswear that provides the excellent fit, fashion and quality of its regular sportswear lines. The gambit has paid off, and Liz Claiborne, Inc., has plans to continue extending the "Elisabeth" line. In yet another ploy to extend its markets and increase its sales, Liz Claiborne, Inc., has ignored the industry standard of four seasons and has opted for six seasonal lines to offer women clothes they can wear right away and to allow for a constant flow of new merchandise to generate consumer interest. The net result of the company's versatility and market savvy: Liz Claiborne outfits more women than any other designer.

To stay on top of the huge volume of its business, Liz Claiborne uses both direct customer feedback and a unique computerized system, SURF (System Updated Retail Feedback), which provides weekly sales trends reports on what is and isn't selling nationwide. At the end of each week, data on sales, styles, sizes, and colors are reviewed by division heads to determine both short and long term planning needs. Most importantly, SURF allows the company to respond quickly to mistakes. For example, for the spring, 1988 season, Liz Claiborne had decided to fall in line with current trends—and market miniskirts. When it became obvious through SURF that

■ **Exhibit 1**

Liz Claiborne, Inc.'s
Product Line Overview

Sportswear:

Includes Collection, Lizsport, Lizwear and Petite Sportswear.

Liz Claiborne, Inc., launched into the fashion industry with its sportswear line in 1976. Designed to be modern classic rather than trendy so as to ensure fashion longevity, the sportswear division divided into three distinct lines. The first, COLLECTION, is primarily a career-oriented, tailored, and professional line. LIZSPORT provides sportswear for leisure time as well as for more casual work environments, while LIZWEAR is a highly denim-driven sportswear division. Our PETITE sportswear was developed in 1982 to fulfill an unmet need in the market for the 5'4" and under customer. Petite sizes are offered in all three sportswear lifestyles.

Dresses:

Misses and Petite.

Misses' dresses were launched in 1982, followed by Petite in 1985. Our dresses include a wide range of fabrications and styles, from career to knit to social occasion dresses. Furthermore, the dress division offers a large selection of dresses that can be worn from day-to-dinner, encompassing the ease and professionalism necessary for a work environment with the style and fun for an evening on the town.

Suits:

In 1991 Liz Claiborne, Inc., ventured into the Suits market. The division differentiates itself by offering a wide variety of skirt and jacket lengths, seasonless fabrics, pant suits, and day-to-dinner designs.

Liz & Co.:

Liz & Co., launched in 1989, consists primarily of comfortable and coordinated knitwear separates with a relaxed fit and a youthful attitude.

Dana Buchman:

Sportswear, Petite Sportswear, and Dresses.

Founded in 1987, Dana Buchman is our bridge sportswear division with prices that range from better sportswear to designer merchandise. It offers sophisticated styles of the highest quality fabrics with an exceptional attention to detail. Dana Buchman's distribution is selective.

Elisabeth:

Sportswear, Petite Sportswear, and Dresses.

In response to a previously neglected market, Liz Claiborne, Inc., developed its large size division called Elisabeth in 1989. The line includes a wide range of products from activewear to career clothing to evening dressing in sizes 14–24 and 14P–22P. Through Elisabeth's high attention to design, quality, and fit, it has become a market leader.

Claiborne:

Men's Sportswear and Men's Furnishings.

Liz Claiborne, Inc., launched into the men's market in 1985 with our Claiborne sportswear division and in 1987 with men's furnishings. Furnishings include men's dress shirts and ties, while our men's sportswear incorporates the same high level of fashion and quality as offered in our women's sportswear areas.

Crazy Horse:

Acquired in 1992, Crazy Horse is a casual line with a young and modern attitude that is merchandised in department and specialty stores. Its fashion-forward appearance appeals to a younger customer.

Russ:

Also acquired in 1992, Russ offers career as well as casual dressing and is displayed in the moderate areas of department stores.

(continued)

The Villager:

The Villager, acquired in 1992 along with Crazy Horse and Russ, focuses on career clothing but offers some casual wear as well. It will be distributed to national and regional chain department stores. Thus, with these three new labels, Liz Claiborne, Inc., has expanded both its product offerings and its distribution to include moderate career and casual dressing.

Accessories:

Includes Handbags/Small Leather Goods and Fashion Accessories.

Our fashion accessories, organized in 1980, include scarves, belts, hats, tights, socks, and hair accessories. Also introduced in 1980 were Liz Claiborne handbags and small leather goods. Many of the Liz Claiborne accessories are designed and developed to coordinate with our sportswear and can be used for anything from work to play. Recently, the Accessories division launched our bodywear, offering the same fit, fashion, and quality of all Liz Claiborne products.

Shoes:

Shoes and Sportshoes.

Also designed to coordinate and complement our sportswear, Liz Claiborne, Inc., moved into the shoe market in 1981. This division includes casual shoes, dress shoes, and as of 1991, fashionable and athletic sportshoes. Of course, like all our apparel divisions, all styles are comfortable and of the highest fashion sense.

Jewelry:

Liz Claiborne Inc. also offers a wide range of fashion jewelry designed for both casual and go-to-work. Many of the designs coordinate with the seasonal apparel trends and color ways. Introduced in 1990, this division offers a full range of jewelry including earrings, necklaces, bracelets, and pins.

Cosmetics:

Our Cosmetics division was launched in 1987 and consists of a collection of fragrances that captures and completes the whole Liz Claiborne attitude. The first, our signature fragrance, is entitled LIZ CLAIBORNE and is bottled in Liz Claiborne's trademark triangle. CLAIBORNE for men was developed in 1989, followed by REALITIES in 1990. In the Fall of 1993, Liz Claiborne, Inc., will be launching its new fragrance, VIVID. Various complementary fragrance items are also carried in the lines, including shampoo, conditioners, and body lotion to name a few.

the company's regular customers had no intention of baring their thighs, Liz Claiborne was able to adjust its fall 1988 designs quickly and order longer skirts for the fall fashion season to avoid losing loyal customers.

Nevertheless, Liz Claiborne, Inc., has had a few disappointments, such as its girls' line for 5–12 year olds begun in 1984, but phased out in 1987. Also, 1992 sales of the men's sportswear and furnishings lines were a big disappointment, falling 24.6 percent; as a result, the "Claiborne" collection of men's sportswear, originally styled for young customers, has shifted to a more upscale, conservative look.

While saturation is always a possibility, especially as the core sportswear line matures, Liz Claiborne works hard to stay one step ahead of the game. Recently the company saw in the moderate market, which targets working women with more sophisticated, yet reasonably priced clothes than those at the GAP or Limited stores, the potential for new business and a broadened customer base. In 1992 Liz Claiborne entered the moderate women's sportswear market by acquiring Russ Togs (Russ, Crazy Horse and The Villager labels), which broadened their distribution by expanding Liz Claiborne's position in both national and regional chain department stores, in addition to the moderate areas of traditional department stores.

◼ Liz Claiborne: 1993

Liz Claiborne, Inc., markets its various lines primarily through 3,500 leading department stores such as Bloomingdale's, Filenes, Lord & Taylor, Macy's, and Jordan Marsh, delivering a consistent product at a fair price. The company usually sets up "Liz Claiborne boutiques" within these stores which carry the full line of Liz merchandise to allow for one-stop shopping for women who don't have time to shop (the store within a store concept pioneered by Ralph Lauren).

However, because many of its best retailers were in financial trouble, Liz Claiborne made an ambitious move into retailing. By 1993, the company had opened 16 Liz Claiborne company-owned retail stores, 39 First Issue stores, and 55 outlet stores nationwide. The 16 company-owned retail stores help give "Liz Claiborne" fashions a unique identity, and play an important role in testing new products and new merchandising ideas, functioning as "laboratories" to observe consumer taste and measure reactions to such elements as fit, selling, size, group, and fabric. The company also owns three Elisabeth retail stores.

The 39 First Issue stores, opened in 1993, are designed to compete with retailers like The Limited and The Gap. The stores exclusively market First Issue merchandise, related separates and basics similar to Liz Claiborne sportswear but less career oriented, designed by a separate team and priced approximately 15 percent lower than the Liz Claiborne label lines.

Liz Claiborne also has 55 outlet stores where they sell unsold merchandise from previous seasons, providing the company with control over the disposition of unsold inventories. The outlets are deliberately located at some distance from the department and specialty stores where Liz products are regularly sold in order to preserve brand image.

Since many segments of the U.S. fashion industry are maturing, overseas markets represent new and substantial sources of growth for U.S. designers. An internationally recognized brand name and worldwide advertising campaign are critical to competing successfully in European and Asian markets. To effectively market its products outside the United States, Liz Claiborne, Inc., is tailoring its sales strategies specifically for each country. To date, Liz Claiborne has met with some success in Canada and England, where women tend to shop and dress like Americans, but less success in other parts of the world. One problem lies in the fact that Liz Claiborne is essentially a department store line in the United States, while in Europe most business is done in small boutiques. In some British stores, Liz Claiborne is leasing space and selling their goods themselves. In Japan the company is selling through a mail order catalog in addition to the two Liz Claiborne stores that were opened in Tokyo during fall, 1993. International expansion has, however, suffered the adverse impact of recessions in both Europe and Japan.

◼ International Manufacturing

Currently, 100 percent of Liz Claiborne's product lines are manufactured overseas. Global outsourcing is widespread in the textile industry to capitalize on lower labor and production costs at overseas manufacturing sites. Outsourcing creates the flexibility to shift production to various sites depending on wage differentials. Yet many of these sites are high risk due to the political and economic instability of developing and Third World countries. Nevertheless, very few firms have manufacturing facilities in the United States, so they vary their sources by using a combination of domestic, Caribbean and foreign sources to insure minimal instability. However, scattered production sites can jeopardize quality control. In addition, reliance on foreign suppliers is not without its disadvantages, since those suppliers are not always consistent, and cannot be easily relied upon to operate on the tight schedules necessitated by the time pressures of an industry that turns around four to six seasonal lines a year.

United States import regulations are currently favorable for retailers, which further contributes to the marketing of goods made overseas; however, these conditions are subject to change. As imports rise, quota restrictions are more strictly enforced; and recently, the government has shifted to a more protectionist policy. The garment industry has been criticized both for exporting U.S. manufacturing jobs and for exploiting foreign labor. Indeed, the shift of clothing production to overseas sites has been economically significant for the United States because "apparel production alone employs more people than the entire printing and publishing field and more than the automobile manufacturing industry."

■ Women's Work

Liz Claiborne, Inc., has a long-standing commitment to the welfare of others, especially women. In the past, the Liz Claiborne Foundation, funded by company profits, actively assisted organizations involved in social welfare programs, e.g., helping the homeless, serving people with AIDS and their families, and enhancing opportunities for underprivileged children. The company also strongly encourages its employees to volunteer and support local non-profit organizations.

Over the years Liz Claiborne has learned a great deal about the lives of the women who buy their products—about their careers, their dreams, and their struggles outside of work. The company wanted both to give something back to the millions of women who had contributed to the company's success, and to contribute to social change by making a difference in people's lives. To do so, Liz Claiborne, Inc., recently developed "Women's Work." "Women's Work" develops and funds multiyear, nationwide programs designed to heighten awareness of social problems and encourage positive social change with regard to issues of particular concern to women and their families, such as domestic violence and work-family conflicts.

The specific "Women's Work" project supported in each target community is based on issues of particular concern to that community: domestic violence in San Francisco, Boston, and Miami; the needs and concerns of working mothers in Chicago. In each city, Liz Claiborne builds innovative, collaborative partnerships with organizations active in confronting domestic violence. In Chicago, a local artist and children from a local elementary school published a book that addresses the impact of working mothers on their families, especially their children. All proceeds resulting from the sale of the book are donated to literacy programs nationwide.

In 1993, to coincide with National Domestic Violence Awareness Month, Liz Claiborne launched domestic violence awareness programs in Boston and Miami, and formed a partnership with the Jane Doe Safety Fund sponsored by the Massachusetts Coalition of Battered Women. To raise money for the fund, Claiborne solicited the help of Barbara Kruger, a contemporary artist whose work advocates

■ **Exhibit 2A**

Photo by Scott Lane

■ **Exhibit 2B**

social change. The Fund's public awareness campaign on domestic violence includes billboards, city bus signs, transit stop posters, and educational brochures (Exhibits 2A and 2B), as well as broadcast and print public service announcements. Additionally, Liz Claiborne launched a collection of special commemorative products (Exhibit 3), which can be purchased at local Liz Claiborne stores, participating department stores, or through a special toll-free number, whose proceeds will be donated to domestic violence programs such as the Jane Doe Safety Fund in Boston. Liz Claiborne has also donated money to establish the first centralized 24-hour domestic violence hot line, which the company hopes will become permanent with the support of local foundations and organizations.

■ **Exhibit 3**

WOMEN'S WORK
Liz claiborne, inc.

Contact: Maria Kalligeros/Lisa Schmidt
Patrice Tanaka & Company, Inc.
(212) 505-9332

LIZ CLAIBORNE, INC. TO LAUNCH COMMEMORATIVE COLLECTION; PROCEEDS WILL BENEFIT DOMESTIC VIOLENCE ORGANIZATIONS

Items Feature Special Images by Artist Barbara Kruger

COMMEMORATIVE COLLECTION

To increase awareness of domestic violence, Liz Claiborne, Inc. will be launching a special collection of products, proceeds from which will raise funds for domestic violence organizations. Each piece in the collection features contemporary artist **Barbara Kruger's** striking red, black and white images and the message, "DON'T DIE FOR LOVE – STOP DOMESTIC VIOLENCE," specially commissioned by Liz Claiborne, Inc. for this program. Startling statistics, running across the top and bottom of the image, read – "Every 12 seconds a woman is beaten in the U.S." and "52% of female murder victims are killed by their partners."

(continued)

"Women's Work" is a way for Liz Claiborne, Inc., to give something back to communities and the American women who have contributed to Liz Claiborne's success by funding programs for the future welfare of women. In addition, Liz Claiborne, Inc., is exploring the possibility of sponsoring educational programs about the detection and treatment of breast cancer, and already offers free mammograms to all its women employees. While the company acknowledges that they do not expect sales to increase as a result of the Liz Claiborne Foundation or "Women's Work," they hope that by responding to concerns important to women and their families, "Women's Work" will reinforce Liz Claiborne, Inc.'s reputation as a company that cares.

■ **Exhibit 3**
(*concluded*)

	Baseball Cap ($10) in black twill with the Kruger message silk screened in red and white above the brim. Available in adjustable one-size-fits-all.
PHONE ORDERING INFORMATION	The collection can be ordered by calling 1-800-449-STOP (1-800-449-7867). American Express, VISA, Mastercard, checks or money orders will be accepted; New York/New Jersey residents must add sales tax. Shipping is <u>not</u> included. Consumers should allow four to six weeks for delivery.
ITEMS AVAILABLE AT RETAIL	The T-shirt, tote bag, baseball cap *and*: Mug ($6) in white featuring the Kruger image in red and black. Sunglasses ($15) are a classic black frame with the Kruger message displayed on the outside of each lens. View is unobstructed for the wearer.

RETAIL LOCATIONS	• several Boston-area Filene's
	
	• Burdines stores in Miami's Dade and Broward Counties
	
	• Museum shops nationwide
	
	• Liz Claiborne Stores:
	  -Copley Place, Boston, MA
	  -Town Center, Boca Raton, FL
	
	• Selected campus stores

WHO DO PROCEEDS BENEFIT?	• <u>Through 800 #</u>: The Family Violence Prevention Fund, a national, non-profit organization devoted to public policy, education and advocacy. • <u>In Miami</u>: The Women's Fund of Dade County which will administer grants to local domestic violence programs. • <u>In Boston</u>: The Jane Doe Safety Fund, a statewide fundraising and public education campaign of the Massachusetts Coalition of Battered Women Service Groups.

# # #

■ 1993: The Wrong Product—And Too Much Of It

By the late 1980s, Liz Claiborne had branched beyond clothes for working women into petites, large sizes, accessories, fragrances, men's clothing, and other lines. With so much to watch over, managers began to lose their focus on the core merchandise. Customers yawned at many outfits, which too often repeated past styles. Retailers, who had allowed Liz Claiborne's presence in their stores to reach King Kong-like proportions, say top managers were slow to admit the problem. According to a former senior Claiborne executive: "If the product didn't sell, it was always someone else's fault.

The buyers didn't show it right, or it wasn't delivered in the right way. They didn't allow themselves to think that maybe they just weren't listening to the customer."

1993 was a difficult year for Liz Claiborne. A weak retail environment, conservative buying by customers, the start-up costs associated with the Russ Division, and the surprise resignation of Jay Margolis in July 1993 led industry analysts to question the strength of Liz Claiborne, Inc. Sales were flat for the first nine months of 1993 and earnings dropped by 40 percent in the third quarter after double-digit declines in the first and second quarters. The consensus opinion on the problem: the wrong product and too much of it.

The following excerpt appeared in the January, 1994 edition of *Smart-Money Magazine:*

> In late 1992, Louis Lowenstein, a Claiborne director, bragged that the apparel maker's balance sheet was so solid it would bring tears to [his] mother's eyes. Save the hanky. Investors watched Liz's earnings slide all year. The company overestimated shoppers' appetites after a strong 1992 Christmas season and made too many clothes. Then its uninspired 1993 fashion collections failed to entice thrift shoppers. The inventory overload prevented Liz from being able to react quickly to the slow retail environment, causing profits to slide an estimated 40% for the year. Liz Claiborne's stock traded at $42.38 on January 7, 1993, and was $18.13 on October 21, 1993.

Clearly, 1993 was a disappointing year for Liz Claiborne, Inc.

■ The Outlook for the Future

Consumers today are demanding more and are adamant about paying less. A global economy has given them a "sultan's power to command exactly what they want, the way they want it, when they want it, and at a price that will make [companies] weep." Companies will have to either meet these expectations or be forced out of business by those competitors that do.

The prolonged recession, low consumer confidence, a four year national decline in per capita clothing spending and numerous bankruptcies among several of the nation's largest department stores have wreaked havoc in the apparel industry. Many companies are cutting costs through sophisticated inventory control systems and computer aided design and manufacturing, as well as enhanced fabric production systems. But the industry must also comply with federal legislation which regulates competition and requires product labeling with content and care instructions designed to protect consumers, both of which contribute to higher costs.

At the same time, Americans are changing the way they shop. Many designers, including Liz Claiborne, rely on large department stores located in shopping malls for a large percentage of their sales. However, the appeal of shopping malls is diminishing and the trend is toward specialty stores. Consumers, especially women, have less time to shop, so convenience is becoming even more important than it already was.

Clearly, for 1994, questions abound. Liz Claiborne, Inc., must rethink both its product lines and its entire marketing strategy, considering whether it has grown too fast, spread itself too thin, and/or set itself up to compete with itself by branching out into retailing lines under other labels which are too similar to its own name-brand lines. And the company must consider how best to fill the void left by the departure of Liz Claiborne herself, clearly a visionary who carved out a fashion empire which may now be on the brink of decline.

■ **Exhibit 4**

Consolidated balance Sheets Liz Claiborne, Inc., and Subsidiaries (all amounts in thousands except share data)

	December 25, 1993	December 26, 1992
Assets		
Current Assets:		
Cash and cash equivalents	$ 104,720	$ 130,721
Marketable securities	204,571	294,892
Accounts receivable—trade	174,435	200,183
Inventories	436,593	385,879
Deferred income tax benefits	15,065	13,907
Other current assets	69,055	55,384
Total current assets	1,004,439	1,080,966
Property and Equipment—Net	202,068	145,695
Other Assets	29,831	29,647
	$1,236,338	$1,256,308
Liabilities and Stockholders' Equity		
Current Liabilities:		
Accounts payable	$ 141,126	$ 138,738
Accrued expenses	97,765	87,330
Income taxes payable	15,547	22,109
Total current liabilities	254,438	248,177
Long-Term Debt	1,334	1,434
Deferred Income Taxes	2,275	8,922
Commitments and Contingencies		
Stockholders' Equity:		
Preferred stock, $.01 par value, authorized shares—50,000,000, issued shares—none	—	—
Common stock, $1 par value, authorized shares—250,000,000, issued shares—88,218,617	88,219	88,219
Capital in excess of par value	56,699	55,528
Retained earnings	1,123,413	1,034,280
Cumulative translation adjustment	(1,279)	(1,410)
	1,267,052	1,176,617
Common stock in treasury, at cost—9,371,217 shares in 1993 and 5,436,864 shares in 1992	(288,761)	(178,842)
Total stockholders' equity	978,291	997,775
	$1,236,338	$1,256,308

■ **Exhibit 5** Consolidated Statements of Income Liz Claiborne, Inc., and Subsidiaries (all dollar amounts in thousands except per common share data)

	Fiscal Years Ended		
	December 25, 1993	December 26, 1992	December 28, 1991
Net Sales	$2,204,297	$2,194,330	$2,007,177
Cost of goods sold	1,453,381	1,364,214	1,207,502
Gross Profit	750,916	830,116	799,675
Selling, general and administrative expenses	568,286	507,541	471,060
Operating Income	182,630	322,575	328,615
Investment and other income—net	16,151	19,349	22,133
Income before Provision for Income Taxes and Cumulative Effect of a Change in Accounting Principle	198,781	341,924	350,748
Provision for Income Taxes	73,500	123,100	128,000
Income before Cumulative Effect of a Change in Accounting Principle	125,281	218,824	222,748
Cumulative effect of a change in the method of accounting for income taxes	1,643	—	—
Net Income	$ 126,924	$ 218,824	$ 222,748
Earnings per Common Share:			
Income before Cumulative Effect of a Change in Accounting Principle	$ 1.54	$ 2.61	$ 2.61
Cumulative effect of a change in the method of accounting for income taxes	.02	—	—
Net Income per Common Share	$1.56	$ 2.61	$ 2.61
Dividends Paid per Common Share	$ .44	$ .39	$ .33

■ **Exhibit 6**
Liz Claiborne   Five Year Sales, Net Income, and EPS Summary (000)

Year	Sales	Net Income	EPS
1993	$2,204,297	$126,924	$1.56
1992	2,194,330	218,824	2.61
1991	2,007,177	222,748	2.61
1990	1,728,868	205,800	2.37
1989	1,410,677	164,591	1.87
5-year Growth Rate	11.8	−6.2	−4.4

■ **References**

Anonymous, "Underachiever's Club Disappointments of 1993: These Wall Street Favorites Burned Investors Bad," *Smart Money,* January 1994, p. 29

Better, Nancy Marx, "The Secret of Liz Claiborne's Success," *Working Women,* April 1992, p. 68

Caminiti, Susan, "Liz Claiborne: How to Get Focused Again," *Fortune,* January 24, 1994, p. 85

Gillam, M., First Call Industry Report, June 16, 1993

Guenciro, Miriam, and Jeannette Jarnow, *Inside the Fashion Industry,* Macmillan Publishing Company, New York, 5th Edition, 1991, p. 5

Jacob, p. 8

Jacob, Rahul, "Beyond Quality and Value," *Fortune,* Autumn/Winter 1993, p. 8

Liz Claiborne Inc., *Current Biography,* June 1989, p. 8

Morris, Michele, "The Wizard of Working Women's Wardrobe," *Working Women,* June 1988, p. 74

Smith, Adam, "How Liz Claiborne Designed an Empire," *Esquire,* January 1986, p. 78–89

Case 22　Wal-Mart Stores, Inc.: Strategies for Market Dominance

James W. Camerius
Northern Michigan University

It was dusk in the foothills of the Ozark mountains in north central Arkansas. One of the most successful retailing entrepreneurs in modern history was driving a battered red 1980 Ford pickup minus two hubcaps down a rural road. A hunting dog named Buck was seated next to him, inside the cab. Some coffee and conversation with friends awaited at Fred's Hickory Inn in Bentonville.

Sam Walton was "down-to-earth and old fashioned in his views of the past, the present and the future," noted the *Arkansas Gazette:*

> I didn't sit down one day and decide that I was going to put a bunch of discount stores in small towns and set a goal to have a billion-dollar company some day. I started out with one store and it did well, so it was a challenge to see if I could do well with a few more. We're still going and we'll keep going as long as we're successful.

From this beginning, Wal-Mart Stores, Inc., has emerged as a modern retail success story.

An Emerging Organization

Wal-Mart Stores, Inc., in 1993, had completed its 29th consecutive year of growth in both sales and earning records. The firm, with corporate offices in Bentonville, Arkansas, operated stores under a variety of names and retail formats including: Wal-Mart Stores, which existed as discount department stores; Sam's Wholesale Clubs, which were wholesale/retail membership warehouses; and Hyper-market* USA, which were combination grocery and general merchandise stores in excess of 200,000 square feet. It operated Wal-Mart Supercenters, scaled-down versions of hypermarkets; dot Discount Drugstores, a super discount drug chain; and Bud's, off-price outlet stores. It was not only the nation's largest discount department store chain, but had recently surpassed the retail division of Sears, Roebuck & Co. in sales volume as the largest retail company in the United States.

The Sam Walton Spirit

Much of the success of Wal-Mart was attributed to the entrepreneurial spirit of its founder and Chairman of the Board, Samuel Moore Walton. One of the most influential retailers of the century, Walton died on April 5, 1992, at the age of 74 years. Sam Walton or "Mr. Sam," as some referred to him, had traced his down-to-earth, old-fashioned, homespun, evangelical ways to growing up in rural Okla-homa, Missouri, and Arkansas. Although he was remarkably blasé about his roots, some suggested that it was a simple belief in hard work and ambition that had "un-locked countless doors and showered upon him, his customers, and his employees . . . the fruits of . . . years of labor in building [this] highly successful company."

"Our goal has always been in our business to be the very best," Sam Walton once said in an interview, "and, along with that, we believe that in order to do that, you've got to make a good situation and put the interests of your associates first. If we really do that consistently, they in turn will cause . . . our business to be successful, which is what we've talked about and espoused and practiced." "The reason for our suc-cess," he noted, "is our people and the way that they're treated and the way they feel about their company." Many have suggested it is this "people first" philosophy which guided the company through the challenges and setbacks of its early years and allowed the company to maintain its consistent record of growth and expansion in later years.

There was little about Walton's background that reflected his amazing success. He was born in Kingfisher, Oklahoma, on March 29, 1918, to Thomas and Nancy Walton. Thomas Walton was a banker at the time and later entered the farm mort-gage business and moved to Missouri. Sam Walton, growing up in rural Missouri in the depths of the Great Depression, discovered early that he "had a fair amount of ambition and enjoyed working," he suggested in a company interview. He com-pleted high school at Columbia, Missouri, and received a Bachelor of Arts Degree in Economics from the University of Missouri in 1940. "I really had no idea what I would be," he said, adding as an afterthought, "at one point in time, I thought I wanted to become president of the United States."

A unique, enthusiastic, and positive individual, Sam Walton was called "just your basic homespun billionaire" by *Business Week* magazine. One source suggested that: "Mr. Sam is a life-long small-town resident who didn't change much as he got richer than his neighbors." He had tremendous energy, enjoyed bird hunting with his dogs, and flew a corporate plane. When the company was much smaller, he could boast that he personally visited every Wal-Mart store at least once a year. A store visit usually included Walton leading Wal-Mart cheers that began "Give me a W, give me an A. . . ." To many employees, he had the air of a fiery Baptist preacher. Paul R. Carter, a Wal-Mart executive vice-president, said: "Mr. Walton has a calling." He became the richest man in America, and by 1991 had created a personal fortune for his family in excess of $21 billion.

For all that Walton's success had been chronicled, its magnitude was hard to comprehend. Sam Walton was selected by the investment publication, *Financial World,* in 1989 as the "CEO of the Decade." He had honorary degrees from the Uni-versity of the Ozarks, the University of Arkansas, and the University of Missouri. He also received many of the most distinguished professional awards of the industry like "Man of the Year," "Discounter of the Year," "Chief Executive Officer of the Year," and was the second retailer to be inducted into the Discounting Hall of Fame. He was recipient of the Horatio Alger Award in 1984 and acknowledged by *Discount Stores News,* as "Retailer of the Decade" in December of 1989. "Walton does a remarkable job of instilling near-religious fervor in his people," says analyst Robert Buchanan of A. G. Edwards. "I think that speaks to the heart of his success." In late 1989, Sam Walton was diagnosed to have multiple myeloma, or cancer of the bone marrow. He planned to remain active in the firm as Chairman of the Board of Directors.

■ The Marketing Concept

Genesis of an Idea

Sam Walton started his retail career in 1940 as a management trainee with the J. C. Penney Co. in Des Moines, Iowa. He was impressed with the Penney method of doing business and later modeled the Wal-Mart chain after many Penney principles including "The Penney Idea" as reviewed in Exhibit 1. In a manner similar to Penney's, Wal-Mart employees were called "associates" rather than "clerks." As a "main street merchant" founded in Kemerer, Wyoming, Penney had found strength in the cultivation of rural markets.

Following service in the U.S. Army during World War II, Walton acquired a Ben Franklin variety store franchise in Newport, Arkansas, which he operated successfully until losing the lease in 1950. He opened another store under the name of Walton's 5 & 10 in Bentonville, Arkansas, the following year. By 1962 he was operating a chain of 15 stores.

The early retail stores owned by Sam Walton in Newport and Bentonville, Arkansas, and later in other small towns in adjoining southern states, were variety store operations. They were relatively small operations of 6,000 square feet, were located on "main street," and displayed merchandise on plain wooden tables and counters. Operated under the Ben Franklin name and supplied by Butler Brothers of Chicago and St. Louis, they were characterized by a limited price line, low gross margins, high merchandise turnover and concentration on return on investment. The firm, operating under the Walton 5 & 10 name, was the largest Ben Franklin franchisee in the country in 1962. The variety stores were phased out by 1976 to allow the company to concentrate on the growth of Wal-Mart Stores.

Foundations of Growth

The original Wal-Mart discount concept was not a unique idea. Sam Walton became convinced in the late 1950s that discounting would transform retailing. He traveled extensively in New England, the cradle of "off-pricing." "He visited just about every discounter in the United States," suggested William F. Kenney, the retired president of the now-defunct Kings Department Stores. He tried to interest Butler Brothers executives in Chicago in the discount store concept. The first Kmart, as a "conveniently

■ **Exhibit 1**
The Penney Idea,
1913

1. To serve the public, as nearly as we can, to its complete satisfaction.
2. To expect for the service we render a fair remuneration and not all the profit the traffic will bear.
3. To do all in our power to pack the customer's dollar full of value, quality, and satisfaction.
4. To continue to train ourselves and our associates so that the service we give will be more and more intelligently performed.
5. To improve constantly the human factor in our business.
6. To reward men and women in our organization through participation in what the business produces.
7. To test our every policy, method, and act in this wise: "Does it square with what is right and just?"

SOURCE: Vance H. Trimble, *Sam Walton: The Inside Story of America's Richest Man*, New York: Dutton, 1990.

located one-stop shopping unit where customers could buy a wide variety of quality merchandise at discount prices" had opened in 1962 in Garden City, Michigan. His theory was to operate a discount store in a small community and in that setting, he would offer name brand merchandise at low prices and would add friendly service. Butler Brothers executives rejected the idea. The first "Wal-Mart Discount City" opened in late 1962 in Rogers, Arkansas.

Wal-Mart stores would sell nationally advertised, well-known brand merchandise at low prices in austere surroundings. As corporate policy, they would cheerfully give refunds, credits, and rain checks. Management conceived the firm as a "discount department store chain offering a wide variety of general merchandise to the customer." Early emphasis was placed upon opportunistic purchases of merchandise from whatever sources were available. Heavy emphasis was placed upon health and beauty aids (H&BA) in the product line and "stacking it high" in a manner of merchandise presentation. By the end of 1979, there were 276 Wal-Mart stores located in eleven states.

The firm developed an aggressive expansion strategy as it grew from its first, 16,000 square foot discount store in Rogers. New stores were located primarily in towns of 5,000 to 25,000 population. The stores' sizes ranged from 30,000 to 60,000 square feet with 45,000 being the average. The firm also expanded by locating stores in contiguous areas, town by town, state by state. When its discount operations came to dominate a market area, it moved to an adjoining area. While other retailers built warehouses to serve existing outlets, Wal-Mart built the distribution center first and then spotted stores all around it, pooling advertising and distribution overhead. Most stores were less than a six-hour drive from one of the company's warehouses. The first major distribution center, a 390,000 square foot facility, opened in Searcy, Arkansas, outside Bentonville in 1978.

National Perspectives

At the beginning of 1991, the firm had 1,573 Wal-Mart stores in thirty-five states with expansion planned for adjacent states. The stores offered a wide variety of general merchandise to the customer. They were designed to offer one-stop shopping in 36 departments which included family apparel, health and beauty aids, household needs, electronics, toys, fabric and crafts, automotive supplies, lawn and patio, jewelry, and shoes. In addition, at certain store locations, a pharmacy, automotive supply and service center, garden center, or snack bar were also operated. "Everyday low prices" were stressed as opposed to putting heavy emphasis on special price promotions. Each store was expected to "provide the customer with a clean, pleasant, and friendly shopping experience."

Although Wal-Mart carried much the same merchandise, offered similar prices, and operated stores which looked much like the competition, there were many differences. In the typical Wal-Mart store, employees wore blue vests to identify themselves, aisles were wide, apparel departments were carpeted in warm colors, a store employee followed customers to their cars to pick up their shopping carts, and the customer was welcomed at the door by a "people greeter" who gave directions and struck up conversations. In some cases, merchandise was bagged in brown paper sacks rather than plastic bags because customers seemed to prefer them. A simple Wal-Mart logo in white letters on a brown background on the front of the store served to identify the firm. In consumer studies, it was determined that the chain was particularly adept at striking the delicate balance needed to convince customers its prices were low without making people feel that its stores were too cheap. In many ways, competitors like Kmart sought to emulate Wal-Mart by introducing people greeters, by upgrading interiors, by developing new logos and signage, and by introducing new inventory response systems. In 1989, sales per square foot of retail space at Wal-Mart were $227. Kmart, in contrast, sold only $139 per square foot that year.

A "Satisfaction Guaranteed" refund and exchange policy was introduced to allow customers to be confident of Wal-Mart's merchandise and quality. Technological advancements like scanner cash registers, hand held computers for ordering of merchandise, and computer linkages of stores with the general office and distribution centers improved communications and merchandise replenishment. Each store was encouraged to initiate programs which would make it an integral part of the community in which it operated. Associates were encouraged to "maintain the highest standards of honesty, morality, and business ethics in dealing with the public."

■ The External Environment

Industry analysts had labeled the 1980s as an era of economic uncertainty for retailers. Some firms faced difficulty upon merger or acquisition. After acquiring United States based Allied Department Stores in 1986 and Federated Department Stores in 1988, Canadian developer Robert Campeau was declared bankrupt with over $6 billion in debt. Several divisions and units of the organization upon reevaluation were either sold or closed. The flagship downtown Atlanta store of Rich's, a division of Federated, was closed after completing a multimillion dollar remodeling program. Specific merchandise programs, in divisions like Bloomingdale's, were reevaluated to lower inventory and to raise cash. The notion of servicing existing debt became a significant factor in the success or failure of a retailing organization in the later half of the decade. Selected acquisitions of U.S. retailers by foreign firms over the past decade are reviewed in Exhibit 2.

Other retailers experienced changes in ownership. The British B.A.T. Industries PLC sold the Chicago-based Marshall Field department store division to the Dayton Hudson Corporation. L. J. Hooker Corporation, the U.S. arm of Australia's Hooker Corporation, sold its Bonwit Teller and Sakowitz stores; it liquidated its B. Altman chain after fruitless sale efforts. The R. H. Macy Company saddled itself with $4.5

■ **Exhibit 2**
Selected Acquisitions
of U.S. Retailers by
Foreign Firms,
1980–1990

U.S. Retailer	Foreign Acquirer	Country of Acquirer
Allied Stores (gen. merch.)	Campeau	Canada
Alterman Foods (supermarkets)	Delhaie-Le Leon	Belgium
Bonwit Teller (gen. merch.)	Hooker Corp.	Australia
Brooks Brothers (apparel)	Marks & Spencer	Great Britain
Federated Department Stores (diversified)	Campeau	Canada
Great Atlantic & Pacific (supermarkets)	Tengelmann	West Germany
Herman's (sporting goods)	Dee Corp.	Great Britain
International House of Pancakes (restaurants)	Wienerwald	Switzerland
Talbots (apparel)	Jusco Ltd.	Japan
Zale (jewelry)	PS Associates	Netherlands

SOURCE: Barry Berman and Joel R. Evans, *Retail Management: A Strategic Approach*, New York: Macmillan Publishing Company, 4th Edition, 1989.

billion in debt as a result of acquiring Bullock's and I. Magnin specialty department stores. Chicago-based Carson, Pirie, Scott & Company was sold to the P. A. Bergner & Company, operator of the Milwaukee Boston Store and Bergner Department Store. Bergner declared a Chapter 11 bankruptcy in 1991.

Many retail enterprises confronted heavy competitive pressure by lowering prices or changing merchandise strategies. Sears, Roebuck & Company, in an effort to reverse sagging sales and less than defensible earnings, unsuccessfully introduced a new policy of "everyday low pricing" (ELP) in 1989. It later introduced name brand items such as Whirlpool alongside its traditional private label merchandise like Kenmore and introduced the "store within a store" concept to feature the name-brand goods. Montgomery Ward and to a lesser extent Kmart and Ames Department Stores followed similar strategies. The J. C. Penney Company, despite repositioning itself as a more upscale retailer, felt an impending recession and concerns about the Persian Gulf War had combined to erode consumer confidence. "As a result," the company noted in its 1990 Annual Report, "sales and profits within the industry were more negatively impacted than at any time since the last major recession of 1980–82."

The discount department store industry by the early 1990s had changed in a number of ways and was thought to have reached maturity by many analysts. Several formerly successful firms like E. J. Korvette, W. T. Grant, Atlantic Mills, Arlans, Federals, Zayre, Heck's, and Ames had declared bankruptcy and as a result either liquidated or reorganized. Regional firms like Target Stores and Shopko Stores began carrying more fashionable merchandise in more attractive facilities and shifted their emphasis to more national markets. Specialty retailers such as Toys 'R' Us, Pier 1 Imports, and Oshmans were making big inroads in toys, home furnishing, and sporting goods. The "superstores" of drug and food chains were rapidly discounting increasing amounts of general merchandise. Some firms like May Department Stores Company with Caldor and Venture, and the F. W. Woolworth Co. with Woolco had withdrawn from the field by either selling their discount divisions or closing them down entirely.

Several new retail formats had emerged in the marketplace to challenge the traditional discount department store format. The superstore, a 100,000–300,000 square foot operation, combined a large supermarket with a discount general-merchandise store. Originally a European retailing concept, these outlets were known as "malls without walls." Kmart's Super Kmart, American Fare, and Wal-Mart's Super Center Store and Hypermarket were examples of this trend toward large operations. Warehouse retailing, which involved some combination of warehouse and showroom facilities, used warehouse principles to reduce operating expenses and thereby offer discount prices as a primary customer appeal. Home Depot combined the traditional hardware store and lumber yard with a self-service home improvement center to become the largest home center operator in the nation.

Some retailers responded to changes in the marketplace by selling goods at price levels (20 to 60 percent) below regular retail prices. These off-price operations appeared as two general types: (1) factory outlet stores like Burlington Coat Factory Warehouse, Bass Shoes, and Manhattan's Brand Name Fashion Outlet, and (2) independents like Loehmann's, T. J. Maxx, Marshall's, and Clothestime, which bought seconds, overages, closeouts, or leftover goods from manufacturers and other retailers. Other retailers chose to dominate a product classification. Some super specialists like Sock Appeal, Little Piggie, Ltd., and Sock Market, offered a single narrowly defined classification of merchandise with an extensive assortment of brands, colors, and sizes. Others, as niche specialists, like Kids Mart, a division of F. W. Woolworth, and McKids, a division of Sears, targeted an identified market with carefully selected merchandise and appropriately designed stores. Some retailers like Silk Greenhouse (silk plants and flowers), Office Club (office supplies and equipment), and Toys 'R' Us (toys) were called "category killers" because they had achieved merchandise dominance in their respective product categories. Firms like The Limited, Victoria's Secret, and The Banana Republic became mini-department specialists by showcasing new lines and accessories alongside traditional merchandise lines.

Wal-Mart became the nation's largest retailer and discount department store chain in sales volume in 1991. Kmart Corporation, now the industry's second largest retailer and discount department store chain, with over 2,300 stores and $37,724,000 in sales in 1992, was perceived by many industry analysts and consumers in several independent studies as a laggard, even though it had been the industry sales leader for a number of years. In the same studies, Wal-Mart was perceived as the industry leader even though according to *The Wall Street Journal:* "they carry much the same merchandise, offer prices that are pennies apart and operate stores that look almost exactly alike." "Even their names are similar," noted the newspaper. The original Kmart concept of a "conveniently located, one stop shopping unit where customers could buy a wide variety of quality merchandise at discount prices," had lost its competitive edge in a changing market. As one analyst noted in an industry newsletter: "They had done so well for the past 20 years without paying attention to market changes. Now they have to." Wal-Mart and Kmart sales growth over 10 years is reviewed in Exhibit 3. A competitive analysis is shown of four major retail firms in Exhibit 4.

Some retailers like Kmart had initially focused on appealing to professional, middle-class consumers who lived in suburban areas and who were likely to be price sensitive. Other firms like Target, which had adopted the discount concept early,

■ **Exhibit 3**
Competitive Sales & Store Comparison, 1980–1992

| Year | Kmart | | Wal-Mart[1] | |
	Sales (000)	Stores[2]	Sales (000)	Stores[2]
1992	$37,724,000	2,435	$55,483,771	1,880
1991	34,580,000	2,391	43,886,902	1,720
1990	32,070,000	2,350	32,601,594	1,573
1989	29,533,000	2,361	25,810,656	1,402
1988	27,301,000	2,307	20,649,001	1,259
1987	25,627,000	2,273	15,959,255	1,114
1986	23,035,000	2,342	11,909,076	980
1985	22,035,000	2,332	8,451,489	859
1984	20,762,000	2,173	6,400,861	745
1983	18,597,000	2,160	4,666,909	642
1982	16,772,166	2,117	3,376,252	551
1981	16,527,012	2,055	2,444,997	491
1980	14,204,381	1,772	1,643,199	330

[1]Wal-Mart Fiscal Year ends January 31. Figures are assigned to previous year.
[2]General merchandise stores. Sales figures are net sales for the firm.

	Wal-Mart	**Sears**	**Kmart**	**J.C. Penney**
Sales (thousands)	$55,483,771	$ 31,961,000	$37,724,000	$18,009,000
Net income (thousands)	$ 1,994,794	$(2,977,000)	$ 941,000	$ 777,000
Net income per share	$ .87	$ —	$ 2.06	$ 2.95
Dividends per share	$ .11	$ —	$ 1.72	$ 1.32
# Stores (see note)	2,136	1,701	4,792	3,862
% Sales change	26.0%	1.7%	9.1%	11.2%

NOTE: Wal-Mart & subsidiaries (number of outlets)
  Wal-Mart Stores—1,880
  Sam's Wholesale Club—256
Sears, Roebuck & Company (all divisions)
  Sears Merchandise Group (number of outlets)
    Multi-line stores—813
    Small hard-line stores—46
    Western Auto—595
    Paint and hardware stores—103
    Homelife furniture stores—34
    Appliance stores—37
    Free-standing tire and auto centers—20
    Retail outlet and other—53
Kmart Corporation (number of outlets)
  General merchandise—2,435
  Specialty retail stores—2,357
    PACE membership warehouse—114
    Builders Square—165
    Payless Drug Stores—552
    Waldenbooks—179
    The Sports Authority—56
    Borders—31
J.C. Penney Company, Inc. (number of outlets)
  Stores—1,312
    Metropolitan market stores—697
    Geographic market stores—615
  Catalog units—2,090
    J.C. Penney Stores—1,312
    Free-standing sales centers—626
    Drug stores—136
    Other, principally outlet stores—16
  Drugstores (Thrift Drug or Treasury Drug)—487

attempted to go generally after an upscale consumer which had an annual house-hold income of $25,000 to $44,000. Fleet Farm and Menard's served the rural consumer, while firms like Chicago's Goldblatt's Department Stores returned to their immigrant heritage to serve blacks and Hispanics in the inner city.

In rural communities, Wal-Mart success often came at the expense of established local merchants and units of regional discount store chains. Hardware stores; family department stores; building supply outlets; and stores featuring fabrics, sporting goods, and shoes were among the first to either close or relocate elsewhere. Regional discount retailers in the Sunbelt states like Roses, Howard's, T. G. & Y., and Duckwall-ALCO, who once enjoyed solid sales and earnings, were forced to reposition themselves by renovating stores, opening bigger and more modern units, remerchandising assortments, and offering lower prices. In many cases, stores like Coast-to-Coast, Pamida, and Ben Franklin closed upon a Wal-Mart announcement to build in a specific community. "Just the word that Wal-Mart was coming made some stores close up," indicated a local newspaper editor.

■ Corporate Strategies

The corporate and marketing strategies that emerged at Wal-Mart to challenge a turbulent and volatile external environment were based upon a set of two main objectives which had guided the firm through its growth years in the decade of the 1980s. In the first objective, the customer was featured, "customers would be provided what they want, when they want it, all at a value." In the second objective, the team spirit was emphasized, "treating each other as we would hope to be treated, acknowledging our total dependency on our Associate-partners to sustain our success." The approach included: aggressive plans for new store openings; expansion to additional states; upgrading, relocation, refurbishing, and remodeling of existing stores; and opening new distribution centers. The plan was to not have a single operating unit that had not been updated in the past seven years. The 1990s were considered in the 1991 annual report: "A new era for Wal-Mart; an era in which we plan to grow to a truly nationwide retailer, and should we continue to perform, our sales and earnings will also grow beyond where most could have envisioned at the dawn of the '80s."

Several new retail formats were introduced by Wal-Mart in the 1980s. The first, Sam's Wholesale Club, opened in Oklahoma City, Oklahoma, in 1983. The wholesale club was an idea which had been developed by other firms earlier but which found its greatest success and growth in acceptability at Wal-Mart. Sam's Wholesale Club's featured a vast array of product categories with limited selection of brand and model; cash-and-carry business with limited hours; large (100,000 square foot), barebone facilities; rock-bottom wholesale prices; and minimal promotion. The limited membership plan permitted wholesale members who bought membership and others who usually paid a percentage above the ticket price of the merchandise. At the beginning of 1991, there were 148 Sam's Wholesale Clubs open in twenty-eight states. Effective February 2, 1991, Sam's Clubs merged the twenty-eight units of The Wholesale Club, Inc., of Indianapolis, Indiana, into the organization.

The first Hypermarket*USA, a 222,000 square foot superstore, which combined a discount store with a large grocery store; a food court of restaurants; and other service businesses such as banks or video tape rental stores, opened in 1988 in the Dallas suburb of Garland. A scaled-down version of Hypermarket*USA was called the Wal-Mart Super Center, similar in merchandise offerings, but with about half the square footage of hypermarts. These expanded store concepts also included convenience stores and gasoline distribution outlets to "enhance shopping convenience." The company proceeded slowly with these plans and later suspended its plans for building any more hypermarkets in favor of the super-center concept.

The McLane Company, Inc., a provider of retail and grocery distribution services for retail stores, was acquired in 1991. In October of 1991, management announced that it was starting a chain of stores called Bud's, which would sell damaged, outdated, and overstocked goods at discounts even deeper than regular Wal-Mart stores.

Several programs were launched to "highlight" popular social causes. The "Buy American" program was a Wal-Mart retail program initiated in 1985. The theme was "Bring It Home To The USA," and its purpose was to communicate Wal-Mart's support for American manufacturing. In the program, the firm directed substantial influence to encourage manufacturers to produce goods in the United States rather than import them from other countries. Vendors were attracted into the program by encouraging manufacturers to initiate the process by contacting the company directly with proposals to sell goods which were made in the United States. Buyers also targeted specific import items in their assortments on a state-by-state basis to encourage domestic manufacturing. According to Haim Dabah, president of Gitano Group, Inc., a maker of fashion discount clothing which imported 95 percent of its clothing and now makes about 20 percent of its products here: "Wal-Mart let it be known loud and clear that if you're going to grow with them, you sure better have some products made in the U.S.A." Farris Fashion, Inc. (flannel shirts), RoadmasterCorporation (exercise bicycles), Flanders Industries, Inc. (lawn chairs), and Magic Chef (microwave ovens) were examples of vendors that chose to participate in the program.

From the Wal-Mart standpoint the "Buy American" program centered around value—producing and selling quality merchandise at a competitive price. The promotion included television advertisements featuring factory workers, a soaring American eagle, and the slogan: "We buy American whenever we can, so you can too." Prominent in-store signage, and store circulars were also included. One store poster read: "Success Stories—These items formerly imported, are now being purchased by Wal-Mart in the U.S.A."

Wal-Mart was one of the first retailers to embrace the concept of "green" marketing. The program offered shoppers the option of purchasing products that were better for the environment in three respects: manufacturing, use, and disposal. It was introduced through full-page advertisements in *The Wall Street Journal* and *USA Today*. In-store signage identified those products which were environmentally safe. As Wal-Mart executives saw it, "Customers are concerned about the quality of land, air, and water, and would like the opportunity to do something positive." To initiate the program, 7,000 vendors were notified that Wal-Mart had a corporate concern for the environment and to ask for their support in a variety of ways. Wal-Mart television advertising showed children on swings, fields of grain blowing in the wind, and roses. Green and white store signs, printed on recycled paper, marked products or packaging that had been developed or redesigned to be more environmentally sound.

Wal-Mart had become the channel commander in the distribution of many brand-name items. As the nation's largest retailer and in many geographic areas the dominant distributor, it exerted considerable influence in negotiation for the best price, delivery terms, promotion allowances, and continuity of supply. Many of these benefits could be passed on to consumers in the form of quality name-brand items available at lower than competitive prices. As a matter of corporate policy, management often insisted on doing business only with a producer's top sales executives rather than going through a manufacturer's representative. Wal-Mart had been accused of threatening to buy from other producers if firms refused to sell directly to it. In the ensuing power struggle, Wal-Mart executives refused to talk about the controversial policy or admit that it existed. As a representative of an industry association representing a group of sales agencies representatives suggested, "In the Southwest, Wal-Mart's the only show in town." An industry analyst added, "They're extremely aggressive. Their approach has always been to give the customer the benefit of a corporate saving. That builds up customer loyalty and market share."

Another key factor in the mix was an inventory control system that was recognized as the most sophisticated in retailing. A high-speed computer system linked virtually all the stores to headquarters and the company's distribution centers. It electronically logged every item sold at the checkout counter, automatically kept the warehouses informed of merchandise to be ordered, and directed the flow of goods to the stores and even to the proper shelves. Most important for management, it helped detect sales trends quickly and speeded up market reaction time substantially.

■ Decision Making in a Market-Oriented Firm

One principle that distinguished Wal-Mart was the unusual depth of employee involvement in company affairs. Corporate strategies put emphasis on human resource management. Employees of Wal-Mart became "associates," a name borrowed from Sam Walton's early association with the J.C. Penney, Co. Input was encouraged at meetings at the store and corporate level. The firm hired employees locally; provided training programs; and through a "Letter to the President" program, management encouraged employees to ask questions and made words like "we," "us," and "our" a part of the corporate language. A number of special award programs recognized individual, department, and division achievement. Stock ownership and profit-sharing programs were introduced as part of a "partnership concept."

The corporate culture was recognized by the editors of the trade publication, *Mass Market Retailers,* when it recognized all 275,000 associates collectively as the 1989 "Mass Market Retailers of the Year." The editors noted, "In this decade the term 'The Wal-Mart associate,' has come to symbolize all that is right with the American worker, particularly in the retailing environment and most particularly at Wal-Mart." The "store within a store" concept, as a Wal-Mart corporate policy, trained individuals to be merchants by being responsible for the performance of their own departments as if they were running their own businesses. Seminars and training programs afforded them opportunities to grow within the company. "People development, not just a good 'program' for any growing company but a must to secure our future," is how Suzanne Allford, Vice President of the Wal-Mart People Division explained the firm's decentralized approach to retail management development.

"The Wal-Mart Way," was a phrase that was used by management to summarize the firm's unconventional approach to business and the development of the corporate culture. As noted in the 1991 annual report referring to a recent development program: "We stepped outside our retailing world to examine the best managed companies in the United States in an effort to determine the fundamentals of their success and to 'benchmark' our own performances." The name "Total Quality Management" (TQM) was used to identify this "vehicle for proliferating the very best things we do while incorporating the new ideas our people have that will assure our future."

■ The Growth Challenge

David Glass, 53 years old, had assumed the role of President and Chief Executive Officer at Wal-Mart, the position previously held by Sam Walton. Known for his hard-driving managerial style, Glass gained his experience in retailing at a small supermarket chain in Springfield, Missouri. He joined Wal-Mart as executive vice president for finance in 1976. He was named president and chief operating officer in 1984.

And what of Wal-Mart without Mr. Sam? "There's no transition to make," said Glass, "because the principles and the basic values he used in founding this company were so sound and so universally accepted." "As for the future," he suggested, spinning around in his chair at his desk in his relatively spartan office at corporate headquarters in Bentonville, "there's more opportunity ahead of us than behind us. We're good students of retailing and we've studied the mistakes that others have made. We'll make our own mistakes, but we won't repeat theirs. The only thing constant at Wal-Mart is change. We'll be fine as long as we never lose our responsiveness to the customer."

Wal-Mart Stores, Inc., had for over twenty-five years experienced tremendous growth and as one analyst suggested, "been consistently on the cutting edge of low-markup mass merchandising." Much of the forward momentum had come from the entrepreneurial spirit of Samuel Moore Walton. The company announced on Monday, April 6, 1992, following Walton's death, that his son, S. Robson Walton, vice chairman of Wal-Mart, would succeed his father as chairman of the board. David Glass would remain president and CEO. A new management team was in place. Management felt it had positioned the firm as an industry leader to meet the challenges of the next decade.

■ Epilogue

The post–Sam Walton era in the company's history brought a number of new challenges. In early 1993, Wal-Mart management confirmed that sales growth for stores open more than a year would likely slip into the 7 percent to 8 percent range in 1993. Analysts were also concerned about the increased competition in the warehouse club business and the company's move from its roots in Southern and Midwestern small towns to the more competitive and costly markets of the Northeast. Wal-Mart Super Centers faced more resilient rivals in the grocery field. Unions representing supermarket workers delayed and in some cases killed expansion opportunities. Some analysts said that, "The company is simply suffering from the high expectations its stellar performance over the years has created."

Questions for Discussion

1. Identify and evaluate the marketing strategies that Wal-Mart pursued to maintain its growth and marketing leadership positions. What factors should a firm consider in the development of its marketing strategy?
2. Discuss the importance of changes in the external environment to an organization like Wal-Mart.
3. What conclusions can be drawn, from a review of Wal-Mart's financial performance over the decade of the 1980s? From this review, what can you conclude about the financial future of the firm?
4. Speculate on how much impact the "absence" of Samuel Moore Walton will have on the forward momentum of the organization. What steps should be taken by management to continue Mr. Sam's formula for success?
5. What evidence is there to suggest that the marketing concept was understood and applied at Wal-Mart?

Appendix A Wal-Mart Stores, Inc. Financial Performance 1993–1984
1993 Annual Report[1]

Ten-Year Financial Summary (dollar amounts in thousands except per share data)	1993	1992	1991	1990	1989
Earnings					
Net sales	$55,483,771	$43,886,902	$32,601,594	$25,810,656	$20,649,001
Licensed department rentals and other income, net	500,793	402,521	261,814	174,644	136,867
Cost of sales	44,174,685	34,786,119	25,499,834	20,070,034	16,056,856
Operating, selling, and general and administrative expenses	8,320,842	6,684,304	5,152,178	4,069,695	3,267,864
Interest costs:					
Debt	142,649	113,305	42,176	20,346	36,286
Capital leases	180,049	152,558	125,920	117,725	99,395
Taxes on income	1,171,545	944,661	751,736	631,600	488,246
Net income	1,994,794	1,608,476	1,291,024	1,075,900	837,221
Per share of common stock:					
Net income	.87	.70	.57	.48	.37
Dividends	.11	.09	.07	.06	.04
Stores in operation at the end of the period					
Wal-Mart Stores	1,880	1,720	1,573	1,402	1,259
Sam's Wholesale Clubs	256	208	148	123	105
Financial Position					
Current assets	10,197,590	8,575,423	6,414,775	4,712,616	3,630,987
Net property, plant, equipment, and capital leases	9,792,881	6,433,801	4,712,039	3,430,059	2,661,954
Total assets	20,565,087	15,443,389	11,388,915	8,198,484	6,359,668
Current liabilities	6,754,286	5,003,775	3,990,414	2,845,315	2,065,909
Long-term debt	3,072,835	1,722,022	740,254	185,152	184,439
Long-term obligations under capital leases	1,772,152	1,555,875	1,158,621	1,087,403	1,009,046
Preferred stock with mandatory redemption provisions					
Shareholders' equity	8,759,180	6,989,710	5,365,524	3,965,561	3,007,909

(continued)

■ **Appendix A** *(concluded)*

Ten-Year Financial Summary
(dollar amounts in thousands except per share data)

	1988	1987	1986	1985	1984
Earnings					
Net sales	$15,959,255	$11,909,076	$ 8,451,489	$ 6,400,861	$ 4,666,909
Licensed department rentals and other income, net	104,783	84,623	55,127	52,167	36,031
Cost of sales	12,281,744	9,053,219	6,361,271	4,722,440	3,418,025
Operating, selling, and general and administrative expenses	2,599,367	2,007,645	1,485,210	1,181,455	892,887
Interest costs:					
Debt	25,262	10,442	1,903	5,207	4,935
Capital leases	88,995	76,367	54,640	42,506	29,946
Taxes on income	441,027	395,940	276,119	230,653	160,903
Net income	627,643	450,086	327,473	270,767	196,244
Per share of common stock:					
Net income	.28	.20	.58	.48	.35
Dividends	.03	.02	.57	.0525	.035
Stores in operation at the end of the period					
Wal-Mart Stores	1,114	980	859	745	642
Sam's Wholesale Clubs	84	49	23	11	3
Financial Position					
Current assets	2,905,145	2,353,271	1,784,275	1,303,254	1,005,567
Net property, plant, equipment, and capital leases	2,144,852	1,676,282	1,303,450	870,309	628,151
Total assets	5,131,809	4,049,092	3,103,645	2,205,229	1,652,254
Current liabilities	1,743,763	1,340,291	992,683	688,968	502,763
Long-term debt	185,672	179,234	180,682	41,237	40,866
Long-term obligations under capital leases	866,972	764,128	595,205	449,886	339,930
Preferred stock with mandatory redemption provisions			4,902	5,874	6,411
Shareholders' equity	2,257,267	1,690,493	1,277,659	984,672	737,503

[1]Wal-Mart Annual Report, January 31, 1993.

Case Group E
Pricing Strategy

■ **Case 23   Little Caesars**

J. Paul Peter
University of Wisconsin–Madison

Pizza is fun food that can also be nutritious if topped with the right ingredients. Consumers have a variety of ways they can obtain this tasty meal; they can make their own pizza favorites from scratch, buy boxed pizza mixes to prepare at home, or buy frozen pizza to have on hand for a present or future meal or snack; microwavable pizza also cuts down preparation time. Consumers can also buy hot, prepared pizza from supermarkets or family restaurants where pizza is a supplement to other foods or products.

The largest segment of the pizza market involves the purchase of hot, prepared pizza which consumers either eat at the pizzeria or take home. One estimate suggests that pizzeria pizza sales are ten times larger than frozen pizza sales. There are over 60,000 pizzerias in the United States. As shown in Exhibit 1 the three largest pizza chains are Pizza Hut, Domino's, and Little Caesars.

PepsiCo-owned Pizza Hut has the largest sales of any pizzeria chain, $4.45 billion, and a market share of 27.8 percent in 1992. A competitive advantage for Pizza Hut is that it offers sit-down dining with a reasonably pleasant atmosphere and a good salad bar. It is more of a family restaurant—a place to eat and chat—than other national pizza chains. It also features a variety of menu items for diners not interested in pizza, important when one in a group who doesn't want pizza could lead the others to a different type of restaurant altogether.

Little Caesars' second largest competitor is Domino's, whose sales in 1992 were $2.36 billion with a market share of 14.8 percent and over 5,000 outlets. The company made millions of dollars in the 1980s when it was the only national pizzeria company that delivered fresh, hot pizza to a buyer's home or office guaranteed to arrive within thirty minutes of an order. While this guarantee helped build Domino's sales, there has been some backlash since delivery drivers may drive too fast or recklessly in order to make the half-hour deadline.

Although it is the third largest company with sales of $2.16 billion in 1992 and a market share of 13.8 percent, Little Caesars has been taking market share from the other competitors. The chain consists of 4,500 restaurants. Its competitive advantage

---

This case prepared by J. Paul Peter, University of Wisconsin–Madison.

Source: Based on Gary Strauss, "Pizza Makers Spice Up War with Value," *USA Today*, May 26, 1993, pp. 1B, 2B; Julia Produs, "Little Caesars Sets Tone in Pizza War," *Wisconsin State Journal*, May 1993, p. 7C.

Company	Sales	Market Share
Pizza Hut	$4.45 billion	27.8%
Domino's	2.36 billion	14.8
Little Caesars	2.16 billion	13.5
Chuck E. Cheese's	343.6 million	2.2
Round Table	315.0 million	2.0
Sbarro	300.6 million	1.9
Godfather's	242.0 million	1.5
Pizza Inn	193.0 million	1.2
All others (includes regional chains and local restaurants)	5.64 billion	35.0

is that it provides larger quantities of pizza at lower prices and has well-located, convenient pick-up counters. Little Caesars is famous for offering two pizzas for the price of one on a regular basis.

The success of Little Caesars has not gone unnoticed by its competitors. In fact, a senior vice president for Domino's commented that "In the past the decision making was based on what Domino's was doing with free delivery. Now, decision making is based on what Little Caesars is doing with inexpensive pizza."

Some of the competitive advantages of these firms have already been diluted. For example, all three now offer free delivery which mitigates Domino's delivery advantage. All three now offer special huge pizzas at reduced prices. For example, backed by a $1 million advertising campaign, Pizza Hut introduced the "Big Foot," a two foot by one foot 21-slice pizza selling for $9 to $11. However, this pizza is only available as a carryout item and could be 15 to 20 percent less profitable than other pizzas. Domino's brought out the "Dominator" for $8.99 to $11.99 (price varies depending on location) which offers 30 slices of pizza (2 by 2 1/2 feet) with one topping. Little Caesars, several months before, began offering the Big Big Cheese pizza, which for $8.88, offers 24 slices of a thick pan cheese pizza.

Competitors are also trying a number of new menu items. Pizza Hut is offering more varieties of pizza and testing items such as chicken platters. Domino's has added salad, submarine sandwiches, and breadsticks. Little Caesars may launch pasta dishes such as lasagna to bolster its menu.

Discussion Questions

1. Considering price, quantity, and quality of the supersize pizzas, how do you think consumers choose among each of these alternatives? In more general terms, what variables are involved in making a purchase decision for pizza?

2. A top executive at Pizza Hut stated that "We aren't targeting people. We are targeting occasions for when people want a lot of pizza for a little money." How important do you think the usage occasion is for pizza purchases?

3. If variable cost for Little Caesar's Big Big Cheese Pizza were $1.88, and fixed cost per store for this product were $7,000, what is the breakeven point for this product per store? What is the breakeven point for the whole pizza chain?

4. What recommendations do you have for Little Caesars management to increase sales, market share, and profits?

Case 24 Schwinn Bicycles

J. Paul Peter
University of Wisconsin–Madison

Inside a plain, brown building in Boulder, Colorado, is a shrine to an American icon: the Schwinn bicycle. Some mud-caked from daily use, some shiny museum pieces—dozens of bikes stand atop file cabinets and lean against cubicles. Amid the spokes and handlebars, a group of zealots is working to pull off the turnaround of the century in the bike business. Brimming with energy, they're determined to resurrect the best known brand on two wheels. But as Schwinn celebrates its 100th anniversary, its management team faces a long uphill climb. Just two years ago, once-mighty Schwinn had a near-death experience in bankruptcy court. Now it's trying to rise to the top of the crowded mountain bike market.

For years, Schwinn was the top U.S. brand, with as much as 25 percent of the market. Now, it has less than 5 percent of the $2.5 billion annual retail bike market. The new Schwinn will sell about 400,000 redesigned bikes—many of them Asian-made models—that sell for $200 to $400 retail, the lower end of the adult bike market. Those models are catching on. But the turnaround won't be a success unless Schwinn persuades cyclists to fork over $700 or more for its newer bikes. Below are market shares of manufacturers for bikes retail-priced $400 and up:

Trek	24%
Cannondale	12%
Specialized	12%
Schwinn	7%
Giant	6%
Diamondback	6%
GT	6%
Scott	4%
Mongoose	3%
Pro Flex	3%

The mass market for low-priced bikes and those made for children is dominated by three U.S. manufacturers: Huffy, Murray, and Roadmaster. The mass market accounts for about 8.5 million of the 12 million bikes sold in the nation annually.

Schwinn's history as a maker of sturdy, low-cost bikes is no longer the asset it once was. Many under-30 cyclists see Schwinns as the bikes their parents rode. They prefer trendier mountain bikes, with their padded seats, upright handlebars, fat tires and additional gears for climbing.

"We have an image challenge," admits Schwinn Marketing Director Gregg Bagni. That's clear from a walk around the University of Colorado campus a half-mile away. Outside dorms and classrooms, racks are filled with bikes made by Trek Bicycle, Specialized Bicycle Components, Cannondale and Giant. Waterloo, Wisconsin-based

This case prepared by J. Paul Peter of the University of Wisconsin–Madison.

Source: Patrick McGeehan, "Biking Icon Wants to Lose Training Wheels," *USA Today*, August 8, 1995, pp. 1B, 2B; "Hard Pedaling Powers Schwinn Uphill in Sales, Toward Profits," *Chicago Tribune*, June 22, 1995, p. 2N; " 'New Schwinn' Bike Has Gone Full Cycle," *Chicago Tribune*, May 16, 1995, p. 3N.

Trek is the leader. This year it expects about $300 million in revenue on sales of more than 900,000 bikes.

"When I was a kid, if you had a Schwinn, you were the luckiest kid in the world," says Scott Montgomery, a Cannondale marketing chief. "Ask a college kid now and they'll say, 'Oh, Schwinn? They're toast.'"

For decades, the Schwinn brand, synonymous with durability, ruled the road. Generations of kids clamored for the company's Excelsiors, Phantoms, Sting-Rays and 10-speed Varsitys. "Schwinn used to be number one and you could hardly find number two," says industry consultant Bill Fields. But in the late '70s and early '80s, cyclists veered off the road into the woods and mountains. Schwinn ignored the mountain bike craze for most of the '80s. By 1992, two-thirds of bikes sold were mountain bikes and Schwinn was in bankruptcy court. Unable to pay lenders or suppliers, the descendants of company founder Ignaz Schwinn sold the company to the Zell/Chilmark Investment fund for $43 million. Zell/Chilmark appointed new management and funded the company, Scott Sports Group, with an additional $7 million.

So far, the Schwinn turnaround is being attempted on a shoestring. Schwinn's workforce shrank from 300 employees to about 180 when the company was reorganized and moved from Chicago to Boulder. The move west was calculated to attract young workers plugged into the mountain-biking community. Once assembled, the managers focused on product design. They had inherited a Schwinn line whose only mountain bikes were priced at the low end of the bike-shop range, between $200 and $400.

"Previous management wouldn't believe anybody would buy a $1500 mountain bike with the Schwinn name on it," one Schwinn executive stated. Now, Schwinn is emblazoned on everything from $100 kids' bikes to $2,500 mountain bikes. Its top-of-the-line, American-made Homegrown model starts at $1,750. One of its hottest products is a decidedly low-tech, retro-style, one-speed Cruiser with a wide seat and balloon tires. It's selling fast in Sunbelt states for up to $250. The Cruiser appeals to retirees and snowbirds in beach communities and to college students who call them "bar bikes" because they are ridden to bars and back.

"They want to position this company as high-end, high-tech," says Cannondale's Montgomery. "And what they've got is this traditional, old-fashioned Harley-Davidson type of product. That's their greatest marketing challenge."

Today's bike business is quite different from the one Schwinn dominated so long ago. Exclusive dealerships like Schwinn uses are disappearing, being replaced by independent bike shops. The typical bike shop carries four brands, so Schwinn bikes are subjected to side-by-side comparisons with competing products. Some of the other brands, such as Trek and Cannondale, have built reputations for cutting-edge technology. Cannondale makes aluminum-frame bikes in U.S. plants, and Trek, a pioneer in carbon fiber frames, is moving production back from Taiwan. All but a few thousand Schwinns are made in Asia.

"Handmade in the USA is a tremendous marketing feature," says Brett Hahn, manager of Yeti Cycles in Durango, Colorado. "Bottom line: Mountain biking is a U.S. sport." Yeti makes hundreds of frames for Schwinn's top-of-the-line Homegrown models. Schwinn is considering buying Yeti or another U.S. manufacturer.

Discussion Questions

1. What are the strengths and weaknesses of Schwinn?
2. What opportunities and threats face the company?
3. How important is it for mountain bikes to be made in America?
4. Evaluate Schwinn's strategy of selling bikes for prices from $100 to $2500.
5. Evaluate Zell/Chilmark's decision to invest $50 million in Schwinn. What did it get for it's money? Calculate the breakeven point and the payback period for this investment given the following assumptions: Schwinn has 4 percent of the retail bike market; Schwinn bikes are marked up an average of 20 percent at retail; Schwinn has a 25 percent profit margin on its bikes.
6. Noting that 80 percent of Trek's sales are for bikes priced $400 and over, how many bikes does Schwinn sell in this category?

Case 25 America Online (AOL)

Natalya V. Delcoure, Lawrence R. Jauch, and John L. Scott
Northeast Louisiana University

Introduction

America Online, Inc. (NYSE: AOL) was founded in 1985. This media company, with headquarters in Dulles, Virginia, has more than 10 million members and currently operates in the United States, Canada, the United Kingdom, France and Germany. AOL provides online services including electronic mail, online conferencing, Internet access, news, magazines, sports, weather, stock quotes, mutual fund transactions, software files, games, computing support and online classes.

According to the company, its mission is "to lead the development of a new interactive medium that eliminates traditional boundaries between people and places to create a new kind of interactive global community that holds the potential to change the way people obtain information, communicate with one another, buy products and services, and learn."

To accomplish this mission, the company's strategy is to continue investment in the growth of its subscriber base, pursue related business opportunities often through joint ventures and acquisitions, provide a full range of interactive services and maintain technological flexibility.

AOL's rapid growth and community orientation have made it the most popular, easiest, and well-known way for consumers to get online. In December 1996, AOL had 8.5 million member sessions a day; 7 million e-mails sent to 12 million recipients a day; and it accounted for approximately $750,000 per day in merchandise transactions.

But AOL has not been trouble-free. On August 7, 1996, AOL threw 6 million subscribers off line for 19 hours due to software problems. America Online revealed that the glitch resulted from an error made by its working subsidiary, ANS Co., in reconfiguring software, and from a bug in router software. The error cost AOL $3 million in rebates. On January 8, 1997 America Online suffered a partial outage that forced it to shut down half of its system for four hours to find a problem. The problem was with an interface in a router device, which manages the flow of data in the network. The outage drew front-page headlines around the world, as millions of users were unable to access electronic mail, the Internet, and a variety of services and publications online for nearly a day.

America Online—Company Profile

America Online emerged from a firm founded in the early 1980s as Control Video Corp., aimed to create an online service that specialized in games. It failed to meet strong competition from the Apple II and Commodore 64. Control Video was

This case was written based on published documents. It is intended to be used as a basis for class discussion rather than to illustrate either effective or ineffective handling of an administrative situation. Copyright © Lawrence R. Jauch and John L. Scott, 1997.

reorganized as Quantum Computer Services and became a custom developer of online services for other companies. Over time, Quantum managed to persuade Tandy Corp. and Apple Computers to offer a new service called Applelink Personal Edition. At the last minute, Apple withdrew from the deal and left Quantum holding software it had developed expressly for Applelink. In 1989 Quantum was only scraping by, and it did not have much money for splashy ad campaigns to attract computer users to their new service—America Online. So it came on the market with a unique approach, which was to blanket the countryside with diskettes containing America Online software. As the years went by, the company changed the way it accounted for the costs of acquiring subscribers and its pricing plans, but America Online had never actually made any money in its entire life. At the same time America Online has tried to position itself as the first "digital media company."

AOL Organization

AOL Corporation now oversees the operations of several subsidiaries and three divisions: AOL Networks, ANS Access and AOL Studios. The Corporate Division comprises the core business functions of Finance, Human Resources, Legal Affairs, Corporate Communications, Corporate Development, and Technology. The Technology group is responsible for delivering research, development, network/data center operations and member support to the other America Online divisions, technology licensees and joint venture partners. The group is also responsible for support functions—including technical support, billing, and sales.

AOL Networks is responsible for extending the AOL brand into the market, developing new revenue streams, advertising and online transactions. AOL Networks is led by Robert Pittman, President, formerly managing partner and CEO of Century 21 and co-founder of MTV Network.

ANS Access is responsible for the telecommunication network. The network consists of more than 160,000 modems connecting 472 cities in the U.S. and 152 cities internationally. Nearly 85 percent of the American population can dial into AOLNet on a local number. For America Online's members who travel, GlobalNet offers access in approximately 230 additional cities in 83 countries. The ANS technical team is responsible for architecture, design, development, installation, management and maintenance of hardware and software for the nationwide corporate data networks and Internet backbone by which communications take place.

AOL Studios runs AOL's innovative chat (iChatco), games (INN), local (Digital City), and independent (Greenhouse) programming properties. AOL Studios is the newest division in AOL. It is working on development of leading-edge technology for broadband and mid-band distribution, interactive brands that can be extended into other media properties such as TV and radio, and managing joint ventures with companies including Time-Warner and CapCities/ABC. Imagination Network Inc. is the provider of computer online entertainment services for AOL.

Digital City provides local programming, news, services, chat rooms, and commerce to AOL members as well as to the Internet at large. To date, Digital City has been launched nationally in Washington DC, Boston, Philadelphia, Atlanta, San Francisco and Los Angeles. Digital City planned to expand to over 40 cities in 1997. Digital City, Inc., is owned by Digital City LP. AOL owns a majority interest in that entity, and the Tribune Company owns the remaining interest.

Advanced CO+RE Systems, Inc., is a wholly owned subsidiary of America Online, which provides network services for AOLnet, together with Sprint Corporation and BBN Corporation. Through this subsidiary, America Online designs, develops, and operates high performance wide-area networks for business, research, education and government organizations.

In February 1996, AOL merged with the Johnson-Grace Company, a leading developer of compression technology and multimedia development and delivery tools. Using the Johnson-Grace technology, America Online is able to deliver the data-intensive graphics and audio and video capabilities using narrow-band technologies, even over the slower speed modems currently used by most AOL members.

In fiscal 1996 AOL combined its key production areas to form AOL Productions, Inc., a wholly owned subsidiary. AOL Productions has emerged as a leading studio system with expertise in all phases of interactive content development for online, World Wide Web, Internet, and CD-ROM delivery.

2Market, Inc., is a joint venture between America Online, Apple Computer and Medior. It provides retail catalog shopping CD-ROMs that include online ordering capabilities. In 1997 America Online, along with Netscape Communications and Disney's ABC unit, announced their plans to launch ABCNEWS.com, a 24-hour news service.

Since the beginning of 1995, the Company also acquired Advanced Network and Services, Inc., Ubique, Ltd., Navisoft, Inc., Global Network Navigator, Inc., Book-Link Technologies, Inc., and Redgate Communications Corporation. AOL is also planning to go into the bookselling business in a joint venture with Barnes & Noble, but the timing is still uncertain.

AOL Marketing

The goals of the firm's consumer marketing programs are to increase the general visibility of America Online and to make it easy for customers to experiment with and subscribe to its services. AOL attracts new subscribers through independent marketing programs such as direct mail, disk inserts and inserts in publications, advertising and a variety of co-marketing efforts. The company has entered into co-marketing agreements with numerous personal computer hardware, software and peripheral production companies, and also with certain of its media partners. These companies bundle America Online software with their products and cater to the needs of a specific audience.

America Online has also been expanding into business-to-business markets, using AOL's network to provide customized network solutions to both individual businesses and to professional communities and industries. These private AOLs (the "PAOLs") offer the ease of use America Online is known for, as well as customized features and functionality accessible only by pre-authorized users, access to the fleet of AOL distribution platforms, secure communications and information. The company offers these products using a direct sales force and direct marketing, and through resellers and system integrators.

America Online utilizes specialized retention programs designed to increase customer loyalty and satisfaction and to maximize customer subscription life. These retention programs include regularly scheduled online events and conferences; the regular addition of new content, services and software programs; and online promotions of upcoming online events and new features. The firm also provides a variety of support mechanisms such as online technical support and telephone support services.

In May 1995 America Online introduced its web browser, which provides integrated World Wide Web access within the AOL services. The integrated approach allows the user to seamlessly use the full suite of America Online features, including chat room, e-mail gateways and mailing lists, file transfer protocol, USENET Newsgroups, WAIS and Gopher.

In the summer of 1997 America Online, Inc. planned to offer its 8 million members a three-dimensional gaming world, CyberPark. The company will try to compete with such heavyweights as Microsoft, Internet Gaming Zone site, and MCI, which will launch a service in 1997 that allows computer users to play their favorite CD-ROM games. The projected earnings are expected to reach $127 million in 1997, but there are still some technical problems to overcome and the uncertainty of how much to charge future users.

America Online has included international market expansion in its strategy to gain competitive advantage. In April 1995, AOL entered into a joint venture with Bertelsmann, one of the world's largest media companies, to offer interactive services in Europe: Germany (November 1995), the United Kingdom (January 1996), and France (March 1996). Bertelsmann agreed to contribute up to $100 million to fund the launch of the European services, provided access to its book and music club membership base of over 30 million, and offered its publishing content to the joint venture on a most favored customer basis. In addition, Bertelsmann acquired approximately a 5 percent interest in America Online and designated a member of the company's Board of Directors. AOL contributed interactive technology and management expertise, proprietary software licenses and development services, staff training and technical support in order to develop, test and launch the interactive services in Europe. Subscribers to the European services enjoy access to America Online's services in the United States, and United States subscribers enjoy access to the European services.

AOL Canada, launched in January 1996, features local content and services. In October 1996, AOL Canada offered Canadian members software, thirteen local channels, billing in Canadian dollars, e-mail, message boards, and easy access to the Internet through a Web browser. AOL Canada's key partners include Citytv, an internationally renowned broadcaster and program producer; MuchMusic, Canada's first national music television channel; Shift Magazine, Canada's hottest publication in media; Intuit Canada, makers of the world's leading personal finance software, Quicken; and Southam New Media, a wholly-owned subsidiary of Southam Inc., Canada's largest news organization.

In May 1996, America Online announced a partnership with Mitsui & Co., one of the world's largest international trading companies, and Nikkei, one of Japan's leading media companies with respected business and computer publications. The joint venture consists of Mitsui & Co. owning 40 percent, Nikkei 10 percent and AOL 50 percent. Japanese partners contributed more than 120 years of experience and credibility in the Japanese market, a strong management team and $56 million to fund the launch of the Japanese service. America Online brings to the venture its ability to develop, manage, and execute interactive online services in the U.S., Europe, and Canada.

America Online's wildly successful marketing ploy of flat rate pricing in the U.S. turned out to contribute to AOL's latest problem. About 75 percent of AOL's customers took the flat-rate offer. As a result, total daily AOL customer use soared from 1.6 million hours online in October 1996 to more than 4 million hours in January 1997. (These problems are more fully described later in this case.)

Meeting Customer Needs

The company provides tools to its members so that they can control their child's or teen's experience online without cramping the adults who enjoy using AOL's services to talk to other adults. Parental controls can block or limit the use of chat, Instant Messages, e-mail, binary files, news groups, or the Web. Different online areas support different values. For instance:

- ACLU forum: encourages lively yet responsible debate. Illegal activities (harassment, distribution of illegal materials) are not permitted in this area.
- Womens' Network: is a women-friendly and safe space for chatting, learning, teaching and networking, but men are still welcome to join the communication.
- Christian Chat room: allows fellowship among Christian members. In this space, proselytizing is forbidden.
- Kids Only: gives children their own space online for searching help with homework, sending e-mail, and hanging out in chat rooms. Parental control can be set up in this area.

The average adult spends about an hour per day on line, but the average child spends three. Currently, there are 4.1 million kids surfing the Net. By 2000, it is expected there will be 19.2 million. Kids, who spent $307 million in 1996 on online services, will spend $1.8 billion by 2002, and that is why media and Web giants are scrambling to offer new kid-friendly sites. Fox TV features cartoons and kid shows. Disney gave AOL first crack at hosting Daily Blast, which offers kids games, comics, and stories for $4.95 per month or $39.95 per year. But, says Rob Jennings, vice-president for programming for AOL networks, "we felt we had a good mix already." Yahooligans! offers kids-friendly Web-sites for free. AOL still has partnerships with other media giants such as Disney rival Viacom Inc.'s Nickelodeon unit, for other offerings.

Since 1994, AOL has offered a Kids Only area featuring homework help, games, and online magazines, as well as the usual fare of software, games, and chat rooms. The area gets about 1 million 8- to 12-year-old visitors monthly.

In April 1996, America Online began to see the effect of seasonality in both member acquisitions and in the amount of time spent by customers using its services. The company expects that member acquisition is to be highest in the second and third fiscal quarters, when sales of new computers and computer software are highest due to holiday seasons. Customer usage is expected to be lower in the summer months, due largely to extended daylight hours and competing outdoor leisure activities.

AOL Employees

As of June 30, 1996, America Online had 5,828 employees, including 1,058 in software and content development; 3,271 in customer support; 199 in marketing; 1,099 in operations; and 291 in corporate operations. None of AOL's employees is represented by a labor union, and America Online has never experienced a work stoppage.

AOL employs numerous part-time workers around the world known as remote staff. These are volunteer staff who develop content and provide both marketing and operations functions. Remote staff write informational articles, produce graphics, host chat rooms, provide technical assistance, and fulfill various support functions. Remote staff duties vary. Some may work as little as ten hours per week or more than forty hours per week.

AOL's remote staff are compensated for these services with "community leader accounts"—a membership for which the staff members are not charged. Relatively few remote staff are paid as independent contractors.

AOL's flat rate pricing plan had a serious impact on its remote staff. Prior to the flat rate, members paid about $3 per hour of online access. Hence, a "free account" would have a value of approximately $300 for a staff member who spent three hours per day online. After the flat rate pricing plan, this account's value fell to $20. This enormous decrease in incentives led many remote staff to resign their positions. The positions hardest hit were those for which the job pressures were highest. AOL's once touted "Techlive" is now all but invisible.

AOL Finance

Exhibits 1 and 2 present the financial statements for fiscal years 1995 and 1996. About 90 percent of the firm's revenues are generated from online subscription fees. AOL's other revenues are generated from sales of merchandise, data network services, online transactions and advertising, marketing and production services and development and licensing fees. The increase of over $600 million in service revenues from 1995 to 1996 was primarily attributed to a 93 percent increase in AOL subscribers.

This is expected to undergo radical change, due to flat rate pricing, with much less revenue coming from subscriber fees, which AOL hopes to make up by increases in the other revenue streams.

Cost of revenue, which includes network-related costs, consists of data and voice communication costs, costs associated with operating the data centers and provid-

■ **Exhibit 1**
Income Statement,
Year Ended June 30
(amounts in
thousands, except per
share data)

	1996	1995
Revenues:		
Online service revenues	$ 991,656	$344,309
Other revenues	102,198	49,981
Total revenues	1,093,854	394,290
Costs and expenses:		
Cost of revenues	627,372	229,724
Marketing	212,710	77,064
Product development	53,817	14,263
General and administrative	110,653	42,700
Acquired research and development	16,981	50,335
Amortization of goodwill	7,078	1,653
Total costs and expenses	1,028,611	415,739
Income (loss) from operations:	65,243	(21,449)
Other income (loss) from operations	(2,056)	3,074
Merger expenses	(848)	(2,207)
Income (loss) before provision for income taxes	62,339	(20,582)
Provision for income taxes	(32,523)	(15,169)
Net income (loss)	$ 29,816	$(35,751)
Earnings (loss) per share:		
Net income (loss)	$ 0.28	$ (0.51)
Weighted average shares outstanding	108,097	69,550

■ Exhibit 2
Consolidated Balance
Sheets, June 30
(amounts in
thousands, except per
share data)

	1996	1995
Assets		
Current assets:		
Cash and cash equivalents	$118,421	$ 45,877
Short-term investments	10,712	18,672
Trade accounts receivable	42,939	32,176
Other receivables	29,674	11,381
Prepaid expenses and other current assets	68,832	25,527
Total current assets	270,578	133,633
Property and equipment at cost, net	101,277	70,919
Other assets:		
Product development costs, net	44,330	18,949
Deferred subscriber acquisition costs, net	314,181	77,229
License rights, net	4,947	5,579
Other assets	35,878	9,121
Deferred income taxes	135,872	35,627
Goodwill, net	51,691	54,356
Total assets	$958,754	$405,413
Liabilities and Stockholders' Equity		
Current liabilities:		
Trade accounts payable	$105,904	$ 84,640
Other accrued expenses and liabilities	127,898	23,509
Deferred revenue	37,950	20,021
Accrued personnel costs	15,719	2,863
Current portion of long-term debt	2,435	2,329
Total current liabilities	289,906	133,362
Long-term liabilities:		
Notes payable	19,306	17,369
Deferred income taxes	135,872	35,627
Other liabilities	1,168	2,243
Total liabilities	$446,252	$188,601
Stockholders' Equity:		
Preferred stock, $.01 par value; 5,000,000 shares authorized; 1,000 shares issued and outstanding at June 30, 1996	1	—
Common stock, $.01 par value; 300,000,000 and 100,000,000 shares authorized, 92,626,000 and 76,728,268 shares issued and outstanding at June 30, 1996 and 1995, respectively	926	767
Additional paid-in capital	519,342	252,668
Accumulated deficit	(7,767)	(36,623)
Total stockholders' equity	512,502	216,812
Total liabilities and equity	$958,754	$405,413

ing customer support. These increased almost $400 million from 1995 to 1996. This increase was related to a growth of data communication cost, customer support cost and royalties paid to information and service providers.

For fiscal 1996, marketing expenses increased 176 percent over fiscal 1995. This was primarily attributed to an increase in the size and number of marketing programs designed to expand the subscriber base.

Product development costs include research and development and the amortization of software. For fiscal 1996, these costs increased 277 percent over fiscal 1995, and increased as a percentage of total revenues from 3.6 percent to 4.9 percent. The increases in product development costs were primarily attributable to an increase in the number of technical employees. Product development costs, before capitalization and amortization, increased by 242 percent.

For fiscal 1996, general and administrative costs increased 159 percent over fiscal 1995 and decreased as a percentage of total revenues from 10.8 percent to 10.1 percent. The increase in general and administrative costs was related to higher personnel, office and travel expenses related to an increase in the number of employees. The decrease in general and administrative costs as a percentage of total revenues was a result of the substantial growth in revenues, which more than offset the additional general and administrative costs, combined with the semi-variable nature of many of the general and administrative costs.

Acquired research and development costs relate to in-process research and development purchased with the acquisition of Ubique, Ltd., in September 1995. Acquired research and development costs relate to in-process research and development purchased as part of the acquisitions of BookLink Technologies, Inc. ("Booklink"), and Navisoft, Inc. ("Navisoft").

The amortization of goodwill increase relates primarily to the America Online's fiscal 1995 acquisitions of Advanced Network & Services, Inc., and Global Network Navigator, Inc., which resulted in approximately $56 million of goodwill. The goodwill related to these acquisitions is being amortized on a straight-line basis over periods ranging from five to ten years. The increase in amortization of goodwill results from a full year of goodwill recognized in fiscal 1996 compared to only a partial year of goodwill recognized in fiscal 1995.

Other income (expenses) consists of interest expense and nonoperating charges net of investment income and nonoperating gains. The change in other income (expense) was attributed to the $8 million settlement of a class action lawsuit partially offset by an increase in investment income.

Nonrecurring merger expenses totaling $848,000 were recognized in fiscal 1996 in connection with the merger of America Online with Johnson-Grace Company. Nonrecurring merger expenses totaling $2,207,000 were recognized in fiscal 1995 in connection with the mergers of AOL with Redgate Communications Corporation, Wide Area Information Servers, Inc., and Medior, Inc.

In December 1993, the Company completed a public offering of 8,000,000 shares of common stock, which generated net cash proceeds of approximately $62.7 million. In April 1995, the joint venture with Bertelsmann to offer interactive online services in Europe, netted approximately $54 million through the sale of approximately 5 percent of its common stock to Bertelsmann. In October 1995, AOL completed a public offering of 4,963,266 shares of common stock, which generated net cash proceeds of approximately $139.5 million. In May 1996, America Online sold convertible preferred stock to Mitsui in its joint venture with Mitsui & Co., Ltd., and Nohon Keizai Shimbun, Inc., to offer interactive online services in Japan. The

For the Quarter Ended	High	Low
September 30, 1994	$10.28	$ 6.88
December 31, 1994	14.63	7.47
March 31, 1995	23.69	12.31
June 30, 1995	24.06	16.75
September 30, 1995	37.25	21.38
December 31, 1995	46.25	28.25
March 31, 1996	60.00	32.75
June 30, 1996	71.00	36.63
September 30, 1996	37.75	34.65
December 31, 1996	33.38	32.25

preferred stock has an aggregate liquidation preference of approximately $28 million and accrues dividends at a rate of 4 percent per annum. Accrued dividends can be paid in the form of additional shares of preferred stock. Exhibit 3 shows the history of share prices of AOL's common stock.

America Online has financed its operations through cash generated from operations and the sale of its capital stock. AOL has financed its investments in facilities and telecommunications equipment principally through leasing. America Online leases the majority of its facilities and equipment under non-cancelable operating leases. The communication network requires a substantial investment in telecommunications equipment, which America Online plans to finance principally through leasing. The company has never declared, nor has it paid, any cash dividends on its Common Stock. AOL currently intends to retain its earnings to finance future growth.

The company uses its working capital to finance ongoing operations and to fund marketing and content programs and the development of its products and services. America Online plans to continue to invest in computing and support infrastructure. Additionally, AOL expects to use a portion of its cash for the acquisition and subsequent funding of technologies, products or businesses complementary to the company's current business. For example, America Online is investing in the development of alternative technologies to deliver its services. AOL has entered into agreements with several manufacturers of PDAs, including Sony, Motorola, Tandy and Casio, to bundle a palmtop edition of America Online's client software with the PDAs sold by such manufacturers. AOL is participating in early cable trials using cable as the conduit into PCs, and has announced future support of ISDN and wireless. In the paging market, AOL has entered into agreements with AT&T Wireless Services and MobileMedia to provide their paging customers who subscribe to AOL with mobile access to certain America Online services.

■ AOL's Environment

For a long time such companies as AT&T, Western Union and RCA dominated the telecommunication industry. The courts deregulated the telephone industry in the 1980s. Although technology and market development made passage of new telecommunications legislation inevitable, it took about ten years to frame it. Even though the Telecommunications Reform Act of 1996 meant to remove many of the regulatory barriers and make it easier for telecom companies to invest in the information superhighway, so far it has made little difference. The Department of Commerce and the U.S. Trade Representative has pushed the World Trade Organization to open up the telecom sector to more service and equipment competition. As the result of trade negotiations in Singapore, tariffs on many telecommunications products and services will be reduced with great potential benefit to U.S. firms. Additional talks were under way in Switzerland in 1997, which may permit U.S. Telecommunications companies to compete on equal footing with providers in Europe and elsewhere.

America Online must pay particular attention to changes in the regulatory environment relating to telecommunications and the media. Additional legislative proposals from international, federal and state government bodies in the areas of content regulations, intellectual property, privacy rights and state tax issues, could impose additional regulations and obligations upon all online service providers.

Telephone companies are collecting high revenues as computer and online services expand. One study found that local carriers collected revenues totaling $1.4 billion in 1995 from second phone lines used mainly for Net links, while spending only $245 million to upgrade their networks for the additional usage. Phone companies experienced 8 percent to 9 percent profit growth in 1996 since second phone line installations at homes grew 25 percent. Both local carriers and online service providers agree that there is a necessity to build higher capacity networks to satisfy the increasing demand for public phone networks to meet the growing trend in cybersurfing.

The future of technology is difficult to predict, but can affect AOL's future strategy. Some speculate that interactive TV is going to be replaced by network computers (such as those from Sun). Some argue that Internet connections should be available for people who want to use them, and that public monies should be provided to ensure access for all. There is a growing place for satellite and fiber in the new communication system. Technology trends are sometimes born of social change. Here are some of the most important trends to watch for the next five years.

- The world phone could be a satellite wireless phone that uses digital technology. A combination of Global System for Mobilization (GSM) and satellite technologies could be the model for the world phone. Pioneers such as Wildfire Communications, Lucent Technologies, Dialogic, and VDOnet are among hundreds of alternative carriers that try to unite PCs, phone, e-mail, fax, and video into a seamless fabric. They are designing software that sends phone calls around the world on the Internet very cheaply. The line dividing computers and telephones, voice and data is blurring. Building on the union of data networks and computers, the Internet has become the new global communications infrastructure for businesses.

- Personal Communication Systems (PCS) could broadside local telecom carriers. Projections are that local exchange carriers must brace for a loss of 35 percent of high-margin business customers and 25 percent or more of their residential shares to PCS providers. Mobile subscribers could represent 17 percent of traditional wireline carrier business by 2010. VocalTec Ltd., leading maker of Internet telephone products, recently broadened the appeal by introducing gateways that connect the Internet to standard phone systems—allowing PC users to call non-PC users on their phones and vice versa. VocalTec claims it saves $10,000 a month on phone bills between the company's New Jersey and Israeli offices.

- Wireless convergence: commercial mobile wireless will include mobile satellite, and satellite communication will overlap coverage and mobility with cellular/PCS. Cordless telephony will play major roles. Several years ago, Microsoft Corp. and

Novell Inc. tried to apply computer-telephony integration technology to any desktop by creating competing standards for connecting phone systems to PC networks. But the products, TAPI and TSAPI, which allowed desktop computers to receive and manage phone calls through their PCs, went nowhere. Now, a wave of products built on TAPI and TSAPI that works with standard telecom equipment is hitting the market. Users can select a handful of names from a database and command the phone switch to set up a conference call with all of them. Pacific Bell is testing a sophisticated messaging service on 300 wireless-phone customers in San Diego. It answers incoming phone calls, screens them, and automatically routes them to wherever you are—a conference room, your home office, or a shopping mall. For a richer media experience, many companies are concentrating on desktop videoconferencing products from Intel, C-Phone, and VDOnet, among others. Those products are very cost efficient and price compatible.

- Asynchronous transfer mode: ATM carrier services are still expensive. Originally developed by Bell Laboratories for high-speed voice networks, ATM has now been adapted for data applications. They are able to move data at 155 mbps, whereas advanced modems top out at 56 kbps. The Defense Department uses a fiber-optic ATM network between the U.S. and Germany. The Mayo Clinic in Rochester, Minn., uses ATM for "tele-medicine"—doctors can video conference with patients. ATM switches account for an estimated savings of $200,000 per month for American Petroleum Institution which uses this tool to transmit drilling-site data over satellite. This technology is moving quickly into the public phone network, which increases the speed of the global communication network.
- Residential gateways: will let customers plug in telecom carriers and cable companies' networks and give users more control.

Increased competition makes it hard to make money on selling unlimited online access. Service providers have to upgrade their equipment to handle higher modem speeds and install separate equipment and phone lines for rival technologies. Sales of new modems are expected to be huge, driven by the Internet boom. AOL signed a deal with U.S. Robotics, which was scheduled to start turning on telephone access numbers on February 27, 1997, to give subscribers log-on access at a faster speed. Currently, the only high speed (56 kbps) modems that America Online customers can use are made by U.S. Robotics, which now controls a quarter of the market. Modems from the Open 56K Forum group—available in March 1997—can't talk to those of U.S. Robotics. Most of the Open 56K group will have modems out in March, 1997. The No. 2 modem maker, Hayes Microcomputer Products Inc. registered more than 40,000 people for a deal it offered on the company's Web page: customers can get their high-speed modems for $99 by sending in any brand modem. U.S. Robotics sells its superfast modems for $199 for a version that is installed into the computer, or $239 for an external model.

Use of the Net has dramatically increased the demand for techies. An estimated 760,000 people are working for Net-related companies alone. The Internet is full of companies' ads wanting programmers. A new study by the Information Technology Association of America estimates that 190,000 infotech jobs stand vacant in U.S. companies—half in the information industry. The situation can get worse, because the number of college students in computer science has fallen 43 percent in the past decade. Net-related companies are spending millions of dollars recruiting employees. In 1996, pay for info-tech workers rose by 12 percent to 20 percent, while average annual pay for software architects rose to $85,600.

The online services market is highly competitive. Major direct competitors include Prodigy Services Company, a joint venture of IBM and Sears; e-World, a service of Apple Computer, Inc.; GEnie, a division of General Electric Information Services; Delphi Internet Services Corporation, a division of News Corp.; Interchange, a service of AT&T Corp.; and, Microsoft Corp., which launched its online service under the name Microsoft Network. Microsoft has been devoting considerable resources and energy to focus the firm and its products squarely on the Internet. The Internet directory services are another source of competition, including NETCOM On-Line Communication Services, Inc.; Bolt, Beranek & Newman, Inc.; Performance System International, UUNET Technologies with Internet MCI; Yahoo, Inc.; Excite, Inc.; Infoseek Corporation; and, Lycos, Inc. Finally, software providers such as Intuit Inc., and Netscape Communication Corporation are another category of competitors.

America Online is, by far, the largest online service, with 10 million American members, as of September 1997. Compuserve was the second largest service prior to AOL acquiring it. The Microsoft Network is now the second largest online service, with 2.3 million subscribers. But a great deal of the competition comes from the small local Internet providers, who were the catalyst that drove AOL to the flat rate pricing plan.

The imperatives for global communications look very promising. Telecom and data networks should become a lifeline for nations, businesses, and individuals. The Internet is pushing world financial markets, and the flow of goods and services. The Net has the potential to revolutionize business and human lives, but it also has the danger that the network can be a vehicle of isolation. Communication by fax, modem, wireless handset, video conferencing, or telecommuting can create personal isolation. A high-tech world may need to be counterbalanced by community, family and person-to-person contacts. The Internet and more advanced computing plus training for people to understand and participate in the network have obvious educational potential.

The Flat Rate Debacle

Through December 31, 1994, the Company's standard monthly membership fee for its service, which included five hours of services, was $9.95, with a $3.50 hourly fee for usage in excess of five hours per month. Effective January 1, 1995, the hourly fee for usage in excess of five hours per month decreased from $3.50 to $2.95, while the monthly membership fee remained the same.

In October 1995, AOL launched its Internet Service, Global Network Navigator, (GNN), which was aimed at consumers who wanted a full-featured Internet-based service, but without the full service quality of AOL. The monthly fee for GNN was $14.95. This fee included 20 hours of service per month with a $1.95 hourly fee for usage in excess of 20 hours per month. In May 1996, AOL announced an additional pricing plan, which was oriented to its heavier users and called "Value Plan." It became effective July 1, 1996, and included 20 hours of services for $19.95 per month, with a $2.95 hourly fee for usage in excess of 20 hours per month.

AOL usage increased dramatically when the company announced its plans to offer flat rate unlimited pricing in October 1996. AOL switched its more than 7 million members at that time to unlimited access for $19.95 a month. Its network was deluged by subscribers, many of whom could not log onto the system during peak evening hours or on weekends. Exhibit 4 shows comparative data before and after this new pricing policy.

Following the second shutdown of its system in January 1997, the company's Chairman and CEO, Steve Case, emphasized that AOL took full responsibility for the "busy signals." "When we decided . . . to introduce unlimited use pricing, we were well aware that usage would increase substantially. We did some consumer testing and operations modeling to generate usage forecast, and we began building extra capacity in advance of the December launch of unlimited pricing. We thought that there would be some problems with busy signals during our peak periods in some cities. . . . But we expected those problems to be modest, and not too long in duration."

AOL has tried to decrease the "busy signal" by increasing the size and the pace of the system capacity expansion, by bringing in new hardware, installing circuits, adding 150,000 new modems, increasing the number of customer service representatives to 4,000, offering a toll-free line, and reducing marketing efforts. Mr. Case even asked the customers for help by moderating their own use of AOL during peak hours.

Even so, AOL became fodder for comics and lawsuits. In one comic strip, the customer is shown on the telephone conversing with "customer service":

Caller: "I am not getting my money's worth with your online service."
Service: "Good news, sir! We have just cut our rates."
Caller: "Your lines are always busy . . . I can't get online!"
Service: "Don't forget you get unlimited time online for no extra charge."

A number of AOL customers filed lawsuits against the company in more than 37 states, charging the firm with civil fraud, breach of contract, negligence and violation of state consumer-protection statutes. The negative publicity from the "busy signals" allowed other online providers the opportunity to expand their number of subscribers, and increase their revenues from advertising and merchandising fees.

America Online began a refund offer to its members and the Attorneys General in several states agreed to support its proposed plan to members. The plan gives customers a refund policy: customers had a choice of a free month online or up to $39.90—the cost of two months of its unlimited service. In addition, AOL increased customer service staffing to handle member cancellations so that calls were answered within two minutes. Also, AOL gave customers the opportunity to cancel their membership through mail, fax or toll-free number.

■ **Exhibit 4** AOL System Use before and after Flat Rate Pricing

Average AOL	January 1997	September 1996
Member daily usage	32 minutes	14 minutes
Daily sessions	10 million	6 million
Total hours daily	4.2 million	1.5 million
Total hours per month	125 million (est.), (Dec.: 102 million)	45 million
Peak simultaneous usage	260,000	140,000
Ave. minutes per session	26 minutes	16 minutes

In the meantime America Online was facing another legal problem, this time from its shareholders. On February 24, 1997, shareholders sued in U.S. District Court in Virginia alleging that AOL directors and outside accountants violated securities laws in the way the company did its accounting. The online giant took a $385 million charge in October 1996 for marketing expenses it had capitalized.

The various problems facing America Online raised serious doubts among analysts about its ability to meet its goal to earn $60 million in fiscal year 1998 (ending in June) without more revenues from sources outside of operations. An analyst with Smith, Barney & Company believed that the $1.7 billion company has a cash flow problem which could force AOL to raise cash through bank loans or another stock offering—which would be the company's fourth. "The worst time to go to the market—is when you need to," notes Abe Mastbaum, money manager of American Securities.

Prior to 1997, AOL was able to maintain its positive cash flow through the addition of new members. Due to overload of the system, brought on by flat-rate pricing, new members cannot be added as aggressively as needed. The company will have to develop new sources of revenue, such as online advertising and fees on electronic transfers, or charge additional fees for premium channels. AOL launched its first premium channel in July of 1997. Its premium games channel allows people from around the world to play both traditional games, such as hearts, and new games against each other. It charges $2 per hour for the premium games channel.

Since AOL did not have the infrastructure in place to handle the increased usage that came with the revised pricing structure, America Online planned to hold its membership at 8 million and spend $350 million to expand system capacity and customer support. At least that was the plan before the Compuserve acquisition.

In April 1997, rumors were heard about AOL acquiring CompuServe from H&R Block. America Online declined to comment. CompuServe said the company is in "external discussions" regarding a deal. Buying CompuServe would add much-needed network capacity to AOL's strained system. Those speculations gave a boost to both companies' stock: CompuServe's shares jumped 12 percent to $11; AOL's stock was up 7.6 percent to $45.75. A month before, CompuServe Corp. had quietly cut 500 jobs, or 14 percent of its work force, which was the latest evidence of the online company's troubles as it lost members in an intense competition with America Online and other rivals. The cuts left CompuServe's home office in Columbus, Ohio, with about 3,200 employees who are primarily online content and service specialists. At the same time CompuServe posted a $14 million quarterly loss and three days later the company's president and chief executive, Robert J. Massey, resigned. In September 1997, AOL traded ANS Access from Worldcom for CompuServe's online service.

Case 26 United Airlines: The Shuttle Introduction

David Guenthner and J. Paul Peter
both of University of Wisconsin–Madison

On October 1, 1994, United Airlines, the nation's largest airline, introduced its new airline service, Shuttle by United (Shuttle). Shuttle began service to a network of 11 cities on the West Coast. The introduction of Shuttle marked a major move for United from an airline that solely offered a traditional, longer-distance, hub-based service to one that offers both a traditional service and a high-frequency, shorter-distance (flights shorter than 750 miles), low-frills, low-cost, point-to-point-based service.[1]

United's decision to introduce Shuttle was based on the need to respond to the short-haul carrier Southwest Airlines' increasing strength in the intra-California flight market and to bolster United Airlines' profitability overall. United Airlines had not posted a profit since 1990, sustaining losses of $332 million in 1991, almost $1 billion in 1992, and $50 million in 1993.[2] With the domestic passenger airline industry shrinking as a whole in the last few years, United targeted the short-haul West Coast market as a means to regain profitability.

Facilitating Shuttle's introduction was the agreement struck by United and the unions representing its pilots and machinists in July 1994. In exchange for future benefit, work rules, and wage concessions, United pilots, machinists, and salaried and management employees received over 50 percent of the voting and equity interests in the company. The significant concessions made by its employees enabled United to establish Shuttle and enter the short-haul market.

The Short-Haul Market and Shuttle's Predecessors

Success in the short-haul market is highly dependent on remaining price competitive while simultaneously meeting the needs and wants of short-haul travelers. Inextricably linked to these issues is cost reduction. While significant cost reduction does not ensure success in the short-haul market, a lack of it can lead to failure, as other short-haul carriers can attest. Shuttle's major predecessors in the short-haul market include Southwest Airlines, Continental Lite by Continental Airlines, and USAir.

Southwest Airlines

Southwest Airlines, since its inception in 1971, has primarily served short-haul city pairs offering unassigned single class seating to both business and leisure travelers alike. Its flights primarily serve cities in the southwest, west, and midwest parts of the

This case was prepared by David Guenthner, Nielsen Scholar at the University of Wisconsin–Madison under the supervision of J. Paul Peter, James R. McManus Bascom Professor in Marketing. Copyright by J. Paul Peter.

[1] Hub-based routing involves directing originating flights to a regional hub city at which another flight is taken to a final destination. Point-to-point routing involves directing a flight from the originating city to the final destination.

[2] Kenneth Labich, "Will United Fly?" *Fortune,* August 22, 1994, p. 72.

United States. As the pioneer in the short-haul industry, Southwest has been the only major airline to be consistently profitable and was the only large carrier to post profitable numbers for 1994.

Southwest has prided itself as the low-cost leader in the airline industry, citing its commitment to its principal market niche which allows it to streamline marketing and operations costs. In addition, Southwest is the only airline ever to win the triple crown of airline customer service (best on-time performance, best baggage handling, and highest customer satisfaction), and, in fact, did so from 1992 to 1994.[3]

Continental Airlines

Continental Airlines introduced its short-haul service Continental Lite in October 1993. Lite, unlike Southwest, has tried to blend the hub-and-spoke routing system with a point-to-point routing system. But like Southwest, Lite has tried to lower costs by serving no food and offering a single seating class. Continental concentrated Lite's service in East Coast markets where Southwest had almost no presence. Continental's commitment to the Lite system was such that as of January 1995, this system constituted 998 of the 1,675 daily flights that Continental offered.[4]

However, since its introduction, Lite has failed to achieve profits even though it did reduce costs significantly. The cost cuts were not enough to make up for low revenues. Some analysts have cited unpopular routes and Continental's weak presence on the East Coast prior to Lite's introduction for the lack of revenue.[5] Performance was so poor for Lite that in October 1994 Continental ousted its CEO, and finally in April 1995, Continental announced that it would dissolve Lite with the exception of short-haul flights to selected hubs.

USAir

At the time of Shuttle's introduction, USAir teetered on the brink of bankruptcy, especially with respect to the California intra-state market where Southwest and Shuttle were competing. As USAir Chairman Seth Schofield stated, "[California] has become a battleground between low-cost, low-fare carriers." It has become such a battlefield that USAir reduced the number of intra-California daily round-trip flights from 16 to 4.5 in October 1994.[6]

■ United Airlines

In addition to the introduction of Shuttle, 1994 was a year of immense change for United Airlines including the employee buyout and the hiring of a new CEO. Both of these changes will ultimately affect the ability of Shuttle to survive.

The employee buyout created the world's largest employee-owned corporation. The goals of the employee buyout were to reduce costs, to facilitate the introduction of Shuttle, and to align the interests of the public stockholders and the new employee

---

[3]Southwest Airlines 1994 Annual Report.

[4]Bridget O'Brian, "Who's News: Flying Continental Through Turbulent Times," *The Wall Street Journal*, October 27, 1994, p. B1.

[5]Perry Flint, "United in Battle," *Air Transport World*, October 1994, p. 33.

[6]"Marketwatch: USAir," *Travel Agent*, October 3, 1994, p. 12.

owners. Ultimately, the goals of the buyout were to unite and empower United's employees and to link employee reward with United's financial performance.[7]

The employee buyout allowed United to reduce costs. As can be seen in Exhibit 1, the buyout is projected to save United over $5 billion between 1994 and 2006 via salary, benefit, and work rules changes.[8]

In addition, terms of the buyout agreement created special allowances for the establishment of Shuttle including an additional 7 percent pay cut to be taken on by the United pilots who fly Shuttle. Exhibit 2 presents the additional cost savings United expected from the introduction of Shuttle under the terms of the buyout agreement. However, there were also stipulations imposed by employees that may limit the effectiveness of Shuttle. For example, the number and type of aircraft that United is allowed to allocate to Shuttle is 130 737s in Shuttle's first five years of operation. Expansion of Shuttle to other markets is limited since it is not allowed to operate from or to any United hub excluding the Los Angeles and San Francisco/Oakland markets. Also, the length of a Shuttle flight is limited to under 750 miles. And finally, the proportion of United's total flight hours that Shuttle can account for was limited to between 20–25 percent for the first five years.[9]

After the buyout was finalized, there still remained doubts as to whether it would succeed in uniting and empowering United's employees. In spite of approval of the buyout by the International Association of Machinists (IAM) and the Air Line Pilots Association (ALPA), only 54 percent of the IAM voted for the buyout, and there

■ **Exhibit 1** Labor Cost Savings from Employee Buyout (figures in millions)

	1994	1995	1996	1997	1998	1999	2000	Total 1994–2006	NPV*
Salary reductions	$190	$396	$420	$433	$452	$488	$204	$3,095	$2,150
Benefit reductions	62	129	139	149	158	171	78	1,222	801
Potential midterm increase	0	0	0	(32)	(90)	(119)	(44)	(302)	(189)
Work-rule changes	12	39	73	101	120	134	138	1,501	792
Contract improvements	(33)	(53)	(41)	(43)	(46)	(47)	(25)	(377)	(240)
Total	$231	$511	$591	$608	$594	$627	$351	$5,179	$3,313

*Net present value of savings.

SOURCE: UAL Corp. Proxy and Prospectus as featured in *Air Transport World*, October 1994, p. 30.

■ **Exhibit 2** Additional Cost Savings from Shuttle (figures in millions)

	1994	1995	1996	1997	1998	1999	2000	Total 1994–2006	NPV*
Improved utilization	$11	$33	$ 53	$ 70	$ 80	$ 81	$ 85	$1,066	$ 557
Limited product	10	32	52	67	77	78	82	1,028	538
Reduced distribution	10	28	26	60	69	70	73	917	478
Total	$31	$93	$151	$197	$226	$229	$240	$3,011	$1,573

*Net present value of savings.

SOURCE: UAL Corp. Proxy and Prospectus as featured in *Air Transport World*, October 1994, p. 30.

[7]UAL 1994 Annual Report

[8]Flint, p. 30.

[9]Ibid.

were reports that some 1,250 of 1,700 pilots questioned in a survey were not in favor of the agreement. In addition, the Association of Flight Attendants (AFA) failed to approve the buyout, and consequently, made no wage or benefit concessions. Finally, over a third of United's workforce are nonunion employees who were not eligible to negotiate the buyout; however, they were forced to take an 8.25 percent pay cut to become stockholders.[10]

A lack of enthusiasm and empowerment among employees was reflected in some of the comments made after the buyout was finalized:

- "My worst fear is that employees end up bickering among themselves. I know there's some animosity against the pilots. . . . As for management, I don't know if they can change their culture. There's a lot of dinosaurs over there at headquarters. There are a lot of power struggles over there, and they worry more about those than they do about running the airline."—David Sharp, 737 Captain
- "There's a lot of unhappiness, a lot of anxiety and underlying resentment. Taking a pay cut is not good news; you can't sugarcoat that. That's the basic perception at headquarters, where the majority of employees are in management. The idea that you'll have labor unions running the company suggests that perhaps not the best business decisions will be made."—Arnie Canham, Crew Schedules Planner
- "I do not feel any regrets that we are not participating in this buyout plan because we made a good-faith effort to negotiate our position. I keep hearing that people who are taking pay cuts will resent us, but I don't believe that because we make far less than the other groups anyway. . . . The irony, of course, is that the bosses ought to think a lot harder about how we feel if they want to keep their customers happy. We're the people who spend all the time with the passengers. To the public, we are United."—Kevin Lum, Flight Attendant[11]

New CEO Gerald Greenwald took a more positive outlook on the buyout. The former Chrysler vice chairman who helped turn around Chrysler in the 1980s and who was selected to head United by its unions stated, "We are going to be a part of history."[12]

Whether Shuttle can thrive within the new structure created by the buyout is an issue debated among experts. Some feel that Shuttle is too restricted by the limitations placed on it by the buyout agreement to compete effectively. Analyst John Eichner stated, "One hand is sort of tied behind (United). Here's Southwest, with more than 160 aircraft and these guys—in five years—can't get more than 130 planes." Another analyst voiced his doubts more strongly saying, "The Shuttle is a sideshow, a burlesque. It is eyewash to make investors think United is like Southwest."[13]

However, United insists that the buyout has created more of a team atmosphere between labor and management that will allow Shuttle to react to competition effectively. Vice President of Shuttle Development Rono Dutta claims that "When we were building these [Shuttle] task teams, there were a lot of union representatives, and earlier, they would have said: 'You can't do this, you can't do that.' Now, it is, 'tell us what you need and we'll work it out.' "[14]

---

[10]Labich, p. 72.

[11]Ibid, pp. 73–78.

[12]Michael J. McCarthy and Carl Quintanilla, "Holders of UAL Approve Bold Buyout That Gives Workers Majority Control," *The Wall Street Journal*, July 13, 1994, p. A3.

[13]Flint, p. 30.

[14]Ibid, p. 33.

■ The California/West Coast Market

The California flight market is the fastest growing in the nation, and some analysts predict that it is large enough to support two or even three major short-haul carriers. Before Shuttle's introduction, 45 percent of United's business either originated, terminated, or flowed through the West Coast.[15] Short-haul competitor Southwest had established an extremely strong market share in California, but prior to the introduction of Shuttle, United already had a significant presence in many of the California markets. Exhibit 3 gives a preintroduction breakdown of market share in nine of the markets that Shuttle began serving in October 1994. These types of numbers were attractive to United, because they were indicative of an opportunity to grow further from a strong current position.

In spite of United's pre-Shuttle strength in market share, its traditional full service product generated losses. However, Shuttle is projected to have costs that are extremely competitive with Southwest's. In addition to savings from the buyout, Shuttle hopes to cut other costs by offering no meals, flying more hours, and by reducing ground times via boarding people in window seats first in an effort to reduce aisle traffic before takeoff. Shuttle is also planning to have stricter carry-on restrictions that will reduce ground times. Exhibit 4 compares the projected costs comparisons of Shuttle and Southwest.

■ **Exhibit 3**   United/Southwest Intra-California Market Shares (selected markets)

City Pair	Airline	Market Share (%)			
		1993	1992	1991	1990
Sacramento–Los Angeles	Southwest	0.0	0.0	0.0	0.0
	United	58.2	49.8	48.6	32.7
Sacramento–San Diego	Southwest	97.5	72.4	29.4	0.0
	United	0.8	3.2	22.4	25.3
San Francisco–Burbank	Southwest	0.0	0.0	0.0	0.0
	United	97.4	99.2	83.7	
San Francisco–Los Angeles	Southwest	0.0	0.0	0.0	0.0
	United	61.4	50.5	45.1	31.5
San Francisco–Ontario	Southwest	0.0	0.0	0.0	0.0
	United	98.3	96.2	93.3	61.9
San Francisco–San Diego	Southwest	58.3	43.9	33.8	20.1
	United	35.6	28.7	36.8	28.6
Oakland–Los Angeles	Southwest	74.7	61.2	42.1	0.0
	United	25.1	36.4	49.9	42.9
Oakland–Burbank	Southwest	99.8	85.4	57.8	43.3
	United	0.2	13.6	32.7	18.0
Oakland–Ontario	Southwest	99.9	93.8	49.6	49.4
	United	0.1	8.1	50.1	49.2

SOURCE: Roberts, Roach, and Associates as featured in *Air Transport World,* October 1994, p. 33.

---

[15]Ibid.

■ **Exhibit 4**
Southwest/Shuttle
Cost Comparisons
(projected costs in
cents per available
seat mile)

	Southwest	Shuttle
Wages and benefits	2.4	2.6
Fuel and oil	1.1	1.1
Aircraft ownership	0.7	0.7
Aircraft maintenance	0.6	0.2
Commissions	0.5	0.6
Advertising	0.2	0.3
Food and beverage	0.0	0.0
Other	1.7	1.9
Total	7.2	7.4

SOURCE: UAL Corp. Proxy and Prospectus as featured in *Air Transport World*, October 1994, p. 30.

■ Shuttle's Entry into the Market and Southwest's Reactions

United's strategy for positioning Shuttle in the West Coast market was reflected in a memo to employees: "The Shuttle is being positioned to create the image of an airline that offers the lowest price in the market, is highly efficient and reliable, and offers more service than the other guys. This positioning intends to cause customers to think of the Shuttle as inexpensive but not cheap. The Shuttle is the same, only better."[16]

Supporting Shuttle's positioning in the West Coast market are its attempts to gain competitive advantage over Southwest by offering assigned seating as well as a higher fare first-class seating for business travelers. Perhaps its most highly touted advantage over Southwest is its Mileage Plus frequent-flier program which will allow passengers to earn trips on United's more expansive global flight network, as opposed to Southwest's program which is limited to domestic short-haul flights. In addition, United is offering a special bonus to frequent fliers of Shuttle.

In October 1994, Southwest was ready to compete aggressively with Shuttle for control of the West Coast market. Southwest Chairman Herb Kelleher foreshadowed this position when in an address to employees he said, "United Shuttle is like an intercontinental ballistic missile targeted directly at Southwest."[17]

In response to Shuttle's introduction, Southwest immediately announced that it was offering, for a limited time, one-day advance purchase fares with discounts up to 50 percent. In addition, Southwest announced the return of its 21-day advance purchase "Fun Fares" promotion which also allows fliers to receive discounts approaching 50 percent.

United was forced to respond by matching Southwest's fares. For example, along the Los Angeles–Oakland route United matched Southwest's $69 one way price and $39 one way advance purchase price.

Southwest escalated competition in November 1994 when it increased its advertising and added two planes and 15 flights to its California routes. When United responded by adding more flights to Shuttle's service, the percentage of seats

---

[16]Ibid, p. 34.

[17]Michael J. McCarthy, "Travel: New Shuttle Incites a War Between Old Rivals," *The Wall Street Journal*, December 1, 1994, p. B1.

filled on the Shuttle system dropped 8 percent through the first three weeks of November.[18] However, operational figures for Shuttle at the end of 1994 included promising signs such as an on-time arrival rate of 88 percent and the fact that over 87 percent of Shuttle's passengers rate the customer service as very good to excellent. Both figures were comparable to or exceeded United's non-Shuttle services.[19]

In spite of the intense competition, Shuttle President A.B. "Sky" Magary insisted, "The Shuttle is working well."[20]

Discussion Questions

1. What issues should United consider when responding to Southwest's price cuts?

2. Will United's efforts to reduce costs risk alienating full-service customers who wish to fly Shuttle's routes? If so, how, and what actions should it take to rectify the situation?

3. Is it reasonable to believe that an employee-owned company as large as United can react quickly and effectively to competitive action, especially with respect to Shuttle and Southwest?

4. How will operating Shuttle as a separate "airline within an airline" affect United's full-service non-Shuttle marketing strategy?

5. Will the restrictions placed on Shuttle by the employee buyout agreement inhibit its abilities to compete in the West Coast market?

6. Will the lack of an agreement between United and the AFA adversely affect Shuttle's operations?

7. Consider the one-way Shuttle flight from Oakland to Los Angeles mentioned in the case. Suppose Shuttle decides to use the B737-300 to service the 470 mile trip. The B737-300 has 126 available seats to be sold. By using the information provided in Exhibit 4, determine the percentage of the B737-300's seats that need to be sold for Shuttle to break even on the flight if all the seats are priced at the advance purchase price of $39. If Shuttle can expect to fill 70 percent of the B737-300's seats, what price should it charge per seat to break even?

---

[18]Ibid.

[19]UAL 1994 Annual Report

[20]McCarthy, p. B1.

Case 27 Sun Microsystems: A High Growth, Loosely Organized Giant in a Constrained, Technology Intensive Environment

Walter E. Greene
University of Texas Pan American

William C. House
University of Arkansas–Fayetteville

Introduction

In 1982, four individuals, who were 27 years old, combined forces to found Sun Microsystems, with the objective of producing and marketing computer workstations to scientists and engineers. Two of the four were Stanford MBA graduates—Michigan born Scott McNealy, and Vinod Khosla, a native of India. They were joined by Andreas Bechtolsheim, a Stanford engineering graduate who had constructed a computer workstation with spare parts in order to perform numerical analysis, and Unix software expert William Joy from the Berkeley campus. Sun's founders believed there was demand for a desktop computer workstation costing between $10,000 and $20,000 in a market niche ignored by minicomputer makers IBM, Data General, DEC, and Hewlett-Packard.

Sun Microsystems is the market leader in the fast-growing workstation industry, expecting sales revenue growth of 30 percent annually during the next five years compared to 5 to 10 percent for the personal computer industry. Workstations can be used in stand-alone fashion or as part of networked configurations. The product lines produced range from low priced diskless units to higher powered graphics oriented stations at the top of the line.

In contrast to personal computers, workstations are characterized by 32-bit instead of 16-bit microprocessors, a strong tendency to use the UNIX operating system instead of MS/DOS, more sophisticated software and graphics capabilities, larger storage capacities, faster processing speeds and the ability to function effectively in a networking environment. The principal users of workstations have been engineers and scientists. However, price reductions and technological improvements have broadened the appeal of workstations so that they are finding use in financial trading, desktop publishing, animation, mapping, and medical imaging applications.

Sun, the fastest growing company in the computer hardware industry, has revenues that are increasing at a five year compounded rate of 85 percent and income increasing at a 67 percent rate from 1985 to 1990.[3] For fiscal year 1991, Sun's revenues were $3.2 billion and net income was $190 million.[13] The company's rapid growth rate has severely drained its cash resources.

The research and written case information was prepared by Wm. C. House of the University of Arkansas–Fayetteville, and Walter E. Greene, Professor, University of Texas Pan American for presentation at the North American Case Research Association Symposium (Atlanta, 1991).

■ Chairman and CEO of Sun Microsystems

Scott McNealy, the current chairman of Sun, is a native of Detroit and grew up on the fringes of the U.S. automobile industry. Originally rejected by both Harvard and Stanford Business Schools, he graduated from Harvard with a major in economics. In 1981, at the age of 26, McNealy became manufacturing director at Onyx systems, a small minicomputer maker. The company was faced with serious quality problems. In two months, the operation showed drastic improvement as McNealy probed work rules and production bottlenecks, encouraging workers to identify problems and overcome obstacles on the way toward improving workplace efficiency.

In 1982, former Stanford classmates Andy Bechtolsheim and Vinod Khosla asked him to join them as Director of Operations in a new company to be called Sun Microsystems. Two years later, McNealy was chosen by the Board of Directors to be CEO over Paul Ely, now executive vice president of Unisys. During the first month after he became CEO, one of the three cofounders resigned, the company lost $500,000 on $2 million in sales, and two-thirds of its computers didn't work.

He is a workaholic, working from daylight to dark, seven days a week, rarely finding time for recreation activities. The frantic pace at Sun engendered by McNealy is sometimes referred to as Sunburn. There is a tendency for Sun executives to take on too many projects at once, thereby creating tremendous internal pressure and organizational chaos.

McNealy's philosophy can be capsuled in these company sayings[9]:

1. On Decision-making—Consensus if possible, but participation for sure.
2. On Management Cooperation—Agree and commit, disagree and commit, or just get the hell out of the way.
3. On Market Response—The right answer is the best answer. The wrong answer is second best. No answer is the worst.
4. On Individual Initiative—To ask permission is to seek denial.

He has stated that the company is trying to achieve four goals—significant increases in revenue and book value, improved product acceptance, and higher profit margins.

■ Chief Computer Designer

Andreas Bechtolsheim, chief computer designer, was one of Sun's cofounders. At age 35 he has the title of vice president of technology. A native of West Germany, Bechtolsheim designed his first computer in 1980 while still a graduate student at Stanford University. It was a workstation designed for scientists and engineers. However, he was unable to sell the idea to any computer company then in existence. Shortly thereafter, he joined Joy, Khosla, and McNealy in founding Sun Microsystems and the company's first product was based on his machine.

Initially, Bechtolsheim persuaded Sun to use off-the-shelf products to develop its workstations instead of following the usual industry practice of utilizing proprietary components. This meant that company products would be easy for competitors to copy, but it also allowed quick entry into the market place. As nonproprietary open systems came to be more widely accepted, competitors such as Apollo, DEC, and IBM encountered problems in keeping pace with product lines that lacked the flexibility and performance of Sun's products. When Steve Jobs formed Next, Inc., and announced the development of a desktop workstation, Bechtolsheim urged Sun officials to build a truly desktop computer. There was considerable resistance to the project, and he almost left the company at that point. Because the company has had a culture based on building bigger boxes, the new sparcstation was widely criticized within the company as being too small. However, Bechtolsheim stubbornly refused to change the specifications and eventually prevailed.

■ Field Operations Director

Carol Bartz, National Sales Director and the number two executive at Sun Microsystems, has about half of the company's 12,000 employees reporting to her. Bartz attended the University of Wisconsin, receiving a Bachelor of Computer Science degree in 1971. After that, she spent seven years with Digital Equipment Corporation. Since joining Sun in 1983, she has become intimately involved in supervising field support activities and a subdivision that sells to federal governmental agencies. According to Bob Herwick, an investment analyst, Bartz is a very effective problem solver, turning around a sluggish service organization and ensuring that the company fully exploited the market potential in the government market.[5]

■ Team and Consensus Management At Sun

McNealy, current Sun chairman, attended Cranbrook, a North Detroit prep school. While there, he excelled in a variety of activities including music, tennis, golf, and ice hockey. According to Alan De Clerk, a high school classmate, McNealy developed a strong self-image and competitive spirit as a result of participating in sports activities and competing with two brothers and a sister. Through the years he has approached all activities as if they were team sports.

McNealy's efforts to build consensus among executives before a decision is made have become famous throughout the company. As he has stated, "Give me a draw and I'll make the decision but I won't issue an edict if a large majority is in favor of an alternative proposal."[9] A frequently quoted example occurred in 1988 when he stubbornly resisted changing prices at a time when rapidly increasing memory costs were reducing profit margins. With a consensus arrayed against him, he finally agreed to some product price increases which were enacted without reducing sales. In fact, he has a hard time saying no to any project pushed by one or more company groups. He demands complete loyalty within his concept of teamwork and becomes very angry if he believes that individuals or teams have let him down.[9]

■ Product Line Focus

The Sparcstation I was introduced in April 1989 at a stripped down price of $9,000. A lower priced version was introduced in May of 1990, costing $5,000. The machine processes data at 12 mips and runs about twice as fast as personal computers. Sun expected the lower price to facilitate sales to large companies who base computer purchases on quantity discounts. However, the low end sparcstation does not have

■ **Exhibit 1**
A Comparison of
Performance Measures
for Major Workstation
Makers

	Price	Specmarks	Price per Specmark
Hewlett Packard 9000	11,990	55.5	216.00
Sun Sparcstation ELC	4,995	20.1	248.50
IBM RS/6000	13,992	32.8	426.50
Sun Sparcstation IPX	13,495	24.2	557.60

SOURCE: J. A. Savage, "Price Takes Backseat with Users," *Computerworld*, September 2, 1991, p. 4.

disk drives, color monitors, or add in slots. Therefore, it must be networked and cannot be used as a stand alone unit.

An improved version of Sparc I was introduced in the summer of 1990 with an improved graphical interface, a color monitor, and sales price of $10,000. Sun has asserted that a personal computer with the same characteristics as the IPC would cost $15,000 to $20,000 and would have only about one third the processing power of this workstation model. The Sparcstation is now Sun's top seller among all its product lines and Sparcstation products produce 80 to 90 percent of total company revenues.

Exhibit 1 shows prices, specmarks (a measure of processing power and speed) for two Sun models as well as for the latest Hewlett Packard and IBM workstation models. From this table, the relative performance of the Sun computers in terms of computing power per dollar can be compared with its major competitors.

■ Company Strategy

Early on, Sun executives believed that they only had a short time to focus on growing demand for computer workstations from scientists and engineers before large companies such as IBM, DEC, and Hewlett Packard would aggressively move into that market niche. Therefore, company strategy was designed to emphasize gaining market share, concentrating on all out sales growth, no matter what the cost. At one point, the organization was adding more than 300 employees and a new sales office each month. Company engineers developed a steady stream of innovative but sometimes impractical prototypes. Products were sold largely by word of mouth with virtually no formal sales promotion programs.

As part of the market share focus, in the mid-80s the company began creating autonomous divisions to develop and market its products. This policy allowed rapid movement into such market areas as sales to government agencies, universities, and financial institutions. The autonomous groups did create unnecessary duplication and contributed to development costs that were almost twice the industry average. When attempts were made to consolidate functions, fierce turf battles resulted and top executives were forced to step in and referee the conflicts.

The market share/sales growth emphasis created many unexpected problems. Needed investments in customer service and data processing activities had to be postponed. The existence of independent, autonomous divisions caused numerous difficulties for both sales and manufacturing activities. At one point, the company had more than 10,000 computer and option combinations to keep track of. Three different product lines based on three different microprocessors—Sparc, Motorola 68000, and Intel 386—required excessive investment and extensive coordination to ensure that they all worked on the same network. Overlaps and duplications in marketing and finance made forecasting all but impossible. At its current size the company can no longer scramble madly to meet shipping deadlines at the last minute.

By the summer of 1989, the company was experiencing production bottlenecks as discounted sales of older products mushroomed. Demand for newer products also increased faster than expected. Large backlogs of sales orders were not being entered in the inventory control system, preventing the company from knowing how many or what kinds of products it needed to produce.

In the last quarter of 1989, Sun experienced a $20 million loss due to misjudging consumer demand for its new Sparcstation and incurring parts shortages. A new management information system produced inaccurate parts forecasts which contributed to order snafus and lower earnings. However, it posted a $5 million profit in the first quarter of 1990. Sun produced revenues of $2.5 billion in fiscal 1990 and expected to achieve revenues of $3.3 billion in 1991.[8] Sun is now changing its approach to place more emphasis on profitability and less on growth, on expanding customer service and hiring fewer employees. Sun President McNealy has recently tied executive pay to before tax return on investment. In the 1989 annual report he stated that he desired performance to be judged on the basis of significant increases in revenues, acceptance of new products, improvements in profit margins, and increases in book value.

McNealy was one of the early pioneers pushing open systems which would allow computers of many different manufacturers to be linked together in networks. In fact, Sun has actually encouraged competition with itself through its focus on open systems development and invited the industry to build Sparc based clones in order to expand the position of the workstation industry. As the percentage of total Sparc based computers sold by Sun has begun to decline, Sun appears to be changing its position on clones. Recently, it told its own dealers they would incur Sun's displeasure if they sold Sun clones along with Sun workstations. Many of these dealers are angry at what they perceive to be Sun's arrogance.

Sun has consistently maintained a narrow product line focus. It has gradually phased out all microprocessors except Sparc and has concentrated on low-end workstations with the greatest market share growth possibilities. It has avoided entering markets for higher priced lines and the personal computer segment with emphasis on low price and compactness. However, recently Sun announced plans to move into high end workstation markets where processing speed and power requirements necessitate linking a series of microprocessors and using sophisticated software. Sun may encounter problems in this market similar to those it experienced in product upgrades of its lower level models, since it does not have a good record in managing product introductions.

As workstations become more powerful and less expensive, workstation manufacturers face a serious challenge in maintaining profit margins. Current models now combine high functionality with high volume, in contrast to an earlier focus on producing highly functional units in small quantities. Extensive use of application specific integrated circuits with fewer components reduces system size, increases reliability, and lowers product costs. Sun and other companies increasingly follow the practice of involving manufacturing representatives in the design process as early as possible in order to minimize manufacturing problems. Increased attention is also being paid to maintaining product quality and improving product testing before systems are shipped.

In past years, Sun's strategies have included focusing on lower prices, well developed marketing programs and third party software development. From 1,500 to 2,000 applications are available for the Sun Sparcstation compared to approximately 1,000 for Hewlett Packard and DEC. The company is licensing its Sparc chip to third party clone companies with the desire of expanding the installed RISC computer base. The overall company goal is to deliver a complete processing solution, including graphics, input/output, software, and networking.

■ Distribution Channels and Customer Service

Workstation makers have traditionally sold their units using manufacturers sales forces and specialized hardware resellers, who repackage specialized software with other companies' workstations. Sun has about 300 VARS (i.e., value added resellers) compared to more than 500 for Hewlett Packard with Digital and IBM falling somewhere in between. Some authorities think the majority of VARs are not capable of selling workstations.[11] Sun is now considering the possibility of selling some of its models through retailers such as Microage in a manner similar to personal computer sales now made by IBM, COMPAQ, and Apple. Such a move would reduce selling and inventory costs but is meeting initial resistance from dealers unaccustomed to handling complex workstation models.

Sun still sells a large number of workstations through its 1,000 person salesforce. In July 1990, Sun selected 200 dealers from three retail chains and gave them training in selling workstations. The company expects to sell $30 million of workstations through retail dealers in fiscal 1990, but a full-fledged dealer network may require several years to develop. Because of the higher average selling prices and of greater product differentiation and uniqueness of workstations compared to personal computers, many PC vendors are expressing interest in handling workstations in spite of the small volumes generated.

One area of concern has been Sun's field service organization, which has not been very effective in supporting customer software. Bartz has stated that the company wants to improve on customer service without making large monetary expenditures or building a dinosaur service group.[2] In line with this, Sun has announced plans to start using company trained, third party service personnel who can be dispatched to customer locations on demand.

■ Customer Categories

The workstation market for engineers and scientists is rapidly becoming saturated. About one-third of Sun's customers now come from the commercial side, up from only 10 percent several years ago. The company is now concentrating more of its efforts on airlines, banks, insurance and finance companies, trying to persuade users to utilize Sun workstations to solve new problems. Sun Vice-President Eric Schmidt says that Sun tends to get early adopters of new technology.[7] Often, by starting with a pilot program that proves successful, workstations can be expanded to other areas in a customer's operations. Eastman Kodak began using Sun workstations in engineering design and soon expanded their use of marketing databases and mailroom operations.

Sun machines are being used by Wall Street firms Merrill Lynch, Shearson/Lehman/Hutton and Bear/Sterns on the trading floor. Northwest Airlines uses 500 workstations in Minneapolis to monitor ticket usage, checking the correctness of air fare charges and the impact of flight delays or cancellations on revenues and profits. To increase customer satisfaction, Sun has had to change product designs, to make its machines easier to install, and to improve understandability of product manuals. As Sun has discovered, commercial customers need more help than engineers.

Dataquest says that by 1994, 29.1 percent of workstation sales will be made to commercial users as opposed to Scientific/Engineering users in a market expected to reach $22 billion.[16] Workstation makers are moving into the personal computer area by offering Unix versions that will run on both workstations and on personal computers. Workstations provide much greater computing power at a lower cost than would be required to enhance a personal computer so that it possessed the equivalent capability of a typical workstation. Workstations seem to be making their biggest inroads into CPU intensive applications formerly done on mainframes (e.g., stock transactions, airline reservations).

Sun's first major TV advertising effort occurred in April 1991 and took the form of a 30-second commercial seen on CNN, ESPN, and the three major TV networks. The commercial was not directed specifically at a consumer audience, but instead was an attempt to get broad exposure for a new message beamed at the business market. Sun expected the advertisement to reach 59 percent of U.S. households and 42 percent of the target market of senior level corporate and computer executives. The campaign also included an eight-page insert in *The Wall Street Journal.*

Sun's advertising budget of approximately $4.6 million in 1990 was spent on computer and general interest business publications. Sun's advertising budget is only about 0.25 percent of sales revenues compared to 1.0 to 1.5 percent spent by its major competitors. Some observers have questioned the cost-effectiveness of a high priced TV advertisement by a company which sells high priced computers to a limited group of customers.

■ Software Developments

Availability of software still remains a major problem in expanding sales of workstations. Only about 5 to 10 percent of UNIX based software is designed for business and commercial applications. Sun is trying to sign up software developers to produce UNIX based versions of many common personal computer products. It now has UNIX based versions of popular PC software, including Lotus 1–2–3 and DBASE IV. It hopes the increased availability of software plus the narrowing cost gap between low end workstations and high end personal computers will help it penetrate the personal computer market. However, it must sell users on the benefit/cost performance of workstations compared to personal computers and also needs to expand its existing base of software developers.

The type of software to be run is often the determining factor in deciding between a personal computer or workstation. For productivity and business applications, PCs can be more cost efficient. For technical and graphics applications, workstations are more appropriate. Differences in costs are no longer a differentiating factor.

An entrenched personal computer MS/DOS operating system base and lack of commercial workstation software have hampered a switch from high end personal computers to workstations. MS/DOS based computers appear adequate for a majority of user needs, especially with the advent of the Windows operating environment. PC users are more likely to change if complex applications such as multimedia, integrated data base, or windowing become desirable rather than on the basis of price alone. Workstations may become less attractive if 80846-based personal computers with considerably more computing power than today's systems become more widely available.

Product/price performance is no longer as important a differentiating factor as it used to be. Software availability and usability are increasing in importance. In recognition of this, Sun has formed two software subsidiaries—one for application software and one to concentrate on improvements in the Unix operating system. The Open Look Graphical Interface has been added to make Sun products more user friendly. The key to maintaining market position seems to be improving systems software and selling software developers and users on the benefits of workstations over other hardware options.

Sun has announced that it will release a new version of its operating system designed to run on Intel based personal computers. Some analysts say that Sun will face a stiff test in competing with Microsoft's DOS/Windows combination and that it is a defensive move, made in realization that Sun no longer can generate enough revenue from its own machines to meet its growth goals. McNealy denies that the Sun announcement is defensive, saying that high powered PC owners will move to Sun's operating systems to take advantage of advanced capabilities (e.g., running multiple programs simultaneously) which is something that has been vaguely promised by Microsoft's Windows new NT versions.[13] McNealy has sharply criticized Windows NT version, referring to it as illusionary or not there.

Sun's Solaris operating system will not be available until mid-1991, and will work on both Intel's X86 series and Sun's Sparc processors. The new operating system will make it easier for Sun's customers to link Sun workstations with other computers in a network and increase the number of Sun users. Sun hopes that this will encourage independent software houses to write new programs for Sun OS. So far, approximately 3,500 application programs are available for Sun OS compared with more than 20,000 for IBM-compatible personal computers.[12]

■ Competition in the Marketplace

Although still the market leader, Sun is facing increasing competition from much larger computer companies. Sun shipped 146,000 workstations in 1990 (39 percent of the market) out of a total of 376,000 and is expected to ship 200,000 in 1991.[4] Having fully absorbed Apollo into its organization, Hewlett Packard is selling about two-thirds as many workstations as Sun, with about 20 percent of the market and DEC, which has completely reworked its product lines, has about 17 percent of the workstation market. Hewlett Packard has also introduced a new work station model comparable in price to the sparcstation which runs about twice as fast as Sun's current model. Exhibit 2 shows the 1989 and 1990 market shares for the major firms in the workstation market.

Company	1989	1990
Sun Microsystems	30.4%	38.8%
Hewlett Packard	26.1	20.1
Digital Equipment	26.6	17.0
Intergraph	7.0	3.8
IBM	1.2	4.5
Silicon Graphics	5.1	2.6
Sony	—	3.3
Next	—	2.6
Other	3.6	7.0
Total	100.0%	100.0%

IBM has made a significant comeback in the workstation market with the RS/6000, after its first workstation model proved to be a slow seller. In 1990, IBM shifted more than 25,000 workstations, producing revenue of 1 billion dollars and attaining a market share of 6.6 percent or more than double its 1989 market share.[4] In 1991, some analysts estimate IBM will sell between $2 and $3 billion of workstations. IBM has a stated goal of overtaking Sun by 1993, achieving a 30 percent market share, although some experts predict it is more likely to achieve a 15 percent market share by that date.[14]

With the workstation market expected to exceed 20 billion dollars by the mid-1990s, competition is expected to be fierce. IBM's late entry, entrenched positions of competitors in the market, lack of a low-priced entry level model, and the use of nonstandard operating and graphics environments are likely to hamper its efforts to achieve a market share much above 15 percent.[6] IBM's service and sales reputation, its large reseller base, and strong position in commercial markets should give the company leverage to enter the fast growing markets for network servers and small or branch office multiuser systems. However, if IBM focuses its efforts on penetrating these markets with its RS/6000, it runs a serious risk of undercutting sales of the AS/400.

Cost no longer seems to be the primary factor in decisions to acquire workstations. Workers must become more accustomed to graphic as opposed to character based systems before adoption by current PC becomes more widespread. Some companies feel that workstations have yet to demonstrate significant productivity advantages over personal computers. The biggest shortcomings of workstations are lack of application software and integration difficulties.

■ Financial Analysis

Exhibit 3 shows revenues, expenses, and income for the five-year period 1986 to 1990. Revenues have increased at a more rapid rate than net income during the period being considered. Return on sales has declined significantly to 4.5 percent from the peak of almost 7 percent in 1987 with revenue per shipment also declining in 1990 compared to 1989 and 1988. Book value per share and unit shipments have increased significantly during the five years.

■ **Exhibit 3**   Revenues, Expenses, and Income for Five Years (billions of $)

	1990	1989	1988	1987	1986
Net revenues	2,466	1,765	1,052	538	210
Cost of sales	1,399	1,010	550	273	102
Gross profit	1,067	755	502	265	108
R&D outlays	302	234	140	70	31
Selling, adm. & general expenses	588	433	250	127	57
Total	890	667	390	197	88
Operating income	177	88	111	68	20
Interest income	(23)	(10)	(302)	834	369
Income taxes	43	17	44	33	9
Net income	111	61	66	36	11
Net income/sales	4.5%	3.4%	6.3%	6.8%	5.3%
Net income/share	1.21	0.76	0.89	0.55	0.21
Book value/share	9.82	7.77	4.75	3.57	2.04
Unit shipment (000'S)	118.3	80.7	48.4	24.6	9.9
Revenue/unit shipped (000'S)	20.8	21.9	21.7	21.8	21.2

SOURCE: Adapted from 1990 Annual Report.

■ **Exhibit 4**   Computer Industry Data for Years 1989 and 1990

Company	Sales Growth		Income Growth		Asset Growth		Net Inc./Sales		Mkt. Value/Equity	
	1990	1989	1990	1989	1990	1989	1990	1989	1990	1989
Apple	1.07	1.21	1.14	1.05	1.12	1.24	8.7	8.2	4.81	3.21
Compaq	1.25	1.39	1.36	1.31	1.30	1.31	12.6	11.6	3.26	3.31
Dec	1.01	1.05	0.00	0.72	1.03	1.10	−.72	6.8	1.21	1.13
Hew Pck	1.10	1.20	0.95	0.97	1.09	1.31	5.7	6.6	1.83	1.98
Intrgrph	1.21	1.07	0.79	0.80	1.06	0.97	6.0	9.2	1.79	1.73
IBM	1.10	1.05	1.60	0.68	1.30	1.06	8.7	6.0	1.75	1.62
NCR	1.06	0.99	0.90	0.94	1.01	0.95	5.9	6.9	3.54	3.40
Silgrphs	1.41	1.73	1.97	1.94	1.37	0.94	8.3	5.9	3.57	4.30
Sun Mcrs	1.34	1.41	318.	0.40	1.49	1.50	5.5	1.8	2.72	1.41
Wang	0.87	0.90	0.00	0.00	0.72	0.87	−6.7	−13.9	1.27	0.87
Avg.	1.14	1.20	32.7	0.88	1.15	1.12	5.4	4.9	2.58	2.37

SOURCE: *Business Week*, 1000 Companies, 1991, 1990.

Exhibit 4 indicates that Sun's sales, income and asset growth are higher than the industry average in 1990 and 1989 with the market value/equity ratio also above the industry average. However, the net income/sales ratio was below the industry average in 1989 and slightly above the industry average in 1990. As Exhibit 5 indicates, Sun appears to be very close to the industry average in terms of two common productivity measures, sales/assets and sales/employee. In reviewing the common leverage measures, Sun is well above the industry average for R&D expenses/revenues and R&D expenses/employee.

■ **Exhibit 5** Computer Industry Data for Years 1989 and 1988

Company	Sales/Assets		Sales/Employee		Adv. Exps./Sales		R&D Exps./Sales		R&D Exps./Employee	
	1990	1989	1989	1988	1989	1988	1989	1988	1989	1988
Apple	1.82	1.91	364	377	7.34	8.30	8.0	6.7	28,937	25,233
Compaq	1.32	1.38	303	289	1.75	2.87	4.6	3.6	13,945	10,849
Dec	1.13	1.15	101	94	1.38	1.01	12.0	11.4	12,123	10,753
Hew Pck	1.22	1.21	125	113	2.69	2.35	10.7	10.4	13,358	11,713
Intrgrph	1.20	1.07	105	110	1.00	1.00	10.6	11.1	11,157	12,216
IBM	0.79	0.81	164	154	1.17	0.44	8.3	7.4	13,572	11,415
NCR	1.38	1.32	106	100	1.06	0.53	7.5	7.0	7,964	6,940
Silgrphs	1.22	1.19	180	105	1.00	1.00	11.9	15.8	21,150	21,908
Sun Mcrs	1.27	1.41	172	148	1.00	0.74	13.3	13.3	22,934	19,733
Wang	1.35	1.12	109	97	1.00	1.02	9.8	8.7	10,543	8,510
Avg.	1.27	1.26	173	159	2.64	1.93	9.7	9.5	15,568	14,027

SOURCE: *Business Week* 1000 Companies, 1991; Innovation in America, Special *Business Week* Issues, 1990, 1988.

■ **End Notes**

1. Susan E. Fisher, "Vendors Court Reseller Partners As Workstations Go Mainstream," *PC Week,* July 30, 1990.
2. Jonathan B. Levine, "High Noon for Sun," *Business Week,* July 24, 1989, pp. 71, 74.
3. John Markoff, "The Smart Alecs at Sun Are Regrouping," *New York Times,* April 28, 1991.
4. Andrew Ould, "IBM Challenges Sun in Workstation Market," *PC Week,* February 28, 1991.
5. Andrew Ould, "Carol Bartz: Star Is Still Rising for Hard Driving Executive," *PC Week,* September 3, 1990.
6. Andrew Ould, "What's Behind Lower Workstation Prices," *UNIX World,* July 1990.
7. Julie Pitta, "The Trojan Horse Approach," *Forbes,* April 15, 1991.
8. Kathy Rebello, "Sun Microsystems on the Rise Again," *USA Today,* April 20, 1990.
9. "Sun Microsystems Turn on the Afterburners," *Business Week,* July 18, 1988.
10. G. Paschal Zachary, "Sparc-station's Success Is Doubly Sweet for Sun Microsystem's Bechtolsheim," *The Wall Street Journal,* May 29, 1990.
11. Fisher, op. cit.
12. Robert D. Hof, "Why Sun Can't Afford to Shine Alone," *Business Week,* September 9, 1991.
13. G. Paschal Zachary, "Sun Challenges Microsoft's Hold Over Software," *The Wall Street Journal,* September 4, 1991.
14. Bob Francis, "Big Blue's Red Hot Workstation," *Datamation,* October 15, 1990.
15. Lawrence Curran, "HP Speeds Up Workstation Race," *Electronics,* April 1991.
16. "Getting Down to Business," *Information Week,* January 14, 1991.

Case Group F

Social and Ethical Issues in Marketing Management

■ **Case 28** **Notetakers Company**
Selling Class Notes and Instructional
Notes to Students

S. J. Garner and Judy Spain
both of Eastern Kentucky University

■ Company Background

Kevin and Jennifer own a business called Notetakers which is located in a strip mall near the campus of a major mid-western university. They started their business a year ago with start-up funds of $5,000. The small storefront contains a counter, a price board, a leased copier, a cabinet full of copier paper, a telephone and three file cabinets. Their product? Class notes.

Each semester, Kevin and Jennifer recruit honor students who are enrolled in large auditorium sections of popular general education classes and some business courses such as beginning marketing and beginning management. The honor students are paid to take and transcribe notes of the classes in which they are enrolled. Each student receives $50 for each "module" of class notes which are delivered to Notetakers one week before a course exam is scheduled. Most courses contain three or four modules (each of which is several weeks long). The honor students also receive a royalty of five percent of the gross sales of each module.

Kevin and Jennifer make copies of the class notes and sell them to students enrolled in the classes. Each module sells for six to ten dollars, depending on the length of the notes. Each module is printed with a cover sheet containing the name of the university, the name and section number of the course, room number, professor's name and time that the class meets. Copies are also included of any handouts given by that particular professor in class.

This case was written by professors Garner and Spain of Eastern Kentucky University, Department of Management and Marketing.

Kevin originally had the idea for this service because he is dyslexic and had difficulty taking coherent notes when he was in school. He had also noticed that students with ADD (attention deficit disorder) had similar problems. Jennifer estimates that thirty to forty percent of the note copies they sell are to disabled students. Students who have missed class due to illness or for other reasons also purchase note modules.

Notetakers offers no guarantee as to the accuracy of the notes they sell. They do place a written notice on each module warning students that they should compare the notes to others taken in class and the textbook materials.

Modules are available for around thirty-six classes currently. But more are added as honor students are recruited and class sizes increase. Currently, each notetaker makes around $300 per course per semester.

The business is open from 8:00 to 5:00 five days a week. Kevin and Jennifer split the counter duties, each spending approximately four and a half hours a day receiving, copying and selling notes. They currently have 20 honor students employed as notetakers.

Business expenses include storefront rental, utilities, supplies, copier lease costs, royalties and base payments to employee notetakers. These expenses total 55 percent of gross receipts. The other 45 percent is split between Kevin and Jennifer.

Notetakers has relied on two promotional methods during its first year of operation. Promotional flyers, designed by Jennifer, are handed out to students visiting the strip center during the first two weeks of class. Kevin and Jennifer merely stand in the door of their shop and hand the flyers to passing students. Secondly, as a condition of their shop lease, they have the strip center's permission to place their flyers on every car parked at the center which has a university parking tag hung on its mirror. So far, these two methods have generated some word-of-mouth among the student population.

Kevin feels that some additional promotion would increase their store traffic and also assist them in recruiting more notetakers to cover more classes. He feels that an advertisement in the student newspaper would be cost-effective and generate maximum exposure to their specific target market without adding waste circulation. Jennifer has designed a six inch by two column ad for use in the newspaper (see Exhibit 1). Kevin has discovered that the base rate for black and white ads is four dollars per column inch for a single insertion. Each insertion will therefore cost $48. (Two columns $\times$ six inches $\times$ $4 = $48.)

Kevin plans to insert the advertisement four times during the coming semester in the weekly college newspaper. The first two insertions will be during the first two weeks of class, the third insertion will be the week before midterm exams and the fourth the week before final exams take place. He has written a check for the first two insertions and mailed it along with a camera ready copy of the ad to the student newspaper.

■ Bad News Arrives

A week after mailing the ad to the student newspaper, Notetakers received the following letter in the mail.

Dear Owners of Notetakers:

I am returning your check and advertisement. It is my feeling that the service you provide has the effect of encouraging students to cut classes and thus miss a large part of their

Miss a few classes?
Have trouble taking notes?

Let
NOTETAKERS
help!!!

We have notes available for over 36 auditorium section classes. All our notes are taken and transcribed by currently entrolled honor students. Call today for prices and sections available.

NOTETAKERS
31 Oak St. in the Campus Strip Center
8–5 Monday through Friday
555 - 706 - NOTE

education. I do not feel it is ethical for you to provide this service and I certainly do not feel it would be ethical of me to allow this ad to be run in the student newspaper.

Sincerely,

Bob Richardson
Retail Advertising Manager

Kevin showed the letter to Jennifer and said, "This isn't fair at all! I've seen ads for beer and adult movies and videos in the newspaper—why are they picking on us? To say our business is unethical is very hypocritical!" Jennifer replied, "It was probably the faculty advisor who rejected the ad. Why don't you call and ask to speak with the advisor. Maybe you can change his mind."

Two days later Kevin told Jennifer that he had spoken to the newspaper's faculty advisor. The advisor told Kevin that he had not banned the ad. He left the decision up to the newspaper advertising manager and told him that he would have to stand behind his own decision. He also said that this was not the first ad to be rejected by the newspaper. Other ads which had been turned down included one from a group that wanted people to appear in a documentary "debunking" the Holocaust as a myth and another for a "stripper" pen featuring a woman who disrobed whenever the pen was tilted.

Kevin went on to say that the advisor also told him that he thought that Notetakers was doing a disservice to students by selling these notes, that it is a well-known fact that students who attend class learn more and make better grades and that Notetakers was encouraging negative behavior. To top it all off, the advisor said he had sent a copy of the Notetakers ad to the university lawyers to see if they could do anything to prevent Notetakers from stealing the intellectual property of the professors teaching these classes and using the name of the University!

■ More Bad News Arrives

Four weeks after the rejection letter arrived, Jennifer called Kevin at home and said, "You better get down here in a hurry to meet with our lawyer. We're being sued! The University just had us served with papers. As near as I can tell, they are saying we have infringed on their trademarks by having the name of the university, the course numbers, sections and dates on our covers. There is also something about some of the professors who teach the courses we have notes for having contracts with publishers to produce study guides based on their class notes. The publishers hold the copyrights on these materials. What are we going to do?"

Kevin and Jennifer met with their attorney, Steve King. Steve reviewed the advertisement, the cover sheet, and samples of the note packets. He told Kevin and Jennifer that the University was alleging a violation of the Lanham Trade-Mark Act of 1964, 15 U.S.C. sec. 1125(a).

The Lanham Act prohibits anyone from engaging in misrepresentation of origin and deceptive advertising regarding the origin of the notes. Specifically, Steve stated that the University is contending that because Notetakers used the course number, name, etc., on the cover sheet, it created confusion as to the actual source of the notes.

After talking to the attorney, Kevin and Jennifer were really confused. What should they do? Should they stop producing the notes and close their business? Were they really in violation of the law? If not in violation of the law, were they really acting unethically as the Advertising Manager said?

■ Case 29   Sarah Norton and Wise Research

Ronald L. Coulter, D. Michael Fields, and Mary K. Coulter
All of Southwest Missouri State University

Rebecca J. Gordon-Runyan
WRG Inc.

When Jeff Baird knocked on the Dallas motel room door on an early August evening in 1995, he expected to see his bubbling and enthusiastic girlfriend. He expected her to be excited, both because it was her birthday and because she was nearing completion of the first week in a two-week training program for the new job she had recently accepted. Instead, the young woman who answered looked troubled and tired.

"Sarah, you don't look very happy," said Jeff.

"I'm not," explained Sarah. "This week has not gone exactly as I expected, and I am seriously questioning whether or not I should even be here."

Although the tone of the meeting had obviously changed dramatically, Jeff was glad he had made the trip. Sarah was extremely troubled and clearly needed to talk to someone about her concerns. Jeff was happy that he was there to listen as Sarah tried to put in perspective the events of the last four days.

■ Initiating the Job Search

Sarah Norton was nearing the point where she had just one semester remaining before obtaining her MBA degree from a large state university in Hammonsville, Missouri. She was preparing, with some concern, to begin her job search. Sarah had identified at least three factors that would make finding a job in her field difficult. First, from a general perspective, American industry was still in the process of its most substantial downsizing. Much of the downsizing was at the expense of lower levels of management—which had depressed the hiring environment for MBAs across the nation. Second, Sarah's area of specialization was market research. Although many companies expressed a continued dependence on research in order to be effective in the mature markets that dominated the U.S. marketplace, the research industry was not considered to be a growth industry. This situation was further complicated for MBA students because many undergraduates were in competition for the same jobs and could be employed at lower salaries. Finally, Sarah preferred to remain in Hammonsville. The city of 150,000 was close to her parents, and Jeff was there. The location issue might prove to be particularly limiting because a city of 150,000 would generate a smaller market for researchers. Although the situation was less than encouraging, Sarah still felt that she had some advantages in pursuing and getting a job in her field.

■ Sarah's Background

Sarah was known to her professors and friends as a mature 32-year-old woman who had grown up in central Missouri in a strong family with loving parents. She had a strong religious background that helped to guide her when she had to make tough personal decisions. She was a very pleasant person to be around, and she was both liked and respected by her colleagues and friends. While her personal philosophy was to respect and treat others as she would like to be treated, she never pushed her moral, ethical, or religious views on others. She was genuine and personable in her relationships and was considered to be a fun person to be around.

Sarah had one younger sister with whom she remained very close. Sarah's first job had been with the state of Missouri in the Professional Registration office of the Board of Healing Arts. She enjoyed working there; the office was operated in a very professional manner, and the employees showed a genuine appreciation for each other. After several years in this job, Sarah realized that she wanted to complete her college degree. At the urging of her sister, Sarah transferred to Hammonsville to work in the local state vocational rehabilitation office. Here Sarah assisted several vocational rehabilitation counselors and took classes at the local state university. Sarah was known for her positive work ethic, strong moral values, and intelligence. She received her undergraduate degree in marketing and management (a double major) and graduated with high honors. During her coursework, Sarah was especially taken with the research classes and decided that she wanted to pursue a career in marketing research.

With this sense of direction, Sarah openly sought opportunities in several research projects with her professors in order to develop her research skills. As a result, she was competent and confident of her ability to do all phases of a research project. She could design questionnaires, input data, analyze and interpret statistical tests, and write reports. She was a proficient statistician. Sarah was also very aware of the importance of collecting and reporting unbiased data. The ethical handling of data had been stressed in her research courses, and such an approach was consistent with her personality and personal values. While no industrywide standards existed for the collection and handling of data, Sarah was aware of the code of ethics developed by the Marketing Research Association, Inc. (see Exhibit 1). This organization consisted of approximately 2,100 members from across the United States. Members used the organization for education and training and for networking opportunities in the field of marketing research.

Sarah knew from her professors' lectures, and from her assigned research readings, that corporations annually spend millions of dollars on research. The results of that research are used to influence multimillion-dollar decisions regarding new product lines, manufacturing employment, and promotional strategies. Sarah was also aware that marketing research conducted by outside research suppliers was a growing industry concern. Articles she had read on the subject reinforced this concern regarding the ethical collection of marketing research data.

When Sarah completed her undergraduate degree in 1994, the job market was particularly tight. Several of her professors suggested that she consider an MBA degree, so Sarah applied to the graduate school and was accepted into the MBA program. This allowed her to remain in Hammonsville. She also was given a graduate assistantship in the marketing department which paid her tuition and living expenses. While working on her MBA, Sarah continued to develop her marketing research skills. She took 12 hours in her graduate program specifically in research

The Code of Professional Ethics and Practices

1. To maintain high standards of competence and integrity in marketing and survey research.
2. To maintain the highest level of business and professional conduct and to comply with federal, state, and local laws, regulations, and ordinances applicable to my business practice and those of my company.
3. To exercise all reasonable care and to observe the best standards of objectivity and accuracy in the development, collection, processing, and reporting of marketing and survey research information.
4. To protect the anonymity of respondents and hold all information concerning an individual respondent privileged, such that this information is used only within the context of the particular study.
5. To thoroughly instruct and supervise all persons for whose work I am responsible in accordance with study specifications and general research techniques.
6. To observe the rights of ownership of all materials received from and/or developed for clients, and to keep in confidence all research techniques, data and other information considered confidential by their owners.
7. To make available to clients such details on the research methods and techniques of an assignment as may be reasonably required for proper interpretation of the data, providing this reporting does not violate the confidence of respondents or clients.
8. To promote the trust of the public for marketing and survey research activities and to avoid any procedure which misrepresents the activities of a respondent, the rewards of cooperation, or the uses of data.
9. To refrain from referring to membership in this organization as proof of competence, since the organization does not so certify any person or organization.
10. To encourage the observance of principles of this code among all people engaged in marketing and survey research.

SOURCE: Used with permission of the Marketing Research Association, Inc., Rocky Hill, CT.

classes and also worked on several special projects for the College of Business for publication and classroom instruction purposes. She also helped acquire secondary data from the library. Sarah had fully expected to return to her assistantship position in the fall of 1995; she had already been offered the head graduate assistant position.

Sarah had agreed to take on the additional responsibilities of head graduate assistant in her final semester of graduate school in the fall—coordinating the schedules and activities of the five graduate assistants who worked in the marketing department. She was confident that the additional time needed would not interfere with either her preparation for classes or what she considered to be her most important activity—finding an entry-level position in the marketing research field. By mid-summer, Sarah had updated her résumé and was ready to begin aggressively pursuing the job market.

■ Reacting to the Position Announcement

Sarah had been casually looking through the employment section of the Hammonsville *News Monitor* on Sunday, July 9, 1995, when she noticed a position announcement for a market research manager. She eagerly read the balance of the ad copy to get more details about the opportunity. The advertisement did not give any specific job requirements, but the copy did provide a catchy reference to details, dilemmas, and deadlines as they related to an entry-level management position. The advertisement gave a post office box number in Hammonsville and asked potential applicants to send a cover letter with their résumés. No company name was provided in the advertisement.

Sarah thought long and hard about applying for the position. If she applied and was offered the position, she thought she might get to stay in Hammonsville. She liked the city, and very few managerial positions ever became available in her specialized area of marketing research. She would likely have to wait to finish the last nine hours on her MBA degree, but she could still finish the degree at the university. She would also have to give up her head graduate assistant position. She especially wanted her professors to know what she was contemplating so they could hire a replacement before the fall semester began. The local university had been good to her, and she did not want to do anything that would appear improper to her professors or to herself. She discussed the situation with her major professor, who encouraged her to look seriously at the position. If it did not appear to be the type of position she wanted, she could simply withdraw from the interview process. Sarah agreed and mailed in her résumé and cover letter.

■ The Initial Response and Sarah's Preparation

Within a week of mailing her application letter, Sarah received a phone call from a woman named Katie. Katie said that Mr. Bill Wise, the company's president, would be arriving in Hammonsville from Dallas to do interviews and that he wanted to interview her. Sarah agreed to meet with Mr. Wise on Thursday, July 27. Sarah inquired as to the name of the organization and was told "Wise Research." A follow-up call was to be made by Katie at a later date to verify the interview time.

Sarah tried to get some background information about the organization so that she could intelligently discuss the company and how she might fit into its plans. She found the company listed in the Hammonsville telephone directory under market research firms. Her professor recommended that she call the number to inquire about the operation prior to the interview, but not to indicate why the call was being made. Sarah called the number and spoke with a young man who said he was the office manager. She asked what type of research they conducted and was informed that the company, located in the Westfield Mall, was strictly involved in fieldwork. The company did not generate any questionnaires, nor did it analyze any of the data it collected. The company simply collected data for other marketing research firms that were providing information to their own clients, such as Procter & Gamble, Ragu, or Campbell's. Sarah, remembering her marketing research text, classified the company as a field service organization (see Exhibit 2); this meant that the firm concentrated on collecting data for research projects. The office manager also indicated that the staff at his facility were not college educated.

The manager, who sounded apprehensive, then asked Sarah why she was interested in this information. Sarah truthfully answered that the president of the company was coming to Hammonsville to interview her for a position, but she did not have any information about the company. The manager seemed upset that the president of the company was coming to Hammonsville and he had not been notified. Sarah specifically indicated that she did not know anything about the position.

■ **Exhibit 2**   Types of Marketing Research Service Suppliers

Customized research services	Companies that work with individual clients from developing the problem/opportunity through the entire research process. They are also referred to as full-service suppliers.
Field research services	These companies concentrate only on collecting data on research projects. They may specialize in various interviewing methodologies such as mail surveys, telephone surveys, personal surveys, focus groups, or mall intercept surveys.
Data analysis research services	These firms specialize in data coding, data editing, and data analysis. They are sometimes referred to as "tab houses," although some specialize in sophisticated data analysis techniques.
Syndicated research services	Companies that routinely collect information to provide to other firms who subscribe to their services.
Branded products research services	These companies have developed specialized data collection and analysis techniques, which are relevant to address specific types of research problems. Their research is branded and marketed like branded products.
Standardized research services	Firms which do marketing research projects conducted in a standard, prespecified manner; the results are then supplied to several different clients.

■ The Interview Process

The Initial Interview

When Katie called several days later to confirm Sarah's interview, she indicated that the interviews were to be held at a local hotel in Hammonsville. Sarah was somewhat surprised because she had expected to be interviewed at the local office in the mall. When she arrived at the hotel, she dialed the extension number Katie had provided. Karen Wise, Bill Wise's wife, answered the phone. She indicated that she also worked at Wise Research. Karen Wise came to the hotel lobby and gave Sarah an application to complete. This was a standard form with a space for annual salary requirement. Sarah responded $25,000–$35,000, knowing that it was a high request for the local market conditions.

After completing the application, Sarah went upstairs to the Wise's hotel room. The interview with Mr. and Mrs. Wise was informal and was held at a small table set in the center of a large room. Mr. Wise sat on one side, his wife sat on his side of the table but more to the end, and Sarah sat on the other side. Mr. Wise was dressed in a lightweight, short-sleeve shirt without a tie or jacket, and Mrs. Wise wore a dress. Sarah did not get the impression from their appearance or the interview process that either of them had much formal education or training. Both were very pleased with the sample paperwork Sarah had brought.

Sarah brought with her a copy of a marketing plan she had done as a student and three questionnaires she had developed to collect data for various projects. During her interview she discussed her data-entry skills and her knowledge of various statistical packages to analyze data. She also discussed her work on several special projects with professors in the College of Business. She explained that for the past year she had been employed as a graduate assistant in the marketing department. She indicated that she had expected to return to this position in the fall since she had already been offered the head graduate assistant position. She also discussed her undergraduate employment at a popular local restaurant where she had been responsible for operations in the absence of the owner. She had often managed the restaurant when the owner was away for several days.

The Wises discussed the deadlines necessary for different projects and how the manager might sometimes have two projects going one day and eight working the next. They gave Sarah a short history of the company. The organization had been in business for about 25 years and operated five mall research offices. Three of the offices were located in Dallas; one was located in Tulsa; and the Hammonsville office was the newest, having been in existence for about 10 years.

Sarah was then told that the local manager was being let go because he was unable to achieve the required production levels. The person the Wises chose would be trained in Dallas for two weeks and then returned to Hammonsville where he or she would be responsible for the Westfield Mall office. The interview was spent primarily discussing the job requirements. Sarah was given the impression that while there would be some contact between the Dallas office and the Hammonsville office, the manager they hired would have direct contact with the clients and autonomy to work with the employees as he or she saw fit.

Sarah's next question was about validating surveys. Survey validation is a procedure where supervisors, or other objective individuals, recontact a small random sample of respondents to check the accuracy of the fieldwork being done. Validation is particularly needed when the temptation for interviewer cheating may be present. Sarah was told that the clients did the validations and that the supervisor also did some. The context of the interview led Sarah to believe that the Wise's organization was contracting to provide valid survey data. Sarah was then told that callbacks for second interviews would be made that afternoon.

The Second Interview

Karen Wise called and left Sarah a message on her answering machine that Thursday evening. Sarah returned the call later in the evening. Karen told Sarah that the pay was $11 per hour with time and a half paid for any overtime work. Sarah specifically asked if it was 40 hours per week, and Karen replied in the affirmative. Karen Wise said this would come out to be $25,000 per year with benefits that Bill Wise would tell her about the next day. Sarah accepted the second interview and then calculated that it would take about 42.5 hours per week to make $25,000 per year.

The second interview was held in the same hotel and was as casual as the first interview. The Wises told Sarah that they were leaving on vacation as soon as they were done in Hammonsville. Again, no mention was made of touring the local Hammonsville facilities or of meeting the staff. The benefit package presented to Sarah included health insurance premiums paid on a plan of Sarah's choice, up to the amount that the company paid for Dallas employees. This was done because the Wise Research insurance plan did not cover Missouri employees. One week of vacation was offered after one year of employment. A performance review would be scheduled after three months, and then another review would be held nine months later. Mr. Wise stated that it didn't behoove them to give raises in that interim.

In preparation for the second interview, Sarah had compiled a list of 17 questions that she considered to be important. Much of the second interview consisted of Sarah's questions and the corresponding answers (see Exhibit 3), as she sought to gain more information about the research firm.

■ **Exhibit 3**   The Second Job Interview: Sarah Norton's Questions and Her Notes on Wise Research's Answers

1. How is the staff paid?
   The staff was paid on an hourly basis.
2. Is there a budget for incentives?
   No, but they were considering one on a trial basis and would possibly use the Hammonsville office to try out a new program. They felt there were problems with incentives based just on completions of surveys as some people screen potential respondents while others actually do the interviews. The Wises seemed to be concerned with the fairness of this method.
3. Are paychecks distributed from Dallas?
   The paychecks come from Dallas (verified at a later date).
4. Are the staff paid weekly or monthly?
   Twice a month.
5. What are the benefits? Health insurance? Profit sharing? Bonuses for production?
   Insurance was provided by the company; there was no profit sharing plan; and bonuses for production might include a pizza party on the company for all the employees, but no specific program was in place.
6. If the Hammonsville office was extremely busy and needed more production, could the manager help do the fieldwork?
   Yes.
7. How do you support your managers?
   Sarah never specifically asked this question but tried to discern information from her conversations. The Wises seemed supportive of their managers. Frequent communication between offices was discussed. They felt that the open lines for assistance from other mall managers would help. Overall, Sarah felt that they would support their managers regarding decisions and actions as long as they were keeping up production.
8. How often are performance reviews done? 3 months? 6 months?
   Reviews were done after the third month and then again at one year.
9. What is the average overtime for a manager?
   No specific time was given, but the Wises did feel that there would be plenty of overtime opportunities. It was mentioned that if the manager frequently had excessive overtime that they would look for either inefficiencies or the need for an additional assistant. Requests for overtime were required prior to actually working. Approval was mandatory.
10. How are the employees trained? Does the manager have latitude in the content of employee training?
    No specific training program had been designed and Sarah would be responsible for how the Hammonsville employees were trained within some guidelines.
11. How does Wise Research get its referrals?
    Companies come to them, and much of their business is repeat. If a mall office does a good job, the client may again specifically ask for that office. The client and mall manager will be able to communicate directly without going through the Dallas office every time. It was mentioned that Hammonsville had a bad reputation and that many clients did not want to use them. The Wises felt this problem could be overcome with time and a new manager.
12. If Sarah increased production in the Hammonsville office, would Wise Research have enough business to keep the office busy?
    Yes, the Wises did not feel that this would be any problem.
13. Would Sarah have autonomy and authority over her office (to set up an evaluation system, to tie bonuses to performance, to specify dress, approach, etc.)?
    The Wises would not directly answer this question. Sarah did not feel that the Wises were willing to let the manager operate completely and independently. The manager did have the authority over his or her office to a certain extent, with the final word coming from Dallas.
14. Were any promotion dollars budgeted to raise the image of the Hammonsville office?
    In preparing for the interview, Sarah had spoken to a variety of Hammonsville people about being interviewed in the mall. The typical first response she received was always negative toward mall interviewers. They were viewed as interruptive, and most people did not like to talk with them. Sarah felt that some efforts to change people's perceptions about the interviewers' work would enable the Hammonsville office to raise production. The Wises indicated that their organization does not budget for any self-promotion efforts.

(continued)

■ **Exhibit 3** (*concluded*)

15. Where in the mall can interviewers go?
    Interviewers are allowed to go anywhere in the original section of the mall. This is quite a large area, but most interviewers were staying primarily by the research office. Interviewers were typically not going farther into the mall because interviews were typically conducted in the research office and the original section of the mall was so large that it could be a long trip back to the office. The people Sarah talked with often tried to avoid the original mall areas where the interviewers typically stood. The Wises did want to see the interviewers branch out further into the mall.
16. How are focus group participants solicited?
    A file of willing participants was maintained to be used when needed.
17. During the Dallas training what would Sarah be provided with?
    The Wises indicated that the company would provide a room close to the mall, and they would provide a rental car if needed. Airfare would be provided from Hammonsville, and Sarah would also receive reimbursement for her expenses.

After completing the interview, the Wises indicated that they would make their decision later that afternoon. They also told Sarah they would call her either that afternoon or the following Monday.

Karen Wise called Sarah from her car phone later that afternoon and offered Sarah the position. Sarah accepted the position and indicated that she could fly out on Monday, August 7, 1995, for training in Dallas. The following week Sarah withdrew from her fall graduate program courses, informed the marketing department that she would not be returning for the fall semester, wrapped up her summer work as a research assistant, and prepared her personal calendar to be in Dallas from August 7 to August 21, 1995.

■ The Dallas Training

Sarah arrived at the Dallas Love Field airport around noon on Monday, August 7, and was picked up at the gate by Mark Wise, the son of Mr. and Mrs. Wise. Mark, who was in his early 20s, was very personable and open about the organization. He also spoke very highly of Cindy Brewster, the supervisor with whom Sarah was to train. Mark did bring up the fact that someone had called their Hammonsville office and asked about the position; he was very curious. The first time he discussed it, Sarah let it go without response. He brought the subject up again during the drive and at lunch. He mentioned that they had received a résumé from another employee in the Hammonsville office. They were confused as to how that could have happened because they had just listed a post office box number in the advertisement. Sarah simply commented that Hammonsville was a small town in many respects, even though the population was around 150,000, and that it would not be unusual for word to get around.

Mark also commented that his parents were tired of the Hammonsville situation. They were determined to hire someone who could make the office work, and they wanted to keep that person in Hammonsville no matter what it required. Mark said that the company had received a large number of résumés, and he thought they had interviewed nearly 100 applicants. When Sarah looked at him in disbelief, he quickly added that his statement might not be exactly accurate, but that they had interviewed for two days. He also stated that they felt happy with their decision and excited about her employment.

Sarah and Mark also had a conversation about her educational background. Mark was interested in research and said what he really wanted to know was how to design the questionnaires in order to get the data they wanted. Sarah briefly discussed some of the aspects of questionnaire design and data collection. It seemed very odd to Sarah that Mark had very little understanding of the research process as a whole, but she chalked it up to his being the younger son who did not work full-time at the company.

Mark took Sarah to lunch and then to a car rental agency where the Wises' other son had rented a car for Sarah to use during her two-week training program. Sarah was lodged in a hotel across the parking lot from a shopping mall which housed the research office where she would be training. Mark then took Sarah to the hotel and on to the mall where he gave her an envelope containing $200 in cash and a hand-written note, asking for her signature to indicate that she had received the $200 for expenses.

At the Chesterfield Mall, Sarah was introduced to the office supervisor, Cindy Brewster, and Mark left to return to the main office. Cindy immediately informed Sarah that she had been instructed by the main office not to disclose why Sarah would be in their office for two weeks. Cindy had told the employees that Sarah was an auditor and monitor who would be watching her. Cindy had Sarah complete another standard personnel form, which again requested simple information such as name, address, emergency contact, and salary. Upon completion of the form, Cindy faxed it to the main office.

Cindy then took Sarah on a tour of the facility. It soon struck Sarah that she had seen no evidence of a computer or typewriter. Later she did see a computer sitting on a shelf in the storage room. Sarah asked if they were computerized, and Cindy replied no. Cindy added that only the main office had computers.

In further conversations with Cindy, Sarah discovered that Wise Research considered 37.5 hours as a full-time week. Katie, the office manager at the main office, had sent an envelope for Sarah which Cindy gave to her. Sarah was surprised the front of the envelope was marked For Cindy's Eyes Only and Top Secret. The envelope contained copies of the routine paperwork that supervisors were responsible for completing. Cindy then mentioned that someone had called the Hammonsville office for information about the position. Again, Sarah did not reveal any information, but it seemed very peculiar to Sarah that the organization was so concerned about this incident, particularly if they had interviewed as many people as Mark had indicated.

Sarah and Cindy also discussed the story that Cindy had been ordered to tell her employees concerning Sarah's presence in the office. Cindy said that Wise Research had not yet notified the Hammonsville manager that he was being released, and she asked Sarah if that bothered her. Sarah was vague in her response, and Cindy made it clear that it *did* bother her. Cindy said that if the organization could treat the Hammonsville manager that way, they would also likely do it to her.

Day Two

Work began on Tuesday at 9 A.M. Sarah was told to carry her time card in her purse so no one would know that she was clocking in and out. To do this, Sarah arrived before the other employees. Cindy began by showing Sarah the paperwork that was to be completed before 10 A.M. At 10 A.M. Cindy held a briefing where the interviewers were brought up to speed on the outstanding projects and were taken through the steps of preparing for new projects. Cindy introduced Sarah as the auditor and monitor that she had told them about.

As the week progressed, Sarah was shown how to check the completed questionnaires and how to report daily progress to the client. When Wise Research began a project, each interviewer received a sheet that contained (1) an estimate of how many completed questionnaires they should be able to get per hour; (2) what percent of people they would approach (called *net incidence*) who would be eligible to respond based on general criteria, such as age or job; and (3) criteria which were specific (called *category incidence*) to the survey, such as "Do you use body shampoo?" Clients were sent a daily report, and Sarah was told that, in preparing this report, supervisors started with the actual production numbers and worked from them. For example, if interviewers were expected to complete two questionnaires per hour and four were actually completed in one day, the supervisor reported that two hours were worked on the job. This way budgeted hours always matched actual hours. They then took the number four and applied the net incidence and category incidence percentages to come up with a fictional number of people they screened out during the day so the final number showed four completions. This total was then distributed over the categories purely at supervisor discretion. They would just manipulate the data until the numbers totaled those estimated by the client. This report was then faxed to the client. Sarah asked Cindy about this practice, and Cindy said it was the way that everyone did it. She then told Sarah a story about how Karen Wise once was discussing one of the numbers with her and Cindy asked her why it bothered her because the numbers were all fabricated anyway. Karen said she was right, and they both had a good laugh. Cindy indicated that she did feel that it was wrong, though, and Sarah questioned how clients could make good decisions based on potentially biased data.

Sarah learned that the actual jobs each office worked on could vary from a home placement of body shampoo (where the client would use the product and then evaluate it) to a mall taste test of liqueurs. Sarah was concerned by some of these practices, so she asked Cindy what would happen if it appeared that a survey was not going to be completed on time. Cindy replied that first you would call the main office for more time. If that wasn't possible, they were often told to get it done no matter what it takes. This might involve calling uncles, nieces, or anyone demographically acceptable to provide the required data. The main office was also likely to tell the supervisor to write it up. Cindy later told Sarah that some of the other mall offices had interviewers who had been caught so many times with invalidated surveys that they were working under three or four different names so the clients would not recognize them.

Day Three

As training continued, another incident occurred that concerned Sarah. Cindy received a call from another mall supervisor. The other mall supervisor heard Sarah's voice in the background and immediately asked if Karen Wise had brought in the new Hammonsville supervisor for training. Cindy immediately denied that Sarah was the new manager, as she had been instructed to do from the main office. The comment from the other mall supervisor seemed strange to Sarah, since each office has four to six, primarily female, interviewers scheduled per day. She realized that there was a high rate of turnover for interviewers, but it seem suspicious that the other mall supervisor immediately asked if Sarah was a new supervisor instead of an interviewer. Sarah questioned Cindy about this, and they talked about the grapevine that was in place at Wise Research. Sarah asked if the grapevine was used mainly for information or power within the organization. Cindy's reply was "For both."

Day Four

By Thursday of the first week, Sarah was directing the briefings on new projects for the interviewers. Cindy sat back and supervised Sarah's efforts. As they went through the questionnaire, one of the interviewers asked about the coding numbers. This led to a discussion about data entry, and one of the interviewers asked Sarah what would happen if a question was not answered. Sarah indicated they would leave it blank when inputting that response and then continue. Sarah explained that one blank response would not invalidate the entire interview. This seemed very annoying to the interviewers, and again Sarah was surprised at the lack of knowledge the employees had about the whole data collection process.

Throughout the daily training sessions, Cindy and Sarah had discussed the culture of the Wise Research organization and again, on Thursday, they began another conversation. Cindy recounted examples of her experiences. She believed that when she was hired for the supervisor's position, Bill Wise had known that she badly needed the job. She had been out of work for several months and her elderly mother needed care, so an income was imperative. Cindy's background was in psychology, and she had worked for mental health institutions prior to being out of work.

They also discussed many of the things that Cindy's boss had told her to do, such as being dishonest with her employees. Cindy told Sarah that there were things that she had been asked to do that she had refused. Sarah was very concerned about Cindy's comment and asked what those things were. Sarah felt that if Cindy had been asked to do these things then she would probably be asked to do them, too. Sarah was becoming upset at the thought of so much dishonesty in the office. What else could they want? Cindy was not specific in her response to Sarah's direct question and implied other things *were* currently happening, but that she had chosen not to be a part of those activities.

In her supervisory position, which she had held for over eight months, Cindy immediately stood out as a Wise Research leader. She was educated and perceived by the interviewers as a fair supervisor. But Cindy was bothered: although she had received notification of her three-month raise earlier, Wise Research had withheld the monetary rewards until just a few weeks before Sarah's arrival. Cindy had made attempts to gain raises for herself and for her assistant, but her attempts had been ignored. When the main office informed Cindy that she was going to receive a pay increase, she was happy, but she also wondered what the Wises might be wanting from her. When she was told she would be supervising Sarah's training, Cindy felt she understood the timing of her raise.

Cindy was aware of Sarah's training benefits. Sarah had been flown in for two weeks and provided with a car, a nice hotel, and $200 in cash for spending money. When Sarah's personnel records were completed and returned to Cindy, she commented on Sarah's starting pay. Apparently, Sarah's starting pay was more than Cindy was receiving even after having been with the company for more than eight months. Cindy explained that when she was hired, training was provided in Dallas-area malls and that she was responsible for all transportation costs. Every single weekday for what was supposed to be one month and ultimately turned into three, Cindy drove 85 miles round trip for her training. She admitted to feeling slighted by the company when Sarah was being treated so well.

By now Sarah did not have the positive feeling that she had when she first accepted her new position with Wise Research. The final straw came when Sarah and Cindy were discussing pay, and Cindy shared an experience she'd had on the Monday morning of Sarah's arrival. Apparently Cindy and others had worked the previous Saturday and had been loaned a couple of interviewers from another Dallas-area mall. One of Cindy's interviewers had been befriended by one of these women, and a conversation had ensued about how long each had been with the company and what salary was made per hour. On Monday, the visiting interviewer had gone back to work and complained that Cindy's employee made more money than she did although Cindy's employee had been with the company a shorter time. Cindy had received a phone call from Katie at the main office. Katie told her that she was to fire her interviewer because the interviewer had discussed her salary with another employee. Sarah asked Cindy if the employee had known about this rule or had been shown an employee handbook where this rule was stated. Cindy said that only supervisors and their assistants had employee handbooks and, to her knowledge, her assistant had never seen one. She did say that she felt that discussion of wages was inappropriate, and Sarah stated that she did not feel that way. Sarah said that her salary was hers, it was based on her skills, and that she should be able to discuss it with whomever she wanted.

Cindy had called the employee into the office, told her about the main office's stand, and told the employee that she must be fired. The interviewer began to cry and tried to change Cindy's mind. Cindy explained that it was not her decision and that she had been ordered to do this. The employee asked to talk with someone in the main office; Cindy felt that she should be able to do that, so she placed the call. When she told Katie that the employee wanted to talk with her, Katie responded that she did not know what more could be said but that she would speak to the employee.

The employee was crying and asked to keep her job. Cindy indicated that she literally said, "I beg you for my job." Cindy then heard the employee say that she would talk to Cindy. This surprised Cindy because she'd had no say in the firing. When the employee got off the phone, Cindy told her that she did not have to beg her for her job. She would have to formally write her up, but that she could still work. When Cindy called Katie back to tell her what she had done, she was asked why. Cindy explained that the woman worked several jobs to support a husband who didn't work and three children and that she needed the income. Katie responded that it wasn't their problem. Apparently, however, the interviewer was allowed to remain because she was still working when Sarah was in training.

Sarah had only been in the office for four days, but her winning personality and sincerity had made an impression on other employees. Sarah felt comfortable with Cindy and her staff. Thursday was also Sarah's birthday, and she received a fax from the main office and a card from Cindy. Cindy also said that her brother was making Sarah a handcrafted gift and that it would be done before she left town. One of the interviewers brought Sarah a cupcake, which might not have been so unusual had it not been the employee's day off. However, the kindness shown by the employees of the Chesterfield Mall research office was being overshadowed by concerns that engulfed Sarah.

◼ Sarah's Dilemma

Thursday night was Sarah's chance to evaluate the events of the last four days. After another week of training, Sarah would be returning to her hometown. She would return to Hammonsville to take over the research office in the Westfield Mall. She had already sacrificed her graduate assistantship and would now have to complete her

MBA degree at a later time. Even though she felt the new company was pleased with her efforts and knowledge, Sarah wondered if she had made a mistake in accepting the position.

This was Sarah's mindset as she anxiously awaited Jeff's arrival. As she waited, she began to consider her options. Should she resign immediately and return to Hammonsville? Would her concerns likely be alleviated in the second week of her training? Should she complete her training, report to the Hammonsville office, attack her work, and simply refuse to do anything that she considered to be unethical? Or, was she simply overreacting to a normal situation in which a company's culture sometimes conflicts with an individual's personal moral philosophies? Sarah was glad that Jeff was coming to Dallas that evening. He could help her sort through her emotions and decide what action would be in her best interest in the long run. The knot in her stomach signaled a sense of urgency in working through her concerns and arriving at a decision sometime before she reported to work the next morning.

■ Case 30   Nintendo versus SEGA: Sex, Violence, and Videogames

Romuald A. Stone
James Madison University

Violence in America in 1994 was considered by many people to have reached epidemic proportions. All across the United States—in cities and towns large and small—citizens were increasingly fearful and concerned that violence was out of control. What was causing this violent behavior? There was no easy answer. But many experts said that the pervasive violence in television programming, films, and videogames was one seed that promoted physical aggression in some individuals and helped create a culture tolerant of violence.

Just as television emerged as a powerful social and cultural force in the early 1950s, videogames were said to be emerging as a potentially powerful influence on children's behavior in the 1990s. While the impact of the growing violence in videogames was debatable, the years of research on violence in television programming provided instructive warning. According to Parker Page, president of the Children's Television Resource and Education Center, "years of research indicate that children who watch a steady diet of violent programming increase their chances of becoming more aggressive towards other children, less cooperative and altruistic, more tolerant of real life violence and more afraid of the world outside their homes."[1] The advent of virtual reality technology in videogame programming led Page to express a special concern in his testimony before a joint Senate subcommittee hearing held in December 1993.

> Mortal Kombat is simply the first in a new generation of video games that allows software designers to combine high levels of violence with fully digitalized human images. No more cute hedge hogs or cartoonish Super Mario Brothers—increasingly, the characters that a young player beheads, disembowels or crushes will look more and more like the kids at school, the neighbor who lives down the street or the young woman heading for aerobics class.[2]

Alarmed by the violent content of many videogames, parents and concerned citizens started lobbying for a comprehensive, industrywide videogame rating system that would give parents the information they needed to make informed choices. To address these concerns, Senators Lieberman and Kohl sponsored legislation to establish the National Independent Council for Entertainment in Video Devices as an independent agency of the federal government to oversee the development of "voluntary" standards to alert parents to the content of videogames. In his testimony before the hearing, Robert Chase, vice president of the National Education Association, expressed the collective concern of educators, children's advocates, and parents:

> America's children are faced with a bewildering set of messages from television, movies, music, electronic games, and print media. Too often, the almost unrelenting assault on the senses encouraging aggression and irresponsibility are in direct opposition to the values

---

[1]U.S. Senate, Violence in Videogames: Joint Hearing of the Judiciary Subcommittee on Juvenile Justice and Government Affairs Subcommittee on Regulation and Government Information (testimony of Parker Page, PhD.), 103rd Cong., 1993.

[2]Ibid.

families hope to instill and the mores our society struggles to preserve. Parents, social scientists, and the community at large share deep trepidation about the fruits of this ever widening dispersal of negative images. The explosion of media in the latter half of this century has made the problem all the more pervasive and the challenges for parents and community leaders all the more difficult.[3]

At the same hearing, the Software Publishers Association (SPA) provided a counter argument:

> In our attempt to protect our children from those relatively few video games which contain unacceptable violence, however, we must not lose sight of the fact that the vast majority of videogames are appropriate for children, and have the potential for developing many important and socially desirable skills. As stated so eloquently by Bob Keeshan, otherwise known as Captain Kangaroo, "Video games . . . provide the potential for heretofore unknown opportunities for information, education and delightful entertainment. . . . The technology is to be encouraged because, used appropriately, such games can be a tool for education as well as entertainment."[4]

The SPA indicated in its testimony that the software entertainment industry was committed to moving quickly and decisively on this issue. The SPA was in the process of working with a coalition of concerned parties to establish a rating system that would be easy for consumers to understand and one that the industry could implement. Nintendo and SEGA had also initiated moves toward a rating system.

■ Nintendo's Position

When Nintendo entered the U.S. videogame industry in 1985, the company established written Game Content Guidelines requiring games marketed under the Nintendo Seal of Quality to meet the following standards:

- No sexually suggestive or explicit content.
- No sexist language or depictions.
- No random, gratuitous, or excessive violence.
- No graphic illustration of death.
- No domestic violence or abuse.
- No excessive force in sports games.
- No ethnic, racial, religious, or sexual stereotypes.
- No profanity or obscenity.
- No use of drugs, smoking materials, or alcohol.
- No subliminal political messages or overt political statements.

As an example of Nintendo's pledge to control and monitor its game content, the company insisted that one of its largest licensees, Acclaim Entertainment, remove objectionable material from the controversial arcade game "Mortal Kombat." In its original form, the game included scenes in which characters' heads were ripped off, their spines were pulled out, they were impaled on spikes, and they splurted blood when hit. All of these graphics were deemed unacceptable and removed from the Nintendo version of the game. SEGA released the game in its entirety.

---

[3]Ibid. (testimony of Robert Chase).

[4]Ibid. (testimony of Ilene Rosenthal).

Some games had been simply rejected outright, since no amount of modification would make them acceptable to Nintendo. One such game was "Night Trap," which contained full motion videos of young, scantily-clad females being attacked by hooded men who drilled holes in their bodies to suck out blood.

Howard Lincoln, Nintendo's then senior vice president (and later chairman), reiterated his company's continued commitment to wholesome family entertainment that was both challenging and exciting to youth while remaining nonoffensive to parents:

> This will remain our philosophy despite the fact we have been criticized by both video game players and others in our industry for taking what we feel is the only responsible approach . . . we believe our game guidelines have served us and our customers well for the past eight years. And we have no intention of abandoning this approach.[5]

However, Nintendo apparently decided to moderate its position following a raft of angry letters from users. Nintendo's 1994 holiday season new version of the "Mortal Kombat" game was just as gruesome as the arcade version.

■ Sega's Position[6]

In 1993, SEGA established a three-pronged approach designed to help parents determine the age-appropriateness of its stable of interactive video software. It included a rating classification system, a toll-free hotline, and an informational brochure. Building on the motion picture industry model, the SEGA rating system applied one of three classifications to each interactive video program it released:

GAF   For general audiences.
MA-13   For mature audiences age 13 and over.
MA-17   Adult appropriate, not suitable for those under age 17.

SEGA's toll-free hotline was staffed by professionals who could supplement the rating classification by informing parents about the specific content of each SEGA product. SEGA also offered its "Everybody Wins" brochure that provided additional information to shoppers at more than 2,800 retail stores. In addition, SEGA formed an independent Videogame Rating Council consisting of experts in the areas of psychology, sociology, cinema, and education to evaluate games and assign appropriate rating classifications. By the end of 1993, 173 SEGA titles had been rated with the following distribution: 86 percent rated for general audiences (GA); 10 percent earned an MA-13 rating; and only 4 percent were targeted for exclusively adult (MA-17) audiences. To make SEGA's rating system work, the company decided that products bearing the MA-17 label should not be distributed to retail toy stores.

■ Progress Report[7]

In July 1994, the U.S. Senate subcommittee endorsed rating guidelines issued by an industry trade group, the Interactive Digital Software Association (IDSA)—see Exhibit 1. The IDSA ratings provided age guidance with five categories similar to

---

[5]Ibid. (testimony of Howard C. Lincoln).

[6]Ibid. (testimony of William White, vice president, SEGA of America Inc.).

[7]M. Moran, "Retailers See Videogame Ratings as a Helpful Guide," *Video Business* 14, no. 32 (1994), pp. 12, 16.

■ **Exhibit 1**   Rating Guideline

Interactive Digital Software Association (IDSA) is using five categories by age to rate video game cartridges such as Nintendo, Sega, Atari. They are:

- Early childhood, ages 3 and up
- Kids to adult, ages 6 and up
- Teen, ages 13 and up
- Mature, ages 17 and up
- Adults only

The Software Publishers Association (SPA) is using a label that shows the level of violence, sex, and strong language used in a computer software or CD-ROM game. Games with no offensive material receive a "Suitable for all audiences" label.

SOURCE: *The Washington Post.*

those used by the Motion Picture Association of America. The ratings were expected to appear on videogame packages by mid-November, in time for the holiday season. Retailers who rent games planned to adhere to the ratings guidelines. Some mass merchants (Sears, Wal-Mart, Toys 'R' Us) had vowed to carry only rated videogames. An informal survey of retailers, however, revealed that large numbers of unrated games were on retailers' shelves for the 1994 seasonal buying rush.[8] Although the IDSA had rated more than 280 titles, the ratings were apparently completed after game packages were printed.

The SPA encountered similar problems. At the end of 1994, only 40 CD-ROM and other software game titles had been rated. Exhibit 1 depicts SPA rating guidelines. Ken Wasch, executive director of the SPA, commented: "I wish more had been rated, but it took longer than we expected to get products submitted, to get them rated, and to get them out to the stores."[9]

There was no agreement among game producers on an industrywide rating system. Some observers believed the existence of several rating systems would confuse consumers. There also appeared to be a debate emerging whether widespread dissemination of rated products would ultimately hurt or help sales.

---

[8]P. Farhi, "A Waiting Game for Rating Games," *The Washington Post*, December 24, 1994, p. D1.

[9]Ibid.

Case 31   E. & J. Gallo Winery

A. J. Strickland III and Daniel C. Thurman
both of The University of Alabama

In the mid-1980s, alcohol consumption in the United States had been declining in virtually every category except low-priced wines. A number of producers in the wine industry did not believe they should be producing what they called skid-row wines (wines fortified with additional alcohol and sweetener and sold in screwtop, half-pint bottles). Richard Maher, president of Christian Brothers Winery in St. Helena, California, who once was with E. & J. Gallo Winery, said he didn't think Christian Brothers should market a product to people, including many alcoholics, who were down on their luck. "Fortified wines lack any socially redeeming values," he said.

Major producers of the low-end category of wines, called "dessert" or "fortified" (sweet wines with at least 14 percent alcohol), saw their customers otherwise. Robert Hunington, vice president of strategic planning at Canandiaqua (a national wine producer whose product, Wild Irish Rose, was the number one low-end wine), said 60 percent to 75 percent of its "pure grape" Wild Irish Rose was sold in primarily black, inner-city markets. Hunington described Wild Irish Rose's customer in this $500 million market as "not super-sophisticated," lower middle-class, and low-income blue-collar workers and mostly men. However, Canandiaqua also estimated the annual national market for dessert category wine to be 55 million gallons; low-end brands accounted for 43 million gallons, with as much as 50 percent sold in pints (typically the purchase choice of winos—alcoholics with a dependency on wine). Daniel Solomon, a Gallo spokesman, said Gallo's Thunderbird had lost its former popularity in the black and skid-row areas and was consumed mainly by retired and older people who didn't like the taste of hard distilled products or beer.[1]

Tony Mayes, area sales representative for Montgomery Beverage Company, Montgomery, Alabama, said one-third of the total revenue from wine sales in the state of Alabama was from the sale of one wine product—Gallo's Thunderbird. Sales crossed all demographic lines. According to Mayes, a consumer developed a taste for wine through an education process that usually began with the purchase of sweet wines from the dessert category. He attributed the high sales of Thunderbird to the fact that the typical wine drinker in Alabama was generally not the sophisticated wine drinker found in California or New York.

Company History and Background

The E. & J. Gallo Winery, America's biggest winery, was founded by Ernest and Julio Gallo in 1933. More than 55 years later, the Gallo Winery was still a privately owned and family-operated corporation actively managed by the two brothers. The Gallo family had been dedicated to both building their brands and the California wine industry.

Prepared by Daniel C. Thurman, doctoral student, under the supervision of A. J. Strickland III, both of The University of Alabama.

[1]Alix M. Freedman, "Misery Market—Winos & Thunderbird Are a Subject Gallo Doesn't Like to Discuss," *The Wall Street Journal*, February 25, 1988, pp. 1, 18.

The Gallos started in the wine business working during their spare time in the vineyard for their father, Joseph Gallo. Joseph Gallo, an immigrant from the Piedmont region in northwest Italy, was a small-time grape grower and shipper. He survived Prohibition because the government permitted wine for medicinal and religious purposes, but his company almost went under during the Depression. During the spring of 1933, Joseph Gallo killed his wife and chased Ernest and Julio with a shotgun. He killed himself following their escape. Prohibition ended that same year, and the Gallos, both in their early '20s and neither knowing how to make wine, decided to switch from growing grapes to making wine. With $5,900 to their names, Ernest and Julio found two thin pamphlets on wine-making in the Modesto Public Library and began making wine.[2]

The Gallos had always been interested in quality and began researching varietal grapes in 1946. They planted more than 400 varieties in experimental vineyards during the 1950s and 1960s, testing each variety in the different growing regions of California for its ability to produce fine table wines. Their greatest difficulty was to persuade growers to convert from common grape varieties to the delicate, thin-skinned varietals because it took at least four years for a vine to begin bearing and perhaps two more years to develop typical, varietal characteristics. As an incentive, in 1967, Gallo offered long-term contracts to growers, guaranteeing the prices for their grapes every year, provided they met Gallo quality standards. With a guaranteed long-term "home" for their crops, growers could borrow the needed capital to finance the costly replanting, and the winery was assured a long-term supply of fine wine grapes. In 1965, Julio established a grower relations staff of skilled viticulturists to aid contract growers. This staff still counsels growers on the latest viticultural techniques.[3]

Private ownership and mass production were the major competitive advantages contributing to Gallo's success. Gallo could get market share from paper-thin margins and absorb occasional losses that stockholders of publicly held companies would not tolerate. Gallo was vertically integrated, and wine was its only business. While Gallo bought about 95 percent of its grapes, it virtually controlled its 1,500 growers through long-term contracts. Gallo's 200 trucks and 500 trailers constantly hauled wine out of Modesto and raw materials in. Gallo was the only winery to make its own bottles (2 million a day) and screw-top caps. Also, while most of the competition concentrated on production, Gallo participated in every aspect of selling its product. Julio was president and oversaw production, while Ernest was chairman and ruled over marketing, sales, and distribution. Gallo owned its distributors in about a dozen markets and probably would have bought many of the more than 300 independents handling its wines if laws in most states had not prohibited it.

Gallo's major competitive weakness over the years had been an image associated with screw tops and bottles in paper bags that developed because of its low-end dessert wine, Thunderbird.[4] There were stories, which Gallo denied, that Gallo got the idea for citrus-flavored Thunderbird from reports that liquor stores in Oakland, California, were catering to the tastes of certain customers by attaching packages of lemon Kool-Aid to bottles of white wine to be mixed at home.[5]

---

[2]Jaclyn Fierman, "How Gallo Crushes the Competition," *Fortune*, September 1, 1986, pp. 24–31.

[3]"The Wine Cellars of Ernest & Julio Gallo, a Brief History," a pamphlet produced by Ernest & Julio Gallo, Modesto, Calif.

[4]Fierman, "How Gallo Crushes the Competition."

[5]Freedman, "Misery Market."

Thunderbird became Gallo's first phenomenal success. It was a high-alcohol, lemon-flavored beverage introduced in the late 1950s. A radio jingle sent Thunderbird sales to the top of the charts on skid rows across the country: "What's the word? Thunderbird. How's it sold? Good and cold. What's the jive? Bird's alive. What's the price? Thirty twice." Thunderbird has remained a brand leader in its category ever since. In 1986, Ernest Gallo poured $40 million into advertising aimed at changing Gallo's image to one associated with quality wines.

Information on Gallo's finances was not publicly available, and the brothers maintained a tight lid on financial details. In a 1986 article, *Fortune* estimated that Gallo earned at least $50 million a year on sales of $1 billion. By comparison, the second leading winery, Seagram's (also the nation's largest distillery), had approximately $350 million in 1985 wine revenues and lost money on its best-selling table wines. *Fortune* stated that several of the other major Gallo competitors made money, but not much.[6]

Gallo produced the top-selling red and white table wines in the country. Its Blush Chablis became the best-selling blush-style wine within the first year of its national introduction. Gallo's award-winning varietal wines were among the top sellers in their classification. The company's Carlo Rossi brand outsold all other popular-priced wines. Gallo's André Champagne was by far the country's best-selling champagne, and E & J Brandy has outsold the number two and three brands combined. Gallo's Bartles & Jaymes brand was one of the leaders in the new wine cooler market.[7]

■ The U.S. Wine Industry

Wine sales in the United States grew from about 72 million gallons in 1940 to over 600 million gallons, accounting for retail sales in excess of $9 billion (see Exhibit 1). This retail sales volume had exceeded such major established grocery categories as detergents, pet foods, paper products, and canned vegetables. While wine consumption had grown at an astonishing rate, trends toward moderation and alcohol-free life-styles made this growth rate impossible to maintain. Nevertheless, annual growth was projected to be 3.2 percent through 1995.

Per capita consumption of wine was low in the late 1950s and early 1960s because wine drinking was perceived as either the domain of the very wealthy or the extreme opposite. "Fortified" dessert wines were the top-selling wines of the period. The first surge in consumption in the late 1960s was the result of the introduction of "pop" wines, such as Boones Farm, Cold Duck, and Sangrias. These wines were bought by baby boomers, who were now young adults. Their palates were unaccustomed to wine drinking and these wines were suited to them. By the mid-1970s, the pop wine drinkers were ready to move up to Lambruscos and white wine "cocktails," and per capita consumption increased (see Exhibit 2). The wine spritzer became the trend, still the alternative to more serious wines for immature palates. Just as this surge began to wane, wine coolers were introduced in 1982 and exploded on the market in 1983. Wine coolers were responsible for a 5 percent market surge in 1984 and

---

[6]Fierman, "How Gallo Crushes the Competition."

[7]"Gallo Sales Development Program," a pamphlet produced by Ernest & Julio Gallo, Modesto, Calif.

Marketing Management Cases

■ **Exhibit 1**
The National Wine
Market (1977–86)

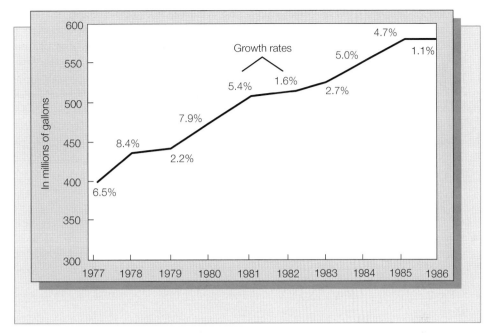

SOURCE: *National Beverage Marketing Directory*, 10th ed., 1988.

■ **Exhibit 2**
Per Capita
Consumption of Wine
in the U.S.

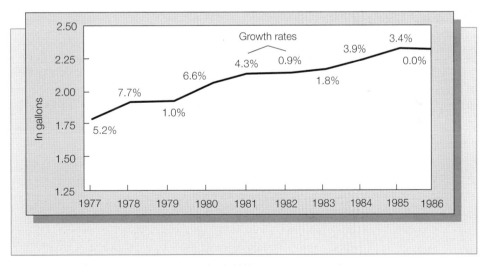

SOURCE: *National Beverage Marketing Directory*, 10th ed., 1988.

experienced four consecutive years of very high growth rates, rising 6 percent in
1987 to 72.6 million nine-liter cases.

The imported wines category enjoyed an upward growth rate from 6.6 percent of
the market in 1960 to a high of 27.6 percent in 1985 (see Exhibits 3 and 4). The category lost market share to 23.1 percent in 1986 primarily because of the shift from
Lambruscos to wine coolers. Additional factors were the weakening dollar and an
overall improved reputation for domestic wines.

■ **Exhibit 3**   Wine Production by Place of Origin (millions of nine-liter cases)

| Origin | 1970 | 1975 | 1980 | 1985 | 1986 | Average Annual Compound Growth Rate | | | Percent Change |
						1970–75	1975–80	1980–85	1985–86
California	82	115	139.5	133.2	133.3	7.0%	3.9%	−0.9%	−0.1%
Other states*	18	19	18.7	16.9	17.3	1.4	−0.3	−2.0	2.4
United States	100	134	158.2	150.1	150.6	6.1	3.3	−1.0	0.3
Imports	13	21	43.1	57.2	45.3	10.5	15.8	5.8	−20.8

*Includes bulk table wine shipped from California and blended with other state wines.
NOTE: Addition of columns may not agree because of rounding.
SOURCE: *Impact* 17, no. 11 (June 1, 1987), p. 4.

■ **Exhibit 4**   Market Share Trends in Wine Production

| Place Produced | 1970 | 1975 | 1980 | 1985 | 1986 | Share Point Change | | |
						1970–80*	1980–85	1985–86
California	73%	74%	69.3%	64.3%	68.0%	4	−5.0	3.8
Other states	16	12	9.3	8.2	8.8	− 7	1.1	0.7
United States	88	86	78.6	72.4	76.9	−10	−6.2	4.5
Imports	12	14	21.4	27.6	23.1	9	6.2	−4.5
Total†	100%	100%	100.0%	100.0%	100.0%	—	—	—

*1980 based on unrounded data.
†Addition of columns may not agree because of rounding.
SOURCE: *Impact* 17, no. 11 (June 1, 1987), p. 4.

■ **Exhibit 5**   1985 Share of U.S. Wine Market

Company	Percent
E. & J. Gallo Winery	26.1%
Seagram & Sons	8.3
Canandiaqua Wine	5.4
Brown-Forman	5.1
National Distillers	4.0
Heublein	3.7
Imports	23.4
All others	24.0
Total	100.0%

SOURCE: Jaclyn Fierman, "How Gallo Crushes the Competition," *Fortune,* September 1, 1986, p. 27.

There were about 1,300 wineries in the United States. *Fortune* identified the major market-share holders in the U.S. market in a September 1986 article. It showed Gallo as the clear leader, nearly outdistancing the next five competitors combined (see Exhibit 5).

A number of threats had faced the wine industry, not the least of which had been the national obsession with fitness and the crackdown on drunken driving. Americans drank 6.5 percent less table wine in 1985 than in 1984 (see Exhibits 6 and 7),

■ **Exhibit 6**   Shipments of Wine Entering U.S. Trade Channels by Type (millions of nine-liter cases)

Type	1970	1975	1980	1984	1985	1986	Average Annual Compound Growth Rate 1970–75	1975–80	1980–85	Percent Change* 1985–86
Table	55.9	88.9	150.8	170.9	159.2	147.1	9.9%	11.2%	1.1%	−7.4%
Dessert	31.1	28.2	19.1	15.5	14.3	14.7	−2.0	− 7.5	−5.7	3.2
Vermouth	4.2	4.2	3.7	3.0	2.9	2.7	—	− 2.5	−4.8	−6.9
Sparkling	9.3	8.4	12.7	19.7	19.4	18.7	−1.9	8.6	8.6	−4.5
Special natural	11.8	24.0	13.6	10.9	10.7	10.9	15.3	−10.7	−4.7	1.9
Imported specialty[†]	0.3	1.0	1.5	1.0	0.9	1.8	25.4	8.1	−9.7	104.7
Total[‡]	112.6	154.7	201.3	220.1	207.3	195.9	6.6%	5.4%	0.6%	−5.5%

*Based on unrounded data.
[†]Imported fruit wines and wine specialties (includes sangria and fruit-flavored wines).
[‡]Addition of columns may not agree because of rounding.

SOURCE: *Impact* 17, no. 11 (June 1, 1987), p. 3.

■ **Exhibit 7**   Share of Market Trends in Shipments of Wine Entering U.S. Trade Channels, by Type

Type	1970	1975	1980	1984	1985	1986	Share Point Change 1970–80*	1980–85	1985–86
Table	50%	57%	74.9%	77.2%	76.8%	75.1%	25	1.9	−1.7
Dessert	28	18	9.5	7.0	6.9	7.5	−18	−2.6	0.6
Vermouth	4	3	1.8	1.4	1.4	1.4	− 2	−0.4	[‡]
Sparkling	8	5	6.3	9.0	9.4	9.5	− 2	3.0	0.2
Special natural	10	16	6.8	5.0	5.2	5.6	− 3	−1.6	0.4
Imported specialty[†]	[‡]	1	0.7	0.5	0.4	0.9	+	−0.3	0.5
Total[†]	100%	100%	100.0%	100.0%	100.0%	100.0%	—	—	—

*1980 based on unrounded data.
[†]Addition of columns may not agree because of rounding.
[‡]Less than 0.05%.

SOURCE: *Impact* 17, no. 11 (June 1, 1987), p. 3.

and consumption was projected to be down another 5 percent in 1986. The industry answer to this problem had been introduction of wine coolers. Gallo's Bartles and Jaymes Coolers were number one until they lost the lead by only a slight margin to a Seagram's brand in 1987.

Another trend had been a shift toward a demand for quality premium wines made from the finest grapes. Premium wines increased market share from 8 percent in 1980 to 20 percent in 1986. Again, Gallo had sold more premium wine than any other producer, but Gallo's growth had been limited by its lack of snob appeal.[8]

Although more than 80 percent of the U.S. adult population enjoyed wine occasionally, Gallo's research indicated most Americans were still infrequent wine drinkers by global standards. Only about one in four Americans drank wine as often as once a week. Per capita consumption in the United States was less than 2.5 gallons per year, compared to about 20 gallons in some Western European countries.[9]

---
[8]Fierman, "How Gallo Crushes the Competition."
[9]"Gallo Sales Development Program."

Though the health-consciousness and alcohol-awareness of the 1980s had a moderating influence on wine growth patterns as consumers traded up in quality and drank less, long-term growth was expected to be steady but slower than that of the 1970s and early 1980s. Exhibit 8 provides drinking patterns for 1986. Personal disposable income was expected to grow in the United States through 1995; busy lifestyles contributed to more dining out; and sale of wine in restaurants was expected to increase. As the aging baby boomers grew in number and importance, their wine purchases were expected to increase. All these factors contributed to the projected average yearly increase in growth rate of 3.2 percent through 1995.[10]

■ **Exhibit 8**   Beverage Consumption Patterns

1986 National Beverage Consumption by Gender (Percent of volume):

Gender	Malt Beverages	Wine	Distilled Spirits	Coolers	Total Nonalcoholic Beverages	Total Beverages
Male	80.8%	51.6%	62.6%	44.9%	51.1%	52.7%
Female	19.2	48.4	37.4	55.1	48.9	47.3
Total	100.0%	100.0%	100.0%	100.0%	100.0%	100.0%

1986 National Alcoholic Beverage Consumption by Household Income (Percent of volume):

Household Income	Malt Beverages	Wine	Distilled Spirits	Coolers	Total Alcoholic Beverages
Under $15,000	26.1%	11.7%	19.7%	22.3%	26.5%
$15,000–$24,999	19.1	13.9	18.1	19.5	21.3
$25,000–$29,999	10.8	14.2	6.6	10.9	12.1
$30,000–$34,999	11.7	9.9	14.7	7.9	10.3
$35,000 & over	32.3	50.3	40.9	39.4	29.8
Total	100.0%	100.0%	100.0%	100.0%	100.0%

1986 National Beverage Consumption by Time of Day (Percent of volume):

Time of Day	Malt Beverages	Wine	Distilled Spirits	Coolers	Total Nonalcoholic Beverages	Total Beverages
Breakfast/morning	2.7%	2.1%	4.6%	1.5%	32.7%	30.6%
Lunch	6.8	5.8	4.2	4.4	20.8	19.8
Snack	27.5	19.0	31.9	27.0	10.9	12.0
Dinner	14.2	45.8	15.5	13.7	22.9	22.6
Evening	48.8	27.3	43.8	53.4	12.7	15.0
Total	100.0%	100.0%	100.0%	100.0%	100.0%	100.0%

1986 National Beverage Consumption by Location of Consumption (Percent of volume):

Location	Malt Beverages	Wine	Distilled Spirits	Coolers	Total Nonalcoholic Beverages	Total Beverages
Total home	64.6%	75.8%	61.4%	76.9%	76.1%	75.5%
Total away from home	35.4%	24.2%	38.6%	23.1%	23.9%	24.5%

SOURCE: *Impact* 17, no. 18 (September 15, 1987), pp. 3–4.

---

[10] "Coolers Providing Stable Growth," *Beverage Industry Annual Manual*, 1987.

■ The Dessert Wine Industry

Dessert wine represented a 55 million-gallon, $500 million industry. The dessert wine category, also called fortified wines, included wines that contained more than 14 percent alcohol, usually 18 percent to 21 percent. They were called fortified because they usually contained added alcohol and additional sugar or sweetener. This category included a group of low-end priced brands that had been the brunt of significant controversy. Canandiaqua's Wild Irish Rose had been the leading seller in this category, with Gallo's Thunderbird claiming second place, followed by Mogen David Wine's MD 20/20.[11]

Dessert wines had shown a decreasing trend both in amount of wine consumed and in market share from 1970 through 1985. However, the trend changed in 1986 when dessert wine's market share rose six-tenths of a share point to 7.5 percent of the total wine market (see Exhibit 7). The rise was attributed in large measure to the 19 percent federal excise tax increase on distilled spirits. An additional factor in the increase in the dessert wine category was the shift to fruit-flavored drinks, which also affected the soft drink industry and wine coolers.[12]

A number of factors indicated that the growth trend would continue for the $500 million dessert-wine category. The desire to consume beverages that contained less alcohol than distilled spirits and were less expensive than distilled spirits, the desire for fruit flavor, and the American trend toward eating out at restaurants more often contributed to the trend toward increased consumption of dessert wines. Additionally, the dessert wine category had survived relatively well with virtually no promotion or advertising. This had been possible because, of the category's 55 million gallons, low-end brands accounted for 43 million gallons, approximately 50 percent of which was sold in half pints; and this market had not been accessible by traditional advertising or promotion.

The dessert wine category had been a profitable venture because many of the wines in this category were made with less expensive ingredients, packaged in less expensive containers, and had usually been sold without promotion. Canandiaqua estimated that profit margins in this category were as much as 10 percent higher than those of ordinary table wines. Gallo said this was not true for its products, but it would not reveal the figures.

The low-end dessert wines were a solid business. *The Wall Street Journal* reported that, of all the wine brands sold in America, Wild Irish Rose was the number six best seller, Thunderbird was 10th, and MD 20/20 was 16th. In contrast to the growth expectations of other brands and categories, sales of these low-end brands were expected to be up almost 10 percent. Yet the producers of these top-selling wines distanced themselves from their products by leaving their corporate names off the labels, obscuring any link to their products. Paul Gillette, publisher of the *Wine Investor,* was quoted in a discussion of this unsavory market as saying: "Makers of skid-row wines are the dope pushers of the wine industry."[13]

---

[11]Freedman, "Misery Market."

[12]U.S. News and Research for the Wine, Spirits and Beer Executive," *IMPACT* 17, no. 11 (June 1, 1987): and *IMPACT* 17, no. 18 (September 15, 1987).

[13]Freedman, "Misery Market."

Case 32 Philip Morris Companies

Keith Robbins
George Mason University

Philip Morris (PM) is best known as a manufacturer and marketer of cigarettes. In fact, PM is the largest cigarette company in the United States, with a 42 percent share of the $70 billion industry.[1] However, over the past 30 years the company has been pursuing such a systematic diversification strategy that, in addition to cigarettes, the company now ranks as the second largest beer brewer in the United States and the second largest food processing company in the world.[2] The company's brands include Clark Chewing Gum, Louis Kemp Seafood, Miller, Miller Lite, Lowenbrau, Jell-O, Oscar Mayer, Sealtest, Maxwell House, Oroweat Baked Goods, Light Touch Desserts, and Marlboro, Virginia Slims, Bucks, Benson & Hedges, Merit, and Parliament (see Exhibit 1).

Philip Morris Companies was incorporated in Virginia on March 1, 1985, as the holding company for the diverse businesses of Philip Morris, Inc.[3] Today, the company is the largest private employer in Richmond.[4,5] The company's ambition has been and remains to be the most successful consumer packaged goods company in the world.[6]

This ambition is reflected in the company's mission statement presented in its 1991 annual report to shareholders: "We are a global consumer products company, manufacturing and marketing tobacco, food, and beer brands around the world. Our broad-based operations generate strong and growing returns for investors by answering consumer needs with low-priced, high-volume, quality products. We are committed to the highest standards of ethics and fairness in all of our activities and operations."

Current CEO Michael Miles (the first nonsmoking CEO at Philip Morris in 145 years) describes the company's strategy for meeting its goal as developing new products to meet emerging consumer trends, expanding geographically, and manufacturing and marketing globally.[7] The strategy appears to be working, as PM remains the largest and most profitable consumer products company in the world. In 1990, Philip Morris had risen to seventh on *Fortune*'s list of largest U.S. manufacturers, with sales approaching $50 billion.[8]

This case was prepared by Keith Robbins of the School of Business Administration at George Mason University. Development of this case was made possible by a grant from the Funds for Excellence Program of the State Council of Higher Education in Virginia.

[1] Standard & Poor's, *Industry Survey*, 1992.

[2] P. Sellers, "Can He Keep Philip Morris Growing?" *Fortune* 125, no. 7 (1992), pp. 86–92.

[3] Moody's *Industrial Manual*, 1991.

[4] "The Forbes 500 Ranking," *Forbes* 149, no. 9 (April 29, 1992), pp. 190–396.

[5] "The Fortune 500 Largest Industrial Corporations," *Fortune* 125, no. 8, 1991.

[6] PM, annual report, 1991.

[7] Ibid.

[8] "The Fortune 500."

■ **Exhibit 1**
PM Brands

Cigarettes: *Philip Morris U.S.A., Philip Morris International*
   Marlboro Brands
   Virginia Slims
   Benson & Hedges
   Merit
   Parliament

Beer: *The Miller Brewing Company*
   Miller Lite
   Miller High Life
   Milwaukee's Best
   Lowenbrau
   Sharp's

Food: *Kraft General Foods, Kraft International, General Foods International*
   Kraft Cheeses
   Maxwell House Coffees
   Louis Rich Turkey
   Oscar Mayer Luncheon Meats, Hot Dogs, and Bacon
   Louis Kemp Seafood Products
   Post Cereals
   Jell-O Brand Gelatin
   Kool-Aid
   Sealtest Dairy Products
   Breyers Dairy Products
   Light'n Lively Dairy Products

Financial: *Philip Morris Capital Corporation*
   Major equipment leasing programs for customers and suppliers

■ A History of Diversification VIA Acquistion

The company has a distinct heritage among U.S. tobacco companies; it is the only major company that was not formed when the Supreme Court broke up the James Duke American Tobacco Trust in 1912.[9] Since its inception in England, Philip Morris has emphasized growth through acquisitions (see Exhibit 2). The success of Philip Morris in growing the purchased companies into industry leaders is legendary.

In 1957, Philip Morris was sixth and last in the U.S. cigarette market. Under the leadership of Joseph F. Cullman III and by emphasizing the Marlboro brand, the company climbed to first place by the end of 1983. In 1970, it bought Miller Brewing, which at the time ranked seventh among U.S. brewers. By 1977, the company had leapfrogged up to second place behind Anheuser-Busch.[10]

Philip Morris has been able to fund its numerous acquisitions through its high-margin tobacco products, which continue to contribute a disproportionate share of corporate earnings. According to U.S. Labor Department statistics, retail tobacco

---

[9]R. Levering, M. Moskowitz, and M. Katz, *The 100 Best Companies to Work for in America* (Reading, Mass.: Addison-Wesley, 1984).

[10]Ibid.

■ **Exhibit 2**
PM's History of
Acquisitions

June 1944	Purchased cigarette-producing assets from Axton-Fisher Tobacco Company, Louisville, Kentucky, for $8.9 million cash.
Feb. 1945	Acquired 99% interest in Benson & Hedges through common stock exchange on a share-for-share basis.
Dec. 1959	Acquired an interest in C.A. Tabacalera Nacional Venezuela.
Dec. 1963	Acquired a substantial interest in Fabriques de Tabac Reunies, S.A., Swiss cigarette manufacturer and licensee.
April 1967	Acquired an interest in Kwara Tobacco Company, Ilorin, Nigeria.
June 1969	Purchased 53% interest in Miller Brewing Company for $130 million.
Jan. 1970	Acquired control of Mission Viejo, Cal., new city and land developer for $20 million.
Feb. 1977	Acquired Wisconsin Tissue Mills, Menasha, Wis., for 314,000 shares of common stock.
Feb. 1977	Purchased 97% of common stock of The Seven-Up Company, a soft-drink extract manufacturer, for $520 million.
June 1978	Purchased the international cigarette business of Liggett Group, Inc., (consisting of rights to sell L&M, Lark, Chesterfield, Eve, and Decade outside of United States) for $45 million.
Nov. 1985	Purchased General Foods Corporation for $5.6 billion.
Dec. 1988	Acquired, through merger with a subsidiary, Kraft, Inc., for approximately $12.9 billion.
Aug. 1990	Acquired Swiss-based coffee and confectionery company Jacobs Suchard AG for $4.1 billion.

SOURCE: Moody's *Industrial Manual,* 1991.

prices have increased on average 10 percent over the past 11 years. This rate of increase exceeds that of any other product, including hospital rooms and prescription drugs, over this period.[11,12] Cigarette manufacturers have found demand for tobacco to be price inelastic—smokers do not seem to decrease consumption despite price increases.

The acquisition spree has been motivated by the company's desire to lessen its dependence on tobacco. Many senior executives openly express concern about the company's heavy dependence on tobacco.[13] Thus, the central issue facing management at Philip Morris is the careful selection of the correct portfolio of consumer packaged goods that will allow the company to protect and build upon global operations. This mixture of businesses must smooth the transition away from tobacco dependence to avoid adverse consequences in an increasingly hostile environment.

■ Industry Segments

Philip Morris's significant industry segments consist of tobacco products, food products, beer, and financial services, including real estate. Operating revenues and operating profits for each of the segments over the past three years are detailed in Exhibit 3.

---

[11]J. Dagnoli, "Philip Morris Keeps Smoking," *Advertising Age* 61, no. 48 (1990), p. 20.

[12]E. Giltenan, "Profits Keep Rollin' in . . . ," *Forbes* 146, no. 1 (1992), pp. 152–53.

[13]Sellers, "Can He Keep."

■ **Exhibit 3**

Company Income and
Revenue Contribution
by Industry Segment
(in millions of dollars)

	1990	1989	1988
Operating revenues:			
Tobacco	$21,090 (41%)	$17,849 (40%)	$16,576 (53%)
Food	26,085 (51)	22,373 (51)	10,898 (35)
Beer	3,534 (7)	3,342 (7)	3,177 (10)
Financial services	460 (1)	516 (2)	622 (2)
Total operating revenues	$51,169	$44,080	$31,273
Operating profit:			
Tobacco	$ 5,596 (67%)	$ 5,063 (72%)	$3,846 (84%)
Food	2,205 (27)	1,580 (23)	392 (9)
Beer	285 (4)	226 (3)	190 (4)
Financial services	196 (2)	172 (2)	162 (3)
Total operating revenues	$ 8,282	$ 7,041	$ 4,590

The company's dependence on tobacco is evidenced by the fact that tobacco revenues account for 41 percent of the company's revenue and 68 percent of its income, though this dependence has lessened somewhat recently. Tobacco's profits represented 72 percent of the company's operating income in 1989. Food products accounted for approximately 27 percent of the company's operating profit in 1990, compared with 23 percent in 1989. In 1990, beer accounted for 7 percent of company revenues and 4 percent of income from operations.[14]

Tobacco Products

Philip Morris U.S.A. is responsible for the manufacture, marketing, and sale of tobacco products in the United States (including military sales), and Philip Morris International is responsible for the manufacture, marketing, and sale of such products outside the United States and for tobacco product exports from the United States.

Domestic Tobacco

Philip Morris sold 220.5 billion units of cigarettes in 1990, an increase of 1 billion units over 1989. Industry sales decreased 0.3 percent in 1990, compared to 1989. Over the past three years, Philip Morris has increased its sales and market share in the United States even though industry revenues have declined:

Year	Industry (billions of units)	Philip Morris	Market Share (%)
1990	522.1	220.5	42.2%
1989	523.9	219.5	41.9
1988	558.1	219.3	39.3

SOURCE: Wheat, First Securities, Inc.

---

[14]Moody's *Industrial Manual,* 1990, 1991, and 1992.

The major industry rivals in domestic tobacco are American Brands; RJR Nabisco, Inc.; B.A.T. Industries (parent of Brown and Williamson); Loews Corporation (parent of Lorillard); and the Liggett Group. The tobacco companies typically are operated as a subsidiary of diverse parent corporations. American Brands, in addition to its Pall Mall and Carlton cigarettes, markets Titleist golf balls, Jim Beam whiskey, and Master Locks. RJR Nabisco, in addition to its Winston, Salem, and Camel cigarettes, markets Oreos cookies, Planter's Peanuts, Del Monte Fruits, and Grey Poupon mustard. Loews Corporation, in addition to its Newport, Kent, and True cigarettes, owns CNA Financial Services, Inc.; Loews' theaters and hotels; and the Bulova Watch Company.

Philip Morris is the overwhelming leader in domestic market share, achieving 1.5 times the sales of its closest rival, RJR Nabisco (see Exhibit 4).

The Maxwell Consumer Report issued by Wheat, First Securities, Inc., has ranked Philip Morris U.S.A. as the leading cigarette company in the United States market since 1983. The company's best-selling brands are Marlboro, Benson & Hedges, Merit, Virginia Slims, and Cambridge. Philip Morris produces 4 of the top 10 selling brands in the United States, including best-selling Marlboro, which garnered 26 percent of the market in 1990 (see Exhibit 5).

Cigarette Industry Segments

Premium and Discount Brands.
Philip Morris premium brands consist of top 10 performers Marlboro, Benson & Hedges, Merit, and Virginia Slims. In the summer of 1991, PM spent a record $60 million to advertise Marlboro Medium, the

■ **Exhibit 4**
Domestic Cigarette Producers' Market Shares (percentage of industry units sold)

Company	1990	1989	1988	1987
Philip Morris	42.0%	42.2%	39.3%	37.8%
Reynolds	28.9	28.7	31.8	32.5
Brown & Williamson	10.8	11.4	10.9	11.0
Lorillard	7.8	7.1	8.2	8.2
American	6.8	7.0	7.0	6.9
Liggett	3.7	3.4	2.8	3.6

SOURCE: Standard & Poor's *Industry Surveys,* 1991.

■ **Exhibit 5**
Top 10 Domestic Cigarette Brands, 1990

Rank	Brand	Company	Units (billions)	Mkt. Share
1	Marlboro	Philip Morris	135.6	26%
2	Winston	Reynolds	46.4	9
3	Salem	Reynolds	32.0	6
4	Kool	Brown & Williamson	32.0	6
5	Newport	Lorillard	25.1	5
6	Camel	Reynolds	21.2	4
7	Benson & Hedges	Philip Morris	20.5	4
8	Merit	Philip Morris	20.3	4
9	Doral	Reynolds	19.2	4
10	Virginia Slims	Philip Morris	16.8	3

SOURCES: Moody's, Standard & Poor's.

first spinoff from the Marlboro brand in 20 years.[15] According to Marlboro VP Nancy Brennan Lund, the brand's 26 percent domestic market share should increase, though its volume probably will not.

A growing industry segment consists of the discount brands. After initially rejecting the idea of selling less-profitable brands, Philip Morris decided to enter the discount segment in 1985. This was prompted by the realization that many of its customers were switching to cheap cigarettes.[16,17] By 1991, Philip Morris became the market leader in the low-priced segment. Now, 17 percent of PM's U.S.A. sales are discount brands, such as Cambridge, Alpine, Bristol, and Bucks.

Industrywide discount brand sales have risen from 11 percent of sales in 1989 to 25 percent today and are expected to double again over the coming five years. Although Philip Morris is performing well in the discount segment, it is unable to put its formidable advertising might behind these brands for fear of cannibalizing its higher-margin premium brands. Recently tobacco companies have raised prices on the discount brands—for example, PM increased its prices by 20 percent on the discount brands.

According to industry analysts,[18,19,20] William Campbell, CEO of Philip Morris U.S.A., is determined to compete in every major cigarette category. The result is that the company now produces low-profit generic cigarettes. Generics, sometimes referred to as *black and whites,* are sold in places like Wal-Mart bearing such names as Best Buy, Basic, and Gridlock: The Commuter's Cigarette—a California brand. Campbell's predominant goal is to increase PM's domestic market share a point a year.

Low Tar. The low tar segment of the market consists of cigarettes delivering 15 milligrams (mg) or less of "tar" per cigarette. In 1990 and 1989, this market accounted for 57.4 percent and 55.5 percent of U.S. industry sales, respectively.[21,22] Philip Morris's low tar brands comprised 42.1 percent of the low tar market in 1990 and 42.8 percent in 1989. The low tar market includes a subsegment referred to as *ultra-low tar* that consists of brands that deliver 6 mg. or less of tar per cigarette. Ultra-low tar brands accounted for 11.3 percent of industry sales in 1990, compared with 10.8 percent in 1989. Philip Morris's ultra-low tar brands garnered 32.9 percent of this market in 1990 and 33.4 percent in 1989.

The low tar and ultra-low tar segments are growing, whereas the industry is in general decline. Philip Morris must ensure that its brands competing in these segments are able to achieve market share positions at least commensurate with its non-low tar cigarettes. This is currently not the case in the rapidly expanding ultra-low tar category, where Philip Morris lost market share during 1990.

---

[15]Sellers, "Can He Keep."

[16]C. Leinster, "Is Bigger Better for Philip Morris?" *Fortune* 119, no. 10 (1989), pp. 66–68+.

[17]A. Farnham, "From Soup to Nuts," *Fortune* 119, no. 1 (1989), pp. 43–47.

[18]S. Chakravraty, "Philip Morris Is Still Hungry," *Forbes* 145, no. 7 (1990).

[19]J. Dagnoli, "CEO Miles Sees International Growth for Philip Morris," *Advertising Age* April 8, 1991.

[20]Sellers, "Can He Keep."

[21]Moody's *Industrial Manual,* 1990 and 1991.

[22]S&P's *Industry Surveys,* 1990 and 1991.

International Tobacco

Worldwide tobacco industry sales have been growing at approximately 2 percent per year for the past several years. The United States exported $5 billion of tobacco products in 1990.[23] Philip Morris International's share of this market was 7.6 percent in 1990, compared with 6.7 percent in 1989. Marlboro is the leader. Its sales increased 13.2 percent in 1990. Its 206.9 billion units accounted for over 4.3 percent of the non-United States cigarette market. In particular, Philip Morris International has strong market share positions in Argentina, Australia, Finland, France, Germany, Hong Kong, Italy, Mexico, Saudi Arabia, and Switzerland, holding at least a 15 percent market share position in each.

Philip Morris is the leading cigarette exporter. Total cigarette exports to 111 foreign countries in 1990 were valued at $4.75 billion. The leading destinations were Asian (58 percent) and European (38 percent) countries. Two factors were primarily responsible for the growth in international sales: the lowering of trade barriers in Japan, Taiwan, and South Korea, and the weakened dollar.[24]

The market for cigarettes outside the United States in 1980 was 3.9 trillion units, with only 40 percent open to Western companies. Currently, international (non-U.S.) consumption stands at 4.9 trillion cigarettes a year, and Western companies now can deal with 95 percent of this market. PM sold 640 billion, or 11.6 percent of the world's cigarettes last year. That places PM second behind the Chinese government (1.5 trillion) in terms of total cigarette sales.

It is interesting that the company's global perspective largely resulted from its inability to penetrate domestic markets. When it was No. 6 among U.S. tobacco companies during the '50s, PM was the first U.S. manufacturer to begin selling its products in duty-free shops in foreign countries. It focused on those countries most frequented by U.S. travelers. Because many of these markets were closed to imports, the company was forced to license the sale of its cigarettes in the areas. The company reasoned that foreign-domestic managers could best oversee these foreign operations. As a result of this early emphasis on international operations, PM's management is more globally diverse than most: Miles and Mayer are Americans, Maxwell is a Scot, Campbell is Canadian, David Dangoor (PM U.S.A. marketing head) is Iranian. Two of the three bosses Miles vied with for the CEO position are Australian; the third is German.[25]

Though many foreign markets recently have opened access to U.S. firms, many protectionist policies are mitigating penetration. Many governments control prices, levy huge taxes, and even market state-owned brands (Taiwanese government's Long Life cigarettes; Japan's Dean cigarettes). Last year in Hong Kong, a 200 percent tax increase on imported cigarettes effectively doubled the price of a pack of Marlboros and cut PM's sales by 80 percent. The government later cut the tax in half after Philip Morris International employees and friends gathered 75,000 signatures.

In Italy, the company was implicated in a government investigation of cigarette imports that illegally avoided Italian taxes. Consequently, Italy imposed a one-month ban on Marlboro, Merit, and Muratti, a popular local blend.

---

[23]M. Levin, "U.S. Tobacco Firms Push Easily into Asian Markets," *Marketing News* 25, no. 2 (January 21, 1991), pp. 2, 14.

[24]Sellers, "Can He Keep."

[25]Ibid.

International tobacco's profit margins are half those of the United States. These margins are improving—they rose 24 percent in 1991 on a 14 percent increase in revenues. In the European community, sales volume has risen 25 percent during the past three years. PM management views Turkey as the "gateway to the east," particularly the former Soviet Union and Central Asia. PM recently broke ground on a $400 million cigarette factory there.[26]

In 1990, PM bought three deteriorating East German factories that churn out the leading local cigarette, F6. In a recent year, PM shipped 22 billion cigarettes to the former Soviet Union.[27]

Food

CEO Miles was formerly head of Kraft General Foods (KGF), which was formed after PM bought Kraft. He was instrumental in the successful implementation of Hamish Maxwell's diversification strategy. Miles's promotion to chief executive helped ease the tension between PM and General Foods that had existed since the latter's hostile takeover. Miles's insight into the food business permitted him to ignore pessimistic forecasts for traditionally strong brands, such as Maxwell House and Post. Many insiders felt that these brands could expect, at best, marginal increases in volume. Miles reemphasized growth and, as a consequence, sales of such leading products as Kool-Aid, Jell-O, and Grape Nuts cereal are expanding again.[28,29] Operating profits in General Foods exceeded $700 million in 1991, versus $433 million in 1989.

Kraft's cheese division has not fared as well. Sales have stagnated. Analysts blame this on Miles's continued price hikes in the face of stable prices for private label cheeses. During 1991, Kraft began cutting prices in an attempt to regain lost market share from the private labels. However, the retailers—who profit quite nicely off their own private label brands—were naturally reluctant to pass the cuts on down to the consumers.[30] The division experienced a shortfall of $125 million between anticipated and realized cheese profits. The problems of the cheese division also have resulted from increased health consciousness among consumers. Cheese products are notoriously high in saturated fat and cholesterol. As more consumers become sensitive to nutritional guidelines espoused by leading health agencies, overall demand for cheese likely will continue to decline. Kraft's products in general and cheese products in particular typically are not purchased by health conscious consumers due to their high fat content.

Richard Mayer, president and CEO of KGF, has two primary ideas for stimulating the food division: (1) to get market research and computer people working in teams with brand managers to make better use of scanner-generated sales data and (2) to distribute all KGF products within a particular region from a single warehouse location to serve customers better.[31] Presently, grocers buy 10 percent of all their grocery items from KGF but draw from many warehouses. These strategies should help KGF respond more expeditiously to market trends and competitors' moves.

---

[26]Moody's *Industrial Manual,* 1992.

[27]PM, annual reports, 1991 and 1992.

[28]Dagnoli, "CEO Miles Sees."

[29]Sellers, "Can He Keep."

[30]Ibid.

[31]Dagnoli, "CEO Miles Sees."

■ Philip Morris as an Employer

Philip Morris consistently is ranked as one of the more progressive employers in the United States. Levering, Moskowitz, and Katz included PM among their listing of *The 100 Best Companies to Work for in America.*

According to James Bowling, director of public relations and public affairs, caring about its employees is what distinguishes Philip Morris: "everybody bought tobacco competitively at auction; manufactured cigarettes in Kentucky, Virginia, and North Carolina; used essentially the same machinery; paid the same union wages; and sold through the same wholesalers and retailers. Therefore, they said that, if there is going to be a difference, it will have to be in the people. As simplistic and corny as that seems, it has been the guiding principle here since that day. We have always tried to treat our people better—by being the first or among the first with amenities and working pleasantries."

One survey of senior managers conducted by an independent auditor, showed very high satisfaction with the company. The benefits package includes long- and short-term disability compensation. Employees automatically are insured for twice their annual salary, and there is a survivor income benefit that, in the event of employee death, would start paying, after four years, 25 percent of last base pay to surviving spouses every month plus 5 percent of your last base pay to each surviving child. There is an employee stock ownership plan and employees who smoke—and the majority do—are entitled to one free carton of cigarettes per week.[32]

Philip Morris was one of the first companies to employ blacks in sales positions. One out of every four persons who works for the company is a minority-group member—and minorities hold 14 percent of positions classified as "officials and managers."[33]

The Richmond cigarette factory is a futuristic plant completed in 1974 at a cost of over $200 million—at the time the largest capital investment in the company's history. The plant boasts of parquet floors and floor-to-ceiling windows overlooking elaborate ornamental gardens.[34]

■ 1991 Performance and Future Prospects

Philip Morris currently sells more than 3,000 items. The value of the shares of stock outstanding reached $74 billion in December 1991 (trading at $75 per share) exceeding the value of all other U.S. companies except Exxon. Among the 1991 highlights: revenues increased 10 percent to $56.5 billion; operating income grew 14 percent to $9.9 billion; unit sales increased nearly 200 million in the United States over 1990, whereas U.S. industry volume decreased by 13 billion units.

Despite many bright spots, particularly in fat-free products, beverages, and breakfast cereals, overall results in North American food businesses were lower than expected. Volume in the brewing business grew 0.4 percent despite a doubling of the federal excise tax at the beginning of the year. Performance in 1991 allowed the

---

[32]Levering et al., *The 100 Best.*

[33]PM, annual report, 1991.

[34]Levering et al., *The 100 Best.*

company to increase dividends by 22.1 percent to an annualized rate of $2.10 per share, the 24th consecutive year of dividend increases.[35]

According to Miles, the company will throw off free cash of more than $21 billion. This is the excess after capital expenditures, dividends, and taxes—and Philip Morris can use it either to pay for acquisitions or to buy back stock, or both. The company currently realizes $15 billion annually from international operations (more than Coca-Cola, PepsiCo, and Kellogg combined). Marlboro is especially strong internationally in Asia, Eastern Europe, and the former Soviet Union.[36]

As portrayed in the company's consolidated income statement (Exhibit 6), Philip Morris U.S.A.'s sales went up 9 percent to $9.4 billion in 1991, and operating profits rose even faster to reach $4.8 billion. Operating margin rose a fabulous 51 percent, up from 42 percent seven years ago. Philip Morris's gains in market share are impressive, too—43.3 percent of total U.S. cigarette sales today, versus 35.9 percent in 1985.

The primary objective at Philip Morris traditionally has been to achieve 20 percent annual earnings growth. Hamish Maxwell hit the mark each of the last five years, but Miles is facing a more maleficent marketplace.

The company is in a very solid financial position as it remains one of the more liquid U.S. companies. It often is referred to as the "King of Cash" (see Exhibit 7).

■ **Exhibit 6**   Philip Morris Companies, Inc: Consolidated Income (in millions of dollars)

	1991	1990	1989	1988	1987
Operating revenues	$56,458	$51,169	$44,080	$31,273	$27,650
Cost of sales	25,612	24,430	21,868	13,565	12,183
Excise taxes on products	8,394	6,846	5,748	5,882	5,416
Gross profit	22,452	19,893	16,464	11,826	10,051
Marketing, admin., & research	13,331	11,499	9,290	7,304	5,956
Amortization of goodwill	499	448	385	125	105
Operating income	8,622	7,946	6,789	4,397	3,990
Interest & other debt expense	1,651	1,635	1,731	670	646
Earnings before income taxes	6,971	6,311	5,058	3,727	3,344
Provision for income taxes	3,044	2,771	2,112	1,663	1,502
Earnings before cumulative effect of acct. change	3,927	3,540	2,946	2,064	1,842
Cumulative effect of acct. change for income taxes	(921)			273	
Net earnings	3,006	3,540	2,946	2,337	1,842
Retained earnings (B.O.Y.)	10,960	9,079	7,833	6,437	5,344
Common dividends	(1,765)	(1,432)	(1,159)	(941)	(749)
Four-for-one stock split			(478)		
Exercise of stock options	(172)	(218)	(63)		
Other	9	(9)			
Retained earnings (E.O.Y.)	12,038	10,960	9,079	7,833	6,437

[35]PM, annual report, 1992.

[36]Sellers, "Can He Keep."

■ **Exhibit 7**   Comparative Consolidated Balance Sheet as of December 31 (in millions of dollars)

	1991	1990	1989	1988	1987
Assets					
Consumer products:					
Cash & equivalents	$ 126	$ 146	$ 118	$ 168	$ 90
Receivables, net	4,121	4,101	2,956	2,222	2,065
Inventories	7,445	7,153	5,751	5,384	4,154
Other current assets	902	967	555	377	245
Total current assets	12,594	12,367	9,380	8,151	6,554
Property, plant, & equipment	15,281	14,281	12,357	11,932	9,398
Less accum. depreciation	5,335	4,677	3,400	3,284	2,816
Property account net	9,946	9,604	8,951	8,648	6,582
Other assets	20,306	20,712	17,251	16,992	5,411
Total consumer products assets	42,846	42,683	35,588	33,791	18,547
Total financial & real estate assets	4,538	3,886	3,440	3,169	2,890
Total assets	$47,384	$46,569	$39,028	$36,960	$21,437
Liabilities					
Total current liabilities	11,824	11,360	8,943	7,969	5,164
Total consumer products liabilities	31,344	31,460	26,108	26,664	12,234
Total financial & real estate assets	3,528	3,162	2,849	2,617	2,330
Stockholders' Equity					
Common stock ($1, par)		935	935	240	240
Additional paid-in capital				252	272
Earnings reinvested in business		10,960	9,079	7,833	6,437
Currency translation adj.		561	143	117	146
Net stockholders' equity	12,512	11,344	9,871	8,208	6,803
Total	$47,384	$45,956	$38,828	$37,489	$21,367

■ Threats To Philip Morris's Traditional Level of Performance

The Declining American Cigarette Industry

Domestic cigarettes contributed $4.8 billion in operating income last year, roughly half the corporate total. But the American cigarette industry is declining 2 to 3 percent per year. Additionally, the trend is toward budget brands with smaller profit margins and away from premium products, such as Marlboro, Merit, Virginia Slims, and Benson & Hedges. According to industry analysts, the bargain brands—including those marketed by Philip Morris—pose more of a threat to the 20 percent target than the product liability litigation now pending Supreme Court review.[37]

Slowing Processed Food Sales

Recession intensifies price elasticity, so shoppers are moving toward less-costly private label brands. Increasing consumer awareness of ingredients has invited comparison between the private labels and national brands, such as Kraft General Foods (KGF). In many cases, there is no substantive difference. KGF's North American revenues rose only 1 percent last year. Excluding special charges, operating income increased a disappointing 8 percent.

---

[37]S&P's *Industry Survey,* 1992.

Antismoking Litigation and Legislation

Investors remain concerned about tobacco's legal status. This hinged on a Supreme Court ruling expected during the summer of 1992. The court will decide whether the federally mandated warning labels on cigarette packs—required since 1966—insulate tobacco companies from liability claims in state courts.

■ Smoking and Health Related Issues

Since 1964, the Surgeon General of the United States and the Secretary of Health and Human Services have released reports alleging a correlation between cigarette smoking and numerous physical maladies, including cancer, heart disease, and chronic diseases of the respiratory system. Recent reports continue to emphasize the health warnings from the earlier studies and additionally focus on the addictive nature of smoking and the demographics of smokers. In particular, the prevalence and growth rates of smoking among women and African-Americans have received much publicity.[38]

Federal law requires marketers of cigarettes in the United States to include one of four warnings on a rotating basis on cigarette packages and advertisements:

SURGEON GENERAL'S WARNING: Smoking Causes Lung Cancer, Heart Disease, Emphysema, and May Complicate Pregnancy.
SURGEON GENERAL'S WARNING: Quitting Smoking Now Greatly Reduces Serious Risk to Your Health.
SURGEON GENERAL'S WARNING: Smoking by Pregnant Women May Result in Fetal Injury, Premature Birth, and Low Birth Weight.
SURGEON GENERAL'S WARNING: Cigarette Smoke Contains Carbon Monoxide.

In addition to the warnings, federal regulations require that cigarettes sold in the United States disclose the average tar and nicotine deliveries per cigarette.

A more recent concern has been the alleged health risks to nonsmokers from what is most often referred to as *passive smoking* or *environmental tobacco smoke* (ETS). In 1986, the U.S. Surgeon General issued a report claiming that nonsmokers were at increased risk of lung cancer and respiratory illness due to ETS. The Environmental Protection Agency is currently at work on a report detailing the risks of ETS. The findings concerning ETS have been instrumental in the passage of legislation that restricts or bans cigarette smoking in public places and places of employment.

Television and radio advertising of cigarettes has been prohibited in the United States since 1971. Since this time, regulatory agencies have acted to further restrict or prohibit smoking in certain public places, on buses, trains, and airplanes, and in places of employment.

Such restrictions are not exclusive to the United States. Many foreign countries have restricted or prohibited cigarette advertising and promotion, increased taxes on cigarettes, and openly campaigned against smoking. Thailand, Hong Kong, France, Italy, and Portugal all have implemented cigarette advertising bans. This virtually precludes successful introduction of new brands in these countries. The European Economic Community (EEC) is contemplating a ban on tobacco advertising

---

[38]Ibid.

in newspapers, magazines, and billboards.[39] More recently, the Asian Consultancy on Tobacco Control, a 14-nation consortium, has been formed to combat smoking in this region. Thus, some countries have tighter restrictions than the United States.

■ Litigation

Approximately 50 court cases are pending, wherein plaintiffs are seeking damages from leading United States cigarette manufacturers. The litigation involves alleged cancer and other health maladies directly resulting from cigarette smoking. Philip Morris was a defendant in 23 actions pending as of March 1, 1991, compared with 24 at the same point in 1990 and with 32 in 1989. The number of court cases appears to have stabilized.

Philip Morris's primary defense tactic has been based on seeking a preemption of liability based on the Federal Cigarette Labeling and Advertising Act. Five federal courts have ruled that the cigarette labeling act does protect cigarette manufacturers from some liability claims. Conversely, the Supreme Court of New Jersey and one of the Texas appellate courts ruled that the cigarette labeling act does not limit the liability of the cigarette manufacturers.

As with any court case the outcome is uncertain. A finding in favor of the plaintiff would have the effect of denying preemption of liability on the basis of the existence of the cigarette warning labels. This could entice additional litigation against cigarette manufacturers. Philip Morris remains confident that, even in this worst-case scenario, the lawsuits will not pose a substantive threat to its overall financial health.

■ The Company's Position

No tobacco company has ever lost a liability case or paid a penny to settle; juries thus far have ruled that smokers have been adequately warned cigarettes can ruin their health. According to John McMillin of Prudential Securities: "A Supreme Court ruling against the industry has limited downside for the stock because worries have already pulled down the price. A tobacco victory could mean the end of major litigation risk and take Philip Morris's stock up 15 to 20 percent."

Tobacco use is one of the most widely discussed health issues around the world. The company's position was stated by CEO Miles in a letter to shareholders in 1992: "Given the general availability of information concerning the health issue, we regard smoking as a voluntary lifestyle decision that need not be subjected to new marketing or use restrictions."

He added: "While we believe that consumers are aware of the claimed health risks of smoking, nonetheless in February 1992 we took actions to begin placing the U.S. Surgeon General's health warning on all our cigarette packages worldwide where warnings are not currently required. This initiative applies to brands manufactured in the United States for export, as well as to those produced overseas by our affili-

---

[39]P. Engardio, "Asia: A New Front in the War on Smoking," *Business Week* (Industrial/Technical Edition), no. 3201 (February 25, 1991), p. 66.

ates and affected licensees. We are taking these steps because the lack of warning on a relatively small number of packages—approximately 10 percent of our volume—has become an issue out of proportion to its importance."

Continuing, Miles stated: "Moreover in the United States we are acting to increase awareness and enforcement of minimum age purchase restrictions on our tobacco products through multimillion-dollar programs involving advertising, trade relations, and family education."

■ Future Prospects

According to Miles, the company has no plans to diversify outside of packaged goods. Since acquisition opportunities in tobacco are limited, most analysts predict a major food acquisition, probably in Western Europe within the coming year or so. In 1990, PM bought one of Europe's largest coffee and chocolate companies, Jacobs Suchard, well known for Toblerone candy bars. The $4.1 billion deal made PM the third-largest food marketer in Europe, behind Nestlé and Unilever. The company's European revenues today are approaching $10 billion in food. Nestlé has about $15 billion in European sales but, with acquisitions, PM figures it will grow faster.

There is much speculation centered on acquisition targets. One is rumored to be H. J. Heinz, a European powerhouse. PepsiCo is not considered a likely target but Cadburry Schweppes is. Another suspected target is Paris-based BSN, which would help PM penetrate the lucrative French cheese market with its Velveeta, Cracker Barrel, and Kraft Natural brands.

For Miles to meet the company's goals, PM must reach $85 billion in sales by 1995, with net income of $9 billion.[40] The future of the tobacco industry, particularly domestically, is cloudy. With numerous product liability lawsuits pending and increasing antismoking sentiments, PM must face the increasingly realistic possibility that cigarette smokers will become virtually nonexistent. As pessimistic as this may sound, a more threatening though less-likely scenario exists: cigarette manufacturing could be banned by the FDA. Within the coming five years, Miles must reposition the firm so it may withstand the effects of declining tobacco income.

---

[40]Sellers, "Can He Keep."

Case 33 Black Diamond Equipment, LTD.

Steven J. Maranville
University of St. Thomas

Madeleine E. Pullman
Colorado State University

Jeff Jamison looked above at the glistening ice and snow of the frozen waterfalls. He had waited three weeks for the ice to get to this perfect condition, thick enough to support his weight, and the correct consistency for holding the picks of the two axes in his hands and the tooth-covered crampons on his feet. On this Saturday in early January of 1993, he was trying out a new axe, the Black Prophet, a state-of-the-art climbing tool with a light weight, composite handle, and innovative head design produced by Black Diamond Equipment, Ltd. Everyone in the mountaineering world was talking about the Black Prophet's novel design and waiting for the tool to enter the stores in the coming months. Jeff was lucky enough to have a connection with one of Black Diamond's sales representatives and thus had access to the new Black Prophet before its formal release to the market.

At the top of the last pitch of the climb, he sank the Black Prophet in the ice and suddenly felt a disconcerting snap. Jeff watched with disbelief as pieces of the broken axe plummeted thousands of feet to the canyon floor. As he fought off panic, Jeff realized that he would be forced to descend with only one axe, a doable but challenging feat. During the long, arduous descent, all Jeff could think about was how a tool like that one could have left Black Diamond's factory.

The following Monday, January 4, 1993, Mellie Abrahamsen, Black Diamond's new quality assurance manager, a recent MBA graduate from the University of Utah, entered her office and turned on her computer to scan her e-mail. The news of the axe incident was echoing throughout the plant. Research and Development, Production, Customer Service, Marketing, and the president were all demanding an explanation and a plan. With all the excitement over the new design, preseason orders for the Black Prophet had exceeded expectations. Although the tool was on back order for many customers, the first production run of the axe had already been shipped to mountaineering stores throughout the world. Highlighted at the top of Abrahamsen's e-mail listing was a priority message from Peter Metcalf, president of Black Diamond, calling an emergency meeting with all department heads to develop a plan for handling the crisis.

Monday Morning Meeting

By 9:00 A.M. Black Diamond's top management team was huddled around the square butcher-block table that filled the center of Metcalf's congested corner office. As Mellie Abrahamsen approached, she could see into Metcalf's office through the two large windows that faced the shop floor. Because she was new to the company, many of the artifacts peculiar to Black Diamond still caught her attention.

Metcalf's office walls were decorated with framed photographs of mountain-climbing and skiing adventures. The management team members sitting around the table were dressed casually; many were wearing Black Diamond sportswear—T-shirts and sweaters with the Black Diamond insignia. Abrahamsen squeezed through the office and found a seat next to Metcalf, from which she had a view out the windows.

Metcalf spoke anxiously to the group: "This incident is a devastating blow. Thank goodness the guy didn't get hurt; but now every one of our axes out there is suspect. If we have to issue a recall on the product, that will kill our axe business. If we have to discontinue our axe program, all the European competitors will step in and copy the technology that we worked so long to perfect. Yet think of the liability implications of an accident from this tool! How could this have happened? I thought this axe had the latest and greatest technology! We've never had problems like this with our regular mountaineering axes."

Maria Cranor, the marketing manager, added to Metcalf's fervent speech: "If customers see this axe as being of poor quality, we'll be forced to cease the axe program. But worse, if customers think Black Diamond is a company that markets unsafe products, our whole business is in jeopardy! Black Diamond must not lose its leadership image."

"My sales representatives are having a fit," Stan Smith, manager of customer service, proclaimed loudly. "They have huge back orders for the axe, and the retail shops have several customers a day asking about the tool. You folks know how this industry is—rumors about tool failures and accidents get around fast."

In a despondent tone, the designer of the Black Prophet, Chuck Brainard, said, "I can't believe this nightmare. Just as we were sitting on top of the world with the most innovative design to enter the market in years—all the competition taken by surprise, and a good ice-climbing season ahead—a major stroke of bad luck hits."

"I can't help but think," said Stan Brown, the production manager, "that the cause of the axe's failure is in its design. It's great to be innovative, but I think the design is so innovative that it just doesn't work."

"Now wait a minute, Stan," Metcalf interjected. "I don't want this to deteriorate into finger pointing."

Brainard spoke up. "No, no, that's all right, Peter. Stan might be right. Maybe we did go too far."

Metcalf went on: "We don't know all the facts. So let's stay focused and not jump to conclusions. This is a companywide problem."

Trying to refocus the group, Cranor said, "We tried to cut the lead time on this project so that we would have at least a year of sales before the French, Swiss, and other U.S. competitors could copy our concept and steal our market share. We have a reputation as a high-quality and innovative design company. This incident is potentially very damaging to our reputation as the market leader for innovation."

"We've got to nip this one in the bud and find a way to reassure our customer base," contended Smith. "I need an answer as soon as possible."

John Bercaw, manager of research and development, said, "Stan, I appreciate the urgent need that you're feeling with regard to handling customer concerns, but we need more than a quick fix. We need to find out why the failure occurred and to put systems in place to prevent this from happening again."

"I agree," Metcalf said. "As I said, this is a companywide problem."

Brainard attempted to clarify the situation. "As I see it, the possible sources of the failure are design, materials, and/or assembly."

"I can speak about the development phase of the project," stated Bercaw. "We worked hard to develop this axe and cut down on the lead time between the conceptualization and production of the final tool. Peter, you know we've been under tremendous pressure to have this new axe into the production phase and on the market in under two years."

Metcalf nodded. "That's been our strategy," he said, "being the 'firstest with the mostest.'"

Bercaw continued. "This project has been a real struggle: we've been working with all sorts of new technologies, like composite construction and modular tool design. The vendors normally don't make tools for these types of applications. They've had a hard time meeting our specifications, and many of the vendors don't want to work on our products because of potential liability implications."

"What about the assembly?" asked Metcalf.

Brown answered, "Well, the shop worked like crazy to get those axes out for the winter season and I put my best people on the rush assembly. The shop has been really taxed, what with the increasing growth rate for all our climbing and mountaineering products. We're always scrambling to meet the back orders. We need more people and new machines to keep up with this demand and improve our quality."

Metcalf persisted. "Do you know of anything in particular that may have been out of the ordinary during assembly?"

Brown replied, "I'd have to talk to Brian, our lead assembler, to see if he has any clues about why that axe could have failed in the field."

Metcalf turned to his left, where Black Diamond's newest management team member was sitting. "I realize that this is all new to you and that you came in after the fact, so I doubt the Quality Assurance Department can do much about this situation now."

Caught somewhat by surprise, Abrahamsen pulled her thoughts together and said, "Since this job is a newly created position, I wasn't here during the design development and testing phase. I would like to see the procedures and testing information on the production lot of axes. Black Diamond wants to be ISO 9000-certified, and we would need to have all those documents for ISO 9000 certification anyway, so this is a good starting place. Meanwhile, I think we should bring all the field axes back for inspection to reinforce customer confidence and prevent what happened on Saturday from happening again."

Looking out of his office's windows, Metcalf pointed to the shop floor and remarked, "Isn't that Brian walking through the shop? Ask him to come in."

Brian Palmer, the lead assembler, entered Metcalf's office. There was no place to sit, so he remained standing. Metcalf explained to Brian the purpose for bringing him into the meeting. Brian indicated that he had heard about the climbing incident involving the Black Prophet.

Metcalf continued. "Brian, we're not on a witch hunt; we're trying to understand the full range of factors that could have contributed to the tool's failure. What can you tell us about the assembly?"

Brian spoke frankly: "I personally put together all of those axes. We didn't have any procedures, because it was the first time we had made a production lot. Normally when we work on a new product, we go through a learning curve trying to figure out the best assembly method. We make so many different types of products in the shop, it's really like a craft shop. And I'm not even sure if I have the most up-to-date prints right now. The vendor had a lot of trouble casting all those parts to the exact dimensions. But I was able to find enough parts that seemed to fit, and with a little extra elbow grease, I hammered the pieces together. I had to work overtime to meet the deadline and get all the preliminary orders out to the customers. But that's what matters—pleasing the customer."

"But is creating a defective axe really pleasing the customer?" questioned Abrahamsen. "What good is it to be first to market if the product fails in the field? Sure, we have to get to market fast; but we also have to make the axe right the first time. The way we deal in the short term with the Black Prophet situation will have some long-term implications for Black Diamond's strategy. I think we should examine the new-product introduction process as well as the ongoing production processes to see how we can prevent this type of thing from happening in the future."

■ The Market for Mountaineering Equipment

The established customer for mountaineering products, including mountaineering skis, had traditionally been the serious international mountaineer—professionals as well as expert amateurs. Some dedicated mountaineers worked as professional guides and explorers; nonprofessionals had other jobs, but both professionals and amateurs spent their vacations and weekends climbing in their local areas and traveling throughout the world attempting to conquer remote peaks. This traditional customer base had been primarily in North America, eastern and western Europe, Japan, and Korea, although limited numbers of participants were from other countries.

Mountaineering was as popular in Europe as basketball was in the United States, with mountaineering stars earning high incomes through competitions, product endorsements, and other media exposure. Because of the long history of climbing in Europe, the European market was the biggest segment in the world climbing market, with 10 percent of the market in France alone. Not only did the adult urban European population prefer to spend vacations in mountain villages, but increasingly younger generations of Europeans were forsaking crowded beaches for mountain holidays revolving around mountain sports.

Starting in the 1980s, media exposure had brought mountain sports to previously ignored market segments throughout the world. Rock climbing and mountaineering images had become popular for advertising many types of products and for adding "color" to music videos and movie plots. Because of this exposure, teenage and recreational customers—predominantly in the U.S. market—represented high-growth segments, with the noticeable growth rate in the mid-1980s erupting into an explosive rate of 40 percent in the early 1990s. Customers in this growing market segment had no intention of traveling the world looking for untouched and ever more challenging peaks; instead, they climbed and skied purely for fun in their local and national resort areas.

Customarily, people wishing to learn mountain sports would employ guide services and schools for acquiring the necessary skills. The newer converts, however, were bypassing this conventional route by going to indoor climbing gyms or learning skills from friends. Many industry experts speculated that the breakdown of the conventional training methods would contribute to an increased lack of knowledge regarding mountaineering safety and lead to increased accident rates. In turn, accidents would increase the chances of litigation for all firms involved in the industry. These trends concerned mountain-sports firms worldwide.

■ Competition in the Mountaineering Equipment Industry

Located in Salt Lake City, Utah, Black Diamond Equipment, Ltd., was a major player in the burgeoning international mountaineering industry, on both domestic and global fronts. Black Diamond manufactured and distributed a full range of products for mountain sports, from rock-climbing gear to mountaineering and backcountry skis, and faced few domestic or global competitors whose business was on a similar scale. (Exhibit 1 offers a company/product profile of the mountaineering industry.)

The industry that served the mountaineering market consisted of three groups: retailers, wholesalers, and manufacturers.

Retailers

The retail businesses serving the market's diverse variety of mountaineering customers were one of three types. The first group, the "core" mountaineering shops, were small retail operations specializing in products specific to mountaineering such as ropes, climbing protection, climbing axes, expedition clothing, packs, harnesses, and information guides for local and national sites. Because these shops were usually located in mountain areas such as the Rocky Mountains or the Alps, the shop personnel were experts in the special tools and applications for their regions. In addition, these employees often had personal knowledge of other locations around the world.

Mountaineering shops usually carried products made in their region with specialized products from other countries. The core shops competed on the basis of the expertise of their personnel and their stock of technically appropriate tools. These retailers specialized in high-quality, cutting-edge-technology products. Prices were relatively high. The majority of their customers were highly skilled mountaineers. Black Diamond operated a small retail shop in this category located next to its Salt Lake City manufacturing facility. Black Diamond's full product range sold well in its own shop as well as in other core shops.

Because of their remote locations, many core shops made effective use of catalogs as a direct-marketing tool. Several mail-order companies, including Black Diamond's mail-order division, competed in this core area, selling products both nationally and internationally.

The second group, mom-and-pop stores, were also small retail outlets, but they sold all types of equipment, from camping and backpacking equipment to bikes and skis. The product mix varied depending on the geographical location. Most of these stores carried a limited assortment of climbing products—usually ropes, harnesses, and carabiners (small clips used in all climbing applications to attach the climber to rock or snow). The personnel in mom-and-pop stores usually had limited technical knowledge of the products being sold.

The third group consisted of sporting goods and department store chains, ranging in size from regional chains such as Eastern Mountain Sports (seven stores) to national chains such as Recreational Equipment Inc. (REI) (40 stores). These stores, which were located in major cities with access to mass markets, had extensive outdoor clothing departments, tents, stoves, canoes and kayaks, sleeping bags, bikes, skis, and so on. Products in each category were selected for volume sales. Thus, in the climbing department, the product line covered the needs of entry-level or intermediate recreational climbers. The expertise of department store personnel was, however, generally limited.

■ **Exhibit 1**
Comparative Market
Shares of
Mountaineering
Industry Competitors,
by Product

Product Category	Manufacturers	National Market Share %	International Market Share %
Carabiners	Black Diamond	50	10
	Omega	10	3
	SMC	10	3
	Wild Country	10	20
	DMM	10	20
	Petzl	5	30
	MSR (REI)	5	4
Climbing protections	Black Diamond	50	20
	Metolius	20	10
	Lowe	10	10
	Wild Country	10	25
	DMM	10	25
Harnesses	Black Diamond	45	10
	Petzl	20	50
	REI	20	
	Blue Water	10	10
	Wild Country	5	20
Plastic boots	Scarpa*	40	30
	Merrell	25	5
	Koflach	25	40
	Lowe	15	5
Adjustable ski poles	Black Diamond	60	5
	Life Link	40	5
Mountaineer skis	Rossignol	30	50
	Hagen*	20	10
Climbing accessories	Black Diamond	55	15
	Omega	25	10
	Petzl	20	75
Gloves	Black Diamond	50	5
Axes			
Snow climbing	Charlie Moser	50	10
	Black Diamond	20	5
Ice climbing	Black Diamond	30	10
	Charlie Moser	30	16
	DMM	25	30
	Grivel	15	30
Rock shoes	Scarpa*	25	20
	Sportiva	25	35
	Boreal	25	35
	Five Ten	15	5
Ropes	Mamutt	30	50
	PMI*	20	40
	New England	20	0
	Blue Water	20	10

*European manufacturers producing Black Diamond designs.

SOURCE: Estimates of industry representatives.

In the United States, REI was the dominant firm in this group of retailers. REI operated department stores in Seattle, Boston, Los Angeles, and Washington, DC, with limited national competition on this level. Because of its large size and wide scope, REI could buy in volume for all its stores and could offer very competitive prices. The Canadian retailer Mountain Equipment Co-op (MEC) served a similar market in Canada, with a large store in each of Canada's major cities. In France, Au Vieux Campeur owned multiple department stores in major French cities, serving a broad customer base.

Wholesalers

Retail outlets bought their product lines from wholesalers during semiannual outdoor equipment shows held throughout the world. The wholesaler category of firms consisted of (1) companies that either manufactured their own products or subcontracted the manufacturing of their designs and distributed their own product lines, (2) companies licensed to distribute the products of other companies in certain geographic areas, and (3) companies that represented various combinations of the two types. Black Diamond was in this last category. The company distributed equipment designed and manufactured in its Utah plant, equipment manufactured for Black Diamond by other firms, and merchandise designed by Black Diamond and distributed under other manufacturers' names. In all, Black Diamond offered over 250 different items, covering most mountain sports (see Exhibit 2).

REI was Black Diamond's biggest wholesale customer, making up almost 10 percent of Black Diamond's total sales. The next biggest customer, Lost Arrow—Japan, was a Japanese distributor comprising 5 percent of Black Diamond's sales. The other major wholesale customers were North American outdoor sports department store chains, mail-order companies, and Black Diamond's own retail shop and mail-order

■ **Exhibit 2**
Black Diamond's
Product Line

Climbing Protection	**Packs**
Camming devices	Hip packs
Nuts	Backpacks
Stoppers	
Pitons	**Tents**
Piton hammers	
Slings	**Snow and Ice Tools**
Runners	Axes
Daisy chains	Crampons
Etriers	Ice screws and hooks
Webbing	
Belay devices	**Ski Tools**
Carabiners	Skis
	Bindings
Harnesses	Poles
Sport climbing	
Alpine mountaineering	**Climbing Clothing**
Big wall	T-shirts
	Sweatshirts
Footwear	Shorts
Mountaineering boots	Pants
Ski boots	Hats
Rock-climbing shoes	Belts
	Chalk bags
Ropes and Rope Bags	

business. Combined, the top 20 percent of Black Diamond's retail customers—roughly 60 companies—accounted for about 80 percent of total sales.

Domestically, Black Diamond's wholesaling competition came from Omega Pacific, which manufactured and distributed its own metal products, and Blue Water, which wholesaled its own lines of ropes and harnesses. Neither of these companies, however, carried a product line as extensive as Black Diamond's.

The international wholesaling segment included strong competition from two British firms, Denny Morehouse Mountaineering and Wild Country, and a French company, Petzl. These firms wholesaled a full range of mountaineering products manufactured by companies with strong international reputations. Additional competition came from regional firms. Most countries had several smaller manufacturers of specific products such as carabiners or climbing axes that were successful in wholesaling their own products.

Several issues influenced sales in the international marketplace. First, the International Organization for Standardization had mandated that by 1997 "personal protective equipment" would have to meet ISO 9000 quality certification standards in order to be sold in Europe. Companies that had been granted certification stamped their products with a symbol showing that the product's manufacturer had met the relevant ISO 9000 standards. The certification was intended to give consumers more confidence in a product's quality. Most of the European mountaineering manufacturers had initiated the certification process and were well on their way to obtaining certification. In contrast, very few American companies had even begun the certification process. Black Diamond had begun the process but was not yet near completion. (Exhibit 3 provides an overview of the ISO 9000 standards.)

■ **Exhibit 3**   ISO 9000 Standards

The ISO 9000 standards provide the requirements for documenting processes and procedures. The intent of the standards is to ensure that organizations "do what they say and say what they do." The standards offer three quality system models—ISO 9001, ISO 9002, and ISO 9003—with increasing levels of stringency. ISO 9003 covers documentation and procedure requirements for final inspection and testing, ISO 9002 adds production and installation, and ISO 9001 includes design and development. An organization chooses the appropriate standard depending on the strategically important functional areas requiring quality procedures. In most cases, manufacturers use ISO 9001 for covering all areas.

In order to receive ISO 9000 certification, a company will spend several years complying with the requirements in the standards. This compliance usually requires extensive documentation of the company's existing quality program and training for all employees involved in processes related to quality. Individual auditors, who work for the international ISO registration organization, evaluate the company for requirement compliance. The certified companies are reevaluated every two years to ensure continuing compliance.

The following is a brief overview of the ISO 9001 requirements:

* The entire quality system must be defined and documented to ensure that each product meets specifications.
* The contractual requirements for quality between the company and the customer must be defined and documented.
* Procedures are required to ensure that critical processes are under control.
* Procedures are required for inspection at all levels and for identification of nonconforming parts or products.
* Procedures are required to prevent nonconforming parts from getting damaged in storage, delivery, or packing.
* Training is required for all personnel affecting quality.
* The quality system must be audited internally to ensure effectiveness and compliance.

Second, some European countries had a long history of climbing and moun-taineering, and certain manufacturers, Grivel, for example, dated back to the late 1800s. Although several European companies had well-established worldwide repu-tations for quality and innovative products, others relied on home-country support, producing relatively low-quality, low-priced products. All mountainous European countries had small factories for carabiners, skis, axes, or shoes that produced, at relatively low cost, simple products in high volume for domestic consumption.

Third, the European market was predominantly ethnocentric in purchasing be-havior. French climbers preferred to buy French products, while German climbers preferred German products. Because of the risks involved in climbing and moun-taineering, customers chose equipment they knew the most about and had the most confidence in. Usually, these products were from the buyers' respective countries.

Manufacturers

As a manufacturer, Black Diamond faced both domestic and international competi-tion. Domestic manufacturing firms ran the gamut from small garage operations to large machine shops with 50 or more employees, and most produced either "soft-ware" or "hardware." The software firms worked with textile products such as ropes and harnesses. The majority of the software firms, including Blue Water, Sterling Rope, and Misty Mountain, were located in the southeastern United States. These more specialized manufacturing firms expanded their market by catering to the needs of nonmountaineering industries, such as construction safety, military appli-cations, and spelunking. The hardware group manufactured or assembled metal products such as carabiners and other climbing tools and protection. This group of manufacturers included Friends, Rock Hardware, and Rock Exotica. These firms had reputations as producers of innovative and high-quality equipment.

REI had recently started up a small manufacturing facility for carabiners. The manager of the facility had many years of engineering experience with Boeing Aircraft and had designed a highly automated manufacturing system capable of both production and quality testing.

Because Black Diamond had begun as a machine shop, the company had strong capabilities in metalworking. Specifically, the Salt Lake City facility manufactured cold-forged metal parts associated with carabiners, axes, and other climbing acces-sories and protection. Hot-forging and casting were subcontracted by Black Dia-mond to manufacturers specializing in this area. Black Diamond was beginning to expand into simple soft goods, such as slings and other webbing products, and in-tended to continue developing its in-house sewing capabilities.

Black Diamond had plans to become vertically integrated. Management believed that in-house performance of operations related to core products would enhance Black Diamond's competitiveness. Consequently, Black Diamond had started re-viewing some of its subcontracting practices to determine what functions could be brought in-house. In particular, the company wanted to bring in-house all sewing of climbing gear and some metal treatments such as heat-treating.

Other products, such as skis, ski poles, foot gear, and ropes, required very specific technologies, production skills, and economies of scale for competitive pricing and quality. Black Diamond entered into subcontracting agreements with international manufacturers to design and manufacture such products. The company also sub-contracted the production of its harnesses to a technically sophisticated harness manufacturer located next door to the Salt Lake City facility that made the harnesses on a semiautomated assembly line. This process required minimal human involvement, in contrast to a "garment industry" sewing process by which one person sews the complete harness from start to finish.

By the late 1980s, European competition was becoming a more significant factor in the U.S. market. In particular, Petzl, a French company with a full range of products, had taken an aggressive position in the U.S. market. Like several of the European competitors, Petzl had a well-established reputation as a producer of high-quality, innovative products. Petzl had set up a manufacturing facility in the United States within 60 miles of Black Diamond's manufacturing facility and had sponsored several professional U.S. climbers. Black Diamond, of course, was making efforts to sell its own products in Europe, but faced the problem of ISO 9000 certification.

Some international manufacturing activity went on in Korea and Japan. Products produced by these manufacturers were marketed and distributed through other international companies. The majority of these products were low-cost, mass-produced items such as carabiners.

The continuing growth of copyright violations and product piracy—especially prevalent within international markets—added a further dimension to global competition. Several U.S. and European companies had used machine shops in Korea and Japan as subcontractors, supplying dies and other technological know-how. Consequently, unlicensed clones of more expensive items were expected to appear soon in the international market.

■ Black Diamond's Operations

Black Diamond Equipment, Ltd., opened for business in 1989 after a group of former managers, with employee support, bought the assets of Chouinard Equipment from Lost Arrow Corporation during Chapter 11 bankruptcy proceedings. The bankruptcy resulted from four lawsuits related to climbing equipment accidents during the 1980s. Chouinard Equipment was the first U.S. company to develop and manufacture rock-climbing gear. From its inception and for the following decade, Chouinard Equipment had a reputation for innovation and quality unmatched by any national competitors.

After the purchase, the new owners chose a new name for the company that would reflect its roots yet would project a fresh beginning. Chouinard Equipment's previous logo had been a diamond. The new company decided to keep the diamond image and chose the name Black Diamond because of the different associations the name might evoke: diamond in the rough, rogue, bad boy, unusual. (See Exhibit 4 for the Black Diamond logo.) Furthermore, a black diamond was used to identify the most difficult type of run in ski areas, and the company owners hoped the name would appeal to the "extreme" athlete, their primary targeted customer base. Black Diamond's management believed that "if you target the extremists, the recreational customers will follow."

The mission of Black Diamond was "to design, manufacture, and bring to market, in a profitable and on-time manner, innovative and technical products of high quality, high performance, and exemplary durability that are targeted toward our primary customers—climbers and backcountry skiers." The company was committed to 10 guiding principles:

1. Being the market leader, synonymous with the sports we serve and are absolutely passionate about;

■ **Exhibit 4**
Black Diamond Logo

2. Having a truly global presence;
3. Supporting the specialty retailer;
4. Creating long-term partnerships with companies we do business with;
5. Being very easy to do business with;
6. Being a fierce competitor with the highest ethical standards;
7. Developing sustainable, competitive advantage;
8. Sharing the company's success with its employees;
9. Creating a safe, personally fulfilling work environment for all employees;
10. Championing the preservation of and access to our mountain environments.

In 1991, the owner-employees relocated the business from Ventura, California, to Salt Lake City, Utah, where they would be closer to the targeted customer. Black Diamond began operations with a staff of roughly 40, covering all functional areas. (See Exhibit 5 for Black Diamond's organizational structure.) Black Diamond was 50 percent owned by employees; the remaining 50 percent of the stock was held by outside investors, predominantly distributors, customers, and friends and family of the main employee stockholders. Of the 50 percent that was employee owned, 75 percent was held by Peter Metcalf, the CEO; Maria Cranor, head of marketing; and Clark Kawakami, the chief financial officer.

In 1993, Black Diamond's annual sales were expected to be approximately $12 million, with a gross profit margin of about 40 percent (around $4.8 million) and a net profit margin of about 10 percent (around $1.2 million). From 1990 through 1993, the climbing industry had experienced tremendous sales growth of 20 to 40 percent per year. The market demanded more innovative products and faster delivery. Black Diamond struggled to keep up with the exploding customer demand by hiring more employees and upgrading shop machinery to increase productivity. Slowly, the original machinery was being replaced by automated machining centers and testing devices. By 1993, the company employed more than 100 people.

Like other metalworking shops, Black Diamond specialized in certain types of metalworking; its areas of specialization consisted of cold-forging metal parts, stamping and forming, computer numerically controlled (CNC) machining, and assembly or fabrication. Forging, stamping, and forming, along with the assembly processes, had been done for 20 years by the original Chouinard company, and these

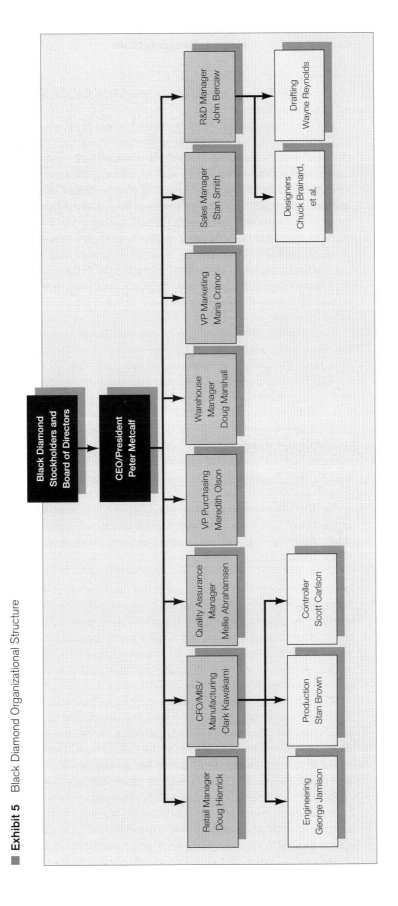

Exhibit 5 Black Diamond Organizational Structure

processes were considered to be Black Diamond's technical core. These core processes used the same multiton presses that forced metal stock into a die or mold to obtain the desired shape.

Since moving to Salt Lake City, the company had expanded into CNC machines—large programmable machine tools capable of producing small-to-medium-sized batches of intricate parts—in an effort to reduce costs and to move more production processes in-house. These machines were expensive, but they provided the advantages of capacity and product flexibility. Many of Black Diamond's processes, however, required machinery that was too costly to justify purchase for the manufacturing of a limited number of parts. Consequently, Black Diamond subcontracted with other vendors for aluminum hot-forging, investment casting, laser-cutting steel, preshearing metals, anodizing, heat treating, welding, screw machining, wire forming such as springs, and aluminum extrusion. These processes were subcontracted to achieve economies of scale (e.g., aluminum extrusion) or because the specialized equipment and skills required were beyond Black Diamond's capabilities (e.g., hot-forging).

Black Diamond's production facility was divided into several functional areas: the machine shop, which built prototypes and constructed and maintained tool and die apparatus; the punch press room, where parts were pressed out at a rate of one per second by several multiton presses; a room with assorted machines (including CNC machines), each operated by one person doing drilling, milling, or grinding; a tumbling and polishing room, where large batches of parts were polished; the assembly room, where parts were assembled by individuals or teams; and, finally, a room for materials and shipping.

Supported by a material requirements planning (MRP) system, materials were ordered several months in advance for a full batch of products—for example, 5,000 carabiners or 500 axes. When fairly common parts such as springs and aluminum rod stock were involved, the orders arrived on time and met standard quality requirements. The more complex and customized parts, such as investment-cast axe parts, were difficult for vendors to make to specifications and thus often did not meet the assembly deadline.

When the parts arrived in the materials supply area, one person was responsible for spot-checking the order to see if the parts met specifications. For example, when 500 axe heads arrived, the inspector would randomly select 15 parts and would measure 20 key dimensions on each part to determine if the tolerances met specifications. If one dimension was out of tolerance, the quality manager was summoned for an evaluation. Depending on how much impact the flaw would have on other assembly processes, a larger meeting, involving all potentially affected parties, might be necessary to determine a course of action.

Most of Black Diamond's products began as a sheet of steel or aluminum rod. After receiving the metal, the incoming inspector would pull a sample to check hardness and dimensions. When production on an order was ready to begin, the metal was moved from a hallway to the press room. The press operator would receive an order for 5,000 parts and would set up the press to begin cutting and smashing parts to shape. Once the dies were in place, the operator would smash a few sample parts and check with an inspector for approval.

As the dies wore down, the parts might turn out to have excess metal, or the logo engraving might be substandard. Depending on the demand for the parts, the inspector might feel pressure to pass on cosmetically imperfect parts. Once approval was given, the operator would proceed to press out as many parts as possible in the shortest time. Often chips of metal would settle in the die and become imbedded in many parts before being discovered by the operator. When this occurred, thousands of parts needed to be scrapped.

After the smashing process, the parts were usually sent out for heat-treating to harden the metal. The heat-treatment plant was located in California, so this procedure had a turnaround time of several weeks. When the parts returned, they went to the tumbling and drilling rooms for further processing. When color was needed, the parts would be shipped out again for anodizing, an electrolytic process by which metal is covered with a protective and/or decorative oxide film.

Finally, when the main body of a product was finished, the materials department would issue batches of all the other components needed to finish that product. All of these parts would proceed to a group of assemblers, seated around tables, who were responsible for putting together the final product. The assembly room was the epitome of a craft shop environment. Large and expensive products such as axes were assembled in small batches by one individual, while products such as carabiners were assembled in larger batches by teams of people who often rotated jobs. The finished products would go through individual testing and inspection before passing to the shipping area. One inspector might evaluate thousands of parts in a day.

Originally, the company had one employee who was responsible for quality assurance and several shop employees who performed quality control functions. The quality assurance person worked for the R&D department and focused on testing new products, prototypes, and work in production. As the company grew and ISO 9000 certification loomed in the future, several members of the management team decided that quality issues needed more prominent attention. Black Diamond needed not only testing but also a plantwide program to ensure that defects did not occur in the first place.

Black Diamond's original quality assurance officer had left the company to guide climbing expeditions, after which Black Diamond's management created a stand-alone quality assurance department and hired Mellie Abrahamsen as the manager. At the time of Abrahamsen's hiring, the members of R&D and the shop functioned along craft-shop lines. Product designers built prototypes on the shop floor, iterating between field testing and lab testing until they felt the design was ready. When the new design went into production, the shop personnel used trial and error to develop an assembly procedure. Out-of-tolerance parts were often accepted by shop personnel, who invented creative ways of adapting the parts or the procedures for assembling the products.

Implementing a quality-control program would mean introducing formal testing and assembly procedures for both designers and shop workers. As Andrew McLean, a head designer, said, "We are like artists here, and you just can't restrain or rush creativity and get good results." Chuck Brainard complained, "If we have to write procedures for every step of production, we'll be changing those things a million times."

Like most machine-shop workers, Black Diamond's shop employees labored under comparatively unglamorous working conditions, involving, for example, noise, grease, and monotony. Many shop workers lacked a high school education and some could not read or write in English. Although the shop workers were the lowest-paid employees at Black Diamond, the company offered them a generous profit-sharing bonus and tried to involve them in monthly meetings concerning the financial performance of the company. Despite these measures, the shop had a high rate of employee turnover.

Because quality control programs require procedure writing, blueprint reading, and statistical techniques, the shop employees needed elementary math and language training so that they could learn the more complicated subjects. Stan Brown acknowledged that the workers needed training, but said, "I can't let those people miss too much work for training. We really need everyone working nonstop to get products out the door."

Many of the professional employees at Black Diamond were avid climbers and users of the products, taking great pride in trying to make the very best products available. Marketing was concerned about keeping up the company's innovative image with new products every season. Production worried about vendor costs, delivery of parts, and the shop's ability to meet sales forecasts. R&D attempted to simultaneously develop buildable new products, reduce lead time for new-product development, and improve existing products. Customer service tried to keep retailers pacified with partial deliveries and promises.

Finally, the new quality assurance department was charged with implementing quality control procedures, conducting training, testing products, and resolving problems attributed to parts or products not meeting specifications. All functional areas faced the problems inherent in trying to achieve the simultaneous goals of meeting customer demand and ensuring the highest-quality products, and the different areas often clashed on the best means and methods of achieving these goals.

■ The Black Prophet

The concept for the Black Prophet axe was originally developed to round out Black Diamond's product line of axes. The product line had two other axes: the Alpamayo, a glacier-walking and snow-climbing axe; and the X-15, a versatile axe for both snow and ice climbing. The Black Prophet was designed specifically for ice climbing and incorporated an innovative ergonomic shape to reduce arm fatigue, a composite, rubber-bounded shaft construction for gripability and weight reduction, and interchangeable modular components that allowed the use of different types of tools—a hammer head, picks, or an adze—for miscellaneous ice applications. (Exhibit 6 is a drawing of the Black Prophet and its component parts.)

Designing and producing the axe entailed several years of working with different vendors to develop the appropriate production process for each component. The axe was designed as a prototype and field-tested with different constructions until R&D agreed on a specific configuration. This configuration was then reviewed by sales representatives considered to be mountaineering experts and by other company members at the quarterly meetings. If the tool did not pass the scrutiny of those examiners, R&D would begin a new phase of prototype development and field tests. This development process would continue until a companywide consensus was reached.

The axe required five parts: shaft, head, hammer, pick, and adze. Three parts were cast metal, requiring a casting subcontractor with the ability to meet strict specifications. The composite shaft was produced by a composite and bonding manufacturer, and the pick was manufactured in Black Diamond's plant. Black Diamond received the parts from each vendor, inspected them for conformance to specifications, and assembled the axes.

The Black Prophet, which cost approximately $80 to produce, sold at retail for $200; the wholesale price was $140. The initial shipment of Black Prophets for the

■ **Exhibit 6**
The Black Prophet

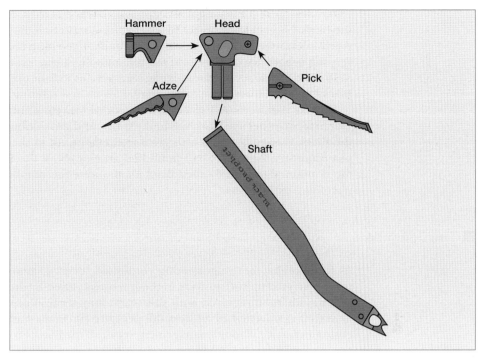

(a) Component Parts

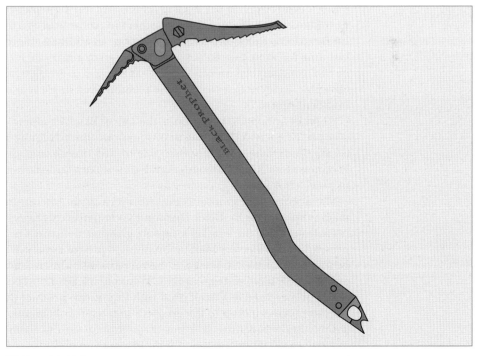

(b) Complete Unit

winter season of 1993 comprised approximately 200 axes. Management expected the Black Prophet to be one of Black Diamond's top 10 selling winter products, with yearly sales projected to be at least 2,500 units. The entire company regarded it as a very big image item on the world mountaineering scene. Every competitor in the industry had an axe for glacier walking; axes were especially popular in Europe, where Black Diamond foresaw superb potential for its new offering.

The axe had been well received at the previous year's outdoor product show. At that time, no other axe like it was in the wings, and the climbing industry anticipated the Black Prophet's arrival with great excitement. All of the major U.S. and European industry magazines had published articles about the Black Prophet, and famous mountaineers had called Black Diamond requesting Black Prophets for their upcoming expeditions.

■ The Dilemma

As the Monday morning meeting continued, Black Diamond's top management team struggled to find answers to the questions raised by the axe crisis. They knew that the situation required both short- and long-term solutions. In the short term, management needed to address the pressure for immediate delivery confronting customer service. Should management recall all the Black Prophet axes currently on the market? A recall would come with high shipping, testing, and opportunity costs. Or should Black Diamond ignore the incident, assuming the accident was a one-time freak, and continue to sell the axes while refuting any rumors about the product's questionable performance? The possibility of lawsuits had to be considered. For any accident causing injury, legal fees could be expected to run $500,000, and a catastrophic accident could bring a suit for several million dollars. While Black Diamond's insurer would pay legal expenses and any settlement involved, with a cap of $1 million, Black Diamond could expect to pay at least $25,000—the company's insurance deductible—for each legal action. In addition, there would be the costs of lost time for those employees who had to go to court (such costs might involve one or two managers' salaries for a year—at $40,000 to $60,000 per person). Several catastrophic accident cases won by the plaintiffs in a single year could put the company into bankruptcy.

Another option was to continue the sale of Black Prophets—including the axes already released as well as those in production—but to require all units to be sold with a cautionary label. Still another was to just quietly and quickly sell those Black Prophets already in retail outlets and undertake a critical review only of the axes still in production.

Management's response to the short-term issue of customer service would have major implications for Black Diamond's competitive strategy. Would Black Diamond be able to meet the market's rapidly growing demand for all products while improving—or at the very least maintaining—product quality? Would Black Diamond be able to maintain an image as the recognized industry leader in the manufacture of innovative tools and equipment? Would Black Diamond be able to balance the realities of increased risk associated with innovative product design and of increased liability corresponding to the greater potential for accidents, while still establishing a dominant competitive position? Even though various members held strong—and in some cases, divergent—opinions, the management team was willing to consider enterprising alternatives.

Nevertheless, management also knew that a more long-term plan needed to be put into place. "When crises strike," Metcalf said, "there will always be some degree of needing to react to the surprise of the situation. But we need to institute a system of managing crises proactively—that means organizing the business to prevent the preventable crises."

Even though the management team thought the quality assurance department should be a constructive resource in this long-term effort, the department was so new that no one had a clear idea of its role. Abrahamsen also questioned her role: "I was hired to implement a plantwide quality control program and to specifically work on ISO 9000 certification. Representing QA, I'm supposed to improve the efficiency of the company by reducing or eliminating defects in the whole production chain, but I'm not sure that a TQM (total quality management) approach will completely solve Black Diamond's problems. Perhaps the whole process of new-product development and ongoing operations would be more effective if a BPR (business process reengineering) approach were used. Either way, my challenge is to get all these other employees and departments to change the way they do things so they're both more efficient and effective."

(Black Diamond's Web address is **www.bdel.com.**)

Section VI

Strategic Marketing Cases

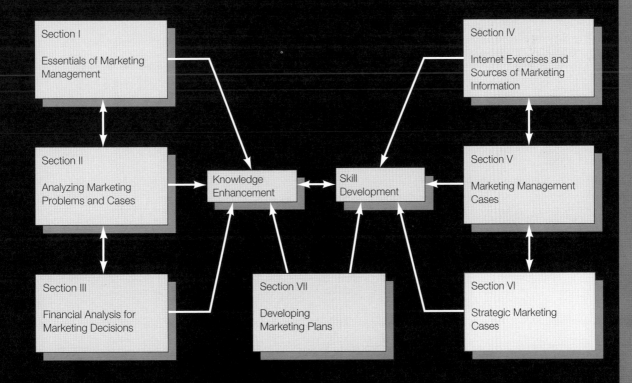

■ Note to the Student

The 11 cases in this section emphasize the role of marketing in developing successful business or organizational strategies. While marketing is critical in these cases, successful analysis and strategy formulation will often involve other areas in the organization as well.

The knowledge and skills you've developed in the analysis of the cases in the previous section provide a useful foundation for analyzing the cases in this section. However, these cases are intended to broaden your knowledge of marketing and your skills at analyzing various strategic problems.

■ Case 1   Dell Computer Corporation

Arthur A. Thompson
The University of Alabama

John E. Gamble
University of South Alabama

In 1984, at the age of 21, Michael Dell founded Dell Computer with a simple vision and business concept—that personal computers could be built to order and sold directly to customers. Michael Dell believed his approach to PC manufacturing had two advantages: (1) bypassing distributors and retail dealers eliminated the markups of resellers, and (2) building to order greatly reduced the costs and risks associated with carrying large stocks of parts, components, and finished goods. While Dell Computer sometimes struggled during its early years in trying to refine its strategy, build an adequate infrastructure, and establish market credibility against better-known rivals, its build-to-order and sell-direct approach proved appealing to growing numbers of customers in the mid-1990s as global PC sales rose to record levels. And, just as important, the strategy gave the company a substantial cost and profit-margin advantage over rivals that manufactured PCs in volume and kept their distributors and retailers stocked with ample inventories.

Going into 1998, Dell Computer had a 12 percent share of the PC market in the United States, trailing only Compaq Computer and IBM, which held first and second place in the market, respectively. Worldwide, Dell Computer had nearly a 6 percent market share (see Exhibit 1). And the company was gaining market share quickly in all of the world's markets. The company's fastest growing market for the past several quarters was Europe. Even though Asia's economic woes in the first quarter of 1998 resulted in a slight decline in Asian sales of PCs, Dell's sales in Asia rose 35 percent. Dell's sales at its Internet Web site were averaging $5 million a day and were expected to reach $1.5 billion annually by year-end 1998. Dell Computer had 1997 revenues of $12.3 billion, up from $3.4 billion in 1994—a compound average growth rate of 53 percent. Over the same period, profits were up from

■ Exhibit 1   World's Top Five PC Vendors, Based on Factory Shipments, 1996 and 1997

1997 Rank	Vendor	1997 Market Shipments of PCs*	1997 Market Share	1996 Market Shipments of PCs*	1996 Market Share	Percent Growth 1996–1997
1	Compaq Computer	10,064,000	12.6%	7,211,000	10.4%	40%
2	IBM	7,239,000	9.1	6,176,000	8.9	17
3	Dell Computer	4,648,000	5.8	2,996,000	4.3	55
4	Hewlett-Packard	4,468,000	5.6	2,984,000	4.3	50
5	Packard Bell NEC	4,150,000	5.2	4,230,000	6.1	(2.0)
	Others	49,369,000	61.8	45,727,000	66.0	8
	All vendors	79,938,000	100.0%	69,324,000	100.0%	15%

*Includes branded shipments only and excludes original equipment manufacturer (OEM) sales for all manufacturers.

SOURCE: International Data Corporation.

This case was prepared by Arthur A. Thompson, The University of Alabama, and John E. Gamble, University of South Alabama.

$140 million to $944 million—an 89 percent growth rate. Since 1990, the company's stock price had exploded from a split-adjusted price of 23 cents per share to $83 per share in May 1998—a 36,000 percent increase. Dell Computer was the top-performing big company stock so far during the 1990s and seemed poised to become the stock of the decade.

Dell's principal products included desktop PCs, notebook computers, workstations, and servers. The company also marketed a number of products made by other manufacturers, including CD-ROM drives, modems, monitors, networking hardware, memory cards, storage devices, speakers, and printers. The company's products and services were sold in more than 140 countries. Sales of desktop PCs accounted for about 65 percent of Dell's total revenues; sales of notebook computers, servers, and workstations accounted for about 33 percent of revenue. In early 1998, the company had 16,000 employees.

■ Company Background

At age 13, Michael Dell was running a mail-order stamp-trading business, complete with a national catalog, and grossing $2,000 per month. At 16, he was selling subscriptions to the *Houston Post,* and at 17 he bought his first BMW with money he had earned. He enrolled at the University of Texas in 1983 as a premed student (his parents wanted him to become a doctor) but soon became immersed in computers and started selling PC components out of his college dormitory room. He bought random-access memory (RAM) chips and disk drives for IBM PCs at cost from IBM dealers, who often had excess supplies on hand because they were required to order large monthly quotas from IBM. Dell resold the components through newspaper ads (and later through ads in national computer magazines) at 10–15 percent below the regular retail price.

By April 1984 sales were running about $80,000 per month. Dell dropped out of college and formed a company, PCs Ltd., to sell both PC components and PCs under the brand name PCs Limited. He obtained his PCs by buying retailers' surplus stocks at cost, then powering them up with graphics cards, hard disks, and memory before reselling them. His strategy was to sell directly to end users; by eliminating the retail markup, Dell's new company was able to sell IBM clones (machines that copied the functioning of IBM PCs using the same or similar components) at about 40 percent below the price of an IBM PC. The price discounting strategy was successful, attracting price-conscious buyers and producing rapid growth. By 1985, the company was assembling its own PC designs with a few people working on six-foot tables. The company had 40 employees, and Michael Dell worked 18-hour days, often sleeping on a cot in his office. By the end of fiscal 1986, sales had reached $33 million.

During the next several years, however, PCs Ltd. was hampered by a lack of money, people, and resources. Michael Dell sought to refine the company's business model, add needed production capacity, and build a bigger, deeper management staff and corporate infrastructure while at the same time keeping costs low. The company was renamed Dell Computer in 1987, and the first international offices were opened that same year. In 1988 Dell added a sales force to serve large customers, began selling to government agencies, and became a public company—raising $34.2 million in its first offering of common stock. Sales to large customers quickly became the dominant part of Dell's business. By 1990 Dell Computer had sales of $388 million, a market share of 2–3 percent, and an R&D staff of over 150 people. Michael Dell's vision was for Dell Computer to become one of the top three PC companies.

Thinking its direct sales business would not grow fast enough, in 1990–93, the company began distributing its computer products through Soft Warehouse Superstores (now CompUSA), Staples (a leading office-products chain), Wal-Mart, Sam's Club, and Price Club (now Price/Costco). Dell also sold PCs through Best Buy stores in 16 states and through Xerox in 19 Latin American countries. But when the company learned how thin its margins were in selling through such distribution channels, it realized it had made a mistake and withdrew from selling to retailers and other intermediaries in 1994 to refocus on direct sales. At the time, sales through retailers accounted for only about 2 percent of Dell's revenues.

Further problems emerged in 1993. Dell reportedly had $38 million in second-quarter losses that year from engaging in a risky foreign-currency hedging strategy. Also, quality difficulties appeared in certain PC lines made by the company's contract manufacturers, profit margins declined, and buyers were turned off by the company's laptop PC models. To get laptop sales back on track, the company took a charge of $40 million to write off its laptop line and suspended sales of laptops until it could get redesigned models into the marketplace. The problems resulted in losses of $36 million for the company's fiscal year ending January 30, 1994.

Because of higher costs and unacceptably low profit margins in selling to individuals and households, Dell did not pursue the consumer market aggressively until sales on the company's Internet site took off in 1996 and 1997. Management noticed that while the industry's average selling price to individuals was going down, Dell's was going up—people who were buying their second and third computers, who wanted powerful computers with multiple features, and who did not need much technical support were choosing Dell. It became clear that PC-savvy individuals liked the convenience of buying direct from Dell, ordering exactly what they wanted, and having it delivered to their door within a matter of days. In early 1997, Dell created an internal sales and marketing group dedicated to serving the individual consumer segment and introduced a product line designed especially for individual users.

By late 1997, Dell had become the industry leader in keeping costs down and wringing efficiency out of its direct sales and build-to-order business model. Industry observers saw Dell as being in strong position to capitalize on several forces shaping the PC industry—sharp declines in component prices, rapid improvements in PC technology, and growing customer interest in having PCs equipped with the power, components, and software they wanted.

Exhibit 2 through Exhibit 5 contain a five-year review of Dell Computer's financial performance and selected financial statements contained in the company's 1998 annual report.

■ Michael Dell

Michael Dell was widely considered one of the mythic heroes within the PC industry and was labeled "the quintessential American entrepreneur" and "the most innovative guy for marketing computers in this decade." He was the youngest CEO ever to guide a company to a Fortune 500 ranking. His prowess was based more on an astute combination of technical knowledge and marketing know-how than on being a technowizard. In 1998 Michael Dell owned about 16 percent of Dell Computer's common stock, worth about $10 billion.

■ **Exhibit 2** Financial Performance Summary, Dell Computer, 1994–1998 (in millions, except per share data)

	February 1, 1998	February 2, 1997	January 28, 1996	January 29, 1995	January 30, 1994
Results of Operations Data					
Net revenue	$12,327	$7,759	$5,296	$3,475	$2,873
Gross margin	$ 2,722	$1,666	$1,067	$ 738	$ 433
Operating income (loss)	$ 1,316	$ 714	$ 377	$ 249	$ (39)
Income (loss) before extraordinary loss	$ 944	$ 531	$ 272	$ 149	$ (36)
Net income (loss)	$ 944	$ 518	$ 272	$ 149	$ (36)
Income (loss) before extraordinary loss per common share					
Basic	$ 1.44	$ 0.75	$ 0.36	$ 0.23	$ (0.07)
Diluted	$ 1.28	$ 0.68	$ 0.33	$ 0.19	$ (0.07)
Weighted average shares					
Basic	658	710	716	618	597
Diluted	738	782	790	750	597
Balance Sheet Data					
Working capital	$ 1,215	$1,089	$1,018	$ 718	$ 510
Total assets	$ 4,268	$2,993	$2,148	$1,594	$1,140
Long-term debt	$ 17	$ 18	$ 113	$ 113	$ 100
Total stockholders' equity	$ 1,293	$ 806	$ 973	$ 652	$ 471

SOURCE: 1998 annual report.

Once pudgy and bespectacled, Michael Dell wore expensive suits and contact lenses, ate only health foods, attended executive seminars at Stanford, and was a frequent speaker at industry conferences. He lived in a three-story 33,000-square-foot home on a 60-acre estate. The company's glass-and-steel headquarters building in Round Rock, Texas (an Austin suburb), had unassuming, utilitarian furniture, abstract art, framed accolades to Michael Dell, laudatory magazine covers, industry awards plaques, bronze copies of the company's 11 patents, and a history wall that contained the hand-soldered guts of the company's first personal computer.[1]

In the company's early days Michael Dell hung around mostly with the company's engineers. He was so shy that some employees thought he was stuck up because he never talked to them. But people who worked with him closely described him as a likable young man who was slow to warm up to strangers.[2] He was a terrible public speaker and wasn't good at running meetings. A *Business Week* reporter labeled him "the enfant terrible of personal computers" in a June 13, 1988, article and quoted a former executive who said, "Dell's got an ego like God."[3] But Lee Walker, a 51-year-

---

[1]As described in *Business Week*, March 22, 1993, p. 82.

[2]"Michael Dell: On Managing Growth," *MIS Week*, September 5, 1988, p. 1.

[3]Kevin Kelly, "Michael Dell: The Enfant Terrible of Personal Computers," *Business Week*, June 12, 1988, p. 61.

■ **Exhibit 3** Consolidated Statement of Income, Dell Computer, 1996–1998 (in millions, except per share data)

	Fiscal Year Ended		
	February 1, 1998	**February 2, 1997**	**January 28, 1996**
Net revenue	$12,327	$7,759	$5,296
Cost of revenue	9,605	6,093	4,229
Gross margin	2,722	1,666	1,067
Operating expenses			
Selling, general and administrative	1,202	826	595
Research and development	145	88	62
Engineering	59	38	33
Total operating expenses	1,406	952	690
Operating income	1,316	714	377
Financing and other	52	33	6
Income before income taxes and extraordinary loss	1,368	747	383
Provision for income taxes	424	216	111
Income before extraordinary loss	944	531	272
Extraordinary loss, net of taxes	—	(13)	—
Net income	944	518	272
Preferred stock dividends	—	—	(12)
Net income available to common stockholders	$ 944	$ 518	$ 260
Basic earnings per common share (in whole dollars)			
Income before extraordinary loss	$ 1.44	$ 0.75	$ 0.36
Extraordinary loss, net of taxes	—	(.02)	—
Earnings per common share	$ 1.44	$ 0.73	$ 0.36
Diluted earnings per common share (in whole dollars)			
Income before extraordinary loss	$ 1.28	$ 0.68	$ 0.33
Extraordinary loss, net of taxes	—	(.02)	—
Earnings per common share	$ 1.28	$ 0.66	$ 0.33
Weighted-average shares outstanding			
Basic	658	710	716
Diluted	738	782	790

SOURCE: 1998 annual report.

old venture capitalist brought in by Michael Dell to provide much-needed managerial and financial experience during the company's organization-building years, became Michael Dell's mentor, built up his confidence, and was instrumental in turning him into a polished executive.[4] Walker served as the company's president and chief operating officer during the 1986–90 period; he had a fatherly image, knew

---

[4]"The Education of Michael Dell." *Business Week,* March 22, 1993, p. 86.

■ **Exhibit 4** Consolidated Statement of Financial Position, Dell Computer, 1997–1998 (in millions)

Assets	February 1, 1998	February 2, 1997
Current assets		
Cash	$ 320	$ 115
Marketable securities	1,524	1,237
Accounts receivable, gross	1,514	934
Less allowance for doubtful accounts	(28)	(31)
Net accounts receivable	1,486	903
Inventories of production materials	189	223
Work-in-process and finished goods inventories	44	28
Other	349	241
Total current assets	3,912	2,747
Property, plant, and equipment		
Land and buildings	$ 137	$ 133
Computer equipment	135	104
Office furniture and fixtures	45	32
Machinery and other equipment	126	59
Leasehold improvements	66	46
Total property, plant, and equipment	509	374
Less accumulated depreciation and amortization	(167)	(139)
Net property, plant, and equipment	342	235
Other assets	14	11
Total assets	$4,268	$2,993
Liabilities and Stockholders' Equity		
Current liabilities		
Accounts payable	$1,643	$1,040
Accrued and other	1,054	618
Total current liabilities	2,697	1,658
Long-term debt	17	18
Deferred revenue on warranty	225	219
Other	36	13
Commitments and contingent liabilities	—	—
Total liabilities	2,975	1,908
Put options	—	279
Stockholders' Equity		
Preferred stock and capital in excess of $.01 par value; shares issued and outstanding: none	—	—
Common stock and capital in excess of $.01 par value; shares issued and outstanding: 644 and 692, respectively	747	195
Retained earnings	607	647
Other	(61)	(36)
Total stockholders' equity	1,293	806
Total liabilities and equity	$4,268	$2,993

SOURCE: 1998 annual report.

■ **Exhibit 5**   Geographic Area Information, Dell Computer, 1996–1998 (in millions)

	Fiscal Year 1998				
	Americas	Europe	Asia-Pacific and Japan	Eliminations	Consolidated
Sales to unaffiliated customers	$8,531	$2,956	$840	$ —	$12,327
Transfers between geographic areas	67	17	—	(84)	—
Total sales	$8,598	$2,973	$840	$ (84)	$12,327
Operating income	$1,152	$ 255	$ 33	$ —	$ 1,440
Corporate expenses					(124)
Total operating income					$ 1,316
Identifiable assets	$1,363	$ 605	$172	$ —	$ 2,140
General corporate assets					2,128
Total assets					$ 4,268

	Fiscal Year 1997				
	Americas	Europe	Asia-Pacific and Japan	Eliminations	Consolidated
Sales to unaffiliated customers	$5,279	$2,004	$476	$ —	$ 7,759
Transfers between geographic areas	50	32	—	(82)	—
Total sales	$5,329	$2,036	$476	$ (82)	$ 7,759
Operating income (loss)	$ 609	$ 193	$ (6)	$ —	$ 796
Corporate expenses					(82)
Total operating income					714
Identifiable assets	$ 903	$ 390	$125	$ —	$ 1,418
General corporate assets					1,575
Total assets					$ 2,993

	Fiscal Year 1996				
	Americas	Europe	Asia-Pacific and Japan	Eliminations	Consolidated
Sales to unaffiliated customers	$3,474	$1,478	$344	$ —	$ 5,296
Transfers between geographic areas	66	192	—	(258)	—
Total sales	$3,540	$1,670	$344	$(258)	$ 5,296
Operating income (loss)	$ 285	$ 171	$ (21)	$ —	$ 435
Corporate expenses					(58)
Total operating income					377
Identifiable assets	$ 867	$ 409	$123	$ —	$ 1,399
General corporate assets					749
Total assets					$ 2,148

SOURCE: 1998 annual report.

everyone by name, and played a key role in implementing Michael Dell's marketing ideas. Under Walker's tutelage, Michael Dell became intimately familiar with all parts of the business, overcame his shyness, learned to control his ego, and turned into a charismatic leader with an instinct for motivating people and winning their loyalty and respect. When Walker had to leave the company in 1990 because of health reasons, Dell turned to Morton Meyerson, former CEO and president of Electronic Data Systems, for advice on how to transform Dell Computer from a fast-growing medium-sized company into a billion-dollar enterprise.

Though sometimes given to displays of impatience and a strong temper, Michael Dell usually spoke in a quiet, reflective manner and came across as a person with maturity and seasoned judgment far beyond his age. He became an accomplished public speaker. He delegated authority to subordinates, believing that the best results came from "[turning] loose talented people who can be relied upon to do what they're supposed to do." Business associates viewed Michael Dell as an aggressive personality, an extremely competitive risk-taker who had always played close to the edge. Moreover, the people he hired were aggressive and competitive, traits that translated into an aggressive, competitive, intense corporate culture with a strong sense of mission and dedication.

Developments in Early 1998

Dell's sales were up strongly in the first quarter of 1998, even in product areas where the company had previously lagged, pushing its global market share to 7.9 percent and its U.S. share to 11.8 percent. Unit shipments were 1.6 million units, compared to 978,000 in the first quarter of 1997. In laptop PCs, Dell moved into third place in U.S. sales and fifth place worldwide. And it climbed into second place in higher-margin products like servers and Windows NT-based workstations. Dell announced the formation of an alliance with Data General Corporation to enter the market for data storage equipment.

In the first quarter of 1998, about half of the industry's PC sales consisted of computers selling for less than $1,300. Dell's average selling price was $2,500 per unit, down 9 percent from the prior quarter. The company was planning to broaden its product line to include lower-priced PCs equipped with Intel's low-end Celeron chip; Dell's new budget models were priced in the $1,200 range.

■ Competing Value Chain Models in the Personal Computer Industry

When the personal computer industry first began to take shape in the early 1980s, the founding companies manufactured many of the components themselves—disk drives, memory chips, graphics chips, microprocessors, motherboards, and software. Believing that they had to develop key components in-house, companies built expertise in a variety of PC-related technologies and created organizational units to produce components as well as to handle final assembly. While certain "noncritical" items were typically outsourced, if a computer maker was not at least partially vertically integrated and an assembler of some components, then it was not taken seriously as a manufacturer.

But as the industry grew, technology advanced quickly in so many directions on so many parts and components that the early personal computer manufacturers could not keep pace as experts on all fronts. There were too many technological innovations in components to pursue and too many manufacturing intricacies to master for a vertically integrated manufacturer to keep its products on the cutting edge. As a consequence, companies emerged that specialized in making particular com-

■ **Exhibit 6**　Comparative Value Chains of PC Manufacturers

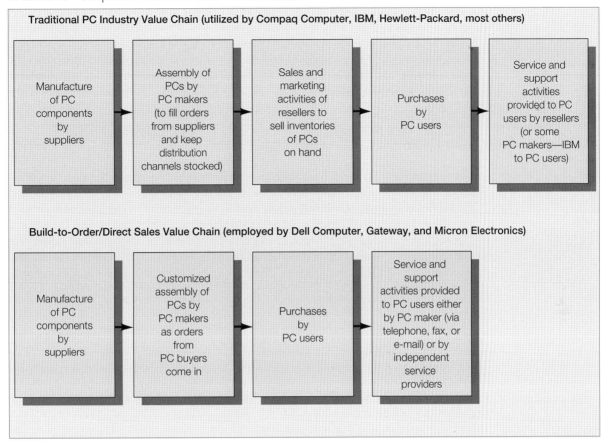

Traditional PC Industry Value Chain (utilized by Compaq Computer, IBM, Hewlett-Packard, most others)

Manufacture of PC components by suppliers → Assembly of PCs by PC makers (to fill orders from suppliers and keep distribution channels stocked) → Sales and marketing activities of resellers to sell inventories of PCs on hand → Purchases by PC users → Service and support activities provided to PC users by resellers (or some PC makers—IBM to PC users)

Build-to-Order/Direct Sales Value Chain (employed by Dell Computer, Gateway, and Micron Electronics)

Manufacture of PC components by suppliers → Customized assembly of PCs by PC makers as orders from PC buyers come in → Purchases by PC users → Service and support activities provided to PC users either by PC maker (via telephone, fax, or e-mail) or by independent service providers

ponents. Specialists could marshal enough R&D capability and resources to either lead the technological developments in their area of specialization or else quickly match the advances made by their competitors. Moreover, specialist firms could mass-produce a component and supply it to several computer manufacturers far cheaper than any one manufacturer could fund the needed component R&D and then make only whatever smaller volume of components it needed for assembling its own brand of PCs.

Thus, in recent years, computer makers had begun to outsource most all components from specialists and to concentrate on efficient assembly and marketing of their brand of computers. Exhibit 6 shows the value chain model that such manufacturers as Compaq, IBM, Hewlett-Packard, and Packard-Bell used in the 1990s. It featured arm's-length transactions between specialist suppliers, manufacturer/ assemblers, distributors and retailers, and end-users. However, Dell, Gateway, and Micron Electronics employed a shorter value chain model, selling direct to customers and eliminating the time and costs associated with distributing through independent resellers. Building to order avoided (1) having to keep many differently-equipped models on retailers' shelves to fill buyer requests for one or another configuration of options and components and (2) having to clear out slow-selling models at a discount before introducing new generations of PCs. Selling direct eliminated retailer costs and markups (retail dealer margins were typically in the 4 to 10 percent range). Dell Computer was far and away the world's largest direct seller to large companies and government institutions, while Gateway was the largest direct seller to individuals and small businesses. Micron Electronics was the only other PC maker that relied on the direct sales and build-to-order approach for the big majority of its sales.

■ Dell Computer's Strategy

Dell Computer's strategy was built around a number of core elements: build-to-order manufacturing, mass customization, partnerships with suppliers, just-in-time components inventories, direct sales, market segmentation, customer service, and extensive data and information sharing with both supply partners and customers. Through this strategy, the company hoped to achieve what Michael Dell called "virtual integration"—a stitching together of Dell's business with its supply partners and customers in real time such that all three appeared to be part of the same organizational team.[5]

Build-to-Order Manufacturing and Mass Customization

Dell built its computers, workstations, and servers to order; none were produced for inventory. Dell customers could order custom-built servers and workstations based on the needs of their applications. Desktop and laptop customers ordered whatever configuration of microprocessor speed, random access memory (RAM), hard-disk capacity, CD-ROM drive, fax/modem, monitor size, speakers, and other accessories they preferred. The orders were directed to the nearest factory. Until recently Dell had operated its assembly lines in traditional fashion, with workers each performing a single operation. An order form accompanied each metal chassis across the production floor; drives, chips, and ancillary items were installed to match customer specifications. As a partly assembled PC arrived at a new workstation, the operator, standing beside a tall steel rack with drawers full of components, was instructed what to do by little red and green lights flashing beside the drawers. When the operator was finished, the components were automatically replenished from the other side of the drawers and the PC chassis glided down the line to the next workstation. However, Dell reorganized its plants in 1997, shifting to "cell manufacturing" techniques whereby a team of workers operating at a group workstation (or cell) assembled an entire PC according to customer specifications. The result had been to reduce assembly times by 75 percent and to double productivity per square foot of assembly space. Assembled computers were tested, then loaded with the desired software, shipped, and typically delivered within five to six business days of the initial order.

This sell-direct strategy meant, of course, that Dell had no in-house stock of finished goods inventories and that, unlike competitors using the traditional

---

[5]This was the term Michael Dell used in an interview published in the *Harvard Business Review*. See Joan Magretta, "The Power of Virtual Integration: An Interview with Dell Computer's Michael Dell," *Harvard Business Review*, March–April 1998, pp. 73–84.

value chain model (Exhibit 6), it did not have to wait for resellers to clear out their own inventories before it could push new models into the marketplace. (Resellers typically operated with 60–70 days' inventory.) Equally important was the fact that customers who bought from Dell got the satisfaction of having their computers customized to their particular liking and pocketbook.

Dell had three PC assembly plants—in Austin, Texas; Limerick, Ireland; and Penang, Malaysia. The company was constructing another plant in Ireland to serve the European market as well as a new plant in China (the company expected the market for PCs in China to soon be huge). Both of the new plants were expected to come into use at the end of 1998.

Partnerships with Suppliers

Michael Dell believed it made much better sense for Dell Computer to partner with reputable suppliers of PC parts and components rather than to integrate backward and get into parts and components manufacturing on its own. He explained why:

> If you've got a race with 20 players all vying to make the fastest graphics chip in the world, do you want to be the 21st horse, or do you want to evaluate the field of 20 and pick the best one?[6]

Management believed long-term partnerships with reputable suppliers yielded several advantages. First, using name-brand processors, disk drives, modems, speakers, and multimedia components enhanced the quality and performance of Dell's PCs. Because of the varying performance of different brands of components, the brand of the components was as important or more important to some buyers than the brand of the overall system. Dell's strategy was to partner with as few outside vendors as possible and to stay with those vendors as long as they maintained their leadership in technology, performance, and quality. Second, because Dell committed to purchase a specified percentage of its requirements from each of its long-term suppliers, Dell was assured of getting the volume of components it needed on a timely basis even when overall market demand for a particular component temporarily exceeded the overall market supply. Third, Dell's formal partnerships with key suppliers made it feasible to have some of their engineers assigned to Dell's product design teams and for them to be treated as part of Dell. When new products were launched, suppliers' engineers were stationed in Dell's plant. If early buyers called with a problem related to design, further assembly and shipments were halted while the supplier's engineers and Dell personnel corrected the flaw on the spot.[7] Fourth, Dell's long-run commitment to its suppliers laid the basis for just-in-time delivery of suppliers' products to Dell's assembly plants in Texas, Ireland, and Malaysia. Some of Dell's vendors had plants or distribution centers within a few miles of Dell's Texas assembly plant and could deliver daily or even hourly if needed. To help suppliers meet its just-in-time delivery expectations, Dell openly shared its daily production schedules, sales forecasts, and new-model introduction plans with vendors.

Michael Dell explained one aspect of the information-sharing relationship with suppliers as follows:

---

[6]As quoted in Magretta, "The Power of Virtual Integration."

[7]Ibid., p. 75.

We tell our suppliers exactly what our daily production requirements are. So it's not, "Well, every two weeks deliver 5,000 to this warehouse, and we'll put them on the shelf, and then we'll take them off the shelf." It's, "Tomorrow morning we need 8,562, and deliver them to door number seven by 7 AM."[8]

Dell also did a three-year plan with each of its key suppliers and worked with suppliers to minimize the number of different stock-keeping units of parts and components in designing its products.

Why Dell Was Committed to Just-in-Time Inventory Practices.
Dell's just-in-time inventory emphasis yielded major cost advantages and shortened the time it took for Dell to get new generations of its computer models into the marketplace. New advances were coming so fast in certain computer parts and components (particularly microprocessors, disk drives, and modems) that any given item in inventory was obsolete in a matter of months, sometimes quicker. Having a couple of months of component inventories meant getting caught in the transition from one generation of components to the next. Moreover, there were rapid-fire reductions in the prices of components—most recently, component prices had been falling as much as 50 percent annually (an average of 1 percent a week). Intel, for example, regularly cut the prices on its older chips when it introduced newer chips, and it introduced new chip generations about every three months. And the prices of hard-disk drives with greater and greater memory capacity had dropped sharply as disk drive makers incorporated new technology that allowed them to add more gigabytes of hard-disk memory very inexpensively.

The economics of minimal component inventories were dramatic. Michael Dell explained:

If I've got 11 days of inventory and my competitor has 80 and Intel comes out with a new 450-megahertz chip, that means I'm going to get to market 69 days sooner.

In the computer industry, inventory can be a pretty massive risk because if the cost of materials is going down 50 percent a year and you have two or three months of inventory versus eleven days, you've got a big cost disadvantage. And you're vulnerable to product transitions, when you can get stuck with obsolete inventory.[9]

Collaboration with suppliers was close enough to allow Dell to operate with only a few days of inventory for some components and a few hours of inventory for others. Dell supplied data on inventories and replenishment needs to its suppliers at least once a day—hourly in the case of components being delivered several times daily from nearby sources. In a couple of instances, Dell's close partnership with vendors allowed it to operate with no inventories. Dell's supplier of monitors was Sony. Because the monitors Sony supplied with the Dell name already imprinted were of dependably high quality (a defect rate of fewer than 1,000 per million), Dell didn't even open up the monitor boxes to test them.[10] Nor did it bother to have them shipped to Dell's assembly plants to be warehoused for shipment to customers. Instead, utilizing sophisticated data exchange systems, Dell arranged for its shippers (Airborne Express and UPS) to pick up computers at its Austin plant, then pick up the accompanying monitors at the Sony plant in Mexico,

---

[8]Ibid.

[9]Ibid., p. 76.

[10]Ibid.

match the customer's computer order with the customer's monitor order, and deliver both to the customer simultaneously. The savings in time, energy, and cost were significant.

The company had, over the years, refined and improved its inventory-tracking capabilities and its procedures for operating with small inventories. In 1993, Dell had $2.6 billion in sales and $342 million in inventory. In fiscal year 1998, it had $12.3 billion in sales and $233 million in inventory—an inventory turn ratio of seven days. By comparison, Gateway, which also pursued a build-to-order strategy, had 1997 sales of $6.3 billion and inventories of $249 million—an inventory turn ratio of 14 days. Compaq had inventories of $1.57 billion at year-end 1997, and 1997 sales of $24.6 billion (thus turning its inventories about every 23 days). Dell's goal was to get its inventory turn down to three days before the year 2000.

Direct Sales

Selling direct to customers gave Dell firsthand intelligence about customer preferences and needs, as well as immediate feedback on design problems and quality glitches. With thousands of phone and fax orders daily, $5 million in daily Internet sales, and daily contacts between the field sales force and customers of all types, the company kept its finger on the market pulse, quickly detecting shifts in sales trends and getting prompt feedback on any problems with its products. If the company got more than a few similar complaints, the information was relayed immediately to design engineers. When design flaws or components defects were found, the factory was notified and the problem corrected within a matter of days. Management believed Dell's ability to respond quickly gave it a significant advantage over rivals, particularly over PC makers in Asia, that made large production runs and sold standardized products through retail channels. Dell saw its direct sales approach as a totally customer-driven system that allowed quick transitions to new generations of components and PC models.

Despite Dell's emphasis on direct sales, industry analysts noted that the company sold 10–15 percent of its PCs through a small, select group of resellers.[11] Most of these resellers were systems integrators. It was standard for Dell not to allow returns on orders from resellers or to provide price protection in the event of subsequent declines in market prices. From time to time, Dell offered its resellers incentive promotions at up to a 20 percent discount from its advertised prices on end-of-life models. Dell was said to have no plans to expand its reseller network, which consisted of about 50–60 dealers.

Market Segmentation

To make sure that each type of customer was well served, Dell had made a special effort to segment the buyers of its computers into relevant groups and to place managers in charge of developing sales and service programs appropriate to the needs and expectations of each market segment. Until the early 1990s, Dell had operated with sales and service programs aimed at just two market segments—(1) corporate and governmental buyers who purchased in large volumes and (2) small buyers

---

[11]"Dell Uses Channel to Move System Inventory," *Computer Reseller News,* January 12, 1998.

■ **Exhibit 7**
Rapid Expansion of
Dell Computer's Target
Customer Segments,
1995–1997

Target Customer Segments, 1995	**Target Customer Segments, 1996**	**Target Customer Segments, 1997**
• Large customers (both corporate and governmental buyers)	• Large companies • Midsize companies • Government agencies and educational institutions	• Global enterprise accounts • Large companies • Midsize companies • Federal agencies • State and local government agencies • Educational institutions
• Small customers (both small businesses and individuals)	• Small customers (both small businesses and individuals)	• Small companies • Individual consumers

SOURCE: Joan Magretta, "The Power of Virtual Integration: An Interview with Dell Computer's Michael Dell," *Harvard Business Review,* March–April 1998, p. 78.

(individuals and small businesses). But as sales took off in 1995–97, these segments were subdivided into finer, more homogeneous categories (see Exhibit 7).

In 1998, 90 percent of Dell's sales were to business or government institutions and of those 70 percent were to large corporate customers who bought at least $1 million in PCs annually. Many of these large customers typically ordered thousands of units at a time. Dell had hundreds of sales representatives calling on large corporate and institutional accounts. Its customer list included Shell Oil, Exxon, MCI, Ford Motor, Toyota, Eastman Chemical, Boeing, Goldman Sachs, Oracle, Microsoft, Woolwich (a British bank with $64 billion in assets), Michelin, Unilever, Deutsche Bank, Sony, Wal-Mart, and First Union (one of the 10 largest U.S. banks). However, no one customer represented more than 2 percent of total sales. Because corporate customers tended to buy the most expensive computers, Dell commanded the highest average selling prices in the industry—over $1,600 versus an industry average under $1,400.

Dell's sales to individuals and small businesses were made by telephone, fax, and the Internet. It had a call center in the United States with toll-free lines; customers could talk with a sales representative about specific models, get information faxed or mailed to them, place an order, and pay by credit card. Internationally, Dell had set up six call centers in Europe and Asia that customers could dial toll free.[12] The call centers were equipped with technology that routed calls from a particular country to a particular call center. Thus, for example, a customer calling from Lisbon, Portugal, was automatically directed to the call center in Montpelier, France, and connected to a Portuguese-speaking sales representative. Dell began Internet sales at its Web site (**www.dell.com**) in 1995, almost overnight achieving sales of $1 million per day. In 1997 Internet sales reached an average of $3 million daily, hitting $6 million some days during the Christmas shopping period. In the first quarter of 1997, Dell's Internet sales averaged nearly $4 million daily; and the

---

[12]"Michael Dell Rocks," *Fortune,* May 11, 1998, p. 66.

company expected that 1998 sales at its Web site would reach $1.5 billion. The fastest growing segment of Dell's international segment was on the Internet in Europe, where sales were running at a weekly volume of $5 million in early 1998. Internet sales were ramping up rapidly from Asian buyers. In early 1998, Dell's Internet sales were about equally divided between sales to individuals and sales to business customers. Nearly 1.5 million people visited Dell's Web site weekly to view information and place orders, about 20 times more than called to talk with sales representatives over the telephone.

In 1997, 31 percent, or $3.8 billion, of Dell's sales came from foreign customers. Europe, where resellers were strongly entrenched and Dell's direct sales approach was novel, was Dell's biggest foreign market. Dell's European sales were growing at 50 percent annually. The market leader in Europe was Compaq, with a 14.8 percent market share, followed by IBM with 8.3 percent, Dell with 7.8 percent, Hewlett-Packard with 7.6 percent, and Siemens Nixdorf (Germany) with 5.6 percent. In Britain, which Dell had entered in the late 1980s, Dell had a 12 percent share, trailing only Compaq. Sales of PCs in Europe were expected to reach 22–24 million in 1998 and 28.5 million in 1999. Total European sales in 1997 were 19.7 million units.

Customer Service

Service became a feature of Dell's strategy in 1986 when the company began providing a guarantee of free on-site service for a year with most of its PCs after users complained about having to ship their PCs back to Austin for repairs. Dell contracted with local service providers to handle customer requests for repairs; on-site service was provided on a next-day basis. Dell also provided its customers with technical support via a toll-free number, fax, and e-mail. Dell received close to 40,000 e-mail messages monthly requesting service and support and had 25 technicians to process the requests. Bundled service policies were a major selling point for winning corporate accounts. If a customer preferred to work with his or her own service provider, Dell gave that provider the training and spare parts needed to service the customer's equipment.

Selling direct allowed Dell to keep close track of the purchases of its large global customers, country by country and department by department—information that customers found valuable. Maintaining its close customer relationships allowed Dell to become quite knowledgeable about its customers' needs and how their PC network functioned. Aside from using this information to help customers plan their PC needs and configure their PC networks, Dell used its knowledge to add to the value it delivered to its customers. For example, Dell recognized that when it delivered a new PC to a corporate customer, the customer's PC personnel had to place asset tags on it and then load the software from an assortment of CD-ROMs and diskettes—a process that could take several hours and cost $200–$300.[13] Dell's solution was to load the customer's software onto one of its own very large Dell servers at the factory and, when a particular version of a customer's PC came off the assembly line, to use its high-speed server network to load that customer's software onto the PC's hard disk in a few seconds. If the customer so desired, Dell would place asset tags on the PC at the factory. Since Dell charged customers only an extra $15 or $20 for the software-loading and asset–tagging services, the savings to customers were considerable. One large customer reported savings of $500,000 annually from having

---

[13]Magretta, "The Power of Virtual Integration," p. 79.

Dell load its software and place asset tags on its PCs at the factory.[14] In 1997, about 2 million of the 7 million PCs Dell sold were shipped with customer-specific software already loaded on the PCs.

Corporate customers paid Dell fees to provide support and service. Dell then contracted with third-party providers to make the necessary service calls. When a customer with PC problems called Dell, the call triggered two electronic dispatches—one to ship the needed parts from Dell's factory to the customer sites and one to notify the contract service providers to prepare to make the needed repairs as soon as the parts arrived.[15] The service providers sent the bad parts back to Dell. Dell then endeavored to diagnose what went wrong and what could be done to see that the problem wouldn't happen again. Problems relating to faulty components or flawed components design were promptly passed along to the relevant supplier, who was expected to improve quality control procedures or redesign the component. Dell's strategy was to manage the flow of information gleaned from customer service activities both to improve product quality and speed execution.

Dell had plans in place to build Application Solutions Centers in both Europe and North America to assist its customers and independent software providers in migrating their systems and applications to Intel's new next-generation, 64-bit computing technology. Dell was partnering with Intel, Microsoft, Computer Associates, and other prominent PC technology providers to help customers make more effective use of the Internet and the latest computing technologies. Dell, which used Intel microprocessors exclusively in its computers, had been a consistent proponent of standardized Intel-based platforms because the company believed those platforms provided customers with the best total value and performance. Dell management considered both Intel and Microsoft as long-term strategic partners in mapping out its future.

In recent months Dell, following Compaq's lead, had created a capital services group to assist customers with financing their PC networks.

Virtual Integration and Information-Sharing

But what was unique about Dell's latest incarnation of its strategy was how the company was using technology and information-sharing with both supply partners and customers to blur the traditional arm's-length boundaries in the supplier–manufacturer–customer value chain that characterized Dell's earlier business model and other direct-sell competitors. Michael Dell referred to this feature of Dell's strategy as "virtual integration."[16] On-line communications technology made it easy for Dell to communicate inventory levels and replenishment needs to vendors daily or even hourly.

Boeing offers an example of how the lines were becoming blurred between Dell and its customers. Boeing, which had 100,000 Dell PCs, was served by a staff of 30 Dell employees who resided on-site at Boeing facilities and were intimately involved in planning Boeing's PC needs and the configuration of Boeing's network. While Boeing had its own people working on what the company's best answers for using PCs were, Dell and Boeing personnel worked closely together to understand Boeing's needs in depth and to figure out the best ways to meet those needs.

---

[14]"Michael Dell Rocks," p. 61.

[15]Kevin Rollins, "Using Information to Speed Execution," *Harvard Business Review*, March–April, 1998, p. 81.

[16]Magretta, "The Power of Virtual Integration," p. 74.

A number of Dell's corporate accounts were large enough to justify dedicated on-site teams of Dell employees. Customers usually welcomed such teams, preferring to focus their time and energy on the core business rather than being distracted by PC purchasing and servicing issues.

In addition to using its sales and support mechanisms to stay close to customers, Dell had set up a number of regional forums to stimulate the flow of information back and forth with customers. The company formed Platinum Councils composed of its largest customers in the United States, Europe, Japan, and the Asia-Pacific region; regional meetings were held every six to nine months.[17] In the larger regions, there were two meetings—one for chief information officers and one for technical personnel. As many as 100 customers and 100 Dell executives and representatives, including Michael Dell himself, attended the three-day meetings, at which Dell's senior technologists shared their views on the direction of the latest technological developments, what the flow of technology really meant for customers, and Dell's plans for introducing new and upgraded products over the next two years. There were also breakout sessions on such topics as managing the transition to Windows NT, managing the use of notebooks by people out in the field, and determining whether leasing was better than buying. Customers were provided opportunities to share information and learn from one another (many had similar problems) as well as exchange ideas with Dell personnel. Dell found that the information gleaned from customers at these meetings assisted in forecasting demand for the company's products.

Dell had developed customized intranet sites (called Premier Pages) for its 3,000 largest global customers; these sites gave customer personnel immediate on-line access to purchasing and technical information about the specific configurations of products that their company had purchased from Dell or that were currently authorized for purchase.[18] The Premier Pages contained all of the elements of Dell's relationship with the customer—who the Dell sales and support contacts were in every country where the customer had operations, detailed product descriptions, what software Dell loaded on each of the various types of PCs the customer purchased, service and warranty records, pricing, and the available technical support.[19] Dell was readying Premier Page software improvements for introduction in the second half of 1998 with even greater functionality. One new feature made it easy for a customer to specify what types of machines and options their personnel should be authorized to purchase. Other features included allowing customer personnel to access detailed information about Dell products on-line, view all the different machines and options the customer had authorized for its personnel, obtain the price of the particular PC they wanted, place an order, and have the order automatically routed to higher-level managers for approval. These features eliminated paper invoices, cut ordering time, and reduced the internal labor needed to staff corporate purchasing functions. Dell was said to have the most comprehensive Web-based PC commerce capability of any PC vendor. The company's goal was to generate 50 percent of its sales on the Internet within the next two or three years by setting up Premier Pages for virtually all of its large customers and adding more

---

[17]Magretta, "The Power of Virtual Integration," p. 80.

[18]Ibid.

[19]"Dell Turns to Servers—Chairman and CEO Michael Dell Discusses the Vendor's Plans for High-End Servers and Online," *Information Week*, April 27, 1998.

features to further improve functionality. So far, customer use of Premier Pages had boosted the productivity of salespeople assigned to these accounts by 50 percent.

The company also gave its large customers access to Dell's own on-line internal technical support tools, allowing them to go to **www.dell.com,** enter some information about their system, and gain immediate access to the same database and problem-solving information that Dell's support personnel used to assist call-in customers.[20] This tool was particularly useful to the internal help-desk groups at large companies.

Demand Forecasting

Management believed that accurate sales forecasts were key to keeping costs down and minimizing inventories, given the complexity and diversity of the company's product line. Because Dell worked diligently to maintain a close relationship with its large corporate and institutional customers, and because it sold direct to small customers via telephone and the Internet, it was possible for the company to keep a finger on the pulse of demand—what was selling and what was not. Moreover, the company's market segmentation strategy paved the way for in-depth understanding of its customers' evolving requirements and expectations. Having credible real-time information about what customers were actually buying and having first hand knowledge of large customers' buying intentions gave Dell strong capability to forecast demand. Furthermore, Dell passed that knowledge on to suppliers so they could plan their production accordingly. The company worked hard at managing the flow of information it got from the marketplace and seeing that it got to both internal groups and vendors in timely fashion.

Forecasting was viewed as a critical sales skill. Sales-account managers were coached on how to lead large customers through a discussion of their future needs for PCs, workstations, servers, and peripheral equipment. Distinctions were made between purchases that were virtually certain and those that were contingent on some event. Salespeople made note of the contingent events so they could follow up at the appropriate time. With smaller customers, there was real-time information about sales, and direct telephone sales personnel often were able to steer customers toward configurations that were immediately available to help fine-tune the balance between demand and supply.

Research and Development

Company management believed that it was Dell's job to sort out all the new technology coming into the marketplace and help steer customers to options and solutions most relevant to their needs. The company talked to its customers frequently about "relevant technology," listening carefully to customers' needs and problems and endeavoring to identify the most cost-effective solutions. Dell had about 1,600 engineers working on product development and spent about $250 million annually to improve users' experience with its products—including incorporating the latest and best technologies, making its products easy to use, and devising ways to keep costs down. The company's R&D unit also studied and implemented ways to control quality and to streamline the assembly process. Much time went into tracking all the new developments in components and software to ascertain how they would prove

---

[20]Interview with Michael Dell, *Internet Week*, April 13, 1998.

useful to computer users. For instance, it was critical to track vendor progress in making longer-lasting batteries because battery life was important to the buyers of portable computers. Dell was the first company to put lithium ion batteries with a life of 5.5 to 6 hours in all of its laptop models.

Advertising

Michael Dell was a strong believer in the power of advertising and frequently espoused its importance in the company's strategy. Thus, Dell was the first computer company to use comparative ads, throwing barbs at Compaq's higher prices. Although Compaq won a lawsuit against Dell for making false comparisons, Michael Dell was unapologetic, arguing that "[the ads were] very effective. We were able to increase customer awareness about value."[21] Dell insisted that the company's ads be communicative and forceful, not soft and fuzzy.

The company regularly had prominent ads in such leading computer publications as *PC Magazine* and *PC World,* as well as in *USA Today, The Wall Street Journal,* and other business publications. In the spring of 1998, the company debuted a multi-year worldwide TV campaign to strengthen its brand image.

Entry into Servers

Dell entered the market for low-end PC servers (those priced under $25,000) in the second half of 1996. The company had opened a 23,000-square-foot plant dedicated to server production, trained 1,300 telemarketers to sell servers, assigned 160 sales reps with systems know-how to big customer accounts, and recruited a staff of systems experts to help the sales reps. It had contracted with companies such as Electronic Data Systems, which had in-depth systems and networking expertise, to help provide service to large customers with extensive server networks. Dell's server plant used "cell" manufacturing instead of an assembly line to permit faster product updates and keep costs low; there were 30 cells at the plant, each with a self-contained work team that performed the entire assembly process from a kit of components and a customized motherboard.

Dell's entry into servers had several purposes. The use of servers by corporate customers was growing rapidly. The margins on servers were large. Moreover, purchase price was not as significant a factor in selecting which brand of server to buy because servers required far more in the way of service, support, and software. Several of Dell's rivals, most notably Compaq, were using their big margins on server sales to subsidize price cuts on desktops and notebooks in an attempt to win corporate PC accounts away from Dell. According to Michael Dell, "To neutralize that, Dell needs to be in the server market." The company expected that sales of servers would grow to about 50 percent of corporate revenues by 2001.

Dell's build-to-order and sell-direct strategies gave it a significant pricing advantage over rivals. Servers from such competitors as Compaq, IBM, and Hewlett-Packard, all of which relied on networks of resellers, were estimated to cost 15 to 20 percent more than Dell servers. However, analysts were skeptical about whether Dell could provide the same quality of service and support to server customers that resellers could. To counter that perception, Dell had bolstered its field sales and

---

[21]"The Education of Michael Dell," p. 85.

support staff to 600 employees and created an in-house consulting group to assist customers. For customers that required extensive system support and integration, Dell partnered with systems experts that were not resellers, such as Electronic Data Systems and Arthur Andersen.

■ Recent Developments in the PC Industry

There were an estimated 250 million PCs in use in 1997, and sales of PCs were approaching 100 million annually (see Exhibit 8). Michael Dell believed there would be 1.4 billion PCs in use within 10 years. Going into 1998, household penetration of PCs was estimated to be 45 percent. There were over 5 million new PC-owning households in 1997, many lured by the introduction of reasonably equipped sub-$1,000 PCs. The three most influential factors in home ownership of PCs were education, income, and the presence of children in the household. Household penetration was expected to exceed 50 percent by the year 2000.

A number of factors were affecting the competitive structure of the world market for PCs in 1998: declining component prices, the troubled economies of several Asian countries, potential slowdowns in the industry growth rate, the attempts of Dell's rivals to shift to build-to-order manufacturing, continuing advances in PC technology, and the moves of several PC makers to expand into marketing more than just PCs to their customers.

Declining Component Prices

Sharp drops in the prices of a number of PC components (chiefly, disk drives, memory chips, and microprocessors) starting in late 1997 had allowed PC makers to dramatically lower PC prices—sales of PCs priced under $1,500 were booming by early 1998. Compaq, IBM, Hewlett-Packard, and several other PC makers had begun marketing sub-$1,000 PCs in 1997. In December 1997, the average purchase price of a desktop computer fell below $1,300 for the first time. It was estimated that about half of all PC sales in 1998 were of computers carrying price tags under $1,500. Growth in unit volume was being driven largely by sub-$1,000 PCs. The low prices were attracting first-time buyers into the market and were also causing second- and third-time PC buyers looking to upgrade to more powerful PCs to forgo top-of-the-line machines priced in the traditional $2,000–$3,500 range in favor of lower-priced PCs that were almost as powerful and well-equipped. Powerful, multifeatured notebook computers that had formerly sold for $4,000 to $6,500 in November 1997 were sell-

■ **Exhibit 8**
Actual and Projected
Worldwide Shipments
of PCs

Year	PC Volume
1980	1 million
1985	11 million
1990	24 million
1995	58 million
1996	69 million
1997	80 million
2000	118 million (projected)

SOURCE: International Data Corporation.

ing for $2,000 to $4,500 in April 1998. The profits of many PC makers slipped in early 1998 because of the need to discount unsold higher-priced machines still in inventory and on retailers' shelves.

Economic Problems in Asia

Economic woes in a number of Asian countries (most notably, Japan, South Korea, Thailand, and Indonesia) were putting a big damper on PC sales in Asia. Asian sales of PCs in 1998 were expected to grow minimally, if at all, and some analysts expected unit volume to fall below 1997 levels. Sharp appreciation of the U.S. dollar against Asian currencies had made U.S.–produced PCs more expensive to Asian buyers. In contrast, sales in the United States and Europe were quite robust, mainly because of lower PC prices.

Disk-drive manufacturers and the makers of printed circuit boards, many of which were in Asia, were feeling the pressures of declining prices and skimpy profit margins. Industry observers were predicting that competitive conditions in the Asian-Pacific PC market favored growing market shares by the top four or five players and the likely exit of PC makers that could not compete profitably.

Slowing Industry Growth

Most industry observers were warning of a global slowdown in the sales of PCs in 1998, partly due to the economic difficulties in several Asian countries and partly due to the potential for market maturity for PCs. Industry growth rates were projected to be close to 15 percent annually for the remainder of the decade, down from the average annual growth rate of 20 percent during the 1990–96 period. However, U.S. shipments of PCs in 1997 had risen 21 percent, to 31 million units, a much higher rate than most industry analysts had expected. Sales of servers were the fastest growing segment of the PC industry; in 1997 revenues jumped 35 percent, to $10.5 billion, on shipments of 1.7 million units.

Attempts to Clone Dell's PC Strategy

Dell's competitors—Compaq, IBM, Packard Bell NEC, and Hewlett-Packard—were shifting their business models to build-to-order manufacturing to reduce their inventories and speed new models to market. Compaq launched its build-to-order initiative in July 1997 and hoped to cut costs by 10 to 12 percent. Compaq's revamped assembly plants could turn out a custom-built PC in three to four hours and could load the desired software in six minutes. Packard Bell NEC's program allowed customers to place orders by phone. But all three were finding that it was hard to duplicate Dell's approach because of how long it took to develop just-in-time delivery schedules with suppliers, to coordinate their mutual production schedules, and to shift smoothly to next-generation parts and components as they appeared on the market. Extensive collaboration was needed to plan smooth technology transitions. Compaq and Hewlett-Packard had spent 18 months planning their build-to-order strategies and expected it would take another 18 or more months to achieve their inventory and cost-reduction goals.

At the same time, such computer retailers as Tandy Corporation's Computer City, CompUSA, OfficeMax, and Wal-Mart had gotten into the build-to-order and sell-direct business. CompUSA was offering customers two lines of desktop computers that could be ordered at any of its 134 stores, by phone, at its Web site, or through its corporate sales force; its goal was to undercut Dell's price by $200 on each configuration. Wal-Mart was offering build-to-order PCs made by a contract manufacturer at its Web site.

Dell was seen as having the right strategy to appeal to customers well versed in PC technology who knew what options and features they wanted and who were aware of the price differentials among brands. According to one industry analyst, "Dell is everybody's target. No matter who you talk to in the industry, Dell is the brand to beat."[22]

The Moves of PC Makers to Broaden Their Business

Several leading players in the PC industry made moves in late 1997 and early 1998 to expand into selling more than just PCs in an effort to improve profitability. The sharp declines in the prices of PCs had crimped gross profit margins and prompted such companies as Compaq, Gateway, Hewlett-Packard, and IBM to view selling PCs as an entrée to providing a bigger lineup of products.

To move beyond simple PC manufacturing, Compaq in late 1997 acquired Digital Equipment Company (DEC), which derived $6 billion in revenues from providing a range of PC services to corporate customers. Gateway announced in May 1998 that it would start bundling into the sale of its PCs to individuals and households a wide range of software, peripheral devices like printers and scanners, maintenance and troubleshooting services, and even its own Internet service. Gateway's CEO Ted Waitt explained, "We're about customer relations a lot more than we are about PCs. If we get a 5 percent margin on a $1,500 PC, we make $75. But if we can make $3 a month on Internet access, that's another $100 over three years. Three years from now, I don't think just selling PC hardware will allow anyone to have a great business."[23] Gateway had begun asking customers ordering a PC to identify their major interests and hobbies; if a customer identified gardening or sports or investing, Gateway offered to include related software packages with the PC. Gateway had also announced a plan to lease PCs to individuals and households and to finance PCs on low monthly payment plans in hopes of getting the customer to trade in the old PC for a new PC later when the lease expired or the last payment was made. Both Hewlett-Packard and IBM had always viewed the PC business as part of a larger portfolio of products and services they offered customers. A substantial portion of Hewlett-Packard's revenues and profits came from sales of servers and printers. IBM derived a big portion of its revenues from mainframe computers, software, and technical and support services.

■ Profiles of Selected Competitors in the PC Industry

Dell's principal competitors in the global PC market had varying strategies and resource capabilities.

Compaq Computer (**www.compaq.com**)

Compaq was the world's leading PC manufacturer, with a global market share of approximately 13 percent. It had overtaken IBM to become the market leader in PCs in 1994. Compaq had revenues of $24.6 billion and profits of $1.9 billion in 1997. Compaq's strategy was to sell almost exclusively through resellers—distributors and

---

[22]As quoted in *Business Week,* September 29, 1997, p. 38.

[23]David Kirkpatrick, "Old PC Dogs Try New Tricks," *Fortune,* July 6, 1998, pp. 186–88.

PC retailers, particularly large computer stores like CompUSA. It was starting to build computers to order and operate its factories with smaller inventories of parts and components, but it had to soft-pedal direct sales so as not to alienate its world-wide reseller network. Because Compaq had bigger components inventories than Dell and because its resellers sometimes had sizable inventories of Compaq's models on hand, Compaq was slower than Dell in getting new generations of its PCs into the marketplace.

Compaq offered a full line of desktop PCs, from sub-$1,000 PCs to top-of-the-line models. It was the most aggressive seller of PCs priced under $1,000 and in recent months had averaged over a 60 percent share of the sub-$1,000 segment. It also offered a broad line of laptop PCs, but its 9 percent share of the laptop segment put it in third place behind Toshiba, the global market leader in laptop PCs (with a 20 percent share), and IBM (with an 11 percent share). Compaq shipped a total of 10 million desktop and laptop PCs worldwide in 1997, up from 7.2 million in 1996. Compaq was also the market leader in PC servers priced under $25,000 and was a strong third (behind IBM and Hewlett-Packard) in low-end or entry servers (those priced under $100,000). Compaq executives expected that sales of PCs to individuals and households would continue to account for about 15 percent of revenues, sales of desktop PCs to corporate customers would fall from 48 percent of revenues in 1997 to about 32 percent in 2000, and sales of servers and workstations would grow to 50 percent of revenues from 35 percent in 1997. Compaq's goal was to have $50 billion in revenues in 2000.

Compaq's market strength was greatest among Fortune 1000 companies; it had weaker penetration in the small and medium business segments. To combat the volume discounts that Dell and other direct vendors typically used to help win the accounts of small and medium businesses, Compaq had recently begun working more closely with its resellers on special pricing to make the Compaq brand more competitive in the bidding process. To boost its subpar 3 percent share of the Japanese market for PCs, Compaq had recently signed a deal that gave Canon Sales Company exclusive distribution and sales rights to Compaq's consumer-oriented Presario models.

In early 1998, Compaq acquired floundering Digital Equipment Company (DEC) for $9.6 billion, a move intended to turn Compaq into more of a full-spectrum global supplier of computer hardware and services and put it into better position to challenge IBM as a "global enterprise computing company." DEC had 1997 revenues of $13 billion (versus $14.5 billion in 1996) and net earnings of $141 million (versus a loss of $112 million in 1996). The merged companies would have combined revenues of $37.6 billion, making Compaq the second largest computer company in the world.

DEC considered itself to be a "network solutions company" with strengths in multi-vendor integration, Internet security, continuous computing, high-availability data, and high-performance networked platforms. Its chief products were large servers (those priced over $1 million), entry servers (those priced under $100,000), large computers and workstations, and personal computers (55 percent of revenues). Services accounted for 45 percent of revenues (about $6 billion); DEC had 25,000 engineers and support people in the field working with customers (Compaq had 8,000 sales and support people in the field, many of whom spent much of their time servicing retailers of Compaq PCs). DEC's gross margins on services averaged 34 percent, compared to Compaq's 25 percent margins on PC sales. Compaq's corporate customers had been requesting the company to provide more service for years.

In May 1998, Compaq announced plans to cut about 15,000 jobs at DEC when the acquisition was completed; the layoffs were expected to come mainly in DEC's personal computer division, portions of its sales force, and corporate computer operations—where there were significant overlaps with Compaq's business. DEC had a total of 53,500 employees, down from a peak of 130,000 in the 1980s. Despite recent workforce downsizings, DEC still employed about 65 percent more people than Compaq to produce about half the volume of sales revenues. DEC management indicated that the company's selling, general, and administrative costs of $3.18 billion in 1997 (24 percent of total 1997 revenues) would likely be cut in half following the merger. Compaq had selling, general, and administrative expenses of $2.95 billion on sales of $24.6 billion in 1997 (equal to 12 percent of revenues).

Compaq believed that DEC's expertise in networking and information systems integration, coupled with the combined product lines, would give it an advantage with large corporate customers over companies like Dell that offered mainly PC-related services. Compaq also believed that DEC's worldwide service and support capabilities would help it win corporate business for PCs, workstations, and servers away from IBM. (Prior to the Compaq–DEC merger, Dell had contracted with DEC's service organization to maintain its PowerEdge line of servers at a number of corporate accounts; Dell was expected to sign Unisys or Wang to replace DEC.)

IBM (www.ibm.com)

IBM was considered to be a "computer solutions" company and operated in more segments of the overall computer industry than Dell. PC sales accounted for $15.7 billion of IBM's 1997 revenues of $68 billion. IBM had 1997 sales of $1.3 billion in workstations; $4.3 billion in entry servers (those priced under $100,000), where it was the market leader; and $6.0 billion in midrange servers (those priced between $100,000 and $1 million), where it was also the market leader. The company had for many years been the global leader in mainframe computers, and it derived $19.3 billion in revenues from providing technical service and support to customers—the company had 160,000 technical support personnel in the field to service customers. In 1997 IBM introduced a long-awaited generation of mainframe computers based on PC-type microprocessors that offered the speed of traditional mainframes at lower purchase and operating costs.

During the 1990s IBM had experienced 2 percent annual revenue growth—revenues rose from $69.7 billion in 1990 to $78.5 billion in 1997. Net income of $6.1 billion in 1997 was barely above the 1990 level of $6.0 billion and well below the company's record earnings of $6.6 billion in 1984. The company was struggling to reinvent itself as the growing use of PCs continued to erode corporate dependence on mainframe computers. IBM's sales of computer hardware were flat; its fastest growing businesses were in services and software. To boost its growth potential and add attractive new products to its lineup, the company had purchased spreadsheet software pioneer Lotus Development in 1995 for $3.5 billion and Edmark, a publisher of educational software for children, in 1997. Also in 1997, IBM sold its ownership interest in Prodigy (an on-line service provider that had once enjoyed a dominant position against rival America Online) for $250 million after investing $1.2 billion.

IBM's market share in PCs was eroding—it had lost more market share in the 1990s than any other PC maker. Its main strengths in PCs were in laptop computers and in desktop sales to corporate customers, many of which also had IBM mainframe computers and had been longtime IBM customers. IBM was regarded as a high-cost producer of PCs and, traditionally, had commanded a premium price for its PCs. IBM saw notebook computers as the key to winning corporate accounts due to the need of many corporate personnel for mobile computing capability. The company's laptop PCs, while highly rated for their performance features and quality, were typically higher priced than comparably equipped models of rival sellers. IBM competed against PC rivals by emphasizing confidence in the IBM brand and the company's long-standing strengths in software applications, service, and technical support. IBM had responded to the direct-sales inroads Dell had made in the corporate market by allowing some of its resellers to custom-assemble IBM PCs to buyer specifications; it was hoping this effort would cut costs up to 10 percent. IBM's PC division was believed to be operating at breakeven or a slight loss in the first quarter of 1998.

Hewlett-Packard (www.hp.com)

Dell regarded Hewlett-Packard (H-P) as a strong competitor because of H-P's global leadership in printers (a 52 percent market share), strong reputation with corporate customers in most all parts of the world, and growing strategic emphasis on the PC segment. Since 1995 H-P's share of the PC market had been rising almost as quickly as Dell's. H-P was co-designing the next-generation microprocessor with Intel—code-named the Merced and scheduled for introduction in late 1999 and full-market rollout in 2000. H-P's partnership with Intel on the Merced was expected to put H-P on the cutting edge of PC technology for the next several years and boost its brand image in PCs.

H-P marketed its PC line through resellers that had the capability to deliver orders to major corporate accounts within 12 to 24 hours. Despite rapidly growing sales, HP's PC division had not yet achieved profitability; the division recorded a small loss in the first quarter of 1998.

H-P was the market leader in revenue, units, and growth in the Windows NT–based workstation market. Compaq was a close second. H-P marketed over 25,000 products that included desktop and notebook PCs, printers, workstations, servers, digital cameras, scanners, calculators, storage devices, networking software and equipment, test and measurement equipment, and medical electronics products.

Gateway (www.gateway.com)

Gateway, formerly called Gateway 2000, was a South Dakota–based company with 1997 revenues of $6.3 billion and profits of $110 million. Founder and chairman Ted Waitt, 34, who wore his hair in a ponytail, owned 46 percent of the company; his brother owned 9 percent. Waitt had dropped out of college in 1985 to go to work for a computer retailer in Des Moines, Iowa; after nine months, he quit to form his own company. The company, operating out of a barn on his father's cattle ranch, sold add-on parts by phone for Texas Instruments PCs. In 1987, the company, using its own PC design, started selling fully-equipped PCs at a price near that of other PC makers. Sales took off and in 1991 Gateway topped *Inc.* magazine's list of the nation's fastest growing private companies. The company went public in 1993, achieving sales of $1.7 billion and earnings of $151 million. The company had differentiated itself from rivals with eye-catching ads; some featured white-and-black-spotted cows while others featured company employees (including one with Waitt dressed as Robin Hood).

Despite growing at a rate of nearly 38 percent annually since 1993, Gateway was struggling to achieve acceptable profitability—the company's profit margin had eroded steadily from a high of 9.6 percent in 1992 to only 1.7 percent in 1997. Gateway, like Dell, built to order and sold direct. But its market strengths were concentrated in the individual, small-business, and school segments, where it outsold Dell. It was the market leader in the education segment. At the beginning of 1997 Gateway's consumer line of desktop PCs was priced on average 12 percent below comparable Dell consumer models; by December 1997, Dell had an average price advantage of 5 percent over Gateway in the consumer segment. One of Gateway's strategies to boost profit margins was to strengthen its appeal to medium-sized and large corporations. The company had recently hired 80 salespeople to court new corporate customers and was strengthening its efforts to sell to corporate customers through dealers as well.

Gateway had entered the server segment in 1997 by purchasing Advanced Logic Research, Inc. (ALR). ALR's server manufacturing facility in California began making servers for Gateway for direct sale to Gateway customers. However, in 1998 ALR was continuing to make ALR servers for sale through its network of resellers.

Toshiba

Toshiba was a $48-billion Japanese electronics and electrical equipment manufacturer with 303 subsidiaries and affiliates worldwide; it ranked as the world's 37th largest corporation in terms of revenues. Its Toshiba America Information Systems division was the leading vendor in the U.S. market for portable computers, with a 20.4 percent share in 1997. The division offered the widest array of portable PCs of any manufacturer, selling both direct and through dealers and having a commanding lead over rivals in both channels. In addition to Toshiba portable PCs in all price ranges, the division also marketed desktop PCs, disk drives, plain-paper copiers, facsimile systems, voice-mail systems, digital key telephones, optical-fiber modems, and digital cameras under the Toshiba brand name. Headquartered in Irvine, California, it had $4 billion in annual sales.

Providers of House-Label Brands

There were about 35,000 resellers of generic, or "white-box," PCs in North America alone. This house-label segment constituted a $7.6-billion market in the United States and Canada, representing shipments of 6.4 million units and 30 percent of sales through resellers. No single no-name brand, however, accounted for more than 0.25 percent market share, and most accounted for far less. Generic PCs assembled in "screwdriver shops" had been a part of the PC business since its inception—Steve Wozniak and Steve Jobs launched Apple from a garage using purchased components. Rising technological savvy about how PCs worked and the widespread availability of individual components made it fairly easy for an enterprising operation to assemble a generic PC. To keep costs and prices low, the makers of generic PCs typically incorporated components from low-end suppliers and their products did not match name-brand PCs in performance and dependability. White-box PCs appealed mainly to very price-conscious buyers; most businesses that had tried generic brands had learned the hard way that the cheapest PC was not always the least expensive in the long run due to problems with quality and reliability.

Roughly two-thirds of the resellers who built their own systems for sale under their own brand also carried name brands. In 1998 resellers expected the sales of generic PCs to rise to about 35 percent of their total PC sales.

■ Case 2   Caterpillar Inc.

Sara L. Pitterle and J. Paul Peter
both of the University of Wisconsin–Madison

After a record year in 1988, Caterpillar's profits declined steadily, culminating in a $404 million loss ($4.00 per share of common stock) in 1991. The loss was attributed to a number of factors, including a prolonged global recession and one-time charges associated with facility closings, consolidation, and employment reductions. These cutbacks were designed to reduce Caterpillar's manufacturing costs over the long term. On April 23, 1992, Caterpillar announced a $132 million loss for the first quarter. Although a strike by the United Auto Workers had disrupted production for the entire quarter, management attributed the loss solely to lower sales. (Appendix A contains a summary of Caterpillar's recent financial performance.)

These losses were incurred by a company which had made unprecedented changes over the past decade in response to the changing industrial equipment market. These changes include a multibillion dollar plant modernization program begun in 1985 and a company reorganization undertaken in 1990. These two changes were designed to ensure Caterpillar's profitability for the 1990s and beyond. However, the 1991 and 1992 profit results led management to wonder whether the changes would be successful.

■ History

Caterpillar is a multinational corporation headquartered in Peoria, Illinois, that competes in three principal business segments. The company designs, manufactures, and markets engines for a wide range of applications including: electrical power generation systems, on-highway trucks, and industrial machinery. The company also designs, manufactures, and markets earthmoving, construction, and materials-handling machinery. (See Appendix B for a complete listing of Caterpillar equipment.) In addition, Caterpillar provides financial products to assist customers in purchasing Caterpillar and noncompetitive related equipment.[1] The company has manufacturing facilities and/or marketing offices in fifteen countries besides the United States.[2]

Caterpillar, the largest manufacturer of engines and construction equipment in the world, traces its origins to two inventors, Daniel Best and Benjamin Holt, who in the late 1800s, independently developed mechanized agricultural equipment. In February 1889, Daniel Best introduced the first steam-powered harvester, replacing the 40-horse-drawn combine with an 8-man, 11-ton, self-propelled tractor using wheels eight feet in diameter. Around the same time, Benjamin Holt began field testing the first crawler-type equipment, built simply by replacing the wheels on existing equipment with new "track" structures—pairs of treads comprised of wooden slats linked loosely together.

This case was prepared by Sara L. Pitterle, Nielson Fellow at the University of Wisconsin–Madison, under the supervision of J. Paul Peter.

[1]Caterpillar Inc. Annual Report for 1991.

[2]Taken from speech by Ed Terrel, Manager of Human Resources for Caterpillar Inc., at the University of Wisconsin–Madison, September 23, 1992.

The two companies prospered, driven by increasing demand in agriculture, road building, military equipment, and industrial construction. The introduction of the internal-combustion engine provided yet another boost for the evolving heavy-equipment industry. In 1925, the Holt and Best companies merged to form Caterpillar Tractor Company, setting the stage for several decades of uninterrupted growth through technological leadership and a commitment to total quality.

In 1931, the first Caterpillar diesel tractor was introduced. This product initiated a six-year sales growth from $13 million to $63 million and launched the track-type tractor into prominence as the single largest user of diesel power. Caterpillar's growing reputation for industry leadership and technological superiority was further strengthened during World War II by U.S. government defense contracts. These contracts included demand for both existing equipment (e.g., bulldozers and graders) and special government requests for revolutionary and sophisticated equipment such as air-cooled diesel engines for advanced military operations.

Throughout the postwar years, and into the 1970s, Caterpillar generally concentrated on the development of large industrial-sized machines and engines. During this time the company purchased the Trackson Company of Milwaukee to produce hoists, pipe layers, and hydraulically operated tractor shovels for Caterpillar crawlers. Later, Towmotor Corporation was acquired to continue the company's expansion into heavy equipment with forklift trucks and straddle carriers for a wide range of materials-handling applications. By the early 1970s, Caterpillar had achieved at least foothold positions in a variety of heavy equipment product lines, with the objective of achieving industry leadership in each of the new areas.

In 1977, Caterpillar unveiled the single largest, most technologically advanced tractor in the world—the D-10. Foremost among its advantages were an elevated drive sprocket and modular-designed major components. The elevation of the drive sprocket removed it from high-wear and shock-load areas, reduced overall stress on the undercarriage, and produced a smoother ride. The modular design of major components not only permitted faster and more efficient servicing, but also provided the opportunity to pretest components before final assembly. Modular designs thereby reduced repair and overall downtime in some cases by as much as 80 percent.[3] Caterpillar rapidly introduced other new products which incorporated the modular design concept.

In the early 1980s, after 50 years of uninterrupted profits, Caterpillar appeared to be invincible because of its ability to continually introduce technologically superior machines that became the industry standard. The company built the biggest and the best equipment in the world for which customers were willing to pay hefty premiums. Then, during 1982, in the words of past Caterpillar chairman and chief executive officer George Schaefer, "Almost overnight the world changed for us."[4]

The construction industry collapsed. Oil and other commodity prices fell, eliminating demand for Caterpillar equipment in mining, logging, and other heavy equipment markets. The dollar strengthened against the yen, giving Japanese equipment makers, especially Komatsu, an opportunity to aggressively pursue the United States' equipment market with cost advantages of up to 40 percent.[5] If these factors

---

[3]Donald Eckrich, "Caterpillar Tractor Company," in J. Paul Peter and James H. Donnelly, Jr., *Marketing Management: Knowledge and Skills,* 3rd ed. (Homewood, IL: Richard D. Irwin, 1991), pp. 702–4.

[4]Ronald Henkoff, "This Cat Is Acting Like a Tiger," *Fortune,* December 19, 1988, p. 72.

[5]Allan J. Magrath, "Eight Ways to Avoid Marketing Shock," *Sales & Marketing Management,* April 1989, p. 55.

were not enough to disrupt the "profits as usual" pattern at Caterpillar, the United Auto Workers, Caterpillar's largest union, went out on strike for seven months during 1982. After making record profits of $579 million in 1981, the company lost $953 million over the next three years.

■ Realignment Strategies

Some of Caterpillar's financial problems during the early '80s were a result of management's failure to react to the changing world environment. Caterpillar was increasing its plant capacity at a rate of 5 percent a year as late as 1982, even though expansion in the world heavy-equipment market ended in 1980. In fact, Caterpillar had pursued expansion until less than half of existing capacity was needed. As a result of this overcapacity, the company reduced plant space by one-third, closing 10 plants (8 in the United States) between 1983 and 1987. During this same time period, 28 percent of the company's equity and 40 percent of its labor force, more than 30,000 jobs, were eliminated.[6]

New Products

With the realization that world demand for large heavy equipment would expand only marginally in the future, the company began to consider other market opportunities. The company recognized that it had been ignoring small contractors who did not need such massive equipment, but who represented a growing market segment. The company responded by introducing new multipurpose products for the owner/operator or small construction contractor. These products included tractor mounted backhoes, front-end loaders, and even farm tractors.[7] While Caterpillar has gained market share in these segments quite successfully (11 percent by 1987), these smaller products also have smaller profit margins and more competition from both domestic manufacturers, such as Deere & Company and Tenneco's J. I. Case, and Japanese companies such as Komatsu, Kawasaki, and Kubota.[8]

Price Changes

Because of Caterpillar's leadership position in product quality and innovation, the company was able to obtain a premium price for its equipment. However, when Komatsu began offering comparable equipment at a 40 percent lower price in the early 1980s, Caterpillar was forced to cut prices to match those of a competitor for the first time in its history. The company decided to sacrifice profits to protect market share and ensure the company's long-term survival. Even using this strategy, Caterpillar's North American market share dropped 11 points from 1981 to 1986. Most analysts agree the figures would have been worse had the company not slashed prices and profits in response to its competitors.[9]

---

[6]Robert S. Eckley, "Caterpillar's Ordeal: Foreign Competition in Capital Goods," *Business Horizons,* March–April 1989, p. 80.

[7]Henkoff, p. 73.

[8]Kathleen Deveny, "For Caterpillar, the Metamorphosis Isn't Over," *Business Week,* August 31, 1987, p. 73.

[9]Henkoff, p. 72.

In addition, Caterpillar recognized that pricing was just one part of the overall revenue-generating strategy for the corporation. Caterpillar pursued other strategies to generate income. For example, the company capitalized on its recognized strength in distribution of products, and sold logistic services to a variety of corporations including Land Rover and Chrysler.[10]

Production Changes

In response to Japanese competition, Caterpillar also broke with its traditional policy of manufacturing everything it sells. The company's paving equipment, sold under the Cat name, was manufactured by CMI Corp. Caterpillar also began a joint venture with Mitsubishi Heavy Industries Ltd., to make excavation equipment in Japan, as well as light construction equipment and forklifts for the U.S. market. In addition, almost all of the equipment sold with the Caterpillar name in the Pacific Rim was manufactured jointly with Mitsubishi.

Plant with a Future Program

Although Caterpillar was profitable in 1985, management had no illusions about the company's ability to remain profitable for the long term with its historically high cost structure. For this reason, the company decided to concentrate on driving costs down and improving quality standards. To achieve these objectives, Caterpillar completed a massive six-year, $1.2 billion plant modernization program called *Plant with a Future (PWAF)*. At the heart of PWAF were automation, new factory layouts, and continuous work flow. The program meant a complete remake of Caterpillar's tooling and manufacturing methods, as well as a change to global sourcing to achieve the lowest possible costs on components.

The first priority for the Plant with a Future program was to simplify and integrate assembly-line processes. This objective was accomplished using a cell manufacturing concept in which plants and equipment are arranged to process families of components from start to finish. For example, machining, welding, heat treating, and painting might all be functions within a single cell. Work flow is continuous because all cells feed the assembly line just in time. Thus, the entire plant requires just-in-time (JIT) delivery schedules.

For Caterpillar to integrate just-in-time delivery to each cell, computer integrated manufacturing (CIM) was utilized. CIM links self-contained manufacturing cells (independent islands of automation) to a material tooling and information network. The program allows and enhances electronic communication between engineering, logistics, and the factory floor. At the completion of the modernization program, interplant communication flowed through a corporate information center coupled with global marketing and financial databases. All systems, from the plant's host computer to personal computers on the shop floor, were linked—resulting in unprecedented coordination and optimization of all manufacturing functions.

An example of what Plant with a Future accomplished can be found at the East Peoria, Illinois, transmission factory. Modernization took five years and cost $200 million. While workers put together gears and clutch assemblies, construction crews worked to build an underground chamber the size of a high school gymnasium. The

---

[10]Allan J. MaGraph, "Ten Timeless Truths about Pricing," *Journal of Consumer Marketing*, Winter 1991, pp. 5–13.

chamber became a computer-controlled heat treatment system, just one part of the modernization program that touched every corner of this 20-acre factory. Transmission assembly, formerly performed in five different buildings, has been consolidated under one roof. Nearly every one of the 500 machine tools has been moved or replaced, and all of this modernization was accomplished without slowing down production lines.

Efficiency at the East Peoria plant increased even during modernization. By installing a computerized inventory control system, the time it took to run components through the plant was cut dramatically. The parts for a clutch housing used to take 20 days to assemble and ship under the old system. With the new system, this same process took just four hours. Quality standards were maintained by shifting quality-control responsibilities to the workers themselves. Costs at this plant were expected to drop 19 percent.[11]

Company Reorganization

In addition to the plant modernization program, Caterpillar tried to reduce costs and maintain a competitive advantage by restructuring the entire company. In 1990, the company announced a plan to change the company from its functional structure to a modern product orientation. The new matrix revolves around 13 profit centers spread throughout the world. Each profit center is divided into specific product groups and four service divisions. This new structure has streamlined processes to such an extent that the company has been able to eliminate 1,000 positions that were no longer necessary.[12]

Caterpillar's new structure tied the entire company much more closely to its customers. For example, although Caterpillar has always had an impressive global dealer network, the old structure required countless phone calls to multiple functional areas in order to receive assistance from the company. Under the new structure, customers and dealers are able to contact each product group directly. The ability to effectively communicate with dealers and customers enabled Caterpillar to guarantee delivery of replacement parts in 48 hours or there was no charge.

This enhanced ability to communicate directly with customers and dealers enabled Caterpillar to respond to customer suggestions more rapidly, and allowed the company to exploit product niches. Under the new structure, decisions were pushed down to lower level management throughout the company. This simplification of the decision making chains enabled the company to introduce new models every two years instead of every five as it had under the old system.[13]

Labor Agreements

Caterpillar's responses to foreign competitors and sliding market share in the '80s assumed that personnel, both salaried and hourly, would give full support to each new program. The plant-modernization program and the company's reorganization into strategic profit centers required unequivocal labor support to be successful. Caterpillar assumed personnel support through these changes. The company endured a decade of tumultuous relations with its largest union, the United Auto Workers.

---

[11]Henkoff, p. 74.

[12]Tracy E. Benson, "Caterpillar Wakes Up," *Industry Week,* May 20, 1991, p. 33.

[13]Gary Slutsker, "Cat Claws Back," *Forbes,* February 17, 1992, p. 46.

The company weathered two prolonged strikes, a seven-month strike in 1982 and a five-month strike beginning in late 1991. In between these strikes, the company managed to increase its production flexibility by winning union approval to cut the number of union job classifications from 418 to 150 in 1986.

During the 1991 strike, Caterpillar steadfastly refused to accept another "pattern agreement" with the United Auto Workers as it has done since 1950.* The company maintained that such pattern agreements provided Japanese competitors with a 25 percent wage cost-advantage. While the union never accepted this position, the strike was broken when Caterpillar announced plans to replace all striking workers. The company hoped to gain productivity increases by avoiding job security clauses that were traditionally part of union contracts.

By breaking the union's strike, Caterpillar had an opportunity to negotiate favorable wage and benefit terms but also had to manage a disgruntled and disheartened workforce. The company, at this writing, has not been able to regain workers' trust. In November 1992, the union cancelled all worker involvement programs. These worker involvement programs had been a successful and critical part of both the factory modernization and company reorganization programs. At a single plant in Aurora, Illinois, the worker involvement programs had saved the company in excess of $4 million. Now, many workers view these programs as management's attempt to weaken the influence of the UAW at Caterpillar.[14]

■ Dealers

While Caterpillar substantially changed its manufacturing systems, philosophy, and corporate structure, the company did not change its distribution system. Caterpillar's channel involved a network of independent dealers. Caterpillar's dealer network handled all sales and service worldwide, with the exception of direct sales to the U.S. government, the Soviet Union, and the People's Republic of China. Caterpillar's 215 independent dealers represented an enterprise almost as large as the company itself; it included operating, sales, parts, and service outlets in more than 140 countries, and employed approximately 72,000 people. A typical dealership sold and serviced Caterpillar equipment exclusively and was likely to be in a second- or third-generation affiliation with the company. Caterpillar's dealer network has long been recognized as the strongest in the industry.

In the early '80s, Caterpillar responded to Komatsu's entrance into the U.S. market by capitalizing on the area where it had a strong competitive advantage—its extensive global dealer network. Caterpillar chose to compete with a total product concept by providing the services that customers deemed most important, which included postsales support and responsiveness to equipment malfunction. Typically, the purchaser of industrial equipment can expect to spend three to four times the

---

*Pattern bargaining is a potent negotiating tactic for the United Auto Workers, although it was abandoned long ago by unions in other industries like communications and steel. Under pattern bargaining, a union negotiates a new contract with one company and that contract then becomes the pattern for contracts with the company's competitors. In Caterpillar's case, its UAW contract would be patterned on contracts negotiated with both Deere and Tenneco's J. I. Case.

[14]Robert L. Rose and Alex Kotlowitz, "Strife between UAW and Caterpillar Blights Promising Labor Idea," *The Wall Street Journal*, November 23, 1992, Section A: p. 1.

original investment on repair and maintenance costs over the life of the machine. While equipment breakdown is a normal part of using this equipment, customers expect quick service and replacement parts for machinery; downtime is extremely costly for them. Caterpillar, through its dealers, has been able to provide unequaled postsales service to the end users.

Caterpillar expects its dealers to be experts in the industry in which they compete. The dealers must know which Caterpillar equipment is required by what market segments and how best to reach these market segments in their own territories. Dealers decide on the best marketing strategy to reach potential customers in their territory. Dealers can elect to reach their customers through direct-mail campaigns, electronic media, trade shows, or some unique combination of the above. The company supports each dealer's marketing plans through merchandising plans, inventory plans, and assistance in pricing and advertising.

Caterpillar recognizes that to sustain its competitive advantage in the industry, it must provide an aggressive program of ongoing training and support for its dealers. Caterpillar provides training for dealership personnel, both sales and service, to make them more responsive to the market and to improve total product image. As the company's product line broadens and deepens, it has to ensure that dealers are aware of each new product and its potential market. In 1985, Caterpillar initiated a program known as the *Sales Team Development System (STDS)*. The aim of the program was to provide professional assistance in utilizing all the resources that are available through Caterpillar. The results from STDS were impressive: 80 percent of the participating dealers felt they significantly improved their planning skills, product/technical knowledge, and general marketing sales skills. Dealers participating in the program increased their net revenues by 102 percent during a time of contraction in global markets.[15]

Caterpillar also increased its support for dealers through improved information flow and communications. The company modernized its communications capabilities with the purchase of advanced computer equipment that allowed for more accurate record and inventory keeping. During the 1991 strike at Caterpillar's U.S. plants, the ability to communicate effectively with dealers enabled Caterpillar to meet the needs of the majority of customers. Equipment was moved between dealers as needed, and some used equipment was leased to customers until new equipment could be made available. Domestic dealers, who normally received most of their inventory from manufacturing plants in the United States, received equipment from Japan, Belgium, and Brazil to meet their customers' orders. Caterpillar management stated repeatedly that they could not identify a single sale lost due to the strike.[16]

Caterpillar's distinct advantage lies not only in its control of the largest market share in the United States, but also in having the most extensive and competent dealership organization in the industry. Its customer offering goes beyond the equipment to a complete package of unique benefits. Caterpillar was able to break away from the competition because of its stronger distribution network. Caterpillar's dealers compete directly and effectively with competitors' dealers, especially Komatsu's and Deere's, by being able to respond to individual customer needs more effectively.

---

[15]S. Tamer Cavusgil, "The Importance of Distributor Training," *Industrial Marketing Management*, February 1990, p. 5.

[16]Robert L. Rose, "Caterpillar Reports First-Quarter Loss Plays Down Strike," *The Wall Street Journal*, April 23, 1992, Section A: p. 6.

■ Competition

Caterpillar is striving to remain the dominant manufacturer in a mature industry that has many competitors. One competitor, Japan's Komatsu, has aggressively pursued Caterpillar for the last decade. Its motto has been "Encircle Cat."[17] Long before the crisis in the early 1980s, management had identified Komatsu as deadly serious in its quest to become the new industry leader. While management had identified the risk, it failed to act upon this information. In 1982, Komatsu began to aggressively pursue market share in the United States. The strong dollar allowed Komatsu to offer prices 40 percent below Caterpillar's prices and still remain profitable.

In 1983, Komatsu continued its aggressive entry into Caterpillar's home market by adding five lines to the crawler tractor and loaders already being sold in the United States. Two years later, the company established a manufacturing plant in Tennessee and bought an old Caterpillar plant in England. In 1988, Komatsu and Dresser formed a 50/50 joint venture for their operations in the United States, Canada, and Latin America. The joint venture combined the two companies' manufacturing, financial, and distribution functions but maintained the companies' separate product lines. The joint venture did not change the dealership network of either company. Komatsu dealers still competed with Dresser dealers in most territories.

Komatsu's surge in the U.S. market slowed in 1987 when it lost its price advantage. Komatsu began to lose market share in the following year, and by 1991 its market share in the United States had fallen from a high of 20 percent to 18 percent. During this same period, Caterpillar increased its market share from 34.5 percent to 36.4 percent.[18]

In addition to losing its price advantage, Komatsu had problems with the Dresser joint venture from the beginning. After the joint venture was established, Dresser executives felt left out of decision making, and most U.S. employees could not understand the work ethic or culture of Japanese personnel. Another major problem for the Komatsu-Dresser venture was that the dealers of both companies struggled against each other for sales, instead of focusing on the major competition from Caterpillar dealers. As a solution to this problem, Komatsu-Dresser began encouraging dealers to combine operations and sell both lines of equipment. Currently, over 50 percent of dealers have combined operations. Komatsu-Dresser's sixty independent U.S. and Canadian dealers have a net worth of $300 million. In comparison, Caterpillar's 65 full-line U.S. dealers have a net worth of $1.72 billion.[19]

Komatsu reported its first annual loss of $14.4 million in 1990. It was followed by a $74 million operating loss in 1991. Both of these losses were attributed to low sales volume as a result of a severe recession. Komatsu began to diversify away from construction equipment, which accounted for 63 percent of the company's total sales. Company executives said publicly that they were no longer trying to overtake Caterpillar as industry leader and that Komatsu's future lies in robotics and machine

---

[17]Robert L. Rose and Masayoshi Kanabayashi, "Corporate Focus: Komatsu Throttles Back on Construction Equipment; Japanese Company, Lagging Rival Caterpillar, Eyes Other Areas for Growth," *The Wall Street Journal*, May 13, 1992, Section B: p. 4.

[18]Ibid.

[19]Kevin Kelly, "A Dream Marriage Turns Nightmarish," *Business Week*, April 29, 1991, p. 94.

tools. To underline this shift away from construction equipment, the bulldozer was removed from atop the corporate headquarters in Tokyo.[20]

While Komatsu states that it is no longer going head-to-head with Caterpillar, the companies are still arch rivals in all markets. Although Komatsu has lost many of its competitive advantages, the company has been able to maintain a better relationship with blue-collar workers in its North American factories. In addition, its per unit labor costs are lower than Caterpillar's. In the international market arena, when Caterpillar was constrained by U.S. foreign policy from selling to many former communist countries, Komatsu was able to develop strong trading relationships with them. For example, when Caterpillar was prohibited by the Carter administration from making sales to the Soviet Union, Komatsu was able to provide the necessary equipment.

Major Domestic Competitors

While Caterpillar and Komatsu battle for the number one and two positions in the heavy equipment market around the world, Caterpillar also competes with a number of domestic manufacturers. These include Deere & Company and Tenneco's J. I. Case in selected product lines. While Deere is more commonly known for its major share of the farm equipment market, it does manufacture and market a line of industrial equipment. Caterpillar has met more competition from Deere & Company since introducing backhoes and front-end loaders for smaller construction companies. These are areas that have traditionally been serviced by Deere and others.

Deere & Company has gone through a turbulent decade much the same as Caterpillar. The company has survived strikes by its largest union and a decade-long slump in its farm-equipment markets. Deere responded by trimming its payroll by 29,000 jobs, which included both salaried and hourly positions. The company restructured and modernized its manufacturing facilities to be able to react more quickly and efficiently to changing customer requirements. Deere expects to compete aggressively in all market segments, but sees its best growth potential in the farm equipment segment of its business.

Tenneco's J. I. Case was primarily a manufacturer of tractors and industrial equipment until it acquired International Harvester and Steiger Tractor Company. Case now has a full line of agricultural equipment and has the number two position for the farm equipment market behind Deere & Company. Case competes with Caterpillar primarily in the smaller construction lines and the farm equipment segment.

■ International Sales

Caterpillar has traditionally sold approximately 50 percent of its products in countries other than the United States. Sales outside of the United States are projected to increase in the future. Many of Caterpillar's greatest opportunities lie in developing countries that are not able to pay for products in hard currency. Caterpillar established the Caterpillar World Trade Corporation in response to these payment

---

[20]Robert L. Rose and Masayoshi Kanabayashi, "Corporate Focus: Komatsu Throttles Back on Construction Equipment; Japanese Company, Lagging Rival Caterpillar, Eyes Other Areas for Growth," *The Wall Street Journal,* May 13, 1992, Section B: p. 4.

difficulties. The World Trade Corporation negotiates payment for Caterpillar equipment in commodities or other finished goods that are then resold to obtain hard currency.

An example of how the World Trade Corporation facilitates Caterpillar's equipment sales can be seen in a recent sale of mining equipment to a Brazilian corporation. Instead of paying for the equipment in an agreed-upon currency, the Brazilian company traded iron ore for it. Caterpillar's World Trade Corporation sold the iron ore to a company in Hungary for men's suits. These suits were then sold in London for hard currency. Although this is a complex means of receiving payment for construction equipment, it allows Caterpillar to take advantage of opportunities in developing countries.[21]

Africa

Caterpillar is one of the largest exporters to Africa. The company has been successful on this continent because it has exploited the expertise of its local dealers. In addition, the company has been extremely flexible in arranging sales terms. The company will sell to governments under existing international loans programs, or establish long-term leasing arrangements. Counter-trade options have also been used with success.* The company has met with success on this continent on its own terms. The company, while adopting the local business practices, will not indulge in bribery or other kickbacks, which are a common means of facilitating business exchanges in many parts of this continent. In the future, Africa is expected to be an area of continued growth for mining equipment because of the continent's mineral wealth.

Brazil

The decline in the company's overall profits during 1990 was due in large part to difficulties in the Brazilian unit. The unit was profitable through 1989 and the first quarter of 1990, but incurred an operating loss for the year overall. The Brazilian government in March 1990, introduced austerity programs that curtailed government spending and reduced sales volume for Caterpillar. The Brazilian currency weakened substantially, which meant that sales that were finalized translated into fewer dollars for the parent company.[22] In 1991, due to continuing economic turmoil in Brazil, Caterpillar Brasil S.A. announced the planned closing of its facility in Sao Paulo and the consolidation of all operations in Piracicaba. Business conditions are expected to continue to be affected by political and economic factors in the short term.

Eastern Europe and Countries of the Former Soviet Union

While there are definite opportunities for industrial equipment manufacturers in the countries that made up Eastern Europe and the former Soviet Union, in all these countries some means of payment for imported equipment must be established.

---

[21]Taken from speech by Ed Terrel, manager of human resources for Caterpillar Inc., at the University of Wisconsin–Madison, September 23, 1992.

*Counter-trade options are defined as the selling company accepting commodities in lieu of cash payment. Caterpillar's World Trade Corporation specializes in counter-trade options.

[22]James P. Miller, "Caterpillar Shares Tumble as Firm Says Profit Will Drop Substantially in 1990," *The Wall Street Journal*, June 26, 1990, Section C: p. 15.

Counter-trade arrangements and international loan programs are expected to play a major role in these countries. Caterpillar pursued these opportunities with caution because of continued political instability. The company has tried to extend its distribution network into these countries. However, establishing dealerships in these countries is difficult because most interested parties do not meet Caterpillar's criteria, which include a stable financial position and the ability to do business with Caterpillar in English.

Southeast Asia, China, and Pacific Rim Countries

Caterpillar has been quite successful in pursuing opportunities in these countries. The company has established a special Far East trading company to focus on the opportunities and special problems associated with transacting business in many of these countries. Caterpillar already has a manufacturing plant in Indonesia and has been successful in selling heavy equipment in China. To take advantage of many of these sales, the company has had to establish complex counter-trade arrangements. In the future, there should be additional opportunities in Cambodia if the recently signed peace agreement is successful.

Counter trade has not been necessary when dealing with the developed countries of Australia and New Zealand. Caterpillar had been extremely successful in selling equipment, particularly large mining equipment, in these two countries. Recently, environmental concerns in both these countries have reduced sales. In Australia, large new mining developments in the Northern Territory have been rejected because of environmental concerns and complaints from indigenous people. In addition, the government has been prohibiting the expansion of even existing mining operations in all regions of the country.

■ Caterpillar's Future

Slow growth in the industrial equipment market is projected for the short term because of continued global recession. In the United States, industrial equipment market growth is closely linked to expansion in the national economy. The need to upgrade and maintain the public infrastructure in older cities is expected to increase and stimulate growth in the construction equipment segment of this market. In addition, highway and bridge repair may continue to provide a major source of market demand, as will the continued construction of new power plants and water supply facilities.

Environmental issues are affecting the demand of industrial equipment. Demand for products used primarily in large mining operations will be most affected by the increased awareness of environmental issues. The world's recent focus on the environment has forced many existing mining operations to downsize, and in some countries, mining projects which would utilize industrial equipment are not being approved.

The equipment market is expected to be stimulated by the growing versatility of products in which attachments are designed to be changed quickly. For example, excavators can now be equipped with bucket or rock-breaker attachments for a wide range of applications. In addition, higher productivity is being achieved through computerized power transmissions that automatically control the engine speed and hydraulic output to maximize productivity and achieve fuel savings.

■ **Appendix A**   Four-Year Financial Summary (Dollars in millions except per share data)

Years Ended December 31	**1991**	**1990**	**1989**	**1988**
Sales and revenues	$ 10,182	$ 11,436	$ 11,126	$ 10,435
Sales	9,838	11,103	10,882	10,255
Percent inside U.S.	41%	45%	47%	50%
Percent outside U.S.	59%	55%	53%	50%
Revenues	344	333	244	180
Profit (loss)	(404)	210	497	616
As a percent of sales and revenue	(4.0%)	1.8%	4.5%	5.9%
Profit (loss) per share of common stock	(4.00)	2.07	4.90	6.07
Dividends per share of common stock	1.05	1.20	1.20	.86
Return on average common stock equity	(9.4%)	4.7%	11.6%	16.0%
Capital expenditures:				
Land, buildings, etc.	653	926	984	732
Equipment leased to others	121	113	105	61
Depreciation and amortization	602	533	471	434
R&E expense	441	420	387	334
As a % of sales and revenue	4.3%	3.7%	3.5%	3.2%
Provision (credit) for income taxes	(152)	78	162	262
Wages, salaries, and employee benefits	3,051	3,032	2,888	2,643
Average number of employees	55,950	59,662	60,784	57,954
December 31				
Total receivables:				
Trade and other	2,133	2,361	2,353	2,349
Finance	2,145	1,891	1,498	1,222
Inventories	1,921	2,105	2,120	1,986
Total assets:				
Machinery and engines	9,346	9,626	9,100	8,226
Financial products:	2,696	2,325	1,826	1,460
Long-term debt due after one year:				
Machinery and engines	2,676	2,101	2,561	1,428
Financial products	1,216	789	491	525
Total debt:				
Machinery and engines	3,136	2,873	2,561	2,116
Financial products	2,111	1,848	1,433	1,144
Ratios—excluding financial products:				
Ratio of current assets to current liabilities	1.74 to 1	1.67 to 1	1.78 to 1	1.76 to 1
Percent of total debt to total debt and stockholders' equity	43.7%	38.8%	36.4%	34.0%

*Data taken from Caterpillar's 1991 Annual Report, pp. 28–29.

These product improvements promote higher product-replacement rates in the near term.[23]

Caterpillar responded to the challenges of the 1980s better than many other U.S. manufacturers. The company made unprecedented changes and learned from previous mistakes. Even with all these changes, the company still recorded losses in recent years and continues to be troubled by severe labor problems. The company must decide whether there is a profitable future for it as a U.S.–based manufacturer of heavy construction equipment and diesel engines.

---

[23]1991 U.S. Industrial Outlook.

■ **Appendix B**
Caterpillar Product
Line

Type of Equipment	Number of Models
Wheel loaders	10
Integrated tool carriers	4
Backhoe loaders	5
Pavement profilers	4
Asphalt pavers	5
Road reclaimer/soil stabilizer	2
Compaction equipment	15
Wheel tractors	3
Compactors	2
Landfill compactors	4
Track loaders	10
Track-type tractors	22
Motor graders	6
Excavators	18
Pipelayers	4
Scrapers	12
Trucks	6
Tractors	4
Articulated trucks	8
Forest machines	4
Skidders	4
Engines	7
Lift trucks	8

SOURCE: Tabulated from Caterpillar's 1991 Annual Report.

Case 3   Kmart Corporation

John E. Gamble
University of South Alabama

In 1997 Kmart Corporation was the second largest full-line discount retailer in North America—operating more than 2,200 stores in the United States, Canada, Puerto Rico, Guam, and the U.S. Virgin Islands. But the company was struggling, having lost $200 million on sales of $33.5 billion in 1996, and having posted losses in two of the three previous years. Revenues had only grown at a modest 4.5 percent annually since 1992. So far, the company's turnaround strategy, initiated in 1995 and directed at eliminating the company's operating inefficiencies and making it more competitive with Wal-Mart—the discount chain industry leader—had not produced positive bottom-line results. Wal-Mart still led Kmart on every one of the discount retail industry's important performance indicators during 1996 (sales growth, net profit margins, and sales per square foot), just as it had during the entire 1990s when it became obvious that Kmart was struggling.

In March 1995 Kmart's CEO, Joseph Antonini, facing mounting criticism from investors and pressure from board members, resigned. In June 1995, the company's board of directors recruited Floyd Hall away from Grand Union Supermarkets and appointed him as chairman, chief executive officer, and president. The board charged Hall with turning around the ailing company. Hall and his top management team promptly launched a number of new initiatives to restore the company to profitability and to compete more effectively with Wal-Mart. However, the main hurdle for Hall and his management team was the effective execution of their plan, since in years past, Kmart had established a reputation for poorly implementing strategies crafted by its previous managers.

Company History and Background

In 1897 Sebastian S. Kresge and John McCrory formed a partnership to own and operate two five-and-dime stores—one in Detroit, Michigan, and the other in Memphis, Tennessee. Sebastian Kresge operated the partnership's store in downtown Detroit while McCrory operated the company's Memphis store. The two men, failing to see any advantage to the partnership after two years, dissolved their business relationship in 1899 and went their own ways—Kresge assuming sole ownership of the Detroit store and McCrory the Memphis store. By 1912, Sebastian Kresge had expanded his five-and-dime variety store operation into a chain of 85 stores with annual sales of more than $10 million, making the S. S. Kresge Company the second largest chain of variety stores in the United States at the time.

In 1929, S. S. Kresge expanded into Canada, opening 19 Canadian five-and-dime stores. That same year, the company opened a Kresge five-and-dime in the world's first suburban shopping center—the Country Club Plaza in Kansas City, Missouri. When suburban shopping started to grow dramatically during the 1950s, and shoppers became increasingly attracted to full-line discount stores that carried a wider variety of household items and apparel at lower prices than five-and-dimes, Kresge responded by opening 18 Kmart full-line discount department stores in 1962. At the

This case was prepared by John E. Gamble of the University of South Alabama.

time of Sebastian Kresge's death in 1966, the S. S. Kresge Company operated 735 Kresge variety stores and 162 Kmart full-line discount stores with combined annual sales of over $1 billion. Throughout the remainder of the 1960s and 1970s, Kresge management increased the number of Kmart stores and replaced existing Kresge stores with Kmart stores. The company's name was changed to Kmart Corporation in 1977, a reflection of the fact that over 95 percent of the company's sales were generated by Kmart units. In 1981 the company opened its 2,000th Kmart location.

Diversification into Other Types of Retail Businesses

During the 1980s and early 1990s, Kmart management began to diversify the company into other businesses rather than continue to emphasize and rely on growing simply by expanding the number of Kmart locations and boosting sales at existing store locations. Kmart purchased two cafeteria chains in 1980 and 1983, but divested both of them in 1986 because of disappointing results. In 1984 Kmart acquired Builders Square (a chain of warehouse-style home centers) and Walden Book Company, which operated Waldenbooks stores in all 50 states. PayLess Drug Stores and Bargain Harold's Discount Outlets (a Canadian retailer) were acquired in 1985. In 1988 three start-up businesses—American Fare hypermarts (giant stores carrying a huge variety of household, apparel, and supermarket merchandise), Pace Membership warehouse clubs, and Office Square warehouse-style office supply stores—were added to the corporation's portfolio of retail chain businesses.

The Sports Authority (a 10-store chain of sporting goods superstores) was acquired in 1990 to complement and strengthen Kmart's own Sports Giant stores started in 1989; the Sports Giant stores were subsequently renamed and integrated into The Sports Authority chain. Kmart also acquired a 22 percent interest in OfficeMax office supply superstores in 1990 and increased its interest in the business to over 90 percent in 1991. In 1992, Kmart management acquired Borders, Inc. (a chain of 22 book superstores in the Midwest and northeast United States), purchased a chain of 13 discount stores in the Czech Republic and Slovakia, acquired Bizmart (a 105-store chain of office supply stores), and announced that it would open up to 100 Kmart stores in Mexico in a 50-50 joint venture with Mexican retailer El Puerto de Liverpool. The company also entered into a joint venture with Metro Limited to open discount stores in Singapore in 1994. Exhibits 1–3 present statements of Kmart's recent financial performance.

■ Overview of the U.S. Discount Retail Industry

The U.S. discount retail industry grew 6 percent in 1996, accounting for an estimated $332 billion in sales. The industry included full-line discount stores (e.g., Wal-Mart, Kmart, and Target); specialty discounters (e.g., Toys 'R' Us and Office Depot); warehouse clubs (e.g., Sam's and PriceCostco); off-price apparel chains (e.g., T. J. Maxx and Marshalls); jewelry and hard line discount retailers (e.g., Service Merchandise and Best Products); and discount mass merchants (e.g., Sears and Montgomery Ward). Exhibit 4 shows the sales for each of these segments for 1994–1996.

The specialty discount segment was the fastest growing segment of the retail discount industry, with a projected sales increase of almost 15 percent in 1996. In 1995 the specialty segment grew by 22.5 percent, with many categories within the segment growing much more rapidly. For example, sales at book superstores grew 45.9 per-

■ **Exhibit 1**   Selected Financial and Operating Statistics, Kmart Corporation, 1992–1996
(dollars in millions, except per share data)

	1996	1995	1994	1993	1992
Summary of operations					
Sales	$31,437	$31,713	$29,563	$28,039	$26,470
Cost of sales, buying, and occupancy	24,390	24,675	22,331	20,732	19,087
Selling, general and administrative expenses	6,274	6,876	6,651	6,241	5,830
Interest expense, net	453	434	479	467	411
Continuing income (loss) before income taxes	330	(313)	102	(306)	1,142
Net income (loss) from continuing operations	231	(230)	96	(179)	745
Net income (loss)	$ (220)	$ (571)	$ 296	$ (974)	$ 941
Per share of common stock					
Net income (loss) from continuing operations	$ 0.48	$ (0.51)	$ 0.19	$ (0.41)	$ 1.63
Dividends declared	—	0.36	0.96	0.96	0.92
Book value	10.51	10.99	13.15	13.39	16.64
Financial data					
Total assets	$14,286	$15,033	$16,085	$15,875	$16,769
Long-term debt	2,121	3,922	1,989	2,209	2,995
Long-term capital lease obligations	1,478	1,586	1,666	1,609	1,612
Capital expenditures	343	540	1,021	793	1,187
Depreciation and amortization	654	685	639	650	566
Ending market capitalization	5,418	2,858	6,345	9,333	10,837
Weighted average share outstanding (millions)	486	460	457	457	456
Number of stores					
United States	2,134	2,161	2,316	2,323	2,281
Canada	123	127	128	127	127
Other	4	22	37	36	27
Total Stores	2,261	2,310	2,481	2,486	2,435
Selling space and sales per square foot					
U.S. Kmart selling space (millions of sq. ft.)	156	160	166	182	181
U.S. Kmart store sales per comparable selling square foot	$ 201	$ 195	$ 181	$ 160	$ 152

SOURCE: 1996 Kmart Corporation Annual Report.

cent; pet supply chains grew 38.4 percent; office supplies superstores grew by 33.7 percent; computer chains grew 34.5 percent; baby superstores grew 29.1 percent; consumer electronics chains grew 27.7 percent; and the sales of home furnishings chains grew by 27.7 percent. Two categories, crafts and sporting goods, grew at a rate substantially lower than that of other specialty categories, but still at a rate faster than the overall discount retail industry.

The growth in specialty discount chains was attributed to the wide selection of merchandise that the stores carried in their one specialty category and to their attractive everyday-low-pricing strategy. Home furnishing stores such as Waccamaw, Bed Bath & Beyond, and Linens 'n Things experienced growth rates that approached 40 percent in 1996. Full-line chains looked upon specialty chains as "category killers" because full-line chains with their wide-ranging merchandise lineup could not devote the same amount of shelf space and square footage to any one product category. Research indicated that many consumers believed they were more likely to find what

■ **Exhibit 2**   Consolidated Statement of Operations for Kmart Corporation, 1994–1996
(dollars in millions, except per share data)

	Fiscal Year Ended January		
	1996	**1995**	**1994**
Sales	$31,437	$31,713	$29,563
Cost of sales, buying and occupancy	24,390	24,675	22,331
Gross margin	7,047	7,038	7,232
Selling, general and administrative expenses	6,274	6,876	6,651
Other (gains) losses	(10)	41	—
Continuing income before interest, income taxes, and dividends on convertible preferred securities of subsidiary	783	121	581
Interest expense, net	453	434	479
Income tax provision (credit)	68	(83)	6
Dividends on convertible preferred securities of subsidiary, net of income taxes of $16	31	—	—
Net income (loss) from continuing operations before extraordinary item	231	(230)	96
Discontinued operations, net of income taxes of $(3), $(139), and $64	(5)	(260)	83
Gain (loss) on disposal of discontinued operations, net of income taxes of $(240), $88, and $282	(446)	(30)	117
Extraordinary item, net of income taxes of $(27)	—	(51)	—
Net income (loss)	$ (220)	$ (571)	$ 296
Earnings (loss) per common share:			
Continuing retail operations	$ 0.48	$ (0.51)	$ 0.19
Discontinued operations	(0.01)	(0.57)	0.19
Gain (loss) on disposal of discontinued operations	(0.92)	(0.06)	0.25
Extraordinary item	—	(0.11)	—
Net income (loss)	$ (0.45)	$ (1.25)	$ 0.63
Weighted average shares (millions)	486.1	459.9	456.6

SOURCE: 1996 Kmart Corporation Annual Report.

they were looking for at a specialty store, with its wide-ranging selection of brands, styles, colors, and so on, than they would at full-line discount stores having a more limited selection of brands and styles in any one product category.

The full-line discount segment was the only retail segment, other than the specialty discount segment, that was growing faster than the U.S. economy. The full-line discount segment was projected to grow by 4.1 percent in 1996, following growth of 9.2 percent in 1995. The full-line discount segment and the entire discount retail industry were both rapidly consolidating through merger and acquisition, liquidation, and bankruptcy. From January 1995 through June 1996, 9 regional full-line discount chains and 13 chains competing in other segments were liquidated, an additional 20 discount chains were either acquired or merged with another chain, and 23 discount retail chains filed for Chapter 11 bankruptcy protection. Regional chains with annual sales of less than $500 million were expected to become casualties of industry consolidation in the near future.

Competitive success within the full-line discount segment of the industry hinged primarily upon store location, store appeal and shopping atmosphere, merchandise selection and availability, and everyday low pricing. Everyday low pricing squeezed

■ **Exhibit 3**   Kmart's Consolidated Balance Sheets, Fiscal Years 1995 and 1996 (in millions of dollars)

	January 29, 1997	January 31, 1996
Assets		
Current assets:		
Cash and cash equivalents	$ 406	$ 1,083
Merchandise inventories	6,354	6,022
Other current assets	973	894
Net current assets of discontinued operations	—	554
Total current assets	7,733	8,553
Property and equipment, net	5,740	5,365
Property held for sale or financing	200	434
Other assets and deferred changes	613	526
Net long-term assets of discontinued operations	—	55
Total assets	$14,286	$15,033
Liabilities and Shareholders' Equity		
Current liabilities:		
Long-term debt due within one year	$ 153	$ 7
Trade accounts payable	2,009	1,793
Accrued payrolls and other liabilities	1,298	1,019
Taxes other than income taxes	139	176
Total current liabilities	3,602	2,995
Long-term debt and notes payable	2,121	3,922
Capital lease obligations	1,478	1,586
Other long-term liabilities	1,013	1,250
Company obligated mandatorily redeemable convertible preferred securities of subsidiary trust holding solely 7¾ %convertible junior subordinated debentures of Kmart (Redemption value of $1,000 at January 29, 1997).	980	—
Shareholders' equity:		
Common stock	486	486
Capital in excess of par value	1,608	1,624
Retained earnings	3,105	3,326
Treasury shares and restricted stock	(37)	(92)
Foreign currency translation adjustment	(70)	(64)
Total shareholders' equity	5,092	5,280
Total liabilities and shareholders' equity	$14,286	$15,033

SOURCE: 1996 Kmart Corporation Annual Report.

■ **Exhibit 4**

Retail Discount Industry Sales by Type of Store, 1994–1996 (in billions of dollars)

	1994	1995	1996[4]
Full-line discount stores[1]	$138.3	$151.1	$157.3
Specialty discounters[2]	55.6	68.1	77.7
Warehouse clubs	39.0	41.1	42.3
Other discount mass merchants[3]	33.3	31.4	32.6
Off-price apparel chains	17.0	15.4	15.5
Jewelry/hard lines retailers	7.2	6.9	6.8
Total market	$290.4	$314.0	$332.2

[1]Includes full-line discount department stores, supercenters, closeout liquidators, and single-price retailers.
[2]Includes home, automotives, crafts, toys office supplies, book, computer superstores, baby superstores, pet supplies, consumer electronics and sporting goods specialty stores.
[3]Includes Sears, Ward, QVC, HSN, and variety stores.
[4]Estimated.

SOURCE: *Discount Store News,* July 1, 1996, p. 38.

■ **Exhibit 5**
Full-Line Discount
Store Sales, by Prod-
uct Category, 1995

Category	Sales (in billions)	Growth rate (1994–1995)	Gross Margin	Percent of Store Sales
Apparel	$ 38.0	1.7%	33.6%	25.1%
Food	13.1	38.0	19.2	8.6
Consumer electronics	11.9	23.3	16.5	7.8
Housewares	10.7	15.7	29.1	7.1
Health and beauty care	9.3	18.3	19.8	6.2
Domestics	8.1	6.8	33.9	5.4
Toys	7.8	0.0	28.1	5.2
Lawn and garden	6.1	34.4	28.2	4.0
Sporting goods	5.4	12.5	27.2	3.6
Stationery	5.3	18.5	40.4	3.5
Pharmacy	4.8	0.0	24.6	3.2
Furniture	4.7	40.3	32.2	3.1
Household cleaners	4.6	19.6	19.6	3.0
Hardware	4.5	18.0	34.2	3.0
Automotives	4.0	15.5	22.0	2.7
Miscellaneous*	3.5	7.7	40.4	2.3
Jewelry/watches	2.6	(1.5)	41.5	1.7
Cosmetics	2.5	14.9	25.0	1.7
Photo	2.3	(11.3)	16.9	1.5
Crafts	1.9	(1.6)	38.0	1.3
Total	$151.1			100.0%

*Includes snack bar, video rental and other categories not listed.

SOURCE: *Discount Store News,* August 5, 1996, p. 46.

store profit margins, but the industry's leading practitioners of everyday low pricing, Wal-Mart, Kmart and Target, were adding consumables (such as food) to boost store traffic and were adding more high-margin items (better grades of apparel and ready-to-assemble furniture) to bolster store margins. Full-line discount stores had to monitor buyer preferences carefully and respond quickly to changing buying patterns, stocking new items growing in favor and giving less shelf and display space to slower-selling items; otherwise, store sales languished and shopper interest waned. Exhibit 5 lists the sales, growth rates, gross margins, and percentage of store sales for major merchandise categories carried by full-line discount stores.

Wal-Mart, Kmart, and Target were all adding to their selection of lawn and garden equipment and power tools. Sears dominated these merchandise categories with its Craftsman line of hand tools and power tools and its selection of professional-grade power tools such as Makita, Milwaukee, and DeWalt. Kmart and Wal-Mart carried primarily Black & Decker power tools and their own private-label brands of power tools. Wal-Mart had licensed the names of three magazines to add name appeal to its own merchandise lines—it was selling tools under the *Popular Mechanics* brand name, its better paint line was branded *House Beautiful,* and its lawn and garden products were sold under the *Better Homes and Gardens* brand name. Generally, private-label brands offered consumers lower prices and retailers higher margins than national brands.

Successful discount stores were most likely to be located near a major highway or interstate—to make the store readily accessible to shoppers over a wide retail trade area. The major trend among full-line discount retailers was to build larger stores stocked with a broader line of merchandise, particularly groceries and traditional supermarket items. Newly constructed discount stores were often double the size of stores constructed in the 1980s. Wal-Mart Supercenters and Super Kmart Centers were as large as 180,000 square feet and included products typically found in full-line grocery stores, department stores, auto supply stores, and hardware stores. In rural areas, the supercenter-type stores generally offered a wider selection of food items than competing supermarkets.

Aside from just carrying a wider selection of merchandise, Wal-Mart Supercenters, Super Kmart Centers, and other full-line merchandisers were giving food items a more prominent placement in their stores, selling a growing number of food items under their own private-label brands—Wal-Mart's "Sam's American Choice," Kmart's "American Fare," and Target's "Archer Farms." Kmart had recently developed a store-within-a-store concept for both its traditional stores and its supercenter stores that allocated 8,700 square feet to convenience items; the new area was located near the store entrance to make it convenient for shoppers to stop in and get a few items. Both regional and national chains had begun to experiment with meals-to-go that were intended to appeal to two-income families who did not have time to cook at home.

■ Kmart Under Joseph Antonini, 1987–1995

Antonini's Strategy to Grow Kmart

Kmart's strategy of growth via diversification into a variety of retail businesses was initiated by Bernard Fauber, the company's chief executive officer from 1980 to 1987. However, most of Kmart's acquisitions were orchestrated by Joseph Antonini, who succeeded Fauber as Kmart's chairman, CEO, and president in 1987. Both Fauber and Antonini believed that entry into specialty retail stores would provide the company with greater growth opportunities than would be possible with only the Kmart chain of discount stores. The move to expand Kmart's scope of retail operations was intended to position the company in such faster growing product categories as drugstore merchandise, office supplies, books, building materials, and sporting goods. Antonini also believed it made good strategic sense for Kmart to be involved in warehouse clubs and hypermarts because such stores were simply a larger-scale and slightly modified version of the retailing format that traditional discount stores like Kmart were already operating. Antonini saw the purchase of the discount stores in the Czech Republic and Slovakia and the joint ventures in Mexico and Singapore as valuable ways to begin positioning Kmart more aggressively in international retail markets.

Antonini's second strategic initiative to stimulate revenue growth focused on a $3.5 billion "renewal" program in 1991 to modernize, expand, or relocate Kmart's 2,435 discount stores. Most of these stores were built during the company's dramatic growth period in the 1960s and 1970s and had undergone little or no remodeling or renovation since they were constructed. Antonini wanted to increase the size of Kmart stores from a typical 80,000 square feet to about 100,000 square feet so that a wider variety of merchandise could be offered to consumers. The modernized Kmart stores provided brighter lighting, wider aisles, more modern and colorful interior signs, and more attractive merchandise displays. In 1992 he announced that the company would launch as many as 500 Super Kmart Centers that, like American Fare, would include both a discount store and a grocery store in a 160,000–180,000 square-foot building. By 1994 the sales of the renovated and new Super Kmart Centers were 23 percent above the sales of the chain's older, unrefurbished stores.

Antonini also initiated efforts to increase the volume of apparel sold in Kmart stores. He believed that increased sales of high-margin apparel would provide the stores with better operating margins and allow the company to offer lower everyday pricing on nonapparel items, like household items and health and beauty products. The company improved the styling and quality of its private-label apparel and began to include more natural fibers and less polyester in its garments. Kmart used endorsements from Jaclyn Smith and Kathy Ireland to create private-label-branded lines of apparel to appeal to fashion-conscious and designer-conscious shoppers. Antonini also added national brands of apparel and footwear like Wrangler, Hanes, L.A. Gear, and Britannia to the company's merchandise mix.

Attempts to Cure Kmart's Long-Standing Inventory Management Problems

Joseph Antonini also believed that the company needed to correct its long-running inability to maintain proper inventory levels in its stores. Kmart had been confronted with this problem for years, but the company had never really been able to resolve it. Most Kmart stores either stocked out of popular-selling items relatively frequently and/or were burdened with excess stocks of slow-moving items that eventually had to be marked down significantly to clear the items from the stores. Antonini believed that Kmart's decentralized buying and merchandising process was at the root of the company's poor inventory management practices. Typically, Kmart buyers negotiated purchases with manufacturers, distribution people shipped products to stores, advertising specialists coordinated the company's advertising, and a separate marketing staff was responsible for promotions. Additionally, the company's store managers were authorized to purchase merchandise specific to their geographic locale and to place special ads in local area newspapers.

Antonini and Chief Information Officer David Carlson implemented a number of state-of-the-art information systems to correct the inventory management problems in the company's 2000-plus stores. In 1990 Kmart launched the GTE Spacenet satellite-based network that linked individual Kmart stores with the Kmart corporate office in Troy, Michigan, and some suppliers. The system allowed Kmart management to eliminate its traditional decentralized inventory management process and adopt a centralized process that was intended to reduce escalating inventory costs while meeting local preferences and price sensitivities. The GTE Spacenet communication system allowed management to implement its Central Merchandising Automated Replenishment (CMAR) system that was jointly developed by Kmart's information systems staff and Electronic Data Systems, a leading supplier of data-processing services. The CMAR system allowed Kmart's corporate office to keep track of every sale in each store. All scanner data was transmitted via a local area network to a UNIX server in the back room of each individual store. At the end of every day, the server transmitted sales data to the corporate headquarters via the GTE Spacenet satellite.

The next morning Kmart product-category managers studied the sales data from each store and later that day placed orders with vendors to replenish each store's inventory. Vendors that were members of Kmart's Partners in Merchandise Flow Program were allowed to monitor the scanner data themselves and ship to Kmart distribution centers when they determined it was necessary to maintain Kmart's desired inventory levels. The distribution centers used a cross-docking system that helped keep inventory levels at the distribution center to a minimum. A senior executive at Kmart explained how centralized category management allowed the company to reduce expenses and keep products that consumers wanted on the shelves.[1]

> Category management has been very successful for us. It's shifted our entire focus to the front door. Years ago we were busy with shipments—looking at what was coming in the back door from our suppliers. Today we have a front-door focus in that we are focusing on the consumer and what the register tape tells us she's taking out the front door. We've seen dramatic improvements in turnover. In fact, we used to call our distribution centers "warehouses" because products would come in and sometimes just sit there. Now they are truly distribution centers with goods flowing in and right out, often within a day or two.

Kmart identified about 1,500 hard lines categories and several hundred soft lines categories and selected managers to make all buying and merchandising decisions, including pricing, assortments, and promotions, for their assigned category of products. Each category manager used the scanner data available from CMAR and demographic profiles and consumer purchasing behavior data provided by third parties such as Nielsen Marketing Research to make their purchasing decisions. Each category manager was required to develop a sales plan, a gross margin plan, and a turnover plan that was presented to the senior marketing executives at the beginning of the financial year.

Kmart spent about $160 million annually to create and implement information systems like CMAR technology and other state-of-the-art computer systems during Antonini's tenure as Kmart's top executive. The company implemented electronic data interchange (EDI) systems with some suppliers that attempted to reduce the company's dependence on paper-based transaction processing. The company also developed the ShopperTrack system, utilized in its newest stores, that used backroom computers and ceiling-mounted sensors to monitor how many customers were in each department throughout the day. The system used the tracking data to project store and department customer counts at 15-minute intervals. Store managers were instructed to use this information to schedule employee staffing at the store's checkout stations and merchandise departments.

Difficulties in Implementing and Executing Antonini's Strategy

At the outset, both Wall Street and Kmart investors reacted favorably to Antonini's moves to diversify the corporation into a number of attractive discount retail segments, to renovate and enlarge Kmart stores, to improve merchandise selection, quality and availability, and to improve information systems. The consensus was that these moves would allow the company to grow faster and to compete more effectively against its major rivals. However, as efforts to implement the strategy continued to unfold, events made it increasingly clear that Kmart was being outmaneuvered by its rivals; Wal-Mart, in particular, was leaving Kmart far behind (see Exhibits 6 and 7). Kmart's sales per store continued to run close to $185 per square foot in 1992, 1993, and 1994, despite the merchandising efforts initiated by Antonini and other Kmart executives. Kmart's pricing continued to average 10 to 15 percent above its chief competitors, as Kmart sought to boost its subpar store margins and make up for the higher selling, general, and administrative expenses brought on by relatively low sales volumes per square foot of selling space.

---

[1]"Kmart's Category Approach," *Discount Merchandiser*, May 1994, p. 118.

Exhibit 6 Comparative Financial Performance of Sears, Kmart, and Wal-Mart, 1980, 1985, 1987–1996

Year	Sales (in millions of dollars)			Net Income (in millions of dollars)			Net Income as a Percentage of Sales		
	Sears*	Kmart	Wal-Mart**	Sears*	Kmart	Wal-Mart**	Sears*	Kmart	Wal-Mart**
1980	$18,675	$14,118	$ 1,643	$ 229	$ 429	$ 56	1.2%	3.0%	3.4%
1985	26,552	22,035	8,451	776	757	327	2.9	3.4	3.9
1987	28,085	25,627	15,959	787	1,171	627	2.8	4.6	3.9
1988	30,256	27,301	20,649	524	1,244	837	1.7	4.6	4.1
1989	31,599	29,150	25,811	647	261†	1,076	2.1	3.9	4.2
1990	31,986	28,607	32,602	257	673	1,291	0.8	2.4	4.0
1991	31,433	29,488	43,887	486	752	1,608	1.5	2.6	3.7
1992	31,961	26,470	55,484	(2,977)	941	1,995	(9.3)	2.8	3.6
1993	29,565	28,039	67,345	752	(974)††	2,333	2.5	(0.8)	3.5
1994	29,608	29,563	82,494	875	296	2,681	2.7	0.3	3.2
1995	31,188	31,713	93,627	1,025	(571)	2,740	2.9	(1.4)	2.9
1996	33,512	31,437	104,859	1,271	(220)	3,056	3.8	(0.7)	2.9

*Sears' data represents Merchandise Group Operations only.

**Wal-Mart's fiscal year ends January 31 of each year; data for the period January 31, 1980 through January 31, 1981, are reported in Wal-Mart's annual report as 1981 results. Because Wal-Mart's fiscal year results really cover 11 months of the previous calendar year, this exhibit shows Wal-Mart's 1981 fiscal results in the 1980 row, its 1986 results in the 1985 row, and so on. This adjustment makes Wal-Mart's figures correspond more to the same time frame as the calendar year data for Sears and Kmart.

†After a pretax provision of $640 million for restructuring.

‡After a pretax provision of $904 million for restructuring.

SOURCE: Company annual reports, 1980, 1985, 1987–1996.

Exhibit 7 Selected Operating Statistics for the Leading North American Discount Retailers

Top Discount Department Stores and Discount Mass Merchants

		Sales (in millions)			Net Profit Margin			1995 Sales per Square Foot	SG&A as a Percent of 1995 Sales	Number of Stores as of Dec. 1995
Rank	Company	1995	1994	Percent Change	1995	1994	Percent Change			
1	Wal-Mart Stores[a]	$54,330	$53,350	1.8%	2.9%	3.25%	(10.0)%	$379	16.0%	2,943
2	Sears[b]	31,188	29,608	5.3	2.9	2.7	7.4	261	21.7	810
3	Kmart[a]	26,779	26,986	(0.8)	(1.65)	0.90	(283.0)	185	21.8	2,326
4	Target[a]	15,807	13,600	16.2	*	*	*	282	*	670
5	Montgomery Ward[b]	6,219	6,218	0.0	0.2	2.0	(90.0)	141	25.5	340

[a]Discount department store.
[b]Discount mass merchandiser.
*Data unavailable

Top Supercenter Chains

		Sales (in millions)			Number of Stores			1995 Sales per Square Foot	1996 Average Store Size (in square feet)
Rank	Company	1995	1994	Percent Change	January 1995	January 1996	January 1997 (projected)		
1	Wal-Mart Supercenters	$11,500	$4,650	147.3%	143	247	350	$314*	188,000
2	Meijer	5,600	5,600	0.0	99	99	109	283	200,000
3	Super Kmart Centers	3,650	1,400	160.7	67	93	104	285*	160,000
4	Fred Meyer	3,429	3,128	9.6	131	136	142	237	109,000
5	Smitty's	675	670	0.8	28	29	28	358	65,000

*Estimated by dividing 1995 sales by the average number of stores between January 1995 and January 1996.
SOURCE: *Discount Store News*, July 1, 1996; company annual reports.

Moreover, while Fauber and Antonini built Kmart's retailing portfolio far beyond its core discount store base, Kmart management never was able to transform any of its acquisitions into enterprises able to compete successfully against key segment rivals in terms of sales, net income, or efficient inventory management. In almost every retailing business that Kmart diversified into, it trailed the industry leader by a considerable distance. Builders Square stores achieved sales volumes only one-third the per-store sales volume of industry leader, Home Depot. The company's Pace warehouse clubs never were able to match the selection and pricing of Sam's warehouse clubs and, in the end, many of Pace's store locations were eventually sold to Wal-Mart. Knowledgeable retail analysts attributed the failure of Kmart's American Fare stores in part to poor store design and poor store management. Payless Drugs, Waldenbooks, and OfficeMax were all weak-performing businesses under Kmart's management, posting either operating losses or minimal operating profits.

Joseph Antonini attributed some of Kmart's difficulties in the apparel segment of its core retail discount business to rapidly shifting market conditions rather than weak strategy on Kmart's part. For example, while, as the company had planned, the Kathy Ireland and Jaclyn Smith apparel lines were successfully positioned as national brands in the minds of shoppers, the initial success proved short-lived. By 1994, sales of the two apparel lines were sagging because of changing buyer preferences. Antonini, whose background and experience had been largely in apparel and soft lines, explained the reasons for the downturn: "Substantial shifts are taking place. For example, clothes just don't mean as much as they did five years ago, focus groups tell us. Designer names are not driving shoppers to stores, but in many ways have the opposite effect. Today, Mom is usually the last family member to get a new outfit. She is sacrificing for her family."[2] Antonini, in a 1994 *Forbes* interview, said that the U.S. economy played a role in undermining some of Kmart's merchandising efforts: "The economy is hurting, disposable income is down, and people are spending money only on essential products. The fringe items—and I consider apparel to be a fringe item—aren't selling anywhere across the country like they used to."[3]

Antonini's expectation that sales of higher-margin apparel items would allow the company to offer lower prices on thousands of other items sold in Kmart stores didn't pan out either. As it turned out, Kmart was at a cost disadvantage relative to Wal-Mart and was not able to meet Wal-Mart's pricing on many items. In addition, Wal-Mart management was intent on being the low-price leader and chose not to allow competitors to price popular items below what Wal-Mart charged. A Wal-Mart executive gave the following explanation of the importance of the company's five-point operating cost advantage and its pricing strategy: "It's very simple. We're not going to be undersold. What that means is, that in an all-out price war, [our competitors] will go broke 5% before we will."[4]

When asked about Wal-Mart's meteoric climb to the top of the full-line discount industry, Antonini stated that Wal-Mart management, who he at times referred to as "snake oil salesmen,"[5] came across as successful largely because Wal-Mart was new to the industry and consumers were inclined to try out a new store. In 1994 he commented that, "They have enjoyed the advantage of being the new show in town in

---

[2]"Antonini, On Changes in the Marketplace," *Discount Merchandiser,* December 1994, p. 12.

[3]"The Best-Laid Plans . . . ," *Forbes,* January 3, 1994, p. 44.

[4]"The High Cost of Second Best," *Fortune,* July 26, 1993, p. 99.

[5]Ibid.

many of our markets."[6] Antonini suggested that Wal-Mart's newcomer advantage was very similar to the new retail shopping excitement that Kmart was able to create during its period of rapid growth in the 1960s and 1970s.

Kmart's Super Kmart Centers.

Kmart's new Super Kmart Centers were having marginally greater success competing against Wal-Mart's Supercenters than older Kmart stores were having in competing with Wal-Mart's regular discount stores. Super Kmart Centers were approximately the same size as Wal-Mart Supercenters and, like Wal-Mart Supercenters, included a full-line grocery, discount store, and specialty departments like automobile service, photo centers, pharmacies, video rentals, floral departments, and hair salons. Super Kmart Centers were developed as a response to Wal-Mart's Supercenters, with little originality or creativity on the part of Kmart headquarters, and had their own unique culture and policies. When the first group of Super Kmart Center stores were opened, employees were proud of the stores' open "no walls" management style and culture that facilitated free and open communication; moreover, they saw their stores as Wal-Mart killers and worked hard to deliver better customer service than Wal-Mart. However, a manager of a rival to Super Kmart Centers noted that the impressively strong and vibrant entrepreneurial spirit of Super Kmart Center store employees (evident in the first group of stores opened) had waned because such cultures had not been firmly implanted in the nearly 100 new Super Kmart Centers that were opened between 1992 and 1995.

Kmart management indicated that annual sales per square foot at Super Kmart Centers were almost 60 percent greater than the annual sales at the company's regular Kmart discount stores. (see Exhibit 7). However, the profitability of the supercenter stores was not materially different than that of the traditional stores, since as much as 40 percent of the sales at the supercenters consisted of low-margin grocery items.

Kmart's Image with Consumers.

Surveys of U.S. discount store shoppers commissioned by *Chain Store Age Executive* found three consistent negative images that customers attributed to Kmart: out-of-stock merchandise, poor housekeeping, and indifferent service. Additionally, the consumers surveyed found Wal-Mart's locations more convenient and believed that Wal-Mart offered better pricing and product selection than Kmart. Antonini's store renovation and remodeling strategy was directed at eliminating Wal-Mart's pricing and selection advantage. However, in 1995—the company's fourth year into its renovation, relocation, and remodeling strategy—sales per square foot at Kmart remained flat at around $185, resulting in S, G, & A expense ratios that were far above Wal-Mart's because the typical Wal-Mart store had sales per square foot of over $375. The higher expense ratios kept Kmart's bottom-line performance from materially improving.

Kmart's Store Renovation and Renewal Program.

Wall Street analysts were very critical of Kmart's efforts at upgrading its stores. Many investors were displeased with Kmart management's use of the proceeds of a $1 billion equity issue in 1991. At the time the new shares of stock were sold, management had indicated that the capital was to be used to renovate and refurbish older Kmart stores. As it turned out,

---

[6]"Kmart's Agenda for Recovery," *Discount Merchandiser,* July 1994, p. 14.

a sizable portion of the money spent in its "renewal" program went into acquiring new specialty retail stores rather than renovating older Kmart stores. Wall Street analysts made the following comments about Kmart's store renewal efforts.[7]

> They aren't doing full renovations, just repainting or putting in new linoleum instead of gutting the stores entirely and redesigning them. And that has hurt them. It's back to the old Kmart culture where it's better to spend money on new stores and expand the chain.
>
> Even Betty Crocker got a new hair-do. I just drove by a Kmart store sign and it looked like a Howard Johnson should be next to it, circa 1957. They have a long way to go before getting rid of the popcorn smell when you walk in the door.
>
> It's not as if they started their remodeling program six months ago. We should have seen a more positive effect on earnings by now.
>
> By the time they're done, it will be time to start all over again.

Some shareholders and industry analysts suggested that the lack of management commitment to the store "renewal" program was a result of the company's past strategies. Kmart had achieved great success during the 1960s and 1970s as a result of its rapid addition of stores. The company's stock jumped from $0.50 per share when the first Kmart store was opened in 1962 to $32 in 1972. Some investors believed that the era of store growth at Kmart helped mold a managerial mind-set that favored putting more emphasis on store expansion than on proper management of existing stores and on merchandising efforts to boost annual sales at each existing store.

Continuing Inventory Problems.   Even though Kmart had invested far more than its industry rivals on developing systems and procedures to correct its inventory-related problems, the problems still existed. Kmart stores still were faced with frequent stockouts of merchandise and some of Kmart's vendors had criticized Kmart's buying procedures, stating that the corporate office frequently placed orders for merchandise and then later canceled the orders. A Kmart executive explained the difficulties of implementing its centralized merchandising strategy:[8]

> Bringing this decision-making power to the desktop is a hurdle. Category management evolved with computer systems, but it's still a challenge to get these high-powered PCs on everyone's desktops and to have them linked together via local area networks. Furthermore, some buyers may not be computer literate or used to dealing with scanner and syndicated data. So it can be an educational process as well as a hardware installation process. Most of our buyers started out as store managers, so to them it's attractive to think, "Oh, I'll call my old store to see how this product is doing." We have to get them additionally looking at and relying on this internal computer data, syndicated third party data, and quantitative information. It also takes a certain kind of person, someone who knows merchandising, who knows computer processing, who knows about financing, who knows a little about advertising—someone who knows enough about everything, as opposed to being a specialist in just one area. The information and the software available are just tools. You still need an experienced person who can tie it all together.

Customer Service Problems.   Some Kmart stores were plagued with unresponsive customer service. A 1994 *Forbes* article cited customer complaints of indifferent Kmart employees who, when asked for a specific item in the store, would wave their

---

[7]"Attention Bottom Fishers," *Financial World*, March 28, 1995, p. 31.

[8]Ibid., pp. 119–20.

hand in a general direction. Another disgruntled shopper complained that, "At the superstores in Farmington Hills or Southfield, the help is surly and uncooperative and you can never find the products that you need and have to have."[9] Commenting to the *Forbes* reporter on that particular complaint, Antonini said:

> Last year Kmart did $34 billion in sales. We had 180 million shoppers come through our doors. We had 1.3 billion transactions. Kmart's fine. We did the business. We did the sales. Now obviously this one shopper wasn't happy, but the store you're referring to is the Super Kmart store, I imagine. That store will do $80 million. Unfortunately this customer wasn't happy and obviously we don't like that. But when you get the amount of customers we get into a store, obviously we're not going to please everybody, but we try, we try.[10]

Morale Problems. Under Antonini, Kmart had continuing internal morale problems. Some employees believed these problems stemmed from the way that Antonini treated subordinates. One Kmart employee told *Forbes* reporters that frequently Antonini would publicly berate other senior executives and use epithets like "stupid," "jerk," or "inept" when addressing them. The Kmart employee also stated that Antonini would tell store personnel that they disgusted him and would frequently tell executives that they weren't worth the salaries they were paid. Antonini denied the charges cited by *Forbes*. "Remember, we're changing culture, and not everyone is happy with change. Am I a tough taskmaster? Yes. Do I challenge people? Yes. Am I demanding? Yes. But to say I'm abusive is an outright lie."[11]

Growing Pressure for Better Performance. In January 1994, rumors were circulating that Kmart's board was pressuring Antonini to show more progress in improving Kmart's competitiveness and financial performance. Responding to queries about whether the board had given him a deadline to get things turned around and had urged revisions in the company's strategy, Antonini said, "Absolutely not true. Because of two down quarters, people would say that? It's unequivocally not true. . . . While the economy is going to be difficult, while competition will continue to be fierce, we feel our strategy is right for the future."[12]

In March 1995, following eight consecutive quarters of lower earnings, Antonini resigned as Kmart's chairman of the board, CEO, and president.

■ Floyd Hall's Turnaround Efforts, June 1995–March 1997

Kmart's board of directors appointed Floyd Hall as the company's new chairman, chief executive officer, and president in June 1995. Hall, who was recruited from Grand Union Supermarkets, had engineered Target's growth during the 1980s and had recently gotten Grand Union back on track. Floyd Hall accepted the position with the intention of turning around Kmart within three years and then moving on to other ventures. "I'm just trying to build a team . . . get a good succession plan and new policies and practices in place. By the way, I do expect to go out on top."[13] Hall

[9]"The Antonini Transcript," *Discount Store News,* April 17, 1995, p. 12.

[10]Ibid.

[11]"The Best-Laid Plans . . . ," p. 45.

[12]Ibid.

[13]"Kmart Is Down for the Count," *Fortune,* January 15, 1996, p. 103.

and the board quickly assembled a new top-level management team—with 12 new vice presidents in marketing and product development; strategic planning, finance, and administration; merchandising; information systems; and other key areas. The 12 new vice presidents had an average of 27 years of retail experience. When Hall asked his new management team to review and evaluate Kmart's competitive position, he found that Kmart trailed Wal-Mart by a considerable distance on every key performance indicator. Wal-Mart's customers averaged 32 store visits per year, while Kmart's customers averaged 15 visits per year. Kmart's sales per square foot in 1994 were $185, compared to Wal-Mart's $379 and Target's $282. Only 19 percent of Kmart shoppers considered themselves loyal to the chain, while 46 percent of Wal-Mart shoppers considered themselves loyal Wal-Mart shoppers. Hall stated, "The most devastating news I saw in all the research was that 49 percent of Wal-Mart's shoppers drive past a Kmart to get to Wal-Mart."[14]

Hall believed that Kmart must be fixed "department by department" and that management must not try to "put a Band-Aid on our problems. This requires surgery."[15] Hall's first priority was to close nearly 400 Kmart stores and divest all noncore businesses from the company's portfolio between 1995 and 1997. Hall also initiated over $900 million in cost reductions during 1995 and 1996 by consolidating the company's Canadian operations with its U.S. operations, consolidating the company's payroll functions (payroll was previously handled by two companies), clearing out $700 million in old inventory, and using the company's volume buying power to reduce the cost of benefits for its 300,000 employees.

Some of the portfolio restructuring actually had taken place in the months just before Antonini's departure. Kmart sold PayLess Drugs in 1993 and spun off OfficeMax and Sports Authority as independent stand-alone companies in late 1994. The initial public offerings of stock in OfficeMax and in Sports Authority were completed in December 1994, with Kmart retaining a 25 percent equity ownership in OfficeMax and a 30 percent equity ownership in Sports Authority. In addition, the company's 21.5 percent interest in Cole Myer, an Australian retailer, was sold in 1994. These transactions provided the company with an approximate after-tax gain of $250 million.

In 1995 and 1996, Hall and Kmart's new management team sold the company's Czech and Slovak stores for $115 million; completed public offerings of stock to divest the company's remaining interests in OfficeMax and Sports Authority (netting the company an after-tax gain of $155 million); sold the assets of the Kmart auto centers to Penske for $84 million; completed a public stock offering of Border's Bookstores group (that resulted in an after-tax loss of $185 million); and sold the Rite Aid drugstore chain for $257 million. The company also discontinued its joint ventures in Singapore and Mexico and entered into a strategic alliance with Cardinal Health to manage the pharmacies in all Kmart and Super Kmart stores.

While Kmart executives believed that these divestitures, store closings, and cost-cutting efforts gave Kmart a stronger balance sheet, more business focus, and improved cost-competitiveness versus Wal-Mart, they were well aware that long-term success in turning Kmart around hinged on dramatically boosting sales and bringing shoppers into Kmart stores more frequently. In late 1996 Marv Rich, Kmart's executive vice-president of strategic planning and finance, stated "Our problem is

---

[14]Ibid., p. 102.

[15]"Kmart: Who's in Charge Here?" *Business Week*, December 4, 1995, p. 107.

not expenses—and we're getting a better handle on them. Our real problem is sales. If we had double the sales, our expense ratio would be half of what it is today, all things being equal."[16]

Kmart's Financial Crisis

Floyd Hall and the other members of Kmart's top management team were confronted with a potentially devastating financial crisis during the last half of 1995 that was a result of Kmart's poor cash flow and the financial decisions made by previous Kmart management. As was common with most retailers, Kmart management had a long-standing preference for financing new store construction off of the company's balance sheet. Groups of newly constructed stores were sold to such organizations as pension funds and insurance companies, who then leased the stores back to Kmart on long-term lease agreements. This was a hidden financial obligation, since long-term lease payment obligations were not required, under accounting rules then prevailing, to be shown as a long-term liability on Kmart's balance sheet; the company only had to report current-year lease payments as an operating expense on its annual income statement.

In the early-1990s, Kmart's financial officers had agreed to special "put provisions" in a number of Kmart's store-leasing agreements in exchange for better lease terms from the financing organizations. The "put provisions" stipulated that if Kmart's bond rating was downgraded to junk-bond status, then Kmart would immediately be obligated to buy back the leased stores from the lease-owner and eliminate any risk of potential default on the remaining years of the leasing agreement. In July 1995—just one month after Hall became Kmart's CEO—Kmart was placed on credit watch by various credit-rating agencies as an indication that they were considering downgrading Kmart's bond rating. The credit watch placement had the effect of preventing Kmart from borrowing on 30-to-60-day commercial paper over the October–November period to pay suppliers for shipping the volume of goods needed to build its Christmas inventory. In order to have ample warehouse and store inventories for the Christmas season, Kmart was forced to activate a $2 billion backup revolving line of credit held by a consortium of 70 banks, adding interest costs and further straining Kmart's already precariously thin profit margins and cash flows.

In October 1995, rumors began on Wall Street that Kmart would consider bankruptcy protection because of the pending bond rating downgrade and the put provisions agreed to during the Antonini era; a number of stories concerning the company's financial difficulties appeared in *The Wall Street Journal* in October 1995. As the rumors took hold, many Wall Street analysts began to debate whether the leaseholders would exercise their "put options" and require Kmart to buy back the leased stores, thus triggering a financial catastrophe for Kmart and forcing it to declare bankruptcy. Kmart's store buyback obligation with leaseholders amounted to $600 million—money that it did not have and might well not be able to raise, according to Wall Street speculation. To make matters worse, the covenants of Kmart's $2 billion revolving line of credit stated that if the leaseholders exercised their put options, any borrowings under the line of credit would immediately become due and payable. Kmart's accounts payable to its vendors already exceeded $3.5 billion

---

[16]"Leaner, Meaner, Cleaner: Nearly $1 Billion in Cost Cutting Has Goosed Earnings and Improved Efficiencies," *Discount Store News*, December 9, 1996, p. 28.

for its purchases for Christmas inventory. The potential for Kmart to be faced with obligations to its vendors and creditors totaling $6 billion, compounded by swirling rumors, drove the company's stock price down to $5 3/4 per share—50 percent of its book value.

As Wall Street expected, Kmart's long-term debt was downgraded to junk bond status in January 1996. Hall and Kmart financial officers had already visited with the leaseholders in late December 1995 and negotiated an agreement for them not to immediately exercise the put options and demand payment. Hall and Kmart financial executives knew from past experiences of other troubled retailers that vendors would not ship Kmart additional merchandise if they were not paid for what had already been shipped. Hall also knew that the company would not survive if there was a broad pullback by vendors and Kmart had to go without merchandise in its stores, so the decision was made to use the available cash to pay vendors in a manner sufficiently timely to ensure continued shipments.

As Kmart paid its suppliers, management continued talks with the 70 banks that funded Kmart's line of credit. The negotiations were difficult, since Kmart did not have sufficient cash to make the required repayments on its revolving line of credit, and the banks' primary concern was how quickly their exposure on the outstanding loans could be covered. Kmart's creditors agreed to allow the company to suspend principal payments on its debt for 18 months while Hall and Kmart's financial officers negotiated a new financing proposal with a consortium of banks led by Chemical Bank. Chemical Bank agreed to put a consortium of lenders together to provide Kmart with $3.7 billion to refinance its obligations under the revolving line of credit and the leased-store debt associated with "put options"—contingent on the company's ability to raise $750 million through an equity issue.

The crisis came to an end in June 1996, when Kmart issued $1 billion in convertible preferred shares and signed a new $3.7 billion financing agreement with Chemical Bank. Because these funds were essential to keeping Kmart from declaring bankruptcy, Hall and Kmart's financial officers agreed to attractive interest rates on the bank loans and to substantial fees for the investment brokers to ensure that buyers were found for the $1 billion in convertible preferred stock.

Attracting Customers to Kmart

Floyd Hall and his new management team determined that there were a number of underlying problems that made it difficult for the company to compete against Wal-Mart:

- Items in high demand were frequently out of stock in Kmart stores.
- The company's pricing was above that of Wal-Mart.
- Kmart had a limited selection of merchandise in some categories.
- Some merchandise stocked in Kmart stores was of inferior quality.
- Many Kmart stores had very poor housekeeping and customer service.

Hall's management team concluded that a combination of new strategies and improved implementation of existing strategies were required to correct Kmart's shortcomings.

A New Merchandising and Distribution Strategy. Kmart had been confronted with serious inventory management problems as far back as the early 1980s, and the new management team saw inventory management as the single biggest problem that had to be corrected. A big part of the solution, they believed, lay in eliminating many slow-selling items and unpopular brands and reducing the number of vendors. Under Antonini's centralized merchandising strategy, Kmart carried one or two national brands, an assortment of second- and third-tier brands, and some private-label brands. The new top management team found that many of the second- and third-tier brands cluttered store shelves and frequently did not sell without deep markdowns.

Kmart's new merchandising executives eliminated some second-tier brands and most third-tier brands and began to develop its private-label brands to fill the gaps in its merchandise mix left by the removal of the lesser-known brands. Kmart reengineered its buying process so that category managers were no longer making buying decisions in isolation from those in other functional areas. Under the reengineered process, Kmart set up buying teams made up of specialists in merchandising, planning, finance, inventory control, logistics, distribution, and advertising. The new process was designed to ensure that merchandise was available when demanded and would sell without regular or deep markdowns.

Studies indicated that most customers shopped in Kmart stores primarily during weekend sales and only occasionally at other times. Management decided that store traffic during nonsale times could be increased by stocking a wider variety of popular national brands like Rubbermaid and Wrangler. Kmart's sales of Rubbermaid products increased by 25 percent after it began to carry a wider assortment of the company's products. To fill gaps left by eliminated brands, Kmart extended its BenchTop do-it-yourself hardware line, began offering a wider variety of American Fare food products, introduced its new line of Route 66 denim apparel, and increased the number of K-Gro horticultural products available in its stores.

Kmart also completely redesigned the Martha Stewart Everyday bed and bath collection and planned a relaunch of the brand in 1997. The Martha Stewart private-label line of linens, towels, and other bed-and-bath products had been created during the Antonini era; however, under Antonini, the brand had not done particularly well because of inadequate promotion and a limited product line. The reintroduced Martha Stewart bed-and-bath collection included a wider variety of products—linens, bath towels, beach towels, draperies, pillows, blankets, and paint. The collection was manufactured by WestPoint Stevens and Springs and used high-quality materials such as 200-thread-count fabrics. The Martha Stewart paint line was manufactured by Sherwin-Williams and featured 256 colors that were similar to colors available in Martha Stewart's $80 per gallon line of paints offered by high-end retailers.

Stephen Ross, Kmart's general merchandise manager of soft lines, stated that the company would extend the Martha Stewart line to include household items in other store departments so as to allow customers to give their homes a decorator look. "We're going to make a case for her [our customer] to do something to freshen up her home—whether her bedroom or bathroom—give her a reason to do it because we've given her some décor tips and we're making it easy to do."[17] Ross believed that having a coordinated Martha Stewart line across store departments, offering decorator tips, and pricing the line competitively would prompt customers to make multiple purchases of Martha Stewart branded products.

Company management took a series of steps to improve its working relationships with suppliers, to correct out-of-stocks, and to reduce its distribution costs. Warren

---

[17]"The Martha-ization of Kmart's Home," *Discount Store News,* December 9, 1996, p. 4.

Flick, Kmart's COO, said, "You can't say enough about the importance of our relationships with our key suppliers in terms of finding efficiencies which are so necessary to take zero-value-added processes out of the system."[18] Kmart began a Collaborative Forecasting and Replenishment program with Warner-Lambert and several technology firms. The program was designed to share Kmart's customer and product information with its suppliers over the Internet. The company also upgraded its IBM Inventory Forecasting and Replenishment Modules system to shorten its replenishment cycle by a full day. Kmart's chief information officer Donald Norman said that the company had reduced the amount of time to replenish some merchandise from 40 hours to 18 hours.

The company also attempted to improve and expand its cross-docking capabilities in its distribution centers. Products that were delivered to its distribution centers were unloaded from suppliers trucks, audited for proper quantity, and then placed on a conveyor belt where they were loaded onto trucks headed for Kmart stores. The improved process was beneficial to both Kmart and its suppliers. The process shortened merchandise delivery time to Kmart stores, reduced inventory held in distribution centers, and improved the company's cash flow. Suppliers who had previously shipped to individual Kmart stores reduced their shipping costs by delivering to fewer destination points, and they received payment earlier since Kmart paid invoices upon receipt of the order at the warehouses rather than at the time of delivery to its stores.

Improving Kmart's Store Productivity and Relative Cost Position.

Despite the efforts of Kmart executives, at year-end 1996 Kmart's store productivity still trailed Wal-Mart's by a wide margin. Kmart had sales of $201 per square foot of retail space compared to sales of $379 per square foot for Wal-Mart. While Kmart's new superstores achieved higher sales volume than the company's older stores, they did not attract customers in sufficient volume to come close to matching sales per square foot at Wal-Mart. Kmart executives saw increased store traffic as the key to improving store productivity and lowering prices. Increased store traffic meant greater economies of scale in distribution and store operations—cost reductions that could then be passed along to shoppers in the form of lower and more competitive prices.

Hall developed and rolled out a redesign of existing stores that was intended to attract more customers to Kmart stores. The company tested its high-frequency Pantry concept during 1995 in selected stores and announced in January 1997 that it would expand the Pantry concept to 1,800 stores during the next three years. The Pantry concept was a redesign of existing stores that took items typically found in a convenience store and placed them in an 8,700-square-foot-area at the front of Kmart stores. Merchandise that was already sold in Kmart stores like diapers, paper towels, bread, milk, dog food, beverages, and snack foods was gathered and placed in one department, then supplemented by additional dry grocery items. Kmart rearranged remaining store merchandise so that frequently purchased items like small appliances and soft lines (underwear, T-shirts, socks, and fleece products) were placed near the Pantry area.

Kmart management expected that the high-frequency Pantry concept would increase store traffic by more than 10 percent and that many shoppers searching for

---

[18]"Flick Unveils Plan to Revamp Kmart," *HFN: The Weekly Newspaper for the Home Furnishing Network,* November 11, 1996, p. 2.

convenience-store items would purchase other items while at Kmart. Warren Flick argued that the new Pantry concept would successfully increase sales per square foot because, "If you have the consumables, you'll get the customers."[19] Kmart management was attracted to the Pantry concept because convenience-store sales were growing rapidly across the United States and because Kmart could implement the feature in its stores at relatively modest incremental costs. The cost to convert an existing Kmart store to the new Pantry concept was $600,000 versus $10 million for a new 100,000-square-foot Kmart store or $20 million for a new 180,000 Super Kmart Center. One Kmart executive doubted that the strategy would, by itself, boost Kmart's bottom-line performance significantly since most of the high-frequency convenience store items carried very low margins. "The Pantry has all the earmarks of something that can increase our sales. Not our profits."[20]

Changes in Structure, Communications, Culture, and Rewards. Concerned that the attitudes and performance of Kmart store managers and associates were adversely impacting shopper visits and loyalty, Hall brought in every Kmart store manager for a five-day meeting in September 1996. Kmart had never had a store managers' meeting, and Hall wanted to emphasize how important the store managers were to the company's success, to reiterate the company's strategic themes and initiatives, and to discuss how store managers could do their jobs better. At the meeting, the executive team explained the company's mission and strategy, and what individual store managers' roles were in implementing the strategy. The executive team also made it clear that they intended to end Kmart's historically insular, turf-wary organizational culture and adopt a more team-oriented atmosphere at both corporate headquarters and in the stores. The company also announced its new management development program to help the company develop future store-level and corporate-level managers from within its ranks. The company had always promoted from within, but had never attempted to build career paths for its managerial employees.

Kmart corporate-level managers also used the five-day conference to unveil its new store and field organizational structure and incentive compensation plan for store managers. One feature of the reorganization involved reducing the number of stores that each district manager was responsible for from 28 to 11. This reduction was intended to allow district managers to have the time necessary to visit every store in their districts more frequently and to provide better coaching to store managers. Within the stores, associates no longer had at-large responsibility, but were assigned to departments. Depending on the size of the store, as many as 14 departments and department managers were created in Kmart stores. Kmart executives believed that giving associates defined areas of responsibility would create a feeling of ownership within their department and encourage employees to offer better service in their departments. The establishment of department heads was also intended to improve customer service and to help associates begin a career as a Kmart manager.

A new incentive compensation plan for store managers was developed to replace Kmart's old managerial pay plan. Previously, Kmart managers were paid a salary plus a bonus based on store sales. Under the new compensation plan, store managers were eligible for both bonuses and stock options. The new bonus plan tied 50 per-

---

[19]"Kmart's Aim: Steal Market Share Away from Wal-Mart," *Daily News Record*, December 13, 1996, p. 1.

[20]"Kmart Is Down for the Count," p. 103.

cent of a store manager's bonus to meeting the store's budget objectives for the year and 50 percent to the store's customer satisfaction rating. The customer satisfaction rating was determined by the results of independent mystery shoppers who visited each store 28 times per year. Mystery shoppers rated each store on customer service provided in specialty departments, the general product knowledge of associates, associate friendliness and willingness to provide assistance, the speed of the checkout process, and all aspects of store cleanliness—from parking lots to fixtures.

Kmart also initiated efforts to improve communications between corporate-level management and its store managers. The company began weekly satellite feeds to discuss merchandising and operations and to provide training in vendor relations and human resources management. The idea was not so much to communicate frequently with stores, but rather to communicate effectively. Kmart's head of merchandise presentation and communications stated that in the past Kmart management put out so many directives to store managers that few could be implemented with real effectiveness. "There's never been a person in Troy [the company's headquarters] who didn't think that their program wasn't the most important one. But if you add them all up at the end of the day, there are 42 programs, and we're capable of doing two."[21]

Kmart established a corporate-level committee to review proposals for new programs, to determine how much time each program would take to implement, and to determine if individual stores had sufficient staffing to execute the plan successfully. Once the corporate-level committee determined that a plan could be implemented, it became the responsibility of a store-level committee to put the plan into place. A new program called All Hands On Deck required each store to have a committee made up of a replenishment manager and all department managers to coordinate merchandise stocking and new program implementation. The All Hands On Deck committee met each morning to determine what was needed to ensure that every department had its displays set up and was properly stocked. The All Hands On Deck committee was empowered to shift associates from departments who had little to do to prepare for the day over to help associates from departments that had to set up new displays or stock large amounts of inventory on its shelves or racks.

■ Kmart's Future Prospects

As Kmart Corporation approached the second anniversary of Floyd Hall's turnaround strategy in June 1997, Kmart executives could point to improved strategic and financial performance in a number of areas. The new $3.7 billion financing agreement and $1 billion convertible preferred equity issue had restored the company's solvency, the company had eliminated close to $1 billion in non-value-adding expenses, and the company's sales per square foot of floor space had increased modestly to $201 from $185 in 1994. In March 1997, the company was able to repay a $1.2 billion term loan that was part of its $3.7 billion financing arrangement concluded in June 1996. The term loan was paid two years ahead of schedule. The company had successfully divested all of its specialty businesses except Builders Square and was currently attempting to find a buyer for that business after its discussions with Waban, Inc., broke down in March 1997.

---

[21]"All Hands On Deck: Teamwork Initiates from the Buyer Level to the Stock Room Focus on Improving Operations," *Discount Store News,* December 9, 1996, p. 25.

The company had also improved its level of customer service and its in-stock position—two areas that Hall and other top-level managers believed to be strategically important to the company's turnaround. Between year-end 1994 and April 1997, the company's customer satisfaction index rating had improved from 68 percent to 87 percent. Its in-stock position on hard lines had improved from 88 percent to 95 percent and from 88 percent to 96.5 percent on soft lines. The company was clearly making progress toward correcting its weaknesses associated with the management of its full-line discount stores and achieving Floyd Hall's vision of operational excellence. Hall commented:

> All I want is a perfect store. The parking lot would be paved, striped and well lit. There would be no chewing gum on the sidewalks and no fingerprints on the doors. And when you stepped inside, the store would be brighter, the sight lines would be low with clear airport-type signage. The merchandise would be more fashion-forward and deliver a strong value message. It would be a place that would be a pleasure to shop in with warm, friendly and knowledgeable people and enough of them to help you when you need it.[22]

Floyd Hall was pleased with his management team's efforts and at year-end 1996 predicted that "1997 is going to be a banner year for Kmart and 1998 will be the [company's] biggest growth year."[23]

(Kmart's Web address is **www.kmart.com**)

---

[22]"O.K.mart Now It's Time for Results," *Discount Store News,* December 9, 1996, p. 25.
[23]Ibid.

◼ Case 4   Harley-Davidson, Inc.—Motorcycle Division

J. Paul Peter
University of Wisconsin–Madison

Harley-Davidson, Inc., is a diversified company with corporate headquarters at 3700 Juneau Avenue, Milwaukee, Wisconsin. Its three major business segments include (1) motorcycles and related products, (2) transportation vehicles including both recreational and commercial vehicles, and (3) defense and other businesses. In 1990, the company experienced another record year of growth. In the *Business Week 1,000* ranking of the top U.S. companies, Harley-Davidson, Inc., with a market value of $515 million, moved from the 973rd to the 865th largest U.S. company. Richard F. Teerlink, president and chief executive officer of the company, offered the following introduction to the company's 1990 annual report:

> Fellow Shareholder: I am again pleased to announce a record year at Harley-Davidson, Inc. in terms of revenues, profits and earnings. I'm especially proud this year because we were able to deliver very impressive results despite the fact that 1990—the third and fourth quarters, especially—was tough on most American manufacturers.
>
> Revenues for 1990 totaled $864.6 million, an increase of 9.3 percent over 1989. Net income was $37.8 million, a 14.8 percent increase and net earnings per share increased 11.0 percent to $2.12. Since 1987, revenues, net income, and net earnings per share have increased 33.8, 78.3, and 29.3 percent, respectively. Considering where we were as recently as five years ago, these are tremendous results.

Indeed, these were tremendous results given that the company is the only U.S. motorcycle manufacturer still in business, although there were once more than 140 competitors. In addition, the company had tremendous difficulties surviving the 1970s and early '80s and few analysts thought it would survive. In fact, the company would have gone bankrupt in 1985 had it not gotten refinancing with only days to spare.

◼ Company Background and Operations

Harley-Davidson was established in 1903 and had a virtual monopoly on the heavyweight motorcycle market by the 1960s.[1] In the early '60s Japanese manufacturers entered the marketplace with lightweight motorcycles that did not directly compete with Harley-Davidson. The influx of the Japanese products backed by huge marketing programs caused the demand for motorcycles to expand rapidly.

Recognizing the potential for profitability in the motorcycle market, American Machine and Foundry (AMF, Inc.) purchased Harley-Davidson in 1969. AMF almost tripled production to 75,000 units annually over a four-year period to meet the increases in demand. Unfortunately, product quality deteriorated significantly as over half the cycles came off the assembly line missing parts and dealers had to fix them up in order to make sales. Little money was invested in improving design or

---

This case was prepared by J. Paul Peter, University of Wisconsin–Madison. All factual information in the case is taken from public sources. Copyright 1991 by J. Paul Peter.

[1]This section is based on "How Harley Beat Back the Japanese," *Fortune*, September 25, 1989, pp. 155–64.

engineering. The motorcycles leaked oil, vibrated, and could not match the excellent performance of the Japanese products. While hard-core motorcycle enthusiasts were willing to fix up their Harleys and modify them for better performance, new motorcycle buyers had neither the devotion nor skill to do so. If Harley-Davidson was to remain in business, it desperately needed to improve quality and update its engine designs. Japanese manufacturers also moved into the heavyweight motorcycle market and began selling Harley look-alike motorcycles. Yamaha was the first company to do so and was soon followed by the three other major Japanese manufacturers, Honda, Suzuki, and Kawasaki. Their products looked so similar to Harley's that it was difficult to tell the difference without reading the name on the gas tank. The Japanese companies also copied the style of the Harley advertisements. As one Harley executive put it, "We weren't flattered."

In late 1975, AMF appointed Vaughn Beals in charge of Harley-Davidson. He set up a quality control and inspection program that began to eliminate the worst of the production problems. However, the cost of the program was high. For example, the company had to spend about $1,000 extra per bike to get the first 100 into shape for dealers to sell at around $4,000. Beals along with other senior managers began to develop a long-range product strategy—the first time the company had looked 10 years ahead. They recognized the need to upgrade the quality and performance of their products to compete with the faster, high-performance Japanese bikes. However, they also recognized that such changes would require years to accomplish and a huge capital investment.

In order to stay in business while the necessary changes in design and production were being accomplished, the executives turned to William G. Davidson, Harley's styling vice president. Known as "Willie G." and a grandson of one of the company founders, he frequently mingled with bikers, and with his beard, black leather, and jeans was well accepted by them. Willie G. understood Harley customers and stated that:

> They really know what they want on their bikes: the kind of instrumentation, the style of bars, the cosmetics of the engine, the look of the exhaust pipes, and so on. Every little piece on a Harley is exposed, and it has to look just right. A tube curve or the shape of a timing case can generate enthusiasm or be a total turnoff. It's almost like being in the fashion business.[2]

Willie G. designed a number of new models by combining components from existing models. These included the Super Glide, the Electra Glide, the Wide Glide, and the Low Rider. Each model was successful and other Harley executives credit Davidson's skill with saving the company. One senior executive said of Willie G., "The guy is an artistic genius. In the five years before we could bring new engines on-stream, he performed miracles with decals and paint. A line here and a line there and we'd have a new model. It's what enabled us to survive."

Still, Harley-Davidson was losing market share to its Japanese competitors, who continued to pour new bikes into the heavyweight market. By 1980, AMF was losing interest in investing in the recreational market and decided to focus its effort on its industrial product lines. Since AMF could not find a buyer for Harley-Davidson, it sold the company to 13 senior Harley executives in an $81.5 million leveraged buyout financed by Citicorp on June 16, 1981.

---

[2]Ibid., p. 156.

In 1982 things turned worse than ever for Harley-Davidson. Overall demand for motorcycles dropped dramatically and Harley's market share of this smaller market also continued to drop. The company had a large inventory of unsold products and could not continue in business with its level of production and expenses. Production was cut drastically, and more than 1,800 of the 4,000 employees were let go.

The Japanese manufacturers continued producing and exporting to the United States at rates well above what the market could endure. Harley-Davidson was able to prove to the International Trade Commission (ITC) that there was an 18-month finished-goods inventory of Japanese motorcycles that fell well below fair market value and asked for protection. The ITC can offer protection to a U.S. industry being threatened by a foreign competitor. In 1983, President Reagan increased the tariffs on large Japanese motorcycles from 4.4 percent to 49.4 percent, but these would decline each year and be effective for only five years. While this did decrease the imports somewhat and gave Harley some protection, Japanese manufacturers found ways to evade most of the tariffs, for example, by assembling more of their heavyweight bikes in their U.S. plants. Harley-Davidson's market share in the 1983 heavyweight motorcycle market slipped to 23 percent, the lowest ever, although it did earn a slight profit. By 1984, it had sales of $294 million and earned $2.9 million; it has continued to increase sales and profits through the early 1990s.

Manufacturing Changes

From the late 1970s Harley-Davidson executives recognized that the only way to achieve the quality of Japanese motorcycles was to adopt many of the manufacturing techniques used by them. The manufacturing systems changes that were instituted included a just-in-time manufacturing program and a statistical operator control system.[3]

The just-in-time manufacturing program was renamed MAN which stood for Materials As Needed. When the program was discussed with managers and employees at the York, Pennsylvania manufacturing facility, many of them reacted in disbelief. The York plant already had a modern computer-based control system with overhead conveyors and high-rise parts store and the new system would replace all of this with push carts! However, the MAN system eliminates the mountains of costly parts inventory and handling systems, speeds up set-up time, and can solve other manufacturing problems. For example, parts at the York facility were made in large batches for long production runs. They were stored until needed and then loaded on a 3.5 mile conveyor that rattled endlessly around the plant. In some cases, parts couldn't be found, or when they were, they were rusted or damaged. In other cases, there had been engineering changes since the parts were made and they simply no longer fit. The MAN system consists of containers that travel between the place where the parts are made and where they are to be used. The containers serve as a signal at each end to either "feed me" or "empty me." This system is credited with reducing work-in-process inventory by $22 million.

The statistical operator control (SOC) system allows continuous process improvements to reduce costs. The system involves teaching machine operators to use simple statistics to analyze measurements taken from parts to determine dimen-

---

[3]This section is based on Thomas Gelb, "Overhauling Corporate Engine Drivers Winning Strategy," *Journal of Business Strategy*, November/December 1989, pp. 8–12.

sional accuracy and quality. The system helps identify problems that occur during production early enough that they can be corrected before many parts are produced.

Human Resource Changes

In designing the new manufacturing processes, Harley executives recognized the importance of employee involvement.[4] In 1978 the company was among the first in the United States to institute a companywide employee involvement program. Harley-Davidson was the second U.S. company to begin a quality circles program which permits employees to contribute their ideas, solve problems, and improve the efficiency and quality of their work. Prior to these changes, engineers would figure out how to improve the manufacturing process and then tell operating employees what changes they needed to make. Naturally, the engineering plans were not flawless but the operating employees would not lift a finger to help solve the problems and would simply blame the engineers for screwing up again.

The changes in manufacturing and human resource strategy were credited with a 36 percent reduction in warranty costs; a 46 percent increase in defect-free vehicles received by dealers since 1982; inventory turnover up 500 percent; and productivity per employee up 50 percent.

Marketing Changes

By 1983 Harley executives recognized that they had become too internally-oriented and needed to pay greater attention to customers.[5] They recognized that they would not be able to compete effectively with the Japanese manufacturers by offering a complete product line of motorcycles but rather would have to find a niche and defend it successfully. They decided to focus all of their efforts on the superheavyweight motorcycle market (850cc or greater) and adopted a "close-to-the-customer" philosophy. This involved several unique marketing strategies. First, Harley executives actively sought out and discussed motorcycle improvement issues with customers. Second, it started the Harley Owner Group (HOG) to bring together Harley riders and company management in informal settings to expand the social atmosphere of motorcycling. The club is factory sponsored and is open to all Harley owners. It sponsors national rallies and local events and gives customers a reason to ride a Harley and involves them in a social group whose main activities revolve around the product.

Third, it began a Demo Ride program in which fleets of new Harleys were taken to motorcycle events and rallies and licensed motorcyclists were encouraged to ride them. This program was felt to be critical for convincing potential new customers that Harley-Davidson motorcycles were of excellent quality and not the rattling, leaking bikes of the 1970s. The program was renamed SuperRide and $3 million was committed to it. A series of TV commercials was purchased to invite bikers to come to any of Harley's over 600 dealers for a ride on a new Harley. Over three weekends, 90,000 rides were given to 40,000 people, half of whom owned other brands. While sales from the program did not immediately cover costs, many of the riders came back a year or two later and purchased a Harley.

---

[4]Ibid.

[5]Ibid.

Fourth, the company invited several manufacturing publications to visit the plant and publish articles on quality improvement programs. These articles reached the manufacturing trade audience and the national media as well. Finally, recognizing that many dealers viewed their business as a hobby and did not know how to sell, the company increased its sales force by 50 percent to give sales representatives more time to train dealers in how to sell Harleys.

Financial Changes

Although Harley-Davidson was improving its quality, reducing its breakeven point, catching up with competitors in the superheavyweight market, and marketing more aggressively, Citicorp was concerned about the economy and what would happen to Harley-Davidson when the tariffs on Japanese bikes were lifted in 1988.[6] The bank decided it wanted to recover its loans and quit being a source of funds for the company. After a number of negotiations, Citicorp took a $10 million write-off which might have facilitated Harley obtaining new financing. However, other bankers felt that the company must have been in really bad shape if Citicorp took a write-off and refused financial assistance. While lawyers were drawing up a bankruptcy plan, Harley executives continued to seek refinancing. Finally, several banks did agree to pay off Citicorp and refinance the company with $49.5 million.

Harley-Davidson went public with a stock sale on the American Stock Exchange in 1986. The company hoped to raise an additional $65 million and obtained over $90 million with the sale of common stock and high-yielding bonds. It then was in an excellent cash position and purchased Holiday Rambler Corporation, at that time the largest privately held recreational vehicle company in the United States. Holiday Rambler is similar to Harley-Davidson in that it is a niche marketer that produces premium-priced products for customers whose lives revolve around their recreational activities. In 1987 the company moved to the New York Stock Exchange and made two additional stock market offerings. Selected financial data for Harley-Davidson is contained in Exhibits 1 through 4.

By 1987, Harley-Davidson was doing so well that it asked to have the tariffs on Japanese bikes removed a year ahead of schedule. On its 85th birthday in 1988, the company held a huge motorcycle rally involving over 40,000 motorcyclists from as far away as San Francisco and Orlando, Florida. All attenders were asked to donate $10 to the Muscular Dystrophy Association and Harley memorabilia was auctioned off. The event raised over $500,000 for charity. The final ceremonies included over 24,000 bikers whose demonstration of product loyalty is unrivaled for any other product in the world.

■ Motorcycle Division—Early 1990

Exhibit 5 shows the motorcycle division's growth in unit sales. In 1990, Harley-Davidson dominated the superheavyweight motorcycle market with a 62.3 percent share while Honda had 16.2 percent, Yamaha had 7.2 percent, Kawasaki had 6.7 percent, Suzuki had 5.1 percent, and BMW had 2.5 percent. Net sales for the division were $595.3 million with parts and accessories accounting for $110 million of this

---

[6]Ibid.

■ **Exhibit 1**   Harley-Davidson, Inc., Selected Financial Data (in thousands, except share and per share amounts)

	1990	1989	1988	1987	1986
Income statement data:					
Net sales	$864,600	$790,967	$709,360	$645,966	$295,322
Cost of goods sold	635,551	596,940	533,448	487,205	219,167
Gross profit	229,049	194,027	175,912	158,761	76,155
Selling, administrative, and engineering	145,674	127,606	111,582	104,672	60,059
Income from operations	83,375	66,421	64,330	54,089	16,096
Other income (expense):					
Interest expense, net	(9,701)	(14,322)	(18,463)	(21,092)	(8,373)
Lawsuit judgment	(7,200)	—	—	—	—
Other	(3,857)	910	165	(2,143)	(388)
	(20,758)	(13,412)	(18,298)	(23,235)	(8,761)
Income from continuing operations before income taxes and extraordinary items	62,617	53,009	46,032	30,854	7,335
Provision for income taxes	24,309	20,399	18,863	13,181	3,028
Income from continuing operations before extraordinary items	38,308	32,610	27,169	17,673	4,307
Discontinued operation, net of tax	—	3,590	(13)	—	—
Income before extraordinary items	38,308	36,200	27,156	17,673	4,307
Extraordinary items	(478)	(3,258)	(3,244)	3,542	564
Net income	$ 37,830	$ 32,942	$ 23,912	$ 21,215	$ 4,871
Weighted average common shares outstanding	17,787,788	17,274,120	15,912,624	12,990,466	10,470,460
Per common share:					
Income from continuing operations	$ 2.15	$ 1.89	$ 1.70	$ 1.36	$ 0.41
Discontinued operation	—	0.21	—	—	—
Extraordinary items	(.03)	(.19)	(.20)	0.28	0.05
Net income	$ 2.12	$ 1.91	$ 1.50	$ 1.64	$ 0.46
Balance sheet data:					
Working capital	$ 50,152	$ 51,313	$ 74,904	$ 64,222	$ 38,552
Total assets	407,467	378,929	401,114	380,872	328,499
Short-term debt, including current maturities of long-term debt	23,859	26,932	33,229	28,335	18,090
Long-term debt, less current maturities	48,339	74,795	135,176	178,762	191,594
Total debt	72,198	101,727	168,405	207,097	209,684
Stockholders' equity	198,775	156,247	121,648	62,913	26,159

In December 1986, the Company acquired Holiday Rambler Corporation. Holiday Rambler Corporation's results of operations are not included in the income statement data for 1986.

SOURCE: Harley-Davidson, Inc., Annual Report 1990, p. 29.

figure. Production could not keep up with demand for Harley-Davidson motorcycles although a $23 million paint center at the York, Pennsylvania plant was nearing completion and would increase production to 300 bikes per day.[7]

Approximately 31 percent of Harley-Davidson's 1990 motorcycle sales were overseas. The company worked hard at developing a number of international markets. For example, anticipating the consolidation of Western European economies in 1992, a European parts and accessories warehouse was established in Frankfurt, Germany, in 1990. After entering a joint venture in 1989 with a Japanese distributor, the company bought out all rights for distribution in Japan in 1990. Revenue from international operations grew from $40.9 million in 1986 to $175.8 million in 1990.

[7]Harley-Davidson, Inc. Annual Report 1990, p. 12.

■ **Exhibit 2**   Harley-Davidson, Inc., Consolidated Statement of Income (in thousands except per share amounts)

Years Ended December 31	1990	1989	1988
Net sales	$864,600	$790,967	$709,360
Operating costs and expenses:			
Cost of goods sold	635,551	596,940	533,448
Selling, administrative, and engineering	145,674	127,606	111,582
	781,225	724,546	645,030
Income from operations	83,375	66,421	64,330
Interest income	1,736	3,634	4,149
Interest expense	(11,437)	(17,956)	(22,612)
Lawsuit judgment	(7,200)	—	—
Other-net	(3,857)	910	165
Income from continuing operations before provision			
for income taxes and extraordinary items	62,617	53,009	46,032
Provision for income taxes	24,309	20,399	18,863
Income from continuing operations before extraordinary time	32,610	27,169	38,308
Discontinued operation, net of tax:			
Income (loss) from discontinued operation	—	154	(13)
Gain on disposal of discontinued operation	—	3,436	—
Income before extraordinary items	38,308	36,200	27,156
Extraordinary items:			
Loss on debt repurchases, net of taxes	(478)	(1,434)	(1,468)
Additional cost of 1983 AMF settlement, net of taxes	—	(1,824)	(1,776)
Net income	$ 37,830	$ 32,942	$ 23,912
Earnings per common share:			
Income from continuing operations	$ 2.15	$ 1.89	$ 1.70
Discontinued operation	—	.21	—
Extraordinary items	(.03)	(.19)	(.20)
Net income	$ 2.12	$ 1.91	$ 1.50

SOURCE: Harley-Davidson, Inc., Annual Report 1990, p. 34.

Product Line

For 1991, Harley-Davidson offered a line of 20 motorcycles shown in Exhibit 6. Other than the XLH Sportster 883 and XLH Sportster 883 Hugger which had chain drives, all models were belt driven; all models had a five speed transmission. Three of the Sportster models had an 883cc engine and one had a 1200cc engine; all of the remaining models had a 1340cc engine. The first five models listed in Exhibit 6 were touring models while the remaining bikes were standard and cruising types. All of the models exhibited impressive painting and classic styling attributes visually reminiscent of Harley-Davidson motorcycles from the '50s and '60s.

Motorcycle magazine articles commonly were favorable toward Harley-Davidson products but pointed out weaknesses in various models. For example, a review of the XLH Sportster 1200 in the December 1990 edition of *Cycle* reported that

> But Harley undeniably has its corporate finger on the pulse of Sportster owners, and knows what they want. All of the complaints—poor suspension, high-effort brakes, awkward riding position, short fuel range, engine vibration, and poor seat—have echoed through the halls of 3700 Juneau Ave. for more than a decade, yet have had seemingly little effect on XL sales. H-D sold 24,000 Sportsters over the past two years, and these complaints have been common knowledge to anyone who's cared enough to listen.[8]

---

[8]"Harley-Davidson 1200 Sportster," *Cycle*, December 1990, p. 90.

■ **Exhibit 3** Harley-Davidson, Inc., Consolidated Balance Sheet (in thousands except share amounts)

December 31	1990	1989
Assets		
Current assets:		
Cash and cash equivalents	$ 14,001	$ 39,076
Accounts receivable, net of allowance for doubtful accounts	51,897	45,565
Inventories	109,878	87,540
Deferred income taxes	14,447	9,682
Prepaid expenses	6,460	5,811
Total current assets	196,683	187,674
Property, plant and equipment, net	136,052	115,700
Goodwill	63,082	66,190
Other assets	11,650	9,365
	$407,467	$378,929
Liabilities and Stockholders' Equity		
Current liabilities:		
Notes payable	$ 22,351	$ 22,789
Current maturities of long-term debt	1,508	4,143
Accounts payable	50,412	40,095
Accrued expenses and other liabilities	72,260	69,334
Total current liabilities	146,531	136,361
Long-term debt	48,339	74,795
Other long-term liabilities	9,194	5,273
Deferred income taxes	4,628	6,253
Commitments and contingencies (Note 6)		
Stockholders' equity:		
Series A Junior Participating preferred stock, 1,000,000 shares authorized, none issued	—	—
Common stock, 18,310,000 and 9,155,000 shares issued in 1990 and 1989, respectively	183	92
Additional paid-in capital	87,115	79,681
Retained earnings	115,093	77,352
Cumulative foreign currency translation adjustment	995	508
	203,386	157,633
Less:		
Treasury stock (539,694 and 447,091 shares in 1990 and 1989, respectively), at cost	(771)	(112)
Unearned compensation	(3,840)	(1,274)
Total stockholders' equity	198,775	156,247
	$407,467	$378,929

SOURCE: Harley-Davidson, Inc., Annual Report 1990, p. 33.

The article, however, was very complimentary of the newly designed engine and new five speed transmission and concluded that "This is the best Sportster ever to roll down an assembly line."

A review of the same model in *Cycle World's 1991 Motorcycle Buyer's Guide* pointed out a number of the same problems but concluded that

> Yet the bike's appeal is undeniable. A stab at the starter button rumbles it into instant life, and as the engine settles into its characteristically syncopated idle, the bike is transformed into one of the best platforms anywhere from which to Just Cruise. And that means everything from cruising your immediate neighborhood to cruising (with appropriate gas and rest stops) into the next state.
>
> This the bike is more than willing to do, with its premium tires and seemingly bullet-proof reliability. The important thing is to not ask the Sportster 1200 to be something it isn't. What it is, is a Sportster, much as Sportsters always have been.
>
> This is merely the best one yet.[9]

---

[9]"Harley-Davidson Sportster 1200—Improving on Tradition," *Cycle World 1991 Motorcycle Buyer's Guide,* April–May 1991, p. 27.

■ **Exhibit 4**　Harley-Davidson, Inc., Business Segments and Foreign Operations

A. Business Segments (in thousands)

	1990	1989	1988
Net sales:			
Motorcycles and related products	$595,319	$495,961	$397,774
Transportation vehicles	240,573	273,961	303,969
Defense and other businesses	28,708	21,045	7,617
	$864,000	$790,967	$709,360
Income from operations:			
Motorcycles and related products	$ 87,844	$ 60,917	$ 49,688
Transportation vehicles	825	12,791	20,495
Defense and other businesses	2,375	2,236	755
General corporate expenses	(7,699)	(9,523)	(6,608)
	83,375	66,421	64,330
Interest expense, net	(9,701)	(14,322)	(18,463)
Other	(11,057)	910	165
Income from continuing operations before provision for income taxes and extraordinary items	$ 62,617	$ 53,009	$ 46,032

	Motorcycles and Related Products	Transportation Vehicles	Defense and Other Businesses	Corporate	Consolidated
1988					
Identifiable assets	$180,727	$215,592	$2,863	$1,932	$401,114
Depreciation and amortization	10,601	6,958	3	396	17,958
Net capital expenditures	14,121	6,693	66	29	20,909
1989					
Identifiable assets	192,087	176,813	7,018	3,011	378,929
Depreciation and amortization	9,786	7,282	1,125	1,814	20,007
Net capital expenditures	18,705	3,524	1,190	200	23,619
1990					
Identifiable assets	220,656	177,498	7,163	2,150	407,467
Depreciation and amortization	13,722	6,925	1,166	618	22,431
Net capital expenditures	34,099	2,547	1,257	490	38,393

There were no sales between business segments for the years ended December 31, 1990, 1989, and 1988.

B. Foreign Operations

	1990	1989	1988
Assets	$25,853	$18,065	$ 6,557
Liabilities	17,717	15,814	3,761
Net sales	82,811	39,653	22,061
Net income	5,555	2,281	1,941

Export sales of domestic subsidiaries to nonaffiliated customers were $93.0 million, $75.4 million and $56.8 million in 1990, 1989, and 1988, respectively.

SOURCE: Harley-Davidson, Inc., Annual Report 1990, p. 43.

■ **Exhibit 5**
Harley-Davidson
Motorcycle Unit Sales
1983–1990

Year	Total Units	Domestic Units	Export Units	Export Percentage
1990	62,458	43,138	19,320	30.9
1989	58,925	43,637	15,288	25.9
1988	50,517	38,941	11,576	22.9
1987	43,315	34,729	8,586	19.8
1986	36,735	29,910	6,825	18.6
1985	34,815	29,196	5,619	16.1
1984	39,224	33,141	6,083	15.5
1983	35,885	31,140	4,745	13.2

SOURCE: Adapted from Harley-Davidson, Inc., Annual Report 1990, p. 20.

Pricing

The suggested retail prices for 1991 Harley-Davidson motorcycles are also shown in Exhibit 6. These products were premium-priced although the low-end XLH Sportster 883 and XLH Sportster 883 Hugger were less so in order that new motorcyclists could buy them and then trade up at a later time to larger, more expensive models. In fact, in 1987 and 1988, the company offered to take any Sportster sold in trade on a bigger Harley-Davidson at a later time.

The prices for Harleys can be compared with competitive products.[10] For example, the three 1991 Honda Gold Wing touring models with larger 1520cc engines had suggested retail prices of $8,998, $11,998 and $13,998. A Harley look-alike, the Kawasaki Vulcan 88, had a 1470cc engine and a suggested retail selling price of $6,599; a Kawasaki Voyager XII with a 1196cc engine had a suggested retail selling price of $9,099. Another Harley look-alike, the Suzuki Intruder 1400, had a 1360cc engine and a suggested retail selling price of $6,599. The Yamaha Virago 1100, another Harley look-alike, had a 1063cc engine and also had a suggested retail selling price of $6,599.

Promotional Activities

Kathleen Demitros, vice president of marketing for the Motorcycle Division, discussed a problem in designing advertising for Harley-Davidson motorcycles:

> One of the problems was that we had such a hard-core image out there that it was turning off a lot of people, even though people basically approved of Harley-Davidson. We had to find a way to balance our image more, without turning it into 'white bread' and making it bland. Our goal was to get as close to our Harley riders as possible and communicate with them very personally.[11]

In addition to print advertising in general magazines, and Harley's own quarterly magazine, called *Enthusiast,* Harley has its own catalogs with full color pictures and descriptions of each model and discussions of Harley-Davidson products. For example, following is an excerpt from the 1991 Harley-Davidson catalog:

---

[10]All prices are taken from the same reference as footnote 9.

[11]Kate Fitzgerald, "Kathleen Demitros Helps Spark Comeback at Harley-Davidson," *Advertising Age,* January 8, 1990, p. 3.

Model	Suggested Retail Price
FLTC Tour Glide Ultra Classic	$13,895
FLHTC Electra Glide Ultra Classic	$13,895
FLTC Tour Glide Classic	$11,745
FLHTC Electra Glide Classic	$11,745
FLHS Electra Glide Sport	$10,200
FXDB Sturgis	$11,520
FLSTC Heritage Softail Classic	$11,495
FLSTF Fat Boy	$11,245
FXSTS Springer Softail	$11,335
FXSTC Softail Custom	$10,895
FXLR Low Rider Custom	$10,295
FXRT Sport Glide	$10,595
FXRS Low Rider Convertible	$10,445
FXRS SP Low Rider Sport Edition	$10,295
FXRS Low Rider	$10,195
FXR Super Glide	$ 8,995
XLH Sportster 1200	$ 6,095
XLH Sportster 883 Deluxe	$ 5,395
XLH Sportster 883 Hugger	$ 4,800
XLH Sportster 883	$ 4,395

SOURCE: Adapted from *Cycle World 1991 Motorcycle Buyer's Guide,* pp. 76–82.

To the average citizen, it's a motorcycle. To the average motorcyclist, it's a Harley. To the Harley owner, it's something else entirely, something special. Once you've got your Harley, it's much more than a piece of machinery or a way to get around. In a sense, it actually owns you. It occupies you even when you're not riding it. It's part of your life. And while you might not ever be able to explain it to anyone who doesn't know, you know; the trip certainly doesn't end after the road does. Different? Most wouldn't have it any other way.

In 1990 the Harley Owner Group had 650 chapters and 134,000 members with expected growth in 1991 of 15 percent and an additional 55 chapters.[12] In addition to national, regional, and state rallies and other events, meetings between HOG members and Harley management continued to provide suggestions for product improvements. HOG groups have "adopted" various scenic highways and have taken responsibility for their upkeep. In the 10 years Harley-Davidson and its owner groups have been involved, they have raised over $8.6 million for the Muscular Dystrophy Association.

Dealer Improvements

Several years earlier Harley-Davidson instituted a Designer Store program to improve the appearance, image, and merchandising of its products at the retail level. By the end of 1990, more than 310 of the company's 851 domestic and international motorcycle dealerships had completed major store renovation projects or had agreed to do them in 1991. Some dealers reported receiving full return on the renovation investment within 12 to 18 months due to increased sales brought about by a more inviting shopping environment.

---

[12]This discussion is based on Harley-Davidson, Inc., Annual Report 1990, pp. 15–26.

Market Information

The traditional U.S. motorcyclist is an 18- to 24 year-old male.[13] Since 1980, the number of men in this age group has declined from 42.4 million to 35.3 million. By 2000 the number is expected to be only slightly higher, at 36.1 million. Women are buying motorcycles in increasing numbers and sales to them have doubled. However, they still account for only 6 percent of the total motorcycles purchased. Motorcycle manufacturers have responded to this market, however, by designing bikes that are lower slung and easier for women to ride. The Harley-Davidson XLH Sportster 883 Hugger was designed in part for this market.

The sale of motorcycles, including three- and four-wheel off-road vehicles, peaked in 1984 at 1,310,240 units. Five years later sales had dropped to 483,005 units. Sales dropped in all categories, although dirt bikes had the largest sales losses. Sales of larger motorcycles, which tend to be purchased by older buyers for use on highways, represented 12.2 percent of sales in 1984 but increased to 21.3 percent of sales five years later.

As less affluent young men have drifted away from motorcycling, the sport has been taken up by professionals and businesspeople in their 40s and 50s. Likely, the late Malcolm S. Forbes, motorcycle enthusiast and wealthy magazine publisher, influenced this market which is older, more conservative, and often rides long distances with their spouses on luxury vehicles.

There is some evidence that many motorcycle owners do not use their bikes very often, some only for a ride or two in the summer. Although the number of fatal accidents involving motorcycles declined 9 percent in a recent year, this decrease was likely because of decreased usage. The Insurance Institute for Highway Safety reported that in a crash, a person was 17 times more likely to die on a motorcycle than in a car.

Competition

Exhibit 7 shows changes in overall market share percentages for the five major competitors in the U.S. motorcycle market.[14] Honda clearly lost the greatest share and its sales decreased from $1.1 billion in fiscal 1985 to $230 million in fiscal 1990. However, motorcycle sales represent less than 1 percent of Honda's worldwide revenues.

■ **Exhibit 7**
U.S. Motorcycle Market Shares for Major Manufacturers

Company	1985	1987	1989
Honda	58.5	50.8	28.9
Yamaha	15.5	19.8	27.7
Kawasaki	10.2	10.2	15.6
Suzuki	9.9	11.6	14.2
Harley-Davidson	4.0	6.3	13.9

SOURCE: R. L. Polk & Co., as reported in "That 'Vroom!' You Hear Is Honda Motorcycles," *Business Week*, September 3, 1990, p. 74.

---

[13]This discussion is based on Doron P. Levin, "Motorcycle Makers Shift Tactics," *The New York Times*, September 16, 1989.

[14]This discussion is based on "That 'Vroom!' You Hear Is Honda Motorcycles," *Business Week*, September 3, 1990, pp. 74, 76.

Honda's plan to battle its sagging sales involved the introduction of more expensive, technologically-advanced bikes. However, with an increase in the value of the yen from 250 to the dollar in 1987 to 120 by 1988, all Japanese competitors had to raise prices. Honda had to raise their prices even more to cover their new expensive models and became less price competitive. In fact, nearly 600 Honda motorcycle dealers went out of business since 1985, leaving the company with 1,200 dealers in North America. Honda's Maryville, Ohio, plant had so much excess capacity that executives considered transforming much of it to production of auto parts.

Honda's 1990 strategy included cutting back prices and a $75 million advertising campaign to reintroduce the "wholesome" angle of cycling to reach new market segments. Promotional emphasis was also given to encouraging Americans to use motorcycles for commuting as an alternative to cars as is done in Europe and the Far East. High levels of air pollution, increased traffic, and rising fuel costs supported Honda's strategy. The advertising campaign was oriented less to selling individual products than to selling the idea that motorcycling is fun. Honda also offered free rides in shopping malls, sponsors races, and paid for Honda buyers to be trained at Motorcycle Safety Centers throughout the country.

In 1991, Honda's motorcycle product line included 25 models with displacements from 49 to 1520cc's including sportbikes, touring, cruisers, standards, and dual purpose types. It also included four models of 4-wheel all terrain vehicles (ATVs). Kawasaki's line included 23 motorcycle models in a variety of types and four 4-wheel models. Suzuki offered 24 models of motorcycles and 8 4-wheel models. Yamaha offered 25 motorcycle models and 7 4-wheel models. Other smaller competitors in the U.S. market included ATK, BMW, Ducati, Husqvarna, KTM, and Moto Guzzi.

The Future

Rich Teerlink and the other Harley executives have much to be proud of in bringing back the company to a profitable position. However, they must also plan for the future, a future that is uncertain and frought with problems. For example, the company faces much larger, well-financed competitors in the industry. The company faces increasing legislation on motorcycle helmet use and noise abatement laws that could decrease industry sales.

The company clearly recognizes the fact that the motorcycle industry has contracted greatly since the mid-1980s. It faces the problem of judging how much to increase supply of Harley-Davidson motorcycles given that it is a mature product whose future is uncertain. It faces decisions concerning how much should be invested in such an uncertain market and what marketing approaches are the most appropriate given this situation.

Case 5   Carnival Corporation: 1998

Michael J. Keeffe, John K. Ross, III, and Bill J. Middlebrook
All of Southwest Texas State University

Carnival Corporation, in terms of passengers carried, revenues generated, and available capacity, is the largest cruise line in the world and considered the leader and innovator in the cruise travel industry. Given its inauspicious beginnings, Carnival has grown from two converted ocean liners to an organization with two cruise divisions, a joint venture to operate a third cruise line, and a chain of Alaskan hotels and tour coaches. Corporate revenues for fiscal 1997 reached $2.4 billion with net income from operations of $666 million. And the growth continues with May 1998 revenues up $100 million over the same quarter 1997 to $1.219 billion. Carnival has several "firsts" in the cruise industry, with over one million passengers carried in a single year and the first cruise line to carry five million total passengers by fiscal 1994. Currently, their market share of the cruise travel industry stands at approximately 26 percent overall.

Carnival Corporation CEO and Chairman, Mr. Micky Arison, and Carnival Cruise Lines President, Mr. Bob Dickinson, are prepared to maintain a reputation as the leader and innovator in the industry. They have assembled one of the newest fleets catering to cruisers, with the introduction of several "superliners" built specifically for the Caribbean and Alaskan cruise markets, and expect to invest over $3 billion in new ships by the year 2002. Additionally, the company has expanded their Holland American Lines fleet to cater to more established cruisers and plans to add three of the new ships to their fleet in the premium cruise segment. Strategically, Carnival Corporation seems to have made the right moves at the right time, sometimes in direct contradiction to industry analysts and cruise trends.

Cruise Lines International Association (CLIA), an industry trade group, has tracked the growth of the cruise industry for over 25 years. In 1970, approximately 500,000 passengers took cruises for three consecutive nights or more, reaching a peak of five million passengers in 1997, an average annual compound growth rate of approximately 8.9 percent (this growth rate has declined to approximately 2 percent per year over the period from 1991 to 1995). At the end of 1997, the industry had 136 ships in service with an aggregate berth capacity of 119,000. CLIA estimates that the number of passengers carried in North America increased from 4.6 million in 1996 to five million in 1997, or approximately 8.7 percent. CLIA expects the number of cruise passengers to increase to 5.3 million in 1998, and with new ships to be delivered, the North American market will have roughly 144 vessels with an aggregate capacity of 132,000 berths.

Carnival has exceeded the recent industry trends, and the growth rate in the number of passengers carried was 11.2 percent per year over the 1992–1996 period. The company's passenger capacity in 1991 was 17,973 berths and had increased to 31,078 at the end of fiscal 1997. Additional capacity will be added with the delivery of several new cruise ships already on order, such as the *Elation*, which went into ser-vice in early 1998 adding 2,040 to the passenger capacity.

This case was prepared by Professors Michael J. Keeffe, John K. Ross III, and Bill J. Middlebrook of Southwest Texas State University. The case was prepared for classroom purposes only, and is not designed to show effective or ineffective handling of administrative situations.

Even with the growth in the cruise industry, the company believes that cruises represent only 2 percent of the applicable North American vacation market, defined as persons who travel for leisure purposes on trips of three nights or longer, involving at least one night's stay in a hotel. The Boston Consulting Group, in a 1989 study, estimated that only 5 percent of persons in the North American target market have taken a cruise for leisure purposes and estimated the market potential to be in excess of $50 billion. Carnival Corporation (1996) believes that only 7 percent of the North American population has ever cruised. Various cruise operators, including Carnival Corporation, have based their expansion and capital spending programs on the possibility of capturing part of the 93 percent to 95 percent of the North American population who have yet to take a cruise vacation.

■ The Evolution of Cruising

With the replacement of ocean liners by aircraft in the 1960s as the primary means of transoceanic travel, the opportunity for developing the modern cruise industry was created. Ships no longer required to ferry passengers from destination to destination became available to investors with visions of a new vacation alternative to complement the increasing affluence of Americans. Cruising, once the purview of the rich and leisure class, was targeted to the middle class, with service and amenities similar to the grand days of first-class ocean travel.

According to Robert Meyers, Editor and Publisher of *Cruise Travel* magazine, the increasing popularity of taking a cruise as a vacation can be traced to two serendipitously timed events. First, television's *Love Boat* series dispelled many myths associated with cruising and depicted people of all ages and backgrounds enjoying the cruise experience. This show was among the top ten shows on television for many years according to Nielsen ratings, and provided extensive publicity for cruise operators. Second, the increasing affluence of Americans and the increased participation of women in the work force gave couples and families more disposable income for discretionary purposes, especially vacations. As the myths were dispelled and disposable income grew, younger couples and families "turned on" to the benefits of cruising as a vacation alternative, creating a large new target market for the cruise product which accelerated the growth in the number of Americans taking cruises as a vacation.

■ Carnival History

In 1972 Ted Arison, backed by American Travel Services, Inc. (AITS), purchased an aging ocean liner from Canadian Pacific Empress Lines for $6.5 million. The new AITS subsidiary, Carnival Cruise Line, refurbished the vessel from bow to stern and renamed it the *Mardi Gras* to capture the party spirit. (Also included in the deal was another ship later renamed the *Carnivale.*) The company start was not promising, however, as on the first voyage the *Mardi Gras,* with over 300 invited travel agents aboard, ran aground in Miami Harbor. Because the ship was slow and guzzled expensive fuel, limiting the number of ports of call and lengthening the minimum stay of passengers on the ship was necessary in order to break even. Mr. Arison then bought another old ocean vessel from Union Castle Lines to complement the *Mardi Gras* and the *Carnivale* and named it the *Festivale.* To attract customers,

Mr. Arison began adding on-board diversions such as planned activities, casinos, nightclubs, discos, and other forms of entertainment designed to enhance the shipboard experience.

Carnival lost money for the next three years and in late 1974, Ted Arison bought out the Carnival Cruise subsidiary of AITS, Inc., for $1 cash and the assumption of $5 million in debt. One month later, the *Mardi Gras* began showing a profit and through the remainder of 1975 operated at more than 100 percent capacity. (Normal ship capacity is determined by the number of fixed berths available. Ships, like hotels, can operate beyond this fixed capacity by using rollaway beds, pullmans, and upper bunks.) Ted Arison (then Chairman), along with Bob Dickinson (who was then Vice President of Sales and Marketing), and his son Micky Arison (then President of Carnival), began to alter the current approach to cruise vacations. Carnival went after first-time and younger cruisers with a moderately priced vacation package that included air fare to the port of embarkation and home after the cruise. Per diem rates were very competitive with other vacation packages and Carnival offered passage to multiple exotic Caribbean ports, several meals served daily with premier restaurant service, and all forms of entertainment and activities included in the base fare. The only things not included in the fare were items of a personal nature, liquor purchases, gambling, and tips for the cabin steward, table waiter, and busboy. Carnival continued to add to the shipboard experience with a greater variety of activities, nightclubs, and other forms of entertainment and added varied ports of call to increase its attractiveness to potential customers. They were the first modern cruise operator to use multimedia advertising promotions and established the theme of "Fun Ship" cruises, promoting the ship as the primary destination and ports of call as secondary. Carnival told the public that it was throwing a shipboard party and everyone was invited. Today, the "Fun Ship" theme still permeates all Carnival Cruise ships.

Throughout the 1980s, Carnival was able to maintain a growth rate of approximately 30 percent, about three times that of the industry as a whole, and between 1982 and 1988 its ships sailed with an average of 104 percent capacity (currently they operate at 104 percent to 105 percent capacity, depending on the season). Targeting younger, first-time passengers by promoting the ship as a destination proved to be extremely successful. Carnival's 1987 customer profile showed that 30 percent of the passengers were between the ages of 25 and 39 with household incomes of $25,000–$50,000.

In 1987, Ted Arison sold 20 percent of his shares in Carnival Cruise Lines and immediately generated over $400 million for further expansion. In 1988, Carnival acquired the Holland America Line which had four cruise ships with 4,500 berths. Holland America was positioned to the higher-income travelers with cruise prices averaging 25–35 percent more than similar Carnival cruises. The deal also included two Holland America subsidiaries, Windstar Sail Cruises and Holland America Westours. This success, and the foresight of management, allowed Carnival to begin an aggressive "superliner" building campaign for their core subsidiary. By 1989, the cruise segments of Carnival Corporation carried over 750,000 passengers in one year, a "first" in the cruise industry.

Ted Arison relinquished the role of Chairman to his son Micky in 1990, a time when the explosive growth of the 1980s began to subside. Higher fuel prices and increased airline costs began to affect the industry as a whole, and the Persian Gulf war caused many cruise operators to divert ships from European and Indian ports to the Caribbean area of operations, increasing the number of ships competing directly with Carnival. Carnival's stock price fell from $25 in June of 1990 to $13 late in the year. The company also incurred a $25.5 million loss during fiscal 1990 for the operation of the Crystal Palace Resort and Casino. In 1991 Carnival reached a settlement with the Bahamian government (effective March 1, 1992) to surrender the 672-room Riveria Towers to the Hotel Corporation of the Bahamas in exchange for the cancellation of some debt incurred in constructing and developing the resort. The corporation took a $135 million write-down on the Crystal Palace for that year.

The early 1990s, even with industry-wide demand slowing, were still a very exciting time. Carnival took delivery of its first two "superliners"; the *Fantasy* (1990) and the *Ecstasy* (1991), which were to further penetrate the three- and four-day cruise market and supplement the seven-day market. In early 1991, Carnival took delivery of the third "superliner" *Sensation* (inaugural sailing November 1, 1993) and later in the year contracted for the fourth "superliner" to be named the *Fascination* (inaugural sailing 1994).

In 1991, Carnival attempted to acquire Premier Cruise Lines, which was then the official cruise line for Walt Disney World in Orlando, Florida, for approximately $372 million. The deal was never consummated since the involved parties could not agree on price. In 1992, Carnival acquired 50 percent of Seabourn, gaining the cruise operations of K/S Seabourn Cruise Lines and formed a partnership with Atle Byrnestad. Seabourn serves the ultra-luxury market with destinations in South America, the Mediterranean, Southeast Asia, and the Baltics.

The 1993–1995 period saw the addition of the "superliner" *Imagination* for Carnival Cruise Lines and the *Ryndam* for Holland America Lines. In 1994, the company discontinued operations of Fiestamarina Lines which attempted to serve Spanish-speaking clientele. Fiestamarina was beset with marketing and operational problems and never reached continuous operations. Many industry analysts and observers were surprised at the failure of Carnival to successfully develop this market. In 1995, Carnival sold a 49 percent interest in the Epirotiki Line, a Greek cruise operation, for $25 million and purchased $101 million (face amount) of senior secured notes of Kloster Cruise Limited, the parent of competitor Norwegian Cruise Lines, for $81 million. Kloster was having financial difficulties and Carnival could not obtain common stock of the company in a negotiated agreement. If Kloster were to fail, Carnival Corporation would be in a good position to acquire some of the assets of Kloster.

Carnival Corporation is expanding through internally generated growth as evidenced by the number of new ships on order (see Exhibit 1). Additionally, Carnival seems to be willing to continue with its external expansion through acquisitions if the right opportunity arises.

In June 1997, Royal Caribbean made a bid to buy Celebrity Cruise Lines for $500 million and assumption of $800 million in debt. Within a week, Carnival had responded by submitting a counter offer to Celebrity for $510 million and the assumption of debt, then two days later raising the bid to $525 million. However, Royal Caribbean seems to have had the inside track and announced on June 30, 1997, the final merger arrangements with Celebrity. The resulting company will have 17 ships with approximately 30,000 berths.

However, not to be thwarted in their attempts at continued expansion, Carnival announced in June 1997 the purchase of Costa, an Italian cruise company and the largest European cruise line, for $141 million. External expansion continued when on May 28, 1998, Carnival announced the acquisition of Cunard Line for $500 million from Kvaerner ASA. Cunard was then merged with Seabourn Cruise Line (50 percent owned by Carnival) with Carnival owning 68 percent of the resulting Cunard Line Limited.

■ **Exhibit 1**   Carnival and Holland America Ships under Construction

Vessel	Expected Delivery	Shipyard	Passenger Capacity*	Cost (millions)
Carnival Cruise Lines				
Elation	03/98	Masa-Yards	2,040	$ 300
Paradise	12/98	Masa-Yards	2,040	300
Carnival Triumph	07/99	Fincantieri	2,640	400
Carnival Victory	08/00	Fincantieri	2,640	430
CCL Newbuild	12/00	Masa-Yards	2,100	375
CCL Newbuild	2001	Masa-Yards	2,100	375
CCL Newbuild	2002	Masa-Yards	2,100	375
Total Carnival Cruise Lines			15,912	$2,437
Holland America Line				
Volendam	6/99	Fincantieri	1,440	274
Zaandam	12/99	Fincantieri	1,440	286
HAL Newbuild	9/00	Fincantieri	1,440	300
Total Holland America Line			4,260	$ 860
Windstar Cruises				
Wind Surf	5/98	Purchase	312	40
Total all vessels			20,484	$3,337

*In accordance with industry practice all capacities indicated within this document are calculated based on two passengers per cabin even though some cabins can accommodate three or four passengers.

■ The Cruise Product

Ted and Mickey Arison envisioned a product where the classical cruise elegance along with modern convenience could be had at a price comparable to land-based vacation packages sold by travel agents. Carnival's all-inclusive package, when compared to resorts or a theme park such as Walt Disney World, often is priced below these destinations, especially when the array of activities, entertainment, and meals are considered.

A typical vacation on a Carnival cruise ship starts when the bags are tagged for the ship at the airport. Upon arriving at the port of embarkation, passengers are ferried by air-conditioned buses to the ship for boarding, and luggage is delivered by the cruise ship staff to the passenger's cabin. Waiters dot the ship offering tropical drinks to the backdrop of a Caribbean rhythm, while the cruise staff orients passengers to the various decks, cabins, and public rooms. In a few hours (most ships sail in the early evening), dinner is served in the main dining rooms where wine selection rivals the finest restaurants and the variety of main dishes are designed to suit every palate. Diners can always order double portions if they decide not to save room for the variety of desserts and after-dinner specialties.

After dinner, cruisers can choose between many forms of entertainment, including live music, dancing, nightclubs, and a selection of movies; or they can sleep through the midnight buffet until breakfast. (Most ships have five or more distinct nightclubs.) During the night, a daily program of activities arrives at the passengers' cabins. The biggest decisions to be made for the duration of the vacation will be what to do (or not to do), what to eat and when (usually eight separate serving times not including the 24-hour room service), and when to sleep. Service in all areas, from dining to housekeeping, is upscale and immediate. The service is so good that a common shipboard joke says that if you leave your bed during the night to visit the head (sea talk for bathroom), your cabin steward will have made the bed and placed chocolates on the pillow by the time you return.

After the cruise, passengers are transported back to the airport in air-conditioned buses for the flight home. Representatives of the cruise line are on hand at the airport to help cruisers in meeting their scheduled flights. When all amenities are considered, most vacation packages would be hard pressed to match Carnival's per diem prices that range from $125–$250 per person per day, depending on accommodations. (Holland America and Seabourn are higher, averaging $300 per person per day.) Occasional specials allow for even lower prices and special suite accommodations can be had for an additional payment.

■ Carnival Operations

Carnival Corporation, headquartered in Miami, is composed of Carnival Cruise Lines, Holland America Lines which includes Windstar Sail Cruises as a subsidiary, Holland America Westours, Westmark Hotels, Airtours, and the newly created Cunard Line Limited. Carnival Cruise Lines, Inc., is a Panamanian corporation and its subsidiaries are incorporated in Panama, the Netherlands Antilles, the British Virgin Islands, Liberia, and the Bahamas. The ships are subject to inspection by the U.S. Coast Guard for compliance with the Convention for the Safety of Life at Sea (SOLAS), which requires specific structural requirements for safety of passengers at sea, and by the U.S. Public Health Service for sanitary standards. The company is also regulated in some aspects by the Federal Maritime Commission.

At its helm, Carnival Corporation is led by CEO and Chairman of the Board Micky Arison and Carnival Cruise Lines President and COO Bob Dickinson. Mr. A. Kirk Lanterman is the President and CEO of the Holland America cruise division which includes Holland America Westours and Windstar Sail Cruises. (A listing of corporate officers is presented in Exhibit 2.)

The company's product positioning stems from its belief that the cruise market is actually comprised of three primary segments with different passenger demographics, passenger characteristics, and growth requirements. The three segments are the contemporary, premium, and luxury segments. The contemporary segment is served by Carnival ships for cruises that are seven days or shorter in length and feature a casual ambiance. The premium segment, served by Holland America, serves the seven day and longer market and appeals to more affluent consumers. The luxury segment, while considerably smaller than the other segments, caters to experienced cruisers for seven day and longer sailings and is served by Seabourn. Specialty sailing cruises are provided by Windstar Sail Cruises, a subsidiary of Holland America.

Corporate structure is built around the "profit center" concept and is updated periodically when needed for control and coordination purposes. The cruise subsidiaries of Carnival give the corporation a presence in most of the major cruise segments and provides for world-wide operations.

Carnival has always placed a high priority on marketing in an attempt to promote cruises as an alternative to land-based vacations. It wants customers to know that the ship in itself is the destination and the ports of call are important, but secondary, to the cruise experience. Education and the creation of awareness are critical to corporate marketing efforts. Carnival was the first cruise line to successfully break away from traditional print media and use television to reach a broader market. Even

Carnival Corporation
Micky Arison
Chairman of the Board and Chief Executive Officer
Howard S. Frank
Vice Chairman and Chief Operating Officer
Gerald R. Cahill
Senior Vice President Finance and CFO
Roderick K. McLeod
Senior Vice President Marketing
Lowell Zemnick
Vice President and Treasurer
Carnival Cruise Lines
Robert H. Dickinson
President and COO
Meshulam Zonis
Senior Vice President Operations
Holland America Lines
A. Kirk Lanterman
Chairman of the Board and CEO
Peter T. McHugh
President and COO

SOURCE: Carnival Corporation, 1998.

though other lines have followed Carnival's lead in selecting promotional media and are near in total advertising expenditures, the organization still leads all cruise competitors in advertising and marketing expenditures.

Carnival wants to remain the leader and innovator in the cruise industry and intends to do this with sophisticated promotional efforts, by gaining loyalty from former cruisers, by refurbishing ships, by varying activities and ports of call, and by being innovative in all aspects of ship operations. Management intends to build on the theme of the ship as a destination given their historical success with this promotional effort. The company capitalizes and amortizes direct-response advertising and expenses other advertising costs as incurred. Advertising expense totaled $112 million in 1997, $109 million in 1996, $98 million in 1995 and $85 million in 1994.

■ Financial Performance

Carnival retains Price Waterhouse as independent accountants, the Barnett Bank Trust Company–North America as the registrar and stock transfer agent, and their Class A Common stock trades on the New York Stock Exchange under the symbol CCL. In December 1996, Carnival amended the terms of its revolving credit facility primarily to combine two facilities into a single one-billion-dollar-unsecured-revolving-credit facility due 2001. The borrowing rate on the One Billion Dollar Revolver is a maximum of LIBOR[1] plus 14 basis points and the facility fee is six basis points. Carnival initiated a commercial paper program in October 1996, which is supported by the One Billion Dollar Revolver. As of November 30, 1996, the Company had $307 million outstanding under its commercial paper program and $693 million available for borrowing under the One Billion Dollar Revolver.

The consolidated financial statements for Carnival Cruise Lines, Inc. are shown in Exhibits 3 and 4 and selected financial data are presented in Exhibit 5.

Customer cruise deposits, which represent unearned revenue, are included in the balance sheet when received and recognized as cruise revenues on completion of the voyage. Customers are also required to pay the full cruise fare (minus deposit) 60 days in advance with the fares being recognized as cruise revenue on completion of the voyage.

Property and equipment on the financial statements is stated at cost. Depreciation and amortization is calculated using the straight line method over the following estimated useful lives: vessels 25–30 years, buildings 20–40 years, equipment 2–20 years and leasehold improvements at the shorter of the "term of lease" or "related asset life." Goodwill of $275 million resulting from the acquisition of HAL Antillen, N.V. (Holland America Lines) is being amortized using the straight line method over 40 years.

During 1995, Carnival received $40 million from the settlement of litigation with Metra Oy, the former parent company of Wartsila Marine Industries, related to losses suffered in connection with the construction of three cruise ships. (Wartsila declared bankruptcy in late 1994.) Of this amount, $14.4 million was recorded as "other income" with the remainder used to pay legal fees and reduce the cost basis of the three ships.

---

[1]"LIBOR Rate" means, for an Interest Period for each LIBOR (London Interbank Offer Rate) Rate Advance comprising part of the same Borrowing, the rate determined by the Agent to be the rate of interest per annum rounded upward to the nearest whole multiple of 1/100 of 1 percent per annum, appearing on Telerate screen 3750 at 11:00 A.M. (London time) two Business Days before the first day of such Interest Period for a term equal to such Interest Period and in an amount substantially equal to such portion of the Loan, or if the Agent cannot so determine the LIBOR Rate by reference to Telerate screen 3750, then (ii) equal to the average (rounded upward to the nearest whole multiple of 1/100 of 1 percent per annum, if such average is not such a multiple) of the rate per annum at which deposits in United States Dollars are offered by the principal office of each of the Reference Lenders in London, England, to prime banks in the London Interbank market at 11:00 A.M. (London time) two Business Days before the first day of such Interest Period for a term equal to such Interest Period and in an amount substantially equal to such portion of the Loan. In the latter case, the LIBOR Rate for an Interest Period shall be determined by the Agent on the basis of applicable rates furnished to and received by the Agent from the Reference Lenders two Business Days before the first day of such Interest Period, subject, however, to the provisions of Section 2.05. If at any time the Agent shall determine that by reason of circumstances affecting the London Interbank market (i) adequate and reasonable means do not exist for ascertaining the LIBOR Rate for the succeeding Interest Period or (ii) the making or continuance of any Loan at the LIBOR Rate has become impracticable as a result of a contingency occurring after the date of this Agreement which materially and adversely affects the London Interbank market, the Agent shall so notify the Lenders and the Borrower. Failing the availability of the LIBOR Rate, the LIBOR Rate shall mean the Base Rate thereafter in effect from time to time until such time as a LIBOR Rate may be determined by reference to the London Interbank market.

Exhibit 3 Carnival Corporation, Consolidated Statements of Operations (in thousands)

	Six Month Comparison		Years Ended November 30						
	May 31, 1998	May 31, 1997	1997	1996	1995	1994	1993	1992	1991
Revenues	$1,219,196	$1,117,696	$2,447,468	$2,212,572	$1,998,150	$1,806,016	$1,556,919	$1,473,614	$1,404,704
Costs and Expenses:									
Operating expense	669,951	634,622	1,322,669	1,241,269	1,131,113	1,028,475	907,925	865,587	810,317
Selling and administrative	163,784	156,219	296,533	274,855	248,566	223,272	207,995	194,298	193,316
Depreciation and amortization	89,266	82,658	167,287	144,987	128,433	110,595	93,333	88,833	85,166
	923,001	493,564	1,786,489	1,661,111	1,508,112	1,362,342	1,209,253	1,148,718	1,088,799
Operating income before affiliated	296,195	244,197	660,979	551,461					
Income from affiliated	(13,034)	11,694	53,091	45,967					
Operating income	283,161	232,503	714,070	597,428	490,038	443,674	347,666	324,896	315,905
Other income (expense):									
Interest income	5,885	3,382	8,675	18,597	14,403	8,668	11,527	16,946	10,596
Interest expense, net of capitalized interest	(24,735)	(31,536)	(55,898)	(64,092)	(63,080)	(51,378)	(34,325)	(53,792)	(65,428)
Other income (expense)	(662)	2,105	5,436	23,414	19,104	(9,146)	(1,201)	2,731	1,746
Income tax expense	6,861	6,353	(6,233)	(9,045)	(9,374)	(10,053)	(5,497)	(9,008)	(8,995)
	(12,651)	(19,696)	(48,020)	(31,126)	(38,947)	(61,909)	(29,496)	(43,123)	(62,081)
Income before extraordinary item	270,510	212,807	666,050	566,302	451,091	381,765	318,170	281,773	253,824
Extraordinary item									
Loss on early extinguishment of debt	—	—	—	—	—	—	—	(5,189)	
Discontinued operations									
Hotel Casino operating loss	—	—	—	—	—	—	—	—	(33,173)
Loss on disposal of Hotel Casino	—	—	—	—	—	—	—	—	(135,463)
Net income	$270,510	$212,807	$ 666,050	$566,302	$451,091	$ 381,765	$ 318,170	$276,584	$ 84,998

SOURCE: 1997 and 1998 10K and 10Q's.

■ **Exhibit 4** Carnival Corporation, Consolidated Balance Sheets (in thousands)

	May 31, 1998	1997	1996	1995	1994	1993	1992
				Years Ended November 30			
Assets							
Current assets:							
Cash and cash equivalents	$ 120,600	$139,989	$ 111,629	$ 53,365	$ 54,105	$ 60,243	$ 115,014
Short-term investments	9,414	9,738	12,486	50,395	70,115	88,677	111,048
Accounts receivable	66,503	57,090	38,109	33,080	20,789	19,310	21,624
Consumable inventories [average cost]	76,226	54,970	53,281	48,820	45,122	37,245	31,618
Prepaid expenses and other	102,754	74,238	75,428	70,718	50,318	48,323	32,120
Total current assets	375,497	336,025	290,933	256,378	240,449	253,798	311,424
Property and equipment [at cost]							
Less accumulated depreciation & amortization	5,469,814	4,327,413	4,099,038	3,414,823	3,071,431	2,588,009	1,961,402
Other assets							
Goodwill [less accumulated amortization]	403,077	212,607	219,589	226,571	233,553	237,327	244,789
Long-term notes receivable	425,715	479,329	430,330	78,907	76,876	29,136	38,439
Investment in affiliates and other assets	425,715	479,329	430,330	128,808	47,514	21,097	38,439
Net assets of discontinued operations	37,733	71,401	61,998	89,553		89,553	89,553
	$6,711,836	$5,426,775	$5,101,888	$4,105,487	$3,669,823	$3,218,920	$2,645,607
Liabilities and shareholders' equity							
Current liabilities:							
Current portion of long-term debt	$58,457	$59,620	$66,369	$72,752	$84,644	$91,621	$97,931
Accounts payable	187,897	106,783	84,748	90,237	86,750	81,374	71,473
Accrued liabilities	169,048	154,253	126,511	113,483	114,868	94,830	69,919
Customer deposits	755,890	420,908	352,698	292,606	257,505	228,153	178,945
Dividends payable	44,619	44,578	32,416	25,632	21,190	19,763	19,750
Reserve for discontinued operations						34,253	36,763
Total current liabilities	121,911	786,142	662,742	594,710	564,957	549,994	474,781
Long term debt	1,557,016	1,015,294	1,277,529	1,035,031	1,046,904	916,221	776,600
Convertible notes			39,103	115,000	115,000	115,000	
Other long-term liabilities	23,907	20,241	91,630	15,873	14,028	10,499	9,381
Shareholders' equity:							
Class A Common stock [1 vote share]	5,949	2,972	2,397	2,298	2,276	2,274	1,136
Class B Common stock [5 votes share]			550	550	550	550	275
Paid in capital	871,676	866,097	819,610	594,811	544,947	541,194	539,622
Retained earnings	2,912,499	2,731,213	2,207,781	1,752,140	1,390,589	1,089,323	850,193
Other	1,799	4,816	546	(4,926)	(9,428)	(6,135)	(6,381)
Total shareholders' equity	3,791,923	3,605,098	3,030,884	2,344,873	1,928,934	1,627,206	1,384,845
	$6,711,836	$5,426,775	$5,101,888	$4,105,487	$3,669,823	$3,218,920	$2,645,607

SOURCE: 1997 and 1998 10K and 10Q's.

703

■ **Exhibit 5**   Carnival Corporation, Selected Financial Data by Segment (in thousands)

| | **Years Ended November 30** | | | | | |
	1997	**1996**	**1995**	**1994**	**1993**	**1992**
Revenues						
Cruise	$2,257,567	$2,003,458	$1,800,775	$1,623,069	$1,381,473	$1,292,587
Tour	242,646	263,356	241,909	227,613	214,382	215,194
Intersegment revenues	(52,745)	(54,242)	(44,534)	(44,666)	(38,936)	(34,167)
	2,447,468	2,212,572	1,998,150	1,806,016	1,556,919	1,473,614
Gross operating profit						
Cruise	1,072,758	913,880	810,736	726,808	598,642	552,669
Tour	52,041	57,423	56,301	50,733	50,352	55,358
	1,124,799	971,303	867,037	777,541	648,994	608,027
Depreciation and amortization						
Cruise	157,454	135,694	120,304	101,146	84,228	79,743
Tour	8,862	8,317	8,129	9,449	9,105	9,090
Corporate	971	976				
	167,287	144,987	128,433	110,595	93,333	88,833
Operating income						
Cruise	656,009	535,814	465,870	425,590	333,392	310,845
Tour	13,262	21,252	24,168	18,084	14,274	23,051
Corporate	44,799	40,362				
	714,070	597,428	490,038	443,674	347,666	333,896
Identifiable assets						
Cruise	4,744,140	4,514,675	3,967,174	3,531,727	2,995,221	2,415,547
Tour	163,941	150,851	138,313	138,096	134,146	140,507
Discontinued resort and casino	518,694				89,553	89,553
Corporate		436,362				
	5,426,775	5,101,888	4,105,487	3,669,823	3,218,920	2,645,607
Capital expenditures						
Cruise	414,963	841,871	456,920	587,249	705,196	111,766
Tour	42,507	14,964	8,747	9,963	10,281	11,400
Corporate	40,187	1,810				
	$497,657	$858,645	$465,667	$597,212	$715,477	$123,166

SOURCE: 1997 and 1998 10K and 10Q's.

On June 25, 1996, Carnival reached an agreement with the trustees of Wartsila and creditors for the bankruptcy which resulted in a cash payment of approximately $80 million. Of the $80 million received, $5 million was used to pay certain costs, $32 million was recorded as other income and $43 million was used to reduce the cost basis of certain ships which had been affected by the bankruptcy.

By May 31, 1998, Carnival had outstanding long term debt of $1.55 billion with the current portion being $58.45 million. This debt is primarily composed of $306.8 million in commercial paper and a number of unsecured debentures and notes of less than $200 million each at rates ranging from 5.65 percent to 7.7 percent.

According to the Internal Revenue Code of 1986, Carnival is considered a "controlled foreign corporation (CFC)" since 50 percent of its stock is held by individuals who are residents of foreign countries and its countries of incorporation exempt shipping operations of U.S. persons from income tax. Because of CFC status, Carnival expects that all of its income (with the exception of U.S. source income from the transportation, hotel, and tour businesses of Holland America) will be exempt from U.S. federal income taxes at the corporate level.

The primary financial consideration of importance to Carnival management involves the control of costs, both fixed and variable, for the maintenance of a healthy profit margin. Carnival has the lowest break-even point of any organization in the cruise industry (ships break even at approximately 60 percent of capacity) due to operational experience and economies of scale. Unfortunately, fixed costs, including depreciation, fuel, insurance, port charges, and crew costs, which represent more than 33 percent of the company's operating expenses, cannot be significantly reduced in relation to decreases in passenger loads and aggregate passenger ticket revenue. Major expense items are air fares (25–30 percent), travel agent fees (10 percent), and labor (13–15 percent). Increases in these costs could negatively affect the profitability of the organization.

Principal Subsidiaries

Carnival Cruise Line

At the end of fiscal 1996, Carnival operated 11 ships with a total berth capacity of 20,332. Carnival operates principally in the Caribbean and has an assortment of ships and ports of call serving the three-, four- and seven-day cruise markets (see Exhibit 6).

Each ship is a floating resort including a full maritime staff, shopkeepers, casino operators, entertainers, and complete hotel staff. Approximately 14 percent of corporate revenue is generated from shipboard activities such as casino operations, liquor sales, and gift shop items. At various ports-of-call, passengers can also take advantage of tours, shore excursions, and duty-free shopping at their own expense.

Shipboard operations are designed to provide maximum entertainment, activities, and service. The size of the company and the similarity in design of the new cruise ships have allowed Carnival to achieve various economies of scale, and management is very cost-conscious.

Although the Carnival Cruise Lines division is increasing their presence in the shorter cruise markets, their general marketing strategy is to use three-, four- or seven-day moderately priced cruises to fit the time and budget constraints of the middle class. Shorter cruises can cost less than $500 per person (depending on accommodations) up to roughly $3,000 per person in a luxury suite on a seven-day cruise, including port charges. (Per diem rates for shorter cruises are slightly higher, on average, than per diem rates for seven-day cruises.) Average rates per day are approximately $180, excluding gambling, liquor and soft drinks, and items of a personal nature. Guests are expected to tip their cabin steward and waiter at a suggested rate of $3 per person per day, and the bus boy at $1.50 per person per day.

Some 99 percent of all Carnival cruises are sold through travel agents who receive a standard commission of 10 percent (15 percent in Florida). Carnival works extensively with travel agents to help promote cruises as alternatives to a Disney or European vacation. In addition to training travel agents from nonaffiliated travel/vacation firms to sell cruises, a special group of employees regularly visits travel agents posing as prospective clients. If the agent recommends a cruise before another vacation option, he or she receives $100. If the travel agent specifies a Carnival cruise before other options, they receive $1,000 on the spot. During fiscal 1995, Carnival took

■ **Exhibit 6**   The Ships of Carnival Corporation

Name	Registry	Built	First in Company	Service Capacity*	Gross Tons	Length /Width	Areas of Operation
Carnival Cruise Lines							
Carnival Destiny	Panama	1996	1997	2,642	101,000	893/116	Caribbean
Inspiration	Panama	1996	1996	2,040	70,367	855/104	Caribbean
Imagination	Panama	1995	1995	2,040	70,367	855/104	Caribbean
Fascination	Panama	1994	1994	2,040	70,367	855/104	Caribbean
Sensation	Panama	1993	1993	2,040	70,367	855/104	Caribbean
Ecstasy	Liberia	1991	1991	2,040	70,367	855/104	Caribbean
Fantasy	Liberia	1990	1990	2,044	70,367	855/104	Bahamas
Celebration	Liberia	1987	1987	1,486	47,262	738/92	Caribbean
Jubilee	Panama	1986	1986	1,486	47,262	738/92	Mexican Riviera
Holiday	Panama	1985	1985	1,452	46,052	727/92	Mexican Riviera
Tropicale	Liberia	1982	1982	1,022	36,674	660/85	Alaska, Caribbean
Total Carnival ships capacity				20,332			
Holland America Line							
Veendam	Bahamas	1996	1996	1,266	55,451	720/101	Alaska, Caribbean
Ryndam	Netherlands	1994	1994	1,266	55,451	720/101	Alaska, Caribbean
Maasdam	Netherlands	1993	1993	1,266	55,451	720/101	Europe, Caribbean
Statendam	Netherlands	1993	1993	1,266	55,451	720/101	Alaska, Caribbean
Westerdam	Netherlands	1986	1988	1,494	53,872	798/95	Canada, Caribbean
Noordam	Netherlands	1984	1984	1,214	33,930	704/89	Alaska, Caribbean
Nieuw Amsterdam	Netherlands	1983	1983	1,214	33,930	704/89	Alaska, Caribbean
Rotterdam IV	Netherlands	1997	1997	1,316	62,000	780/106	Alaska, Worldwide
Total HAL ships capacity				10,302			
Windstar Cruises							
Wind Spirit	Bahamas	1988	1988	148	5,736	440/52	Caribbean, Mediterranean
Wind Song	Bahamas	1987	1987	148	5,703	440/52	Costa Rica, Tahita
Wind Star	Bahamas	1986	1986	148	5,703	440/52	Caribbean, Mediterranean
Total Windstar ships capacity				444			
Total capacity				31,078			

*In accordance with industry practice passenger capacity is calculated based on two passengers per cabin even though some cabins can accommodate three or four passengers.

reservations from about 29,000 of the approximately 45,000 travel agencies in the U.S. and Canada, and no one travel agency accounted for more than 2 percent of Carnival revenues.

On-board service is labor-intensive, employing help from some 51 nations—mostly third world countries—with reasonable returns to employees. For example, waiters on the *Jubilee* can earn approximately $18,000 to $27,000 per year (base salary and tips), significantly greater than could be earned in their home countries for similar employment. Waiters typically work ten hours per day with approximately one day off per week for a specified contract period (usually three to nine months). Carnival records show that employees remain with the company for approximately eight years and that applicants exceed demand for all cruise positions. Nonetheless, the American Maritime union has cited Carnival (and other cruise operators) several times for exploitation of its crew.

Holland America Lines

On January 17, 1989, Carnival acquired all the outstanding stock of HAL Antillen N.V. from Holland America Lines N.V. for $625 million in cash. Carnival financed the purchase through $250 million in retained earnings (cash account) and borrowed the other $375 million from banks at .25 percent over the prime rate. Carnival received the assets and operations of the Holland America Lines, Westours, Westmark Hotels, and Windstar Sail Cruises. Holland America currently has seven cruise ships with a capacity of 8,795 berths with new ships to be delivered in the future.

Founded in 1873, Holland America Lines is an upscale line (it charges an average of 25 percent more than similar Carnival cruises) with principal destinations in Alaska during the summer months and the Caribbean during the fall and winter, with some world-wide cruises of up to 98 days. Holland America targets an older, more sophisticated cruiser with fewer youth-oriented activities. On Holland America ships, passengers can dance to the sounds of the Big Band era and avoid the discos of Carnival ships. Passengers on Holland America ships enjoy more service (a higher staff-to-passenger ratio than Carnival) and have more cabin and public space per person, and a "no tipping" shipboard policy. Holland America has not enjoyed the spectacular growth of Carnival cruise ships, but has sustained constant growth over the decade of the 1980s and early 1990s with high occupancy. The operation of these ships and the structure of the crew is similar to the Carnival cruise ship model, and the acquisition of the line gave the Carnival Corporation a presence in the Alaskan market where it had none before.

Holland America Westours is the largest tour operator in Alaska and the Canadian Rockies and provides vacation synergy with Holland America cruises. The transportation division of Westours includes over 290 motor coaches comprised of the Gray Line of Alaska, the Gray Line of Seattle, Westours motorcoaches, the McKinley Explorer railroad coaches, and three-day boats for tours to glaciers and other points of interest. Carnival management believes that Alaskan cruises and tours should increase in the future due to a number of factors. These include the aging population wanting relaxing vacations with scenic beauty coupled with the fact that Alaska is a U.S. destination.

Westmark Hotels consist of 16 hotels in Alaska and the Yukon territories, and also provides synergy with cruise operations and Westours. Westmark is the largest group of hotels in the region providing moderately-priced rooms for the vacationer.

Windstar Sail Cruises was acquired by Holland America Lines in 1988 and consists of three computer-controlled sailing vessels with a berth capacity of 444. Windstar is very upscale and offers an alternative to traditional cruise liners with a more intimate, activity-oriented cruise. The ships operate primarily in the Mediterranean and the South Pacific, visiting ports not accessible to large cruise ships. Although catering to a small segment of the cruise vacation industry, Windstar helps with Carnival's commitment to participate in all segments of the cruise industry.

Seabourn Cruise Lines

In April 1992, the company acquired 25 percent of the capital stock of Seabourn. As part of the transaction, the company also made a subordinated, secured ten-year loan of $15 million to Seabourn and a $10 million convertible loan to Seabourn. In December 1995, the $10 million convertible loan was converted by the company into an additional 25 percent equity interest in Seabourn.

Seabourn targets the luxury market with three vessels providing 200 passengers per ship with all-suite accommodations. Seabourn is considered the "Rolls Royce" of the cruise industry and in 1992 was named the "World's Best Cruise Line" by the prestigious Condé Naste Traveler's Fifth Annual Readers Choice poll. Seabourn cruises the Americas, Europe, Scandinavia, the Mediterranean, and the Far East.

Airtours

In April 1996, the Company acquired a 29.5 percent interest in Airtours for approximately $307 million. Airtours and its subsidiaries is the largest air inclusive tour operator in the world and is publicly traded on the London Stock Exchange. Airtours provides air-inclusive packaged holidays to the British, Scandinavian, and North American markets. Airtours provides holidays to approximately five million people per year and owns or operates 32 hotels, two cruise ships, and 31 aircraft.

Airtours operates 18 aircraft (one additional aircraft is scheduled to enter service in the spring of 1997) exclusively for its U.K. tour operators providing a large proportion of their flying requirements. In addition, Airtours' subsidiary Premiair operates a fleet of 13 aircraft (one additional aircraft is also scheduled to enter service with Premiair in the spring of 1997), which provides most of the flying requirements for Airtours' Scandinavian tour operators.

Airtours owns or operates 32 hotels (6,500 rooms) which provide rooms to Airtours' tour operators principally in the Mediterranean and the Canary Islands. In addition, Airtours has a 50 percent interest in Tenerife Sol, a joint venture with Sol Hotels Group of Spain, which owns and operates three additional hotels in the Canary Islands providing 1,300 rooms.

Through its subsidiary Sun Cruises, Airtours owns and operates two cruise ships. Both the 800-berth MS *Seawing* and the 1,062-berth MS *Carousel* commenced operations in 1995. Recently, Airtours acquired a third ship, the MS *Sundream,* which is the sister ship of the MS *Carousel.* The MS *Sundream* is expected to commence operations in May 1997. The ships operate in the Mediterranean, the Caribbean and around the Canary Islands and are booked exclusively by Airtours' tour operators.

Costa Crociere S.p.A.

In June 1997, Carnival and Airtours purchased the equity securities of Costa from the Costa family at a cost of approximately $141 million. Costa is headquartered in Italy and is considered Europe's largest cruise line with seven ships and 7,710 passenger capacity. Costa operates primarily in the Mediterranean, Northern Europe, the Caribbean, and South America. The major market for Costa is southern Europe, mainly Italy, Spain, and France. In January 1998, Costa signed an agreement to construct an eighth ship with a capacity of approximately 2,100 passengers.

Cunard Line

Carnival's most recent acquisition has been the Cunard Line, announced on May 28, 1998. Comprised of five ships, the Cunard Line is considered a luxury line with strong brand name recognition. Carnival purchased 50 percent of Cunard for an estimated $255 million with the other 50 percent being owned by Atle Brynestad. Cunard was immediately merged with Seabourn and the resulting Cunard Cruise Line Limited (68 percent owned by Carnival) with its now eight ships, will be headed by the former President of Seabourn, Larry Pimentel.

Joint Venture with Hyundai Merchant Marine Co. Ltd.

In September 1996, the Carnival and Hyundai Merchant Marine Co. Ltd. signed an agreement to form a 50/50 joint venture to develop the Asian cruise vacation market. Each have contributed $4.8 million as the initial capital of the joint venture. In addition, in November 1996, Carnival sold the cruise ship *Tropicale* to the joint venture for approximately $95.5 million cash. Carnival then chartered the vessel from the joint venture until the joint venture is ready to begin cruise operations in the Asian market, targeting a start date in or around the spring of 1998. The joint venture borrowed the $95.5 million purchase price from a financial institution and Carnival and HMM each guaranteed 50 percent of the borrowed funds.

This arrangement was, however, short lived as in September 1997, the joint venture was dissolved and the Company repurchased the *Tropicale* for $93 million.

■ Future Considerations

Carnival's management will have to continue to monitor several strategic factors and issues for the next few years. The industry itself should see further consolidation through mergers and buy outs, and the expansion of the industry could negatively affect the profitability of various cruise operators. Another factor of concern to management is how to reach the large North American market, of which only 5 percent to 7 percent have ever taken a cruise.

With the industry maturing, cruise competitors have become more sophisticated in their marketing efforts and price competition is the norm in most cruise segments. (For a partial listing of major industry competitors, see Exhibit 7.) Royal Caribbean Cruise Lines has also instituted a major shipbuilding program and is successfully challenging Carnival Cruise Lines in the contemporary segment. The announcement of the Walt Disney Company entering the cruise market with two 80,000-ton cruise liners by 1998 should significantly impact the "family" cruise vacation segment.

With competition intensifying, industry observers believe the wave of failures, mergers, buyouts and strategic alliances will increase. Regency Cruises ceased operations on October 29, 1995, and has filed for Chapter 11 bankruptcy. American Family Cruises, a spin-off from Costa Cruise Lines failed to reach the family market and Carnival's Fiestamarina failed to reach the Spanish-speaking market. EffJohn International sold its Commodore Cruise subsidiary to a group of Miami-based investors which then chartered one of its two ships to World Explorer Cruises/Semester At Sea. Sun Cruise Lines merged with Epirotiki Cruise Line under the name of Royal Olympic Cruises and Cunard bought the Royal Viking Line and its name from Kloster Cruise Ltd., with one ship of its fleet being transferred to Kloster's Royal Cruise Line. All of these failures, mergers and buyouts occurred in 1995, which was not an unusual year for changes in the cruise line industry.

The increasing industry capacity is also a source of concern to cruise operators. The slow growth in industry demand is occurring during a period when industry berth capacity continues to grow. The entry of Disney and the ships already on order by current operators will increase industry berth capacity by over 10,000 per year for the next three years, a significant increase. The danger lies in cruise operators using the "price" weapon in their marketing campaigns to fill cabins. If cruise operators cannot make a reasonable return on investment, operating costs will have to

■ **Exhibit 7** Major Industry Competitors

Celebrity Cruises, 5200 Blue Lagoon Drive, Miami, FL 33126

Celebrity Cruises operates four modern cruise ships on four-, seven- and ten-day cruises to Bermuda, the Caribbean, the Panama Canal and Alaska. Celebrity attracts first-time cruisers as well as seasoned cruisers. Purchase by Royal Caribbean on July 30, 1997.

Norwegian Cruise Lines, 95 Merrick Way, Coral Gables, FL 33134

Norwegian Cruise Lines (NCL), formally Norwegian Caribbean Lines, was the first to base a modern fleet of cruise ships in the Port of Miami. It operates ten modern cruise liners on three-, four- and seven-day Eastern and Western Caribbean cruises and cruises to Bermuda. A wide variety of activities and entertainment attracts a diverse array of customers. NCL has just completed reconstruction of two ships and is building the *Norwegian Sky,* a 2,000 passenger ship to be delivered in the summer of 1999.

Disney Cruise Line, 500 South Buena Vista Street, Burbank, CA 91521

Disney has just recently entered the cruise market with the introduction of the *Disney Magic* and *Disney Wonder.* Both ships will cater to both children and adults and will feature 875 staterooms each. Each cruise will include a visit to Disney's private island, Castaway Cay. Although Disney currently has only two ships and the cruise portion of Disney is small, their potential for future growth is substantial with over $22 billion in revenues and $1.9 billion net profits in 1997.

Princess Cruises, 10100 Santa Monica Boulevard, Los Angeles, CA 90067

Princess Cruises, with its fleet of nine "Love Boats," offers seven-day and extended cruises to the Caribbean, Alaska, Canada, Africa, the Far East, South America, and Europe. Princess's primary market is the upscale 50-plus experienced traveler, according to Mike Hannan, Senior Vice President for Marketing Services. Princess ships have an ambiance best described as casual elegance and are famous for their Italian-style dining rooms and onboard entertainment.

Royal Caribbean Cruise Lines, 1050 Caribbean Way, Miami, FL 33132

RCCL's nine ships have consistently been given high marks by passengers and travel agents over the past 21 years. RCCL's ships are built for the contemporary market, are large and modern, and offer three-, four- and seven-day as well as extended cruises. RCCL prides itself on service and exceptional cuisine. With the purchase of *Celebrity,* RCCL becomes the largest cruise line in the world with 17 ships and a passenger capacity of over 31,100. Plans include the introduction of six additional ships by the year 2002. In 1997 RCCL had net income of $175 million on revenues of $1.93 billion.

Other Industry Competitors (Partial List)

American Hawaii Cruises	(2 ships—Hawaiian Islands)
Club Med	(2 ships—Europe, Caribbean)
Commodore Cruise Line	(1 ship—Caribbean)
Cunard Line	(8 ships—Caribbean, Worldwide)
Dolphin Cruise Line	(3 ships—Caribbean, Bermuda)
Radisson Seven Seas Cruises	(3 ships—Worldwide)
Royal Olympic Cruises	(6 ships—Caribbean, Worldwide)
Royal Cruise Line	(4 ships—Caribbean, Alaska, WW)

SOURCE: Cruise Line International Association, 1996 and company 10k's and annual reports.

be reduced (affecting quality of services) to remain profitable. This will increase the likelihood of further industry acquisitions, mergers, and consolidations. A worst-case scenario would be the financial failure of weaker lines.

Still, Carnival's management believes that demand should increase during the remainder of the 1990s. Considering that only 5 percent to 7 percent of the North American market has taken a cruise vacation, reaching more of the North American target market would improve industry profitability. Industry analysts state the problem is an "assessment of market potential" is only an "educated guess"; not to mention the possibility that the current demand figures are reflective of the future.

Case 6   L.A. Gear, Inc.

A. J. Almaney, S. Green, S. Slotkin, and H. Speer
All of DePaul University

■ Overview

In February 1989, Robert Y. Greenberg stood on the floor of the New York Stock Exchange and watched as the letters "LA" flashed across the ticker tape for the very first time after L.A. Gear was listed on the Big Board. "It was my proudest moment. It was my dream," Greenberg said. "You see, I always wanted to be the president of a company on the New York Stock Exchange,"[1] he added.

For over 14 years, L.A. Gear promoted the Southern-California lifestyle with attractively styled shoes designed primarily for women. Later, however, the company altered its focus to include products that appealed to the men's performance athletic market. The company continued to produce fashion shoes for women, but its core business became the performance athletic market where sales were not as dependent on swings in consumer tastes. The company achieved its position as the number three brand maker of footwear products when it surpassed Converse, Inc. in 1989. Greenberg set his sights at the number one position in the industry by challenging Nike and Reebok.

However, L.A. Gear began to experience financial difficulties in 1991. Its market share dropped from a high of 12 percent in 1990, to 8 percent in 1991, and to 5 percent in 1992. And its net sales declined from $820 million in 1990, to $619 million in 1991, and to $430 million in 1992. The company incurred losses of $45 million in 1991 and $72 million in 1992. As a result, L.A. Gear was unable to obtain credit from its lenders. To enhance its credit rating, L.A. Gear managed to lure a new investor, Trefoil Capital Investors L.P. who, in September 1991, paid $100 million for a 34 percent stake in the company.

Since the Trefoil deal, L.A. Gear's internal operations underwent major restructuring. As part of the restructuring, the Trefoil team replaced L.A. Gear's top management—including the company's founder, Robert Y. Greenberg. Stanley P. Gold, managing director of Trefoil Capital Investors L. P., and Mark R. Goldston, former Reebok executive, took over. Gold succeeded Greenberg as the company's new chairman and chief executive officer, and Goldston was appointed president and chief operating officer.

Gold and Goldston developed a survival strategy to nurse the ailing L.A. Gear back to health. At the core of the turnaround strategy was a new advertising campaign built around the theme, "Get in Gear." In an effort to create a clear identity for L.A. Gear, Goldston reorganized product lines into three groups: athletic, lifestyle, and children. The new management also launched a restructuring program aimed at paring the company's costs.

Presented and accepted by the refereed Midwest Society for Case Research. All rights reserved to the authors and the MSCR. Copyright ©1993 by A. J. Almaney (312) 362-6785. This case was prepared by A. J. Almaney, S. Green, S. Slotkin, and H. Speer of DePaul University and is intended to be used as a basis for class discussion rather than to illustrate either effective or ineffective handling of the situation. A. J. Almaney is Professor of Management at DePaul University.

In their letter to the shareholders, Gold and Goldston stated, "We believe that the accomplishments of the past year have laid the groundwork upon which we can build to achieve our ultimate objective—to make L.A. Gear a leader in the footwear industry and one of the most admired companies in America." But, will they be able to accomplish their objective in this highly competitive industry?

■ History

Robert Y. Greenberg, L.A. Gear's founder, had a knack for selling. First, it was wigs. Later it was roller skates and jeans for the trendy residents of Venice Beach, California. Then it was sneakers. As one analyst described him, "Greenberg is the quintessential salesman."[2]

Greenberg's story is a 1980s financial fairy tale with a 1990s climax: A streetsmart shoemaker who always feared being poor would create a pair of sneakers that brought him fortune. As a kid working in the Brooklyn's family produce business and reading his father's copies of *Forbes* magazine, Greenberg set his sights on starting his own company. He took his first step toward that goal by enrolling in a beauty school. After graduation, he opened a chain of hair salons in Brooklyn in the mid 1960s. Later, he started a wig-importing business. As that venture petered out, Greenberg spotted another trend—fashion jeans—and began importing them from South Korea. By 1979, the jeans business had started to fade, and Greenberg decided to pack up for Southern California.

His next inspiration came soon after his arrival in Los Angeles, as he waited three hours at Venice Beach to rent roller skates for his wife and kids. "I figured the guy must be taking in $4,000 to $5,000 a day," he said. So, Greenberg walked out of that skate shop and immediately plunked $40,000 into his own, which soon expanded to nine locations. Not only did he sell skates through the stores, but he established a skate-manufacturing business. The market for skates quickly soured, though. As a result, Greenberg opened a clothing store on Melrose Avenue which he named L.A. Gear. By 1985, the L.A. Gear store was losing money.

Greenberg started looking for the next trend to ride. Having watched Reebok storm the market a year earlier with its fashionable aerobics shoes, Greenberg went chasing after Reebok with his own candy-colored sneakers, all aimed at a market he knew: trend-conscious teenage girls. In what proved to be a brilliant marketing strategy, he opted to sell his shoes not just to sporting-goods stores but to big department stores like Nordstrom, May Co, and Bullock's. L.A. Gear's big break came the following year, 1987, when Reebok underestimated the demand for its wildly popular black-and-white athletic shoes. Greenberg stepped in to meet the demand by marketing "The Workout," a simple canvas shoe that became the flagship of the company.

During Greenberg's Venice Beach tenure, he had become friends with Sandy Saemann, who was making skating safety equipment while Greenberg was hawking skates. After Saemann launched his own advertising agency, Greenberg brought him into the company to help craft L.A. Gear's frothy image of sun and sex.

The Greenberg-Saemann combination worked. L.A. Gear soon became a highly profitable operation. Sales mushroomed from $200,000 per month at the beginning of 1985 to 1.8 million per month by mid-year. As the company grew to an operation of 51 employees, it needed outside funds for more development and opted for an initial public offering which was completed on July 1, 1986.

The company used the $16.5 million in proceeds from the offering to fund its growing working capital requirements and to fund a hefty advertising and promotion budget. The initial single style of footwear developed into 150 styles, and L.A. Gear's preeminence in the youth market expanded to include footwear for customers of all ages. In 1986, L.A. Gear launched lines for men, children, and infants and expanded its women's line to include athletic shoes for basketball, aerobics, and crosstrainers.

In 1989, sales rocketed to $617 million from $71 million in 1987, and the company surpassed Converse Inc. to become the nation's third-largest seller of athletic shoes. In 1989, L.A. Gear's stock switched from trading in the over-the-counter market to the Big Board. L.A. Gear's stock price in 1988 was $10.94 with $224 million in sales. By early December 1989, L.A. Gear's stock had climbed more than 178 percent, more than any Big Board stock.[3] *The Wall Street Journal, Business Week,* and *Fortune* named L.A. Gear the best performing stock on the New York Stock Exchange in 1989. Greenberg boasted that he would push L.A. Gear past Reebok and Nike by 1991. Mark R. Goldston, L.A. Gear's current president, described the company's early success as a phenomenon achieved by innovative styling and a unique ability to have their ear to the market and respond quickly.

In 1990, however, the company's stock price started to decline, and investors became concerned that L.A. Gear was losing its appeal to fashion-conscious young women. Some analysts marked the beginning of L.A. Gear's troubles with the failure of its Michael Jackson shoes.[4] In 1989, Sandy Saemann, executive vice president, signed a $20 million contract with Michael Jackson for endorsement of a line of black, silver-buckled shoes. But the shoes proved to be a failure. Other signs of trouble included reports of stock selling by insiders as well as the Justice Department's investigation of alleged underpayment of custom duties.[5]

In April 1991, L.A. Gear posted a fiscal first-quarter loss of $12.5 million. Sales fell 8.8 percent to $171 million from $187 million. L.A. Gear posted a tangible net worth of $193 million as of February 28, 1991.[6]

In May 1991, L.A. Gear agreed to sell a 30 percent stake to Roy E. Disney's Trefoil Capital Investors L.P. for $100 million. Under the agreement, Trefoil would also receive three seats on L.A. Gear's board of directors and the opportunity to have first option to buy shares of Greenberg's 3.5 million in common shares should Greenberg decide to sell. L.A. Gear also agreed to hire Disney's Shamrock Capital Advisors Inc. as consultants for three years, paying fees of $500,000 the first year, $600,000 the second year, and $700,000 the third year.

Shortly after the Trefoil agreement was initiated, Sandy Saemann—a flamboyant, gold-chain decked executive vice president—resigned. Saemann was the architect of L.A. Gear's sexy marketing campaign which often featured scantily clad models. He was also credited with gathering celebrity endorsers for L.A. Gear. Saemann agreed to provide consulting services to L.A. Gear for 2.5 years. Analysts said Saemann resigned because his flamboyant personality conflicted with the Trefoil team.[7] Kevin Ventrudo, 32, senior vice president of administration and a board member, also resigned. Mark R. Goldston succeeded Robert Greenberg as president. Greenberg remained chairman and chief executive.

On January 27, 1992, Robert Greenberg, L.A. Gear's founder, was eased out as chairman and chief executive and a director, along with Gil N. Schwartzberg, vice chairman. Stanley P. Gold, 50, managing director of Trefoil was appointed as the new chairman and chief executive officer of L.A. Gear.

Stanley P. Gold
*Chairman of the Board and Chief
    Executive Officer*
L.A. Gear, Inc.
President and Managing Director
Trefoil Investors, Inc. and Shamrock
    Capital Advisors, Inc.

Mark R. Goldston
President and Chief Operating Officer
L.A. Gear, Inc.

Richard W. Schubert
General Counsel and Secretary
L.A. Gear, Inc.

Alan E. Dashling
*Chairman of the Board and Chief
    Executive Officer*
Sterling West Bancorp.

Willie D. Davis
President and Chief Executive Officer
All-Pro Broadcasting

Stephen A. Koffler
*Executive Vice President and Director
    of Investment Banking*
Sutro & Co., Inc.

Ann E. Meyers
Sports Commentator
KMPC Radio, Prime Ticket, ESPN,
    Sportschannel, and ABC

Clifford A. Miller
Chairman
The Clifford Group, Inc.

Robert G. Moskowitz
Managing Director
Trefoil Investors, Inc. and Shamrock
    Capital Advisors, Inc.

R. Rudolph Reinfrank
Executive Vice President
Shamrock Holdings, Inc.

Vappalak A. Ravindran
Chief Executive Officer
Paracor Company
President
Elders Finance, Inc.

SOURCE: L.A. Gear, 1992 Annual Report, p. 29.

■ Board of Directors

As shown in Exhibit 1, the board of directors was composed of 11 members. Three of them were insiders, while the others were outsiders. One of the outside directors was a woman, Ann E. Meyers, who worked as a sports commentator. The chairman of the board was Stanley P. Gold who also served as the chief executive officer (CEO) of the firm. The board carried out its duties through the Executive and Nominating Committees. The Executive Committee consisted of Stanley Gold, R. Rudolph Reinfrank, and Mark Goldston. Reinfrank served as chairman of the Executive Committee. The Nominating Committee consisted of Stephen A. Koffler, Robert G. Moskowitz and Mark Goldston. Koffler served as the chairman of the Nominating Committee.

■ Top Management

L.A. Gear's top management underwent major changes since the consummation of Trefoil's $100 million investment in the company. Below is a profile of each of the key executives.

Stanley P. Gold.   Stanley Gold, 50 years old, succeeded Greenberg as chairman and chief executive officer of L.A. Gear, Inc. Formerly, he was president and chief executive officer of Shamrock Holdings, Inc., a Burbank, California-based company wholly owned by the Roy Disney Family. Gold was considered to be a turnaround expert. He proved himself by helping revive Walt Disney Co., oil driller Enterra, and soybean processor Central Soyal. Prior to assuming his positions at Shamrock, Gold was a managing partner of Gange, Tyre, Ramer & Brown, Inc., a prominent Los Angeles law firm he joined in 1968. For a number of years, he specialized in corporate acquisitions, sales, and financing. Earlier in his legal career, he served as a trial lawyer in major corporate and civil litigation.[8]

A native of Los Angeles, California, Gold first studied at the University of California at Berkeley and subsequently graduated from the University of California at Los Angeles with an A.B. degree in political science. After receiving his J.D. degree from the University of Southern California Law School in 1967, he did postgraduate work at Cambridge University in England.[9] Gold's professional and civic affiliations included the American Bar Association and the Copyright Society. He served as a guest lecturer at the Wharton School at the University of Pennsylvania. He was Chairman of the Board of Governors of Hebrew Union College, a Trustee of the Center Theater Group in Los Angeles, the George C. Marshall Foundation, and a member of the USC Law Center Board of Councilors.

Mark R. Goldston.   Mark Goldston, 38 years old, succeeded Robert Y. Greenberg, the company's founder, as president and chief operating officer. Greenberg was also eased out as chairman, chief executive, and a director at a board meeting in an apparent effort by the company's largest investor, Trefoil Capital Investors L.P., to bury the "old" L.A. Gear.[10] Despite Greenberg's assertions that "the company is left in great hands," the ouster capped a four-month battle between the laid-back Greenberg and the buttoned-down Trefoil team for the soul of L.A. Gear.[11]

Goldston was a principal of Odyssey partners, a leverage buyout and investment firm. At Odyssey, Goldston was part of an internal operating unit that supervised the management of certain portfolio companies. His responsibilities included the development, execution, and management of operating plans and the evaluation of strategic alternatives for those portfolio companies. Prior to joining Odyssey, Goldston was senior and chief marketing officer of Reebok International, Ltd. where he spearheaded the marketing effort for "The Pump," a $500 million line of athletic footwear products. As one of the inventors of the Reebok "Visible Energy Return System Technology," Goldston was on the U.S. patent for that technology. Additionally, Goldston was involved in the development of the Hexalite and Energaire product lines for Reebok. Prior to joining Reebok, Goldston was president of Faberge USA, Inc., a cosmetics and personal care products company. During his tenure there, the company's U.S. sales increased about 50 percent.

Goldston was on the J.L. Kellogg Graduate School of Management Dean's Advisory Board at Northwestern University. In addition, he sat on the board of directors of Revel/Monogram, Inc., ABCO Markets, and Collection Clothing Corp. Goldston's book, entitled *The Turnaround Prescription*, detailing a step-by-step blueprint for effecting a corporate marketing turnaround was published in 1992.[12]

In his new position as president and chief operating officer, Goldston brought in fresh talent by hiring former Reebok employees—Gordie Nye, Robert Apatoff and Christopher Walsh. Gordie Nye, Vice President of Marketing Athletic Footwear, joined the company in December 1991. Previously, he was at Reebok where he was Senior Director of Fitness Marketing, with responsibility for marketing men's and women's fitness products.

Christopher Walsh. Christopher Walsh was 43 years old. He joined L.A. Gear as senior vice president of operations in December 1991. Previously, he was vice president of production at Reebok for three years, where he was in charge of worldwide supply sources. Prior to joining Reebok, he spent two years at Toddler University, a children's shoe manufacturer as vice president of operations. Prior to that, he worked as a senior consultant for Kurt Satmon Associates for two years, focusing on strategic planning. Earlier in his career, he worked at Nike for ten years in production and sourcing.[13]

William L. Benford. William L. Benford, 50 years old, was appointed chief financial officer in September 1991.[14] Prior to that, he was senior vice president and chief financial officer of Central Soya company. Before that he was vice president and treasurer of Dekalb, Inc. He was also affiliated with Shamrock Holdings, Inc., an investment company for the Roy E. Disney Family. Shamrock Holdings, Inc., bought Central Soya company in 1985, turned it around, and sold the company two years later at a profit of about $125 million.

■ Mission

L.A. Gear defined its mission as follows:

> The Company's principal business activity involves the design, development, and marketing of a broad range of quality athletic and casual/lifestyle footwear. Since its inception, the Company has expanded its product line from its original concentration on fashionable women's footwear to diversified collections of footwear for men, women, and children. The Company is organized into two primary marketing divisions: Athletic (including men's and women's basketball, fitness, walking, tennis, and aerobics) and Lifestyle (casual footwear styles intended for non-athletic use). All of the Company's footwear products are manufactured to its specifications by independent producers located primarily in South Korea, Indonesia, Taiwan and the People's Republic of China.[15]

■ Objectives and Strategies

L.A. Gear's short-term objective was to streamline its operations over the next two years. In the long-term, the company would attempt to achieve the following objectives:

- To provide a broad range of quality athletic and casual/lifestyle footwear, primarily in the "mid" price range (i.e., $30 to $65 retail).
- To improve relations with, and increase shelf space at, full-margin retailers.
- To improve production and quality control practices.
- To increase international sales and profitability.

In attaining these objectives, L.A. Gear adopted a retrenchment/turnaround strategy that involved a comprehensive restructuring of its operations. Thus, in 1992 the company's staff was reduced by 613 employees, or about 45 percent. In addition, the company reduced its occupancy of about 200,000 square feet of leased office space in five buildings to about 116,000 square feet in two buildings. Further, the general and administrative expenses were reduced in 1992 by $42.7 million, or 21.2 percent, to $158.7 million from $201.4 million in 1991. The company also discontinued its apparel marketing and design operations which had a pre-tax operating loss of $14.2 million in 1991.

The company's restructuring was augmented with a product development strategy. The product strategy involved developing a broad range of innovative new products for the athletic, lifestyle, and children's line. Grouping products into three well identified divisions was well received by analysts of the footwear industry. Bob McAllister, West Coast market editor for *Footwear News,* said, "In the past, there was no rhyme or reason to L.A. Gear's different styles. Now, the company has introduced new lines that are cleanly divided into athletic, lifestyles and kids."[16]

The company also sought to differentiate its products from its competitors. Goldston was confident that L.A. Gear would increase its market share by using materials in a unique way to carve a specific niche for its products. According to Goldston, "L.A. Gear is committed to designing shoes that do not resemble its competition."[17] While pursuing retrenchment and product development strategies, L.A. Gear launched a marketing campaign that focused on projecting a consistent brand image across varying retail price points and distribution channels.

■ Production

L.A. Gear's footwear was manufactured to its specifications by independent producers located primarily in The People's Republic of China, Indonesia, South Korea, and Taiwan. In 1992, manufacturers in these countries supplied 34, 32, 30, and 4 percent of total pairs of footwear purchased by the company respectively.

The footwear products imported into the United States by the company were subject to customs duties, ranging from 6 to 48 percent of production costs. Duty rates depended on the construction of the shoe and whether the principal component was leather or some other material.

The use of foreign manufacturing facilities subjected the company to the customary risks of doing business abroad, including fluctuations in the value of currencies, export duties, import controls, trade barriers, restrictions on the transfer of funds, work stoppage, and political instability. Thus far, these factors, however, did not seem to have had an adverse impact on the company's operations.

■ Products

L.A. Gear's product lines were organized into three marketing categories: Athletic, Lifestyle, and Children's. Athletic footwear included fitness, walking, tennis, cross-training, and basketball shoes, as well as the recently introduced Light Gear Cross-Runner and Dance Training shoes. These products were marketed under two brand names: L.A. Gear, with suggested domestic retail prices under $70; and L.A. Tech, the newly released, which were a higher priced premium brand.

The Lifestyle lines included men's and women's casual footwear styles that included the Street Hiker, Vintage Series, and Fashion Athletic and Casual Collections. The Children's footwear incorporated features from the Athletic and Lifestyle lines plus products specifically developed for children. L.A. Lights, lighted shoes for children introduced in June 1992, became one of the largest selling children's shoes in the company's history. The age of the company's target market for the adult products was 14 to 35 years, and for children 5 to 13.[18] Some of L.A. Gear's products and the technologies incorporated in the Athletic, Lifestyle, and Children's lines are described in Exhibit 2.

Athletic	Description
Catapult	A midsole system consisting of a carbon graphite spring to provide cushioning and shock absorption
Encapsole Air	A cushioning system which uses air chambers built into the outsole to provide shock absorption
Light Gear	Shoes incorporating battery-powered lights in the outsole that flash upon impact

Lifestyle	Description
Street Hiker	A light-weight casual hiking shoe
Vintage Series	Footwear based on classic athletic styles

Children's	Description
L.A. Gear (Galactica for boys; L.A. Twilight for girls; Nightcrawlers for infants)	Shoes incorporating motion activated battery-powered lights in the outsole that flash with movement
Regulator	Shoes with an adjustable fit and support system using an air inflation device to cushion the foot over the midfoot area
Bendables	Flexible shoes for infants
Clear Gear	Shoes with a clear outsole in flexible plastic with an assortment of designs printed on the midsole

SOURCE: L.A. Gear, 1992 10-K Form, p. 4.

■ Product Quality

In 1990, L.A. Gear committed a grave marketing blunder in the process of launching its new line of basketball shoes. In a scramble to launch the new shoes, the company outfitted the Marquette University team with handmade pairs, since molds were not completed yet for the large sizes the team members required. As TV cameras zeroed in on one player, the bottom of his sneaker peeled away from the top. This and other cases of poor quality served to seriously tarnish the company's brand image. In an effort to improve quality, L.A. Gear reduced the number of foreign manufacturers from 44 in 1991 to 29 in 1992, retaining only those known for their quality products. The company also engaged a "sourcing" agent with the responsibility of inspecting finished goods prior to shipment by the manufacturer, supervising production management, and facilitating the shipment of goods.

■ Advertising

Sandy Saemann, Greenberg's second in command, was the architect of L.A. Gear's early advertising campaign. His success in signing such celebrities as Paula Abdul and Kareem Abdul-Jabbar was responsible for the phenomenal increase in the company's sales between 1985 and 1990. Saemann fit the image of the laid-back California executive perfectly—right down to the silver necklace. And his flamboyant vision proved perfect for peddling flashy sneakers. Saemann represented L.A. Gear's brash, entrepreneurial roots by producing virtually all of the company's ads and commercials himself without the help of Madison Avenue. However, L.A. Gear's tumble began, ironically, with its biggest advertising deal ever. In 1989, Saemann was able to sign megastar Michael Jackson in what was described as the largest endorsement contract ever: $20 million. L.A. Gear had hoped to time the release of a new line of shoes to an upcoming Michael Jackson greatest-hits album, but the album never materialized. Teenagers everywhere thumbed their noses at the black, buckle-laden shoes. The company was eventually forced to discontinue the entire line, taking a loss of several million dollars.

Since the failure of the Michael Jackson advertising campaign, L.A. Gear stopped contracting for the endorsement of its products by entertainment celebrities. Instead, the company chose to contract endorsements with athletic stars such as Karl "The Mailman" Malone of the Utah Jazz, Hakeem Olajuwon of the Houston Rockets, and Joe Montana of the San Francisco Forty-Niners. A new slogan, "Get in Gear," was used in the campaign.

Under the new management, L.A. Gear changed the focus of many of its advertising campaigns from promoting a fashionable shoe to promoting a performance shoe. Performance was emphasized with the advertisement tag line for the Catapult performance shoe, "It's not just a shoe, it's a machine."[19] L.A. Gear's most successful commercial was the use of the tag line "Anything else is just hot air" to promote the Catapult shoe, with its hightech, carbon-fiber soles. The ad was an indirect attack at Nike who made the Air Jordan shoes, endorsed by Chicago Bulls' star Michael Jordan. NBC refused to run the television ads, and the ensuing exposure received by coverage of NBC's refusal was worth millions to L.A. Gear.[20] In promoting the $110 Catapult shoe, the new management decided to drop the L.A. Gear logo, believing that the L.A. Gear name was a liability in performance shoes.

The new management team subdivided the marketing of the company's products on the basis of price. Shoes costing less than $70 per pair retained the L.A. Gear name and logo, and shoes priced over $70 per pair carried the L.A. Tech name. L.A. Gear's management believed that the L.A. Tech name would help establish the line as a high technology and performance product. The lowest-cost L.A. Gear shoe retailed for approximately $30 per pair, whereas the top of the line L.A. Tech shoe, the Catapult, topped out at about $150 per pair.[21] L.A. Gear's budget amounted to between 10 and 15 percent of total sales.

■ Research and Development

In designing its products, L.A. Gear conducted comprehensive market research, using a variety of conventional research techniques. Primarily, the company depended on focus groups, product testing, and interviews with consumers and retailers. These methods allowed the company to accurately gauge the image and reputation of L.A. Gear's products and to incorporate changes demanded by the public.

■ Sales

The phenomenal rise in L.A. Gear's sales between 1985 and 1990 was due to Greenberg's ability to create a clear-cut image for the company with brightly colored shoes and sexy ads aimed at teenage girls. The company's spectacular success led Greenberg to set a higher objective for the company, $1 billion in sales. To achieve this objective, Greenberg tried to challenge Nike and Reebok directly by adding a line of

	1992		1991		1990	
	$	%	$	%	$	%
Domestic footwear						
Women's	112,990	26	178,481	29	285,709	35
Men's	104,593	24	176,238	28	196,969	24
Children's	90,997	21	134,485	22	174,486	21
Other	2,688	1	2,517	—	4,217	1
Total domestic net sales	311,268	72	491,721	79	661,381	81
International footwear	118,926	28	127,454	21	158,220	19
Total net sales	430,194	100	619,175	100	819,601	100

SOURCE: L.A. Gear, 1992 10-K Form, p. 5.

men's performance shoes. The move was too much, too fast. Venturing into the men's performance shoes blurred L.A. Gear's image. According to one analyst, "When L.A. Gear moved into the performance side, it lost its way." Greenberg, however, was unwilling to lay the company's problems on the men's shoes. Instead, he maintained that "in any battle you're gonna get a little bruised or battered. And we're playing with a couple of billion-dollar companies that don't need us around."

The rapid growth also placed an enormous strain on the company. Employees had to push hard to attain the new growth objective. As a result, the company's internal controls got out of hand. A shareholders' class action lawsuit called those controls "chaotic and virtually nonexistent."

As a result of the relentless push for fast growth, product-quality problems, and the attendant bad publicity, L.A. Gear saw its share of the overall athletic shoe market drop from a high of 12 percent in 1990 to 5 percent in 1992. The company net sales, as shown in Exhibit 3, declined from $820 billion in 1990 to $619 billion in 1991 and to $430 in 1992. The 1992 sales figure represented a 31 percent decline from 1991. The company incurred losses of $72 million in 1992 and $45 million in 1991. Net international sales, which accounted for about 28 percent of the company's total net sales, decreased by 6.7 percent from 1991.

According to management, the overall decline in net sales for 1992 was principally due to a drop in the number of pairs sold worldwide resulting from decreased customer demand, and, to a lesser extent, to an average decrease of $1.52 in the selling price per pair. The decline was also due to the continuing effects of the recession and price reductions by the company's principal competitors, which resulted in increased competition at lower prices.

Another factor that contributed to the drop in the 1992 sales volume was delivery delays. As part of its restructuring program in 1992, the company changed the manufacturers from which it purchased products. These changes contributed to the company's difficulties in meeting its delivery deadlines on orders for its back-to-school season.

■ International Strategy

In recent years, sales of athletic and casual/lifestyle footwear in many international markets grew at a faster rate than in the United States. However, L.A. Gear's own sales in the international market declined from $158 million in 1990, to $127 million in 1991, and to $119 million in 1992.

In an effort to stem this decline in sales, L.A. Gear decided to increase its investment in the international market through joint ventures, acquisitions of distributors, and the creation of wholly owned foreign subsidiaries. By selling its products directly abroad (as opposed to the company's historical reliance on independent distributors in those markets), the company sought to increase sales by adopting more competitive marketing and distribution programs. In March 1992, the company established its first foreign subsidiary to conduct direct sales of its products in France.

L.A. Gear also began to focus on Asia for its potential as a retail sales market. "We see Asia as a huge market. You have basically got two billion pairs of feet out here," said Goldston. Consequently, the company began investigating promotional alliances and equity partnerships with Asian companies.

■ Distribution

L.A. Gear distributed its products out of a one million square foot warehouse/distribution center in Ontario, California. The company's products were sold in the U.S. to about 4,000 distributors that included department, sporting goods, athletic footwear and shoe stores, and wholesale distributors.

In recent years, L.A. Gear relied on extensive distribution through wholesale distributors who sold into deep-discount outlets. This policy tarnished the company's image and, as a result, several key retail accounts ceased or reduced their business with the company in 1991. To improve relations with full-margin retailers, the company began to distribute its products through specific channels, using what it called the "Gear Strategy Classification System." In line with this system, distribution channels were grouped in terms of "Image," "Mainstream," "Volume," and "Value." The Image channels were used to market the most technologically advanced and expensive high-performance products such as the L.A. Tech. The Mainstream and Volume channels were used to market "2nd Gear" and "1st Gear" products which incorporated fewer technological and aesthetic features. The Value channels were intended only for the distribution of inventory that could not be sold through the other channels. As part of the Value channels, the company planned to open a limited number of outlet stores.

Under Greenberg, the company maintained a next-day (at once) open stock system, where retailers could order products and have them shipped within 24 hours. This system forced inventory expenses to skyrocket. To mitigate this problem, the company also adopted a "futures" ordering system which provided discounts to retailers who ordered products four to six months in advance of shipment. It was hoped that the new program would enable the company to improve inventory management.

Internationally, L.A. Gear distributed its product in about 60 countries, primarily through agreements with independent distributors. The distribution agreements were intended to maintain a consistent product offering and brand image throughout the world. However, this arrangement afforded the company little or no control over the ultimate retail price of its footwear. It also restricted both profit and growth potential.

■ Research and Development

L.A. Gear maintained close ties with firms that conducted basic materials research. For example, L.A. Gear had an alliance with U.T.I. Chemicals Corporation of California. U.T.I. developed a new outsole material known as Z-thane which was a patented plastic compound that outlasted similar materials already in the marketplace.[22] L.A. Gear also applied older materials to their shoe lines, such as the innovative use of carbon fiber heel protectors in its performance shoes. With the Catapult, L.A. Gear hoped to challenge the high performance image of Nike and Reebok by luring the performance oriented buyer away from these market leaders.

L.A. Gear, however, lagged behind its competitors in product innovation. For example, the company introduced a "pump" style shoe almost two years after Nike and Reebok introduced their versions of this technology. Ironically, former CEO Robert Greenberg once boasted that the company spent a fraction of what its competition spent on research and development.[23] The company's "catch-up" R&D practices damaged its relations with retailers. For example, one shoe buyer to a large department-store chain said: "We saw Nike and Reebok 1993 spring lines in May or June of 1992 and started committing for product in July. We didn't see L.A. Gear's product until mid-August."[24]

■ Human Resources

L.A. Gear employs 753 full-time employees. In 1991, the company embarked on a restructuring program to reduce its workforce. By 1992, 613 employees ceased employment with the company, 152 of whom were associated with the company's discontinued apparel design and marketing operations. This represented a 45 percent reduction in staff and reduced the company's monthly payroll expense from $4.8 million in 1991 to $3.4 million in 1992. The company's employees were not covered by any collective bargaining agreement, but management considered the company's relations with its employees to be satisfactory. The company offered its employees 401(k) retirement savings programs and had an employee stock option plan (ESOP) in place. The ESOP program was instituted as an incentive program for employees and management.

■ Communication and Corporate Culture

As L.A. Gear grew bigger, it had to hire more employees to handle the new functions. In 1985, 50 people turned out the product; by 1992, that figure swelled to 1,200. As a result, the company which was characterized by an informal communication system and corporate culture, splintered into departmental fiefdoms scattered in several buildings. The new structure eroded the informal relationships that existed among L.A. Gear's management and employees. In the early days, for instance, Greenberg and Saemann worked just across the hall from each other, and their basic form of communication was to yell back and forth. Greenberg, who had a passion for tropical fish and kept a large tank in his office, would often march across the hall to see Saemann with a dripping net in one hand and a new sneaker design in the other.

The new management brought with it buttoned-down seriousness. Coats and ties were now a regular sight at L.A. Gear. Gone were the days when Greenberg would slip each of his employees $100 bills in pink envelopes whenever the company turned a profit. Now, employees carried around black coffee mugs that read ATTACK BUSINESS COSTS.

■ Legal Issues

In 1990 and 1991, three class action lawsuits were brought against L.A. Gear by shareholders. The shareholders claimed that the company violated the U.S. securities laws by inflating sales by tens of millions of dollars in 1990 when it counted as revenues merchandise that was being stored in L.A. Gear's warehouses and docks. In settling these lawsuits, the company recorded a $23 million pre-tax charge against its 1992 earnings.

In October 1992, L.A. Gear reached an agreement with the U.S. Attorney for the District of Massachusetts regarding the resolution of all customs claims arising from the importation of footwear from Taiwan in 1986 and 1987. Accordingly, L.A. Gear entered a guilty plea with respect to two counts charging underpayment of duties on such shipments. A sentencing hearing was scheduled in 1993. In addition, the company paid $1.3 million in settlement of all potential civil claims arising from underpayment of duties on the 1986 and 1987 shipments from Taiwan.

In November 1992, L.A. Gear settled a patent infringement lawsuit brought against it by Reebok International Ltd, alleging that certain footwear products marketed by the company infringed on a patent issued to Reebok covering "inflatable bladder" shoe technology. L.A. Gear paid Reebok $1 million to settle the lawsuit. As part of the settlement, L.A. Gear entered into a license agreement under which Reebok granted the company a four-year non-exclusive worldwide license to manufacture, use, and sell footwear utilizing the "inflatable bladder." The license agreement, however, did not grant L.A. Gear access to Reebok's technology.

Another legal issue involved L.A. Gear's relationship with entertainer Michael Jackson. In September 1992, the company filed a complaint against Jackson alleging, among other things, fraud, breach of contract, and breach of good faith. The company's claims arose from contracts between the company and the defendant which granted the company the exclusive right to use Jackson's name and likeness in advertising and promoting the company's shoes and apparel as well as the right to develop and market a Michael Jackson athletic shoe line. Michael Jackson countered with a lawsuit, alleging fraud and breach of good faith on the part of the company. No settlement of this dispute has been reached yet.

■ Finance and Accounting

L.A. Gear's gross profit declined from $286 million in 1990, to $170 million in 1991, and to $109 million in 1992. While the company earned a net income of $31 million in 1990, it lost $66 million and $72 million in 1991 and 1992 respectively.

Because of an imbalance between inventory purchases and sales, L.A. Gear accumulated inventory greater than that necessary for its business. The introduction of the company's new product lines also resulted in a greater number of styles being discontinued than would otherwise have been the case. As a result, as part of an inventory reduction program, the company sold inventory at significant discounts resulting in lower margins. As was the custom in the footwear industry, substantial changes to the current product lines were made at least twice a year (i.e., for the spring and back-to-school seasons). As a result, a certain number of styles were usually discontinued.

In September 1991, Trefoil Capital Investors, L.P. invested $100 million in L.A. Gear in the form of a new issue of Series A Cumulative Convertible Preferred Stock, the net proceeds of which were used to repay indebtedness. In November 1992, the company had cash and cash equivalent balances of $84 million. In addition, the company expected to receive income tax refunds in 1993 of about $25 million.

■ Industry

The U.S. general footwear market was valued at about $12 billion. The athletic shoe market comprised about $6 billion. According to *Footwear News,* the domestic retail shoe market was expected to continue to grow at a rate of 5.5 percent at least until the year 2000.[25]

A 1987 Census of Manufacturers conducted by the U.S. Bureau of the Census revealed that over 100 companies participated in the men's and women's footwear industries.[26] During 1992 there were two dozen companies competing in the U.S. branded footwear market.[27] Domestically, the two largest athletic shoe makers were Nike and Reebok with a combined share of the market totaling 50 percent.[28] Although Nike and Reebok, as well as L.A. Gear, were headquartered in the U.S., the majority of their products was manufactured in Asian, European, and South American countries. A shoe that retailed for $100 cost the company between $20 and $25 if manufactured in foreign countries. Markups to the retailer and consumer were nearly 100 percent.

The footwear industry was not cyclical but did show some seasonality with back-to-school sales in August and September. Although profitability and sales for footwear companies fluctuated, these fluctuations were attributable not to economic cycles but to changes in advertising expenditures, price, product quality, and overall market trends such as consumer preferences for fashion versus performance shoes.

Entry into the footwear industry was rather difficult. This was due to the fact that success in this industry depended to a great extent on heavy advertising, brand awareness, and intensive research and development. In the high-performance athletic shoe market, advertising was critical to footwear producers as a means of promoting new styles and creating brand awareness. Footwear companies spent vast sums to get popular athletes to endorse certain shoes. Nike and Reebok, for example, spent $200 million on advertising and promotion in 1992. This medium was cost prohibitive to smaller firms whose revenues were often too small to mount effective marketing campaigns. Another barrier to entry was brand awareness. Consumers purchased shoes based on either how well they perceived a brand to perform or on its fashion characteristics. On the average, when selecting a shoe, men tended to look at sole cushioning and how well an inner structure supported the foot—not fashion or style. Women's purchases, however, were determined more by the design or style of the shoe.[29]

An even greater entry barrier in the footwear industry was the excessive capital required for research and development. Nike, Reebok, and L.A. Gear allocated large budgets toward R&D. Each of the top three competitors had a highly advanced technology. Nike had its Air Jordan; Reebok had the Pump and Insta Pump; and L.A. Gear had its Catapult and Regulator shoes that incorporated high-tech carbon fiber soles.

In the highly competitive discount-athletic footwear market, barriers to entry were less formidable. Volume companies (mass producers) tended to carve out a niche through brands they licensed or created on their own. According to *Footwear News,* "the mass market usually followed where the better-grade merchandise had already beaten a path. Volume sources capitalized on the consumer appetite for branded-athletic footwear generated by the sophisticated marketing of companies such as Nike, Reebok, and L.A. Gear." According to the Sporting Goods Manufacturers Association, discount stores commanded $3.4 billion of the athletic shoe market.[30]

The U.S. footwear industry was maturing and analysts expected that consumers would purchase more non-athletic footwear than athletic footwear. With the domestic market maturing, many footwear companies began expanding overseas where the market was expected to grow at a rate of 23 percent a year in the next decade.[31]

The appeal of overseas markets to U.S. footwear companies stemmed not only from their sheer size but also from the cheap advertising common in such markets. Furthermore, a growing number of consumers overseas were becoming increasingly interested in U.S. sports generally and in basketball in particular. Actually, U.S. basketball was now a close second to soccer in worldwide popularity.[32] As a result, footwear companies discovered that their big endorsers, like Michael Jordan for Nike, translated well across borders.

■ Competitors

The athletic and athletic-style footwear industry was highly competitive in the United States and on a worldwide basis. L.A. Gear's competitors included both specialized athletic shoe companies and companies with diversified footwear product lines. The company's primary competitors in the domestic athletic and athletic-style markets were Nike and Reebok. These companies were more established than L.A. Gear and had greater financial, distribution, and marketing resources, as well as greater brand awareness, than the company. Internationally, L.A. Gear's major competitor was Adidas. Below is a brief profile of each of L.A. Gear's major competitors.

Nike

Nike was a publicly held sports and fitness company with a 26 percent share of the domestic market. Nike was the first company in the sports and fitness industry to exceed $2 billion in U.S. revenues and $3 billion worldwide. The company accomplished this in 1991. The diversity of Nike's product lines was far reaching. The company designed and marketed athletic footwear, apparel, and related items for competitive and recreational uses. To promote this breadth of product line, Nike was successful with advertisements that used high-profile athletes. Nike had an impressive stable of endorsers with Michael Jordan, Bo Jackson, David Robinson, and Andre Agassi. The success of these advertising campaigns enabled Nike to command a higher price for its shoes than its competitors.

To add to their image as one of the premier athletic footwear companies, Nike began to open a series of high-tech futuristic looking, company-owned outlets around the world called Nike Town. This outlet was a tribute to Nike's innovative flair and marketing genius.[33] The design concept incorporated sports, fitness, entertainment, history, and product innovation.

Nike spent more than its competitors on research and development. Nike learned the hard way to push its technology. In 1987, Nike was surpassed by rival Reebok as the number one domestic footwear company. At this time, Nike was concentrating on marketing its apparel and fashion shoes instead of promoting its air cushioning system. Within eighteen months of being surpassed by Reebok, Nike regained the number one spot by marketing its Nike Air Jordan shoes. Now, Nike's engineers began to call the shots—not its fashion designers.

Reebok

Reebok International Ltd. was a designer and marketer of active lifestyle and performance products, including footwear and apparel. Reebok held 24 percent of the domestic footwear market. According to industry sources, Reebok was the company best positioned to take advantage of the developing worldwide sneaker market.[34] Reebok announced in early 1992 that it had established a new worldwide sports marketing unit and that it would spend 25 percent more on advertising. Additionally, international sales soared 75 percent to $832.6 million from $475.2 in 1990. The sports marketing unit worked in conjunction with the fitness and casual units to deliver the best products and programs to consumers and retailers worldwide.

In 1988, Reebok acquired Avia and Rockport—two fast-growing companies. Paul Fireman, chairman and chief executive officer, believed that Avia and Rockport exemplified a "sense of aliveness" which was a characteristic of Reebok.[35] In 1991, Avia's sales rose 4.3 percent to $161 million, and Rockport's sales grew 8.5 percent to $251.3 million. Rockport produced products primarily for the walking shoe market while Avia competed directly with the Reebok brand for the athletic footwear market.

Reebok replaced its ineffective advertising with a cause-related campaign aimed at supporting philanthropic organizations while promoting its own products. In 1990, industry sources noted that Reebok was lacking a winning advertising campaign. In that year, two consecutive advertising campaigns flopped. In 1991 and 1992, Reebok reversed this trend with its cause-related advertising. Practitioners maintained that cause-related advertising could be risky, but when handled carefully, could supply the best of all promotional worlds: higher visibility, a unique image niche resulting from association with worthy projects, and stronger ties to the community.[36] As part of its cause-related marketing, Reebok gave financial support to Amnesty International's Human Rights Now tour. Angel Martinez, vice president of business development at Reebok's Los Angeles office, said that, "the tour was an extension of our value system as a company. We believe in freedom of expression and wanted to do something of importance, beyond selling sneakers."[37] Reebok's President, Joseph LaBonte, added: "We both believe very strongly in the freedom to do what you want."

To remain competitive with Nike, Reebok also planned to contract endorsements with high-profile athletes. Even though the Insta-Pump would not be available to consumers until January 1993, Reebok hoped to get a lot of promotional mileage by putting the shoes on several Olympic track-and-field stars at the 1992 summer games in Barcelona, Spain.

Adidas and Puma

A decade ago, most athletic shoes sold in Europe were made by Adidas or its smaller rival, Puma. For years, the two German companies controlled about 75 percent of Europe's athletic shoe and apparel market, and they were also strong in the U.S. Things changed, however. Now, Nike and Reebok, and to a lesser degree L.A. Gear, made spectacular inroads in Europe. Although Adidas continued to be No. 1 with $1.6 billion in revenues, Nike ranked second with $500 million and Reebok ranked third with $380 million. L.A. Gear's sales were less than $119 million.

Both Nike and Reebok profited from long-term problems at Adidas and Puma. In the past five years, both German companies reported steady streams of losses because of unfocused marketing, high costs, and a glut of products. At Adidas, the confusion was acute: In footwear alone, it had 1,200 different variations and styles. "We had everything," said Michel Perrauding, Adidas' manager for logistics, "even shoes for left-handed bowlers."

Adidas' poorly coordinated marketing in Europe angered many distributors who started to desert to Nike and Reebok. And in the United States where Adidas was once No. 1 in athletic shoes, chronic delivery problems and a failure to spot the trend to more comfortable shoes led to huge losses and a dramatic drop in market share.

Nike and Reebok, however, might have to confront the possibility that Adidas and Puma might fight back. A Swedish company took full control of Puma and planned to pump cash into it. At Adidas, a new French owner slashed its product range in shoes and apparel to several hundred from several thousand, retired hundreds of employees, and started a network of more efficient purchasing and production facilities in Asia. Adidas launched a new line, Equipment, featuring no-frills shoes for such sports as soccer, tennis, and track. There was also a new Adidas series of hiking and outdoors shoes. Nevertheless, Adidas and Puma lacked the deep pockets of Nike and Reebok to enable them to spend as much on advertising as the two U.S. companies.

■ Customers

L.A. Gear sold to retail stores, specialty shoe stores, and sporting goods stores but their ultimate customer was the individual retail consumer. L.A. Gear's customers historically were young fashion minded girls. Under Greenberg, the company promoted the young Southern-California lifestyle. Its advertisements were of young blondes on the beach in stylish L.A. Gear shoes. Under the new management, the company repositioned itself. Former CEO Robert Greenberg said that they knew that in order to grow they would eventually have to enter the men's market and that meant more technically-oriented footwear.[38] Fashion athletics was now only a part of L.A. Gear.

■ Government Regulations

In 1990, the U.S. Congress passed the Textile, Apparel, and Footwear Trade Act (the "Textile Act") which would have set highly restrictive global quotas on imported textile, apparel, and footwear products. This legislation was vetoed by President Bush, and the veto was sustained by the House of Representatives.

There was a possibility that a similar legislation would be proposed in the future. If such a legislation was enacted into law, L.A. Gear could face restrictions on its ability to import into the U.S. its footwear products manufactured abroad.

In 1992, the U.S. placed L.A. Gear's suppliers in Taiwan, China, Indonesia, and South Korea on a "priority watch list" for engaging in unfair trade practices. If such countries were proved to be engaged in unfair trade practices, the U.S. might retaliate against them, which could result in increases in the cost, or reductions in the supply, of footwear generally and L.A. Gear's footwear in particular.

■ Demographics

The U.S. population, which totaled 250 million in 1990, was expected to reach 283 million by the year 2010. That was an increase of about 13 percent. Perhaps more significant to the footwear industry was the rise in the size of the baby boom generation, born between 1946 and 1964. A prime target of footwear companies, this segment, which comprised 18 percent of the population in 1990, was expected to grow by about 9 percent by the year 2010.

■ Culture

Lifestyle changes in the United States, as well as in many other countries, were propitious for footwear producers. An increasing segment of the population was becoming more health conscious, engaging in athletic activities such as jogging and walking. Because of the increasing popularity of walking, the walking-shoes market was expected to be the largest growth segment of the footwear industry. According to industry sources, 75 percent of the walking-shoes market consisted of women in their mid-30s and up.[39]

■ Economy

In 1991 and 1992, the Federal Reserve Board laid the groundwork for an economic recovery by keeping prime interest rates low and gradually expanding the money supply. The Fed was able, at the same time, to keep inflation at less than 4 percent. Depressed consumer confidence in economic recovery, however, continued to be a major obstacle to increased consumer and business spending. The slow start of President Clinton's economic program served only to slow a long-awaited growth in the nation's economy.

■ Technology

Counterfeiting is the perennial enemy of brand-name producers in Asia. Recognizing the danger to his company's technology, Goldston, L.A. Gear's president said, "The major focus of our agreements with new manufacturers is on integrity. Our technology innovation will be protected."[40] However, an L.A. Gear executive said the means available to foreign shoe manufacturers for protecting patents were limited. As a result, athletic-shoe makers could find their most nagging competitors were not each other but the companies who filled their orders. Such companies as L.A. Gear "tend to stumble when faced with competition, and this time it will come from say, . . . a factory in Indonesia that has acquired the technology to make a good jogging shoe."[41]

■ Politics

With political changes occurring in Eastern Europe and the Soviet Union, markets that were previously closed to Western companies were now fairly wide open.

The enactment of NAFTA (North American Free Trade Agreement) among the U.S., Canada, and Mexico, was likely to strengthen U.S. exports. According to estimates made by the U.S. Trade Representative, the tariff reductions alone, if undertaken by all countries, could raise U.S. real GNP by 3 percent by the year 2000.[42]

■ Conclusion

As they implement their turnaround strategy, Gold and Goldston have their work cut out for them. What should they do next? And will their strategic moves be sufficient to restore L.A. Gear to its heyday or will they cause the company to disappear?

■ Endnotes

1. "L.A. Gear," *Los Angeles Magazine,* December 1991, p. 116.
2. "L.A. Gear Calls in a Cobbler," *Business Week,* September 16, 1991, p. 78.
3. "L.A. Gear +184.6%," *Institutional Investor,* March 1990, pp. 52, 53.
4. "L.A. Gear Co-Founder Saemann Quits in Wake of Firms Deal with Trefoil," *The Wall Street Journal,* June 13, 1991, p. B1.
5. "The Best and Worst Stocks of 1989," *Fortune,* January 29, 1990, p. 114.
6. "L.A. Gear Inc.," *The Wall Street Journal,* April 4, 1991, p. B1.
7. "L.A. Gear Co-Founder Saemann Quits in Wake of Firms Deal with Trefoil," *The Wall Street Journal,* June 13, 1991, p. B1.
8. "Stanley P. Gold L.A. Gear Chairman & Chief Executive Officer," L.A. Gear Press Release, January 24, 1992.
9. Ibid.
10. "L.A. Gear Inc. Investor Steps in With New Team," *The Wall Street Journal,* January 27, 1992, pp. B1, B5.
11. Ibid.
12. "L.A. Gear Inc. Investor Steps in With New Team," *The Wall Street Journal,* January 27, 1992, pp. B1, B5.
13. Ibid.
14. "L.A. Gear, Several Changes at Senior Level," *The Wall Street Journal,* September 17, 1991, p. A22.
15. L.A. Gear, Form 10-K, 1991, p. 2.
16. Ibid.
17. Ibid.
18. L.A. Gear Inc., 1990 Annual Report (Los Angeles, CA: L.A. Gear Inc.), p. 7.
19. B. Horivitz, "Some Companies Find They Get More," *Los Angeles Times,* February 5, 1991, p. D6.
20. "L.A. Gear Says High Inventories May Affect 1992 Earnings," *Bloomberg News,* March 3, 1992.
21. Ibid., p. B5.
22. L.A. Gear Inc., 1990 Annual Report (Los Angeles, CA: L.A. Gear Inc.), p. 8.
23. "The Goldston Prescription," *Footwear News,* January 27, 1992, pp. 11–12.
24. "L.A. Gear Still Looks Like an Also-Ran," *Business Week,* December 21, 1992, p. 37.

■ **Appendix A** L.A. Gear, Inc. Consolidated Balance Sheet, as of November 30 (in thousands)

	1992	1991
Assets		
Current assets:		
Cash and cash equivalents	$ 55,027	$ 1,422
Collateralized cash	28,955	—
Accounts receivable, net	56,369	111,470
Inventories	61,923	141,115
Prepaid expenses and other current assets	2,557	8,506
Refundable income taxes	25,269	22,795
Deferred income taxes	—	11,763
Total current assets	230,100	297,071
Property and equipment, net	17,667	26,869
Other assets	1,735	1,631
Total assets	$249,502	$325,571
Liabilities, Mandatorily Redeemable		
Preferred Stock and Shareholders' Equity		
Current liabilities:		
Borrowing under line of credit	$ —	$ 20,000
Accounts payable and accrued liabilities	49,753	55,856
Dividends payable on mandatorily redeemable preferred stock	7,746	—
Costs related to discontinued operations	4,552	18,000
Total current liabilities	62,051	93,856
Mandatorily redeemable preferred stock:		
7.5% Series A Cumulative Convertible Preferred Stock,		
$100 stated value; 1,000,000 shares authorized, issued and		
outstanding; redemption value of $100 per share	100,000	100,000
Shareholders' equity:		
Common stock, no par value;		
80,000,000 shares authorized; 22,898,182 shares issued		
and outstanding at November 30, 1992 (19,542,513 shares		
issued and outstanding at November 30, 1991)	127,714	92,331
Preferred stock, no stated value; 9,000,000 shares authorized;		
no shares issued	—	—
Retained earnings (accumulated deficit)	(40,263)	39,384
Total shareholders' equity	87,451	131,715
Commitments and contingencies	—	—
	$249,502	$325,571

SOURCE: L.A. Gear, 1992 Annual Report, p. 17.

25. "Footwear (Men's, Women's, Boys' and Girls')," *Fairchild Fact File,* 1990, pp. 5–9.

26. Ibid., pp. 5–9.

27. F. Meeds, "The Sneaker Game," *Forbes,* October 22, 1990, p. 114.

28. J. Schlax, "The Shoe as Hero," *Forbes,* August 20, 1990, p. 77.

29. K. Kerwin, "L.A. Gear Is Going Where the Boys Are," *Business Week,* June 19, 1989, p. 54.

30. Ibid., p. 52.

31. M. Grimm, "To Munich and Back with Nike and L.A. Gear," *Adweek's Marketing Week,* February 18, 1991, p. 21.

32. Ibid., p. 22.

33. M. Wilson, "Nike Town Goes Back to the Future," *Chain Store Age Executive,* February, 1991, pp. 82–83.

■ **Appendix B** L.A. Gear, Inc. Consolidated Statements of Cash Flows, as of November 30 (in thousands)

	1992	1991	1990
Operating activities:			
Net income (loss)	$(71,901)	$(66,200)	$31,338
Adjustment to reconcile net income (loss) to net cash provided by (used in) operating activities: Shareholders' litigation settlements	17,075	—	—
Depreciation and amortization	7,107	7,182	3,394
Provision for loss on discontinued operations	—	18,000	—
Loss on sale or abandonment of property and equipment	1,871	4,146	—
Issuance of shares to employee stock savings plan	233	382	—
(Increase) decrease in: Accounts receivable, net	55,101	44,431	(52,969)
Inventories	79,192	19,553	(21,152)
Prepaids and other assets	6,343	1,565	(998)
Refundable and deferred income taxes	8,791	(26,174)	(3,795)
Increase (decrease) in:			
Accounts payable and accrued liabilities	(6,103)	(8,222)	3,143
Costs related to discontinued operations	(8,343)	—	—
Net cash provided by (used in) operating activities	89,366	(5,337)	(41,039)
Investing activities-capital expenditures	(4,881)	(14,188)	(18,939)
Financing activities:			
Net proceeds from issuance of mandatorily redeemable preferred stock	—	92,511	—
Payment of dividends on mandatorily redeemable preferred stock	—	(1,265)	—
Exercise of stock options and warrants	1,986	414	908
Tax benefits arising from the disposition/exercise of incentive stock options	2,089	356	5,408
Proceeds from issuance of common stock	14,000	—	—
Net borrowing (repayment) under line of credit agreement	(20,000)	(74,000)	56,600
Net cash provided by (used in) financing activities	(1,925)	17,656	62,916
Net increase (decrease) in cash and cash equivalents	82,560	(1,869)	2,938
Cash at beginning of year	1,422	3,291	353
Cash and cash equivalents at end of year, including collateralized cash	$83,982	$ 1,422	$ 3,291

SOURCE: L.A. Gear, 1992 Annual Report, p. 17.

34. M. Tedeschi, "Reebok Splits U.S. Int'l Setups," *Footwear News,* November 26, 1990, p. 12.

35. S. Gannes, "America's Fastest-Growing Companies," *Fortune,* May 23, 1988, p. 37.

36. A. Shell, "Cause-Related Marketing: Big Risks, Big Potential," *Public Relations Journal,* July, 1989, pp. 8, 13.

37. Ibid., p. 8.

38. M. Rottman, "L.A. Gear Catapults into Technology," *Footwear News,* February 18, 1991, pp. 12, 14.

39. D. McKay, "Walk This Way," *Footwear News,* September 9, 1991, pp. 14–15.

40. "L.A. Gear President Says Shoe Maker Will Recover and Will Focus on Asia," *The Wall Street Journal,* October 16, 1992, p. B7.

41. Ibid.

42. OECD Economic Survey, United States, 1990/1991, pp. 60–65.

■ Case 7   Kentucky Fried Chicken and the Global Fast-Food Industry in 1998

Jeffrey A. Krug
University of Illinois at Urbana–Champaign

In 1998, Kentucky Fried Chicken Corporation (KFC) was the world's largest chicken restaurant chain and third largest fast-food chain. KFC held over 55 percent of the U.S. market and operated over 10,200 restaurants worldwide. It opened 376 new restaurants (more than one restaurant a day) and operated in 79 countries.

One of the first fast-food chains to go international during the late 1960s, KFC developed one of the world's most recognizable brands. Japan, Australia, and the United Kingdom accounted for the greatest share of KFC's international expansion during the 1970s and 1980s. During the 1990s, KFC turned its attention to other international markets that offered significant opportunities for growth: China, with a population of over 1 billion, and Europe, with a population roughly equal to that of the United States. Latin America offered a unique growth opportunity because of the size of its markets, its common language and culture, and its geographical proximity to the United States. Mexico was of particular interest because of the North American Free Trade Agreement (NAFTA), which went into effect in 1994.

Prior to 1990, KFC expanded into Latin America primarily through company-owned restaurants in Mexico and Puerto Rico. By 1995, KFC had also established company-owned restaurants in Venezuela and Brazil, as well as franchised units in numerous Caribbean countries. During the early 1990s, KFC shifted to a two-tiered strategy in Latin America. First, it established 29 franchised restaurants in Mexico following the enactment of Mexico's new franchise law in 1990. This allowed KFC to expand outside of its company restaurant base in Mexico City, Guadalajara, and Monterrey. KFC was one of many U.S. fast-food, retail, and hotel chains to begin franchising in Mexico following the new franchise law. Second, KFC began an aggressive franchise-building program in South America. By 1998, it was operating franchised restaurants in 32 Latin American countries. Much of this growth was in Brazil, Chile, Colombia, Ecuador, and Peru.

■ Company History

Fast-food franchising was still in its infancy in 1952 when Harland Sanders began his travels across the United States to speak with prospective franchisees about his Colonel Sanders Recipe Kentucky Fried Chicken. By 1960, "Colonel" Sanders had granted KFC franchises to over 200 take-home retail outlets and restaurants across the United States. He had also succeeded in establishing a number of franchises in Canada. By 1963, the number of KFC franchises had risen to over 300 and revenues had reached $500 million.

By 1964, at the age of 74, the Colonel had grown tired of running the day-to-day operations of his business and was eager to concentrate on public relations issues. Therefore, he sought out potential buyers, eventually deciding to sell the business to two Louisville businessmen—Jack Massey and John Young Brown Jr.—for $2 mil-

This case was prepared by Jeffrey A. Krug, University of Illinois at Urbana–Champaign.

lion. The Colonel stayed on as a public relations representative and goodwill ambassador for the company.

During the next five years, Massey and Brown concentrated on growing KFC's franchise system across the United States. In 1966, after being taken public, KFC was listed on the New York Stock Exchange. By the late 1960s, the company had gained a strong foothold in the United States, and Massey and Brown turned their attention to international markets. In 1969, KFC signed a joint venture with Japan's Mitsuoishi Shoji Kaisha, Ltd., and acquired the rights to operate 14 existing KFC franchises in England. Subsidiaries were also established in Hong Kong, South Africa, Australia, New Zealand, and Mexico. By 1971, KFC had 2,450 franchises and 600 company-owned restaurants worldwide, and was operating in 48 countries.

Heublein, Inc.

In 1971, KFC entered negotiations with Heublein, Inc., to discuss a possible merger. The decision to seek a merger candidate was partially driven by Brown's desire to pursue other interests, including a political career (Brown was elected governor of Kentucky in 1977). Several months later, Heublein acquired KFC. Heublein was in the business of producing vodka, mixed cocktails, dry gin, cordials, beer, and other alcoholic beverages. However, Heublein had little experience in the restaurant business. Conflicts quickly erupted between Colonel Sanders, who continued to act in a public relations capacity, and Heublein management. Sanders became increasingly distraught over quality control issues and restaurant cleanliness. By 1977, new restaurant openings had slowed to about 20 per year; few restaurants were being remodeled, and service quality had declined.

In 1977, Heublein sent in a new management team to redirect KFC's strategy. The team immediately implemented a back-to-the-basics strategy and discontinued new-unit construction until existing restaurants could be upgraded and operating problems eliminated. KFC then refurbished restaurants, placed emphasis on cleanliness and service, cut out marginal products, and reestablished product consistency. By 1982, KFC's strategic focus had proved successful and the company was again aggressively building new units.

R. J. Reynolds Industries, Inc.

In 1982, R. J. Reynolds Industries, Inc. (RJR), merged Heublein into a wholly owned subsidiary. The merger with Heublein represented part of RJR's overall corporate strategy of diversifying into unrelated businesses, including energy, transportation, food, and restaurants. RJR's objective was to reduce its dependence on the tobacco industry, which had driven RJR sales since the company's founding in North Carolina in 1875. Sales of cigarettes and tobacco products, while profitable, were declining because of reduced consumption in the United States. This was mainly the result of an increased awareness among Americans about the negative health consequences of smoking.

RJR had no more experience in the restaurant business than did Heublein. However, it decided to take a hands-off approach to managing KFC. Whereas Heublein had installed its own top management at KFC headquarters, RJR left KFC management largely intact, believing that existing KFC managers were better qualified to operate KFC's businesses than its own managers were. In doing so, RJR avoided many of the operating problems that plagued Heublein. This strategy paid off as KFC continued to expand aggressively and profitably under RJR ownership. In

1985, RJR acquired Nabisco Corporation for $4.9 billion. Nabisco sold a variety of well-known cookies, crackers, cereals, confectioneries, snacks, and other grocery products. The merger with Nabisco represented a decision by RJR to concentrate its diversification efforts on the consumer foods industry. It subsequently divested many of its non-consumer food businesses. RJR sold KFC to PepsiCo, Inc., one year later.

■ PepsiCo, Inc.

Corporate Strategy

In 1965 the merger of the Pepsi-Cola Company and Frito-Lay, Inc., created one of the largest consumer products companies in the United States: PepsiCo, Inc. Pepsi-Cola's traditional business was the sale of soft drink concentrates to licensed independent and company-owned bottlers that manufactured, sold, and distributed Pepsi-Cola soft drinks. Pepsi-Cola's best known trademarks were Pepsi-Cola, Diet Pepsi, Mountain Dew, and Slice. Frito-Lay manufactured and sold a variety of snack foods, including Fritos corn chips, Lay's potato chips, Ruffles potato chips, Doritos, Tostitos tortilla chips, and Chee-tos cheese-flavored snacks. PepsiCo quickly embarked on an aggressive acquisition program similar to that pursued by RJR during the 1980s, buying a number of companies in areas unrelated to its major businesses. Acquisitions included North American Van Lines, Wilson Sporting Goods, and Lee Way Motor Freight. However, these businesses failed to live up to expectations, mainly because the management skills required to operate them lay outside of PepsiCo's area of expertise.

Poor performance in these businesses led then-chairman and chief executive officer Don Kendall to restructure PepsiCo's operations in 1984. First, the company divested itself of businesses that did not support PepsiCo's consumer product orientation, such as North American Van Lines, Wilson Sporting Goods, and Lee Way Motor Freight. Second, PepsiCo sold its foreign bottling operations to local businesspeople who better understood the culture and business environment in their respective countries. Third, Kendall reorganized PepsiCo along three lines: soft drinks, snack foods, and restaurants.

Restaurant Business and Acquisition of Kentucky Fried Chicken

PepsiCo first entered the restaurant business in 1977 when it acquired Pizza Hut's 3,200-unit restaurant system. Taco Bell was merged into a division of PepsiCo in 1978. The restaurant business complemented PepsiCo's consumer product orientation. The marketing of fast-food followed many of the same patterns as the marketing of soft drinks and snack foods. PepsiCo therefore believed that its management skills could be easily transferred among its three business segments. This was compatible with PepsiCo's practice of frequently moving managers among its business units as a way of developing future top executives. PepsiCo's restaurant chains also provided an additional outlet for the sale of Pepsi soft drinks. Pepsi-Cola soft drinks and fast-food products could also be marketed together in the same television and radio segments, thereby providing higher returns for each advertising dollar. To complete its diversification into the restaurant segment, PepsiCo acquired Kentucky Fried Chicken Corporation from RJR-Nabisco for $841 million in 1986. The acquisition of KFC gave PepsiCo the leading market share in chicken (KFC), pizza (Pizza Hut), and Mexican food (Taco Bell), three of the four largest and fastest-growing segments within the U.S. fast-food industry.

Management

Following the acquisition by PepsiCo, KFC's relationship with its parent company underwent dramatic changes. Whereas RJR had operated KFC as a semi-autonomous unit, satisfied that KFC management understood the fast-food business better than its own management did, PepsiCo acquired KFC in order to complement its already strong presence in the fast-food market. Rather than allowing KFC to operate independently, PepsiCo undertook sweeping changes: Negotiating a new franchise contract to give PepsiCo more control over its franchisees, reducing staff in order to cut costs, and replacing KFC managers with its own. In 1987, a rumor spread through KFC's headquarters in Louisville that the new personnel manager, who had just relocated from PepsiCo's headquarters in New York, had said "There will be no more home-grown tomatoes in this organization."

Such rumors indicated a more serious morale problem, created by several restructurings that led to layoffs throughout the KFC organization, the replacement of KFC personnel with PepsiCo managers, and conflicts between KFC and PepsiCo's corporate cultures. KFC's culture was built largely on Colonel Sanders's laid-back approach to management, under which employees enjoyed relatively good job stability and security. Over the years, a strong loyalty had been created among KFC employees and franchisees, mainly because of Colonel Sanders's efforts to meet his employees' benefits, pension, and other non-income needs. In addition, the friendly, relaxed atmosphere at KFC's corporate offices in Louisville had mirrored the company's corporate culture, which had been left essentially unchanged during the Heublein and RJR years.

In stark contrast, PepsiCo's corporate culture was characterized by a strong emphasis on performance. Top performers expected to move up through the ranks quickly. PepsiCo used its KFC, Pizza Hut, Taco Bell, Frito Lay, and Pepsi-Cola divisions as training grounds for its top managers, rotating its best managers through its five divisions on average every two years. This practice created immense pressure on managers to continuously demonstrate their prowess within short periods, in order to maximize their potential for promotion. This practice also left many KFC managers with the feeling that they had few career opportunities with the new company. One PepsiCo manager commented, "You may have performed well last year, but if you don't perform well this year, you're gone, and there are 100 ambitious guys with Ivy League MBAs at PepsiCo who would love to take your position." An unwanted effect of this performance-driven culture was that employee loyalty was often lost and turnover became higher than in other companies.

When asked about KFC's relationship with its corporate parent, Kyle Craig, president of KFC's U.S. operations, commented:

> The KFC culture is an interesting one because I think it was dominated by a lot of KFC folks, many of whom have been around since the days of the Colonel. Many of those people were very intimidated by the PepsiCo culture, which is a very high-performance, high-accountability, highly driven culture. People were concerned about whether they would succeed in the new culture. Like many companies, we have had a couple of downsizings, which further made people nervous. Today, there are fewer old KFC people around and I think to some degree people have seen that the PepsiCo culture can drive some pretty positive results. I also think the PepsiCo people who have worked with KFC have modified their cultural values somewhat and they can see that there were a lot of benefits in the old KFC culture.

PepsiCo pushes its companies to perform strongly, but whenever there is a slip in performance, it increases the culture gap between PepsiCo and KFC. I have been involved in two downsizings over which I have been the chief architect. They have been probably the two most gut-wrenching experiences of my career. Because you know you're dealing with peoples' lives and their families, these changes can be emotional if you care about the people in your organization. However, I do fundamentally believe that your first obligation is to the entire organization.

A second problem for PepsiCo was its poor relationship with KFC franchisees. A month after becoming president and chief executive officer in 1989, John Cranor addressed KFC's franchisees in Louisville, in order to explain the details of the first contract change in 13 years. The new contract gave PepsiCo greater power to take over weak franchises, relocate restaurants, and make changes in existing restaurants. In addition, it no longer protected existing restaurants from competition with new KFC units, and it gave PepsiCo the right to raise royalty fees as contracts came up for renewal. After Cranor finished his address, the attending franchisees jumped to their feet to protest the changes. The franchisees had long been accustomed to relatively little interference from management in their day-to-day operations (a policy begun by Colonel Sanders). Interference, of course, was a strong part of PepsiCo's philosophy of demanding change. KFC's franchise association later sued PepsiCo over the new contract. The dispute remained unresolved until 1996, when the most objectionable parts of the contract were removed by KFC's new president and CEO, David Novak. A new contract was ratified by KFC's franchisees in 1997.

PepsiCo's Divestiture of KFC, Pizza Hut, and Taco Bell

PepsiCo's strategy of diversifying into three distinct but related markets—soft drinks, snack foods, and fast-food restaurants—created not only one of the world's largest consumer products companies but also a portfolio of some of the world's most recognizable brands. Between 1990 and 1996, PepsiCo grew at an annual rate of over 10 percent, surpassing $31 billion in sales in 1996. However, this sales growth masked troubles in PepsiCo's fast-food businesses. Operating margins (profit as a percentage of sales) at Pepsi-Cola and Frito Lay averaged 12 and 17 percent, respectively, between 1990 and 1996. During the same period, margins at KFC, Pizza Hut, and Taco Bell fell from an average of over 8 percent in 1990 to a little more than 4 percent in 1996. Declining margins in the fast-food chains reflected increasing maturity in the U.S. fast-food industry, more intense competition, and the aging of KFC and Pizza Hut's restaurant base. As a result, PepsiCo's restaurant chains absorbed nearly one-half of the company's annual capital spending during the 1990s while generating less than one-third of PepsiCo's cash flows. Therefore, cash was diverted from PepsiCo's soft drink and snack food businesses to its restaurant businesses. This reduced PepsiCo's return on assets and its stock price, and made effective competition with Coca-Cola (PepsiCo's leading rival) more difficult. In 1997, PepsiCo spun off its restaurant businesses into a new company called Tricon Global Restaurants, Inc. (see Exhibit 1). The new company was based in KFC's Louisville headquarters. PepsiCo's objectives were to reposition itself as a packaged goods company, to strengthen its balance sheet, and to create more consistent earnings growth. PepsiCo received a one-time distribution from Tricon of $4.7 billion, $3.7 billion of which was used to pay off short-term debt. The balance was earmarked for stock repurchases.

■ **Exhibit 1**   Tricon Global Restaurants, Inc., Organization, Chart, 1998

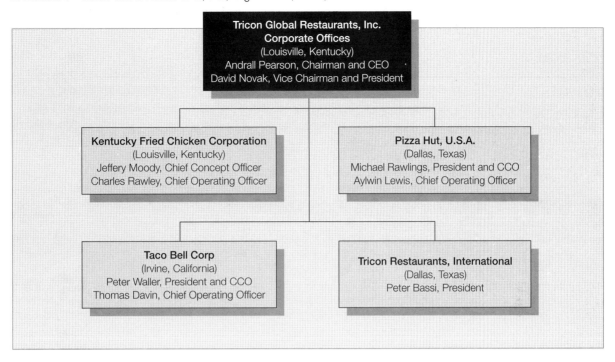

■ Fast-Food Industry

According to the National Restaurant Association (NRA), food-service sales topped $320 billion for the approximately 500,000 restaurants and other food outlets making up the U.S. restaurant industry in 1997. The NRA estimated that sales in the fast-food segment of the food-service industry grew 5.2 percent, to $104 billion, up from $98 billion in 1996. This marked the fourth consecutive year that fast-food sales either matched or exceeded sales in full-service restaurants, which in 1997 grew 4.1 percent, to $104 billion. The growth in fast-food sales reflected the gradual change in the restaurant industry, in which independently operated sit-down restaurants were becoming dominated by fast-food restaurant chains. The U.S. restaurant industry as a whole grew by approximately 4.2 percent in 1997.

Major Fast-Food Segments

Six major business segments made up the fast-food segment of the food-service industry. Sales data for the leading restaurant chains in each segment are shown in Exhibit 2. Most striking is the dominance of McDonald's, which had sales of over $16 billion in 1996. This represented 16.6 percent of U.S. fast-food sales, or nearly 22 percent of sales among the nation's top 30 fast-food chains. Sales at an average McDonald's restaurant totaled $1.3 million per year, compared to about $820,000 for the average U.S. fast-food restaurant. Tricon Global Restaurants (KFC, Pizza Hut, and Taco Bell) had U.S. sales of $13.4 billion in 1996. This represented 13.6 percent of U.S. fast-food sales and 17.9 percent of the top 30 fast-food chains.

■ **Exhibit 2**
Leading U.S. Fast-
Food Chains (Ranked
by 1996 Sales,
$ millions)

Sandwich chains	Sales	Share
McDonald's	$16,370	35.0%
Burger King	7,300	15.6
Taco Bell	4,575	9.8
Wendy's	4,360	9.3
Hardee's	3,055	6.5
Subway	2,700	5.8
Arby's	1,867	4.0
Dairy Queen	1,225	2.6
Jack in the Box	1,207	2.6
Sonic Drive-In	985	2.1
Carl's Jr.	648	1.4
Other chains	2,454	5.2
Total	$46,745	100.0%

Dinner houses		
Red Lobster	$ 1,810	15.7%
Applebee's	1,523	13.2
Olive Garden	1,280	11.1
Chili's	1,242	10.7
Outback Steakhouse	1,017	8.8
T.G.I. Friday's	935	8.1
Ruby Tuesday	545	4.7
Lone Star Steakhouse	460	4.0
Bennigan's	458	4.0
Romano's Macaroni Grill	344	3.0
Other dinner houses	1,942	16.8
Total	$11,557	100.0%

Grilled buffet chains		
Golden Corral	$ 711	22.8%
Ponderosa	680	21.8
Ryan's	604	19.4
Sizzler	540	17.3
Western Sizzlin'	332	10.3
Quincy's	259	8.3
Total	$3,116	100.0%

Family restaurants		
Denny's	$1,850	21.2%
Shoney's	1,220	14.0
Big Boy	945	10.8
International House of Pancakes	797	9.1
Cracker Barrel	734	8.4
Perkins	678	7.8
Friendly's	597	6.8
Bob Evans	575	6.6
Waffle House	525	6.0
Coco's	278	3.2
Steak 'n Shake	275	3.2
Village Inn	246	2.8
Total	$8,719	100.0%

(continued)

Pizza chains	Sales	Share
Pizza Hut	$ 4,927	46.4%
Domino's Pizza	2,300	21.7
Little Caesars Pizza	1,425	13.4
Papa John's Pizza	619	5.8
Sbarro	400	3.8
Round Table Pizza	385	3.6
Chuck E. Cheese's	293	2.8
Godfather's Pizza	266	2.5
Total	$10,614	100.0%
Chicken chains		
KFC	$ 3,900	57.1%
Boston Market	1,167	17.1
Popeye's Chicken	666	9.7
Chick-fil-A	570	8.3
Church's Chicken	529	7.7
Total	$ 6,832	100.0%

SOURCE: *Nation's Restaurant News.*

Sandwich chains made up the largest segment of the fast-food market. McDonald's controlled 35 percent of the sandwich segment, while Burger King ran a distant second, with a 15.6 percent market share. Competition had become particularly intense within the sandwich segment as the U.S. fast-food market became more saturated. In order to increase sales, chains turned to new products to win customers away from other sandwich chains, introduced products traditionally offered by other types of chains (such as pizza, fried chicken, and tacos), streamlined their menus, and upgraded product quality. Burger King recently introduced its Big King, a direct clone of the Big Mac. McDonald's quickly retaliated by introducing its Big 'n Tasty, a direct clone of the Whopper. Wendy's introduced chicken pita sandwiches, and Taco Bell introduced sandwiches called wraps, breads stuffed with various fillings. Hardee's successfully introduced fried chicken in most of its restaurants. In addition to offering new products, chains lowered prices, improved customer service, co-branded with other fast-food chains, and established restaurants in nontraditional locations (e.g., McDonald's installed restaurants in Wal-Mart stores across the country).

The second largest fast-food segment was dinner houses, dominated by Red Lobster, Applebee's, Olive Garden, and Chili's. Between 1988 and 1996, dinner houses increased their share of the fast-food market from 8 to over 13 percent. This increase came mainly at the expense of grilled buffet chains, such as Ponderosa, Sizzler, and Western Sizzlin'. The market share of such chains (also known as steak houses) fell from 6 percent in 1988 to under 4 percent in 1996. The rise of dinner houses during the 1990s was partially the result of an aging and wealthier population that increasingly demanded higher quality food and more upscale settings than those of sandwich chains. However, rapid construction of new restaurants, especially among relative newcomers—such as Romano's Macaroni Grill, Lone Star Steakhouse, and Outback Steakhouse—resulted in overcapacity within the dinner house segment. This reduced average restaurant sales and further intensified competition. In 1996,

8 of the 16 largest dinner houses posted growth rates in excess of 10 percent. Romano's Macaroni Grill, Lone Star Steakhouse, Chili's, Outback Steakhouse, Applebee's, Red Robin, Fuddruckers, and Ruby Tuesday grew at rates of 82, 41, 32, 27, 23, 14, 11, and 10 percent, respectively.

The third largest fast-food segment was pizza, long dominated by Pizza Hut. While Pizza Hut controlled over 46 percent of the pizza segment in 1996, its market share slowly eroded thereafter because of intense competition and its aging restaurant base. Domino's Pizza and Papa John's Pizza have been particularly successful. Little Caesars is the only pizza chain to remain predominantly a take-out chain, though it recently began home delivery. However, its policy of charging $1 per delivery damaged its reputation among consumers as a high-value pizza chain. Home delivery, successfully introduced by Domino's and Pizza Hut, was a driving force for success among the market leaders during the 1970s and 1980s. However, the success of home delivery drove competitors to look for new methods of increasing their customer bases. Pizza chains diversified into nonpizza items (e.g., chicken wings at Domino's and Italian cheese bread at Little Caesars), developed nontraditional units (e.g., airport kiosks and college campuses), offered special promotions, and offered new pizza variations with an emphasis on high-quality ingredients (e.g., Roma Herb and Garlic Crunch pizza at Domino's and Buffalo Chicken Pizza at Round Table Pizza).

Chicken Segment

KFC continued to dominate the chicken segment, with 1997 sales of $4 billion (see Exhibit 3). However, rather than building new restaurants in the already saturated U.S. market, KFC focused on building restaurants abroad. (In fact, the number of KFC restaurants in the United States declined slightly, from 5,128 in 1993 to 5,120 in 1998.) In the United States, KFC focused on closing unprofitable restaurants, upgrading existing restaurants with new exterior signage, and improving product quality. The strategy paid off. While overall U.S. sales during the 10 years up to 1998 remained flat, annual sales per unit increased steadily in 8 of the 9 years up to 1998.

Despite KFC's continued dominance within the chicken segment, it lost market share to Boston Market, which by 1997 had become KFC's nearest competitor, with $1.2 billion in sales. Emphasizing roasted chicken rather than fried, Boston Market successfully created the image of an upscale deli offering healthy, home-style alternatives to fast foods. It has broadened its menu beyond rotisserie chicken to include ham, turkey, meat loaf, chicken pot pie, and deli sandwiches. In order to minimize its image as a fast-food restaurant, Boston Market had refused to put drive-thrus in its restaurants and had established most of its units in outside shopping malls rather than in the freestanding units at intersections so characteristic of other fast-food restaurants.

In 1993, KFC introduced its own rotisserie chicken, called Rotisserie Gold, to combat Boston Market. However, it quickly learned that its customer base was considerably different from that of Boston Market's. KFC's customers liked KFC chicken despite the fact that it was fried. In addition, customers did not respond well to the concept of buying whole chickens for take-out. They preferred instead to buy chicken by the piece. KFC withdrew its rotisserie chicken in 1996 and introduced a new line of roasted chicken called Tender Roast, which could be sold by the piece and mixed with its Original Recipe and Extra Crispy Chicken.

Other major competitors within the chicken segment included Popeye's Chicken and Church's Chicken (both subsidiaries of AFC Enterprises in Atlanta), Chick-fil-A, Bojangle's, El Pollo Loco, Grandy's, Kenny Rogers Roasters, Mrs. Winner's, and

■ **Exhibit 3**
Top U.S. Chicken
Chains

U.S. Sales ($ millions)	1992	1993	1994	1995	1996	1997	Annual Growth Rate
KFC	$3,400	$3,400	$3,500	$3,700	$3,900	$4,000	3.3%
Boston Market	43	147	371	754	1,100	1,197	94.5
Popeye's Chicken	545	569	614	660	677	727	5.9
Chick-fil-A	356	396	451	502	570	671	11.9
Church's Chicken	414	440	465	501	526	574	6.8
Total	$4,758	$4,952	$5,401	$6,118	$6,772	$7,170	8.5%
Number of U.S. Restaurants							
KFC	5,089	5,128	5,149	5,142	5,108	5,120	0.1%
Boston Market	83	217	534	829	1,087	1,166	69.6
Popeye's Chicken	769	769	853	889	894	949	4.3
Chick-fil-A	487	545	534	825	717	762	9.0
Church's Chicken	944	932	937	953	989	1,070	2.5
Total	7,372	7,591	8,007	8,638	8,795	9,067	4.2%
Sales per Unit ($ 000s)							
KFC	$ 668	$ 663	$ 680	$ 720	$ 764	$ 781	3.2%
Boston Market	518	677	695	910	1,012	1,027	14.7
Popeye's Chicken	709	740	720	743	757	767	1.6
Chick-fil-A	731	727	845	608	795	881	3.8
Church's Chicken	439	472	496	526	531	537	4.1
Average	$ 645	$ 782	$ 782	$ 782	$ 782	$ 782	3.9%

SOURCE: Tricon Global Restaurants, Inc., 1997 annual report; Boston Chicken, Inc., 1997 annual report; Chick-fil-A, corporate headquarters, Atlanta; AFC Enterprises, Inc., 1997 annual report.

Pudgie's. Both Church's and Popeye's had similar strategies—to compete head-on with other "fried chicken" chains. Unlike KFC, neither chain offered rotisserie chicken, and both chains limited non-fried-chicken products. Chick-fil-A focused exclusively on pressure-cooked and char-grilled skinless chicken breast sandwiches, which it served to customers in sit-down restaurants located predominantly in shopping malls. As many malls added food courts, often consisting of up to 15 fast-food units competing side-by-side, shopping malls became less enthusiastic about allocating separate store space to food chains. Therefore, in order to complement its existing restaurant base in shopping malls, Chick-fil-A began to open smaller units in shopping mall food courts, hospitals, and colleges. It also opened freestanding units in selected locations.

Demographic Trends

A number of demographic and societal trends in the United States contributed to increased demand for food prepared away from home. Because of the high divorce rate and the fact that people married later in life, single-person households represented about 25 percent of all U.S. households in 1998, up from 17 percent in 1970. This increased the number of individuals choosing to eat out rather than eat at home. The number of married women working outside of the home also increased dramatically during the 25 years up to 1998. About 59 percent of all married women had careers. According to the Conference Board, 64 percent of all married households will be double-income families by 2000. About 80 percent of households headed by individuals between the ages of 25 and 44 (both married and unmarried) will be double-income. Greater numbers of working women increased family incomes. According to *Restaurants & Institutions* magazine, more than one-third of all households had incomes of at least $50,000 in 1996, and about 8 percent of all households had annual incomes over $100,000. The combination of higher numbers of dual-career families and rising incomes meant that fewer families had time to prepare food at home. According to Standard & Poor's *Industry Surveys,* Americans spent 55 percent of their food dollars at restaurants in 1995, up from 34 percent in 1970.

Fast-food restaurant chains responded to these demographic and societal changes by expanding their restaurant bases. However, by the early 1990s, the growth of traditional free-standing restaurants slowed as the U.S. market became saturated. The major exception was dinner houses, which continued to proliferate in response to Americans' passion for beef. Since 1990, the U.S. population has grown at an average annual rate of about 1 percent; the total reached 270 million people in 1997. Rising immigration in the 1990s dramatically altered the ethnic makeup of the U.S. population. According to the Bureau of the Census, Americans born outside of the United States made up 10 percent of the population in 1997. About 40 percent of that number were Hispanic, while 24 percent were Asian. Nearly 30 percent of Americans born outside of the United States arrived since 1990. As a result of these trends, restaurant chains expanded their menus to appeal to the different ethnic tastes of consumers, expanded into nontraditional locations such as department stores and airports, and made food more available through home delivery and take-out service.

Industry Consolidation and Mergers and Acquisitions

The slowdown in growth in the U.S. fast-food market intensified competition for market share among restaurant chains and led to consolidation, primarily through mergers and acquisitions, during the mid-1990s. Many restaurant chains found that market share could be increased quicker and more cheaply by acquiring an existing company rather than building new units. In addition, fixed costs could be spread across a larger number of restaurants. This raised operating margins and gave companies an opportunity to build market share by lowering prices. An expanded restaurant base also gave companies greater purchasing power over suppliers. In 1990, Grand Metropolitan, a British company, purchased Pillsbury for $5.7 billion. Included in the purchase was Pillsbury's Burger King chain. Grand Met (which in 1988 had purchased Wienerwald, a West German chicken chain, and the Spaghetti Factory, a Swiss chain) strengthened the franchise by upgrading existing restaurants and eliminating several levels of management in order to cut costs. This gave Burger King a long-needed boost in improving its position against McDonald's, its largest competitor.

Perhaps most important to KFC was Hardee's acquisition of 600 Roy Rogers restaurants from Marriott Corporation in 1990. Hardee's converted a large number of these restaurants to Hardee's units and introduced Roy Rogers fried chicken to its menu. By 1993, Hardee's had introduced fried chicken into most of its U.S. restaurants. Hardee's was unlikely to destroy the customer loyalty that KFC long enjoyed. However, it did cut into KFC's sales, because it was able to offer consumers a widened menu selection that appealed to a variety of family eating preferences. In 1997, Hardee's parent company, Imasco Ltd., sold Hardee's to CKE Restaurants, Inc. CKE owned Carl's Jr., Rally's Hamburgers, and Checker's Drive-In. Boston Chicken, Inc., acquired Harry's Farmers Market, an Atlanta grocer that sold prepared meals. The acquisition was designed to help Boston Chicken develop distribution beyond its Boston Market restaurants. AFC Enterprises, which operated Popeye's and Church's, acquired Chesapeake Bagel Bakery of McLean, Virginia, in order to diversify away from fried chicken and to strengthen its balance sheet.

The effect of these and other recent mergers and acquisitions on the industry was powerful. The top 10 restaurant companies controlled almost 60 percent of fast-food sales in the United States. The consolidation of a number of fast-food chains within larger, financially more powerful parent companies gave restaurant chains strong financial and managerial resources that could be used to compete against smaller chains in the industry.

International Quick-Service Market

Because of the aggressive pace of new restaurant construction in the United States during the 1970s and 1980s, opportunities to continue such expansion in the 1990s were limited. Restaurant chains that did build new restaurants found that the higher cost of purchasing prime locations resulted in immense pressure to increase annual sales per restaurant. Many restaurants began to expand into international markets as an alternative to continued domestic expansion. In contrast to the U.S. market, international markets offered large customer bases with comparatively little competition. However, only a few U.S. restaurant chains had defined aggressive strategies for penetrating international markets by 1998; key among these were McDonald's, KFC, Pizza Hut, and Taco Bell.

McDonald's operated the largest number of restaurants. In 1998 it operated 23,132 restaurants in 109 countries (10,409 restaurants were located outside the United States). In comparison, KFC, Pizza Hut, and Taco Bell together operated 29,712 restaurants in 79, 88, and 17 countries, respectively (9,126 restaurants were located outside the United States). Of these four chains, KFC operated the greatest percentage of its restaurants (50 percent) outside of the United States. McDonald's, Pizza Hut, and Taco Bell operated 45, 31, and 2 percent of their units outside the United States, respectively. KFC opened its first restaurant outside the United States in the late 1960s. By the time of its acquisition by PepsiCo in 1986, KFC was already operating restaurants in 55 countries. KFC's early expansion abroad, strong brand name, and managerial experience in international markets gave it a strong competitive advantage vis-à-vis other fast-food chains that were investing abroad for the first time.

Exhibit 4 shows *Hotels'* list of the world's 30 largest fast-food restaurant chains at year-end 1993 (*Hotels* discontinued reporting these data after 1994). Seventeen of these chains (ranked by number of units) were headquartered in the United States. There were a number of possible explanations for the relative scarcity of fast-food restaurant chains outside the United States. First, the United States represented the largest consumer market in the world, accounting for over one-fifth of the world's gross domestic product. Therefore, the United States was the strategic focus of the largest restaurant chains. Second, Americans were quick to accept the fast-food

■ Exhibit 4

The World's 30 Most Global Fast-Food Chains (year-end 1993, ranked by number of countries)

Rank	Franchise	Location	Units	Countries
1	Pizza Hut	Dallas, Texas	10,433	80
2	McDonald's	Oakbrook, Illinois	23,132	70
3	KFC	Louisville, Kentucky	9,033	68
4	Burger King	Miami, Florida	7,121	50
5	Baskin-Robbins	Glendale, California	3,557	49
6	Wendy's	Dublin, Ohio	4,168	38
7	Domino's Pizza	Ann Arbor, Michigan	5,238	36
8	TCBY	Little Rock, Arkansas	7,474	22
9	Dairy Queen	Minneapolis, Minnesota	5,471	21
10	Dunkin' Donuts	Randolph, Massachusetts	3,691	21
11	Taco Bell	Irvine, California	4,921	20
12	Arby's	Fort Lauderdale, Florida	2,670	18
13	Subway	Milford, Connecticut	8,477	15
14	Sizzler International	Los Angeles, California	681	14
15	Hardee's	Rocky Mount, North Carolina	4,060	12
16	Little Caesars	Detroit, Michigan	4,600	12
17	Popeye's Chicken	Atlanta, Georgia	813	12
18	Denny's	Spartanburg, South Carolina	1,515	10
19	A&W Restaurants	Livonia, Michigan	707	9
20	T.G.I. Friday's	Minneapolis, Minnesota	273	8
21	Orange Julius	Minneapolis, Minnesota	480	7
22	Church's Chicken	Atlanta, Georgia	1,079	6
23	Long John Silver's	Lexington, Kentucky	1,464	5
24	Carl's Jr.	Anaheim, California	649	4
25	Loterria	Tokyo, Japan	795	4
26	Mos Burger	Tokyo, Japan	1,263	4
27	Skylark	Tokyo, Japan	1,000	4
28	Jack in the Box	San Diego, California	1,172	3
29	Quick Restaurants	Berchem, Belgium	876	3
30	Taco Time	Eugene, Oregon	300	3

SOURCE: *Hotels,* May 1994; 1994 PepsiCo, Inc., annual report.

concept, whereas many other cultures had strong culinary traditions that were difficult to break down. Europeans, for example, had long preferred to frequent more mid-scale restaurants, where they spent several hours in a formal setting enjoying native dishes and beverages. While KFC was again building restaurants in Germany by the late 1980s, it previously failed to penetrate the German market, because Germans were not accustomed to take-out food or to ordering food over the counter. McDonald's had greater success penetrating the German market, because it made a number of changes in its menu and operating procedures, in order to better appeal to German culture. For example, German beer was served in all of McDonald's German restaurants. KFC had more success in Asia and Latin America, where chicken was a traditional dish.

Aside from cultural factors, international business carried risks not present in the U.S. market. Long distances between headquarters and foreign franchises often made it difficult to control the quality of individual restaurants, as well as to solve servicing and support problems. Transportation and other resource costs were higher than in the domestic market. In addition, time, cultural, and language differences increased communication and operational problems. Therefore, it was reasonable to expect U.S. restaurant chains to expand domestically as long as they achieved corporate profit and growth objectives. As the U.S. market became saturated and companies gained expertise in international markets, however, more companies could be expected to turn to profitable international markets as a means of expanding restaurant bases and increasing sales, profits, and market share.

■ Kentucky Fried Chicken Corporation (**www.kfc.com**)

KFC's worldwide sales, which included totals from both company-owned and franchised restaurants, grew to $8 billion in 1997. U.S. sales grew 2.6 percent over 1996 and accounted for about one-half of KFC's sales worldwide. KFC's U.S. share of the chicken segment fell 1.8 points, to 55.8 percent (see Exhibit 5). This marked the sixth consecutive year that KFC sustained a decline in market share. In 1998, KFC's market share had fallen by 16.3 points since 1988, when it held a 72.1 percent market share. Boston Market, which established its first restaurant in 1992, increased its market share from 0 to 16.7 in the same period. On the surface, it appeared as though Boston Market achieved its market share gain by taking customers away from KFC. However, KFC's sales growth had remained fairly stable and constant over the previous 10 years. Boston Market's success was largely a function of its appeal to consumers who did not regularly patronize KFC or other fried-chicken chains. By appealing to a market niche that was previously unsatisfied, Boston Market was able to expand the existing consumer base within the chicken segment of the fast-food industry.

■ Exhibit 5

Market Shares of Top U.S. Chicken Chains, 1988–1997

	KFC	Boston Market	Popeye's	Chick-fil-A	Church's	Total
1988	72.1%	0.0%	12.0%	5.8%	10.1%	100.0%
1989	70.8	0.0	12.0	6.2	11.0	100.0
1990	71.3	0.0	12.3	6.6	9.8	100.0
1991	72.7	0.0	11.4	7.0	8.9	100.0
1992	71.5	0.9	11.4	7.5	8.7	100.0
1993	68.7	3.0	11.4	8.0	8.9	100.0
1994	64.8	6.9	11.3	8.4	8.6	100.0
1995	60.5	12.3	10.8	8.2	8.2	100.0
1996	57.6	16.2	10.0	8.4	7.8	100.0
1997	55.8	16.7	10.1	9.4	8.0	100.0
Change 1988–1997	(16.3)%	+16.7%	(1.9)%	+3.6%	(2.1)%	

SOURCE: *Nation's Restaurant News.*

Refranchising Strategy

The relatively low growth rate in sales in KFC's domestic restaurants during the 1992–97 period was largely the result of KFC's decision in 1993 to begin selling company-owned restaurants to franchisees. When Colonel Sanders began to expand the Kentucky Fried Chicken system in the late 1950s, he established KFC as a system of independent franchisees. This was done in order to minimize his involvement in the operations of individual restaurants and to concentrate on the things he enjoyed the most—cooking, product development, and public relations. This resulted in a fiercely loyal and independent group of franchisees. As explained earlier, when PepsiCo acquired KFC in 1986, PepsiCo's strategy demanded increased involvement in decisions over franchise operations, menu offerings, restaurant management, finance, and marketing. KFC franchisees were fiercely opposed to increased control by the corporate parent. One method for PepsiCo to deal with this conflict was to expand through company-owned restaurants rather than through franchising. PepsiCo also used its strong cash flows to buy back unprofitable franchised restaurants, which could then be converted into company-owned restaurants. In 1986, company-owned restaurants made up 26 percent of KFC's U.S. restaurant base. By 1993, they made up about 40 percent (see Exhibit 6).

While company-owned restaurants were relatively easier to control compared to franchised outlets, they also required higher levels of investment. This meant that high levels of cash were diverted from PepsiCo's soft drink and snack food businesses into its restaurant businesses. However, the fast-food industry delivered lower returns than the soft drink and snack foods industries. Consequently, increased investment in KFC, Pizza Hut, and Taco Bell had a negative effect on PepsiCo's consolidated return on assets. By 1993, investors became concerned that PepsiCo's return on assets did not match returns delivered by Coca-Cola. In order to shore up

■ **Exhibit 6**
KFC Restaurant Count
(U.S. Restaurants),
1986–1997

	Company-Owned	Percent of Total	Franchised/Licensed	Percent of Total	Total
1986	1,246	26.4%	3,474	73.6%	4,720
1987	1,250	26.0	3,564	74.0	4,814
1988	1,262	25.8	3,637	74.2	4,899
1989	1,364	27.5	3,597	72.5	4,961
1990	1,389	27.7	3,617	72.3	5,006
1991	1,836	36.6	3,186	63.4	5,022
1992	1,960	38.8	3,095	61.2	5,055
1993	2,014	39.5	3,080	60.5	5,094
1994	2,005	39.2	3,110	60.8	5,115
1995	2,026	39.4	3,111	60.6	5,137
1996	1,932	37.8	3,176	62.2	5,108
1997	1,850	36.1	3,270	63.9	5,120
1986–93 compound annual growth rate					
	7.1%		(1.7%)		1.1%
1993–97 compounded annual growth rate					
	(2.1%)		1.5%		0.1%

SOURCE: Tricon Global Restaurants, Inc., 1997 annual report; PepsiCo, Inc., annual report, 1994,1995,1996,1997.

its return on assets, PepsiCo decided to reduce the number of company-owned restaurants by selling them back to franchisees. This strategy lowered overall company sales, but it also reduced the amount of cash tied up in fixed assets, provided PepsiCo with one-time cash flow benefits from initial fees charged to franchisees, and generated an annual stream of franchise royalties. Tricon Global continued this strategy after the spinoff in 1997.

Marketing Strategy

During the 1980s, consumers began to demand healthier foods, greater variety, and better service in a variety of nontraditional locations such as grocery stores, restaurants, airports, and outdoor events. This forced fast-food chains to expand menu offerings and to investigate nontraditional distribution channels and restaurant designs. Families also demanded greater value in the food they bought away from home. This increased pressure on fast-food chains to reduce prices and to lower operating costs in order to maintain profit margins.

Many of KFC's problems during the late 1980s surrounded its limited menu and inability to quickly bring new products to market. The popularity of its Original Recipe Chicken had allowed KFC to expand without significant competition from other chicken competitors through the 1980s. As a result, new-product introductions were never an important element of KFC's overall strategy. One of the most serious setbacks came in 1989 as KFC prepared to add a chicken sandwich to its menu. While KFC was still experimenting with its chicken sandwich, McDonald's test-marketed its McChicken sandwich in the Louisville area. Shortly thereafter, it rolled out the McChicken sandwich nationally. By beating KFC to the market, McDonald's was able to develop strong consumer awareness for its sandwich. This significantly increased KFC's cost of developing awareness for its own sandwich, which KFC introduced several months later. KFC eventually withdrew its sandwich because of low sales.

In 1991, KFC changed its logo in the United States from Kentucky Fried Chicken to KFC, in order to reduce its image as a fried chicken chain. (It continued to use the Kentucky Fried Chicken name internationally, however.) It then responded to consumer demands for greater variety by introducing several products that would serve as alternatives to its Original Recipe Chicken. These included Oriental Wings, Popcorn Chicken, and Honey BBQ Chicken. It also introduced a dessert menu that included a variety of pies and cookies. In 1993, it rolled out Rotisserie Chicken and began to promote its lunch and dinner buffet. The buffet, which included 30 items, was introduced into almost 1,600 KFC restaurants in 27 states by year-end. In 1998, KFC sold three types of chicken—Original Recipe and Extra Crispy (fried chicken) and Tender Roast (roasted chicken).

One of KFC's most aggressive strategies was the introduction of its Neighborhood Program. By mid-1993, almost 500 company-owned restaurants in New York, Chicago, Philadelphia, Washington, D.C., St. Louis, Los Angeles, Houston, and Dallas had been outfitted with special menu offerings to appeal exclusively to the black community. Menus were beefed up with side dishes such as greens, macaroni and cheese, peach cobbler, sweet-potato pie, and red beans and rice. In addition, restaurant employees wore African-inspired uniforms. The introduction of the Neighborhood Program increased sales by 5 to 30 percent in restaurants appealing directly to the black community. KFC followed by testing Hispanic-oriented restaurants in the Miami area, offering such side dishes as fried plantains, flan, and tres leches.

One of KFC's most significant problems in the U.S. market was that overcapacity made expansion of freestanding restaurants difficult. Fewer sites were available for new construction and those sites, because of their increased cost, were driving profit margins down. Therefore, KFC initiated a three-pronged distribution strategy. First, it focused on building smaller restaurants in nontraditional outlets such as airports, shopping malls, universities, and hospitals. Second, it experimented with home delivery, beginning in the Nashville and Albuquerque markets in 1994. By 1998, home delivery was offered in 365 of KFC's U.S. restaurants. Other nontraditional distribution outlets being tested included units offering drive-thru and carry-out service only, snack shops in cafeterias, scaled-down outlets for supermarkets, and mobile units that could be transported to outdoor concerts and fairs.

A third focus of KFC's distribution strategy was restaurant co-branding, primarily with its sister chain, Taco Bell. By 1997, 349 KFC restaurants had added Taco Bell items to their menus and displayed both the KFC and Taco Bell logos outside their restaurants. Co-branding gave KFC the opportunity to expand its business dayparts. While about two-thirds of KFC's business was dinner, Taco Bell's primary business occurred at lunch. By combining the two concepts in the same unit, sales at individual restaurants could be increased significantly. KFC believed that there were opportunities to sell the Taco Bell concept in over 3,900 of its U.S. restaurants.

Operating Efficiencies

As pressure continued to build from price-conscious consumers, restaurant chains searched for ways to reduce overhead and other operating costs, in order to improve profit margins. In 1989, KFC reorganized its U.S. operations in order to eliminate overhead costs and to increase efficiency. Included in this reorganization was a revision of KFC's crew training programs and operating standards. A renewed emphasis was placed on clean restaurants, fast and friendly service, and product quality. In 1992, KFC reorganized its middle-management ranks, eliminating 250 of the 1,500 management positions at KFC's corporate headquarters. More responsibility was assigned to restaurant franchisees and marketing managers, and pay was more closely aligned with customer service and restaurant performance. In 1997, Tricon Global signed a five-year agreement with PepsiCo Food Systems (which was later sold by PepsiCo to AmeriServe Food Distributors) to distribute food and supplies to Tricon's 29,712 KFC, Pizza Hut, and Taco Bell units. This provided KFC with significant opportunities to benefit from economies of scale in distribution.

■ International Operations

Much of the early success of the top 10 fast-food chains was the result of aggressive building strategies. Chains were able to discourage competition by building in low-population areas that could only support a single fast-food chain. McDonald's was particularly successful at quickly expanding into small towns across the United States, thereby preempting other fast-food chains. It was equally important to beat a competitor into more densely populated areas where location was of prime importance. KFC's early entry into international markets placed it in a strong position to benefit from international expansion as the U.S. market became saturated. In 1997, 50 percent of KFC's restaurants were located outside of the United States. While 364 new restaurants were opened outside the United States in 1997, only 12 new restaurants were added to the U.S. system. Most of KFC's international expansion was through franchises, though some restaurants were licensed to operators or jointly operated with a local partner. Expansion through franchising was an important strategy for penetrating international markets, because franchises were owned and operated by local entrepreneurs who understood local language, culture, and customs, as well as local law, financial markets, and marketing characteristics. Franchising was particularly important for expansion into smaller countries such as the Dominican Republic, Grenada, Bermuda, and Suriname, which could only support a single restaurant. Costs of operating company-owned restaurants in these smaller markets were prohibitively high. Of the 5,117 KFC restaurants located outside the United States in 1997, 68 percent were franchised, while 22 percent were company-owned and 10 percent were licensed restaurants or joint ventures.

In larger markets such as Japan, China, and Mexico, there was a stronger emphasis on building company-owned restaurants. By coordinating purchasing, recruiting and training, financing, and advertising, KFC could spread fixed costs over a large number of restaurants and negotiate lower prices on products and services. KFC was also better able to control product and service quality. In order to take advantage of economies of scale, Tricon Global Restaurants managed all of the international units of its KFC, Pizza Hut, and Taco Bell chains through its Tricon International division, located in Dallas, Texas. This enabled Tricon Global Restaurants to leverage its strong advertising expertise, international experience, and restaurant management experience across all three chains.

Latin American Strategy

KFC's primary market presence in Latin America during the 1980s was in Mexico, Puerto Rico, and the Caribbean. KFC established subsidiaries in Mexico and Puerto Rico, from which it coordinated the construction and operation of company-owned restaurants. A third subsidiary in Venezuela was closed because of its high fixed costs. Franchises were used to penetrate countries in the Caribbean whose market size prevented KFC from profitably operating company restaurants. In Mexico, KFC, like most other fast-food chains there, relied exclusively on the operation of company-owned restaurants through 1989. While franchising was popular in the United States, it was virtually unknown in Mexico until 1990, mainly because of the absence of a law protecting patents, information, and technology transferred to the Mexican franchise. In addition, royalties were limited.

In 1990, Mexico enacted a new law that provided for the protection of technology transferred into the country. Under the new legislation, the franchisor and franchisee were free to set their own terms and to collect royalties. Royalties were taxed at 15 percent on technology assistance and know-how, and at 35 percent for other royalty categories. The advent of the new franchise law resulted in an explosion of franchises in fast-food, services, hotels, and retail outlets. In 1992, franchises had an estimated $750 million in sales in over 1,200 outlets throughout Mexico. Prior to passage of Mexico's franchise law, KFC limited its Mexican operations primarily to Mexico City, Guadalajara, and Monterrey, in order to better coordinate operations and minimize costs of distribution to individual restaurants. The new franchise law gave KFC and other fast-food chains the opportunity to expand their restaurant bases into rural regions of Mexico, where responsibility for management could be handled by local franchisees.

After 1990, KFC altered its Latin American strategy in a number of ways. First, it opened 29 franchises in Mexico to complement its company-owned restaurant base. It then expanded its company-owned restaurants into the Virgin Islands and reestablished a subsidiary in Venezuela. Third, it expanded its franchise operations into South America. In 1990 a franchise was opened in Chile, and in 1993 one was opened in Brazil. Franchises were subsequently established in Colombia, Ecuador, Panama, and Peru, among other South American countries. A fourth subsidiary was established in Brazil, in order to develop company-owned restaurants. Brazil was Latin America's largest economy and McDonald's primary Latin American investment location. By June 1998, KFC operated 438 restaurants in 32 Latin American countries. By comparison, McDonald's operated 1,091 restaurants in 28 countries in Latin America.

Exhibit 7 shows the number of KFC and McDonald's operations in Latin America. KFC's early entry into Latin America during the 1970s gave it a leadership position in Mexico and the Caribbean. It had also gained an edge in Ecuador and Peru, countries where McDonald's had not yet developed a strong presence. McDonald's focused its Latin American investment in Brazil, Argentina, and Uruguay, countries where KFC had little or no presence. McDonald's was also strong in Venezuela. Both KFC and McDonald's were strong in Chile, Colombia, Panama, and Puerto Rico.

■ **Exhibit 7**   Latin America Restaurant Count—KFC and McDonald's (as of December 31, 1997)

	KFC Company Restaurants	KFC Franchised Restaurants	KFC Total Restaurants	McDonald's
Argentina	—	—	—	131
Bahamas	—	10	10	3
Barbados	—	7	7	—
Brazil	6	2	8	480
Chile	—	29	29	27
Colombia	—	19	19	18
Costa Rica	—	5	5	19
Ecuador	—	18	18	2
Jamaica	—	17	17	7
Mexico	128	29	157	131
Panama	—	21	21	20
Peru	—	17	17	5
Puerto Rico and Virgin Islands	67	—	67	115
Trinidad and Tobago	—	27	27	3
Uruguay	—	—	—	18
Venezuela	6	—	6	53
Other	—	30	30	59
Total	207	231	438	1,091

SOURCE: Tricon Global Restaurants, Inc.; McDonald's, 1997 annual report.

Economic Environment and the Mexican Market

Mexico was KFC's strongest market in Latin America. While McDonald's had aggressively established restaurants in Mexico since 1990, KFC retained the leading market share. Because of its proximity to the United States, Mexico was an attractive location for U.S. trade and investment. Mexico's population of 98 million people was approximately one-third that of the United States and represented a large market for U.S. companies. In comparison, Canada's population of 30.3 million people was only one-third as large as Mexico's. Mexico's proximity to the United States meant that transportation costs between the two were significantly lower than those between the United States and Europe or Asia. This increased the competitiveness of U.S. goods in comparison to European and Asian goods, which had to be transported to Mexico across the Atlantic or Pacific Ocean at substantial cost. The United States was, in fact, Mexico's largest trading partner. Over 75 percent of Mexico's imports came from the United States, while 84 percent of its exports went to the United States (see Exhibit 8). Many U.S. firms invested in Mexico in order to take advantage of lower wage rates, which meant that goods produced in Mexico could be shipped back into the United States or to third markets and sold at lower cost.

While the U.S. market was critically important to Mexico, Mexico still represented a small percentage of overall U.S. trade and investment. Since the early 1900s, the portion of U.S. exports to Latin America had declined. Instead, U.S. exports to Canada and Asia, where economic growth outpaced growth in Mexico, increased more quickly. Canada was the largest importer of U.S. goods. Japan was the largest exporter of goods to the United States, with Canada a close second. U.S. investment in Mexico was also small, mainly because of past government restrictions on foreign investment. Most U.S. foreign investment was in Europe, Canada, and Asia.

The lack of U.S. investment in and trade with Mexico during this century was mainly the result of Mexico's long history of restricting trade and foreign direct investment. The Institutional Revolutionary Party (PRI), which came to power in Mexico during the 1930s, had historically pursued protectionist economic policies in order to shield Mexico's economy from foreign competition. Many industries

■ **Exhibit 8**
Mexico's Major Trading Partners, 1992, 1994, and 1996

	1992		1994		1996	
	Exports	**Imports**	**Exports**	**Imports**	**Exports**	**Imports**
U.S.	81.1%	71.3%	85.3%	71.8%	84.0%	75.6%
Japan	1.7	4.9	1.6	4.8	1.4	4.4
Germany	1.1	4.0	0.6	3.9	0.7	3.5
Canada	2.2	1.7	2.4	2.0	1.2	1.9
Italy	0.3	1.6	0.1	1.3	1.2	1.1
Brazil	0.9	1.8	0.6	1.5	0.9	0.8
Spain	2.7	1.4	1.4	1.7	1.0	0.7
Other	10.0	13.3	8.0	13.0	9.6	12.0
Total	100.0%	100.0%	100.0%	100.0%	100.0%	100.0%
Value (in millions)	$46,196	$62,129	$60,882	$79,346	$95,991	$89,464

SOURCE: International Monetary Fund, Direction of Trade Statistics Yearbook, 1997.

were government-owned or controlled, and many Mexican companies focused on producing goods for the domestic market without much attention to building export markets. High tariffs and other trade barriers restricted imports into Mexico, and the Mexican government prohibited or heavily restricted foreign ownership of assets in Mexico.

Additionally, a dictatorial and entrenched government bureaucracy, corrupt labor unions, and a long tradition of anti-Americanism among many government officials and intellectuals reduced the motivation of U.S. firms to invest in Mexico. The nationalization of Mexico's banks in 1982 led to higher real interest rates and lower investor confidence. Afterward, the Mexican government battled high inflation, labor unrest, and lost consumer purchasing power. However, investor confidence in Mexico improved after 1988, when Carlos Salinas de Gortari was elected president. Following his election, Salinas embarked on an ambitious restructuring of the Mexican economy. He initiated policies to strengthen the free-market components of the economy, lowered top marginal tax rates to 36 percent (down from 60 percent in 1986), and eliminated many restrictions on foreign investment. Foreign firms can now buy up to 100 percent of the equity in many Mexican firms, instead of the previous limit of 49 percent.

Privatization

The privatization of government-owned companies came to symbolize the restructuring of Mexico's economy. In 1990, legislation was passed to privatize all government-run banks. By the end of 1992, over 800 of some 1,200 government-owned companies had been sold, including Mexicana and AeroMexico, the two largest airline companies in Mexico, as well as Mexico's 18 major banks. However, more than 350 companies remained under government ownership. These represented a significant portion of the assets owned by the state at the start of 1988. Therefore, the sale of government-owned companies, in terms of asset value, was moderate. A large number of the remaining government-owned assets were controlled by government-run companies in certain strategic industries such as steel, electricity, and petroleum. These industries had long been protected by government ownership. As a result, additional privatization of government-owned enterprises until 1993 was limited. However, in 1993, when President Salinas opened up the electricity sector to independent power producers, Petroleos Mexicanos (Pemex), the state-run petrochemical monopoly, initiated a program to sell off many of its nonstrategic assets to private and foreign buyers.

North American Free Trade Agreement (NAFTA)

Prior to 1989, Mexico levied high tariffs on most imported goods. In addition, many other goods were subjected to quotas, licensing requirements, and other nontariff trade barriers. In 1986, Mexico joined the General Agreement on Tariffs and Trade (GATT), a world trade organization designed to eliminate barriers to trade among member nations. As a member of GATT, Mexico was obligated to apply its system of tariffs to all member nations equally and therefore dropped tariff rates on a variety of imported goods. In addition, import license requirements were dropped for all but 300 imported items. During President Salinas's administration, tariffs were reduced from an average of 100 percent on most items to an average of 11 percent.

On January 1, 1994, the North American Free Trade Agreement (NAFTA) went into effect. The passage of NAFTA, which included Canada, the United States, and

Mexico, created a trading bloc with a larger population and gross domestic product than those of the European Union. All tariffs on goods traded among the three countries were scheduled to be phased out. NAFTA was expected to be particularly beneficial for Mexican exporters, because reduced tariffs made their goods more competitive in the United States compared to goods exported to the United States from other countries. In 1995, one year after NAFTA went into effect, Mexico posted its first balance of trade surplus in six years. Part of this surplus was attributed to reduced tariffs resulting from the NAFTA agreement. However, the peso crisis of 1995, which lowered the value of the peso against the dollar, increased the price of goods imported into Mexico and lowered the price of Mexican products exported to the United States. Therefore, it was still too early to assess the full effects of NAFTA.

Foreign Exchange and the Mexican Peso Crisis of 1995

Between 1982 and 1991 in Mexico, a two-tiered exchange rate system was in force that consisted of a controlled rate and a free-market rate. The controlled rate was used for imports, foreign debt payments, and conversion of export proceeds. An estimated 70 percent of all foreign transactions were covered by the controlled rate. The free market rate was used for other transactions. In 1989, President Salinas instituted a policy of allowing the peso to depreciate against the dollar by one peso per day. The result was a grossly overvalued peso. This lowered the price of imports and led to an increase in imports of over 23 percent in 1989. At the same time, Mexican exports became less competitive on world markets.

In 1991, the controlled rate was abolished and replaced with an official free rate. In order to limit the range of fluctuations in the value of the peso, the government fixed the rate at which it would buy or sell pesos. A floor (the maximum price at which pesos could be purchased) was established at Ps 3,056.20 and remained fixed. A ceiling (the maximum price at which the peso could be sold) was established at Ps 3,056.40 and allowed to move upward by Ps 0.20 per day. This was later revised to Ps 0.40 per day. In 1993, a new currency, called the new peso, was issued with three fewer zeros. The new currency was designed to simplify transactions and to reduce the cost of printing currency.

When Ernesto Zedillo became Mexico's president in December 1994, one of his objectives was to continue the stability of prices, wages, and exchange rates achieved by Salinas during his five-year tenure as president. However, Salinas had achieved stability largely on the basis of price, wage, and foreign exchange controls. While giving the appearance of stability, an overvalued peso continued to encourage imports, which exacerbated Mexico's balance of trade deficit. Mexico's government continued to use foreign reserves to finance its balance of trade deficits. According to the Banco de Mexico, foreign currency reserves fell from $24 billion in January 1994 to $5.5 billion in January 1995. Anticipating a devaluation of the peso, investors began to move capital into U.S. dollar investments. In order to relieve pressure on the peso, Zedillo announced on December 19, 1994, that the peso would be allowed to depreciate by an additional 15 percent per year against the dollar compared to the maximum allowable depreciation of 4 percent per year established during the Salinas administration. Within two days, continued pressure on the peso forced Zedillo to allow the peso to float freely against the dollar. By mid-January 1995, the peso had lost 35 percent of its value against the dollar and the Mexican stock market plunged 20 percent. By November 1995, the peso had depreciated from 3.1 pesos per dollar to 7.3 pesos per dollar.

	Annual Percentage Change (%)				
	1993	**1994**	**1995**	**1996**	**1997**
GDP growth					
Canada	3.3%	4.8%	5.5%	4.1%	n.a.
United States	4.9	5.8	4.8	5.1	5.9%
Mexico	21.4	13.3	29.4	38.2	n.a.
Real GDP growth					
Canada	2.2%	4.1%	2.3%	1.2%	n.a.
United States	2.2	3.5	2.0	2.8	3.8
Mexico	2.0	4.5	(6.2)	5.1	n.a.
Inflation rate					
Canada	1.9%	0.2%	2.2%	1.5%	1.6%
United States	3.0	2.5	2.8	2.9	2.4
Mexico	9.7	6.9	35.0	34.4	20.6
Depreciation (appreciation) against U.S. dollar					
Canada (C$)	4.2%	6.0%	(2.7)%	0.3%	4.3%
Mexico (NP)	(0.3)	71.4	43.5	2.7	3.6

SOURCE: International Monetary Fund, *International Financial Statistics,* 1998.

The continued devaluation of the peso resulted in higher import prices, higher inflation, destabilization within the stock market, and higher interest rates. (See Exhibit 9 for selected economic data for Canada, the United States and Mexico.) Mexico struggled to pay its dollar-based debts. In order to thwart a possible default by Mexico, the U.S. government, International Monetary Fund, and World Bank pledged $24.9 billion in emergency loans. Zedillo then announced an emergency economic package, called the *pacto,* which reduced government spending, increased sales of government-run businesses, and placed a freeze on wage increases.

Labor Problems

One of KFC's primary concerns in Mexico was the stability of labor markets. Labor was relatively plentiful and wages were low. However, much of the workforce was relatively unskilled. KFC benefitted from lower labor costs, but labor unrest, low job retention, high absenteeism, and poor punctuality were significant problems. Absenteeism and poor punctuality were partially cultural. However, problems with worker retention and labor unrest were also the result of workers' frustration over the loss of their purchasing power due to inflation and government controls on wage increases. Absenteeism remained high, at approximately 8 to 14 percent of the labor force, though it was declining because of job security fears. Turnover continued to be a problem and ran at between 5 and 12 percent per month. This made employee screening and internal training important issues for firms investing in Mexico.

Higher inflation and the government's freeze on wage increases led to a dramatic decline in disposable income after 1994. Further, a slowdown in business activity, brought about by higher interest rates and lower government spending, led many businesses to lay off workers. By the end of 1995, an estimated 1 million jobs had been lost as a result of the economic crisis sparked by the peso devaluation. Industry groups within Mexico called for new labor laws giving them more freedom to hire and fire employees and increased flexibility to hire part-time rather than full-time workers.

■ Risks and Opportunities

The peso crisis of 1995 and resulting recession in Mexico left KFC managers with a great deal of uncertainty regarding Mexico's economic and political future. KFC had benefitted from economic stability between 1988 and 1994. Inflation was brought down, the peso was relatively stable, labor relations were relatively calm, and Mexico's new franchise law had enabled KFC to expand into rural areas using franchises rather than company-owned restaurants. By the end of 1995, KFC had built 29 franchises in Mexico. The foreign exchange crisis of 1995 had severe implications for U.S. firms operating in Mexico. The devaluation of the peso resulted in higher inflation and capital flight out of Mexico. Capital flight reduced the supply of investment funds and led to higher interest rates. In order to reduce inflation, Mexico's government instituted an austerity program that resulted in lower disposable income, higher unemployment, and lower demand for products and services.

Another problem was Mexico's failure to reduce restrictions on U.S. and Canadian investment in a timely fashion. Many U.S. firms had trouble getting approvals for new ventures from the Mexican government. A good example was United Parcel Service (UPS), which sought government approval to use large trucks for deliveries in Mexico. Approvals were delayed, forcing UPS to use smaller trucks and putting the company at a competitive disadvantage vis-à-vis Mexican companies. In many cases, UPS was forced to subcontract delivery work to Mexican companies that were allowed to use larger, more cost-efficient trucks. Other U.S. companies, such as Bell Atlantic and TRW, faced similar problems. TRW, which signed a joint venture agreement with a Mexican partner, had to wait 15 months longer than anticipated before the Mexican government released rules on how it could receive credit data from banks. TRW claimed that the Mexican government slowed the approval process in order to placate several large Mexican banks.

A final area of concern for KFC was increased political turmoil in Mexico during the last several years. On January 1, 1994, the day NAFTA went into effect, rebels (descendants of the Mayans) rioted in the southern Mexican province of Chiapas on the Guatemalan border. After four days of fighting, Mexican troops had driven the rebels out of several occupied towns. Around 150 people—mostly rebels—were killed. The uprising symbolized many of the fears of the poor in Mexico. While President Salinas's economic programs had increased economic growth and wealth in Mexico, many of Mexico's poorest felt that they had not benefited. Many of Mexico's farmers, faced with lower tariffs on imported agricultural goods from the United States, felt that they might be driven out of business because of lower priced imports. Social unrest among Mexico's Indians, farmers, and the poor could potentially unravel much of the economic success achieved in Mexico during the last five years.

Further, President Salinas's hand-picked successor for president was assassinated in early 1994 while campaigning in Tijuana. The assassin was a 23-year-old mechanic and migrant worker believed to be affiliated with a dissident group upset with the PRI's economic reforms. The possible existence of a dissident group raised fears of political violence in the future. The PRI quickly named Ernesto Zedillo, a 42-year-old economist with little political experience, as their new presidential candidate. Zedillo was elected president in December 1994. Political unrest was not limited to Mexican officials and companies. In October 1994, between 30 and 40 masked men attacked a McDonald's restaurant in the tourist section of Mexico City to show their opposition to California's Proposition 187, which would have curtailed benefits to illegal aliens (primarily from Mexico). The men threw cash registers to the floor, cracked them open, smashed windows, overturned tables, and spray-painted the walls with slogans such as "No to Fascism" and "Yankee Go Home."

KFC thus faced a variety of issues in Mexico and Latin America in 1998. KFC halted openings of franchised restaurants in Mexico; all restaurants opened there since 1995 were company-owned. KFC began aggressively building restaurants in South America, which had remained largely unpenetrated by KFC through 1995. Of greatest importance was Brazil, where McDonald's had already established a strong position. Brazil was Latin America's largest economy and a mostly untapped market for KFC. The danger in KFC's ignoring Mexico was that a conservative investment strategy could jeopardize its lead over McDonald's in a large market where KFC had long enjoyed enormous popularity.

Briggs & Stratton Corporation: Competing in the Outdoor Power Equipment Industry

Richard C. Hoffman
Salisbury State University

John E. Gamble
Auburn University–Montgomery

Edwin W. Arnold
Auburn University–Montgomery

Since introducing its first small aluminum engine in 1953, Briggs & Stratton had consistently led the industry in manufacturing small gasoline engines for outdoor power equipment such as lawn mowers, rotary tillers, snow throwers, and lawn vacuums (see Exhibit 1). During the 1980s, Briggs & Stratton, like many other U.S. manufacturing companies, found itself confronted with a new group of rivals—Japanese companies with the strategic intent of capturing the U.S. market. In 1994, Briggs & Stratton president and chief executive officer Frederick P. Stratton observed:

> We began the 1980s as the world's leading producer of small engines. We began the 1990s as the world's leading producer. These two statements belie the intervening difficulties. . . . Responding to reduced demand and a weakening yen, the four Japanese motorcycle manufacturers threw resources into an effort to conquer the small engine market. We recognized that we had to do a lot of things differently if we were to maintain our leadership position in the face of this threat. The combination of a stronger yen and the things we did stemmed the tide. The Japanese thrust has been parried, and the experience made us in many ways a stronger company.

To maintain its leadership position, the company broadened its product line, reduced costs, improved quality, and invested in new plants and processes. One of the outcomes combating the Japanese invasion was a clearer vision of the firm's strategy in a period characterized by strong competitive rivalry. As Stratton described it:

> We reaffirmed our traditional strategic direction, agreeing to commit major resources only to our traditional mass market core business and to serve other market segments with limited resources or in partnerships with other companies with appropriate capabilities.

■ **Exhibit 1**
Outdoor Power
Equipment Products

Lawn mowers	Lawn edger-trimmers
Garden tractors	Shredder-grinders
Rotary tillers	Lawn vacuums
Snow throwers	Leaf blowers
Flexible line trimmers	

SOURCE: *Profile of the Outdoor Power Equipment Industry,* 1993.

This case was prepared by Richard C. Hoffman, Salisbury State University; John E. Gamble, Auburn University–Montgomery; and Edwin W. Arnold, Auburn University–Montgomery.

■ Company History

Briggs & Stratton (B&S) began conducting business in Milwaukee in 1908. The company's first product was a six-cylinder, two-cycle engine that Stephen F. Briggs had developed during his engineering courses at South Dakota State College. After he graduated in 1907, he was eager to produce his engine and enter the rapidly expanding automobile industry. Through a mutual friend, Stephen F. Briggs, the inventor, met Harold M. Stratton, the successful businessman. With that introduction, the Briggs & Stratton Corporation was born. Unfortunately, the engine cost too much to produce, as did their second product, an automobile called the Superior. The partners were out of money and out of the automobile assembly business.

However, in 1909 Briggs filed a patent for a gas engine igniter to replace the existing magneto ignition system in automobiles. This product set the stage for the company to later become the largest U.S. producer of switch and lock apparatus used in automobiles. By 1920, the company was widely recognized as a major producer of ignition switches for cars and trucks.

In 1920, Briggs & Stratton acquired the patents and manufacturing rights to the Smith motor wheel and the Flyer, a buckboardlike motor vehicle powered by the Smith motor wheel. The Smith motor wheel was a wheel with a small engine attached for propulsion. It could also be used on bicycles. The price for the two-passenger Flyer was $150, but it still could not compete with Ford's Model T. The Model T was higher priced but also more technologically advanced.

As sales of the motor wheel slowed, the company found that a stationary version, the model PB, provided a good power source for washing machines, garden tractors, and lawn mowers. By 1936, engines were being mass produced at the rate of 120 units per hour. During World War II, Briggs & Stratton produced bomb fuses and aircraft ignitions.

After the war, Briggs & Stratton set out to capture a larger share of the growing lawn and garden equipment market. Recognizing the lawn mower market as a potential growth area, the company set out to make a lighter weight, low-cost engine. Briggs developed and introduced the aluminum alloy engine in 1953, which achieved a 40 percent reduction for both weight and price. The aluminum engine was a huge success, with initial demand outstripping supply. In response to demand, the company opened a new engine plant in Wauwatosa, Wisconsin, on an 85-acre site.

In November 1975, some 56 years after the motor wheel opened the way into the small engine business, the 100 millionth Briggs & Stratton engine came off the assembly line. In 1990, revenues reached $1 billion for the first time, and in 1995, B&S ranked 717th in sales on the Fortune 1000 list of the largest U.S. industrial and service corporations. Over 90 percent of the company's revenues came from the sale of small gasoline-powered engines; the remainder came from selling ignition switches and locks for motor vehicles to the auto manufacturers. Exhibits 2–5 present the company's recent financial performance.

■ Outdoor Power Equipment Industry

In 1995, the outdoor power equipment (OPE) industry consisted of a diverse group of various-sized manufacturers of finished goods and components. The $7.5 billion industry had experienced considerable attrition and consolidation since the mid-1970s. The number of lawn mower manufacturers had declined from around 80

■ **Exhibit 2**   Briggs & Stratton Corporation Income Statements, 1992–1994

	1994	1993	1992
Net sales	$1,285,517,000	$1,139,462,000	$1,041,828,000
Cost of goods sold	1,018,977,000	926,861,000	867,780,000
Gross profit on sales	266,540,000	212,601,000	174,048,000
Engineering, selling, general, and administrative expenses	94,795,000	83,176,000	78,736,000
Income from operations	171,745,000	129,425,000	95,312,000
Interest expense	(8,997,000)	(11,283,000)	(11,246,000)
Other income (expense), net	6,973,000	(3,737,000)	(3,863,000)
Income before provision for income taxes	169,721,000	114,405,000	80,203,000
Provision for income taxes	67,240,000	44,060,000	28,700,000
Net income before cumulative effect of accounting changes	102,481,000	70,345,000	51,503,000
Cumulative effect of accounting changes for:			
Postretirement health care, net of income taxes of $25,722,000	(40,232,000)	—	—
Postemployment benefits, net of income taxes of $430,000	(672,000)	—	—
Deferred income taxes	8,346,000	—	—
	(32,558,000)	—	—
Net income	$ 69,923,000	$ 70,345,000	$ 51,503,000

SOURCE: 1994 company annual report.

competitors in the mid-1970s to 25 major manufacturers of walk-behind lawn mowers and 15 manufacturers of garden tractors in 1995. The four largest companies accounted for nearly 70 percent of total outdoor power equipment production. The surviving OPE manufacturers were faced with consumers demanding value— higher quality products with greater horsepower at a relatively low price.

Outdoor power equipment manufacturing was not vertically integrated to any significant extent. Industry members manufactured components or assembled finished goods. Component manufacturers supplied one or more of the parts listed in Exhibit 6 to the OPE finished goods manufacturers. Most OPE manufacturers fabricated the metal housings and frames of the lawn mowers, garden tractors, snow throwers, and other outdoor power equipment and then assembled their products from the various parts supplied by the components manufacturers. The cost of components accounted for 47 percent of the value of all finished OPE shipments. Honda and Toro were the only power equipment manufacturers that had vertically integrated backward into components. Honda manufactured engines, housings, frames, and components at its Sweponsville, North Carolina, lawn mower assembly plant. Toro's vertical integration resulted from its 1989 acquisition of Lawn-Boy from Outdoor Marine Corporation. Most Lawn-Boy models were equipped with the brand's own two-cycle engines. Exhibit 7 presents industry-average costs and profit margins for outdoor power equipment manufacturers.

Distribution in the industry had undergone a major shift during the late 1980s and early 1990s. Traditionally, approximately 50 percent of outdoor power equipment produced by manufacturers was shipped to independent wholesalers who in

■ **Exhibit 3**   Briggs & Stratton Corporation Consolidated Balance Sheets, 1993–1994

	July 3, 1994	June 27, 1993
Assets		
Current assets:		
Cash and cash equivalents	$221,101,000	$ 39,501,000
Short-term investments	—	70,422,000
Receivables, less reserves of $1,678,000 and $754,000, respectively	122,597,000	124,981,000
Inventories:		
Finished products and parts	55,847,000	46,061,000
Work in process	27,078,000	25,320,000
Raw materials	2,745,000	2,684,000
Total inventories	85,670,000	74,065,000
Future income tax benefits	32,868,000	27,457,000
Prepaid expenses	20,548,000	16,537,000
Total current assets	482,784,000	352,963,000
Prepaid pension cost	8,681,000	7,602,000
Plant and equipment:		
Land and land improvements	10,279,000	10,991,000
Buildings	111,966,000	114,066,000
Machinery and equipment	530,701,000	516,565,000
Construction in progress	16,647,000	16,498,000
Less: Accumulated depreciation and unamortized investment tax credit	383,703,000	362,578,000
Total plant and equipment, net	285,890,000	295,542,000
Total assets	$777,355,000	$656,107,000
Liabilities and Shareholders' Investment		
Current liabilities:		
Accounts payable	$ 56,364,000	$ 39,357,000
Foreign loans	21,323,000	15,927,000
Accrued liabilities:		
Wages and salaries	48,545,000	34,668,000
Warranty	29,800,000	28,318,000
Taxes, other than income taxes	6,772,000	6,003,000
Other	34,837,000	23,079,000
Total accrued liabilities	119,954,000	92,068,000
Federal and state income taxes	9,103,000	10,592,000
Total current liabilities	206,744,000	157,944,000
Deferred income taxes	12,317,000	49,900,000
Accrued employee benefits	15,423,000	13,305,000
Accrued postretirement health care obligation	64,079,000	—
Long-term debt	75,000,000	75,000,000
Shareholders' investment:		
Common stock—authorized 30 million shares $0.01 par value, issued and outstanding 14,463,500 shares in 1994 and 1993	145,000	145,000
Additional paid-in capital	42,358,000	42,883,000
Retained earnings	362,136,000	318,247,000
Cumulative translation adjustments	(847,000)	(1,317,000)
Total shareholders' investment	403,792,000	359,958,000
Total liabilities and shareholders' investment	$777,355,000	$656,107,000

SOURCE: 1994 company annual report.

■ **Exhibit 4** Briggs & Stratton's Performance by Business Segment, 1990–1994 (in thousands of dollars)

| | **Year Ended June 30** | | | | |
	1994	**1993**	**1992**	**1991**	**1990**
Sales					
Engines and parts	$1,197,744	$1,066,053	$ 967,802	$885,930	$ 931,638
Locks	87,773	73,409	74,026	64,817	71,219
	$1,285,517	$1,139,462	$1,041,828	$950,747	$1,022,857
Operating income					
Engines and parts	$ 158,900	$ 128,079	$ 90,781	$ 61,081	$ 61,246
Locks	12,845	1,346	4,531	2,335	5,035
	$ 171,745	$ 129,425	$ 95,312	$ 63,416	$ 66,281
Assets					
Engines and parts	$ 467,561	$ 458,369	$ 455,691	$432,345	$ 456,927
Locks	46,832	49,557	45,713	46,994	39,698
Unallocated	262,962	148,181	112,449	77,452	38,415
	$777,355	$ 656,107	$ 613,853	$556,791	$ 535,040
Depreciation expense					
Engines and parts	$ 40,605	$ 44,895	$ 38,808	$ 34,521	$ 38,080
Locks	2,345	2,327	2,305	1,926	1,809
	$ 42,950	$ 47,222	$ 41,113	$ 36,447	$ 39,889
Expenditures for plant and equipment					
Engines and parts	$ 37,398	$ 34,251	$ 37,035	$ 28,760	$ 35,010
Locks	3,406	3,859	3,189	3,276	2,787
	$ 40,804	$ 38,110	$ 40,224	$ 32,036	$ 37,797

SOURCE: 1994 company annual report.

turn distributed it to general merchandisers, home centers, lawn and garden stores, and other OPE retailers. By 1992, only 20 percent of OPE products on their way to market passed through wholesalers, 18 percent were handled by exporters, and the balance were shipped factory-direct to the retailer. At the retail level, home centers (Home Depot, Lowe's), national merchandisers such as Sears, and discounters (Wal-Mart, Kmart, and Target) were gaining a larger share of the OPE market. The five largest retailers of OPE products accounted for nearly half of all walk-behind and riding mowers sold in the United States. Outdoor power equipment market share by retail channel is presented in Exhibit 8.

Retail sales of outdoor power equipment tended to vary with the ups and downs in housing starts and the general condition of the national economy. During the late 1970s, industry sales had grown rapidly, driven by the growth in new housing starts and the U.S. economy, allowing many components producers and OPE makers to prosper. Shipments of walk-behind rotary lawn mowers approached 6 million units in 1979 and then tumbled to 4.4 million in 1983 as a result of recessionary effects on the U.S. economy. As the economy improved, sales of walk-behind mowers improved to 5 million units throughout the late 1980s. Exhibit 9 provides shipments of outdoor power equipment by category for recent years and shipment forecasts for 1995 and 1996.

Exhibit 5 Briggs & Stratton's Sales, Earnings, and Statistical Data, 1985–1994 (in thousands of dollars except per share data)

				For the Years Ended June 30						
	1994	1993	1992	1991	1990	1989	1988	1987	1986	1985
Summary of operations										
Net sales	$1,285,517	$1,139,462	$1,041,828	$950,747	$1,002,857	$ 876,379	$914,057	$784,665	$745,831	$717,773
Gross profit on sales	266,540	212,601	174,048	132,431	132,438	59,629	115,113	111,618	124,408	111,248
Provision for income taxes	67,240	44,060	28,700	16,500	18,290	(13,980)	12,950	18,950	27,850	28,990
Net income	$ 69,923	$ 70,345	$ 51,503	$ 36,453	$ 35,375	$(20,032)	$ 30,211	$ 26,614	$ 34,080	$ 33,517
Average number of shares of common stock outstanding	14,464	14,464	14,464	14,464	14,464	14,464	14,464	14,464	14,464	14,464
Per share of common stock:										
Net income	$ 4.84	$ 4.86	$ 3.56	$ 2.52	$ 2.45	$ (1.39)	$ 2.09	$ 1.84	$ 2.36	$ 2.32
Cash dividends	1.80	1.70	1.60	1.60	1.60	1.60	1.60	1.60	1.60	1.60
Shareholders' investment	27.92	24.89	21.60	19.69	18.76	17.92	20.97	20.48	20.29	19.59
Other data										
Shareholders' investment	$ 403,792	$ 359,958	$ 312,404	$ 284,715	$ 271,383	$ 259,226	$303,305	$296,260	$293,517	$283,399
Total assets	777,355	656,107	637,853	556,791	535,040	560,816	510,600	451,879	436,622	411,598
Plant and equipment	669,593	658,120	643,433	632,488	606,863	580,184	513,700	470,586	427,672	390,657
Plant and equipment net of reserves	285,890	295,542	309,698	320,364	326,288	330,198	295,573	273,903	248,347	230,240
Provision for depreciation	42,950	47,222	41,113	36,447	39,889	38,995	29,955	24,502	21,508	17,914
Expenditures for plant and equipment	40,804	38,110	40,224	32,036	37,797	79,513	57,001	52,235	46,288	58,443
Working capital	276,040	195,019	137,008	105,298	84,082	63,757	63,372	77,281	93,854	92,522
Current ratio	2.3 to 1	2.2 to 1	1.9 to 1	1.8 to 1	1.7 to 1	1.4 to 1	1.4 to 1	1.8 to 1	2.0 to 1	2.0 to 1
Number of employees at year-end	8,628	7,950	7,799	7,242	7,994	7,316	9,827	8,611	8,299	8,203
Number of shareholders at year-end	6,228	6,651	7,118	7,943	8,466	9,222	6,923	7,206	7,924	8,959
Quoted market price:										
High	$ 90 1/4	$ 68 5/8	$ 54 3/4	$ 33 3/4	$ 34	$ 34 3/4	$ 41 7/8	$ 42	$ 40 1/4	$ 31 1/8
Low	64 7/8	42 1/8	32 7/8	20 1/2	24 1/8	24 3/4	20 1/4	31 1/2	25 3/4	25 1/2

SOURCE: 1994 company annual report.

Exhibit 6
Components Used in
the Assembly of
Outdoor Power
Equipment, 1992,
1988, and 1983

Component	Percent of Total Value of Components Sold to OPE Finished Goods Assemblers		
	1992	1988	1983
Engines	50.6%	52.4%	58.0%
Wheels	4.2	4.6	6.0
Transmissions	8.9	7.6	9.0
Blades	1.1	NA	NA
Brakes/steering	1.0	NA	NA
Belts	1.3	1.8	NA
Tires	3.1	2.9	NA
Plugs/filters	0.6	NA	NA
Grass-catching bags	1.4	1.2	2.0
Seats	1.3	1.4	NA
Batteries	1.4	1.4	2.0
Decks	2.9	NA	NA
Engine parts	1.3	NA	NA
Electrical motor parts	1.2	NA	NA
Pulleys	1.3	NA	NA
Tines and augers	0.6	NA	NA
Fuel tanks	0.8	NA	NA
Cables and controls	1.6	NA	NA
Other	15.4	26.7	23.0
Total	100.0%	100.0%	100.0%

SOURCE: *Profile of the Outdoor Power Equipment Industry,* 1993.

Exhibit 7
Costs and Profit
Margins for Outdoor
Equipment, 1992

Cost Area	Percent
Materials	9.6%
Components	47.6
Wages and benefits	18.3
Transportation	1.7
Advertising	2.8
Selling and administration	9.2
Other	7.5
Total costs	96.7
Net income before taxes	3.3
Total	100.0%

SOURCE: *Profile of the Outdoor Power Equipment Industry,* 1993.

Exhibit 8
U.S. Outdoor Power
Equipment Retail
Distribution, 1995,
1992, and 1983

Retail Outlet	1995	1992	1983
Hardware stores	5.0%	6.3%	12.0%
Home centers	12.0	8.7	3.0
National merchandisers	30.0	27.2	22.0
Discount department stores	17.0	12.0	8.0
Lawn and garden stores	15.0	16.9	17.0
OPE/farm equipment stores	16.0	20.2	19.0
Other	5.0	8.7	19.0
Total	100.0%	100.0%	100.0%

SOURCES: Compiled by the case researchers from a number of sources, including interviews with company personnel; 1983 and 1992 data is based on information contained in the *Profile of the Outdoor Power Equipment Industry,* 1993.

■ **Exhibit 9**
Shipments of Outdoor Power Equipment, 1985, 1990–1994, with Forecasts for 1995–1996 (units in thousands)

| | Equipment | | | | | |
| | Walk-Behind | | | Riding | | |
Year	Rotary Mowers	Rotary Tillers	Snow Throwers	Rear-Engine Mowers	Front Engine Mowers	Garden Tractors
1985	5,015	430	258	322	479	153
1990	5,700	300	355	247	885	156
1991	5,350	296	285	209	840	128
1992	5,150	343	285	205	847	133
1993	5,720	343	265	185	1,060	163
1994*	6,030	315	248	177	1,086	189
Extended forecasts						
1995	6,170	341	NA	158	1,168	199
1996	6,078	352	NA	149	1,170	207

*Estimated.

SOURCE: Outdoor Power Equipment Institute.

■ **Exhibit 10**
U.S. Trade Patterns for the Outdoor Power Equipment Industry, 1991 (in millions of dollars)

| | U.S. Exports of OPE Products | | Source of U.S. Imports of OPE Products | |
Country	Dollar Value	Percent	Dollar Value	Percent
Canada and Mexico	$166	30.8%	$27	36.9%
European Community	223	41.4	7	10.1
Japan	20	3.6	29	39.5
East Asia	15	2.8	6	7.7
South America	11	2.0	1	1.7
Other	104	19.4	3	4.1
World total	$539	100.0%	$74	100.0%

SOURCE: *Profile of the Outdoor Power Equipment Industry*, 1993.

■ **Exhibit 11**
Currency Exchange Rates per U.S. Dollar, 1985, 1990–1995

Currency	1995	1994	1993	1992	1991	1990	1985
Canada (dollar)	1.35	1.31	1.29	1.21	1.15	1.17	1.32
Germany (mark)	1.38	1.74	1.61	1.51	1.49	1.68	3.15
Japan (yen)	84	112	111	127	135	145	251
Mexico (peso)*	6.29	3.10	3.10	3,089	2,948	2,683	224

*The Mexican government has revalued the country's currency a number of times during the 1980s and 1990s due to the currency's devaluation against the U.S. dollar.

SOURCE: *The Wall Street Journal*, various years.

In 1974, U.S. exports of OPE products amounted to $85 million versus imports of a meager $2 million. By 1985, U.S. exports had grown to $127 million, with imports reaching $118 million—giving the U.S. OPE industry a slim $9 million trade surplus. While most of the 1985 exports were to Canada, over 40 percent of the imports were from Japan. Imports of OPE products peaked in 1988 at $273 million and were only $74 million in 1991. Exports by the U.S. OPE industry in 1991 were $539 million, giving U.S. manufacturers a $465 million trade surplus. Exhibit 10 summarizes trade patterns for outdoor power equipment in 1991. Exchange rates played a big role in whether foreign-made OPE products could be price competitive in the U.S. market and whether U.S.-made OPE products could compete in foreign markets. Currency exchange rates for selected countries for the years 1985 and 1990–95 are displayed in Exhibit 11.

Industry Regulation

Prior to 1982, manufacturers of OPE were not regulated by the Consumer Products Safety Commission (CPSC); compliance was voluntary. Voluntary standards were promulgated by the Outdoor Power Equipment Institute (OPEI) and had been supported by the industry trade association since the mid-1950s. The standards were primarily concerned with improved product performance and safety. Safety standards involved both the protection from thrown objects and noise level. About 90 percent of the industry's products were in compliance with these voluntary standards. Products complying with the standards were affixed with a triangular OPEI seal.

A number of CPSC regulations went into effect in 1982. These standards called for increased safety restrictions for walk-behind power mowers, including shields to protect people from thrown objects, deflectors and drain holes to prevent ignition of spilled fuel, the deadman blade control system, and labeling requirements. Mowers built after July 1, 1982, had to have blades that stopped within three seconds after the operator released a deadman control at the handle of the mower. Meeting this standard involved either installing a blade brake or the addition of a rechargeable, battery-powered electric starter. The CPSC estimated that compliance with the deadman blade control system would cost approximately $35 per unit.

Many engine manufacturers, including Briggs & Stratton, had successfully developed technology to make manual starting much easier, with engines usually starting on the first or second pull. The lawn mower industry asked Congress to amend the safety standard to allow engine stop with manual restart as a third method of compliance with the blade control requirement. President Reagan signed the amendment despite the CPSC's strong opposition. As of 1995, there were no federal regulations concerning riding mowers, and no additional regulation of walk-behind mowers had been initiated since 1982.

The industry also had to comply with the Magnuson-Moss Act of 1975 requiring that all products with a written warranty and costing the consumer $15 or more come with either a statement concerning the duration of the warranty or a limited warranty. The industry, from time to time, also faced state and local regulations concerning noise and pollution levels of outdoor power equipment.

Environmental regulations emanating from California and the U.S. Environmental Protection Agency (EPA) were of utmost concern to the industry. In 1994, the California Air Resources Board (CARB) and the EPA jointly proposed stringent national emission standards for small utility engines—those typically used in lawn mowers and other outdoor power equipment. Phase I EPA regulations enacted in 1994 required that all utility engines manufactured after August 1996 be modified to reduce the emissions of hydrocarbons and nitrogen oxides by 70 percent from 1990 levels. The California regulations were effective January 1, 1995. The EPA and CARB cited ozone formation (smog) as the motivation for Phase I regulations. In 1995, the industry was involved with the EPA in "regulatory-negotiation" of Phase II regulations that, if implemented, would ultimately require utility engines to meet the same emission standards as automobiles. Phase II regulations also concerned evaporation and spillage from gasoline tanks and containers. Phase I regulations were expected to increase the cost of utility engines by $5 to $10 per engine. In 1993, the outdoor power equipment industry incurred expenses of $10.6 million related to EPA requirements and expenses of $725,000 related to CPSC compliance.

Competition: Domestic

Competition in the OPE industry occurred mainly within two broad strategic groups—finished goods producers and components producers. The finished goods manufacturers represented the largest group of competitors. The major producers of premium-priced lawn mowers included Toro Company, Snapper, and John Deere and Company. MTD Products, Murray Ohio Manufacturing, and American Yard Products (AYP) were the chief producers of outdoor power equipment for the medium-priced and discount markets. The latter three firms also produced equipment for retailers selling OPE products under their own private label. Exhibit 12 shows the major domestic players in the OPE industry in the United States.

The largest assembler of outdoor power equipment for the premium-priced segment was the Toro Company, Inc., headquartered in Minneapolis. Toro was also the leading manufacturer of snow-throwing equipment. Toro Company had sales of $794 million and net income of $22 million in 1994. Toro's total revenue included over $300 million in commercial-grade OPE and other lawn and garden equipment such as irrigation systems. Toro had recently increased its share of the high-end segment by acquiring Wheel Horse and Lawn-Boy; Wheel Horse primarily manu-

■ **Exhibit 12**
Selected U.S. Outdoor Power Equipment Manufacturers (sales in millions of dollars)

Company	1994 Main OPE Sales	Products
American Yard Products	600*	Finished goods
Bolens/Troy-Bilt	50	Finished goods
Briggs & Stratton Corp.	1,197	Engines
John Deere & Co.	1,305[†]	Finished goods
Kohler Co.	200*	Engines
MTD Products Co.	700*	Finished goods
McLane Manufacturing Co.	20*	Finished goods
Murray Ohio Mfg. Co.	500*	Finished goods
Snapper	248	Finished goods
Tecumseh Products Co.	427	Engines
Toro Company Inc.	794[†]	Finished goods
Yazoo Mfg. Co. Inc.	25*	Finished goods

*Estimated from interviews with industry participants.
[†]Includes revenue from sources other than consumer OPE.

SOURCES: Company annual reports; *Ward's Business Directory of U.S. Private and Public Companies,* 1994; *Standard & Poor's Register,* Vol. 1, 1995.

factured and marketed riding mowers and garden tractors and Lawn-Boy's strength was in walk-behind lawn mowers. Lawn-Boy was one of the few vertically integrated producers and even made its own engines, designing them with a distinctive integrated look (i.e., the engine cowling lines matched the lines of the blade housing) that appealed to some consumers in the premium-priced segment. Lawn-Boy was the only domestic manufacturer to produce its own engines. Lawn-Boy models were equipped with either the brand's "in-house" two-cycle engine or Tecumseh's four-cycle engine. The two-cycle design provided additional power, which was useful for self-propelled models used on hilly terrain, but it required that gasoline and oil be mixed in the fuel tank. Lawn-Boy's top-of-the-line models were equipped with an oil injection system, where oil and gasoline were stored in separate reservoirs and then electronically mixed. Other major engine manufacturers in the industry produced four-cycle engines that required no mixing of gasoline and oil. So far, Toro had not opted to use Lawn-Boy's two-cycle engines on its Toro or Wheel Horse product lines.

The Snapper division of Actava Group, Inc., marketed a full line of premium-priced lawn mowers, tillers, and snow blowers. Snapper competed in North America and Europe and achieved sales of $248 million in 1994. Snapper emphasized after-the-sale service, and even though it had its own small sales force, it generally marketed through distributors to a network of independent lawn and garden stores. The company maintained large parts inventories and conducted factory service schools that dealers were required to attend once or twice each year.

Deere and Company, Inc., also produced top-of-the-line products. Deere's garden tractors ranged from $2,000 to $10,000 and were considered by industry rivals to have "Mercedes-Benz" quality. Much of Deere's OPE sales were in the farming segment. Deere's OPE sales in 1994 amounted to approximately $1.3 billion. For several years, Deere had chosen B&S engines to power its mowers, but recently it had signed an agreement to purchase the majority of its garden tractor engines from Kawasaki. Kawasaki gained Deere's business by supplying an engine with higher specifications and a lower price than the Briggs & Stratton engines previously used by John Deere. Deere had recently acquired the Jacobsen/Homelite division of Textron, Inc., which produced high-quality walk-behind lawn mowers, chain saws, blowers, and flexible line trimmers sold under the Homelite and Jacobsen brand names.

The producers of lower-priced mowers included the three largest U.S. lawn mower manufacturers—MTD, Murray, and AYP. MTD Products, Inc., of Valley City, Ohio, was closely held and had estimated sales of $700 million. MTD bought its engines from Briggs & Stratton and Tecumseh, manufactured the frames and housing, and assembled the units for sale. The company sold its products to private-label distributors and marketed nationally in the discount department stores and home centers under its MTD and Yardman brands. The company also marketed through lawn and garden stores under its newly acquired brands—Cub Cadet and White. MTD had the distinction of being the nation's largest producer of walk-behind lawn mowers and Briggs & Stratton's largest customer.

American Yard Products was the nation's second-largest producer of lawn mowers, with estimated sales of $600 million. AYP, a subsidiary of Electrolux, was Sears's primary supplier of Craftsman label walk-behind mowers, riding mowers, and garden tractors. The Craftsman brand accounted for approximately 25 percent of all lawn mower sales. AYP was also a private-label supplier to other discount chains and manufactured Poulan's line of lawn mowers. AYP used Tecumseh and Briggs & Stratton engines on its equipment.

The Murray Ohio Manufacturing Co., owned by British conglomerate Tomkins PLC and located in Brentwood, Tennessee, was a major producer of both OPE and bicycles for the medium-priced and discount segments. The company produced a broad line of walk-behind mowers, riding mowers, and garden tractors marketed under its Murray brand. Murray was the primary supplier to Wal-Mart until 1995, when MTD acquired the contract to supply all walk-behind and riding mowers offered by the nation's leading discounter. Murray had recently acquired Noma, a private-label manufacturer, to expand its capability to supply private-label buyers. Total corporate sales approximated $500 million in 1994. Murray, like its primary rivals MTD and AYP, sourced engines from both B&S and Tecumseh.

The single biggest cost component of lawn mowers was the engine. The three largest producers of mower engines were Briggs & Stratton, Tecumseh Products Co., and Kohler Company. Tecumseh was Briggs & Stratton's chief domestic competitor in engines ranging from 3 to 20 horsepower and had actually strengthened its position in the industry as a result of price competition in the finished goods segment of the industry. Many OPE manufacturers such as MTD, AYP, and Murray had utilized multiple sourcing as a strategy to minimize components costs. Until retailers began to pressure for lower prices, most finished goods manufacturers found it more convenient to purchase all or most of their engines from a single source—usually Briggs & Stratton.

Tecumseh Products Company was the largest U.S. producer of refrigerator compressors and the second-largest producer of small, gasoline-powered engines. The company also produced gear assemblies and related transmission parts. In 1994, Tecumseh's operating income on engine sales of $427 million (32 percent of total sales) was $41 million (32 percent of total operating income). The largest customers of Tecumseh engines were Toro Company and AYP. Tecumseh engines were used exclusively on Toro's snow-throwing equipment and on about 50 percent of Craftsman walk-behind mowers. Sears advertisements regularly touted the reliability of its Craftsman Eager-1 engines, which were all supplied by Tecumseh.

Kohler Company was privately held, had estimated sales of $1 billion, and employed 12,500 workers. The majority of the company's revenues came as a result of its plumbing fixtures business. Kohler was a distant third in small engine sales, behind B&S and Tecumseh. Kohler's engine business was strongest in segments requiring greater horsepower. Kohler engines were more commonly found on garden tractors and industrial products than on walk-behind mowers.

Competition: Foreign

Japan was the primary exporter of OPE products to the United States. The value of Japanese exports of lawn mowers and parts to the United States had increased from less than $3 million in 1978 to $36.1 million in 1985, representing 41 percent of the total value of OPE goods imported into the United States that year. As of 1992, Japanese imports still accounted for 40 percent of all outdoor power equipment imported into the United States. Most foreign imports of OPE products into the United States were high-quality walk-behind mowers and garden tractors. Garden tractors were imported as agricultural machinery and were exempted from paying U.S. tariffs. The three leading import brands of garden tractors were all Japanese: Kubota, Yanmar, and Satoh.

The Japanese small gasoline engine manufacturers—Honda, Yamaha, Kawasaki, and Suzuki—maintained their strongest foothold in the market for engines with industrial applications. Honda was widely acknowledged as the leading global supplier of industrial engines. In the lawn mower segment, Honda mowers were the only foreign brand that was a factor in the U.S. market. Competition from Japanese imports had become much less of a problem for U.S.-based manufacturers since the late 1980s because of the strong increases in the value of the yen against the dollar.

A softening of the motorcycle business in the 1980s had forced Japanese motorcycle manufacturers to look to other markets in order to maintain full use of their production facilities. All four Japanese motorcycle manufacturers (Honda, Kawasaki, Suzuki, and Yamaha) identified outdoor power products as appropriate new business opportunities.

Honda had stated publicly that it intended to become a leader in the powered products field and had transferred resources from its motorcycle division to its powered products division. In many respects, OPE products represented a natural business diversification for Honda because the company was founded in 1948 to produce small internal combustion engines. Honda's production capacity for small utility engines was about 2.1 million units a year in 1995. The company sold its mowers in the United States through a network of 2,000 established OPE lawn and garden store dealers.

Honda's U.S. Strategy

Honda had targeted the high end of the U.S. market for OPE products. Similar to Lawn-Boy, it manufactured both the lawn mower engine and the lawn mower body, which resulted in equipment having an integrated look. Honda engines were noted for their light weight and dependability. Professional users of OPE had casually dubbed Honda's engines "Briggs-Hondas" because of their dependability. Heavy users often replaced worn-out Briggs & Stratton engines with Honda engines. Honda's product strength was based on its extensive R&D expenditures and its speedy incorporation of cutting-edge technological developments. Honda marketed its products with the aid of extensive advertising and promotion and priced its products competitively, sometimes setting prices below the other premium-priced brands to gain market share. Honda had been extremely successful in both the U.S. motorcycle and automobile markets using similar strategies and possessed extensive resources to support similar efforts in the OPE market (see Exhibit 13).

In 1994, Honda sold approximately 150,000 lawn mowers in the United States—up from 10,000 mowers in 1983. Honda also sold replacement engines compatible with many makes of mowers. Until 1984, Honda lawn mowers bound for the United States had been manufactured in Japan. When its level of U.S. sales made it economical to establish a production base in the United States, Honda built a $26 million manufacturing plant for engines and lawn mowers in Sweponsville, North

■ **Exhibit 13**

Honda Motor Company, Financial Summary, 1985, 1990–1994 (in millions of U.S. dollars)

1994	1993	1992	1991	1990	1985
Sales	$39,927	$35,798	$33,370	$30,567	$27,070	$10,753
Net income	619	220	307	540	572	532
Assets	34,708	28,526	26,374	21,005	18,018	5,974
Stockholders' equity	$11,715	$ 9,447	$ 9,085	$ 7,736	$ 6,872	$ 2,806
Number of employees	92,800	91,300	90,900	85,500	79,200	50,609

SOURCE: Compiled from: "The Global 500," *Fortune*, various years.

■ **Exhibit 14**
Honda Motor
Company, U.S.
Outdoor Power
Equipment Product
Line, 1995

Product	Number of Models
Lawn mowers	18
Riding mowers	3
Lawn tractors	3
Multipurpose tractors	4
Tillers	7
Generators	26
Snow blowers	6
Commercial mowers	5
Engines	69

SOURCE: *Honda Motor Company Fact Book.*

Carolina. The plant produced all Honda lawn mowers offered in the global market. Honda produced approximately 175,000 mowers and 200,000 engines annually and employed 350 workers in its U.S. facility. Honda had exported over 225,000 lawn mowers and engines from its Sweponsville plant to 16 countries since 1986.

Honda's products had been well received in the United States, drawing excellent ratings from consumer magazines. A list of Honda outdoor power equipment offered in the United States is provided in Exhibit 14. Comparisons with domestic models were generally quite favorable. The main disadvantages listed in a 1992 *Consumer Reports* review were difficulty of oil changes and the need to substitute blades when changing from bagging clippings to mulching. Honda mowers received high marks for convenience, performance, and safety. The starting controls were simple, easy to reach, and had an automatic choke that eliminated the need for a choke control on the throttle. The cutting performance of Honda mowers was usually rated excellent; they provided a level cut, even in tall heavy grass, and efficiently bagged clippings. Honda's mowers met or exceeded safety standards, including a deadman clutch that stopped the blade one second after the control was released, well within the three-second requirement.

■ The Briggs & Stratton Corporation

In 1995, Briggs & Stratton (B&S), headquartered in Wauwatosa, Wisconsin, was the world's largest producer of both small, gas-powered engines used primarily for outdoor power equipment and ignition systems and locks used by the automobile industry. B&S had an estimated 75 percent of the small engine market in the United States and over 50 percent of the worldwide market. Engines and parts accounted for 93 percent of Briggs's total revenues in 1994 (see Exhibit 15). The other 7 percent was from the sale of automotive lock and key sets through B&S Technologies. Both industries that the company competed in were characterized by strong rivalry. Briggs management decided to spin off the automobile ignition system and lock division to its shareholders in 1995. A subsidiary corporation was to be established with shares distributed to B&S shareholders as a tax-free dividend.

Eighty-five percent of Briggs's engine sales were to manufacturers of lawn mowers and other outdoor power equipment (shredders-grinders, snow blowers, tillers, etc.). Approximately 15 percent of its engine sales were to manufacturers of construction and agricultural equipment. Briggs's top three customers for small engines

■ **Exhibit 15**
Briggs & Stratton
Corporation's Sales of
OEM and Air-Cooled
Engines by End User,
1990–1994

End Uses	Percent of Engine Sales				
	1994	**1993**	**1992**	**1991**	**1990**
Lawn and garden equipment	85%	85%	86%	86%	86%
Industrial/agricultural equipment	15	15	14	14	14
All exports of engines	21	25	21	21	23
Total engine sales as a percent of corporate revenues	93%	92%	93%	93%	93%

SOURCE: Company annual reports.

were MTD (18 percent of sales), Murray Ohio Manufacturing (12 percent of sales), and American Yard Products (12 percent of sales). Other large customers included Toro and Snapper.

In 1989, B&S's engine sales declined 4 percent, and the firm recorded its first unprofitable year in over two decades. The next year, the firm returned to profitability and sales increased at an average annual rate of 3.1 percent between 1990 and 1994. The improved performance was due in part to lower interest rates, improved housing starts, and good weather. Management expected to maintain annual growth in revenues of 3 percent during the 1995–97 period.

International Activities

B&S estimated that 35 to 40 percent of its total engine business resulted from exports, either through the company's direct sales or through the sales of U.S. OPE manufacturers who chose Briggs as a supplier. Frederick P. Stratton, the company's CEO, observed:

> The market for products powered by our engines is increasingly international. The flow of material around the world is truly amazing. For example, we know of cases where engines we ship to customers in Australia are mounted on equipment destined for Europe, and engines we ship to customers in Europe are mounted on equipment destined for the U.S.

B&S realized that simply defending its domestic market share was not sufficient and that, in the long run, new growth would come from increased sales abroad. During the past decade, B&S gradually expanded its presence in international markets. The company targeted its engines to Europe's established lawn and garden equipment market and concentrated on providing engines for agricultural, marine, and light industrial applications to developing Asian nations. The primary competitors in the overseas markets included smaller local firms and eight Japanese competitors (Honda, Kawasaki, Suzuki, Yamaha, Fuji, Mitsubishi, Kubota, and Yanmar). Tecnamotor S.p.A. of Italy was a major European competitor and was owned by Tecumseh.

In major foreign markets sales were handled by direct customer contact, whereas in smaller markets independent sales representatives were used. B&S had established sales and service offices in Switzerland, Norway, United Arab Emirates, Australia, New Zealand, and China. Wholly owned distributed centers were located in Canada, the United Kingdom, France, Germany, the Netherlands, Australia, and New Zealand.

Briggs & Stratton had used strategic alliances to establish overseas manufacturing capabilities. The first of these was a 1986 joint venture with Daihatsu Motor Co. to produce V-twin (two cylinders) overhead valve engines for B&S's Vanguard line (a premium engine line) in Osaka, Japan. This was a less expensive approach to broadening the product line than developing a new product on its own. In 1993, B&S signed a marketing agreement whereby Daihatsu would produce and market a new line of three-cylinder, water-cooled diesel and gasoline engines for the Vanguard line. Another joint venture existed with the Puling Machinery Works and the Yimin Machinery Plant in China to produce cast-iron engines for industrial/construction use in markets outside the United States. In 1992, B&S contracted with Mitsubishi Heavy Industries to supply a line of single-cylinder engines to add to B&S's Vanguard line.

Products

B&S had the widest engine product line of the small engine manufacturers located throughout the world. Briggs's most popular engines were air-cooled, four-cycle aluminum alloy engines that ran on straight gas (not mixed with oil) and ranged in size from 3 to 20 horsepower. Less than 5 percent of the company's engines were of the older air-cooled, cast-iron design, but it still made cast-iron models ranging from 9 to 16 horsepower for selected OPE products sold mainly in foreign markets. B&S also produced air- and water-cooled diesel engines ranging from 3 to 28.5 horsepower. Walk-behind lawn mowers generally were equipped with a 3- to 5.5-HP engine.

Since 1984, B&S had launched four new styles of engines to respond to changing demand and to combat increased competition from Japan. The first of these new lines was the MAX series of 3.5- to 4-HP engines offering better styling, easier starting, and quiet/low maintenance performance. This new line represented the first major engine redesign since 1967. The Quantum line was introduced two years later. It also featured low-profile styling, improved durability, and improved operating convenience—Quantum engines had fewer parts and were assembled with the aid of robotic technology. In 1987, B&S launched the Vanguard line—overhead valve engines ranging from 8 to 18 horsepower and intended for the premium-priced OPE market and for industrial applications. Subsequent additions of larger engines to this line were made through strategic alliances with two Japanese manufacturers, Daihatsu and Mitsubishi. In 1993, the Diamond series of engines was introduced for commercial lawn and garden equipment. These engines ranged from 5.5 to 20 horsepower and had extended life features for durability and rugged power.

Improvements were made to two of B&S's smaller engine lines used for lower-priced equipment. These were renamed the Classic and Sprint lines. In addition to introducing new engine lines, B&S made improvements in ignitions, noise reduction, and pollution abatement. Exhibit 16 presents B&S's track record in new product development.

Marketing and Promotion

For most of its history, B&S sold engines directly to OPE manufacturers, relying on its quality image and reputation to gain sales. This changed during the 80s when B&S assembled its first marketing staff to market engines to consumers and retailers of finished goods. B&S wanted consumers to ask for their engines by name when buying a lawn mower. The company began a television advertising campaign for the first time using the slogan "Briggs & Stratton: the power in power equipment." Newer versions of these ads were still being aired in the 1990s during the spring season and were shown during sporting events. However, most of B&S's advertising expenditures were devoted to paying for cooperative ads with dealers to promote

1953	Aluminum Alloy Gasoline Engine: Reduced weight and cost of small engines.
1961	Easy Spin Starting: Engine starting effort cut in half by a simple cam-controlled, fault-proof compression release.
1962	Oil Foam Air Cleaner: Dirt banned from engine for its life by an easy-to-clean polyurethane foam filter.
1966	Syncho Balance Design: Engine and riding equipment vibrations smoothed out by a synchronized counterweight system.
1968	Automatic Vacuum Controlled Choke: Replaced manual choke, providing extra power when needed for heavy loads.
1971	12-Volt Gear-Type Starter with Dual Circuit Alternator: Provided quick starting at low temperatures. Alternator provides both D/C battery charging and A/C for light or external loads.
1977	Quiet Power: The 16-HP twin-cylinder engine prompted by noise abatement guidelines provided quiet running and low vibration levels.
1982	Magnetron Ignition: A self-contained transistor with no moving parts. Provides more consistent spark for dependable starting. Can be installed on existing engines.
1983	The small electric motor was introduced for power mowers. The new 120-volt, 1,000-watt motor weighed 11 lbs., had a 10-year life, and met CPSC standards for deadman blade control.
1984	MAX Series of 3.5- to 4-HP engines featuring improved durability and appearance.
1986	Quantum Series of 3.5- to 8-HP engines for the premium market.
1987	Vanguard OHV line of medium engines 8 to 18 horsepower for premium market and industrial/construction applications.
1993	Diamond Series of premium 5.5- to 20-HP engines for the commercial lawn care market.

SOURCE: Compiled from company pamphlets and annual reports.

OPE products equipped with B&S engines and to promote dealer-certified repair and maintenance services to owners of products with B&S engines. A 1992 survey indicated that B&S's marketing efforts had been successful, as 72 percent of the surveyed customers specified Briggs & Stratton as the engine they preferred to power their lawn and garden equipment.

Distribution and Service

B&S sold about 70 percent of its engines via annually negotiated contracts with OPE manufacturers. To attract new customers and regain former customers lost to foreign rivals, B&S abandoned its long-standing policy of a single price for all buyers, regardless of quantity purchased or other conditions. The company now offered pricing incentives to its customers who ordered standardized engines, accepted delivery during the off season, or who committed early to specific delivery times during the peak season. However, B&S was committed to its long-standing policy of not integrating forward into the finished goods market and competing with the buyers of its engines.

The growing strength of discount chain retailers had resulted in greater pressure on the prices that OPE producers and parts suppliers could command. Large retailers buying in volume were bargaining hard for favorable prices from OPE producers. Frederick Stratton observed, "For some segments it significantly reduced the price premium our brand equity could command. This increased the importance of being a low-cost producer." Briggs's network of over 25,000 authorized service centers in North America and another 7,000 overseas made B&S engines attractive to OPE producers, since the large retailers did not offer outdoor power equipment repair or service.

Production

Manufacturing and assembly of outdoor power equipment was driven by the need to deliver new lawn mowers and tractors for retail sale in early spring and summer. As a result, demand from B&S's customers was at its peak in winter and spring. Most engines were produced from December to March. Briggs & Stratton manufactured almost all of its components used in assembling engines, including aluminum and iron castings, carburetors, and ignitions. It purchased parts such as piston rings, spark plugs, valves, and smaller plastic and metal parts. Global sourcing was used for these purchases when economically feasible. Over the past few years, B&S had increased its use of recycled or recyclable material, especially steel and aluminum. Currently, 60 percent (by weight) of the firm's engines was made from recycled materials. Recycled materials tended to be cheaper and contributed to lowering material costs.

Briggs & Stratton had begun to use materials requirement planning (MRP), an inventory reduction program (EOQ), and statistical process control in its new production facilities. The purpose of the MRP system was to provide the correct parts in the right quantities when they were needed in the manufacturing process. This system took advantage of information stored in a computer for timely response and scheduling. The goal of EOQ was to cut inventory in half while still meeting demand requirements. The statistical process control system was intended to detect any trend toward making bad parts before the parts were even produced. In addition, "quality centers" were created to ensure a constant flow of ideas from the bottom up on how to improve inventory and other production management activities.

Since 1985, Briggs had begun to move its plant operations out of Wisconsin. B&S management intended to cut production costs by building state-of-the-art facilities located in nonunion areas. The company's first non-Wisconsin plant opened in 1986 in Murray, Kentucky. This fully automated plant produced the Classic and Sprint engine lines. In 1990, a new "focused factory" was opened in Poplar Bluff, Missouri, to produce the premium Quantum engine line. Both production processes and employee training at Poplar Bluff were specifically designed for this engine line to ensure the high quality demanded of premium-quality engines. B&S's largest engine factory was still located in Wauwatosa, Wisconsin. Most other engine lines as well as single-cylinder, overhead-valve Vanguard engines were produced in Wisconsin. Two other Wisconsin factories produced engines and engine parts. Other B&S engines were produced in Asia at the plants of strategic allies in Japan and China. Two foundries in West Allis, Wisconsin, produced castings for B&S engines and also sold to outside customers.

At the end of 1994, B&S employed 8,628 employees, the highest number since 1988, when employment had peaked at 9,827. Productivity per employee improved over the years. In 1985, sales per employee averaged $87,500; by the end of 1994, sales per employee averaged $148,993. Despite this improvement, B&S management still believed that the company had a labor cost disadvantage relative to its foreign and domestic rivals. In 1994, Briggs & Stratton announced a major restructuring of manufacturing operations.

As part of its low-cost strategy, the company planned to construct three new U.S. plants at an estimated cost of $112 million. The new plant construction would result in the transfer of approximately 2,000 jobs from production facilities in Milwaukee, Wisconsin, to new facilities in Statesboro, Georgia, Auburn, Alabama, and a third southern site that had not yet been determined. The plan also provided for the expansion of the Kentucky and Missouri plants and the eventual closing of some of the Wisconsin plants. B&S management anticipated that the plant relocation strategy would result in annual cost savings of approximately $12 million—primarily due to reductions in labor expenses.

Frederick Stratton stated that the hourly compensation costs at the company's Wisconsin manufacturing facilities placed it at a competitive disadvantage in regard to its ability to compete on price. B&S management estimated that its wage and benefit costs were 20 percent higher than its primary domestic rival, Tecumseh. The company had found that labor-related expenses in its new Poplar Bluff, Missouri, and Murray, Kentucky, plants were considerably lower than in the Milwaukee, Wisconsin, facility. The average wage and benefit cost in the two southern U.S. plants was approximately $11.00 per hour, whereas the hourly wage and benefit cost averaged $21.27 in Milwaukee. The Bureau of Labor Statistics estimated the 1993 U.S. average hourly compensation cost for the industry at $17.86. A contributing factor to the labor cost differential between Briggs & Stratton's plants was the reluctance by the United Paperworkers International Union to agree to productivity improvement processes that had been successful in the southern facilities. Briggs & Stratton management intended to operate the new plants on a nonunion basis.

■ Future Outlook

The threat of competition from the Japanese had made Briggs & Stratton a much stronger company. The company responded to the challenge by introducing innovative new product lines, improving product quality, and lowering its relative cost position. In addition, the company was helped by a strong U.S. economy and a strengthening Japanese yen. The economic conditions and the changes at B&S helped the company attract new customers and regain some old ones. Going into 1995, B&S had regained Toro's business that had been lost to Suzuki, gotten Snapper to switch from Fuji back to B&S, and recaptured some of John Deere's business. Frederick Stratton commented on the company's success:

> There are two ways to judge the health of a business: its current financial performance and its long-term strategic position. We believe that our recent good financial performance is to a great degree a result of strategic decisions made three to five years ago. We recognize that our financial performance three to five years from now will reflect the decisions we made in 1994.

■ Case 9   PepsiCo and the Fast-Food Industry

Joseph Wolfe
University of Tulsa

As the PepsiCo Corporation entered the early 1990s, Wayne Calloway, the company's Board Chairman and Chief Executive Officer, had every right to be optimistic. From 1991 to 1992 sales had increased 14 percent, earnings were up 21 percent, and per share dividends increased 20 percent. Moreover the firm's major industry segments of soft drinks, snack foods, and restaurants had obtained respective 10 percent, 17 percent, and 16 percent sales hikes. Taking a five-year perspective, since 1987 PepsiCo's compounded annual sales had increased 16.8 percent, and its income from continuing operations had grown at an 18.4 percent rate. With these results Calloway now set a new goal for the corporation's 338,000 employees by asking the question "How does a $20 billion company add another $20 billion in just five years?"

Based on his review of the situation, the CEO identified two major growth opportunities. PepsiCo's $20.0 billion growth was to come from (1) global expansion, and (2) a redefinition of the company's basic businesses. As Calloway stated,

> Not too long ago we would have described ourselves as a company in the business of soft drinks, snack chips and quick service restaurants. Today, we're in the business of beverages, snack foods and quick service food distribution. A soft drink company sells only carbonated colas and the like; a beverage company might sell things like water and tea or fruit based drinks. Also, a restaurant company is constricted to certain physical locations. A food distribution company can take its products wherever there's a customer, without necessarily making an investment in a large restaurant. We also reconsidered our geographic limitations. Up until a few years ago, we were basically a strong U.S. company with a solid but limited international presence. Not so today. In 1991, nearly one out of every four sales dollars came from our international operations. When you consider that 95.0 percent of the world's population is outside the U.S., you can see what that means in terms of opportunity. And this is doubly true for our kinds of products, which are in great demand everywhere on earth, with almost no economic or cultural barriers.

Although numerous opportunities appear to exist for PepsiCo, many industry observers have noted overall domestic soft drink industry sales increases have been marginal and the cola segment has just about been played out. Even though the cola market amounted to $34 billion in 1992, its growth was only 1.5 percent, far lower than the 5 to 7 percent annual growth rates experienced in the 1980s, despite changes in packaging, logotypes and advertising campaigns by both Coke and Pepsi. The market share for diet soft drinks, for years a growth segment, showed its first annual drop from 29.8 percent in 1991 to 29.4 percent in 1992, and overall consumption rose only marginally from 47.8 gallons to 48.0 gallons per capita. In the United States, Coca-Cola maintained its 40.7 percent share of the soft-drink market, while PepsiCo slipped from 31.5 percent to 31.3 percent in 1992. Additionally, the first mover advantages claimed by Pepsi in the former Warsaw Pact nations quickly evaporated after Coca-Cola began its 18-month, $400 million assault in Central Europe's post-Socialist countries in "Operation Jumpstart." Health concerns have generally affected the sales of both snack foods and fast-food dining and have strong implications for PepsiCo's other two divisions. Although new product formulations

---

This case prepared by Joseph Wolfe, Professor of Management at the University of Tulsa.

have been introduced by snack chip and cracker manufacturers, and new, leaner burgers and menu assortments have been launched by all of America's national chains, these innovations have met with mixed success.

In charting his company's future, Wayne Calloway knows he must interpret the source of PepsiCo's growth prospects while carefully balancing the resource needs of the various divisions, businesses, and products at his disposal. Known worldwide for its soft drinks, in reality more sales, or about 36 percent of its revenues, are obtained from its restaurant operations. Although these operations increased their sales, the division's costs and profit performances have been spotty. What can be done to correct this situation? Again Calloway is optimistic for at least his company's Pizza Hut and Taco Bell systems:

> A steadily growing interest in eating away from home and the continued gravitation to convenience foods are creating an atmosphere of excitement for our restaurants. Our strategy is to take advantage of these trends by accelerating our growth in existing markets and introducing our products to new markets. At Pizza Hut, we'll continue to expand delivery aggressively. We're testing alternatives to our traditional dine-in concept and we're adding innovative distribution channels. Taco Bell is also continuing its break with tradition. Alternative distribution points and the increasing use of technology to drive costs down make Taco Bell the market innovator. The situation at KFC in the U.S. is challenging. We're in the process of restructuring our business to greatly improve productivity and customer service. We're reorganizing our kitchens, upgrading our units and adding nontraditional distribution points.

■ PepsiCo Inc.

PepsiCo is an international company currently operating in three industries—soft drinks, snack foods, and restaurants. As shown in Exhibit 1, it has followed an evolutionary path to its current status as an annual $20 billion revenue giant. Begun in 1893 as a soda fountain drink known in New Bern, North Carolina, as "Brad's drink," the trademark Pepsi-Cola was created in 1902 when the Pepsi-Cola Company became a North Carolina corporation. Profitable operations ensued until heavy losses on sugar inventories caused its bankruptcy in 1922. A new "Pepsi-Cola Corporation" was formed the following year and all operations were moved to Richmond, Virginia. The new Virginia corporation lost money for the next five years and then was only marginally profitable until it too went bankrupt in June 1931.

Using the assets and borrowing power of the New York-based Loft, Inc., candy company, Charles Guth subsequently purchased Pepsi-Cola's proprietary rights for $10,500. The drink was reformulated to Guth's tastes, Pepsi's syrup was sold mainly to Loft's own candy stores, but the operation continued to lose money. Mired in the depths of the Great Depression, the company began to bottle its soft drink in used 12-ounce beer bottles and promoted the slogan "Two large glasses in each bottle." Through this move Pepsi offered almost twice as much for the same 5¢ price charged by Coca-Cola in its 6½-ounce container. Sales and profits rose dramatically. With this revival in profits, court battles were soon waged against the firm on two fronts. The Loft Company's management, with the help of its major stockholder Phoenix Securities, sued Guth for the company's control, while Coca-Cola simultaneously filed a trademark infringement suit over Pepsi's use of the word "Cola." After four years of court-appointed management, Charles Guth lost all his claims. In the intervening period Coca-Cola also lost its lawsuit against Pepsi after successfully

■ **Exhibit 1**   Significant Company Events

1893	"Brad's Drink" concocted in Caleb B. Bradham's pharmacy in New Bern, North Carolina.
1902	Pepsi-Cola Company Incorporated in North Carolina.
1908	First bottling franchise created.
1920	Sugar prices rise dramatically from 5¼¢ to 26¼¢ per pound. Bradham invests heavily in sugar inventories. Prices drop to 3½¢ per pound in December and the company reports a $150,000 loss on operations.
1922	Company files for bankruptcy. Bradham forced to resign and R.C. Megargel & Company forms "The Pepsi-Cola Company" as a wholly owned Delaware Corporation. This company lapses on March 18, 1925 for nonpayment of taxes.
1923	Craven Holding Corporation of North Carolina purchases all of Pepsi-Cola's assets and trademark. Roy C. Megargel forms the "Pepsi-Cola Corporation" in Richmond, VA after purchasing Pepsi's trademark, business, and goodwill from the Craven Holding Corporation for $35,000. Operations in New Bern closed and moved to Richmond.
1928	Company is merged with the "National Pepsi-Cola Corporation" which was 90% owned by Megargel.
1931	Company goes bankrupt. Charles Guth uses $10,500 from the Loft, Inc. candy and candy store company to buy Pepsi's proprietary rights. A new Pepsi-Cola Company is founded in Long Island City and loses money for the next three years.
1933	Company begins to bottle its soft drinks in used 12 oz. beer bottles. Within five months over 1,000 cases a day are being sold.
1935	Loft, with support from Phoenix Securities Corporation, sues Guth for control of Pepsi-Cola. Guth loses the suit but appeals the decision. Company is managed by a court-appointed team during the appeal process.
1938	Coca-Cola files a trademark violation suit against Pepsi over its use of the word Cola. Coke loses the lawsuit.
1939	Charles Guth loses his appeal. All legal and financial control of the company reverts to Phoenix Securities which has a dominant stock interest in Loft. "Pepsi-Cola hits the spot" jingle created.
1941	Pepsi jingle played on over 469 radio stations and voted America's best-known tune in 1942.
1946	Sales level off at about $45.0 million for the next few years and earnings drop 70%.
1950	Pepsi nears bankruptcy. Alfred N. Steele leaves Coca-Cola to become Pepsi's President and vows to "Beat Coke." Pepsi's Cuban sugar plantation sold for $6.0 million. Over the next five years $38.0 million is invested in new plants and equipment.
1955	Steele marries film star Joan Crawford. Pepsi's advertising budget is $14 million or 18% of the industry's total. Advertising theme is "Be Sociable with Light Refreshment." Sales have risen 112% since 1950. Company owns 120 plants in over 50 countries.
1958	Steele attempts to merge company with Pabst Brewing Company.
1959	Steele dies of a heart attack after completing "Adorama," a $200,000 national sales promotion tour. Donald Kendall, head of Pepsi's overseas operations, photographs Nikita Khrushchev drinking six cupfuls of Pepsi at a Moscow trade fair. Drink becomes an instant hit with the Russians and the East European world.
1962	Advertising theme is "Now, it's Pepsi, for those who think young."
1963	Coke introduces diet Tab and Pepsi-Cola introduces Patio Diet Cola and later Diet Pepsi to fill low calorie segment pioneered by Royal Crown's Diet Rite Cola.
1964	Advertising theme is "Come Alive, You're in the Pepsi Generation." Company establishes the Pepsi-Cola Equipment Corp. to lease trucks and equipment to bottlers. Company later acquires and adds to this unit Lease Plan International, a trucking concern, National Trailer Convoy, North American Van Lines, Lee Way Motor Freight, and Chandler Leasing. Pepsi-Cola United Bottlers buys Rheingold Breweries for $26 million; PepsiCo later acquires a 51% interest in the United Bottlers operation. Company acquires Tip Corp., the Virginia manufacturer of Mountain Dew.
1965	Develops Devil Shake to compete with the Yoo-Hoo chocolate drink. Company attempts to buy controlling interest in Miller Brewing Co. Company purchases Wilson Sporting Goods from LTV. Pepsi-Cola Company merges with Frito-Lay of Dallas to become PepsiCo, Inc. Herman W. Lay becomes PepsiCo's largest stockholder and Chairman of its Board.
1966	Advertising theme is "Taste That Beats the Others Cold . . . Pepsi Pours It On." Company closes its up-state New York sugar refinery after losing $12 million on operations.

(continued)

■ **Exhibit 1**   *(concluded)*

1969	Pepsi's late-year advertising theme becomes "You've Got a Lot to Live, and Pepsi's Got a Lot to Give." Soft drink sales are $940 million compared to Coke's $1.3 billion.
1970	Corporation moves from its Manhattan Headquarters to the suburb of Purchase, New York.
1974	Company fined $50,000 for conspiring to fix sugar cane prices in 1972 and 1973.
1977	Company acquires Pizza Hut for about $300 million. Coca-Cola outbids PepsiCo for Taylor Wines of New York for $96 million. Pepsi's management admits that its overseas executives have made $1.7 million in questionable payments to local officials; Coke's questionable payments had been $1.3 million.
1978	Company acquires Taco Bell, Inc., the nation's largest Mexican fast food chain, for $148 million in stock.
1982	Lee Way Motor Freight loses $12.8 million.
1984	Taco Bell unit experiments with La Petite Boulangerie, a franchised chain of bakeries. Introduces Slice to compete in the "natural fruit" drink segment. Sells Lee Way Motor Freight for a $15 million after tax loss.
1985	Sells North American Van Lines for an after tax gain of $139 million. Sells Wilson Sporting Goods for an $18 million after tax loss.
1986	Acquires Kentucky Fried Chicken, the world's largest chicken chain. Acquired Mug Root Beer, and 7UP for distribution in all non-U.S. markets.
1989	Acquires the United Kingdom's Smiths Crisps Limited and Walkers Crisps Holdings Limited for $1.34 billion. Acquires General Cinema's domestic bottling operations for $1.77 billion.
1991	Taco Bell acquires Hot'n Now hamburger franchiser.
1992	Acquires Evercrisp Snack Productos de Chile SA and Mexico's Kas SA and Knorr Elorza SA. Buys out joint venture partners Hostess Frito-Lay in Canada and Gamesa Cookies in Mexico. Acquired a 50% interest in California Pizza Kitchen Inc. and an equity position in Carts of Colorado, Inc.
1993	Pepsi-Cola International begins to distribute Cadbury Schweppes products in Central Europe through a franchise partnership. Increased distribution of H2Oh! sparkling water and Avalon still water in the United States. PepsiCo creates a $600.0 million European snack food joint venture with General Mills after failing in its bid to purchase the company's European operations. PepsiCo's snack companies in Spain, Portugal and Greece are joined with General Mills' French, Belgium, and Dutch operations into Snack Ventures Europe.

suing many other soft drink manufacturers for the same violation and having seen more than 1,100 other cola manufacturers go out of business.

For the next 20 years the company operated as a soft drink firm battling against the firmly entrenched Coca-Cola company. Another bankruptcy was narrowly averted in 1950, and various conglomerate diversifications were attempted or consummated from the late 1950s to the mid-1960s. Upon its merger with Frito-Lay in 1965, the company became PepsiCo, Incorporated, and obtained its subsequent growth through concentric acquisitions, new product introductions, and product line extensions.

In 1993 PepsiCo's soft drink division markets Pepsi-Cola, Mountain Dew, and Slice in regular and diet versions in both the American and international market, and 7UP in non-American markets. In this division the company also operates various soft drink joint bottling and distribution ventures such as those with Ocean Spray and Lipton Tea in the United States, Canada's Avalon spring water on the U.S. eastern seaboard, A&W's root beer and cream soda, Squirt and Vernors brands in Asia, and Kas brands with Knorr Elorza SA in Spain. Crystal Pepsi and Diet Crystal Pepsi, the firm's clear, uncolored "New Age" soft drink, was introduced during Super Bowl XXVII with 90 seconds of advertising at $28,000 a second, and it slowly rolled out All Sport as it tried to crack America's $800 million-a-year sports drink category.

The company's snack foods division makes and distributes its products throughout the world. Its major offerings are Lay's Potato Chips, Cheetos, Doritos, Crunch

Tators, Tostitos, Ruffles, Rold Gold Pretzels, Fritos, and Santitas Tortilla Chips. New snack and chip products include Sunchips multigrain snacks, Suprimos wheat-based snack chips, McCracken's cracker crisps, and the Sonric sweet snack in Mexico. In a related move, Frito-Lay has introduced a line of salsa and picante sauces which garnered an 11 percent share of 1992's $496.8 million market. In spring 1993 the division rolled out a premium brand of salsa and picante named after its popular Tostitos restaurant-style chips. Major manufacturing and processing operations can be found in the United Kingdom, Spain, Mexico, Portugal, and Brazil. Joint ventures are underway in various countries such as in Mexico with the Gamesa Company in the cookie business, with Poland's Wedel in the sweet snack segment, and the complete ownership of the Arnotts snacks and cracker company in Australia after initially operating as a joint venture.

PepsiCo also operates the world's largest system of restaurants through its Pizza Hut, Taco Bell, and KFC chains. Included in this division are the sales of PepsiCo Food Systems Worldwide (PFS), which supplies all company-owned and franchised units with everything from food, paper goods, and equipment to promotional materials. The division's revenues come from company-owned store sales, initial franchising fees, royalty and rental payments from franchisees, and net wholesale sales to franchisees by PFS. Although already a worldwide presence, new markets for Pizza Hut have been opened in Aruba, Cyprus, and Gibraltar, for KFC in France and Chile, and Taco Bell in Aruba, Korea, and Saudi Arabia. In total Pizza Hut and KFC each operate in over 60 countries, and Taco Bell is in eleven countries with 20 more countries being investigated. Within the United States Taco Bell is experimenting in Charleston, South Carolina, and Fresno, California, with its Hot'n Now acquisition, an express drive through burger concept, as well as additions to the fare served in its three major restaurant systems. Exhibits 2–3 present the corporation's Income Statements and Balance Sheets for the fiscal years 1989–1992, Exhibit 4 indicates PepsiCo's degree of international sales involvement, and Exhibits 5–6 present each

■ **Exhibit 2**
PepsiCo Corporation
Income Statements
(000,000)

	Years Ending			
	12/26/92	**12/28/91**	**12/29/90**	**12/31/89**
Net sales	$21,970.9	$19,607.9	$17,802.7	$15,242.4
Cost of goods sold	10,492.6	9,395.5	8,549.4	7,421.7
Gross profit	11,477.4	10,212.4	9,253.3	7,820.7
Selling and general administration	8,840.3	7,880.8	7,008.6	5,887.4
Pretax operating income	2,637.1	2,331.6	2,244.7	1,933.3
Non-operating income	113.7	(45.4)	111.2	26.8
Interest expense	586.1	615.9	688.5	609.6
Pretax income	2,164.7	1,670.3	1,667.4	1,350.5
Provision for taxes	597.1	590.1	576.8	449.1
Less exceptional item and discontinued operations*	1,193.3	-0-	13.7	-0-
Net income	$ 374.3	$ 1,080.2	$ 1,076.9	$ 901.4

*1990 net charges for discontinued operations; 1992 net charges for required accounting changes for retiree health benefits and income taxes.

SOURCE: Adapted from company 10-K report and *News from PepsiCo Inc.*, (February 2, 1993), p. 2.

■ **Exhibit 3**   PepsiCo Corporation Balance Sheets (000,000)

	Years Ending			
	12/26/92	**12/28/91**	**12/29/90**	**12/31/89**
Assets				
Cash	$ 169.6	$ 186.7	$ 170.8	$ 76.2
Marketable securities	1,888.5	1,849.3	1,644.9	1,457.7
Receivables	1,588.5	1,481.7	1,414.7	1,239.7
Inventories	768.8	661.5	585.8	546.1
Other current assets	426.6	386.9	265.2	231.1
Total current assets	4,842.3	4,566.1	4,081.4	3,550.8
Property, plant and equipment	7,442.0	6,594.7	5,710.9	5,130.2
Advances to subsidiaries	1,707.0	1,681.9	1,505.9	970.8
Intangibles	6,959.0	5,932.4	5,845.2	5,474.9
Total assets	$20,951.2	$18,775.1	$17,143.4	$15,126.7
Liabilities				
Notes payable	$ 706.8	$ 228.2	$ 1,626.5	$ 866.3
Accounts payable	1,164.8	1,196.6	1,116.3	1,054.5
Income taxes	387.9	492.4	443.7	313.7
Other current liabilities	2,064.9	1,804.9	1,584.0	1,457.3
Total current liabilities	4,324.4	3,722.1	4,770.5	3,691.8
Deferred charges	1,682.3	1,070.1	942.8	856.9
Long term debt	7,964.8	7,806.2	5,600.1	5,777.1
Other long term liabilities	1,624.0	631.3	925.8	909.8
Total liabilities	15,595.5	13,229.7	12,239.2	11,235.6
Common stock	14.4	14.4	14.4	14.4
Capital surplus	667.6	476.6	365.0	323.9
Retained earnings	5,439.7	5,470.0	4,753.0	3,978.4
Less treasury stock	667.0	745.9	611.4	491.8
Currency adjustment	(99.0)	330.3	383.2	66.2
Shareholder equity	5,355.7	5,545.4	4,904.2	3,891.1
Total liabilities and net worth	$20,951.2	$18,775.1	$17,143.4	$15,126.7
Dividends paid	$ 395.5	$ 343.2	$ 293.9	$ 241.9

SOURCE: Adapted from company 10-K report and 1992 Stockholder's Report, pp. 32 and 46.

■ **Exhibit 4**   PepsiCo Sales and Profits by Geographic Area (000,000)

	Net Sales				**Operating Profit**			
Area	**1992**	**1991**	**1990**	**1989**	**1992**	**1991**	**1990**	**1989**
United States	$16,551.0	$15,167.8	$14,046.9	$12,519.4	$2,059.6	$1,842.2	$1,853.3	$1,601.9
Europe	1,349.0	1,486.0	1,057.5	771.7	52.6	61.8	108.5	53.8
Canada and Mexico	2,214.2	1,434.7	1,089.2	899.0	251.0	198.7	164.2	117.1
Other	1,855.8	1,519.4	1,321.9	1,052.3	138.6	123.8	98.4	122.9
Total	$21,970.0	$19,607.9	$17,515.5	$15,242.4	$2,501.8	$2,226.5	$2,224.4	$1,895.7

SOURCE: 1990 and 1991 Stockholder's Reports, p. 35 and 1992 Stockholder's Report, p. 29.

■ **Exhibit 5**   Domestic and International Segment Sales and Profits (000,000)

	Net Sales				Operating Profit			
Segment	1992	1991	1990	1989	1992	1991	1990	1989
Beverages								
Domestic	$ 5,485.3	$ 5,171.5	$ 5,034.5	$ 4,623.3	$ 686.3	$ 746.2	$ 673.8	$ 577.6
International	2,120.4	1,743.7	1,488.5	1,153.4	112.3	117.1	93.8	98.6
Total	7,605.6	6,915.2	6,523.0	5,776.7	798.6	863.3	767.6	676.2
Snack foods								
Domestic	3,950.4	3,737.9	3,471.5	3,211.3	775.5	616.6	732.3	667.8
International	2,181.7	1,827.9	1,295.3	1,003.7	209.2	271.0	202.1	137.4
Total	6,132.7	5,565.8	4,766.8	4,215.0	984.7	787.6	934.4	805.2
Restaurants								
Domestic	7,115.4	6,258.4	5,504.0	4,684.8	597.8	479.4	447.2	356.5
International	1,116.9	868.5	684.8	565.9	120.7	96.2	75.2	57.8
Total	8,232.3	7,126.9	6,225.7	5,250.7	718.5	575.6	522.4	414.3
Total								
Domestic	16,551.0	15,167.8	14,046.9	12,519.4	2,059.6	1,842.2	1,853.3	1,601.9
International	5,419.0	4,440.1	3,468.6	2,723.0	442.2	384.3	371.1	293.8
Grand Total	$21,970.0	$19,607.9	$17,515.5	$15,242.4	$2,501.8	$2,226.5	$2,224.4	$1,895.7

SOURCE: 1990 and 1991 Stockholder's Reports, p. 35 and News from PepsiCo, Inc., (February 2, 1993), p. 5.

■ **Exhibit 6**

Identifiable Assets by Division and Geographic Area (000,000)

Division and Area	1992	1991	1990	1989
Soft drinks	$ 7,857.5	$ 6,832.6	$ 6,465.2	$ 6,198.1
Snack foods	4,628.0	4,114.3	3,892.4	3,310.0
Restaurants	5,097.1	4,254.2	3,448.9	3,070.6
Total	$17,582.6	$15,201.1	$13,806.5	$12,578.7
United States	$11,957.0	$10,777.8	$ 9,980.7	$ 9,593.4
Europe	1,948.4	2,367.3	2,255.2	1,767.2
Canada and Mexico	2,395.2	917.3	689.5	409.5
Other	1,282.0	1,138.7	881.1	808.6
Total	$17,582.6	$15,201.1	$13,806.5	$12,578.7

SOURCE: 1990 and 1991 Stockholder's Reports, p. 35 and 1992 Stockholder's Report, p. 29.

■ **Exhibit 7**

Assorted Restaurant Division Charges (000,000)

Pizza Hut	1990—$9.0 for closing underperforming domestic units; $8.0 to consolidate domestic field operations; $2.4 to relocate headquarters
Taco Bell	1989—$5.5 to consolidate domestic field operations 1990—$4.0 for closing underperforming domestic units

KFC	1989—$8.0 reorganization
	1990—$4.0 for closing underperforming domestic units
	    $0.6 for closing underperforming international units
	1991—$32.8 to restructure domestic operations
	    $1.2 to restructure international operations
	    $9.0 for delay of Skinfree Crispy introduction

SOURCE: 1990 and 1991 Stockholder's Reports, p. 35.

segment's overall performance and their assigned assets and geographic areas of concentration. Exhibit 7 indicates recent one-time and unusual expenditures associated with PepsiCo's industry segments.

■ The Fast-Food Industry

Americans eat about 750 million meals a day, but over the years the proportion of food consumed in the home has declined. In the battle for "stomach share," Exhibit 8 shows by 1991 almost as much, or about $262 billion, was spent on restaurant fare as was spent for prepared and nonprepared grocery store food. Considering prepared food, which is a growth industry because of the two-person working family and the provision of an escape from cooking chores, Exhibit 9 demonstrates fast-food restaurants have increased their market share, while the table-service or "white linen" restaurant share has declined. In 1993 restaurant spending will amount to more than $268 billion and meals will be served both on and off the restaurant's premises as displayed in Exhibit 10.

The 1980s was a decade of high industry growth with average sales increases amounting to 8.7 percent a year. Lately, however, real growth and the industry's returns on net worth have declined. See Exhibit 11 for the combined actual and estimated operating profits for a number of restaurant chains. After adjusting for

■ **Exhibit 8**
U.S. Consumer Food
Expenditures

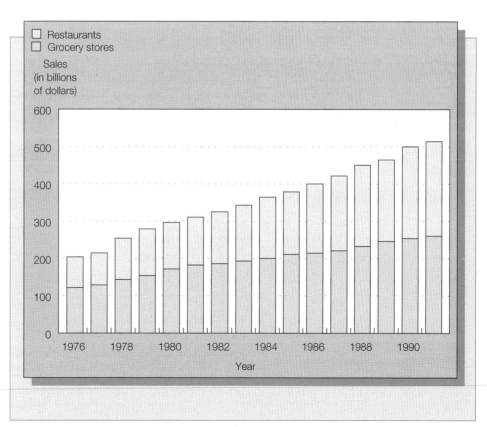

SOURCE: Derived from graph data presented in Eben Shapiro, "A Page From Fast-Food's Menu," *New York Times* (October 14, 1991), p. Dl.

■ **Exhibit 9**
America's Sources of
Prepared Food

	Food Source			
Year	**Fast-Food Restaurants**	**Table-Service Restaurants**	**Supermarkets**	**Other**
1991	51.0%	23.0%	14.0%	12.0%
1990	46.0	27.0	14.0	13.0
1989	41.0	33.0	12.0	14.0

SOURCE: Adapted from Charles S. Clark, "Fast-Food Shake-Up," *CQ Research* 1, no. 25 (November 8, 1991), p. 837.

■ **Exhibit 10**
Where America Ate Its
Restaurant Food in
1991

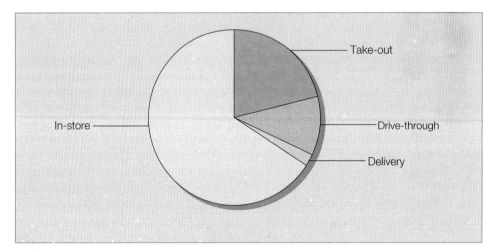

SOURCE: From data and graphs in "Forget Candlelight, Flowers—and Tips: More Restaurants Tout Takeout Service," *The Wall Street Journal* (June 18, 1992), p. B1.

■ **Exhibit 11**   Restaurant Industry Income and Expenses (000,000)

	1989	**1990**	**1991**	**1992***	**1993***	**1995–1997***
Sales	$12,048.0	$12,943.0	$13,330.0	$14,085.0	$15,315.0	$21,275.0
Cost of sales	9,445.6	10,017.9	10,277.4	10,845.5	11,716.0	16,062.6
Gross profit	2,602.4	2,925.1	3,052.6	3,239.6	3,599.0	5,212.4
Adm. overhead	426.0	459.1	473.0	325.8	401.0	640.7
Depreciation	604.9	758.9	800.8	845.0	895.0	1,155.0
Pretax profit	1,571.5	1,707.1	1,778.1	2,068.7	2,303.0	3,416.7
Less taxes	573.6	602.6	601.2	713.7	783.0	1,161.7
Net profit	$ 997.9	$ 1,104.5	$ 1,177.5	$ 1,355.0	$ 1,520.0	$ 2,255.0
Net worth	$ 4,937.7	$ 5,762.3	$ 6,624.8	$ 7,640.0	$ 8,860.0	$13,075.0

*Estimated per year.

NOTE: Summary results for Bob Evans Farms, Carl Karcher Enterprises, Frisch's Restaurants, International Dairy Queen, JB's Restaurant, Luby's Cafeterias, McDonald's, Morrison Restaurant, National Pizza, Perkins Family Restaurant, Piccadilly Cafeterias, Ryan's Family Steak Houses, Shoney's, Sizzler International, TCBY Enterprises, Vicorp Restaurants, and Wendy's International.

SOURCE: William G. Barr, "Restaurant Industry," *Value Line* (September 25, 1992), p. 295.

inflation, total 1991 to 1992 industry sales increased only 1.8 percent, and price wars have periodically broken out in response to outlet proliferation and the lingering 1991 recession. Discounting has been employed extensively to generate traffic, but the major chains are now redefining the nature of a "bargain." This new definition regards "value" through the use of combination meals which guide the customer to higher markup food items while simultaneously emphasizing the food's quality and the restaurant's service and atmosphere.

While overall growth has declined, various growth segments and food delivery concepts exist. From 1985 to 1990 the fast-food industry's sandwich segment rose from 4.9 percent of total sales to 5.7 percent of sales, while hamburger chain sales fell from 53.4 percent to 50.5 percent of all sales. Sandwich segment sales amounted to about $5.3 billion in 1992, or .8 percent more than in 1991. In 1991 America's 100 largest restaurant chains added only 413 hamburger outlets, but pizza makers opened 1,095 additional restaurants. By the beginning of 1992 the nation had about 18,600 pizza and 26,600 burger restaurants. Ice cream and yogurt outlets were ranked third in number, but this food segment had a net loss of 142 outlets in 1991. Contributing to the pizza category's growth are a number of factors. Technomic President Ronald Paul says "Pizza's a very friendly product." He observes crusts can vary in thickness and can be crunchy or chewy, the pizza's cheese base is rich in protein, and a great variety of toppings can be applied. Moreover, given the trend to more takeout and home delivery, pizza holds up better over further distances than either burgers or fries. Exhibit 12 displays the current high growth food segments while Exhibit 13 lists America's fastest growing fast-food chains.

Although the upscale, casual dining segment has lost market share in recent years, each unit generates relatively high profits. Rather than relying on the fast-food restaurant's "table turn" for profits, white linen restaurants obtain profits by serving more highly marked up meals, generating bar and table liquor sales, and the serving of multi-course meals rather than finger food and limited combos. General

■ Exhibit 12
Growth Food
Segments in 1991

Segment	Growth
Pizza	5.4%
Chicken	6.8
Fish	11.6
Mexican	12.6
Oriental	28.4

SOURCE: Adapted from 1991 PepsiCo, Inc. Stockholder's Report, p. 31.

■ Exhibit 13
Fastest Growing
Fast-Food Chains

Chain	Menu/Theme	1990 Sales ($000,000)
Taco Bell	Inexpensive Mexican food	2,600.0
Subway	Deli-style submarine sandwiches	1,400.0
Sonic	1950s-style drive-ins	515.0
Sbarro	Fast Italian food	277.0
Rally's	Double drive-through burgers	216.0

SOURCE: Lois Therrien, "The Upstart's Teaching McDonald's a Thing or Two," *Business Week* (October 21, 1991), p. 122.

■ **Exhibit 14** Selected National Restaurant Chains by Type

<table>
<tr><td colspan="2" align="center">Family Restaurants</td></tr>
<tr><td>Big Boy</td><td>963 units. Originally known for its hamburgers but now offers a variety of meals and a soup, salad, and fruit bar. Worst rated restaurant in this category. Value and prices were average.</td></tr>
<tr><td>Denny's</td><td>1,391 units. 24-hour service, well-known for breakfast menu and grilled sandwiches. Menus for senior citizens and children. Alcohol served at many locations. Food taste and selection rated less than average for average-priced fare.</td></tr>
<tr><td>Int. House of Pancakes</td><td>500 units. Traditional breakfast stop with a wide variety of all day meals of average value and price. Menus for seniors and children. Most patrons were seated immediately.</td></tr>
<tr><td>Po Folks</td><td>137 units. Large portions of "home style cookin'." Special menus for seniors and children. Has a takeout service and catering facilities. Considered a good value with lower than average prices. Received the highest overall rating in this category of restaurants.</td></tr>
<tr><td>Village Inn</td><td>229 units. Focuses mainly on breakfast with a limited selection of lunch and dinner meals. Senior citizen discount and low fat/calorie breakfasts. Most diners were seated immediately.</td></tr>
<tr><td colspan="2" align="center">Steak/Buffet Restaurants</td></tr>
<tr><td>Golden Corral</td><td>458 units. Mostly steak but limited grilled chicken and seafood. Food, salad, and dessert bar with over 100 items. Menus for seniors and children. Bar. Prices and food value judged better than average.</td></tr>
<tr><td>Mr. Steak</td><td>60 units. Steak, chicken, and seafood. Takeout service and a children's menu. Received the highest rating for this type of restaurant.</td></tr>
<tr><td>Sizzler</td><td>634 units. Features chicken, steak, and seafood with a large salad, soup, taco, and pasta bar. Senior citizen and children's menus. Entertainment lounge and wine. Takeout service. Taste, food selection, price and value rated average.</td></tr>
<tr><td colspan="2" align="center">Casual Dinner Houses</td></tr>
<tr><td>Bennigan's</td><td>223 units. Menu varies throughout the U.S. but emphasizes Southwestern dishes and finger foods. Children's menu. Takeout. Bar. Received the lowest ratings for this type of restaurant. Value and prices were much worse than average although the atmosphere was rated much better than average.</td></tr>
</table>

(continued)

Mills, Inc. has been especially successful in the casual dining, ethnic food restaurant segment. To supplement its aging Red Lobster seafood restaurant chain, in 1982 General Mills simultaneously created the Olive Garden based on an Italian theme, purchased Darryl's, a North Carolina fern-bar restaurant chain, a California health-food restaurant called The Good Earth, and Casa Gallardo, a Mexican-food chain. Of the four concepts, the Olive Garden appeared to have the greatest potential, as market research found that Italian cuisine was America's most identifiable ethnic food. In 1985 seven more restaurants were opened and by 1992 the chain had grown to 320 stores with sales of $808 million. Success did not come easily, however, as management spent five years and about $28 million before settling on the chain's optimal recipes, flavorings, and decor. Although uniformity and consistency are the hallmarks of fast-food operations, the Olive Garden found it had to recognize regional taste differences if it was to cater to the white-collar, evening dinner crowd. It discovered through taste tests and trial menus that chunky tomato sauce did not do very well in St. Louis but patrons in California loved it and customers in Rhode Island uniquely favored veal saltimbocca.

■ **Exhibit 14**   (*concluded*)

Chili's	267 units. Southwest grill, Tex-Mex, burgers, and salads. Seniors and children's menus. Bar. Fare was rated above average in tastiness. Rated about average for this group.
El Torito	169 units. Clearly Mexican featuring fajitas, quesadillas, and chimichangas and daily specials. Sunday brunch. Bar. Dinner portions were considered larger than average.
Houlihan's	54 units. Steaks, burgers, and fajitas. Kids' menu. Bar and lounge. Value and prices were rated much worse than average for this group.
Olive Garden	Homemade pasta, regional Italian meat and seafood specialties. Large Italian wine list. Children's menu, takeout service and catering. The highest rated restaurant in this category with much better than average taste and better than average menu selection. Dinner portions were larger than average and the food's quality was more consistent. At least 25 percent of the raters had to wait more than 10 minutes to be seated for dinner.
Red Lobster	550 units. Seafood, chicken, and steak with catch-of-the-day specials. Children's menu, takeout service, and bar. Prices rated much higher than average although its fare was rated above average in taste and selection. 25 percent of the raters had to wait more than 10 minutes to be seated.
Ruby Tuesday	151 units. Menu varies throughout the U.S. with international appetizers and main courses. Salad bar and weekend brunch. Senior citizen discounts and children's menus. Bar. Rated below average for price and value.
Steak and Ale	158 units. Well appointed atmosphere featuring steak, seafood, pasta, and chicken. Salad bar. Bar. Food rated much tastier than average and above average in selection. Prices were much higher than average. Rated the second highest restaurant in this group.
T.G.I. Friday's	202 units. Very eclectic menu. Also has "lite" and children's menus. Takeout service and bar. Prices were much higher than average although tastiness and selection were better than average.
Tony Roma's	122 units. Barbecued ribs and chicken entrées. Takeout, bar, and children's menu. Food rated higher than average in tastiness although rated below average in value and cost.

SOURCE: Adapted from "Best Meals Best Deals," *Consumer Reports* 57, no. 6 (June, 1992), pp. 361–362.

Based on General Mills' success with its Olive Garden, it is now in its third year of testing Chinese cuisine at its China Coast restaurant in Orlando, Florida. The company first tried oriental cuisine with its Minneapolis-based Leeann Chin buffet and takeout chain seven years ago after extensive testing. When this failed the company hired Terry Cheng, a Chinese-American chef and food biologist, to produce a more satisfying menu for American tastes. The result has been the creation of six main dishes revolving around moo goo gai pan, fried rice, egg rolls, and sweet-and-sour chicken but definitely not authentic Chinese dishes such as chicken feet, jellyfish, and bird's nest soup. Exhibit 14 presents an array of national chains employing various ethnic segments and upscaled dining accommodations along with their ratings from a 1992 *Consumer Reports* reader survey.

In addition to price wars and niche hunting as strategies for dealing with the fast-food industry's declining growth, other methods are being tried to continue the industry's development. These strategies entail the creation of more convenient outlets, alternative food delivery methods, greater attempts to capture the after-six eating crowd, and an increasing reliance on foreign or internationally derived sales.

Because so many people need and want to avoid spending time preparing meals in their own kitchens, more meals are purchased in restaurants, more people are buying prepared and semiprepared foods in grocery stores, and more are using restaurant takeout, drive-through, and delivery service. This latter service group is called off-premises dining which grew 5.9 percent in 1991 while the fast-food restaurant industry's on-premises sales were flat. Prepared foods represented a $63.5 billion business in 1989, and the market research firm Find/SVP projects this market will increase to $88.7 billion by the mid-90s with the supermarkets' share increasing to 16.5 percent at the expense of fast-food restaurant sales.

Over the years certain chains have been more successful than others in obtaining off-premises sales. These sales accounted for 65 percent of Wendy's volume in 1992, a 30 percent increase since 1988, and they accounted for 70 percent of Burger King's sales. Despite the growth of this food delivery method certain dangers are involved. As George Rice, chairman of GDR Enterprises says, "Off-premises sales are a great opportunity, but they can also screw up your business." He recommends owners should view it as a separate business and ask such questions as "Who's going to take orders? How's the kitchen going to integrate takeout with on-premises orders? Where are takeout customers going to stand while they wait? Will they make the restaurant look crowded?" Other sit-down restauranteurs resist doing takeouts as they have been using their ambiance as a competitive weapon against the plastic-boothed and spartan-appearing fast-food chains. Ann Durning of the Olive Garden chain observes "We make takeout available, but our feeling is that there's more to a full service restaurant than food. There is also good service, Italian music and fresh flowers on the table."

An innovation that eliminates the problems of offering both on and off-premises dining from the same location is the creation of restaurants that prepare meals exclusively for off-premises consumption. Pizza Hut has opened Fastino's, a chain that sells pasta and pizza on a takeout and drive-through basis only. Pizza Hut's Vice President of Development Pat Williamson predicts Fastino's will eventually become as big as its 8,000-unit Pizza Hut chain. A variant of this concept is the use of double drive-throughs. McDonald's is experimenting with this concept in Raleigh, NC which uses tandem drive-through windows on the side of a small food preparation and cashiering building. The store has no counter or seating, is one-third the size of a typical McDonald's 4,500 square foot outlet, and the number of employees per unit falls from 60 to about 35. To accelerate food preparation and simplify order-taking, a limited menu is used that excludes salads and breakfast entrees such as pancakes. Other companies experimenting with this concept are Taco Bell and Arby's which, respectively, bought the Hot'n Now and Daddy-O's Express Drive-Thru chains in 1991.

Other trends attempting to capitalize on the desire for off-premises dining, as well as compensating for the scarcity of prime sites for full-scale restaurants in various markets, are the creation of smaller outlets and greater access to fast-food from alternative locations. One smaller outlet form is the use of kiosks and portable food carts. Basically a one-person operation, Taco Bell has operated kiosks in supermarkets in Phoenix, and Taco Bell's first Mexico City outlet was a two-person food cart started in June 1992, with two more locations planned for Mexico City and one in Tijuana. Pizza Hut, which already has 500 carts in operation, has plans to set up more than 10,000 carts in the United States and more than 100,000 in overseas locations. KFC opened a cart unit in a General Motors plant in January 1992 with plans for carts in train stations, office buildings, sports stadiums, and amusement parks. PepsiCo is also negotiating with Wal-Mart to put its units in the mass merchandiser's chain throughout the United States. As an indication of the company's commitment to this concept, PepsiCo purchased a strong minority interest in Carts of Colorado Inc. in February 1992.

Others are also looking for additional stores. McDonald's is attempting to develop "niche" outlets in such places as airports and hospitals, as well as in small, rural towns by opening smaller-sized units called Golden Arch Cafes. These cafes are about half the size of a standard McDonald's, seat about 50 people, and offer counter service. Other examples of the "niche" location are the presence of Wendy's in the downtown Atlanta Day's Inn lobby and Marriott Hotels' provision of Pizza Hut room service from its own kitchens despite the fact that most of its hotels have restaurants and it once owned the Gino's and Roy Rogers restaurant chains. Hotels and motels find they can charge more for the franchised products they offer than their own because of their instant brand name recognition. As of early 1992, Pizza Hut's offerings were available in about 40 Marriott Hotels with 25 more scheduled for July 1992. Economy hotels, which usually do not have dining facilities or are losing money on them, are now the fast-food industry's target. Economy or budget hotels account for about 38 percent of the nation's 44,500 hotels and motels and are the lodging industry's fastest growing segment.

Another attempt to increase sales in the fast-food industry has come with its revival of its attack on attracting the dinner crowd and to profit from the rise of the "casual dining out experience." Many customers want to relax and spend more time over dinner than they do at breakfast or lunch. Norman K. Stevens, former marketing chief for Hardee's, explains "People's expectations at dinner are totally different than at lunch" and that dinner is more of a leisurely event, a destination, and not something to be gotten over with as quickly as possible. As an example of this trend 1991 sales at sit-down ethnic restaurants totaled $8 billion, a 10 percent increase over 1990's sales. It is difficult, however, to change a nation's fast-food eating habits or to change a chain's food delivery system or concept. McDonald's attempted to expand upon its successful lunch trade by offering its Egg McMuffin in 1975 to the breakfast segment. It was unsuccessful with the category until 11 years later when it introduced a variety of breakfast sandwiches. Upon the establishment of its breakfast menu the chain created a "Mac Tonight" promotion featuring a piano-playing Moonman character in 1987 to induce customers to have an evening meal at a McDonald's. The campaign was not very successful, as only about 20 percent of McDonald's sales come after 4:00 PM.

Burger King has initiated a dinner menu and table service to revive its stagnant sales and attract a different dinner customer. Although it serves about 2 million Whoppers a day, it realized its customers were switching to other menu items late in the day. Burger King's Cory Zywotow also found their customers said "They'd like to relax and spend more time" over dinner. In certain outlets tablecloths and napkin rings are provided to heighten the ambiance. Starting at 4:00 PM, each Burger King offers four main courses priced between $3.00 to $5.00—a hamburger, steak sandwich, fried shrimp, or fried chicken filet in a dinner basket with either a baked potato or french fries, and a salad or cole slaw. Customers are given a tray, beverage cups and a numbered plastic marker along with free popcorn. When their order is ready it is brought to them at their table. Management believes its sit-down dinner service was a major factor in increasing the company's operating profit over 9 percent from 1991 to 1992. While table service is an innovation for a fast-food restaurant the role of a different evening menu should not be overestimated, as about 65 percent and 73 percent of KFC's and Pizza Hut's respective sales are at the dinner hour despite the lack of both table service and special dinner items.

Because of the decline in industry sales growth and saturation in various food segments and geographic markets, many chains have turned to overseas operations. Looking at the franchising field in general, a survey of 366 franchisers conducted by

Arthur Andersen & Co. in 1992 found that only about one-third of them have foreign outlets but nearly half of those without foreign operations intend to grow internationally in the next five years. Gary L. Copp, President of Spee-Dee Oil Change Systems, Inc. speaks for many when he reasons, "Why take on Chicago when I can go to Brazil and find a virgin market?"

In the fast-food industry international sales have become very important and very profitable. McDonald's first-quarter 1992 international sales rose 14 percent to $1.9 billion, or 39 percent of its total revenue and 42 percent of its total operating profits. Steven A. Rockwell of Alex. Brown & Sons estimates the company's overseas profits will surpass domestic profits by 1995 due to both the number of units operated and the high unit volumes they produce. In early 1992 McDonald's added 50 restaurants to its system of which most were in foreign countries and as many as 450 new overseas units were planned for the year. By April 1992 McDonald's had 8,772 American and 3,696 foreign restaurants. In that month it also opened its biggest store—a 700 seat facility in Beijing.

Other chains have also profited from foreign operations. KFC posted a 26 percent third-quarter world-wide profit increase while its same-store U.S. sales declined 1 percent. Its first East European store was opened in Budapest, Hungary, in partnership with the Hungarian franchisee Hemingway Holding AG, in October 1992 after working nearly two years to develop local suppliers. Pizza Hut opened two restaurants in Moscow in September 1990 with one selling pizzas for hard currency and the other selling them for rubles. About 20,000 customers are served a week, about the amount sold by 10 American-based Pizza Huts.

As profitable as foreign operations are for the fast-food franchisers, numerous problems accompany the application of their global strategies and standardized operating systems in foreign cultures. McDonald's American success has come from its routinized manufacturing and operating skills. Its operations manual is 600 pages long and the company demands mass production techniques and absolute uniformity. A crew person must get a manager's approval before replacing a malted drink order or a spilled soft drink. Dressing a hamburger is always done in the same order—mustard first, then ketchup, then onions, and then two pickles. The result is a Big Mac that looks and tastes the same in Tokyo as in Tacoma. In coming to Hungary, however, McDonald's found the country's native potatoes were dark and did not fry "golden brown," and the requisite iceberg lettuce was not home-grown. To replicate the chain's eye appeal and taste standard entire B-747 airplane loads of potatoes and shredded lettuce were initially flown to Budapest when it opened its first restaurant on the corners of V. Aranykéz and Régiposta streets.

While the fast-food industry's participants have employed numerous strategies to accommodate its lower growth, two long-term concerns have continued to haunt the industry. One concern deals with fast-food's nutritional value and this concern has accelerated with America's greater awareness of the health and diet issues associated with its aging population. The other concern deals with franchisee/franchisor relations. Although these relations have often been contentious, many franchisees have been hit hard by franchiser actions taken to maintain sales growth at the unit level. Accordingly, in the early 1990s they have developed a new militancy which often frustrates the designs of the national chains.

To many consumers fast-food has always meant "bad food." PepsiCo has attempted to avoid this stereotype of fast not being good by calling their chains "quick service" restaurants. Others, such as McDonald's, emphasize the enjoyment of eating fast, tasty meals with friends, family, and coworkers. America's health concerns are real, however, and the national chains have begun to introduce low-fat and low-calorie items to their standard fare as well as emphasizing the nutritional value of fast-food dining. In early 1990 McDonald's introduced its McLean Deluxe, a 91 percent fat-free hamburger containing carrageenan, a seaweed-based additive, to wide acclaim. Unfortunately its sales were not sizzling. Two years later, as part of a nutritional, public information effort, the company aired a dozen animated 55-second televised spot announcements called "What's on Your Plate." These announcements attempted to explain the basics of well-balanced eating and how it could be accomplished. In each restaurant McDonald's posts nutritional information on all its fare, and leaflets about its food are available for the asking. Burger King displays posters with the calorie, fat, cholesterol, and sodium content of all its food. The company is also test marketing menus in 350 of its stores exclusively based on Weight Watchers foods as well as experimenting with foods under 300 calories, including chicken on angel-hair pasta and chocolate mocha pie. About 60 percent of Taco Bell's company-owned outlets offer complete nutritional product information, while Wendy's has taken the position of matching its competition regarding the amount of information it supplies.

Many critics, however, are dissatisfied with the industry's efforts at providing a healthy diet. Michael Jacobson, Executive Director of the Center for Science in the Public Interest, feels the fast-food industry could do more. "The charts and posters don't convey much to the average person. The information is presented as a matrix with 10 or 15 numbers for every food. Most people aren't going to lose their places in line to read about nutritional values."

Both nutritionists and industry participants emphasize the role of self-choice in making food purchases mixed with a bit of cynicism regarding America's eating intentions versus its actions. Sandwich shops have capitalized on the desire for greater nutrition. Many customers believe deli meats sandwiched between two slices of fresh bread is healthier than a quarter-pound burger on a bun. Subway's "fattiest" sandwich is a six-inch meatball sub. "[I]t's not particularly healthy," observes Bonnie Liebman, Director of Nutrition at the Center for Science in the Public Interest, "but it has only half as much fat as a McDonald's Big Mac." As another example of the role of self-choice, Michael Evans of Burger King notes that by eating a Whopper without mayonnaise the customer saves 140 calories. With mayonnaise, which is the way most people have it served, it has 619 calories. Accordingly, many chain operators are frustrated regarding the health issue. Maurice Bridges, Hardee's Director of Public Affairs says, "After spending millions on research, we found, just by listening to the consumer, that people are talking nutrition, but they buy on taste." And industry observer Rajan Chaudhry of *Restaurants and Institutions* magazine believes, "People talk healthy but what they're really looking for is something to let them off the hook and let them believe they're eating healthier than they were otherwise."

Exhibit 15 displays the results of eating typical fast-food restaurant fare for an entire day. The average adult needs between 1,200 and 3,000 daily calories for weight maintenance. Approximately 50–60 percent of those calories should come from carbohydrates, 15–20 percent from protein, and 25–30 percent should come from fat. It is also recommended that healthy adults limit their sodium intake to 3,000 milligrams per day and cholesterol to 300 daily milligrams.

Since the early 1960s McDonald's has exemplified the virtues of franchising as a form for rapid business development. Frandata Corp. of Washington, DC, estimates there are more than 3,000 franchisers in the United States operating about 540,000 franchised outlets. And according to the International Franchise Association a new

■ **Exhibit 15**

A Day of Fast-Food Dining

Meal	Nutrition				
	Carbo-hydrates	Protein	Fat	Choles-terol	Calories
Breakfast at McDonald's					
Orange juice	19	1	0	0	80
McMuffin sausage/egg	28	23	27	263	440
Hashbrown potatoes	15	1	7	9	130
Total	62	25	34	272	650
Lunch at Pizza Hut					
3 slices medium size pepperoni pizza	75	42	36	75	750
1 regular pepsi	40	0	0	0	159
Total	115	42	36	75	909
Supper at KFC					
3 drumsticks	12	39	27	201	438
Cole slaw	13	2	7	5	119
2 buttermilk biscuits	56	10	24	2	470
1 regular pepsi	40	0	0	0	159
Total	121	51	58	208	1,186
Grand Total	298	118	128	555	2,745

NOTE: Carbohydrates, protein, fat, and cholesterol listed in grams.

SOURCE: *Eating Out Made Simple.* (Tulsa, OK: St. Francis Hospital, 1991), pp. 16–17, 22, 25–26.

outlet of some type opens about every 16 minutes. Accordingly, franchised business sales have risen dramatically and rose 6.1 percent in 1991 to $757.8 billion, or more than 35 percent of all retail sales. Although some franchisees experience long hours, hard work, and often little profits, franchising makes business sense in many cases. In four of five industries surveyed by Francorp, an Olympia Fields, Illinois, consulting firm, a franchisee's 1991 per-store sales grew faster or declined less than their industry's national average. Restaurants, which constitute the franchising industry's largest single group, found their 1991 per-store sales increased 6.2 percent versus an overall restaurant industry growth rate of 3 percent.

Despite these generally favorable results, many restaurant franchisees have become increasingly dissatisfied with their franchisers. When Britain's Grand Metropolitan PLC purchased Burger King from the Pillsbury Co. in 1989, it ordered changes in floor tile designs, background music, and cutbacks in field management help. It also created an advertising campaign that many franchisees felt was unsuccessful. Burger King's management group faced a very disgruntled, 1,300-member National Franchisee Association, Inc., which it met in 1991 for the first time in seven years. The association's grievances were so great it even explored buying Burger King from Grand Met.

Other militant franchisee associations have entered the fray. Almost all of Taco Bell's franchisees joined an independent group in January 1992 to oppose PepsiCo's aggressive price-cutting strategy and to challenge a contract clause which allows PepsiCo to open company-owned stores within a franchisee's market. In protest against the advertised prices PepsiCo sets for their company-owned stores, about 30 percent of the franchised units priced their products higher than the nationally promoted prices in September 1992. Taco Bell officials said in March 1992, however, it would maintain the 59-cent, low-price strategy that many believed started the industry's price war in late 1988. Although the chain rang up 50 percent sales increases to $2.4 billion in two years, its profit growth dropped rapidly. Earnings increases of 108 percent and 19 percent for 1991's first two quarters sank to 2 percent and 5 percent in the following two quarters. As a result of Taco Bell's discounting, McDonald's engaged in retaliatory price-cutting in 1991, and in Joseph S. Capser's experience, a Tampa, Florida, licensee with 29 McDonald's restaurants, price-cutting increased his customer count 15 percent but overall sales increased only 4 percent to 5 percent, and profits fell 10 to 15 percent.

Accordingly, many franchisees feel they are bearing the brunt of the price wars being conducted at their chains' headquarters level. The Taco Bell franchisees want higher-priced items featured in its advertisements, but Tim Ryan, the system's senior vice president of marketing, says "Our customers' focus on price is unchanged. Value continues to be the primary driver." Accordingly he is testing a Value Menu that is priced 10 cents lower. Actions by Taco Bell's Hot'n Now management group have engendered a similar response by some of its franchisees. All Hot'n Now units have been encouraged to feature 39¢ prices for hamburgers, french fries, and soft drinks, which has upset many of the chain's independent franchisees. Because they say they cannot make a profit with these prices and the company's advertisements are confusing, 15 franchisees formed an independent association to stand up to PepsiCo in October 1992.

■ PepsiCo's Quick Service Restaurant Division

Under Wayne Calloway's leadership, PepsiCo's success has been attributed to the philosophy, "Love change. Learn to dance. And leave J. Edgar Hoover behind." By this he means change is inevitable, so it is better to initiate change rather than reacting to a situation. "The worst rule of management is 'If it ain't broke, don't fix it.' In today's economy, if it ain't broke, you might as well break it yourself, because it soon will be." By "learning to dance" the CEO wants PepsiCo to deal with customers in new ways, and "leaving J. Edgar Hoover behind" means practicing a "hands off" management style the former FBI chief would have detested. This loose style has allowed each chain a wide degree of latitude, although Calloway is not against moving people around when necessary and setting high financial goals for each operation. He brought John Cranor over from Frito-Lay in 1991 to fix the Kentucky Fried Chicken operation and sent Pepsi's Worldwide Beverages chief Roger Enrico to head the snack division after he suffered a mild heart attack in Turkey. To accomplish this latter move, he created a new unit for Michael Jordan after Enrico replaced him, and within the past eight years three senior soft drink sales and marketing vice presidents have left the company after falling off their career ladders.

Although much of the public's attention has been focused on the cola wars, Calloway has set his mind on a different priority, which is to double his company's quick service business within the decade. "For us the restaurant business is the most compelling action around. We're not going to prosper if we just wait for busy people to come to our restaurants. We want to move toward the day when pizzas, chicken, and tacos are as convenient and readily available as a bag of Doritos is now." To help accomplish his goals, the following top executives have been assembled, and they are dealing with the operating results found in Exhibits 16–19.

■ **Exhibit 16**
Same-Store Sales
Growth by Chain

Chain	1992	1991	1990	1989
Pizza Hut	0.0%	0.5%	5.5%	9.2%
Taco Bell	6.0	4.1	11.5	15.3
KFC	0.0	0.0	7.0	2.0

SOURCE: Derived from E. S. Ely, "Some High Hurdles Loom for Pepsico's Fast-Food Hotshots," *New York Times* (February 16, 1992), Section 3, p. 5 and *News from PepsiCo, Inc.,* (February 2, 1993), pp. 7–9.

■ **Exhibit 17**
Restaurant Division's
1992 U.S. Market
Shares by Food
Category

PepsiCo Chain	Food Category	Market Share	Total Market (In billions)
KFC	Chicken	48.6%	$ 7.4
Pizza Hut	Italian	26.2%	$16.4
Taco Bell	Mexican	69.6%	$ 4.6

SOURCE: Based on data presented in 1992 Stockholder's Report, p. 23.

■ **Exhibit 18**
1992 Unit Ownership
by Area and Chain

Area	Pizza Hut	Taco Bell	KFC
United States:			
Company-owned	4,301	2,498	1,994
Licensed	402	134	21
Franchised	2,905	1,446	3,074
Total	7,264	3,616	5,056
Overseas:			
Company-owned	539	51	726
Joint venture	370	0	474
Franchised	937	24	2,440
Total	1,846	75	3,640
Grand total	9,454	4,153	8,729

NOTE: Unit totals include 477 primarily Pizza Hut kiosks and 293 other special concept units. Taco Bell U.S. unit count includes 99 company-owned and 38 franchised Hot'n Now restaurants. U.S. count does not include 29 California Pizza Kitchen, Inc. units.

SOURCE: Abstracted from 1992 Stockholder's Report, p. 24.

■ **Exhibit 19**   Results by Restaurant Chain (000,000)

	Net Sales				Operating Profit			
Chain	1992	1991	1990	1989	1992	1991	1990	1989
Pizza Hut	$3,603.5	$3,258.3	$2,949.9	$2,453.5	$335.4	$314.5	$245.9	$205.5
Taco Bell	2,460.0	2,038.1	1,745.5	1,465.9	214.3	180.6	149.6	109.4
KFC	2,168.8	1,830.5	1,530.3	1,331.3	168.8	80.5	126.9	99.4
Total	$8,232.3	$7,126.9	$6,225.7	$5,250.7	$718.5	$575.6	$522.4	$414.3

SOURCE: Data found in 1990 and 1991 Stockholder's Reports, p. 35 and *News from PepsiCo, Inc.,* (February 2, 1993), p. 6.

Kentucky Fried Chicken Corporation   *Louisville, Kentucky*
John M. Cranor III   *President and Chief Executive Officer*   *Age: 46*   *Years of service: 15*
Taco Bell Worldwide   *Irvine, California*
John E. Martin   *President and Chief Executive Officer*   *Age: 47*   *Years of service: 9*
Pizza Hut Worldwide   *Wichita, Kansas*
Steven S. Reinemund   *President and Chief Executive Officer*   *Age: 44*   *Years of service: 8*

Kentucky Fried Chicken Corporation. As shown in Exhibit 16 this chain's same-store sales have not risen for the past two years and it has met with a number of failures as it has attempted to diversify its offerings away from fried chicken-on-the-bone. A number of factors, however, should help John Cranor in his attempts to turn this operation around. Michael Mueller, restaurant analyst with Montgomery Securities observes, "Regular hamburger customers, for health and variety, are switching to chicken." Within the restaurant industry itself, chicken entree and sandwich sales climbed to 12.4 percent of all transactions in 1990 from 10.9 percent in 1987 while hamburgers fell from 19.0 percent to 17.0 percent during the same period. Moreover the chain's nearest rivals, Church's and Popeye's, recently merged and were ultimately forced into bankruptcy.

KFC dominates America's chicken segment with at least a 50 percent market share, as shown in Exhibit 17, but many fast-food chains have entered the marketplace with their own chicken-based meals. Wendy's has introduced a grilled chicken sandwich and Burger King has come out with its BK Broiler. McDonald's began offering chicken fajitas in mid-year 1991, and it has been testing both grilled sandwiches and oven-baked chicken-on-the-bone. Closer to home additional competition is coming from within the PepsiCo family itself. Taco Bell introduced four chicken products in April 1991, and Pizza Hut began testing marinated, rotisserie-cooked chicken in mid-1992. Two of Taco Bell's items were 79¢ chicken tacos and 99¢ chicken-and-cheese filled tortillas called MexiMelts. Elliot Bloom of Taco Bell insisted his chicken products would not steal business from KFC. "You're talking about apples and oranges. What we're offering fills a void, a different niche."

Many see KFC's reliance on fried chicken products as its main menu problem. Although chicken itself is lean and potentially healthy, the batters and frying processes employed usually offset those advantages. The chain has renamed itself KFC to eliminate the "fried" from its logotype and a new skinless, but still fried, product called

Lite 'N Crispy was introduced in Spring, 1991. It suffered a number of embarrassing marketplace setbacks as it was too expensive, tasteless, and the division's franchisees protested its low margins. Initially announced as a phased national introduction, it had to be renamed Skinfree Crispy and withdrawn until 1992 due to its production and taste problems. The delay ultimately resulted in charges of $9 million against domestic operations in 1991. For some industry observers, Lite 'N Crispy's flop is indicative of the entire KFC operation. "There doesn't seem to be a strategic direction. There is a disjointedness, and the skin-free chicken is a microcosm of that" states Emanuel Goldman of Paine Webber Inc. Moreover, Lite 'N Crispy's failure is particularly significant as John Cranor intended it to be the bridge from flavored chicken, such as lemon, barbecue, and teriyaki, to other nonfried fare.

This experience has also caused the division to back off from other new product introductions although it introduced Popcorn Chicken in July 1992. Popcorn Chicken consists of small pieces of marinated, breaded and fried chicken. The Center for Science in the Public Interest, however, in its *Nutrition Action Healthletter* described it as "nuggets of grease-drenched breading that are oozing with fat and salt." A standard 5.3-ounce serving contains 45 grams of fat, almost twice as much as in two Big Macs, and 1,775 mg of sodium. Other new products have been stalled in KFC's test kitchens and a line of eight new sandwiches failed while in test market. The sandwiches, including barbecue, spicy, and chicken salad designed for the lunch trade, increased sales only when heavily promoted. Moreover, they cannibalized KFC's higher-margin chicken-on-the-bone sales.

William McDonald, KFC's senior marketing vice president, says reformulating the chicken is not easy. "It's not a no-brainer. We've learned a product has got to be unbelievably indulgent, special and unique and not eminently substitutable at home." The chain has been trying hard to come up with a non-fried chicken—first trying to bake it, then trying open-hearth grilling. When those two methods were unsatisfactory, KFC tried char-grilling and then broiling the product. It has recently scrapped Monterey Broil, its most recent effort, and is starting over again to make it stand out from home-prepared chicken by spicing up its flavor. Doctoring this product's recipe could take another one and a half years to complete.

The chain has also been working on its image in addition to making menu changes. By early 1992, 85 percent of its U.S. stores had invested an average of $7,500 for new landscaping, new atriums, a coat of fresh red roof paint, and brighter wallpaper. John McDonald says, "KFC has a '60s image and it's the '90s. We've got to turbo-charge." Beginning in Spring 1992, KFC's advertising became focused on the make-believe town of Lake Edna and its single KFC restaurant. The campaign's purpose was to capture the positive, feel-good aspects associated with good food and the traditional values and security found in small towns. Colin Moore, KFC's senior marketing vice president, said in defense of the campaign's strategy, "Clearly we were looking for a 'campaign-able' idea. And we think we've found it. Lake Edna is obviously a fictitious place that is simultaneously nowhere and everywhere. This notion of a small town is as much a state of mind as a physical location." KFC spent almost $120 million on advertising in 1991. In that same year McDonald's spent $387.3 million; $118.4 and $92.7 million was paid by Pizza Hut and Taco Bell.

Various economy and efficiency actions have also been undertaken, and John Cranor has recruited a number of Pizza Hut executives to teach him the fast-food business. As a first step, KFC has begun to use more frozen products in its cooking to reduce in-house chicken preparation labor costs. At the chain's administrative level, $43.0 million was spent in 1991 on a restructuring that could save the division up to $25.0 million a year. The move eliminated about 750 or one-half the company's managers and support staff at both the 800-employee Louisville, Kentucky headquarters and its 700-employee field management offices. After the restructuring, the remaining middle managers supervised more stores, and headquarters became more involved in field operations. Although KFC admitted the restructuring was necessary and the division had become bloated, Ron Paul, president of Technomic Inc. observes "All this does is improve their margins in the short run. It does not fundamentally change the menu and the way consumers view the store."

In attempting to turn the KFC operation around, John Cranor has been faced by another source of problems. Its franchisees, who own about two-thirds of KFC's American outlets, are an independent minded group with many of their outlets in middle- or low-income neighborhoods where customers are less concerned about nutrition and are partial to fried food. Besides, many are loyal to Col. Sanders' original Kentucky Fried Chicken concept, which is why they initially purchased their franchises, and are antagonistic towards some of the new products headquarters has created for them. Their antagonism has been expressed many ways, and they have had PepsiCo in court for three years over various contract disputes. PepsiCo has begun to buy out some of its franchisees as at least a partial method for dealing with these frustrations.

When asked how KFC's turnaround has progressed under his leadership Cranor responded, "I didn't expect turning KFC around was going to be an easy proposition. We're all impatient with everything. We need direction, we need a unified focus. We just want to make sure we don't screw up a $6 billion business while we decide how to get from there to $10 billion." Gary Stibel, of the New England Consulting Group, agrees the division's president has the right idea. For KFC "the marketing challenge is a matter of attracting new users without losing their current loyal following."

Pizza Hut Worldwide.   Steven S. Reinemund, division president and former Marriott Corporation executive, believes he heads a pizza distribution company. Accordingly, Pizza Hut has been very creative in finding alternative methods for obtaining off- and on-premises pizza sales. It began delivering pizza in 1987 and has built the most units dedicated to delivery and carryout. Says George Rice, chairman of a food-service consulting firm, "Since 1984 the entire growth in restaurant sales has been in takeout, delivery, and other consumption outside the stores. That makes Pizza Hut one of the industry's best-positioned companies." Although Pizza Hut has captured about 25 percent of the pizza delivery market it is well behind Domino's and just even with Little Caesars in the number of stores devoted to takeout and delivery service. Moreover, Little Caesars is adding domestic units of this type to its chain at a faster rate than is Pizza Hut.

In 1992 a strategic shift was implemented by Steven Reinemund in reaction to a long-term trend in operating results. By the third quarter of 1991 Pizza Hut's delivery sales increases were not compensating for the declining sit-down sales it was experiencing. Therefore it began to refocus on its in-store business. Part of this effort has been the installation of all-you-can-eat buffets.

The buffets were tested for four months at Pizza Huts in Dallas, Indianapolis, Savannah, and Tulsa, and were later installed in 2,000 restaurants in 1992 at a cost of tens of millions of dollars. "We're into it hot and heavy" said Reinemund. "It is phase one of our effort to revitalize our dine-in business." For $3.99, patrons can load their plates at a 14-foot table spread with pastas, salads, and pizza. Although its buffets were initially open only for lunch, it is possible that dinner buffets will be added. Certain risks, however, are involved with buffet service. As observed by Michael Mueller, a restaurant analyst with Montgomery Securities, "It's not an easy business to operate well. The risk is the quality of the food you offer." To maintain product quality Pizza Hut designed a screen that sits inside a pan and allows air to circulate around the pizza. By this method pizzas can stay hot and fresh at the buffet table for as long as 20 minutes.

Steven Reinemund is also exploring the upscale pizza market with a concept called Pizza Hut Cafes. The chain believes a market exists for this concept, although the field is already crowded with others offering pastas, desserts, and gourmet pizzas in casual dining atmospheres. Its cafe, which has been tested in Wichita, Kansas, featured tablecloths, desserts, sauteed chicken, and a wider variety of pizzas than found in regular Pizza Huts.

Taco Bell Worldwide.   Under John Martin's leadership Taco Bell has become the fast-food industry's value leader. In late 1988 the chain introduced its 59¢ Value Menu. Sales rose 50 percent in two years to $2.4 billion, causing McDonald's and Burger King to retaliate in late 1990, but to their disadvantage as their operations are not as efficient as Taco Bell's. Continuing the trend of offering everyday bargains, in fall 1990 Martin reorganized most of his menu into three price tiers—59¢, 79¢ and 99¢. Although he ultimately had to back off the rigid enforcement of these tiers due to franchisee pressures for margins, he believes offering value menus is his chain's key to success and he feels Taco Bell alone can be as big as the entire PepsiCo corporation is today. In responding to questions about his low price strategy, Martin responds, "Radical thought, huh? Low prices are what got our business started. The other guy has gotten away from it."

To be a low-cost producer Taco Bell began to shift as much food preparation to outside suppliers as possible and to rationalize its production methods in the mid-1980s. Its ground beef is precooked outside the store and then reheated, its tortillas are already fried, precooked dishes are placed in boil bags, and all its onions are prediced in a factory. The result of these actions has been the slicing of 15 daily man-hours from every outlet and the reduction of kitchen space from 70 percent to 30 percent of a typical building. "Our entire Taco Bell restaurant can fit into a McDonald's kitchen," says Elliot Bloom.

Other operating efficiencies have come from greater automation and simplified food production. This has enabled Taco Bell to permanently slash prices on its 69¢ 29-item core menu. Martin has refigured the menu to emphasize plain tacos and burritos, which take only eight seconds to make, versus the 20 seconds needed to make a Mexican pizza or a taco salad. Through various efficiencies a new Taco Bell restaurant can handle twice the volume of five years ago with half the labor and it is currently testing taco-making robots in its quest for lower operating costs.

While being the industry's low-price leader, various industry analysts question Taco Bell's strategy. They point out that low pricing hurts profit margins, cannibalizes the sales of full meals, can leave customers unfilled, and creates an image of low quality. Hugh Zurkuhlen of Weiss, Peck & Greer says the chain is "a potential victim of their own success" and would have a difficult time abandoning that image when facing the ultimate pressures of rising ingredient and labor costs.

■ 1993 and Beyond

As 1993 begins, Wayne Calloway's overall goal for PepsiCo "is simply to be the best consumer products company in the world." He went on to explain, "In 1992 we took dramatic steps to keep us on a strong growth path. Our domestic beverage division is being completely restructured to serve our customers better. And our aggressive acquisition activity, over 50 in all, is doing a lot to expand and strengthen our core businesses. We're entering 1993 with solid momentum and well positioned to address changing consumer needs. Low cost Mexican food is still a novelty to most Americans, there are more ways to sell pizza, and new products and value combinations at KFC will bring customers back more often." Jay Nelson, an analyst with Brown Brothers Harriman, observes that "PepsiCo doesn't participate in rapid-growth industries with favorable demographic trends. But managers there think it's their destiny to win." The question is what must PepsiCo do to continue its phenomenal growth in sales and profits? What contributions can PepsiCo's restaurant operations make as the corporation attempts to double its sales in the next five years?

■ **Appendix A**   Annual per Capita Consumption of Various Consumer Goods and Wealth for Selected Countries

Country	Soft Drinks[a]	Income[b]	TVs[c]	Newspapers[d]	Literacy[e]
United States	770	$19,678	769	255	99.0%
Mexico	512	2,222	123	142	88.0
Australia	403	14,994	500	308	99.0
Germany[f]	255	19,637	385	417	99.0
Japan	75	21,845	244	569	99.0
CIS	46	3,606	313	345	99.0
India	3	339	16	16	36.0

[a]1991 Per capita 8 oz. servings per year.
[b]1988 GDP per capita in U.S. dollars.
[c]Television sets per 1,000.
[d]Newspaper circulation per 1,000.
[e]Percent literacy rate.
[f]Former Federal Republic of Germany.

SOURCES: Adapted from data in *1992 PepsiCo Stockholder's Report,* pp. 9, 15; *The World Almanac and Book of Facts,* NY: Pharos Books (1991,) pp. 687, 712, 718, 723, 733, 760, 765; "Indicators of Market Size for 117 Countries," *Business International* (July 30, 1990), pp. 248, 250.

■ **Appendix B**   Current and Estimated PepsiCo Sales and Operating Results from Continuing Operations

	1988	1989	1990	1991	1992*	1993*	1995–1997*
Sales	$13,007.0	$15,242.0	$17,803.0	$19,608.0	$22,200.0	$24,500.0	$32,500.0
Cost of sales	11,016.9	12,681.3	14,847.7	16,274.6	18,426.0	20,212.5	26,650.0
Operating profit	1,990.1	2,560.7	2,955.3	3,333.4	3,774.0	4,287.5	5,850.0
General overhead	598.6	902.3	1,021.3	1,098.7	1,234.0	1,357.5	1,775.0
Depreciation	629.3	772.0	884.0	1,034.5	1,100.0	1,250.0	1,600.0
Pretax profit	762.2	886.4	1,050.0	1,200.2	1,440.0	1,680.0	2,475.0
Income taxes	251.5	295.2	346.5	417.7	504.0	588.0	866.3
Posttax profit	$ 510.7	$ 591.2	$ 703.5	$ 782.5	$ 936.0	$ 1,092.0	$ 1,608.8

*Estimate.
SOURCE: Stephen Sanborn, "PepsiCo, Inc.," *Value Line,* (November 20, 1992), p. 1539.

Case 10   Outback Goes International

Marilyn L. Taylor and Madelyn Gengelbach
Both of the University of Missouri at Kansas City

George M. Puia
Indiana State University

Krishnan Ramaya
University of Southern Indiana

■ Outback Goes International

In early 1995 Outback Steakhouse enjoyed the position as one of the most successful restaurant chains in the U.S. Entrepreneurs Chris Sullivan, Bob Basham, and
Tim Gannon, each with more than 20 years experience in the restaurant industry,
started Outback Steakhouse with just two stores in 1988. In 1995 the company was
the fastest growing U.S. steakhouse chain with over 200 stores throughout the
United States.

Outback achieved its phenomenal success in an industry that was widely considered as one of the most competitive in the U.S. Fully 75 percent of entrants
into the restaurant industry failed within the first year. Outback's strategy was
driven by a unique combination of factors atypical of the food service industry. As
Chairman Chris Sullivan put it, "Outback is all about a lot of different experiences that has been recognized as entrepreneurship." Within six years of com-
mencing operations, Outback was voted as the best steakhouse chain in the country. The company also took top honors along with Olive Garden as America's
favorite restaurant. In December 1994, Outback was awarded *Inc.*'s prestigious
Entrepreneur of the Year award. In 1994 and early 1995 the business press hailed
the company as one of the biggest success stories in corporate America in recent
years.

The authors express deep appreciation to the following individuals at the Ewing Marion Kauffman
Foundation which underwrote the expenses for the development of the case and a video on the
company: Dr. Ray Smilor, Vice President, and Dr. Mabel Tinjacha, Program Specialist for the Center for
Entrepreneurial Leadership. In addition, the authors also wish to express special appreciation to
Outback executives Bob Merritt, CFO and Treasurer, Nancy Schneid, Vice President of Marketing; and
Hugh Connerty, President (of Outback International) who contributed special time and attention to
this particular case. The research team has had sustained commitment from all the senior executives
including Chris Sullivan, Chairman and CEO; Bob Basham, President and COO; Tim Gannon, Sr. Vice
President, and Ava Forney, Assistant to the Chairman and CEO; as well as other Outback officers,
executives, and employees. Numerous "Outbackers" have given generously of time, knowledge, and
skills to make this case study possible.

This case was prepared by Marilyn L. Taylor and Madelyn Gengelbach, both of the Bloch School of
Business and Public Administration at the University of Missouri at Kansas City, George M. Puia of the
College of Business Administration at Indiana State University, and Krishnan Ramaya of the School of
Business Administration at the University of Southern Indiana.

In late 1994 Hugh Connerty was appointed President of Outback International. In early 1995 Connerty, a highly successful franchisee for Outback, explained the international opportunities facing Outback Steakhouse as it considered its strategy for expansion abroad:

> We have had hundreds of franchise requests from all over the world. [So] it took about two seconds for me to make that decision [to become President of Outback International] . . . . I've met with and talked to other executives who have international divisions. All of them have the same story. At some point in time the light goes off and they say, "Gee we have a great product. Where do we start?" I have traveled quite a bit on holiday. The world is not as big as you think it is. Most companies who have gone global have not used any set strategy.

Despite his optimism, Connerty knew that the choice of targeted markets would be critical. Connerty wondered what strategic and operational changes the company would have to make to assure success in those markets.

History of Outback Steakhouse, Inc.

Chris Sullivan, Bob Basham, and Tim Gannon met in the early 1970s shortly after they graduated from college. The three joined Steak & Ale, a Pillsbury subsidiary and restaurant chain, as management trainees as their first post-college career positions. During the 1980s Sullivan and Basham became successful franchisees of 17 Chili's restaurants in Florida and Georgia with franchise headquarters in Tampa, Florida.[1] Meanwhile Tim Gannon played significant roles in several New Orleans restaurant chains. Sullivan and Basham sold their Chili's franchises in 1987 and used the proceeds to fund Outback, their start-from-scratch entrepreneurial venture. They invited Gannon to join them in Tampa in fall, 1987. The trio opened their first two restaurants in Tampa in 1988.

The three entrepreneurs recognized that in-home consumption of meat, especially beef, had declined.[2] Nonetheless, upscale and budget steakhouses were extremely popular. The three concluded that people were cutting in-home red meat consumption, but were still very interested in going out to a restaurant for a good steak. They saw an untapped opportunity between high priced and budget steakhouses to serve quality steaks at an affordable price.

Using an Australian theme associated with the outdoors and adventure, Outback positioned itself as a place providing not only excellent food but also a cheerful, fun, and comfortable experience. The company's Statement of Principles and Beliefs referred to employees as "Outbackers" and highlighted the importance of hospitality, sharing, quality, fun, and courage.

Catering primarily to the dinner crowd,[3] Outback offered a menu that featured specially seasoned steaks and prime rib. The menu also included chicken, ribs, fish, and pasta entrees in addition to the company's innovative appetizers.[4] CFO Bob Merritt cited Outback's food as a prime reason for the company's success. As he put it:

> One of the important reasons for our success is that we took basic American meat and potatoes and enhanced the flavor profile so that it fit with the aging population. . . . Just look at what McDonald's and Burger King did in their market segment. They (have) tried to add things to their menu that were more flavorful (for example) McDonald's put the Big Mac on the menu . . . as people age, they want more flavor . . . higher flavor profiles. It's not happenstance. It's a science. There's too much money at risk in this business not to know what's going on with customer taste preferences.

The company viewed suppliers as "partners" in the company's success and was committed to work with suppliers to develop and maintain long term relationships. Purchasing was dedicated to obtaining the highest quality ingredients and supplies. Indeed, the company was almost fanatical about quality. As Tim Gannon, Vice President and the company's chief chef, put it, "We won't tolerate less than the best." One example of the company's quality emphasis was its croutons. Restaurant kitchen staff made the croutons daily on site. The croutons had 17 different seasonings, including fresh garlic and butter. The croutons were cut by hand into irregular shapes so that customers would recognize they were handmade. At about 40 percent of total costs, Outback had one of the highest food costs in the industry. On Friday and Saturday nights customers waited up to two hours for a table. Most felt that Outback provided exceptional value for the average entree price of $15–$16.

Outback focused not only on the productivity and efficiency of "Outbackers" but also their long term well-being. Executives referred to the company's employee commitment as "tough on results, but kind with people." A typical Outback restaurant staff consisted of a general manager, an assistant manager, a kitchen manager, plus 50–70 mostly part time hourly employees. The company used aptitude tests, psychological profiles, and interviews as part of the employee selection process. Every applicant interviewed with two managers. The company placed emphasis on creating an entrepreneurial climate where learning and personal growth were strongly emphasized. As Chairman Chris Sullivan explained:

> I was given the opportunity to make a lot of mistakes and learn, and we try to do that today. We try to give our people a lot of opportunity to make some mistakes, learn, and go on.

In order to facilitate ease of operations for employees, the company's restaurant design devoted 45 percent of restaurant floor space to kitchen area. Wait staff were assigned only three tables at any time. Most Outback restaurants were only open 4:30–11:30 P.M. daily. Outback's wait staff enjoyed higher income from tips than in restaurants that also served lunch. Restaurant management staff worked 50–55 hours per week in contrast to the 70 or more common in the industry. Company executives felt that the dinner-only concept had led to effective utilization of systems, staff, and management. "Outbackers" reported that they were less worn out working at Outback and that they had more fun than when they worked at other restaurant companies.

Outback executives were proud of their "B-locations (with) A-demographics" location strategy. They deliberately steered clear of high-traffic locations targeted by companies that served a lunch crowd. Until the early 1990s most of the restaurants were leased locations, retrofits of another restaurant location. The emphasis was on choosing locations where Outback's target customer would be in the evening. The overall strategy payoff was clear. In an industry where a sales-to-investment ratio of 1.2-to-1 was considered strong, Outback's restaurants generated $2.10 for every $1 invested in the facility. The average Outback restaurant unit generated $3.4 million in sales.

In 1995 management remained informal. Headquarters were located on the second floor of an unpretentious building near the Tampa airport. There was no middle management—top management selected the joint venture partners and franchisees who reported directly to the President. Franchisees and joint venture partners in turn hired the general managers at each restaurant.

Outback provided ownership opportunities at three levels of the organization: at the individual restaurant level, through multiple store arrangements (joint venture and franchise opportunities), and through a stock ownership plan for every employee. Health insurance was also available to all employees, a benefit not universally available to restaurant industry workers. Outback's restaurant-level general managers' employment and ownership opportunities were atypical in the industry. A restaurant general manager invested $25,000 for a 10 percent ownership stake in the restaurant, a contract for five years in the same location, a 10 percent share of the cash flow from the restaurant as a yearly bonus, opportunity for stock options, and a 10 percent buyout arrangement at the end of the five years. Outback store managers typically earned an annual salary and bonus of over $100,000 as compared to an industry average of about $60,000–70,000. Outback's management turnover of 5.4 percent was one of the lowest in its industry in which the average was 30–40 percent.

Community involvement was strongly encouraged throughout the organization. The corporate office was involved in several non-profit activities in the Tampa area and also sponsored major national events such as the Outback Bowl and charity golf tournaments. Each store was involved in community participation and service. For example, the entire proceeds of an open house held just prior to every restaurant opening went to a charity of the store manager's choice.

Early in its history the company had been unable to afford any advertising. Instead, Outback's founders relied on their strong relationships with local media to generate public relations and promotional efforts. One early relationship developed with Nancy Schneid who had extensive experience in advertising and radio. Schneid later became Outback's first Vice President of Marketing. Under her direction, the company developed a full-scale national media program that concentrated on television advertising and local billboards. The company avoided couponing and its only printed advertising typically came as part of a package offered by a charity or sports event.

Early financing for growth had come from limited partnership investments by family members, close friends, and associates. The three founders' original plan did not call for extensive expansion or franchising. However, in 1990 some friends, disappointed in the performance of several of their Kentucky-based restaurants asked to franchise the Outback concept. The converted Kentucky stores enjoyed swift success. Additional opportunities with other individuals experienced in the restaurant industry arose in various parts of the country. These multi-store arrangements were in the form of franchises or joint ventures. Later in 1990 the company turned to a venture capital firm for financing for a $2.5 million package. About the same time, Bob Merritt joined the company as CFO. Merritt's previous IPO[5] experience helped the company undertake a quick succession of three highly successful public equity offerings. During 1994 the price of the company's stock ranged from $22.63 to a high of $32.00. The company's income statements, balance sheets, and a summary of the stock price performance appear as Exhibits 1, 2, and 3 respectively.

Outback's International Rollout

Outback's management believed that the U.S. market could accommodate at least 550–600 Outback steakhouse restaurants. At the rate the company was growing (70 stores annually), Outback would near the U.S. market's saturation within 4–5 years. Outback's plans for longer-term growth hinged on a multi-pronged strategy. The company planned to roll out an additional 300–350 Outback stores, expand into the lucrative Italian dining segment through its joint venture with the successful Houston-based Carrabbas Italian Grill, and develop new dining themes.

■ **Exhibit 1** Outback Steakhouse, Inc., Consolidated Statements of Income

	Years Ended December 31		
	1994	1993	1992
Revenues	$451,916,000	$309,749,000	$189,217,000
Costs and Expenses			
Costs of revenues	175,618,000	121,290,000	73,475,000
Labor and other related expenses	95,476,000	65,047,000	37,087,000
Other restaurant operating expenses	93,265,000	64,603,000	43,370,000
General and administrative expenses	16,744,000	12,225,000	9,176,000
(Income) from oper. of unconsol. affl.	(1,269,000)	(333,000)	
Total	$379,834,000	$262,832,000	$163,108,000
Income from operations	$ 72,082,000	$ 46,917,000	$ 26,109,000
Non-operating income (expense)			
Interest income	512,000	1,544,000	1,428,000
Interest expense	(424,000)	(369,000)	(360,000)
Total	$ 88,000	$ 1,175,000	$ 1,068,000
Income before elimination of			
minority partners' interest and income taxes	$ 72,170,000	$ 48,092,000	$ 27,177,000
Elimination of minority partners' interest	11,276,000	7,378,000	4,094,000
Income before provision for income taxes	60,894,000	40,714,000	23,083,000
Provision for income taxes	21,602,000	13,922,000	6,802,000
Net income	$ 39,292,000	$ 26,792,000	$ 16,281,000
Earnings per common share	$0.89	$0.61	$0.39
Weighted average number of			
common shares outstanding	43,997,000	43,738,000	41,504,000
Pro forma			
Provision for income taxes	22,286,000	15,472,000	8,245,000
Net income	$ 38,608,000	$ 25,242,000	$ 14,838,000
Earnings per common share	$0.88	$0.58	$0.36

At year-end 1994 Outback had 164 restaurants in which the company had direct ownership interest. The company had six restaurants which it operated through joint ventures in which the company had a 45 percent interest. Franchisees operated another 44 restaurants. Outback operated the company-owned restaurants as partnerships in which the company was general partner. The company owned from 81 percent to 90 percent. The remainder was owned by the restaurant managers and joint venture partners. The six restaurants operated as joint ventures were also organized as partnerships in which the company owned 50 percent. The company was responsible for 50 percent of the costs of these restaurants.

The company organized the joint venture with Carrabbas in early 1993. The company was responsible for 100 percent of the costs of the new Carrabba's Italian Grills although it owned a 50 percent share. As of year end 1994 the joint venture operated ten Carrabba's restaurants.

The franchised restaurants generated 0.8 percent of the company's 1994 revenues as franchise fees. The portion of income attributable to restaurant managers and joint venture partners amounted to $11.3 million of the company's $72.2 million 1994 income.

■ **Exhibit 2**   Outback Steakhouse, Inc., Consolidated Balance Sheets

	Years Ended December 31				
Assets	**1994**	**1993**	**1992**	**1991**	**1990**
Current Assets					
Cash and cash equivalents	$ 18,758,000	$24,996,000	$60,538,000	$17,000,700	$2,983,000
Short-term municipal securities	4,829,000	6,632,000	1,316,600		
Inventories	4,539,000	3,849,000	2,166,500	1,020,800	319,200
Other current assets	11,376,000	4,658,000	2,095,200	794,900	224,100
Total current assets	$ 39,502,000	$40,135,000	$66,116,700	$18,816,400	$3,526,300
Long-term municipal securities	$ 1,226,000	$ 8,903,000	$ 7,071,200		
Property, fixtures, and equipment, net	162,323,000	101,010,000	41,764,500	15,479,000	6,553,200
Investments in and advances					
to unconsolidated affiliates	14,244,000	1,000,000			
Other assets	11,236,000	8,151,000	2,691,300	2,380,700	1,539,600
Total	$228,531,000	$159,199,000	$117,643,700	$36,676,100	$11,619,100
Liabilities and Stockholders' Equity					
Current Liabilities					
Accounts payable	$ 10,184,000	$1,053,000	$3,560,200	$ 643,800	$ 666,900
Sales taxes payable	3,173,000	2,062,000	1,289,500	516,800	208,600
Accrued expenses	14,961,000	10,435,000	8,092,300	2,832,300	954,800
Unearned revenue	11,862,000	6,174,000	2,761,900	752,800	219,400
Current portion of long-term debt	918,000	1,119,000	326,600	257,000	339,900
Income taxes payable			369,800	1,873,200	390,000
Total current liabilities	$ 41,098,000	$20,843,000	$16,400,300	$6,875,900	$2,779,600
Deferred income taxes	$ 568,000	$ 897,000	$ 856,400	$ 300,000	$ 260,000
Long-term debt	12,310,000	5,687,000	1,823,700	823,600	1,060,700
Interest of minority partners in					
consolidated partnerships	2,255,000	1,347,000	1,737,500	754,200	273,000
Total liabilities	$ 56,231,000	$28,774,000	$20,817,900	$8,753,700	$4,373,300
Stockholders' Equity					
Common stock $0.01 par value.					
100,000,000 shares authorized for					
1994 and 1993; 50,000,000					
authorized for 1992; 42,931,344					
and 42,442,800 shares issues and					
outstanding as of December 31, 1994					
and 1993, respectively; 39,645,995					
shares issued and outstanding					
as of December 31, 1992	$ 429,000	$ 425,000	$ 396,500	$ 219,000	$ 86,300
Additional paid-in capital	83,756,000	79,429,000	74,024,500	20,296,400	4,461,100
Retained earnings	88,115,000	50,571,000	22,404,800	7,407,000	2,698,400
Total stockholders' equity	172,300,000	130,425,000	96,825,800	27,922,400	7,245,800
	$228,531,000	$159,199,000	$117,643,700	$36,676,100	$11,619,100

■ **Exhibit 3**   Outback Steakhouse, Inc., Selected Financial and Stock Data

Year	Systemwide Sales	Company Revenues	Net Income	EPS	Company Stores	Franchise and JVS	Total Stores
1988	2,731	2,731	47	0.01	2	0	2
1989	13,328	13,328	920	0.04	9	0	9
1990	34,193	34,193	2,260	0.08	23	0	23
1991	91,000	91,000	6,064	0.17	49	0	49
1992	195,508	189,217	14,838	0.36	81	4	85
1993	347,553	309,749	25,242	0.58	124	24	148
1994	548,945	451,916	38,608	0.88	164	50	214

Outback Stock Data

1991	High	Low
Second quarter	$ 4.67	$ 4.27
Third quarter	6.22	4.44
Fourth quarter	10.08	5.5
1992		
First quarter	13.00	9.17
Second quarter	11.41	8.37
Third quarter	16.25	10.13
Fourth quarter	19.59	14.25
1993		
First quarter	22.00	15.50
Second quarter	26.16	16.66
Third quarter	24.59	19.00
Fourth quarter	25.66	21.16
1994		
First quarter	29.50	23.33
Second quarter	28.75	22.75
Third quarter	30.88	23.75
Fourth quarter	32.00	22.63

By late 1994 Outback's management had also begun to consider the potential of non-U.S. markets for the Outback concept. As Chairman Chris Sullivan put it:

> . . . we can do 500–600 (Outback) restaurants, and possibly more over the next five years. . . . [However] the world is becoming one big market, and we want to be in place so we don't miss that opportunity. There are some problems, some challenges with it, but at this point there have been some casual restaurant chains that have gone (outside the United States) and their average unit sales are way, way above the sales level they enjoyed in the United States. So the potential is there. Obviously, there are some distribution issues to work out, things like that. But we are real excited about the future internationally. That will give us some potential outside the United States to continue to grow as well.

In late 1994 the company began its international venture by appointing Hugh Connerty as president of Outback International. Connerty, like Outback's three founders, had extensive experience in the restaurant industry. Prior to joining Outback he developed a chain of successful Hooter's restaurants in Georgia. He used the proceeds from the sale of these franchises to fund the development of his franchise of Outback restaurants in Northern Florida and Southern Georgia. Connerty's success as a franchisee was well recognized. Indeed, in 1993 Outback began to award a large crystal trophy with the designation "Connerty Franchisee of the Year" to the company's outstanding franchisee.

Much of Outback's growth and expansion were generated through joint venture partnerships and franchising agreements. Connerty commented on Outback's franchise system:

> Every one of the franchisees lives in their areas. I lived in the area I franchised. I had relationships that helped with getting permits. That isn't any different than the rest of the world. The loyalties of individuals that live in their respective areas [will be important]. We will do the franchises one by one. The biggest decision we have to make is how we pick that franchise partner. . . . That is what we will concentrate on. We are going to select a person who has synergy with us, who thinks like us, who believes in the principles and beliefs.

Outback developed relationships very carefully. As Hugh Connerty explained:

> . . . trust . . . is foremost and sacred. The trust between (Outback) and the individual franchisees is not to be violated. . . . Company grants franchises one at a time.[6] It takes a lot of trust to invest millions of dollars without any assurance that you will be able to build another one.

However, Connerty recognized that expanding abroad would present challenges. He described how Outback would approach its international expansion:

> We have built Outback one restaurant at a time. . . . There are some principles and beliefs we live by. It almost sounds cultish. We want international to be an opportunity for our suppliers. We feel strongly about the relationships with our suppliers. We have never changed suppliers. We have an undying commitment to them and in exchange we want them to have an undying commitment to us. They have to prove they can build plants (abroad).

He explained:

> I think it would be foolish of us to think that we are going to go around the world buying property and understanding the laws in every country, the culture in every single country. So the approach that we are going to take is that we will franchise the international operation with company-owned stores here and franchises there so that will allow us to focus on what I believe is our pure strength, a support operation.

U.S. Restaurants in the International Dining Market

Prospects for international entry for U.S. restaurant companies in the early 1990s appeared promising. Between 1992 and 1993 alone international sales for the top fifty restaurant franchisers increased from U.S. $15.9 billion to U.S. $17.5 billion. Franchising was the most popular means for rapid expansion. Exhibit 4 provides an overview of the top U.S. restaurant franchisers including their domestic and international revenues and number of units in 1993 and 1994.

International expansion was an important source of revenues for a significant number of players in the industry. International growth and expansion in the U.S. restaurant industry over the 1980s and into the 1990s was largely driven by major fast food restaurant chains. Some of these companies, for example, McDonald's, Wendy's, Dairy Queen, and Domino's Pizza, were public and free-standing. Others, such as Subway and Little Caesars, remained private and free-standing. Some of the largest players in international markets were subsidiaries of major consumer products firms such as Pepsico[7] and Grand Metropolitan PLC.[8] In spite of the success enjoyed by fast-food operators in non-U.S. markets, casual dining operators were slower about entering the international markets. (See Appendix A for brief

■ **Exhibit 4**   Top 50 U.S. Restaurant Franchises Ranked by Sales

Rank	Firm	Total Sales		International Sales		Total Stores		International Stores	
		1994	1993	1994	1993	1994	1993	1994	1993
1	McDonald's	25,986	23,587	11,046	9,401	15,205	13,993	5,461	4,710
2	Burger King	7,500	6,700	1,400	1,240	7,684	6,990	1,357	1,125
3	KFC	7,100	7,100	3,600	3,700	9,407	9,033	4,258	3,905
4	Taco Bell	4,290	3,817	130	100	5,615	4,634	162	112
5	Wendy's	4,277	3,924	390	258	4,411	4,168	413	377
6	Hardee's	3,491	3,425	63	56	3,516	3,435	72	63
7	Dairy Queen	3,170	2,581	300	290	3,516	3,435	628	611
8	Dominos'	2,500	2,413	415	275	5,079	5,009	840	550
9	Subway	2,500	2,201	265	179	9,893	8,450	944	637
10	Little Caesar	2,000	2,000	70	70	4,855	4,754	155	145
		Non-fast Food in Top 50							
11	Denny's	1,779	1,769	63	70	1,548	1,515	58	63
13	Dunkin' Donuts	1,413	1,285	226	209	3,453	3,047	831	705
14	Shoney's	1,346	1,318	0	0	922	915	0	0
15	Big Boy	1,130	1,202	100	0	940	930	90	78
17	Baskin-Robbins	1,008	910	387	368	3,765	3,562	1,300	1,278
19	T.G.I. Friday's	897	1,068	114	293	314	NA	37	NA
20	Applebee's	889	609	1	0	507	361	2	0
21	Sizzler	858	922	230	218	600	666	119	116
23	Ponderosa	690	743	40	38	380	750	40	38
24	Int'l House of Pancakes	632	560	32	29	657	561	37	35
25	Perkins	626	588	12	10	432	425	8	6
29	Outback Steakhouse	549	348	0	0	NA	NA	NA	NA
30	Golden Corral	548	515	1	0	425	425	2	1
32	TCBY Yogurt	388	337	22	15	2,801	2,474	141	80
37	Showbiz/Chuck E Cheese	370	373	7	8	332	NA	8	NA
39	Round Table Pizza	357	340	15	12	576	597	29	22
40	Western Sizzlin	337	351	3	6	281	NA	2	NA
41	Ground Round	321	310	0	0	NA	NA	NA	NA
42	Papa John's	297	NA	0	NA	632	NA	0	NA
44	Godfather's Pizza	270	268	0	0	515	531	0	0
45	Bonanza	267	327	32	47	264	NA	30	NA
46	Village Inn	266	264	0	0	NA	NA	NA	NA
47	Red Robin	259	235	27	28	NA	NA	NA	NA
48	Tony Roma's	254	245	41	36	NA	NA	NA	NA
49	Marie Callender	251	248	0	0	NA	NA	NA	NA
	Average of firms 11–20	1,222	1,223	99	144	2,030	1,915	163	251
	Average of firms 21–30	647	594	51	26	717	730	37	36
	Average of firms 31–40	382	358	7	9	502	495	26	20
	Average of firms 41–50	270	257	17	23	345	363	26	43

NA: Not ranked in the top 50 for that category.

SOURCE: "Top 50 Franchises," *Restaurant Business* (November 1, 1995), pp. 35–41.

overviews of the publicly available data on the top ten franchisers and casual dining chains that had ventured abroad as of early 1995.)

One of the major forces driving the expansion of the U.S. food service industry was changing demographics. In the U.S. prepared foods had become a fastest-growing category because they relieved the cooking burdens on working parents. By the early 1990s, U.S. consumers were spending almost as much on restaurant fare as for prepared and non-prepared grocery store food. U.S. food themes were very popular abroad. U.S. food themes were common throughout Canada as well as Western Europe and East Asia. As a result of the opening of previously inaccessible markets like Eastern Europe, the former Soviet Union, China, India, and Latin America, the potential for growth in U.S. food establishments abroad was enormous.

In 1992 alone, there were more than 3,000 franchisers in the U.S. operating about 540,000 franchised outlets—a new outlet of some sort opened about every 16 minutes. In 1992, franchised business sales totaled $757.8 billion, about 35 percent of all retail sales. Franchising was used as a growth vehicle by a variety of businesses including automobiles, petroleum, cosmetics, convenience stores, computers, and financial services. However, food service constituted the franchising industry's largest single group. Franchised restaurants generally performed better than free-standing units. For example, in 1991, franchised restaurants experienced per-store sales growth of 6.2 percent versus an overall restaurant industry growth rate of 3.0 percent. However, despite generally favorable sales and profits, franchisor–franchisee relationships were often difficult.

Abroad franchisers operated an estimated 31,000 restaurant units. The significant increase in restaurant franchising abroad was driven by universal cultural trends, rising incomes, improved international transportation and communication, rising educational levels, increasing numbers of women entering the work force, demographic concentrations of people in urban areas, and the willingness of younger generations to try new products.[9] However, there were substantial differences in these changes between the U.S. and other countries and from country to country.

Factors Impacting Country Selection

Outback had not yet formed a firm plan for its international rollout. However, Hugh Connerty indicated the preliminary choice of markets targeted for entry:

> The first year will be Canada. . . . Then we'll go to Hawaii. . . . Then we'll go to South America and then develop our relationships in the Far East, Korea, Japan, . . . the Orient. At the second year we'll begin a relationship in Great Britain and from there a natural progression throughout Europe. But we view it as a very long-term project. I have learned that people think very different than Americans.

There were numerous considerations which U.S. restaurant chains had to take into account when determining which non-U.S. markets to enter. Some of these factors are summarized in Exhibit 5. Issues regarding infrastructure and demographics are expanded below. Included are some of the difficulties that U.S. restaurant companies encountered in various countries. Profiles of Canada, South Korea, Japan, Germany, Mexico, and Great Britain appear as Appendix B.

Infrastructure.   A supportive infrastructure in the target country is essential. Proper means of transportation, communication, basic utilities such as power and water, and locally available supplies are important elements in the decision to introduce a particular restaurant concept. A restaurant must have the ability to get resources to its location. Raw materials for food preparation, equipment for manufacture of food served, employees, and customers must be able to enter and leave the establishment. The network that brings these resources to a firm is commonly called a supply chain.

■ **Exhibit 5**   Factors Affecting Companies' Entry into International Markets

External Factors

Country Market Factors

Size of target market, competitive structure—atomistic, oligopolistic to monopolistic, local marketing infrastructure (distribution, etc.).

Country Production Factors

Quality, quantity and cost of raw materials, labor, energy and other productive agents in the target country as well as the quality and cost of the economic infrastructure (transportation, communications, port facilities and similar considerations).

Country Environmental Factors

Political, economic and socio-cultural character of the target country—government policies and regulations pertaining to international business.
Geographical distance—impact on transportation costs.
Size of the economy, absolute level of performance (GDP per capita), relative importance of economic sectors—closely related to the market size for a company's product in the target country.
Dynamics including rate of investment, growth in GDP, personal income, changes in employment. Dynamic economies may justify entry modes with a high break-even point even when the current market size is below the break-even point.
Sociocultural factors—cultural distance between home and country and target country societies. Closer the cultural distance, quicker entry into these markets, e.g., Canada.

Home Country Factors

Big domestic market allows a company to grow to a large size before it turns to foreign markets. Competitive structure. Firms in oligopolistic industries tend to imitate the actions of rival domestic firms that threatens to upset competitive equilibrium. Hence, when one firm invests abroad, rival firms commonly follow the lead. High production costs in the home country is an important factor.

Internal Factors

Company Product Factors

Products that are highly differentiated with distinct advantages over competitive products give sellers a significant degree of pricing discretion.
Products that require an array of pre and post purchase services makes it difficult for a company to market the product at a distance.
Products that require considerable adaptation.

Company Resource/Commitment Factors

The more abundant a company's resources in management, capital, technology, production skills, and marketing skills, the more numerous its entry mode options. Conversely, a company with limited resources is constrained to use entry modes that call for only a small resource commitment. Size is therefore a critical factor in the choice of an entry mode. Although resources are an influencing factor, it must be joined with a willingness to commit them to foreign market development. A high degree of commitment means that managers will select the entry mode for a target from a wider range of alternative modes than managers with a low commitment.

The degree of a company's commitment to international business is revealed by the role accorded to foreign markets in corporate strategy, the status of the international organization, and the attitudes of managers.

SOURCE: Franklin Root, *Entry Strategies for International Markets* (Lexington, MA: D.C. Heath, 1987).

The level of economic development is closely linked to the development of a supportive infrastructure. For example, the U.S. International Trade Commission said:

> Economic conditions, cultural disparities, and physical limitations can have substantial impact on the viability of foreign markets for a franchise concept. In terms of economics, the level of infrastructure development is a significant factor. A weak infrastructure may cause problems in transportation, communication, or even the provision of basic utilities such as electricity. . . . International franchisers frequently encounter problems finding supplies in sufficient quantity, of consistent quality, and at stable prices. . . . Physical distance also can adversely affect a franchise concept and arrangement. Long distances create communication and transportation problems, which may complicate the process of sourcing supplies, overseeing operations, or providing quality management services to franchisees.[10]

Some food can be sourced locally, some regionally or nationally, and some must be imported. A country's transportation and distribution capabilities may become an element in the decision of the country's suitability for a particular restaurant concept.

Sometimes supply chain issues require firms to make difficult decisions that affect the costs associated with the foreign enterprise. Family Restaurants Inc. encountered problems providing brown gravy for its CoCo's restaurants in South Korea. "If you want brown gravy in South Korea," said Barry Krantz, company president, "you can do one of two things. Bring it over, which is very costly. Or, you can make it yourself. So we figure out the flavor profile, and make it in the kitchen." Krantz concedes that a commissary is "an expensive proposition but the lesser of two evils."[11]

In certain instances a country may be so attractive for long term growth that a firm dedicates itself to creating a supply chain for its restaurants. An excellent illustration is McDonald's expansion into Russia in the late 1980s:

> . . . supply procurement has proved to be a major hurdle, as it has for all foreign companies operating in Russia. The problem has several causes: the rigid bureaucratic system, supply shortages caused by distribution and production problems, available supplies not meeting McDonald's quality standards. . . . To handle these problems, McDonald's scoured the country for supplies, contracting for such items as milk, cheddar cheese, and beef. To help ensure ample supplies of the quality products it needed, it undertook to educate Soviet farmers and cattle ranchers on how to grow and raise those products. In addition, it built a $40 million food-processing center about 45 minutes from its first Moscow restaurant. And because distribution was (and still is) as much a cause of shortages as production was, McDonald's carried supplies on its own trucks.[12]

Changing from one supply chain to another can affect more than the availability of quality provisions—it can affect the equipment that is used to make the food served. For example:

> . . . Wendy's nearly had its Korean market debut delayed by the belatedly discovered problem of thrice-frozen hamburger. After being thawed and frozen at each step of Korea's cumbersome three-company distribution channel, ground beef there takes on added water weight that threw off Wendy's patty specifications, forcing a hasty stateside retooling of the standard meat patty die used to mass-produce its burgers.[13]

Looking at statistics such as the number of ports, airports, quantity of paved roads, and transportation equipment as a percentage of capital stock per worker can give a bird's-eye view of the level of infrastructure development.

Demographics.   Just like the domestic market, restaurants in a foreign market need to know who their customers will be. Different countries will have different strata in age distribution, religion, and cultural heritage. These factors can influence the location, operations, and menus of restaurants in the country.

A popular example is India, where eating beef is contrary to the beliefs of the 80 percent of the population that is Hindu.[14] Considering India's population is nearly one billion people, companies find it hard to ignore this market even if beef is a central component of the firm's traditional menu. "We're looking at serving mutton patties," says Ann Connolly, a McDonald's spokeswoman.[15]

Another area where religion plays a part in affecting the operation of a restaurant is the middle east. Dairy Queen expanded to the region and found that during the Islamic religious observance of Ramadan no business was conducted; indeed, the windows of shops were boarded up.[16]

Age distribution can affect who should be the target market. "The company (McDonald's in Japan) also made modifications (not long after entering the market), such as targeting all advertising to younger people, because the eating habits of older Japanese are very difficult to change."[17] Age distribution can also impact the pool of labor available. In some countries over 30 percent of the population is under 15 years old; in other countries, over 15 percent is 65 or older. These varying demographics could create a change in the profile for potential employees in the new market.

Educational level may be an influence on both the buying public and the employee base. Literacy rates vary, and once again this can change the profile of an employee as well as who comprises the buying public.

Statistics can help compare countries using demographic components like literacy rates, total population and age distribution, and religious affiliations.

Income.   Buying power is another demographic that can provide clues to how the restaurant might fare in the target country, as well as how the marketing program should position the company's products or services. Depending on the country and its economic development, the firm may have to attract a different segment than in the domestic market. For example in Mexico:

> . . . major U.S. firms have only recently begun targeting the country's sizable and apparently burgeoning middle class. For its part, McDonald's has changed tactics from when it first entered Mexico as a prestige brand aimed almost exclusively at the upper class, which accounts for about 5 percent of Mexico's population of some 93 million. With the development of its own distribution systems and improved economies of scale McDonald's lately has been slashing prices to aid its penetration into working-class population strongholds. "I'd say McDonald's pricing now in Mexico is 30 percent lower, in constant dollar terms, than when we opened in '85," says Moreno [Fernando Moreno, now international director of Peter Piper Pizza], who was part of the chain's inaugural management team there.[18]

There are instances where low disposable income does not translate to a disinterest in dining out in a Western-style restaurant. While Americans dine at a fast food establishment such as McDonald's one or two times per week, lower incomes in the foreign markets make eating at McDonald's a special, once a month occurrence. "These people are not very wealthy, so eating out at a place like McDonald's is a dining experience."[19] China provides another example:

> . . . at one Beijing KFC last summer, [the store] notched the volume equivalent of nine U.S. KFC branches in a single day during a $1.99 promotion of a two-piece meal with a baseball cap. Observers chalk up that blockbuster business largely to China's ubiquitous "spoiled-brat syndrome" and the apparent willingness of indulgent parents to spend one or two months' salaries on splurges for the only child the government allows them to rear.[20]

Statistics outlining the various indexes describing the country's gross domestic product, consumer spending on food, consumption and investment rates, and price levels can assist in evaluating target countries.

Trade Law.   Trade policies can be friend or foe to a restaurant chain interested in expanding to other countries. Trade agreements such as NAFTA (North American Free Trade Agreement) and GATT (General Agreement on Tariffs and Trade) can help alleviate the ills of international expansion if they achieve their aims of "reducing or eliminating tariffs, reducing non-tariff barriers to trade, liberalizing investment and foreign exchange policies, and improving intellectual property protection. . . . The recently signed Uruguay Round Agreements [of GATT] include the General Agreement on Trade in Services (GATS), the first multilateral, legally enforceable agreement covering trade and investment in the services sector. The GATS is designed to liberalize trade in services by reducing or eliminating governmental measures that prevent services from being freely provided across national borders or that discriminate against firms with foreign ownership."[21]

Franchising, one of the most popular modes for entering foreign markets, scored a win in the GATS agreement. For the first time franchising was addressed directly in international trade talks. However, most countries have not elected to make their restrictions on franchising publicly known. The U.S. International Trade Commission pointed out:

> Specific commitments that delineate barriers are presented in Schedules of Commitments (Schedules). As of this writing, Schedules from approximately 90 countries are publicly available. Only 30 of these countries specifically include franchising in their Schedules. . . . The remaining two-thirds of the countries did not schedule commitments on franchising. This means that existing restrictions are not presented in a transparent manner and additional, more severe restrictions may be imposed at a later date. . . . Among the 30 countries that addressed franchising in the Schedules, 25 countries, including the United States, have committed themselves to maintain no limitations on franchising except for restrictions on the presence of foreign nationals within their respective countries.[22]

Despite progress, current international restaurant chains have encountered a myriad of challenges because of restrictive trade policies. Some countries make the import of restaurant equipment into their country difficult and expensive. The Asian region possesses "steep tariffs and (a) patchwork of inconsistent regulations that impede imports of commodities and equipment."[23]

Outback's Growth Challenge

Hugh Connerty was well aware that there was no mention of international opportunities in Outback's 1994 Annual Report. The company distributed that annual report to shareholders at the April 1995 meeting. More than 300 shareholders packed the meeting to standing room only. During the question and answer period a shareholder had closely questioned the company's executives as to why the company did not pay a dividend. The shareholder pointed out that the company made a considerable profit in 1994. Chris Sullivan responded that the company needed to reinvest the cash that might be used as dividends in order to achieve the targeted growth. His response was a public and very visible commitment to continue the company's fast-paced growth. Connerty knew that international had the potential to play a critical role in that growth. His job was to help craft a strategy that would assure Outback's continuing success as it undertook the new and diverse markets abroad.

Appendix A

Profiles of Casual Dining and Fast Food Chains[1]

This appendix provides summaries of the 1995 publicly available data on: (1) the two casual dining chains represented among the top 50 franchisers that had operations abroad (Applebee's and T.G.I. Friday's/Carlson Companies, Inc.) and (2) the top ten franchisers in the restaurant industry all of which are fast-food chains (Burger King, Domino's, Hardee's, International Dairy Queen, Inc., Little Caesar's, McDonald's, Pepsico including KFC, Taco Bell and Pizza Hut, Subway, and Wendy's).

■ (1) Casual Dining Chains with Operations Abroad

Applebee's

Applebee's was one of the largest casual dining chains in the United States. It ranked 20th in sales and 36th in stores for 1994. Like most other casual dining operators, much of the company's growth had been fueled by domestic expansion. Opening in 1986, the company experienced rapid growth and by 1994 had 507 stores. The mode of growth was franchising, but in 1992 management began a program of opening more company-owned sites and buying restaurants from franchisees. The company positioned itself as a neighborhood bar and grill and offered a moderately priced menu including burgers, chicken, and salads.

In 1995 Applebee's continued a steady program of expansion. Chairman and CEO Abe Gustin set a target of 1,200 U.S. restaurants and had also begun a slow push into international markets. In 1994 the company franchised restaurants in Canada and Curacao and signed an agreement to franchise 20 restaurants in Belgium, Luxembourg, and the Netherlands.

Most of Carlson's revenues came from their travel group. The company experienced an unexpected surprise in 1995 when U.S. airlines announced that they would put a cap on the commissions they would pay to book U.S. flights. Because of this change, Carlson decided to change their service to a fee-based arrangement and expected sales to drop by US $100 million in 1995. To make up for this deficit, Carlson began to focus on building their hospitality group of restaurants and hotels through expansion in the U.S. and overseas. The company experienced significant senior management turnover in the early 1990s and founder Curtis Carlson, age 80, had announced his intention to retire at the end of 1996. His daughter was announced as next head of the company.

[1]Unless otherwise noted the information from this appendix was drawn from: "Top 50 Franchisers," *Restaurant Business.* November 1, 1995, pp. 35–41, and Hoover's Company Profile Database, 1996, The Reference Press, Inc., Austin, TX, from American Online Service, various company listings.

Year	1989	1990	1991	1992	1993	1994
Sales*	29.9	38.2	45.1	56.5	117.1	208.5
Net income*	0.0	1.8	3.1	5.1	9.5	16.9
EPS ($)	(0.10)	0.13	0.23	0.27	0.44	0.62
Stock price—close($)	4.34	2.42	4.84	9.17	232.34	13.38
Dividends ($)	0.00	0.00	0.01	0.02	0.03	0.04
# Employees	1,149	1,956	1,714	2,400	16,600	8,700

*$M. 1994: debt ratio, 20.1%; ROE, 19.2; cash, $17.2M; current ratio, 1.13; LTD, $23.7.

T.G.I. Friday's/Carlson Companies, Inc.

T.G.I. Friday's was owned by Carlson Companies, Inc., a large, privately held conglomerate that had interests in travel (65 percent of 1994 sales), hospitality (30 percent) plus marketing, employee training and incentives (5 percent). Carlson also owned a total of 345 Radisson Hotels and Country Inns plus 240 units of Country Kitchen International, a chain of family restaurants. T.G.I. Friday's grew 15.7 percent in revenue and 19.4 percent in stores in 1994. With 37 restaurants overseas, international sales were 12.7 percent of sales and 11.8 percent of stores systemwide. Carlson operated a total of 550 restaurants in 17 countries. About one third of overall sales came from activities outside the U.S.

Year	1985	1986	1987	1988	1989	1990	1991	1992	1993	1994
Sales*	.9	1.3	1.5	1.8	2.0	2.2	2.3	2.9	2.3	2.3

*$B; no data available on income; excludes franchisee sales.

■ (2) The Top Ten Franchisers in the Restaurant Industry

Burger King

In 1994 Burger King was number two in sales and number four in stores among the fast-food competitors. Burger King did not have the same presence in the global market as McDonald's and KFC. For example, McDonald's and KFC had been in Japan since the 1970s. Burger King opened its first Japanese locations in 1993. By that time, McDonald's already had over 1,000 outlets there. In 1994 Burger King had 1,357 non-U.S. stores (17.7 percent of systemwide total) in 50 countries, and overseas sales (18.7 percent) totaled $1.4 billion USD.

Burger King was owned by the British food and spirits conglomerate Grand Metropolitan PLC. Among the company's top brands were Pillsbury, Green Giant, and Haagen-Dazs. Grand Met's situation had not been bright during the 1990s, with the loss of major distribution contracts like Absolut vodka and Grand Marnier liqueur, as well as sluggish sales for its spirits in major markets. Burger King was not a stellar performer, either, and undertook a major restructuring in 1993 to turn the tide including reemphasis on the basic menu, cuts in prices, and reduced overhead. After quick success, BK's CEO James Adamson left his post in early 1995 to head competitor Flasgston Corporation.

Year	1985	1986	1987	1988	1989	1990	1991	1992	1993	1994
Sales*	5,590	5,291	4,706	6,029	9,298	9,394	8,748	7,913	8,120	7,780
Net income*	272	261	461	702	1,068	1,069	616	412	450	
EPS($)	14	16	19	24	28	32	33	28	30	32
Stock price—close($)	199	228,225	215	314	329	328	441	465	476	407
Dividend/share($)	5.0	5.1	6.0	7.5	8.9	10.2	11.4	12.3	13.0	14.0
Employees(K)	137	131	129	90	137	138	122	102	87	64

*Millions of Sterling. 1994: debt ratio, 47.3%; ROE, 12.4%; cash (Ster.), 986M; LTD (Ster.), 2,322M. 1994 segments sales (profit): North America, 62% (69%); U.K. and Ireland, 10% (10%); Africa and Middle East, 2% (1%); other Europe, 21% (18%); other countries, 5% (2%). Segment sales (profits) by operating division: drinks, 43% (51%); food, 42% (26%); retailing, 14% (22%); other, 1% (1%).

Domino's

Domino's Pizza was eighth in sales and seventh in stores in 1994. Sales and store unit growth had leveled off; from 1993 to 1994 sales grew 3.6 percent, and units only 1.4 percent. The privately held company registered poor performance in 1993, with a 0.6 percent sales decline from 1992. Observers suggested that resistance to menu innovations contributed to the share decline. In the early 1990s the company did add deep dish pizza and buffalo wings.

Flat company performances and expensive hobbies were hard on the owner and founder Thomas Monaghan. He attempted to sell the company in 1989 but could not find a buyer. He then replaced top management and retired from business to pursue a growing interest in religious activities. Company performance began to slide, and the founder emerged from retirement to retake the helm in the early 1990s. Through extravagant purchases of the Detroit Tigers, Frank Lloyd Wright pieces, and antique cars, Monaghan put the company on the edge of financial ruin. He sold off many of his holdings (some at a loss), reinvested the funds to stimulate the firm, and once again reorganized management.

Despite all its problems, Domino's had seen consistent growth in the international market. The company opened its first foreign store in 1983 in Canada. Primary overseas expansion areas were Eastern Europe and India. By 1994 Domino's had 5,079 stores with 823 of these in 37 major international markets. International brought in 17 percent of 1994 sales. Over the next 10–15 years the company had contracts for 4,000 additional international units.[24] These units would give Domino's more international than domestic units. International sales were 16.6 percent of total, and international stores were 16.5 percent of total in 1994.

Year	1985	1986	1987	1988	1989	1990	1991	1992	1993	1994
Sales*	1,100	1,430	2,000	2,300	2,500	2,600	2,400	2,450	2,200	2,500
Stores	2,841	3,610	4,279	4,858	5,185	5,342	5,571	5,264	5,369	5,079
Employees (K)	na	na	na	na	na	100	na	na	na	115

*$000,000.

Hardee's

Hardee's was number six in sales and eleven in stores for 1994. In 1981 the large diversified Canadian company, Imasco purchased the chain. Imasco also owned Imperial Tobacco (Player's and du Maurier, Canada's top two sellers), Burger Chef, two drugstore chains, the development company Genstar, and CT Financial.

Hardee's had pursued growth primarily in the U.S. Of all the burger chains in the top 10 franchises, Hardee's had the smallest international presence with 72 stores generating $63 million USD (1.8 percent and 2.0 percent of sales and stores, respectively) in 1994.

Hardee's sales grew by about 2 percent annually for 1993 and 1994. A failed attempt by Imasco to merge their Roy Rogers restaurants into the Hardee's chain forced the parent company to maintain both brands. Hardee's attempted to differentiate from the other burger chains by offering an upscale burger menu, which received a lukewarm reception by consumers.

Year	1985	1986	1987	1988	1989	1990	1991	1992	1993	1994
Sales*	3,376	5,522	6,788	7,311	8,480	9,647	9,870	9,957	9,681	9,385
Net income*	262	184	283	314	366	205	332	380	409	506
EPS ($)	1.20	0.78	1.12	1.26	1.44	1.13	0.64	0.68	0.74	0.78
Stock price—close ($)	13.94	16.25	12.94	14.00	18.88	13.81	18.25	20.63	20.06	19.88
Dividends ($)	0.36	0.42	0.48	0.52	0.56	0.64	0.64	0.68	0.74	0.78
Employees (K)	na	na	na	na	190	190	180	na	200	200

*$M—all $ in Canadian. 1994: debt ratio, 38.4%; ROE, 16.1%; current ratio; 1.37; LTD(M), $1,927. 1994 segment sales (operating income): CT Financial Services, 47%; (28%); Hardees, 32% (11%), Imperial Tobacco, 16% (0%); Shoppers Drug Mart, 2% (9%); Genstar Development, 1% (2%).

International Dairy Queen, Inc.

Dairy Queen was one of the oldest fast-food franchises in the United States: the first store was opened in Joliet, Illinois, in 1940. By 1950, there were over 1,100 stores, and by 1960 Dairy Queen had locations in 12 countries. Initial franchise agreements focused on the right to use the DQ freezers, an innovation that kept ice cream at the constant 23 degrees (F) necessary to maintain the soft consistency. In 1970 a group of investors bought the franchise organization; but, the group has been only partly successful in standardizing the fast-food chain. In 1994 a group of franchisees filed an antitrust suit in an attempt to get the company to loosen its control on food supply prices and sources. DQ franchises cost $30,000 initially plus continuing payments of 4 percent of sales.

The company's menu consisted of ice cream, yogurt, and Brazier (hamburgers and other fast food) items. Menu innovations had included Blizzard (candy and other flavors mixed in the ice cream). The company had also acquired several companies including the Golden Skillet (1981), Karmelkorn (1986) and Orange Julius (1987).

In 1994, Dairy Queen ranked number seven in sales and six in stores. By that same year the company had expanded its presence into 19 countries with 628 stores and $300 million USD in international sales. 1994 was an excellent year for DQ: sales were up 22.8 percent over 1993. This dramatic change (1993 scored an anemic 3.0 percent gain) was fueled by technology improvements for franchisees and international expansion. In 1992 Dairy Queen opened company-owned outlets in Austria, China, Slovenia, and Spain. DQ announced in 1995 that they had a plan to open 20 stores in Puerto Rico over a four year period.

Year	1985	1986	1987	1988	1989	1990	1991	1992	1993	1994
Sales*	158	182	210	254	282	287	287	296	311	341
Net income*	10	12	15	20	23	27	28	29	30	31
EPS ($)	0.33	0.42	0.51	0.70	0.83	0.97	1.05	1.12	1.79	1.30
Stock price—close ($)	5.20	7.75	8.00	11.50	14.75	16.58	21.00	20.00	18.00	16.25
Dividends ($)	0	0	0	0	0	0	0	0	0	0
Employees (K)	430	459	503	520	549	584	592	672	538	564

*M. 1994: debt ratio, 15.3%; ROE, 24.4%; current ratio, 3.04; LTD, $23M. 1994 restaurants: U.S., 87%; Canada, 9%; other, 4%. Restaurants by type: DQ's: franchised by company. 62%; franchised by territorial operators, 27%; foreign, 3%, Orange Julius, 7%; Karmelkorn, 1%; Golden Skillet, less than 1%. Sales by source: good supplies and equipment to franchises, 78%; services fees, 16%; franchise sales and other fees, 3%; real-estate finance and rental income, 3%.

Little Caesar's

Little Caesar's ranked 10th in sales and eighth in stores for 1994. Sales growth had slowed to a halt: a 92–93 increase of 12.2 percent evaporated into no increase for 93–94.

These numbers were achieved without a significant overseas presence. Of the top 10 franchises, only Hardee's had a smaller number of stores in foreign lands. Little Caesar's received 3.5 percent of sales from foreign stores. Only 3.2 percent of the company's stores were in non-U.S. locations, namely, Canada, Czech and Slovak Republics, Guam, Puerto Rico, and the U.K.

Year	1985	1986	1987	1988	1989	1990	1991	1992	1993	1994
Sales*	340	520	725	908	1,130	1,400	1,725	2,050	2,150	2,000
# of stores	900	1,000	1,820	2,000	2,700	3,173	3,650	4,300	5,609	4,700
Employees	18,000	26,160	36,400	43,600	54,000	63,460	73,000	86,000	92,000	95,000

*$M.

McDonald's

At the top in 1994 international sales and units, McDonald's Inc. was the most profitable retailer in the U.S. during the 1980s and into the 1990s. The company opened its first store in California in 1948, went public in 1965, and by 1994 had over 20 percent of the U.S. fast-food business. McDonald's opened its first international store in Canada in 1967. Growing domestic competition in the 1980s gave impetus to the company's international expansion. By 1994 there were over 15,000 restaurants under the golden arches in 79 countries. The non-U.S. stores provided about one third of total revenues and half of the company's profits. McDonald's planned to open 1,200–1,500 new restaurants in 1995—most outside the U.S. International markets had grown into an attractive venue for the burger giant because there was "less competition, lighter market saturation, and high name recognition" in international markets.

The company's growth was fueled by aggressive franchising. In the early 1990s two thirds of the McDonald's locations were franchised units and franchisees remained with the company an average of 20 years. McDonald's used heavy advertising ($1.4B in 1994) and frequent menu changes and other innovations (1963: Filet-O-Fish sandwich and Ronald McDonald; 1968 Big Mac and first TV ads; 1972: Quarter Pounder, Egg McMuffin (breakfast); 1974: Ronald McDonald House; 1975: drive thru; 1979: Happy Meals; 1983: Chicken McNuggets; 1986: provided customers with list of products' ingredients; 1987: salads; 1980s "value menus"; 1991: McLean DeLuxe a low-fat hamburger (not successful) and experimentation with decor and new menu items at local level; 1993: first restaurants inside another store (Wal-Mart). The company planned to open its first restaurants in India in 1996 with menus featuring chicken, fish sandwiches, and vegetable nuggets. There would be no beef items.

From 1993–1994, McDonald's grew 10.2 percent in sales and 8.7 percent in stores. Because of their extensive experience in international markets, international sales had grown to 42.5 percent of their total revenues, and half its profits. Indeed, McDonald's was bigger than the 25 largest full-service chains put together.

Year	1985	1986	1987	1988	1989	1990	1991	1992	1993	1994
Sales*	3,695	4,144	4,894	5,566	6,142	6,640	6,695	7,133	7,408	8,321
Net income*	433	480	549	656	727	802	860	959	1,083	1,224
EPS($)	0.56	0.63	0.73	0.86	0.98	1.10	1.18	1.30	1.46	1.68
Stock price—close ($)	9.00	10.16	11.00	12.03	17.25	14.56	19.00	24.38	28.50	29.25
Dividends ($)	0.10	0.11	0.12	0.14	0.16	0.17	0.18	0.20	0.21	0.23
Employees (K)	148	159	159	169	176	174	168	166	169	183

*$M. 1994: Debt ratio, 41.2%; ROE, 20.7%; cash, $180M; current ratio, 0.31; LTD, $2.9M; market value, $20B.

Pepsico: KFC and Taco Bell—Also Includes Pizza Hut (Latter Is Not in the Top 50)

Pepsico owned powerful brand names such as Pepsi-Cola and Frito-Lay and was also the world's number one fast-food chain—with its ownership of KFC, Taco Bell, and Pizza Hut.

KFC was third in sales and stores of the top 50 franchises in 1994. Active in the international arena since the late 1960s, KFC had been a major McDonald's competitor in non-U.S. markets. In 1994, the company had $3.6 billion USD in sales and 4,258 stores in other countries. McDonald's had been commonly number one in each country it entered, but KFC had been number two in international sales and had the number one sales spot in Indonesia. In 1994, KFC international revenues were 50.7 percent of sales with 45.3 percent of stores in international locations.

Taco Bell was fourth in sales and fifth in stores of the top 50 franchises in 1994. This ranking had been achieved with minimal international business to date. Taco Bell had $130 million USD sales and 162 stores internationally. The company attempted to enter the Mexican market in 1992 with a kiosk and cart strategy in Mexico City. The venture did not fare well, and Taco Bell soon pulled out of Mexico.[25] In 1994, international revenues were 3 percent of sales and 2.9 percent of stores were international locations.

Year	1985	1986	1987	1988	1989	1990	1991	1992	1993	1994
Sales*	8,057	9,291	11,485	13,007	15,242	17,803	19,608	21,970	25,021	28,474
Net income*	544	458	595	762	901	1,077	1,080	1,302	1,588	1,784
EPS ($)	0.65	0.58	0.76	0.97	1.13	1.35	1.35	1.61	1.96	2.22
Stock price—close ($)	8.06	8.66	11.11	13.15	21.31	26.00	22.88	3.40	40.88	36.25
Dividend/share ($)	0.15	0.21	0.22	0.25	0.31	0.37	0.44	0.50	0.58	0.68
Employees (K)	150	214	225	235	266	308	338	372	423	471

*$M. 1994: debt ratio, 48.1%; ROE, 27.0%; cash (M), $1,488; current ratio, 0.96; LTD (M), $8,841. 1994 segment sales (operating income): restaurants, 37% (22%); beverages, 34% (37%); snack foods, 29% (41%).

Subway

Founded more than 29 years ago, Subway remained privately held in 1994.[26] The company had experienced explosive growth during the 1990s. It ranked ninth in sales and second in stores for 1994. Sales grew 13.6 percent from 1993 to 1994, and 26 percent from 1992 to 1993. Stores grew 17.1 percent from 1993 to 1994, and 15.3 percent from 1992 to 1993. In 1994, Subway overtook KFC as the number two chain in number of stores behind McDonald's. The company attributed its growth at least partially to an exceptionally low-priced and well-structured franchise program. In addition store sizes of 500–1500 square feet were small. Thus, the investment for a Subway franchise was modest.

The company's growth involved a deliberate strategy. The formula involved no cooking on site, except for the baking of bread. The company promoted the "efficiency and simplicity" of its franchise and advertised its food as "healthy, delicious, (and) fast." The company advertised regularly on TV with a $25 million budget and planned to increase that significantly. All stores contributed 2.5 percent of gross sales to the corporate advertising budget. Subway's goal was to equal or exceed the number of outlets operated by the largest fast-food company in every market that it entered. In most cases the firm's benchmark was burger giant McDonald's.

International markets played an emerging role in Subway's expansion. In 1994, international sales were 10.6 percent of sales, compared to 8.9 percent the previous year. International stores were 9.5 percent of total in 1994, and 7.5 percent in 1993. Subway boasted a total of 9,893 stores in all 50 states and 19 countries.[27]

Wendy's

Wendy's was number five in sales and number nine in stores for 1994. In 1994, after 25 years of operation, Wendy's had grown to 4,411 stores. This growth had been almost exclusively domestic until 1979, when Wendy's ventured out of the U.S. and Canada to open its first outlets in Puerto Rico, Switzerland, and West Germany. Wendy's granted J. C. Penney the franchise rights to France, Belgium, and Holland, and had one store opened in Belgium by 1980.

Wendy's still saw opportunities for growth in the U.S. Industry surveys had consistently ranked Wendy's burgers number one in quality, but poor in convenience (Wendy's had one store for every 65,000 people while McDonald's, in contrast had one for every 25,000). Growth was driven primarily by franchising. In 1994 71 percent of the stores were operated by franchisees and 29 percent by the company. Company restaurants provided 90 percent of total sales while franchise fees provided 8 percent. The company had made menu and strategic changes at various points in its history. For example in 1977 the company first began TV advertising; 1979 introduced its salad bar; 1985 experimented with breakfast; 1986 and 1987 introduced Big Classic and SuperBar buffet (neither very successful); 1990 grilled chicken sandwich and 99 cent Super Value Menu items; and 1992 packaged salads.

Wendy's planned to add about 150 restaurants each year in foreign markets. With a presence of 236 stores in 33 countries in 1994, international was 9.1 percent of sales and 9.4 percent of stores in 1994.

Year	1985	1986	1987	1988	1989	1990	1991	1992	1993	1994
Sales*	1,126	1,140	1,059	1,063	1,070	1,011	1,060	1,239	1,320	1,398
Net income*	76	(5)	4	29	24	39	52	65	79	97
EPS ($)	0.82	(0.05)	0.04	0.30	0.25	0.40	0.52	0.63	0.76	0.91
Stock price close ($)	13.41	10.25	5.63	5.75	4.63	6.25	9.88	12.63	17.38	14.38
Dividend/share ($)	0.17	0.21	0.24	0.24	0.24	0.24	0.24	0.24	0.24	0.24
Employees (K)	40	40	45	42	39	35	39	42	43	44

*$M; 1994: debt ratio, 36.6%; ROE, 5.2%; current ratio, 0.98,; LTD (M), $145.

Appendix B

Country Summaries[1]

Canada

In the 1990s Canada was considered an ideal first stop for U.S. business seeking to begin exporting. Per capita output, patterns of production, market economy, and business practices were similar to the U.S. U.S. goods and services were well received in Canada: 70 percent of all Canadian imports were from the United States. Canada's market conditions were stable, and U.S. companies continued to see Canada as an attractive option for expansion.

Canada had one of the highest real growth rates among the OECD during the 1980s, averaging about 3.2 percent. The Canadian economy softened during the 1990s, but Canadian imports of U.S. goods and services were expected to increase about 5 percent in fiscal year 1996.

Although Canada sometimes mirrored the U.S., there are significant cultural and linguistic differences from the U.S. and between the regional markets in Canada. These differences were evident in the mounting friction between the English- and French-speaking areas of Canada. The conflict had potential for splitting of territory between the factions, slicing Canada into two separate countries. The prospect of this outcome left foreign investors tense.

Germany

In the mid-1990s Germany was the largest economy in Europe, and the fifth largest overall importer of U.S. goods and services. Since reunification in 1990, the eastern part of Germany had continued to receive extensive infusions of aid from western Germany, and these funds were only just beginning to show an impact. The highly urbanized and skilled Western German population enjoyed a very high standard of living with abundant leisure time. In 1994, Germany emerged from a recession, and scored a GDP of $2 trillion USD.

A unique feature of Germany was the unusually even distribution of both industry and population—there was no single business center for the country. This was a challenge for U.S. firms. They had to establish distribution networks that adequately covered all areas of the country. In Germany there was little opportunity for regional concentration around major population centers as in the United States.

The country was a good market for innovative high tech goods and high quality food products. Germans expected high quality goods, and would reject a less expensive product if quality and support were not in abundance. Strongest competition for U.S. firms were the German domestic firms not only because of their homegrown familiarity of the market, but also because of the consumers' widely held perception that German products were "simply the best."

---

[1]Note: the material in this appendix is adapted from the Department of Commerce Country Commercial Guides and the *CIA World Fact Book*.

A recurring complaint from Germans was the prevalent "here today, gone tomorrow" business approach of American firms. Germans viewed business as a long term commitment to support growth in markets, and did not always receive the level and length of attention necessary from U.S. companies to satisfy them.

Conditions in the former area of East Germany were not the doomsday picture often painted, nor were they as rosy as the German government depicts. It would take 10–15 years for the eastern region of the country to catch up to the western region in terms of per capita income, standard of living, and productivity.

Japan

Japan had the second largest economy in the world. Overall economic growth in Japan over the past 35 years had been incredible: 10 percent average annual growth during the 1960s, 5 percent in the 1970s and 1980s. Growth ground to a halt during the 1990s due to tight fiscal policy. The government tightened fiscal constraints in order to correct the significant devaluation of the real estate markets. The economy posted a 0.6 percent growth in 1994 largely due to consumer demand. The overall economic outlook remained cloudy, but the outlook for exports to Japan remained positive.

Japan was a highly homogeneous society with business practices characterized by long-standing close relationships among individuals and firms. It took time for Japanese businessmen to develop relationships and for non-Japanese business people the task of relationship building in Japan was formidable. It was well known that Japan's market was not as open as the United States but the U.S. government had mounted multi-faceted efforts to help U.S. business people to "open doors." While these efforts were helpful, most of the responsibility in opening the Japanese market to U.S. goods or services remained with the individual firm. Entering Japan was expensive and generally required four things: (1) financial and management capabilities and a Japanese-speaking staff residing within the country, (2) modification of products to suit Japanese consumers, (3) a long term approach to maximizing market share and achieving reasonable profit levels, and (4) careful monitoring of Japanese demand, distribution, competitors, and government. Despite the challenges of market entry, Japan ranked as the second largest importer of U.S. goods and services.

Historically Japanese consumers were conservative and brand conscious, although the recession during the 1990s nurtured opportunities for "value" entrants. Traditional conformist buying patterns were still prominent, but more individualistic habits were developing in the younger Japanese aged 18–21. This age cohort had a population of 8 million people, and boasted a disposable income of more than $35 billion USD.

Japanese consumers were willing to pay a high price for quality goods. However, they had a well-earned reputation for having unusually high expectations for quality. U.S. firms with high quality, competitive products had to be able to undertake the high cost of initial market entry. For those that were willing, Japan could provide respectable market share and attractive profit levels.

Mexico

Mexico had experienced a dramatic increase in imports from the United States since the late 1980s. During 1994 the country experienced 20 percent growth over 1993. In 1994, Mexico's peso experienced a massive devaluation brought on by investor anxiety and capital flight. Although the Mexican government implemented tight fiscal measures to stabilize the peso, their efforts could not stop the country from plunging into a serious recession.

Inflation rose as a result of the austerity policies and it was expected to be between 42–54 percent in 1995. Negative economic growth was anticipated in 1995 as well. The U.S. financial assistance package (primarily loans) provided Mexico with nearly $50 billion USD and restored stability to the financial markets by mid-1995. The government was taking measures to improve the country's infrastructure. Mexico's problems mask that its government had, on the whole, practiced sound economic fundamentals.

Mexico was still committed to political reform despite the current economic challenges. After ruling the government uninterrupted for 60 years, the PRI party had begun to lose some seats to other political parties. Mexico was slowly evolving into a multi-party democracy.

Despite the economic misfortunes of recent years, Mexico remained the United States' third largest trading partner. Mexico still held opportunities for U.S. firms able to compete in the price-sensitive recessionary market. Mexico had not wavered on the NAFTA agreement since its ratification and in the mid-1990s 60 percent of U.S. exports to Mexico entered duty free.

South Korea

South Korea had been identified as one of the U.S. Department of Commerce's 10 "Big Emerging Markets." The country's economy overcame tremendous obstacles after the Korean War in the 1950s left the country in ruins. The driving force behind South Korea's growth was export-led development and energetic emphasis on entrepreneurship. Annual real GDP growth from 1986–1991 was over 10 percent. This blistering pace created inflation, tight labor markets, and a rising current account deficit. Fiscal policy in 1992 focused on curbing inflation and reducing the deficit. Annual growth, reduced to a still enviable 5 percent in 1992, rose to 6.3 percent in 1993. Fueled by exports, 1994's growth was a heady 8.3 percent. South Korea's GDP was larger than Russia, Australia, or Mexico.

The American media had highlighted such issues as student demonstrations, construction accidents, and North Korean nuclear problems and trade disputes. Investors needed to closely monitor developments related to North Korea. However, the political landscape in S. Korea had been stable enough over the 1980s to fuel tremendous economic expansion. The country was undertaking significant infrastructure improvements. Overall, S. Korea was a democratic republic with an open society and a free press. It was a modern, cosmopolitan, fast-paced and dynamic country with abundant business opportunities for savvy American businesses.

There had been staggering development of U.S. exports to S. Korea: $21.6 billion USD in 1994 and over $30 billion USD expected in 1995. While S. Korea was 22 times smaller than China in terms of population, it imported two times more U.S. goods and services than China in 1994!

Although S. Korea ranked as the United States' sixth largest export market, obstacles for U.S. firms still remained. Despite participation in the Uruguay Round of GATT and related trade agreements, customs clearance procedures and regulations for labeling, sanitary standards, and quarantine often served as significant non-tariff barriers.

The United Kingdom (or Great Britain)

The United Kingdom (U.K.) was the United States' fourth largest trading partner and the largest market for U.S. exports in Europe. Common language, legal heritage, and business practices facilitated U.S. entry into the British market.

The U.K. had made significant changes to their taxation, regulation, and privatization policies that changed the structure of the British economy and increased its overall efficiency. The reward for this disciplined economic approach had been sustained, modest growth during the 1980s and early 1990s. GDP grew 4.2 percent in 1994, the highest level in six years. The U.K. trimmed its deficit from $75 billion USD in fiscal 1994 to $50 billion in fiscal 1995.

The U.K. had no restrictions on foreign ownership and movement of capital. There was a high degree of labor flexibility. Efficiencies had soared in the U.K. and in the mid-1990s the country boasted the lowest real per unit labor cost of the Group of Seven (G7) industrialized countries.

The U.K.'s shared cultural heritage and warm relationship with the United States translated into the British finding U.S. goods and services as attractive purchases. These reasons, coupled with British policy emphasizing free enterprise and open competition, made the U.K. the destination of 40 percent of all U.S. investment in the EU.

The U.K. market was based on a commitment to the principles of free enterprise and open competition. Demand for U.S. goods and services was growing. The abolition of many internal trade barriers within the European Common market enabled European-based firms to operate relatively freely. As a result, U.S. companies used the U.K. as a gateway to the rest of the EU. Of the top 500 British companies, one in eight was a U.S. affiliate. Excellent physical and communications infrastructure combined with a friendly political and commercial climate were expected to keep the U.K. as a primary target for U.S. firms for years to come.

■ Endnotes

1. All three Outback founders credited casual dining chain legend and mentor Norman Brinker with his strong mentoring role in their careers. Brinker played a key role in all of the restaurant chains Sullivan and Basham were associated with prior to Outback.

2. American consumption of meat declined from the mid-1970s to the early 1990s primarily as a result of health concerns about red meat. In 1976 Americans consumed 131.6 pounds of beef and veal, 58.7 pounds of pork, and 12.9 pounds of fish. In 1990 the figures had declined to 64.9 pounds of beef and veal, 46.3 of pork, and 15.5 of fish. The dramatic decrease was attributed to consumer attitudes toward a low fat, healthier diet. Menu items that gained in popularity were premium baked goods, coffees, vegetarian menu items, fruits, salsa, sauces, chicken dishes, salad bars, and spicy dishes. [George Thomas Kurian, *Datapedia of the United States 1790–2000* (Maryland: Bernan Press, 1994), p. 113.]

3. Outback's original Henderson Blvd. (Tampa, Florida) Restaurant was one of the few open for lunch. By 1995 the chain had also begun to open in some locations for Sunday lunch or for special occasions such as Mother's Day lunch.

4. Outback's signature trademark was its best-selling "Aussie-Tizer," the "Bloomin' Onion." The company expected to serve nine million "Bloomin' Onions" in 1995.

5. Merritt had worked as CFO for another company which had come to the financial markets with its IPO (initial public offering).

6. Outback did not grant exclusive territorial franchises. Thus, if an Outback franchisee did not perform the company could bring additional franchisees into the area. Through 1994 Outback had not had territorial disputes between franchisees.

7. PepsiCo owned Kentucky Fried Chicken, Taco Bell, and Pizza Hut.

8. Grand Met owned Burger King.

9. Ref. AME 76 (KR).

10. "Industry and Trade Summary: Franchising," U.S. International Trade Commission, Washington, DC, 1995, pp. 15–16.

11. "World Hunger," *Restaurant Hospitality,* November 1994, p. 97.

12. *International Business Environments and Operations,* seventh edition, 1995, pp. 117–119.

13. "U.S. Restaurant Chains Tackle Challenges of Asian Expansion," *Nation's Restaurant News,* February 14, 1994, p. 36.

14. *CIA World Factbook,* India, 1995.

15. "Big McMuttons," *Forbes,* July 17, 1995, p. 18.

16. Interview with Cheryl Babcock, Professor, University of St. Thomas, October 23, 1995.

17. "Franchise Management in East Asia," *Academy of Management Executive* 4, no. 2 (1990), p. 79.

18. "U.S. Operators Flock to Latin America," *Nation's Restaurant News,* October 17, 1994, p. 47.

19. Interview with Cheryl Babcock, Professor, University of St. Thomas, October 23, 1995.

20. "U.S. Restaurant Chains Tackle Challenges of Asian Expansion," *Nation's Restaurant News,* February 14, 1994, p. 36.

21. "Industry and Trade Summary: Franchising," U.S. International Trade Commission, Washington, DC, 1995, p. 30.

22. Ibid.

23. "U.S. Restaurant Chains Tackle Challenges of Asian Expansion," *Nation's Restaurant News,* February 14, 1994, p. 36.

24. "Big News Over There!" *Restaurants and Institutions,* July 1, 1994.

25. "U.S. Operators Flock to Latin America," *Nation's Restaurant News,* October 17, 1994.

26. There is, thus, no publicly available financial data on Subway.

27. Subway's site on the Internet, accessed March 24, 1996.

Case 11   OfficeMax and the Office Supply Industry

Margaret J. Naumes and William Naumes
both of University of New Hampshire

The good news, in September 1996, was that OfficeMax was poised to become the number two firm in the highly competitive office supply industry. The bad news was that this promotion from third place in the industry would occur due to the planned merger of firm number two, Staples, and firm number one, Office Depot. If allowed by the Federal Trade Commission (FTC), the merger would result in a firm with about 1,100 stores and annual sales of more than $10 billion. OfficeMax, by contrast, had just under 500 stores and sales in 1995 of $2.54 billion. Its CEO, Michael Feuer, put a positive spin on the situation: "I view this situation as good news . . . Fewer is always better. This will position us with a unique opportunity in the marketplace."[1]

Nine months later, the situation was still unclear. In February 1997, the FTC had asked for additional information. It appeared to be concerned about the impact on customers if the merger was allowed to proceed, in particular about prices in markets where Staples and Office Depot competed directly. In March, the FTC voted to ask for a court order to block the merger. To allay the FTC's concerns about competition, Staples then put together a plan to sell 63 of its stores (in areas where it currently competed only with Office Depot) to OfficeMax in order to preserve competition in those markets. This proposal was sufficient to cause the FTC to reconsider. On the eve of the rescheduled vote, news services quoted "a source familiar with the situation" who predicted that the merger would be approved.[2] However, on Friday, April 4, the FTC voted 4 to 1 to challenge the merger on the grounds that it would violate federal antitrust laws. Staples' CEO, Thomas Stemberg, reacted with astonishment, and replied, "If I were a betting man, I would say this matter is likely to wind up in litigation."[3]

For OfficeMax, the on-again, off-again merger created some uncertainty. One issue was whether the company would be able to acquire the 63 stores Staples offered it. The major issue, however, was the nature of future competition in the office supply industry. Whether or not its merger with Office Depot was allowed to occur, Staples had made it clear that it would no longer settle for the number two spot in the industry. How would this even more aggressive competitor affect OfficeMax's ability to continue its rapid, and finally profitable, growth?

■ The Competitive Structure of the Office Supply Industry

One of the key points of debate between Staples and the FTC concerned the size of the office supply industry. If the industry's annual sales were $185 billion, as Staples argued, the combined Staples/Office Depot's $10 billion would represent only 5 percent of the market.[4] The FTC, on the other hand, argued that superstores

---

[1]"Staples/Office Depot Merger: The Timing Is Right," *Discount Store News,* September 16, 1996, p. 131.
[2]Chris Reidy, "FTC Seen Endorsing Staples Buy," *Boston Globe,* April 3, 1997, p. D1.
[3]Aaron Zitner and Chris Reidy, "Staples' $4 Billion Merger Rejected," *Boston Globe,* April 5, 1997, p. A4.
[4]"Deal Places Staples Back at Top of Industry," *The Patriot Ledger* (Quincy, MA), September 5, 1996.

such as Office Depot, Staples, and OfficeMax constituted a market of their own, with annual sales of $23 billion. In this more narrowly defined market, the Staples/Office Depot combination would have 44 percent of the market. Superstores were much more focused than traditional discount retail chains. A superstore carried a wide variety of merchandise in one category such as toys (Toys 'R' Us), books (Barnes & Noble), sports (Sports Authority), or office supplies. Due to purchasing power, the superstore chain could set prices equal to or lower than those of stores with diverse product/merchandise lines. The superstores' strategy of wide selection and low price was alleged to make it difficult for retailers with broad product lines and less selection within each line to compete, hence the superstores' nickname *category killers.*

"Office supplies" was not a clearcut category. Products such as paper for printers and copiers, envelopes, notebooks, paper clips, and file folders are used in offices of all sizes. File cabinets, desks, lamps, computer tables, and other office furniture represented another product line. Computer software and accessories, and potentially computers themselves, were also used in modern offices. In addition, services such as custom printing (stationery, order forms, business cards, etc.) could be included as part of the office supply industry. Thus, the superstores were in competition not only with the mom-and-pop office supply stores serving a local community but also with any store selling office supplies, including WalMart and warehouse stores such as Price/Costco or Sam's Warehouse Clubs. Furniture stores sold desks, sofas, and cabinets appropriate for office use. Entire chains, such as ComputerTown, were devoted to computers, accessories, and software. Kinko's and Sir Speedy advertised themselves as solving office problems by providing comprehensive photocopying services. All three superstore companies carried a full line of office supplies, business machines, computer accessories, and office furniture, and offered some type of business services. See Exhibit 1 for a breakdown of U.S. manufacturers' shipments of office supplies to different resellers, from the annual survey for the Business Products Industry Association.[5]

■ **Exhibit 1**

Percentage Breakdown of U.S. Domestic Manufacturers' Shipments of Office Supplies to Different Resellers, 1989–1994

	1994	1993	1992	1991	1990	1989
Mass market	10.1%	10.9%	12.4%	7.6%	10.2%	10.4%
Warehouse clubs	4.3	4.1	4.0	4.0	4.0	3.5
Superstores	18.7	15.0	11.4	10.2	7.3	4.3
National wholesalers	15.6	18.4	18.2	19.2	17.3	18.3
Regional wholesalers	4.0	4.5	5.0	5.0	5.1	6.5
Total wholesalers	19.6	22.9	23.2	24.2	22.4	24.8
Mail order	3.4	4.5	4.7	4.3	4.6	4.4
Largest dealers	17.3	14.5	14.9	14.8	13.1	12.7
Large dealers	6.1	7.9	8.1	8.1	10.6	9.2
Total large dealers	23.4	22.4	23.0	22.9	23.7	21.9
Small/medium dealers	10.2	9.3	9.3	11.1	12.5	14.0
Direct and government	3.5	3.2	4.1	6.2	6.6	5.7
Other	6.8	7.7	7.9	9.5	8.7	11.0

SOURCE: Independent Office Products and Furniture Dealers Association.

---

[5]"Superstores Swallow a Bigger Piece of the Pie," *Purchasing,* April 25, 1996, p. 86S7.

Changes in the Office Supply Industry

Prior to the 1980s, most small businesses bought their typing paper, adding machine tape, and file folders from small, local office supply stores. Customers walking into such stores would see greeting cards, small gift items, and even toys or collectibles (Smurfs or china figurines). On the shelves farther back would be posterboard, three-ring notebooks, and lined paper, as well as products aimed primarily at businesses. The store might also have a desk or window for ordering custom photocopying and printing, anything from a company's letterhead to engraved wedding invitations. The store might deliver orders to its larger customers, for whom it might also offer direct billing. Anyone wanting a desk or a file cabinet would need to go to a store specializing in office furniture, or place an order through a catalog. Business machines consisted of typewriters (by the 1970s, electric had replaced manual typewriters in the typical office) and adding machines; copiers were leased; and only a few companies and individuals had seen the possibilities in desktop computers.

By the 1990s, the industry had changed. Superstores purchased less than 1 percent of U.S. manufacturers' shipments of office supplies in 1986; this figure grew to 4.3 percent in 1989, to 11.4 percent in 1992, and to 18.7 percent in 1994. Office Depot led the industry, with 526 stores and $5.3 billion in sales in fiscal 1995, followed by Staples, with 574 stores and $3.1 billion in sales, and OfficeMax, with 564 stores and $2.5 billion in sales. Warehouse clubs, although accounting for only about 4 percent of sales, also targeted business customers by offering low prices for bulk purchases.[6]

The primary impact of these two new channels—superstores and warehouse clubs—was on small office supply retailers. One source estimated that the number of independent dealers nationwide had decreased from more than 12,000 to about 2,000.[7] Certainly, this trend was evident in many urban areas; in Indianapolis, for example, the number of independent office supply dealers fell from 15–20 in 1979 to 5 in 1996.

Competitive Strategies in Office Supplies

Both superstores and warehouse clubs offered customers low prices. This had the effect of lowering margins for everyone in the office supply industry, from 40 percent to 15 percent. Some of the independent retailers discovered that they were able to match prices with the superstores on most products. Brian Morford, owner of a small office supply company, explained: "Every discount store has loss leaders to bring in customers. . . . We don't offer loss leaders, but we offer pretty much the same discounts otherwise. We feel that we're competitive."[8]

In order to remain competitive, independent stores adopted a variety of strategies. Many joined purchasing clubs or cooperatives, and some looked for close ties with key suppliers. Careful inventory management became important. This could take the form of just-in-time deliveries from suppliers or, more commonly, of eliminating items that turned over slowly. Some independent stores concentrated on

---

[6]Ibid.

[7]Dean Boyer, "Independent Office Supply Dealers Perfect Strategies," *Pierce County Business Examiner* (Tacoma, WA), October 28, 1996.

[8]Ibid.

products that the superstores did not carry, such as specialized paper-handling equipment or computer peripherals. Some focused on service to their customers, particularly small businesses, providing small lots and delivery services. Another approach was to increase, or add, more profitable lines of business, often greeting cards and gifts. Bob Franzen, co-owner of Coast Office Equipment Company in Olympia, Washington, summarized his strategy for survival: "What we have left is a company that does what it does well and stays out of areas we don't."[9]

Disposable supplies and business forms made up less than half of industry sales. The Business Products Industry Association estimated 1994 sales of supplies at $24.4 billion, and of business forms at $6.9 billion.[10] However, a typical office superstore sold not only these products but also computers, software, business machines (such as calculators, copiers and fax machines), and furniture. This also put the superstore in competition with a variety of other specialized retailers, some of them also superstores. Computers and computer accessories, for example, were available from specialized chains as well as electronic superstores such as Circuit City, and from warehouse stores and even Wal-Mart. There were also catalogs devoted to software and peripherals; and Dell and Gateway, among others, offered computers by phone. Estimated sales of microcomputers and peripherals amounted to $42.8 billion in 1994, with an additional $8.0 billion in software. Desks, chairs, file cabinets, and other furniture for the modern office, with annual sales amounting to $8.5 billion, were also available from both furniture and specialty stores, as well as through catalogs. Sales of machines such as typewriters, calculators, copiers, phones, and fax equipment amounted to an additional $12.5 billion; these products were available from a variety of sources, including Service Merchandise and similar discount stores. Even drugstores and supermarkets sold school supplies, an important seasonal sales category.

Some companies specialized in contract sales to large businesses, operating without any retail operations. This was the strategy followed by U.S. Office Products Company, which had grown by acquisition from its first company in 1994 to more than 100 acquired contract stationers and total annual sales of $2.1 billion.[11] Some office products manufacturers, such as Boise Cascade, had their own office products divisions. Most office supply stores contracted out orders for custom printing, but did offer copying services, putting them in competition with chains such as Kinko's and Sir Speedy.

New Developments in the Office Supply Industry

Two trends gaining in importance in the office supply industry were catalog sales and on-line shopping. Catalogs enabled shoppers to compare prices without leaving work. Michael Feuer, CEO of OfficeMax, pointed out, "Shoppers are much less patient than they were just a couple of years ago. They want a wide selection. Price is the ticket for admission."[12] OfficeMax and Staples both offered catalogs, as did a number of smaller companies. For example, the stores of W. B. Mason, a Boston regional supplier dating back to 1898, contained only office furniture, while the

---

[9]Ibid.

[10]All sales estimates in this paragraph are from "Superstores Swallow," p. 86S8.

[11]Peter Spiegel, "Supplies Surprise," *Forbes*, November 4, 1996, pp. 98, 100.

[12]Michael Feuer, "Bullish on the Internet," *Discount Merchandiser*, December 1996, p. 42.

company's full line of supplies was available through its catalog. To compete, W. B. Mason promised overnight delivery within the region via its own fleet of trucks, and "the absolute lowest prices" on all its products. This combination of price and service helped W. B. Mason's sales grow from $30 million in 1993, the first year of the catalog, to $70 million in 1996.[13]

Electronic retail, although still relatively small, was seen as the next major growth area. Dan Sweeney, of IBM's Consulting Group, argued, "Who would have ever thought that you could sell jewelry on television? Or fashion apparel through the mail? I think electronic shopping is inevitable and will represent a significant share of retail activity."[14] Predictions on the number of Americans who would be connected to the Internet in the year 2000 ranged from 32.9 million to 50 million. On-line retail sales were estimated to be $6.9 billion or more.[15] OfficeMax was one of many retailers already developing Web sites and other sales tools, including on-line catalogs. While there were still concerns about security and payment, new technology would continue to make shopping on-line more common and convenient.

■ OfficeMax

Background

OfficeMax, founded in Cleveland, Ohio, in 1988, originally targeted small businesses. Initially it was financed by individuals and private venture capitalists. Within two years, it had attracted the attention of Kmart, which purchased 90 percent of the new company's stock during 1990 and 1991. Co-founder and CEO Michael Feuer described the acquisition as extremely valuable for OfficeMax: "Kmart was one of the best financial partners I ever had in my business career. They never interfered with our business strategy. We had a unique opportunity to build a new paradigm of doing business."[16] He felt that the freedom from reporting publicly to shareholders every quarter had enabled the company to invest and grow rapidly.[17] Sales grew at a compound annual rate of 141 percent in fiscal years 1990 through 1993. This was the result of both new-store openings and acquisitions such as that of the 96 BizMart superstores, purchased in March 1993. By late 1994, OfficeMax had 345 stores and sales of over $1.4 billion.

The company also had a history of losses, not earning its first profit until fiscal year 1994. In November 1994, as part of a program to refocus on its core discount store business, Kmart sold 75 percent of its OfficeMax stock, spinning off the office supply chain as an independent company. As part of the arrangement, Kmart freed OfficeMax from all its debt, and provided a pool of cash. The following July, Kmart sold the rest of its OfficeMax stock; OfficeMax received an additional $110 million from this sale, which was used to fund further expansion.

During the 1995 fiscal year, which ended in January 1996, OfficeMax reached $2.54 billion in net sales and $125 million in net income, achieving its goals despite

[13]Chris Reidy, "A Question of Competition," *The Boston Globe*, May 23, 1997, pp. E1–2.

[14]Jennifer Pellet, "The Future of Electronic Retail," *Discount Merchandiser*, January 1996, p. 36.

[15]Ibid.

[16]Jay L. Johnson, "OfficeMax: Maximizing the Office Products Superstore," *Discount Merchandiser*, November 1995, p. 38.

[17]Ibid., p. 40.

bad weather over much of the United States and a federal government shutdown in January, affecting in particular sales to small businesses.[18] (See Exhibits 2 and 3 for financial statements.) Sales from ongoing operations earned a profit of $56.6 million, with the remainder coming from the sale of the company's stock in Corporate Express, a contract stationery supplier. OfficeMax also opened 80 new superstores, a variety of stores with more specialized formats, and launched its first national advertising campaign. Some store sales increased 16.7 percent during the year. The company had also focused on internal issues, including increased efficiency at existing stores and improved productivity of new stores, as well as improved inventory turnover.

Aggressive growth continued during 1996 and into 1997. By September 1996, when the Staples/Office Depot merger was announced, OfficeMax had 425 stores and projected revenues for the 1996 fiscal year of $3.3 billion. The company planned to open a total of 160 superstores in 1996 and 1997, in addition to expanding the number of catalog/delivery centers, CopyMax and mini-CopyMax stores, and FurnitureMax office furniture outlets. Two stores were scheduled to

■ **Exhibit 2**   OfficeMax Balance Sheet, 1993–1996 (in thousands of $)

	Fiscal Year Ending			
	1/27/96	1/21/95	1/22/94	1/23/93
Assets				
Cash	$ 365,863	$ 174,250	$ 31,744	$ 14,100
Receivables	27,039	28,021	25,211	11,000
Inventories	636,211	468,177	409,028	178,200
Other current assets	20,009	20,898	20,310	3,800
Total current assets	1,049,122	691,346	486,293	207,100
Property, plant, and equipment	256,171	178,884	138,696	52,400
Accumulated depreciation	75,795	46,674	22,897	6,000
Net property and equipment	180,376	132,210	115,799	46,400
Intangibles	343,134	352,548	361,976	193,900
Deposits and other assets	15,236	11,367	22,154	1,200
Total assets	$1,587,868	$1,257,467	$1,009,712	$448,600
Liabilities				
Accounts payable	$ 348,605	$ 331,161	$ 239,048	$119,300
Accrued expenses	156,306	120,105	133,668	57,200
Other current liabilities	44,802	27,197	NA	NA
Total current liabilities	549,713	479,463	372,716	176,500
Other long-term liabilities	47,266	29,428	28,486	13,900
Total liabilities	596,979	508,891	401,202	190,400
Common stock net	850,557	736,551	187,198	187,200
Capital surplus	NA	NA	410,307	70,900
Retained earnings	141,814	16,051	11,005	100
Other equities	(1,482)	(4,026)	NA	NA
Shareholder equity	990,889	748,576	608,510	258,200
Total liabilities and net worth	$1,587,868	$1,257,467	$1,009,712	$448,600

---

[18]"President's Letter," OfficeMax annual report, 1996.

■ **Exhibit 3**   OfficeMax Income Statement, 1993–1996 (in thousands of $)

	Fiscal Year Ending			
	1/27/96	1/21/95	1/22/94	1/23/93
Net sales	$2,542,513	$1,841,212	$1,421,794	$528,205
Cost of goods	1,970,536	1,422,400	1,108,992	411,429
Gross profit	571,977	418,812	312,802	116,776
Selling, general, and administrative expenses	476,310	353,755	284,146	111,742
Income before depreciation and amortization	$ 95,667	$ 65,057	$ 28,656	$ 5,034
Nonoperating income	117,976	(8,725)	(8,734)	(3,874)
Income before taxes	213,643	56,332	19,922	1,160
Provision for income taxes	87,880	25,975	9,073	1,881
Net income before extraordinary items	125,763	30,357	10,849	(721)
Outstanding shares	82,331	76,418	50,945	23,381

open in Mexico City, and the company planned to expand into Asia. OfficeMax continued to experiment with new formats, including BatteryMax, and new technologies, including offering its full product line via an on-line catalog.

Management

"A lot has changed over the past eight years, but the basis on which we operate has not—customer service, great values, exciting store formats. These are the simple secrets to our success and our success lies with effective execution at every level of the business, every day of the week," reported Feuer in his 1996 "President's Letter" to OfficeMax shareholders.[19] Feuer described the company's objective as "to layer-in growth initiatives well into the turn of the century, creating business vehicles that will contribute significant comparable store sales gains year after year. . . . The winners during the balance of this century will be the low-cost providers with the strongest balance sheets."[20]

One important thrust of OfficeMax's activities was to improve operating efficiencies and, consequently, profitability. While still owned by Kmart, the company had invested heavily in computer systems. All district and regional managers, as well as top management, had access to a large pool of information, including data for specific stores and product lines. As a result, the company was able to reduce costs "because [it had] fewer people using better technologies to perform fewer manual chores."[21] Management believed that the company's general and administrative expenses were the lowest in the industry, estimating OfficeMax's at 1.86 percent, compared with competitors' 3 percent.

In order to further reduce inventory costs, the company had developed its own logistics system. This was based on the five ThruMax cross-docking facilities, opened in 1995. These took in bulk shipments from suppliers and broke them down into quantities usable by individual stores or distribution centers (hence the term *cross-docking*, as the merchandise was transferred from one loading dock to another).

---

[19]Ibid.

[20]Ibid.

[21]Johnson, "OfficeMax," p. 38.

Top executives met first thing every morning, and there were regular Saturday-morning executive meetings where everyone present talked about what he or she had done during the week. This was part of the culture, which Feuer described as one that continually found a way to solve problems: "Our philosophy is very simple. Get exceedingly bright, capable people. Hold them accountable. Give them the authority to do their job. Then keep careful track of them, so no one stumbles."[22] Between the rapid growth and top management's high expectations, managers could easily work 11 or 12 hours a day, six or more days a week.

Retail Operations

By 1997, the company had developed five basic formats and was experimenting with several more. The mainstay was the OfficeMax superstore, now found nationwide. The appearance and floor plans of OfficeMax stores had changed several times over the company's eight-year history. Currently, the older stores were being remodeled, many for the second or third time, to have wider aisles and a better sight line, making it easier for customers to find merchandise on their own, or to find employees for assistance. The company continued to open stores in new markets, entering locations such as central California with multiple stores and other, smaller markets with only one.

In addition to carrying a limited amount of office furniture in its superstores, and a more extensive line in its catalog, OfficeMax opened its first 22 FurnitureMax stores in 1995, and added another 65 in 1996. These stores targeted customers ranging from home offices to larger companies. They allowed customers to browse among and compare a variety of chairs, desks, conference tables, filing systems, and other furniture.

Another new concept launched in 1995 was CopyMax, a center within the superstore offering digital printing. Begun with only eight units, CopyMax appeared so successful that the company had begun adding mini-CopyMax units to its superstores during remodeling. This combination was known as a BiMax store. The company also had begun building TriMax stores, incorporating both a CopyMax or mini-CopyMax and a FurnitureMax under the same 40,000 square foot roof within an OfficeMax superstore. Many of the company's new stores were being constructed in the TriMax format.

OfficeMax's product line was also available through a catalog. Customers could place an order at the store for items that were not in stock, or could order direct from one of the three catalog call centers. Items were then delivered from one of 15 delivery centers nationwide.

Areas for Expansion

Although not yet profitable, the CopyMax stores within the superstores had proven interesting enough that the company planned to experiment with freestanding CopyMax stores, starting with three in Cleveland, its headquarters city. This could lead to further expansion into other settings, such as banks and office buildings. Another store-within-a-superstore experiment was BatteryMax, which was first opened in mid-1996.

---

[22]Ibid., p. 40.

Late in 1996, the company opened its first two stores in Mexico City. These were the first results of a joint venture with Grupo Oprimax, a Mexican company. In December, OfficeMax announced that it had formed a joint venture with Jusco Co. Ltd., a prominent retail company headquartered in Tokyo, to open 200 OfficeMax stores in Japan. This agreement was structured so that OfficeMax would initially own only 19.9 percent of the joint venture, with the possibility of increasing its stake to 50 percent whenever it wanted.[23] This kept OfficeMax below the 20 percent threshold at which generally accepted accounting procedures would require the company to include the venture, including its start-up costs and losses, as part of OfficeMax's consolidated financial statements, essentially allowing the company to treat the venture as an investment during its early stages.[24] The OfficeMax/Jusco partnership enabled the companies to also explore other locations throughout Asia. Competitor Staples' international operations were concentrated in Europe, where it was expanding its holdings of companies in the United Kingdom and in Germany.

A major area for growth was provided by OfficeMax's on-line connections. The company was the only one of the office supply superstores to have sites on all major computer service providers, including America Online and the Microsoft network. Several of these deals were written to prohibit competitors from being part of the service's on-line shopping. OfficeMax was also accessible via the Internet. These sites included information about the company, a service to help customers locate the nearest store, information about customer service, and even a complete catalog. Customers could order electronically, with the order being routed to the nearest delivery center for overnight delivery. This enabled OfficeMax to reach customers in areas where there was not yet an OfficeMax store, and ultimately to locate potential new retail store locations.[25] Other potential applications for the on-line site included assistance with editorial and office problems, including tips on how to do a presentation—with a "by the way, we have all these items, click here if you'd like to buy them from us now," at the end of the help session.[26]

One future idea, code-named CyberMax, was an electronic OfficeMax kiosk, to be located in the lobbies of banks, office buildings, even post offices and airports. These kiosks could provide CopyMax services and could also potentially allow a customer to plug in her laptop computer and print, or even go on-line to order products from the catalog.[27]

OfficeMax was continuing to experiment with its merchandise mix. The company expected sales of computers to continue to grow as a percentage of sales; unfortunately, computers carried a lower margin than many of the company's other products. One evolving product line was known as TechMax.[28] This would boost the stores' range of copiers, fax machines, cellular phones, electronic organizers, and other such "productivity tools" increasingly being demanded by individuals as well as businesses of all sizes.

---

[23]Laura Liebeck, "Staples, OfficeMax Look Abroad," *Discount Store News,* January 6, 1997, p. 88.

[24]Johnson, "OfficeMax," p. 37.

[25]Jennifer Pellet, " 'OfficeMax Is Everywhere!', " *Discount Merchandiser,* January 1996, p. 40.

[26]Pellet, "The Future of Electronic Retail," p. 37.

[27]Johnson, "OfficeMax," pp. 37–38.

[28]Feuer, "Bullish on the Internet," p. 42.

The company was also beginning to move into the business contract stationery market. OfficeMax had first entered this market in 1993, when it purchased 19 percent of the stock in Corporate Express and Feuer took a seat on Corporate Express's board. Although OfficeMax increased its investment to 20 percent in 1994, the company quickly realized that the contract stationer business was similar to its own delivery business: "Not only does our catalog and delivery center business perform the same functions as a contract stationer, OfficeMax was, in reality, already providing merchandise to larger corporate customers that were being served by contract stationers."[29] In September 1995, the company sold its shares of Corporate Express for an estimated $200 million, although the two companies continued to participate in joint buying and marketing programs. OfficeMax then developed its own version of a contract stationer, OfficeMax Corporate Direct, targeting medium-sized firms with 100–200 employees.

■ OfficeMax and the Merger

Looking to the future, OfficeMax saw both threats and opportunities. "We can go into new markets in a pre-emptive strike," said Feuer.[30] Office Depot and Staples had reduced their expansion plans in order to allow time to digest the merger and to rationalize the combined network of stores. The uncertainties provided by the long FTC investigation process had allowed OfficeMax additional time to carry out its 1996 and 1997 plans, relatively unopposed. However, the threat of a combined Staples/Office Depot was formidable, in penetration and number of stores, in marketing, and in buying power. Even if the merger was not allowed to take place, Staples had effectively announced that it was intent on future aggressive growth. For OfficeMax, the future appeared to be even more competitive than the past.

(OfficeMax's Web address is **www.officemax.com**.)

---

[29]"President's Letter."

[30]Paulette Thomas, "OfficeMax Sees Opportunity in Plight," *The Wall Street Journal*, September 1996.

Section VII

Developing Marketing Plans

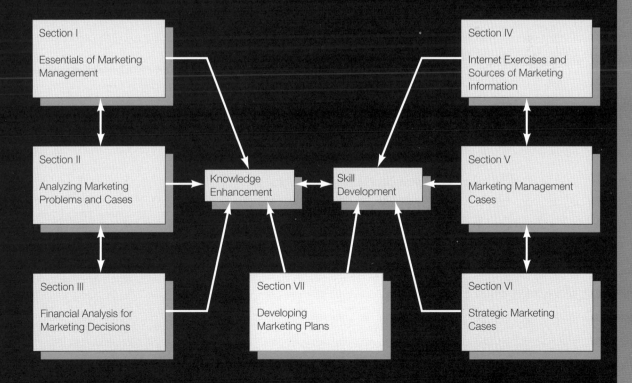

Section I

Essentials of Marketing Management

Section II

Analyzing Marketing Problems and Cases

Section III

Financial Analysis for Marketing Decisions

Knowledge Enhancement

Section VII

Developing Marketing Plans

Skill Development

Section IV

Internet Exercises and Sources of Marketing Information

Section V

Marketing Management Cases

Section VI

Strategic Marketing Cases

Imagine this scenario.   After receiving your bachelor's or master's degree in marketing, you are hired by a major consumer goods company. Because you've done well in school, you are confident that you have a lot of marketing knowledge and a lot to offer to the firm. You're highly motivated and are looking forward to a successful career.

After just a few days of work you are called in for a conference with the vice president of marketing. The vice president welcomes you and tells you how glad the firm is that you have joined them. The vice president also says that, since you have done so well in your marketing courses and have had such recent training, he wants you to work on a special project.

He tells you that the company has a new product, which is to be introduced in a few months. He also says, confidentially, that recent new product introductions by the company haven't been too successful. Suggesting that the recent problems are probably because the company has not been doing a very good job of developing marketing plans, the vice president tells you not to look at marketing plans for the company's other products.

Your assignment, then, is to develop a marketing plan for the proposed product in the next six weeks. The vice president explains that a good job here will lead to rapid advancement in the company. You thank the vice president for the assignment and promise that you'll do your best.

How would you feel when you returned to your desk? Surely, you'd be flattered that you had been given this opportunity and be eager to do a good job. However, how confident are you that you could develop a quality marketing plan? Would you even know where to begin?

We suspect that many of you, even those who have an excellent knowledge of marketing principles and are adept at solving marketing cases, may not yet have the skills necessary to develop a marketing plan from scratch. Thus, the purpose of this section is to offer a framework for developing marketing plans. In one sense, this section is no more than a summary of the whole text. In other words, it is an organizational framework based on the text material that can be used to direct the development of marketing plans.

Students should note that we are not presenting this framework and discussion as the only way to develop a marketing plan. While we believe this is a useful framework for logically analyzing the problems involved in developing a marketing plan, other approaches can be used just as successfully.

Often, successful firms prepare much less detailed plans, since much of the background material and current conditions are well known to everyone involved. However, our review of plans used in various firms suggests that something like this framework is not uncommon.

We would like to mention one other qualification before beginning our discussion. Students should remember that one important part of the marketing plan involves the development of a sales forecast. While we have discussed several approaches to sales forecasting in the text, we will detail only one specific approach here.

■ A Marketing Plan Framework

Marketing plans have three basic purposes. First, they are used as a tangible record of analysis so the logic involved can be checked. This is done to ensure the feasibility and internal consistency of the project and to evaluate the likely consequences of implementing the plan. Second, they are used as roadmaps or guidelines for directing appropriate actions. A marketing plan is designed to be the best available scenario and rationale for directing the firm's efforts for a particular product or brand. Third, they are used as tools to obtain funding for implementation. This funding may come from internal or external sources. For example, a brand manager may have to present a marketing plan to senior executives in a firm to get a budget request filled. This would be an internal source. Similarly, proposals for funding from investors or business loans from banks often require a marketing plan. These would be external sources.

Figure 1 presents a format for preparing marketing plans. Each of the 10 elements will be briefly discussed. We will refer to previous chapters and sections in this text and to other sources where additional information can be obtained when a marketing plan is being prepared. We also will offer additional information for focusing particular sections of the plan as well as for developing financial analysis.

Title Page

The *title page* should contain the following information: (1) the name of the product or brand for which the marketing plan has been prepared—for example, Marketing Plan for Little Friskies Dog Food; (2) the time period for which the plan is designed—for example, 2000–01; (3) the person(s) and position(s) of those submitting the plan—for example, submitted by Amy Lewis, brand manager; (4) the persons, group, or agency to whom the plan is being submitted—for example, submitted to Lauren Ellis, product group manager; and (5) the date of submission of the plan—for example, June 30, 2000.

While preparing the title page is a simple task, remember that it is the first thing readers see. Thus, a title page that is poorly laid out, is smudged, or contains misspelled words can lead to the inference that the project was developed hurriedly and with little attention to detail. As with the rest of the project, appearances are important and affect what people think about the plan.

Executive Summary

The *executive summary* is a two- to three-page summary of the contents of the report. Its purpose is to provide a quick summary of the marketing plan for executives who need to be informed about the plan but are typically not directly involved in plan approval. For instance, senior executives for firms with a broad product line may not have time to read the entire plan but need an overview to keep informed about operations.

■ **Figure 1**
A Marketing Plan
Format

- Title page
- Executive summary
- Table of contents
- Introduction
- Situational analysis
- Marketing planning
- Implementation and control of the marketing plan
- Summary
- Appendix: Financial analysis
- References

The executive summary should include a brief introduction, the major aspects of the marketing plan, and a budget statement. This is not the place to go into detail about each and every aspect of the marketing plan. Rather, it should focus on the major market opportunity and the key elements of the marketing plan that are designed to capitalize on this opportunity.

It is also useful to state specifically how much money is required to implement the plan. In an ongoing firm, many costs can be estimated from historical data or from discussions with other executives in charge of specific functional areas. However, in many situations (such as a class project), sufficient information is not always available to give exact costs for every aspect of production, promotion, and distribution. In these cases, include a rough estimate of total marketing costs of the plan. In many ongoing firms, marketing cost elements are concentrated in the areas of promotion and marketing research, and these figures are integrated with those from other functional areas as parts of the overall business plan.

Table of Contents

The *table of contents* is a listing of everything contained in the plan and where it is located in the report. Reports that contain a variety of charts and figures may also have a table of exhibits listing their titles and page numbers within the report.

In addition to using the table of contents as a place to find specific information, readers may also review it to see if each section of the report is logically sequenced. For example, situational analysis logically precedes marketing planning as an activity, and this ordering makes sense in presenting the plan.

Introduction

The types of information and amount of detail reported in the *introduction* depend in part on whether the plan is being designed for a new or existing product or brand. If the product is new, the introduction should explain the product concept and the reasons it is expected to be successful. Basically, this part of the report should make the new idea sound attractive to management or investors. In addition, it is useful to offer estimates of expected sales, costs, and return on investment.

If the marketing plan is for an existing brand in an ongoing firm, it is common to begin the report with a brief history of the brand. The major focus here is on the brand's performance in the last three to five years. It is useful to prepare graphs of the brand's performance that show its sales, profits, and market share for previous years and to explain the reasons for any major changes. These exhibits can also be extended to include predicted changes in these variables given the new marketing plan. A brief discussion of the overall strategy followed in previous years also provides understanding of how much change is being proposed in the new marketing plan.

Also useful in the introduction is to offer a precise statement of the purpose of the report as well as a roadmap of the report. In other words, tell readers what this report is, how it is organized, and what will be covered in the following sections.

Situational Analysis

The *situational analysis* is not unlike the analysis discussed in Chapter 1 and Section II of this text. The focus remains on the most critical and relevant environmental conditions (or changes in them) that affect the success or failure of the proposed plan. While any aspect of the economic, social, political, legal, or cooperative envi-

Understanding an industry and the actions of competitors is critical to developing successful marketing plans. Below is a list of some questions to consider when performing competitive analysis. Thinking about these questions can aid the marketing planner in developing better marketing strategies.

1. Which firms compete in this industry, and what is their financial position and marketing capability?
2. What are the relative market shares of various brands?
3. How many brands and models does each firm offer?
4. What marketing strategies have the market leaders employed?
5. Which brands have gained and which have lost market share in recent years, and what factors have led to these changes?
6. Are new competitors likely to enter the market?
7. How quickly do competitive firms react to changes in the market?
8. From which firms or brands might we be able to take market share?
9. What are the particular strengths and weaknesses of competitors in the industry?
10. How do we compare with other firms in the industry in terms of financial strength and marketing skills?

ronments might deserve considerable attention, there is seldom if ever a marketing plan in which the competitive environment does not require considerable discussion. In fact, the competitive environment may be set off as a separate section called *industry analysis*. The strengths and weaknesses of major competitors, their relative market shares, and the success of various competitive strategies are critical elements of the situation analysis.

Section IV of the text offers some sources of information for analyzing the competitive environment. In addition, trade association publications, *Fortune, Business Week,* and *The Wall Street Journal* frequently have useful articles on competitive strategies. Firms' annual reports often provide considerable useful information.

Marketing Planning

Marketing planning is, of course, a critical section of the report. As previously noted, it includes three major elements: marketing objectives, target markets, and the marketing mix.

Marketing Objectives. Marketing objectives are often stated in plans in terms of the percentage of particular outcomes that are to be achieved; for example, 80 percent awareness of the brand in particular markets, increase in trial rate by 30 percent, distribution coverage of 60 percent, or increase in total market share by 3 percent over the life of the plan. Similarly, there may also be objective statements in terms of sales units or dollars or increases in these. Of course, the reasons for selection of the particular objectives and rationale are important points to explain.

Target Markets. The *target markets* discussion explains the customer base and rationale or justification for it. An approach to developing appropriate target markets is contained in Chapter 5 of this text, and a useful source of secondary data for segmenting markets is the *National Purchase Diary Panel.*

This section also includes relevant discussion of changes or important issues in consumer or organizational buyer behavior; for example, what benefits consumers are seeking in this products class, what benefits does the particular brand offer, or what purchasing trends are shaping the market for this product. Discussions of consumer and organizational buyer behavior are contained in Chapters 3 and 4 of this text.

Marketing Mix.   The *marketing mix* discussion explains in detail the selected strategy consisting of product, promotion, distribution and price, and the rationale for it. Also, if marketing research has been done on these elements or is planned, it can be discussed in this section.

Product.

The *product* section details a description of the product or brand, its packaging and attributes. Product life-cycle considerations should be mentioned if they affect the proposed plan.

Of critical importance in this discussion is the competitive advantage of the product or brand. Here it must be carefully considered whether the brand really does anything better than the competition or is purchased primarily on the basis of brand equity or value. For example, many brands of toothpaste have fluoride, yet Crest has the largest market share primarily through promoting this attribute of its brand. Thus, does Crest do anything more than other toothpastes, or is it Crest's image that accounts for sales?

Discussion of product-related issues is contained in Chapters 6 and 7, and services are discussed in Chapter 12 of this text. For discussion of marketing plans for products marketed globally, see Chapter 13.

Promotion.

The *promotion* discussion consists of a description and justification of the planned promotion mix. It is useful to explain the theme of the promotion and to include some examples of potential ads as well as the nature of the sales force if one is to be used. For mass-marketed consumer goods, promotion costs can be large and need to be considered explicitly in the marketing plan.

Discussion of promotion-related issues is contained in Chapters 8 and 9 of this text. Secondary sources, such as *Standard Rate and Data, Simmons Media/Market Service, Starch Advertising Readership Service,* and the *Nielsen Television Index,* provide useful information for selecting, budgeting, and justifying media and other promotional decisions.

Distribution.

The *distribution* discussion describes and justifies the appropriate channel or channels for the product. This includes types of intermediaries and specifically who they will be. Other important issues concern the level of market coverage desired, cost, and control considerations. In many cases, the channels of distribution used by the firm, as well as competitive firms, are well established. For example, General Motors and Ford distribute their automobiles through independent dealer networks. Thus, unless there is a compelling reason to change channels, the traditional channel will often be the appropriate alternative. However, serious consideration may have to be given to methods of obtaining channel support, for example, trade deals to obtain sufficient shelf space.

Discussion of distribution-related issues is contained in Chapter 10 of this text. Useful retail distribution information can be found in the *Nielsen Retail Index* and the *Audits and Surveys National Total-Market Index.*

Price.

The pricing discussion starts with a specific statement of the price of the product. Depending on what type of channel is used, manufacturer price, wholesale price, and suggested retail price need to be listed and justified. In addition, special deals or trade discounts that are to be employed must be considered in terms of their effect on the firm's selling price.

Marketing
Highlight 2

Stating Objectives: How to Tell a Good One from a Bad One

For the direction-setting purpose of objectives to be fulfilled, objectives need to meet five specifications:

1. An objective should relate to a single, specific topic. (It should not be stated in the form of a vague abstraction or a pious platitude—"we want to be a leader in our industry" or "our objective is to be more aggressive marketers.")
2. An objective should relate to a result, not to an activity to be performed. (The objective is the result of the activity, not the performing of the activity.)
3. An objective should be measurable (stated in quantitative terms whenever feasible).
4. An objective should contain a time deadline for its achievement.
5. An objective should be challenging but achievable.

Consider the following examples:

1. *Poor:* Our objective is to maximize profits.

   Remarks: How much is "maximum"? The statement is not subject to measurement. What criterion or yardstick will management use to determine if and when actual profits are equal to maximum profits? No deadline is specified.

   Better: Our total profit target in 2000 is $1 million.
2. Poor: Our objective is to increase sales revenue and unit volume.

   Remarks: How much? Also, because the statement relates to two topics, it may be inconsistent. Increasing unit volume may require a price cut, and if demand is price inelastic, sales revenue would fall as unit volume rises. No time frame for achievement is indicated.

Better: Our objective this calendar year is to increase sales revenues from $30 million to $35 million; we expect this to be accomplished by selling 1 million units at an average price of $35.

3. *Poor:* Our objective in 2000 is to boost advertising expenditures by 15 percent.

   Remarks: Advertising is an activity, not a result. The advertising objective should be stated in terms of what result the extra advertising is intended to produce.

   Better: Our objective is to boost our market share from 8 percent to 10 percent in 2000 with the help of a 15 percent increase in advertising expenditures.
4. *Poor:* Our objective is to be a pioneer in research and development and to be the technological leader in the industry.

   Remarks: Very sweeping and perhaps overly ambitious; implies trying to march in too many directions at once if the industry is one with a wide range of technological frontiers. More a platitude than an action commitment to a specific result.

   Better: During the 2000–2010 decade, our objective is to continue as a leader in introducing new technologies and new devices that will allow buyers of electrically powered equipment to conserve on electric energy usage.
5. *Poor:* Our objective is to be the most profitable company in our industry.

   Remarks: Not specific enough by what measures of profit—total dollars, or earnings per share, or unit profit margin, or return on equity investment, or all of these? Also, because the objective concerns how well other companies will perform, the objective, while challenging, may not be achievable.

   Better: We will strive to remain atop the industry in terms of rate of return on equity investment by earning a 25 percent after-tax return on equity investment in 2000.

SOURCE: Adapted from Arthur A. Thompson, Jr., and A. J. Strickland, *Strategic Management: Concepts and Cases*, 5th ed. (Burr Ridge, IL: Irwin/McGraw-Hlll, 1990), pp. 23–34.

Discussion of price-related issues is contained in Chapter 11. In addition to a variety of other useful information, the *Nielsen Retail Index* provides information on wholesale and retail prices.

Marketing Research. For any aspect of marketing planning, there may be a need for marketing research. If such research is to be performed, it is important to justify it and explain its costs and benefits. Such costs should also be included in the financial analysis.

If marketing research has already been conducted as part of the marketing plan, it can be reported as needed to justify various decisions that were reached. To illustrate, if research found that two out of three consumers like the taste of a new formula Coke, this information would likely be included in the product portion of the report. However, the details of the research could be placed here in the marketing research section. Discussion of marketing research is contained in Chapter 2.

Implementation and Control of the Marketing Plan

This section contains a discussion and justification of how the marketing plan will be implemented and controlled. It also explains who will be in charge of monitoring and changing the plan should unanticipated events occur and how the success or failure of the plan will be measured. Success or failure of the plan is typically measured by a comparison of the results of implementing the plan with the stated objectives.

For a marketing plan developed within an ongoing firm, this section can be quite explicit, since procedures for implementing plans may be well established. However, for a classroom project, the key issues to be considered are the persons responsible for implementing the plan, a timetable for sequencing the tasks, and a method of measuring and evaluating the success or failure of the plan.

Summary

This *summary* need not be much different than the executive summary stated at the beginning of the document. However, it is usually a bit longer, more detailed, and states more fully the case for financing the plan.

Appendix—Financial Analysis

Financial analysis is a very important part of any marketing plan. While a complete business plan often includes extensive financial analysis, such as a complete cost breakdown and estimated return on investment, marketing planners frequently do

Marketing
Highlight 4

Some Questions to Consider in Marketing Planning

Below is a brief list of questions about the marketing planning section of the report. Answering them honestly and recognizing both the strengths and weaknesses of the marketing plan should help to improve it.

1. What are the key assumptions that were made in developing the marketing plan?
2. How badly will the product's market position be hurt if these assumptions turn out to be incorrect?
3. How good is the marketing research?
4. Is the marketing plan consistent? For example, if the plan is to seek a prestige position in the market, is the product priced, promoted, and distributed to create this image?
5. Is the marketing plan feasible? For example, are the financial and other resources (such as a distribution network) available to implement it?
6. How will the marketing plan affect profits and market share, and is it consistent with corporate objectives?
7. Will implementing the marketing plan result in competitive retaliation that will end up hurting the firm?
9. Is the marketing mix designed to reach and attract new consumers or increase usage among existing users or both?
9. Will the marketing mix help to develop brand-loyal consumers?
10. Will the marketing plan be successful not just in the short run but also contribute to a profitable long-run position?

not have complete accounting data for computing these figures. For example, decisions concerning how much overhead is to be apportioned to the product are not usually made solely by marketing personnel. However, the marketing plan should contain at least a sales forecast and estimates of relevant marketing costs.

Sales Forecast. As noted, there are a variety of ways to develop sales forecasts. Regardless of the method, however, they all involve trying to predict the future as accurately as possible. It is, of course, necessary to justify the logic for the forecasted figures, rather than offer them with no support.

One basic approach to developing a sales forecast is outlined in Figure 2. This approach begins by estimating the total number of persons in the selected target market. This estimate comes from the market segmentation analysis and may include information from test marketing and from secondary sources, such as *Statistical Abstracts of the United States*. For example, suppose a company is marketing a solar-powered watch that is designed not only to tell time but to take the pulse of the wearer. The product is targeted at joggers and others interested in aerobic exercise. By reviewing the literature on these activities, the marketing planner,

■ Figure 2
A Basic Approach to Sales Forecasting

Total number of people in target markets (a)	a
Annual number of purchases per person (b)	$\times$ b
Total potential market (c)	$=$ c
Total potential market (c)	c
Percent of total market coverage (d)	$\times$ d
Total available market (e)	$=$ e
Total available market (e)	e
Expected market share (f)	$\times$ f
Sales forecast (in units) (g)	$=$ g
Sales forecast (in units) (g)	g
Price (h)	$\times$ h
Sales forecast (in dollars) (i)	$=$ i

847

Marketing
Highlight 5

Some Questions to Consider in Implementation and Control

Implementation and control of a marketing plan require careful scheduling and attention to detail. While some firms have standard procedures for dealing with many of the questions raised below, thinking through each of the questions should help improve the efficiency of even these firms in this stage of the process.

1. Who is responsible for implementing and controlling the marketing plan?
2. What tasks must be performed to implement the marketing plan?
3. What are the deadlines for implementing the various tasks, and how critical are specific deadlines?
4. Has sufficient time been scheduled to implement the various tasks?
5. How long will it take to get the planned market coverage?
6. How will the success or failure of the plan be determined?
7. How long will it take to get the desired results from the plan?
8. How long will the plan be in effect before changes will be made to improve it based on more current information?
9. If an ad agency or other firms are involved in implementing the plan, how much responsibility and authority will they have?
10. How frequently will the progress of the plan be monitored?

John Murphy, finds that the average estimate of this market on a national level is 60 million persons and is growing by 4 million persons per year. Thus, John might conclude that the total number of people in the target market for next year is 64 million. If he has not further limited the product's target market and has no other information, John might use this number as a basis for starting the forecast analysis.

The second estimate John needs is the annual number of purchases per person in the product's target market. This estimate could be quite large for such products as breakfast cereal or less than one (annual purchase per person) for such products as automobiles. For watches, the estimate is likely to be much less than one since people are likely to buy a new watch only every few years. Thus, John might estimate the annual number of purchases per person in the target market to be .25. Of course, as a careful marketing planner, John would probably carefully research this market to refine this estimate. In any event, multiplying these two numbers gives John an estimate of the *total potential market,* in this case, 64 million times .25 equals 16 million. In other words, if next year alone John's company could sell a watch to every jogger or aerobic exerciser who is buying a watch, the company could expect sales to be 16 million units.

Of course, the firm cannot expect to sell every jogger a watch for several reasons. First, it is unlikely to obtain 100 percent market coverage in the first year, if ever. Even major consumer goods companies selling convenience goods seldom reach the entire market in the first year and many never achieve even 90 percent distribution. Given the nature of the product and depending on the distribution alternative, John's company might be doing quite well to average 50 percent market coverage in the first year. If John's plans call for this kind of coverage, his estimate of the total available market would be 16 million times .5, which equals 8 million.

A second reason John's plans would not call for dominating the market is that his company does not have the only product available or wanted by this target market. Many of the people who will purchase such a watch will purchase a competitive brand. He must, therefore, estimate the product's likely market share. Of all the estimates made in developing a sales forecast, this one is critical, since it is a reflection of the entire marketing plan. Important factors to consider in developing this estimate include (1) competitive market shares and likely marketing strategies; (2) competitive retaliation should the product do well; (3) competitive advantage of the product, such as lower price; (4) promotion mix and budget relative to competitors; and (5) market shares obtained by similar products in the introductory year.

Overall, suppose John estimates the product's market share to be 5 percent, since other competitive products have beat his company to the market and because the company's competitive advantage is only a slightly more stylish watch. In this case, the sales forecast for year one would be 8 million times .05, which equals 400,000 units. If the manufacturer's selling price was $50, then the sales forecast in dollars would be 400,000 times $50, which equals $20 million.

This approach can also be used to extend the sales forecast for any number of years. Typically, estimates of most of the figures change from year to year, depending on changes in market size, changes in distribution coverage, and changes in expected market shares. The value of this approach is that it forces an analyst to carefully consider and justify each of the estimates offered, rather than simply pulling numbers out of the air. In developing and justifying these estimates, many of the sources listed in Section IV provide a good place to start searching for information—for example, *Selling Areas Marketing Inc.* (SAMI) data.

Estimates of Marketing Costs.   A complete delineation of all costs, apportionment of overhead, and other accounting tasks are usually performed by other departments within a firm. All of this information, including expected return on investment from implementing the marketing plan, is part of the overall business plan.

However, the marketing plan should at least contain estimates of major marketing costs. These include such things as advertising, sales force training and compensation, channel development, and marketing research. Estimates may also be included for product development and package design.

For some marketing costs, reasonable estimates are available from sources such as *Standard Rate and Data.* However, some cost figures, such as marketing research, might be obtained from asking various marketing experts for the estimated price of proposed research. Other types of marketing costs might be estimated from financial statements of firms in the industry. For example, Morris's *Annual Statement Studies* offers percentage breakdowns of various income statement information by industry. These might be used to estimate the percentage of the sales-forecast figure that would likely be spent in a particular cost category.

References

The *references* section contains the sources of any secondary information that was used in developing the marketing plan. This information might include company reports and memos, statements of company objectives, and articles or books used for information or support of the marketing plan.

References should be listed alphabetically using a consistent format. One way of preparing references is to use the same approach as is used in marketing journals. For example, the format used for references in *Journal of Marketing* articles is usually acceptable.

■ Conclusion

Suppose you're now back sitting at your desk faced with the task of developing a marketing plan for a new product. Do you believe that you might have the skills to develop a marketing plan? Of course, your ability to develop a quality plan will depend on your learning experiences during your course work and the amount of practice you've had; for example, if you developed a promotion plan in your advertising course, it is likely that you could do a better job on the promotion phase of the marketing plan. Similarly, your experiences in analyzing cases should have sharpened your skills at recognizing problems and developing solutions to them. But inexperience (or experience) aside, hopefully you now feel that you understand the process of developing a marketing plan. You at least know where to start, where to seek information, how to structure the plan, and what are some of the critical issues that require analysis.

■ Additional Readings

Abratt, Russell, Maria Beffon, and John Ford. "Relationship between Marketing Planning and Annual Budgeting." *Marketing Intelligence & Planning* 12, no. 1 (1994), pp. 22–28.

Cohen, William A. *The Marketing Plan.* New York: John Wiley & Sons, 1995.

Goetsch, Hal. "Are Marketing Plans Passé? Does the Sun Rise?" *Marketing News,* December 5, 1994, pp. 4–5.

Hartman, John W. "Unplanned Events Wreak Havoc on Business Plans." *Business Marketing,* February 1994, p. 10.

Hudson, Phil. "Communicate Your Marketing Plan." *Bank Marketing,* October 1994, p. 64.

Lehmann, Donald R., and Russell S. Winer. *Analysis for Marketing Planning.* 3d ed. Burr Ridge, IL: Irwin/McGraw-Hill, 1994.

Manaktala, Vin. "Marketing: The Seven Deadly Sins." *Journal of Accountancy,* September 1994, pp. 67–72.

Rifken, Glenn. "Information Technology: The Client/Server Challenge." *Harvard Business Review,* July–August 1994, pp. 9–10.

Shark, Alan R. "Orchestrating a Strategic Marketing Plan." *Association Management,* November 1994, pp. 46–59.

Stephens, Nancy J. "Plan First." *Manager's Magazine,* November 1994, pp. 6–9.

Weber, John A. "Using Purchase Influence Niching for Better Focus in Industrial Marketing Plans." *Industrial Marketing Management,* December 1994, pp. 419–38.

Weylman, C. Richard. "Making Sure Your Marketing Plan Becomes Reality." *National Underwriter,* January 2, 1995, p. 18.

Chapter Notes

Section I

Chapter 1

1. See Reinhard Angelmar and Christian Pinson, "The Meaning of Marketing," *Philosophy of Science*, June 1975, pp. 208–14.

2. Peter D. Bennett, *Dictionary of Marketing Terms*, 2d ed. (Chicago: American Marketing Association, 1995), p. 166.

3. Much of this section is based on J. H. Donnelly, Jr., J. L. Gibson, and J. M. Ivancevich, *Fundamentals of Management*, 9th ed. (Burr Ridge, IL: Irwin/McGraw-Hill, 1998), chap. 7.

4. The process may differ depending on the type of organization or management approach, or both. For certain types of organizations, one strategic plan will be sufficient. Some manufacturers with similar product lines or limited product lines will develop only one strategic plan. However, organizations with widely diversified product lines and widely diversified markets may develop strategic plans for units or divisions. These plans usually are combined into a master strategic plan.

5. For a discussion of this topic, see Gerald E. Ledford, Jr., Jon R. Wendenhof, and James T. Strahely, "Realizing a Corporate Philosophy," *Organizational Dynamics*, Winter 1995, pp. 4–19; and Stephan Cummings and John Davies, "Mission, Vision, Fusion," *Long Range Planning*, December 1994, pp. 147–50.

6. Philip Kotler and Gary Armstrong, *Principles of Marketing*, 6th ed. (Englewood Cliffs, NJ: Prentice Hall, 1994), chap. 2.

7. Philip Kotler, *Marketing Management: Analysis, Planning, Implementation and Control*, 8th ed. (Englewood Cliffs, NJ: Prentice Hall, 1994), chap. 3.

8. Norton Paley, "A Sign of Intelligence," *Sales & Marketing Management*, March 1995, pp. 30–31.

9. Peter Drucker, *Management: Tasks, Responsibilities, Practices* (New York: Harper & Row, 1974), pp. 77–89; Kotler, *Marketing Management*, chap. 3.

10. Much of the following discussion is based on Drucker, *Management*, pp. 79–87.

11. Noel B. Zabriskie and Alan B. Huellmantel, "Marketing Research as a Strategic Tool," *Long Range Planning*, February 1994, pp. 107–18.

12. Originally discussed in the classic H. Igor Ansoff, *Corporate Strategy* (New York: McGraw-Hill, 1965).

13. For complete coverage of this topic, see Michael E. Porter, *Competitive Advantage: Creating and Sustaining Superior Performance* (New York: The Free Press, 1985). Material in this section is based upon discussions contained in Steven J. Skinner, *Marketing*, 2d ed. (Boston: Houghton Mifflin Co., 1994), pp. 48–50; and Thomas A. Bateman and Carl P. Zeithaml, *Management Function & Strategy*, 2d ed. (Burr Ridge, IL: Irwin/McGraw-Hill, 1993), pp. 152–53.

14. For a complete discussion of this topic see Michael Treacy and Fred Wiersma, *The Discipline of Market Leaders* (Reading, MA: Addison-Wesley, 1995); and Michael Treacy and Fred Wiersma, "How Market Leaders Keep Their Edge," *Fortune*, February 6, 1995, pp. 88–98.

15. Philip Kotler, *Marketing Management*, p. 13.

16. For a discussion of this issue and other mistakes marketers frequently make, see Kevin J. Clancy and Robert S. Shulman, "Breaking the Mold," *Sales & Marketing Management*, January 1994, pp. 82–84.

17. George S. Day and David B. Montgomery, "Diagnosing the Experience Curve," *Journal of Marketing*, Spring 1983, pp. 44–58.

18. P. Rajan Varadarajan, Terry Clark, and William M. Pride, "Controlling the Uncontrollable: Managing Your Market Environment," *Sloan Management Review*, Winter 1992, pp. 39–47.

19. Reed E. Nelson, "Is There Strategy in Brazil?" *Business Horizons*, July–August 1992, pp. 15–23.

20. Peter S. Davis and Patrick L. Schill, "Addressing the Contingent Effects of Business Unit Strategic Orientation on the Relationship between Organizational Context and Business Unit Performance," *Journal of Business Research*, 1993, pp. 183–200.

21. J. Scott Armstrong and Roderick J. Brodie, "Effects of Portfolio Planning Methods on Decision Making: Experimental Results," *International Journal of Research in Marketing*, January 1994, pp. 73–84.

22. Michel Roberts, "Times Change but Do Business Strategies?" *Journal of Business Strategy*, March–April 1993, pp. 12–15.

23. Donald L. McCabe and V. K. Narayanan, "The Life Cycle of the PIMS and BCG Models," *Industrial Marketing Management*, November 1991, pp. 347–52.

Chapter 2

1. Based on Peter D. Bennett, ed., *Dictionary of Marketing Terms*, 2d ed. (Chicago: American Marketing Association, 1995), p. 77.

2. Gilbert A. Churchill, Jr., and J. Paul Peter, *Marketing: Creating Value for Customers*, 2d ed. (Burr Ridge, IL: Irwin/McGraw-Hill, 1998), p. 116.

3. For a discussion of some general problems in marketing research, see Alan G. Sawyer and J. Paul Peter, "The Significance of Statistical Significance Testing in Marketing Research," *Journal of Marketing Research*, May 1983, pp. 122–33.

4. This section is based on Churchill and Peter, *Marketing*, pp. 114–16.

Chapter 3

1. A. H. Maslow, *Motivation and Personality* (New York: Harper & Row, 1954); also see James F. Engel, Roger D. Blackwell, and Paul W. Miniard, Consumer Behavior, 8th ed. (Fort Worth, TX: Dryden Press, 1995), chap. 5, for further discussion of need recognition.

2. For a detailed review of research on external search, see Sharon E. Beatty and Scott M. Smith, "External Search Effort: An Investigation across Several Product Categories," *Journal of Consumer Research*, June 1987, pp. 83–95. Also see Narasimhan Srinivasan and Brian T. Ratchford, "An Empirical Test of a Model of External Search for Automobiles," *Journal of Consumer Research*, September 1991, pp. 233–42; and Julie L. Ozanne, Merrie Brucks, and Dhruv Grewal, "A Study of Information Search Behavior during the Categorization of New Products," *Journal of Consumer Research*, March 1992, pp. 452–63.

3. For further discussion of information processing, see J. Paul Peter and Jerry C. Olson, *Consumer Behavior and Marketing Strategy*, 4th ed. (Burr Ridge, IL: Irwin/McGraw-Hill, 1996), chap. 3.

4. For a summary of research on attitude modeling, see Blair H. Sheppard, Jon Hartwick, and Paul R. Warshaw, "The Theory of Reasoned Action: A Meta-Analysis of Past Research with Recommendations for Modification and Future Research," *Journal of Consumer Research*, December 1988, pp. 325–43.

5. For further discussion of postpurchase feelings, see Richard L. Oliver, "Cognitive, Affective, and Attribute Bases of the Satisfaction Response," *Journal of Consumer Research*, December 1993, pp. 418–30; and Haim Mano and Richard L. Oliver, "Assessing the Dimensionality and Structure of the Consumption Experience: Evaluation, Feeling, and Satisfaction," *Journal of Consumer Research*, December 1993, pp. 451–66.

6. See William O. Bearden and Michael J. Etzel, "Reference Group Influence on Product and Brand Purchase Decisions," *Journal of Consumer Research*,

September 1982, pp. 183–94; and Terry L. Childers and Akshay R. Rao, "The Influence of Familial and Peer-Based Reference Groups on Consumer Decisions," *Journal of Consumer Research*, September 1992, pp. 198–211.

7. See Rosann L. Spiro, "Persuasion in Family Decision Making," *Journal of Consumer Research*, March 1983, pp. 393–402.

8. See Janet Wagner and Sherman Hanna, "The Effectiveness of Family Life Cycle Variables in Consumer Expenditure Research," *Journal of Consumer Research*, December 1983, pp. 281–91. Also see Charles M. Schanninger and William D. Danko, "A Conceptual and Empirical Comparison of Alternative Household Life Cycle Models," *Journal of Consumer Research*, March 1993, pp. 580–94.

9. Russell W. Belk, "Situational Variables and Consumer Behavior," *Journal of Consumer Research*, December 1975, pp. 156–64. Also see Jacob Hornik, "Situational Effects on the Consumption of Time," *Journal of Marketing*, Fall 1982, pp. 44–55; C. Whan Park, Easwer S. Iyer, and Daniel C. Smith, "The Effects of Situational Factors on In-Store Grocery Shopping Behavior: The Role of Store Environment and Time Available for Shopping," *Journal of Consumer Research*, March 1989, pp. 422–33; and Mary Jo Bitner, "Servicescapes: The Impact of Physical Surroundings on Customers and Employees," *Journal of Marketing*, April 1992, pp. 57–71.

Chapter 4

1. This discussion is based on Gilbert A. Churchill, Jr., and J. Paul Peter, *Marketing: Creating Value for Customers*, 2d ed. (Burr Ridge, IL: Irwin/McGraw-Hill, 1998), pp. 182–84. Also see Michele D. Bunn, "Taxonomy of Buying Decision Approaches," *Journal of Marketing*, January 1993, pp. 38–56.

2. This discussion is based on Eric N. Berkowitz, Roger A. Kerin, Steven W. Hartley, and William Rudelius, *Marketing*, 4th ed. (Burr Ridge, IL: Irwin/McGraw-Hill 1994), p. 184.

3. For research on influence strategies in organizational buying, see Gary L. Frazier and Raymond Rody, "The Use of Influence Strategies in Interfirm Relationships in Industrial Product Channels," *Journal of Marketing*, January 1991, pp. 52–69; and Julia M. Bristor, "Influence Strategies in Organizational Buying," *Journal of Business-to-Business Marketing*, 1993, pp. 63–98.

4. For research on the role of organizational climate in industrial buying, see William J. Qualls and Christopher P. Puto, "Organizational Climate and Decision Framing: An Integrated Approach to Analyzing Industrial Buying Decisions," *Journal of Marketing Research*, May 1989, pp. 179–92.

Chapter 5

1. Russell I. Haley, "Benefit Segmentation: A Decision-Oriented Research Tool," *Journal of Marketing,* July 1968, pp. 30–35; Russell I. Haley, "Benefit Segmentation—20 Years Later," *Journal of Consumer Marketing,* 1983, pp. 5–13; and Russell I. Haley, "Benefit Segments: Backwards and Forwards," *Journal of Advertising Research,* February–March 1984, pp. 19–25.

2. Roger J. Calantone and Alan G. Sawyer, "The Stability of Benefit Segments," *Journal of Marketing Research,* August 1978, pp. 395–404; also see James R. Merrill and William A. Weeks, "Predicting and Identifying Benefit Segments in the Elderly Market," in *AMA Educator's Proceedings,* eds. Patrick Murphy et al. (Chicago: American Marketing Association, 1983), pp. 399–403; Wagner A. Kamakura, "A Least Squares Procedure for Benefit Segmentation with Conjoint Experiments," *Journal of Marketing Research,* May 1988, pp. 157–67; and Michel Wedel and Jan-Benedict E. M. Steenkamp, "A Clusterwise Regression Method for Simultaneous Fuzzy Market Structuring and Benefit Segmentation." *Journal of Marketing Research,* November 1991, pp. 385–96.

3. John L. Lastovicka, John P. Murry, Jr., and Eric Joachimsthaler, "Evaluating the Measurement Validity of Lifestyle Typologies with Qualitative Measures and Multiplicative Factoring," *Journal of Marketing Research,* February 1990, pp. 11–23.

4. This discussion is taken from J. Paul Peter and Jerry C. Olson, *Consumer Behavior and Marketing Strategy,* 5th ed. (Burr Ridge, IL: Irwin/McGraw-Hill, 1999), pp. 361–63.

5. See Al Ries and Jack Trout, *Positioning: The Battle for Your Mind* (New York: Warner Books, 1981); and Al Ries and Jack Trout, *Marketing Warfare* (New York: McGraw-Hill, 1986).

Chapter 6

1. Material for this section is based on discussions contained in Louis E. Boone and David L. Kurtz, *Contemporary Marketing,* 8th ed. (Fort Worth, TX: Dryden, 1995), chap. 2; Gilbert A. Churchill, Jr., and J. Paul Peter, *Marketing: Creating Value for Customers* (Burr Ridge, IL: Irwin/McGraw-Hill, 1995), chap. 1, p. 634; James H. Donnelly, James L. Gibson, and John M. Ivancevich, *Fundamentals of Management,* 9th ed. (Burr Ridge, IL: Irwin/McGraw-Hill 1995), p. 501; Joseph M. Juran, "Made in the U.S.A.: A Renaissance in Quality," *Harvard Business Review,* July–August 1993, pp. 42–47, 50; and Valerie A. Zeithaml, "Consumer Perceptions of Price, Quality, and Value: A Means End Model and Synthesis of Evidence," *Journal of Marketing,* April 1988, pp. 35–48.

2. For a discussion on this topic, see Andrew J. Bergman, "What the Marketing Professional Needs to Know about ISO 9000 Series Registration," *Industrial Marketing Management,* 1994, pp. 367–70.

3. The material for this section comes from Glenn L. Urban and Steven H. Star, *Advanced Marketing Strategy* (Englewood Cliffs, NJ: Prentice Hall, 1991), chap. 16.

4. For a detailed discussion of this topic, see Anne Perkins, "Product Variety Beyond Black," *Harvard Business Review,* November–December 1994, pp. 13–14; and "Perspectives: The Logic of Product-Line Extensions," *Harvard Business Review,* November–December 1994, pp. 53–62.

5. Mats Urde, "Brand Orientation—A Strategy for Survival," *Journal of Consumer Marketing,* 1994, pp. 18–32.

6. James Lowry, "Survey Finds Most Powerful Brands," *Advertising Age,* July 11, 1988, p. 31.

7. Peter H. Farquhar, "Strategic Challenges for Branding," *Marketing Management,* 1994, pp. 8–15.

8. Peter D. Bennett, ed., *Dictionary of Marketing Terms,* 2d ed. (Chicago: American Marketing Association, 1995), p. 27.

9. Terance Shimp, *Promotion Management and Marketing Communications,* 2d ed. (Hinsdale, IL: Dryden Press, 1990), p. 67.

10. David A. Aaker and Kevin Lane Keller, "Consumer Evaluations of Brand Extensions," *Journal of Marketing,* January 1990, pp. 27–41.

11. Aaker and Keller, "Consumer Evaluations of Brand Extensions."

12. For a detailed discussion of brand equity, see David Aaker, *Managing Brand Equity* (New York and London: Free Press, 1991).

13. For a complete discussion of this topic, see Geoffrey L. Gordon, Roger J. Calantone, and C. A. di Benedetto, "Brand Equity in the Business-to-Business Sector: An Exploratory Study," *Journal of Product & Brand Management,* 1993, pp. 4–16.

14. Jeffrey D. Zbar, "Industry Trends Hold Private-Label Promise," *Advertising Age,* April 3, 1995, p. 31.

15. Pam Weisz, "Contac Looks for Relief in Re-design," *Brandweek,* February 6, 1995, p. 18.

16. Karen Benezra, "Frito Bets 'Reduced' Pitch Is in the Chips," *Brandweek,* January 23, 1995, p. 18.

17. Thomas Hine, "Why We Buy," *Worth,* May 1995, pp. 80–83.

18. For a discussion of problems related to this issue, see Geoffrey L. Gordon, Roger J. Calantone, and C. Anthony di Benedetto, "Mature Markets and Revitalization Strategies: An American Fable," *Business Horizons,* May–June 1991, pp. 39–50.

19. Barry L. Bayus, "Are Product Life Cycles Really Getting Shorter?" *Journal of Product Innovation Management,* September 1994, pp. 300–08.

20. The discussion on benchmarking is based on Stanley Brown, "Don't Innovate—Imitate," *Sales & Marketing Management,* January 1995, pp. 24–25; Charles Goldwasser, "Benchmarking: People Make the Process," *Management Review,* June 1995, pp. 39–43; and L. S. Pryor and S. J. Katz, "How Benchmarking Goes Wrong (and How to Do It Right)," *Planning Review,* January–February 1993, pp. 6–14.

Chapter 7

1. "Face Value: The Mass Production of Ideas, and Other Impossibilities," *The Economist,* March 18, 1995, p. 72.

2. Greg Erickson, "New Package Makes a New Product Complete," *Marketing News,* May 8, 1995, p. 10.

3. Zina Mouhkheiber, "Oversleeping," *Forbes,* June 15, 1995, pp. 78–79.

4. The material on the five categories of new products is from C. Merle Crawford, *New Products Management,* 5th ed. (Burr Ridge, IL: Irwin/McGraw-Hill, 1997), chap. 1.

5. H. Igor Ansoff, *Corporate Strategy* (New York: McGraw-Hill, 1965), pp. 109–10.

6. Richard Stroup, "Growing in a Crowded Market Requires Old and New Strategies," *Brandweek,* August 22, 1994, p. 19.

7. These two examples came from Justin Martin, "Ignore Your Customers," *Fortune,* May 1, 1995, pp. 121–26.

8. "Where Do They Get All Those Ideas?" *Machine Design,* January 26, 1995, p. 40.

9. This section is based on Daryl McKee, "An Organizational Learning Approach to Product Innovation," *Journal of Product Innovation Management,* September 1992, pp. 232–45.

10. The discussion on risk is from Thomas D. Kuczmarski and Arthur G. Middlebrooks, "Innovation Risk and Reward," *Sales & Marketing Management,* February 1993, pp. 44–51.

11. For a more complete discussion on the advantages and disadvantages or strategic alliances, see Richard N. Cardozo, Shannon H. Shipp, and Kenneth J. Roering, "Proactive Strategic Partnerships: A New Business Markets Strategy," *Journal of Business and Industrial Marketing,* Winter 1992, pp. 51–63; and Frank K. Sonnenberg, "Partnering: Entering the Age of Cooperation," *Journal of Business Strategy,* May/June 1992, pp. 49–52.

12. James Quinn, "Managing Innovation: Controlled Chaos," *Harvard Business Review,* May–June 1985, pp. 73–84; and Hirotaka Takeuchi and Ikujiro Nonaka, "The New Product Development Game," *Harvard Business Review,* January–February 1986, pp. 137–46.

13. For a discussion of this issue, see Eric M. Olson, Orville C. Walker, Jr., and Robert W. Ruekert, "Organizing for Effective New Product Development: The Moderating Role of Product Innovativeness," *Journal of Marketing,* January 1995, pp. 48–62; and Cristopher Meyer, "How the Right Measures Help Teams Excel," *Harvard Business Review,* May–June 1994, pp. 95–97.

14. For a detailed discussion on these stages, see Karl T. Ulrich and Steven D. Eppinger, *Product Design and Development* (New York: McGraw-Hill, 1995); and Glen Rifken, "Product Development: Emphatic Design Helps Understand Users Better," *Harvard Business Review,* March–April 1994, pp. 10–11.

15. The material on test marketing is from C. Merle Crawford, *New Products Management,* 5th ed. (Burr Ridge, IL: Irwin/McGraw-Hill, 1997), chaps. 17 and 18.

16. Patricia W. Meyers and Gerald A. Athaide, "Strategic Mutual Learning between Producing and Buying Firms during Product Innovation," *Journal of Product Innovation Management,* September 1991, pp. 155–69.

17. For a discussion of this issue, see Christina Brown and James Lattin, "Investigating the Relationship between Time in Market and Pioneering Advantage," *Management Science,* October 1994, pp. 1361–69; Robin Peterson, "Forecasting for New Product Introduction," *Journal of Business Forecasting,* Fall 1994, pp. 21–23; and Tracy Carlson, "The Race Is On," Brandweek, May 9, 1994, pp. 22–27.

18. For a discussion of reasons why products fail, see Betsy Spellman, "Big Talk, Little Dollars," *Brandweek,* January 23, 1995, pp. 21–29.

19. For a discussion of the pitfalls associated with using traditional financial techniques to evaluate new product decisions, see George T. Haley and Stephen M. Goldberg, "Net Present Value Techniques and Their Effects on New Product Research," *Industrial Marketing Management,* June 1995, pp. 177–90.

Chapter 8

1. This discussion is adapted from material contained in Gilbert A. Churchill, Jr., and J. Paul Peter, *Marketing: Creating Value for Customers* (Burr Ridge, IL: Irwin/McGraw-Hill, 1995), chap. 18.

2. Peter D. Bennett, ed., *Dictionary of Marketing Terms* (Chicago: American Marketing Association, 1988), p. 4.

3. For a description of ad spending by leading companies and brands, see "The Top 200 Brands," *Advertising Age,* May 1, 1995, pp. 33–34.

4. Material for this section is largely based on the discussion of advertising tasks and objectives contained in William Arens and Courtland Bovée, *Contemporary*

Advertising, 5th ed. (Burr Ridge, IL: Irwin/McGraw-Hill, 1994), chap. 7.

5. Much of the material for this section is based on Phillip Jones, "Ad Spending: Maintaining Market Share," *Harvard Business Review*, January–February 1990, pp. 38–42; and James C. Schroer, "Ad Spending: Growing Market Share," *Harvard Business Review*, January–February 1990, pp. 44–48.

6. For a discussion of developing effective advertising, see Jeffrey F. Durgee, "Qualitative Methods for Developing Advertising That Makes Consumers Feel, 'Hey, That's Right For Me,' " *Journal of Consumer Marketing*, Winter 1990, pp. 15–21.

7. For more comprehensive coverage of this topic, see George E. Belch and Michael A. Belch, *Introduction to Advertising and Promotion: An Integrated Communications Perspective*, 3d ed. (Burr Ridge, IL: Irwin/McGraw-Hill, 1995), chap. 12.

8. Bennett, *Dictionary of Marketing Terms*, p. 253.

9. George E. Belch and Michael A. Belch, *Introduction to Advertising and Promotion: An Integrated Communications Perspective*, 3d ed. (Burr Ridge, IL: Irwin/McGraw-Hill, 1995), p. 478.

10. Definition of push marketing and its activities is from Arens and Bovée, *Contemporary Advertising*, p. G17.

11. For a fuller explanation of the pros and cons associated with push marketing strategies, see Betsy Spellman, "Trade Promotion Redefined," *Brandweek*, March 13, 1995, pp. 25–34; and John McManus, " 'Lost' Money Redefined as 'Found' Money Won't Connect the Disconnects," *Brandweek*, March 25, 1995, p. 16.

12. This discussion is based on Donald R. Glover, "Distributor Attitudes toward Manufacturer-Sponsored Promotions," *Industrial Marketing Management*, August 1991, pp. 241–49.

13. For a further discussion of the dangers involved in using sales promotions, see John P. Jones, "The Double Jeopardy of Sales Promotions," *Harvard Business Review*, September–October 1990, pp. 145–52.

14. For a discussion of this topic, see Murray Raphel, "Frequent Shopper Clubs: Supermarkets' Newest Weapon," *Direct Marketing*, May 1995, pp. 18–20; Richard G. Barlow, "Five Mistakes of Frequency Marketing," *Direct Marketing*, March 1995, pp. 16–17; and Alice Cuneo, "Savvy Frequent-Buyer Plans Build on a Loyal Base," *Advertising Age*, March 20, 1995, pp. S10–11.

Chapter 9

1. Warren Keegan, Sandra Moriarty, and Thomas Duncan, *Marketing*, 2d ed. (Englewood Cliffs, NJ: Prentice Hall, 1994), p. 654.

2. Eric von Hipple, "The Sources of Innovation," *The McKinsey Quarterly*, Winter 1988, pp. 72–79.

3. Terance A. Shimp, *Promotion Management and Marketing Communication*, 2d ed. (Chicago, IL: Dryden Press, 1990), p. 602.

4. Material for this discussion came from Ronald B. Marks, *Personal Selling: An Interactive Approach*, 5th ed. (Boston, MA: Allyn and Bacon, 1994), pp. 12–13.

5. Material for the discussion of objectives is adapted from Joel R. Evans and Barry Berman, *Marketing*, 6th ed. (New York: Macmillan, 1994), pp. 640–42.

6. Unless otherwise noted, the discussion on the relationship-building process is based largely on material contained in Barton A. Weitz, Stephen B. Castleberry, and John F. Tanner, Jr., *Selling: Building Partnerships*, 3d ed. (Burr Ridge, IL: Irwin/McGraw-Hill, 1998); and Rolph Anderson, *Essentials of Personal Selling: The New Professionalism* (Englewood Cliffs, NJ: Prentice Hall, 1995). For an in-depth discussion of this topic, readers should consult these references.

7. Material for this discussion is from Thomas Leech, "Getting It Right the First Time," *Sales & Marketing Management*, March 1995, p. 49.

8. Material for the discussion on closing guidelines is drawn from "Don't Forget to Ask for the Sale," *Sales & Marketing Management*, June 1995, p. 37.

9. Terry G. Vavra, "Selling after the Sale," *Bank Marketing*, January 1995, pp. 27–30.

10. Bill Kelley, "From Salesperson to Manager: Transition and Travail," *Sales & Marketing Management*, February 1992, pp. 32–36.

11. For a discussion of this topic, see Saul W. Gellerman, "The Tests of a Good Salesperson," *Harvard Business Review*, May–June 1990, pp. 64–69.

12. William J. Stanton, Richard H. Buskirk, and Rosann L. Spiro, *Management of a Sales Force*, 9th ed. (Burr Ridge, IL: Irwin/McGraw-Hill, 1995), pp. 319–20.

13. Michael Kelley, "Replace Sales Management with Sales Leadership," *Marketing News*, June 19, 1995, p. 10.

14. The discussion on national account management is from James S. Boles, Bruce K. Pilling, and George W. Goodwyn, "Revitalizing Your National Account Marketing Program," *Journal of Business & Industrial Marketing* 9, no. 1 (1994), pp. 24–33.

15. Based on a survey by the National Industrial Conference Board: "Forecasting Sales," *Studies in Business Policy*, no. 106.

16. Much of the discussion in this section is based on material contained in Gilbert A. Churchill, Jr., Neil M. Ford, and Orville C. Walker, Jr., *Sales Force Management*, 4th ed. (Burr Ridge, IL: Irwin/McGraw-Hill, 1993), and Stanton, Buskirk, and Spiro, *Management of a Sales Force*.

17. For additional discussions, see David J. Good and Robert W. Stone, "How Sales Quotas Are Developed," *Industrial Marketing Management*, February 1991, pp. 51–55.

18. For a complete discussion of the skills and policies utilized by successful sales leaders in motivating salespeople, see David W. Cravens, Thomas N. Ingram, Raymond W. LaForge, and Clifford E. Young, "Hallmarks of Effective Sales Organizations," *Marketing Management*, Winter 1992, pp. 57–66; Thomas R. Wortruba, John S. Mactie, and Jerome A. Colletti, "Effective Sales Force Recognition Programs," *Industrial Marketing Management*, February 1991, pp. 9–15; and Ken Blanchard, "Reward Salespeople Creatively," *Personal Selling Power*, March 1992, p. 24.

19. Robert G. Head, "Restoring Balance to Sales Compensation," *Sales & Marketing Management*, August 1992, pp. 48–53.

Chapter 10

1. Peter D. Bennett, *Dictionary of Marketing Terms*, 2d ed. (Chicago: American Marketing Association, 1995), p. 242.

2. For further discussion of relationship marketing, see Jan B. Heide, "Interorganizational Governance in Marketing Channels," *Journal of Marketing*, January 1994, pp. 71–85; Robert M. Morgan and Shelby D. Hunt, "The Commitment-Trust Theory of Relationship Marketing," *Journal of Marketing*, July 1994, pp. 20–38; and Manohar U. Kalwani and Narakesari Narayandas, "Long-Term Manufacturer-Supplier Relationships: Do They Pay Off for the Supplier Firm?" *Journal of Marketing*, January 1995, pp. 1–16.

3. This section is based on Donald J. Bowersox and M. Bixby Cooper, *Strategic Marketing Channel Management* (New York: McGraw-Hill, 1992), pp. 104–7; Bert Rosenbloom, *Marketing Channels: A Management View*, 4th ed. (Hinsdale, IL: Dryden Press), pp. 440–65; and Eric N. Berkowitz, Roger A. Kerin, Steven W. Hartley, and William Rudelius, *Marketing*, 3d ed. (Burr Ridge, IL: Irwin/McGraw-Hill, 1992), pp. 387–90.

4. This section is based on Gilbert A. Churchill, Jr., and J. Paul Peter, *Marketing: Creating Value for Customers*, 2d ed. (Burr Ridge, IL: Irwin/McGraw-Hill, 1998), pp. 392–98.

5. This section is based on Churchill and Peter, *Marketing: Creating Value for Customers*, pp. 414–18.

6. This classification is taken from Michael Levy and Barton A. Weitz, *Retailing Management*, 3d ed. (Burr Ridge, IL: Irwin/McGraw-Hill, 1998), chap. 3.

Chapter 11

1. Kent B. Monroe, "Buyers' Subjective Perceptions of Price," *Journal of Marketing Research*, February 1973, pp. 70–80; also see Donald R.

Lichtenstein and Scot Burton, "The Relationship between Perceived and Objective Price—Quality," *Journal of Marketing Research*, November 1989, pp. 429–43.

2. For research concerning the effects of price and several other marketing variables on perceived product quality, see Akshay R. Rao and Kent B. Monroe, "The Effect of Price, Brand Name, and Store Name on Buyers' Perceptions of Product Quality: An Integrative Review," *Journal of Marketing Research*, August 1989, pp. 351–57; and William B. Dodds, Kent B. Monroe, and Dhruv Grewal, "Effects of Price, Brand, and Store Evaluations on Buyers' Product Evaluations," *Journal of Marketing Research*, August 1991, pp. 307–19.

3. For further discussion of price elasticity see Stephen J. Hoch, Byung-Do Kim, Alan L. Montgomery, and Peter Rosi, "Determinants of Store-Level Price Elasticity," *Journal of Marketing Research*, February 1995, pp. 17–29.

4. For further discussion of legal issues involved in pricing, see Louis W. Stern and Thomas L. Eovaldi, *Legal Aspects of Marketing Strategy* (Englewood Cliffs, NJ: Prentice Hall, 1984), chap. 5.

5. For more detailed discussions, see Frederick E. Webster, *Marketing for Managers* (New York: Harper & Row, 1974), pp. 178–79; also see Thomas T. Nagle and Reed K. Holden, *The Strategy and Tactics of Pricing* (Englewood Cliffs, NJ: Prentice Hall, 1995); and Kent B. Monroe, *Pricing: Making Profitable Decisions*, 2d ed. (New York: McGraw-Hill, 1990).

Chapter 12

1. Much of the material for this introduction came from Ronald Henkoff, "Service Is Everybody's Business," *Fortune*, June 27, 1994, pp. 48–60; and Tim R. Smith, "The Tenth District's Expanding Service Sector," *Economic Review*, Third Quarter 1994, pp. 55–66.

2. Peter D. Bennett, ed., *Dictionary of Marketing Terms*, 2d ed. (Chicago: American Marketing Association, 1995), p. 261.

3. Carolyn R. Fryer, "What's Different about Services Marketing," *Journal of Services Marketing*, Fall 1991, pp. 53–58.

4. Harry N. Shycon, "Improved Customer Service Measuring the Payoff," *Journal of Business Strategy*, January–February 1992, pp. 13–17.

5. Ibid.

6. For a discussion of customer service in product companies, see A. Lynn Daniel, "Overcome the Barriers to Superior Customer Service," *Journal of Business Strategy*, January–February 1992, pp. 18–24; and James Brian Quinn, Thomas L. Doorley, and Penny C. Paquette, "Beyond Products: Services-Based Strategies," *Harvard Business Review*, March–April 1990, pp. 58–67.

7. Craig Cina, "Five Steps to Service Excellence," *Journal of Services Marketing*, Spring 1990, pp. 39–47.

8. Frank Sonnenberg, "Service Quality Forethought, not Afterthought," *Journal of Business Strategy,* September–October 1989, pp. 54–57.

9. Susan J. Devlin and H. K. Dong, "Service Quality from the Customer's Perspective," *Marketing Research 6,* no. 1 (1995), pp. 4–13.

10. Joan O. Fredericks and James M. Salter II, "Beyond Customer Satisfaction," *Management Review,* May 1995, pp. 29–32.

11. The material in this section draws from research performed by Leonard L. Berry, Valerie A. Zeithaml, and A. Parasuraman, "Quality Counts in Services, Too," *Business Horizons,* May–June 1985, pp. 44–52; A. Parasuraman, Valerie A. Zeithaml, and Leonard L. Berry, "A Conceptual Model of Service Quality and Its Implications for Future Research," *Journal of Marketing,* Fall 1985, pp. 41–50; Leonard L. Berry, A. Parasuraman, and Valerie A. Zeithaml, "The Service-Quality Puzzle," *Business Horizons,* September–October 1988, pp. 35–43; Stephen W. Brown and Teresa A. Swartz, "A Gap Analysis of Professional Service Quality," *Journal of Marketing,* April 1989, pp. 92–98; Leonard L. Berry, Valerie A. Zeithaml, and A. Parasuraman, "Five Imperatives for Improving Service Quality," *Sloan Management Review,* Summer 1990, pp. 29–38; A. Parasuraman, Leonard L. Berry, and Valerie A. Zeithaml, "Understanding Customer Expectations of Service," *Sloan Management Review,* Spring 1991, pp. 39–48; and Leonard L. Berry, *On Great Service: A Framework for Action* (New York: Free Press, 1995).

12. Rick Berry, "Define Service Quality so You Can Deliver It," *Best's Review,* March 1995, p. 68.

13. Material for this section is drawn from John T. Mentzer, Carol C. Bienstock, and Kenneth B. Kahn, "Benchmarking Satisfaction," *Marketing Management,* Summer 1995, pp. 41–46; and Alan Dutka, *AMA Handbook for Customer Satisfaction: A Complete Guide to Research, Planning and Implementation* (Lincolnwood, IL: NTC Books, 1994). For detailed information on this topic, readers are advised to consult these sources.

14. Much of the material for this section was taken from Karl Albrecht and Ron Zemke, *Service America* (Burr Ridge, IL: Irwin/McGraw-Hill, 1985); and Ron Zemke and Dick Schaaf, *The Service Edge 101 Companies That Profit from Customer Care* (New York: New American Library, 1989).

15. Chip R. Bell and Kristen Anderson, "Selecting Super Service People," *HR Magazine,* February 1992, pp. 52–54.

16. James A. Schlesinger and James L. Heskett, "Breaking the Cycle of Failure in Services," *Sloan Management Review,* Spring 1991, pp. 17–28.

17. Leonard L. Berry and A. Parasuraman, "Services Marketing Starts from Within," *Marketing Management,* Winter 1992, pp. 25–34.

18. Ibid.

19. Leonard L. Berry and A. Parasuraman, "Prescriptions for a Service Quality Revolution in America," *Organizational Dynamics,* Spring 1992, pp. 5–15.

20. Bob O'Neal, "World-Class Service," *Executive Excellence,* September 1994, pp. 11–12.

21. This example is from David E. Bowen and Edward E. Lawler III, "The Empowerment of Service Workers: What, Why, How, and When," *Sloan Management Review,* Spring 1992, pp. 31–39.

22. Judith Waldrop, "Spending by Degree," *American Demographics,* February 1990, pp. 22–26.

23. Howard Schlossberg, "Study: U.S. Firms Lag in Using Customer Satisfaction Data," *Marketing News,* June 1992, p. 14.

24. Andrew E. Serwer, "The Competition Heats Up in Online Banking," *Fortune,* June 26, 1995, pp. 18–19.

25. Material on bank consolidations is from Kelly Holland, "Why Banks Keep Bulking Up," *Business Week,* July 31, 1995, pp. 66–67; and Amy Dunkin, "Investing in a Bank-Eat-Bank World," *Business Week,* July 31, 1995, pp. 92–93.

26. Tom Harvey, "Quality: The Only Profit Strategy," *Bank Marketing,* January 1995, pp. 43–46.

27. Material for the discussion of Columbia/HCA was provided courtesy of Off the Record Research, a San Francisco–based institutional investment research company.

28. John Labate, "Chronimed," *Fortune,* February 20, 1995, p. 118.

29. Elaine Underwood, "Airlines Continue Flight to E-Ticketing," *Brandweek,* May 8, 1995, p. 3.

30. Peter L. Ostrowski, Terrence V. O'Brien, and Geoffrey L. Gordon, "Determinants of Service Quality in the Commercial Airline Industry: Differences between Business and Leisure Travelers," *Journal of Travel & Tourism Marketing 3,* no. 1 (1994), pp. 19–47.

31. Material for the discussion on the lodging industry came from Elaine Underwood, "Joined at the Hip," *Adweek's Marketing Week,* June 1, 1992, pp. 22–23; and Sak Onkvisit and John L. Shaw, "Service Marketing: Image, Branding, and Competition," *Business Horizons,* January–February 1989, pp. 13–18.

Chapter 13

1. Karen Pennar, "America: Losing Out on Exports," *Business Week,* July 31, 1995, p. 30.

2. Material on McDonald's and PepsiCo is from Jeanne Whitman, "McDonald's Cooks Worldwide Growth," *Advertising Age International,* July 17, 1995, p. 14.

3. Brian Zajac, "Weak Dollar, Strong Results," *Forbes,* July 17, 1995, pp. 274–76.

4. Jason Vogel, "Chicken Diplomacy," *Financial World,* March 14, 1995, pp. 46–49.

5. For a full explanation on cultural differences, see Rose Knotts, "Cross-Cultural Management: Transformations and Adaptations," *Business Horizons,* January–February 1989, pp. 29–33.

6. Claudia Penteado, "Pepsi's Brazil Blitz," *Advertising Age,* January 16, 1995, p. 12.

7. Karen Benezra, "Fritos 'Round the World,'" *Brandweek,* March 27, 1995, pp. 32, 35.

8. Material for this section is from Craig Mellow, "Russia: Making Cash from Chaos," *Fortune,* April 17, 1995, pp. 145–51; and Peter Galuszka, "And You Think You've Got Tax Problems," *Business Week,* May 29, 1995, p. 50.

9. Mir Magbool Alam Khan, "Enormity Tempts Marketers to Make a Passage to India," *Advertising Age International,* May 15, 1995, p. 112.

10. This section was taken from James F. Bolt, "Global Competitors: Some Criteria for Success," *Business Horizons,* January–February 1988, pp. 34–41.

11. For a complete discussion of the risks associated with pursuing a global strategy, see Barrie James, "Reducing the Risks of Globalization," *Long Range Planning,* February 1990, pp. 80–88.

12. This section is based on George S. Yip, Pierre M. Loewe, and Michael Y. Yoshino, "How to Take Your Company to the Global Market," *Columbia Journal of World Business,* Winter 1988, pp. 37–48.

13. Ibid.

14. The introductory material on foreign research is based on Michael R. Czintoka, "Take a Shortcut to Low-Cost Global Research," *Marketing News,* March 13, 1995, p. 3.

15. Donald B. Pittenger, "Gathering Foreign Demographics Is No Easy Task," *Marketing News,* January 8, 1990, pp. 23, 25.

16. Debbie Klosky, "Pepsi, Coke Usher in New Age in Spain," *Advertising Age,* June 5, 1995, p. 45.

17. This discussion is based on John Burnett, *Promotion Management* (Boston: Houghton-Mifflin Co., 1993), chap. 19.

18. The material for this section on market entry and growth approaches is based on Philip R. Cateora, *International Marketing,* 8th ed. (Burr Ridge, IL: Irwin/McGraw-Hill, 1993), pp. 325–34; Charles W. L. Hill, *International Business: Competing in the Global Marketplace* (Burr Ridge, IL: Irwin/McGraw-Hill, 1994), pp. 402–8; and William M. Pride and O. C. Ferrell, *Marketing: Concepts and Strategy,* 9th ed. (Boston: Houghton-Mifflin, 1995), pp. 111–14.

19. Bruce A. Walters, Steve Peters, and Gregory G. Dess, "Strategic Alliances and Joint Ventures: Making Them Work," *Business Horizons,* July–August 1994, pp. 5–10.

20. Joel Bleeke and David Ernst, "Is Your Strategic Alliance Really a Sale?" *Harvard Business Review,* January–February 1995, pp. 97–105.

21. Material in this section is based on Subhash C. Jain, "Standardization of International Marketing Strategy: Some Research Hypotheses," *Journal of Marketing,* January 1989, pp. 70–79.

Section II

1. Michael E. Porter, *Competitive Strategy* (New York: Free Press, 1980). Also see Michael E. Porter, *Competitive Advantage: Creating and Sustaining Superior Performance* (New York: Free Press, 1985); and Michael E. Porter, *The Competitive Advantage of Nations* (New York: Free Press, 1990).

Section III

1. For methods of estimating the cost of capital, see Charles P. Jones, *Introduction to Financial Management* (Burr Ridge, IL: Irwin/McGraw-Hill, 1992), chap. 14.

2. See Eugene F. Brigham, *Fundamentals of Financial Management* (Hinsdale, IL: Dryden Press, 1986).

3. It is useful to use average inventory rather than a single end-of-year estimate if monthly data are available.

4. For a discussion of ratio analysis for retailing, see Joseph B. Mason and Morris L. Mayer, *Modern Retailing: Theory and Practice,* 6th ed. (Burr Ridge, IL: Irwin/McGraw-Hill, 1993), chap. 8.

Name Index 1

(Names in References)

Name Index 2

(Names in Text)

Case Index

Subject Index